Nineteenth-Century Literature Criticism

Topics Volume

Guide to Gale Literary Criticism Series

For criticism on	Consult these Gale series
Authors now living or who died after December 31, 1999	*CONTEMPORARY LITERARY CRITICISM (CLC)*
Authors who died between 1900 and 1999	*TWENTIETH-CENTURY LITERARY CRITICISM (TCLC)*
Authors who died between 1800 and 1899	*NINETEENTH-CENTURY LITERATURE CRITICISM (NCLC)*
Authors who died between 1400 and 1799	*LITERATURE CRITICISM FROM 1400 TO 1800 (LC)* *SHAKESPEAREAN CRITICISM (SC)*
Authors who died before 1400	*CLASSICAL AND MEDIEVAL LITERATURE CRITICISM (CMLC)*
Authors of books for children and young adults	*CHILDREN'S LITERATURE REVIEW (CLR)*
Dramatists	*DRAMA CRITICISM (DC)*
Poets	*POETRY CRITICISM (PC)*
Short story writers	*SHORT STORY CRITICISM (SSC)*
Literary topics and movements	*HARLEM RENAISSANCE: A GALE CRITICAL COMPANION (HR)* *THE BEAT GENERATION: A GALE CRITICAL COMPANION (BG)*
Asian American writers of the last two hundred years	*ASIAN AMERICAN LITERATURE (AAL)*
Black writers of the past two hundred years	*BLACK LITERATURE CRITICISM (BLC)* *BLACK LITERATURE CRITICISM SUPPLEMENT (BLCS)*
Hispanic writers of the late nineteenth and twentieth centuries	*HISPANIC LITERATURE CRITICISM (HLC)* *HISPANIC LITERATURE CRITICISM SUPPLEMENT (HLCS)*
Native North American writers and orators of the eighteenth, nineteenth, and twentieth centuries	*NATIVE NORTH AMERICAN LITERATURE (NNAL)*
Major authors from the Renaissance to the present	*WORLD LITERATURE CRITICISM, 1500 TO THE PRESENT (WLC)* *WORLD LITERATURE CRITICISM SUPPLEMENT (WLCS)*

ISSN 0732-1864

Volume 180

Nineteenth-Century Literature Criticism

Topics Volume

Criticism of Various
Topics in Nineteenth-Century Literature,
including Literary and Critical Movements,
Prominent Themes and Genres, Anniversary
Celebrations, and Surveys of National Literatures

Kathy D. Darrow
Russel Whitaker
Project Editors

THOMSON

GALE

Detroit • New York • San Francisco • New Haven, Conn. • Waterville, Maine • London

THOMSON

GALE

Nineteenth-Century Literature Criticism, Vol. 180

Project Editors
Russel Whitaker and Kathy D. Darrow

Editorial
Jeffrey W. Hunter, Jelena O. Krstović, Michelle Lee, Thomas J. Schoenberg, Noah Schusterbauer, Lawrence J. Trudeau

Data Capture
Frances Monroe, Gwen Tucker

Rights and Acquisitions
Emma Hull, Barb McNeil, Tracie Richardson

Composition and Electronic Capture
Tracey L. Matthews

Manufacturing
Rhonda Dover

Associate Product Manager
Marc Cormier

LIBRARY OF CONGRESS CATALOG CARD NUMBER 84-643008

ISBN-13: 978-0-7876-9851-5
ISBN-10: 0-7876-9851-2
ISSN 0732-1864

Printed in the United States of America
10 9 8 7 6 5 4 3 2 1

Contents

Preface vii

Acknowledgments xi

Literary Criticism Series Advisory Board xiii

Preface

Since its inception in 1981, *Nineteenth-Century Literature Criticism* (*NCLC*) has been a valuable resource for students and librarians seeking critical commentary on writers of this transitional period in world history. Designated an "Outstanding Reference Source" by the American Library Association with the publication of is first volume, *NCLC* has since been purchased by over 6,000 school, public, and university libraries. The series has covered more than 500 authors representing 38 nationalities and over 28,000 titles. No other reference source has surveyed the critical reaction to nineteenth-century authors and literature as thoroughly as *NCLC*.

Scope of the Series

NCLC is designed to introduce students and advanced readers to the authors of the nineteenth century and to the most significant interpretations of these authors' works. The great poets, novelists, short story writers, playwrights, and philosophers of this period are frequently studied in high school and college literature courses. By organizing and reprinting commentary written on these authors, *NCLC* helps students develop valuable insight into literary history, promotes a better understanding of the texts, and sparks ideas for papers and assignments. Each entry in *NCLC* presents a comprehensive survey of an author's career or an individual work of literature and provides the user with a multiplicity of interpretations and assessments. Such variety allows students to pursue their own interests; furthermore, it fosters an awareness that literature is dynamic and responsive to many different opinions.

Every fourth volume of *NCLC* is devoted to literary topics that cannot be covered under the author approach used in the rest of the series. Such topics include literary movements, prominent themes in nineteenth-century literature, literary reaction to political and historical events, significant eras in literary history, prominent literary anniversaries, and the literatures of cultures that are often overlooked by English-speaking readers.

NCLC continues the survey of criticism of world literature begun by Thomson Gale's *Contemporary Literary Criticism* (*CLC*) and *Twentieth-Century Literary Criticism* (*TCLC*).

Organization of the Book

An *NCLC* entry consists of the following elements:

- The **Author Heading** cites the name under which the author most commonly wrote, followed by birth and death dates. Also located here are any name variations under which an author wrote, including transliterated forms for authors whose native languages use nonroman alphabets. If the author wrote consistently under a pseudonym, the pseudonym will be listed in the author heading and the author's actual name given in parenthesis on the first line of the biographical and critical information. Uncertain birth or death dates are indicated by question marks. Single-work entries are preceded by a heading that consists of the most common form of the title in English translation (if applicable) and the original date of composition.

- The **Introduction** contains background information that introduces the reader to the author, work, or topic that is the subject of the entry.

- The list of **Principal Works** is ordered chronologically by date of first publication and lists the most important works by the author. The genre and publication date of each work is given. In the case of foreign authors whose works have been translated into English, the list will focus primarily on twentieth-century translations, selecting those works most commonly considered the best by critics. Unless otherwise indicated, dramas are dated by first performance, not first publication. Lists of **Representative Works** by different authors appear with topic entries.

- Reprinted **Criticism** is arranged chronologically in each entry to provide a useful perspective on changes in critical evaluation over time. The critic's name and the date of composition or publication of the critical work are given at the beginning of each piece of criticism. Unsigned criticism is preceded by the title of the source in which it appeared. All titles by the author featured in the text are printed in boldface type. Footnotes are reprinted at the end of each essay or excerpt. In the case of excerpted criticism, only those footnotes that pertain to the excerpted texts are included. Criticism in topic entries is arranged chronologically under a variety of subheadings to facilitate the study of different aspects of the topic.

- A complete **Bibliographical Citation** of the original essay or book precedes each piece of criticism.

- Critical essays are prefaced by brief **Annotations** explicating each piece.

- An annotated bibliography of **Further Reading** appears at the end of each entry and suggests resources for additional study. In some cases, significant essays for which the editors could not obtain reprint rights are included here. Boxed material following the further reading list provides references to other biographical and critical sources on the author in series published by Thomson Gale.

Indexes

Each volume of *NCLC* contains a **Cumulative Author Index** listing all authors who have appeared in a wide variety of reference sources published by Thomson Gale, including *NCLC*. A complete list of these sources is found facing the first page of the Author Index. The index also includes birth and death dates and cross references between pseudonyms and actual names.

A **Cumulative Nationality Index** lists all authors featured in *NCLC* by nationality, followed by the number of the *NCLC* volume in which their entry appears.

A **Cumulative Topic Index** lists the literary themes and topics treated in the series as well as in *Classical and Medieval Literature Criticism, Literature Criticism from 1400 to 1800, Twentieth-Century Literary Criticism,* and the *Contemporary Literary Criticism* Yearbook, which was discontinued in 1998.

An alphabetical **Title Index** accompanies each volume of *NCLC*, with the exception of the Topics volumes. Listings of titles by authors covered in the given volume are followed by the author's name and the corresponding page numbers where the titles are discussed. English translations of foreign titles and variations of titles are cross-referenced to the title under which a work was originally published. Titles of novels, dramas, nonfiction books, and poetry, short story, or essay collections are printed in italics, while individual poems, short stories, and essays are printed in roman type within quotation marks.

In response to numerous suggestions from librarians, Thomson Gale also produces an annual paperbound edition of the *NCLC* cumulative title index. This annual cumulation, which alphabetically lists all titles reviewed in the series, is available to all customers. Additional copies of this index are available upon request. Librarians and patrons will welcome this separate index; it saves shelf space, is easy to use, and is recyclable upon receipt of the next edition.

Citing *Nineteenth-Century Literature Criticism*

When citing criticism reprinted in the Literary Criticism Series, students should provide complete bibliographic information so that the cited essay can be located in the original print or electronic source. Students who quote directly from reprinted criticism may use any accepted bibliographic format, such as University of Chicago Press style or Modern Language Association style.

The examples below follow recommendations for preparing a bibliography set forth in *The Chicago Manual of Style,* 14th ed. (Chicago: The University of Chicago Press, 1993); the first example pertains to material drawn from periodicals, the second to material reprinted from books:

Franklin, J. Jeffrey. "The Victorian Discourse of Gambling: Speculations on *Middlemarch* and *The Duke's Children*." *ELH* 61, no. 4 (winter 1994): 899-921. Reprinted in *Nineteenth-Century Literature Criticism*. Vol. 168, edited by Jessica Bomarito and Russel Whitaker, 39-51. Detroit: Thomson Gale, 2006.

Frank, Joseph. "*The Gambler*: A Study in Ethnopsychology." In *Freedom and Responsibility in Russian Literature: Essays in Honor of Robert Louis Jackson,* edited by Elizabeth Cheresh Allen and Gary Saul Morson, 69-85. Evanston, Ill.: Northwestern University Press, 1995. Reprinted in *Nineteenth-Century Literature Criticism*. Vol. 168, edited by Jessica Bomarito and Russel Whitaker, 75-84. Detroit: Thomson Gale, 2006.

The examples below follow recommendations for preparing a works cited list set forth in the *MLA Handbook for Writers of Research Papers,* 6th ed. (New York: The Modern Language Association of America, 2003); the first example pertains to material drawn from periodicals, the second to material reprinted from books:

Franklin, J. Jeffrey. "The Victorian Discourse of Gambling: Speculations on *Middlemarch* and *The Duke's Children*." *ELH* 61.4 (Winter 1994): 899-921. Reprinted in *Nineteenth-Century Literature Criticism*. Eds. Jessica Bomarito and Russel Whitaker. Vol. 168. Detroit: Thomson Gale, 2006. 39-51.

Frank, Joseph. "*The Gambler*: A Study in Ethnopsychology." *Freedom and Responsibility in Russian Literature: Essays in Honor of Robert Louis Jackson*. Eds. Elizabeth Cheresh Allen and Gary Saul Morson. Evanston, Ill.: Northwestern University Press, 1995. 69-85. Reprinted in *Nineteenth-Century Literature Criticism*. Eds. Jessica Bomarito and Russel Whitaker. Vol. 168. Detroit: Thomson Gale, 2006. 75-84.

Suggestions are Welcome

Readers who wish to suggest new features, topics, or authors to appear in future volumes, or who have other suggestions or comments are cordially invited to call, write, or fax the Associate Product Manager:

Associate Product Manager, Literary Criticism Series
Thomson Gale
27500 Drake Road
Farmington Hills, MI 48331-3535
1-800-347-4253 (GALE)
Fax: 248-699-8054

Acknowledgments

The editors wish to thank the copyright holders of the criticism included in this volume and the permissions managers of many book and magazine publishing companies for assisting us in securing reproduction rights. Following is a list of the copyright holders who have granted us permission to reproduce material in this volume of *NCLC*. Every effort has been made to trace copyright, but if omissions have been made, please let us know.

COPYRIGHTED MATERIAL IN *NCLC*, VOLUME 180, WAS REPRODUCED FROM THE FOLLOWING PERIODICALS:

ATQ, v. 19, March 2005. Copyright © 2005 by The University of Rhode Island. Reproduced by permission.—*Cross Currents,* v. 37, summer-fall, 1987. Copyright © 1987 by Cross Currents Inc. Reproduced by permission.—*ELH,* v. 56, fall, 1989. Copyright © 1989 The Johns Hopkins University Press. Reproduced by permission.—*Essays in Criticism,* v. 47, October, 1997 for "Henry James's Permanent Adolescence" by John R. Bradley. Copyright © 1997 Oxford University Press. Reproduced by permission of the publisher, conveyed through Copyright Clearance Center.—*Essays in Poetics,* v. 20, autumn, 1995. Reproduced by permission.—*Feminist Studies,* v. 3, spring-summer, 1976. Copyright © 1976 by Feminist Studies, Inc. Reproduced by permission of Feminist Studies, Inc., Department of Women's Studies, University of Maryland, College Park, MD 20724.—*GLQ: Journal of Lesbian and Gay Studies,* v. 2, 1995 for "Lesbian Panic and Mary Shelley's 'Frankenstein,'" by Frann Michel. Copyright © 1995 by Overseas Publishers Association. All rights reserved. Used by permission of the current publisher, Duke University Press.—*The Midwest Quarterly,* v. 46, spring, 2005. Copyright © 2005 by *The Midwest Quarterly,* Pittsburgh State University. Reproduced by permission.—*The Mississippi Quarterly,* v. 46, spring, 1993; v. 48, spring, 1995; v. 56, summer, 2003. Copyright © 1993, 1995, 2003 by Mississippi State University. All reproduced by permission.—*Neophilologus,* v. 74, April, 1990 for "'Common Dawn': Wordsworth and the Philosophy of Democracy" by Gordon K. Thomas. Reproduced by permission of the author.—*Persuasions: The Jane Austen Journal,* v. 25, 2003. Reproduced by permission.—*Proceedings of the Western Society for French History: Selected Papers of the 1998 Annual Meeting,* v. 26, 2000. Copyright © 2000 Western Society for French History. All rights reserved. Reproduced by permission.—*Raritan: A Quarterly Review,* v. 22, fall, 2002. Copyright © 2002 by *Raritan: A Quarterly Review.* Reproduced by permission.—*Slavic and East European Journal,* v. 37, winter, 1993. Copyright © 1993 by AATSEEL of the U.S., Inc. Reproduced by permission.—*Studies in American Fiction,* v. 28, spring, 2000. Copyright © 2000 Northeastern University. Reproduced by permission.—*Studies in the Novel,* v. 12, summer, 1980; v. 34, fall, 2002. Copyright © 1980, 2002 by North Texas State University. Both reproduced by permission.—*Walt Whitman Quarterly Review,* v. 21, summer, 2003. Copyright © 2003 by The University of Iowa. Reproduced by permission.—*Wordsworth Circle,* v. 36, winter, 2005. Copyright © 2005 Marilyn Gaull. Reproduced by permission of the editor.

COPYRIGHTED MATERIAL IN *NCLC*, VOLUME 180, WAS REPRODUCED FROM THE FOLLOWING BOOKS:

Adolph, Robert. From "Whitman, Tocqueville, and the Language of Democracy," in *The Delegated Intellect: Emersonian Essays on Literature, Science, and Art in Honor of Don Gifford.* Edited by Donald E. Morse. Peter Lang, 1995. Copyright © 1995 Peter Lang Publishing, Inc., New York. All rights reserved. Reproduced by permission.—Davies, Ann. From "The 'Seer': The Democratic Poet's Recognition and Transcendence," in *Seers and Judges: American Literature as Political Philosophy.* Edited by Christine Dunn Henderson. Lexington Books, 2002. Copyright © 2002 by Lexington Books. All rights reserved. Reproduced by permission.—De Sherbinin, Julie W. From "Chekhov and Christianity: The Critical Evolution," in *Chekhov Then and Now: The Reception of Chekhov in World Culture.* Edited by J. Douglas Clayton. Peter Lang, 1997. Copyright © 1997 Peter Lang Publishing, Inc., New York. All rights reserved. Reproduced by permission.—Gohdes, Clarence. From "An American Author as Democrat," in *Literary Romanticism in America.* Edited by William L. Andrews. Louisiana State University Press, 1981. Copyright © 1981 by Louisiana State University Press. All rights reserved. Reproduced by permission.—Hallock, John W. M. From *The American Byron: Homosexuality and the Fall of Fitz-Greene Halleck.* University of Wisconsin Press, 2000. Copyright © 2000 by the Board of Regents of the University of Wisconsin System. All rights reserved. Reproduced by permission.—Jenkins, Ruth Y. From *Reclaiming Myths of Power: Women Writers and the Victorian Spiritual Crisis.* Bucknell University Press, 1995. Copyright © 1995 by Associated University Presses, Inc. All rights reserved. Reproduced by permission.—Keegan, Abigail F. From *Byron's Othered Self and*

Thomson Gale Literature Product Advisory Board

The members of the Thomson Gale Literature Product Advisory Board—reference librarians from public and academic library systems—represent a cross-section of our customer base and offer a variety of informed perspectives on both the presentation and content of our literature products. Advisory board members assess and define such quality issues as the relevance, currency, and usefulness of the author coverage, critical content, and literary topics included in our series; evaluate the layout, presentation, and general quality of our printed volumes; provide feedback on the criteria used for selecting authors and topics covered in our series; provide suggestions for potential enhancements to our series; identify any gaps in our coverage of authors or literary topics, recommending authors or topics for inclusion; analyze the appropriateness of our content and presentation for various user audiences, such as high school students, undergraduates, graduate students, librarians, and educators; and offer feedback on any proposed changes/enhancements to our series. We wish to thank the following advisors for their advice throughout the year.

Christianity in Nineteenth-Century Literature

The following entry provides critical commentary on the treatment of Christianity in nineteenth-century literature. For discussion of Catholicism in nineteenth-century American literature, see *NCLC,* Volume 64; for discussion of the Oxford Movement, see *NCLC,* Volume 72.

INTRODUCTION

During the nineteenth century, there was a pronounced focus on the ancient world in general, and on ancient Christianity in particular. This interest stemmed from the desire to discern and promote a unified, original Christian vision within the fragmented world of Victorian Christianity, which included, among others, Anglicans, Protestants, Roman Catholics and Eastern Orthodox Christians. The interpretation of Christian doctrine, as an intellectual controversy, was displayed in literature as well as in religious and political journals of the nineteenth century. Not only were Christian religious leaders articulate and impassioned authors, but the ideas spawned by their debate inspired many novelists and poets to espouse a particular interpretation of Christian ideology in their works. Victorian women writers approached the topic of Christianity in a manner that often differed from that of Christian society at large, and critics have clashed over the meaning of these gender-specific differences. Russian authors' treatment of Christianity and Christian themes often involved debates between faith and atheism, the presence of Christian ideals and artifacts in everyday life, and the interpretation of Christianity in view of Enlightenment-era scholarship.

The Oxford Movement, a revival of Roman Catholic doctrine within the Anglican Church in the first half of the nineteenth century, has been understood as a reaction against the conventional understanding of religion in Victorian Britain, governmental involvement in ecclesiastical life, the increasing secularism that accompanied the rising importance of economic structures, and the rationalist thought that sprang from the Enlightenment. Calling for a return to the beliefs of early Christianity, the leaders of the Oxford Movement emphasized religious dogma, the centrality of faith, and its practice in daily life. The Oxford Movement remained a minority faction within Anglicanism, and many of its members eventually left the national Church; nevertheless, its challenges to complacent spirituality—its com-

mitment to a more fervent, mindful, and almost ascetic engagement with the divine, and stringent protections of religious life from the authority of the state—spurred intense intellectual controversy and contributed to the reform of the Anglican Church. John Keble, John Henry Newman, and Edward Bouverie Pusey were the best-known figures in the Oxford Movement. All of these men saw the Anglican Church as undergoing a period of crisis and resolved to take action to rejuvenate its authority through sermons and religious tracts. A series of printed pamphlets, called *Tracts for the Times* (1833-41), attracted attention both within and outside Oxford, and its writers would come to be known as Tractarians. These works engendered a great deal of controversy within the Church, and the leaders of the Oxford Movement gained increasing influence at the University.

The revivalist excitement generated by the Tractarians' publications and sermons spread to the United States and the Continent. Over the entire course of the Oxford Movement, its proponents were forced to reiterate their loyalty to Anglicanism, an insistence that grew sharper with Newman's decision to convert to Catholicism and the younger leaders' deep criticisms of the Anglican Church. In 1844 W. G. Ward wrote *The Ideal of a Christian Church, Considered in Comparison with Existing Practice,* in which he argued openly for the supremacy of Roman doctrine. The leaders of the Oxford Movement swifly condemned the work and distanced their position from that of Ward. With increasing secessions to Rome and attacks from moderate Anglicanism, the Tractarians were forced to reform their movement throughout the remainder of the nineteenth century. Under Pusey's leadership, which succeeded that of Newman, the Oxford Movement moved into increasing mysticism and ritualism, as well as continuing doctrinal orthodoxy. "Puseyism," as it came to be known, was deeply unpopular among Anglicans, who were profoundly suspicious of extremist faiths of all varieties. Most scholars agree that the Oxford Movement failed to attain popular support within the Anglican Church and, after its brief heyday, devolved into extreme ritualism that existed on the periphery of Anglicanism. Tractarianism, however, successfully challenged the disintegration of Church authority and impacted the Anglican Church in a more subtle way by challenging the secularist leanings of Victorian England. Many commentators claim that the Oxford Movement prefigured issues that confront current religious institutions, and generated impassioned and articulate responses to the central conflicts of nineteenth-century thought.

Insofar as the American colonies were settled, and the nation was founded, predominantly by Protestants, the culture of America in the nineteenth century was mainly characterized by the Protestant spirit. Despite a period of toleration immediately following the Revolutionary War when Protestant-Catholic relations were cordial, anti-Catholic sentiment escalated in the early nineteenth century and took on a definite shape and direction with the nativist movement, which waged war against Mormonism, the Masonic Order, and Catholicism. Historians offer various explanations for the phenomenon of nativism occurring at that point in American history, as well as for its vast sweep and exceptional virulence. But it is generally agreed that nativism, particularly anti-Catholicism, developed through the convergence of the political ideals and religious beliefs by which most Americans defined themselves, and the sudden, dramatic increase in the number of Catholic immigrants. The Roman Catholic Church seemed to nativists to be the antithesis of America's democratic ideals; deemed conspicuously hierarchical and authoritarian, the Roman Church was assumed to be politically anti-democratic as well. Its belief in celibacy for clergy made it appear anti-social; its rites were mystical and, therefore, ran counter to the purely ethical religion and natural theology prevalent in the Protestant churches of the nineteenth century; and the highly cultured and learned Roman Magesterium clashed with strong egalitarian instincts, especially during the era of Jacksonian democracy.

Commentators have discussed how Victorian women writers offered their own particular interpretations of Christian ideals in their works. In her novel *Ruth* (1853), Elizabeth Cleghorn Gaskell rejects the patriarchal Christian hierarchy, depicting instead an alternative Christian world in which her women characters are endowed with rights and are afforded respect that women are denied in the real world. Similarly, Charlotte Brontë's *Jane Eyre* (1847) highlights the close relationship between religion and gender roles in Victorian society, and, according to such critics as Maria Lamonaca, conveys how difficult it was for Christian women to promote feminist ideals and still remain "good Christians." The extent to which Christianity is thematically germane in reading Jane Austen's works is a topic of considerable debate among literary scholars. While many critics characterize Austen as a devout Christian whose religion plays a central role in her works, others argue that Austen's Anglican faith has no bearing on or presence in her works.

Scholars have studied nineteenth-century Americans' strong identification with and devotion to Jesus Christ. Commentator Richard Wightman Fox illustrates that even such staunchly secular thinkers as Thomas Jefferson and Ralph Waldo Emerson espoused the philosophy of Jesus Christ, both out of genuine regard for his teaching, which corresponded to their own liberal democratic ideology, and as a means of communicating with their religious colleagues and constituents in a common language. Critic Charles Swann maintains that Mark Rutherford's story "Did He Believe?," which appears in Rutherford's novel *Catherine Furze* (1893), is an attack of Walter Pater's portrayal of the history of Christianity as an undirected, organically evolving theology that serves its leaders and reinforces social hierarchies. Rutherford presents, according to Swann, a view of Christianity as an essential and leading force in civilizing society, offering empowerment to the world's disenfranchised and downtrodden.

Victorian-era Russian authors, many influenced by literary naturalism, have often been characterized as either those who purport a tenuous, but hopeful, faith in Christianity, and those who are staunch atheists. Critic Luigi Pareyson maintains that in *Brat'ya Karamazovy* (1880; *The Brothers Karamazov*), Fyodor Dostoevsky provides numerous responses to the questions of how a just and loving God could allow children to suffer, and to what purpose. Pareyson illustrates that Dostoevsky allows various characters in the novel to express their individual responses to these questions: Ivan utterly rejects Christianity and denies God's existence; Dmitry dreams that an adult's willingness to suffer is called for in response to a child's pointless suffering; Father Zossima asserts that suffering is an integral aspect of humankind's universal condition; and ultimately, Alexey affirms God's existence but rejects the necessity of pointless suffering. Pareyson and other critics interpret Dostoevsky's treatment of suffering as an endorsement of the Christian approach to this mystery of human existence. Numerous critics, from the nineteenth century to the present day, have debated Anton Chekhov's views on Christianity, using his works to argue for or against the author's Christian faith or atheism. Critic Julie De Sherbinin maintains that Chekhov, unlike his Russian contemporaries, does not present an opinion on the merits or validity of Christianity in his works, but rather presents a detailed and well-informed portrait of the cultural artifacts of Christianity in nineteenth-century Russia. Alexander Pushkin's views of Christianity and his treatment of the topic in his works have also been widely studied by literary critics. While many critics assert that Pushkin's works embody a firmly atheist vision of the world, other critics, such as Olga Sedakova, argue that Pushkin's works present a complex world vision that allows for ambiguity and the freedom of individual interpretation.

REPRESENTATIVE WORKS

Thomas Arnold

The Christian Duty of Granting the Claims of the Roman Catholics (essay) 1829
Sermons. 3 vols. (sermons) 1829-34
Principles of Church Reform (essay) 1833
Christian Life; Its Course, Its Hindrances, Its Helps (sermons) 1841
Christian Life; Its Hopes, Its Fears, and Its Close (sermons) 1842
Sermons Chiefly on the Interpretation of the Scripture (sermons) 1845

Jane Austen

Sense and Sensibility (novel) 1811
Pride and Prejudice (novel) 1813
Emma (novel) 1816

Charlotte Brontë

Jane Eyre; an Autobiography [as Currer Bell] (novel) 1847

Robert Browning

Christmas-Eve and Easter-Day (poetry) 1850

Thomas Carlyle

Sartor Resartus (prose) 1833-34; published in the journal *Fraser's Magazine*; published in book form, 1836
On Heroes, Hero-Worship, and the Heroic in History (lectures) 1841

Anton Chekhov

Skazki Mel'pomeny (short stories) 1884
Pestrye rasskazy (short stories) 1886
Nevinnye rechi (short stories) 1887
V sumerkakh: Ocherki i rasskazy (short stories) 1887
Rasskazy (short stories) 1888
Detvora (short stories) 1889
The Black Monk, and Other Stories [translated by R. E. C. Long] (short stories) 1903
The Kiss, and Other Stories [translated by Long] (short stories) 1908
Stories of Russian Life [translated by Marian Fell] (short stories) 1914
The Bet, and Other Stories [translated by S. S. Koteliansky, J. M. Murry, and J. W. Luce] (short stories) 1915
Russian Silhouettes: More Stories of Russian Life [translated by Fell] (short stories) 1915

The Steppe, and Other Stories [translated by Adeline Lister Kaye] (short stories) 1915
The Darling, and Other Stories (short stories) 1916
The Duel, and Other Stories (short stories) 1916
The Tales of Tchehov. 13 vols. (short stories) 1916-23
Collected Works. 5 vols. (short stories) 1987
Anton Chekhov: Later Short Stories, 1888-1903 (short stories) 1999
The Comic Stories (short stories) 1999
The Complete Early Short Stories of Anton Chekhov (short stories) 2001
The Undiscovered Chekhov: Fifty-One New Stories (short stories) 2001

Charles Dickens

*The Life of Our Lord (juvenilia) 1934

Benjamin Disraeli

Tancred; or, The New Crusade. 3 vols. (novel) 1847

Fyodor Dostoevsky

Zapiski iz podpol'ya [*Notes from Underground*] (novel) 1862; also translated as *Letters from the Underworld*
Brat'ya Karamazovy [*The Brothers Karamazov*] (novel) 1880

George Eliot

The Life of Jesus, Critically Examined. Translated from the Fourth German Edition. 3 vols. [translator; as Marian Evans] (essay) 1846
"The Essence of Christianity" [translator; as Evans] (essay) 1854
Scenes of Clerical Life (novel) 1858
Romola (novel) 1863

Ralph Waldo Emerson

Essays (essays) 1838; also published as *Essays: First Series,* 1854
Essays: Second Series (essays) 1844

Elizabeth Cleghorn Gaskell

Mary Barton: A Tale of Manchester Life (novel) 1848
Ruth (novel) 1853
North and South (novel) 1855
The Letters of Mrs. Gaskell (letters) 1967

Thomas Hughes

Tom Brown's School Days [published anonymously] (novel) 1857; also published as *Schooldays at Rugby*

Anna Jameson

Sacred and Legendary Art. 2 vols. (criticism) 1848
Legends of the Monastic Orders, as Represented in the Fine Arts (nonfiction) 1850
Legends of the Madonna, as Represented in the Fine Arts (nonfiction) 1852
The History of Our Lord (nonfiction) 1864

John Keble

The Christian Year: Thoughts in Verse for the Sundays and Holydays throughout the Year. 2 vols. [published anonymously] (poetry) 1827

National Apostasy Considered in a Sermon Preached in St. Mary's, Oxford before His Majesty's Judge of Assize, on Sunday, July 14, 1833 (lecture) 1833

Tracts for the Times by Members of the University of Oxford. 6 vols. [with John Henry Newman, Alfred Menzies, Edward Bouverie Pusey, R. Hurrell Froude, and several others] (pamphlets) 1833-41

Lyra Apostolica (lectures) 1836

John Henry Newman

The Arians of the Fourth Century: Their Doctrine, Temper, and Conduct (history) 1833

An Essay on the Development of Christian Doctrine (essay) 1845

Apologia pro Vita Sua: Being a Reply to a Pamphlet Entitled "What, Then, Does Dr. Newman Mean?" (autobiography) 1865; also published as *History of My Religious Opinions*

An Essay in Aid of a Grammar of Assent (essay) 1870

The Via Media of the Anglican Church, Illustrated in Lectures, Letters, and Tracts Written between 1830 and 1841. 2 vols. (theology) 1877

Florence Nightingale

Suggestions for Thought to Searchers after Religious Truth. 2 vols. [published anonymously] (essays) 1860

Suggestions for Thought to the Searchers after Truth among the Artizans of England [published anonymously] (essays) 1860

Walter Pater

Marius the Epicurean: His Sensations and Ideas. 2 vols. (novel) 1885

Edward Bouverie Pusey

Remarks on the Prospective and Past Benefits of Cathedral Institutions, in the Promotion of Sound Religious Knowledge, Occasioned by Lord Henley's Plan for Their Abolition (lectures) 1833

A Letter to His Grace the Archbishop of Canterbury, on Some Circumstances Connected with the Present Crisis in the English Church (letter) 1842

The Holy Eucharist: A Comfort to the Penitent (sermon) 1843

The Royal Supremacy Not an Arbitrary Authority But Limited by the Laws of the Church, of Which Kings Are Members (theology) 1850

The Real Presence of the Body and Blood of Our Lord Jesus Christ, the Doctrine of the English Church, with a Vindication of the Reception by the Wicked and of the Adoration of Our Lord Jesus Christ, Truly Present (theology) 1857

Alexander Pushkin

Kapitanskaia dochka [*The Captain's Daughter; or, The Generosity of the Russian Usurper Pugatscheff*] (novella) 1836

Table Talk (essays) 1857

Poems by Alexander Pushkin (poetry) 1888

The Poems, Prose, and Plays of Alexander Pushkin (poetry, plays, short stories, and novellas) 1936

Polnoe sobranie sochienii. 16 vols. (poetry, plays, short stories, novellas, novels, essays, criticism, and letters) 1937-49

Pushkin's Poems (poetry) 1945

Mark Rutherford

Catharine Furze (novel) 1893

Isaac Taylor

Natural History of Enthusiasm (history) 1829

Ancient Christianity, and the Doctrines of the Oxford Tracts for the Times. 2 vols. (history) 1839-42

Alfred, Lord Tennyson

In Memoriam (poem) 1850

Mrs. Humphry Ward

Robert Elsmere. 3 vols. (novel) 1888

W. G. Ward

The Ideal of a Christian Church Considered in Comparison with Existing Practice; Containing a Defence of Certain Articles in the British Critic in Reply to Remarks on Them in Mr. Palmer's "Narrative" (theology) 1844

Nicholas Wiseman

"Anglican Claims to Apostolical Succession" (essay) 1839; published in the journal *Dublin Review*

*This work was written in 1848.

OVERVIEWS

Royal W. Rhodes (essay date 1995)

SOURCE: Rhodes, Royal W. "Introduction: The Church of the Fathers and Victorian Religious Controversy." In *The Lion and the Cross: Early Christianity in Victorian Novels,* pp. 1-29. Columbus: Ohio State University Press, 1995.

[*In the following essay, an introduction to his book, Rhodes traces the various stages in the Victorian debate over interpretations of Christianity.*]

For all who might wish to acquire the current controversial small-talk without the labor of reading grave
works of theology, the press was about to provide abundant instruction in the shape of novels and story-books,
illustrating the doctrines and practices of the newly-
risen "ism." And now a very extensive literature of this
kind has grown up among us, exhibiting the "movement" and the "development" in all their phases, and
adding largely to the materials which must be mastered
by the future Church historian who would qualify himself for describing the workings of the late controversies on the mind of our generation.

—George Eliot, "Religious Stories," *Fraser's
Magazine* (1848)

So wrote the Victorian author George Eliot (Mary Ann
Evans, 1819-80) in surveying the growing number of
didactic novels and tales by writers of different religious persuasions. Within that body of literature, the
Early Church novel is a distinct subgenre that has been
commented upon by a variety of literary historians and
critics. As helpful as their work is, their understanding
of the Victorian religious novel needs revision. A neglected aspect of this literature, but one that remains the
chief reason for undertaking the continued study of
these novels, is their preoccupation with the controverted doctrines and partisan religious issues of the period, masked by antique settings. No Victorian writer
was untouched by these contemporary issues, whether
they identified themselves or have been identified as
"religious" authors. A number of writers, however, can
be identified in terms of their specific churchmanship.
The disputed theological questions of the day became
in the hands of such authors—Anglicans, Dissenters,
and Roman Catholics—the substance of novels meant
to portray the distinctive features of the ideal Church,
conceived variously by the contending religious parties.
Delineating the polemical and propaganda value of the
many novels in this category, showing their links to
particular issues, and marking the shifting stances of individual authors and religious groups within the period
put a strain on both the writer and the reader of this
study. If one approaches the novels in terms of the
churchmanship of their authors, however, one can use
this material as an array of highly significant and articulate documents for the study of Church history, documents that show vividly the rapid pace of movements
of thought within the Victorian Age and the highly
charged emotional pulse of the religious debate. Those
churchly issues grew, root and branch, as a direct result
of the Oxford Movement, blending theology and Romanticism and raising the level of religious disputation
by its heightened historical consciousness. In the Early
Church novel High Church Anglican writers found a
valuable instrument for their program of religious reform; it is necessary, therefore, to examine the complex
relationships between the Oxford Movement and the literary program undertaken by various theological writers. For authority they appealed to Scripture and the

tradition of antiquity; it is necessary, then, to discuss
their understanding of those sources, of antiquity, and
of contemporary criticism of that appeal.

The Oxford Movement and Literature

The Oxford Movement (1833-45), that flowering of the
Anglo-Catholic Revival in the Church of England, continues to be a rich source of scholarly investigation as a
religious, social, and political phenomenon. This is true
partly because the movement attracted the attention and
sometimes the allegiance of the best minds and most
dynamic personalities of nineteenth-century Britain.
The important historiographical interpretations of the
movement, beginning in the Victorian era itself, re-
emerging with new vigor for the centennial, and continuing with altered perspectives to our own day, demonstrate the range of approaches to the study of the
Anglo-Catholic Revival as a dramatic episode in Church
history. The movement has also been seen by both its
adherents and opponents as an exercise of formidable
literary virtuosity; Walter E. Houghton's masterful elu-
cidation of the rhetorical toils of John Henry Newman's
Apologia, for example, confirmed that evaluation. Although some critics have stressed discontinuity with the
literary aspirations of the epoch, generally the movement is now readily understood as an influential channel, in both its aesthetic forms and sensibilities, for
transmitting Romanticism throughout the nineteenth
century. In the partisan view of Newman's close friend
Frederic Rogers, Tractarianism offered, in place of the
aesthetic and emotional famine of the Evangelical
school, "a religion which did not reject, but aspired to
embody in itself, any form of art and literature . . .
which could be pressed into the service of Christianity."[1] Therefore, an important task of the Church historian, investigating those personal, confessional, and
ecclesiastical questions that shaped the revival, remains
to examine portions of that massive literary productiv-
ity and to relate it to the personal and religious concerns of the various authors and to their culture and society at large. This is exactly the challenge set by
George Eliot in 1848.

The present investigation will deal with specific examples of religious-historical novels in Victorian England, novels and tales depicting the Roman Empire
and the Early Church from New Testament times down
to the sixth-century mission of Augustine to Britain.
This sub-genre of Romantic literature, popularized by
Edward Bulwer-Lytton and Walter Pater among others,
has received some attention from those literary historians interested in the development of the novel. This has
been part of a more extensive critical examination of
the theoretical base of historical fiction and the revolutionary development of historical consciousness in the
nineteenth century with its new historical outlook: historicism. It is enough to remark that historical trends

played a crucial role in enlivening the understanding of Victorian England about its organic unity with the historical phenomena of its past. Thus, in 1850 Lord Palmerston defended in Parliament his gunboat diplomacy by voicing this Romantic sense of national identity and imperial aspiration in the ringing phrase: "Civis Romanus sum." The mantle of empire had been transferred to the last outpost of that empire; in some respects the Britons were more Roman than the Romans. Such an awareness, fed by popular culture as well as by the traditions of classical education, merged with religious interests to promote a wide readership for this type of novel, in which the Victorians "looked upon the face of Caesar."[2]

While recognizing religious elements in many of the novels produced during this period, only a few investigators have tried to relate systematically this fictionalized material to the theological concerns of their authors or to the pressing religious questions of the day. Some have related these questions only in general terms to major movements and trends of ideas, for example, Raymond Chapman's theoretical identification of such fiction with the Oxford Movement. But historical novels, rooted not only in historiographical works but also in "tracts for the times," pamphlets, sermons, cautionary tales, personal memoirs, and converts' confessions, should be aligned with the particular concerns of the Victorian pulpit and political platform.[3]

From the great number of religious-historical novels produced during the Victorian era, this study treats selectively re-creations of the Ancient or Primitive Church from Apostolic and Subapostolic times down through the first six Christian centuries, the Church of the Fathers, East and West. These examples are used as literary-historical sources to track shifts in the religious understanding and sensibilities of the nineteenth century. They share concerns found in secular or nonconfessional examples of historical fiction: criticism of contemporary culture and society, a sense of historical nostalgia, a deep sense of nationhood, various Romantic literary devices, and a proclivity toward sensationalism, to name a few corresponding elements. But the religious or churchly novels reflect much more their authors' theological concerns and the changing questions of the contemporary religious debate: the authority of Church and Scripture, tradition and apostolic succession, conversion and apostasy, faith and doubt, and the relation of Church and State. Regarding the question of authority alone, the important, though not exclusive, appeal to Christian antiquity and the Apostolic Church finds dynamic, imaginative response in these works. This has to be related, not only to the broad movements of thought, such as the Oxford Movement or Ritualism, but also to the specific concerns of the various authors, concerns and study not purely theological but historical as well. The ecclesiastical authors ex-

amined here should be viewed as literary witnesses, sometimes programmatic, sometimes unwitting, to controverted theological positions, to the deepest concerns within their own or other Church parties, and specifically to various aspects of the Anglican/Roman Catholic debate. Religious issues, not purely historiographical or literary ones, generated this literature and set it inevitably in a polemical context.[4]

In the Victorian era earlier historical epochs had become badges of religious party; for example, the seventeenth-century Civil War and the figures of King Charles I and Oliver Cromwell functioned in that emblematic way, as did the Reformation period and the perennially riveting personalities of the Tudor dynasty. On one side, James Anthony Froude, sometime Tractarian sympathizer, in the first of four volumes of his *History of England from 1529 to the Death of Elizabeth* (1856-70) defended the English Reformers against the Whig interpretations of Hallam and Macaulay and the disdain of some Tractarians, including his deceased older brother Hurrell, the close friend of Newman. Froude, largely innocent of dogmatic theology, saw the Reformation in political and philosophical terms as England's unshackling from a foreign potentate and from intellectual enslavement.[5] Against Norman and Stewart absolutism, Froude and later historians, at times quite tendentiously, raised the standard of Saxon democratic institutions down through English history.[6] Later in the century, E. A. Freeman reiterated this view: "We have reformed by calling to life again the institutions of earlier and ruder times, by setting ourselves free from the slavish subtleties of Norman lawyers, by casting aside as an accursed thing the innovations of Tudor tyranny and Stewart usurpation."[7] Therefore, reform, whether of the sixteenth or nineteenth century, was viewed by many influential Victorians in politicized terms, not without definite repercussions for the state of religion in the land. On the other side of the question, the appeal to the Caroline divines and beyond them to antiquity became the particular badge of the Tractarians, who were intent on fostering a "new Reformation" in the State Church. Various historical projects, for example, the Library of the Fathers of the Holy Catholic Church (St. Bartholomew's Day, 1838 to 1885), begun under the joint editorship of John Henry Newman, John Keble, and Edward Bouverie Pusey, provided an enduring contribution to theological scholarship. At times uncritical and unhistorical in their use of the past,[8] the Tractarians sought to defend a particular historical view, contributing to the general appeal to history. Although Newman in 1844 admonished himself in the front of the preliminary notebooks for his *Essay on Development,* "Write it historically, not argumentively," the use of history by him and others was inherently and by necessity polemical.[9]

As religiously minded people in the Victorian era looked for the bases of belief and religious authority, concerned with certainty and security, an anachronistic view and portrayal of the Ancient Church played an important role. Even as tastes changed through this period, readers looked for no mere costume dramas, but for the type of tales of religious introspection and confession they were enjoying in other "theological romances" and even "boilers down."[10] On the other hand, this return to the Early Church was mutually understood as an attempt to judge, respectively, the Roman and Reformation churches against the purity of the ancient and undivided Christian community: "Our appeal was to antiquity—to the doctrine which the Fathers and Councils and Church universal had taught from the creeds."[11] Such historical appeals were sometimes viewed by Evangelicals as an ignominious betrayal of Protestant principles. Liberal churchmen considered them irrelevant to the pressing social and religious needs of the nineteenth century.

These novels, however, cannot be viewed merely as tendentious history or sentimental expressions of piety. Although many of them are both, they are also important glosses on the diverse theological and historical books of their authors, on the popular and critical views of religious issues, on the hagiographical style and archaeological interests of the nineteenth century, and on the spirituality of the age. In terms of what peculiar insights they give into this age generally, they provide fresh evidence for the view that Newman's departure from the Anglican church in 1845 was only a false ending to the Oxford Movement. What had begun as a defense of the high Anglican doctrine of the Church vis-à-vis its subjection to the parliamentary State took on new colors in a continuing theological and ecclesiastical effort to develop the Anglo-Catholic understanding of the English Church. That understanding, shaped by confrontation with an intellectually combative Roman Catholicism and renewed hierarchy in England and by party debate within the Anglican Church, continued to turn to antiquity for justification, just as did the opponents of both groups. That historical appeal, satirized by Newman in the alleged titles of books appropriate for an Anglo-Catholic library—"Lays of the Apostles," "The English Church Older Than the Roman," and "Anglicanism of the Early Martyrs"—developed and sharpened after 1845.[12] This study examines those ecclesiastical motivations which have been incompletely explained or ignored in purely literary studies and will treat a variety of little known Anglican and Roman Catholic authors. Because the Non-Conformists stressed Scripture alone, their spokesmen were not conspicuously involved in the development of literary treatments of the Subapostolic age, although a few will be mentioned in passing.

In particular, the novels provide valuable information not immediately identifiable in the other theological and historical works of the authors. They show the angle, sometimes direct, more often oblique, at which Victorians pursued the major religious questions of the day through crisis and calm. One ready example is the Gorham case (1848-50), which is not so important for an understanding of Victorian belief about baptismal regeneration in infants, the doctrinal point that initiated the dispute, but is essential for understanding the Erastian relationship of State and Established Church, whether bishops or Parliament should decide which doctrines must be affirmed by a duly ordained priest in the Church of England. The dynamics of the claim to apostolic, independent spiritual authority that occupied a variety of church bodies in Britain and the Continent during this period appears in the novels in terms of the doctrines, ritual, and polity of the Christian Church confronting the Roman Empire and the emerging barbarian nations. The rival religions to Christianity in that empire, pagan cults, Hellenistic philosophy, and proselytizing Judaism are transmogrified in the novels from the secularism, philosophical humanism, and Jewish/Zionist questions of the day. The contemporary Victorian debate over asceticism, ritualism, and biblical-historical criticism is articulated afresh with an appeal to antiquity. And just as Edward Gibbon and the Enlightenment had largely deeschatologized the Christian message, so the novels reflect in a unique way the nineteenth century's reeschatologizing of that gospel, raising new perspectives on the questions of prophecy, revelation, miracles, and martyrdoms by using a variety of literary skills to introduce apocalyptic themes and images into Victorian religious discourse. Perhaps most important, the novels document a historic shift in the consciousness of Christian believers facing the growing secularism and humanistic challenge to orthodoxy; the appeal to the ancient apologetics of a minority church is seen as a direct parallel to the Victorian condition. The Early Church of the Fathers, then, addresses Christians across the millennia with a new immediacy. Like the Victorians themselves, we must now turn to the Fathers in order to examine the varied methods and complex motives that pressed the churchly authors to re-create the Early Church in novels. Why, apart from treatments in sermons, tracts, and theological treatises, were the authors compelled to portray the Church of the Fathers in this genre? What gains and losses did this strategy engender? To answer these questions it will be necessary to survey briefly the positions of Victorian proponents and opponents of an appeal to antiquity and then comment on possible reasons why the novel was chosen as a suitable vehicle for ecclesiastical programs and propaganda.

The appeal to antiquity, formulated during the Victorian religious debate, can be mapped in two distinct ways. First, one can catalogue the tremendously important discoveries of new texts, which provided fresh information about the past. The discovery in 1875 of the *Didache,* rich in detailed instructions for the life and liturgy of an Early Christian community, is one prime example. The information from such discoveries, however, did not always enter into the novels. An extensive bibliography could also be done showing the new editions and translations made available to the informed Victorian public. For this learned circle the Church of the Fathers as a concept changed significantly between 1845 and 1875. The second way to penetrate into this area is to trace the shifting meanings that contemporary writers applied to such key terms as *the Primitive Church, the Apostolic Church,* and *the Church of the Fathers.* What this study will refer to generally as Early Christianity was referred to by Victorian writers in several ways, undergoing redefinition throughout the period. There is, moreover, a pronounced oscillation in their use of such language. Whereas High Church novelists used the *Ancient Church, Primitive Church,* and *Church of the Fathers* interchangeably—as did Roman Catholic writers, who also employed the term *Patrology* almost exclusively—Evangelicals and the more liberal Broad Churchmen had long adopted the vocabulary and distinctions used on the Continent in Protestant circles. In referring to the Primitive Church, what German theologians called the "Urkirche," the Evangelical and Broad Church novelists meant the Christian Church up to the close of the New Testament Canon. The place of the second-century Apologists, such as Justin Martyr and Irenaeus, is hard to define without the modern understanding of strata in Scripture, even strata in the strata shown by form criticism and redaction criticism. Broad Churchmen, however, were more willing than their Evangelical colleagues to argue for the continued inspiration of the Apologists. The High Church inclusiveness in terminology was part of a doctrinal stance in regard to the apostolicity of the entire epoch of the Early Church; Evangelicals and Broad Churchmen demonstrated by their exclusive distinctions their leaning toward Scripture alone and their opposition to Anglo-Catholic beliefs.

A striking feature of the Oxford Movement, a feature commented on in studies and interpretations of the era, was its appeal to the Fathers, a bipartite appeal immediately to the seventeenth-century Caroline divines and mediately through them to the Fathers of the Primitive Church.[13] They were by no means the first or sole advocates of such an appeal. Thomas Chalmers, the leader of the Great Disruption in Scotland (1843), argued from similar authorities in *On Respect Due to Antiquity* as his basis for the church's independence from Erastian programs, which placed the church in the control of the State. The spiritual heirs of the Scottish Non-Jurors, the Hutchinsonians, and later the Hackney Phalanx, all historic opponents to state control, were the fathers of the Tractarians in such appeals. Even the rationalist prime minister Lord Melbourne (1779-1848) dabbled in patristic literature as a hobby. With an earnest intensity characteristic of the age, the thought of the Fathers was mined to answer the burning new questions of the day, questions on the best form of church government, on the nature of prophecy and revelation, and on the nature and function of Christ. Any investigation of the sort presented here should remind the reader of how much still remains to be known about the Victorian use of the Fathers in terms of sources and texts available, methods of interpretation, and theological utility as they conceived it.

Using an inverted form of the canon found in the *Commonitory* of Vincent of Lerins (ca. 434), "quod semper, quod ubique, quod ab omnibus" [what is believed always, everywhere, and by all],[14] as the criteria for what constituted orthodox tradition, the Tractarians attempted to make the English branch of the Catholic Church a *via media* between what they regarded as Protestant neglect of tradition and Roman Catholic innovations. Another signal contribution of the Tractarians in this regard was the extensive publication of extracts of the Fathers, *catenae* of quotations addressing controverted doctrinal points, and the larger enterprise of patristic translations, The Library of the Fathers, continued under the editorship of Dr. Pusey and Charles Marriott after Newman's departure. The Library constituted the first comprehensive corpus of patristic texts in English translation.[15] A wide audience could thus read the Fathers for themselves and test the doctrines and practices contained therein.

What were the Victorians finding when they did look into the storehouse of antiquity? First of all, they thought they could without difficulty grasp the "mind and purpose of the old Fathers" and from this clear perspective establish the measure by which to judge or vindicate controverted theological points in the present age. Of equal importance, they found that the Fathers confirmed the Articles, liturgy, and canons of the Anglican Church in terms of its "Antiquity, Catholicity, and Universality." While the Church of England diverged from this ancient model on some points, felt by the investigators to be therefore external and not of the *esse,* the vital essence, of the church, they found the Fathers and the Church of England speaking with one voice on the continuity of received truth in Scripture, protected and maintained by the apostolic succession of bishops, dubbed the "historic episcopate" later in the century.

Based on the patristic sources, the Tractarians, Evangelicals, and Broad Churchmen, with varying degrees of emphasis, accepted one canon of Scripture, two testaments of equal authority and plenary inspiration, three creeds (the Apostles', Nicene, and Athanasian), and four Ecumenical Councils (Nicaea, Constantinople, Ephesus, and Chalcedon). To this array Tractarians added emphasis on five centuries of purity, the *consensus quinquesaecularis* down to the mission of Augustine of Canterbury in 597, six Ecumenical Councils "allowed and received" (Constantinople II and III were added to the earlier list), seven ecclesiastical centuries "of great authority and credit," and eleven centuries of Christian unity between East and West.

Richard Hooker's (ca. 1554-1600) understanding of the intimate relationship of Scripture, reason, and tradition was a convenient shorthand for these Victorians sorting out the respective claims of Fathers and Reformers. The Fathers were honored because they came in time near the composition of Scripture, demonstrated the mind of that Scripture, and received uncorrupted the apostolic traditions. Although by the 1850s Anglicans recognized the divergence in local traditions of the historic pentarchy, the five ancient patriarchates, an awareness brought by research into and contact with the Eastern Orthodox churches, they still tended to homogenize their view of the several centers of early Christianity under the rubric *the undivided Church.* Along with the Vincentian canon and the Ecumenical Councils, the consensus of the Fathers was seen as a representative guide but not an infallible one. In contrast to the company of the apostles, there was no parity of authority among respective Fathers. Moderate Churchmen picked up and read Augustine with more impact than when they might chance to read Ephraem the Syrian. Even the language of orthodox Fathers was thought to present dangers in the Victorian age, since it could be misconstrued to encompass Roman "corruptions." Pusey's university sermon (14 May 1843) on the "Real Objective Presence of Christ in the Eucharist," written chiefly in the language of the Fathers—in particular Cyril of Jerusalem and John Chrysostom—was condemned by university authorities and Pusey was suspended from preaching for two years.

The position of the Council of Trent (1545-63), which Anglicans understood to set up the Fathers as an authoritative source independent of Scripture, was rejected. Nor were the Fathers to be viewed as providing an exact pattern of church life and worship binding for all time. Even the old High Church liturgiologists had freely deviated from ancient usages to create their own patterns of celebration. The Fathers were considered a positive force in shaping the English Reformation but were not a binding theological authority. This attitude was vividly expressed in the decision of Stephen Lushington, Dean of Arches, the magistrate in the case of Rowland Williams under prosecution for his allegedly heterodox article regarding biblical criticism in *Essays and Reviews* (1860). The earlier ecclesiastical censure

was nullified, since the court could make a determination only on the basis of the legal formularies of the Establishment, and not on the basis of Scripture, the doctrines of the Ancient Church, or the consensus of divines.[16] For decades controversialists had asked whether the Anglican Church could be said to possess the Christian faith as transmitted by the Fathers. In 1846 T. W. Allies, a Tractarian, had resolved the question in the affirmative in his work *The Church of England Cleared from the Charge of Schism,* and then turned dramatically volte-face in 1850. The final legal decisions over the Gorham case (1848-50), involving the linked questions of baptismal regeneration and Erastianism; the Denison case (1856-58), concerning eucharistic worship and belief in a real presence; and the turmoil over *Essays and Reviews* (1860-62), involving the new criticism, forced a number of Anglicans to accept Newman's verdict that the via media and its continuity with the Church of the Fathers was only a "paper system," at best a mere creature of the State. They were forced to this extreme because it seemed to them that the courts had systematically excluded the Fathers as a basis for Anglican belief; and it was believed by some that Church authorities in condemning the Tractarians had inadvertently condemned the Fathers. Other Anglicans, however, continued to implement changes based on patristic models that had not been immediately conceptualized or systematized into a theology of Anglo-Catholicism of the type seen later in Charles Gore (1853-1932), Henry Scott Holland (1847-1918), Darwell Stone (1859-1941), and Charles Lindley Wood— Viscount Halifax (1839-1934).

FROUDE, KEBLE, AND PUSEY

The Tractarians and their early sympathizers were far from unanimous about the appeal to the consensus of Anglican divines and the Early Church. Samuel Wilberforce, the bishop of Oxford (1845-69) and termed by some "the High Church incarnate," agreed for a time with the Tractarians and admitted the validity of such an appeal to the Caroline divines and the initial three centuries of the Christian era, before cautiously reconsidering.[17]

R. Hurrell Froude (1803-36), the Fellow of Oriel who brought Newman and John Keble to understand each other and sealed their mutual friendship, was, according to Frederic Rogers, the one who first christened the members of the movement "Apostolicals." Along with another Oriel Fellow, John Davison, Froude sought from the early Fathers a general perspective as well as specific vindication of his own theological ideas. In 1827 he found support for his affirmation of celibacy in the works of Ignatius of Antioch; the Fathers were seen, then, as supportive and regulative insofar as they confirmed the present religious outlook of the inquirer.[18] Although he encouraged Newman's own patristic research,

Froude diverged on the prominence of the role to be played by the Church of the Fathers. "[H]e was," says Newman, "powerfully drawn to the Medieval Church, but not to the Primitive."[19]

John Keble (1792-1866), whose Assize Sermon of 1833 defending the "successors of the Apostles" in the suppressed Irish bishoprics is credited with launching the Oxford Movement, believed the Anglican Church was the one true representative in England of the whole Church, Catholic and Apostolic; it was not an impersonal institution but "one's own Nursing Mother and one-third of Christendom." On the other hand, since he admitted the broken nature of that Catholic identity, it is sometimes easy to caricature Keble's position as a defense of "the one true parish." His Assize Sermon was not, however, merely an attack on the "National Apostasy" resulting from or causing the government's suppression of redundant dioceses in Ireland. It was a declaration of the "external security" served by the apostolic succession, safeguarding an unwavering communion with the Church of the Apostles and preventing Roman "novelties" (e.g., the doctrine of transubstantiation) and Protestant infidelity, which were both due to excessive "rationalism."[20] After 1827 enforced leisure permitted him to study the early Fathers, such as Cyprian, and allusions to these authors appeared in his momentously best-selling collection of verses, *The Christian Year* (1827).[21] That verse, likened by some critics to Wordsworth rewritten for pious ladies, and his Latin lectures as professor of poetry at Oxford (1831-41) point out the relationship between Romantic epistemology and Keble's sometimes quirky brand of Tractarian sacramentalism.

The theory of language and symbol contained in the works of Bishop Butler and William Wordsworth (a historical and hereditary usage transmitted in analogy, metaphor, and symbol, compared to the ahistoric, analytic use of language in Bacon and Hobbes) was for Keble preparation for a reclamation of the symbolic mode of thought of the Fathers, especially the Alexandrians.[22] Along with his editorship of The Library of the Fathers, Keble also published a translation of Irenaeus' *Against Heresies* (1872). Early on he was requested to do the volume on Bede in the Lives of the English Saints.[23] Keble was, of course, more actively engaged in the new edition of Richard Hooker, praising the judicious Elizabethan divine who withdrew from Thomas Cranmer's position and drew near William Laud: through that latter worthy archbishop, Providence, by overruling the *sola scriptura* excesses of the Reformation, left the way open to a restoration of ante-Nicene antiquity.[24] Apostolic succession, the sacrificial nature of the Eucharist, and the triune God were doctrines not found systematically manifest in Scripture, but nonetheless binding on the faithful. In the summer of 1836 Keble preached his famous sermon at Winchester Ca-

thedral "Primitive Tradition Recognized in Holy Scripture." He declared that the tradition of the Fathers was parallel to, and not merely derivative from, Scripture. It was the Fathers who provided the context of the composition and reception of those writings; "the Scriptures themselves," he stated, "do homage to the tradition of the Apostles."[25] For Keble that tradition was complete and authoritative from primitive times. He followed the understanding of both the Magdeburg *Centuries* and the *Annales*: truth is immutable; it has not, indeed cannot, improve, evolve, change, or develop. The modern age only rediscovers that original deposit of faith. He criticized Robert Isaac Wilberforce in 1850 for adopting the "abstract," "metaphysical," and "legal" theory of development of Newman "instead of clinging to Scripture and to primitive antiquity."[26] When Keble finally did read Newman's *Essay on Development* for himself in 1863, his horror was confirmed: "It must come to development after all . . . to a pretty theory instead of Catholic Tradition."[27] The vicar of Hursley had reworked Newman's charge that the via media was not real but only a "paper system" into what, for Keble, was a telling argument against Newman.

The Library of the Fathers remains a monument, *aere perennius,* to the financial sacrifice as well as to the scholarly care of Edward Bouverie Pusey (1800-82), the first "name" to be joined to the Tracts, since he was then professor of Hebrew at Oxford (1828-82). For many the name of Pusey itself meant antiquity, as Keble explained to Bishop Wilberforce in 1851.[28] The Fathers illuminated for Pusey correct theological opinion but were not themselves authoritative. In Tract 18, "Thoughts on the Benefits of the System of Fasting, Enjoined by Our Church" (1833), Pusey viewed the 1549 Edwardian Prayer Book as a visible link uniting the English Church with "the Primitive Catholic Church." Like the Fathers, the Prayer Book had no independent authority but transmitted faith and devotions to the contemporary Church. This connection between the Fathers and the formularies and authorized texts of the English Church is reiterated in Pusey's reason for choosing selections from the Fathers to be read by the Anglican Sisterhood revived under his direction. The Fathers are those "whom our Homilies so praise."[29] On this point Pusey and most of the other Tractarians parted ways. To Pusey, as to the Reverend Sir George Prevost among others, the Reformation was a true reform, repudiating Roman corruption and recalling the purity of the Primitive Church. Pusey could with equanimity offer to subscribe to the Martyrs' Memorial (1838-41) to the sixteenth-century bishops Cranmer, Latimer, and Ridley, looked upon by most as a scheme to exalt the Reformation and deliberately embarrass the Tractarians; he showed none of Froude's shuddering contempt for the Reformers. As he told Newman: "We owe our peculiar position as adherents of primitive antiquity to them."[30] There were certain elements Pusey unearthed in the fervid course of his "high-pitched devoted patristicism," such as the prayers of ancient martyrs to and for the dead, that ran counter to Reformation principles and that shocked his Anglican contemporaries.[31] But late in the century, especially as he mulled over the dangerous principles he detected in the First Vatican Council decrees, Pusey lamented the "lull" in theological debate and the general neglect of the Fathers by "the young clergy so ignorant of antiquity as not to know the difficulty."[32] When the vast publishing project of the Library of the Fathers reached its conclusion, fewer people were bothering to read the Fathers provided for them.

NEWMAN AND THE ROMAN CATHOLICS

When Ignaz Döllinger (1799-1890), the scholarly Roman Catholic opponent of Ultramontanism, described John Henry Newman (1801-90) as the greatest living authority on the first three centuries of the Christian era, it was in response to the latter's *Essay on Development* and the seventeen years of patristic research behind it, research that exploded the unhistorical notions of the reactionary Catholic Ultramontanists.[33] Since boyhood Newman had been fascinated with the Fathers; at the time of his conversion in 1816, a conversion to Evangelical faith, a copy of Joseph Milner's five-volume *History of the Church of Christ* (1794-1819) had delighted him with extensive extracts from Augustine, Ambrose, and others.[34] At the same time, a reading of Thomas Newton's *Dissertations on the Prophecies* (1754) convinced him that the pope was the predicted Antichrist. Renewing his interest in these sources in the late 1820s, he started to read chronologically, beginning with Ignatius and Justin Martyr. But as he later observed, he approached them the wrong way: "I had read them simply on Protestant ideas, analyzed and catalogued them on Protestant principles of division, and hunted for Protestant doctrines and usages in them." The one vivid impression he kept from that initial foray into the dense patristic literature had profound meaning for contemporary ecclesiological questions: the divine institution of the episcopate.

In 1831, requested by Hugh Rose, the High Church rector of Hadleigh, to write on the early Councils, Newman concentrated on Nicaea, the beginning of a "drama in three acts."[35] The result was published in 1833 as *The Arians of the Fourth Century*. That same year, after the Assize Sermon, he likened John Keble confronting the power of the State to Ambrose opposing the emperor Theodosius. This dramatic use of "realized' analogy, where likeness becomes identity, simile becomes symbol, was Newman's distinctive style in treating the Fathers. No other Anglican was startled awake from haunted dreams to see in his own looking glass the grim visage of an Arian or Monophysite.[36] What had startled Newman, he later claimed, was the aggressive Catholic apologetics of Nicholas Wiseman, beginning

in 1836 and culminating in an article in the *Dublin Review,* "Anglican Claims to Apostolical Succession" (1839), which contained the magical phrase of Augustine, "securus judicat orbis terrarum." To Newman this appeared as a simpler method of deciding ecclesiastical questions, but he responded publicly to Wiseman that Augustine's principle was not a rigorous regulation without damaging exceptions. The only sure guide for the English Church, Newman decided, was its own traditional via media in adhering to Scripture and Christian antiquity alone. After his conversion he included a contradictory note in the revised edition (1877, 1883) of his work the *Via Media* that "history and patristical writings do not absolutely decide the truth and falsehood of all important theological propositions, any more than Scripture decides it . . . all that we can say is that history and the Fathers look in one determinate direction. The definition of the Church is commonly needed to supply the defects of logic."[37]

By 1840 Newman saw his task as one of adversary to Protestants who opposed the Church of the Fathers to the Apostolic Church or to those who said the Apostolic system was irretrievably lost. At the same time, since the Anglican Church was a branch of the one Catholic Church, it was necessary to demonstrate that its formularies could be interpreted according to the doctrine and practice of the Catholic Church since antiquity. He took it for granted that because the Church was founded by Christ, there never was a time since antiquity when it was not. "The Catholic Fathers and Ancient Bishops" had been lauded by the formulators of the Thirty-Nine Articles, so that formulary had to be at least "patient" of Catholic understanding. The explosive Tract XC resulted. The document and its hostile reception launched Newman and his disciples Romeward. Because the Anglican episcopate condemned the tract and seemingly its Catholic understanding of antiquity, Newman concluded that they had disinherited the English Church from the Early Church and broken the apostolic bond of antiquity, the rule of inward holiness and divine faith that had for so long been "miraculously preserved." Newman later unctuously criticized his Anglo-Catholic colleagues as "Patristico-Protestants" who had to use "private judgment" (the name at which every High Church knee quaked) in regard to the Fathers, since there was no formal ecclesial approbation by their bishops.[38]

In order to lay the ghost of his turmoil and to account for the apparent variations in the history of Christian dogma, during his retirement at Littlemore he began work on the *Essay on Development* (1845). He concluded that Protestantism was not historic Christianity, but the historical evidence was too fragmentary to identify it positively with Roman Catholicism. Using seven rigorous "tests" that he later amended to "notes," he concluded, "Primitive Christian history could only be understood in the light of later Christian history . . . isolated, the [early] expressions formed no system and pointed no where."[39] But since Christ founded an unfailing Divine Society, there must exist a visible Church in the nineteenth century that was historically the successor of the Church of the Fathers. That had to be the Church of Rome. Moving from intimations to accumulated probabilities to certainty, a process he later codified in his *Grammar of Assent* (1870), Newman made his leap of faith from this platform. It should be noted in passing that this process is a theological movement and not a strictly historical one. That is confirmed in the *Essay on Development* (chap. 2, sec. 3:5) by the introduction of those divine twins Ambrose and Athanasius, who are marvelously resuscitated to pass judgment hypothetically on the Victorian Church. Both were properly orthodox and both had bearded the State for interfering in ecclesiastical matters. Newman undoubtedly chose them as *examples* of the living "mind" of the Church; they would recognize not Canterbury but Rome as the living Catholic system. Newman substituted this "mind" for the Anglican use of the canon of Vincent of Lerins.

On the Continent, Roman Catholics were also deeply engaged in the study of the Fathers and Christian antiquities as part of a widespread Catholic Revival. The textual work of J.-P. Migne's *Patrologia* of Latin (1844-55) and Greek (1857-66) Fathers—built on and continuing the work of the Maurists Mabillon, Martène, and Ruinart and the archaeological discoveries and publications of J. B. DeRossi (1822-94), including the famed excavation of the catacomb of St. Callistus in 1852—provided the raw material for generations of other scholars.[40] Both Catholics and Protestants could warmly applaud Ignaz Döllinger's encyclopedic survey of the world of antiquity, his *Vestibule of Christianity,* which Newman had had translated at the Oratory, and his conservative study *The First Age of Christianity and the Church* (1860).[41] On the other hand, the Fathers of the Church were of particular usefulness in the confessional apologetics of this revived Continental Catholicism. Albert DeBroglie composed his painstaking history, *The Church and the Empire in the Fourth Century* (1856-66), because contemporary France required conversion, he thought, like the Roman Empire.[42] And François Auguste, vicomte de Chateaubriand (1768-1848), the grand Romantic author and statesman, used the literary and architectural remains of antiquity to "prove" the incompatibility of Protestantism with Primitive Christianity.[43]

The most famous name in this apologetic endeavor was, of course, Johann Adam Möhler (1796-1838), whose reading of the Fathers had been a personal revelation of an organic, spontaneous Christianity. Möhler made a mystical identification of contemporary believers and the Fathers and saw Enlightenment Deism as Arianism

and Romantic Pantheism as Sabellianism.[44] He wrote in 1825, "He who truly lives in the Church will also live in the first age of the Church and understand it; and he who does not live in the present Church will not live in the old and will not understand it, for they are the same."[45] In his *Symbolik* (1832) he aimed to prove that Protestantism was unfaithful to primitive Christianity. Although Newman cites Möhler in the *Essay on Development* (introduction, sec. 21) as a distinguished example of the use of the Fathers in controversial works, it seems unlikely that Newman read much of the Tübingen scholar during his Anglican career.[46] Newman's Romanizing disciples, W. G. Ward and Frederic Oakeley, whom Tom Mozley likened to the pugilistic Castor and Pollux, read the Romantic *Einheit* and dogmatic *Symbolik* with enthusiasm, finding there the notion that the only true test of Catholic doctrine was the moral experience to be had living that teaching.[47] It was this idea of a living and authoritative Church, in which the past was absorbed, perhaps consumed, by the present, that set off the understanding of dogma and ecclesiology of Continental Roman Catholicism from the movement in England. W. G. Ward's inflammatory *Ideal of a Christian Church* (1844) was as far from William Palmer's *Treatise on the Church* (1838) as the nineteenth century was from the fourth.

THE ARNOLDS, TAYLOR, SAVILLE

Of course not everyone was as sanguine as the Tractarians about the usefulness of patristic texts and study. Thomas Gaisford, dean of Christchurch and a director of the Oxford University Press, called the volumes of the Fathers in the House Library "sad and rubbish."[48] Benjamin Jowett (1817-93), master of Balliol and Broad Church Platonist, thought Voltaire had contributed more than all the Fathers. In 1839 Mark Pattison, who later contributed with Jowett to *Essays and Reviews,* lamented the time he squandered on "degenerate and semi-barbarous Christian writers of the Fourth Century."[49] The bitterness in Pattison's observation betrays the intensity of emotions involved in his own spiritual movement from Newmanism to skepticism, a movement critics of the Tracts claimed was inevitable. Even the publication of patristic texts, albeit with forceful, even tendentious notes, elicited sharp responses. The foundation of the Parker Society in 1844, named for the staunchly Protestant Matthew Parker (1504-75), archbishop of Canterbury, was with the Martyrs' Memorial a move to set the Reformers against the Fathers. Perhaps a desire to avoid such theological entanglements, as well as a scholarly bias, prompted the Oxford Press to print only Latin and Greek texts, but no English translations, of the Fathers.[50]

Other opponents saw this appeal as a "limited historicism," which seemed to be "a fear of development as a stubborn refusal to consider different opinions."[51] To these critics the appeal to the Fathers appeared as an inability to address or cope with the modern age, just as surely as the revived cult of asceticism was merely a mask for morbid hatred of the body and life, destroying the family and the State. Charles Kingsley satirized the archaicizing influence of the Tractarians in the fictional character Lord Vieuxbois, who states, "I do not think that we have any right in the nineteenth century to contest an opinion which the fathers of the Church gave in the fourth."[52] In such a case liberal churchmen believed that backward-glancing Victorian Christianity would become only a dead letter.

The Tractarian quest *ad fontes* enlisted the interest, if not always the allegiance, of numerous thoughtful enquirers into religious topics. Such immersion in the sources had profound effects, since it forced the investigators to "reflect on the psychology of historians and chroniclers; . . . exposed mere hagiography and pious tradition; . . . increased the student's sensitiveness to historic evidence and its presentation."[53] Primitive Christianity could appear to such minds as so much chaos as well as cosmos, horror as well as holiness. George Eliot (1819-80)—who among numerous accomplishments translated David Strauss's *Das Leben Jesu* (1846) and wrote a historical novel, *Romola* (in *Cornhill*, 1862-63) about Savonarola's Florence—attempted to construct, based on a linear theory of history, a chart of Early Church history with dates and names. Her research proved personally unedifying and undercut for her the notion of the absolute truth of Christianity.[54] For Eliot, as for other Victorians, once the received sense of the unity and coherence of the Early Church was disturbed, all ground of authority and truthfulness fell away. The supposed purity of the Early Church was taken quite literally; when evidence contradicted it they threw off the entire system. Newman had recognized the danger inherent in such total immersion in the sources: "To imbibe into the intellect the ancient Church as a fact, is either to be a Catholic or an infidel."[55] Two works by Isaac Taylor, *Natural History of Enthusiasm* (1829), a rationalistic critique of Evangelicalism continued in his book *Fanaticism* (1833), and *Ancient Christianity and the Doctrines of the Oxford Tracts for the Times* (1839-40), a progressively more shrill reply to the Puseyites, inadvertently helped Eliot slip the restraints of orthodoxy.[56] The doubts Taylor raised in her mind about the security of using the Fathers as a moral or doctrinal guide were pushed by Eliot back to the apostles. Were they any safer? That question of authority pressed through Fathers to Scripture and the apostles to Jesus himself is characteristic of the age, especially after the 1860s and the rise of biblical criticism.

Not all Anglicans were ready or willing to throw out the Fathers because of reputed Puseyite excesses or inapplicability of patristic doctrine to the present age. Thomas Arnold (1795-1842), for one, believed that while the Primitive Church, even less the post-Nicene Church, had little special authority in current circumstances, it still played a valuable role in the preservation of Christianity.[57] There were, he concluded in his *Fragment on the Church* (published 1844), three, perhaps overlapping, phases in Church history: (1) the first and perfect state of purity when institutions were subordinate to the Spirit; (2) an intermediate phase when forms, such as Councils and Creeds (Arnold himself rejected the Athanasian Creed), were provisionally necessary to preserve the initial Spirit; and (3) ossification of these temporary forms. But in his own day, at least following 1830, the Spirit of Christianity was self-evident, he believed, and older forms must be discarded as unnecessary. His descendants took opposing sides in relation to the Church of the Fathers. Tom Junior (1823-1900), who converted back and forth between Anglicanism and Roman Catholicism, was attracted by the stories of the martyrs of Lyons and the heroic deaths of Ignatius and Polycarp; he saw the "idea" of the Church as a historical fact in the lives of ordinary people being schooled in holiness. Tom's eldest daughter, Mary—Mrs. Humphry Ward (1851-1920), the author of the successful novel of religious crisis *Robert Elsmere* (1888)—was, much like Eliot, turned against traditional Christianity on historical grounds, based on her own systematic and intense reading of fourth- and fifth-century authors in the course of her research on Visigothic Spain.[58]

Isaac Taylor (1787-1865), a former Dissenter regarded by some contemporaries as the most important English lay theologian since Samuel Taylor Coleridge and credited with coining the English term *patristic,* had become convinced of the corruptions of the Primitive Church after reading the graphic accounts in the works of Sulpicius Severus, the fifth-century biographer of Martin of Tours.[59] In *Ancient Christianity and the Doctrines of the Oxford Tracts for the Times* (originally published 1838-40) Taylor assembled his private reading to oppose the Tracts in general and Newman in particular with "the present UNITY, purity, and spiritual vitality of protestant christendom," embodied in the English Church.[60] He also attacked "the Paparchy," the "'bible alone' outcry," and latitudinarian infidelity (which was the reason in 1863 he berated John William Colenso, bishop of Natal, for his revolutionary critical approach to the Pentateuch). The Church of England and the Fathers themselves hold forth the sole authority of the canon of Scripture (the "WRITTEN CANONICAL REVELATION," as Taylor impressed on his audience, 2:151). This was the only sure guide, since "preposterous errors and sad delinquencies" had crept into both the Early Church and the present one, errors to be expunged by "our *modern* good sense." The Tractarians, he felt, had sought "GENUINE APOSTOLIC TRADITIONS," on the basis of the "Scanty (not to say vapid) writings" of the Subapostolic age, and in place of "Catholic truth," embraced "every element of papal tyranny, cruelty, profligacy, and spiritual apostasy" (2:143, 1:426). The Newmanites had begun "not indeed to *cleanse* the stables of monkish pietism, but to deluge the land with their filth" (1:64). The result was a reexcrescence of "Monkery and Miracle." The "ascetic institute of the nicene Church" and the "ghostly tyranny of unmarried priests," set against the simple idea of the Church in the Sermon on the Mount, were related to a disordered social condition. Taylor amplified Thomas Arnold's position that such visible and arbitrary distinctions among Christians were necessarily fatal to piety and morals. Miracles were directly linked to Monkery, since a taste for the marvelous was characteristic of the ascetic life. Jerome, the prime mover in such corruption, is seen as the cause of more human misery than the hordes of Tamerlane (1:346). Taylor ominously indicates that miracles and the cult of saints and martyrs "were employed as the means of COAXING THE MOB TO SUPPORT THE CHURCH IN OPPRESSING THE SEVERAL BODIES OF SEPARATISTS" (2:376). Such saint worship ("demolatry"), which is conducive to unbounded credulity or universal skepticism, is carried over into the modern age in the "gaudy polytheism" observed by every "rightminded traveller" in Spain, Italy, and Ireland (2:376). Taking the age of Pope Gregory the Great as the undisputed *terminus ad quem* of accumulated corruption and superstition, Taylor divides Church history into stages—from Gregory to the Nicene Age, the Nicene Age to Cyprian, and Cyprian to the Apostolic Age—positing on the basis of "historical *probability,* a proportionate corruption" for the various stages. Opposed to this progressive idolatry and degeneracy is the patriarchal/Mosaic/prophetic witness of the Protestant ministry. Whereas the Tractarians attempt to Judaize the Church in external practices and forms, the Protestant clergy are the true continuators of the Aaronic hierarchy, "modestly observant of its subordinate place in the social system."[61] Scripture, again, is the proof of this in its apocalyptic predictions, sustaining the true Aaronic structures and denouncing Roman usurpations and political intrigues. Taylor was an important and influential early critic of the Tractarians, respected as an authority because of his knowledge of patristic sources.[62] Questions and objections he raised were used by various authors later in the century who shared his indignation, if not his scholarship.

An example of that is found in Bourchier Wrey Saville (1817-88), the Evangelical rector of Shillingford Exeter, who composed his work *The Primitive and Catholic Faith* (1875) in response to both Ritualism and Vaticanism. He writes: "The chief object of this present work is to show the resemblance between the doctrines of the Reformed Church of England, as interpreted by the 'Evangelical' party, and those held and taught by the Primitive Church in the earliest and purest days of her existence; as well as to urge upon all the duty of cultivating a closer communion with other Protestant Churches who hold the same faith with ourselves, though not under Episcopal government."[63] That primitive faith is summarized in a quotation from Cyril of Alexandria: "Evangelical teaching is grace by faith; justification in Christ; and sanctification through the power of the Holy Ghost" (x, 10). The pan-Protestantism this faith nourishes is "the Gospel of the grace of God" described in Ephesians, while the Ritualistic preach "another Gospel" described in Galatians. The Vatican Council (1869-70) was manifestly predicted by the Holy Ghost as Babylon the Great, the Mother of Harlots. Papists unable to recognize the Pope as Antichrist similarly would not have recognized Christ as the Messiah; Saville cites Christopher Wordsworth, the conservative bishop of Lincoln (1869-85), as the authority that the prophecies linking the bishop of Rome to Apocalyptic Babylon were as true as the Old Testament predictions of the Messiah fulfilled in Jesus.[64] Saville's emphasis is always on apocalyptic texts and evidence. Likening the Ritualists themselves to the forty assassins pursuing Paul (Acts 23:21), Saville construes Ritualism as an unacceptable return to Jewish ordinances. The analogy he uses is that of a weak Peter of Antioch confronting Paul, who was "better taught in the truth of Evangelical religion." Saville spurns any Jewish connections, just as he later did in *Anglo-Israelism and the Great Pyramid* (1880), a rejection of the alleged Jewish origin of the English nation. On the other hand, he supports the Pauline foundation of Christianity in England: *The Introduction of Christianity into Britain: An Argument on the Evidence in Favour of St. Paul Having Visited the Extreme Boundary of the West* (1861). Arthur P. Stanley, the Broad Church dean of Westminster (1864-81), had warned in the same year about attaching too much importance to missionaries before Augustine, but the idea of the apostolic foundation of the ancient British Church as a remedy to Romanism had a wide and continuing appeal. Until the year 600, the British Church enjoyed purity and independence; then Augustine introduced syncretistic practices and demonology (i.e., saint worship) in order to win over the Saxons, as reported by Bede (*Eccl. Hist.* 1.30), thus bringing on the "Egyptian darkness" of the Middle Ages.[65]

The variety of authors and of positions taken on the Church of the Fathers tells a great deal. A large number of clergy and laity of all church parties and those who finally rejected any church affiliation were searching the Fathers, as well as the Scriptures, to justify or condemn contemporary religious movements. Even those who proclaimed "the Bible alone" as the guide to faith and practice were compelled to bolster their position by an appeal to the Early Church. By the 1870s no one could simply ignore the mass of patristic evidence; this was the lasting effect brought by the Oxford Movement's appeal to the Primitive Church.

THE EARLY CHURCH

With such a varied and complex appropriation of the Fathers, constructed over time by a multitude of sermons and other theological works, the question remains why Victorian authors chose the novel to present the Church of the Fathers to their readership. Granted the immense popularity of the novel form during this period, was there something special the religious-historical novelist felt could be accomplished in that form with more facility than in the standard genres of theological discourse? And what, if any, was the theological justification they made of such use of novels?

When Thomas Carlyle and other eminent Victorians isolated the basis of the immense popularity of Sir Walter Scott's Waverley novels, they concluded with the truism that historical novels taught the modern age that the past was filled with "living men." In Christian terms, representatives of various church parties believed that "faith is illustrated more by the life of the character described than by mere theological terms by which it may be expressed."[66] Thus followed the literary galleries of portraits, memorials, and biographies illustrating the spirit and effects of Christianity since antique times. In 1840 Newman published the essays of *The Church of the Fathers* in order to present, as he says, in biographical sketches "the atmosphere, the sentiments, and customs of the Early Church." But these fragments did not prove artistically or theologically satisfying; a longer format, capable of presenting the varied richness of the congeries of atmosphere, sentiments, customs, and beliefs, seen as they were lived and as they affected living agents in history, was necessary. The novel, religious writers found, was particularly suited to that end, since without excessive dryness (or perhaps even objectivity) they could present what they called the "facts" (the opposite of hypotheses and thus "objective") and the "ethos" of the Early Church. A "fact" was a snapshot of antiquity, the essence of "ethos" a moving picture.

The word *ethos,* or at least its freighted meaning, was minted and circulated by the Anglo-Catholics, replacing the term used by older High Churchmen: "the *genius* of Anglicanism." The term connotes for the modern reader, perhaps, the vague notion of Common Prayer piety and the cluttered tea-time atmosphere of John Keble's parsonages. For the Tractarians and Anglo-Catholics it denoted much more. The ethos of the Early Church they hoped to instill was not a mere "servile imitation of the past, but such a reproduction of it as is really new, while it is old."[67] By various means they sought the total "consciousness" of orthodoxy, not merely subscription to orthodox expressions. The modality of that reproduction was to be through holiness and prayer. Tractarians were concerned with the "notes" of the Church not only as "Catholic" and "Apostolic" but also

as "Holy," the note left out of the Prayer Book version of the Nicene Creed. They shared this advertised quest for holiness as constitutive of the Church with Evangelicals and Methodists who cherished the classic model of Wesley's "Holiness Club." The publication of martyrs' and saints' lives was to them no mere pious exercise but a practical pattern of moral examples for contemporary imitation. They also helped give historic meaning to the proper understanding of the early creeds, confessions, and Scripture itself. Both R. Hurrell Froude and Thomas Arnold Jr. found this pure ethos of the Early Church exemplified in the character of the second-century Polycarp.[68]

The connection between Newman's Tract XC, demonstrating the Catholic sense of the official formularies of the English Church, and his projected Lives of the English Saints (1844-45), demonstrating the Catholic sense of the spirituality and holiness of the English Church, is direct and formally necessary. Martyrology tales, "spiced with sensationalism," enjoyed along with hagiographical collections an extended vogue. First, martyrs were employed by opposing churchmen as well to demonstrate the horrific effects of the Catholic system; in 1875 John Foxe's sixteenth-century *Book of Martyrs* was published in London in yet another edition and used in the ongoing antipopery campaign. Second, liturgy was a source and expression of this ethos and was painstakingly recreated in the novels. A distinction often made in this regard between the Tract writers and the later Ritualists or Ecclesiologists is hard to maintain. Härdelin and others have convincingly demonstrated the importance of the liturgy to the early Tractarians. They felt that liturgical customs were visible signs of Catholic doctrine, both expressing and preserving that doctrine and its continuity with the Primitive Church's understanding of Scripture, since liturgy is doctrine and Scripture lived out.[69] The historic visibility of the Church and its doctrine is another vital component of ethos. Third, for men such as Frederic Oakeley and W. G. Ward, ethos had an ethical edge; since the religious experience is historical and societal in nature, conscience and its necessary concomitant, a living moral guide, must exist and so constitute the ground of any appeal to authority. They found this in a spiritually independent, authoritatively teaching Church: *ubi auctoritas, ibi ecclesia.* This combination of Romantic feeling and communal conscience—more in harmony, they felt, with the mysteriousness of the living, revealed truth—was opposed by them to the spartan logical reason of the Oxford Noetics and other liberalizing theologians. Fourth, the sense of ethos must be seen in terms of contemporary considerations of propriety. The "reserve in communicating religious knowledge," the *disciplina arcani* of the Early Church, was an idea Tractarians revamped, causing such great misunderstanding. This sense of reserve was as much revulsion at the enthusiastic methods and interminable, emotional witnessing of new waves of Evangelicalism as anything else. And the notion of ethos constituted an equal revulsion toward the present supposed worldliness of the Church of England. Figures as diverse as James Anthony Froude and Richard W. Church viewed with sad eye the "lazy carriages and fashionable families" of English bishops and the "'smug parsons,' and pony-carriages for their wives and daughters" against the Tractarian ideal of "holy life, prayer, fasting, the confessional."[70] This multileveled understanding of ethos, then, exemplified the life of the Church of England and the consequences of the appeal to antiquity much more articulately than any formal theory of authority. But even that most formal theory, the Vincentian Canon, was looked upon basically as a test of that ethos, a "moral or spiritual principle," displayed in the "outward manifestations of a holy community."[71]

This quest for a holy "ethos" that characterized the movement in general had particular importance for Newman. In 1837 he wrote that he found a defect in the novels of Jane Austen: "What vile creatures her parsons are! She has not a dream of the high Catholic ἦθος."[72] This sense of ethos as a comprehensive worldview was articulated later when, speaking of his historical work, he wrote:

> What I should like would be to bring out the ἦθος of the Heathen from St. Paul's day down to St. Gregory, when under the process, or in the sight of the phenomenon, of conversion; what conversion *was* in those times, and what the position of a Christian in that world of sin, what the sophistries of philosophy viewed as realities influencing men. But besides the great difficulty of finding time, I don't think I could do it from History. I despair of finding facts enough—as if an imaginary tale could alone embody the conclusions to which existing facts *lead*.[73]

While recognizing the incompleteness of any depiction and the need to rely on the Church as a doctrinal guide, the search for the proper expression of ethos was phrased in his continual personal query "What would the Fathers have done?"[74] It was his attempt to see what the Fathers *had* done in analogous situations that turned him to the straight "record of facts" in his three-volume translation of Claude Fleury's *Ecclesiastical History*. In a memorable phrase, Newman commented that Fleury "presented a sort of photograph of ecclesiastical history" with a minutely detailed narrative not found in the Church histories of Johann Mosheim (1693-1755), August Neander (1789-1850), Joseph Milner (1744-97), or Henry H. Milman (1791-1868).[75] And although Fleury's presentation "unsettled" him, Newman was personally convinced that holiness was possible in the English Church, apart from the specific Catholic doctrines which it seemed only Rome visibly manifested. Newman saw in the age of the martyrs a visible sign of this demonstration of principles even before the formulation of

doctrines. By 1839 in his essay "Prospects of the Anglican Church" he had already moved from the general Tractarian understanding of ethos to the developing "*mind* of the church." "We cannot," he wrote, "if we would, move ourselves literally back into the times of the Fathers: we must in spite of ourselves, be churchmen of our own era, not of any other, were it only for this reason, that we are born in the nineteenth century, not in the fourth."[76] But in Newman's response to Nicholas Wiseman following 1839 he concluded that he had aligned himself with the Donatists, who made the unity of the Church depend on holiness, whereas now, following Augustine, he believed the only sure way to salvation was the reverse, the dependence of holiness on formal unity in the Church. This was the new "mind" he put on while composing the *Essay on Development*. Decades later in response to Kingsley's query "What does Dr. Newman mean?" he went beyond the simple question in terms that help us unravel his perception of both "ethos" and "mind." In the *Apologia* he wrote: "He asks what I mean; not about my words, not about my arguments, not about my actions, as his ultimate point, but about that living intelligence, by which I write, and argue, and act. He asks about my Mind and its Beliefs and its sentiments; and he shall be answered."[77] The progressive use of the terms *ethos, Mind,* and *meaning* recapitulates important stages in Newman's own development. *Ethos* pertains to the present reduplication of a standard established in the past, which is recovered or rediscovered for the present. *Mind* reflects the near suppression of the past for a present, living authority, such as Ward's "Ideal" Church. And *meaning* signifies a shift to an emphasis on persons and human experiences, connecting past and present, memory and observation, using personalist terms and historical analogy. That larger *meaning,* a grammar of belief and practice, behaving, as it were, as though a living intelligence, generated by the theological disputes of the Oxford Movement, intimately linked in its unfolding Newman's novel of the Early Church with other religious forms used by Roman Catholics, Anglo-Catholics, and their opponents.

Notes

1. Frederic Rogers (Lord Blachford), quoted by Raymond Chapman, *The Victorian Debate,* 258.

2. Raymond Chapman, *Faith and Revolt,* 147, 148.

3. See Samuel Pickering Jr., *The Moral Tradition in English Fiction, 1785-1850* (University Press of New England, 1977). The Evangelical tales of Hannah More, Rowland Hill, and Mrs. Sherwood are considered important precursors of the Victorian religious novel: Margaret Maison, *The Victorian Vision: Studies in the Religious Novel,* 89.

4. Maison, *Victorian Vision,* 5.

5. George P. Gooch, *History and Historians in the Nineteenth Century,* 333.

6. Avrom Fleishman, *The English Historical Novel,* 27; Christopher Hill, "The Norman Yoke," *Democracy and the Labour Movement: Essays in Honour of Donna Tor,* ed. John Saville (London: Lawrence & Wishart, 1954).

7. E. A. Freeman, *The Growth of the English Constitution* (London: Macmillan, 1872), 17-21, quoted in H. J. Hanham, ed., *The Nineteenth-Century Constitution, 1815-1914: Documents and Commentary* (Cambridge: Cambridge University Press, 1969), 20.

8. Vernon F. Storr, *The Development of English Theology in the Nineteenth Century, 1800-1860* (London: Longmans, 1913). Brilioth also points out unhistorical methods employed; see Yngve Brilioth, *Evangelicalism and the Oxford Movement* (London: Oxford University Press, 1934).

9. John Henry Newman, Papers on Development: Newman MSS in the Oratory of St. Philip Neri, Birmingham, B2.I and B2.II, batch 135, cited by Jaroslav Pelikan, *Development of Christian Doctrine: Some Historical Prolegomena* (New Haven: Yale University Press, 1969), 37.

10. Maison, *Victorian Vision,* 1, 6, 224-25; Chapman, *Victorian Debate,* 261. Randall T. Davidson, later archbishop of Canterbury (1903-28), while yet dean of Windsor, described Mrs. Humphry Ward's best-seller *Robert Elsmere* (1888) as a "boiler down," attacking her misinterpretation of B. F. Westcott's understanding of the affinity of Christianity to its Jewish and Hellenistic antecedents and her "Unitarian" idea of a "New Gospel of Brotherhood": Davidson, "Religious Novels," *Contemporary Review* (November 1888), 674-82. *Elsmere* remains a classic statement of the religious doubt and upheaval of the late Victorian period.

11. William Palmer, *A Narrative of Events Connected with the Publication of the Tracts for the Times* (Oxford, 1843), 44. In a later edition Palmer was more sharply critical of attitudes and personalities connected with the early tracts.

12. Chapman, *Faith and Revolt,* 146. Newman creates these titles in his first novel, *Loss and Gain* (1848); see 1962 ed., 199.

13. F. L. Cross, *The Oxford Movement and the Seventeenth Century* (London: SPCK, 1933). For a more recent introduction to the question, see Owen Chadwick, *The Mind of the Oxford Movement.* Ecumenical discussions among Anglicans, Lutherans, and Roman Catholics have generated some important surveys: Gareth Bennett, "Patristic Tradition in Anglican Thought, 1660-1900"; and Stanley Greenslade, "The Authority of the Tradition of the Early Church in Early Anglican Thought." An early ecumenical essay from the Roman Catholic perspective is provided by George Tavard, *The Quest for Catholicity.*

14. Vincent of Lerins, *Commonitorium,* ed. R. S. Moxon (Cambridge: Cambridge University Press, 1915), [2.3] 10. The original reads: "quod ubique, quod semper, quod ab omnibus." The Tractarians placed the test of "antiquity" first as part of their anti-Roman argumentation.

15. Richard Pfaff, "The Library of the Fathers"; "Anglo-American Patristic Translations 1866-1900," *Journal of Ecclesiastical History* 28 (January 1977), 39-55. The first Hampden controversy occurred in 1836 when Melbourne appointed the Whig clergyman Renn Hampden Regius Professor of Divinity at Oxford, a man Tractarians and Evangelicals alleged was doctrinally unorthodox. The second controversy involved Hampden's election as bishop of Hereford in 1848. See Owen Chadwick, *The Victorian Church,* 1:112-21.

16. Chadwick, *Victorian Church,* 2:80-81.

17. Chapman, *Faith and Revolt,* 143.

18. Frederic Rogers (Lord Blachford), quoted in Chapman, *Faith and Revolt,* 281. Piers Brendon, *Hurrell Froude and the Oxford Movement,* 71; see also 76-77.

19. John McNeill, *Modern Christian Movements,* 113.

20. Alf Härdelin, *The Tractarian Understanding of the Eucharist,* 121, 186. Keble developed this theme of "security" later in Tract 52.

21. Georgina Battiscombe, *John Keble,* 99, 105. By 1873 it had sold 379,000 copies.

22. See W. J. A. M. Beek, *John Keble's Literary and Religious Contributions to the Oxford Movement* (Nijmegen: Centrale Drukk., 1959). Keble's Tract 89, "On the Mysticism of the Fathers" (1840, although writing had begun by 1837), showed the influence of the Alexandrian school and Samuel Taylor Coleridge on imagination; Battiscombe, *John Keble,* 214-15. See also John Coulson, *Newman and the Common Tradition: A Study in the Language of Church and Society* (London: Oxford University Press, 1971).

23. Battiscombe, *John Keble,* 211, 242. Pfaff assigns Keble a very little part in the work of the Library of the Fathers series ("Library of the Fathers," 341 n. 27).

24. McNeill, *Modern Christian Movements,* 128. See *The Works of . . . Mr. Richard Hooker: With an*

Account of His Life and Death by Isaac Walton, ed. John Keble, 3 vols. (Oxford: Clarendon, 1836).

25. Quoted by Brendon, *Hurrell Froude,* 149.

26. Letter to Robert Isaac Wilberforce (10 July 1850), criticizing the latter's Archdeacon's Charge. In 1854 he criticized Wilberforce again for adopting "a philosophical dream," quoted in Battiscombe, *John Keble,* 306-7.

27. Letter to Mrs. Armstrong (12 January 1863), quoted in Battiscombe, *John Keble,* 335.

28. Letter of John Keble to Bishop Samuel Wilberforce (13 June 1851), quoted by Anonymous (author of "Charles Lowder"), *The Story of Dr. Pusey's Life,* 2d ed. (London: Longmans, Green, 1900), 363.

29. Letter of E. B. Pusey to John Keble (18 February [1848?]), quoted in *Pusey's Life,* 336.

30. Quoted in Meriol Trevor, *Newman,* vol. 1: *The Pillar of the Cloud,* vol. 2: *Light in Winter* (Garden City, N.Y.: Doubleday, 1962-63), 1:216.

31. W. Tuckwell, *Reminiscences of Oxford* (1900), quoted in W. L. Burn, *The Age of Equipoise: A Study of the Mid-Victorian Generation* (New York: W. W. Norton, 1965), 72. In 1898 William Temple, archbishop of Canterbury, declared that prayers for the dead were lawful but not compulsory; see Chadwick, *Victorian Church,* 2:356.

32. Letter of E. B. Pusey (1881), quoted in *Pusey's Life,* 534.

33. Wilfrid Ward, *Life of Newman,* 2 vols. (London: Longmans, 1912), 1:444. See the important article that sets this biography in the context of the Modernist controversy in the reign of Pius X: Sheridan Gilley, "Wilfrid Ward and His Life of Newman," *Journal of Ecclesiastical History* 29 (April 1978), 177-93.

34. Charles Stephen Dessain, *John Henry Newman* (London: Nelson, 1966), 10-11. The late Father Dessain of the Oratory gives an admirable, brief survey of Newman's grounding in Scripture and the Fathers. He relates how Newman later inserted references in pencil in the first edition copies of his sermons, showing how dependent he was on these sources (17). Coming late to the Caroline divines, Newman found the immediate "standard of Christian doctrine" in Ambrose, Augustine, Jerome, John Chrysostom, the Cappadocians (especially on the question of celibacy), Athanasius, Cyril of Jerusalem, the Alexandrians, Lactantius, and Sulpicius Severus. For a helpful survey of articles concerning Newman's use of the Fathers, especially the Alexandrians, in the formula-

tion of his educational theories, see Martin Svaglic, "John Henry Newman, Man and Humanist," *Victorian Prose: A Guide to Research,* ed. David DeLaura, 115-65, esp. 138 ff.

35. John Henry Newman, *Lectures on Certain Difficulties Felt by Anglicans in Submitting to the Catholic Church,* 293; "The Church of the Fathers" (1833), *Essays and Sketches,* ed. Harrold, 3:3.

36. Newman followed this manner in both his Anglican and Roman Catholic careers. Archbishop Laud was Cyprian, Jeremy Taylor was Chrysostom, and conversely Augustine against the Donatists was a recapitulation of the Non-Juror dispute ("Primitive Christianity" [1833-36]); William Palmer writing on the Jansenists in his *Essay on the Church* (1838) was a "Nestorian" writing on the relationship of Rome and the Monophysites (*Certain Difficulties,* 249); and Anglicans in general were Nestorians, Monophysites, Eutychians, Eusebians, Donatists, and Arians. It was not a matter of doctrinal identity in this final list but a question of the relationships of the rival religious bodies of the fourth and fifth centuries to the State.

37. John Henry Newman, *Via Media,* vol. 1, rev. ed. (1877), 38, quoted in Thomas Bokenkotter, *Cardinal Newman as an Historian,* 41 n. 1.

38. Newman, *Certain Difficulties,* lecture 5.

39. J. Derek Holmes, "Newman, History and Theology," *Irish Theological Quarterly,* n.s., 36 (January 1969), 34-45, 42-43. See John Henry Newman, *An Essay on the Development of Christian Doctrine,* 99-121; Owen Chadwick, *From Bossuet to Newman* (Cambridge: Cambridge University Press, 1957), 144-49. Later Newman characterized the differences between Rome and the Early Church as being only "in a few matters of discipline and tone," while Protestants differed in "all"; see Newman, *Certain Difficulties,* 287.

40. See David Knowles, "The Maurists," *Great Historical Enterprises* (London and New York: Nelson, 1963), 34-62; Robert Aubert et al., *The Christian Centuries,* vol. 5: *The Church in a Secularised Society* (New York: Paulist Press, 1978), 165-85; Aubert, "Un demi-siècle de revues d'histoire ecclésiastique," *Rivista di storia della Chiesa in Italia* 14 (1960), 173-202; and G. Fereto, *Note storicobibliografiche di archeologia cristiana* (Vatican City, 1942).

41. Gooch, *History and Historians,* 552. The English translation of *The First Age of Christianity* was completed in 1866 by Henry N. Oxenham and dedicated to Newman.

42. Ibid., 556.

43. See H. G. Schenk, *The Mind of the European Romantics,* 95 ff.

44. Jaroslav Pelikan, *Historical Theology,* 56. Newman, while making similar analogies, politicized the context in which his identifications are made; Church/State relations rather than doctrinal content were the key.

45. Johann Adam Möhler, *Die Einheit in der Kirche oder das Prinzip des Katholizismus dargestellt im Geiste der Kirchenväter der drei ersten Jahrhunderte* (Tübingen, 1825), quoted in Gooch, *History and Historians,* 549-50.

46. Chadwick, *Bossuet to Newman,* 119; see Johann Adam Möhler, *Symbolism; or, Exposition of the Doctrinal Differences between Catholics and Protestants as Evidenced by Their Symbolical Writings,* trans. J. R. Robertson, 2 vols. (London: Charles Dolman, 1843).

47. David Newsome, *The Wilberforces and Henry Manning,* 286. In the 1840s Edward Manning was reading up on Möhler and other Roman Catholic polemicists (ibid., 328). Ward's insistence on experiential religion sounds quite similar to John Wesley's abandonment in 1738 of "Primitive" for "real" Christianity; see Eamon Duffy, "Primitive Christianity Revived, Religious Renewal in Augustan England," *Studies in Church History 14: Renaissance and Renewal in Christian History* (Oxford: Basil Blackwell, 1977), 287-300.

48. Thomas Mozley, *Reminiscences Chiefly of Oriel College and the Oxford Movement,* 2 vols. (London: Longmans, 1882), 1:356.

49. Peter Sutcliffe, *The Oxford University Press: An Informal History* (Oxford and New York: Oxford University Press, 1978), 8-11.

50. Brendon, *Hurrell Froude,* 192. See H. Gough, *A General Index to the Publications of the Parker Society* (Cambridge: Parker Society, 1855), preface; and also Sutcliffe, *Oxford University Press,* 8-11.

51. Chapman, *Faith and Revolt,* 261.

52. Charles Kingsley, *Yeast* (1848), quoted in Chapman, *Faith and Revolt,* 142. The name Vieuxbois may indicate "old-fashioned timber," something quite obsolete.

53. Andrew Drummond, *The Churches in English Fiction,* 173.

54. Chapman, *Victorian Debate,* 286-90.

55. Newman, *Certain Difficulties,* 310.

56. Drummond, *Churches in English Fiction,* 21-22.

57. See Thomas Arnold, *The Life and Correspondence of Thomas Arnold D.D.,* ed. Arthur P. Stanley (1844), quoted in Chapman, *Faith and Revolt,* 144.

58. Meriol Trevor, *The Arnolds: Thomas Arnold and His Family* (London: Bodley Head, 1973), 41, 101-2, 195.

59. The German *patristisch* was in use before Taylor's time, but in England *patrological* or *patrologic* was the commonly used adjectival form (*OED*).

60. Isaac Taylor, *Ancient Christianity and the Doctrines of the Oxford Tracts,* 1: preface, vi-vii.notes to pages x-xnotes to pages x-x

61. See ibid., 1:413. Taylor, accusing the Tractarians of judaizing, quotes Erasmus' *Antidote* on ascetic practices: "Quae magis ad judaeos pertinent, quam ad Christianos, et superstitiosum facere possunt, pium non possunt." See also ibid., 2:402-22.

62. Newman refers to Taylor's work in his "Prospects of the Anglican Church" (1839), *Essays and Sketches,* 1:364. Taylor's reference (2:367) to "a few astute and sinuous minds" who want to subvent the intention of the framers of the Thirty-nine Articles and who thus forgo "the comforts of a 'good conscience'" is clearly aimed at Newman and Tract XC.

63. Bouchier Wrey Saville, *The Primitive and Catholic Faith,* vi.

64. Ibid., 6. See Saville's other works: *The First and Second Advent, with Reference to the Jew, the Gentile, and the Church of God* (1858); *Turkey; or, The Judgment of God upon Apostate Christendom under the Three Apocalyptic Woes* (1877); and *Prophecies and Speculations Respecting the End of the World* (1883).

65. Saville, *Primitive and Catholic Faith,* 84.

66. Review in the Anglo-Catholic periodical *Christian Remembrancer* (July 1860), quoted in Chapman, *Faith and Revolt,* 87. See also John O. Waller, "A Composite Anglo-Catholic Concept of the Novel, 1841-1868," *BNYPL* (1966), which traces changing perspectives in the Anglo-Catholic periodicals *Christian Remembrancer* (1851-68) and the *Ecclesiastic* (1845-68).

67. Newman, quoted in Bokenkotter, *Newman as Historian,* 41.

68. Brendon, *Hurrell Froude,* 71; Trevor, *The Arnolds,* 101-2.

69. The lectures of Charles Lloyd, bishop of Oxford (1827-29), played a vital role in demonstrating to

the movement's leaders the importance of liturgical study and its use in apologetics for the Church of England; see Tract 85, treated in Härdelin, *Tractarian Understanding*, 228. Even in his early ministry at St. Clement's, Oxford, Newman preached about the "visibility" as well as the "Catholicity" and "Apostolicity" of the Church; see Dessain, *Newman*, 8.

70. James Anthony Froude, *The Nemesis of Faith* (1848), quoted in Robert Lee Wolff, *Gains and Losses*, 399-400; R. W. Church, *Occasional Papers*, 2 vols. (London: Macmillan, 1897), 2:470-74, quoted in Dessain, *Newman*, 86. The observation by Church, made two days after Newman's death, implies that Newman left the English Church because of this endemic worldliness, a view with which Newman himself was not in agreement, according to Dessain. But one should remember the famous scene in Newman's *Loss and Gain* in which the hero is physically sickened by the sight of a married curate who had sworn celibacy (198). For a balanced psychological interpretation of this often discussed scene, see Wolff, *Gains and Losses*, 46-47.

71. Bennett, "Patristic Tradition," 79.

72. Letter to Mrs. John Mozley (19 January 1837), quoted in Baker, *Novel and the Oxford Movement*, 67.

73. Letter to Frederich Capes (28 February 1849), quoted in ibid., 55.

74. Newman's comments in 1874 on "The Catholicity of the Anglican Church" (1840), quoted in Dessain, *Newman*, 83.

75. *Apologia*, chap. 2, 87; Bokenkotter, *Newman as Historian*, 46.

76. Newman, *Essays and Sketches*, 1:355.

77. *Apologia*, preface, 16.

Abbreviations

PRIMARY MATERIAL

A   James, *Attila: A Romance*

Ac   Farrie, *Acte: A Novel*

An   Collins, *Antonia; or, The Fall of Rome*

AO   Jacobs, *Jesus as Others Saw Him: A Retrospect, A.D. 54*

Ap   Neale, *The Farm of Aptonga: A Story of the Times of St. Cyprian*

B   Corelli, *Barabbas: A Dream of the World's Tragedy*

BG   Pottinger, *Blue and Green; or, The Gift of God*

C   Newman, *Callista: A Tale of the Third Century*

D   Baring-Gould, *Domitia*

DB   Tucker, *Daybreak in Britain*

E   Moore, *The Epicurean: A Tale*

EH   Neale, *English History for Children*

Es   Mossman, *Epiphanius: The History of His Childhood and Youth as Told by Himself*

F   Wiseman, *Fabiola; or, The Church of the Catacombs*

G   Whyte-Melville, *The Gladiators*

GC   Farrar, *Gathering Clouds: A Tale of the Days of St. Chrysostom*

H   Kingsley, *Hypatia; or, New Foes with an Old Face*

HC   Mossman, *A History of the Catholic Church of Jesus Christ from the Death of Saint John to the Middle of the Second Century*

I   Holt, *Imogen: A Tale of the Early British Church*

J   Kingston, *Jovinian: A Story of the Early Days of Papal Rome*

M   Hoppus, *Masters of the World*

N   Graham, *Neara: A Tale of Ancient Rome*

Ns   Carpenter, *Narcissus: A Tale of Early Christian Times*

O   Mercier, *Our Mother Church: Being Simple Talk on High Topics*

P   Bulwer-Lytton, *The Last Days of Pompeii*

Pp   Baring-Gould, *Perpetua: A Story of Nîmes in A.D. 213*

R   Wilberforce, *Rutilius and Lucius; or, Stories of the Third Age*

S   Yonge, *The Slaves of Sabinus, Jew and Gentile*

SW   Croly, *Tarry Thou till I Come; or, Salathiel, the Wandering Jew*

V   Lockhart, *Valerius: A Roman Story*

Z   Smith, *Zillah: A Tale of the Holy City*

JOURNALS

AQ   *American Quarterly*

BNYPL *Bulletin of the New York Public Library*

MLR   *Modern Language Review*

PQ   *Philological Quarterly*

VN   *Victorian Newsletter*

Works Cited

Altick, Richard D. *The English Common Reader: A Social History of the Mass Reading Public, 1800-1900.* Chicago: University of Chicago Press, 1957.

Baker, Ernest A. *History in Fiction: A Guide to the Best Historical Romances, Sagas, Novels, and Tales.* 2 vols. London: George Routledge & Sons, 1907.

Baker, Joseph E. *The Novel and the Oxford Movement.* Princeton: Princeton University Press, 1932.

Battiscombe, Georgina. *John Keble: A Study in Limitations.* New York: Alfred A. Knopf, 1964.

Baumgarten, Murray. "The Historical Novel: Some Postulates," *Clio* 4 (February 1975), 173-82.

Bennett, Gareth V. "Patristic Tradition in Anglican Thought, 1660-1900." *Oecumenica* (1971-72), 63-87.

Berger, Morroe. *Real and Imagined Worlds: The Novel and Social Science.* Cambridge, Mass.: Harvard University Press, 1977.

Bokenkotter, Thomas S. *Cardinal Newman as an Historian.* Louvain: Bibliothèque de l'Université, 1959.

Brendon, Piers. *Hurrell Froude and the Oxford Movement.* London: Paul Elek, 1974.

Buckley, Jerome H., ed. *The Worlds of Victorian Fiction.* Harvard English Studies 6. Cambridge, Mass.: Harvard University Press, 1975.

Butterfield, H. *The Historical Novel: An Essay.* Cambridge: Cambridge University Press, 1924.

Chadwick, Henry. *The Early Church.* Harmondsworth: Penguin Books, 1976.

Chadwick, Owen. *The Mind of the Oxford Movement.* London: Adam and Charles Black, 1960.

———. *The Secularization of the European Mind in the Nineteenth Century.* Cambridge: Cambridge University Press, 1975.

———. *The Victorian Church.* 2 vols. New York: Oxford University Press, 1966, 1970.

Chapman, Edward M. *English Literature in Account with Religion, 1800-1900.* Boston and New York: Houghton Mifflin, 1910.

Chapman, Raymond. *Faith and Revolt: Studies in the Literary Influence of the Oxford Movement.* London: Weidenfeld & Nicolson, 1970.

———. *The Victorian Debate: English Literature and Society, 1832-1901.* London: Weidenfeld & Nicolson, 1968.

Chitty, Susan. *The Beast and the Monk: A Life of Charles Kingsley.* New York: Mason & Charter, 1975.

Church, R. W. *The Oxford Movement, Twelve Years, 1833-1845.* Edited by G. F. A. Best. Chicago: University of Chicago Press, 1970.

Cockshut, A. O. J. *Anglican Attitudes: A Study of Victorian Religious Controversies.* London: Collins, 1959.

Cruse, Amy. *After the Victorians.* London: George Allen & Unwin, 1938.

———. *The Victorians and Their Books.* London: George Allen & Unwin, 1935.

Cunningham, Valentine. *Everywhere Spoken Against: Dissent in the Victorian Novel.* Oxford: Clarendon Press, 1975.

Dahl, Curtis. "Pater's Marius and Historical Novels on Early Christian Times." *Nineteenth-Century Fiction* 28 (June 1973), 1-24.

Dalziel, Margaret. *Popular Fiction 100 Years Ago: An Unexplored Tract of Literary History.* London: Cohen & West, 1957.

Darton, F. J. H. *Children's Books in England: Five Centuries of Social Life.* Cambridge: Cambridge University Press, 1958.

Davies, Horton. *Worship and Theology in England.* Vol. 3: *From Watts and Wesley to Maurice, 1690-1850.* Princeton: Princeton University Press, 1961.

DeLaura, David J. *Hebrew and Hellene in Victorian England: Newman, Arnold, and Pater.* Austin: University of Texas Press, 1969.

———, ed. *Victorian Prose: A Guide to Research.* Essays by Fellows of the Royal Society of Literature. New York: Modern Language Association, 1973.

Dorman, S. "*Hypatia* and *Callista*: The Initial Skirmish between Kingsley and Newman," *Nineteenth Century Fiction* 34 (1979), 173-93.

Drinkwater, John, ed. *The Eighteen-Sixties.* Essays by Fellows of the Royal Society of Literature. Cambridge: Cambridge University Press, 1932.

Drummond, Andrew L. *The Churches in English Fiction: A Literary and Historical Study.* Leicester: Edgar Backus, 1950.

Elliott-Binns, L. E. *Religion in the Victorian Era.* Greenwich, Conn.: Seabury Press, 1953.

Fleishman, Avrom. *The English Historical Novel: Walter Scott to Virginia Woolf.* Baltimore: Johns Hopkins University Press, 1971.

Frend, W. H. C. *Martyrdom and Persecution in the Early Church.* New York: New York University Press, 1967.

Glucksmann, Hedwig L. "Die Gegenüberstellung von Antike-Christentum in der englischen Literatur des 19. Jahrhunderts." Inaugural dissertation. Hannover, 1932.

Gooch, George P. *History and Historians in the Nineteenth Century.* Boston: Beacon Press, 1959.

Greensalde, Stanley L. "The Authority of the Tradition of the Early Church in Early Anglican Thought." *Oecumenica* (1971-72), 9-33.

Härdelin, Alf. *The Tractarian Understanding of the Eucharist.* Uppsala: Studia Historico-ecclesiastica Upsaliensa, 1965.

Hill, Alan G. "Originality and Realism in Newman's Novels," *Newman after a Hundred Years,* ed. Ian Ker and A. G. Hill, 21-42. Oxford: Clarendon Press, 1990.

James, Louis. *Fiction for the Working Man, 1830-1850.* London: Oxford University Press, 1963.

Kaye, James R. *Historical Fiction: Chronologically and Historically Related.* Chicago: Snowdon Publishing, 1920.

Kelly, Doris B. "A Checklist of Nineteenth-Century English Fiction about the Decline of Rome." *BNYPL* 72 (1968), 400-13.

Knoepflmacher, U. C. *Religious Humanism and the Victorian Novel: George Eliot, Walter Pater, and Samuel Butler.* Princeton: Princeton University Press, 1965.

Kumar, Shiv K., ed. *British Victorian Literature: Recent Revaluations.* New York: New York University Press, 1969.

Longford, Elizabeth. *Queen Victoria: Born to Succeed.* New York: Harper & Row, 1974.

Lukács, Georg. *The Historical Novel.* London: Merlin Press, 1962.

McAdoo, Henry R. *The Spirit of Anglicanism: A Survey of Anglican Theological Method in the Seventeenth Century.* New York: Scribners, 1965.

Machin, G. I. T. *Politics and the Churches in Great Britain, 1832 to 1868.* Oxford: Clarendon Press, 1977.

McNeill, John T. *Modern Christian Movements.* New York: Harper & Row, 1968.

Maison, Margaret M. *The Victorian Vision: Studies in the Religious Novel.* New York: Sheed & Ward, 1961.

Newsome, David. *The Wilberforces and Henry Manning: The Parting of Friends.* Cambridge, Mass.: Harvard University Press, Belknap Press, 1966.

Nield, Jonathan. *A Guide to the Best Historical Novels and Tales.* London: Elkin Mathews & Marrot, 1902 (rev. ed., 1929).

Norman, E. R. *Anti-Catholicism in Victorian England.* New York: Barnes & Noble, 1968.

Pelikan, Jaroslav. *The Emergence of the Catholic Tradition, 100-600.* Vol. 1 of *The Christian Tradition.* Chicago: University of Chicago Press, 1971.

———. *Historical Theology: Continuity and Change in Christian Doctrine.* New York: Corpus; Philadelphia: Westminster, 1971.

Pfaff, Richard W. "The Library of the Fathers: The Tractarians as Patristic Translators." *Studies in Philology* 70 (1973), 329-44.

Rance, Nicholas. *The Historical Novel and Popular Politics in Nineteenth-Century England.* London: Vision Press, 1975.

Roth, Cecil. *A History of the Jews in England to 1858.* 3d ed. Oxford: Clarendon Press, 1964.

Sadleir, Michael. *Excursions in Victorian Bibliography.* London: Chaundy & Cox, 1922.

Schenk, H. G. *The Mind of the European Romantics: An Essay in Cultural History.* London: Constable, 1966.

Sheppard, A. T. *The Art and Practice of Historical Fiction.* London: Humphrey Toulmin, 1930.

Showalter, Elaine. *A Literature of Their Own: British Women Novelists from Brontë to Lessing.* Princeton: Princeton University Press, 1976.

Shuster, George N. *The Catholic Spirit in Modern English Literature.* New York: Macmillan, 1922.

Simmons, James C. *The Novelist as Historian: Essays on the Victorian Historical Novel.* The Hague: Mouton, 1973.

Slack, Robert C., ed. *Bibliographies of Studies in Victorian Literature: For the Ten Years 1955-1964.* Urbana: University of Illinois Press, 1967.

Smith, Warren S. *The London Heretics, 1870-1914.* New York: Dodd, Mead, 1968.

Soloway, R. A. *Prelates and People: Ecclesiastical Social Thought in England, 1783-1852.* London: Routledge & Kegan Paul, 1969.

Stang, Richard. *The Theory of the Novel in England, 1850-1870.* New York: Columbia University Press, 1959.

Stevenson, Lionel, ed. *Victorian Fiction: A Guide to Research.* Cambridge, Mass.: Harvard University Press, 1964.

Steward, Herbert L. *A Century of Anglo-Catholicism.* New York: Oxford University Press, 1929.

Tarr, Sr. Mary Muriel. *Catholicism in Gothic Fiction: A Study of the Nature and Function of Catholic Materials in Gothic Fiction in England, 1762-1820.* Washington, D.C.: Catholic University of America Press, 1946.

Tavard, George H. *The Quest for Catholicity: A Study in Anglicanism.* London: Catholic Book Club, 1963.

Templeman, William D., ed. *Bibliographies of Studies in Victorian Literature for the Thirteen Years 1932-1944.* Urbana: University of Illinois Press, 1945.

Vargish, Thomas. *Newman: The Contemplation of Mind.* Oxford: Clarendon Press, 1970.

Wolff, Robert L. *Gains and Losses: Novels of Faith and Doubt in Victorian England.* New York: Garland Publishing, 1977.

Wright, Austin, ed. *Bibliographies of Studies in Victorian Literature for the Ten Years 1945-1954.* Urbana: University of Illinois Press, 1956.

Ziolkowski, Theodore. *Fictional Transfigurations of Jesus.* Princeton: Princeton University Press, 1972.

Appendix A

<small>COLLECTIONS OF SAINTS' LIVES</small>

Adams, D. C. O. *The Saints and Missionaries of the Anglo-Saxon Era.* 2d series. Oxford, 1897-1901.

Baring-Gould, Sabine. *The Lives of the Saints.* 16 vols. London, 1897-98.

Bedjan, Paul. *Acta martyrum et sanctorum Syriace.* 7 vols. Paris, 1890-97.

Bell, Mrs. Arthur George. *The Saints in Christian Art.* 3 vols. London, 1901-4.

Butler, Alban. *The Lives of the Fathers, Martyrs, and Other Principal Saints.* 4 vols. London, 1756-59.

Challoner, Richard. *Britannia Sancta; or, The Lives of the Most Celebrated British, English, Scottish, and Irish Saints.* 2 parts. London, 1745.

Faber, F. W., et al. *The Saints and Servants of God.* 42 vols. London, 1847-56.

Forbes, Alexander P. *Kalendars of Scottish Saints.* Edinburgh, 1874.

Godescard, J. F. *Vies des pères, des martyrs, et autres principaux saints, traduit librement de l'anglais d'Alban Butler.* 12 vols. Paris, 1763-.

Guérin, Paul. *Les Petits Bollandistes.* 7th ed. 18 vols. Paris, 1876.

Hyvernat, H. *Les Actes des martyrs de l'Égypte.* Paris, 1886-.

Mabillon, J., et al. *Acta Sanctorum ordinis S. Benedicti.* 9 vols. Paris, 1668-1701.

Martinov, J. E. *Annus ecclesiasticus Graeco-Slavicus.* Brussels, 1863.

Newman, J. H. *Lives of the Irish Saints.* 12 vols. Dublin, 1875-.

Owen, Robert. *Sanctorale Catholicum, or Book of Saints.* London, 1880.

Pétin, Abbé. *Dictionnaire hagiographique.* 2 vols. Paris, 1850.

Räss, A., and N. Weiss. *Leben der Heiligen.* 23 vols. Mainz, 1823-.

Rees, W. J. *Lives of the Cambro-British Saints of the Fifth and Immediat Succeeding Centuries.* Llandovery, 1853.

Stadler, J. E., and F. J. Heim. *Vollständiges Heiligen Lexikon.* 5 vols. Augsburg, 1858-.

Stanton, Richard. *A Menology of England and Wales.* London, 1887, 1892.

Sue Zemka (essay date 1997)

SOURCE: Zemka, Sue. "Christ and the Holy Family: Two Victorian Sites of Subject Constitution." In *Victorian Testaments: The Bible, Christology, and Literary Authority in Early-Nineteenth-Century British Culture,* pp. 100-16. Stanford, Calif.: Stanford University Press, 1997.

[*In the following essay, Zemka surveys the debate in nineteenth-century British society surrounding the literary and artistic representation of Jesus Christ and the Holy Family.*]

Between 1845 and 1850, [Charles] Dickens, [Benjamin] Disraeli, George Eliot, [Alfred, Lord] Tennyson, and [Robert] Browning produced works that invoke, in a variety of genres and with mixed success, the image of Christ. As either a literary allusion or a quasi-mythical figure, Christ appears in Dickens's *Life of Our Lord* (1848), Disraeli's *Tancred* (1847), Eliot's translation of Strauss's *Das Leben Jesu* (1846), Tennyson's *In Memoriam* (1850), and Browning's *Christmas-Eve and Easter-Day* (1850). That writers of a comparable stature from the previous and following centuries did not, with such frequency and in such a concentrated period of time, make similarly explicit uses of Christology should alert us to the overdetermined—or at least overextended—nature of this Victorian trope. At mid-century Hunt and Millais also turned their attentions toward the figure of Christ, representing him as child, worker, man, and God; in all instances, as an icon of the hopes and dilemmas of an artistic movement that aspired, in Hunt's words, to "resurrect" the moribund aesthetics and semiotics of British painting. Such interest in the aesthetic potential of figures that straddled myth and history was not uncommon in Victorian art: commenting upon Pickersgill's *Burial of Harold,* a prize-winning painting of 1847, a reviewer in *Punch* expressed hope that the mania in English art for finding the body of the last Saxon king had expended itself, and that "British artists would leave off finding [Harold's] body anymore, which they have been doing, in every exhibition, these fifty years" (Strong 118). The reviewer's hopes were rewarded; during the next few years, Harold became a less frequent subject in British painting. However, with the advent of Pre-Raphaelitism, the subject anticipated by this, one of Harold's last and most successful appearances, was just emerging: Pickersgill's Harold was based directly on a Lamentation over the Dead Christ.

The resurgence of interest in Christ was largely the result of the birth of the modern period in Christian theology, a period dominated less by supernatural articulations of faith than by scientific and historial ones.[1] The Higher Criticism, Comtism, philological and ethnological research, manuscript studies, and travel writings were among the influences that reintroduced European imaginations to Christ and mandated a realistic, sober approach, as if the style of treatment, whether literary or iconographic, could somehow confer historical verisimilitude on the subject. Hence the life of Christ became an important subgenre of the nineteenth century, one practiced by [David Friedrich] Strauss, Renan, John Seeley, F. W. Farrar, and, one might add, [Friedrich] Nietzsche, although his work bears little resemblance to that of the others.[2] Throughout England and much of Europe, the life of Christ was one of the battlefields on which the pious contended with skeptics over the role that religion should play in modern society. But changing images of Christ also reflected another, ancillary battle over the perceived generational and gendered nature of religious authority.[3] As we saw in [chapter 2 of *Victorian Testaments*], there was the Christology of Arnold's Broad Church tradition, with its emphasis on a modern-day secular supplement to Christ, the manly English character. Approaching the topic of Victorian masculinity from a different angle, Herbert Sussman's study pays considerable attention to the dilemmas that a manly Christ posed to the artists of the Pre-Raphaelite Brotherhood. Norman Vance analyzes the specifically Christological tradition in more detail, exploring the nuances of the concept of manliness as it was appended to a practical ethic of male Christian behavior. And yet, even at the height of Kingsley and Hughes's manly Christian movement, the associations between Christ and femininity or Christ and childhood were also quite visible in Victorian art and literary culture. The readiness with which Christ might be transposed onto images of women is evidenced by examples of a feminine Christology from the mid-nineteenth century—by Sarah Stickney Ellis's comparison of women to Christ in the conclusion of *The Daughters of England*, for example, or by Florence Nightingale's quite different vision of a female messiah with distinctly feminist inclinations. Indeed, the rhetoric of Muscular Christianity was partly a reaction against perceptions that Christian faith had become, via the influences of sentimentality and Evangelicalism, a mode of thought and behavior arguably more proper to women than to men.[4]

The subject of this [essay and chapters 4 and 5 of *Victorian Testaments*] is Victorian Christology. Chapter 4 [explores] a set of issues in Dickens's mid-century representations of women and children that I have framed around the figure of Christ. Chapter 5 [explores] the ramifications of the Victorian alliance between Christ and femininity for one Victorian woman, Florence Nightingale. Consequently, it may be a source of some dismay to the reader that as much attention will be devoted in these chapters to the rhetoric surrounding women and children as to that surrounding Christ. In this brief [essay], I hope to make clear the reasons for frequently neglecting my announced topic. [Chapters 1 and 2 of *Victorian Testaments* narrate] instances in which problems of scriptural interpretation are resolved

with appeals to the incarnation as a revelation in the flesh, a distillation of the idea of truth into what was a definitive trope of nineteenth-century philosophy, the anthropomorphic form. In this uniquely Victorian cultural enactment of the incarnation, the body of the human divine functions less as a fulfillment of the Scriptures than as an attempt at a symbolic replacement for the Scriptures, and this implicit modification of traditional Christian theology occurs, I have suggested, because print culture dominates to an unprecedented degree, and in a manner that reveals its inability to supply the ideological coherence desired of it—an ideological coherence nostalgically, if illusively, associated with the Bible. [Chapters 4, 5, and 6 of *Victorian Testaments*] follow a different pathway, where the efficacy of the incarnation to resolve uncertainties of biblical meaning is undercut by problems raised by the idea of the incarnation itself. These problems arise once the authority of Christ's image as the realization of the Word in a human identity is interjected into social contexts where authority is also managed by a careful but tenuous economy of gendered and generational roles.

As with so many dilemmas of the Victorian age, one way to narrativize the tensions inherent in the Christology of the period is to cite Carlyle. With uncharacteristic reserve, Carlyle omitted Christ from the list of luminaries touched upon in *On Heroes and Hero-Worship*: "The greatest of all Heroes is One—whom we do not name here! Let sacred silence meditate that sacred matter" (11). Such was a more pious but no less mystifying approach than the one he took in *Sartor Resartus,* where he proclaimed Christ the highest symbol of the godlike, albeit a symbol "whose significance will ever demand to be anew inquired into, and anew made manifest" (179). In both instances, Carlyle refuses to enframe the human divine, refuses to arrest a dynamic spiritual process that is ongoing in history in what must paradoxically be understood as a most material way. But the problem with this paradox as Carlyle presents it is that the idea of Christ resists iconic and narratological representation even as it incites the desire for such representation. The results become evident in Carlyle's response to *The Light of the World*. After William Holman Hunt used Christina Rossetti as a model for the painting, Carlyle accused him of selling out to Royal Academy tastes by making Christ "a puir, weak, girl-faced nonentity, bedecked in a fine silken sort of gown" when he should have made him in the image of a "Man toiling along in the hot sun . . . tired, hungry often and footsore. . . . His rough and patched clothes bedraggled and covered with dust" (quoted in Hunt 1: 358).[5] And yet, even Carlyle, as the above quotation from *On Heroes* demonstrates, was unwilling to attempt such a depiction himself. As Sussman states, the image of Christ forced together two incompatible cultural standards, "the traditional representation of the life of Jesus" and "the norms of early Victorian bourgeois manhood"

(120). In this regard, Hunt's feminization of Christ might be understood as a remedy for a dilemma that Carlyle had aggravated when he encouraged both an advance upon and a retreat from the idea of Christ as an adult male. The other remedy was to embrace a masculine but spiritually diluted Christ, as in the apotheosization of Arnold's character, or in F. J. Foxton's *Popular Christianity* (1849), which makes Christ the master type of other prophetic geniuses such as Shakespeare and Homer (160-61), or in one of Hunt's anecdotes of Pre-Raphaelite beginnings, in which during a studio break in 1848 the Brotherhood composes a "list of immortals" that distinguishes Christ from other personages by virtue of assigning him four asterisks instead of three (the number assigned to Shakespeare) or two (the number assigned to Chaucer, Keats, Browning, and King Alfred) (Hunt 1: 159). Such a Christ was hardly a god at all, so thoroughly was his story recontextualized into that of men gifted with genius in a rare but by no means exclusive way. He was, to quote Vance's adjectives, "vigorously" and "intensely" human (6). But he was also lacking in supernatural spiritual powers, powers which it seems could only be conveyed by the use of symbolism (as Hunt would do in *The Shadow of Death*), or, more problematically, by the use of a female model.

The source of ambivalence toward representing Christ as a man lay in a psychological effect of Christianity itself: human subjectivity of the nineteenth century was often predicated on guilt, and according to the plot of sentimental fantasy, guilt was a male prerogative, a dubious entitlement linked to sexual and monetary appetites that neither children nor women in their ideal forms shared. Hence the recurrent artistic attraction to the image of the prostitute, whose scandalous passage between the differential realms of a feminine and a sexual nature presented a unique opportunity for conferring fuller subjectivity on women characters, of allotting them the ontological status of a subject rather than an object in a salvation narrative. Hence also the artist's habitual withdrawal from the image of Christ as an adult male, an image which suggested a disturbing convergence of guilt and divinity, of dependency and power. Indeed, this convergence was all the more disturbing for being true, since it captured an impossible but efficient formula of authority in Victorian culture, the formula that wedded men to their images of women and children as purifying displacements of their own power and authority.

Carlyle's desire for the image of a working Christ, of an emphatically embodied Christ, is remembered as a call-to-arms of the proponents of manly Christianity, Kingsley and Hughes the chief among them. The relationship between Kingsley's Christology and his ideology of gender has been explored in detail, not only by Vance but more recently by John Maynard. Neither

critic takes notice of a review of Anna Jameson's *Sacred and Legendary Art* that Kingsley contributed to *Fraser's* in March 1849—a forgivable omission, as the review does nothing to further our understanding of Kinglsey's ideas. However, because it sets Kingsley's thoughts on gender and Christology in the framework of aesthetic appreciation, and because in so doing it divides quite clearly, even simplistically, the symbolic functions of viewer and viewed, I would like to discuss briefly this review and the book that occasioned it.

Sacred and Legendary Art (1848) was the first in Anna Jameson's four-part study of medieval and early Renaissance European art. The second volume in the series, *Legends of the Monastic Orders,* was published in 1850; the third volume, titled *Legends of the Madonna,* appeared in 1852; and the last volume, *The History of Our Lord,* was published posthumously in 1860, after being completed by Lady Eastlake. Jameson's decision to undertake a volume on artistic representations of Christ at the culmination of her twelve-year attempt to mediate the iconography of Mary and the saints to the Protestant world was sensible enough; it is also, we might note, consistent with the Protestant tradition of avoiding a direct treatment of the human divine. In *Sacred and Legendary Art* Jameson establishes the objectives and approach that will inform her entire series. She presents herself as a critic who is anxious to defend Italian Renaissance painting, even as she acknowledges the need for caution in the study of Catholic hagiography. Frequently, she makes reference to the English commonplace that the idolatrous veneration of saints in medieval and early Renaissance Europe was a symptom of the religious perversions caused by withholding the Bible from the poor. But this, she argues, is no reason to deny the beauty and pathos of the art produced in Roman Catholic countries. The Catholic Church's management of Christ's divinity she considers more misguided than deliberately malevolent, suggesting that in their solicitude for orthodoxy, the church fathers altogether removed Christ's personal character "far away from the hearts of the benighted and miserable people . . . into regions speculative, mysterious, spiritual, whither they could not, dared not, follow Him" (*Sacred* 3). And yet, these speculative, mysterious, and spiritual qualities are precisely what English Protestantism, she fears, misses entirely. Like the Pre-Raphaelites, she accuses English aesthetics of lacking the beauty and brilliance of early Renaissance art because of stale conventions, narrow prejudices, and repressive tendencies. In these habits, she suggests, the English art public are encouraged by their fear that religious superstition is a disease transmitted by familiarity. Thus the time has come to master this fear and decipher impartially the symbols of late medieval and early Renaissance art. For the English to do otherwise is to "seal up a fountainhead of the richest poetry, and to shut out a thousand ennobling and inspiring thoughts" (*Sacred* 12).

The review essay that Kingsley wrote upon the appearance of *Sacred and Legendary Art* is laudatory and discursive. The arguments of the essay typify the hybridity of Kingsley's beliefs, which included a faith in the propriety of gender roles, a faith in the evils of Catholicism, and a faith in the sanctity of sexual pleasure in married life. Thus he warns against the Catholic threat to English Protestant culture but, like Jameson, suggests that the best defense is a cautious appropriation of Catholic culture's superior sense of the beautiful. "The deepest cravings of the human heart" continue to be left unsatisfied by Protestant art, he states, reiterating Jameson's preface, and hence English youth "are looking for themselves at the ante-Raphaellic artists" (285). This should serve as admonishment to their Protestant elders for starving the imagination and the desire for beauty, all on the misguided assumption that "the Gospel had nothing to do with art, [that] art was either Pagan or Popish" (284). As a counterbalance to this erroneous tendency, Kingsley finds Mrs. Jameson's work irreproachable, because it "is enthusiastic but not idolatrous, discriminating but not captious" (289). If the separate identities of Protestant and Catholic Christians were to turn on nothing more than the difference between enthusiasm and idolatry, reactionary Englishmen might with some justification be alarmed. But Kingsley has additional reason to trust Jameson in this venture: because she is an "English wife and mother," she can approach the subject of Christian iconography with "tender and admiring sympathies" that are held in check by "her Protestant education to unsullied purity of thought" (289).[6] Kingsley's Christian beliefs, Maynard explains, were uniquely wedded to his endorsement of human sexuality, and two precepts that enabled him to accommodate both carnal pleasure and Protestantism were marital monogamy and the fulfillment of gendered identities.[7] The ideological axes that connected Protestantism to a sacramental sexuality in marriage and idealized gender roles could also be connected to national personality traits, and thus Kingsley lists among Jameson's qualifications not only a Protestant sensibility and a feminine nature but also "the birthright of English honesty" (290).

By invoking this ideological continuum in almost everything he wrote, Kingsley lent energy and a sense of exigency to the tradition that Thomas Arnold enlisted against the demons of rationalism and Tractarianism—the tradition of constructing an English national personality. However, these attitudes certainly extended beyond the Broad Church movement, and the pervasiveness of the associations that obtain in Kingsley's imagination is exemplified by their similar appearance among the Pre-Raphaelite Brotherhood. According to William Holman Hunt's retrospective account, he and Millais initially thought themselves capable of exploring early Christian art because they possessed an "English honesty" rounded out by certain inspiring qualities: their childlike approach to nature and their youthful, revolutionary stance toward the patriarchy of the Reynolds school. Moreover, it is worth noting that their seminal conversation occurred over Hunt's rendering of Christ in his painting *Christ and the Two Maries*.[8] Coming to the Brotherhood's defense in 1853, Ruskin took up the Brotherhood's conception of themselves as possessing a childlike genius, lamenting that of all great societies, "it is reserved for England to insult the strength of her noblest children—to wither their warm enthusiasm in patient battle" ("Lectures" 164). In the case of the Pre-Raphaelites, as in the case of Kingsley's review of Jameson's work, the future of English religious art is entrusted to sensibilities deemed not only English but also feminine and childlike. These examples signal the fact that the Catholic infection which Kingsley feared has already taken place; the English already have the disease, which in their case is an idolatrous treatment not of art objects but of discursive objects. For Kingsley's desperate attempt to distinguish between Catholic idolatry and Protestant enthusiasm is no doubt inspired by the even more tenuous distinction that it hides, the distinction between a Catholic worship of the Madonna and Child and the Protestant worship of mothers and children.

However, in what appears to be a diversion from the anti-Catholic bent of Kinsgley's rhetoric, the differences between Catholicism and Protestantism are made in his review to be less significant than the difference between Christianity and Paganism. To the peremptory importance of this latter distinction he is willing to sacrifice the grievances between the two main sects of Western Christianity. Paganism is a worship of power and evil, and hence the merger of Catholic iconography and Protestant belief is a less grievous error than that of "[tracing] malevolent likenesses" between a Cecilia and an Isis, or a Magdalene and a Venus (291). The separation of Christianity from religions that worship brute power is also metonymically connected to gender, for insofar as the chief Christian deity ennobles humanity, Kingsley suggests, he does so by imparting to it attributes that are presumably divine but also, within his discourse, gendered feminine. The first mention of Christ follows a discussion of Jameson's treatment of the story of Saint Dorothea:

> Is there not heroism in it greater than of all the Ajaxes and Achilles who ever blustered on earth? Is there not power greater than of kings—God's strength made perfect in woman's weakness? Tender forgiveness, the Saviour's own likeness; glimpses, brilliant and true at the core, however distorted and miscoloured, of that spiritual world where the wicked cease from troubling, where the meek alone shall inherit the earth, where, as Protestants too believe, all that is spotless and beautiful in nature as well as in man shall bloom forever perfect?

(292)

Of course, Kingsley acknowledges, the danger run by this religious aesthetic and religious sensibility is that it becomes, like the works by Giotto and Raffaello, "altogether effeminate" and wholly banishes the "masculine" Greek virtues "of sex, of strength, of activity, of grandeur of all forms" (294). The "passive spiritual faculties" (innocence, devotion, meekness, resignation) are all good, "but not the whole of humanity" (295). And yet, rather than including these missing attributes in the objects of artistic representation, Kingsley assigns them to the viewers of past history, men who are willful and brutal before they are ennobled by the alterior attributes in the masterworks they behold:

> [Raffaello and Giotto] were faithful preachers of the great Christian truth, that devoted faith, and not fierce self-will, is man's glory. Well did their pictures tell to brutal peasants, and to still more brutal warriors, that God's might was best shewn forth, not in the elephantine pride of a Hercules, or the Titanic struggles of a Laocoon, but in the weakness of martyred women, and of warriors who were content meekly to endure shame and death, for the sake of Him who conquered by sufferings, and who bore all human weaknesses.
>
> (295-96)

Hence the subject who views works of high religious art is neither complete nor redeemable without the edifying and seductive virtues objectified therein. At the same time, the weakness and meekness of the women martyrs and Christian warriors portrayed in the paintings are—according to Kingsley's dichotomous definition of human nature—similarly incomplete without the brutal and martial subjects that stand before them. Not only is Christ unrepresented in the scene (his image only metonymically invoked as the original of the virtue of long-suffering), but the impossibility of his representation is also implied, insofar as Kingsley's desire to rewed power and meekness in an image of the Christian savior has been accomplished with great indirection, via the distribution of these qualities among viewing subjectivities and the glorified objects of their perception. Christian identity, and with it the identity of Christ, is thus made into a necessarily social phenomenon, one which appears to privilege the individual but in fact depends entirely on the interdependent symbolic functions performed by a cast of characters.

Anna Jameson develops the concern with the gendering of the viewers and subjects of Christian art in a slightly different vein. In *Legends of the Madonna* she focuses on the subject of Catholic "Virgin worship," beginning her discussion by noting the theological difficulties that have historically accompanied the subject of Christ's gender. Adele M. Holcomb notes that Jameson's choice of subject matter for the third title in her series was probably influenced by two conflicting currents in women's history of the period: the rise of interest in Mariolatry that preceded Pius IX's proclamation of the doc-

trine of the Immaculate Conception in 1854 (the doctrine according to which Mary was conceived without sin in her mother's womb), and the advent of organized feminism in England and North America (113). The historical context goes some way in explaining the odd confluence of chivalric and feminist sentiments in Jameson's treatment of the role of women in early Christian history. She praises Christ for elevating the moral status of women (so does Nightingale in *Cassandra*), but she also wrestles with the tradition that God chose a male incarnation. Since true Protestant Christianity denies the divinity of Mary, Jameson laments, it is still troubled "by the want of a new type of womanly perfection." Jameson attributes this problem to what she considers the relatively recent historical preoccupation with gendered dichotomies. "Christ, as the model man, united the virtues of the two sexes," she conjectures, "until the idea that there are essentially masculine and feminine virtues intruded itself on the higher Christian conception" (24). And yet, there is no returning to the androgynous ideal of Christ, for the bifurcation of gender is also a sign of evolutionary progress. Consequently, she reaches a conclusion common to such dissimilar figures as Florence Nightingale, Sarah Stickney Ellis, and Auguste Comte: the future of the human ideal will manifest itself, Jameson proclaims, through women—women seen not simply as spiritual and physical conduits of the race, but as the embodiments of its higher nature.[9] Defending the iconography of the Madonna, she writes:

> Others will have it that these scattered, dim, mistaken—often gross and perverted—ideas which were afterwards gathered into the pure, dignified, tender, image of the Madonna, were but as the voice of a mighty prophecy, sounded through all the generations of men, even from the beginning of time, of the coming moral regeneration, and complete and harmonious development of the whole human race, by the establishment on a higher basis, of what has been called the "feminine element" in society. And let me speak for myself. In that perpetual iteration of that beautiful image of THE WOMAN highly blessed—*there,* where others saw only pictures or statues, I have seen this great hope standing like a spirit beside the visible form: in this fervent worship once given to that gracious presence, I have beheld an acknowledgment of a higher as well as gentler power than that of the strong hand and the might that makes the right, and in every earnest votary who, as he knelt, was in this sense pious beyond the reach of his own thought, and "devout beyond the meaning of his will."
>
> (*Legends* 22)

Unlike her reviewer Kingsley, Jameson stresses the attenuation of the act of worship across an evolutionary time frame that prophesies a more active role for the "feminine element." However, like Kingsley, she divides the Christian ideal of human nature into a masculine votary and an elevated feminine icon, the latter a source of ennobling and beneficent instincts for a human nature that is, at base, at once brutal, benighted, and male.

Once again, the Protestant suspicion of an iconography of Christ is corroborated for reasons more logical than pious. For in a culture preoccupied with the gendered division of signifying functions, the project of merging human and divine consciousness into one form is unthinkable. Or, more accurately, where it was thinkable, as in the Madonna or female Christ, it was dangerous, and this on three scores. First, the implicit deification of women resulted in a form of sentimental idolatry that could only function in Protestant culture as long as the fact that it was idolatrous was denied. Second, this deification could be turned into a challenge to the patriarchal order of Victorian belief, as it had been in Joanna Southcott's day, and as it would be again in Nightingale's *Cassandra*. Finally, the merger of sacred and profane powers into one human form defeats the ideological efficacy of a social construction of human nature, which maintains a patriarchal economy of power by distributing various forms of power and powerlessness among three symbolic participants: fathers, mothers, and children.

Another set of passages relevant to these aspects of Victorian Christology occurs in a better remembered art historical opus of the 1840s, *Modern Painters II*. In the second and final section, Ruskin presents his delineation of the imaginative faculty, the faculty that mediates to human perception the external forms of beauty, the forms which he analyzed in the preceding section under the rubric of the theoretic faculty. Nowhere, Ruskin suggests, do we observe the theoretic and imaginative faculties working together so completely as in representations of "the superhuman ideal." The problem with such representations, as Ruskin describes them, echoes the problem of divine incarnation, since they "attempt at realization to the Bodily senses of the Beauty supernatural and divine" (314). Because their powers are not equal to God, Ruskin withholds from artists the ability to portray Christ successfully. In human works the supernatural ideal necessarily diverts from its perfect culmination, manifesting itself instead in various indirect and peripheral means of representation: the depiction of God assuming a nonhuman form, such as the dove or the lamb; the depiction of a form properly belonging to the supernatural ideal, but not necessarily seen, such as the risen Christ appearing to his disciples behind closed doors; and the depiction of the supernatural ideal's operation on human forms, such as in the shining of Moses's face (315). Through these metonymic representations artists have gained greater success than in their portraiture of Christ, Ruskin determines, and indeed "all who are acquainted with the range of sacred

art will admit not only that no representation of Christ has ever been partially successful, but that the greatest painters fall therein below their accustomed level" (317).

As in the passages from Kingsley and Jameson, Ruskin's opinions here are no doubt assisted by a residual Protestant conviction that Catholic iconography is idolatrous. However, what is for our purposes more striking is that Ruskin explicitly averts the artist's gaze from the body of Christ and fixes it instead on certain peripheral means of representing the superhuman ideal—pictures of angels, for example, or, what is by now a familiar substitute, of the Madonna: "We need reason no farther, but may limit ourselves to the purest modes of giving a conception of superhuman but still creature forms, as of angels; in equal rank with whom, perhaps, we may place the mother of Christ" (318). The passage exemplifies Paul Sawyer's diagnosis of a tendency that connects the first and second volumes of *Modern Painters*: "The acceptance of human imperfection produces the vision of a transcendent feminine Other" (81).[10] It also exemplifies a tendency that connects Ruskin to a broader cultural discourse, since by turning away from Christ and toward the secondary embodiments of God, Ruskin demonstrates the tendency of his generation to deify images of women—or, perhaps more precisely, of women and children, since the Madonna alluded to here is identified with her function as the bearer of a child. And yet, these secondary representations of an incarnational ideal are hardly an escape from the paradoxes of the primary incarnation, insofar as deified women are models at once preferable to a male Christ (for Victorian culture enforced, often at the expense of masculine sanctity, a direct bond between femininity and Christian holiness) and regrettably inferior (for within this discourse female images cannot fully realize the incarnation of God into man).

Here and elsewhere in *Modern Painters II*, the hidden face of God is the absent center of Ruskin's eschatological narrative of Renaissance art, a narrative that traces one thread of the *res extensia* of God through creation, even as it looks forward to the return of God and man to a *res cogitans* of heavenly apprehension. Throughout, the voice of the narrator imparts certainty that the study of beauty and the structure of aesthetic perception are not unlike the study of God and the structure of heavenly worship. For the reader ensconced in the above concluding details of Ruskin's epistemology of beauty, this certainty is likely to be an encouragement, all the more so since Ruskin has already reached his true conclusion some chapters before.[11] At the end of section 1, Ruskin explains how "theoria" or the theoretic faculty works in the service of a beneficent Deity, and as if to prove the point he conveys with the virtuosity of his scripturally resonant prose a foretaste of his imagined heaven:

We cannot say how far it is right or agreeable with God's will, while men are perishing round about us, while grief, and pain, and wrath, and impiety, and death, and all the powers of the air, are working wildly and evermore, and the cry of the blood going up to heaven, that any of us should take hand from the plough; but this we know, that there will come a time when the service of God shall be in the beholding of him, and though in these stormy seas, where we are now driven up and down, his Spirit is dimly seen on the face of the waters, and we are left to cast anchors out of the stern, and wish for the day, that day will come, when, with the evangelists on the crystal and stable sea, all the creatures of God shall be full of eyes within, and there shall be "no more curse, but his servants shall serve him, and shall see his face."

(217-18)

In a sense, this conclusion is a visionary resolution to a question that Gary Wihl affiliates with the entire volume of *Modern Painters II*—a continuation of the first volume's attempt to decide "between the externally given and the internal, imaginative modification" (43). For if, at the culmination of time we are, as Ruskin paraphrases Revelation 22.3-4, "full of eyes within," it is unclear if the God we behold is within ourselves or without.

Importantly, the collapse of subject and object is here situated in an apocalyptic moment, as it was in Coleridge's prose, and as it was in the Irvingite glossolalists' belief that the possession of their bodies by God signaled an imminent Second Coming. We cannot know to what extent those earlier visionaries found in their self-shattering experiences an efficacious sense of escape or renewal. We can determine, however, from the textual record, that their experiences were tightly situated within the social and political structures of their lives, and that the heavenly impulse toward a catastrophic surrender of their identities also worked as a weapon in their contestations of and for religious authority. Set in this context, the ambiguous difference between the subject and object of worship in the above paragraph is far from being a momentary nuance of Ruskin's prose; it goes to the heart of mid-Victorian concepts of humanity, and to the divisions of power (social, sexual, and psychological) that structured those concepts. For, as we know, once Ruskin turns (in the following chapter) to the subject of this-wordly visions of the divine, the nondifferentiated apocalypse wherein sacred beauty extends both inward and out will divide itself into the more distinct and socially provocative form of a holy family.

In this way, the social and psychological patterns of Victorian worship were structured by the impossibility of the condition that Ruskin defines as heaven—the perception of a God at once internal and external, of a ubiquitous God who claims all space, both social and psychological, in the name of divine beauty. Likewise, one of the modern Christs of the nineteenth century was a character split internally between an awareness of his godhead and the awareness of himself as a mortal man. Versions of this psychologized Christ appear in the biographies of Renan, Strauss, and Farrar. Arguably, it is also a concern of some Pre-Raphaelite depictions of Christ—of Millais's *Christ in the Home of His Parents*, for example, where the boy Jesus displays a wound in his hand, a signifier in the flesh of his shocking corporal vulnerability, but also a typological reference to the antitype of his crucifixion, of the uncanny certainty of his sacrificial destiny as a god. His divided consciousness is the center of the painting, defining as it does the positions, attitudes, and functions of those who surround him.[12] It might also be understood as the social and psychological predicament with which an imagined male viewer of the nineteenth century most readily identifies. Separated from perfection by a materiality that was the condition of his being, male Victorian Christians had a primary prerogative to assign moral and psychological qualities to the various members of society, to institute the nuclear family as the whole embodiment of human traits, and to sequester this communal economy of human attributes within an individualistic paradigm of the soul in a state of (so Ruskin would have it in 1846) expectation and deferral, a state of seeking the habitat of its redeemer.

Notes

1. Elinor S. Shaffer exemplifies the renewed interest in Christ in the early nineteenth century with observations on Hegel, Coleridge, Goethe, and finally Jean Paul's dramatic *Rede des toten Christus,* a portion of which Carlyle translated in "Jean Paul Richter Again" (1829). As Shaffer comments, "the more the theology of the age came to stress Christ as the link between man and a distant God, or like Schleiermacher himself, Christ himself as man, the more He too became cut off from God" (61).

2. These more or less canonical representations of Christ emerged against the backdrop of a religious publishing industry that produced Gospel harmonies, New Testament commentaries, New Testament stories for children, and prophetic analyses of Revelation. A sampling of such works that were available at mid-century to pious readers of several denominations includes the following titles: *The Parables of Our Lord,* by the Wife of an Irish Clergyman (1837); *Gospel Stories, illustrative of the incidents in the History of Our Saviour* (1845); *Lectures Explanatory of the Diatessoran, or History of Our Lord Jesus Christ,* by J. D. MacBride (1835); *An Evangelical Life of Our Saviour* (1820); *The Words of Lord Jesus,* by John Reed (1823); *The Life, Doctrine and Sufferings of Our*

Blessed Lord, by Rev. Henry Rutter (1830); *Christ an Example for the Young,* by Robert Mimpriss (1854); *Reflections on the Genealogy of Jesus Christ* (1836); and *Gershem, or, the 33,000 Words of Jesus Christ* (1847). Denominational treatments of Christ differed from one another not so much in content (there being little room for innovation here) as in tone and genre. Even these distinctions, however, were not clear-cut; moreover, religious authors frequently employed the fictional and lyrical modes that were, strictly speaking, considered profane by Evangelical and conservative Non-Conformists. One example is the work of Robert Montgomery, a clown at the Bath theater who also wrote religious lyrics. In 1832 he published a long poem titled *The Messiah.* Despite negative reviews from both secular and religious journals, *The Messiah* passed through eight editions by 1842. The modest popularity of *The Messiah,* attests to the presence of a theologically flexible lower-class readership with some influence in the literary marketplace.

3. While my primary focus in [this essay and in Chapter Four of *Victorian Testaments* is] on the manner in which nineteenth-century Christology interacted with the politics of gender in England, a more explicit and more extensive dialogue between Christology and political issues was occurring at roughly the same time in Germany. Marilyn Chapin Massey has traced the political subtext to the several editions of Strauss's *Das Leben Jesu,* arguing that the "genius" Christ of the third edition of 1838 was ensconced in a complex philosophical discourse, employed primarily by Left and Right Hegelians, wherein a masculine or politically active type of genius was opposed to a feminine and inwardly directed type of genius. These metonymic chains also extended into class, as evidenced by the left-wing Hegelian Arnold Ruge's denunciation of the modified Christ of Strauss's third edition as an "aristocratic" portrayal (Massey 114). By juxtaposing this Christ to that of the earlier 1835 edition, Massey finds in the history of Strauss's book an analogue for German political history of the same decade: while "the 1835 *Life of Christ* caught up and changed the idioms of German culture to present an image of people struggling collectively for their freedom," the altered edition of 1838 "offered the palliative of an aristocratic Christ, a genius Christ, who was the epitome of the perfection of the inner life" (149).

4. If nothing else, the Evangelical movement strengthened the associations between women and religion by virtue of the fact that so many women were active in Evangelical philanthropic and missionary societies and often assumed leadership

roles. However, Vance argues that Kingsley's reasons for objecting to Evangelicalism had less to do with its feminization of religion than with its residual Calvinist disdain for the body. Thus Kingsley lumped Evangelicalism in with Tractarianism as "Manichee" religious beliefs, movements whose "rejection of the physical world . . . ran counter to his insistence on a healthy body and a healthy mind" (30-35). But Vance also notes that at the popular level the muscular Christian notion of manliness was a less sophisticated rejoinder to the notion that, as the Baptist preacher C. H. Spurgeon summarized, "if you become a Christian you must sink your manliness and turn milksop" (quoted in Vance, 26). The writings of Sarah Stickney Ellis exemplify how practical associations between women and religion were verified by an essentialist discourse; among the qualities that Ellis attaches to both women and Christ were self-sacrifice, devotional purity, and "the capacity for . . . intense enjoyment" (156-214). Florence Nightingale seemed to take such advice to heart; as we [Consider in Chapter 5 of *Victorian Testaments*], Nightingale concludes her feminist tract *Cassandra* with the prophecy of a female savior.

5. As Jeremy Maas explains, for the figure of Christ Hunt used a variety of models: Elizabeth Siddal for the hair, Christina Rossetti for the face. Additionally, Maas has uncovered evidence that Hunt might also have employed a third model, Henry Clark, who would have sat, as Maas determines, "primarily for the figure, rather than the features, of Christ" (39-42).

6. Kingsley's characterization of Jameson's religious upbringing is misleading: she was born in Dublin of an Irish father and an English mother, and Jameson claimed that efforts to indoctrinate her in childhood were undercut by her "confused and heterodox" understanding of the Bible (Jameson, *Commonplace Book* 127). Moreover, Jameson later became active in the cause of Catholic and Protestant religious orders for women—a movement that Kingsley did not believe to be consistent with Protestant belief.

7. For Maynard's discussion of Kingsley's views of femininity and female sexuality, see pp. 120-21.

8. Reconstructing events more than fifty years past, Hunt traces the Brotherhood's origins to conversations he had with John Everett Millais in late 1847 and early 1848. One crucial conversation takes place over Hunt's painting *Christ and the Two Maries.* In response to Millais's suggestion that he refer to the prints of the old masters, Hunt is moved to eloquence: with the principles of the old masters he won't be satisfied, for after much cogitation Hunt has developed "scruples" that are

"nothing less than irreverent, heretical, and revolutionary." Against the "paralyzing content" of the Reynolds school—its complacency with "settled laws" that have "no living power"—Hunt opposes the preferability of a long apprenticeship to nature, because "dogma," Hunt affirms, "does not transmit genius." As impertinent toward the authority of the Royal Academy as he would be humble toward that of nature, Hunt concludes on a note that seems to sentence the Pre-Raphaelites to a protracted adolescence: "Children should begin as children," he tells Millais, "and wait for the years to bring them to maturity" (1: 82-86).

9. Comte's late philosophy relinquished the more scientific diction of its earlier phases and established women as the objects of worship in his new "religion of humanity." This form of worship, he insisted, was entirely consistent with the tenets of his positivism: "Positivism . . . encourages, on intellectual as well as moral grounds, full and systematic expression of the feeling of veneration for women." The truly mystified nature of this veneration becomes inescapably apparent in the following paragraph, in which, as in other instances cited in this chapter, women are sources of improvement for male worshipers whose inferiority and dependence are oddly canceled out by their explicit monopoly on power: in the Positivist future, Comte prophesies, "the enervating influence of chimerical beliefs will have passed away; and men in all the vigour of their energies, feeling themselves the masters of the known world, will feel it their highest happiness to submit to the beneficent power of womanly sympathy. In a word, Man will in those days kneel to Woman, and to Woman only" (287-88).

10. The thesis that, within the discourse that Ruskin participates in, normative subjectivity is aligned with human imperfection and is gendered masculine is reinforced by Sawyer's later description of Ruskin's distinction between sublime and visionary art: "For Ruskin, sublime art induces identification with masculine energy, visionary art contemplation of the beautiful as an object; in religious terms one form is 'taken in' like the eucharist, the other beheld as an icon or memorial" (83).

11. In fact, as Gary Wihl observes, the second section of *Modern Painters II* was added to the manuscript during one of its revisions (43).

12. In a similar vein, Sussman suggests that Millais's *Christ in the House of His Parents* demonstrates a concern with picturing the family as "a center of bourgeois value, as the source of economic support and emotional nurturance," but at the same time registers anxieties "about manliness and particularly male sexuality" (121).

Works Cited

Arnold, Matthew. "Rugby Chapel." In *Collected Works of Matthew Arnold: Poetry and Prose,* vol. 1, ed. John Bryson. Cambridge, Mass.: Harvard University Press, 1954.

Arnold, Thomas. "The Bible." In *Miscellaneous Works of Thomas Arnold,* 146-59. New York: D. Appleton & Co., 1845.

———. "The Church." In *Miscellaneous Works of Thomas Arnold,* 1-72. New York: D. Appleton & Co., 1845.

———. "Early Roman History" (1825). In *Miscellaneous Works of Thomas Arnold,* 378-403. New York: D. Appleton & Co., 1845.

———. "The effects of distant Colonization on the Parent State; a prize essay, recited in the theatre at Oxford, June 7, 1815." The Collection of the British Library.

———. "Essay on the Right Interpretation of Scripture." In *Sermons,* 2nd ed., vol. II, 427-78. London: B. Fellowes, 1832-34.

———. *History of Rome* (1838). 2 vols. New York: D. Appleton & Co., 1872.

———. *Introductory Lectures on Modern History* (1842). New York: D. Appleton and Co., 1880.

———. *Principles of Church Reform* (1833). In *Miscellaneous Works of Thomas Arnold,* 73-130. New York: D. Appleton & Co., 1845.

———. *Tracts for the Times.* In *Miscellaneous Works of Thomas Arnold,* 236-89. New York: D. Appleton & Co., 1845.

———. "Two Sermons on the Interpretation of Prophecy" (1838). In *Religious Controversies of the Nineteenth Century,* ed. A. O. J. Cockshut, 93-103. Lincoln: University of Nebraska Press, 1966.

Carlyle, Thomas. "Death of Edward Irving." In *Critical and Miscellaneous Essays,* vol. 3. London: Chapman and Hall, 1899.

———. *On Heroes, Hero-Worship and the Heroic in History* (1840). In *The Works of Thomas Carlyle,* 2nd ed., vol. 5. New York: AMS Press, 1980.

———. *Sartor Resartus* (1833-34). In *The Works of Thomas Carlyle,* 2nd ed., vol. 1. New York: AMS Press, 1980.

Comte, Auguste. *A General View of Positivism* (1875). Trans. J. H. Bridges. New York: Robert Speller and Sons, 1957.

Dickens, Charles. *Dombey and Son* (1846-48). Harmondsworth, England: Penguin Books, 1970.

———. *The Life of Our Lord* (1848). New York: Simon and Schuster, 1934.

———. "Old Lamps for New Ones." *Household Words* 1 (1850): 258-69.

———. *Pilgrim Edition of the Letters of Charles Dickens,* vol. 5, *1847-49.* Ed. Graham and K. J. Fielding Storey. Oxford: Clarendon Press, 1981.

Ellis, Sarah Stickney. *The Daughters of England: Their Position in Society, Character, and Responsibilities.* New York: D. Appleton, 1843.

Foxton, F. J. *Popular Christianity: Its Transition State, and Probable Development.* London: John Chapman, 1849.

Hughes, Thomas. *Tom Brown's Schooldays* (1857). New York: Grosset and Dunlap, 1930.

Hunt, William Holman. *Pre-Raphaelitism and the pre-Raphaelite brotherhood.* 2 vols. London: Macmillan, 1905-6.

Jameson, Anna. *A Commonplace Book of Thoughts, Memories, and Fancies, Original and Selected.* London: Longman's, 1855.

———. *Legends of the Madonna, as Represented in the Fine Arts* (1852). Boston and New York: Houghton, Mifflin, 1885.

———. *Sacred and Legendary Art* (1848). 2 vols. Boston and New York: Houghton, Mifflin, 1885.

[Kingsley, Charles.] "The poetry of sacred and legendary art." *Fraser's* 39 (Mar. 1849): 283-98.

Maas, Jeremy. *Holman Hunt and 'The Light of the World'.* London: Scolar Press, 1984.

Massey, Marilyn Chapin. *Christ Unmasked: The Meaning of the 'Life of Jesus' in German Politics.* Chapel Hill: University of North Carolina Press, 1983.

Maynard, John. *Victorian Discourses on Sexuality and Religion.* Cambridge: Cambridge University Press, 1993.

Nightingale, Florence. "Cassandra" and Other Selections from "Suggestions for Thought". Ed. Mary Poovey. New York: New York University Press, 1992.

———. *Ever Yours, Florence Nightingale: Selected Letters.* Ed. Martha Vicinus and Bea Nergaard. London: Virago Press, 1989.

———. *"I Have Done My Duty": Florence Nightingale and the Crimean War, 1854-56.* Ed. Sue Goldie. Iowa City: University of Iowa Press, 1987.

———. "Introduction" to *Sketch of the History and Progress of District Nursing,* by William Rathbone. London: Macmillan, 1890.

———. *Letters From Egypt: A Journey on the Nile, 1848-1850.* Ed. Anthony Sattin. New York: Weidenfeld and Nicholson, 1987.

———. *Notes on Nursing: What It Is, and What It Is Not* (1859). New York: D. Appleton, 1912.

———. Papers. The Florence Nightingale Museum. London.

———. *Suggestions for Thought to Searchers After Religious Truth Among the Artizans of England.* 3 vols. London: George E. Eyre and William Spottiswoode, 1860.

———. *"Suggestions for Thought" by Florence Nightingale: Selections and Commentaries.* Ed. Michael D. Calabria and Janet A. Macrae. Philadelphia: University of Pennsylvania Press, 1994.

Ruskin, John. "Lectures on Architecture and Painting" (1854). In *The Works of John Ruskin,* vol. 12, ed. E. T. Cook and Alexander Wedderburn, 134-64. London: George Allen, 1903.

———. *Modern Painters II.* In *The Works of John Ruskin,* vol. 4, ed. E. T. Cook and Alexander Wedderburn. London: George Allen, 1903.

Sawyer, Paul L. *Ruskin's Poetic Argument: The Design of the Major Works.* Ithaca: Cornell University Press, 1985.

Shaffer, Elinor S. *'Kubla Khan' and 'The Fall of Jerusalem': The Mythological School in Biblical Criticism and Secular Literature, 1770-1880.* Cambridge: Cambridge University Press, 1975.

Strong, Roy. *'And when did you last see your father?': The Victorian painter and British history.* London: Thames and Hudson, 1978.

Sussman, Herbert. *Victorian Masculinities: Manhood and Masculine Poetics in Early Victorian Literature and Art.* Cambridge: Cambridge University Press, 1995.

Vance, Norman. *Sinews of the Spirit: The Ideal of Christian Manliness in Victorian Literature and Religious Thought.* Cambridge: Cambridge University Press, 1985.

Wihl, Gary. *Ruskin and the Rhetoric of Infallibility.* New Haven: Yale University Press, 1985.

WOMEN WRITERS

Ruth Y. Jenkins (essay date 1995)

SOURCE: Jenkins, Ruth Y. "To 'Stand with Christ against the World': Gaskell's Sentimental Social Agenda." In *Reclaiming Myths of Power: Women Writ-*

ers and the Victorian Spiritual Crisis, pp. 93-116. Lewisburg, Penn., London, and Toronto, Ontario: Bucknell University Press and Associated University Presses, 1995.

[*In the following essay, Jenkins contends that Gaskell offers an alternate interpretation of Judeo-Christian tradition in order to model the empowerment of disenfranchised members of Victorian society.*]

> "An unfit subject for fiction" is *the* thing to say about [*Ruth*]; I knew all this before; but I determined notwithstanding to speak my mind out about it; only how I shrink with more pain than I can tell you from what people are saying, though I wd do every jot of it over again to-morrow. . . . In short the only comparison I can find for myself is to St Sebastian tied to a tree to be shot at with arrows.
>
> —Elizabeth Gaskell, *LG*, 220-21

Near the end of Elizabeth Gaskell's second novel, *Ruth* (1853), Thurston Benson defends his efforts to help the fallen protagonist work out her salvation, telling Mr. Bradshaw that he intends to "stand with Christ against the world."[1] Although declared late in the novel, this conflict—between Christ and man—permeates the work, shaping the story of Ruth Hilton—her seduction by Bellingham (and the worldly values he represents) and her redemption by Benson's charitable beliefs. Through this dissenting minister's compassion and pronouncements, Gaskell "speak[s] [her] mind out," challenging society. Against this model, she contrasts Bradshaw's moral vengeance: although a member of Benson's Dissenting Chapel, Bradshaw is foremost a capitalist whose dependence on his culture's established practices cause his preachments to echo distinctly those dominant ideological agendas. The extent to which he privileges the symbolic order of that culture—clerical and political—over the values represented by the dissenting minister is revealed when Benson refuses to prosecute Bradshaw's son, Richard, for embezzlement. Even when his son is involved, Bradshaw insists to Benson: "If there were more people like me, and fewer like you, there would be less evil in the world, sir. It's your sentimentalists that nurse up sin" (*R*, 402). Through these confrontational dialogues between Bradshaw and Benson, the novel's main plot about Ruth Hilton and its subplot about Bradshaw's son intersect and illuminate each other. With the nexus of these two narratives, Gaskell can expose her culture's gender-based moral codes and hierarchical agenda and present as an alternative a revolutionary, sentimental model for social reform.[2]

The revolutionary potential of this alternative social vision can best be understood by clarifying the period's dominant social order. At the heart of that order is the complicit dynamic between the political and clerical components of Victorian society. Gaskell believed that the powerful Church of England, with its hierarchical

structure and strict dogma, reproduced her culture's ideology: both the sacred and secular spheres separated men and women and subjected women in God's name. Believing such social conditions were man-made and not of divine design, Gaskell charged her culture with appropriating God's word to authorize industrial oppression for greater profit and female subjection for men's vicarious salvation.

Central to Gaskell's conflict with her culture is this appropriation of sacred symbolism for a human enterprise, an appropriation that, she would argue, misconstrues God's word for patriarchal ends. The alternative agenda that she posits would seek to replace her culture's ethical and secular hierarchy with a social vision that recognizes the integral interdependence of humanity— whether worker or master, woman or man. Significantly, by claiming just such authority Gaskell, *re*appropriates sacred imagery to empower and validate those her culture marginalizes.

While Gaskell delineates the tensions between masters and workers inherent in a rapidly industrializing culture more explicitly in *Mary Barton* and *North and South,* no where does she provide such a revolutionary vision for revising gender-based moral codes as she does in *Ruth.*[3] This history of an innocent girl's fall, redemption, temptation, and salvation—a revisionist story of biblical history, replacing Christ's passion as female in patriarchal society—exposes the cultural appropriation of God and His word that Gaskell witnesses. Through this story of social rejection and Christian compassion, Gaskell charges her culture to replace what she sees as a rigid and reductive Old Testament ethic of justice with a charitable and compassionate New Testament ethic of charity. By appropriating the most fundamental myth in Western religion as a narrative strategy to critique and reform Victorian culture, Gaskell challenges her readers to question the doctrines considered sacred and reevaluate standards considered divinely ordained. With her use of religious symbolism in *Ruth,* she challenges her readers to reconsider, like her character Jemima, "Who was true? Who was not? Who was good and pure? Who was not?" (*R*, 322). As with Jemima, "The very foundations of . . . belief [would be] shaken" (*R*, 322). Through this unsettling narrative strategy, Gaskell privileges a New Testament vision built upon a foundation of charity and mercy that grafts what I identify, and will later develop, as the earthly model of mother-love to what she believed to be the sacred law of God the Father.

Gaskell reproduces both the dominant social dynamics of her culture and her competing model in *Ruth;* the tension between these two social patterns not only propels the narrative but also reveals the conservative power Gaskell harnesses to fuel her "sentimental" model. Just as she constructs characters, like Jemima, who must question both their beliefs and the assumptions upon which they rest, Gaskell also foregrounds the anticipated dismissal of this new model by having Bradshaw label it *sentimental*. It is at this self-critical point that Gaskell reveals her text at its most subversive. When Bradshaw names her social vision "sentimental," he uses its pejorative meaning to dismiss Benson and his behavior. Representing the culture's dominant ideology, Bradshaw can only see sentimentalism as negative; Gaskell, however, through Benson and Ruth, reclaims "sentimental" as positive. This reverberation between Bradshaw's negative and Benson's positive naming of sentimental operates in a parallel manner to the text as a whole: not only does Gaskell contrast the dominant social patterns with her radical agenda for human interaction, but she also juxtaposes a reinterpreted symbolic, sacred order to the one appropriated by her patriarchal culture that authorizes the maintenance of established social dynamics.[4]

By reclaiming the power associated with religious imagery to authorize and narrate her story, Gaskell's vision extends beyond the subjection of women or the maltreatment of Victorian workers; Gaskell's revolutionary model is tantamount to collapsing her culture's ideology, replacing it with "sentimental" values. By labeling her own vision sentimental, Gaskell produces two narrative effects. First, because the pharisaical Bradshaw voices this pejorative label, we are forced to question his (and by association the culture's) reliability as an interpreter of either the natural or the supernatural world. Second, with the pejorative connotation of sentimental questioned simply by who voices it, Gaskell subverts the patriarchal energy attempting to disparage and discredit this alternative model of human interaction. Doing so, Gaskell revalues as positive the behavior pejoratively labeled sentimental, and more importantly, she reframes it as a model of behavior to be neither limited to women nor restricted to the domestic sphere.

This chapter will consider in detail the explicit delineation of the *sentimental* vision found in *Ruth*: how Gaskell appropriates religious imagery as a narrative strategy to subvert patriarchal standards and social codes, how she rejects a culturally bifurcated morality. Jane P. Tompkins has recently argued that sentimental fiction, what she describes as a political enterprise halfway between a sermon and social theory, attempts to reorganize culture from a woman's point of view.[5] This revisionist theory of sentimental fiction provides a useful method from which to reconsider Gaskell's fiction. I argue, however, that to understand Gaskell's agenda fully, one must recognize that even if Gaskell's culture domesticated these values, the subculture in which Gaskell lived did not.[6] These values were propagated by her religion—Unitarianism—regardless of gender. Because of this grounding in her spiritual beliefs, a brief consideration of the Victorian Unitarian church is necessary to clarify the extent to which Gaskell's ideology, as it appears in her fiction, reflects not just a woman's perspective, but a social dynamic alternative to that sanctioned and perpetuated by her culture's dominant ideology.

Elizabeth Gaskell grew up in one of the leading Unitarian families of her day and married into another. Because this dissenting sect believed in the importance of individual potential, both men and women were educated. Gaskell, even though raised by her maternal aunts upon her mother's death, received an extensive education.[7] The community in which Gaskell grew up, then, challenged not only the Church of England but also, by educating her, the prevalent gender-based distinctions. The nondoctrinare history of this faith, its intellectual appetite for multiple perspectives, its disbelief in the Trinity or Christ's divinity, and its powerful philanthropic traditions placed it in firm contradiction to the patriarchal hierarchy of the established Church; and just as importantly, it stood in contrast to the prevalent Hebraic and authoritarian element of Victorian religion by embracing and practicing a New Testament ethic.[8]

These differences—this ethic of justice represented by the Church of England and the ethic of Christian charity practiced by the Unitarian faith—echo important gender distinctions that Carol Gilligan has identified in her important study of psychological growth. Reexamining patterns of male and female moral development, she describes the different developmental paradigms as the ethic of justice (for traditional male development) and the ethic of care (for the female), differences that result from either a perspective of separate (male) or connected (female) object relations.[9] Significantly, though, when considering Gilligan's results against the ethical paradigm illustrated in *Ruth*, the division of justice and mercy is not aligned along gender divisions for Gaskell, just as the "sentimental" values are not relegated to the domestic sphere in her subculture. Instead these ethical models parallel what Gaskell saw as differences between Old and New Testament values, between a Hebraic Church of England and dissent. For this reason, the radicalism of Gaskell's social agenda is underscored when one recognizes that these values of empathy and compassion, traditionally associated with women and the domestic sphere, are put forth as the ethical values through which all humanity should interact in both public and private spheres—men and women alike.

The contrast between the beliefs that the Unitarians held and those they ascribed to the Church of England appears in sermons of William Gaskell, Elizabeth's husband. These sermons reveal the important differences between justice and charity: the fundamental importance of God's mercy, not vengeance, for all; the belief that no sinner is damned to everlasting punishment; the contention that the New Testament offers a system of ethics for everyday life; and finally, the commitment to charitable conduct as a mark of the true Christian.[10] But most significantly, his sermons illuminate the conflict between Gaskell's Unitarian values and the Church of England. Shortly after the Gaskells' marriage, William Gaskell

> preached against intolerance by Protestant theologians, and defended Unitarianism on the principle of liberty of interpretation of the Scriptures and on the grounds that no man can claim infallibility for his views . . . his view of the Gospel is that: it is simply the highest teacher of humanity. . . . In a still later sermon . . . while reaffirming his view that errors of interpretation need to be fought against, he points out that intelligent artisans reject orthodoxy and religion altogether because of it. . . . He then goes on to attack the popular interpretations which present a religion based on fear.[11]

Living within this religious environment, Gaskell's ethical perspective placed her *outside* her culture's Established Church but still inside a community that significantly defined itself by challenging that church. While many of her contemporaries, when faced with the limitations of organized religion, found themselves crippled with doubt, Gaskell's beliefs provided her with an alternative vision of society and code of behavior. Unitarianism nurtured the values displayed by Benson in *Ruth* and charged the Victorian culture to replace its Old Testament values with those of the new. And, while other sects such as the Evangelicals endeavored as well to make Victorian Christianity a living religion, preferring deeds to doctrine, Gaskell's vision took this idea further: translocating the values associated with the home into the streets, authorizing women as well as men to be spiritual actors.

The importance of Gaskell's religious beliefs and background in shaping her narrative strategies, then, is twofold: 1) because of this heritage, she stands outside the powerful Church, but within an organized body actively working to change cultural values; and 2) because Unitarianism believed in the cultivation of the intellect regardless of sex, she found the religious authority to challenge patriarchal subjection of women, especially those who failed to fulfill their socially defined roles.[12] So, ironically, in a period nearly defined by its theological doubt, Gaskell's spiritual faith authorizes her revolutionary vision.

The nonhierarchical dogma of her faith, her close political ties with Christian socialists,[13] and the numerous industrialist dissenters who attended her husband's chapel contributed to the complexity of Gaskell's vision of industrialism, capitalism, and the workers' plight. Although she believed in the Carlylean doctrine "Do the

duty that lies nearest to thee" (*LG*, 117), she could not help but also see the impoverished and dreadful conditions in which the workers lived and often worked. And, just as she could see the workers' exploitation from industrialization, she saw parallel exploitation of women in patriarchal culture.[14]

Many women, especially those from the middle and upper classes, rather than be able to work themselves, became a means of capital for men. Mirroring this condition, Gaskell's character Jemima Bradshaw voices anger and frustration at her father's mercenary attitude that projects her as the future wife of his business partner: she "felt as if she would rather be bought openly, like an Oriental daughter, where no one is degraded in their own eyes by being parties to such a contract" (*R*, 238). The increasing pattern of the overt symbol of purity, yet covert role of monetary status that women were expected to play in maintaining the culture's ideology, fueled the condemnation and ostricization of women who failed to do so. Here, especially, the nexus between the political and clerical appropriation of religious imagery is evident. Any woman who radically rejected her assigned position in culture by defying socially determined sexual mores called forth Milton's image of Satan's expulsion from heaven—the fall—and, like Satan, those fallen women possessed a curious subversive energy with which to threaten the dominant ideology.[15]

It is this energy that Gaskell taps in *Ruth* to reshape personal and social dynamics.[16] If, as Tompkins argues, sentimental fiction is an amalgam of sermon and social theory, then Gaskell's narrative exploited the strengths of both modes of discourse in *Ruth*. Unlike the powerful industrialists who contributed to the domestication of Christianity, Gaskell does not separate the "sermon" from the social theory, the shape of her fiction from her vision.[17] Gaskell, along with her husband, worked and shared common beliefs with the Victorian Christian socialists. This intense interest in a philosophy that sought to explode the Church's pacifying myth of a future, heavenly reward to excuse oppressive conditions on earth provided Gaskell with a political ideology akin to her Unitarian beliefs. And because she lived and worked in the heart of industrial Manchester, Gaskell invested her fiction with vivid details from real life, with an energy born from witnessing real suffering.[18] To this realistic portrait of the poor and fallen, Gaskell fuses religious images and myth, but unlike earlier religious discourse, her narrative would be intimately grounded in the sordid realities of secular life.[19] This grafting in Gaskell's fiction worked two ways. The Victorian reader, in contrast to the modern reader, would quickly respond to even obscure biblical allusions,[20] and because Gaskell secularized biblical myth, her readers would be forced to reexamine cultural beliefs when they failed to concur with these stories made parallel. Like Jemima Bradshaw, they should ask: "Who was true? Who was not? Who was good and pure? Who was not?"

Gaskell's use of religious imagery as a narrative strategy enabled her to subvert patriarchal fictions, to tell a different story from those sanctioned by patriarchal values. In *Ruth,* Gaskell produces a revisionist incarnation story, validating and empowering the ostracized and victimized fallen Ruth Hilton. By creating a character who is first condemned and then revered by her culture, Gaskell calls that culture's values into question; by characterizing Ruth as both a Mary Magdalene and a Madonna figure, Gaskell subverts and explodes her culture's and its sanctioned religion's rigid and reductive dichotomous vision of women.

Gaskell's agenda can best be illustrated by examining the narrative's three sections, each of which culminates in a major turning point in Ruth Hilton's history: first, the story of her life from becoming a dressmaker's apprentice until her exposure by Bradshaw as an impostor and fallen woman; the second, her marginalization and ostricization by her culture, her penitence, and subsequent public salvation; and third, her decision to nurse her seducer, Bellingham/Donne, through his fever, an act that brings about her death.[21] Examining Gaskell's choice of narrative structure as well as the importance of the Richard Bradshaw subplot can demonstrate the full impact of her revolutionary agenda for the reader.

Significantly, Gaskell spends most of the novel in detailing this first part of Ruth's story, chronologically carrying the reader through her character's life, beginning with her first night as an orphaned apprentice at Mrs. Mason's dress shop. Forcing us to experience Ruth's life along with her—seeing her world as she sees it, feeling the isolation and loneliness that she feels—Gaskell manipulates our values and preconceived notions of fallen women. The reader sees the naive adolescent, left without mother or father, forced to manipulate a new and impersonal environment; and so, when Ruth allows herself to be seduced, while the reader may have the experience to foresee the outcome, we realize that Ruth does not. Because of this, the reader cannot help seeing the forces that contribute to this seduction, and should not be as willing to judge and condemn Ruth.

Not only does Gaskell portray Ruth's fall and redemption in this first section, but she also tempers the seducer, Bellingham, by presenting him through Ruth's unworldly eyes. This subjective rendering, combined with the portrayal of Ruth working out her salvation through her love for her son, should temper the readers'

cultivated moral reaction. When her past is revealed, then, the reader *should* see the narrow and reductive reaction of her culture. Like the Bensons with whom she lives, the reader has made an investment in Ruth's rehabilitation, has been educated through Gaskell's characterization of this fallen woman—that, although Ruth has "sinned," she is not evil.[22]

In this first section of the novel, which traces the history of Ruth's adolescence, seduction, fall, and redemption, Gaskell provides a revisionist myth of Christian history: from prelapsarian Eve to her seduction and fall, Christ's later temptation, his agony in the garden, and finally his willingness to fulfill prophecy, Ruth's life reenacts (and reinterprets) Christian myth. Like Eve, Ruth struggles with seduction, but unlike Eve, she has not received God's (or even man's) warnings about evil. With the exception of confusing and undefined feelings, Ruth is literally without a symbolic code of values; she was, the narrator tells her readers, "too young when her mother died to have received any cautions or words of advice respecting *the* subject of a woman's life" (*R,* 44).

Ruth has neither the living mother, whose behavior would literalize morality for her, nor the ability to translate the vague memories of her mother's actions into an abstracted code of value—whether for sacred or secular agendas. Consequently, she struggles unsuccessfully to reconcile her instinct that meeting Bellingham might be wrong with the genuine pleasure she receives from his companionship and love. The "strange undefined" feelings that she experiences make her question her walks with him (*R,* 39), but after deciding that she had not been "defrauding Mrs. Mason of any of her time," Ruth even concludes that "there must be something wrong in [her] . . . to feel so guilty when [she has] done nothing which is not right" (*R,* 41). Significantly Ruth turns to the memory of her mother's words to reconcile her feelings: since "dear mamma used to say [the ability to thank God] was a sign when pleasures were innocent and good" and Ruth can "thank God for the happiness [she] has had in [the] charming spring walk," she concludes that these walks could not be bad (*R,* 41). Yet on Ruth's fateful journey to her home, the aging family worker fails in his attempts to warn Ruth of her potential seduction. Old Thomas, unable to speak literally to her of this danger, turns to the abstract language of the Bible. Ruth, never having been taught to manipulate this symbolic language, is left baffled, and "never imagined that the grim warning related to the handsome young man who awaited her with a countenance beaming with love" (*R,* 51). Ruth's knowledge of "right" and "wrong," good and evil, exists only on a personal, concrete level; when she encounters new situations, her behavior is guided by the memory of her mother's finite instructions about how to understand those feelings. Much of the following narrative traces Ruth's learning and mastery of the symbolic language that now leaves her baffled with Old Thomas.

This growing consciousness by Ruth of her culture's value system as revealed through its codes of behavior is demonstrated by her attempts to gain control over her fate. When Mrs. Mason spies her and Bellingham arm in arm returning from Milham Grange and dismisses her on the spot, Ruth suddenly "saw how much she had done that was deserving of blame" (*R*, 55); nonetheless, she still struggles to understand the difference between what is "right" and "wrong," between her desires and the cultural prescriptions that deny them. For instance, after her dismissal by Mrs. Mason, Bellingham convinces Ruth that she is friendless and persuades her to go to London with him; but temporarily left alone, she decides that Old Thomas might take her in, attempts to return to him, but discovers she has no money to pay for the tea Bellingham has ordered for her. With her sexual honor in the balance at this moment, it is ironically her social honor that tips the scale and contributes to her fall. So even though she has genuinely attempted to resist complete seduction—not because she recognizes the social impropriety but because she believes in Old Thomas's friendship—circumstances conspire against her. When Bellingham returns with their carriage secured, he "reasons" with Ruth, and the narrator tells us that "She was little accustomed to oppose the wishes of any one—obedient and docile by nature, and unsuspicious and innocent of any harmful consequences" (*R*, 61). What little socialization she has assimilated into her behavior, her training to be passive finally seals her fate. At this point in her history, then, her understanding of appropriate behavior—albeit incomplete and out of proportion—does her more social harm than good.

The extent to which Ruth remains ignorant of her society's values, even after they live together in London—an unquestionably worldly and sophisticated city—is revealed in the next section of the narrative. While the reader knows she has been seduced, Ruth has neither interpreted nor internalized her culture's moral codes; in fact it is not until a young child refuses her kiss, calls her a "naughty woman," and Ruth sees Benson's sorrowful expression that she begins to comprehend her fallen state as she lives with Bellingham in Wales (*R*, 71).

More concerned with detailing Ruth's growing consciousness of her fallen state than the fact that she is fallen, Gaskell moves her narrative quickly ahead, jumping over their months in London and focusing in, instead, on Ruth's painful epiphany. It is just this kind of experience with the child—interpersonal, not abstract—that teaches her the abstract code of her culture's value system. Eventually, she will learn to combine her instincts and feelings with the symbolic language used to convey secular and sacred values, but first she will need to repeat this lesson in a variety of forms as she works out her salvation. This obligatory recognition on Ruth's part of the moral impropriety of her life as Bellingham's lover reveals an apparently conservative element in Gaskell's vision; even so, Gaskell subsumes that conservatism to her larger, radical agenda by exposing the harm of the unadulterated social rejection of those individuals who do not conform to society's "moral" codes, by asking "What became of such as Ruth, who had no home and no friends" (*R*, 34), and by portraying the harsh and uncharitable conditions Ruth must face even while she struggles to enact "Christian" values.

Once Ruth has seen that she is "fallen" in society's eyes, this aspect of her education complete, Gaskell again propels the story to the point of her abandonment by Bellingham and, subsequently, her complete cultural marginalization. Just as Ruth comprehends her social ostricization, Bellingham falls ill with a fever. His physical deterioration mirroring his weak character, he is convinced by his mother to abandon Ruth. This agent of patriarchal law, this phallic mother,[23] completes her son's desertion of Ruth: arranging secretly to quit the inn, Mrs. Bellingham whisks her son away and secures for Ruth a socially appropriate position—totally outcast from society with no apparent hope for reintegration. This function of the partriarchally complicit mother—to reinforce androcentric values—exists as a powerful opponent to Gaskell's social vision, an aspect of the novel to which I will return.

In contrast to predominant cultural scripts concerning fallen women, Gaskell's narrative provides Ruth with the opportunity to master her community's values and to become reintegrated into her society through her character's relationship with Benson, a charitable action on his part that underscores the nongendered ethic of compassion Gaskell found in Unitarianism. Significantly, it is charitable human interaction that saves *both* Benson and Ruth. After finding Ruth crouched behind a hedge taunted by Welsh children, Benson tries to comfort her. Hearing the river, though, she races off to drown herself; when he tries to stop her, Benson slips and aggravates his painfully deformed back.[24] His agonized cry draws Ruth's attention away from herself and suicide, and once she has returned, Benson pleads with her to stay—first unsuccessfully in God's name, then with success in the name of her mother.

This scene, contrasting the power of the earthly mother to a heavenly father (both of whom are absent), reveals an important aspect of Gaskell's vision. As she has already shown, the early death of Ruth's mother (before she could teach her daughter to decipher symbolic social codes) means that Ruth has neither a guide to interpret the symbolic language of the Father nor the skill to interpret it for herself at this time.[25] "For His sake" means little to Ruth at this point, but "In your mother's name" means everything (*R,* 100).

The important model of mother-love, as opposed to the partriarchally complicit mother, is central to Gaskell's revolutionary vision. Quite the opposite from reinforcing the cultural image of mother as Madonna, Gaskell's vision of mother-love radically subverts those values. The difference also informs the important dissimilarities between the values that Ruth's mother emulated and those endorsed by women complicit in the culture's dominant ideology. At the heart of this difference is the contrast between what Gaskell believed to be God's intentions and her culture's appropriation of His word: Gaskell seeks to differentiate what she believes to be a basic morality from an exaggerated and destructive transformation of that morality into reductive and hegemonic cultural maxims. Whereas the complicit mother reinforces the patriarchal reading of these values, the model of mother-love, in contrast, instructs what Gaskell believes to be the *unappropriated* morality. In this spiritual context, mother-love—human interaction that builds on compassion and care—develops from a communal commitment to Christianity rather than a hierarchical doctrine; traditionally, this model of interaction has been displaced into the home (or to some extent the Church). As long as the behavior identified as mother-love is socially limited to women and the domestic sphere, however, it can be subsumed by the dominant ideology to account for opposing values in a culture without allowing them in the public sphere or even inscribing them with value. By confining this behavior to women, and by extension to the home, a patriarchal culture gains free reign to be competitive and antagonistic in the workplace.

Gaskell's mother-love, however, does not endorse her culture's ideology, even if it appears to enact those patriarchal values sanctioned for women. While the "maternal" qualities were elevated during the Victorian period as the ideal of womanhood, Gaskell's interest in these qualities does not replicate this larger cultural pattern. Rather than advocate the ghettoization of those values to women or the domestic sphere, Gaskell translocates the model of mother-love from an exclusive place in the home out into society at large.[26] In this way, she charges both men and women to embrace the values and behavior represented by Christ, the values and behavior found on earth in mother-love, not in the enshrined Madonna or the phallic mother.

What most distinguishes Gaskell's model of mother-love from the partriarchally complicit model of mother is the differing representations of the values and codes of an absent father: for Gaskell, the model of mother-love represents the Christian Father; that of the phallic mother, the patriarchal. Although bolstered by Estab-lished Church doctrine, the patriarchal values that inform her culture's ideology, Gaskell would contend, not only represent oppressive and self-serving policies but also distort and misrepresent God's word. Mother-love, in contrast, replicates the fundamental values of New Testament Christianity—compassion, charity, forgiveness, and, most of all, a vision built on sympathetic projection.[27]

Importantly, it is through Ruth's literal role as mother, the knowledge of her pregnancy, that Ruth's desire to find her own salvation is sparked; until then, she continues to feel that life is hopeless. Although Benson's sister, Faith, cannot quite agree,[28] both Ruth and Benson see this coming child as Ruth's salvation: she must love rather than be loved; she must be both a model and teacher to instruct her child of God's word. Benson tells his sister, "Faith, do you know I rejoice in this child's advent" (*R,* 118). Through the coming of the child—echoing biblical history of the prophecy—hope is gained; through the coming of one who will allow the sinner to work out his or her sin, Gaskell prepares Ruth for her personal salvation.

At this point the biblical associations that Gaskell creates through her characterizations of Ruth and her son (Eve, Mary Magdalene, the Virgin Mary, Jesus) become conflated. Prior to this, Ruth's character has recreated Eve—the seduction and fall. Now she enacts the second Eve, Mary. Significantly, though, this Mary is not immaculately conceived, let alone virginal. This fallen Mary is more like (and often alluded to as) Mary Magdalene. Yet like the virgin Mary (and Joseph), Ruth is taken into a marginalized place to give birth to her son. And like Christ's, Leonard's birth is seen by Benson as an "advent." Through the birth of the son (named after her mother's father), Ruth will achieve redemption and salvation. Yet from this point in the narrative Ruth's characterization as Eve, or the Virgin Mary, or Mary Magdalene, shifts dramatically to that of Christ Himself—a revolutionary association for a fallen woman. From this point on, the son gains salvation through the mother.

It is through Ruth's ability to turn outward, to project sympathetically, to learn to love more than she may be loved, that she finds her redemption. Through Benson's guidance, Ruth educates herself so that she may teach Leonard; doing so, she learns her God's and her culture's manifestation of symbolic language and codes. Once Ruth has learned the word of the Father through her love for her son, her character is tested, just as the earlier prophets were tested, just as Christ was tempted. For Ruth this temptation takes the form of another encounter with Bellingham: now that she has internalized the symbolic code of law, now that she knows "right" from "wrong," will Ruth have the strength to refuse Bellingham? Indeed, no longer radically naive, will she resist (or be able to resist) Bellingham's temptation? Is the once fallen woman always fallen?

This second temptation and Ruth's ability now to negotiate her culture's codes can best be understood and illustrated by revealing the narrative strategy Gaskell uses to show both Ruth's initial naiveté and her growing assimilation of the law of her spiritual Father. Instead of presenting Bellingham through an omniscient narrator, Gaskell allows readers to see him predominantly through Ruth's eyes, although the readers' experience can foresee what Ruth cannot. Although this presentation of Bellingham's character through Ruth's perspective continues through all three sections of the novel, the vision we see in the first section is especially important in order for readers to project themselves sympathetically into Ruth's naive world. Inexperienced, Ruth sees the world through unsophisticated eyes. Therefore, we see Bellingham's kindness at the ball, offering Ruth a flower in thanks for mending the dress of his condescending partner (*R*, 16); we even see him ride past her like "lightning" to save a drowning child, a boy whom he would eventually employ (*R*, 22, 443). Instructing her to, "Tell [me] everything . . . as you would to a brother; let me help you, if I can, in your difficulties," Bellingham appears to Ruth to be nothing if not a loving and compassionate friend, a good and benevolent man (*R*, 41).

This uncritical presentation of Bellingham through Ruth's eyes is tempered, however, by the narrator's occasional details. Providing another side of Bellingham's character, the narrator reveals the character's thoughts about Ruth's "*naïveté,* simplicity, and innocence"; he feels "It would be an exquisite delight to attract and tame her wildness, just as he had often allured and tamed the timid fawns in his mother's park" (*R*, 33). Whether consciously or not, Bellingham sees Ruth, not as a sister, but as a kind of possession, a wild creature for him to control and manipulate. Yet even when we see the limitations of Bellingham's character, we also see him, to his credit, admit to his mother that while Ruth is no "paragon of virtue," *he* "led her wrong" (*R*, 88). Still his fever in Wales reveals his moral weakness: rather than fight for the treatment he feels due Ruth, he submits to his mother's socializing forces. He gives in not so much because he agrees with her, but because it will "spare [him] all this worry, while [he] is so weak" (*R*, 90) and "get rid of [his] uneasiness" (*R*, 91). Years later, at Eagle's Crag, the Bradshaws' seaside estate, Bellingham, now Mr. Donne, is being wooed by Mr. Bradshaw to be the Eccleston parliamentary candidate. At this point the narrator reveals another aspect of his moral weakness. Struck by the similarity between the Bradshaws' governess, Mrs. Denbigh, and his former lover as they sit across a breakfast table, Bellingham thinks of Ruth "for the first time in several years" but decides that "there was but one thing that could have

happened [to her] . . . perhaps it was as well he did not know her end, for most likely it would have made him very uncomfortable" (*R*, 276).[29]

Significantly, now that Ruth has learned the "Christian" law of the father, her ability to negotiate the patriarchal law will be tested, and she sees Bellingham across that same table with wiser and more critical eyes: "He was changed, she knew not how. In fact, the expression, which had been only occasional formerly, when his worse self predominated, had become permanent. He looked restless and dissatisfied. But he was very handsome still" (*R*, 277). Seeing both his hardened demeanor and his still handsome face, knowing her past was wrong yet nonetheless attracted to Bellingham, Ruth is primed for her temptation: she now knows the consequences, but she is again attracted to her former lover and the father of her child. Faced by genuine temptation, Ruth, like Christ, must confront it, agonize over sacred and secular codes, and then firmly reject that temptation. Reintroduced into each other's life at Eagle's Crag after years of separation, Ruth and Bellingham face their common past and their potentially different futures. Once convinced that Mrs. Denbigh is his former lover, Bellingham connives and manipulates ways to accost Ruth about their past in the hopes of reestablishing their relationship. For Ruth, this encounter is most dangerous because it is so tempting.

Tortured again by her contradictory feelings for Bellingham, Ruth struggles to act on what she has now learned to be God's word and its translation into societal codes. The great difficulty of this struggle is symbolically demonstrated by Bellingham's literal intervention between her and God's word. Having followed Ruth and the young Bradshaw girls to church, Bellingham enters their pew and sits "just opposite to her; coming between her and the clergyman who was to read out the word of God" (*R*, 281). In their encounter after church on the heaving sands below Eagle's Crag, Gaskell interweaves allusions to the parable of the house on the rock and the house on the sand when Ruth finds herself confronted and taunted by Bellingham.[30] Here Ruth struggles with confusion over former passion and future salvation (*R*, 269, 272-73); in contrast, Eagle's Crag, built high on the rocky cliffs, becomes the refuge within which Ruth can regain her strength to resist Bellingham's advances.[31] And like Christ in the Gethsemane Garden, Ruth, wind-swept and rain-soaked from leaning out her room's window into the storm, agonizes over still loving Bellingham; in this blasting storm the words "stormy wind fulfilling his word" (*Psalms* 148:8) echo in her mind (*R*, 274). Hearing this causes Ruth to kneel before God and through tears pray: "Oh, my God, help me, for I am very weak. My God! I pray thee be my rock and my strong fortress, for I of myself am nothing. If I ask in His name, thou wilt give it me. In the name of Jesus Christ I pray for strength to do Thy will!" (*R*,

274). At church she sees her agony as akin to Christ's: "And when they prayed again, Ruth's tongue was unloosed, and she also could pray, in His name, who underwent the agony in the garden" (*R*, 283). Significantly, the very words that Benson had earlier used without effect to prevent Ruth's suicide attempt are now the words from which she finds strength.

With this renewed strength through divine communion, as she now understands "for His sake," Ruth can resist Bellingham's persistent temptation, even when he condescends to offer marriage. She has learned that "the old time would be as white as snow to what it would be now" (*R*, 273), and relying on the presence of a poor fisherman to protect her, refuses, telling Bellingham that "The errors of [her] youth would be washed away by [her] tears—it was so once when the gentle, blessed Christ was upon the earth" (*R*, 301), alluding to Christ's forgiveness of Mary Magdalene. Like the Magdalene, Ruth's past will be forgiven through her penitence, even though, significantly, Bellingham need not go through an equivalent penitence. Here, then, she has won a partial victory over him: she will no longer love Bellingham, and she refuses to be seduced this time.

In this way Gaskell demonstrates what she believes to be Ruth's complete, *personal* redemption: she has learned God's moral code, has taught that code to her son both as a model and through deciphering symbolic word, and has resisted a second temptation. Because of this personal redemption, the story shifts; Gaskell moves from the private to the public sphere. In this arena Ruth must work out her *public* redemption, and her culture must learn to replace its harsh ethical codes with Christian charity.

The conflict between the new social code of ethics that Gaskell calls for and the prevailing Hebraic justice can be clearly illustrated by the Bensons' interaction with the harsh and judgmental public. While Gaskell presents the Bensons as models of Christian charity, even they fear public admonition enough to misrepresent the truth of Ruth's condition, although out of compassion for the unborn child. In this way, both Ruth and the Bensons are at odds with their culture's ideology: Ruth falls from social grace, failing to fulfill its code for women; the Bensons refuse to comply with their culture's standards for dealing with such women. The narrator, interrupting the story, reflects on the inevitable harm that will result from disguising Ruth as a widow, even if done out of Christian charity:

> Ah, tempter! unconscious tempter! Here was a way of evading the trials for the poor little unborn child, of which Mr Benson had never thought. It was the decision—the pivot, on which the fate of years moved; and he turned it the wrong way. But it was not for his own sake. For himself, he was brave enough to tell the truth; for the little helpless baby, about to enter a cruel, biting

world, he was tempted to evade the difficulty. He forgot what he had just said, of the discipline and penance to the mother consisting in strengthening her child to meet, truthfully and bravely, the consequences of her own weakness.

> (*R*, 122)

Compounding this first deception, Benson does not rectify the original deceit when Bradshaw decides that Ruth should be his daughter's governness. Persuaded by Ruth's penitence, her genuine efforts toward goodness, and her model mother-love for Leonard, Benson gives in to his sister's plan not to tell, and once again the narrator intrudes: "The scroll of Fate was closed, and they could not foresee the Future; and yet, if they could have seen it, though they might have shrunk fearfully at first, they would have smiled and thanked God when all was done and said" (*R*, 200).

When the narrative moves from Ruth's personal penitence to her public shame, Gaskell voices most clearly the values that are at the heart of her ethic of compassion through Benson's confrontation with Bradshaw over Ruth's past. Now recognizing all too clearly the impact of hiding the truth about Ruth's past, now faced with the need to live his faith and beliefs overtly on such a controversial issue, Benson takes his "stand with Christ against the world." Reacting to Bradshaw's harsh dismissal of any extenuating circumstances in Ruth's past, Benson bears witness to a higher truth, declaring:

> Now I wish God would give me power to speak out convincingly what I believe to be His truth, that not every woman who has fallen is depraved; that many—how many the Great Judgment Day will reveal to those who have shaken off the poor, sore penitent hearts on earth—many, many crave and hunger after a chance for virtue—the help which no man gives to them—help—that tender help which Jesus gave once to Mary Magdalen.

> (*R*, 350-51)

Again voicing his culture's ideology, Bradshaw responds: "The world has decided how such women are to be treated; and, you may depend upon it, there is so much practical wisdom in the world that its way of acting is right in the long run" (*R*, 351). Erupting with passion, Benson finally voices his values, this time unqualified:

> I state my firm belief, that it is God's will that we should not dare to trample any of His creatures down to the hopeless dust; that it is God's will that the women who have fallen should be numbered among those who have broken hearts to be bound up, not cast aside as lost beyond recall. If this be God's will, as a thing of God it will stand; and he will open a way.

> (*R*, 351)

With this exposure of Ruth's past and the harsh realities of her culture's values made explicit, Gaskell shifts her narrative to demonstrate her character's efforts to maneuver her way through this social marginalization and ostricization. This transfer from domestic to public realms symbolically occurs in the scene where Bradshaw dismisses Ruth, and Jemima literally "bear[s] witness" for her (*R,* 338). Significantly this confrontation occurs in the most fundamental female place of the domestic sphere—the nursery. The verbal (and physical) ejection of Ruth—and the mother-love she has come to represent—out of this female space into the public sphere, traditionally male, sets in motion the translocation of the "sentimental" values from a secondary sphere of influence to a confrontation with those of the dominant. Just as significantly, Bradshaw, who originally labeled these values sentimental, also forces them out of the nursery and into the public arena. By shifting her narrative from the personal to the public, Gaskell impels her readers to see the already penitent Ruth once again required to work out her redemption, this time for a rigid, Old Testament public. Although this section of *Ruth* most visibly displays the conflict between God and His human appropriation, Gaskell has prepared us for this conflict throughout the novel. Earlier, the narrator had told the reader of Old Thomas's concern for Ruth, even though he believed that "God judgeth not as man judgeth," and Benson and his sister decide that Ruth "must strengthen her child to look to God, rather than to man's opinion" (*R,* 121). Even Ruth, when telling her son about his illegitimacy, comforts him by saying that "I think God, who knows all, will judge me more tenderly than men" (*R,* 343).

However comforted by her belief in God's mercy, Ruth still must face her earthly judges, must prove her worthiness for redemption within the public sphere. She achieves this by reenacting her mother-love for Leonard; by transforming that love from private to public in nursing the sick and aged, Ruth begins to work out her public salvation.[32] In this way, Ruth must again learn "that it is more blessed to love than to be beloved" (*R,* 248), this time on a larger scale. To do this, she goes to nurse the poor and sick, and when the town is struck by fever, she volunteers at the fever ward.[33] Her impact here brings about public approval of her; witnesses openly voice her goodness like Benson and Jemima have done earlier. Through her example, her community is forced to reconsider the values and standards applied to fallen women like Ruth. Not only do the townspeople gather around outside the fever ward where "many arose and called her blessed" (*R,* 430), but her son, Leonard, can gain his self-respect. Significantly, this public invocation of her holiness erases her sin; her past has been revised. One witness recalls, "They say she has been a great sinner, and that this is her penance"; but another person insists, "Such a one as her has never been a great sinner; nor does she do her work as a penance, but for the love of God, and of the blessed Jesus" (*R,* 429).[34] This public witness is especially important because it challenges a reading of *Ruth*

that simplistically reduces her behavior as solely motivated by penitence; instead, this witness suggests an alternative, possibly complementary motivation—mother-love, Christian love.

The profound reversal of opinion displayed by the previously Hebraic public and its powerful subversion of dominant ideology can be more fully illuminated by examining Gaskell's application of biblical text to Ruth. When the narrator reports that "many arose and called her blessed," Gaskell subverts her culture's patriarchal appropriation of the Old Testament proverb of the good wife; instead of reinforcing her culture's vision of the good wife, or even echoing texts about Mary Magdalene, Gaskell here applies these words of honor to a fallen woman.[35] Gaskell's narrator praises Ruth's compassion and mother-love, and she portrays a public that has learned through this fallen woman to reinterpret God's words, not to accept uncritically the patriarchal appropriation of them. When the worst of the fever abates, Ruth is sent home with proclamations from the town council and doctors about her worthiness. And just as her sin has been revised and eradicated, so is her literal shame—her son—accepted and acknowledged: genuine offers to educate Leonard arise from Mr. Farquhar and Mr. Davis.

If Gaskell had only wanted to demonstrate Ruth's penitence and salvation, the novel could end here. And many readers believe that it should have. Gaskell's agenda, however, is more extensive than redeeming *a* fallen woman. By including the final section of Ruth Hilton's story (as well as the Richard Bradshaw subplot), Gaskell creates a truly revolutionary tract for social revision. It is in this next section that Gaskell takes her narrative beyond just a critique of her culture's treatment of fallen women, as subversive as that would be.[36] Instead Gaskell presents a radical vision of her culture's need to replace Old Testament values and religion with New Testament charity by her representation of Ruth's death.

Here Gaskell most clearly and boldly presents Ruth as a Christ or prophet figure.[37] Having gained public approval and absolution for her past, Ruth does not need to nurse Bellingham, who has contracted the fever; she does not need to perform this act from which she will eventually die herself. In fact, rather than endorse this self-sacrificial act, both Benson (as spiritual advisor) and Mr. Davis (as social spokesperson) attempt to keep her from going—she has been both morally and socially redeemed. And contrary to what most critics believe (both Gaskell's contemporaries and modern), Gaskell sends Ruth to her inevitable death to portray a radical sentimentalism through the model of mother-love, not to punish Ruth further because her sins cannot be absolved on earth.[38]

Gaskell has Ruth nurse Bellingham to demonstrate the most revolutionary aspect of her social tract: Ruth gains the final victory over her seducer; like Christ, this sacrifice infuses her with a greater power than Bellingham had over her.[39] This embrace with death is neither punishment for her sins nor a variation of her suicide attempt in Wales. While Ruth has too often in the past lived and thought only about her present, looking neither forward nor back (*R,* 420), here she enacts a radical version of her mother-love, putting others before herself because she sees the intricate web of human connectedness. Bellingham's fever is potentially fatal for him, not just morally weakening, and this time he is no longer nursed by his patriarchally complicit mother. (She, like general public sentiment about Ruth, has died [*R,* 320].) With this fever, Bellingham is nursed to health by Ruth, and then she leaves. She no longer waits outside his door, passive and dependent on him for strength or direction.

Having given life to her seducer, Ruth completes the Passion story. In these final pages, Gaskell includes two important images about Ruth's death that solidify her association with Christ. As Mr. Davis and Benson watch over her, Gaskell alludes to the song of Cymbeline, writing that Ruth "home must go, and take her wages" (*R,* 447). To the Victorian reader, who would know this allusion, the significance that Imogen is not dead would evoke important Christian parallels; to that Christian, death would not mean dying, but life everlasting.[40] As if this first allusion to Ruth's resurrection and affinity with Christ is not sufficient, Gaskell unquestionably invokes the crucified Christ by Ruth's death: "'I see the Light coming. . . . The Light is coming,' she said. And raising herself slowly, she stretched out her arms, and then fell back, very still for evermore" (*R,* 448). Gaskell emphasizes this parallel to Christ even further by having Bellingham go to Ruth on the third day after her death—the day of Christ's resurrection. Here Ruth gains her final victory over Bellingham: he is exposed as her seducer, and he and his values are finally and completely rejected by Benson, a triumphant rejection of the culture's ideologies for the new "sentimental" ones.

This final visit of Bellingham foregrounds the revolutionary component of Gaskell's sentimental agenda by revealing that Bellingham has misunderstood Ruth's motives when she nursed him to health. Standing over Ruth's laid out body, Bellingham tells Benson: "I cannot tell you how I regret that she should have died in consequence of her love of me" (*R,* 453). By this he discloses his belief that romantic love, not Christian love, had motivated Ruth's sacrificial act. Significantly, Gaskell has earlier prepared the reader to reject this misinterpretation of Ruth's actions by including the chapter aptly titled "Sally tells of her Sweethearts and Discourses on the Duties of Life." In addition to voicing a challenge to the notion that married life is always preferable to single life for women, Sally dispels the idea that one can die of romantic love by telling the

story of Dixon's proposal of marriage to her. Upon rejecting him, she believes "he'd die for love for [her]," influenced by the romantic "old song of Barbary Allen" (*R,* 169). But, less than three weeks later, Sally hears, via the church bells, of Dixon's wedding. Reinforcing this tale of antiromance, Gaskell juxtaposes this with an image of Ruth "peaceful as death," foreshadowing the actual event (*R,* 170). It is the difference between earthly and religious love that clarifies how Ruth's death is a victory over Bellingham and not punishment for her earlier love for him. Unlike Richardson's Clarissa, who after her rape eventually dies of her integrity, Ruth dies from an active working out of her beliefs and principles. Not a passive victim of patriarchal values, Ruth becomes a victim, like Christ, a female martyr in her male culture as a prophet of God's word, as a model of mother-love.[41]

But if Gaskell so thoroughly calls for society to revise its values through the story of Ruth Hilton, why does she include the sub-plot of Richard Bradshaw's embezzlement of Benson's money? First, this subplot serves as a supplement to extend further Ruth's story from the female and private spheres to the male and public. The sexual double standard that existed in Gaskell's culture presented different codes for men and women: Ruth, not Bellingham, is punished for their relationship. So to explore a male fall from grace in her culture, Gaskell writes Richard Bradshaw's sub-plot about the male equivalent of a moral fall—not living by the established codes of business. Through Benson and Farquhar's compassionate treatment of Richard, the reader sees Gaskell's new code of behavior extended into and enacted in the public arena. Gaskell charges her culture to replace completely its values with those associated with the domestic sphere. And with those concrete domestic values, she forces the rigid Old Testament values so clearly exemplified by Mr. Bradshaw to be replaced by the ethic of care—displayed here both by Benson and Farquhar when faced with Richard's fall.

In this story, the unwavering adherence to a Hebraic God by the father at the expense of his son inverts the thwarted sacrifice of Isaac by Abraham found in the Old Testament. There, the degree of Abraham's faith is tested, and it is his blind faith in God's principles that allows his son to live. Here Gaskell presents a Victorian Abraham, Mr. Bradshaw, whose faith is too blindly obedient to those abstract, impersonal principles; it is this unwavering commitment that nearly causes, not reprieves, his son's death. Although Bradshaw fully intends to sacrifice his son for what he believes to be God's and culture's laws, when he fears that Richard is dead in a coach accident, Bradshaw can no longer operate on that abstract level. Only when faced with the actual loss of his son does Bradshaw begin to understand New Testament compassion. For Gaskell, it is the importance of this interpersonal love, the interdependence of all humanity, that gains power over the abstract code of behavior.

While Richard's fall parallels Ruth's, unlike her, he does not die. Why? He does not need to die in Gaskell's narrative because of the differing codes of his culture for the male crime of abstract principle and the female crime of sexual indiscretion. His sin is not as much a crime against his culture's ideology as Ruth's is; hers is a more subversive rejection of its values because female chastity is the foundation of political and clerical patriarchy.

The main plot and the subplot are also tied together by the concept of salvation through the son, a clear allusion to Christ's sacrifice for humanity. Richard's crime and near death challenge Bradshaw's reductive morality; the very real possibility that Richard has died in a coach accident enables Bradshaw to return to a human, not abstract, level of interaction. Similarly Leonard proves the initial and important focal point for Ruth's redemption; it is his coming birth and his need to be educated as to God's and man's codes that spark Ruth's penitence. But with Leonard and Ruth, the biblical roles blur. He is her salvation, but so she is his. His birth is considered an "advent" by Benson, and Leonard mourns her the way Mary Magdalene mourns Christ. Finally through Leonard, the two stories connect. Bradshaw achieves his greatest salvation through this son of a fallen woman: finding Leonard crying upon his mother's grave, Bradshaw takes him home to the Bensons; this act not only reestablishes ties between Benson and Bradshaw, but also causes Bradshaw to cry, bringing the novel full circle to the motto from which it began—with the image of sin washed away through repentant tears.

With *Ruth,* Gaskell provides a revolutionary model to reform her culture; in the process of doing so, she empowers its marginalized members by asserting a diametrically opposed ideology to that which dominates Victorian society. She gives voice to new social codes by reclaiming the law of the Father through the model of the Son (Christ) and the daughter (as symbolized by mother-love).

Throughout her oeuvre Gaskell rejects an equation of God's words with her culture's ideological vision; she rejects an appropriation of Christianity that serves man and not God. Whether she explicitly uses biblical allusions as she does in her early fiction or veils those values by historical settings or even simply presents this ethic characterized by communities of women enacting mother-love, Gaskell challenges a patriarchal appropriation of God.[42] God the Father may be in heaven, but on earth, his saving words are represented by the mother's love. Seeing a society where both God and mother-love

are absent in the power-wielding public domain, where both—under a guise of deferential worship—have been marginalized, Gaskell subverts her culture's values and produces a competing vision that replaces Old Testament justice with New Testament mercy. By reclaiming the Judeo-Christian myth from patriarchal misinterpretation, Gaskell reappropriates Christian symbolism to empower those the Victorian Church has rejected and reenfranchise those the culture has marginalized.

Notes

1. Elizabeth Gaskell, *Ruth* (Oxford: Oxford University Press, 1985), 351. Subsequent quotations from this work are cited in the text as *R.*

2. This challenge to replace the prevailing Hebraic values with a radical Christian model occurs throughout Gaskell's oeuvre despite the traditional division of her fiction into three categories (the early social-problem novels, the later domestic novels, and the abundance of supernatural stories). With the clamor from industrialists that surrounded *Mary Barton* (1848) and *North and South* (1854-55), the moral uproar that accompanied the publication of *Ruth* (1853), and the biographical challenges that dominated her first edition of *The Life of Charlotte Brontë* (1857), it is not surprising that Gaskell, like Hardy after her, would turn away from such a polemical vision and produce instead less overtly controversial fiction, although maintaining a consistent agenda.

3. Even while foregrounding the social-problem theme in *Mary Barton* and *North and South,* Gaskell still structures these narratives by an explicit appropriation of Christian allusion to criticize her culture. Early in *Mary Barton* John Barton sees the struggles between the masters and workers in distinctly religious terms. He criticizes the masters' "lack of Christian brotherhood" and claims that the "workers and masters are separate as Dives and Lazarus," a theme that gives shape to the unfolding story of Manchester life (*Mary Barton* [Harmondsworth: Penguin, 1985], 45; subsequent quotations from this work are cited as *MB*). The novel even concludes with a reminder of Christ's poverty and "man's responsibility to help those with less" (*MB,* 457).

With a more balanced presentation, Gaskell returns to these problems between masters and workers in *North and South.* Here, though, Gaskell extends her critical vision beyond just the tensions between industrialists and their workers to include the Established Church and the legal and conventional codes that govern England. By an act of conscience, Mr. Hale leaves the Church of England, transplanting his family from the rural South to the industrial North (*North and South*

[Oxford: Oxford University Press, 1982], 33; subsequent quotations from this work are cited as *NS*). His son, Frederick, is falsely accused of mutiny (*NS*, 109), and Margaret lies to the police about her brother's visit to England (*NS*, 283). Outside the Church of England and English law, neither Mr. Hale nor his son will ever be able to be fully reintegrated into their culture; by definition neither can reconcile their moral vision with society's codes. Gaskell does not attempt to provide a solution for these ideological challenges of conscience. She does, however, portray a growing understanding between laborers and masters; through the learned compassion for one another, Higgins (the worker) and Thornton (the owner) begin to understand the plight of the other. Mr. Hale describes the workers' union as having the potential to be "Christianity itself" (*NS*, 233), and Thornton establishes a co-op commissary for his workers (*NS*, 361). The novel concludes, again voicing what Gaskell saw as a New Testament vision, that "we have all of us one human heart" (*NS*, 419).

4. Significantly, Bradshaw's dismissal of Benson's philosophy as sentimental anticipates the label most twentieth-century critics have given Gaskell's fiction. Even while acknowledging the historically explosive and controversial qualities inherent in her fiction, modern criticism continually points to structural flaws, a moralizing tone, and *sentimental* values in her early novels. For instances of her fiction being dismissed as sentimental, see A. B. Hopkins's *Elizabeth Gaskell, Her Life and Work* (New York: Octagon Books, 1971); as pious, see Arthur Pollard's "The Novels of Mrs. Gaskell," *Bulletin of John Rylands Library* 43 (1960-61): 403-25; or as moralizing, see Enid L. Duthie's *The Themes of Elizabeth Gaskell* (Totowa, N.J.: Rowman and Littlefield Press, 1980) and Edgar Wright's *Mrs. Gaskell: The Basis for Reassessment* (London: Oxford University Press, 1965). Consequently, the major project of reexamining Gaskell's fiction remains.

5. Tompkins, "Sentimental Power," 83-85.

6. Tompkins's redefinition of "sentimental" in her reading of *Uncle Tom's Cabin* is an important challenge to patriarchal aesthetics; although using her redefinition as a starting point, my reconsideration of sentimentalism in Gaskell diverges from Tompkins's argument in the crucial nongendered component fundamental to Gaskell's Unitarianism.

7. As a young woman Gaskell attended Avonbank, situated in Stratford-upon-Avon, and when her father became ill, she returned to live with him,

upon which he superintended her studies in Latin, French, and Italian (Hopkins, *Elizabeth Gaskell*, 31, 40).

8. Wright, *Mrs. Gaskell*, 25-26, 43. For further discussion of the nonhierarchical and nondogmatic foundation upon which Unitarianism based its beliefs, see Tessa Brodestsky (*Elizabeth Gaskell* [Oxford: Oxford University Press, 1986], 4). Significantly these qualities find important parallels in feminist readings of theological and literary canons; two important examples of this criticism include Elaine Pagels's *The Gnostic Gospels* and Christine Froula's "When Eve Reads Milton: Undoing Canonical Economy."

9. Carol Gilligan, *In a Different Voice: Psychological Theory and Women's Development* (Cambridge: Harvard University Press, 1982), 167.

10. M. D. Wheeler, "The Sinner as Heroine: A Study of Mrs. Gaskell's *Ruth* and the Bible," *Durham University Journal*, n.s., 5 (1976): 149.

11. Wright, *Mrs. Gaskell*, 25-26.

12. Although her liberal religious heritage enabled Gaskell to challenge her culture's reductive dismissal of female talent, she (as wife and mother) still possessed a mildly conservative perspective of balancing one's domestic responsibilities and one's career. In an 1850 letter to Eliza Fox, she wrote: "One thing is pretty clear, *Women* must give up living an artist's life, if home duties are to be paramount. It is different with men, whose home duties are so small a part of their life. . . . I am sure it is healthy for [women] to have the refuge of the hidden world of Art. . . . I have felt this in writing. . . . I have no doubt that the cultivation of [both "home duties and the development of the Individual"] tends to keep the other in a healthy state" (*LG*, 106). Her genuine commitment to challenge cultural rejections of nonconformist women, however, can best be illustrated through her efforts (enlisting Dickens's assistance) to help a young, orphaned woman who had been seduced by a surgeon when she had been ill emigrate to Australia. For details regarding this effort on Gaskell's part, see *LG*, 98-100. Even with exemplary behavior like Gaskell's own efforts to aid her society's victims, I am not trying to suggest that all Church of England members were pharisaical or that all Dissenters were socially progressive. Significantly the confrontation that illuminates Gaskell's agenda in *Ruth* takes place between two male Dissenters, Benson and Bradshaw. Similarly, some of her husband's congregation, like Bradshaw, could not revise their values to include Gaskell's controversial vision. In an early February 1853 letter to Eliza Fox, Gaskell

writes: "I think I must be an improper woman without knowing it, I do so manage to shock people. Now *should* you have burnt the 1st vol. of Ruth as so *very* bad? even if you had been a very anxious father of a family? Yet *two* men have; and a third has forbidden his wife to read it; they sit next to us in Chapel and you can't imagine how 'improper' I feel under their eyes" (*LG*, 222-23).

13. Hopkins writes that Gaskell's "purpose belongs also with the Christian Socialists, among whom she counted many good friends: Francis William Newman (heterodox brother of the Cardinal), F. D. Maurice, Thomas Hughes, and Charles Kingsley" (*Elizabeth Gaskell,* 131-32). In a letter to William Robson, Gaskell asks him to distribute a pamphlet and two papers authored by Maurice and Kingsley (*LG*, 105), and to Eliza Fox, she copies lines from Kingsley, whom she calls "my *hero*" (*LG*, 90).

14. For a detailed analysis of this phenomenon, see Taylor, *Eve and the New Jerusalem*, 126-27.

15. Nina Auerbach provides a more complete discussion of this hidden power in the myth of Victorian womanhood in both her article "The Rise of the Fallen Woman" and her book *Woman and the Demon.*

16. Gaskell strongly believed that her fiction was a means to "speak [her] mind" (*LG*, 220-21) even though much of the impetus behind the production of her first novel, *Mary Barton,* was to refocus her energies after the death of her young son, William—an activity her husband suggested.

17. The organic quality that Gaskell attributed to her fiction can be seen in a letter in which she tells a young author who solicited her advice about writing that "The plot must grow, and culminate in a crisis; not a character must be introduced who does not conduce to this growth and progress of events. The plot is like the anatomical drawing of an artist; he must have an idea of his skeleton, before he can clothe it with muscle & flesh, much more before he can drape it" (*LG*, 542).

18. In "Elizabeth Gaskell and the Novel of Social Pride," Angus Easson argues for the powerful recreation of the living conditions of Victorian workers in Gaskell's fiction, adding that Gaskell was alone among the period's major novelists in living in an industrial rather than urban area (*Bulletin of John Ryland Library* 67 [1984-85]: 693).

19. For a detailed study of this transfer of biblical allusions from religious to secular discourse, from allegorical to a more realistic presentation, during the Victorian period, see Barry Qualls's *The Secular Pilgrims of Victorian Fiction.*

20. Wheeler, "The Sinner as Heroine," 149.

21. The narrative divisions which I see in *Ruth* do not correspond with the three-volume divisions of the text: the first volume followed Ruth's story until her arrival, with the Bensons, at Eccleston; the second volume ended with Ruth rejecting Bellingham's marriage proposal (Easson, "Elizabeth Gaskell," 109).

22. Much of the Victorian public reaction to *Ruth,* however, was hostile if not outraged (see note 7). When told by his wife that *Ruth* had been burnt in some places, Archdeacon Hares replied: "Well, the Bible has been burnt" (Hopkins, *Elizabeth Gaskell,* 126). While the *Examiner* and the *North British Review* wrote favorably of *Ruth,* and individuals, including the leading Christian Socialists and Richard Monckton Milne, responded favorably to it, many more magazines and individuals condemned the novel as well as the author. In an early February 1853 letter to Eliza Fox, Gaskell writes: "one of your London librarians . . . has had to withdraw it from circulation on account of 'its being unfit for family reading' and Spectator, Lity Gazette, Sharp's Mag; Colborn have all abused it as roundly as may be. Litery [sic] Gazette in every form of abuse 'insufferably dull' 'style offensive from affectation' 'deep regret that we and all admirers of Mary Barton must feel at the author's loss of reputation'" (*LG*, 223).

23. I use the term phallic mother to identify a female complicit in the subjection of women by a patriarchal culture. This term, although originating with Freud (explaining the child's fantasy that the mother has a phallus), has been transformed by the French feminists to the more metaphoric quality I define above. The phallic mother's power results largely from its hidden quality; doubly veiled by both gender and social position, the phallic mother provides a crucial socializing factor in reproducing an androcentric culture. For a more detailed definition and analysis of the phallic mother, see Julia Kristeva's "The Novel as Polylogue" in *Desire in Language* and Jane Gallop's chapter "The Phallic Mother: Fraudian Analysis" in *The Daughter's Seduction.*

24. Significantly, Thurston Benson's religious and ideological marginalization is mirrored by his physical carriage: he is an outsider by appearance as well as belief; when Ruth first meets him in Llan-dhu, she "saw a man [with] the stature of a dwarf . . . he was deformed" (*R*, 67).

25. For a useful theoretical discussion of these issues, see Margaret Homans's *Bearing the Word: Language and Female Experience in Nineteenth-Century Women's Writing* (Chicago: University of

Chicago Press, 1986). Homans's first chapter, "Representation, Reproduction, and Women's Place in Language" (1-39), provides an important discussion in which she uses "Lacanian terms [to] transform Chodorow's psychological theory into a revisionary myth of women and language" (6). From this she proposes that "Articulations of myths of language, and specifically of their relation to the literal and to the literalization, appear generally in the form of four recurrent literary situations or practices," which she designates as "bearing the word" (29). Her theory, and her work on Gaskell, have important implications for this chapter. Writing about Gaskell, Homans asserts that "mother-present language . . . is always and inextricably bound up with and interdependent upon paternal power and its determination of women's subordinate linguistic role as transmitters of men's words" (234-35); I argue, however, that for Gaskell, especially in *Ruth,* this language representation becomes more complex. The figurative/symbolic that reveals the law of the Father replaces not just the absent mother, but also the absent God. The biblical language which Gaskell has her characters learn teaches a code of behavior in contrast to her androcentric culture, not one complicit with it. See also Sara Ruddick's "Maternal Thinking" for a useful delineation of the qualities that characterize this perspective; as part of this description, she identifies "inauthenticity," which she defines as a quality similar to submission and obedience found in "some versions of Christianity" (in *Mothering: Essays in Feminist Theory,* ed. Joyce Treblicot [Totowa, N.J.: Rowman & Allanheld, 1984], 221). In this way, Ruddick establishes the distinction that I argue defines Gaskell's contrast between "mother-love" and the patriarchally complicit women exemplified by Bellingham's mother. Similarly, the "attentive" love present in maternal thinking anticipates the emphasis of sympathetic projection, which, translated into Christian doctrine as the Golden rule, reflects qualities that I see in Gaskell's revisionist social vision (220). See also Virginia Sickbert's "The Significance of Mother and Child in Christina Rossetti's *Sing-Song*" (forthcoming in *Victorian Poetry*) for an important analysis of the role of the mother in Rossetti's poetry.

26. For an insightful analysis of Gaskell's use of metonymy and the significant role of women to connect public and private spheres in *North and South,* see Gallagher's *The Industrial Reformation of English Fiction,* esp. pp. 166-84.

27. Tompkins asserts that one of the important features of sentimental fiction is that salvation is achieved through the model of motherly love ("Sentimental Power," 83).

28. Faith Benson serves an important role as a mirror of public sentiment, reflected by her initial rejection and ultimate acceptance of Ruth. First she shrinks from this fallen woman, but once she develops a history with Ruth she becomes the character's champion. It is also Faith that persuades her brother to allow Ruth to be the Bradshaws' governess, an act which both instigates Ruth's second dismissal and sets in motion the transfer of sentimental values from the domestic to the public arena.

29. Both Bellingham and Ruth have assumed new names when they reencounter each other here: he has taken the family name Donne, which provides him with greater position, property, and financial power (*R,* 440); she has taken the name Mrs. Denbigh (Benson's mother's name), which provides her with requisite respectability for a woman with a child (*R,* 130). The implications of these name changes underscore the significantly different values associated with the culture's gender-based morals. For men, value is abstract and connected to positions of power; for women, value is closely tied to their relation to men and the harnassing of their reproductive capacity within patriarchal constraints.

30. This image also metaphorically reveals the passion Ruth still feels for Bellingham.

31. Wheeler, "The Sinner as Heroine," 154.

32. Although the modern reader would interpret Ruth's choice to nurse the sick as an extension of "woman's work" from private to public mothering, nursing was considered nearly scandalous in the nineteenth century, attracting immodest and intemperate women before Florence Nightingale's transformation of it into what she believed to be, and what Gaskell's character supports, a "blessed" calling. Gaskell conflates the contemporary notion of nursing with that of the nineteenth century by having Ruth, as fallen woman, bring to that vocation a holy and pure quality.

33. Ruth's nursing the sick and dying in the fever ward is much more than what Coral Lansbury has argued it to be—a kind of unconscious modeling of Benson's care of the sick (*Elizabeth Gaskell: The Novel of Social Crisis* [New York: Barnes & Noble, 1975], 80). Instead, Ruth *chooses* to tend the sick partly because Mr. Wynne (the parish doctor) asks her to do so and partly because she needs the employment—she sees it as an opportunity to end her socially imposed idleness while comforting others (*R,* 388-89); the Bensons, in fact, try to talk her out of this endeavor.

34. While this scene outside the fever wards may be one of the most explicit cases, Gaskell, throughout

the novel, has characterized Ruth with biblical allusions; all of the following (with distinct allusions to Christ) occur *after* her seduction. The narrator likens Ruth to Christ while she is at Benson's Sunday school: "Ruth sat on a low hassock, and coaxed the least of the little creatures to her" (*R,* 151). Later, the mutual salvation of Ruth and her son is described: "The child and the mother were each messengers of God—angels to each other" (*R,* 369). Benson, in an attempt to give Ruth strength to face her public detractors, reminds her of Christ's thorny life, paralleling her martyrdom (*R,* 358).

35. The verse that Gaskell revises is: "Her children rise up and call her blessed; / her husband also, and he praises her: / 'Many women have done excellently, / but you surpass them all'" (*Proverbs* 31:28-29).

36. See Rachel Blau duPlessis's *Writing Beyond the Ending* for a useful analysis of similar strategies by modern women writers. Although Gaskell is not included in her project, duPlessis's theory of women writers redefining narrative conventions provides useful insights into Gaskell's strategies. By delineating various narrative strategies that women writers used to write beyond the traditional endings of fiction, duPlessis provides a theory with which to illuminate women authors' conscious rewriting of narrative patterns to include female experience.

37. Because Unitarianism tended not to believe in Christ's divinity, Gaskell's conflation of biblical history (male and female) into Ruth's history becomes more credible; the ability to be a prophet of God's word is opened to those who believe and accurately reveal God's word.

38. Examples of negative critical response to Gaskell's decision to conclude her novel with Ruth's death range from sympathetic incredulousness to simplistic condescension. Charlotte Brontë, for example, wrote "Why should she die? Why are we to shut up the book weeping?" (quoted in Gaskell, *Life of Brontë,* 475). Modern critics have echoed Brontë's question. Patricia Beer writes, "if Ruth is really an innocent victim of circumstances, why does she have to be so severely punished?"; she concludes it can only be because Gaskell believed "sexual intercourse outside marriage was a kind of disease with after effects" (*Reader, I Married Him: A Study of Women Characters of Jane Austen, Charlotte Brontë, Elizabeth Gaskell, and George Eliot* [New York: Macmillan, 1974], 146). In her biography of Gaskell, Hopkins writes, "Ruth was already saved; her death is purely gratuitous" (*Elizabeth Gaskell,* 130). Angus Easson, writing in his *Elizabeth Gaskell,* wonders if Gaskell "in pre-

senting her character sympathetically, contrived to make her sinless in the event and yet to react afterwards as though she has sinned? That is, Gaskell seems to confound society's view of what has happened with God's despite quoting 'God judgeth not as man judgeth'" (118). And Margaret Ganz calls the description of Ruth's death as saintly, "mere mystical twaddle" (*Elizabeth Gaskell: The Artist in Conflict* [New York: Twayne, 1969], 112).

39. Tompkins argues, in her discussion of *Uncle Tom's Cabin,* that one of the defining features of sentimental fiction is the power obtained through a character's death; replicating Christ's example, those who die for someone else's salvation are more powerful than those they die for ("Sentimental Power," 85).

40. The passage alluded to from Shakespeare's *Cymbeline* is "Fear no more the heat o' the sun / Nor the furious winter's rages; / Thou thy worldly task hast done, / Home art gone, and ta'en thy wages. / Golden lads and girls all must, / As chimney-sweepers, come to dust." Wheeler, analyzing the effect of Gaskell's allusion on the Victorian reader, writes "The anticipatory effect of [this] quotation relies upon the reader's knowledge of the play. Imogen is not dead. Nor is Ruth, as a Christian, 'dead' in any final sense at the end of the novel, in the eyes of Thurston Benson, when he reads from Revelation" ("The Sinner as Heroine," 159).

41. Angus Easson sees Ruth's death as that of a conventional victim. Reading the novel's conclusion in this fashion, though, forces him to miss Gaskell's subversion of that literary motif. He writes: "Gaskell's purpose was partly to show that the fallen woman could lead a full and useful life, yet she couldn't escape the conventional idea that Ruth, the heroic dignified expansive creature, is also a victim, who must have her tragedy. She has not yet grasped fully, as she was to in *Sylvia's Lovers,* that to live can be more tragic than to die" (*Elizabeth Gaskell,* 125).

42. This range of Gaskell's narrative strategies can be best illustrated in her shorter works of fiction. With "Lois the Witch" (1861) and *Sylvia's Lovers* (1863) Gaskell continues to detail the conflict between God's and man's laws by using the Salem witch trials and the British press gangs as violent metaphors of oppression against those who deviate from the dominant ideology. These safer veiled challenges, distanced both historically and metaphorically, nonetheless call into question her culture's politics and reveal the tragic outcome of those who defy or reject the established values—Lois, hanged as a witch; and Daniel Robson, Sylvia's father, hanged as a rioter.

This tension between the defiant or victimized and their culture, which occurs throughout Gaskell's fiction, becomes transformed in her later fiction into a presentation of the power of a community of women, the dynamic of which essentially replicates Christian love. In "The Well of Pen-Morfa" (1850), *Cranford* (1851), "The Three Eras of Libbie Marsh" (1853), and "Half a Life-Time Ago" (1855), women help and aid other women, even, as in the case of Susan Dixon, when it is a former lover's widow and children. Through charity to one another, women find their salvation, taking in orphans, "idiots," and lame women—those rejected by patriarchal culture.

Written a few years before *Ruth*, Gaskell's short story "Lizzie Leigh" (1850) can be read as a preliminary engagement with the same issues to which she would later return in her most polemic novel. This narrative of two daughters' falls—one figurative and the other literal—rejects patriarchal codes for an ethical system built on love and forgiveness. Like *Ruth*, this story grafts biblical and religious imagery onto the narrative of a fallen woman and challenges traditional ideological assumptions about men and women. The narrator writes that "Milton's famous line might have been framed and hung up as the rule of [the Leighs'] married life, for he was truly the interpreter, who stood between God and [Mrs. Leigh]" (*Four Short Stories* [London: Pandora Press, 1983], 48). It is significantly Mrs. Leigh's rejection of her husband's harsh translation of God's words about fallen women and their daughter that eventually enables her reunion with Lizzie. Although, unlike Ruth, Lizzie does not die at the story's end, her daughter's death provides the catalyst for Lizzie's redemption. Although this story contains images of female prophets and Christ figures (it concludes with a picture of female compassion likened to Christ's), "Lizzie Leigh" does not present as revolutionary an agenda as does *Ruth*.

Abbreviations

LG Elizabeth Gaskell, *The Letters of Mrs. Gaskell,* ed. J. A. V. Chapple and Arthur Pollard (Cambridge: Harvard University Press, 1967).

MB Elizabeth Gaskell, *Mary Barton* (London: Penguin, 1985).

NS Elizabeth Gaskell, *North and South* (Oxford: Oxford University Press, 1982).

R Elizabeth Gaskell, *Ruth* (Oxford: Oxford University Press, 1985).

Bibliography

Auerbach, Nina. "The Rise of the Fallen Woman." *Nineteenth-Century Fiction* 35 (1980): 29-52.

———. *Woman and the Demon: The Life of a Victorian Myth.* Cambridge: Harvard University Press, 1982.

Beer, Patricia. *Reader, I Married Him: A Study of the Women Characters of Jane Austen, Charlotte Brontë, Elizabeth Gaskell, and George Eliot.* New York: Macmillan, 1974.

Brodestsky, Tessa. *Elizabeth Gaskell.* Oxford: Oxford University Press, 1986.

duPlessis, Rachel Blau. *Writing Beyond the Ending: Narrative Strategies of Twentieth-Century Women Writers.* Bloomington: Indiana University Press, 1985.

Duthie, Enid L. *The Themes of Elizabeth Gaskell.* Totowa, N.J.: Rowman & Littlefield Press, 1980.

Eagleton, Terry. *Myths of Power: A Marxist Study of the Brontës.* London: Macmillan, 1975.

Easson, Angus. *Elizabeth Gaskell.* London: Routledge & Kegan Paul, 1979.

———. "Elizabeth Gaskell and the Novel of Local Pride." *Bulletin of John Ryland Library* 67 (1984-85): 688-709.

Ganz, Margaret. *Elizabeth Gaskell: The Artist in Conflict.* New York: Twayne, 1969.

Gaskell, Elizabeth. *Four Short Stories.* London: Pandora Press, 1983.

———. *The Letters of Mrs. Gaskell.* Edited by J. A. V. Chapple and Arthur Pollard. Cambridge: Harvard University Press, 1967.

———. *The Life of Charlotte Brontë.* Harmondsworth: Penguin, 1983.

———. *Mary Barton.* London: Penguin, 1985.

———. *North and South.* Oxford: Oxford University Press, 1982.

———. *Ruth.* Oxford: Oxford University Press, 1985.

Gilligan, Carol. *In a Different Voice: Psychological Theory and Women's Development.* Cambridge: Harvard University Press, 1982.

Homans, Margaret. *Bearing the Word: Language and Female Experience in Nineteenth-Century Women's Writing.* Chicago: University of Chicago Press, 1986.

Hopkins, A. B. *Elizabeth Gaskell, Her Life and Work.* New York: Octagon Books, 1971.

Kristeva, Julia. *Desire in Language: A Semiotic Approach to Literature and Art.* Translated by Thomas Gora, Alice Jardine, and Leon Roudiez. Edited by Leon S. Roudiez. New York: Columbia University Press, 1980.

Lansbury, Coral. *Elizabeth Gaskell: The Novel of Social Crisis.* New York: Barnes & Noble, 1975.

Pagels, Elaine. *The Gnostic Gospels.* New York: Random House, 1979.

Pollard, Arthur. *Mrs. Gaskell: Novelist and Biographer.* Cambridge: Harvard University Press, 1966.

———. "The Novels of Mrs. Gaskell." *Bulletin of John Rylands Library* 43 (1960-61): 403-25.

Qualls, Barry. *The Secular Pilgrims of Victorian Fiction: The Novel as Book of Life.* Cambridge: Cambridge University Press, 1982.

Ruddick, Sara. "Maternal Thinking." In *Mothering: Essays in Feminist Theory,* edited by Joyce Treblicot, 213-30. Totowa, N.J.: Rowman & Allanheld, 1984.

Sickbert, Virginia. "Dissident Voices in Christina Rossetti's Poetry." Ph.D. diss., State University of New York at Stony Brook, 1990.

———. "The Significance of Mother and Child in Christina Rossetti's *Sing-Song.*" *Victorian Poetry.* Forthcoming.

Taylor, Barbara. *Eve and the New Jerusalem: Socialism and Feminism in the Nineteenth Century.* New York: Pantheon, 1983.

Tompkins, Jane P. "Sentimental Power: *Uncle Tom's Cabin* and the Politics of Literary History." In *The New Feminist Criticism: Essays on Women, Literature and Theory,* edited by Elaine Showalter, 81-104. New York: Pantheon, 1985.

Wheeler, M. D. "The Sinner as Heroine: A Study of Mrs. Gaskell's *Ruth* and the Bible." *Durham University Journal,* n.s., 5 (1976): 148-61.

Wright, Edgar. *Mrs. Gaskell: The Basis for Reassessment.* London: Oxford University Press, 1965.

Maria LaMonaca (essay date fall 2002)

SOURCE: LaMonaca, Maria. "Jane's Crown of Thorns: Feminism and Christianity in *Jane Eyre.*" *Studies in the Novel* 34, no. 3 (fall 2002): 245-63.

[*In the following essay, LaMonaca observes that in* Jane Eyre *Brontë provides insights into the Victorian woman's attempt to reconcile her spiritual and personal beliefs within the confines of the Christian tradition.*]

> St. John is unmarried: he never will marry now. Himself has hitherto sufficed to the toil; and the toil draws near its close: his glorious sun hastens to its setting. . . . And why weep for this? No fear of death will darken St. John's last hour: his mind will be unclouded; his heart will be undaunted; his hope be sure; his faith steadfast. His own words are a pledge of this:—

> 'My Master,' he says, 'has forewarned me. Daily he announces more distinctly—"Surely I come quickly!" And hourly I more eagerly respond—"Amen: even so come, Lord Jesus!"'

Despite the loftiness of its rhetoric and the heroic light it casts on St. John's endeavors, the closing passage of Charlotte Brontë's *Jane Eyre* is more likely to disappoint or confuse readers than inspire them. Perhaps the most perplexing ending of any Victorian novel, Jane's closing tribute to the rigid, patriarchal, and gloomy St. John presents a particular challenge to readings of the novel as a feminist *bildungsroman*. Classic feminist readings have tended to view St. John as one-dimensional patriarchal villain; accordingly, Jane rejects not only her pious cousin, but also the Christian worldview he represents. Since St. John's religious agenda serves only as a vehicle of masculine self-aggrandizement and domination (Gilbert and Gubar 366), Jane ultimately rejects his "patriarchal religious value-system" for an earthly paradise of marital equality with the reformed and chastened Rochester (Rich 490). To interpret the novel's conclusion as an exorcism of religious thought and belief, however, fails to account for St. John's virtual apotheosis on the final page. Nor do such interpretations acknowledge the earnest (if at times unorthodox) religious commitments of the book and its author. Brontë was, after all, a loyal member of the Church of England who firmly defended *Jane Eyre* against charges of immorality and anti-Christian sentiment: "To pluck the mask from the face of the Pharisee," she insisted in a preface to the book's second edition, "is not to lift an impious hand to the Crown of Thorns" (3).

Over the past decade, scholars have begun to read and interpret *Jane Eyre* with far greater attentiveness, both to its religious themes, and the theological and doctrinal controversies of Brontë's era. Consequently, some more recent studies suggest that *Jane Eyre*'s Christian commitments are not necessarily incompatible with the book's presumably feminist emphases. Readings by J. Jeffrey Franklin, Janet L. Larson, Marianne Thormählen, Susan VanZanten Gallagher, and Amanda Witt, for example, all highlight the assertion of Jane's religious and spiritual autonomy as a major component of her *bildungsroman*.[1] By discerning for herself what she perceives to be God's will, Jane effectively resists Rochester's and St. John's attempts to possess her spirit as well as her body. Ultimately, Jane marries Rochester because it is her vocation—the divine call that only she herself can hear. Given the religious resonances of Jane's marriage, as Thormählen and Franklin both suggest, the prominence of St. John (less a patriarchal bogeyman than a sincere if over-zealous Christian) at the novel's end "balances the book" (Thormählen 217). "Both have sought and received Divine guidance and been faithful to the claims of their God-created selves," argues Thormählen (218), while Franklin perceptively suggests that the novel's concluding emphasis on St. John underscores Jane's freely chosen vocation as "a missionary of spiritual love" (482). Gallagher's reading of *Jane Eyre* as a "Christian feminist bildungsroman" suggests a similarly balanced and unproblematic ending: "The novel's religious assertion of a woman's right to self-identity and its depiction of marriage as a relationship of equality," she argues, "anticipate twentieth-century Christian feminism" (68).

So intertwined were discourses of religion and gender in the Victorian period, that a close examination of *Jane Eyre*'s religious themes inevitably furthers our understanding of the novel's gender politics: that is, we see more clearly what is at stake for Jane in her struggle against male control. Yet to read the ending simply as a harmonious "balancing of the book"—with Jane and St. John heeding separate, but equal, divine callings—is to overlook the difficulties Victorian women of faith faced in trying to reconcile their spiritual integrity with cultural norms of domesticity and femininity.[2] To assert, moreover, that the novel embodies "a Christian feminism that . . . advocates the values of love, sexuality, and a marriage of partnership," and that "God's providential care encourages Jane's movement towards freedom and equality" (Gallagher 67) risks flattening the rich discourses, beliefs, and practices of nineteenth-century Evangelical Christianity into little more than a strategy for women to achieve earthly fulfillment and political equality.[3] Certainly, Jane's insistence upon her spiritual and moral integrity enables a stinging critique of society's expectations for women. Jane's religious convictions are presented as the primary force behind her resistance to conventional female subject-positions, whether as Rochester's mistress or as St. John's spiritual helpmate. Moreover, Jane's insistence on a direct, unmediated relationship with her Creator uncovers a glaring inconsistency in Evangelical teaching that posed for women of faith a virtual theological impasse: Evangelicals championed the liberty of discernment and conscience for *all* believers, but *also* prized a model of marriage in which wives were spiritually subordinate to their husbands.

Given the religious and cultural context in which it was written, *Jane Eyre* proclaims what could be considered a message of radical spiritual autonomy for women. Yet feminist scholars must exercise caution: twentieth-century understandings of a woman's freedom and empowerment are not easily applied to the self-conceptions of Victorian women of faith. Rather than flatten out the rich ambiguities of the novel's conclusion, my reading merges feminist and Christian perspectives to highlight theological and domestic tensions left unresolved by the final page. Jane's spiritual *bildungsroman* requires that she develop a moral and ethical agency independent of male control. Yet *Jane Eyre*'s conclusion leaves open

the possibility that Jane, despite her efforts, has failed to reconcile the conflicting demands of domesticity and faith. And although scholars such as Barry Qualls see within Brontë's fiction a privileging of the here-and-now over the hereafter, this reading suggests that *Jane Eyre*'s heroine is, by the novel's conclusion, precariously straddled between this world and the next.

Jane's resistance to male control, as scholars have noted, is vexed by the fact that both Rochester and St. John Cloak their agendas in religious language—that is, both presume that their desire to control Jane is compatible with God's will.[4] Jane's resistance to this control, however, is not merely a refutation of two men's flawed theological arguments. In resisting Rochester and, especially, the pious clergyman St. John, Jane confronts a cherished Evangelical model of female piety—one based directly on Milton's portrayal of Adam and Eve in *Paradise Lost*—that often represented women as *incapable* of discerning God's will for themselves.[5] A survey of eighteenth- and early nineteenth-century conduct books and sermons on the topic of marriage reveals two points in common: first, a pressing concern over the growing secularization of marriage; and second, the extent to which the model of Milton's Eve enchanted male clergymen across religious denominations. Repeatedly, conduct books and sermons urged readers to choose marriage partners who were earnest and upstanding Christians. In his popular treatise, *The Golden Wedding Ring* (1813). Anglican preacher John Clowes, in an attempt "to restore marriage to its primitive sanctity, purity, and bliss, by pointing out its connection with religion" (Foreword), describes "pure conjugal love" as "a representative image or picture, of the union of all divine and heavenly principles, from their SUPREME SOURCE to their lowest state of descent and operation" (13). Not surprisingly, Clowes casts husbands in the role of Supreme Being, while wives represent the "lowest state." "For contemplation he and valour form'd," declares Clowe of the husband, quoting Milton's description of Adam; "For softness she, and sweet attractive grace; / He for GOD only, she for God in him" (10).

To justify this marital hierarchy, clergymen invoked essentialist claims. Clowes states that "every sensible and well-disposed woman attaches herself to a man of *understanding,* and that every sensible and well-disposed man attaches himself most to that woman who *most loves his understanding.* Here then is the true ground of the *union of minds* between two persons of different sexes" (9). Because women's salvation relied so heavily on men's "understanding" of religion and God's will, conduct books and sermons urged women to be especially careful in their choice of a spouse. In his often-reprinted sermon, *The Mutual Duties of Husbands and Wives* (1801), Dissenting minister William Jay (who also quotes Milton) allows that "If the demands of a husband oppose the will of GOD, you are pre-engaged by a law of universal operation, and 'ought [sic] to obey GOD rather than man'" (10). Yet Jay never provides any examples or explanations of such "exceptional" cases. He then goes on to say that although man "is often absurd in his designs, capricious in his temper, tyrannical in his claims, and degrading in his authority," women, by consequence of Eve's original sin, "cannot dispense with this subjection [to husbands] without opposing the express will of GOD, and violating the laws of marriage to which you have acceded" (13).[6]

Charlotte Brontë, as the daughter of an Anglican clergyman with pronounced Evangelical views, undoubtedly was familiar with such pamphlets and sermons on marriage. She was also likely to have read Hannah More's fictionalized sermon on marriage, the phenomenally best-selling novel *Coelebs in Search of a Wife* (1808). As the title suggests, the novel's plot focuses on its hero's travels in search of the ideal Christian mate. Ultimately, Coelebs finds his ideal in Lucilla, a woman whose upbringing has been deliberately patterned on Milton's Eve. Lucilla is virtuous, quiet, and possesses no opinions independent of those she has been taught. She will, the novel assures us, be ideally suited for a Miltonic marriage, in which Coelebs lives "for God alone, and [Lucilla] for God in him." *Jane Eyre* might be considered a rewriting of More's novel. Not only does Brontë's novel focus on the journeying *heroine's* choice of a potential mate, but more importantly, it calls attention to the theological dangers inherent in More's (and Milton's) marital ideal. Brontë explores this threat most forcefully in the novel's insistent concern with idolatry: Jane's idolatry for Rochester, which temporarily "eclipses" God (307), and St. John's arrogant certainty of God's will, suggest a dangerous conflation between male spiritual mediators and the Divine itself. Rather than regard her husband as the mouthpiece of God, the novel suggests, a woman might come to mistake her husband *for* God.[7]

From the first moments of her love for Rochester, Jane is aware of the perils of human idolatry. Jane's passion, as much as Rochester's arguments, distorts her judgment, so that "while he spoke my very Conscience and Reason turned traitors against me, and charged me with crime in resisting him" (356). Jane is particularly susceptible to Rochester's seduction because he makes his appeal on religious and moral grounds. Rochester, that is, puts upon Jane's shoulders the responsibility for his moral rebirth: "Is the wandering and sinful, but now rest-seeking and repentant man," he queries, "justified in daring the world's opinion, in order to attach to him for ever, this gentle, gracious, genial stranger; thereby securing his own peace of mind and regeneration of life?" (246). Rochester insistently describes his roman-

tic desire as a product of God's will when he proposes to Jane in his "Eden-like" orchard [278], contending that "my Maker sanctions what I do" (287).

While Jane recognizes the presumptiveness of Rochester's position, she nonetheless cannot resist the role Rochester has assigned her. In response to his religious arguments, Jane, in a rare burst of sermonizing, retorts: "Sir . . . a Wanderer's repose or a Sinner's reformation should never depend on a fellow-creature. Men and women die; philosophers falter in wisdom, and Christians in goodness: if any one you know has suffered and erred, let him look higher than his equals for strength to amend, and solace to heal." Jane's insistence that an individual's salvation "should never depend on a fellow-creature" is consistent with Evangelicalism's emphasis on a "religion of the heart"—that is, an intimate, direct, and unmediated relationship between the soul and its Creator. Jane's statement is set against a masculine religious rhetoric in the novel that, with a few exceptions, gestures towards error, insincerity, or spiritual failure on the part of the speaker. It comes as no surprise, therefore, that Jane cannot live up to her spoken convictions.[8] Shortly afterwards, she reveals the extent of her spiritual dependence upon Rochester, who has become "almost my hope of heaven" (246). More frequently, however, the text emphasizes Rochester's spiritual dependence upon Jane, who during her stay at Thornfield is the more charismatic figure. Victorian readers, familiar with Christian typology, undoubtedly would have noticed the strong religious resonances of Jane's account of the first Thornfield fire: "I . . . deluged the bed and its occupant, flew back to my own room, brought my own water-jug, baptized the couch afresh, and by God's aid, succeeded in extinguishing the flames which were devouring it" (168). While the flames enveloping Rochester prefigure the second, devastating fire at Thornfield, allegorically, the text depicts Jane throwing the waters of baptism—spiritual rebirth—upon Rochester, ostensibly quenching the fires of Hell which threaten to devour him.

While Rochester's temptation is difficult to resist, Jane nonetheless remains firm in her resolution to leave Thornfield, and expresses little genuine doubt about her decision. Surprisingly, it is St. John Rivers—that ostensibly unattractive, even repulsive character—who poses to Jane the greater temptation, the one she clearly has the more difficulty resisting. The difficulty of Jane's position at this point of the novel only becomes evident once we accept that Jane truly and sincerely regards her cousin as a saintly, devoted Christian. In light of Evangelical tracts and sermons counseling women to think more of religion than love as a foundation for marriage, St. John would have been viewed in many circles as a most eligible bachelor indeed.[9] Thus while Jane has no trouble resisting the sophistry of the religious hypocrite Brocklehurst, and can, with difficulty, see through the machinations of the all-too-human Rochester, how can she repudiate a "good man, pure as the deep sunless source," in possession of a "crystal conscience" (458)? Critics have detailed the reasons why St. John repulses Jane, but although he is clearly self-aggrandizing, manipulative, inflexible, and legalistic, these traits are presented to the reader less as inconsistencies or blemishes within his otherwise sterling character, than as the inevitable result of it. In short, St. John buckles under the weight of his own perfection. His countenance—so perfect and regular it suggests the hard lineaments of Greek statuary—accurately reflects a soul made rigid by its own moral strengths. Despite Jane's recognition of St. John's personal shortcomings, she does not let her awareness of "the corrupt man within him" diminish her veneration for the "pure Christian" (457) side of his nature. Jane even suggests that St. John's faults are part and parcel of a truly great and active nature: "[H]e was," she observes, "of the material from which nature hews her heroes—Christian and Pagan—her law-givers, her statesmen, her conquerors: a steadfast bulwark for great interests to rest upon; but, at the fireside, too often a cold cumbrous column, gloomy and out of place" (438).

Considering Jane's "veneration" of St. John, then, his attractiveness to her—and the difficulty with which she turns down his proposal—is more complex than any Freudian inclination for abjection or self-punishment. As Jane considers St. John's offer, Brontë does not ironise her reflection: "[I]s not the occupation he now offers me truly the most glorious man can adopt or God assign?" (450). That Jane believes in St. John's cause is perhaps best demonstrated by her complete willingness to help spread the Gospel in India, despite all its attendant privations, on the condition that she be allowed to remain single. To complicate matters further, Jane must once again deal with a domineering male character who is firmly convinced of God's will for them both. Because God is all-knowing, St. John seems to believe that he himself, as God's servant, is likewise omniscient. "I am the servant of an infallible master," he exults, "I am not going out under human guidance . . . my lawgiver, my captain, is the All-perfect" (447). Just as Rochester perceives in Jane "an instrument" of God, and tries to convince her that to abandon him would be an act of wickedness, St. John warns Jane, "[I]f you reject [my offer], it is not me that you deny, but God" (455).

If St. John can know God's will for himself, can he not also determine God's will for Jane? St. John determines that his marriage to Rosamond would be a hindrance to his execution of God's divine plan. Although his renunciation of Rosamond Oliver appears at first an unnatural, even cruel, suppression of his feelings—St. John tramples the heads of flowers as he averts his gaze from the lovely maiden—Jane herself soon acknowledges the

wisdom of her cousin's decision: "I understood, as by inspiration, the nature of his love for Miss Oliver; I agreed with him that it was but a love of the senses" (438). St. John's assertion that "she is not the partner suited to me . . . and . . . twelve months' rapture would succeed a lifetime of regret" (417) is supported by Jane's own less-than-complimentary observations of the heiress. Although Jane describes Rosamond as "a vision . . . of perfect beauty" (405) she also considers her "not absolutely spoilt . . . vain . . . unthinking . . . not profoundly interesting or thoroughly impressive" (411-12). In short, she concludes, "I liked her *almost* as [much as] I liked my pupil Adele" (412, italics mine). Considering that Adele is a child, a foreigner, and a Catholic, who will require "a sound English education" to mold her character (499), Jane's comparison is hardly flattering. This beautiful but somewhat childish and superficial woman is not presented as a worthy complement to St. John's greatness of character.

All these elements—Jane's veneration of St. John as a stalwart Christian, her support of his missionary cause, and St. John's unwavering certainty of God's will for them both—appear to cloud and obscure her judgment even more than her passionate love for Rochester had. At this crucial juncture of the narrative, Jane—just moments away from being "chained for life to a man who regarded one but as a useful tool" (463)—cannot bring herself to rely solely on St. John's judgment: "I could decide if I were but certain," she tells him, "were I but convinced that it is God's will I should marry you, I could vow to marry you here and now—come afterwards what would!" (466). At this point in the novel the reader arrives at that notorious "thumping piece of Gothic claptrap" (Prescott 90) which depicts Jane, in response to her frantic prayer, suddenly able to hear Rochester's voice summoning her. By the end of the chapter, Jane has successfully broken away from St. John: "It was *my* time to assume ascendancy," she says. "*My* powers were in play, and in force . . . I desired him to leave me: I must, and would be alone. He obeyed at once. Where there is energy to command well enough, obedience never fails" (467).

Despite a long history of criticism which explains Jane's "mysterious summons" in terms of psychological or natural phenomena, this salvific moment in the novel can be convincingly read as a moment of direct supernatural intervention.[10] Like the great Romantic poets, Jane associates Nature with the transcendent. Yet Romantic engagements with nature, as M. H. Abrams has noted, tend toward celebrating the divinity of humanity rather than reaffirming an otherworldly deity—a tradition which Jane does not seem to invoke. Instead, the natural world reinforces for Jane her conviction of a God far greater than—and hence distinctly separate from—humankind. Out on the heath at night, after her initial flight from Thornfield, Jane's musings about Nature, which she invests with a feminine persona, at first suggest little more than a vague pantheism: "Nature seemed to me benign and good; I thought she loved me, outcast as I was; and I, who from man could anticipate only mistrust, rejection, insult, cling to her with filial fondness. To-night, at least, I would be her guest—as I was her child: my mother would lodge me without money and without price" (363). Yet Jane's pantheistic musings quickly give way to a more conventional theological creed: "Night was come, and her planets were risen . . . We know that God is everywhere; but certainly we feel His presence most when His works are on the grandest scale spread before us: and it is in the unclouded night-sky, where his worlds wheel their silent course, that we read clearest His infinitude, His omnipotence, His omnipresence" (364).

Although Jane, at the time of St. John's proposal and her subsequent mysterious summons, dismisses the voice as merely "the work of nature," she undergoes a sudden change of heart once she returns to Rochester at Ferndean. Rochester describes how—after supplicating God for an end to his torment—he cried out to Jane three times in a fit of despair and longing, and heard in response her voice: "Where are you?" This manifest coincidence astonishes Jane beyond all power of speech:

> Reader, it was on Monday night—near midnight—that I too had received the mysterious summons: those were the very words by which I replied to it. I listened to Mr. Rochester's narrative; but made no disclosure in return. The coincidence struck me as too awful and inexplicable to be communicated or discussed. If I told anything, my tale would be such as must necessarily make a profound impression on the mind of my hearer; and that mind, yet from its sufferings too prone to gloom, needed not the deeper shade of the supernatural. *I kept these things then, and pondered them in my heart.*
>
>   (497, italics mine)

At this point, rather than try to reason herself out of "superstition," Jane simply acknowledges the "awful" and "inexplicable" character of this "supernatural" coincidence. Jane's unwillingness to speak further (in a book where religious talk is cheap) is typical of her recognition of great theological and religious significance. Indeed, Jane's final comment to the reader, "I kept these things then, and pondered them in my heart" echoes Luke's description of Mary's response to the miraculous event of the Incarnation.[11]

Jane, in the course of her moral reflection, eschews both Rochester's and St. John's attempts to dictate God's will to her. Discerning God's will through seemingly direct contact with the supernatural, Jane demonstrates that women—true to one facet of Evangelical doctrine—must experience God directly, "through the heart," despite Evangelical models of femininity and gender which, paradoxically, denied women this very possibility. God's voice doesn't simply fall out of the sky into Jane's lap, however, clearly, she has had to *learn* discernment. *Jane Eyre* levels another subtle criticism against male spiritual authority in the fact that Jane seems to learn her "religion of the heart" not from the male clergymen of the novel, but from the *women.* Despite St. John's apparent sincerity and sterling virtue, both he and Brocklehurst preach a religion of the Letter, or Law. Their God is a supernatural magistrate who damns sinners for disobeying the Word. "Do you know where the wicked go after death?" (41), Brocklehurst asks Jane, before giving her a tract on "the awfully sudden death of Martha G———, a naughty child addicted to falsehood and deceit" (44). After hearing St. John preach for the first time, moreover, Jane describes "a strange bitterness; an absence of consolatory gentleness: stern allusions to Calvinistic doctrines—election, predestination, reprobation . . . each reference to these points sounded like a sentence pronounced for doom" (394).[12]

While Jane has learned to seek God in Nature, as well as in the stillness of her own heart, St. John can look no further than the "letter [that] killeth" (2 Corinthians 3:6). "Nature was not to him," Jane notes, "that treasury of delight it was to his sisters [. . .] never did he seem to roam the moors for the sake of their soothing silence" (393). Unlike the men who attempt to impose their wills upon Jane, women in the novel communicate their theological convictions by example rather than exhortation, thus imposing a feminine silence in contrast to male garrulousness about the Word. Of course, Helen Burns makes some long speeches. Helen's renunciation of earthly happiness represents an aspect of St. John's theology that Jane cannot accept, but Helen, in spite of Adrienne Rich's assertion, cannot fairly be considered a younger and feminine version of St. John Rivers (Rich 487). This is partly because Helen's otherworldly views pose no real threat to Jane, since they are perfectly disinterested. More importantly, although Jane rejects some elements of Helen's spoken doctrine, her example and beliefs serve Jane in good stead later in the novel.[13] It is Helen who advises Jane to study the New Testament and follow Christ's *example,* in particular his injunction to "Love your enemies"—a counsel that clearly influences the forgiveness Jane grants the dying Mrs. Reed. More importantly, however, Helen also tells Jane not to "think too much of the love of human beings" (81) and instead anticipate God's love in the next world. While Jane, in marrying Rochester, obviously does not follow this advice to the letter, it represents to her the necessity of valuing God's love above all earthly passions, and seems to provide her with a moral framework for later resisting an idolatrous relationship which, in violating "the law given by God," would cut Jane off from her Creator.

Most interestingly, however, Helen models for Jane an independence of thought on matters of theology and doctrine. Unable to reconcile her belief in an all-benevolent God with the concept of eternal damnation, Helen professes a personal belief in universal salvation: "I hold another creed; which no one ever taught me, and which I seldom mention . . . it extends hope to all: it makes Eternity a rest—a mighty home, not a terror and an abyss. Besides, with this creed, I can clearly distinguish between the criminal and his crime; I can so sincerely forgive the first while I abhor the last" (70). Helen's willingness to depart in significant ways from hard-line Calvinist doctrine not only distances her further from the rigid St. John, but also seems to prefigure Jane's own attitudes towards religious people and creeds alike. Just as Helen can keep her awareness of sin from destroying her belief in humanity, Jane can keep her recognition of St. John's human frailty from diminishing her regard for him as a stalwart and sincere Christian. She can, moreover, accept some elements of Evangelical Christian doctrine while rejecting those that seem to her incompatible with her own religious convictions. Supporting Jane in her refusal to accept St. John as a husband—the most torturous form of self-renunciation she can imagine—is a belief in a more benign and loving Creator, a Creator closer to Helen Burns's merciful Father than to St. John's vengeful deity. This notion of a gentle, loving Creator seems much more conducive to a "religion of the heart" than masculine visions of an angry, unapproachable Lawgiver.

After Helen Burns, it is Diana and Mary who serve as models of divinely-inspired womanhood for Jane. Diana and Mary demonstrate no trace of the Calvinist morbidity or grim earnestness that consume their brother. Instead, they demonstrate a power which Jane sorely lacks: that of resisting St. John's charismatic power. St. John induces Jane to study Hindostanee, in part, because he cannot convince his sisters to do so. His long sermons upon the nature of Jane's duty, moreover, are set into stark relief by the gentle, loving, and quiet support Diana and Mary provide for their adopted "sister." Significantly, among all the matters these three women discuss among themselves—foreign languages, literature, drawing—religion and theology are not mentioned. As women who veil their religious convictions in silence, they are a pair after Jane's own heart. Most importantly, Diana pronounces St. John's designs upon Jane as "Insupportable—unnatural—out of the question!" (463). Once again, a female character upholds for Jane a sense of Divine will and purpose which is more allied with human nature and human desire.

For all Jane's notions of a gentle, nurturing Creator, paradoxically, her spiritual progress pushes her toward active postures which are anything but conventionally feminine. Indeed, Jane's progress suggests a kind of "muscular Christianity" that thrusts her, for much of the narrative, away from conventional women's roles and domestic spaces. Despite Evangelical visions of the home as a consecrated space, Jane experiences her most direct contact with the supernatural when outdoors—on the open heath after her flight from Thornfield, and at the time of St. John's proposal, in a mossy glen by a waterfall (446). The discernment of God's will, moreover, is no passive exercise; as Jane discovers, it requires a considerable amount of self-reliance and active agency. Contrary to traditional Calvinist notions of Christian grace (which posit the human soul as completely powerless to save itself, relying entirely on divine mercy, forgiveness, and salvation it cannot earn), Jane must actively work to enable her redemption. Aside from active prayer and discernment, Jane must suffer. Jane's suffering is not like Helen Burns's passive endurance of persecution (a mode of suffering typically associated with the feminine), however, but rather an *active* (masculine, heroic) decision to *renounce,* however painful, the thing she most ardently desires—Rochester's love which stands between Jane and her "hope of heaven."[14] After Jane's aborted marriage ceremony, she determines to force herself to adhere to the law and will of God unaided: "[Y]ou shall tear yourself away, none shall help you: you shall, yourself, pluck out your right eye: yourself cut off your right hand: your heart shall be the victim; and you, the priest, to transfix it" (335). Jane's reliance on herself to cast away the adulterous temptation—along with its imagery of self-mutilation—is entirely in accordance with Christ's command in the New Testament: "If thy right eye offend thee, pluck it out, and cast it from thee . . . if thy right hand offend thee, cut it off, and cast it from thee" (Matt. 5:29-30). Although painful, this emotional self-mutilation is infinitely preferable to spiritual ruin: Jane, not Rochester, becomes master of her soul as well as her body. Accordingly, Jane's suffering also manifests itself physically. Upon fleeing Thornfield she conveniently forgets her small store of money and provisions, rendering herself prey to the ravages of rain, cold, hunger, and fatigue.

Although Bertha's death enables Jane to return to Rochester, the couple's happy union seems first to require a mutual spiritual purging. Like Jane, Rochester has been chastised through suffering. Yet while Jane's active suffering (tearing away her own "right eye" and "right hand") frees her from limiting feminine postures, coinciding with her wanderings from hearth and home, Rochester's literal mutilation (interpreted by many critics as a symbolic castration) is forced upon him. Having taken no action in the matter of his own redemption, Rochester's passive suffering—akin to that of Helen Burns—takes on a distinctly feminine quality: "Divine justice pursued its course," he tells Jane, "disasters came thick on me: I was forced to pass through the valley of the shadow of death. *His* chastisements are mighty; and one smote me which has humbled me for ever. You know I was proud of my strength: but what is it now, when I must give it over to foreign guidance, as a child does its weakness?" (495).

Jane's empowering suffering leads her to spiritual victory and domestic bliss—a "happy ending" predicated, however, upon the containment of her muscular spirituality. Interpreted one way, the book's conclusion shows Jane victorious over two spiritual pitfalls: the dangers of human idolatry (suggestive of mere sensual gratification), *and* the lure of excessive self-renunciation. The renunciatory power which renders Rochester's suffering feeble in comparison must ultimately itself be relinquished, lest Jane, like St. John Rivers, become at the fireside "a cold, cumbrous column, gloomy and out of place." Both extremes, self-indulgence and self-restraint, must be purged from the text before Jane and Rochester's domestic paradise can be realized. Just as Bertha, the lascivious madwoman, conveniently falls to her death, St. John, Jane's *other* double, must remove himself to the deadly privations of missionary life in India. Consequently, Jane's marriage is framed as self-gratification (albeit one consistent with "the law given by God; sanctioned by man" [356]) rather than self-renunciation. In response to Rochester's suggestion that Jane's wish to marry him emanates from her "delight in sacrifice," Jane replies, "To be privileged to put my arms round what I value—to press my lips to what I love . . . is that to make a sacrifice? If so, then certainly I delight in sacrifice" (494).

As for a resolution to the problem of human idolatry, the conclusion's implicit association of Jane with the Virgin Mary suggests Jane's acquisition of an autonomous spiritual power. Aside from "keeping and pondering," like Mary, miraculous events in her heart, Jane, when the chastened Rochester first glimpses her, is garbed in a light blue dress, the traditional color of the Virgin. In the very next paragraph, Jane describes Rochester receiving his infant son into his arms. As Rochester holds the infant, and "acknowledged that God had tempered judgment with mercy" (501), the reader is reminded once again of Christ's birth, and of the infant who came to redeem humankind from sin and death. Jane, initially faced with the dilemma of Milton's Eve, has been transformed from a woman relying on her fallen husband as an intermediary between herself and God, to a woman who is figured in Scripture as favored daughter of the Father and the Holy Spirit. Christian theologians have traditionally figured Mary as a Second or New Eve, one who would, by bringing Christ into the world, participate in the atonement of Eve's Original Sin. Mary's obedience to God's will ("be it unto me according to thy word" [Luke 1:38]) atones for Eve's original disobedience; Jane, accordingly, through accepting what *she* perceives as Divine Will, has mastered the temptation to be led astray by others. Although faithfully reflecting scriptural precedent in this regard, Jane's retelling of Eve's story is nonetheless a radical departure from Milton's account: Milton (in common, no doubt, with the original writer(s) of Genesis), had not considered that Adam and the Snake might, for Eve, be one and the same.

However, the Marian allusions also raise questions as to what extent Jane has truly liberated her spiritual self from dependency upon fallible human beings and human relationships. Jane's association with Mary may signify a special, unmediated relationship between herself and the Father; it also suggests, however, that Jane now acts as a Mediatrix for Rochester (or even an idol, considering that Victorian anti-Catholic propaganda depicted Catholics "worshipping" Mary). Keeping in mind the fire-quenching scene earlier in the novel, the reader is left with the impression that Jane has simply reverted to her earlier role as her master's Savior. While Jane is still pondering St. John's marriage offer, she tells him, "[B]efore I definitely resolve in quitting England, I will know for certain, whether I cannot be of greater use by remaining in it than by leaving it" (461). Recalling St. John's dedication to potential Indian converts, Jane invests her relationship to Rochester with redemptive, Evangelical overtones. Although Jane's marriage, framed as an alternative missionary endeavor, could be perceived as "balancing the book," ultimately Jane—having taken upon herself the redemption of her husband—rejects Eve in favor of another conventional female role: that of the Victorian Household angel. Rochester, who is unable fully to recognize God's love and mercy until Jane returns to him, becomes spiritually, as well as physically, dependent upon Jane. Jane, by taking on the role of divine intermediary for Rochester, ironically renounces spiritual autonomy for a reciprocal dependence. Just as St. John cannot follow the will of God and carry out his vocation unless he goes to India, it is only through Rochester, we are led to infer, that Jane can fulfill *her* religious and spiritual destiny.

For all Jane's heroic struggles, she may not have entirely freed herself from the dangers of human idolatry. While the conclusion's double portrait of Jane and St. John suggests two individuals who have found and fulfilled their respective callings, perhaps only one has found a sphere truly suited to his ambition and talent. "Well may he eschew the calm of domestic life," reflects Jane of her cousin at one point, "it is not his element: there his faculties stagnate—they cannot develop or appear to advantage. It is in scenes of strife and danger—where courage is proved, and energy exercised, and fortitude tasked—that he will speak and move, the leader and superior" (438). In the rose-tinted vision of Jane's long-deferred domestic bliss, however, it is easy to overlook the fact that Jane—in so many ways St. John's double—has no lack of ambition herself. Early in the narrative, we see young Jane dreaming of travels to faraway lands. She dreams of "the bleak shores of

Lapland, Siberia . . . Iceland" (14) and upon reading *Gulliver's Travels,* muses how "I might one day, by taking a long voyage, see with my own eyes the little fields, houses, and trees [of Lilliput]" (29). Later on, Jane rebels against the notion of a conventional domestic life of "making puddings and knitting stockings" (126). Yet this is precisely the sort of life she leads at Ferndean.

Given the possibility that Jane—shut away in moldy Ferndean, constantly ministering to the demands of an invalid—may *not* have found her earthly paradise, the rhetoric of Victorian domesticity allows her no means through which to articulate any disappointment. Like any good household angel, Jane "delights in sacrifice"; any pain or suffering, supposedly transformed into pleasure by womanly love and devotion, is thereby negated. In choosing to marry Rochester, Jane has forfeited her ability to perform heroic, *visible* acts of self-renunciation. Deprived of this avenue of self-assertion and autonomous identity, Jane removes herself from the conclusion of her own autobiography, ceding her place to one presumably worthier than herself: "His [St. John's] is the exaction of the apostle, who speaks but for Christ, when he says—'Whosoever will come after Me, *let him deny himself,* and take up his cross and follow Me'" (my italics). Having freed himself from the hearthside, St. John's suffering, unsoftened by domestic sentiment, feeds his "ambition . . . which aims to fill a place in the *first rank* of those who are redeemed from the earth" (501-02, my italics). Jane's veneration of St. John's zeal reflects her own thwarted ambition, and foreshadows the frustration of a housebound St. Teresa in George Eliot's *Middlemarch.*[15]

If Jane and St. John have each discerned God's will for themselves, why is St. John "called, and chosen" (502) to his heroic missionary endeavors—certain of a greater glory awaiting him—while Jane, called to "mind [more] earthly things," is presumably relegated to the second or third ranks of God's faithful? If Jane's religion is—as feminist criticism sometimes presumes—merely a strategy for personal empowerment, then clearly this religion has failed her by novel's end. To Evangelical Victorians, however, "vocation" and "calling" was, if something freely discerned, *not* freely chosen. If Jane's calling as Rochester's wife is (as the conclusion works to convince us) compatible with Jane's own desires, so much the better for Jane. Yet the lingering possibility of Jane's dissatisfaction underscores a cultural breach between our ideas of happiness and Evangelical Christian notions of a life well lived. In *Varieties of Religious Experience* (1901-02), William James described modern religious liberalism as "a victory of healthy-mindedness . . . over the morbidness [of] . . . old hell-fire theology" (88) of the previous century. Thus the "healthy-minded" modern reader (whether or not a believer) might find it difficult to comprehend the mindset of those James labeled as "sick-souled": beliefs which lead individuals to court suffering, accept sacrifice, or make decisions seemingly contrary to personal desire and inclination. Despite Barry Qualls' assertion, then, that Jane in her marriage to Rochester opts for a "healthy-minded" earthly paradise, "an alliance [of nature and religion] which does not oppose . . . a genuinely human and creative life lived in this world" (46), the possible limitations of Jane's choice gestures towards a more traditional, "sick-souled" worldview. Jane's marriage, framed as a vocation in its own right, cannot then be considered a happy *ending,* but rather an arduous process, leading—like St. John's missionary work—to some yet-deferred state of bliss.

Despite Charlotte Brontë's struggles to reconcile her heroine's spiritual integrity with female desire and with the rhetoric of nineteenth-century femininity, she cannot, in the end, give equal weight to all claims. Jane imagines a life that will accommodate both her passionate desires and her ambitious nature; her spiritual integrity, however, ultimately demands that she frame both passion and ambition within the constraints of Victorian domesticity. Numerous critics, of course, have expressed uneasiness with the final pages of *Jane Eyre.* There is much evidence to suggest that the redeemed, glorified figure of Jane is overshadowed, whether by a repressive Victorian culture, or—through the book's closing reference to the Book of Revelation—"a patrilineally mediated structure of authority and voice" (Williams 84). In focusing on the theological and religious significance of the conclusion, however, it is impossible to overlook other, even more ominous hints. While a "sick-souled" notion of stern duty and suffering threatens to darken Jane's domestic idyll, so might an unexpectedly threatening notion of God the Father. For all Jane's suggestions of a benign, gentle, and even maternal God—one whose will is not incompatible with human nature and human desire—it is St. John's coldly just and vengeful deity that looms over the novel's final scenes. God may have "tempered judgment with mercy" in bringing Jane and Rochester together again, but not until He exacted the full Scriptural penalty—an eye and a hand—upon Rochester for his crime of intended adultery. This God, who *enforces* compliance with his will, resembles less the Mother who pleads with Jane to "flee temptation" than the Father who hurled Eve out of paradise for her disobedience. In this light, even the religious faith that has enabled Jane to maintain a sense of autonomy in the face of all attempts at manipulation, suggests yet another constraint upon her freedom. This note of Calvinist panic—evoking the terrors of Brontë's early womanhood, and the specter of a God allowing *no* individual choice in the matter of personal salvation—uncomfortably suggests the final, lingering possibility of a patriarchal force that no amount of renunciation can surmount.

Jane's *bildungsroman,* viewed through the lens of nineteenth-century Evangelical Christian discourse, thus exposes intimate connections between female identity and faith in Victorian England. Victorian women lived in a culture that employed the rhetoric of Christianity to prescribe their role and identity—an identity that many women, paradoxically, perceived as a threat to their moral and spiritual integrity. To obtain power, knowledge, and interpretative authority, as Janet Larson notes, women "had to expose the violence of a dominant ideal and 'kill,' maim, or at the very least convert the Victorian Angel in the House" (46). Brontë, along with many of her female contemporaries, similarly drew upon Christian discourse and theology to challenge existing feminine ideals of Eves and Angels. For these women, however, God was no rhetorical abstraction, but a very real and genuine Other. Throughout the margins of Jane Eyre's final speeches lurks an anxiety that Jane may be confusing her own desires for God's will.[16] And by invoking God's will to support these desires, she may be distorting that Other—a misrepresentation tantamount to idolatry. It should come as no surprise, then, that by novel's end Jane's theology is every bit as conflicted as her new identity as Mrs. Rochester. These ambiguities reflect the tensions real Victorian women of faith experienced in trying to meet multiple, often conflicting demands in their lives. Such challenges were complicated further by the fact that nineteenth-century Evangelical Christianity—attentive to the realities of sin, sorrow, sacrifice, and loss—was no easy creed for women *or* men. Despite the attractive "healthy-mindedness" of so much of Jane's theology in her narrative, the book's tormented ending reminds readers that Brontë, freethinker as she was, nonetheless subscribed to Christianity that cherished Christ's "Crown of Thorns" as its standard. Given, then, the vexed discourses of gender, domesticity, and faith surrounding *Jane Eyre*'s production, an easy reading of the book's ending is neither possible nor desirable.

Notes

1. In the first, long-overdue, book-length study on religion in the Brontës' fiction, Marianne Thormählen regards Jane's religious convictions as the primary motivation for her actions: "Jane . . . withstand[s] temptation not because [the Brontës' heroines] are 'good girls' . . . reluctantly complying with now-outmoded rules for virtuous behavior. They resist because failure to do so would be a betrayal of the Creator who is to them . . . the very fount of love" (59-60). J. Jeffrey Franklin also stresses the centrality of Jane's faith in God in the novel. "[C]ontact with the supernatural," argues Franklin, "appears to contribute directly to Jane's empowerment, to the finding of her own voice" (471-72). Amanda Witt describes Jane's spiritual maturation as an essential part of her *bildungsroman,* noting that Jane finally

acquires "perfect [spiritual] vision" by "looking to God first, rather than to an idolized lover" (33).

2. The model Victorian woman was devoted to husband and family so much so, that some women viewed domestic ideals as a potential threat to their spiritual integrity. "What I complain of the Evangelical party for," wrote Florence Nightingale, "is the degree to which they have raised the claims upon women of 'Family' the idol they have made of it. It is a kind of Fetishism . . . They acknowledge no God, for all they say to the contrary, but this Fetich" (qtd. in Reed 209). Charlotte Yonge, in a letter of 1853, expressed similar concerns about the spiritual pitfall of human idolatry: "I know women have a tendency that way [towards hero-worship], and it frightens me, because the most sensible and strong-minded are liable to be led astray . . . I always remember one of Dr. Pusey's letters that speaks of a desire for guidance, a good thing in itself, turning to be a temptation. I am very much afraid of live Bilds [heroes] . . ." (qtd. in Coleridge 190).

3. Evangelical ideals were at once complicit in and opposed to Victorian constructions of the domestic sphere. On the one hand, Evangelical writers often condemned novels that downplayed concerns about eternal salvation in favor of representing all-too-temporal romantic and domestic bliss. At the same time, Evangelicalism's idyll of the home as a sacred space—a space presided over by perfectly virtuous women-contributed significantly to the formation of the secular cult of the Angel in the House.

4. As Carolyn Williams points out, "St. John convincingly claims to be a 'medium,' to convey God's will and God's voice transparently" (74).

5. My use of the term "Evangelical" throughout this essay is informed by Elisabeth Jay's definition in her book *The Religion of the Heart.* While acknowledging the absence of doctrinal uniformity or theological consistency within Evangelicalism, Jay attempts to outline a "consensus of beliefs held by different individuals" (51) within the Anglican church of the nineteenth century. Chief among these beliefs, according to Jay's definition, is a personal apprehension of God (51), the conviction of innate human depravity (Original Sin), and the authority of Scripture. Some disputed, "non-essential" doctrines were a belief in eternal punishment for sinners, an expectation of the Second Coming, a belief in the active agency of Providence, and personal assurance of salvation. Although Jay focuses on Evangelicalism within the Anglican church, the Evangelical movement significantly influenced all Protestant denomina-

tions in Britain in the late-eighteenth and nine-teenth centuries.

6. Similarly, the Presbyterian minister James Fordyce, in *Sermons to Young Women* (a text that ran through at least fourteen editions between 1765 and 1809) lauds "that obsequious majesty ascribed by [Milton] to innocent Eve" (130). He urges his female readers to "command by obeying, and by yielding to conquer" (131).

7. So might men, apparently, be perceived as gods to their children. In another classic Evangelical novel, Mary Martha Sherwood's *History of the Fairchild Family,* Mr. Fairchild pronounces to his offspring that "I stand in the place of God to you, whilst you are a child" (qtd. in Jay 141).

8. Charlotte Brontë, along with many of her contemporaries, "did not look with favor upon the 'serious conversation' in which many Evangelicals delighted, preferring to keep their religion a matter for private contemplation" (Jay 255).

9. *Considerations on Marriage, Addressed to Christian Professors* (1840) urges women to think of love "as little as possible" (11), and "never to give their hearts to an object, whose heart was not, as far as they could judge, on scriptural grounds, given to God . . . never to arrange, by their own choice an act, to spend a life of unsanctified enjoyment on earth, with one with whom they cannot hope to spend an eternity of hallowed happiness in heaven" (13).

10. Thormählen, who also considers the summons as a supernatural event, places Brontë's use of the miraculous within the context of some trends in early nineteenth-century religious thought. Coleridge and Maurice, she notes, regarded the miraculous not as a rupture with Nature, but as an affirmation of its hidden order (70).

11. Following the visit of the shepherds, the Evangelist reports that "Mary kept all these things, and pondered them in her heart" (Luke 2:19).

12. As both Elisabeth Jay and historian D. W. Bebbington have noted, there was no consensus among Evangelicals on the question of predestination or eternal damnation. Jane, by rejecting St. John's Calvinism, merely rejects one strand of Evangelical thought for another doctrine—that of Arminianism.

13. Helen's "earnest conversation" also differs from that of Brocklehurst and St. John, because she partakes in it only after Jane invites her to do so. Jane, marveling at Helen's example of quiet submission to Miss Scatcherd's torments, asks her to explain her motives Helen's response suggests

that example must accompany legislation: "Read the New Testament, and *observe* what Christ says, and how he acts—make his word your rule, and his conduct your example" (69, my italics).

14. In *Dandies and Desert Saints,* James Eli Adams notes that Victorian heroines often assert independent will through "a virtuoso ascetic regimen" (7)—an exhibition typically "stigmatized" and contained within the course of the narrative by the force of gendered norms.

15. "Many Theresas have been born who found for themselves no epic life wherein there was a constant unfolding of far-resonant action; perhaps only a life of mistakes, the offspring of a certain spiritual grandeur ill-matched with the meanness of opportunity . . . Here and there is born a Saint Theresa, foundress of nothing, whose loving heartbeats and sobs after an unattained goodness tremble off and are dispersed among hindrances, instead of centering in some long-recognisable deed" (Eliot xiv).

16. This ambivalent dimension of *Jane Eyre*'s conclusion seems to echo the spiritual terror expressed by Brontë in a letter of 1837, in which she despairs of ever being able to know or follow God's will: "[I am] smitten at times to the heart with the conviction that ghastly Calvinistic doctrines are true . . . If Christian perfection be necessary to salvation, I shall never be saved; my heart is a very hot-bed for sinful thoughts, and when I decide an action I scarcely remember to look to my Redeemer for direction. . . . I go on constantly seeking my own pleasure, pursuing the gratification of my own desires" (qtd. in Gaskell 152).

Works Cited

Abrams, M. H. *Natural Supernaturalism: Tradition and Revolution in Romantic Literature.* 1973 ed. New York and London: W. W. Norton, 1971.

Adams, James Eli. *Dandies and Desert Saints: Styles of Victorian Masculinity.* Ithaca, NY: Cornell UP, 1995.

Bebbington, D. W. *Evangelicalism in Modern Britain: A History from the 1730's to the 1980's.* London: Unwin Hyman, 1989.

Brontë, Charlotte. *Jane Eyre.* 1847. Ed. Michael Manson. New York and London: Penguin Books, 1996.

Clowes, John. *The Golden Wedding-Ring; or, Thoughts on Marriage, in a Conversation between a Father and His Two Children.* Manchester: J. Gleaye, 1813.

Coleridge, Christabel. *Charlotte Mary Yonge: Her Life and Letters.* 1903. Detroit: Gale Research Company, 1969.

Considerations on Marriage: Addressed to Christian Professors. London: Wright and Albright, 1840.

Eliot, George. *Middlemarch.* 1871-72. Ed. Bert G. Hornback. New York: W. W. Norton, 1977.

Fordyce, James. *Sermons to Young Women.* 1766. Third American from the Twelfth London Edition. Philadelphia: M. Carey, 1809.

Franklin, J. Jeffrey. "The Merging of Spiritualities: Jane Eyre as Missionary of Love." *Nineteenth-Century Literature* 49 (1995): 456-82.

Gallagher, Susan VanZanten. "*Jane Eyre* and Christianity." *Approaches to Teaching Brontë's Jane Eyre.* Ed. Diane Long Hoeveler and Beth Lau. New York: Modern Language Association, 1993.

Gaskell, Elizabeth. *The Life of Charlotte Brontë.* 1857. Ed. and intro. Winifred Gérin. London: The Folio Society, 1971.

Gilbert, Sandra M., and Susan Gubar. *The Madwoman in the Attic: The Woman Writer and the Nineteenth-Century Literary Imagination.* 2nd ed. New Haven: Yale UP, 1979.

James, William. *Varieties of Religious Experience.* In *William James: Writings 1902-1910.* New York: Library of America, 1987.

Jay, Elisabeth. *The Religion of the Heart: Anglican Evangelicalism and the Nineteenth-Century Novel.* New York: Oxford UP, 1979.

Jay, William. *The Mutual Duties of Husbands and Wives: A Sermon, Occasioned by the Marriage of Robert Spear, Esq.* 3rd ed. London: C. Whittingham, 1801.

Larson, Janet L. "Lady-Wrestling for Victorian Soul: Discourse, Gender, and Spirituality in Women's Texts." *Religion and Literature* 23.3 (1991): 43-64.

More, Hannah. *Coelebs in Search of a Wife.* 1808. Ed. Mary Waldron. London: Thoemmes P, 1995.

Prescott, Joseph. "*Jane Eyre*: A Romantic Exemplum with a Difference." *Twelve Original Essays on Great English Novels.* Ed. Charles Shapiro. Detroit: Wayne State UP, 1960. 87-102.

Qualls, Barry V. *The Secular Pilgrims of Victorian Fiction: The Novel as Book of Life.* New York: Cambridge UP, 1982.

Reed, John Shelton. *Glorious Battle: The Cultural Politics of Victorian Anglo-Catholicism.* Nashville: Vanderbilt UP, 1996.

Rich, Adrienne. "Jane Eyre: The Temptations of a Motherless Woman." *Ms.* October 1973: 89-106. Rpt. in *The Brontë Sisters: Critical Assessments.* Vol. 3. Ed. Eleanor McNees. The Banks, England: Helm Information, 1996. 226-39.

Thormählen, Marianne. *The Brontës and Religion.* New York: Cambridge UP, 1999.

Williams, Carolyn. "Closing the Book: The Intertextual End of *Jane Eyre.*" *Victorian Connections.* Ed. Jerome J. McGann. Charlottesville: UP of Virginia, 1989.

Witt, Amanda B. "'I Read It in Your Eye': Spiritual Vision in *Jane Eyre.*" *Victorian Newsletter* (1994): 29-34.

Anne Richards (essay date 2003)

SOURCE: Richards, Anne. "The Passions of Marianne Dashwood: Christian Rhetoric in *Sense and Sensibility.*" *Persuasions: The Jane Austen Journal* 25 (2003): 141-54.

[*In the following essay, Richards stresses the central importance of Christianity in the works of Jane Austen through a close reading of* Sense and Sensibility, *noting particularly Austen's expression of Christian ideals through the words and experiences of the character Marianne Dashwood.*]

> The way Austen and her heroines seek to imitate Jesus is by learning the necessity of loving their enemies, turning their other cheek, denying themselves, fixing their faces on the heavenly Jerusalem, taking up their cross, and making the journey to the place of their metaphorical crucifixion. That place is the place of their atonement, their passion, their "death," their resurrection, and their triumph over the fallenness of "the world."
>
> —*Jane Austen and Religion,* Michael Giffin

AUSTEN AND RELIGION

Taking as its starting point the question of whether Christian ideology plays a major role in Jane Austen's novels, this essay concludes, along with Michael Giffin's *Jane Austen and Religion: Salvation and Society in Georgian England,* that Austen "conducts her critique [of Georgian society] as a devout Christian believer" (2). Critics sympathetic to this view include Gary Kelly, who writes that "Austen's novels can be read as representing the protagonist's destiny according to an Anglican view of the human condition" (166), and Marilyn Butler, who labels Austen a "conservative Christian moralist" (164).

To many readers it may seem self-evident that Austen is a Christian writer. But Giffin observes that historical research and textual criticism in the Twentieth Century illuminated the religious turn of Austen's novels only after the retreat of the academic study of English literature. Such study was, in Giffin's view, "explicitly or implicitly hostile to what one can loosely describe as the traditional western and Christian world-view" (2), and academic critics tended to accuse "those who did try to read [Austen's] novels from a philosophical or theological perspective . . . of either over-reading or misreading." His observation echoes that of Mary Augusta Austen-Leigh, Austen's great niece, who bemoaned the propensity of critics unsympathetic towards Anglicanism to misunderstand Austen's character and especially her religious sensibility. Austen-Leigh noted, for instance, that one French critic characterized Austen's temperament in a way "so mistaken as to be in some respects exactly the reverse of the truth" (93); in fact, Austen possessed a "piety which ruled her in life and supported her in death" (94). Among the many readers who missed this point was G. K. Chesterton, who believed Austen to be "supremely irreligious" (503; cited in Mudrick 150).[1]

Such a claim suggests a profound ignorance of Austen's life, at least. Austen's father, a "scholarly country vicar" (Brown 5), considered it his duty to inculcate in his children an appreciation of Anglicanism. Two of his sons became clergymen, and "[u]nder [his] guidance, Jane learnt to regard Christianity as a reasonable and practical doctrine which made sense in this world as well as offering hope for the next" (Collins xviii). Her life and thoughts were guided by the religious principles he had instilled in her, and the many prayers she composed for her family bespeak a humble devotion, e.g.,

> May we now, and on each return of night, consider how the past day has been spent by us, what have been our prevailing thoughts, words and actions during it, and how far we can acquit ourselves of evil. Have we . . . disobeyed the commandments, have we neglected any known duty, or willingly given pain to any human being? Incline our hearts to ask these questions oh! God, and save us from deceiving ourselves by pride or vanity.
>
> (*Minor Works* 453-54)

By the standards of this century, Austen's every day was overfull of religious duties and rituals, and she developed, not surprisingly, "into an assiduous reader of sermons and a sharp critic of those she heard delivered from the pulpit" (Collins 52). Valerie Grosvenor Myer, who, like other biographers, believes that Austen's Christianity was "sincere" (236; see also James Austen-Leigh, Cecil, and Collins), notes that Austen especially approved of Bishop Sherlock's sermons, which "emphasized self knowledge."[2] She considered herself profoundly indebted to her own religious upbringing (Collins 236), as indicated by a prayer she composed which implored God "above all other blessings . . . to quicken our sense of the value of that holy religion in which we have been brought up, that we may not, by our own neglect, throw away the salvation thou hast given us" (*Minor Works* 454). Like her life, her death was, for the time, an unremarkably pious one. According to Cecil, during the last stages of what probably

was Addison's disease, "she fortified her spirit with frequent prayers and regular religious reading. One or other of her two clergymen brothers, James and Henry, used to read the service with her as an aid to devotion" (196). When informed late in July 1817 that she did not have long to live, she "took the news calmly but asked if she might have the Sacrament administered to her while she was still able to realize its full significance" (198). Her sister-in-law Mary, who nursed the invalid faithfully, reported to a relative that Austen was "resigned and composed, a believing Christian" (Myer 235). Her final words, delivered to Cassandra, were "Pray for me, oh pray for me!" (Cecil 198). At Austen's request, she was buried in Winchester Cathedral. In short, it is consistent with the evidence of her life and death to assert that Austen was "a devout Anglican who [accepted] the canonical truths presented in Jewish and Christian scripture, and who [assented] to the theological truths presented in the *Book of Common Prayer*" (Giffen 162).

Many twentieth-century scholars, however, have "questioned the relevance of Austen's religion to her fictional art" (Kelly 154). For instance, in an exchange of letters in the *Times Literary Supplement* of January and February 1944, Q. D. Leavis argues that "Austen's personal beliefs could only interest the literary critic if they were manifested in the novels." In the same vein, Laurence Lerner (1967) states that "however pious Austen the person may have been, Austen the novelist did not believe in God, because 'a belief or a value only matters artistically if it is artistically present' in the writer's work" (20, cited in Kelly). As the current essay will attempt to demonstrate, Austen's confidence in the spiritual hope cherished by her parents, and her admiration for behavior reflecting Christian morality, are evident in the themes, imagery, and narrative structure of *Sense and Sensibility*.

Wayne Booth attributes to the character "Jane Austen" generosity, penetrating judgment, tenderness, impartiality, an ability to see into the heart, morality, and wisdom (265)—all qualities associated with the Christian God. Indeed, Booth considers "Jane Austen" a "perfect" character:

> When we read [*Emma*] we accept [Austen] as representing everything we admire most. She is as generous as Knightley; in fact, she is a shade more penetrating in her judgment. She is as subtle and witty as Emma would like to think herself. Without being sentimental she is in favor of tenderness. She is able to put an adequate but not excessive value on wealth and rank. She recognizes a fool when she sees one, but unlike Emma she knows that it is both immoral and foolish to be rude to fools. She is, in short, a perfect human being, within the concept of perfection established by the books she writes.
>
> (265)

Christian ideology provides a foundation on which Austen constructs this ethos and is qualified to mete punishment, to bestow reward, and to survey the world with a confident detachment unlooked for in an impoverished, dependent second daughter of a country parson. In this regard, Austen follows the tradition of Margaret Fell and may be seen as a forerunner of writers such as Charlotte and Anne Brontë, and Margaret Fuller and Louisa May Alcott.

Kelly writes that the plots of Austen's novels are "consistent with an Anglican reading of human history as a form of romance journey in which an omniscient yet benevolent deity presides over a historical plot of human error, fall, and redemption by both free will and grace, and which instructs the reader to hope for and aspire to redemption" (165). In the absence of Austen's staunch faith, there would have been no "benevolent diety" of the novels as Kelly intuits it and no "perfect" "Jane Austen" as Booth constructs her. Her spiritual confidence sets her narratives apart from those of Modern novelists such as Henry James (*The Rhetoric of Fiction* passim) and certainly helps account for her enduring popularity. In addition to being a sublime stylist, ironist, and dramatist, Austen deftly conveys the certitude "God's in His heaven: All's right with the world."

Some have ascribed to Austen's novels an overarching irony under which no ideology should be taken seriously. Prefacing *A Rhetoric of Irony* with an anecdote illustrating this misapprehension, Booth relates a discussion he has had with a student who is certain that *Pride and Prejudice* is ironic through and through. Assertions of this type "raise something of a problem," Booth explains, for they indicate "a world in which many critics insist on the value of multiple readings, on the 'open-endedness' of all ironic literature, and on the insecurity, or even relativity, of all critical views" (3). Eschewing this assumption of radical postmodern critique, Booth argues that although an author uses irony episodically within a novel, that novel may yet contain a "sincere" message that ultimately prevails over irony.

Having sketched the likelihood that Austen was a devout Anglican, this essay will examine the subtle ways in which Austen infuses *Sense and Sensibility* with Christian ideology by manipulating theme, imagery, and plot.

Theme

The main characters of *Sense and Sensibility* are believable admixtures of those traits named in the novel's title. Yet there is one place in which individuals are either "sense" or "sensibility" characters—and that is the mind of Marianne Dashwood. Marianne denies as a matter of course the sensibility, and thus the humanity, of any person who is not a convert to her Romantic

cult, who does not feel about feeling precisely as she does. The novel's title, then, depicts Marianne's *Weltanschauung*. By separating herself emotionally from the vast majority of her family and acquaintances, whom she believes cannot feel, Marianne disregards the foundational Christian commandment—love of neighbor, or charity.

For their lack of sensibility, Marianne harshly judges nearly everyone she knows. She tells her mother that she does not believe Edward Ferrars capable of emotion and states, "'It would have broke my heart to hear him read with so little sensibility. Mama, the more I know of the world, the more I am convinced that I shall never see a man whom I can really love. I require so much!'" (18). She finds fault with Edward's personal appearance insofar as she believes it reflects insensitivity: "'His eyes want all that spirit, that fire, which at once announce virtue and intelligence. And besides this; I am afraid, Mama, he has no real taste . . .'" (17). She repeats the accusation of Colonel Brandon: "'He has neither genius, taste nor spirit,'" she pronounces. "'His understanding has no brilliancy, his feelings no ardour, and his voice no expression'" (51). Mrs. Jennings, according to Marianne, "'cannot feel. Her kindness is not sympathy; her good nature is not tenderness'" (201). Marianne even suggests that her sister lacks emotional depth: "'Elinor has not my feelings,'" she tells her mother, and "'therefore she may overlook [Edward's dullness], and be happy with him'" (18). For Marianne, Marianne is the measure of all things:

> With excellent abilities and an excellent disposition, [she] was neither reasonable nor candid. She expected from other people the same opinions and feelings as her own, and she judged of their motives by the immediate effect of their actions on herself.
>
> (201-02)

On first glance, Marianne loves and respects only her mother and Willoughby, but actually, Marianne loves and respects only herself. "The resemblance between her and her mother was strikingly great" (6), and in the final analysis any compliment Marianne pays her mother's sensibility or nobility of spirit has its source in what she admires most in herself. Marianne's egocentrism is clear in her creation of the fantasy of Willoughby, ultimately an extension of her self-love. "'I could not be happy,'" says Marianne, "'With a man whose taste did not in every point coincide with my own. He must enter into all my feelings; the same books, the same music must charm us both'" (17). The two young people have a "general conformity of judgement in all that related to either" (47), but it is clear that this conformity is not authentic: Marianne demands compliance, and Willoughby is enamored enough to ensure it:

> [Marianne's] favorite authors were brought forward and dwelt upon with so rapturous a delight, that any

young man of five and twenty must have been insensible indeed, not to become an immediate convert to the excellence of such works, however disregarded before. Their taste was strikingly alike. The same books, the same passages were idolized by each—or, if any difference appeared, it lasted no longer than till the force of her arguments and the brightness of her eyes could be displayed. He acquiesced in all her decisions [and] caught all her enthusiasms.

(47)

Although Marianne has "'scarcely allowed sorrow to exist but with [herself]'" (346), she awakens morally at the end of the novel and no longer imagines herself separated from the rest of humanity by an extraordinary sensibility. Because she is a character of "sense" as well as "sensibility," and because her "'illness [makes her] think'" (345), she is capable of reform. One example may suffice to illustrate the transformation wrought in Marianne's attitude towards her own and others' sensibilities after her illness. When Marianne learns from Elinor of Willoughby's arrival at the Palmers' and of his confession, she does not seek encouragement "in the violence of her affliction" (7), nor does she consider herself only, regarding the matter. Rather, she considers first the feelings of her mother:

A thousand inquiries sprung up from her heart, but she dared not urge one. . . . As soon as they entered the house, Marianne, with a kiss of gratitude, and these two words just articulate through her tears, "Tell Mama," withdrew from her sister and walked slowly upstairs. Elinor would not attempt to disturb a solitude so reasonable as what she now sought.

(348)

Marianne tells Elinor that "'the future must be [her] proof. . . . [her] feelings shall be governed and [her] temper improved. They shall no longer worry others, not torture [herself]'" (347). Evidence that Marianne's illness and transformation are meant to be understood in terms of a rebirth in Christ appears in Austen's use of religious imagery and allusion throughout the novel, especially in narrating the heroine's involvement with Willoughby.

IMAGERY

Willoughby personifies spiritual ruination, and Austen signifies this by her use of Christian imagery in relating his story. To the extent that self-love corrupts him, Willoughby represents one of the moral alternatives facing Marianne. Because he is addicted to pleasure, he has chosen his god, and it is Mammon. His one distress is his fettered estate; he has no inkling of his spiritual bankruptcy, and he cherishes a faith that "'the death of [his] old cousin, Mrs. Smith, [is] to set [him] free'" (320). When this relation does not die, he abandons Marianne, whom he adores, for Miss Grey, whom he

despises. The fact that he has leagued himself with the devil is the basis of the imagery he uses to describe to Elinor his last meeting with Marianne:

"What a sweet figure I cut. What an evening of agony it was! Marianne, beautiful as an angel, on one side, calling me Willoughby in such a tone!—O God—holding out her hand to me, asking me for an explanation with those bewitching eyes fixed in such speaking solicitude on my face! And Sophia, jealous as the devil, on the other hand looking all that was—well, it does not signify; it is over now."

(327)

When Elinor sees Willoughby for that last time, she starts "back with a look of horror at the sight of him," obeying "the first impulse of her heart in turning instantly to quit the room" (317). Willoughby prevails on her to listen and throughout his speech utters the word *God* four times; *the devil,* twice; *soul,* three times; *heart,* six times; *guilty,* twice; *blessed,* twice; and also *diabolical, saint, heaven, faith, temptation,* and *atonement.* Like Marianne, Willoughby has been called on to make the moral choice, but he chooses darkness. Indeed, the only certain knowledge the reader gains from his confession is that he regrets he is no longer happy and that Marianne is welcome to continue her relationship with him now that he is married.

Marianne's moral journey, too, is punctuated by Christian imagery. When Marianne first meets Willoughby, she is—as the reader learns in an incidental conversation—on "High Church Down" (60). She is running to her family's cottage when she trips and sprains her ankle. "'There, exactly there,'" she tells Elinor, "'On that projecting mound—there I fell; and there I first saw Willoughby'" (344). As the reader infers from the story of the young Eliza, from the moment of meeting him, Marianne has been in danger of slipping from her adolescent self-absorption into his hedonism. Her impetuosity places her at especial risk.[3]

Marianne falls, but she is also resurrected. For Austen's active protagonists, writes Kelly, "the turning point is an act of self-abnegation or humility that could be described as Christian and that seems to occur against the run of the plot and thus to be providential, or the effect of grace" (163). After Marianne contracts an infection during the Easter season, it seems she will not live, but despite the failure of the doctor's medicines and a prolonged fever, she revives. Immediately after Willoughby's exit, Elinor returns to Marianne's room to find her sister "just awaking [from unconsciousness], refreshed by so long and sweet a sleep to the extent of [Elinor's] hopes" (333). What follows is the unveiling of a remarkable change in Marianne. Her emotions have become "too natural . . . to raise anything less tender than pity" in Elinor. Marianne has "'scarcely allowed sorrow to exist but with [herself]" (346), but her "'illness has made [her] think'" (345), and she repents of her former behavior:

> "Long before I was enough recovered to talk, I was perfectly able to reflect. I considered the past: I saw in my own behavior, since the beginning of our acquaintance with him last autumn, nothing but a series of imprudences towards myself and want of kindness to others. I saw that my own feeling had prepared my sufferings, and that my want of fortitude under them had almost led me to the grave. . . . I wonder at my recovery—wonder that the very eagerness of my desire to live, to have time for atonement to my God, and to you all, did not kill me at once."
>
> (345-46)

The language Marianne uses to describe how she envisions her new life with Elinor is, like Willoughby's speech to Elinor, noteworthy for the denseness of its Christian imagery:

> "When the weather is settled, and I have recovered my strength," she said, "we will take long walks together every day. We will walk to the farm at the edge of the [High Church] down, and see how the children go on; we will walk to Sir John's new plantation and Barton Cross, and the Abbeyland; and we will often go to the ruins of the Priory, and try to trace its foundations as far as we are told they once reached. I know we shall be happy."
>
> (343)

Marianne vows that henceforth Willoughby's memory "'shall be regulated, it shall be checked by religion, by reason, by constant employment'" (347), and that she will "'live solely for [her] family'" (347). Marianne's illness is much more than a physical episode: it is a spiritual rebirth.

PLOT

In addition to the general theme of the need to cultivate charity, and the religious imagery used in conjunction with Marianne's illness and her relationship with Willoughby, there is at least one other aspect of *Sense and Sensibility* that points to the centrality of Marianne's Christian journey. The action of the novel can be seen as conforming to one pattern; and this pattern, as having its point of reference in her "rebirth" (see Figure).

The two sets of relationships mapped in [the] Figure mirror each other. Willoughby and Lucy Steele (A) are both avaricious: Willoughby is unusually handsome, and Robert's objections aside, the Dashwood sisters must acknowledge Lucy's "considerable beauty" (120). Willoughby and Lucy are eager, affectedly open communicators: "Long before [Willoughby's first] visit concluded [with Marianne], they conversed with the familiarity of a long-established acquaintance" (47); similarly,

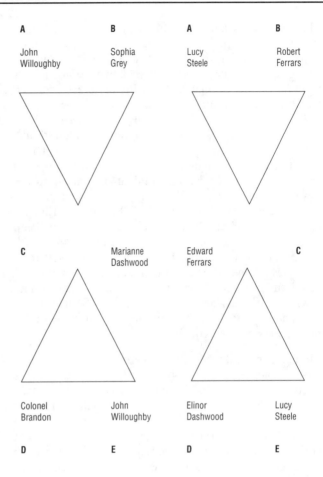

Lucy early singles Elinor out as the target of an "easy and frank communication of her sentiments" (127). Willoughby calculates that the death of his aunt, and later Miss Grey, will secure his fortune and freedom; and Lucy, that the death of Mrs. Ferrars, and then the death of the incumbent at Norland, will secure hers. Finally, Lucy and Willoughby are both associated with frivolity during the Christmas holidays. Willoughby dances from eight to four on the previous Christmas, and Lucy and her sister are "prevailed on to stay nearly two months at the Park, and assist in the due celebration of that festival which requires a more than ordinary share of private balls and large dinners to proclaim its importance" (152).

On first glance, Miss Grey and Robert (B) may seem to have little in common, but in fact they share their most salient characteristic: nondescription, Miss Grey is "a very fashionable-looking young woman" (176) whom even Mrs. Jennings has nothing to say about. "'I never heard any harm of her,'" that good woman tells Elinor, "'Indeed, I hardly ever heard her mentioned'" (194). Robert, too, is a person of fashion and inconsequence. When the Dashwood sisters are introduced to him, his broad stare "imprinted on Elinor the remembrance of a person of strong, natural, sterling insignificance, though adorned in the first style of fashion" (220, 221).[4]

The similarities between Colonel Brandon and Elinor (D) are clear. Neither character ever entertains high hopes of marrying the beloved. Even before Edward's engagement to Lucy is generally known, Elinor is "far from depending on that result of his preference for her, which her mother and sister still considered as certain" (22); and even after Willoughby has married, Mrs. Dashwood tells Elinor that Colonel Brandon thinks "'Marianne's affection too deeply rooted for any change in it under a great length of time, and even supposed her heart again free, is too diffident of himself to believe, that which such a difference of age, and disposition, he could ever attach her'" (338). Despite Elinor's and Edward's realistic appraisals, Elinor cannot keep herself from being secretly and painfully in love with Edward, nor can Colonel Brandon prevent himself from loving Marianne. Most important, both Elinor and Colonel Brandon personify charity, scrupulously performing "'with gentleness and forebearance'" the virtues that Marianne sets for herself upon reformation: "'the civilities, the lesser duties of life'" (347).

Marianne and Edward (C) are the only positive characters who are central to the lives of the others and consequently occupy the focal points of the diagrams. Marianne has been mistakenly attached to Willoughby, for she believes he is a much better man than he is; and Edward has been mistakenly attached, as well—not simply because he has made a promise he must keep but because, like Marianne, he has made an egregious error in judging character:

> Though his eyes had long been opened, even before his acquaintance with Elinor began, to [Lucy's] ignorance and a want of liberality in some of her opinions, they had been equally imputed to him by her want of education; and till her last letter reached him he had always believed her to be a well-disposed, good-hearted girl, and thoroughly attached to himself. Nothing but such a persuasion could have prevented his putting an end to [the] engagement.
>
> (336, 337)

As the plot spins out, the romantic statuses of Edward and Marianne both remain secret. Edward is engaged to Lucy although no one realizes this initially, and Marianne is not engaged to Willoughby although no one realizes this initially, either. The "engagements" end similarly: Edward and Marianne both receive callous letters from the persons they once were attached to, informing them that the attachments are either obsolete or fictitious. When Willoughby writes to Marianne, he returns her letters to him and a lock of her hair; when Lucy writes to Edward, she requests that he burn her letters to him, "'but the ring, with my hair, you are very welcome to keep'" (365).

Furthermore, Marianne is abandoned for Miss Grey, and Edward is abandoned for Robert (A-B). The choices are not remarkable: Willoughby has chosen Miss Grey for her money, and Lucy has chosen Robert for his. Edward's financial position is as attractive to Lucy as Marianne's is to Willoughby, and both replacements are inferior (B-C). When Lucy abandons Edward, his conscience is free to choose Elinor; when Willoughby abandons Marianne, her heart is free to choose Colonel Brandon (C-D).

Willoughby and Colonel Brandon, like Lucy and Elinor, are foils (D-E). Colonel Brandon and Willoughby are jealous of each other, as are Elinor and Lucy. Colonel Brandon suffers because he knows the truth about Willoughby; and Elinor, because she knows the truth about Lucy. Colonel Brandon reveals the history of the younger Eliza to Elinor, summarizing: "'[Willoughby's] character is now before you—expensive, dissipated and worse than both. Knowing all this, as I have known it many weeks, guess what I must have felt on seeing your sister as fond of him as ever'" (120). Elinor does not believe that Edward can ever be happy with Lucy. "Could he, were his affection for herself out of the question, with his integrity, delicacy, and well-informed mind, be satisfied with a wife like her—illiterate, artful, and selfish?" and she weeps "for him more than for herself" (140).

Finally, Willoughby confesses that he had no real love for Marianne when he engaged her regard, and evidently Lucy had no more for Edward when she engaged his honor (C-E).

Austen's structuring of the main action in this manner is not an artifice but points to the centrality of the theme of Marianne's rebirth as Christian penitent. Marianne's conflict with Willoughby is a private battle symbolizing a universal one. The conflict between Edward and Lucy, however, is not internal and has no universal implications. Edward's release from Lucy's power is the result of circumstance alone. And Austen is remarkably clear about this, giving Edward a mock salvation at the hands of his mother, and thereby once again referring the reader to the novel's true salvation story—Marianne's.

> After a proper resistance on the part of Mrs. Ferrars, . . . Edward was admitted to her presence, and pronounced again to be her son. . . .
>
> . . . For many years of her life she had two sons, but the crime and annihilation of Edward, a few weeks ago, had robbed her of one; the similar annihilation of Robert had left her for a fortnight without any; and now, by the resuscitation of Edward, she had one again. . . .
>
> In spite of being allowed once more to live, however, he did not feel the continuance of his existence secure, till he revealed his present engagement; for the publication of that circumstance, he feared might give a sudden turn to his constitution, and carry him off as rapidly as before.
>
> (373)

Edward has never been in danger of alienating a moral God; he has been in danger only of offending his mother. That his mother resurrects him is another circumstance, another exteriority, for which Edward bears no responsibility and harbors little concern. When told that he should write to her and beg her forgiveness, he refuses, saying, "'I am grown neither humble nor penitent by what has passed'" (372). But Marianne's rebirth is deeply heartfelt: she is painfully eager "'to have time for atonement to [her] God'" (346). "'My spirit is humbled,'" she asserts, "'my heart amended'" (347).

The actions of Elinor, Robert, and Lucy find their common reference in Edward, just as the actions of Willoughby, Miss Grey, and Colonel Brandon find theirs in Marianne. But because of Edward's moral maturity, the novel's action strains for the illumination of that struggle taking place in Marianne's young and passionate heart. *Sense and Sensibility* is a novel about Marianne Dashwood—not for the reasons Romantically inclined readers might like to give, but because Marianne's *Christian* passion is the focus of the dramatic action of the novel.

* * *

This essay has supported Giffen's claim that Austen "is a Christian humanist, not a secular humanist—she is an Anglican author who writes Christian stories" (27). And, like Giffen, I have suggested that if Austen's "readers, her biographers, and her literary critics—fail to grasp the centrality of that fact and do not rise to the challenge that it presents to reading and biography and criticism, then we will misunderstand her life and misread her novels at their most profound level of interpretation." A close reading of *Sense and Sensibility* indicates that critical interest in Austen's religious ideology is appropriate, for Marianne's "Christian romance" provides the novel its focus. Marianne is the one character whose worldview embraces the false dilemma of the novel's title, the one character who walks safely through a forest of religious imagery, and the one character who develops internally and around whose pilgrimage Austen structures her story.

Notes

1. Chesterton expounded that Austen's "very virtues glitter with the cold sunlight of the great secular epoch between medieval and modern mysticism." Perhaps his conversion to Roman Catholicism left him unsympathetic towards certain Humanist and Enlightenment elements of the Anglican worldview.

2. Jane's familiarity with the ecclesiastical profession extended far beyond her father and the Bishop. In *Jane Austen: The Parson's Daughter* (1998), Irene Collins suggests the substantial role that clergymen played in the author's experience.

> Her maternal grandfather and her great uncle had been clergymen; so were her godfather, one of her uncles, two of her brothers and four of her cousins. Her sister became engaged to a clergyman and of the young men who are known or believed to have been Jane's suitors three were clergy. She was acquainted with a great many other clergymen, for they were thick on the ground in rural areas, where the rest of the population was small. . . . Jane's published correspondence alone mentions over ninety clergymen with whom she was acquainted.
>
> (xvi)

Austen was as knowledgeable about the clerical life as an unmarried woman of her time was likely to be.

3. Note that the syllables of her name, spoken backwards, read "would dash and marry."

4. The reader, incidentally, first meets Robert in Mr. Gray's shop.

Works Cited

Austen, Jane. *The Novels of Jane Austen.* Ed. R. W. Chapman. 3rd ed. Oxford: OUP, 1986.

Austen-Leigh, James Edward. *A Memoir of Jane Austen.* London: Oxford UP, 1926.

Austen-Leigh, Mary Augusta. *Personal Aspects of Jane Austen.* New York: E. P. Dutton and Company, 1920.

Booth, Wayne C. *A Rhetoric of Irony.* Chicago: UCP, 1974.

———. *The Rhetoric of Fiction.* 2nd ed. Chicago: UCP, 1983.

Brown, Ivor. *Jane Austen and Her World.* London: Henry Z. Walck, Inc., 1967.

Butler, Marilyn. *Jane Austen and the War of Ideas.* Oxford: Clarendon P, 1975.

Cecil, David. *A Portrait of Jane Austen.* Middlesex, England: Penguin Books, 1983.

Chesterton, G. K. "The Evolution of Emma." *Living Age.* 25 August 1917.

Collins, Irene. *Jane Austen: The Parson's Daughter.* London: Hambledon P, 1998.

Giffen, Michael. *Jane Austen and Religion: Salvation and Society in Georgian England.* Houndmills, Hampshire: Palgrave Macmillan, 2002.

Kelly, Gary. "Religion and Politics." In Copeland, Edward, and Juliet McMaster (eds.). *The Cambridge Companion to Jane Austen.* Cambridge: CUP, 1997. 149-69.

Lerner, Laurence. *The Truthtellers: Jane Austen; George Elliot; D. H. Lawrence.* London: Chatto and Windus, 1967.

Mudrick, Marvin. *Jane Austen: Irony as Defense and Discovery.* Princeton: PUP, 1952.

Myer, Valerie Grosvenor. *Jane Austen: Obstinate Heart.* New York: Arcade Publishing, 1997.

SOCIAL AND POLITICAL DISCOURSE

Charles Swann (essay date autumn 1995)

SOURCE: Swann, Charles. "Rutherford versus Pater: Christianity, Politics and History." *Essays in Poetics* 20 (autumn 1995): 152-69.

[*In the following essay, Swann interprets a section of Mark Rutherford's* Catherine Furze *as a negative commentary on the ideas of Walter Pater, particularly upon Pater's presentation of Christianity in* Marius the Epicurean.]

> In the history of the church, as throughout the moral history of mankind, there are two distinct ideals, . . . two conceptions, under one or the other of which we may represent to ourselves men's efforts towards a better life . . . The ideal of asceticism represents moral effort as essentially a sacrifice, the sacrifice of one part of human nature to another, that it may live the more completely in what survives of it; while the ideal of culture represents it as a harmonious development of all the parts of human nature, in just proportion to each other. It was to the latter order of ideas that the church, and especially the church of Rome in the age of the Antonines, freely lent herself . . . Tact, good sense, ever the note of a true orthodoxy, the merciful compromises of the church, indicative of her imperial vocation in regard to all the varieties of human kind, with a universality of which the old Roman pastorship she was superseding is but a prototype, was already become conspicuous . . .
>
> Against that divine urbanity and moderation . . . was a fanatical revolt—sour, falsely anti-mundane, ever with an air of ascetic affectation.
>
> There are two great ethical parties in the world and, in the main, but two. One of them asserts the claims of the senses. Its doctrine is seductive because it is so right. It is necessary that we should in a measure believe it, in order that life may be sweet. But nature has heavily weighted the scale in its favour; its acceptance requires no effort. It is easily perverted and becomes a snare. In our day nearly all genius has gone over to it, and preaching it is rather superfluous. The other party affirms what has been the soul of all religions worth having, that it is by repression and self-negation that men and States live.[1]

In the middle of Mark Rutherford's *Catharine Furze* (1893), there is an interpolated story about early Christianity, entitled "Did He Believe?" It has, of course, its function in the novel as a whole, but I want to argue that it is also to be read specifically as an attack on *Marius the Epicurean*'s presentation of Christianity as eclectic evolution without doctrinal content and more generally as a challenge to Pater's politics of history and his ideas of culture—ideas that, of course, have been traced back especially to Newman and Arnold. Rutherford's dislike of Arnold's "culture" can be easily documented—and my epigraphs indicate, I hope, something of the radical ideological difference between those writers of the '80s and the '90s, Rutherford and Pater.

Rutherford, writing under his own name of William Hale White in the preface to the second edition of his translation of Spinoza's *Ethic* had made clear his disapproval of at least one strand of Pater's thought as well as a puritan preference for plain style:

> It [the doctrine of the One] presents itself once more, now altogether beyond Christian influence, in the hard and ambitious intellectualism of Spinoza; a doctrine of pure repellent substance—substance 'in vacuo,' to be lost in which, however, would be the proper consummation of the transitory individual life. Spinoza's own absolutely colour-less existence was a practical comment on it.
>
> —*Plato and Platonism,* by Walter Pater, p. 33

This characterization of Spinoza seems strange, even after a superficial study of these propositions. The word "colour-less," in one sense, may certainly be applied to him; for sunlight is colourless, for the reason that it includes *all* the rays of the spectrum. The coloured light is that of the priest, the prophet, or the Church. "Repellent" and "in vacuo" are instructive examples of the seductive influence of phrases on an artist in style, and of the danger to which he is continually exposed of lapsing thereby into unintelligibility.[2]

Such dates as we have suggest that Pater might well have been on Rutherford's/White's mind when writing *Catharine Furze* as he seems to have been involved in writing that at much the same time as he was working on the Spinoza preface. The preface seems to have been written roughly between November 1892 and October 1893. *Catharine Furze* was published in December 1893 and *Plato and Platonism* had been published in February of the same year.[3]

If I am right about the question of how to read "Did He Believe?", it would not, I think, be the first time that, Rutherford had, so to speak, argued with another author by presenting a fiction as criticism—and, in both cases, it is the question of the nature of historical change that is central. For example, it is virtually impossible not to read *The Revolution in Tanner's Lane* as, in part, a criticism of the political history in *Felix Holt*. The central character in both novels is a secularized radical who has connections with radical Dissent. Both books include a Dissenting minister (Lyon and Bradshaw) who is at least sympathetic to radical politics, and both have a French connection (Esther and her mother in *Felix Holt,* the Caillauds in *The Revolution*). But the parallels (and the list could be extended) are there to point to contrasts.[4] For instance, the important thing about Esther in terms both of plot and theme is that she is legitimate: one important thing in terms of the theme of (French and other) revolutions about Pauline Caillaud is that she is a bastard. Rutherford, with his background of radical Dissent, remains fascinated with the idea of secularizing the Pauline conversion experience, with the idea of revolutionary change, whether in an individual or a society. George Eliot, on the other hand, privileges legitimacy, inheritance and continuity. She thinks of radical change as dangerous. "The morally chosen future" must unite with the past as Esther Lyon's example shows:

> It seemed to her that she stood at the first and last parting of the ways . . . It is only in that freshness of our time that the choice is possible which gives unity to life, and makes the memory a temple where all relics and all votive offerings, all worship and all grateful joy, are an *unbroken history* sanctified by one religion.
>
> (Ch. XLIV, my emphasis)

This unity is, however, only available to the reasonably pure in heart. This seems a decidedly conservative religion—especially as there is little or no room in it for a middle-aged Saul to have any conversion experience. There is very little room for the repentant sinner in Eliot's moral scheme—continuity is (nearly) all.

Renan's *Life of Jesus,* Eliot claimed, "has so much *artistic* merit that it will do a great deal towards the culture of ordinary minds by giving them a *sense of unity* between that far off past and our present". (My emphasis) It looks as though this sense of unity is one of the key functions of art—and one which has a crucial political dimension. That identity must be preserved at all costs for it may well help to avoid any danger of a revolutionary break appearing between past and present—or present and future: "such books as Renan's have their value in helping the popular imagination to feel that the sacred past is of one woof with that human present which ought to be sacred too."[5]

That image from weaving—that spatialization of history—is one that Pater also uses/misuses. When describing the family burial-place of the Cecilii, Pater comments on the Christian burial inscriptions: "marble taken, in some cases, from older pagan tombs,—the inscription sometimes a *palimpsest,* the new epitaph being woven into the faded letters of an earlier one." (*ME,* II, 99) A moment's visualization suggests that 'superimposed' is the more likely verb. But Pater insists that the past is not rubbed out, not imposed on, not replaced, but is woven into the present. The image recurs in Pater's discussion of Plato's originality:

> It is hardly an exaggeration to say that in Plato, in spite of his wonderful savour of freshness, there is nothing absolutely new: or rather, as in many other very original products of human genius, the seemingly new is old also, a palimpsest, a tapestry of which the actual threads have served before, or like the animal frame itself, every particle of which has already lived and died many times over.

Revolution is a concept that is virtually excluded from Pater's view of history. When it does briefly appear, it is immediately made safe: "Revolution is often impious. . . . But in this nature revolutionism is softened, harmonized, subdued as by distance. It is the revolutionism of one who has slept a hundred years." A majority of such characters would, Pater assures us, be the regeneration of the world. It is a trifle hard to see where the potential for revolutionary—or any other—change lies in a character that is "like the reminiscence of a forgotten culture," or "like a relic from the classical age," especially as it has something of the "eternal outline of the antique."[6]

Those last quotations come, of course, from that very early essay "Diaphaneite," but the more mature *Marius* equally insists on evolution rather than revolution, insists too on Christianity as a religion that offers no threat to society as constituted, that is, above all, conserving:

> All around, in those *well-ordered* precincts, were the quiet signs of *wealth,* and of a *noble* taste—a taste, indeed, chiefly evidenced in the *selection and juxtaposition* of the material it had to deal with, *consisting almost exclusively of the remains of older art,* here arranged and harmonised, with effects, both as regards colour and form, as to seem really *derivative* from some finer intelligence in these matters than lay within the resources of the ancient world. It was the old way of true *Renaissance*—being indeed the way of nature with her roses, the divine way with the body of man, perhaps with his soul—conceiving the new organism by *no sudden and abrupt creation,* but rather by the action of a new principle upon elements, all of which had in truth already lived and died many times.
>
> (*ME,* II, 96-6. With the exception of *Renaissance,* my emphases)

This is, of course, a kind of aestheticism—and I cannot help but regret that Pater's aestheticism is occasionally vulgarly precious—"'the beauty of holiness', nay! the elegance of sanctity" *ME,* II, 123)—and sometimes seemingly tactless. In a letter to a high church Anglican vicar he wrote: "Religion, I sometimes think, is the only way in which poetry can really reach the hard-worked poor; and how largely the movement in which your Church takes part has developed the capacities of our national religion towards that effect."[7] As the letter was read out at a meeting for the parish building fund, the vicar cannot have minded being told that the function of his religion was to introduce the workers to culture—not to save their souls. But then the presentation of Christ in *Marius* is certainly not that of a saviour or moral revolutionary. He is (in one of the very few references to him) merely "a figure which seemed to have absorbed, like some rich tincture in his garment, all that was deep-felt and impassioned in the experiences of the past." (*ME,* II, 134) Christ here seems little more than a selective sponge soaking up the best in history—and Marius, whether or not he is intended as an imitation of Christ, is at most a piece of blotting-paper. He must be the most passive hero in English literature.

The passivity extends from the person to the faith. Pater seems to see it as matter for celebration that the age of conversion is past—which is surely bad history:

> Altogether, in the reign of Antoninus Pius, the time was gone by when men became Christians under some sudden and over-powering impression, and with all the disturbing results of such a crisis. At this period the larger number, perhaps, had been born Christians, had been ever with peaceful hearts in their "Father's house." That earlier belief in the speedy coming of judgement and of the end of the world, with the consequences it so naturally involved in the temper of men's minds, was dying out. Every day the contrast between the church and the world was becoming less pronounced.
>
> (*ME,* II, 118-9)

It is left unclear whether the church is reconciled to the world or vice versa—but the implication seems to be that the church is, thankfully, reconciling itself to the world. Indeed, manners seems to be what Pater particularly privileges—think of his fondness for the term "tact." But think especially of Marius's final departure from Rome. He plans to see the emperor once more "with an appeal for common-sense, for reason and justice." (*ME,* II, 201) Owing to the fact that Marcus Aurelius is entertaining orphan children, and because Marius is too good-mannered to interrupt the Emperor's (and the children's) pleasure, because too he doesn't want to wait around, Marius doesn't make "the chivalrous effort at enlightenment," which, we are told, might have involved "some possible touch of heroism . . . that might have really cost him something."(*ME,* II, 203, 200) It is clear that Pater means no criticism of his hero—he takes only too literally Winchester's motto: "Manners Makyth Man."

Pater offers Christianity as evolutionary, synthetic, syncretic—a religion for ladies and gentlemen. Think for example, of Cecilia who is repeatedly described as wealthy and Cornelius who carries "about with him, in that privileged world of comely usage to which he belonged, the atmosphere of some still more jealously exclusive circle". (*ME,* I, 169) The church of Rome "at that critical period in the development of Christianity . . . was for reason, for common sense, for fairness to human nature, and generally, for what may be called

the naturalness of Christianity."*ME,* II, 122). Christ is a very safe and unthreatening figure: "serene, blithe and debonair, beyond the gentlest shepherd of Greek mythology," notable for his "divine moderation."(*ME,* II, 114, 124) His incarnation is described in terms more appropriate to the Queen dropping in on her tenants: "some immeasurable condescension manifest in a certain historic fact."(*ME,* II, 110-1) Radical Christianity is—damning word—"provincial":

> It was only among the ignorant, indeed, only in the "villages," that Christianity, even in conscious triumph over paganism, was really betrayed into iconoclasm . . . The [city] faithful were bent less on the destruction of the old pagan temples than on their conversion to a newer and higher use; and, with much beautiful furniture ready to hand, they became Christian sanctuaries.
>
> (*ME,* II, 124)

The wise way, for Pater, is then not exclusion or choice but incorporation: "'You fail to recognize your own good intentions,'" the church "seems to say, to pagan virtue, pagan kindness. She identified herself with those intentions and advanced them with an unparalleled freedom and largeness." (*ME,* II, 113) The church had "adopted many of the graces of pagan feeling and pagan custom." (*ME,* II, 125) The point of privileging the pagan thus is to play down the Jewish element in Christianity. Indeed, Judaism is reduced to "an obscure synagogue." (*ME,* II, 125)

I have suggested that Marius is not the most active hero in fiction—and his death-bed "conversion" is of a piece with his life. As Carolyn Williams says, Marius "is *made* a Christian, not exactly against his will, but crucially without his will having been consulted."[8] The comment is an accurate gloss on the conclusion:

> In the moments of his extreme helplessness their mystic bread had been placed, had descended like a snowflake from the sky, between his lips . . . It was the same people who, in the gray, austere evening of that day, took up his remains, and buried him secretly, with their accustomed prayers; but with joy also, holding his death, according to their generous view in this matter, to have been of the nature of a martyrdom; and martyrdom, as the church had always said, a kind of sacrament with plenary grace.
>
> (*ME,* II, 224)

It is against that conclusion that the ending of "Did He Believe?" seems very clearly to have been written. The story concerns a sculptor, Charmides, born in Greece, but living in Rome in about 300 A.D. He encounters Christianity through a Greek slave, Demariste (Demos/ Aristos?), with whom he falls in love. This love leads him to take an interest in Christianity and to something like belief, and eventually to dying for that something. Despite crying when arrested "For Christ and His

Cross!" his faith is ambiguous—or rather it is mediated through his love for Demariste, while her faith is absolute and certain:

> "Look, look, my beloved, there, there!" trying to lift her mangled arm. "Christ the Lord! One moment more and we are with Him!"
>
> Charmides could just raise his head, and saw nothing but Demariste. He was able to turn himself towards her and move her hand to his lips, the second, only the second and the last kiss.
>
> So they died. Charmides was never considered a martyr by the Church. The circumstances were doubtful, and it was not altogether clear that he deserved the celestial crown.[9]

This patently reads as a rebuke to Peter for his low standards of martyrdom.

There is, however, much more in the tale which bears on Peter's fiction. The date of the story and Demariste's conversion rebuts his point about conversion to the church—and the choice of a slave carries too a rebuke. And Rutherford stresses how crucial the Jewish element is to Christianity—which also reads as a criticism of Pater (though here, I think, Rutherford has in mind also Ist Corinthians, Ch. 1, vv.22 and 23: "The Greeks seek after wisdom: But we preach Christ crucified, unto the Jews a stumbling block, and unto the Greeks foolishness"). Charmides is initially prejudiced against Christianity because of its Jewishness:

> The Jews were especially hateful to him and to all cultured people in Rome. They were typical of all the qualities which culture abhorred. No Jew had ever produced anything lovely in any department whatever—no picture, statue, melody, nor poem. Their literature was also barbaric: there was no consecutiveness in it, no reasoning, no recognition in fact of the reason . . . What made the Jews especially contemptible to culture was that they were retrograde . . . There is only one path, so culture affirmed, . . . the path of rational logical progress . . . If our present state is imperfect, it is because we do not know enough . . . These Jews actually believed in miracles; . . . and thought they could regenerate the world by hocus-pocus.
>
> (*CF,* I, 152-153, 154)

I suspect that Rutherford here hopes to hit two birds with one stone—Pater and the Arnold of, particularly, *St. Paul and Protestantism*—given that emphasis on culture's abhorrence of Jewish ideas and their "obscure *disconnected* prophecies." (*CF,* I, 153. My emphasis) Culture may have no place for the Jew or the radical Christian but, as we shall see, such a Christian may interrogate culture's claims to moral, intellectual or even political authority.

Where Pater stresses identity, Rutherford emphasizes difference—the radical difference between the Roman/Greek traditional world-view and that of Judaism and Christianity. From the view-point of the classical world, Rutherford argues, Christianity is genuinely difficult to understand. Charmides, when he reads the Epistle to the Romans, was

> somewhat astonished to find that it was written by a man of learning, who was evidently familiar with classic authors, but surely never was scholarship pressed into such a service! The confusion of metaphor, the suddenness of transition, the illogical muddles were bad enough, but the chief obstacle to comprehension was that the author's whole scope and purpose, the whole circle of his ideas, were outside Charmides altogether.
>
> (*CF,* I, 156)

When Charmides returns the Epistle to Demariste, he questions her:

> "Who is this Christ whom you worship?"
>
> "The Son of God, He who was crucified; the man Jesus; He who took upon Himself flesh to redeem us from our sins; in whom by faith we are justified and have eternal life."
>
> It was all pure Hebrew to him, save the phrase 'Son of God,' which sounded intelligible.
>
> (*CF,* I, 157)

The mild joke makes a serious point: the Christian faith is difficult for the Greek to grasp both intellectually and emotionally. Acceptance of Christianity may, according to Demariste, have to involve a repudiation or, at the mildest, a revaluation of the claims of the (pagan) past and of the claims of culture—another anti-Pater point. As Demariste puts it:

> "I saw that all art, all learning, everything which men value, were as straw compared with God's commands, and that it would be well to destroy all our temples, and statues, and all that we have which is beautiful, if we could thereby establish the kingdom of Good within us, and so become heirs of the life everlasting."
>
> (*CF,* I, 159)

If Christianity is, for Pater, part of an evolutionary history, for Rutherford it involves a revolutionary rupture with the past. The Roman world, as Charmides reads Rome's representative, Lucretius, offers "order and sequence." Charmides "knew where he was; he was at home." And he asks "Was all this nought, were the accumulated labour and thought of centuries to be set aside and trampled on by the crude, frantic inspiration of clowns?" (*CF,* I, 161) The answer is positive. On reading the gospel according to Matthew—a new kind of history—Charmides "was amazed at the *new turn* which was given to life, at the reasons assigned for the curses which were dealt to these Jewish doctors . . . Charmides pondered and pondered, and saw that this Jew had given *a new centre, a new pivot* to society."

(*CF,* I, 162. My emphases) Christianity has supplanted "order and sequence" by a revolutionary break with the past, a "complete rupture" with traditional moral and philosophic thought. If Charmides "could have connected Christianity with his own philosophy; if it had been the outcome, the fulfilment of Plato, his duty would have been so much simpler. "(*CF,* I, 164) Where Charmides cannot go along with the Christians is not so much their belief in a revolutionary transformation in and of history, but in the (related?) belief that this transformation/transfiguration may point to the end of history: the Christians' "fantastic delusions, their expectation that any day the sky might open and their Saviour appear in the body, were impossible to him." (*CF,* I, 163) But he cannot avoid the reflection that "the point was not whether the Christians were absurd, nor was it even the point whether Christianity was not partly absurd." The real point was "whether there was not more certainty in it than was to be found in anything at that time current in the world." And Christianity also provides a new category for thought, emotion and morals, a "new spring for action in the Pauline mystery of justification by faith". (*CF,* I, 163)

But, despite Charmides' desire to take part in making a (moral) history politically, with others, he remains the Greek rationalist: "If he were to enrol himself as a convert his conversion would be due . . . to a theory, to a calculation" and not to "an irresistible impulse." (*CF,* I, 165) Or so he thinks—but, as the narrative tells us, he has been if not converted at least moved towards Christianity not by reasoned argument but by a kind of history—the biography of Christ—and by his love for Demariste. Not entirely unlike Marius, Charmides wants "to have done with isolation, aloofness, speculation." (*CF,* I, 164) However, Charmides is coming (if unconsciously) to a kind of humanistic religion through the nature of his love for Demariste—though an authorial voice is needed to place that religious humanism historically—religious not only because he sees the God in Demariste but also because that love, it is claimed, transforms and transcends history:

> Charmides had fallen in love with this slave, but it was love so different from any love which he had felt before for a woman, that it ought to have had some other name. It was a love of the soul, of that which was immortal, of God in her; it was a love, too, of no mere temporary phenomenon, but of reality outlasting death into eternity . . . It was the new love with which men were henceforth to love women—the love of Dante for Beatrice.
>
> (*CF,* I, 165-6)

At the moment of death, Demariste sees Christ, while—the suggestion is the humanist one—Charmides sees the Christ in Demariste.

And here it looks at first as though there is a parallel between Pater and Rutherford. Pater too looks forward to the Middle Ages. Marius saw

in all its primitive freshness and amid the lively facts of its [Christianity's] coming into the world, as a reality of experience, that regenerate type of humanity, which, centuries later, Giotto and his successors, down to the best and purest days of the young Raphael . . . were to conceive of an artistic ideal.

> (*ME,* II, 109-10)

Pater too sees in Christianity as offering a new kind of relation between the sexes. Marius "felt . . . the unique power of Christianity . . . Chastity, . . . the chastity of men and women . . . is the most beautiful thing in the world and the truest conservation of that creative energy by which men and women were first brought into it." (*ME,* II, 110) He too connects Christianity and art:

> For what Christianity did many centuries afterwards in the way of informing an art, a poetry, of graver and higher beauty, we may think, than that of Greek art and poetry at their best, was in truth conformable to the original tendency of its genius . . . Saint Francis, with his following in the sphere of poetry and of the arts—the voice of Dante, the hand of Giotto—. . . did but re-establish a continuity, only superseded in part by those troublous intervening centuries . . . with the gracious spirit of the primitive church.
>
> (*ME,* II, 117-118)

But Pater, on the one hand, as we have seen offers preservation of previous art as one reason for celebrating Christianity, and, on the other, values it (as in the quotation above) principally because it makes for a better art, not a better ethics. (Note the valuation of St. Francis). Pater seems to value religion as a cause of beauty: Rutherford offers the "love of beauty" as an index of morality. Importantly the following quotation comes from within the story—it is part of the meaning of "Did He Believe?" I must confess I would love to know how Pater or the Wilde of *The Picture of Dorian Gray,* would have responded to it:

> The love of the beautiful itself is moral—that is to say, what we love in it is virtue. A perfect form or a delicate colour are the expression of something which is destroyed in us by subjugation to the baser desires or meanness, and he who has been unjust to man or woman misses the true interpretation of a cloud or falling wave.
>
> (*CF,* I, 152)

Marius may be a writer, but he hardly seems to be a creative artist. Charmides crucially is a sculptor—even though (shades of the 1890s) he too often is offering decadent art to a decadent audience:

> it was sad to think that the Hermes on which he had spent himself . . . should become a mere decoration to a Roman nobleman's villa, valued only because it cost so much . . .
>
> (*CF,* I, 149)

But he is capable of better things:

> There stood the statue [of Pallas Athene], severe, grand
> . . . , and if there was one thing in the world clear to
> him, it was that what he saw was no inanimate mineral
> mass, but something more. It was no mere mineral
> mass with an outline added. Part of the mind of the
> world was in it, actually in it, . . . and that what he
> had done was simply to realize a Divine idea which
> was immortal, no matter what might become of his em-
> bodiment.

(CF, I 149-50)

And it is that intuition which makes him open to what
Rutherford sees Christianity as standing for—
Charmides' willingness to shift from aesthetic production (realizing a "Divine idea") to faith and religion—
equally attempting to realize a Divine idea—but this
time in the realms of love, ethics and politics.

Against Pater's evolutionary conservatism, Rutherford
offers Christianity (whether or not we are or can be
believers) as historically crucial, transforming history
from sequence into something marked by discontinuities and ruptures, transforming the relations between
man and man—egalitarianism against Pater's preference for hierarchy—and, as we have seen, transforming
too the relations between (free) man and (slave) woman.
Rutherford's Christianity, unlike Pater's, is in the best
sense of the term, a slave religion—a religion from and
for the powerless, whether the relatively powerless is
the marginalized artist reduced to the equivalent of an
interior decorator, or the totally disempowered, the slave
woman—who may still represent and embody (Demos/
Aristos) the people's best (the people are best?): Demariste.

Rutherford may have had his disagreements with
George Eliot: he certainly has his quarrels with Pater—
and I suspect that he would have agreed (as should we
all!) with Eliot's judgement on Pater. She is speaking of
The Renaissance but the point can be generalized. She
found that book "quite poisonous in its false principles
of criticism and false conceptions of life."[10] Rutherford
has provided a narrative which questions and repudiates
Pater's ideology of conservative evolution and accommodation.

Notes

1. Walter Pater, *Marius the Epicurean: His Sensations and Ideas,* (London: Macmillan and Co.,
   1903), Vol. II, pp. 120-1. This is the text of the
   heavily revised third edition. I have, of course,
   checked the quotations from that edition against
   the first edition (1885) but have used this text as it
   is the most widely available. All subsequent page
   references are placed parenthetically in the text.

   Mark Rutherford, "A Visit to Carlyle in 1868," in
   Pages from a Journal, (London: T. Fisher Unwin,
   1900), pp. 8-9.

2. Benedict de Spinoza, *Ethic,* translated by W. Hale
   White; translation revised by Amelia Hutchinson
   Stirling, with an introduction by W. Hale White,
   (London: T. Fisher Unwin, 1894), p. xciii.

3. One cannot be sure how long Rutherford sat on
   the manuscripts of the novels. But what evidence
   we have suggests that there is no great gap between completion and publication.

4. See my "Evolution and Revolution: Politics and
   Form in *Felix Holt* and *The Revolution in Tanner's Lane* in *Literature, Society and the Sociology of Literature,* ed. Francis Barker *et al.,*
   (University of Essex, 1977), pp. 75-92.

5. G. S. Haight, (ed.), *The Letters of George Eliot.,*
   (New Haven and London: Yale University Press,
   1954-1966), Vol. iV, p. 95.

6. Walter Pater, *Plato and Platonism,* (London: Macmillan, 1909), p. 8. and *Miscellaneous Studies,*
   (London: Macmillan, 1917), p. 252.

7. L. Evans (ed.), *The Letters of Walter Pater,*
   (Oxford: Oxford University Press, 1970), p. 244.

8. Carolyn Williams, *Transfigured World: Walter Pater's Aesthetic Historicism,* (Ithaca and London:
   Cornell University Press, 1898), p. 180.

9. Mark Rutherford, *Catharine Furze,* 2 Vols.,
   (London: T. Fisher Unwin, 1893), Vol. I, pp. 169-
   70. All subsequent page references are placed parenthetically in the text. My hypothesis that Demariste may be meant to suggest Demos/Aristos is
   one I feel fairly confident about—but Charmides
   is a choice of name that is genuinely puzzling.
   The best known Charmides is surely Plato's in his
   dialogue of that name—and it is not the least
   homo-erotic of the Socratic dialogues, clearly giving the Victorian translator, Jowett, some problems. Hale White owned a copy of this. Things
   don't get easier if we turn to another well-
   known 'Charmides' (1881)—Oscar Wilde's: "Pater's essay on Winckelmann declared that 'Greek
   religion too has its statues worn with kissing', and
   spoke of Winckelmann's 'handling of pagan
   marbles . . . with no sense of shame'. These
   phrases coalesced in Wilde's mind with a story he
   remembered from Lucian, of a young man who
   embraced a statue of Aphrodite. He decided to alter the goddess to Athena, because being virginal
   she would feel particularly violated and vindic-
   tive. Charmides is hot enough . . . Athena re-
   venges herself by luring Charmides to drown himself. His body floats to shore, where a nymph falls
   in love and, after seeking ineffectually to awaken
   him, dies of unrequited passion, giving Wilde full
   scope to describe male beauty. Aphrodite inter-
   venes and arranges for the two, purged of sacri-

lege and necrophilia, to enjoy each other in the fields of Acheron . . . Charmides' love for a statue and the nymph's for a corpse lend the poem a certain gaminess. Wilde lingers like Keats over sweets, and like Swinburne over sours, but what animates the poem is the imagery of psychosexual transgression." (Richard Ellmann, *Oscar Wilde* [London, Penguin, 1988], pp. 134-5). This is accurate and it is hard to see how the poem could appeal to the Puritanical White/Rutherford—yet his Charmides is "excited" by his sculpture of Pallas Athene: "It was no mere mineral mass with an outline added. Part of the mind which formed the world was in it. . . . [I]t came to Charmides . . . that what he had done was simply to realize a Divine idea which was immoral, no matter what might become of its embodiment . . . It was nothing more than he had learned from his Plato . . ." (Vol. I pp. 149-50) Charmides, Athene *and* Plato. It is decidedly odd.

10. *George Eliot Letters,* (op. cit.), V, 455.

Abbreviations

ME *Marius the Epicurean*
CF *Catherine Furze*

Richard Wightman Fox (essay date fall 2002)

SOURCE: Fox, Richard Wightman. "Jefferson, Emerson, and Jesus." *Raritan* 22, no. 2 (fall 2002): 62-75.

[*In the following essay, Fox delineates Emerson's and Jefferson's secularized approach to Christianity and to the doctrine and moral teachings of Jesus Christ.*]

The curious amalgam of piety and worldliness in American culture has intrigued foreign and domestic observers for a long time. Religion was entwined with American democracy, said Alexis de Tocqueville in the 1830s. Democracy spawned an equalizing individualism that "concentrated every man's attention upon himself" and "isolated" one person from another. But the Americans' all-pervasive "democratic and republican Christianity" countered the centrifugal disorder. It supplied effective communal cohesion, ironically, by giving individualism free rein. Max Weber developed the theme two generations later. Protestantism was enmeshed in American capitalism. Weber considered Benjamin Franklin a "colorless deist," but also took him as a pure product of Calvinist piety. Franklin gave the capitalist spirit a religious form and feel. He made "the earning of money . . . the expression of virtue and proficiency in a calling." He turned acquisition away from greed and toward a methodical and impersonal kind of self-fashioning.

Weber underestimated the religious component in Franklin's ethic, but he put the focus where it belongs: on the interpenetrating sacred and profane elements in Christian faith and practice. Too many social analysts follow H. L. Mencken's debunking style of analysis, in which piety is a pretension that cloaks worldly aims. Of course errant American preachers from the liberal celebrity Henry Ward Beecher in the nineteenth century to the televangelist Jimmie Swaggart in the twentieth have offered endless satisfaction to the exposers of hypocrisy. But the harder and no less necessary interpretive task is to illuminate the secular elements that mix with and help constitute religion as a set of beliefs and practices. What Weber grasped is that religion can be secularized in many respects without ceasing to be religion.

The reverse is equally true: secularity can be sacralized in many respects without ceasing to be secularity. Just as religious faith has been molded by secular commitments, so secular faith has been shaped by religious loyalties. Secularity is not simply an absence of religion or a diminution of religion. It is a faith in its own right. Nowhere is this more evident than in the nineteenth-century American secular devotion to Jesus, himself a famed Jewish critic of religious hypocrisy. Jefferson and Emerson gave Jesus a secular career in America at a time when the burgeoning Baptists and Methodists were pressing him into service as the divine companion of the Protestant masses. As Jefferson understood, American revolutionaries diverged from their European peers by preserving an attachment to Jesus. European secularists couldn't keep Jesus because to them Christianity reeked of the Old Regime. "In Europe," wrote Tocqueville, "Christianity has been intimately united to the powers of the earth. Those powers are now in decay, and [Christianity] is, as it were, buried under their ruins." American secularizers could retain Jesus because they associated him with democracy, not reaction.

In a democratic environment suffused with Christ-talk and Christ-worship, it made sense for Jefferson, Emerson, and other anti-clerical agitators to stick with Jesus. He was at the heart of an entire cultural language in which the Protestant majority was fluent. He was a currency one could spend, a type of credit one could store up. Jefferson and Emerson wanted to show that a social critic could stand against certain religious structures and habits of mind without falling into French-style atheism. Appealing to Jesus gave legitimacy to their anticlerical liberalism. Of course the Gospel writers had made it easy for secularizers to sidle up to Jesus by depicting him as a rebel against conservative religious authority. Those like Jefferson and Emerson who wished to dissociate themselves from orthodox conceptions of divinity could proclaim, in effect, "Jesus made me do it."

For all of their many differences of temperament and historical placement, Jefferson and Emerson both took

Jesus as the most eminent philosopher of the human condition. They arrived at this position independently, a sign of how pervasive and serviceable Jesus was in all corners of the early-nineteenth-century American cultural environment. In the revolutionary generation Jefferson was scarcely alone in saluting Jesus' wisdom while denying his divinity. But he shows most clearly why "Enlightened," anticlerical Americans of his time remained so committed to Jesus. Jesus the iconoclast was a sure lever against reactionary clergy, many of whom remained committed to established religion in the states after the First Amendment banned establishment at the federal level. Jefferson set out to rescue Jesus from the churches, and that liberation campaign helped him demonstrate just how dispassionately rational a modern nineteenth-century American could be.

Ever the revolutionary, Jefferson decided during his presidency to modernize the Gospel. Ever the diplomat and politician, however, he shared his campaign of biblical recasting only with a small grapevine of respected gentlemen. His active study of Scripture began during his first term. Jesus was "a master workman," he wrote, whose "system of morality was the most benevolent and sublime probably that has been ever taught; and eminently more perfect than those of any of the antient philosophers." Jefferson said that his views were "very different from that Anti-Christian system imputed to me. . . . To the corruptions of Christianity I am indeed opposed; but not to the genuine precepts of Jesus himself. I am a Christian, in the only sense in which he wished any one to be; sincerely attached to his doctrines, in preference to all others; ascribing to him every human excellence, and believing he never claimed any other."

Jefferson sent several friends a detailed outline of a pamphlet he wished to see written. It would show why Jesus was better than all other thinkers, Greek, Roman, or Hebrew. Although Jesus had never systematized his moral doctrine, still "a system of morals is presented to us, which, if filled up in the true style and spirit of the rich fragments he left us, would be the most perfect and sublime that has ever been taught by man." Jesus was superior because his system of morals combined three indispensable insights. First, it was universal, not parochial. None of the Greeks, Romans, or Hebrews, said Jefferson, had understood that ethical obligation extended to all men. Second, it was pegged to the doctrine of a "future state," a belief essential for ensuring the "moral conduct" of the populace. Third, it located virtue not in action or behavior alone, but in the "heart" and "thoughts." Jesus, Jefferson thought, was the first philosopher to locate virtue in the purity of the initial reflection that contemplated an act. Jesus was perfect for the republican era because he internalized morality. The law lay within the pure soul of each good citizen, not in the top-down commands of self-appointed cler-

ics. During Jefferson's reelection campaign in 1804, when he was again under attack as a French-leaning infidel, he let friends circulate the news that he wished to ground the republic upon the wisdom of Jesus—purged of the supernatural accretions that had piled up over centuries of "mystery-mongering" by the churches.

After his reelection Jefferson set aside the dream of tying the future of the republic to the philosophy of Jesus. What he did not give up was the goal of eventually liberating the authentic Jesus and his message from the mystery-mongers. In retirement in 1820 he obtained two copies of the New Testament in each of four languages—Greek, Latin, French, and English—and created "The Life and Morals of Jesus of Nazareth," a quadrilingual secularization of the Gospels. He wrote no commentary himself. He simply took scissors to the Scriptures, removing any passage that implied or claimed that Jesus was divine, and pasting what remained into a blank book bound in red Morocco leather. (He needed two copies in each language so that he could use both sides of a leaf when necessary.) The result of his cut-and-paste handiwork was four columns of Enlightenment-approved text, moving left to right, in progressive historical order, from Greek to Latin to French to English.

Jefferson's surgical strike on the Gospels is touching testimony to an elderly man's undying faith in reason. He was over seventy-five years old when he padded around his study at Monticello purifying Holy Writ of superstition. He may have realized that this quixotic document was a finger in the dike protecting the scientific Enlightenment from the flood of Methodist and Baptist evangelicals, and from the drip of Christian rationalists in the Unitarian camp. Jefferson was a rationalist Christian too, but more secular than the Unitarians since he saw no point in worshiping a personal Jesus. From his standpoint Unitarians like William Ellery Channing were stuck in a teetering halfway house. They had rightly abandoned Calvinism—which stressed God's sovereignty so one-sidedly that it annulled the individual's natural power to know the truth or do good—but they persisted in heralding Jesus as a personal spirit. What mattered about Jesus was his teaching, not his person. It was his teaching that could save reason from the obscurantism of Calvinists and Methodists and the personalism of Unitarians.

God was essential to Jefferson's scheme (as today's religious right is fond of pointing out), but a divine Jesus wrecked it (as the religious right does not mention). God's superintendence was the protection society needed against disorder. Human beings could safely experiment with new social arrangements because God had built balance into his natural order, an order that included the natural hearts of men. "The practice of morality being necessary for the well-being of society," he wrote, "[God] has taken care to impress its precepts so indelibly on our hearts that they shall not be effaced by the subtleties of our brain." This was not heart-over-head doctrine, not a concession to the "enthusiasm" of the evangelicals, but a declaration that heart and head worked together to stabilize the operation of reason in the world. Jesus was essential not as redeemer or spirit but as sage. He was the greatest teacher of all because he understood that the rational moral sense implanted by God in every person could prompt a revolution in human equality. Jefferson's God wanted people to renew the created world through rational action, and his prophets were men of wisdom like Jesus. Human beings, not God, would do the reconstruction, and they would be inspired by the example of the greatest thinker of them all. Of course Jefferson's imagined revolution in human equality extended only to white men. But in his day—when age-old habits of deference still enforced arbitrary distinctions even among white men—that was a revolution in its own right, however partial it must appear from a later standpoint.

In his old age Jefferson wrote that he never went to bed "without an hour, or half hour's previous reading of something moral, whereon to ruminate in the intervals of sleep." "The Life and Morals" may have been one of his favorite bedtime texts. It would have been a double object of rumination, disclosing the timeless wisdom of Jesus and the enlightened handiwork of Jefferson. If his daily meditation included an expression of gratitude to his creator, he thanked God for the gift of reason. He said as much in 1814 in response to a correspondent named Miles King, who was a recently converted Methodist preacher. King was one of the thousands of ordinary Americans who had found in evangelical religion an affirmation of the spiritual equality of all human beings. He may also have found in Jeffersonian politics an affirmation of the political equality of all white men. King had written Jefferson an eleven-page letter announcing that God had told him to plead with Jefferson to embrace

> the Christian System of Salvation . . . to seek until you shall find Christ Jesus . . . for the place that Knows you now will Soon Know you no More for Ever! and do my friend and illustrious fellow citizen, timely consider, even now lay it close to your heart, that God! hath commanded all men every where to repent, because he hath appointed a day in which he will Judge this world in Righteousness, by that man (God-man) whom he hath Ordained, Jesus Christ! whereof he hath given an assurance to all men in that he hath raised him up from the dead!

Jefferson thanked King for his "kind intentions" toward his "future happiness." He told King they shared a deep faith in reason, for it was only by appealing to his reason that King knew his mandate to proselytize Jefferson was really from God, not "imaginary." Reason was

the only oracle which god has given us to determine between what really comes from him, and the phantasms of a disordered or deluded imagination. When he means to make a personal revelation he carries conviction of its authenticity to the reason he has bestowed as the umpire of truth. You believe you have been favored with such a special communication. Your reason, not mine, is to judge of this: and if it shall be his pleasure to favor me with a like admonition, I shall obey it with the same fidelity with which I would obey his known will in all cases.

In the final account, Jefferson said, people took "different roads . . . to that our last abode: but, following the guidance of a good conscience, let us be happy in the hope that, by these different paths, we shall all meet in the end—and that you and I may there meet and embrace is my earnest prayer."

Jefferson's epistolary encounter with Miles King in 1814 is a nice reminder that the historical path from the Enlightened world of Jefferson to the Transcendentalist world of Emerson (born in 1803, sixty years after Jefferson) was a battlefield occupied by antagonistic and shifting cultural forces. Jefferson and Emerson both ended up as secular devotees of Jesus, and both bemoaned the rampant "mystery-mongering" of evangelicalism. But Emerson's generation also took issue with the rationalism of Jefferson's revolutionary cohort. By the time Emerson and his collegiate peers were introduced to the Enlightenment in the 1820s, it was the prudently "didactic Enlightenment," as historian Henry May called it. The Scottish Common Sense philosophers had been appropriated as official guardians of virtue by Unitarian preachers and college presidents alike. Conservative currents, including the evangelical movement that converted Miles King, had long since washed away the cultural supports for a Jefferson-style life of reason. The radical phase of the French Revolution in the 1790s had persuaded many Americans to turn back to religion as a defense against novel philosophies. Many of the same readers who had cherished Tom Paine's republican tract *Common Sense* in 1776 reviled his antisupernaturalist opus *The Age of Reason* in 1794. For Emerson's cohort a generation later, the Enlightenment was stale. "From 1790 to 1820," Emerson quipped in the 1850s, "there was not a book, a speech, a conversation, or a thought, in the State [of Massachusetts]," and he could easily have extended his remark to include the nation. Reasonable religion had become the prescribed alternative to enthusiastic religion. He and his cohort had to imagine new pathways to a vital life of the mind.

Emerson would reaffirm the life of reason in the 1830s. But the only reason that made sense to him was a reason that drew heavily on the conversionist impulses of the evangelical tradition. The secularist Emerson drew more on the orthodox Calvinist Jonathan Edwards than he did on fellow secularist Thomas Jefferson. It had been Edwards's inspiration in the early eighteenth century to blend Locke and Newton with Paul and Jesus. The point for him was not to choose between reason and faith but to experience a new birth of sensibility and devotion, to catch the utter beauty of God's handiwork, to give him the glory for creating human beings whose inveterate sinfulness was joined to surpassing intelligence. Jefferson's reason, from the Transcendentalist point of view, was thin and abstract—not an eruptive way of life but a merely formal instrument. If Emerson had known that Jefferson had cut up the four Gospels to make them enlightened vessels of rational religion, he would have marveled at the sea change reason itself had undergone between the revolutionary era and his own.

For Jefferson, Jesus was the great wise man, the human being who taught people to criticize their traditions and remake their society while shielding it from moral erosion. Emerson's Jesus was a wise man too, but he was more than a teacher of eternal maxims and a model of principled opposition to tired institutions. He was a man of wisdom who dismantled Jefferson's wall of separation between divine and human. Jefferson wanted to protect the man Jesus from insinuations that he was divine. What made Jesus so vitally human, for Emerson, was his knowledge that divinity was inside as well as outside of humanity. The concepts did not exclude one another. We might want to call Emerson's Jesus the Romantic Jesus to distinguish him from the rational Jesus of Jefferson, but that sort of contrast misses the point that Emerson's Jesus was fully rational too, not to mention fully rooted in the evangelical world of Jonathan Edwards. Emerson certainly drew on Romantic themes and perceptions from his beloved Goethe, Coleridge, and Carlyle, but he wished above all to abolish the line splitting off human from divine, rational from inspired, personal from impersonal, secular from religious. Like Jefferson, Emerson was trying to prevent Jesus from falling into the exclusive hands of evangelicals who considered reason a threat to faith. Unlike Jefferson, Emerson thought the highest form of reason (the "Reason," in Coleridge's formula, as opposed to the efficiency-seeking "Understanding") was suffused with the mysterious dynamism of faith.

Jefferson and Emerson both had to be careful about what they said publicly. To speak of Jesus as anything less than a divine redeemer was to court charges of disloyalty as well as heterodoxy. It was to be a fellow traveler of "European" atheism. So in the first decade of the nineteenth century Jefferson said only privately that people were too busy worshiping Jesus to understand his significance as a philosopher. And in the early 1830s Emerson said only privately that people were too busy praising Jesus to imitate his search for the divine within. Venerating Jesus had gotten in the way of reaching for the fully human stature Jesus had achieved. "Is it not time to present this matter of Christianity exactly as it is," he wrote in his journal in 1834, "to take away all false reverence from Jesus, & not mistake the stream for the source? . . . God is in every man. God is in Jesus but let us not magnify any of the vehicles as we magnify the Infinite Law itself. We have defrauded him of his claim of love on all noble hearts by our superstitious mouth honor. We love Socrates but give Jesus the Unitarian Association."

Emerson finally went public with his views in his Divinity School Address of 1838, a text only slightly less scathing than his journal entries. The church had not taught "the doctrine of the soul," he told the six graduates and their professors and families, "but an exaggeration of the personal . . . [the church] dwells, with noxious exaggeration about the *person* of Jesus. The soul knows no persons. It invites every man to expand to the full circle of the universe, and will have no preferences but those of spontaneous love." The goal of the spiritual life was to escape devotion to externalities, such as the Jesus icon, and experience the eruptive presence of a force so massive, so eternal, and so unpredictable, that it could best be called an "impersonal" law or principle. That law could transform one's own "person," and was thus "personal" as well as "impersonal." The paradox was that finding one's fully personal soul meant reaching the domain of impersonality, hence losing "persons" altogether.

In his journals at the time, and in his great essays of the 1840s, Emerson spelled out his opposition to the Christian infatuation with personality. It led people to clamor after individual immortality, whereas Jesus never "utter[ed] one syllable about the naked immortality of the soul, never spoke of simple duration." Here Emerson inverted Jefferson, who had praised Jesus for focusing on "the future state" more insistently than the Greeks, Romans, or Hebrews did. Emerson lauded Jesus for registering more clearly than the Greeks that the eternal was not coming later, but was already here. To grasp at personal immortality was to miss the whole point of Jesus' preaching. His call was not to a final resting place in eternity, but to the eternal that was ever present in our midst. "The only way," he wrote in 1839, that "Jesus or [any] other holy person helps us is this, that as we advance without reference to persons on a new, unknown, sublime path, we at each new ascent verify the experiences of Jesus & such souls as have obeyed God before. We take up into our proper life at that moment his act & word & do not copy Jesus but really are Jesus, just as Jesus in that moment of his life was us. Say rather, it was neither him nor us, but a man at this & at that time saw the truth & was transformed into its likeness." Jesus deserved imitation because he did not imitate.

Emerson was hitting the Massachusetts Unitarian clergy where it hurt the most. They had put all their chips on Jesus' personality when they turned against Trinitarian orthodoxy, against the idea that the One God was made up of three Persons. Like Jefferson, they had dismissed Trinitarianism as unbiblical and logically ridiculous. Like Jefferson they were making war on mysteries. Yet unlike Jefferson they had wanted to preserve some semblance of Jesus' divinity. His perfect personality was their solution to the dilemma. Jesus was not equal to God, they thought, but uniquely chosen by God, indeed (as the more cosmically minded Unitarians still put it) created by God from the beginning of time for his special vocation: that of embodying the fullest blossoming of human personhood. Emerson had come to see that the Unitarian solution remained trapped in the same pit that their supposed enemies, the Calvinists, had carved out. The Calvinists' other main opponents, the revivalistic Methodists, were marooned there too. They all thought the religious life was about venerating someone else rather than seizing the chance God had given them and experiencing a rebirth of their own. Emerson's rejection of Jesus-worship and endorsement of self-reliant spirituality was not a call for celebrating what we would call "human potential." His popularizers in the late nineteenth century, notably Ralph Waldo Trine, are the true source of twentieth-century religions of self-development. Emerson humanized Jesus as much to protect the sovereignty of God (the original Unitarian goal) as to assert the open-ended growth of human beings. As he made clear in his essay "Experience," growth is always hemmed in by the paralysis of human finitude and self-deception. Trine and other Emerson boosters scrupulously scrubbed that Gospel-based sentiment out of Emerson's legacy.

All the pushing and shoving among Calvinists, revivalists, and Unitarians to get next to Jesus made Emerson sick, and in the safety of his journal he uttered words that Tom Paine himself would have thought sacrilegious. "It might become my duty," he wrote in 1840, "to spit in the face of Christ as a sacred act of duty to the Soul, an act which that beautiful pilgrim in nature would well enough appreciate." "You name the good Jesus," he blurted in 1843, "until I hate the sound of him." In a culture so blinded by its personalized Christ, the only way left to convey the actual teaching of Jesus was to do it round-about, by teaching the cognate ideas of other wise men. "Therefore it is that we fly to the pagans," he wrote in 1838, "& use the name & relations of Socrates, of Confucius, Menu [Manu], Zoroaster; not that these are better or as good as Jesus & Paul (for they have not uttered so deep moralities) but because they are good algebraic terms not liable to confusion of thought like those we habitually use."

Emerson's humanizing and de-divinizing of Jesus (or call it his redivinization of everyone else) informed all of his famous essays of the 1840s. Jesus was "only" human, but he had risen beyond the usual heights of human striving. He was the wondrously gifted individual who grasped, as Emerson wrote in his journal in 1835, that "God must be sought within, not without." God was within each person not as an ingrained moral sense (Jefferson's belief), and not as a personal spirit (the claim of many Christians), but as the ever flowing source of one's self-renewal. In his essay "Circles" (1841), he identified the life course with the perpetual creation of wider and wider circles of experience. "The instinct of man presses eagerly onward to the impersonal and illimitable," and carries "the brave text of Paul's" as its guiding truth: "Then shall also the Son be subject unto Him who put all things under him, that God may be all in all." Letting God live in one's self meant increasing one's openness to surprise, novelty, and, paradoxically, self-forgetting. "When these waves of God flow into me," he wrote, he no longer succumbed to the stewing-in-self that especially afflicted writers like himself. He stopped fretting about all the wasted days and months when he could have been scribbling more prose. In the "divine moments . . . I no longer reckon lost time." As Jesus taught, selves found themselves by losing themselves.

Giving oneself over to the impersonal, giving up niggling, calculating self-improvement, did not mean retreating into contemplative quietism. Emerson tied self-forgetting to the plowing under of atrophied habits and rigid conventions. "The one thing which we seek with insatiable desire," he wrote at the end of "Circles," "is to forget ourselves, to be surprised out of our propriety, to lose our sempiternal memory, and to do something without knowing how or why; in short, to draw a new circle. . . . The way of life is wonderful: it is by abandonment." Emerson's vision was religious as much as it was secular. The irony is that it relied upon a secular Jesus for its religious intensity.

Emerson's final move in de-divinizing Jesus was to see him as one wise man among others, a sage whose central teachings might be the most sublime of all (as Jefferson had also said), but which could nevertheless be understood by thoughtful people anywhere. Jesus was a contingent product of the Middle East and the European West. He was not sovereign, God was. Cultures and languages were historical accidents. No culture was a privileged carrier of truth. The New Testament contained many unchanging truths, "orphic words" such as "God is no respecter of persons," "His kingdom cometh without observation," and "His kingdom is a little child," and they could all be rendered in other languages. Translation was possible because the deepest truths were unchanging; translation was necessary because all words and formulations become wooden. The immutable truths perennially revitalized in translation were immutable, of course, only because they required people to change if they were going to live up to them. They were eternal principles because they mandated self-translation, an open-ended, always incomplete striving for virtue as well as knowledge.

For Emerson Jesus was the greatest authority on the impersonal embrace of God. Jesus established the basic form for all subsequent moral and spiritual aspiration. Jesus was like a great writer, who "established the conventions of composition" that even "the most original" of later authors "feels in every sentence." Self-reliant individuals followed Jesus in looking within, not without, and discovering there new and unexplored terrain. They imitated Jesus by reworking the language of eternal truths to keep them fresh. "Life only avails," Emerson wrote in "Self-Reliance" (1841), "not the having lived. Power ceases in the instant of repose; it resides in the moment of transition from a past to a new state, in the shooting of the gulf, in the darting to an aim. This one fact the world hates, that the soul *becomes;* for that for ever degrades the past, turns all riches to poverty, all reputation to a shame, confounds the saint with the rogue, shoves Jesus and Judas equally aside."

"Shoving Jesus and Judas equally aside" exhibits Emerson's secularizing animus at its most passionate. It is as close as Emerson ever got to publishing the kind of culturally seditious sentiments that dot his journals: spitting on Christ, hating the name of Jesus. Shoving Jesus and Judas equally aside was a double horror in a culture as Christianized as Emerson's: first pushing Jesus away, then equating Jesus and Judas. Of course Emerson was being ironic. His secular salvo was utterly religious. To shove the socially correct Jesus out of the way was to honor the actual Jesus all the more. To attack Jesus the icon was to defend Jesus the visionary. There is a side of Emerson that imagined a pagan society would do better than a Christianized one at hearing and imitating Jesus. In a pagan society Jesus and his message would stand out in bold relief. Emerson turned secular to save religion, to undermine the phony religiosity of his culture. He needed Jesus because Jesus showed him how to be an iconoclast, how to purify and salvage religion. Emerson was a major secularizer of American culture because he helped convince a substantial body of his Protestant compatriots that they could become more deeply religious by becoming more secular, more truly devoted to Jesus by abandoning the conventional worship of him.

Emerson shared with Jefferson the conviction that Jesus was indispensable to modern (and American) minds as they broke free from old structures and systems of thought. Both of these secularizers had put the theology of orthodoxy behind them, but even as they stripped Jesus of his divinity, they continued to pay homage to his moral and spiritual power. Many later secular disciples of Jesus followed them. Like Jefferson and Emerson, figures as varied as Eugene Debs, Elizabeth Cady Stanton, and Jane Addams embraced Jesus as symbol and instigator of what Addams, in a speech in 1892, saw as the merging of "revelation" with "life." "Jesus had no set of truths labeled Religious," she said. His message did not "belong to the religious consciousness, whatever that may be." The secular faith she spelled out meant "seeking for the Christ which lieth in each man." Nineteenth-century America was the century of evangelization led by the Methodists and Baptists, but it was also the century of secularization inaugurated by Jefferson and Emerson. These apparently contradictory developments converged in the veneration of Jesus. Jefferson pacing in his study, scissors poised, and Emerson penning journal entries about "that beautiful pilgrim in nature," were as devoted to Jesus as the Methodist preacher Miles King, Jefferson's God-appointed rescuer.

RUSSIAN LITERATURE

Luigi Pareyson (essay date summer-fall 1987)

SOURCE: Pareyson, Luigi. "Pointless Suffering in *The Brothers Karamazov*." *Cross Currents* 37, nos. 2-3 (summer-fall 1987): 271-86.

[*In the following essay, translated into English by Elizabeth Hughes, Pareyson studies Dostoevsky's treatment of the suffering of innocents in* The Brothers Karamazov, *and asserts that the author affirms the Christian approach to the theological dilemma over the presence of evil in the world.*]

Suffering is the center of Dostoyevski's art, the recurrent theme in virtually all of his work. His approach is unsystematic, but the strength and depth of his meditations are no less remarkable.

His perspective, whatever its complications, is classically Christian. Suffering is the destiny of mankind and the expiation of a common guilt. We are subject to sin, and the evil we harbor in our hearts marks us for pain. There is a way, however, of redeeming suffering, of purifying it, and that is to accept it in conscious expiation. This penance is the highest manifestation of the universal law of expiation. A terrible and necessary mode of self-renewal, it brings with it a deeper understanding of the world and of our authenticity.

This conclusion, regarding the world and the self, bears the imprint of Dostoyevski's original interpretation of these postulates which are the point of departure of his probing; and they conclude with the discovery and elaboration of a dialectic which is as disconcertingly ambivalent as it is profound. De Maistre's characterization of the sentimental Lamennais—"For all of the magnanimity and nobility of his world, virtually all of his books seem to be written on the gallows"—applies much more aptly to the Russian novelist. Dostoyevski sounds the depths of both suffering and freedom. He is keenly aware of the ambiguities in our suffering which, as in the case of Dmitri, can be a longing for atonement, a longing which is part of the Russian experience of Christianity or of its direct opposite, a spurious and unwholesome variety of masochism.

1

Within the central question of suffering, the problem of the apparently pointless suffering of children, however, is the novelist's primary concern. Dostoyevski returns to it again and again, and gives its most appropriate dimensions in *The Brothers Karamazov.*

Pointless or useless suffering is that pain which, because of its intensity or the helplessness of the sufferer, cannot be turned into a means of purification or spiritual growth. The person subject to it is fundamentally passive, an involuntary martyr.

Examples abound in our times of torture, genocide, and concentration camps—but similar horrors, as Dostoyevski's novels document, were hardly wanting in his day. Of all the forms which this anguish can take, that of a mother mourning her dead children is among the most piercing—and Dostoyevski's pages on this theme are not easily forgotten. Rachel weeping "for they are no more," the lamentation for the Innocents in the gospel of Matthew—this world has its counterpart both in the life of Dostoyevski, who felt himself guiltily responsible for his son's death from inherited epilepsy, and likewise in his novels. *The Brothers Karamazov* contains two such passages. The better known is Captain Snegirev's lament over the death of his son Iljusta in the novel's epilogue. Even more striking is the story (Book II, Chapter 3) of the peasant woman desperate to see for one more time—if only for a single minute—her dead child. She has moved from one monastery to another in fruitless despair, like Rachel unconsolable. "Do not be consoled," Father Zosima tells her. "That is not what you need. Do not take consolation but weep." Suffering such as this, Dostoyevski notes, feeds on itself.

In our anguish we reopen wounds, cling desperately to God, deny Him, experience utter isolation and defiance, encounter the apparent absurdity of life—and also its atoning pain.

2

Before we turn to the problem of suffering in children, it might be well to allude briefly to two of Dostoyevski's parallel concerns—the question of suffering in animals and in idiots.

In effect, Dostoyevski's views confirm those of Schopenhauer to whom we are so indebted on this matter. The novelist is deeply aware of the hidden ties that bind together all of creation. He knows that our brutality tends to increase in proportion to the helplessness of the animal; more important, he recognizes in such cruelty a frontal attack on the sacred quality of life. "Love animals," Father Zosima pleads. "God granted them something akin to reason, and an untroubled joy. Do not torment them, do not take away their joy. Do not place yourself higher than the animals. They are without sin whereas you, for all of your greatness, contaminate the earth" (Book VI, Chapter 3).

The suffering of idiots is treated in a similar vein. The seemingly arbitrary cruelty of the idiot's destiny has, through the ages, been countered by the belief that the idiot is in some mysterious way a person touched by God. Balzac's *Medecin de Campagne* portrays that deference in France. It was even stronger in Christian Russia. The idiot lived on public charity and any signs of affection he showed to his benefactors were considered virtually a sign of God's benevolence. This belief, for Dostoyevski, reintegrated the idiot as a person into the human community.

The suffering of idiots and of animals share in the novelist's main preoccupation—the question of the apparently pointless suffering of children. All are victims who do not understand; but children, more than the others, are trustingly passive. They accept what they submit to. They do not renounce their boundless trust. It is precisely their vulnerability which makes them so attractive to Dostoyevski, kindling an empathy which leads him to conceive their suffering in terms that go beyond Dickens' social protest or Hardy's darker psychological probings. Indeed, the novels of Dostoyevski teem with suffering children. The most conspicuous are the victims of "oppressive and brutal spirit of the metropolis," be it London or St. Petersburg. With their "dark and terrifying strength" these cities crush their inhabitants: the children making their way among the weekend crowds of drunkards; the six year old Haymarket girl whose features already bear the stamp of "infinite resignation"; the pale emaciated children in the grimy world of St. Petersburg for whom home is a dismal and squalid basement; the precociously delinquent beggars, sodden with alcohol; the boy who dies of cold on Christmas night after having looked upon a Christmas tree—in sum, children like Iljusa, vilified, degraded, and humiliated by their father, or the adolescent tyrannized into servility by the headmaster. And then there are accounts of raped children driven to suicide, of young girls sold to lecherous old men. We cannot forget the despairing submission of the child destined from her earliest years to become the bride of the respectable and hypocritical Julian Mastakovic; the little boy punished with a stream of boiling water poured out from a samovar over his hands; the unanswered cry for help of the little girl which occasions the remorse of a ridiculous little man and leads finally to suicide. The story of Dmitri encapsulates these sufferings: he could remember only one affectionate gesture from his childhood—that of a doctor who once gave him a handful of walnuts.

In placing his concern for the suffering of children in a more spacious context, Dostoyevski assigns one side of the case to Ivan Karamazov, a thinker who amply deserves mention in any history of philosophy. More persuasively than Nietzsche, he argues the cause of modern nihilism and comes to radical denial of Christianity through his acceptance of Christian postulates as his point of departure. His implacable conclusions make Nietzsche's seem tortuous and labyrinthian. (Razanov argued that, contrary to the novelist's intention, Ivan rather than Alyosha is the principal character in the novel, the one who appears to have the irrefutable last word.)

Ivan confronts the problem of suffering children from the very start—not so much in the "Legend of the Grand Inquisitor," although of course that is central to the question, but in the conversations with Smerdkjakov. Indeed, the legend acquires its meaning within the context of Ivan's position and the positions of his adversaries; it should not be read as an isolated text but as a moment in a single and continuous dialogue. Ivan knows that "the earth is sodden from its crust down to the center with tears." He can understand this of a universe of adults; but not of a world of children who have not "eaten and continued to eat the forbidden fruit." Children are not guilty of anything.

3

In this concern and affection for children, Ivan and Dostoyevski are clearly one. There can be no doubt as to the novelist's response to the evangelical injunction to "be like little children." It is understandable why the admirable Prince Myskin is so much at home in the world of children, as are Father Zosima, Kirilov, and of course Ivan Karamazov.

Dostoyevski's tenderness for children does not conflict with his convictions regarding the universality of hu-

man guilt. He knows very well that children are not consistently candid, that—as a tradition that extends from William Golding, Henry James and Georges Bernanos back to St. Augustine maintains—there is evil in children. Dostoyevski speaks of their corruptibility, on occasion of their depravity; but he stresses their innocence, their confident trust. Ivan is the champion and defender of this innocence. He turns his back on adults. Their suffering is well deserved, he argues; it fits in with the vicissitudes of the human race. The suffering of children, though, is quite another matter. Their virtues and defenselessness make them lovable "even at close range." For this reason their suffering is scandalous. Children are exempt from solidarity in sin and suffering—or more accurately, they ought to be, for manifestly they do suffer.

Are we therefore to suppose that this is the punishment called for by the sins of their fathers, that the suffering of children is necessary? Ivan categorically rejects both propositions. "It is absolutely impossible to understand why they too must suffer," why they too must "serve as raw material and fertilizer to bring about a future harmony for the benefit of who knows whom." If in our world it is necessary that children suffer, then our world is absurd and scandalous.

And the examples with which Ivan buttresses his case are frightening. The cruelty of Turks in Bulgaria—children cut from their mothers' wombs with daggers, nurslings thrown into the air and impaled on bayonet point. The case of the general who, when he discovers that his favorite greyhound is limping, punishes the eight-year-old boy who hurt her inadvertently by forcing him to flee nude before the entire pack until he finally falls and is torn to pieces before his mother's eyes.

4

To dwell on these horrifying cases of useless suffering, Ivan argues, is to rebel against the very idea of God. The doctrine of the ultimate happiness of all offers scant consolation. There is no way to reconcile pointless suffering with an ultimate harmony. No reparation to those who have so suffered is possible, nor can there be adequate punishment. The same holds for the possibility of pardon. Who could pardon the dismemberment of a child by dogs? Nothing appears more repugnant to Ivan than a harmony in which mother, son and tyrant ultimately join in a single and harmonious hymn to the Creator's justice. Far better, Ivan is convinced, to vent rage and refuse consolation. The thought that the suffering of one could bring about the happiness of another is monstrous. (Something of this spirit, "What kind of happiness could ever be founded on the suffering of another?", characterizes Dostoyevski's *Discourse on Pushkin*). The doctrine appears all the more repugnant if the sufferer is poor and defenseless: to act in this way, God would have to be cruel beyond all measure. His crime would be not only against man's natural desire for happiness but against a still deeper human instinct, the striving for justice.

Viewed in this perspective, Rozanov is clearly right in maintaining that Ivan's denial of God is not the usual atheism of his day. Indeed, in arguing that there is an implicit and inescapable conflict between God's justice and his cruelty, Ivan adumbrates for the first time a dialectic with a long tradition behind it—one that is the conclusion of Dostoyevski's meditation: the vision of conflict within God himself.

What will become a moment in the dialectic of Dostoyevski, however, remains a scandal for Ivan. God, for him, could not possibly constitute the meaning of the world. The price, he concludes, is "more than he is willing to afford" and he is ready "to hand back his admission ticket."

Such a conclusion recalls the polemic that the tears of children evoked from Belinsky, who protested against a God deaf to the plight of the poor, an atheism which, as Berdyaev suggests, prides itself on its denial of a God indifferent to human suffering. But the religious overtones of this atheism are no less obvious, and their intensity betrays the strength of the atheist's own anguished memory of a lost God.

"Of what importance is it to me," Ivan asks, "that most men live comfortably if they do so at the expense of one single anguished human being? The destiny of the individual is more important than that of the entire world." And Belinsky: "If I should attain to the highest rung in the evolutionary ladder, I would demand an accounting for all of the poor creatures martyred by history, their wretched destiny. If such an accounting were not given, I would throw myself down head first. I do not want happiness, not even as a gift, without first being reassured on the fate of each of my brothers."

The truth is, however, that Ivan's atheism is more complex than Belinsky's. More important, Dostoyevski is not completely one with his creation, Ivan. The novelist, as he acknowledged in a letter in defense of his Christianity, valued "the power of denial," but after passing through the crucible of doubt, he transformed that power into a hosannah.

Ivan's negations move in a very different direction from Dostoyevski's; nowhere is this more evident than in Ivan's denial of Christ and Christianity. Creation has failed, he feels, and so has redemption. Far from freeing humankind, Christ has succeeded only in increasing its misery, since he has burdened it with the most un-

bearable burden, freedom of choice. In this perspective, not even hope in an ultimate ransom from pain and suffering is spared.

The love of humanity only brings about the opposite of the Redeemer's intent: it increases human suffering. And just as atheism is called for by theism itself, so the inadequacy of Christ's love for humanity calls for anti-Christianity. Out of a true love for humanity—out of the necessity for attainable happiness, Ivan rejects creation and redemption and entrusts the task of its liberation to humanity alone. Or, better, humans claim the right to assign that work to those who by means of a temporal church and socialism will assure that happiness. This is necessary because the signs of God and Christ, Ivan argues, are not love and compassion but injustice and cruelty. Authentic mercy and love are to be found only in those who labor to transform reality and to organize earthly happiness. This is the mission of the Grand Inquisitor.

5

In his chapter on Dostoyevski in *L'homme revolté,* Camus stresses the connection between the suffering of children and the non-existence of God. It is precisely in this convergence that he too sees the common root of faith and nihilism—the point at which all is accepted or denied—the moment of choice documented in the intensely dramatic pages of *La Peste.* Harder, more courageous and more demanding than everyday religion, the religion of the plague is also more robust and resolute: it comes close to hating God in order to love him, however arduous and painful that love may be.

Because we do not understand pointless suffering, we can only will to accept it. This, in effect, is to choose the love of God since only he can ultimately cancel that suffering; we must will that suffering because God wills it. "We must leap into the heart of the unacceptable offered to us in order to make our choice, and from that height we will see truth emerge from what has the appearance of injustice. This is precisely the leap that, in what Camus calls his "rejection of salvation" Ivan refuses to take. "I prefer to hold on to my unappeased rage even if I am wrong," Ivan states; whether or not God—an unjust God—exists.

When all the necessary qualifications have been made, however, and Ivan's thought is clearly understood, one great problem remains: how is that atheism to descend from the heights of Promethean outrage to a lived day-to-day rhythm? can it gain in practical terms what it loses in loftiness? Ivan distinguishes between an objective and a subjective dimension, the first embracing social and political solutions of some magnitude, the other the personal response to such solutions. Ivan fails to recognize the tendency of the personal to slide into a downward spiral. The atheism that has its origin in love of justice outraged by the world's absurdity often descends first to the sphere of amorality, then to ethical indifference, and ultimately to the suppression of all values. At this point, even cannibalism can be moral. This moral agnosticism, in turn, may lead to love of life on the elemental level, a visceral and frantic "thirst for life." Alexey rightly sees this as the form of Ivan's religion: to love life above all else, more than logic and rational thought, in spite of them and despite the chaotic and diabolical nature of reality; and that, as Alexey points out, is already half way to salvation.

Nevertheless, Ivan's atheism continues in a downward spiral, identifying itself more and more with the banality of daily existence, as shown in Ivan's nightmare encounter with the devil. Here, the devil is no longer Lucifer, the fallen angel. He has been transformed into a conventional gentleman, elegantly dressed, at home with reality—practical, a man of the world who prefers the concrete particulars of the human world to the smoky haze of his own kingdom. He has no higher ideal than "to become incarnate for once and for all in an enormous woman shopkeeper who weighs over two hundred pounds, to believe all she believes and then to go to church to light a candle and pray fervently." Banal, the devil renders banal all that he touches: he believes in God and goes to Mass, since God has been reduced to a simple idea, formless and undeveloped enough to make it possible for all to believe; and going to Mass is a mere convention in which anyone may participate. The devil's transformation does not weaken his power; it crowns his triumph. The more the devil's image loses prominence and clarity, the more effective his presence becomes. Indeed, his victory is achieved by convincing all that he does not exist. Then all defenses against him are undone, since there is not point in struggling against a non-existent enemy. The diabolical aspect of Hitler—just one example among many—is confirmed, not denied, by his ordinary dress, his look of being a middle-class clerk, rather small, with a bit of dandruff on his shoulders and a raincoat over his dark suit. The same can be said of his most savage cohorts, who are outwardly diligent civil servants and respectable fathers and husbands. The soporific character of the banal disarms us and weakens our defenses.

The practical forms atheism assumes in day-to-day life do not weaken but perfect it. It gradually loses the frenzy of revolt, but this decline is not decay. Rather, it is the perfect resolution of atheism into nihilism. It is no longer a program but a way of life. In this sense Ivan is no longer the believing atheist who retains a remembrance of the faith, ever ready to take it up again, or in any case bent on finding a substitute. He is more modern: he has gone beyond that religious and nostalgic nihilism to use his destructive force in a subtler, and therefore more radical fashion. His is a nihilism suited for everyday use—easy-going, conformed to a devil who has become banal. The negation is so generalized and total that it becomes identified completely with reality. This may be why it descends from glowing and heroic rebellion, to rootless liberation and submoral satisfaction of daily needs. Conflicting elements of the self are quickly soldered together; and all obstacles and regret disappear. Regeneration is instantaneous—and continuous; it constitutes a perpetual present.

The triumph of everyday nihilism in its final stage cancels the religious spirit. It may attenuate its denials, but they are nonetheless absolute. It may be light-hearted, undramatic, and easy-going, but it is nonetheless lethal. The religious spirit, once it has been banned, however, takes refuge in the depths of the heart—where it is usually transformed into despair. That is the only way in which, exiled from public life, the religious spirit can make itself felt. This is precisely what happens to Ivan. In its dark premonition of the world of today, we see the singular relevance of Ivan's thought.

6

Radical in its denials, complex in its conclusions and implications, Ivan's atheism bypasses two prevailing objections to God's existence—the undemonstrability of his existence, and the scandal of injustice and suffering. Reality, Ivan concedes, need not coincide with the demonstrable; as for an end to suffering, or a rationale for it, Ivan sees no reason why human beings, wicked as they are, have any right to happiness. Thus Ivan accepts, in part, traditional religious concepts; but in so doing he turns their conclusions upside down: for Ivan the only reality is Euclidean thought—an outlook reminiscent of positivism and rationalism—and the other worlds implicit in a religious view are spurious and imaginary. Euclidean thought, by limiting itself to facts and to reasoning, rejects the notion of an ultimate human harmony or happiness, as well as any connection between guilt and suffering. Evil, in this view, is only the effect of certain causes, according to a law of causality which concatenates all the events of the world.

It has been argued, paradoxically, that Ivan accepts God but not the world. More precisely, he accepts God whom he does not know to exist, but not the world which he does know to exist. This may or may not be, since there is no doubt that Ivan, for all of his attraction to certain religious assertions, seems perplexed once he has fully elaborated his atheism. It is also true, however, that Ivan's discourse is not the orderly exposition of a coherent theory. His is a line of reasoning in the making, *in fieri;* its point of departure and its results are clearly distinct and successive. Its end result turns easily into the denial of the point of departure; and in fact it is through the idea of God and the hope of religion that Ivan arrives at his nihilistic conclusions. Indeed, by this logic, God himself, as architect of an absurd world, seems to cry out for his own nonexistence.

Dostoyevski recognizes as much when he argues that atheism is the "negation not of God but of the meaning of His creation." The concept moves logically and inevitably to its own denial, just as traditional religious ideas, mere fictions and projections of man, lead to their own opposites.

In the end, *The Brothers Karamzov* refutes this nihilism; as Dostoyevski points out, the novel reaches its climax not with blasphemy but its rebuttal. That refutation is not a point-by-point discussion of each element in Ivan's thought. Artistic rather than philosophical, it furnishes us with a more eloquent denial of Ivan's thought than rational analysis could provide. The rebuttal is often made by persons and events—Father Zosima's mode of life, Smerdyakov's suicide, Ivan's madness, Alexey's friendship with children, Dmitri's desire to suffer all things in and of themselves. Dialogue, too, looms large—especially Ivan's conversations with Smerdyakov and Alexey's brief but forceful observations.

These arguments, it is often claimed, do not carry the day. The vigor of Ivan's atheism makes his adversaries appear weak and vague. Ivan's sharp and skeptical arguments seem more effective than Alexey's truncated replies and the sweet, devout speeches of Father Zosima.

Many critics allege that the weakness of Dostoyevski's rebuttal springs from his own spirit of negation, which makes him more effective in describing evil than good. That Dostoyevski died before he could fully elaborate his thought does not impress such critics; and they do not doubt that intentionally or not Ivan's is Dostoyevski's voice. Like his hero, they feel, the novelist is rebellious, blasphemous, and destructive; his God—in conformity with his own admission that he was a child of his age, an age of doubt and denial—is the God of an atheist, his Christ the Christ of a non-believer.

Dostoyevski himself felt the force of such allegations. "I have not accomplished one tenth of what I set out to do," he writes. "Until now my novel does not answer all the questions raised by Ivan's atheism and an answer is needed. I have planned *The Russian Monk* as an answer to these denials and now I tremble: will the answers suffice? And I tremble because the answers I offer are not direct as in the *Legend* and other chapters but oblique, and I do not make a point-by-point rebuttal but sum up my case in images, in art. Will I be understood? Will I have nothing but crumbs to show for my intent?"

Dostoyevski's self-criticism may be too severe. Denial is by nature more clamorous and showy than affirmation. In the *Legend*, Christ remains silent in the face of

the Grand Inquisitor's accusations and expectations. The positive does not need to attract attention. Its existence says all. Denial must make itself heard because it seeks to demolish what is established. Real strength belongs to affirmation, since the furor of negation, although exciting and fascinating, has a feigned vigor; its wild restlessness and showy self-confidence barely conceal its deep-rooted insecurity.

The truth about Dostoyevski's own belief is equally obvious. Ivan's voice is not his. The novelist has listened to Ivan. He has traveled along the road with him and there is an atheistic moment which he shared with him; but they do not arrive at the same inn. Where Ivan's journey ends, nihilism, becomes the writer's new point of departure. What Ivan takes as definitive is provisional for Dostoyevski. Ivan's system is Dostoyevski's method, an instrument in the search for God's existence. Just as Ivan with his Euclidean coherence turns traditional religious affirmations into their contraries, so Dostoyevski transforms Ivan's atheism into a renewed theism. God is rediscovered through a coherent atheism, the denial of the world leads to the awareness of its meaning, and the spirit of nihilism is trasmuted into the realization of the value of life. Atheism is turned into a dialectic and becomes "the second last step" which leads to the last. Without this atheism, God's existence would be flat and consolatory; without the existence of God, such atheism would be mere negation and destructiveness. Together, and only together, they reach fullness of meaning. And in so doing, the culmination of the dialectic appears in the last step.

Dostoyevski's approach, then, is to show that ultimately Ivan's atheism leads to theism rather than demolishing it. Just as Ivan's nihilism cannot be reduced to the usual anti-religion of popular atheism, so theism capable of confronting Ivan's thought must know how to adapt doubt, negation and critical inquiry for its own ends. It will emerge victorious over atheism not so much because it has been vaccinated against its denials as because it has mastered a dialectic in which critical enquiry strengthens choice, doubt strengthens faith, and denial reinforces conviction.

7

Three refutations of Ivan's thought stand out: Dmitri's stance, Father Zosima's discourse, and Alexey's brief and telling observations.

That Dmitri is willing, indeed anxious, to go to Siberia for "the little child" is perhaps the most dramatic refutation of all. The suffering of the child in Dmitri's dream embodies the pointless suffering of the world. The child cries, its little bare arms outstretched, blue with cold. He cries out in hunger for the mother who carries him in her arms but has no milk to give him. Dmitri is driven by the need to do something immediately "so that the child will weep no more, nor will the mother, black with hunger, nor will anyone any longer have to weep." And the only way to do this is to suffer, and, although innocent, go to Siberia. Suffering, from this perspective, is the only way to redeem the suffering of the child, to heal the pain of all since "we are all guilty and must answer for the sufferings of others."

Our solidarity in guilt and suffering is the only road by means of which we can redeem the suffering of others. This holds even though the principle of solidarity is inapplicable to children—for how could their suffering be of use to anyone? What is demanded, therefore, is the voluntary suffering of an innocent adult to redeem the pointless suffering of a child. That an innocent person should consent to go to Siberia for the little child, that he should *want* to suffer for him, transforms that suffering into joy. "He fell an innocent victim of the truth!", Kolja says of Dmitri. "What a happy man! He fell, yes, but what happiness he knew!" And with this resolved, the scandal of that pointless suffering is rooted out, redeemed.

With respect to Father Zosima, Dostoyevski appears initially to have planned to center in him the most telling parts of his rebuttal; and indeed the discussion between the two is pivotal. Besieged by despair and madness, Ivan is all intent on defending moral indifferentism and his day-to-day nihilism, while Father Zosima, close to death, exhausts himself in revitalizing traditional religious teaching with ties to the faith of the people and the doctrine of the Church. In this contrast and struggle, the themes of pointless suffering and of divine glory confront one another no longer as contraries but as mediating elements which bind together guilt and pardon, solidarity in guilt and expiation through love—two unsoundable abysses, the depths of human suffering and the heights of divine glory. Inasmuch as they are abysses, they are united: one abyss, that of God and man. The disputants are irreducibly two, each armed against the other, but co-essential in their opposition, collaborating in the counterpoint of the only meaningful opposition. One without the other would be simplistic and incomplete: Ivan bombastic in his revolt, Zosima oversweet in his piety. Only when viewed together does each receive from the other his true meaning.

As a refutation of Ivan's atheism, Father Zosima's discourse is above all an exaltation of love which holds together all segments of the universe and binds them in a cosmotheandric unity. All beings who participate in pain and joy are equally destined for happiness, and this happiness is achieved by the acceptance of man's sinful condition and the need for reciprocal pardon. This cosmic love is not confined to mankind. It embraces all the beings in the universe, adults and children, the beasts of the earth and the birds of the sky, the

grains of sand, and the leaves of the trees. Expressed with singular poetical force in the story of Father Zosima's brother, this concept is crucial to the discussion of pointless suffering. That brother suffers *usque ad mortem,* yet is serene, and blesses life. By his example he manifests how suffering can turn into joy through universal pardon, for if our common guilt will make us accept equal responsibility for our sins and those of others, it will be enough for each of us to ask pardon of all. We forgive and are forgiven. Were this by some miracle to occur instantaneously, universal love would reestablish universal happiness. Each one would have to "count himself responsible for all human sins." This awareness and this intent would suffice to bring "paradise" to immediate realization: "Life is paradise, but we do not want to understand that. If we sought to understand it, the world would be paradise tomorrow." Happiness is thus realizable, without either divine or human manipulation, by the power of love. It alone can banish absurdity from the world and undo every argument against God's existence. The principle of common human guilt and common expiation, far from implying the necessity of useless suffering, takes on another meaning: it is an injunction to accept, and then wish to suffer for the guilt of others. It foreshadows the universal love which will draw all men together. Freedom from suffering is the victory of redemptive love.

It falls to Father Zosima's brother to refute Ivan's other claim, that creation has failed. God is not the creator of an absurd world. It is humanity that corrupts and contaminates all that it touches. Far from attesting to the non-existence of its creator, the world is an incessant hymn of praise in his honor. All beings, even the smallest and least significant, testify to the divine mystery. Thus Ivan's love of life—he is enchanted by "the sticky little leaves that open in the springtime"—finds its true basis and justification in the universal love that draws all beings together, even the blade of grass, even the leaf that "sings its hymn to God and addresses its tearful lament to Christ, and does so all unknowing in the mystery of its innocent existence."

Father Zosima's brother's universal love is the "other half" which, according to Alexey, is missing from Ivan's love of live, the half that will reveal to him the meaning of life. Through it, the universal concatenation of which Ivan speaks—"everything derives simply and directly from something else, and everything flows along and evens out"—breaks through the confines of Euclidean thought and finds its true significance in nature as one whole whose bond is universal love. "Everything, as in the ocean, flows into and is in communion with the rest: touch it in one place and your action is felt at the opposite end of the earth." Love vanquishes all, including suffering, even useless suffering. In that connection, through which everything reverberates through all the rest, "certainly the birds, and even the children and all the animals which surround you, would be happier if you were better than you are now, even if only a bit better."

Certainly, this goes beyond the Euclidean world which does not recognize another world or its possibility. This is the point of Father Zosima's admonition that nothing has meaning if it lacks "the seeds of the other world." Many things are hidden from us in this world, but in exchange we are given "the secret awareness of a living tie which links us with that higher world." At the high point of Father Zosima's cosmotheandric vision, the refutation of Ivan's atheism is all one with the refutation of Euclidean thought. The love that conquers suffering and frees us is aware of the oneness of reality, of universal relationships, of the unity of the earthly and transcendent to which Dostoyevski makes so many allusions: Alexey who embraces the earth after the death of Father Zosima, Kirilov's praise of eternal harmony, the pilgrim Makar's exaltation of the mystery of the universe. In this non-Euclidean universe, useless suffering remains a scandal but has its place. The idea that "my sin is a loss for all of humanity" and that "my suffering helps to expiate the sins of all men" may be absurd on a Euclidean plane, but here it has a clear and precise meaning.

8

The most telling rebuttal to Ivan, however, is Alexey's. His is the first and last word, an answer which goes to the root of the problem and stamps it with Dostoyevski's definitive solution.

There is One who can pardon because he, though innocent, suffered. There is One who "can pardon all things, dispense pardon to everyone and for everyone because he gave his own blood for everyone and for all transgressions." The world is not absurd nor is redemption a failure. The world is based not on the faulty design of an architect but, as the *Legend* shows, on the infinite sufferings of a redeemer. This was the customary defense and Ivan marveled that his brother had not long since invoked it. In fact, Alexey refers to it only after having made two key points: that the general who delivered up the child to the pack of ferocious hounds deserved to be shot, and that he himself would refuse to be the architect of a world that would require pointless suffering as a condition for universal happiness.

The qualifications are telling; and they indicate the direction of Dostoyevski's thought. The sufferings of Christ, Alexey maintains, are not to be used in order to silence the lamentations of those subject to pointless suffering. To do so is indeed to give scandal. Alexey, too, refuses "to accept the world" but that non-acceptance has nothing to do with the rejection of God. That is the point of his comment to Rakitin who took

him by surprise in a moment of doubt: "It is not that I rebel against my God. I simply do not accept his world." The scandal remains but so does belief. Heartfelt indignation at the scandal of pointless suffering, like a sense of wounded justice, does not make belief in God's existence impossible. Alexey can come to this conclusion because he is not confined to the limits of Ivan's Euclidean universe. In that world there is no redeemer for the suffering of children, no one who can pardon sin, no one who can answer humankind's cry for deliverance, the plea for mercy. Only the Redeemer who accepted suffering himself can grant this pardon and offer this redemption without scandal, in spite of the radical and deep incomprehensibility of pain. Human suffering is a black and bottomless abyss. The Redeemer himself has not explained it. He took suffering on himself in order to free man from it.

For Ivan, obviously, the incomprehensibility of suffering has quite another meaning, and leads coherently not to a universal cosmic indifference but to something which resembles a Satanodicy, a vindication of Satan. From this perspective, this incomprehensibility can never be healed, much less dissipated.

All scandal disappears, conversely, if God Himself suffers and wishes to do so. Compared to this mystery, a manifestation of a world which transcends ours, nothing can seem scandalous nor can anything be said on the problem of suffering. God's suffering is the only answer we have to the problem of pointless suffering: the only "explanation" we are given. There is the scandal of the pointless suffering of the one who is without guilt; there is the scandal of the Redeemer who suffers and dies.

9

Dostoyevski stops at this point. But I wish to press on since the ultimate significance of what he says transcends what he states explicitly. We must, that is, seek to elaborate Dostoyevski's fundamental idea, that if the human race has been freed from suffering by God who has taken it upon himself, then our sharing in the Redeemer's suffering, which is the key to the meaning of our suffering, has suppressed our own (I Peter 1:19; 21-24).

Christ's suffering is a monstrous event. It throws light on the human tragedy extending that tragedy to the Godhead. Pointless suffering, in this sense, is an exemplar. The suffering is in God and God must suffer. If this is so, suffering, no longer limited to humankind, becomes infinite. It takes its place at the very heart of reality; it acquires theogonic significance. Suffering is all the more terrible when we believe that God chooses to suffer and does so. Undoubtedly the most appallingly dramatic moment in Christ's suffering occurs when, hanging on the cross, he feels himself abandoned by

God. This is a real abandonment, as Kierkegaard notes, such as could not happen to a human but only to a God-man. God answers Christ's cry with silence—double cruelty of a God who willed that his Son should suffer but abandoned him in the moment of suffering. This means that God is cruel above all to himself and therefore abandons himself to the crucifixion. He did not spare his son—that is, himself—and in a sort of sublime masochism took up arms against himself. There is in God a radical and basic cruelty which leads him to deny himself and to rise up against himself.

A law of expiation bends humanity under the weight of a suffering destiny; we are rescued by unexpected grace, God's pardon. But this pardon is made possible by virtue of a tragedy even more terrible than the human one: the suffering of Christ and his abandonment by God in his most despairing moment. To the human tragedy, dominated by a law of expiation, we see added another, divine and theogonic: God pitted against himself.

When Dostoyevski, with Alexey's words, proposes the suffering Christ as a living denial of the failure of creation and redemption, he is urging, in effect, a renewal of a *theologia crucis.* In its spirit is a central, pivotal truth that refutes Ivan's atheism. On the level of a higher atheism, we can discern in God himself a profound and paradoxical atheistic moment. The agony of Christ which, by introducing suffering into the divine, makes that suffering infinite and makes the human drama divine, also implies a denial in God. God denies God, as in the anonymous phrase, *Nemo contra Deum nisi Deus ipse* (No one against God but God Himself), cited by Goethe.

We are not dealing only with the concept, so typically Dostoyevskian, of an atheistic moment in theism. We are dealing with the idea, no less in conformity with his thought, of an atheistic moment in God. At the culmination of his tragic drama, God denies himself: this is the moment of crucifixion, this unheard of, totally bewildering moment, this "suicide" that is both sublime and terrifying.

10

As we meditate on the suffering Christ, we begin to make our way to a dialectic concept of God who has within himself antinomy and contradiction, opposition and contrast, discord and conflict. We grope towards a God who, out of love, is both cruel and merciful towards humans and towards Himself; who, out of love, is cruel towards himself to the point of wanting to suffer, and towards the Son to the point of abandoning Him; who, out of love, is caught up in death and self-destruction since "Love," in the words of Angelus Silesius, "drags God to death."

Die Liebe reizt Gott in Tod. What an unfathomable convergence of love and cruelty! It is the very love of God that devises the sacrifice of Christ:

O that God is crucified! That one can wound Him!
That He bears the outrage inflicted on Him!
That He endures such fear and dread and that He can die!
Do not be astonished, Love devised this.

Here we have entwined in the divine antinomy the impassivity of the transcendent God and the anguish of the incarnate Christ. We can understand that God is silent and cries out in pain; that his silence is for suffering mankind and for the Son at the height of his agony; that God is impassive and cries out in the anguish of Christ's humanity. On the cross, God abandons the Son, and the Son laments and suffers in his abandonment.

The dialectic God in continual flux between the terms of conflict within him may have a certain ambiguity, but precisely because of this he is less vulnerable to refutation than a non-dialectic God. Useless suffering supplies the means to criticize traditional theodicy. Such a critique has little force against a God who is good, close, living, merciful, and powerless but at the time distant, cruel, silent and awesome.

By virtue of this dialectic, God's triumph over suffering is accomplished precisely at the high point of God's suffering. The moment at which, with the abandonment of Christ on the cross, God's pain reaches its climax, is also the moment in which suffering is defeated and overcome for all time. Negation, introduced in the most scandalous form possible into the dialectic God, is thereby all the more decisively refuted and overcome. If God's conflict with himself has not divided him, neither will the negation annihilate him. The more he is subject to negation, the less harm it inflicts on him. The more he embraces it and gathers it into himself, the more he is its master. God's terrible struggle within himself, far from destroying him, confirms him in his coherence and purges him once and for all of negativity. Divine suffering is at last complete expiation and liberation, the ultimate victory over evil and pain. It is the moment of the highest triumph of denial—that is, of evil and suffering, which very nearly takes possession of God. This is denial's furthermost reach, beyond which it cannot go. And if at this most vulnerable point, God does not crumble under this assault, then denial has been vanquished for all time and the human being has been freed from suffering.

In God's inner struggle with his own atheistic moment, evil and suffering are destroyed, denial demolished, the veil of anguish that enfolds the suffering core of reality dissolved. Evil and suffering are abysses which only God can illuminate, which only he can vanquish by embodying them within himself. This is a great and terrible mystery. In redeeming suffering by taking it on himself, God opposes himself and rises up against himself. He is pitiless towards the Son; in effect, he heightens, magnifies, makes the suffering of the world theogonic. Yet the same God is also the conqueror of suffering, the redeemer of humanity, the God who confirms himself in his being. The atheistic moment in divinity is also its theistic moment. The lowest point of God's powerlessness—the suffering of Christ—is also the high point of his power. Greater omnipotence cannot be imagined than that of a God who does not cease to be powerful in utter helplessness. No sign of omnipotence is as eloquent as a luminous victory won over suffering and evil by utter helplessness. The defeat of evil, suffering and the powers of destruction is the victory of a powerless God, so weak as to incur suffering and death. In his powerlessness, God shows his omnipotence.

Today, as yesterday, the ever-recurring and troubling center of our meditations is the problem of good and evil. In this Christian answer to the problem, the ancient and recurring notion that evil and good remain incomprehensible unless somehow, in a divine drama, they are borne within divinity itself, assumes its most sublime form. Dostoyevski confirms this truth and illuminates it.

The tragedy of humanity's subjection to suffering is also the tragedy of God's conflict with himself. Profoundly Christian, this truth is exceptionally important for a daily rediscovery of Christianity. Nonetheless, this universalist moment ought to win consideration by non-Christians as well. No one today can be a Christian without taking Dostoyevski into account, any more than if he ignores Kierkegaard. But a meditation on this theme, insofar as it sets out to penetrate the mystery of suffering, goes beyond the question of atheism, beyond the problem of the existence of God. It transfigures these problems in the act of restoring them to their true and deepest meaning, on a level such as that on which even a Goethe could affirm that Christianity "disclosed to us the divine depths of suffering," a plane on which the anguished compassion for human suffering and a trembling foreboding of transcendence can draw all thinking people, believers and non-believers, together.

Carol Apollonio Flath (essay date winter 1993)

SOURCE: Flath, Carol Apollonio. "Fear of Faith: The Hidden Religious Message of *Notes from Underground*." *Slavic and East European Journal* 37, no. 4 (winter 1993): 510-29.

[*In the following essay, Flath investigates the Christian themes of Dostoevsky's mature works by focusing on the author's treatment of God and humanity in* Notes from Underground.]

I. The Lost Message

. . . the human soul [. . .] either turns towards God— and thus, for the length of its earthly life, retains deep

within itself an awareness of Him and belief in Him; or turns away from Him—and can then, all its life long, no more remember Him or believe in Him, even if it yearns for Faith or speaks of Faith. Hovering solitary in the void, such a soul finds no true access to men— for only in God can man truly be known by man. It dreams of mankind and of the world, and hates both the dream and its own yearning for the tormenting dream's deception . . .

(Ivanov 18)

Some of the most profound readers of Dostoevskij have focused on the religious message of his fictional works. In the process, though faithful to the author's intent, they have tended to abandon textual analysis in favor of sermonizing; understandably, they have concentrated on Dostoevskij's mature works—those novels in which the religious theme is set forth explicitly and unambiguously. And yet, paradoxically—though appropriately, for Dostoevskij, since the message is so well hidden in it—it is in *Notes from Underground* that the author makes his most profound statement of the human need for Christ; it is here that he initiates the exploration of human separation from God that will dominate all of his mature work.[1] My goal here will be to anchor a discussion of the Christian theme that underlies Dostoevskij's mature work in an investigation of the specific language and plot of this literary text which, in my view, comprises the most perfect unity of genre and message of all the author's works.

The narrator of *Notes from Underground* finds himself in a condition of "fateful/fatal intermediacy" (роковая промежуточность) (Semenova 170) that immobilizes him on several planes: physically, the Underground Man finds himself trapped in his corner, symbolically expressed as the place between the floorboards and the ground (or the ceiling below); temporally he is at middle age (forty, halfway to his self-scheduled death at eighty) or in his "phases (bands)" (полосы)[2]; psychologically,

я не только злым, но даже и ничем не сумел сделаться: ни злым, ни добрым, ни подлецом, ни честным, ни героем, ни насекомым.

(100)

[Not only couldn't I become spiteful, I couldn't become anything at all: neither spiteful nor good, neither a scoundrel nor an honest man, neither a hero nor an insect.]

Dostoevskij's skill at depicting these levels can lead to an overemphasis of their importance ("His illness is not merely physical . . . , it is *psychological* . . . the underground man has strong sado-masochistic tendencies which condition both his 'philosophy' and his behavior" [my emphasis] (Peace 12)). A careful look at the text will reveal that the narrator's illness actually stems from a more profound level of intermediacy, the spiritual crisis that Dostoevskij himself asserted was his primary message in the *Notes*. Because he is unwilling or unable to commit himself to Christ, the Underground Man is trapped between the world of God and that of humanity. The issue bears some resemblance to the notion of limbo in Roman Catholic theology, the exile suffered by children who die before baptism—that is, in a state of original sin; it is a kind of "intermediate damnation."[3] Since the narrator's secular, rational world view will not allow him to identify this as the root cause of his crisis, he refers to it as a disease, using the clichés of medicine, which, together with the other sciences, usurped religion in the 1860s. Although we can find no evidence to indicate that Dostoevskij was consciously thinking about the issue in these terms while working on *Notes from Underground,* the idea of original sin will help us identify the spiritual source for the Underground Man's crisis, and the idea of exile from God's kingdom—its consequence.

The most perceptive readers of *Notes from Underground* have agreed on the work's spiritual message: the narrator's anguished inertia can be relieved only by belief in Christ (Jackson, Frank, Walicki and others). They all quote an external source: the author's famous letter to his brother Mixail written on March 26, 1864, after the first part, the "article," was published:

> Уж лучше было совсем не печатать предпоследней главы (самой главной, где самая-то мысль и высказывается) чем печатать так, как оно есть, т.е. с надерганными фразами и противореча самой себе. но что ж делать? Свиньи цензора, там, где я глумился над всем и иногда богохульствовал для виду,—то пропущено, а где из всего этого я вывел потребность веры и христа,—то запрещено.
>
> (XXVIII, 73)

> [It would have been better not to publish the penultimate chapter at all (the main one, where the essential thought is expressed) than to publish it the way it is, i.e. with its forced sentences and internal contradictions. But what is to be done? The censors are swine; they passed the parts where I ridiculed everything and sometimes blasphemed for show, but they cut the part where I deduced from all this the need for belief and for Christ.]

Dostoevskij's intent is clearly expressed in this letter. But what about the text of the *Notes?* Why have so many perceptive readers (Šestov, Mixailovskij, Baxtin, Wasiolek, Holquist) passed over this message—Dostoevsky's central idea—in the text of the work itself? Even those who focus on it agree that it is only hinted at in the text (with the exception of Frank; see note 12). At best, they point out a passage in Chapter XI of Part I (e.g. Katz' note, p. 26):

> . . . вовсе не подполье лучше, а что-то другое, совсем другое, которого я жажду, но которого никак не найду! к черту подлолье!
>
> (121)

> [. . . it isn't at all the underground that's better, but something different, completely different, something that I long for, but cannot find! The underground can go to the devil!]

If indeed Dostoevskij had intended the Underground Man's conflict to be resolved in belief in Christ, why didn't he restore the censored passage in later editions? Is it simply another example of his characteristic, and somewhat masochistic, technique of giving the strongest arguments—best exemplified in the Grand Inquisitor chapter of *The Brothers Karamazov*—to his antagonist (PSS notes, V, 379)? Or did he leave it out for aesthetic reasons—allowing the fictional plot, rather than the narrator's or author's analysis, to carry the message (Todorov 91)? If so, he overestimated his readers. The reader, like Ivanov's "lost" soul, and like the Underground Man himself, is unable to find the "lost" message, remember it or believe in it. Without attempting to rediscover the author's own motives in leaving the deletion unrestored, I will try to build upon and move beyond Todorov's reliance on plot for his argument, and prove that the very way Dostoevskij presents his message actually does convey it, even as the surface meanings of his words do not.

We are searching for an artistic unity of message and form. Given the contradictory, rough nature of the *Notes* and its ambiguous genre, such a unity would not be expected to be *harmonious*. But if Dostoevskij intended its tensions and contradictions to be resolved in religious belief, surely he would not have isolated this message in a single passage; surely it would have permeated the work in some form or other. In this close reading of the text I will be looking for patterns that, taken together with this famous passage about "something different," would direct us to the deeply spiritual nature of the Underground Man's predicament and the potential for its resolution through Christ.[4]

Investigating genre (Dostoevskij's parody of the confession genre), language (significant ambiguities in the meanings of certain words) and plot (the Underground Man's behavior in part II), we will discover on all three levels a pattern of denial and perversion of Christian grace that, through *reverse* example, directs us back to the religious message that Dostoevskij claimed to have put in the text to begin with. The fact that the message is never stated explicitly is fully consistent with the mature Dostoevsky's pattern of giving eloquence of expression to his atheists (best represented by Ivan Karamozov), while reserving to God's messengers the "last word," which is not a word at all, but a silent eloquence of gesture (the kiss of grace given by Aleša Karamazov and by Christ). In *Notes from Underground,* as in *The Brothers Karamazov,* the embrace (Liza's, Aleša's) fails to bring the nonbeliever (the Underground Man, Ivan) to God's grace, but as our pattern will reveal, the issue will be clear to the reader, if not to the fictional recipient of the message: a choice between God—specifically, Christ—and spiritual nothingness—"intermediate" damnation.

II. THE FALSITY (FAITHLESSNESS) OF LITERARY CONFESSIONS

Confession, as a genre that allows exploration of the deepest secrets of an individual's psychology, has been especially valued by modern writers, beginning with Rousseau (with a glance backwards, of course, to St. Augustine). Dostoevskij used the confession form in some of his greatest works and engaged in a lifelong polemic with Rousseau (Belknap, Howard, Lotman, Miller); *Notes from Underground* itself was originally called "Confession" (*Ispoved'*). Robert Belknap has shown how both Rousseau and Dostoevskij departed from the traditional genre of "repentant confession." Rousseau, he suggests, wrote an apologia; *Notes from Underground* is an "unrepentant confession," a confession that lacks both repentance (an essential part of a true confession) and a justification for the confessor's wrong acts (apologia). In *Notes from Underground* the confessor's refusal to repent allows him to take pleasure in his lack of contrition (as Volkovskij in *The Insulted and Injured* calls it, "the thrill of indecent exposure") and to deny the reader the opportunity to feel self-righteous (as Belknap puts it, "to withdraw authority from the reader" [122]).[5] An exploration of what drives the Underground Man to use confession in this way will lead us directly to the schism that prevents him from accepting religious faith, imprisoning him in his spiritual intermediacy.

Dostoevskij's anti-hero writes an *anti-confession*. He repeatedly casts doubt on the truthfulness of his own words:

> Это я наврал про себя давеча, что я был злой чиновник. . . .

> [I wasn't telling the truth just now when I said that I was a nasty official . . .]

> Ведь через минуту какую-нибудь я уже с злобою соображаю, бывало, что все это ложь, ложь, отвратительная напускная ложь.

> (107)

> [And in a minute I would already be realizing that it was all a lie, a disgusting, pretentious lie.]

and he attacks Rousseau's model explicitly, quoting Heine:

> Гейне утверждает, что верные автобиографии почти невозможны, и человек сам об себе наверно налжет. По его мнению, Руссо, например, непременно налгал на себя в своей исповеди, и даже умышленно налгал, из тщеславия. Я уверен, что Гейне прав . . .

> (122)

[Heine asserts that true autobiographies are nearly impossible, and that a man will surely lie about himself. In his opinion Rousseau, for example, undoubtedly lied about himself, in fact, even lied deliberately, out of vanity. I am sure that Heine is right.]

Why are true autobiographies (confessions) impossible? Why, when he uses the genre, does the Underground Man have to lie?

The answer can be found in our realization that, by appropriating a religious sacrament for secular use, Rousseau has committed sacrilege. His confession addresses *people,* not God[6]. That is why it is false, that is why the Underground Man, though aware at least of the wrongness of Rousseau's apologia, must inevitably lie in his own confession. This is his first denial of the possibility of Grace. He cannot give up the language of rationality and rationalization and submit to the unquestioning faith that would allow him to be truthful in a deeper sense. The very wording of his attack exposes the real issue, lack of faith (вера): <u>верные</u> автобиографии невозможны . . . <u>наверно</u> налжет . . . , я уверен . . .[7].

For the same reason, he cannot identify his readers or communicate meaningfully with them:

> Для чего, в самом деле, называю я вас «господами», для чего обращаюсь к вам, как будто и вправду к читателям? Таких признаний, какие я намерен начать излагать, не лечатают и другим читать не дают.

> (122)

[Why is it that I call you "gentlemen;" why do I address you as though I'm really addressing readers? The kinds of confession I intend to set forth are not published or given to other people to read.]

Misappropriation of the sacrament of confession is analogous to selling one's soul (a theme developed in Part II):

> Вы скажете, что пошло и подло выводить все это теперь на рынок . . .

> (134)

[You will say that it is base and mean to bring all this out now onto the marketplace.]

Realizing that he cannot confess to other people, and unable to address God, as a true ("faithful") confessor must, he turns to himself, initiating the solipsistic pattern that will afflict all Dostoevsky's doubting protagonists:

> Но Гейне судил о человеке, исповедовавшемся перед публикой. Я же пишу для одного себя и раз навсегда объявляю, что если я и пишу как бы обращаясь к читателям, то единственно только

для показу, потому что так мне легче писать. Тут
форма, одна пустая форма, читателей же у меня
никогда не будет.

(122)

[But Heine was judging a man confessing before the
public. As for me, I write for myself alone and announce once and for all that if it seems in my writing
that I am addressing readers, that is only for show, because it's easier for me to write that way. It's just a
form, an empty form, and I never will have readers.]

He claims that he is writing to no one, but we, reading
it, realize this cannot be true. By speaking and writing
at all, the Underground Man is at least trying to address
someone else, and even his excuse (для показу) betrays his orientation to a reader or watcher).[8] He cannot
communicate with his imaginary readers because he
cannot acknowledge the presence in them of God's
grace and recognize his own need to gain it, through
Christ. It remains to us (*Dostoevskij*'s readers) to discover this message in his text.

Thus the Underground Man finds himself trapped *between God and his fellow men,* unable to communicate
with either. Without God, contact with other people is
meaningless, and true confession is impossible
(Likewise, when the Underground Man turns to *exposé*
(обличение), its direct opposite, in his feeble attempt
to escape the trap of literary confession (pp. 129-130),
he inevitably fails.) His improper use of the confession
genre is the underlying reason for the Underground
Man's imprisonment in literary clichés—which has been
thoroughly analyzed in the criticism (notably by Frank
(parody) and Holquist (plot). By drawing attention to
the inability of "secular" language and genre to express
a deeper truth, Dostoevskij paradoxically enables us to
reach an understanding of that truth—without ever hearing its name. In this sense he is justified in not restoring
that censored passage in which he tried to express it directly; the fictional (false) narrator is left to continue
fruitlessly addressing fictional readers, but Dostoevskij
has communicated his message to *us*. In this sense anti-
confession has allowed true confession to take place.

III. Original Sin, The Impossibility of Human Forgiveness and the Need for Gratitude

The theme of forgiveness is as important in Dostoevskij's mature novels as that of confession. But it too
is already fully explored in *Notes from Underground*.
Since the Underground Man cannot confess faithfully,
he also cannot ask honestly for forgiveness. Here, too,
he is trapped. He feels guilty, but the very determinism
he attacks—the "wall" and the "laws of nature"—won't
let him admit his guilt:

. . . как будто чем-то сам виноват, хотя опять-
таки до ясности очевидно, что вовсе не виноват . . .

(106)

. . . as though guilty of something, though then again
obviously not guilty at all . . .

. . . всего обиднее, без вины виноват, и так ска-
зать, по законам природы.

. . . and most insulting of all, guilty without guilt, and,
so to speak, by the laws of nature.

Determinism necessarily absolves people of guilt; where
there is no choice there is no responsibility.[9] Now if we
look beyond the incidental, surface guilts that the narrator is desperately trying to confess, we can identify
their root cause as *original sin*—the guilt that is without guilt—and here again it becomes clear why confession of it, and forgiveness for it, is impossible. The Underground Man suffers for the sins of his entire secular
generation. He and his contemporaries find themselves
in a condition best described by Ivanov:

. . . the operation of Luciferian forces in man—a necessary consequence of that spiritual event, the defection
from God which the Church calls the Fall of Man—is
in this world a natural presupposition and basis of all
our historical and, to this day, largely heathen civilization, and is, in truth, our civilization's Original Sin
. . .

(130)

Original sin denies responsibility, but requires, for
grace, confession and forgiveness. The Underground
Man cannot confess, because, as a representative of the
"age of reason," he is condemned to a vain search for a
rational explanation of his guilt—a secular absolution.
In this context our attention is drawn to a curious passage, where the Underground Man, who apparently has
no family ties whatever, and has not referred to any in
the past, mentions a "dear papa":

Да и вообще терпеть не мог говорить: "Простите,
папаша, вперед не буду."

(107)

[And in general I couldn't bear saying, "Forgive me
Papa, I won't do it again."]

Even accepting the possibility that "papaša" is an empty
"filler" word, and putting aside the issue of possible
Freudian interpretations, the word sounds strange coming from our apparently parentless narrator and is certainly not an accepted cliché in the Russian language.
Couldn't we speculate that, if indeed the guilt he feels
is Original Sin, this is an indirect reference to the only
possible recipient of his confession, God the father?

A blurring of the boundary between God and humanity
is a central theme in Dostoevskij; from it comes the
evil of the Man-God he explores so eloquently in his
later works. In retrospect we can see that his attention
is drawn to it in his earliest works as well, although the
theme is only hinted at in them. In his 1928 article

about "The Nose" and *The Double,* for example, A. L. Bem indirectly shows how Golyadkin makes the mistake of seeing God in any secular figure of authority:

> . . . for him authority is somehow connected with his father and even with the Higher Being, God . . . 'I look upon our benevolent superior as a father,' he says continually. His imagined words to his Excellency sound almost like a prayer. . . . From all this, it is apparent that Dostoevsky gave the episode with the authorities substantial significance in the development of his tale. It is possible only to hint at it here.
>
> (240)

Whatever Bem's reasons for not developing this important idea in his article—and it is tempting to speculate on them—we can suggest that it is indeed this tendency to see God in the person of secular authorities rather than in a sacred realm that is a root cause of Golyadkin's own tragic split. Though *The Double* is not our focus here, the foreshadowing in it of Dostoevskij's later treatment of spiritual *raskol* deserves further attention; this work is too often read on a purely psychological level. In Dostoevskij's mature novels there is no ambiguity: usurpation of God—and God's work—by human beings is what causes the internal division that torments Raskol'nikov and Ivan Karamazov. We will turn to this theme in more detail in our discussion of the plot in Part II of *Notes from Underground.*

The Underground Man cannot ask forgiveness from a God he cannot accept. Instead, he tried to circumvent God, seeking the forgiveness he needs in other people—and naturally fails. This is his second denial of God's grace. When after the disastrous dinner party his companions decide to go to the brothel and he realizes that he must go with them (fate is already leading him to Liza and his chance at salvation), he begs their forgiveness (147-8). Zverkov does not grant it, claiming that the likes of the Underground Man could not possibly insult him. When the roles are reversed and the Underground Man craves for himself the power to forgive others—like his servant Apollon, this too is impossible. He demands that Apollon beg forgiveness from him before he will agree to give him his salary (here trying to *sell* forgiveness just as Rousseau sells confession and Liza sells her purity). The servant's inevitable answer is "Быть того не может!" (170). ["That cannot be!"]

And when the Underground Man turns to Liza for forgiveness, his thoughts and dreams, as well as his actions, take on the forms of religious language and gesture, though, true to pattern, never unambiguously so:

> . . . целовать ее ноги, молить о прощении
>
> (177)
>
> . . . to kiss her feet, to beg/*pray* for forgiveness

But ultimately only God can give true forgiveness. On some level both Liza and the Underground Man understand this, though neither of them can put it into words:

> —Лиза, друг мой, я напрасно . . . ты прости меня,—начал было я,—но она сжала в своих пальцах мои руки с такою силою, что я догадался, что не то говорю, и перестал.
>
> (162) [my emphasis]

> ["Liza, my friend, I shouldn't have . . . forgive me," I began, but she squeezed my hands in her fingers with such force that I realized that I was saying the *wrong thing,* and I stopped.]

Liza has touched him deeply, on a spiritual level, by communicating this "wrongness" to him. But without consciously recognizing his need for God he cannot escape his tragic condition; when he concludes this conversation, could his "farewell"—immediately corrected to "good-bye"—itself be one last plaintive and urgent (imperfective) request for forgiveness, even though he knows it will be in vain? The word farewell in Russian, after all, is identical to the imperfective of the word to forgive:

> —а теперь я уйду, прощай . . . до свидания.
>
> (162)

> ["And now I'll leave, farewell/forgive, . . . goodbye."]

In this context we can make sense of a passage that resists a comfortable interpretation in a purely secular reading of the text. One of the most characteristic traits of humanity, in the Underground Man's opinion, is "ingratitude":

> Господа, положим, что человек не глуп . . . Но если и не глуп, то все-таки чудовищно неблагодарен! Неблагодарен феноменально. Я даже думаю, что самое лучшее определение человека—зто: существо на двух ногах и неблагодарное.
>
> (115-6)

> [Gentlemen, let's assume that man is not stupid . . . But if he's not stupid, still he's monstrously ungrateful! Phenomenally ungrateful. I even think that the best definition of man is: a two-legged creature who is ungrateful.]

The concept of gratitude entails an object—someone to whom it is directed. Given that this quality, in the Underground Man's formulation, defines all of humanity, its intended recipient must necessarily be non-human; in context, we are led to identify him as God, albeit a God the Underground Man cannot let himself recognize.

IV. The Man-God in *Notes from Underground* False and Wrongful Salvation

When the Underground Man attempts to make others ask his forgiveness, or forgive him, he is trying to appropriate, or to grant to humans, a power that rightfully belongs to God. This is essentially what he did with the confession genre, when he claimed that he was writing for himself alone. Given the nature of the confession genre and the Underground Man's rejection of a human audience, we can only presume that, by confessing to himself, he is trying to *take on the identity of God, thereby usurping him.* This desired usurpation of God—even with altruistic motives—человеколюбие, "love of humanity" (Frank 193)—is the true cause of his predicament, and it lies at the root of modern Existentialism. The wrongness of an attempt to replace God (thus becoming the Man-God) is central to Dostoevskij's religious philosophy and has been thoroughly explored in the context of the mature novels. But our analysis of the text will show that the idea is already developed in *Notes from Underground.*

I will not discuss the social and political utopias that Dostoevsky is attacking—in particular the one described by Černyševskij in *What is to be Done;* they have been thoroughly studied (Frank, Walicki). For our purposes, the important idea, from the point of view of the Underground Man's spiritual health, is that utopian philosophies, by presuming that people can create their own ideal societies on earth, implicitly deny God his exclusive power to grant human happiness. The Underground Man, as a representative of the idealistic generation of the '40s, like Stepan Verxovenskij after him, has inexorably moved away from God. In the meantime the idealistic humanism of the '40s has become the atheistic materialism of the '60s. And inevitably the Underground Man, subconsciously denying God but fighting atheism, finds himself "play-acting" a divine role—the Man-God. On one hand, he tries to act as God the Savior; on the other, he play-acts Christ the Martyr. This fruitless imitation of God, taking place in the absence of God, is the Underground Man's third denial of grace. It seems to be an empty "game" (the word игра allows interpretation as both "game" and "play-acting"), but, as the Underground Man admits, it is more than a game. In trying to imitate God, while denying him, the Underground Man's confession turns into travesty, and he inevitably finds himself carrying out the devil's work[10].

This role-playing is a kind of *mimesis,* and, appropriately, it is enacted through the plot of Part II, "On Account of the Wet Snow," which, unlike Part I, is presented in a form that corresponds to conventional narrative. The Nekrasov poem that Dostoevskij chose for the epigraph directs our attention to the by then already hackneyed plot of rescue of a fallen woman by an enlightened man of the forties; for our purposes the word спасение can be translated either "rescue" or "salvation." The relation of the epigraph to the plot of "On Account of the Wet Snow" have given rise to widely varying interpretations. In the most thought-provoking one, Robert Louis Jackson points out the

ironic reversal of roles of the man and woman, arguing that it is the fallen woman, Liza, who is the rescuer (180-83), but that Dostoevsky, deeply respecting the theme of the "restoration of the fallen man" (181) is not attacking the salvation myth itself:

> . . . the reader realizes that it is the Underground Man, not Dostoevsky, who has been savagely parodying Nekrasov and that he has now been trapped by his own parody. Dostoevsky did not abandon the idealistic ethos of the 1840s, but reinvested it with a tragic Christian content.
>
> (182)

Jackson apparently would agree here with Skaftymov that in *Notes From Underground* Dostoevsky reaffirmed the humanistic idealism of the '40s. But if we accept this conclusion, the outcome of the plot brings up an important question: why does Liza not succeed in saving the Underground Man (Jackson's "tragic content")? Does her failure imply that he is beyond salvation, that his sin is so grave that he is doomed? I would suggest that it is not the Underground Man's refusal to accept Liza's forgiveness, but rather his refusal to accept *God's grace* (through her), that causes the failure. Love and forgiveness from another person offers an opportunity for salvation, but it is only the first step (Miller 99); salvation can only come from a conscious acceptance of God himself, not merely from the love and forgiveness of another person. This would explain why the Underground Man experiences momentary relief, but cannot maintain it; he cannot give up his role as the "savior" to accept true salvation for himself.

The language in "On Account of the Wet Snow" reinforces such a conclusion. When he tyrannizes over his servant Apollon and Liza, the Underground Man is actually attempting to take on divine power. To explain his decision to withold Apollon's wages, for example, he refers to his "will as master" (воля господская-168), which we might easily translate as "God's will". But the pattern is most obvious in his two interactions with Liza (Chapters VI-X of Part II).

The Underground Man clearly wants to gain control of Liza's soul. Acting as a Man-God, seemingly attempting to rescue her, he finds himself doing the devil's work:

> Черт возьми, это любопытно, зто—сродни,—думал я,—чуть не потирая себе руки.—Да и как с молодой такой думой не справиться?.
>
> (156)

["Devil take it, this is curious, this is *related*" all but rubbing my hands to gether. "And how could I not manage with such a young soul." (Dostoevsky's emphasis; I would emphasize "Devil take it . . .")]

"И как мало, мало,—думал я мимоходом,—нужно было слов, как мало нужно было идиллии (да и идиллии-то еще напускной, книжной, сочиненной), чтоб тотчас же и повернуть всю уеловеческую душу по-своему. То-то девственностьто! То-то свежесть-то почвы!"

(166)

[And how very few words, thought I in passing, how little idyllic sentiment (and forced, bookish, artificial at that), were needed to immediately bend human soul in my own way. There's innocence for you! There's virgin soil!]

In this "idyllic sentiment," a holdover from a Romantic view of the world, we can detect Dostoevskij's veiled attack on those ideals of the forties that made men think themselves capable of performing a savior's role. The Underground Man makes it quite clear that he is acting; true to his pattern of denial, however, he cannot admit he is playing God. But we can figure it out:

Давно уже предчувствовал я, что перевернул всю ее душу и разбил ее сердце, и, чем больше я удостоверялся в том, тем больше желал поскорее и как можно силбнее достигнуть цели. Игра, чгра увлекла меня; впрочем, не одна чгра . . .

(162) [my emphasis]

[I had already sensed long before that I *had turned her entire soul inside out* and had broken her heart, and the more I became convinced of it, the more I wanted to quickly and as forcefully as possible to achieve my goal. It was the *game/play* that attracted me, *and by the way, not only that* . . .]

In these passages and others throughout Part II, The Underground Man makes it clear that he is attempting to gain control over Liza's soul. Unable to trust God to save human souls, he turns again to himself. The language of "selling souls"—which parallels the language of "selling confession in the marketplace"—permeates these chapters. The Underground Man torments Liza with the thought that she has already sold her soul and brings her to the point where she almost succumbs; she seems to see him as a kind of "higher being" (высшее существо-163)—a God.

Again he does not realize what he is doing; at first he believes (or at least "dreams"/мечтать, 166) he can save her soul; the idea of "rescue/salvation" appears repeatedly throughout the text, as for example when he dreams: я спасаю Лизу (166). [I save Liza]; она бросается к ногам моим и говорит, что я ее спасчмель и что она меня любит больше всего на свеме (167) [my emphasis]. [She throws herself at my feet and says that I am her *savior* and that she loves me more than anything *on earth*]. But it is from this false attempt at salvation that all the evil comes. When the Underground Man seems to realize the gravity of his sin, at least, if not its true nature, he substitutes for the word "savior/rescuer" (спаситель) the more clearly religious/blasphemous one "savior/resurrector" (воскреситель

[174]), in his accusation of himself. He finally understands that it is as impossible for him to save her as it is for him to restore her virginity, and the sad scenario of the weeping prostitute with the fish that he describes in Chapter VII of Part II comes to describe his own, and Liza's, predicament: the fish, a traditional symbol of Christ, is pickled and dead, powerless, and the prostitute, denied its power of salvation (unlike her biblical predecessor), can only beat it against the steps and face her own grim death.

The other aspect of the Underground Man's play-acting is the martyr role; the "passion" with which he embraces his suffering is analogous to Christ's Passion (страсть) (Человек иногда ужасно любит страдание, до страсти . . . [119] Man sometimes terribly loves suffering, to the point of passion). By embracing the suffering of his disease of acute self-consciousness he takes on the sins of humanity, freeing his contemporaries from an awareness of the falsity of their rationalistic world view. In this way, rather than saving them, he deludes them—deluding, I might add, many readers along the way,—into thinking his is the "last word."

It is this level of the text that readers like Mixailovskij or Peace miss when they emphasize the psychological basis of the Underground Man's cruelty. Dostoevskij, unlike his narrator, is playing no game; he is using his characters to enact a deadly serious mystery play about that very struggle between God and the Devil over human souls that Dmitrij Karamazov is to describe in the author's last, and greatest, novel.

V. Real Life

Notes from Underground can be interpreted as the lamentation of a man who cannot participate meaningfully in contemporary social or political life. Such an interpretation would draw on the opposition within the text itself between the Underground Man's debilitating and continual self-analysis and the non-reflective activity of specific men he encounters: the billiard-playing officer, Zverkov, his other former schoolmates and generalized "men of action"—a cliche of the sixties. Words such as "living life" (живая жизнь) "reality" (действительность) and "activity" (деятельность) can be assumed to signify the realm of social activity. The Underground Man becomes pure consciousness; Zverkov ("beast") becomes pure physicality (the *raskol* is externalized), and even such events as the narrator's inability to make physical contact with his "officer" can be explained by an understanding of him as basically incorporeal. The fact that the ("superfluity vs. activity") issue was one of the most hotly debated topics in Russian intellectual and literary circles of the day contributes to the authority of such an interpretation.

In other places "real life" seems intended by the Underground Man to refer to the world of Romantic idealism.

Without rejecting the validity of these two potent lines of thought, we will see that the "real life" the Underground Man craves is something deeper than social action or Romantic ideals. These are simply delusions, distracting his attention from the world of God's grace that lies behind them. It is in his references to "real life" that the narrator comes closest to a direct expression of the true nature of his need and in fact to a reconciliation of the ostensibly conflicting realms of action and ideals[11]. In spite of himself he bears the potential for religious salvation; it lies in his refusal to accept a cheap version of reality (a cheap happiness-[178]), one in which (false) salvation can be gained through mere human activity in an exclusively material world or through empty Romantic dreaming.

The Underground Man will not let himself be content with a diminished dream:

> Зачем же я устроен с такими желаниями? неужели ж я для того только и устроен, чтоб дойти до заключения, что всё мое устройство одно надувание? неужели в этом вся цель? не верю.
>
> [my emphasis] (121)

> [Why was I made with such desires? Can it be that I was made only to come to the conclusion that my entire being is just a fraud? Can the whole purpose be this? *I don't believe* (so).]

Without committing himself to an unambigious statement for religious belief, in this typically double-layered statement (*I don't believe*) the Underground Man has given us the reason for his plight. He must commit himself to believe, but he cannot. The choice is between God and the laws of nature. And he has shown that the laws of nature are not *real life*; they do not demand belief (belief is unnecessary when everything can be proven logically), and they lead only to *death* (ведь дважды два четыре есть уже не жизнь, господа, а начало смерти [118-9]. [After all, twice two is no longer life, gentlemen, but the beginning of death]).

As for Romantic ideals, in Chapter II of Part II the Underground Man describes the content of his youthful dreams:

> Бывали мгновения такого положительного упоения, такого счастья, что даже малейшей насмешки внутри меня не ощущлось, ей-богу. Была вера, надежда, любовь. то-то и есть, что я слаепо верча тогда, что каким-то чудом, каким-нибудь внешним обстоятельством всё это вдруг раздвинется, расширится; вдруг представится горизонт соответственной деятельности, благотворной, прекрасной, и главное, совсем гомовой (каким именно—я никогда не знал, но, главное,—совсем готовой), и вот я выступлю вдруг на свем божчй, чуть ли не на белом коне . . .
>
> [132-3]

[There were moments of such positive ecstasy, such happiness, that I felt not even the slightest mockery, *so help me God*. There was *faith*, hope, love. The fact was, *I believed blindly* then, that by some *miracle*, some kind of external circumstance all that would suddenly part like a curtain, and would expand; suddenly there would appear a horizon of appropriate activity, beneficial, beautiful, and, most importantly, *completely ready-made* [Dostoevsky's emphasis] (what kind exactly, I never knew, but the main thing was that it be completely ready-mady), and here I step out into *God's world*, all but on a white steed.

Though, true to form, the words maintain their ambiguity, and the nature of the Underground Man's crisis ensures that his dream will be masked in literary cliches (for which the age of "enlightenment" is guilty), I would again suggest that this passage, with its repeated (though, here again, double-edged and ambiguous) references to God and faith, also conveys a dream of religious salvation. The object of the dream is obscure, even to the dreamer, because of the very deceptiveness of the Romantic cliches that have usurped religion for the Underground Man's troubled generation. The secularization of religious words begins here, in the Romantic idealism of the forties, and it will inevitably lead to secularization of religious sacraments (represented by the Underground Man's own denials of grace).

In Part II, while preparing for the dinner with his old schoolmates, he misinterprets this religious craving as a desire to become a man of action (physical action).

> Теперь не до думанья; теперь наступает гейсмвчмельносмь . . . Конечно, всего бы лучме совсем не ехать. Но . . . я бы всю жизнь дразнил себя потом: "А что, струсил, струсил дейсмвчмельносмч, струсил!"
>
> (141) [emphasis mine]

> This was no time for thinking; *reality* was setting in. . . . Of course it would have been best not to go at all. But . . . I would have taunted myself afterwards my whole life: "So you were scared, to scared to face *reality!*"

Ironically, the dinner party was to lead to his chance to face true reality, the reality he craved; his encounter with Liza was to serve as his opportunity to accept God. But, crippled by his fear of faith, he was too scared to act on it.

As Dostoevskij wrote his brother Mixail, only faith will release the Underground Man from his imprisonment in determinism and rationalization; in the author's view, as he will make clear in his later works, this is the only true act of free will possible for humanity. But instead of taking this positive step, his narrator persists in his self-analysis, continually diagnosing himself without admitting the possibility of a cure. In one of the most revealing passages in the *Notes,* the paradigm of confession is reversed; the narrator becomes "you" and the words describing his condition are given to his imagined reader. Confession becomes accusation:

> В вас есть и правда, но в вас нет целомудрия; вы из самого мелкого тщеславия несете вашу правду на показ, на позор, на рынок . . . Вы действительно хотите что-то сказать, но <u>из боязнч прячеме баще последнее слово, помому чмо у вас нем рещчмосмч его высказамь,</u> а только трусливое нахальство. Вы хвалитесь сознанием, но вы только колеблетесь, потому что хоть ум у вас и работает, но сердце ваше развратом помрачено. . . .

> (121-2) [my emphasis]

> There's truth in you, but you have no chastity; out of utterly petty vanity you bring out your truth on display, onto the marketplace, to be shamed . . . There really is something you want to say, but *from fear you conceal your last word, because you lack the resolve to say it,* you have only cowardly impudence. You boast about your consciousness, but you only vascillate, because although your mind works, your heart is darkened by depravity.

What can this "last word" be? In the *Notes* the Underground Man has repeatedly expressed both his craving for action and his futile retreat into Romantic dreams. The "last word" must be something that transcends all the words he speaks. Here I would like to suggest that the Underground Man is aware on some level, though his reason and pride will not let him admit it, of his potential to recognize the deeper truth that we are identifying here as God's grace. It is here that we recognize his paralysis as a *fear of faith*. In this passage he is so close to stating this truth directly that he cannot even trust himself with the words and turns them over to his reader. This truth must transcend the truisms of Romantic idealism; after all, our narrator has already tried to live by them and has recognized them as false, as superficial and unsatisfying as the literary plots they give rise to. But a direct statement of the spiritual nature of the truth is impossible: it would be using words for something that Dostoveskij is saying cannot be expressed in words; it would undermine the plot that conveys this impossibility (if the Underground Man is consciously aware of the potential for salvation within him, or if Liza saves him, he can no longer be maintained in his intermediate state); and Dostoevskij's attack, through parody, on the genre of literary confession, would not allow it—the genre itself would immediately cheapen the message. Thus, by not allowing his narrator to express the religious message directly, Dostoevskij maintains the aesthetic unity of the work. This passage along supports the author's decision not to restore the censored section (and in this sense Todorov is right). For the present "strip of time" the Underground Man is trapped by the very determinism he fights, because he is using its own laws as a weapon.

It is the Underground Man's particular location between the spiritual and material worlds that allows him to diagnose his illness in such detail. The diagnosis is equally applicable to his materialist contemporaries, who are without faith, but unlike him, do not realize the seriousness of their state and do not want to be reminded of it. Since they cannot accept the peculiar illogic of the Underground Man's arguments, and since the nature of the confession genre (or any literary form) will not allow a direct, true expression of religious faith in words, he can only babble and moan at them and hope that they will recognize in his moans the reflection of their own delusions[12]. In the closing paragraph of *Notes from Underground,* without relinquishing the ambiguity of his words, he calls his generation (and generations of readers to come) to recognize that they share his plight:

> Мы все отвыкли от жизни, все хромаем, всякий более или менее. Даже до того отвыкли, что чувствуем подчас к настояющей "живой жизни" какое-то омерзение, а потому и терпеть не можем, когда нам напоминают про нее. Ведь мы до то того дошли, что настоящую жизнь чуть не считаем за труд, почти что за службу, и все мы про себя согласны, что по книжке лучше . . . Ведь мы даже не знаем, где и живое-то живет теперь, и что оно такое, как называется.

> (178-79)

> [We all have grown unaccustomed to life, we are all crippled, each of us more or less. We've gotten so unaccustomed to it, that sometimes we feel a kind of loathing for it, and we can't stand it when someone reminds us of it [as the Underground Man is doing at this moment]. We've even reached the point where we consider real life as hard work, something like service, and we all agree that things are better done through books . . . We don't even know where "real life" is living now, and what it is, what it is called.]

The switch to the first person plural is surely significant. Whereas throughout the text the narrator has been isolating himself from his contemporaries, here suddenly he sees himself as *representative* of them. He recognizes that he shares their delusions. "Real life" here cannot be simply the realm of activity in the social and political world of the sixties; after all, the entire text of the *Notes* has been directed at exposing the shallowness of the rational premises on which it is based. It cannot be simply the world of Romantic idealism; through his own example, where every attempt to live according to Romantic ideals turns on itself and corrupts what it was aimed at exalting, the Underground Man has shown that Romantic dreams only lead *away* from "real life." Instead, this passage is an impassioned appeal to an entire generation, an appeal to his contemporaries to regain the faith that they have all lost, together. Like the possessed nihilists who will be Dostoevskij's focus in *The Devils,* the Underground Man and the contemporaries he addresses here are lost in a secular world, a world that has abandoned religious belief in favor of the "twice-two" rationality that is the beginning of "death." How else can we make sense of his heartfelt lamentation for the "real life" that they have all lost—a passage so important that Dostoevskij offers it in the closing paragraph of his narrator's monologue, where we would normally expect to read a conclusion?

It is especially fitting that Stepan Verxovenskij should arrive at this truth by chance, rather than from logical deduction. At the end of *The Devils,* he asks the "gospel seller," Sofija Matveevna, to read a passage at random. The words she reads from the Apocalypse describe perfectly that intermediate state that crippled his (and his predecessor's) generation, and that cleared the way for the devil to "possess" the generation that followed them, impelling them to the destructive activity that the Underground Man knew was wrong, but was powerless to prevent:

> —И ангелу Лаодикийской церкви напиши: так говорит Аминь, свидетель верный и истинный, начало создания божия. Знаю твои дела; ты ни холоден, ни горяч; о, если б ты был холоден или горяч! Но поелику ты тепл, а не горяч и не холоден, то извергну тебя из уст моих. Ибо ты говоришь: я богат, разбогател, и ни в чем не имею нужды, а не знаешь, что ты несчастен, и жалок, и нищ, и слеп, и наг."

(X, 497)

["'And unto the angel of the church of the Laodiceans write: These things saith the Amen, the faithful and true witness, the beginning of the creation of God; I know thy works, that thou art neither cold nor hot; I would thou wert cold or hot. So then because thou art lukewarm, and neither cold nor hot, I will spue thee out of my mouth. Because thou sayest, I am rich and increased with goods, and have need of nothing: and thou knowest not that thou art wretched, and miserable, and poor, and blind, and naked.'"]

Hearing these words that remind us vividly of the Underground Man's description of his own character (ни злым, ни добрым . . . [see above, p. 0]), Stepan Verxovenskij begins to discover here the truth that eluded his predecessor; evil for Dostoevskij comes from a void, from an absence of commitment and faith. The abandonment of God's grace began with humanists like Rousseau, whose confession bypasses God. By sounding the alarm, and by standing like a reproachful image in a crooked mirror before his contemporaries, the Underground Man, paradoxically, is more alive than they, the unreflective men of action: Я, пожалуй, еще "живее" вас выхожу (178). [In fact I may turn out to be more "alive" than you].

The appeal fails; even the one who voices it fails to heed and understand. But we have discovered that the Underground Man is more than a negative example in

Dostoevskij's characteristic "доказание от противного" (proving by negative example) (Pačini). He preaches a religious message as well, though never unambiguously. Dostoevskij certainly must have hoped that the example of his narrator's suffering, like the passion of Christ, would lead people to faith. In *Notes from Underground,* as in his mature works, the author gave the most direct expression, the *words,* to the ideas he was fighting—but here he ensured that the words would be ambiguous. He had not yet fully developed the silent gesture of faith—the kiss, the embrace or the bow to the earth—that in the later novels brings God's grave to people, through people—but he provided an inconclusive gesture that was full of potential (Liza's embrace). Because of his refusal to resolve the crisis of his narrator (as he does—and he is criticized to this day for doing so—two years later with Raskol'nikov), the *Notes,* of all his works, maintains the purest unity—paradoxical, of course, in a work so rough and contradictory—of thought and form. In maintaining at all levels—plot, character, language, argument, genre—an all-encompassing ambiguity, Dostoevskij gave powerful artistic expression to the spiritual paralysis that he diagnosed in his contemporaries.

Notes

1. As I will suggest below, the split begins with Dostoevskij's earliest works (especially *The Double*), but it is in *Notes from Underground* that a consistent pattern begins to take shape. Perhaps because of the ambiguity of its presentation—which is the subject of my discussion here—the religious message of this work has not yet been discussed in detail, even by that generation of critics who concentrated on this dimension in Dostoevskij.

2. Dostoevskij's choice of this word is curious, but appropriate. полоса, in its usual meaning refers to a strip, stripe or band; in the *Notes* полосы are phases (or "flashes"—Katz) the Underground Man goes through. For example, in Chapter I of Part II:

   > Но вдруг ни с того ни с сего наступает полоса скептицизма и равнодушия (у меня всё было полосами)

   (125)

   [But suddenly out of nowhere a "Phase/band/flash" of skepticism and indifference would set in. Everything with me was in ———es(?).]

   The two-dimensionality of the image called up by the word adds its own "flattening effect" to the sense of in-betweenness on all levels in this text; the narrator finds himself limited to two dimensions in a three-dimensional world. In his provocative discussion of "liminality" Roger Anderson sees this state as separating the conscious, secular world from that of *myth.*

3. "The limbo theologians insist that each of us is born with original sin on our souls. We are sinners

not by choice but by heritage; nonetheless, we are "children of wrath." As a result, limbo is a state of damnation. . . . Catholic theologians look upon limbo as an exile." (Dyer 16-17) Theologians debate about the severity of this exile; in Augustine's view, unbaptized children suffer all the torments of hell ("they could not be free of the greatest torment of the lost soul, its anguish over the loss of God." [17]); others have granted the possibility of a milder state. In *Notes from Underground* the narrator's fate is still undecided, and will remain so until he either dies or makes a conscious choice to accept God. In this study I will try to show how he is caught between the lifelessness of a purely secular/rational outlook (twice two is four) and the real life of God's grace.

4. I will not be concentrating here on hints in this text of Dostoevskij's future почвенничество. Of course this is one of the most important aspects of his religious thought, and it presents rich possibilities for analysis of the *Notes* (especially when the "земская сила/force of the earth" (!!), the driver taking the Underground Man to the brothel, reproaches him, causing a "sudden chill"—a realization of his impending sin?—in Part II, Chapter IV (p. 150).

5. Belknap's argument could be seen as a further development of Robin Feuer Miller's; Miller: "Dostoevsky has exposed the literary confession as reflecting alternatively a desire to shock one's audience or to justify oneself before it." (96)

6. Miller reaches a similar insight: "One cannot expose oneself indecently in private—or before God" (91); "The successful confession remains a sacrament, a sacred communication (99)."

7. Svetlana Semenova begins her article "'Высшая идея существования' у Достоевского" with a definition of the difference between the two Russian "truths" (правда and истина): "Истина не может доставить блаженства // *istina* cannot grant blessedness" (166). When she then quotes Rousseau's statement of the goal of his confession: "явить 'человека во всей истине его природы' // to reveal man in all the "truth" of his nature (168), the Russian word she uses is *istina*, rather than *pravda*. Implicitly she refers to the same kind of limitedness, in the deepest sense falseness, that I am trying to expose here.

8. Baxtin, of course, conducted the most thorough analysis of this issue in Dostoevskij's language, but by placing Dostoevskij on the level of his characters, he denies the *author* the *authority* to communicate his message, one that must, in this case, *necessarily* transcend the dialogue of the Underground Man.

9. It has been convincingly demonstrated that, though the Underground Man fights the laws of nature and determinism, he himself is a victim of them; proclaiming freedom, he is utterly unfree (Jackson).

10. It is in this context that we can find deeper meaning in the words that share the root "злой" that reverberate throughout the *Notes*. We are prepared for a discussion of the nature of evil from the very first line: Я человек борьной . . . Я злой человек (99) (I am a sick man. . . . I am an *evil* man) This bold translation should not be seen as a denial of the validity of the other much debated translations of the word: bad-tempered, spiteful, mean, nasty . . . ; I myself would not venture to offer "evil" as a first choice. But in our study of significant ambiguities in this text, surely this is one of the most important.

11. Joseph Frank's similarly directed study shows how the Crystal Palace metamorphises from a symbol of socialist utopia to a promise of Christian paradise (324-331). I believe his is the most detailed critical attempt to delineate the religious message within the text of the *Notes*.

12. His notes are his powerless moans against his spiritual ailment (his metaphysical "toothache") It is significant that the powerless dentists ("Wagenheims", p. 106) are foreigners. After all, his "illness" originates in the corruptive influence of secular Western thought.

Works Cited

Anderson, Roger B. *Dostoevsky: Myths of Duality* (Gainsville, Fla: University of Florida Press, 1986).

Bakhtin, Mikhail. *Problems of Dostoevsky's Poetics.* Trans. Caryl Emerson (Minneapolis: U. of Minnesota Press, 1984).

Belknap, Robert. "The Unrepentant Confession" in *Russianness: Studies on a Nation's Identity* (Ann Arbor: Ardis, 1990), 113-123.

Bem, A. L. "'The Nose' and *The Double*," tr. Peter B. Stetson, in *Dostoevsky and Gogol: Texts and Criticism,* ed. Meyer, Priscilla and Stephen Rudy (Ann Arbor: Ardis, 1979), pp. 229-248.

Dostoevsky, Fyodor. *Notes From Underground,* tr. and ed. Michael R. Katz (New York: W. W. Norton & Co., 1989)

Достоевский, Ф. М. Полное собранче соччненчй в мридцамч момах (Ленинград: наука), V (1973), X (1974) and XXVIII (1985).

Dyer, George J. *Limbo: Unsettled Question* (New York: Sheed and Ward, 1964).

Frank, Joseph. *Dostoevsky: The Stir of Liberation, 1860-1865* (Princeton: Princeton University Press, 1986)

Holquist, Michael. *Dostoevsky and the Novel* (Princeton: Princeton University Press, 1977)

Howard, Barbara F. "The Rhetoric of Confession: Dostoevskij's *Notes From Underground* and Rousseau's *Confessions, Slavic and European Journal,* XXV, 4 (Winter 1981), 16-32.

Ivanov, Vyacheslav. *Freedom and the Tragic Life: A Study in Dostoevsky,* tr. Norman Cameron. New York: The Noonday Press, 196

Jackson, Robert Louis. *The Art of Dostoevsky: Deliriums and Nocturnes* (Princeton: Princeton University Press, 1981)

Лотман, Юрий. "Руссо: Русская культура XVIII-начала XIX века," жан-жак Руссо. Тракмамы. (Ленинград, 1969)

Mikhailovsky, Nikolai K. *A Cruel Talent,* tr. Spencer Cadmus (Ann Arbor: Ardis, 1978)

Miller, Robin Feuer. "Dostoevsky and Rousseau: The Morality of Confession Reconsidered," *Western Philosophical Systems in Russian Literature,* ed. Anthony M. Mlikotin (Los Angeles: Univ. of South Calif. Press, 1979), 89-101.

Пачини, Джанлоренцо. "Духовное завещание Достоевского", Серчя литерамуры ч языка, XL, 4, 1990, 328-340.

Peace, Richard. *Dostoevsky: An Examination of the Major Novels* (Cambridge: Cambridge University Press, 1971).

Семенова, Светлана. "'Высшая идея существования' у Достоевского," Вопросы литературы, 11, 1988, 166-195.

Шестов, Л. Досмоевскчй ч нчмше. Философчя трагедии (Скифы, 1922)

Шкловский, В. За и промчв. Замемкч о Досмоевском (Москва: Советский писатель, 1957)

Julie W. De Sherbinin (essay date 1997)

SOURCE: De Sherbinin, Julie W. "Chekhov and Christianity: The Critical Evolution." In *Chekhov Then and Now: The Reception of Chekhov in World Culture,* edited by J. Douglas Clayton, pp. 285-99. New York: Peter Lang, 1997.

[*In the following essay, De Sherbinin examines critical commentary on Chekhov's treatment of Christianity, maintaining that the author presents a unique view of Christianity—and religion in general—as an expression of "cultural identity."*]

According to a fragment of academic apocrypha, some years ago an erudite Orthodox priest at St Vladimir's Seminary was asked to assess Russian writers according to their knowledge of Church liturgy and scripture. He assigned Dostoevsky a "C," Tolstoy a "B," and Chekhov an "A." The reasons for Chekhov's familiarity with Orthodox ritual, dogma, and custom are well-known: He received a strict religious upbringing at the hands of his father, Pavel Egorych, allusions to which Chekhov makes in his correspondence and some details of which have been supplied in memoirs written by his brothers Aleksandr and Mikhail.[1] The latter reports that Chekhov later maintained a library of liturgical service books to consult as he was writing.[2] Chekhov exhibited as well a verbatim memory of liturgy, undoubtedly gleaned from long hours of choir practice and holiday services in the Taganrog church, and from the rigors of his father's enforced domestic prayer regime. An example of this proficiency is found in a letter to a fellow writer where Chekhov confidently rectifies an error in ecclesiastical usage: "At the end of the story the sacristan (this is very nice and apropos) sings: 'Bless, O my soul, O Lord, and be joyful . . .' There is no such prayer. There is one like this: 'Bless the Lord, O my soul and all that is within me bless his holy Name.'"[3]

Chekhov's own disavowals of faith are frequently cited. Although my aim is hardly to claim Chekhov for Christianity, it bears pointing out that these citations from his correspondence are rarely contextualized. Thus his famous comment to I. L. Leontev (Shcheglov) that "I no longer have religion" must be read, at least in part, as a rhetorical gesture to dissuade his colleague from espousing Rachinsky's Christian pedagogical methodology.[4] It should not be construed as a programmatic statement. In spite of his professed lack of faith, Chekhov demonstrated a keen humanitarianism, a generosity of spirit and charity associated with the tenets of Christian philanthropy. These seeming paradoxes—a man who rejects the Church, yet attends holiday services; a nonbeliever who comports himself in a manner sanctioned by devout Christians; a writer who professes no faith, yet describes its contours profoundly in such stories as "On Holy Night," "The Student," and "The Bishop"—these paradoxes have led to broadly differing critical assessments of Chekhov's relationship to Christianity.[5]

This essay, however, will not simply survey the critical literature concerning this question. Indeed, enough has been written on the subject to preclude such a design.[6] Rather, I would like to suggest that for the better part of the one hundred years since this question first appeared, it has not been posed in the most illuminating manner. Critics have by and large been preoccupied with sculpting Chekhov as a believer or an atheist, as if one or the other designation might best describe, or help account for, his work. While such a discussion is of intrinsic interest in the study of any author, it is ultimately of limited usefulness in understanding the inner world of a Chekhovian text. I will attempt to make the case, instead, that Chekhov understood religion in a thoroughly modern, ethnographic sense as a manifestation of cultural identity.

Russian intellectual history is distinguished by a remarkably consistent bifurcation between the great, if tormented, proponents of Christian thought (Gogol, Dostoevsky, Tolstoy, Leskov, and Soloviev) and ardent defenders of rationalist, utilitarian, atheistic worldviews (Belinsky, Herzen, Bakunin, Chernyshevsky, Pisarev, Mikhailovsky). Clifford Geertz writes that one of the main methodological problems in writing about religion as an observer is "to put aside at once the tone of the village atheist and that of the village preacher, as well as their more sophisticated equivalents, so that the *social and psychological implications* [my emphasis] of particular religious beliefs can emerge in a clear and neutral light."[7] In a subtle yet radical departure from Russian intellectual tradition, Chekhov does exactly that. He observes the mechanisms not only of religious belief, but of a culture thoroughly imbued with traditions, symbols, language, and values shaped by the Orthodox creed. Chekhov, then, has a great deal in common with the cultural ethnographer. Yet his own observations are hardly presented in a scientific light (something he attempted to do, Cathy Popkin suggests, when he donned the ethnographer's hat on his trip to Sakhalin[8]). Rather, Chekhov has left us a body of texts saturated with allusions to Christian scripture, liturgy, iconography, holidays, and saints that serve as signposts pointing to layers of meaning not immediately accessible on the surface. In a sense he has reencoded phenomena of religious culture into literary texts, relying on his reader to exercise skills of cultural analysis in the recognition of these artifacts and discovery of their function. Chekhov thoroughly intuited the "social and psychological implications of particular religious beliefs" of which Geertz speaks. Ironically, Chekhov's own penetrating phenomenological view of religious culture has been frequently translated by purveyors of that culture (Russian and Soviet critics) into the "either"/"or" dichotomies of Christian thought that are often the very subject of his analytical lens. I shall begin with a selective discussion of Chekhov critics who present themselves as detractors or defenders of Chekhov's religious faith. There then follows a brief survey of efforts in Soviet era criticism to address allusions to religion in Chekhov's fiction. Finally, it is within a current American trend of criticism that I situate my own biases.

D. S. Merezhkovsky's acrid commentary on Chekhov's lack of Christian convictions aptly represents the viewpoint of those who regard it the writer's sacred commission to propound spiritual values. Merezhkovsky accuses Chekhov of "walking past Christ without looking back."[9] The chief strategy of his discussion, and one shared by most of those engaged in the "Was Chekhov a Christian?" debate, is to cite the views of Chekhov's characters as evidence of an authorial stance on religion. Thus Chekhov must have seen in Christianity, as does von Koren in "The Duel," "one of the humanitarian sciences" and Chekhov would have preferred, as did von Koren, "never to pose a question on so-called Christian grounds." Conversely, in order to have written "The Student," Chekhov must have 'met Christ face to face' and foregone the opportunity to accept Him."[10] The pitfalls of such subjective selection of textual evidence need hardly be discussed.

The nature of Merezhkovsky's dichotomized conceptualization represents the tenacious hold of such thinking on the Christian mind, one accustomed to the binary opposition between virtue and sin, Heaven and Hell. The extent to which Merezhkovsky's and Chekhov's approaches to this subject diverge may be observed by comparing similar imagery in their works. In his trilogy *Christ and Antichrist,* Merezhkovsky employs polarized Christian symbols: the evil of the beast (Antichrist) and the goodness of the dove (Christ) are literally relayed in black and white imagery.[11] Such straightforward dualistic thinking is rendered highly ambivalent under Chekhov's pen. In "The Teacher of Literature," for instance, the conventional values associated with white and black (perfection/purity/virginity vs. evil/degradation/male conquest) are introduced through indirect allusions to Shakespeare's "Rape of Lucrece" and Pushkin's "Count Nulin," only to be thoroughly subverted and redefined in Nikitin's consciousness as he finds his way out from under the influence of culturally (and religiously) determined values that have blunted his life.[12] Marena Senderovich has demonstrated how the reversal of the meaning of black and white in the story "An Attack of Nerves" coincides with the reversal of Vasilev's beliefs in, first, scholarly methodology and, second, the Christian moral code (represented by the whiteness/purity that Vasilev projects onto the "fallen women" whom he encounters in the brothel). M. Senderovich goes on to suggest that the hero's crisis derives from his own bookishness—i.e., his belief in academic texts and evangelical writings (which find expression in the black and white of a book's page).[13] In Chekhov, then, "black and white" understandings are associated with both the influence of Christian teachings and a "faith" in textual representations of life. Their dismantling is conveyed artistically through the reversal or inversion of values conventionally attached to these colours: for both Nikitin and Vasilev what initially appear to be indisputable truths turn out to be cultural constructs of little use in the forging of an identity. Indeed, Chekhov's subject of analysis here, at least in part, is the very religious consciousness that spawns Merezhkovsky's critique of Chekhov.

It was Merezhkovsky's generation of critics that, perhaps for obvious reasons, was the most interested in Chekhov's religiosity. Thus the theologian Sergei Bulgakov takes up the question in "Chekhov kak myslitel'," followed by the analysis in 1913 of a fellow cleric, M. M. Stepanov, in "Religiia A. P. Chekhova," and A. Izmailov's chapter on Chekhov's religion in his 1916 book.[14] These works stress Chekhov's purported religious feelings and sensitivity while simultaneously attempting to account for his lack of professed faith. This perspective produces interesting conflicts for the authors. Izmailov comes to the dazzling conclusion that "Chekhov wished for faith with his heart, while judging it with his intellect, and envied the faithful."[15]

It is worth dwelling briefly on one aspect of Chekhov's interest in Christianity identified by some of these early critics, his appreciation of the aesthetic splendor of Orthodox services. A. S. Lazarev recalls an occasion at Easter, 1888, when Chekhov persuaded him to go to evening vespers by promising, "today the singing there will be marvellous." Chekhov is said to have embellished on this notion of liturgy as a source of beauty by extolling the village church: "A village's church is the only place where the peasant, not to mention other things, can get even a few aesthetic impressions."[16] Similar commentary appears periodically in Chekhov's correspondence. That this sensory, even sensual, richness and beauty was prized not only explains Chekhov's lifelong habit of attending holiday services, but also figures in his psychological portraits of the Russian religious mind. The church interior, and icons in particular, become an internalized referent point for the external world in the stories "In Passion Week" and "Peasants."

These early apologists for Chekhov's almost-but-not-quite religious faith represent one end of a continuum of criticism that assigns to Chekhov faith of one sort or another—"faith in art," "faith in man," "faith in progress," "faith in science," etc. The cultural impulse that insists on locating in an author's belief system a "faith" in itself comprises a paradigm shaped by religious thinking. Again, these very cultural patterns are the subject of Chekhov's interest. Thus in "On the Road" Likharev says of faith that if a Russian doesn't believe in God, it means that he believes in something else: "For half of my life I numbered myself among the ranks of atheists and nihilists, but there has not been one hour in my life when I did not believe." Savely Senderovich writes that the central theme of the story is "the Russian capacity for faith, the nature of a Russian's faith, and the meaning of faith in Russian life."[17] He demonstrates that Likharev's faith is portrayed in its full ambivalence, for it pertains to a profane world in which sacred value has been displaced. In contrast, failing to distinguish between his own culturally defined beliefs and this culturological commentary on Russia,

Bulgakov regards Likharev's words as evidence of the author's own religiosity.[18] The critical discourse is itself, then, shaped by paradigms of "belief." It is not that Chekhov had religious faith of any ilk; rather, he profoundly understood the psychology behind faith and portrayed it in its variable manifestations.

In the Soviet era we predictably encounter some rather crude ideological statements on the topic of Chekhov and Christianity as well as the beginnings of some more attentive observations about individual texts. To the former belongs E. I. Morozov's statement, "Chekhov felt that it [religion] cripples people spiritually and morally, imposes weighty fetters on their intellect and emotions, and paralyzes their will."[19] In the latter grouping, I. N. Sukhikh suggests that Chekhov critiques hierarchical moral schemes through links between "The Black Monk" and Revelations, allusions that underscore Kovrin's pretensions to the status of an intellectual apostle.[20] Chekhov and the Book of Ecclesiastes have received particular attention. The émigré critic M. Kurdiumov, viewing Chekhov from the angle of Orthodox belief as an unfortunately godless author, claims a typological similarity between the spiritually barren lives of Chekhov's characters and the grief expressed in Ecclesiastes.[21] E. A. Polotskaia advances a sociohistorical interpretation, suggesting that Chekhov's interest in King Solomon and Ecclesiastes represents a philosophical commentary on the conflicts inherent in late-nineteenth century Russian life.[22] Finally, N. V. Kapustin seeks to establish Ecclesiastes as an integral facet of Chekhov's poetics by pointing out both articulated and implied allusions in a number of stories.[23] It should be noted that the Soviet editors of Chekhov's *Complete Works* have significantly facilitated investigation into Christian allusions in Chekhov by conscientiously annotating scriptural citations.

Interesting work by a young Russian scholar deserves special note. In his study of Chekhov's "christmas" stories, P. N. Tolstoguzov offers an engaging interpretation of the early story "Without a Title." The story recounts an elder's return from a neighboring metropolis to his monastery, where he regales the holy brothers with tales of the glittering evils he witnessed there, only to find the next morning that all the monks have left for the city. According to Tolstoguzov, Chekhov reworks the conventions of early Christian didactic literature by setting up the opposition between the Christian *pustyn'* (configured as the grave) and the pagan city, then reversing the terms to make of the harlot (*bludnitsa*) on the table in the tavern, whom the holy father describes in order to decry, a prototype of the sinful woman in Revelations, a biblical personification of the city and symbol of fecundity, an image of life and salvation to which the monks respond. Tolstoguzov carefully maintains that "Chekhov extricates his images from the framework of moral antitheses" and nicely underscores the ambivalent nature of the "maximally semiotic" images in the story.[24]

The intricate play that Tolstoguzov sees in Chekhov's handling of Christian symbols belies A. S. Sobennikov's recent statement that "biblical images and reminiscences, spiritual verses, and the description of church rites and religious holidays comprise a significant 'cultural stratum' in the works of the writer [that] easily submits to scholarly analysis."[25] Current American scholarship, too, seriously challenges the idea that these allusions can be "easily" deciphered, insisting instead on the need for arduous and meticulous investigation into the Christian texts and allusions woven into Chekhov's prose.[26] The principal scholars engaged in this endeavor are Robert Louis Jackson and Savely Senderovich.

The common ground in the analyses of Jackson and Senderovich is a scrupulous attention to the *language* of Chekhov's stories. (We recall here Mayakovsky's attempt to wrest Chekhov from the hands of pedestrian critics by insisting on his status as an aesthete, a "King of the Word."[27]) A humorous tidbit from Chekhov's notebooks illustrates how cultural meaning resides in even his most frivolous play with religious language: "When in the church they sang 'Today is the crux of our salvation,' at home he had soup made from a head, and on the day of the beheading he wouldn't eat anything round, but thrashed his children."[28] In this practically untranslatable play on words, the subject confuses a liturgical phrase, "the crux (*glavizna*) of our salvation" with soup made from an animal's head (*glavizna*), and on the day of St John the Baptist's beheading (*useknovenie*), he refuses to eat anything round (which might resemble a head) and, extrapolating only the root "*sek*" ("to beat"), flogs his children. Obsolete and obscure Church Slavic expressions, so prevalent in the mind of a Russian exposed to the liturgy, are not left behind in church, but leak out into everyday life. The words are "translated" idiosyncratically into actions highly inappropriate to the religious context, but filled with a certain obtuse logic for the agent himself. Thus inversions and distortions of theological messages are manifest in dislocated linguistic functions. These reversals underlie Chekhov's deployment of the Christian idiom.

In his analyses of "Because of Little Apples," "A Woman's Kingdom," "Rothschild's Fiddle," "The Student," and "In Exile," Robert L. Jackson uncovers just such dislocations attending Chekhov's use of Christian subtexts. (It is important to note that these subtexts are by no means self-evident, indeed have eluded notice for almost a century.) Thus Jackson views "Because of Little Apples" as a parody of the biblical scene in the Garden of Eden, a social-historical and mythopoetic allegory in which the corrupted Eden is equated with the omnipo-

tent cruel and sadistic autocratic traditions of tsarist Russia.[29] According to Jackson, reference to another garden appears in "A Woman's Kingdom"—the garden of Gethsemane, where Christ prayed during the night before his detention. By alluding to the garden, Chekhov characterizes Anna Akimovna's preoccupation with fortune-telling and games of chance: she has renounced the principles of freedom and responsibility represented by the "Kingdom of Christ" for the vicissitudes of blind Fate.[30] The 137th psalm ("By the rivers of Babylon") is decoded by Jackson as the unifying symbolic motif in "Rothschild's Fiddle," while he reads "The Student" as a story of spiritual transfiguration modeled on the life of the apostle Peter.[31] Jackson at once brings deeply humanist readings to Chekhov and reveals the extraordinary subtlety of his craft, in which a single detail can be the key to a pivotal subtext. Furthermore, by illuminating Chekhov's philosophical dialogues with such sources as the Bible, Dostoevsky, Pushkin and Dante, Jackson places him alongside the Russian authors conventionally considered more engaged in philosophical discussions with the literary and artistic canons.[32] Jackson's, then, is a landmark discovery of the importance of Christian contexts in Chekhov's prose.

Several recent publications seem to understand Chekhov's allusions to Christianity as an expression of the author's moral, and even spiritual bearings. George Pahomov discusses "The Grasshopper" as a latter-day hagiographic depiction of Dymov, the doctor whose value is recognized only upon his death by his frivolous wife, and understands the motifs of light, hierophany, and apocalypse in "Peasants" as a narrational device to favor the "elect" characters (Nikolai, Olga, Sasha) over the sinners dwelling in darkness (Kiriak, Fekla).[33] Willa Chamberlain Axelrod interprets allusions to scripture and liturgy in "On Holy Night" and "The Duel" as Chekhov's directives toward faith and the triumph of Christian morality.[34] Alexandar Mihailovic reads "Ionych" through Christological references as a story of Startsev's rejection of salvation and capitulation to a tomb-like state of self-mortification and death.[35] Maxim Shrayer also identifies hidden Christological motifs in "On the Night of Christmas Eve," suggesting that the hero replicates Christ's sacrifice in order to liberate his wife from a stifling marriage.[36] These studies bring to our attention many images and citations indisputably coded to Orthodox sources. At the same time, to one extent or another they impute to Chekhov a Christian envisioning of the world that resounds dissonantly. That is, for the most part in these analyses the characters' behaviour is directly keyed to a Christian moral scheme (even if negatively configured) in which Chekhov is implicated as arbiter. Although all of these scholars would probably agree that Chekhov was not a believer, in these readings his sympathies seem to accord with the values of the sacred, of moral judgement, redemption and salvation.

Another vein of recent work concerned with configurations of Orthodox life in Chekhov's prose unearths his profound interest in what might be called Russian "popular culture." Clifford Geertz suggests that culture "denotes an historically transmitted pattern of meanings embodied in symbols, a system of inherited conceptions expressed in symbolic forms by means of which men communicate, perpetuate, and develop their knowledge about and attitudes toward life."[37] It is attention precisely to Chekhov's treatment of symbolic forms widespread in Orthodox life that characterizes the work of Savely Senderovich.

S. Senderovich demonstrates how Christian legends and iconography of St George the Dragon slayer and the Maiden constitute a cultural complex that appears in a variety of transposed forms in Chekhov's prose. The name "George," and its many variations, signals the presence of the paradigm as an important symbolic component of a given story. Senderovich locates this nexus of meaning in over a dozen stories, and shows how "pieces" of the legend are played out in another twenty texts. These, of course, are never direct or moralizing versions of the legend, but rather inversions, a device that "represents a means of penetrating into the other, unapparent side of things."[38] Senderovich's readings are grounded in a theory that privileges the lexeme as the basic component of Chekhov's prose (as it is in poetry)[39], and therefore attend closely to the artfully manipulated cultural language associated with the St George legend. Four modalities through which language of the culture is conveyed suggests the complexity of addressing Christian images in Chekhov, for it can concern the protagonist's conscious manipulation of language to serve his own ends; unconscious usage of a cultural idiom that in fact manipulates the hero; the language of the culture as the author's medium, used by him unconsciously and therefore manipulating him; and motifs of religious language which belong to idiomatic usage, and are distinguished in the context only by the author's artful inclusion of them.[40] Thus, for Senderovich, ascertaining the *function* of a Christian image, motif, or allusion is always the critical step in analysis. His analyses capture the enormous complexity that marks Chekhov's understanding of Russia's Orthodox heritage and the profound impression it has left on the secular and profane worlds with which Chekhov is preoccupied.

Other work, as well, suggests that the St George complex does not stand alone as a network in Chekhov's prose pertaining to Russia's Orthodox legacy. My study of the function of the Marian paradigm of the virgin and the harlot relates to the two "Marys" of Orthodoxy, the Mother of God and the repentant sinner Mary of Egypt, an association that appears in a least fifteen stories and serves to probe Russian cultural perceptions of female identity.[41] Michael Finke's recent observations about the frequency of the motif of the hero's descent

to the underworld in Chekhov's work (a theme borrowed from Antiquity and Christianity) goes even further to establish the idea that whole systems of meaning associated with Christian cultural patterns consciously or unconsciously fascinated Chekhov throughout his career.[42]

In 1891 A. S. Suvorin published a feuilleton in *Novoe vremia* in which he castigated the philosopher V. S. Soloviev for "daring to call himself Orthodox." Chekhov wrote to Suvorin in response: "Can such words as Orthodox, Jew, and Catholic really express some sort of exclusive personal virtues or merits? In my opinion, whether willingly or unwillingly, everyone should consider himself Orthodox who has that word written in his passport. Whether you are a believer or not, whether you are the prince of the world or an exiled convict, according to custom [*v obikhode*] you are still Orthodox."[43] These words well convey Chekhov's understanding of Christianity. Religious identity is regarded here as a culturally determined phenomenon, an affiliation forged by a common *obikhod,* by mutual natural and symbolic languages, a belonging imposed by convention and sealed by the passport. Significantly, faith *per se* has little do with Chekhov's notions of religion—"if you are a believer or not . . . you are still Orthodox."

Chekhov's formulation shares with the writings of his contemporary, Max Weber, who linked Calvinist doctrine to the flourishing of capitalism, the insight that religious belief can serve as a defining factor in the secular activity of a people. Chekhov goes further, however, in averring that even without belief, the inherited contours of a religious mindset create cultural identity. This may be particularly relevant for Russian culture, in which rich Medieval traditions, a predominantly peasant population, and the prolonged alliance between church and state created a peculiarly hardy foundation for Christian modes of thinking. Indeed, one need not search far to find evidence of psycho-social and political patterns derived from religious culture throughout Russia in the twentieth century, ranging from the political arena to the cultural values reproduced in everyday discourse in the private sphere.[44]

The question of Chekhov's relationship to Russia's Orthodox religious heritage is coming into its own. A recent international conference was devoted exclusively to religious and philosophical dimensions in Chekhov's life and work.[45] This ongoing work shows much promise. The countless overt allusions to phenomena of Christian life that saturate Chekhov's text—references that have for nearly a century been regarded as Russian *realia* recorded by the quintessential realist—represent unturned stones that may potentially yield interpretations of great interest. The initial excavation, however, represents only the first step in analysis, for once the allusions are ascertained, be they to scripture or to a saint's life, the more complex task remains of ascertaining the function/s of the citations. These are never direct, usually unanticipated, and always elusive. Moreover, such painstaking work requires not only a familiarity with Chekhov's *oeuvre,* but an intimate knowledge of the Orthodox world in which he lived. Happily, recent scholarship has left behind the unproductive question of Chekhov's espousal or rejection of Orthodoxy and has begun to overturn stones, to understand his immensely penetrating observations about the power of a religion to shape a national psyche.

Notes

1. In an often quoted letter to I. L. Leontev (Shcheglov), Chekhov quips that he and his brothers felt themselves "little convicts" in childhood when church-goers listened to their singing and envied their parents such angelic boys. *Pis'ma,* V, 20. Aleksandr Chekhov embroiders on their father's tyrannical coerciveness in matters of ritual. "Iz detskikh let A. P. Chekhova," *A. P. Chekhov v vospominaniiakh sovremennikov,* ed. N. I. Gitovich and I. V. Fedorova (M., 1960): 39, 63-74. Mikhail Chekhov assesses their childhood religious experience in a much more benevolent manner. *Vokrug Chekhova* (M., 1960): 33.

2. *Sochineniia,* XII, 365.

3. Chekhov excerpts from the first antiphon of the Russian Orthodox liturgy, one based on the 102nd Psalm. See the letter of A. P. Chekhov to N. A. Khlopov, 13 February 1888 (*Pis'ma,* II, 200).

4. A. P. Chekhov to I. L. Leontev, 9 March 1892 (*Pis'ma,* V, 20).

5. Pushkin is the other prominent Russian writer of whom the same can be said. He wrote to Zhukovsky: "Whatever might be my political and religious thinking, I keep it to myself and do not intend to challenge senselessly the accepted order and necessity." Letter cited in Sergei Davydov, "Pushkin i Khristianstvo," *Zapiski russkoi akademicheskoi gruppy,* 25 (1992-93): 68.

6. For a more comprehensive enumeration of sources concerned with the nature of Chekhov's faith, see Willa Chamberlain Axelrod, "Russian Orthodoxy in the Life and Fiction of A. P. Chekhov" (Ph.D. diss., Yale U., 1991): 8-32.

7. Clifford Geertz, "Religion as a Cultural System," in *The Interpretation of Cultures: Selected Essays by Clifford Geertz* (New York, 1973): 123.

8. Cathy Popkin, "Chekhov as Ethnographer: Epistemological Crisis on Sakhalin Island," *Slavic Review* 51, 1 (1992): 36-51.

9. D. S. Merezhkovskii, *Chekhov i Gor'kii* (St Petersburg, 1906; reprint Letchworth Herts., 1975): 49.

10. Merezhkovskii, 43, 48. Sergei Bulgakov goes even further, suggesting in regard to "The Student" that "it is difficult to assess where the student ends and the author begins." See "Chekhov kak myslitel'," *Novyi put',* 11 (1904): 140.

11. A. S. Sobennikov discusses the differences between Merezhkovsky's metaphysical Christian symbols and Chekhov's "interest in the side of Christian teachings that helps man orient himself in the world." See "A. P. Chekhov i D. S. Merezhkovskii (K probleme religioznogo simvola)," *Chekhovskie chteniia v Ialte,* ed. V. Mel'nikova (M., 1990): 96.

12. I briefly consider the importance of black and white imagery in "Life beyond Text: The Nature of Illusion in 'The Teacher of Literature,' *Reading Chekhov's Text,* ed. R. L. Jackson (Evanston, Il., 1993): 115-126.

13. Marena Senderovich, "The Symbolic Structure of Chekhov's Story 'An Attack of Nerves'," *Chekhov's Art of Writing,* ed. P. Debreczeny (Columbus, Ohio, 1977): 11-26.

14. Sergei Bulgakov, "Chekhov kak myslitel'," *Novyi put',* 10, 11 (1904): 32-54, 138-152. M. Stepanov, "Religiia A. P. Chekhova" in *Religiia russkikh pisatelei,* 1 (1913): 3-58. A. Izmailov, *Chekhov. Biograficheskii nabrosok* (Moscow, 1916): 533-559.

15. Izmailov, 555.

16. Both citations are from Izmailov, 552.

17. Savely Senderovich, "Poetics and Meaning in Chekhov's 'On the Road'," *Anton Chekhov Rediscovered,* ed. S. Senderovich and M. Sendich (East Lansing, Mich., 1987): 144.

18. Bulgakov, 39.

19. E. I. Morozov, "Kritika A. P. Chekhovym religioznoi morali," *Sbornik statei i materialov,* 5, ed. L. P. Gromov (Rostov, 1969): 13. See also V. B. Kataev, "O 'vrozhdennoi religii' Chekhova (B. Zaitsev i drugie o rasskaze 'Arkhierei'), *Russkaia literatura v otsenke sovremennoi zarubezhnoi kritiki (Protiv revizionizma i burzhuaznykh kontseptsii)* (M., 1973), 163-76.

20. I. N. Sukhikh, *Problemy poetiki A. P. Chekhova* (L., 1987): 102-116.

21. M. Kurdiumov, *Serdtse smiatennoe* (Paris, 1934): 38.

22. E. A. Polotskaia, *A. P. Chekhov: Dvizhenie khudozhestvennoi mysli* (M., 1979): 58-62.

23. N. V. Kapustin, "O bibleiskikh tsitatakh i reministsentsiiakh v proze Chekhova," *Chekhoviana:*

Chekhov v kul'ture XX veka, ed. V. Lakshin (M., 1993): 17-26.

24. P. N. Tolstoguzov, "Skazka A. P. Chekhova 'Bez zaglavii': K probleme inoskazaniia," *Problema zhanra i stilia* (Vladivostok, 1988): 137-146. See also his dissertation, "Skazka i skazochnost' v tvorchestve A. P. Chekhova 1880-kh godov (Na materiale rozhdestvennykh rasskazov)" (Candidate diss., Herzen Pedagogical U., Leningrad, 1988: UDK 882.092).

25. A. S. Sobennikov, 88.

26. Earlier Western scholarship has not ignored the subject of Christianity in Chekhov, but has tended to focus on related sociological concerns or to re-mark on portraits of spirituality in the stories with obvious Christian themes. See W. H. Bruford, *Chekhov and his Russia* (New York, 1947): 127-41; Boris Zaitsev, *Chekhov: Literaturnaia biografiia* (New York, 1954); George Ivask, "Chekhov and the Russian Clergy," *Anton Chekhov, 1860-1960: Some Essays,* ed. T. Eekman (Leiden, 1960): 83-92; Richard Marshall, "Chekhov and the Russian Orthodox Clergy," *Slavic and East European Journal,* 7 (1963): 375-91. Contemporary studies with a similar bent include Nils Åke Nilsson, "The Bishop: Its Theme," in *Reading Chekhov's Text,* and Thomas Wächter, *Die künstlerische Welt in den späten Erzählungen Cechovs* (New York, 1992). See as well Willy Birkenmaier, "Die Darstellung des Christentums in Werke Cechovs" (Ph.D. diss., Tübingen, 1971).

27. V. V. Maiakovskii, "Dva Chekhova," *Polnoe sobranie sochinenii v dvenadtsati tomakh,* I (M.,1939): 335-344.

28. L. P. Grossman, ed. *Zapisnye knizhki Chekhova* (M., 1927; reprint. Ann Arbor, 1963): 79.

29. R. L. Jackson, "Dostoevsky in Chekhov's Garden of Eden: 'Because of Little Apples'." *Dialogues with Dostoevsky: The Overwhelming Questions* (Stanford, 1993): 83-103.

30. Robert L. Jackson, "Chekhov's 'A Woman's Kingdom: A Drama of Character and Fate," *Russian Language Journal,* 39 (1985): 1-11.

31. Robert L. Jackson, "'If I Forget Thee, O Jerusalem': An Essay on Chekhov's *Rothschild's Fiddle,*" *Anton Chekhov Rediscovered,* 35-49; and "Chekhov's 'The Student'" in *Reading Chekhov's Text,* 127-33.

32. Indeed Chekhov was a consummate pilferer of both. Studies are increasingly focusing on Chekhov's intricate play with the traditions of European and Russian prose, poetry, drama, opera, and painting.

33. George Pahomov, "Chekhov's 'The Grasshopper': A Secular Saint's Life," *Slavic and East European Journal,* 37, 1 (1993): 33-45; and "Religious Motifs in Chekhov's 'Muzhiki,'" *Zapiski russkoi akademicheskoi gruppy v SSHA,* 25 (1992-93): 111-119.

34. Willa Chamberlain Axelrod, "Passage from Great Saturday to Easter Day in 'Holy Night,'" *Reading Chekhov's Text,* 96-102; "The Biblical and Theological Context of Moral Reform in 'The Duel'," *Russian Literature,* 35 (1994): 129-152.

35. Alexandar Mihailovic, "Eschatology and Entombment in 'Ionych,'" *Reading Chekhov's Text,* 103-114.

36. Maxim Shrayer, "Christmas and Paschal Motifs in 'V rozhdestvenskuiu noch'," *Russian Literature,* 35 (1994): 243-55.

37. Geertz, 89.

38. Savely Senderovich, "Anton Chekhov and St George the Dragonslayer," *Anton Chekhov Rediscovered,* 184. An extended version of this study is "Chudo Georgiia o zmie: Istoriia oderzhimosti Chekhova odnim obrazom," *Russian Language Journal,* 39 (1985): 135-225. For the most complete exposition, see *Chekhov—s glazu na glaz: Istoriia odnoi oderzhimosti A. P. Chekhova* (St Petersburg, 1994).

39. See Savely Senderovich, "A Fragment of Semiotic Theory of Poetic Prose (The Chekhovian Type)," *Essays in Poetics,* 14, 2 (1989): 43-63.

40. See Senderovich, *Chekhov—s glazu na glaz,* 137.

41. See my dissertation, "Two Marias in Chekhov: Artistic Functions of the Christian Paradigm of the Virgin and the Harlot" (Ph.D. diss., Cornell U., 1992).

42. Michael Finke, "The Hero's Descent to the Underworld in Chekhov," *The Russian Review,* 53 (1994): 67-80.

43. A. P. Chekhov to A. S. Suvorin, 18 November, 1891 (*Pis'ma,* IV, 296).

44. Aspects of iconography, iconoclasm, confession, communion, and eschatological and apocalyptic belief have played major roles in Soviet era political life, something commented on by a number of scholars, including Richard Stites. Nancy Ries considers underlying religio-cultural configurations in Russian verbal expression in her ethnography of discourse genres in contemporary Russian society: "The Power of Negative thinking: Russian Talk and the Reproduction of Mindset, Worldview, and Society," *The Anthropology of East Europe Review,* 10, 2 (1991): 38-53.

45. A volume of proceedings from the second Baden-weiler Chekhov Symposium (October, 1994) organized by the International Chekhov Society is currently being prepared for publication by R. D. Kluge (U. of Tübingen) and V. B. Kataev (Moscow State U.).

Olga Sedakova (essay date 2004)

SOURCE: Sedakova, Olga. "'Non-Mortal and Mysterious Feelings': On Pushkin's Christianity." In *Two Hundred Years of Pushkin, Volume III: Pushkin's Legacy,* edited by Robert Reid and Joe Andrew, pp. 33-45. Amsterdam and New York: Rodopi, 2004.

[*In the following essay, Sedakova concentrates on the theme of foolishness in Pushkin's works to illuminate the author's commentary on Christianity.*]

One of the most solemn and final of Pushkin's poems, framed as a kind of last word, surveying not only his complete work and its significance, but also its future after the poet's death[1] concludes with a surprising line: 'И не оспаривай глупца' ('Dispute not with a fool'). It is surprising because we have come to expect a summation, a resolution in the concluding line of a poem. And Pushkin usually follows this compositional rule in his completed lyrics. So what is this gesture, that seems so unexpected after the solemn and triumphant tone of the preceding lyrics, supposed to mean? Such a conclusion has led some interpreters to consider *Monument* wholly in terms of a parody of Derzhavin. The 'fool' in that case is the person who takes the lofty style of the poem for real. Indeed, how could Pushkin who had proclaimed the independence of the poet from the people's judgement ('Поэт! не дорожи любовию народной'; 'Зависеть от царя, зависеть от народа—не все ли нам равно?' ['Poet! Hold not dear the people's love'; 'Is it not one to us whether we rely on the tsar or the people?']), have been proud of being loved by the people?

However, Pushkin's irony and use of ambiguity have their limits. We could never doubt the seriousness of the first lines of the poem. The seriousness of the last is also obvious. Is this wretched fool so important to Pushkin, that he concludes his farewell poem with the fool's superfluous 'praise and accusation' ('хвалу и клевету приемли равнодушно / И не оспоривай глупца.' ['Be not swayed by praise and accusation; / Dispute not with a fool.'])? We of course know that Pushkin's relationship with his readership in the last years of his life had been a disaster (one only needs to read what Karamzin wrote about *Monument* in his correspondence) and we can explain such a final line by Pushkin's biographical circumstances. But we also know what kind of filter Pushkin's biographical circumstances had to pass through to become part of an artistic creation.

This final line would not seem so unexpected if we bore in mind the role played by *foolishness* in Pushkin's world. Foolishness is a notion that has not been clearly defined or rationalized. It is equal in scale to Blok's 'пошлость' (triviality; vulgarity): the most hostile and the most hopeless of things. It is the face that evil itself had shown him.

Face to face with foolishness (or 'violence', 'blindness', 'childishness', 'drowsiness' etc.) Pushkin recommends (and not only in the final line of *Monument*) the only *intelligent* tactic: silence, refusal to answer, the indifference of superiority. One can notice, however, that Pushkin never managed to assume the pose of the unruffled aristocrat, and a condescending *laissez-faire*—'do as you are doing'; 'let them be'—could never cover up the immense pain or, as Pushkin himself puts it, the 'immeasurable sadness': 'Доволен? так пускай судьба его бранит / И плюет на алтарь, где твой огонь горит / И в детской радости колеблет твой треножник' ('Are you satisfied? Then let fate curse him / And spit on the altar where your fire burns / And shake your tripod with childish joy').

Yes, it is nothing more than a 'child's playfulness', but the games of such adult children are rather frightening and they play them in the most inappropriate places. 'Procul este, prophani!'—this is Pushkin's sincere reaction to the games of chance played by foolishness. 'Идите прочь! кому какое дело / Поэту мирному до вас.' ('Depart! What business / Can the peaceful poet have with you?') Foolishness, as Pushkin portrays it, is always blasphemous, ever-ready to mock ('ругаться') the upright man: 'над кем ругается слепой и буйный век' ('Whom the blind and unruly age mocks').

It blasphemes both when it bursts on to the altar to desecrate priest and sanctuary (as in the poems quoted, where a symbolic poetic altar [with pagan overtones] is described) and when it acts as custodian of the sacred (as the sentries in *Earthly Power* [мирская власть]).[2] Foolishness does this not because it does not believe, but because it does not understand what is taking place:

Иль мните важности предать царю царей?
Иль покровительством спасаете могучим?
владыку, тернием венчанного колючим . . .
Иль опасаетесь, чтоб чернь не оскорбила
того, чья казнь весь род адамов искупила?

(Or do you think you are adding importance to the
  king of kings?
Or that you are saving him with powerful protection?
The ruler, crowned with prickly thorns . . .
Or do you fear that the rabble may insult
Him whose passion has redeemed all the seed of
  Adam?)

Neither of these ways of treating the sacred—open mockery and ridiculous protection—excludes the other.

'The blind and unruly age' easily makes the transition from unreflecting mockery to absurd protectiveness—something we in Russia have unexpectedly witnessed in recent years.

When discussing Pushkin's Christianity and, more broadly, his 'religious orientation', the principal danger is that we ourselves may succumb to foolishness in the Pushkinian sense, that is, to presumptuousness, over-simplification and moralizing. We may also boldly re-hash run-of-the-mill verities that are 'new' only to us, comparing Pushkin with a standard of morality and piety, which would have fitted Faddei Bulgarin just as well, if not even better.[3] It does not really matter whether we come out with praise or blame. Foolish praise insulted Pushkin much more than reproaches.

I hope that by considering the theme of foolishness and intelligence we may be brought closer to understanding Pushkin's inner world than by other approaches: comparing his views to the school catechism or describing his life in terms of 'the return of the prodigal son'.[4] It is well known that Pushkin's departure from atheism was less a response to any 'call from the heart' or to 'pangs of conscience', than to the demands of *intelligence.* He found atheism unsatisfactory from an intellectual point of view: 'Not admitting the existence of God is more *stupid* than supposing, as do certain nations, that the world is held up by a rhinoceros'.[5] Since his school days the struggle between his heart and his mind had taken a form diametrically opposed to the usual: 'The mind seeks the Godhead, but the heart fails to find' (*Unbelief* [Безверие, 1817]); 'Mon coeur est material-iste, mais ma raison s'y refuse' (diary entry, 1821).

The other possibility has been noted by S. L. Frank, who supposes that the investigation of the religious spirit of Pushkin's lyrics demands a 'formal analysis', the analysis of poetical form.[6] But the matter is not so simple, presupposing as it does an understanding of the *form* of secular (non-ecclesiastical) art, which answers the criteria of 'religious'. Do we have such an understanding? I am afraid not. However, even in the most general essay, even before the analysis, we could say that the elusive characteristics of Pushkinian form are closely connected to our theme, the theme of intelligence and foolishness. I doubt that we could call any other Russian writer's style of writing so unequivocally intelligent.

Let us dwell on the most general characteristics of foolishness in Pushkin's works. First of all, foolishness is not a lack of intellect ('an impertinent know-all' in Pushkin's understanding is also a fool. Consider his well-known distrust of abstract thought; his obvious preference for the English pragmatic attitude over the German metaphysical). Foolishness is rather a delusion of the soul. Probably æsthetic, rather than intellectual, it

is a kind of ontological indelicacy, inappropriateness, or lack of taste (we will talk about the link between taste and intelligence later). Thinking this way, Pushkin denied that the hero of Griboedov's *Woe from Wit* possessed 'wit' (that is, was prudent or sensible).

This is a feature that strikes me as interesting and important. Pushkin was a man of his time—the 'new', the 'enlightened age', the post-Enlightenment era,—that is, sceptical and rational. The Byronic period, as Pushkin clearly sensed (if one compares what Tatiana and One-gin read) was another step in the progressive breaking away from 'wonderful illusions' (a process which in our times is effected by 'demythologization' and 'destructivism') and the peaceful euphoria of sentimentalism. Pushkin was early acquainted with the works of sceptics, cynics and pessimistic moralists like La Roch-efoucauld. Foolishness and intelligence are most certainly the main theme in this line of thought. The contemporary man saw himself, first of all, as cultivated and *thinking,* and this made him consider himself superior to 'the simplicity of yore'. To think meant to be capable of looking at things, including one's self, from the sidelines, ('metaphysically', to use the language of the time), critically, taking nothing on trust and maintaining the safe distance of doubt. It is in this sense that Onegin speaks of the 'thinking man': 'Кто жил и мыслил, тот не может / В душе не презирать людей' ('He who has lived and thought cannot but / Despise people in his soul').

Here foolishness is understood quite distinctly (NB: this popular understanding of foolishness survives to the present): it principally implies naïveté, idealism and unsophistication. Lack of the habit of reflecting. Lack of traumatic experience: 'Ума холодных наблюдений / И сердца горестных замет' ('Cold observations of the mind / And the sorrowful testimonies of the heart').

In this case the *clever* man would be he who already knows that everything in our world is in the worst condition; he knows that this is the unalterable truth and that we only imagine everything to be good and lofty and he is reconciled to this situation as the normal state of affairs. He, who knows that man is not an angel (a mild encapsulation of this anthropology) is effectively incorrigible. ('Our virtues are our disguised defects' said La Rochefoucauld.) To comprehend the entire difference between the New Age and its predecessors, we may remember that Dante saw everything the other way round: he considered sin and vice to be the misapplication of the love which powers all creation. Vice in his ethical system plays the role of the grimace or grotesque of love and theological virtue: love that is mistaken in its choice of subject, in its proportion and degree etc. It errs because it has lost the 'virtue of sense, *il ben dell'inteletto*'.

Moreover, the intelligent man of the New Age relies on the indisputable premise that truth is a traumatic experience. Truth discovers the mean, superficial and vulgar at the foundation of all things. It tears away the patina of wonderful, elevating illusions. For Dante, just as for his educated contemporaries, the reverse was the case: 'la verita che tanto ci sublima' ('The truth that so elevates us': *Paradiso*, XXII, 42). The 'lowly' could never be the 'true' by definition, because the design of Creation is immeasurably lofty. Only a fool cannot see this 'loftiness', having 'given away sense for lust'.

The intelligence of 'contemporary man' is expressed in his resolute disappointment: in his own opinion he has long outgrown the childishness of hope. That which has burnt out may never be lit anew. Faded love may not be revived. That is a painful revelation, but it is truth for the man who has 'lived and thought'. To think differently is to be faint-hearted. This is the general tone of Baratynskii's lyrics. It goes without saying that it is just such an insane hope that constitutes wisdom for Dante. Moreover, the *Comedy* tells the story of a rekindling. For Dante the faint-hearted and vile is he who accepts hopelessness, who never takes on anything impossible.

Of course this is not a complete summary of the widespread New Age understanding of intelligence and foolishness, but I shall stop here and try to describe Pushkin's relationship with this world outlook. The most common quality connected with cleverness is coldness: thus, *warmth* (lack of intelligence) versus *cold*—and ruthless—intelligence.

Pushkin's attitude (in his works intelligence is often accompanied by this epithet) cannot be described as in simple and direct opposition to this point of view. Pushkin does not deny scepticism (nor fatalism, the other face of the Age of Enlightenment) their reality. Sometimes he unites them completely, especially when it comes to social man, whom he views quite hopelessly: 'О люди, жалкий род, достойный слез и смеха, / Жрецы минутного, поклонники успеха . . .' ('O, people, pitiful race, deserving tears and laughter, / Worshippers of the moment, devotees of success . . .') 'The blind and unruly age' remains 'blind and unruly' and this motivates the political views of the mature Pushkin.[7] Such an opinion of the 'people', 'miserable children of the world' would have been simple misanthropy, had Pushkin not known another man, not social man, but he who has 'forgotten the world' and cares about 'the benefits of base life', a man who returns to himself, to the penates, 'to hours of inexpressible pleasures', to the 'power of harmony'. A man sunk in a 'miraculous dream' or miraculously awakened. Pushkin describes this condition of oblivious concentration: 'Душа поэта встрепенется, / как пробудившийся орел' ('The soul of the poet begins to arouse / Like a woken eagle'); 'Я забывая мир, и в сладкой тишине / Я сладко усыплен моим воображеньем' ('And forgetting the world, in sweet silence / I am sweetly lulled to sleep by my imagination'). This man attends a school where 'Любить, лелеять [учат] / Несмертные, таинственные чувства'. ('[He is taught to] love and cherish / Immortal and mysterious feelings').

Pushkin, unlike the sceptics, not only knew this unsocial condition of man, but he also dared to consider it man's authentic, native home, his 'depth of heart' (and above all, of course, his own [Pushkin's] native home, his penates). He undoubtedly looks sceptically at the possibility that such conditions might be available to everyone: as his Mozart says: 'Тогда б не смог / И мир существовать' ('For then / The world itself could not exist').

The world ('the hectic concerns of society') exists as a distraction from harmony, penates and depth of heart. But Pushkin would have been the last person to have wished this world to come to a speedy end. He likes to imagine the continuation of events of everyday life even in his absence—when his grandson 'С приятельской беседы возвращаясь, / Веселых и приятных мыслей полон . . .' ('Returning from friendly conversation / Is full of happy and pleasant thoughts . . .'). His work (I mean of course that of the mature Pushkin) consists in finding amongst these hectic concerns a 'humble prose'—that is poetry's other form of existence.

Pushkin, moreover, in arguing with the New Age, does not say (as did Dante) that truth is lofty. He simply says, that 'elevating lies' are much more dear *to him*. He thus consents to having the reputation of a 'fool' in the eyes of contemporaries, in the eyes of the age (and in his own eyes too, for he is a 'child of society'): 'Но я любя был глуп и нем' ('But loving, I was stupid and dumb').

Generally speaking, unrequited love, devotion to which the poets of Provence saw as the highest truth, is for Pushkin a 'wretched foolishness'. The social licence for such behaviour had ended; nevertheless, Pushkin cannot and does not want to give up this 'wretched foolishness'.

He could have also called foolish his own incapacity for lasting disappointment in the Baratynskian manner—to the end, with no hope of a miraculous revival, an awaking from 'cold sleep' ('Я думал сердце позабыло' ['I thought that my heart had forgotten']). Unlikely revivals of various kinds, as it is well known, form an archeplot in Pushkin's works.[8]

So, Pushkin does not openly refute the sceptical conception of foolishness, he simply corrects it. For example, he demands that a poet—and poetry—should have the right to be foolish: 'Как жизнь поэта простодушна' ('Naive, like the life of a poet'). By the same token beauty—and beautiful women—do not need 'intelligence', that is, ideas.[9] This means that sheer presence is more important than the work of intellect.

But the most significant thing is that Pushkin clearly sees the asymmetry of sceptical theory—and reminds us of the other side of foolishness which the sceptic does not even mention. Pushkin reminds us of what might be called the foolishness of negativism or disbelief, or of total criticism; as Pushkin puts it: 'the foolishness of disapproval, that is less noticeable than the foolishness of praise'.

If we resort to the well-known Gospel advice, we can say that not being as wise as serpents is as foolish as not being as simple as doves. It is foolish because it does not correspond to the way the world is arranged and is doomed to failure. (Pushkin's plots often illustrate the rightness and ultimate good fortune which attend noble simplicity and the failure of calculation and deceit; consider *The Shot* and, in *The Captain's Daughter,* the way in which the 'cunning' Savelich and the naive Grinev relate to Pugachev, who like Pushkin's Peter the Great, represents a sort of elemental power, a 'divine storm'.)

It is foolish to be charmed thoughtlessly—but not to surrender to charm, not to 'be delighted and moved' is much more foolish. These two kinds of foolishness can be illustrated by the conversation between Onegin and Lenskii about the Larin sisters: Lenskii is the first to act foolishly, being charmed by Olga; Onegin, who appreciates Tatiana from a distance and remains cold, does the second foolish thing. It is foolish to trust thoughtlessly—but being 'subtle', that is, calculating and mistrusting (we can find examples in Pushkin's plots), is much more foolish, and, as he puts it, incompatible with a great soul.

It is foolish to take thoughtlessly—but to decline thoughtlessly is much more foolish. The question of taste, that is, of selecting and forming a hierarchy, is one of the most important things for Pushkin and he formulates it as a question of intelligence and the 'consideration of ideas', not of vague preferences. This is an original approach not only in terms of the conventions of his times, but also of ours. After all, we may call a person who admires Ilia Glazunov 'lacking in taste', but would not say the same of someone who can find nothing exceptional in Leonardo's works. And if we deny Zoilos something, it would be kindness or decency but not cleverness, as Pushkin put it in his epigram on the detractor: '"Затейник зол", с улыбкой скажет Глупость. / "Невежда глуп", зевая скажет Ум' ('"The schemer is evil", says Foolishness with a smile. / "The ignoramus is foolish", says Cleverness with a yawn').

We find an interesting example of Pushkin's 'non-polemical' disproof of scepticism in the following extract from 'Table Talk':

> A man by his nature is inclined rather to judge than to praise (says Machiavelli, that great connoisseur of the nature of men). Foolishness of judgment is not so noticeable, as foolish praise; a fool sees nothing of value in Shakespeare's works, and this is put down to his fastidiousness or eccentricity etc. The same fool is delighted by Ducray-Dumenil's novel or Polevoi's history and people look at him with contempt, though to a *thinking man* his foolishness was much more obvious in the first case.

(My italics)

Let us note: not to a kind-hearted man, but to a thinking man! It would seem that Pushkin develops Machiavelli's sceptical viewpoint only to end by attacking 'that great connoisseur of the nature of men'. And the weapon he uses to strike scepticism is thought, that is, that on which it most prides itself! Thought that knows only one thing about man—his impotence—is superficial and incomplete thought. Full thought knows something else: 'Они дают мне знать сердечну глубь / в могуществе и немощах его' ('They let me know the depth of heart / In its strength and infirmities').

Scepticism, in this case, anthropological scepticism—looks like a half-thought, that is, foolishness. It has never discovered anything about the 'power' of the heart. To conceive *intelligence* as merely a critical and negative principle is shown to be insufficiently *intelligent,* unthought through! And as for knowledge of human nature Pushkin, as usual, by chance and in passing conveys his own knowledge to us (disguised as stylized anthology): 'Должно бессмертных молить, да сподобят нас чистою душою / Правду блюсти: ведь оно же и легче'. ('One should pray to the immortals that they should help us with a pure soul / To perceive the truth: for that way is easier'.) It is easier, because it is much closer to nature. But nevertheless: in order 'to be helped' to get so close to nature, 'one should pray'.

That is why Pushkin considers evil and vice foolish, for this is all they have and all that they consist of. The most obvious examples are in Pushkin's fairy-tales: the greedy old woman in *The Tale about a Fisherman and a Fish,* the stingy priest in *Balda.* It is foolish and short-sighted to behave in this way. It is the mark of foolishness to feel that one is master of a situation, both now and in the future. I decide, I judge, I control the course of events. Foolishness does not understand where the sphere with which one may legitimately have dealings ends, and where the irrational, with which no one can argue, starts. (Pushkin, who called himself 'a tired slave' well understands it: 'If there is nothing to do, there is nothing to talk about'.)

Dante, in saying that souls which are placed in hell, have lost *il ben dell'intelleto,* did not contradict his time. He was simply following Thomas Aquinas and the whole traditional understanding of 'folly' (foolishness), antique and Biblical, which preceded him. And when Pushkin presents the foolish and the blind in terms similar to those of the Bible—as intelligence at once utilitarian ('Не подвижуся без зла' ['I cannot move without evil']) and cynical ('Рече безумен в сердце своем: несть Бог' ['The fool has said in his heart, 'There is no God']])—he is running counter to the ideological mainstream of his times. In so doing, he is probably relying only on his own experience of autonomy, of solitary communion with himself: 'Дабы сберечь ваш огнь уединенный, / Беседуя с самим собою') ('Seeking to preserve your solitary fire, / Conversing with myself') about those 'mysterious non-mortal feelings'. Clearly, Pushkin had no Aquinas to follow. His spiritual knowledge had been formed experimentally; he experimented on himself:[10] 'Они меня любить, лелеять учат / Не смертные, таинственные чувства' ('They teach me to love and foster / Mysterious non-mortal feelings . . .')

Here we have to reject the widespread contemporary understanding of 'чувство' as emotion, as something alien to the intellect and merely psychological. In Pushkin's use in this case as in many others (for instance that of 'клевета' mentioned above—accusation, but not lie) the Church-Slavonic and Old-Slavonic meanings are still alive. 'Чувство' is the general ability 'to perceive' ('чуять'), and is both intellectual and emotional; it is an openness. Here are some Biblical examples of the same meaning: 'Благочестие же в Бога, начало чувства; безумии же досады суще желатилие, возненавидеша чувство; устне мудрых связуются чувством: сердца же безумных не тверда' (*Proverbs,* I, 7; 22 and XV, 7: 'The fear of the Lord is the beginning of knowledge; the scorners delight in their scorning, and fools hate knowledge; The lips of the wise disperse knowledge: but the heart of the foolish doeth not so'). This 'чувство' also has its opposite in 'нечувствие', stone-like insensitivity: loss of all receptiveness, irresponsibility.[11]

Pushkin's understanding of 'intelligence' or 'prudence' as correct and pure 'чувство' is remarkably close to the ascetic school (*sophrosyne*: also translatable as 'chastity'). However, this rapprochement may not seem so strange if we are aware that experts on asceticism, for example A. Geronimus, consider it close to 'art', or 'spiritual art': right-thinking or awareness, or, in other words, 'чувство'—a straightforward, living, *pure* relationship with its object, 'Расположение души . . . к быстрому соображению понятий . . .' ('A disposition of the soul . . . towards a quick grasp of concepts . . .').[12] For Pushkin the know-all and the fool are unfeeling, that is, closed, resisting any relationship, igno-

rant of inspiration and intelligence (which, as it had been rightly noted, 'До слуха чуткого коснется' ['Would touch the keen ear']). The change of objects explains Pushkin's famous 'proteanism' (or 'polystylism'); that is, it is foolish and insensitive to address a miller in the same way as one would address one's friend—Prince Viazemskii for example.

Any declaration in Pushkin's world is unfeeling, that is, foolish. So is any final conclusion. For example, let us replace 'non-mortal feelings' in our quotation with 'immortal feelings': it now sounds much more foolish. Why? The labour of naming and comprehension has gone, as has the objection to one's self or to something else. The speaker seems to be looking closely at what is in front of him: mortal? No, non-mortal. The same movement—returning to something that has been said before and responding to it—can be heard in the assertion: 'Нет, весь я не умру' ('Я скоро весь умру') ('No, all of me will not die') ('Soon all of me will die'). This broadens the *time* of the statement; in its meaning it begins to feel less like an aphorism, at once instant and eternal, than a remark made in conversation with one's self, in a dialogue between the present and the past. The summarizing nature of utterance in Pushkin's works is always weak: we can never say whether we are confronting a universal judgement or a particular opinion: 'На свете счастья нет, но есть покой и воля'. ('In the world there is no happiness, but there is repose and freedom'.) (Compare in Onegin's letter: 'Я думал воля и покой / Замена счастью, Боже мой! / Как я ошибся, как наказан!' ['I thought freedom and repose / A fair exchange for happiness, my God! / What a mistake to make, what a punishment!']). Again, compare to this the (doubtless widespread) conceit characteristic of similar statements of other poets: 'Есть в близости людей заветная черта; / Есть бытие, но именем каким . . . etc.' ('There is something hidden and precious in human intimacy; / Being exists, but by what name . . . ?').

In the depth of Pushkin's 'mysterious feelings' (which he never names and never describes) and his knowledge of 'сердечная глубина' ('the depth of the heart') we can discern a respect for freedom. No other poet has envisaged with such equanimity a world in which he is no longer present. There is no melancholy, no wish to return once more (as with Lermontov); only the hope that he will be remembered:

> Но пусть мой внук . . .
> И обо мне вспомянет;
> Скажи: есть память обо мне;
> Укажет будущий невежда
> На мой прославленный портрет.
>
> (But let my grandson . . .
> Remember me;
> You say that I am remembered;

    Some future ignoramus
    Pointing a finger at my celebrated portrait.)

Examples of this, probably the most unique of Push-kin's motifs—homage to a world from which he has already departed—can be quoted again and again. Push-kin leaves the world free of himself. He also leaves love free of himself: 'Как дай Вам Бог любимой быть другим' ('As, God grant, you may be loved by another').

In his writing, antididactic and elusive, Pushkin leaves us 'free of himself'. He leaves his own words free of himself, the composition and the subject of his works and their 'moral'. Or rather he does not *leave*: he grants freedom to everything that has not possessed it before. Pushkin is the author of a unique theodicy: 'За что мне на Бога роптать, / Когда хоть одному творенью / я мог свободу даровать!' ('Why should I murmur against God / When I can grant freedom / To even one of his creations!') This is almost a declaration. But the substance itself, the verbal and rhythmical flesh of his (mature) works does itself represent this 'gift of freedom'.

To grant freedom to others (or another), one needs to possess a surplus of it. This surplus in Pushkin's case is provided by health, flexibility and swiftness of both mind and feeling. Pushkin is the least passionate of Russian poets—'passionate' in the ancient sense of the word. He is not dominated by the inertia of one sensation, one mood, style or idea—he passes over them quickly, as if walking on water—without sinking. In comparison other Russian authors seem obsessed, each by something of his own: some by melancholy, some by irritability, some by a dream and others by disappointment. They are prisoners of their own style and Pushkin manages to slip away from all of his styles.

Many works of literature (Pasternak thought all of them) apart from their immediate plot or subject subtly expound another simultaneously which is in fact the main theme: 'the science of poetry'. Pushkin undoubtedly supposed that he was creating some rules for Russian literature and providing examplars. Possibly he was the only person who was capable of following them.

Mediæval Latin studies of poetry were frequently called *Ars Amandi* (The Art of Love) rather than *Ars Poetica* (The Art of Poetry). Pushkin's 'science of poetry' could be called 'the science of respecting freedom'. And even if no Russian poet has as yet managed to practise that science as consummately as its originator, the 'law of liberty' has remained undisputed and cherished by everyone who has written in Russian since Pushkin. His descendants have made some improvements to this law: Blok spoke of 'covert (тайный) liberty' (where 'тайный' implies both 'covered' and 'mysterious'); Maria Petrovikh in her 'Testament' wrote about the 'silence' of liberty—exactly in the spirit of Pushkin:

    Не шум газетной оды,
    Журнальной болтовни,
    Лишь тишина свободы
    Прославит наши дни.

    (No loud newspaper doggerel
    No journalistic prattle,
    Only the silence of freedom
    Will grant our days their glory.)

It is Mandelshtam who understands this mysterious covert liberty in its entirety—*Pushkin's non-mortal feeling*—as the special gift of Russia, its religious gift, which is as valuable as the constructive and historic gift from the West:[13] 'To that place, where everything appears as a necessity, where each stone is covered up by the patina of time and slumbers, immured in a vault, Chaadaev brought moral freedom, the gift of the Russian land, the best flower that it has ever grown' ('Петр Чаадаев', 1914).

Notes

This line, ["Non-mortal and mysterious feelings,"] from Pushkin's 'еще одной высокой важной песни' is a free translation of a phrase from Southey's *Hymn to the Penates*: 'strange unworldly feelings'.

1. Indeed, its future until the end of times: 'И славен буду я, доколь в подлунном мире / Жив будет хоть один пиит' ('And I will be famous / As long as any poet lives beneath the moon'). This and subsequent translations in this chapter are by Robert Reid. Pushkin, probably, could never imagine the world without a single poet. But neither could Horace have imagined, when defining the extent of his own of immortality, that the Roman pontifex would one day not 'ascend the Capitol accompanied by a silent maiden': 'Crescam laude recens dum Capitolium / Scandet cum tacita virgine pontifex' (Horace, *Carmina,* III, 30).

2. For Pushkin, both the abuser of art—'the barbarian-artist'—and Salieri's 'righteous anger' at the blind violin player, expressed by the same image, are equally ugly. Compare: 'Художник-кварвар кистью сонной / Картину гения чернит' ('The barbarian-artist with somnolent [another synonym for "unwise"—"the cold dream"] brush / Blackens the work of a genius') and 'Мне не смешно, когда маляр презренный / Мне пачкает Мадонны Рафаэля' ('I am not amused when a contemptible house-painter / Bedaubs Raphael's Madonna').

3. Cf. Baratynskii's epigram on Bulgarin:

    Поверьте мне, Фиглярин-моралист
    Нам говорит преумиленным слогом:
    'Не должно красть: кто на руку нечист,

Перед людьми грешит и перед Богом;
Не надобно в суде кривить душой,
Нехорошо живиться клеветой,
Временщику подслуживаться низко;
Честь, братцы, честь дороже нам всего!'
Ну что ж? Бог с ним! все это к правде близко,
А может быть и ново для него.

(Believe me, Foolgarin the moralist
Tells us in tones most touching:
'Do not steal; he who is dishonest
Sins before God and others;
Nor go against your conscience when at law
And it is wrong to prosper by false witness
And it is base to flatter placemen;
Honour, good friends, we prize above all else!'
So what? Good for him! It's all pretty near the truth
Maybe it's new to him, though.)

4. When we hear stories about an artist's repentance and conversion we have to admit that there is something rather sad about them, and thus they do not seem very instructive, at least in a serious way. The appeal to the salvation of one's self is usually feverish and panicked, and it always reveals the shadow of a major downfall of some kind. These stories are sad, because the place of the artist as someone authoritative, speaking neither about himself nor voicing his personal opinions, is taken by a specific personality. The artistic somehow contrives to make this private individual, who is really of no interest to anyone, appear in an entirely different guise, illuminated by an obliviousness to self. Whereas what is audible here is the voice of the naked 'I', the voice of a not very elevating fear and concern for the self. Thank God, this is not so in Pushkin's case. And if we think about what Christian art is—that is, not merely art on Christian themes—it is, first and foremost, an art that gives of itself. I hope that I will not be understood as denying the value of repentance or humility. It is simply that their artistic representations are probably not very close to everyday reality.

5. From a manuscript of 1827-8, quoted by B. Modzalevskii, *Pis'ma Pushkina*, I, Academia, St Petersburg, 1926, p. 314.

6. 'To investigate the religious spirit of Pushkin's poetry in all its depth and true originality would require an æsthetic analysis of his poetry and, moreover, a "formal" one, inasmuch as it would concern itself with poetical form; however it would go far beyond what is normally termed "formal criticism".' See S. L. Frank, *Etiudy o Pushkine,* YMCA Press, Paris, 1987, p. 10.

7. 'Political views' in the sense of Pushkin's conservatism, acceptance of the state system, censorship etc. There is in him a sympathy with the Hobbe-

sian outlook: human imperfection means that a controlling power must participate in the creation of community.

8. See R. Jakobson, 'The Statue in Pushkin's Poetic Mythology' in *Selected Writings,* (*On Verse: Its Masters and Explorers*), The Hague, Paris-New York, 1979, pp. 237-80; also O. Sedakova, '*Mednyi vsadnik*: kompozitsiia konflikta', *Rossiia,* VII, 1991, pp. 39-55.

9. In the same way John Keats speaks of the equation between truth and beauty as a liberation from 'thought': 'Thou, silent form! dost tease us out of thought / As doth eternity. Cold Pastoral! (*Ode on a Grecian Urn*)1

10. 'Благочестие же в Бога, начало чувства; безумнии же досады суще желатилие, возненавидеша чувство; устне мудрых связуются чувством: сердца же безумных не тверда' (Притч., 1, 7; 2; 15, 7). Such a feeling is the opposite of being unfeeling, as cold as stone: the loss of any perception, being beside oneself.

11. V. A. Geronimus rightly perceives a sentimentalist origin in Pushkin's use of 'feeling'. However, this does not invalidate my 'Slavonic' interpretation. It is common for Pushkin to have a double source of meaning—French and Slavonic (or demotic Russian). This is the case with the word 'печаль' (grief) of which I have written elsewhere. (Reference is to a discussion between the author and the Pushkin specialist V. A. Geronimus.)

12. Pushkin's favourite ephitets are *alive* and *pure.* They represent the best he can say about anything that exists. Too many people think that these two things are incompatible and opposed. But separate and in opposition they are of no interest at all!

13. Prot. A. Geronimus, 'Isikhatskoe bogoslovie: poeziia i poetika', in *Problemy asketiki i mistiki pravoslaviia,* Didik, Moscow, 1995, pp. 151-76. There is good reason to see Pushkin less as representing Russian genius, than as transcending the spirit of that genius. In foreign studies of Pushkin remarks about the uniqueness of his writing in Russian literature are widespread: he is considered 'the most un-Russian of all Russian writers'. The grace of Pushkin's genius can seem alien to Russia, to 'Russian inertia', the heaviness, bravery and sentimentality of 'the mysterious Russian soul' if we do not also keep in mind the previous centuries of our culture, the early architecture and icon painting, the ancient Russian language in which *vulgarity* meant 'all things bad', *sin* meant 'to commit vulgarity' and *elegant* meant 'excellent'.

FURTHER READING

Criticism

Barth, J. Robert. "The Sacramental Vision of Gerard Manley Hopkins." In *Seeing into the Life of Things: Essays on Literature and Religious Experience,* edited by John L. Mahoney, pp. 210-25. New York: Fordham University Press, 1998.

> Explores Gerard Manley Hopkins's interpretation and portrayal of Christian sacrament in his poetry.

Fulford, Tim. "Blessed Bane: Christianity and Colonial Disease in Southey's *Tale of Paraguay.*" *Romanticism on the Net* 24 (November 2001): <http://users.ox.ac.uk/~scat0385/24fulford.html>.

> Asserts that the purpose of Robert Southey's *Tales of Paraguay* was "to promote missionary colonialism as a model Britain should follow in its own empire."

Gatta, John. "Godliness Writ Large in John Muir's *Sierra.*" *Religion and Literature* 35, nos. 2-3 (summer-autumn 2003): 11-28.

> Concentrates on John Muir's search for religious truth in the natural world.

Litvack, Leon B. "Callista, Martyrdom, and the Early Christian Novel in the Victorian Age." *Nineteenth-Century Contexts* 17, no. 2 (1993): 159-73.

> Explores the widespread interest in representations of martyrdom in early Victorian literature.

Sinche, Bryan. "Godly Rebellion in *The Bondwoman's Narrative.*" In *In Search of Hannah Crafts: Critical Essays on* The Bondwoman's Narrative, edited by Henry Louis Gates, Jr., and Hollis Robbins, pp. 175-91. New York: Basic Civitas, 2004.

> Considers Hannah Craft's *The Bondwoman's Narrative* in light of the author's desire to denounce the evils of slavery while maintaining faith in the existence of God.

Svaglic, Martin J. "John Henry Newman: The Victorian Experience." In *The Victorian Experience: The Prose Writers,* edited by Richard A. Levine, pp. 47-82. Athens: Ohio University Press, 1982.

> Regards Cardinal John Henry Newman's writings on Christianity within the context of the Victorian intellectual community.

Thomas, Gordon K. "Eros and Christianity: Byron in the Underground Resistance Movement." In *Byron, The Bible, and Religion: Essays from the Twelfth International Byron Seminar,* edited by Wolf Z. Hirst, pp. 101-17. Newark, Del. and London: University of Delaware Press and Associated University Presses, 1991.

> Interprets Byron's treatment of Eros within the Christian tradition as an expression of the poet's search for religious truth.

Democracy in Nineteenth-Century Literature

The following entry provides critical commentary on the treatment of democracy in nineteenth-century literature.

INTRODUCTION

Many nineteenth-century writers cautioned against the rapid advance of democracy in the United States. These writers anticipated problems caused by democracy, such as the tyranny of the majority, the domination of public opinion, and an absence of intellectual freedom. Some nineteenth-century commentators maintained that humankind's struggle for equality, or individuality, would cause the disintegration of society. One of Ralph Waldo Emerson's tenets in support of democracy was that all individuals shared the divine nature of God, and therefore each person was of equal importance. Emerson's opponents countered that with such expansive equality, there could be no variety and specifically, no hierarchy. By engendering such mediocrity, no one of any merit would be fit to run the country. Alexis de Tocqueville anticipated that the materialism and individualism inherent in democracy would isolate people and make them less likely to deny personal gratification for the good of the community. Henry James, in his works, similarly held that a desire for independence would lead individuals into isolation that could result in a selfishness that stemmed from indifference towards society. James, Tocqueville, and Emerson all stressed the importance of individual morals in addressing any challenges presented by a democratic society. James, however, emphasized women's role in this regard, voicing the common belief that women held sway over moral standards, were naturally more concerned with the greater good of society, and therefore would constrain moral lapses.

Other writers conveyed their distrust of democracy and asserted that the power of the majority would threaten individuality. One such author, James Fenimore Cooper, alleged that the domination of public opinion would limit individual freedom of thought and expression. Tocqueville suggested that a loss of intellectual freedom could lead to a decline in the quality of literature, education, and politics. Additionally, he and others felt that commercialism and the mass production of literature for the purpose of entertainment might also diminish literary quality in America. These warnings did not come to fruition; instead, American fiction and poetry came to reflect the growing interdependence between the individual and a democratic society. Nineteenth-century novels and poems celebrate the individual while highlighting the universality of human experience. One of the paradoxes noted in Walt Whitman's poem, "Song of Myself," included in *Leaves of Grass* (1855), is that the poem promotes individuality and a connectedness to society based on equality. Critics such as Ray B. Browne interpret such works as Herman Melville's *Billy Budd* (1924) as affirmations of the common man, and point out that although William Wordsworth eschewed political rhetoric in his works, he openly championed the common man.

REPRESENTATIVE WORKS

Thomas Carlyle
Sartor Resartus (novel) 1836
Latter-Day Pamphlets (pamphlets) 1850

James Fenimore Cooper
Precaution. 2 vols. [published anonymously] (novel) 1820
The Spy: A Tale of the Neutral Ground. [published anonymously] 2 vols. (novel) 1821
The Pioneers; or, The Sources of the Susquehanna: A Descriptive Tale. 2 vols. (novel) 1823
The Last of the Mohicans: A Narrative of 1757. 2 vols. (novel) 1826
The Prairie. 3 vols. (novel) 1827
The American Democrat; or, Hints on the Social and Civic Relations of the United States of America (nonfiction) 1838
The Chainbearer; or, The Littlepage Manuscripts. 3 vols. (novel) 1845
Satanstoe; or, The Family of Littlepage. A Tale of the Colony. 3 vols. (novel) 1845
Ravensnest; or, The Redskins. 3 vols. (novel) 1846

John Dewey
The Ethics of Democracy (philosophy) 1888
The Public and Its Problems (philosophy) 1927

Ralph Waldo Emerson
Essays (essays) 1838; also published as *Essays: First Series,* 1854
Essays: Second Series (essays) 1844
May-Day and Other Pieces (poetry) 1867

Fortune of the Republic. Lecture Delivered at the Old South Church (essay) 1878

Henry James
Daisy Miller (novel) 1879
The Bostonians (novel) 1886
"Pandora" (short story) 1886; published in the journal *New York Sun*
The Princess Casamassima (novel) 1886
The American Scene (travel essays) 1907

Herman Melville
Clarel: A Poem and Pilgrimage in the Holy Land (poetry) 1876
Billy Budd and Other Prose Pieces (novel and short stories) 1924

Edgar Allan Poe
The Man That Was Used Up. A Tale of the Late Bugaboo and Kickapoo Campaign (poem) 1839
Tales of the Grotesque and Arabesque. 2 vols. (short stories) 1840
"Some Words with a Mummy" (short story) 1845; published in the journal *American Review*
"The System of Doctor Tarr and Professor Fether" (short story) 1845; published in the journal *Graham's Magazine*
"Mellonta Tauta" (short story) 1849; published in the journal *Godey's Lady's Book*

Alexis de Tocqueville
De la démocratie en Amérique. 2 vols. [*Democracy in America*] (travel essays) 1840

Anthony Trollope
The Warden (novel) 1855
An Autobiography (autobiography) 1883

Frances Trollope
Domestic Manners of the Americans. 2 vols. (travel essays) 1832

Walt Whitman
Leaves of Grass [published anonymously] (poetry) 1855
Democratic Vistas (essays) 1871
An American Primer [edited by Horace L. Traubel] (essays) 1904

William Wordsworth
*Lyrical Ballads [with Samuel Taylor Coleridge] (poetry) 1798
Memorials of a Tour on the Continent, 1820 (memoirs) 1822
†The Prelude, or Growth of a Poet's Mind, An Autobiographical Poem (poetry) 1850

*Enlarged editions of *Lyrical Ballads* were published in 1801 and 1802. A final edition was published in 1805.

†This work was written between 1799 and 1805.

OVERVIEWS

Reino Virtanen (essay date January 1950)

SOURCE: Virtanen, Reino. "Tocqueville on a Democratic Literature." *The French Review* 23, no. 3 (January 1950): 214-22.

[*In the following essay, Virtanen examines Tocqueville's prophetic assessment of the qualities of literature informed by American democratic principles.*]

Surely one of the most interesting cases in the history of ideas is that of Alexis de Tocqueville. Elected to the French Academy at 35 on the strength of one book, he was to publish only one other in his lifetime. The one was *De la Démocratie en Amérique*; the other, *l'Ancien Régime et la Révolution,* was only part of a projected longer work. After a resounding success, the one on America was to fall from the top ranks of influential books to that dignified level of writings often mentioned but seldom read to the end. And even this measure of esteem was not granted to the second part of *De la Démocratie en Amérique.* The first part, devoted to description of the operation of American political institutions, was what impressed John Stuart Mill, Sainte-Beuve, Laboulaye, Prévost-Paradol and Émile Faguet. None of these nineteenth-century commentators paid much attention to the second part, which seemed vague and abstract to them in contrast to the concrete and factual earlier volumes. It was the later section that Sainte-Beuve had in mind when he cited the quip that Tocqueville had started to think before learning anything.[1]

In our time the fortunes of the two parts, the factually descriptive and the abstractly philosophical, are almost being reversed. It was inevitable that Tocqueville's study of America in the Age of Jackson would meet with neglect as the decades passed. Not all of the features he described in the still largely agrarian, imperfectly industrialized America of 1831 could be found existing and not many could be found unchanged by the next great European student of the American commonwealth, James Bryce. Yet in this still later day of the Gunnar Myrdals and the Harold Laskis, we find a John Gunther, a David Lilienthal, not to mention a *New Yorker* reviewer, all now conjuring with the name of Alexis de Tocqueville. Not only that, he has in recent years been the object of tribute from critics like F. O. Matthiessen, R. P. Blackmur and Eric Bentley, philosophers from Wilhelm Dilthey to Ortega y Gasset, sociologists like Albert Salomon and historians like Gilbert Chinard and Henry Steele Commager.[2] The significant thing is that most of those just named are as interested in the once neglected second part as they are in the first.

A stimulating article by T. V. Smith, entitled "Hindsight on de Tocqueville's Foresight," distinguishes three aspects of Tocqueville's work: "what he saw as a cognizant scientist, what he saw as a clairvoyant philosopher, what he saw as an audacious prophet."[3] What he saw as a scientist has become dated in a hundred years, but these hundred years have thrown into a new perspective certain theories of the philosopher, certain visions of the seer. There is his discovery of the importance in American politics of associations, today often called pressure groups. There is his presentiment of a new aristocracy arising out of industry. He had a sense for world politics. In the afternoon of French power, the noontide of British power, the morning of German power, he looked ahead to a time when two nations on the peripheries, America and Russia, would dominate the world.

Such a record as prophet might well justify studying more attentively those ideas on democratic philosophy and literature which an earlier critic, Henry Sidgwick, found weak and superficial, and which even George W. Pierson in our own day does not take very seriously.[4] Examination of these chapters establishes Tocqueville's right to stand as something like a pioneer of the sociology of culture. With a more modest display of index cards, with less apparatus of demonstration than his debtor Hippolyte Taine, his pages remain suggestive at a time when those of Taine seem to be losing their power.

That does not mean that Tocqueville's ideas on the kind of literature and philosophy to be expected in a democracy have been completely overlooked until the present day. He has been regarded for a century as a leading sponsor of the opinion that American democracy is incompatible with pure thought. Bliss Perry in 1912 explained the defects in our culture in just this way. "For an explanation of these defects", he wrote, "shall we fall back upon a convenient maxim of De Tocqueville's and admit with him that 'a democracy is unsuited to meditation'? We are forced to do so."[5] Another maxim of Tocqueville's has been in circulation for a good while. Van Wyck Brooks found in Mark Twain's *Pudd'nhead Wilson* a paraphrase of Tocqueville's comment: "I know of no country in which there is so little independence of mind and real freedom of discussion as in America." And Brooks recalls Mark Twain's remark: "In our country we have those three unspeakably precious things: freedom of thought, freedom of speech and the prudence never to practice either."[6] Some chapters of the first part do indeed stress this view of America. It is here that Tocqueville expresses his aristocratic dread of a despotism maintained by the majority.

> Si l'Amérique n'a pas eu encore de grands écrivains, nous ne devons pas en chercher ailleurs les raisons: il n'existe pas de génie littéraire sans liberté d'esprit, et il n'y a pas de liberté d'esprit en Amérique.[7]

Tocqueville as critic of American culture has been so completely identified with such observations that many people are unaware of the more penetrating comment presented in the second part.[8] It is here that he emerges as a social philosopher, a forerunner of sociology. It is to be expected that much of this theorizing should be vague and inconclusive, and some of it self-contradictory. But for some of his insights, prophetic is a tempting word. His chapter on the philosophic method of the Americans is a preview of pragmatism, while his *aperçus* on the tendency in a democracy toward pantheism apply to much in Transcendentalism and Walt Whitman.

Without a deep interest in American literature, without a single reference to any American poet or novelist, he put his finger on certain qualities of this literature which only the future would unveil. Many years ago the well-known author of books on Shakespeare and Montaigne, Edward Dowden, pointed out a striking correlation between his characterizations and Walt Whitman's *Leaves of Grass*. Dowden wrote: "It is curious to find de Tocqueville before there existed properly any native American literature, describing in the spirit of philosophical prophecy what we find realized in Whitman's *Leaves of Grass*." Dowden goes on to quote from the chapter on "Sources of Poetry among Democracies": "He who inhabits a democratic country sees . . . men differing but little . . . his thought embraces the whole world. . . . The general similitude of individuals, which renders any one of them taken separately an improper subject of poetry, allows poets to include them all in the same imagery and to take a general survey of the people itself." Whitman's "I celebrate myself" is, as Dowden observes, but the celebration of himself as a man, as an American. The affinity between Tocqueville's formulation and Whitman's *en masse* is evident. Dowden adopts Tocqueville's distinctions between aristocratic and democratic literature. In contrast to aristocratic literature, the art of a democratic age places little value on form, style and tradition. Each new generation is a law unto itself. Individualism is strong and experimentation is common. Turning to Whitman, Dowden perceives that his work corresponds with "the democratic tendencies of the world of thought and feeling in which he moves." He is spontaneous, his sympathies are not selective but multiform. He has a mystic faith in science, with confidence in the future.[9]

In 1932, Charles Cestre was impressed in his turn by Tocqueville's anticipation of Whitman. Cestre itemizes in three packed pages the concordances between Tocqueville's description of the future American poetry and Whitman's actual characteristics, his "barbaric yawp" and war cry, his scorn for the past, his interest in nature more for the symbols it gives than for its own sake, his celebration of man, of fraternity, his pantheism.[10]

How audacious the views of Tocqueville seemed to his contemporaries may be judged from the following remark of the *Blackwood's* reviewer in 1840: "Such a change in the character of poetry, as M. de Tocqueville supposes will come about, appears to us quite impossible, unless a correspondent change, not in governments, not in society, but in human nature itself, takes place at the same time."[11]

But what are the principal features of the change in the character of poetry which he foresees? Democratic society lacks the intermediate powers between God and man which are found depicted in aristocratic times. It lacks the high and low classes whose remoteness from the mean favors an idealized portrayal in aristocratic literature. We recall Henry James' dissatisfaction with the "absence of a variety of types" in America with its lack of a social hierarchy. Democratic literature finds it hard to idealize individual men, for all individuals bear a familiar stamp. There is a distaste for the past as a source for poetry. Hawthorne and James, of course, did not share this distaste with Whitman. Yet even Hawthorne was to make this comment on European art: "I wished that the whole Past might be swept away, and each generation compelled to bury and destroy whatever it had produced."[12] This is also the attitude expressed by Holgrave in *The House of the Seven Gables.*

But if these springs of poetry have nearly ceased to flow, democratic times open new ones. "La démocratie détourne l'imagination de tout ce qui est extérieur à l'homme pour ne la fixer que sur l'homme. . . . Tout ce qui se rapporte à l'existence du genre humain pris en entier, à ses vicissitudes, à son avenir, devient une mine très féconde pour la poésie."

"On peut prévoir," writes Tocqueville, "que les poètes qui vivent dans les âges démocratiques peindront des passions et des idées plutôt que des personnes et des actes." In a democracy, persons and actions are too well known to all to be suitable for poetry. Therefore the poet will seek the soul below its outer covering. "Or, il n'y a rien qui prête plus à la peinture de l'idéal que l'homme ainsi envisagé dans les profondeurs de sa nature immatérielle."[13] Such passages serve to remind us that Tocqueville was writing during the Romantic period, with their echoes of Mme de Staël's *De la Littérature* and Chateaubriand's *Génie du Christianisme.* Among democratic peoples poetry will not be made with legends. Poetry will not attempt to people the world with supernatural beings in whom no one believes. The day of allegory is over. "Toutes ces ressources lui manquent; mais l'homme lui reste et c'est assez pour elle."[14] Tocqueville's conception is reminiscent of William Hazlitt who wrote in his *English Poets*: "There can never be another Jacob's Dream. . . . It is not only the progress of mechanical knowledge, but the necessary advances of civilization, that are unfavourable to

the spirit of poetry. . . . In the United States of America where the philosophical principles of government are carried still further in theory and practice, we find that the *Beggar's Opera* is hooted from the stage. Society, by degrees, is constructed into a machine that carries us safely and insipidly from one end of life to the other in a very comfortable prose style."[15] But Tocqueville does not, as we know, expect the decline of all poetry. "L'homme lui reste, et c'est assez pour elle." He is not subject to the correction which Shelley's *Defense of Poetry* administered to Thomas Love Peacock's *Four Ages of Poetry.* This is clear from Tocqueville's statement:

> Les destinées humaines, l'homme, pris à part de son temps et de son pays, et placé en face de la nature et de Dieu, avec ses passions, ses doutes, ses prospérités inouies et ses misères incompréhensibles, deviendront pour ces peuples l'objet principal et presque unique de la poésie; et c'est ce dont on peut déjà s'assurer si l'on considère ce qu'ont écrit les plus grands poètes qui aient paru depuis que le monde achève de tourner à la démocratie.

And he cites as "poèmes de la démocratie" *Childe Harold, René,* and *Jocelyn.*[16] Tocqueville's translator added *Faust* to this list, and might we not for our purpose add Herman Melville's Captain Ahab from *Moby Dick*? It is interesting that a later French critic, E. D. Forgues, reviewing *Moby Dick* in 1853, was to echo precisely the following remarks of Tocqueville:

> Je n'ai pas peur que la poésie des peuples démocratiques se montre timide ni qu'elle se tienne très-près de terre. J'appréhende plutôt qu'elle ne se perde à chaque instant dans les nuages, et qu'elle ne finisse par peindre des contrées entièrement imaginaires. Je crains que les œuvres des poètes démocratiques n'offrent souvent des images immenses et incohérentes, des peintures surchargées, des composés bizarres, et que les êtres fantastiques sortis de leur esprit ne fassent quelquefois regretter le monde réel.[17]

It has already become clear that what Tocqueville calls democratic literature is almost coextensive with the Romantic movement, though he never uses the term himself. The absence of the word from his book might suggest that he was isolated from the literary controversies of his age. He was insulated perhaps but not entirely isolated. Chateaubriand was his cousin. Comparison of his formulations with texts from Mme de Staël, Lamartine, Hugo and Vigny would reveal parallels between their views on the destiny of poetry. His chapter on commercialism in literature develops the same thesis as Sainte-Beuve's *causerie* on *la Littérature industrielle.*[18]

In addition to his "Whitman," Dowden wrote two other essays involving Tocqueville. His 1871 article on "Edgar Quinet" without mentioning Tocqueville bears the impress of Tocqueville's thinking. In fact the poetic aims of Edgar Quinet are so close to Tocqueville's picture of a democratic poet that Dowden takes over Tocqueville's formulation word for word: "Quinet conceived," writes Dowden, that "the epic should reappear in a new form . . . previously it had celebrated the achievements of a hero or a people; . . . now the human race itself must become the hero. . . . Such must be the epic of a democratic age. In a great democracy, the aristocratic ideal is replaced by one different . . . no individual hero can be the subject of a poem; the entire nation, or humanity itself, becomes the central figure."[19] Though Quinet was not a good enough poet to serve as Whitman's opposite number, they share the same conception of the poet's mission. Dowden's article on the *Transcendental Movement* (1877) reveals more of this common ground. Tocqueville had set down as traits of a democratic period "an almost invincible aversion to the supernatural" and a passion for pantheistic ideas. These are significant traits also of Transcendentalism, which glorifies or deifies humanity. "It will not appear a mere accident," writes Dowden, "that some of the characteristics noted by Tocqueville should show themselves in Wordsworth and Coleridge . . . who had nourished their feelings in ardent youth with the enthusiasm of the French democracy. Shelley, again, is nothing if he is not revolutionary and at the same time transcendental."[20] Thus Dowden, stimulated by Tocqueville's ideas, helps to restore them to their living context in post-revolutionary France.

It would be too much to say that Tocqueville deduced the characteristics of democratic poetry, as he claims to do, from the pure concept of equality. His description is too close to some of the poetry already produced by the Romantic movement. Is it impertinent to apply here his own criticism of the abuses of language in a democracy? He had written: "Un mot abstrait est comme une boîte à double fond: on y met les idées que l'on désire, et on les en retire sans que personne le voie."[21] Undoubtedly his concept of equality suffers from an excessive abstractness. In some contexts it broadens out to encompass bourgeois society itself. In others it narrows down to include only the leveling tendency which is one factor in the America of the Age of Jackson. He could make his predictions of some typical themes of democratic poetry by projecting into an imagined future the lines of development already manifest in contemporary Europe and check them against what could be found, if only in an inchoate form, on the American scene. Why he made so little of American examples—he cited none in his books—is explained by his observation that American writers were as yet mere imitators of the English. His prediction of what American poetry would become proved more significant than a discussion of the Dennies, Willises and Pauldings would have been. Less excusable, perhaps, is his neglect of Cooper,

Irving, and Bryant, but even this omission counts for little when set against his exposition, before the fact, of Transcendentalism, of Whitmanism, of pragmatism.

He found America's journalism more expressive than its literature.[22] This observation of the situation in the 1830's appears largely vindicated by the fact that Whitman and Mark Twain would start out as editors, and also by the journalistic origins of the short story of Hawthorne, Poe and Bret Harte. And it was journalism that provided data for one of his most penetrating formulations. If the concept of equality does not contain enfolded within it all the consequences which he deduced from it, if many of his ideas can be traced instead to the Romantic ambient, there is one corollary for which we must praise both his *esprit de géométrie* and his *esprit de finesse*. We find it in his brief chapter on "Pourquoi les écrivains et les orateurs américains sont souvent boursouflés." He links American grandiloquence and love of general ideas with the social conditions of democratic communities:

> . . . chaque citoyen est habituellement occupé à contempler un très-petit objet, qui est lui-même. S'il vient à lever plus haut les yeux, il n'aperçoit alors que l'image immense de la société, ou la figure plus grande encore du genre humain. Il n'a que des idées très-particulières et très-claires, ou des notions très-générales et très-vagues; l'espace intermédiaire est vide.[23]

We are reminded of Bronson Alcott's *Conversations* with titles like "On Man," "On Character," "On Temperaments and Pursuits." As Odell Shepard observes: "Alcott's topics were by far too large and vague and general. One may see, however, in glancing through the titles of Thoreau's or Emerson's Essays, that this was a common fault of the time." F. O. Matthiessen has pointed to Whitman's "Orbic Chant for all Eventualities" as an instance of the tendency.[24]

We could hardly expect the literature of democratic nations to follow exactly the course which Tocqueville laid out for it. To him its course appeared relatively simple. The themes, he asserted, would be less numerous but more vast. He was far from suspecting the richness and variety, in both form and substance, which the 19th and 20th centuries would unfold. He could not know that so good a Democrat as Hawthorne was to utter the plaint "no shadow, no antiquity," as Henry James was to deplore "the silent past."[25] He foresaw the growth of commercialism in literature, deprecated the lack of taste and indifference to form which he thought inevitable under a democracy. Thus he has provided ammunition for French writers like Georges Batault after the First World War.[26] But to see in him a sort of aristocratic heckler of democratic culture, as Batault did, is to distort his ideas almost completely.

His conception of aristocratic and democratic literature corresponds quite closely to Classicism and Romanticism. He conceives the characteristic theme of democratic poetry to be the problem of man confronting the universe. It is interesting that this conception derives from a great 17th-century writer's thoughts on the ego. And Pascal's presence here is quite in order, for it was the Romantics who re-discovered him. An agonized sense of cosmic exile imbues the final passages of the chapter on the "Sources of Poetry". We cannot help feeling that Tocqueville's formula for a democratic poetry breaks down. Yet though his *esprit de géométrie* is defeated, it is still a sort of victory for Tocqueville. It is a victory for his *esprit de finesse.*

Notes

1. Sainte-Beuve, C. A., "Œuvres et correspondence inédites de M. de Tocqueville," *Causeries du Lundi.* Paris, Garnier, 4ᵉ éd., XV, p. 105 n. For other commentators see: Mill, John Stuart, *Dissertations and Discussions* (Boston, Spencer, 1858), II, pp. 85 f, 123-141; Laboulaye, Édouard, *L'État et ses limites,* (Paris, Charpentier, 1863), pp. 173-174; Prévost-Paradol, *Essais de Politique et Littérature* (Paris, Michel Lévy, 1863), pp. 58-80; Faguet, Émile, *Politiques et Moralistes du XIX siècle* (Paris, Société française d'imprimerie, 1900), 3ᵉ série, pp. 66-114.

2. Matthiessen, F. O., *American Renaissance* (New York, Oxford University Press, 1941), pp. 533-534, 543-544; Blackmur, R. P., in *The Question of Henry James* (ed., Dupee), (New York, Holt, 1945), pp. 195-196; Bentley, Eric, *The Playwright as Thinker* (New York, Reynal and Hitchcock, 1946), pp. 369-370; Dilthey, Wilhelm *Der Aufbau der geschichtlichen Welt in den Geisteswissenschaften* (Gesammelte Werke, VII) (Leipzig, 1927), pp. 104-105; Ortega y Gasset, José, *Toward a Philosophy of History,* trans. (New York, Norton, 1941), pp. 44, 76; Salomon, Albert, "Tocqueville, Moralist and Sociologist," *Social Research,* II, Nov. 1935, pp. 405-427; Chinard, Gilbert, preface, *Tocqueville: de la Démocratie en Amérique. Extraits* (Princeton, Institut Français de Washington, 1943); Commager, Henry Steele, *America in Perspective* (New York, Mentor Books, 1948), pp. 37 ff.

3. Smith, T. V., "Hindsight on de Tocqueville's Foresight," *The University Review,* Autumn 1942, vol. IX, no. 1, pp. 19-26.

4. Sidgwick, Henry, *Miscellaneous Essays and Addresses* (London, 1904), p. 367; Pierson, G. W., *Tocqueville and Beaumont in America* (New York, Oxford University Press, 1938), pp. 150-151, 475-476.

5. Perry, Bliss, *The American Mind* (Boston, Houghton Mifflin, 1912), p. 68.

6. Brooks, Van Wyck, *The Ordeal of Mark Twain* (New York, 1920), p. 100.

7. Tocqueville, Alexis de, *De la Démocratie en Amérique* (Paris, Calmann Lévy, 1888), II, p. 157. Hereinafter designated by *D. A.*

8. Tocqueville, *Correspondance inédite, (Œuvres complètes,* VII) (Paris, Lévy, 1866), pp. 66-67.

9. Dowden, Edward, "The Poetry of Democracy: Walt Whitman," *Studies in Literature, 1789-1877* (London, 1909), pp. 468-521. Katherine Harrison extolled Tocqueville's prophetic qualities in 1926, calling attention to the parallels with Whitman as if unaware of Dowden's essay. See "A Forecast of American Literature," *South Atlantic Quarterly,* Oct. 1926, vol. 25, pp. 350-360.

10. Cestre, Charles, "Alexis de Tocqueville, Témoin et juge de la civilisation américaine," *Revue des Cours et Conférences,* Jan. 15, 1934, XXXV, I, pp. 281-287.

11. Anon., Review of *D. A.,* III, *Blackwood's Magazine,* Oct. 1840, vol. 48, p. 471.

12. Hawthorne, Nathaniel, *The English Notebooks,* ed. Stewart (New York, MLA, 1941), p. 243. The Henry James reference is from his *Hawthorne* (New York, Harper, 1887), p. 40.

13. *D. A.,* III, pp. 117-124.

14. *D. A.,* III, p. 125.

15. Hazlitt, William, *Lectures on the English Poets* (Complete Works, ed. Howe, V), (London, Dent, 1930), pp. 9-10.

16. *D. A.,* III, pp. 125-126.

17. *D. A.,* III, p. 129. Forgues, E. D., "Moby Dick," *Revue des Deux Mondes,* Feb. 1, 1853, I, p. 515.

18. *D. A.,* III, pp. 99-100. Sainte-Beuve, "La Littérature industrielle," *Portraits contemporains* (Paris, Lévy, no date), II, pp. 455-470.

19. Dowden, "Edgar Quinet," *op. cit.,* p. 378.

20. Dowden, "The Transcendental Movement," *op. cit.,* pp. 58-60.

21. *D. A.,* III, p. 115.

22. *D. A.,* III, p. 91.

23. *D. A.,* III, pp. 127-128.

24. Shepard, Odell, *Pedlar's Progress: The Life of Bronson Alcott* (Boston, Little Brown, 1937), p. 244. Matthiessen, *Op. cit.,* pp. 533-534.

25. Hawthorne, Preface, *The Marble Faun* (Boston, Houghton Mifflin, The Riverside Edition, 1888),

p. 15. Cf. Mathew Josephson, *Portrait of the Artist as American* (New York, 1930), p. 46.

26. Batault, Georges, "Tocqueville et la littérature américaine," *Mercure de France,* Sept. 16, 1919, vol. 135, pp. 250-261.

Ann Davies (essay date 2002)

SOURCE: Davies, Ann. "The 'Seer': The Democratic Poet's Recognition and Transcendence." In *Seers and Judges: American Literature as Political Philosophy,* edited by Christine Dunn Henderson, pp. 1-16. Lanham, Md.: Lexington Books, 2002.

[*In the following essay, Davies studies the ways in which de Tocqueville, Dewey, and Whitman relate democracy and poetry.*]

Diverse in their political sympathies and visions, Alexis de Tocqueville, John Dewey, and Walt Whitman nonetheless converge in viewing poetry as an integral force in the democratic experience, shaping and being shaped by its political and social forces. In particular, each writer portrays democratic poetry as simultaneously promoting pluralism *and* unity, able to celebrate democratic individuality while also recognizing the commonality of the human experience. Tocqueville and Dewey take this one step further by arguing that poetry thus promotes social understanding and cooperation as well as political agency, and in his ability to weave together catalogs of diverse and sometimes seemingly mundane experiences into vast statements about the democratic experience, Whitman seems to embody Dewey and Tocqueville's vision of the democratic poet. Dewey himself singles out Whitman as the "seer" of democracy. Yet Whitman and Dewey's ambitious pursuit of democratic individuality and community correspondingly place heavy demands upon poetry, and in the case of Whitman, poetry and politics both seem to suffer as a result. Further, the transcendent experience which makes poetry so appealing to Dewey and Whitman results in the displacement of, or an antipathy toward, political interests, ideals and their conflicts. Thus, what they present as integral to the democratic experience ultimately seems alienated from certain aspects of it. Tocqueville, who of the three seems most skeptical of democracy and its effects on poetry, seems nonetheless more reconciled to democratic *politics* and its working relationship with poetry.

PERSPECTIVES ON DEMOCRACY AND POETRY

Tocqueville's diagnosis of the potential maladies of democracy are well-worn. Concerned that the passion for equality would outpace the love of liberty, he fears that materialism and individualism would isolate citizens from one another, discourage them from participating in politics and lead to a parental despotism, which is comfortable but not free. The counterweight to this horror lies in self-interest rightly understood. By engaging in civic associations, individuals are drawn out of themselves, see the benefits of collective action, acquire the habits of political liberty, and learn to hold off the gratification of their most immediate, shortsighted material interests in favor of a longer-term perspective in which collective and individual interests converge.

Yet while associations play a central role in American democracy, self-organization alone may not be sufficient for healthy civil society. Associational activity may produce identification with the collective and a long-term perspective, but it may just as well bring about factious divisiveness unless supplemented by common values or vision.[1] Religion, patriotism or love of liberty may supply such community, but in Tocqueville's account poetry's appeal to the common human experience may also call us away from our narrow materialistic pursuits and remind us of our commonality, providing a thread that knits together a community or at least a lens through which individuals can view the other and reconcile themselves to one another.

Claiming that poetry involves "the search for and representation of the ideal," Tocqueville first describes the aspects of democracy that seem to work against it: (1) the focus on careers and acquisition, which, if it does not kill imagination, channels it toward the useful; and (2) the lack of subject matter, which Tocqueville traces to differences in religion, a distaste for the past, and the absence of an aristocratic or abjectly miserable class. Sainthood, the past, and socially distant classes all produce a kind of fuzziness around their subjects that potentiates idealization necessary for the poetic. On the other hand, democracy's dismissal of the saints, its preoccupation with the present, and in greater equality, can produce only an individual of "medium size, seen clearly from every angle," which never has the making of an ideal.[2]

Democratic poets casting about for a subject may settle upon descriptive poetry, but this is merely a transitional phase, according to Tocqueville: "Democratic peoples may amuse themselves momentarily by looking at nature, but it is about themselves that they are really excited. Here, and here alone, are the true springs of poetry among them" (*DA,* 484). Although individuals may no longer inspire poetry, the very likeness of individuals invites the poet "to group them in imagination and make a coherent picture of the nation" worthy of poetic treatment. The restlessness, impatience and mixing of cultures within democracy somewhat paradoxically allows one to "form the picture of one vast democracy in which a nation counts as a single citizen" (*DA,* 485-486). Despite his predominant concern that majority tyranny will overwhelm liberty, here he seems to ap-plaud the enveloping of the individual by the nation, with poetry being potentiated by and perhaps contribut-ing to such identification. In poetry, the tension between the individual and the collective seems somehow ame-liorated. Tocqueville ratchets up the rhetoric by em-ploying religious imagery, stating that when every man, "raising his eyes above his country, begins at last to see mankind at large, God shows himself more clearly to human perception in full and entire majesty" and people are able to conceive that the actions of each individual include "a trace of the universal and consistent plan by which God guides mankind" (*DA*, 486).

While this integration of the individual within the larger whole seems central to the fabric of Tocqueville's envi-sioned democracy, how the poet and his readers leap from the individual to the nation, then to humankind and ultimately to God is not initially evident. It be-comes clearer when Tocqueville argues that contempla-tion of the self, the "hidden depths of man's spiritual nature," will produce objects that arouse "piety, wonder, scorn, and terror" (*DA*, 487). In language that Whitman would echo thirty years later, Tocqueville states, "Hu-man destiny, man himself, not tied to time or place, but face to face with nature and with God, with his pas-sions, his doubts, his unexpected good fortune, and his incomprehensible miseries, will for these people be the chief and almost the sole subject of poetry" (*DA*, 487).[3] Suddenly the puzzle of human existence seems not "medium-sized" but vast. Further, this struggle to come to terms with life and death that lies within the depths of the individual lies within the depths of *all* individu-als. Capable of seeing and conveying the uniformity of these passions in a way that Tocqueville suggests was not possible in the poetry of aristocracy, democratic po-etry accesses the experience of all through a consider-ation of the single self. In this instance, equality and the individual do not imperil one another but instead gain a kind of access to themselves and to the other, allowing poets and their readers to gather a deeper understanding of what equality and the realities of the individual are. Through this, the individual and the aggregate—as well as poetry and religion—merge. The demand for self-understanding seems inevitable to Tocqueville but also impossible for the democratic individual to confront alone. The questions and answers posed by poetry (as well as religion) provide not only a kind of existential grounding for the individual but also a means by which individuals can achieve identity with one another and with the aggregate.

Like Tocqueville, Dewey argues that the promise of de-mocracy is not self-fulfilling or automatic; success or failure rests upon the character of "the public," to use Dewey's term, but the problem of the public, according to Dewey, is that it remains largely inchoate and unor-ganized. Technology has built a "great society" without

integrating it. For this Dewey faults not technology it-self, but the absence of ideas addressing technological factors.[4] In the absence of meaningful communication, "man has suffered the impact of an enormously en-larged control of physical energies without any corre-sponding ability to control himself and his own affairs," and such control can only be restored through the "signs and symbols" that can forge shared experience (*Public*, 174).

Without that kind of shared meaning, the public cannot locate and identify itself, and without the formation of such a public, neither meaningful liberty nor equality can exist (*Public*, 141-142). In Dewey's view, liberty involves "the secure release and fulfillment of personal potentialities" that can only take place in "rich and manifold association with others," and equality involves distributing liberty in a manner conducive to the full development of the individuality of each (*Public*, 150). For Dewey, neither liberty nor equality exists as an a priori concept; instead, each rests upon the particular character of the community in which it is embedded. Rather than juxtaposing the demands and obligations of a community and individual liberty, Dewey argues that our relationships with others shape the habits necessary for human action and provide a consciousness that is integral to a morally meaningful freedom (*Public*, 150-161). Further, actions that treat individuals differently are central to Dewey's conception of equality. As an example, he notes that the identical treatment of a child and an adult in a family would serve neither of them well nor, for that matter, fulfill the function of the fam-ily itself. Equality instead involves meeting the child's needs for care and development instead of sacrificing him/her to the superior strength or matured abilities of the other family members. The child receives care not because of some antecedent quality or claim, but be-cause this is its share of the activity toward which the association of the family is directed (*Public*, 150).

Dewey's arguments about the realization of liberty and equality rest upon knowledge of the *character* of the community in question, for without this the interests of the individual cannot be weighed and diverse claims cannot be reconciled. Each association's end is settled upon, and assigned meaning through, "the give-and-take of communication," which facilitates the develop-ment of one's individual distinctiveness but also of an understanding and appreciation of the beliefs, desires, and methods of the group (*Public*, 154-155). Properly understood, liberty and equality thus promote unity rather than jealous competition. Therefore, Dewey looks for a means of constructing in industrial society "the mutual comprehension and appreciation that we experi-ence in 'face-to-face' communities."[5]

Dewey claims that such a democracy had its seer in Walt Whitman and would be fulfilled when free social inquiry and full and moving communication could be conjoined. Whitman thus seems essential to Dewey not just for his vision of democracy but for the means by which he expresses it. Arguing that a knowledge of history is necessary for the connectedness of knowledge, Dewey regrets that history as practiced comes too late to form public opinion around the issues of immediate concern. Yet news alone also seems to be an inadequate means for providing such historical knowledge, because, it is either too highbrow or too superficial. Somehow the triviality of everyday life must be punctured without losing appeal to the masses. The solution, Dewey argues, lies in the ability of art to "break through the crust of conventionalized and routine consciousness." By capturing common things, such as a flower or the song of a bird, poetry, drama and novels act to access the "deeper levels of life," kindling "emotion, perception and appreciation" (*Public,* 183-184).[6] Poetry, and art in general, elicit a sense of the larger whole, attaching us to the common life and allowing us to find fulfillment in it.[7]

Dewey's treatment of poetry is cursory in *The Public and its Problems.* However, in that work he frames ideas that he later develops more substantially in *Art as Experience* (1934), in which he presents art as that which experiences and confronts the conflict between our formed dispositions and the changing circumstances around us, ultimately bridging them.[8] Dewey argues that the aesthetic awakens us—and does so in a way that philosophy and political institutions cannot—because art "enters directly into attitude" and is "the most direct and complete manifestation of experience as experience" (*Art,* 332, 297). Through intuition—the fusing of the old and new and the merging of the intellectual and nonintellectual—the aesthetic consolidates seemingly random and isolated incidents into organized meanings that both philosophy and politics require but cannot themselves solely provide (*Art,* 326). The reasoner, as Keats points out, must nonetheless trust intuitions and fall back upon imagination (*Art,* 33). Those who seek the support of the public must also rely upon imagination. Dewey points out that the Magna Carta holds power over us not as a result of its literal contents, but on the meaning given it in our imagination (*Art,* 326). Effective morals come not from abstract treatises and dry laws, but through the immediacy, intimacy, and energy of artistic expression (although Dewey also assigns art the task of calling into question those morals as well). Art that accesses and expresses this harmony in turn potentiates "mind" and all its connotations—intellectual, affectional, and volitional. Through the aesthetic experience, we come to take note of our situation, to care about it and to be able to act in a purposive way in relation to it (*Art,* 263-265). We are transformed from beings that merely interact with the world into beings that participate and communicate (*Art,* 22).

In his discussion of art, Dewey hits upon some of his favorite themes. First, the aesthetic roots the driving force of human experience in the material, contextualized world of the senses and culture, not abstract, a priori principles. At the same time, it moves beyond mere materialism in that he can maintain that the poetical, for example, is "always a close kin of the animistic" (*Art,* 29). Further, the experience forged by art is both common in its origin and individualistic in its experience. Consequently, it is both universal and subjective. Breaking through "conventional distinctions to the underlying common elements of the experienced world," art and poetry also develop individuality through the ways in which those elements are seen and expressed (*Art,* 248). The "language of art" unites us as it inspires us, but the experience that it forges involves an interaction between the artistic product and the self which will not be the same for two different people or even the same person at different times (*Art,* 331-336). Yet even this individualized experience promotes community. Viewing the world through the lens of imagined possibilities, we are able to see more clearly and critically, to encounter both identity and difference and to redirect our desire and purpose.[9]

DEMOCRATIC TRANSCENDENCE: WHITMAN'S POET

Whitman seems to have viewed himself as the "seer" of democracy as Dewey proclaimed, with the essence of his art lying in the ambiguity or tension that paradoxically results in a burst of democratic recognition, a commonality founded upon diversity and contradiction. In the universe Whitman constructs, time, space and forces collapse together, with the past, present, and future existing simultaneously, the individual and nation embodying one another, the material and immaterial intimately linked, and affirmation and agitation reinforcing one another. Through this, he claims, the poet finds resonance by accessing the ethos while also critiquing particular aspects of a particular age, voicing the present while giving form to the future. Sharing the language of religion with Tocqueville, along with a confidence similar to Dewey's in common experience's ability to bring meaning to our individual and communal lives, Whitman gives some sense of what the two authors may have envisioned, as well as perhaps suggesting the challenges posed by those visions.

Like Tocqueville, Whitman thinks that America will develop its own poetry, arguing that the myth and romance of the poems of the past insult democracy and fail to address its realities. Like Dewey, and Tocqueville as well, he also maintains that the development of such poems and poets is essential to democracy, asserting in his first preface to *Leaves of Grass* in 1855 that the U.S. will most need poets, will have the greatest, and will use them the most.[10] Echoing Tocqueville, Whitman maintains that "a religious and moral character" must undergird the political bases of the state; humanity gives rise to religion and politics, not the reverse (320). Thus poets would displace presidents as the "common referee" (9). Priests and philosophers cannot play this role because philosophy and religion remain distant, failing to penetrate our experiences, thoughts and emotions. While "All truths wait in all things," Whitman writes in "Song of Myself," "Logic and sermons never convince, / The damp of the night drives deeper into my soul" (63). Poetry, on the other hand, offers both vision and judgment to which its audience responds, and in Whitman's claims Dewey's arguments about the power and political necessity of imagination come to mind. A favorite word of Whitman's is "vistas," and he constantly offers these, both of the external world and of the depths within ourselves. From these heights, Whitman thinks the poet can find resonance and thus reveal truth, for "only what proves itself to every man and woman is so / only what nobody denies is so" (63). The poet "sees the solid and beautiful forms of the future where there are now no solid forms" (9). He[11] is able to do so only by "flood[ing] himself with the immediate age as with vast oceanic tides" (24). Yet in plunging into the age, the poet also transfigures it, opening it to "the eternity which gives similitude to all" (1973, 24). Such similitude in turn may give rise to the comradeship that embodies the best form of democracy, counterbalancing a more materialistic and "vulgar" version (369n).[12]

In this, Whitman seems to capture Dewey's desire for a poetry that supplements the news, capturing while at the same time transcending the everyday. Tocqueville also notes the importance of newspapers in democracy, as vehicles for the formation and communication of associations and consequently as the promoters of interest rightly understood. As noted, however, the formation of community requires that such interest be supplemented by a thread of commonality not necessarily supplied by particular interests themselves. While poetry might serve as that vehicle, that which Tocqueville envisions seems to focus more on the general human condition and a fairly maudlin view of it. Whitman's poetry, on the other hand, embraces current events, with his own work as a journalist shaping his poems' content and form. In his notebooks bits of classified ads coexist with poem fragments, and editorials and news articles provided subjects for his poetry. The penny press supplied a vocabulary, an eclectic form and a shared modern experience as a scaffolding for his poetry. His vast catalogs of experiences, occupations, and vignettes themselves resemble a front page on which political news bumps up against reports of murder, domestic scandal, and health tips.[13]

Yet even while swallowing everything, Whitman's poet is still discerning; he is both the equalizer and the arbiter of the diverse, supplying and checking each as needed. His judgment is exercised "as the sun falling around a helpless thing" (9). In shedding such light, the poet cannot just describe beautiful objects. Rather, people "expect him to indicate the path between reality and their souls," and he must recognize the demerits as well as the merits of their age (9-10; 24).[14] In his poetry Whitman asserts that the poet goes beyond the sun, not simply lighting the surfaces but forcing the depths as well (80). Judgment seems to be a matter of shedding light on what is real, not simply apparent; yet this newly lit reality is, it seems, immediately self-evident to all. The poet does not "moralize" because, Whitman argues, the democratic soul never acknowledges any lessons but its own.[15]

Whitman most succeeds, I think, in conveying a central theme of Tocqueville and Dewey—that is, the potentially symbiotic relationship between individualism and democracy. On the one hand, he develops the unbounded nature of the individual within democracy: He could be anyone, and anyone could be him.[16] This allows the poet to "swallow" the experience of others and make it his own while also making it possible for his audience to respond to his portrait of his own interior self or selves. "Song of Myself" opens with the lines, "I celebrate myself, / And what I assume you shall assume, / For every atom belonging to me as good belongs to you" (32).[17] Whitman's celebration of himself does not set him apart from others. Constantly pointing to his own power and immortality, he also repeats that others have this as well, even if they do not realize it. It is the poet's task to point this out, but this also means that what Whitman takes on, others take on as well; what he sees, others will see as well.

Obviously, this is a give-and-take process; if there is no resonance between poet and reader, then somehow what the poet has advanced is not true. Whitman acknowledges as much later in the poem: "What is a man anyhow? What am I? and what are you? / All I mark as my own you shall offset it with your own, / Else it were time lost listening to me" (51). Similarly, he need not take on without comment what others mindlessly put forward. Hence, the narrator of "Song of Myself" imagines that living with animals might be preferable to residing with humans who whine, weep for their sins, sicken him with their talk about God, and maniacally pursue material goods (64-65).

While the membrane of our selves takes on a kind of permeability or boundlessness in democracy, it is not limitless. According to Whitman, our identity with others lies in those things which are eternally human and not simply the passing show. People, surroundings, and experiences come into being and pass away, "But they are not the Me Myself. / Apart from the pulling and hauling stands what I am, / Stands amused, complacent, compassionating, idle, unitary" (35). Shortly after this,

Whitman states that he is not "an earth" but the "mate and companion of all" (38). For him, democracy produces a situated self; if it is not constituted by democracy, its realization is certainly potentiated by it. The self celebrated by Whitman could not exist if there were not other democratic individuals to love. Yet it stands separate and somewhat aloof from the world of appearances, even as it consorts with other selves similar to it. The poet helps to form a "great aggregate Nation" by calling forth these "fully develop'd and enclosing individuals" (308; see also 329-330).

As with Tocqueville, this conjoining of the individual and the collective takes on a religious overtone with Whitman. In his view, "the religious" lies at the heart of democracy, vitalizing individualism and love (337), and poets touch the heart of religion more closely than any clergy. However, to say that there is a religious overtone to Whitman is not to claim that he is conventionally religious, far from it. In his poems, he dismisses priests, prayer, and any concept of time that places perfection anywhere but in the present. As "Song of Myself" comes to a close, Whitman writes, "I hear and behold God in every object, yet I understand / God not in the least. / Nor do I understand who there can be more wonderful / than myself" (93). Whitman claims to offer a new conception of ego: through the celebration of oneself, one can possess both pride and compassion. Worshiping oneself, one also worships others. While this seems as if we would unite around an affirmation of life, it is interesting to note that Whitman precedes the lines just written by saying that he is at peace about God and death, and he maintains in "Democratic Vistas" that the poet must write the great poem of death (376). Like Tocqueville in his discussion of our natural impulse toward religion, Whitman assumes that death preoccupies us; poetry addresses our immortality while somewhat strangely affirming the equity of body and soul as well (57, 93).

The difference between Tocqueville and Whitman in relation to the centrality of death to the poetic idea is that Tocqueville views our relationship with death as an epic struggle, while Whitman presents death as happily vanquished by poetry's assurance of immortality. This would seem to rob democratic poetry of what Tocqueville viewed as its most fertile resource, since he depicts democracy's limited poetic impulse as largely revolving around the fear of death. Further, Whitman's brief farewell to the Puritans raises the issue of Puritanism's effect upon poetry. Tocqueville thinks that the austerity of Puritanism discouraged poetry. Even as the apparent influence of Puritanism faded in the U.S., the influence it exerted in the origins of the colonies continued to shape the mores and habits of Americans, according to his formulation. Whitman, on the other hand, seems confident that Americans would simply shrug off the past. Perhaps the gap here can be explained by Whit-

man's view of the relationship between poetry and history. If Puritanism was an enduring legacy, the job of poetry might be not to acknowledge it, but to boldly undermine it, to dismiss its power and to shine light on our "real" democratic selves. However, this dynamic in turn reveals the tensions between the situated and transcendent self and particularly highlights the difficulties faced by the poet who absorbs and celebrates all while at the same time exercising judgment and achieving democratic resonance. Whitman seemed initially blind to and eventually stymied by the possible inertia of mass public opinion. While celebrating the eternal and immaterial as well as the commonality that results from our participation in it, Whitman also celebrates the common, a theme more favored by Dewey than Tocqueville. Poets should address the mass, but this is not a matter of settling for the lowest common denominator: for Whitman, all are "unspeakably great" (17). Again and again, the metaphor of grass, with its suggestion of ubiquity, subtle beauty, and singularity even in the aggregate's apparent seamlessness appears in Whitman's poetry. One cannot rise above it, but one can speak to it. Poetry involves uncovering the uniqueness, which paradoxically we all share, that lies below the surface of our apparently pedestrian lives. What at first seems uniform and seamless is revealed upon closer inspection to be composed of myriad distinct "leaves"; yet those leaves still continue also to participate in the whole, again simultaneously recognized as individual and fitting within the larger whole, as everyday but also unique.

Such recognition would seem to be a delicate enterprise, but in Whitman's view, revealed truth produces spontaneous acclamation. Therefore, the democratic poet cannot take comfort in being misunderstood as a result of his own greatness: "The proof of the poet is that his country absorbs him as affectionately as he has absorbed it" (27). Yet in his 1888 preface to *Leaves of Grass,* Whitman must acknowledge that he himself had not yet found substantial resonance with the public. He replies that he failed to capture the truth of the moment, that it would take another 100 years for an audience to evolve who could appreciate him. In this, he was largely correct, but it nonetheless seems to raise questions about the relationship between poetry and democracy. If a poet "yawps," and receives a lukewarm response, can he defend his work with a democratic spirit, or is he likely to call into question the public's judgment? Whitman asserts that he should not have embraced the nation as affectionately as he did, suggesting at least some kind of limitation in the ostensibly democratic relationship between the poet and the people (97). Nonetheless, the poet making such a claim would run into problems with the narrator of "Song of Myself," who asserts that he gives voice to the thoughts of all ages and all lands and that without this they are nothing (49).

Whitman blames crass materialism for the resistance he encountered, a factor to which Tocqueville, too, attributed the distraction of Americans' imagination.[18] Writing in 1871, Whitman decries American society's "hollowness of heart" and cites moneymaking as the magic serpent that had eaten all the others (325-326). Even while recognizing that the spirit of acquisition brings the "amelioration" and progress necessary for the results he sought, he also maintains that prosperity doesn't "satisfy the soul" (339, 324). The potential of democracy was still apparent to him, evidenced by the Civil War and the people's lack of terror of death in both the North and the South.[19] Yet that kind of commitment had already quickly disappeared. In "Song of the Exposition," written the same year as "Democratic Vistas," the narrator calls, "Away with themes of war! away with war itself! / . . . And in its stead speed industry's campaigns" (267). Yet Whitman seems unable to muster much enthusiasm for the catalogs of the wonders of industry and technology in the poem. The tone of this poem implies what becomes explicit at the end of "Democratic Vistas": if there is a justification for democracy, it lies in the future, "through the copious production of perfect characters and pervading religiousness" (347). After refusing in his earlier poetry to acknowledge a distinction between present and future or the promise of anything beyond the most immediate, Whitman now resorts to such distinctions as a defense of democracy and his own poetry.

We are reminded again of the impossible task Whitman has set for himself, namely that the test of truth lies in its spontaneous resonance in the heart of each as the poet judges for all. Even if we recognize the hyperbole in Whitman's claims, we need to take seriously the disillusion that he seemed to experience. The 1860s and 1870s seemed uncomfortable times for him, as he seemed neither fully prepared for the viciousness of the sectional conflict nor the apparent mundaneness that followed. While he seemed incapable of expressing the violence that stemmed from democratic commitment in his poetry, regular politics also sickened him. The machinations of Tocqueville's interest rightly understood held absolutely no appeal to him. Describing a political convention, he wrote:

> The members who composed it were, seven-eighths of them, the meanest kind of bawling and blowing office holders, office seekers, pimps, malignants, conspirators, murderers, fancymen, custom house clerks, contractors, kept-editors, spaniels well-train'd to carry and fetch, jobbers, infidels, disunionists, pushers of slavery, creatures of Presidents, creatures of would-be Presidents, spies, bribers, compromisers, lobbyers, sponges, ruin'd sports, expell'd gamblers, policy backers, monte dealers, duelists, carriers of conceal'd weapons, deaf men, pimpled men, scarr'd inside with vile disease, gaudy

> outside with gold chains made from the people's money and harlots money twisted together, crawling serpentine men, the lousy combings and born freedom sellers of the earth.[20]

This is an exhaustive, if despairing, list and apparently one that Whitman was reluctant to swallow. Friendlier to politics, Tocqueville might nonetheless agree that its creatures would not make appealing subjects for democratic poetry. He might, however, have offered the example of American religion to a democratic poet frustrated by the crass commercialism and pettiness of his surroundings: the clergy retained its relevance in democracy by tying its lessons to success in this world. If religion and poetry distract us from our materialistic pursuits, then, they must nonetheless appear relevant to, or at least friendly toward, those pursuits.

However, Whitman's difficulties go beyond the question of his public reception. In claiming to encompass all, Whitman downplays the possibility of conflict, leaving him alternately jingoistic and silent when it occurs. In his early poems and essays he proclaims himself capable of swallowing all experience and making it his own, but there is one character with whom he never directly claims identity. While he can become the hunted slave and feel the bullets that rive him (71), Whitman never presents himself in his poetry as the southern slave owner.[21] This omission is perhaps all the more striking because in an 1847 notebook entry he does claim to be the "poet of slaves and of the master of slaves;" yet somehow this claim never made it into his published poetry. Whitman might reply that the poetry of democracy and liberty need not encounter or embody the impulses of tyranny. The democratic poet, however, must be pressed to answer the question: What if there are disagreements about what constitutes democracy or liberty? In such a case, the problems of democracy do not involve questions of "good heart" but competing and possibly incommensurable claims.[22] In his later poem, "Reconciliation," Whitman acknowledged as much: "my enemy is dead, a man divine as myself is dead" (233). Yet where does enmity arise for a poet who celebrates the divinity in all?[23] Whitman might say in the denial of liberty, but his descriptions of liberty, while full of praise, are also glib and rather contracted. Liberty seems so straightforward to Whitman that he cannot explore its nuances or even its depths. As a result, there can be no conflict about it in his poetry, and when such conflict *does* arise, Whitman is initially rendered dumb. While later able to recognize the divinity of the enemy, his accounts of the democratic experience and liberty are unable to account for the source of that enmity, a significant gap for one who claims to go beyond the sun in "forcing the depths" and for anyone who might be interested in avoiding the mourning of other enemies in the future.

If this seems too demanding a standard or requirement, Whitman still faces contradictory impulses of his own in relation to the potential for conflict. On the one hand, he is obviously concerned about the potential for contending ideals to break apart the union. "Democratic Vistas" opens with Whitman voicing his fear of a conflicting interior and the lack of a "common skeleton." Yet he also closes the essay, as noted, by pointing to the potential for democracy that he sees in northern and southern Americans' willingness to die for their cause. His fear and his sense of hope seem to contradict one another, as conflict appears both dangerous and restorative. Further, the poet of *Leaves of Grass,* who had once seemed to express near-anarchist faith in the spontaneous unity of the people, now embraced as a sign of hope an ideological fervor that would spur the bloodiest conflict in U.S. history.

Can a poet who claims that truth—and, in fact, real democracy—involve appealing to all also fully acknowledge and accommodate fundamental differences? In his first preface to *Leaves of Grass,* Whitman promises that poets should replace presidents as the common referee, but can poets really referee at all? Perhaps Whitman would say that they act as the medium between our internal and external worlds, but this still leaves an open question of how to situate ourselves in relation to one another and to the political demands of the time. Whitman states that the poet praises peace when there is peace and sounds the alarum when there is war, but there is a maudlin and nearly xenophobic quality to his war poems. The union becomes the "dread Mother;" all work and workmen are the union's, "None separate from thee—henceforth One only, we and thou" (270-271). The arbiter of diversity has adopted a more monolithic tone. One might say that this is an accurate reflection, or perhaps even a critique, of the "Yankee Leviathan." However, in the midst of war, Lincoln's "Second Inaugural Address," and even his "Gettysburg Address," capture a much more nuanced approach to the forging of consensus and its costs. Whitman's earlier glibness in discussing liberty and a democracy that so easily captures all experience leaves him with little room for acknowledging competing claims, the possible necessity of compromise or the potential for violent conflict and its tragedy, and as a result his war poetry seems more reactionary than visionary. One is left thinking either that Whitman's concept of individualistic democracy simply gives way upon encountering the breath of hard-felt views which may result in violence and the demand for regimentation, or that in fact his concept of democracy always contained within it a hard-edged nationalistic or even militaristic edge.

Dewey is also open to criticism for having a vision of politics (and art) markedly devoid of conflict. While not denying its potential and in fact maintaining that discord provides the opportunity for reflective thought, he nonetheless seems optimistic about the capacity of organized intelligence to encounter such problems peacefully. Dewey and Whitman shared in common their witness of the carnage of the Civil War: Dewey as the son of a soldier whose family relocated to Virginia, and Whitman as a quasi-nurse in Washington. However, while Dewey's experience as a child likely contributed to his sense of the futility of violence in the pursuit of political objectives, Whitman's experiences and expectations led him in a different direction. Repeatedly describing and lamenting the "butchery" of the war in his notebooks, he nonetheless sanitized the war in his poetry, transforming the particularity of death into something abstract and glorious.[24] If there is a consistency in Whitman's transcendentalism and progressive faith here, it comes at the expense of a sheer divorce between the aesthetic and the grittier realm of politics. Again, Lincoln's "Second Inaugural" may be more successful in acknowledging the ambiguity and brutality of the war while attempting to frame more transcendent forces at work within it.

Yet if Dewey and Whitman both seek to wish or theorize away the age-old problem of violence and coercion, they both attempt to adopt a progressive attitude in their treatment of science and technology. Like Dewey, Whitman refreshingly resists being a knee-jerk reactionary in relation to science and technology, refusing to draw a dichotomy between art and science. In "Song of Myself" he writes, "A word of reality . . . materialism first and last imbuing. / Hurrah for positive science! Long live exact demonstration!" Whitman hails the lexicographer, chemist, physician, and geologist: "The facts are useful and real . . . they are not my / dwelling. . . . I enter by them to an area of the dwelling" (55-56; cf. *Art,* 289-297, 318-319). Whitman does not deny or denounce scientific method or technological development but acknowledges them, gives meaning to them and in the process uses them to arrive at his "dwelling"—the eternal commonality where democracy and individuality converge.

In the 1888 preface to *Leaves of Grass,* Whitman acknowledges that modern science and democracy appear to endanger "that primal and interior something in man," but in reality they prepare for "grander individualities than ever. . . . [T]he elements of courageous and lofty manhood are unchanged" (308). Even if unchanged, Whitman does not give a sense of how that "manhood" should arrange itself in relation to the industrial revolution. In "Song of the Exposition" the narrator claims to raise his voice "To teach the average man the glory of his daily / walk and trade" (368), but the assurance rings rather hollow. In "Democratic Vistas" Whitman asserts that poetry must inspire itself with science and the modern, but as with democracy's justification, this inspiration seems to be put off to the future.

The stakes in this are high because, in rejecting the claim that science will replace poetry, Whitman argues that imagination in modern times would give "ultimate vivification to facts, to science and to common lives, endowing them with glow and glories and final illustriousness which belong to every real thing and to real things only" (299). Without this, he writes, science, democracy and even life itself would be in vain. Dewey may have viewed Whitman as a seer in the way in which he situates the individual within the aggregate, but Whitman's poetic vision seems to fail in relation to the most pressing problem faced by Dewey's public, namely the ways in which modern industrial relations had decimated local societies. Perhaps Dewey thinks that the revival of Whitman's democratic individual could potentiate the community necessary to address such issues. However, this seems a smaller role than Whitman envisioned, and Dewey faces his own problems in this regard. In *Art as Experience* Dewey argues that oligarchical control of the means of production must end if we are to experience the aesthetics of industrial production. Yet with this, he seems to argue workers into a box: The aesthetic experience plays an integral part in forging the "true" experience necessary for assigning the individual and communal meaning which can potentiate community and progressive change. Yet for such an experience to occur, Dewey suggests that industrial relations need to change. What can be the source of that change without the original aesthetic experience that rests upon more democratic social conditions? Dewey may not have escaped Lippmann's phantom public after all.

Tocqueville, Dewey, Whitman all seek from poetry a truth that would unite us, in a sense, prepolitically, by addressing our hopes, fears or some kind of connection between our internal and external realities. Neither Tocqueville nor Dewey requires that this be the only function that poetry serves, but each pays attention to poetry for the political role that it may play, especially in conjoining the experiences and emotions of the individual with the identity of the nation or community. Perhaps inevitably, Whitman's vision is more grandiose. Poetry becomes identified with democracy; one is not possible without the other. This brings a paradoxical combination of the political and the apolitical, or even antipolitical, to his poetry and essays. On the one hand, poetry requires universal acclamation to be recognized as truth; on the other, the poet must call forth our better, truer selves. Can a poet celebrate, affirm and critique and be celebrated, affirmed and critiqued all at the same time? In the first preface to *Leaves of Grass,* Whitman writes that the poet exercises judgment like the sun falling around a helpless thing. The power and inevitability of this image may be captivating, but it also suggests a way in which issues and events may be taken for

granted, glossed over or presented in a unidimensional fashion. In the face of conflict or at least lack of commonality, this may leave both poet and reader feeling like a "helpless thing" with the poet unable to voice the "truth" to which his reader may respond. Although Whitman said that the reader must exercise his own judgment in response to the poet's, he did not offer an avenue for this kind of negotiation. Thus "cheerful simplicity" may leave us all at a loss, and if Whitman is the "seer" of Dewey's democracy, then Whitman's problem may become Dewey's as well. When political agency is most required and faces its stiffest challenges, it may be difficult to root it within the aesthetic that Whitman and Dewey envision. The recognition and transcendence that seem so central to the formation of democratic individuality and community may avoid or short-circuit the dialogue necessary for the construction of shared meanings instead of promoting it.

Tocqueville's notion of poetry and the role it plays seems less demanding than theirs. In it everyday reality is not so much punctured as indulged, albeit on the level of psychological fears and hopes. If poetry is transcendent, the leap seems shorter, and the result more ambiguous, than Whitman and Dewey's. Tocqueville's poetry facilitates democracy by potentiating interest rightly understood; it itself is not "true" democracy, as Whitman might claim, or the forger of "true" experience itself, as Dewey might assert. Tocqueville's explanation of the impulse toward poetry seems stilted and melodramatic, and we can only hope that the poetry produced by it would avoid the same tones. Nonetheless, if his vision of poetry seems more mundane, its rootedness allows us to rise above our petty selves, but then also to return to them and perhaps even reconcile ourselves to them. He is friendlier to egotism and self-interest, even while recognizing the need to supplement them. The poetry he envisions leaves room for politics and political agency, neither displacing nor evading them, and in this Tocqueville's conception of poetry may embody and produce a stronger form of democracy than Dewey and Whitman's.

Notes

1. See Barbara Allen, "Alexis de Tocqueville and the Covenantal Tradition of American Federal Democracy," *Publius* 28:2 (spring 1998), 1-23, and Joshua Mitchell, *The Fragility of Freedom: Tocqueville on Religion, Democracy, and the American Future* (Chicago: The University of Chicago Press, 1995).

2. Alexis de Tocqueville, *Democracy in America,* trans. George Lawrence and ed. J. P. Mayer (Garden City, N.Y.: Doubleday & Co., Inc., 1969). All subsequent references to *Democracy in*

America (hereafter *DA*) will be parenthetical, with page numbers corresponding to this edition.

3. There is a striking parallel between Tocqueville's descriptions of the poetic and the "natural" religious impulses. In his view, opposing instincts co-exist within us. We are disgusted at our existence yet long to continue to exist, and in his view, both of these sentiments drive us toward contemplation of the next world (*DA*, 296-297). Our "scorn" for life leads us toward a disgruntled perspective toward our earthly existence, causing us to wonder, "Is that all there is?" Meanwhile our fear of the loss of our selves in death prompts us to seek everlasting life. Thus these two opposing tendencies push us in the same direction, toward religion, something outside of ourselves and the earthly realm yet at the same time vitally connected to our lives (or deaths). Religious belief in this scenario amounts to a form of hope, that the next life will be better than this one or that we will at least not cease to *be*.

4. John Dewey, *The Public and Its Problems* (Athens: Ohio University Press, 1954), 141. All subsequent references will be parenthetical (as *Public*), with page numbers corresponding to this edition.

5. Alan Ryan, *John Dewey* (New York: W. W. Norton & Co., Inc., 1995), 219. Ryan also notes that in *Individualism Old and New,* Dewey would subsequently pose the issue in the form of a question: "Can a mechanical, industrial civilization be converted into a distinctive agency for liberating the minds and refining the emotions of all who take part in it?" (321).

6. In *Art as Experience,* Dewey expresses the concern that capitalism divorces art from the everyday (*Art*, 8-10). This seems to shape a conundrum for the formation of the Great Community. That which is necessary for seizing control of the Great Society seems itself to require the control of the Great Society. See John Dewey, *Art as Experience* (New York: Minton, Balch and Co., 1934), 8-10. All subsequent references will be parenthetical (as *Art*), with page numbers corresponding to this edition.

7. There is a clever irony to Dewey's reliance upon art in *The Public and Its Problems*. In *The Phantom Public* and *Public Opinion,* Lippmann had made the case that consensus was simply manufactured by elites through the use of vague symbols to unify diverse interests. In replying to this, Dewey does not deny the power of symbols but seeks to relocate them in the art of the everyday.

Consensus continues to have a grass-roots quality; common concerns are translated into common goals by simultaneously "capturing" and puncturing common things.

8. Interestingly, while Dewey calls Whitman the seer of democracy in *The Public and Its Problems,* he does not mention that particular poet in *Art as Experience,* relying instead upon Shelley, Keats, and Wordsworth.

9. Robert B. Westbrook, *John Dewey and American Democracy* (Ithaca: Cornell University Press, 1991), 397-398.

10. Walt Whitman, *The Portable Walt Whitman,* ed. Mark Van Doren (New York: The Viking Press, Inc., 1973), 9. All subsequent references will be parenthetical, with page numbers corresponding to this edition. Whitman suggests a similar theme in his 1888 preface, although there he stresses the need for poetry more than its use and acceptance (311).

11. Whitman repeatedly maintained that poetry should capture the experiences of men and women, but in discussing the *poet,* he consistently used the masculine pronoun.

12. In his "Walt Whitman and the Culture of Democracy" (*Political Theory* 18, 4 [November, 1990]: 545-571), George Kateb seeks to separate out Whitman's democratic individuality from his praise of comradeship. It is a difficult and, I would say, untenable divorce (cf. Michael Mosher, "Walt Whitman: Jacobin Poet of American Democracy," *Political Theory* 18, 4: 587-595).

13. Simon Parker, "Unrhymed Modernity: New York City, the Popular Newspaper Page, and the Forms of Whitman's Poetry," *Walt Whitman Quarterly Review* 14, 1 (summer 1996): 161-167.

14. For a discussion of Whitman's play between reader and poet, see Gale L. Smith, "Reading 'Song of Myself': Assuming What Whitman Assumes," *American Transcendental Quarterly* 6, 3 (September 1992): 158-159.

15. If he seems to come perilously close to a moralistic tone when he discusses the "prudence" suitable for immortality, Whitman would likely reply that the prudence offered by the great poet, the preference for "real long-lived things," is a chant of celebration rather than mortification, to which the democratic individual responds because it "answers at last the craving and glut of the soul" (20-23).

16. For praise of Whitman's democratic receptivity and responsiveness and the role that it can play in

promoting democratic individuality, see Kateb, "Culture." In his view, Whitman points toward the infinite potentiality (and thus strangeness) of our own selves and the intersection and recognition of our own tumultuous self with the potentialities of others.

17. See also 48, where after a long catalog of people, places and things, Whitman writes, "And these one and all tend inward to me, and I tend / outward to them / And such as it is to be of these more or less I am." The membrane between self and world is quite permeable.

18. The irony here is that Whitman's popularity in the twentieth century has hardly punctured the commercial spirit. Thus Whitman's vision seems to have lost even while his poetry has won acclaim.

19. Whitman welcomed the Civil War in that it raised people above "the shallowness and miserable selfism of these crowds of men, with all their minds so blank of high humanity and aspiration" (unpublished manuscript in George M. Fredrickson, *The Inner Civil War* [New York: Harper & Row, 1965], 67).

20. Quoted in Mosher, "Jacobin," 590.

21. He does identify himself as "a planter nonchalant and hospitable," but that image does not reach to the claim or feeling of having a right to own another.

22. Dewey encounters a similar problem in the interplay he outlines between art, politics, the recognition that they supposedly elicit, and the strange absence of conflict in the process. While recognizing that those who are "insensitive to meaning and life" may misjudge new movements, the only potential disputes that he suggests involve the old exerting ascendancy over the new or the egoistic over the truly common experience (*Art,* 303-304; cf. Mark Mattern, "John Dewey, Art and Public Life," *The Journal of Politics* 61, 1 [February 1999]: 54-75). Thus, in his praise of transcendence, Dewey unwittingly supplies fodder for those who want to short-circuit dialogue and debate. One can simply dismiss an opponent by claiming that he/she is narrow, reactionary or obviously doesn't "get it."

23. As Nancy Rosenblum notes, Whitman's unity with others was freighted with history in other ways as well. While apparently able to feel the pain of the hunted slave, he rejected "amalgamation" for free blacks and was willing to deny them civil rights (Nancy Rosenblum, "Strange Attractors: How In-

dividualists Connect to Form Democratic Unity," *Political Theory* 18, 4 [November 1990]: 577).

24. Fredrickson, *The Inner Civil War,* 95.

ANTI-DEMOCRATIC SENTIMENT

Benjamin Evans Lippincott (essay date 1938)

SOURCE: Lippincott, Benjamin Evans. "The Intellectual Protest." In *Victorian Critics of Democracy: Carlyle, Ruskin, Arnold, Stephen, Maine, Lecky,* pp. 244-64. Minneapolis: University of Minnesota Press, 1938.

[*In the following essay, Lippincott outlines the intellectual arguments against democracy that were leveled by Victorian writers and theorists.*]

I

In the eyes of the critics of democracy Victorian society was in danger of disruption. It was, they held, a society without unity; it was divided against itself, divided into opposing classes of rich and poor. It was a society without guidance; the aristocracy failed to lead, and the middle class was giving way to the anarchy of democracy. The aristocracy no longer commanded respect; men no longer admitted that the virtue of the few entitled the few to rule. Nor, in the eyes of these critics, were the mass of men impressed with the middle-class claim to govern; even Stephen, Maine, and Lecky, who were attached to property, were aware that power based upon property so far from inspiring loyalty often inspired discontent.

The critics, with the exception of Arnold, were convinced that the coming of democracy must mean disintegration. If, in their view, democracy did not promise the rule of ignorance and an impoverished culture, it promised dissolution of the social fabric. If the injustice of capitalist democracy, with its freedom to exploit and its freedom to be exploited, did not drive workingmen to revolt, the covetous nature of these men would tempt them to rebel and to destroy the private property order. And if, in their view, democracy led neither to stagnation nor to anarchy, it led rather to what was equally undesirable, to socialism.

In order to combat democracy and its threat of anarchy the critics championed authority and the title of the few to rule. Carlyle and Ruskin looked to authority and to the few for the purpose of combating competitive capitalism as well as democracy. Though Arnold did not surrender to the ideas of a past world and recommend an aristocracy of the military type, he looked to a remnant of the truly civilized to set standards that would curb the excesses of laissez-faire individualism and abolish, through persuasion, the inequality of property. Stephen, Maine, and Lecky, however, did not advocate authority for social ends, but for the purpose of stemming the rising tide of democracy; they looked to authority to maintain middle-class capitalism.

II

The anti-democratic and authoritarian ideas of the intellectuals failed to make any impression on their age; that is to say, the anti-democratic and authoritarian ideas of Carlyle and Ruskin failed to make any impression. For Arnold, Stephen, Maine, and Lecky did not count in the matter of influence. It is not surprising that Carlyle and Ruskin persuaded very few, if any, to accept their anti-democratic and authoritarian ideas, for these ideas were for the most part in direct opposition to the political ideas of the middle class, which formed the main part of their reading public.

In speaking of the political ideas of the middle class, we do not imply a rigid line separating classes, or that all members of the middle class held identically the same views. We imply that, though many members obviously held ideas which other members did not hold, and though the same ideas were held with different intensity, there was a sufficiently common outlook to enable us to characterize their views in general. In order to show the opposition between Carlyle and Ruskin and the thought of the middle class, we will state the ideas of the latter in a more definite and extreme form than that in which most men in this group probably held them. Our only contention is that the ideas of the middle class were opposed to those of the prophets to such an extent that the middle class, when they gave serious consideration to the views of the prophets, could hardly be convinced by them.

It is obvious that there was some common ground between Carlyle and Ruskin and the middle class. The middle class could agree with Carlyle and Ruskin that something should be done to alleviate the suffering of the workers. And if Carlyle and Ruskin did a little something to persuade the more enlightened members of the middle class to modify their views on laissez faire and to support state interference for humanitarian ends, for example, by passing factory acts, they were not able to persuade them to believe in authority for any more thorough-going purposes. The plea that the prophets made on behalf of the common man seems to have engendered more interest in, than well-wishing for him, more pity than genuine respect.

The liberals in the middle class who favored the franchise for workingmen and who helped to promote its realization could have only contempt for the prophets' view that the common man was inferior. The proposal of Carlyle and Ruskin for the regimentation of society, directed by an aristocracy of captains of industry or by an aristocracy of birth, could only be repellent to the middle class. The middle-class view of liberty was profoundly opposed to an emphasis on authority in the political sphere. Traditional English individualism, which the middle class had done so much to foster, could accept almost anything but an authoritarian state. A class that had fought for religious freedom against an overweening authority in the seventeenth century and had established its right to worship as it pleased, a class that still had to fight against religious discrimination at the universities in the nineteenth century, could not believe in giving government extensive power. A class that had been considerably hampered in the eighteenth and in the first half of the nineteenth century by government restrictions against freedom of trade must needs be suspicious of an authoritarian system of government. Moreover, the middle class had become what they were and had risen to power on the theory of as little government as possible, letting each man do as he likes, and letting him be the judge of his own interests. The middle class, then, had found life at its best when they could follow the creed of individualism, the creed of a minimized state. This creed was directly opposed to political authoritarianism, which meant having to do what one was told.

Though the middle class admired the aristocracy and undoubtedly believed that it was the best that the world had ever seen, they could hardly desire to be governed by it or by anything similar to it. It could hardly be expected that a class that had struggled for at least a century and a half against the aristocracy before winning political ascendancy over it would be interested, within a few decades of its victory, in turning the government back to the aristocracy. A class that had witnessed the triumph of its own abilities over a class whose star had set could scarcely think that those whom they had superseded were better fitted to govern. The middle class had seen the aristocracy rule and they had felt the effects of its policy; they denied that rule by a hereditary class was the best way of selecting governors. They could not discern an extraordinary gift for governing in men who accepted privilege irrespective of merit, who permitted a rotten borough system to exist, and who stood out for protection when the interests of the nation clearly demanded free trade. They could not idealize the virtues of the few when the few were identified with privileges from which they were excluded.

Moreover, the middle class believed that they were better qualified to rule than the aristocracy; the nation had made truly great progress under their leadership. Furthermore, the interests of the nation were identified with the middle class rather than with the aristocracy; the nation was primarily industrial, not agricultural; the aristocracy could not know the needs of industry as well as the middle class. And the interests of the middle class itself were better served when they directed the state; not only were their economic interests better secured, but so also their liberties. And to surrender power to the aristocracy would mean a sacrifice of self-respect that the middle class was not prepared to make, especially in virtue of their success.

The middle class, as is shown above, was not convinced that democracy in the sense of universal suffrage would bring about the destruction of society; and they could not take seriously the idea of an authoritarian state ruled by an aristocracy. Neither was the middle class prepared to accept the charge of the prophets that the materialism of Victorian society and the exploitation of the laborer by capitalism threatened to bring about revolution. It is true of this charge, as of the anti-democratic and authoritarian ideas we discussed above, that many who read the prophets were stimulated and went their way, and that others rejected their charge as fantastic. It is also true that many who read their charge sincerely attempted, within the limits of their own way of thought, to see whether or not they could agree with it. It is our contention that the majority of these men of good will could not take the charge of materialism and of exploitation seriously, for it was in profound conflict with their economic and social philosophy.

Again, let it be said that when we refer to the middle class or to their ideas, we speak in general terms. In order to make our argument clear, we will present their position, as we did above, in what is undoubtedly an exaggerated form as regards any single member of the class. For any member of the middle class who admitted the charge of materialism and of exploitation would have to change fundamentally his conception of the private property order. He would have to agree that profit (monopoly profit, the getting of something for nothing) should not be the chief incentive of work; that there should be a principle of justice explaining reward in terms of need, effort, and the quality of effort; and that the application of this principle would involve a great spreading of benefits to the lower classes, to the whole community.

To begin with, we may say that the middle class recognized to some extent the charge of materialism and of exploitation; they realized, for example, that limiting the working hours of women and children was necessary; but they did not recognize the charge in any fundamental way. It could hardly have been otherwise, for a fundamental recognition of the charge would have implied a rejection of their whole background and their social philosophy. The middle class had risen to power

by means of industry and commerce organized under an almost unfettered system of private property. Men are not easily persuaded to reject the property order under which they have risen to the chief place in the state. Men who have become accustomed to power and the benefits it confers are not willing to part with it easily; certainly few are willing to part with it simply because they are admonished to do so by intellectuals. The middle class had great admiration for the social position of the aristocracy, and many aspired to the ranks of the aristocracy as a final crown of success. Wealth was the key that could unlock the gate; to reject the property system that made possible social distinction was not possible to men who would become aristocrats.

The middle class had risen to power under a private property system organized on the profit motive. To admit the charge of materialism and of exploitation was to admit that profit ought not to be the chief incentive to the acquisition of property; and to admit that was to give up the principle that had been at the very heart of their whole activity. It could hardly be expected that a class at the height of its power would surrender a principle that was so fundamental to its success.

The charge of the prophets was fundamentally opposed not only to the philosophy of economic individualism, but also to the spirit of materialism, which was so strong at the time the prophets were most widely read—from the sixties through the nineties. By the eighties the evangelists in religion could no longer appeal to the imagination of the middle class; where Wesley had been received as a prophet, General Booth was received with contempt. It was significant that missionaries left England to save souls. With capitalism at its zenith, the charge of materialism could hardly impress many minds.

Despite appearances to the contrary, humanitarianism aided fundamentally not in opening, but in closing, the minds of the middle class to the charge of exploitation. True enough, it played an important part in making for such needed reforms as the factory acts, prison reform, and the abolition of slavery in the West Indies. But these were minor, not major, reforms. When it came to the latter, humanitarianism acted as a hindrance.

Humanitarianism fortified the conscience against the recognition of vital social obligation, such as was implicit in the charge of exploitation. That the middle class had recognized part of their obligations to those below left them with a sense of having discharged their duty. The fundamental reason for this was that humanitarianism is based not on an idea of justice, but on a feeling of pity. Thus the minor concessions were acts of charity, acts of philanthropy; that is, they were done because the middle class had pity for the lower class, not because they recognized the injustice of the conditions under which the lower class lived, not because they recognized any genuine moral obligation to the lower class. To do that which the middle class believed they were not morally required to do demonstrated their virtue; and they were righteous for having done whatever they had done. Thus the little things done were as worthy as the big things left undone. The extent to which the middle class felt virtuous—and it was not small—measured the extent to which they were immune to the idea of right; measured, that is, the extent to which real obligation to society had been whittled away.

The very fact that humanitarianism was based on a feeling of pity instead of on an idea of justice, on what was so largely emotional instead of on what was rational, tended to dissociate it from reason. This fact tended to make humanitarianism unsympathetic to intellectual inquiry, unsympathetic to a search into the causes of the economic and social conditions that made for suffering among the workers and that made humanitarianism possible. And the very fact that humanitarianism was based on a feeling so personal in character as the feeling of pity meant, as it must do, that it lent itself easily to personal indulgence; very frequently the feeling of pity was held sentimentally, that is, it was held for its own sake. This made for a special concern with feeling, and for a lack of interest in reason. Very frequently, too, humanitarianism was accepted merely because it was fashionable or respectable; to accept anything merely because it is given and merely because it carries prestige is to abandon reason.

With humanitarianism, then, so little a matter of justice and so much a matter of feeling, and so little informed by reason, it is no wonder that it led to a preoccupation with the tangible, immediate, and obvious social evils. Nor, for the same reasons, is it any wonder that humanitarianism was concerned with remedies rather than with cure and prevention. To remove the minor, and to leave undisturbed the major, social and economic diseases is to remove the minor but temporarily. To be concerned with remedies, not with cure and prevention, is to perpetuate the need for basic reform. In fact, it is not too much to say that humanitarianism in a very real sense produces the need for reform, and is an obstacle to its own abolition. The philosophy that lay behind the charge of the prophets was hardly in sympathy with perpetuating reform for the sake of humanitarians.

Humanitarianism, lastly, inhibited the recognition of vital social obligation from another angle. Nothing is more important for the recognition of real social obligation than respect for personality, or for the potential intrinsic worth of the individual; yet humanitarianism made for disrespect of personality, especially in the case of propertyless men. The very condition essential to the existence of humanitarianism is an unequal society; humanitarianism is a function of inequality. If the middle class is to have pity for the many below, the many must be below. Because humanitarianism implies a superior and an inferior, it breeds disrespect among

those better off for those less well off. The fundamental reason for this is not that there is a difference as such between the middle and lower classes, nor that there is a difference based on property, but that there is a difference based on an unjust property system.

When men do not have to justify what they own, they tend to justify whatever they possess. And those who own soon come to develop disrespect for those who do not, for those who own soon come to believe that the accumulation of property is a sign of character and ability, and they are easily persuaded that those without property are also without character and ability. Thus in the eyes of the middle class, those below did not really deserve even the minor benefits, like the factory acts, for they were men of little worth. The final comment on humanitarianism is that it enabled the middle class to keep their property and to claim their humanity.

Puritanism, the characteristic religion of the middle class, did little to open their minds to the charge of materialism and of exploitation; on the contrary, it worked to close them. What mattered fundamentally for the puritan was the communion of his soul with God; his religion was personal, not social, in essence. The emphasis the puritan placed on the individual character of his religion meant, as R. H. Tawney has pointed out, that religion entered relatively little into his social life. Less important for the puritan than the relation of his soul to God was his relation to his fellow human beings; what was important was the perfection of his spirit, not social justice. Puritanism, then, left the social life of the individual untenanted by any fundamental ethical principle; it left his social life open to an easy acceptance of the materialistic ideas of capitalism. In fact, puritanism lived with little difficulty side by side with capitalism, and came in a very real sense to sanction it. Wilhelm Dibelius, an acute observer of English life, has said: "Religion permitted, nay encouraged the massing of money. . . . The Christian altar was in perilous proximity to the Golden Calf."[1] Puritanism tended to set a seal of approval on the pursuit of private gain; God's chosen were those whom He was pleased to favor with success in this lower world. Surely to permit the accumulation of a fortune was a sign of His blessing.

It is clear that the charge of materialism and of exploitation fell for the most part on deaf ears. If a few were convinced of the justice of the charge, very few indeed were prepared to act in order to mitigate it. Most of these few must have thought it impracticable to act in the face of the overwhelming power of the middle class, which stood for property and materialism, and permitted exploitation. However this may be, most men resolve to act, not as a result of reading the books of intellectuals, but as a result of their own experience. Moreover, it is rare that a man transcends the ideas of the class in which he is brought up, and is able to see its defects and to find himself in fundamental disagreement with it. It is still rarer that, because of his fundamental disagreement, he acts in order to remove the defects. To act with a view to mitigating the charge of materialism and of exploitation must mean a great change in the individual's thought and way of life, a far greater change than is possible for most men to make, certainly during a period of prosperity and contentment like that of the Victorian era.

III

The protest of the prophets, Carlyle, Ruskin, and Arnold, and of the technical critics, Stephen, Maine, and Lecky, against democracy was a protest against the rise of the common man. The democratic movement in England in the nineteenth century, as Arnold observed, was above all a movement of expansion on something like a communal scale. With the middle class receiving the franchise in 1832, and universal manhood suffrage all but achieved by 1885, it is clear that the democratic movement meant that the ordinary man was beginning to assert himself. And the social legislation that followed his participation in political power meant that the ordinary man was beginning to assert himself in order to better his lot. That he achieved from time to time somewhat better conditions of life partly satisfied and partly stimulated his craving for freedom, for an opportunity to express himself and to make something of his powers. Along with his desire to explore his personality went the desire for equality; unless opportunities were open to all, the fruits of a free life would not be enjoyed by common men, but would remain the privilege of the few.

The intellectual critics opposed democracy fundamentally because it gave common men too much freedom; to give common men power, they thought, would bring about disorder, a disintegration of society. If Carlyle and Ruskin believed that disorder would come in part from the freedom that democracy gave men, they believed that it would come still more from the fact that common men were incapable of governing. Arnold harbored fears of democracy on the ground that mediocrity might triumph, and perhaps even brutality find a place in affairs; he doubted whether the common man was sufficiently developed to exercise political power creatively.

The technical critics saw democracy threatening society not because it was impotent to act, but because it aggrandized authority too much and was too eager to act. Though Stephen believed that democracy lacked consistent purpose, power of unified action, and a sense of direction, he held that the philosophy of liberty, equality, fraternity was a far greater evil; if this philosophy were put into practice, it would, he feared, loosen all the bonds that held society together. Though Maine insisted

on the difficulty and on the fragility of democracy, he was more concerned with arguing that democracy threatened economic disruption; the desire of common men to feast on milk and honey would bring about an attack on property. Though Lecky held that parliamentary government was becoming an institution for satisfying the greed of special interest groups, he held far more strongly that democracy endangered capitalism, on the ground that the common man wanted his share of the good things and would plunder in order to get them.

Although the prophet and the technical critic were broadly in agreement that democracy led to disorder because the common man was incapable of taking part in government, they came to this conclusion from somewhat different conceptions of the common man. Carlyle and Ruskin held that the ordinary individual was wanting in rational and moral ability to seek a way out by himself; and Arnold held that, though the ordinary individual had great potentialities for the future, and should be admitted to power, he was still insufficiently developed to make the most of it. The technical critics feared not that the common man was helpless or insufficiently developed; they feared that he was too assertive, that he was too selfish and too greedy, that he was too irrational and too rash. It is significant that the prophet-critics were critical of the organization of private property in their day, while the technical critics strongly supported it.

IV

What was the basis of the contention of the intellectual critics that the common man was not really capable of exercising political power? The critics would undoubtedly have replied that it was direct observation. They cited a number of facts and illustrations to support their view that the common man was inferior, and there can be no dispute that some of their facts do show this very thing. Given the conditions in which the upper classes permitted the lower to live, given the slums and the squalor, given a few riots, the revolutions of 1848 and the Paris Commune—given such facts, it was easy for the critics to conceive of the common man as deficient in mind and character. It was easy, however, on one condition, namely, that they thought that the common man was deficient before they looked for the facts; else they could never have found the facts. Since facts must be selected, a notion of what to select must precede the act of selection. The question is, what was the source of the critics' notion of the common man's inferiority? What factors shaped the basic notion of the critics' political philosophy?

The intellectual protest against the rise of the common man was, so far as ideas were concerned, first and foremost a protest of puritanism. Carlyle, Ruskin, Arnold, and Stephen were brought up in puritan households and all were imbued with puritan ideas. They could hardly have escaped the view in some form or other that the mass of men were sinners. All the critics, though Lecky perhaps above all, were undoubtedly affected by the view current in the middle class of the common man's inferiority. If this view, which was given typical expression by Macaulay, was inherited in part from the aristocracy, it also came from middle-class sources; it came very much from the puritan conception of the depravity of human nature, and it came from the natural disposition of men in power to look upon those without as somehow inferior.

The other sources of the notion of the common man's inferiority are best seen in relation to the sources of the doctrine of aristocracy and the doctrine of authority. The special title of the few to rule, which the critics urged against the rule of common men, seems to derive in part from the puritan notion that only the few are elected, and that they are the salt of the earth. It also seems to derive from middle-class ideas of power: the industrial and commercial enterprises of the nation were the pride of the middle class; as of necessity they were managed by the few. There was common agreement in the middle class that these concerns were well managed. A class that set great store upon competition and believed in the survival of the fittest must have respect for the few who survive. Respect for the virtues of the few must also have come to some extent from the very fact that these critics lived in a class that admired aristocracy.

The stand taken for authority by Carlyle, Ruskin, and Stephen, and the lesser stand taken by Arnold, may be traced in part to puritanism. Force has always attracted the puritan mind as an effective weapon for stamping out sin; when God is a stern judge enforcing justice, coercion appears to be the most direct and tangible method of fulfilling the Law against the disobedient. Another source of the emphasis on authority, which may have more bearing on Stephen, Maine, and Lecky than on the prophets, is the respect of the middle class for authority in the economic sphere. In spite of the antagonism of the middle class to an authoritarian state, this class was an exponent of authority in the sphere of industry and commerce. The everyday experience of a great many in the middle class was to exercise authority or to live under it; industrial and commercial institutions were managed on the autocratic principle, however benevolent, of government.

If puritanism and middle-class ideas of power were the main sources, so far as ideas were concerned, of the three leading doctrines of the critics—the common man's inferiority, the title of the few to rule, and authority—if these were the main sources, they were not the only ones. Classical education, to which the critics

were subjected in their youth, is a source that cannot be overlooked. The above doctrines were most perfectly represented in Plato's *Republic,* and the tone of classical education has rather implied Plato's view of these doctrines. And classical history, which showed the populace turning to disorder in Athens and in Rome, could support the view that the common man was inferior.

If Maine was chiefly indebted to the German historical school and to India for his appreciation of the three doctrines, Stephen was indebted to India and a little to Bentham. Carlyle's appreciation of the three doctrines was undoubtedly reinforced by Fichte, Goethe, and Novalis; Ruskin's by Carlyle and Plato; Arnold's to some extent by Plato and Burke; and Lecky's by Burke. It is not unlikely that respect for the special virtues of the few and respect for authority were strengthened a little by the very fact that the critics were members of the upper circles of society; and by the fact that they were themselves among the élite who were expected to give guidance.

The three doctrines of the critics were developed very largely in authoritarian periods, like the Reformation, or in epochs of concentration, like England in the eighteenth century; they were developed by writers like Calvin, and by writers like Burke and Hume. The doctrines of the common man's inferiority, of the special virtue of the few, and of authority were asserted when a few men or a part of the community claimed the title to govern. Those who ruled, whether they were churchmen, aristocrats, or middle-class men, found that the common man's inferiority was proof of their own special virtue and of their right to govern; and they were convinced that they could not deal with the common man and prevent civil disobedience unless they had considerable authority. The protest of the critics of democracy was a protest of the past against the present.

Ernest Barker has said that the literary man in politics is essentially a Platonist.[2] When a mind trained in letters turns from its own world to the social world, it seeks in the latter, as it does in the former, the beauty of order and the charm of definition. Not finding these, but finding disorder, it naturally looks to authority as a corrective. The technical critics as well as the prophets were probably influenced by the conditions under which a writer must work, by the necessity of ordering knowledge and of arranging ideas.

The intellectual critics may have been influenced by another condition necessary to their activity; an undisturbed atmosphere is essential to continuous thinking. That the atmosphere of the nineteenth century was, for the intellectual, not calm, but disturbed, perhaps especially by the growth of the democratic movement, may have augmented their hostility to democracy. Intellectuals do not like to be interrupted in the pursuit of their business any more than do businessmen or administrators in theirs. Security and orderly life are desirable for sustained thought.

The fact, too, that the critics were specialists who went outside their specialties to criticize in the field of social science, where they had not been trained, is undoubtedly significant in explaining their aversion to democracy. The specialist is always impressed with the complexity of his own field, and is easily led to believe that all problems are equally complex; and, in turn, that only the few who are specialists can hope to understand the life of the world. Not only does the specialist tend naturally to be anti-democratic with contempt for common opinion, but he also tends naturally to be skeptical of change. He is impressed with the sinfulness of error, and he fears to tread in the province of the unverified, where change always lies, for the possibility of error, he thinks, is overwhelming. To him novelty is dangerous; change should not be attempted unless there is certainty of a correct result, that is to say, change should not be attempted. The specialist, then, from the very nature of his activity, tends to be unsympathetic to democracy, because, at bottom, he forgets that problems are simple as well as complex, else life as it is lived by the mass of men, and by intellectuals when they are not specialists, could not be lived as we know it.

Again, the fact that the critics were specialists in ideas is perhaps not without some bearing upon their authoritarianism. Men who deal with ideas and men who become exponents of a point of view are prone to assume the cloak of authority. The consciousness that their minds are trained and that they have knowledge easily leads them to indulge in oracular pronouncement. They tend to believe that a trained mind, whatever its training, is entitled to an impressive hearing. Nor is it irrelevant to say that the success of these men in their own pursuits tended to make them a little authoritarian; men who achieve distinction tend to lay down the law. Perhaps this is especially true of intellectuals.

That Carlyle, Ruskin, and Arnold were men of letters, that Stephen was a judge and Maine a lawyer and Lecky a historian, that these men were engaged in professions more or less removed from life, could only strengthen their belief in the three doctrines. That these men lived very largely apart from the world meant that they had little opportunity of testing and correcting the ideas and attitudes that they had acquired in their youth. Their anti-democratic and authoritarian ideas, which they had learned from their parents and taken from their class and from the environment of their class, were never subject, except in the case of Arnold and to some extent in the case of Stephen, to the modifying influence of practical activity.

That they lived in their ivory towers meant more than this; it meant that the three doctrines were held as if they represented ultimate truth. This is not difficult to understand. These critics thought continually with the same assumptions, assumptions which they acquired in their youth, and they found nothing in their own experience to contradict them; thus their assumptions became part of themselves and part of the permanent order of things. Since their life was their thought, their thought was reality; the democratic movement in the world outside, which ran counter to their thought, was the appearance that was false. That their basic ideas remained unaltered in a world of flux made them more certain of their reality; what was permanent was true, and what was changing untrue. As the democratic movement gained momentum and the contradiction between what the critics thought and external events became greater, it did not occur to them to question what they thought. On the contrary, the doctrines of the inferiority of the common man, of the special virtue of the few, and of authority became more vivid in their minds.

That Arnold was much less hostile to democracy and much less authoritarian than the other critics was in part due to his participation in practical affairs. He presents a striking contrast to Carlyle, Ruskin, Stephen, Maine, and Lecky, and stands in relation to these men as the natural law jurists of the seventeenth and eighteenth centuries stood in relation to the historical jurists of the nineteenth. Arnold had a career in the everyday world, and the natural law jurists had careers wholly in that world; the writings of the latter were a by-product of their practical activity. Arnold believed in the possibilities of democratic change, and the natural law jurists had confidence in reason, taught principles of constructive legislation, and believed in action. Carlyle, Ruskin, Stephen, Maine, and Lecky opposed democratic change, and placed their faith in an aristocratic or middle-class utopia of an authoritarian nature; and the jurists of the historical school who had academic careers distrusted legislative change and were averse to action.[3]

Arnold, unlike the other critics, came into vital contact with the lower classes; as an inspector of elementary schools, he saw that human beings come from the slums as well as from Mayfair. His study of the structure, the administration, and the working of English and foreign schools kept him in touch with actual affairs; Arnold's practical activity helped to keep him human. His work as an inspector put him in touch with the life of the community and made him more sympathetic to those who were trying to find themselves. It seems that it is essential for an intellectual to take some active part in the world if he is to retain a sense of the present and its importance, and if he is to understand what the community is thinking and doing.

The source, however, of the three doctrines lies not only in the early family training and social background of the critics, and in the nature and conditions of intellectual work, but also in their temperaments. The egoistical, assertive, and absolutistic temper of Carlyle, Ruskin, and Stephen was probably a main source of their belief in authority and in the superior virtues of the few. Arnold's temperament was also a source of his authoritarian strain. These men had in them the urge of the prophet. Carlyle, Ruskin, and Stephen possessed in a high degree the combative spirit; they were fighters who found their antagonists in the realm of ideas. In argument these men were convinced of the moral rightness of their own views and of the wrongness of their opponents; they asked and gave no quarter. Carlyle and Ruskin were so certain of their inspiration that they could brook no opposition. If Lord Acton is correct, there was in Maine behind his academic calm a tendency to Caesarism. That Lecky stood less strongly for authority than Carlyle, Ruskin, and Stephen was due in part to his more open and more tolerant temperament. Though he could become in his own way as indignant as any of these men, he usually took account of the views of his opponents.

That Arnold could harbor doubts concerning the common man and emphasize authority and the special virtues of the few, and, at the same time, retain his belief in democracy was very largely due to his temperament. His friendliness and his gaiety, his grace and his wit, his ability to see himself in a humorous light, his flexibility and resilience, his refusal to make seriousness a cardinal virtue, his attempt to understand his opponents, his sensitiveness to those subtle attitudes that make the great differences, all these characteristics enabled him to get the upper hand of his tendency to egoism and his tendency to the pontifical manner. In spite of his aristocratic and authoritarian traits, he could identify himself with his fellows, whether they were in the upper or in the lower classes; that is to say, he could see the importance of liberty and equality and maintain a democratic spirit. The importance of temperament as a source of the three doctrines may be illustrated by saying that though Stephen, Maine, and Lecky were men who emphasized the importance of fact and careful reasoning, though they were historians, they asserted their prejudices more strongly than Arnold, and on occasion they gave way to statements as extreme in expression for them as any of Carlyle's were for him. Though Arnold never inquired into the "facts" with such pertinacity as the technical critics, he gave reason and temperate judgment a greater place in his views on contemporary politics than they did in their views. And though Maine set out purposely to apply scientific method to politics, even Carlyle, who stood for intuition, hardly violated it more than he.

As the critics grew older, the liberal strain that was in their temperament tended, except in the case of Ruskin, to disappear. Carlyle, in his early years, was deeply sympathetic with the working class; in his later years he found the working class disobedient. Arnold, in his later years, could find in the common man a tendency to disorder, and could attach no little importance to the virtue of the few and to the doctrine of authority. In the latter part of his life, Stephen's Calvinism dominated the liberal strain he acquired from Bentham. As a young man, Maine supported democracy in France and stood for some elements of socialism; toward the end of his life he distrusted democracy and looked back to aristocracy. Ruskin's liberal side never altered except perhaps to become more liberal; that is to say, his denunciations of the exploitation of the worker increased in his later years.

Finally, it is probably true that the dyspepsia from which Carlyle suffered, the brain fever with which Ruskin was afflicted, the depression that came over Maine and Lecky, had the effect of increasing the distrust these critics felt for the democratic movement.

V

Any criticism of the intellectual protest must begin by attacking it at the base; the critics' view of the common man must in its essentials be rejected. Their attack on democracy was based at bottom on the view that the common man was too inferior to be entrusted with power. It is our contention that the intellectuals were mistaken in holding that the common man monopolized the defects of human nature. The defects of the common man, his want of mind and of character, are not limited to the economic lower classes, but are to be found in all classes. All kinds of individuals and types, H. S. Jennings says, are to be found in any section of society.[4] And he points out that "if one means by democracy such a constitution of society that any part of the mass can in time supply individuals fitted for all its functions—in that sense the biological situation is that of democracy." The intellectual critics, we suggest, distorted the nature of the common man: they emphasized his weaker side and neglected his stronger side; they emphasized his defects and neglected his virtues.

At the same time, the intellectual critics overemphasized the importance, so far as politics is concerned, of the superiorities of the few. Admitting the great value of unusual qualities of mind and character, and admitting that they are rare, they are not so unusual that it would be safe to entrust them with the sole governing authority. A government of the wisest and best, of Plato's philosopher-kings, might be efficient, but never safe. The problem of government is not only a problem of intelligence and character, but also a problem of will and sentiment. The mass of men must be consulted if rulers are to be reasonably certain of the continuous execution of their orders.

Moreover, to withhold political power from the mass of men is to give privilege to the few. Men who are excluded from power are excluded from benefits. Not that the few are wanting in good intentions; they are merely unable to translate them in terms other than their own experience. And their own experience generally leads them to believe that the interests of the community are best served by advancing the interests of their class. Moreover, to leave the mass of men politically inert is to leave the few to become corrupted by their own privilege and the mass of men to suffer from the disadvantage of inferiority.

Since the intellectuals had little respect for the lower classes, they had little understanding of the need of that class for freedom. They did not appreciate that a prime condition of human development is the opportunity of taking a significant part in directing one's own life, for only by taking such a part can men hope to live creatively. It is obviously true that there can be no freedom without authority; freedom for all is impossible without restraints for all, and authority is necessary in maintaining restraints. But the intellectuals put too much emphasis on authority, and too little on freedom. They did not see that the democratic system, which they opposed, is the very best system for achieving their end; they did not see that the best way to make men responsible is to give them some responsibility, and that the best way to humanize them is to educate them.

Notes

1. Wilhelm Dibelius, *England: Her Character and Genius* (London, 1930), p. 125.

2. Ernest Barker, *Political Thought in England, 1848 to 1914* (rev. ed., London, 1928), p. 203.

3. Dean Pound says that it was significant that the historical jurists Savigny, Puchta, Maine, Ames, Thayer, and Bigelow were academic men and were opposed to legislative change and to action, while the natural law jurists Burlamaqui, Montesquieu, Blackstone, Kent, and Story had practical careers and believed in reason and change. *Interpretations of Legal History* (Cambridge, Massachusetts, 1923), p. 17.

4. Herbert S. Jennings, *The Biological Basis of Human Nature* (1st ed., New York, 1930), pp. 220-21. Cf. p. 201 above.

Wilson B. Gragg (essay date December 1958)

SOURCE: Gragg, Wilson B. "Trollope and Carlyle." *Nineteenth-Century Fiction* 13, no. 3 (December 1958): 266-70.

[In the following essay, Gragg compares and contrasts the political views and writings of Anthony Trollope and Thomas Carlyle, and explores the writers' relationship to each other.]

The great political paradox of nineteenth-century England was the advance of democracy against the almost universal opposition of the major political and intellectual leaders.[1] Two of the strangest bedfellows in this antagonism were Anthony Trollope, who associated the ideas "of communism, of ruin, and insane democracy," and Thomas Carlyle, who saw the Reform Bill of 1867 as "Shooting Niagara."

The ghost of the popular novelist stirs disapprovingly at this coupling with the violent pamphleteer. Carlyle's vehemence annoyed the placid novelist of acceptance; his doom-laden thundering angered the confident meliorist. In 1851, Trollope wrote to his mother regarding the *Latter-Day Pamphlets,* which he had just purchased:

> To me it appears that the grain of sense is so smothered up in a sack of sheerest trash, that the former is valueless. . . . I look upon him as a man who was always in danger of going mad in literature and who has now done so.

So strong was this revulsion that Trollope devoted a large portion of chapter xv of *The Warden* to a denunciation of Carlyle as "Dr. Pessimist Anticant."[2] (He justifies this extraneous attack by having Anticant write a pamphlet against Mr. Harding, the warden of Hiram's Hospital.) After identifying Dr. Anticant as "a Scotchman, who had passed a great portion of his early years in Germany," and who "had astonished the reading public by the vigour of his thoughts, put forth in the quaintest language," Trollope cites two examples of Anticant's work as a basis for criticism.

The first of these parodies, from the prophet's earlier period, is suggestive of the *Essay on Burns* and *Sartor Resartus:*

> "Oh, my poor brother," said he, "slaughtered partridges a score of brace to each gun, and poets gauging alebarrels, with sixty pounds a year, at Dumfries, are not the signs of a great era!—perhaps of the smallest possible era yet written of. Whatever economies we pursue, political or other, let us see at once that this is the maddest of the uneconomic: partridges killed by our land magnates at, shall we say, a guinea a head, to be retailed in Leadenhall at one shilling and ninepence, with one poacher in limbo for every fifty birds! our poet, maker, creator, gauging ale, and that badly, with no leisure for drinking, and such like beer-barrel avocations! Truly, a cutting of blocks with fine razors while we scrape our chins so uncomfortably with rusty knives! Oh, my political economist, master of supply and demand, division of labour, and high pressure—oh, my loud-speaking friend, tell me, if so much be in you, what is the demand for poets in these kingdoms of Queen Victoria, and what the vouchsafed supply?"

Trollope comments on this passage with a calm, practical humor which points up the contrast between the two men.

This was all very well: this gave us some hope. We might do better with our next poet, when we got one; and though the partridges might not be abandoned, something could perhaps be done as to the poachers.[3]

The dubious praise which Trollope grants this early style is a criticism of the Kantian Carlyle:

> We all of us could, and many of us did, learn much from the doctor while he chose to remain vague, mysterious, and cloudy.

There is unquestioned condemnation of Carlyle's later style. The doctor, Trollope continues,

> mistook the signs of the times and the minds of men, instituted himself censor of things in general, and began the great task of reprobating everything and everybody, without further promise of any millennium at all. This was not so well; and, to tell the truth, our author did not succeed in his undertaking; . . . when he became practical, the charm was gone.

And the second passage in *The Warden* takes off the style of the *Latter-Day Pamphlets.*

> Could utmost ingenuity in the management of red tape avail anything to men lying gasping—we may say, all but dead; could despatch boxes with never-so-much velvet lining and Chubb's patent, be of comfort to a people *in extremis,* I also, with so many others, would, with parched tongue, call on the name of Lord John Russell; or, my brother, at your advice, on Lord Aberdeen; or, my cousin, on Lord Derby, at yours; being with my parched tongue, indifferent to such matters. 'Tis all one. Oh, Derby! Oh, Gladstone! Oh, Palmerston! Oh, Lord John! Each comes running with serene face and despatch box. Vain physicians! though there were hosts of such, no despatch box will cure this disorder! What! are there no other doctors' new names, disciples who have not burdened their souls with tape? Well, let us call again. Oh, Disraeli, great oppositionist, man of the bitter brow! or, Oh, Molesworth, great reformer, thou who promisest Utopia. They come; each with that serene face, and each—alas, me! alas, my country!—each with a despatch box! Oh, the serenity of Downing Street! My brothers, when hope was over on the battlefield, when no dimmest chance of victory remained, the ancient Roman could hide his face within his toga, and die gracefully. Can you and I do so now? If so, 'twere best for us; if not, oh my brothers, we must die disgracefully, for hope of life and victory I see none left to us in this world below. I for one cannot trust much to serene face and despatch box!

Of this Trollope says summarily that it "was not thought to have much in it," and he derides *Sartor Resartus* as "that attack of his on chip bonnets . . . the anathemas with which he endeavoured to dust the powder out of the bishops' wigs."

In the *Autobiography,* also, Trollope denounces Carlyle as a prophet of doom who declares that "we are all going straight away to darkness and the dogs. But then we don't put much faith in Mr. Carlyle," avers Trollope, we "who cannot but see how comfort has been increased, how health has been improved, and education extended."

These are unequivocal signs of Trollope's strong aversion to Carlyle's violent pessimism. Yet there is a significant lack of broad burlesque in the parodies in *The Warden*; the popular novelist was indubitably influenced by the popular prophet. In March of 1855, the year when *The Warden* appeared, Trollope submitted to Longman's a work entitled *The New Zealander,* in rejecting which the publisher's reader wrote,

> All the good points in the work have already been treated by Mr. Carlyle, of whose *Latter-Day Pamphlets* this work, *both in style and manner,* is a most feeble imitation.

A further note on the relationship between the two men is contained in a letter from G. H. Lewes to Thomas Adolphus Trollope, Anthony's brother, dated 5 July 1861.

> Yesterday Anthony dined with us [Lewes and George Eliot], and, as he had never seen Carlyle, he was glad to go down with us to tea at Chelsea. Carlyle had read and *agreed* with the West Indian book, and the two got on very well together; both Carlyle and Mrs. Carlyle liking Anthony, and I suppose it was reciprocal, though I did not see him afterwards to hear what he thought. He had to run away to catch his train.

Whether or not Trollope had overcome his dislike of Carlyle, *The West Indies and the Spanish Main,* published two years before this meeting, smacks of Carlyle in such specific phrases as "Hispana-Dano-Niggery-Yankee-doodle population" as well as in its general depreciation of the West Indian Negroes.

Furthermore, in Trollope's projected history of fiction, begun in 1866 and never finished, he refers to Carlyle as "one whom I have ever revered as a thinker, and valued as an author, and whom I much esteem as a man—one from whom, perhaps, I have learned more than from any other English writer"; he actually dubs him "our dear old English Homer." Since this statement appeared ten years before the condemnation of Carlyle in the *Autobiography,* one must conclude that Trollope is here acknowledging the influence of the author whose violence he nevertheless found antipathetic.

Like Carlyle and many others of his time, Trollope feared the rapid advance of democracy; like him also, he believed that all happened for the best in the long run. But Trollope, a matter-of-fact realist, did not regard the ruling class whom both trusted for guidance in the same light as did Carlyle, the poet and prophet. He did not see salvation in a hero with a deep-seeing eye—he would have regarded such a concept as romantic nonsense—but in gentlemen born who were real human beings.

The contrast between the two men is strikingly evident in their styles of writing: the calm, pellucid clarity of Trollope; and the turgid, chaotic vehemence of Carlyle. To read the writings of these different men, both representative of and influential upon the thought of their time, is to prove again that there is no typical Victorian.

Notes

1. See Benjamin Evans Lippincott, *Victorian Critics of Democracy* (Minneapolis: University of Minnesota Press, 1938).

2. This chapter contains also an attack on Dickens as "Mr. Popular Sentiment."

3. See the partridge-slayer's epitaph at the end of Book II, chapter iv of *Sartor Resartus*; Trollope refers to this passage in *Marion Fay* also.

Larry J. Reynolds (essay date summer 1980)

SOURCE: Reynolds, Larry J. "Kings and Commoners in *Moby-Dick*." *Studies in the Novel* 12, no. 2 (summer 1980): 101-03.

[*In the following essay, Reynolds illustrates how Herman Melville relates both his democratic and antidemocratic ideals in* Moby-Dick.]

If one examines Herman Melville's sociopolitical thought in detail and depth, he will discover that it consists of two opposing sets of attitudes—one democratic, the other antidemocratic and elitist—that were in irreconcilable conflict throughout Melville's life. His democratic attitudes, what he called his "unconditional democracy," centered upon a high regard for the idea of man and were broadly social, rather than narrowly political, in meaning. For him, democracy meant recognizing the innate dignity and equality of man, in the ideal, and treating all men, particularly the lowly and oppressed, with respect and sympathy. His elitism, on the other hand, which was both social and intellectual, centered upon a low regard for the mass of actual men and meant viewing and treating the mass with dislike and disdain, while according admiration and empathy to a worthy few.[1] Although he had little regard for the wealthy and limited sympathy for feudal hereditary aristocracies, he, nevertheless, applied standards of birth and class along with intelligence and depth of vision in his evaluations of others. Throughout his works, his democracy expresses itself explicitly in a humanitarian concern for Polynesian natives, Negro slaves, Irish immigrants, common sailors, and the poor and outcast in general, while his elitism implicitly informs the attributes, attitudes, and actions of his main characters, who are socially and intellectually superior to the mass of ordinary men.

Unlike James Fenimore Cooper, whose background and thought parallel his own in many ways, Melville did not try to resolve the conflict in his attitudes by professing political democracy while insisting upon social aristocracy; instead, he paraded one set of attitudes and disclaimed the other. In an 1851 letter to Hawthorne, he exhibits the sweeping egalitarianism he liked to assert at the height of his career, declaring that "with no son of man do I stand upon any etiquette or ceremony, except the Christian ones of charity and honesty" and warning his friend: "When you see or hear of my ruthless democracy on all sides, you may possibly feel a touch of a shrink, or something of that sort. It is but nature to by shy of a mortal who boldly declares that a thief in jail is as honorable a personage as Gen. George Washington." In an afterthought, however, he reveals the tension underlying his boldness as he concedes: "It seems an inconsistency to assert unconditional democracy in all things, and yet confess a dislike to all mankind—in the mass."[2]

Recognition of this tension in Melville's thought is not prevalent among his major biographers and critics,[3] and, over the years, only a handful of commentators have pointed it out.[4] Moreover, no one to date, with one exception, has explored its importance in his literary work.[5] This essay is an attempt to show the most important ways it shapes Melville's greatest work, *Moby-Dick*.

In Melville's first five novels, *Typee* (1846), *Omoo* (1847), *Mardi* (1849), *Redburn* (1849), and *White-Jacket* (1850), the democratic-elitist tension can be seen growing stronger as he presents its two sides with more seriousness and force and becomes more concerned with resolving the conflict within his own mind. In *Moby-Dick* (1851), the rich and dark masterpiece he scraped "off the whole brain to get at,"[6] the underlying tension creates a thematic complexity and depth that all readers sense. In a very self-conscious way, *Moby-Dick* is an American book, constructed out of American materials and exploring the plight of the superior individual in American society. Not surprisingly, of all the novel's ideological dimensions, including the philosophical, the psychological, and the religious, none has engaged modern critical attention more consistently than has the sociopolitical. At first, this particular dimension of the work appears dualistic and clear, with democratic attitudes informing Ishmael's conduct and character and elitist attitudes informing Ahab's. In fact, most critics interpret the novel in this manner, taking sides with what they see as Ishmael's democratic liberalism or Ahab's kingly nobility, with the former receiving the admiration of most critics since F. O. Matthiessen's 1941 condemnation of Ahab as a destructive and alienated individualist.

In one of the most influential evaluations of *Moby-Dick* yet made, Matthiessen declares: "Without deliberately intending it, but by virtue of his intense concern with the precariously maintained values of democratic Christianity, which he saw everywhere being threatened or broken down, Melville created in Ahab's tragedy a fearful symbol of the self-enclosed individualism that, carried to its furthest extreme, brings disaster both upon itself and upon the group of which it is part."[7] A multitude of critics have echoed Matthiessen; Milton R. Stern and Ray B. Browne, to cite just two examples, have done so rather clearly. Stern observes that "as forecastle-Ishmael is identified with the history of common humanity, quarterdeck-Ahab is totally isolated," and he finds that the bulk of the novel's materials "work together to suggest that men, in the inescapable democracy of mutual mortality, must give their primary attention to the world they live in."[8] Similarly, Browne finds that in *Moby-Dick* "Melville suggests the eventual tragic failure of the Promethean impulse in the individual but its eventual triumph in massed Prometheanism in humanity—in democracy—in the person of Ishmael." For Browne, Ishmael is "the commonest of the commoners," who at the novel's end "has been apotheosized as a symbol of the rise of the common man."[9]

While such analyses of the novel have a satisfying formal neatness and an appealing liberal emphasis, they unfortunately result in an over-simplification of the complex sociopolitical views represented by Ishmael and, to a lesser extent, those represented by Ahab. As I hope to show, the attributes and attitudes of both characters arise from the tension that characterizes Melville's own thought.

Walter E. Bezanson has pointed out a critically important, but often ignored, feature of *Moby-Dick*: that is, it contains two Ishmaels. "The first Ishmael is the enfolding sensibility of the novel, the hand that writes the tale, the imagination through which all matters of the book pass. He is the narrator. . . . The second Ishmael is not the narrator, not the informing presence, but is the young man of whom, among others, narrator Ishmael tell us in his story. . . . This is forecastle Ishmael or the younger Ishmael of 'some years ago.'"[10] With the younger Ishmael we have indeed a Melvillean main character whose behavior is not elitist or anti-democratic in any discernible way. He eats, sleeps, and works with the "people" without reservation and is willing to be sociable with anyone, regardless of his social or intellectual status; the opening scenes where he befriends a "head-peddling" cannibal serve to dramatize this point. "It is but well to be on friendly terms with all the inmates of the place one lodges in,"[11] narrator Ishmael declares, and this philosophy is not contradicted by the account of his past practice, as it is with all of Melville's other first-person narrators.

When we consider the older Ishmael, the reflecting, brooding, wondering, explaining consciousness, whose voice is often indistinguishable from Melville's own, he seems at first to share the pure democratic sensibilities of his younger self. In his memorable "Knights and Squires" speech, he sings the praises of the crew, the "kingly commons," and celebrates "that democratic dignity which, on all hands, radiates without end from God; Himself! The great God absolute! The centre and circumference of all democracy! His omnipresence, our divine equality!" (p. 104). Elsewhere, like the narrators that precede him in the earlier works, Ishmael reveals his democratic abhorrence of the failure of men and institutions to recognize and value the inherent dignity, equality, and brotherhood of all. In *Moby-Dick,* of course, the most noticeable failure is Ahab's, and in "The Specksynder," Ishmael specifically condemns his captain's "irresistible dictatorship," explaining that "be a man's intellectual superiority what it will, it can never assume the practical, available supremacy over other men, without the aid of some sort of external arts and entrenchments, always, in themselves, more or less paltry and base" (p. 129).

Nevertheless, while many of narrator Ishmael's attitudes are thoroughly democratic, the matter and manner of his narrative itself contain an elitist and antidemocratic bias that ultimately places him closer in attitude and outlook to Ahab than to any member of the crew. Ishmael's high regard for the idea of man and his sympathy for the lowly and oppressed are opposed and balanced by a dislike for the mass of mankind and an admiration for the noble few, among whom he includes himself and his captain. Like Emerson who admitted, "I like man, but not men,"[12] Ishmael acknowledges the paradox in his own thinking when he says, "take high abstracted man alone; and he seems a wonder, a grandeur, and a woe. But . . . take mankind in mass, and for the most part, they seem a mob of unnecessary duplicates . . ." (p. 387).

In the opening pages of the novel, Ishmael specifically disowns aristocratic pretensions by declaring, "when I go to sea, I go as a simple sailor, right before the mast, plumb down into the forecastle, aloft there to the royal mast-head" (p. 14), yet he soon admits that being ordered about "touches one's sense of honor, particularly if you come of an old established family in the land, the Van Rensselaers, or Randolphs, or Hardicanutes" (p. 14). Later, though casual, pretentious references, he further emphasizes his high birth and fallen lot. For example, in "The Town-Ho's Story" he refers to socializing in Lima with the circle of his Spanish friends, and adds that "of those fine cavaliers, the young Dons, Pedro and Sebastian, were on the closer terms with me" (p. 208). Similarly, in "A Bower in the Arsacides" he refers nonchalantly to his "late royal friend Tranquo, king of Tranque" and mentions vacationing "at his retired palm villa at Pupella" (p. 373).

Ishmael's dissatisfaction with his status as a "common" sailor and his pride in past aristocratic associations are complemented by a subtle personal antipathy toward democratic leveling, an antipathy that surfaces in his note on "gally," an English word obsolete except for its use by American whalemen. He laments that "much the same is it with many other sinewy Saxonisms of this sort, which emigrated to the New-England rocks with the noble brawn of the old English emigrants in the time of the Commonwealth. Thus, some of the best and furthest-descended English words—the etymological Howards and Percys—are now democratised, nay, plebeianised—so to speak—in the New World" (p. 322). (This sentiment would be echoed in *Pierre* in Melville's autobiographical lament that "in our cities families rise and burst like bubbles in a vat. For indeed the democratic element operates as a subtle acid among us; forever producing new things by corroding the old. . . .")[13]

Any study of the allusions of *Moby-Dick* reveals that Ishmael not only likes to display his uncommon erudition, but also in his thoughts prefers, like Taji of *Mardi,* to circulate "freely, sociably, and frankly, among the gods, heroes, high-priests, kings, and gentlemen."[14] As his metaphors and similes repeatedly disclose, nobility, royalty, and greatness fascinate him. He compares his captain to King Ahab and King Belshazzar and calls him "a Khan of the plank, and a king of the sea, and a great lord of Leviathans" (p. 114); he compares Queequeg to Czar Peter; Daggoo, the "imperial negro," to King Ahasuerus; the *Pequod* to an Ethiopian emperor; Steelkilt to Mark Anthony and Charlemagne; and Moby Dick to King Antiochus's elephants and to the white bull Jupiter. He associates the whiteness of the whale with royalty and preeminence and claims that "whaling is imperial," noting that by old English law the whale is "a royal fish" (p. 101). Finally, in his discussion of his own vocation, he humorously becomes carried away with the honor and nobility of it all, claiming that Perseus, St. George, Hercules, and Jonah should be considered whalemen, and adding, "Nor do heroes, saints, demigods, and prophets alone comprise the whole roll of our order. Our grand master [Vishnoo] is still to be named; for like royal kings of old times, we find the head-waters of our fraternity in nothing short of the great gods themselves" (pp. 304-6)

Traditionally, critics have tried to reconcile Ishmael's admiration for the noble few with his democratic attitudes in two ways: first, by arguing that he appreciates various heroes and kings not for their own sakes but as metaphors to represent and emphasize the natural excellence of even the common man; and second, by proposing that his regard is artistic, rather than personal, in origin, that is, that it arises from his, or Melville's, attempt to create Shakespearean tragedy out of American materials, an attempt that demands the magnification and aggrandizement of the crew, "the Whale, the Ship, and, OVER ALL, the Captain."[15] Both of these theses, however, are only partially valid.

Although many of Ishmael's "outward majestical trappings and housings" (p. 130) are certainly intended to impart a nobility and grandeur to ordinary men and their disdainfully-regarded profession, this intent should be seen as an effect rather than a cause of his elitism. Like all of Melville's narrators, Ishmael values actual as well as figurative nobility. His reflections on Queequeg effectively reveal this. The younger Ishmael initially admires Queequeg because of the man's frankness, generosity, kindheartedness, and courage. Narrator Ishmael, however, delightedly announces that this friend was no "common" cannibal for "his father was a High Chief, a King; his uncle a High Priest; and on the maternal side he boasted aunts who were the wives of unconquerable warriors" (p. 56). In other words, blood will tell; Queequeg's noble character is explained by his noble lineage. And, although Ishmael makes this point in a humorous manner, the humor should not mislead anyone about Melville's acceptance of its validity, for he had made precisely the same point about King Mehevi in *Typee* and Jack Chase in *White-Jacket,* and he would make it again about the noble foundling Billy in *Billy Budd.*

As for the demands of genre as an explanation for Ishmael's emphasis on nobility and greatness, we need only recall the fascination with and appreciation of birth, rank, and power present in the earlier works, particularly *Mardi,* to realize that part of Melville's enthusiasm for Shakespeare (which he acquired during the spring of 1849 and defined during August of 1850 while in the first stages of writing *Moby-Dick*)[16] followed rather than preceded the formulation of his, and thus Ishmael's, attitudes. Certainly, much of the texture of *Moby-Dick,* including the stage directions, the soliloquies, the prophecies, and the poeticized rantings of Ahab, derives from Melville's recent rereading of Shakespeare, particularly *Macbeth* and *King Lear,* and it establishes the novel's uniqueness among Melville's works; nevertheless, Ishmael's elitist regard for uncommon men, particularly heroes and kings, is shared by Tommo, Omoo, Taji, Redburn, and White-Jacket and thus is not part of this uniqueness. As Nathalia Wright has observed with regard to the whole of Melville's works, "for all his democracy, Melville's world has an aristocratic cast."[17]

Ultimately, I think, narrator Ishmael's democratic attitudes must be viewed as irreconcilably in conflict with his intellectual tendency to align himself with superior individuals and groups. This tendency, however, forms only half of his elitism; his dislike and disdain for the mass of actual men from the other. When Ishmael observes that "men may seem detestable as joint stock-companies and nations" but "man, in the ideal," is "a grand and glowing creature" (p. 104), the qualification "in the ideal" is all-important. Interpretations of the novel that stress its democratic, Democratic, humanistic, or humanitarian aspects tend to overlook or blur the distinction between Ishmael's view of ideal man and his view of the mass of men. Like Ahab, he perceives that the "people" of the *Pequod* measure up to no ideal, and his narrative continually dramatizes the baseness, savagery, and ignorance that lie beneath the surface character of the inhabitants of this shipboard society.

For example, in "Midnight, Forecastle" he presents an account of a drunken fight between Daggoo and a Spanish sailor that reveals the murderous impulses of the crew and suggests that these impulses are God's work. As the fight begins, the sailors cry for a ring and the Old Manx sailor observes, "Ready formed. There! the ringed horizon. In that ring Cain struck Abel. Sweet work, right work! No? Why then, God, mad'st thou the ring?" (p. 154). The wild brutal action of the scene confirms Starbuck's estimate of the men as "a heathen crew that have small touch of human mothers in them! Whelped somewhere by the sharkish sea. The white whale is their demogorgon" (p. 148).

The three sailors shown to respond most willingly and enthusiastically to Ahab's incitements are the harpooners, Daggoo, Tashtego, and Queequeg. Although Queequeg is initially characterized as noble, independent, and kindhearted, he later joins Tashtego and Daggoo "in an eager sympathy with Ahab's murderous purpose," as Merlin Bowen has pointed out.[18] Ahab calls the harpooners "my three pagan kinsmen" (p. 146), and as the novel progresses Ishmael uses them to symbolize the dark, primitive, and savage side of man and nature—the side seen by him as dominant and the only side seen by Ahab. When Ahab baptizes his harpoon in the name of the devil, these three willingly supply the baptismal blood, and when he presides over the black mass in "The Candles," they become, in appearance at least, his fellow devil worshippers. Finally, in "The Try-Works," they again lose their individuality and become "Tartean shapes" revealing the dark and unholy side of mankind.

The three mates, Starbuck, Stubb, and Flask are presented by Ishmael as less noticeably unadmirable than the "people" under their command, yet they, too, fail to live up to any ideal conception of man. The righteous Starbuck is, on the whole, a weak and shallow individual, lacking the intellectual depth necessary to understand Ahab's motives and the courage necessary to resist his designs. He can only naively and pathetically exclaim, "Let faith oust fact" (p. 406). Stubb, good-natured and courageous in his way, shares Starbuck's pragmatic and limited vision. He also displays an occasional insensitivity, and after abandoning the helpless Pip on the ocean justifies his action by hinting that "though man loves his fellow, yet man is a money-making animal" (p. 346). As for the third mate Flask, he can act with an appalling cruelty, as we see in the description of the blind and crippled whale that he needlessly tortures. This conduct, as F. O. Matthiessen has conceded, "becomes a contributing factor to our sense that . . . this crew may deserve something of the retribution that overtakes it."[19] Viewed realistically, then, the men of the *Pequod* are, as narrator Ishmael declares, "mongrel renegades, and castaways, and cannibals—morally enfeebled . . . by the incompetence of mere unaided virtue or right-mindedness in Starbuck, the invulnerable jollity of indifference and recklessness in Stubb, and the prevading mediocrity in Flask" (p. 162). As such they are viewed with dislike and disdain not only by Ahab, but by narrator Ishmael as well.

It has been customary to see in *Moby-Dick* the theme of democratic brotherhood presented as the affirmative alternative to the tragic individualism embodied by Ahab. The friendship that develops between the younger Ishmael and Queequeg, that is, their "marriage" and "hearts' honeymoon" in "A Bosom Friend," is usually accepted as the introduction of the theme; "The Monkey-Rope" and "A Squeeze of the Hand" as the development and extension of it; and "The Epilogue" as its conclusion, with Ishmael appropriately saved by the "coffin life-buoy" of his friend. This view of the novel has obvious merit, and I have no intention of denying its validity; however, I want to stress that the view is limited and often results in an incomplete understanding of Ishmael's attitudes toward himself and others, particularly through the failure to recognize his deep reservations about the goodness and worth of his former fellow sailors, including Queequeg. Furthermore, critics who cite "A Squeeze of the Hand" as evidence of an affirmation of brotherhood in the novel, usually disregard the outrageous sexual implications of the chapter. As Robert Shulman has pointed out, although the chapter "may contain one of Melville's few social affirmations—that brotherhood saves and love redeems—it should be stressed that what is recommended is a peculiarly anti-social sociality."[20]

Although Ishmael as common sailor participates in the democratic society of the forecastle, as narrator, he is more closely allied with the uncommon individual occupying the quarterdeck. While he perceives and abhors Ahab's ruthless manipulation and sacrifice of others, he also sees and admires his "globular brain" and "ponderous heart" (p. 71) and the heroic suffering and courage they inspire. Ishmael's admiration for Ahab's greatness, a greatness that ultimately lies in grief,[21] is often explicit as when he explains that "great hearts sometimes condense to one deep pang, the sum total of those shallow pains kindly diffused through feebler men's whole lives. And so, such hearts, though summary in each one suffering; still, if the gods decree it, in their life-time aggregate a whole age of woe, wholly made up of instantaneous intensities; for even in their pointless centres, those noble natures contain the entire circumferences of inferior souls" (p. 451). At other times, his admiration is implicit and informs his consistent presentation of Ahab as "a mighty pageant creature, formed for noble tragedies" (p. 71) and accounts for the figurative superiority given him in the drama he acts out. In other words, while Ahab in his own right possesses an intellectual superiority accorded him by his rare mind, and tragic vision and a social superiority accorded him by his rank, authority, and power, Ishmael figuratively enhances the latter in tribute to the former. In the process, however, he ironically undercuts his idealization of democracy by presenting the crew as the knights, squires, and commoners of a feudal hierarchy.

Looking at Ahab apart from Ishmael's magnification of him, one sees a man thoroughly convinced of his superiority to all other men and expressing attitudes that, with just one exception, are totally elitist. As Captain Peleg says, "Ahab's above the common; Ahab's been in colleges, as well as 'mong the cannibals" (p. 76), and Ahab is acutely aware of his uncommonness, using it to justify his actions. Convinced that "the permanent constitutional condition of the manufactured man . . . is sordidness" (p. 184) and believing that he "stands alone among the millions of the peopled earth" (p. 452), he disdainfully uses his men as tools in his quest and maintains an "irresistible dictatorship" over them by exploiting their ignorance and depravity. His quarterback speech, his nailing of the doubloon to the mast, his magnetizing the compass needle, and his maintenance of the whaling voyage are some of the "external arts and entrenchments" (p. 129) by which he maintains his supremacy. Although Peleg also tells Ishmael that "Ahab has his humanities" (p. 77), they rarely appear. Except in his relationship with Pip and in his conversation with Starbuck in "The Symphony," Ahab is ruthlessly autocratic and shows no respect or sympathy toward his fellow man. (Ironically, of course, he nevertheless sees himself as a representative of mankind, as a Promethean savior defying "all the subtle demonisms of life and thought" (p. 160), all "the omniscient gods" who are "oblivious of suffering man" (p. 428).

Ahab's attitudes are democratic in one small aspect, however, and it forms his main link with Ishmael and with Melville as well. Starbuck isolates this aspect when he says, "Horrible old man! Who's over him, he cries;— aye, he would be a democrat to all above; look, how he lords it over all below!" (p. 148). Although Ahab's self-serving egalitarianism does not, of course make him democratic in the broad humanitarian sense of the word, the consistent sense of pride that informs his inconsistent attitudes toward "all above" and "all below" does underlie both sides of the democratic-elitist tension found in all of Melville's works. Let me explain this important point, if I can. When Melville's narrators affirm the noble and godlike nature of man, in the ideal,

they are, in effect, proudly asserting their own worth, and when they protest against the indignity and injustice inflicted upon the common man, these protests are inspired by proud indignation. Likewise, when his narrators express dislike and disdain for the mass of ordinary men, and when they identify with the superior few, these attitudes too can be traced to pride.

Although Ishmael's deep involvement in Ahab's tragic quest results in part from his sense of exile and alienation as well as from his acute awareness of the "heartless voids and immensities of the universe" (p. 169), it is his rebellious sense of pride that brings him closest in spirit to his captain. While Ishmael begins his narrative humbly by referring to the "universal thump" and asking, "Who aint a slave?" (p. 15), he later declares, "I believe that much of a man's character will be found betokened in his backbone. . . . A thin joist of a spine never yet upheld a full and noble soul. I rejoice in my spine, as in the firm audacious staff of that flag which I fling half out to the world" (p. 294). Elsewhere, in a similar proud and defiant tone, he boasts, "come a stove boat and stove body when they will, for stave my soul, Jove himself cannot" (p. 41). And, in his famous tribute to Bulkington, he argues for earnest thinking and "the intrepid effort of the soul to keep the open independence of her sea; while the wildest winds of heaven and earth conspire to cast her on the treacherous, slavish shore" (p. 97).[22]

In the climactic "Try-Works" chapter, Ishmael discovers the dangers of looking too long in the face of the hellish fire, of seeing only "the redness, the madness, the ghastliness" (p. 354) around him, and for the first time clearly understands the distinction between his view of the world (which is two-thirds dark) and Ahab's (which is totally dark), between the "wisdom that is woe" and the "woe that is madness" (p. 355); nevertheless, both before and after this discovery, he vicariously participates in Ahab's heroic defiance of the god or gods that have maimed him. He shares Ahab's sense of self-respect and independence that bodies forth in opposition to anyone or anything that threatens to demean the self, and his assertion of Ahab's superiority to the mass of base, shallow, and "inferior souls" is indirectly an assertion of his own.

Melville, like Ishmael, felt a proud sense of superiority that he never abandoned, even in his most democratic moments. He was, as he told Sophia Hawthorne, "of Scotch descent—of noble lineage—of the Lords of Melville & Leven."[23] And although he tried to adjust to his family's fallen state and to the emergence of mass society in America by becoming an ardent democrat, he could not give up his view of himself as déclassé patrician whom birth and genius placed far above the mass of ordinary men, but whom fate placed in lowly circumstances.

After writing *Moby-Dick,* in which his democratic and elitist attitudes conflict more vigorously than in any of his other writings, Melville began to lose his enthusiasm for democratic ideals, and his contempt for the tastes of the reading public (who failed to appreciate either *Moby-Dick* or *Pierre*) developed into contempt for the public itself. *The Confidence-Man* (1856) presents his strongest condemnation of all men, and "Benito Cereno," "The House Top," and parts of *Clarel* (1876) contain conservative views of man and society that could not be much darker. In *Clarel* Mortmain declares "Man's vicious: snaffle him with kings; / Or, if kings cease to curb, devise / Severer bit," while Ungar sees life in America as "Myriads playing pygmy parts— / Debased into equality."[24]

These articulate monomaniacs express the side of Melville's thought that grew stronger in his later years as he bitterly examined American society and its treatment of him. His last work, *Billy Budd,* represents a slight renaissance of his democratic attitudes and can be read as a defense of the dignity and rights of the common man; however, it can also be read, with perhaps more accuracy, as a work that defends the aristocratic Vere and supports his belief that "with mankind . . . forms, measured forms, are everything."[25] In other words, here, as in *Moby-Dick,* the democratic-elitist tension in Melville's thought performs a creative function, endowing his art with engaging complexity, depth, and contradiction.

Notes

1. Regrettably the term "elitism" is often used as a shibboleth in contemporary political rhetoric; I use it here for it is the only word which connotes the social and intellectual dimensions of this side of Melville's thought.

2. *The Letters of Herman Melville,* ed. Merrell R. Davis and William H. Gilman (New Haven: Yale Univ. Press, 1960), pp. 126-27.

3. During the 1920s and 30s, when it was customary to identify Melville with Ahab, scholars such as Raymond Weaver, in *Herman Melville: Mariner and Mystic* (New York: Doran, 1921), and Stanley Geist, in *Herman Melville: The Tragic Vision and the Heroic Ideal* (Cambridge: Harvard Univ. Press, 1939), emphasized Melville's high regard for the superior individual and said little about his democratic sympathy for others. Willard Thorp's Introduction to his *Herman Melville: Representative Selections* (New York: American Book Co., 1938), followed by F. O. Matthiessen's highly influential *American Renaissance: Art and Expression in the Age of Emerson and Whitman* (New York: Oxford Univ. Press, 1941), reversed this trend and focused critical attention on Melville's democratic

humanism and social sympathies while de-emphasizing his elitist disdain for the mass and administration for the superior few. Significantly, the beginning of this trend coincided with the rise of totalitarianism in Europe and new concern for the preservation of American democratic ideals. Today, this concern remains in the consciousness of the post-World War II generation of Melvilleans, and books and articles continue to appear that review his works through Matthiessen's eyes, seeing there—particularly in the early works, *Typee* (1846) through *Moby-Dick* (1851)—liberal democratic attitudes in rather pure form. The 1950s saw a boom in such studies, but the trend remains prominent in the 1970s, as work as Ray B. Browne's, *Melville's Drive to Humanism* (Lafayette, Ind.: Purdue Univ. Studies, 1971), Edward S. Grejda's *Common Continent of Men: Racial Equality in the Writings of Herman Melville* (Port Washington, N.Y.: Kennikat Press, 1974), and H. Bruce Franklin's *Victims as Criminal and Artist: Literature from the American Prison* (New York: Oxford Univ. Press, 1978) amply demonstrate.

4. Lewis Mumford, in his classic biography, *Herman Melville: A Study of His Life and Vision* (1929; rev. New York: Harcourt, Brace, 1962), p. 204, observes that Melville's "own outlook was emotionally patrician and aristocratic; but his years in the forecastle had modified those feelings, and one needs some such compound word as aristodemocracy to describe his dominant political attitude." Eleanor Metcalf, in *Journal of a Visit to London and the Continent by Herman Melville, 1849-1850* (Cambridge: Harvard Univ. Press, 1948), p. 144, also notes the "characteristic conflict in him of aristocratic leanings and democratic urgings." William H. Gilman, in his *Melville's Early Life and "Redburn"* (1951; rpt. New York: Russell and Russell, 1972), p. 15, observes the mingling of patrician and democratic sentiments in Melville's father and sees this mingling as "further curious evidence of the subtle influence extending from father to son." Similarly, Harrison Hayford and Merton M. Sealts, Jr., in the "Notes & Commentary" in *Billy Budd, Sailor (An Inside Narrative)* (Chicago: Univ. of Chicago Press, 1962), p. 180, note that throughout Melville's later works "runs a marked antithesis between . . . his 'ruthless democracy on all sides' and his evident pride of family, respect for tradition, and regard for those men who stand out from the mass, as do his own principal characters."

5. See my "Antidemocratic Emphasis in *White Jacket,*" *American Literature,* 48 (March 1976), 13-28. Hershel Parker, "Melville and Politics: A Scrutiny of the Political Milieux of Herman

Melville's Life and Works," Diss. Northwestern Univ. 1963, does an admirable job of dispelling the notion that Melville was an original political thinker and a prophet of democracy; however, it unfortunately discounts, rather than explores, the tension in Melville's thought by linking him with his shallow and opportunistic brother Gansevoort and claiming that Melville "was capable of elaborating contradictory arguments to fit the rhetorical demands of the work at hand, and to be as untroubled as Ganesvoort had been about the need to 'believe' what he was saying" (p. 186).

6. *Letters,* p. 117.

7. *American Renaissance,* p. 459.

8. "*Moby-Dick,* Millenial Attitudes, and Politics," *Emerson Society Quarterly,* 54 (1st Qt. 1969), 59, 54.

9. *Melville's Drive toward Humanism,* pp. 39, 56. See also Willie T. Weathers, "*Moby Dick* and the Nineteenth-Century Scene," *Texas Studies in Literature and Language,* 1 (Winter 1960), 477-501; Charles H. Foster, "Something in Emblems: A Reinterpretation of *Moby-Dick,*" *New England Quarterly,* 34 (March 1961), 3-35; and Alan Heimert, "*Moby-Dick* and American Political Symbolism," *American Quarterly,* 15 (Winter 1963), 498-534.

10. "*Moby-Dick*: Work of Art," in Moby-Dick: *Centennial Essays,* ed. Tyrus Hillway and Luther S. Mansfield (Dallas: Southern Methodist Univ. Press, 1953), pp. 36-37.

11. *Moby-Dick,* ed. Harrison Hayford and Hershel Parker (New York: Norton, 1967), p. 16. All subsequent references are cited parenthetically in the text.

12. *The Heart of Emerson's Journals,* ed. Bliss Perry (1938; rpt. New York: Dover, 1958), p. 217.

13. Ed. Harrison Hayford, Hershel Parker, and G. Thomas Tanselle (Evanston and Chicago: Northwestern-Newberry, 1971), p. 9.

14. *Mardi,* ed. Harrison Hayford, Hershel Parker, and G. Thomas Tanselle (Evanston and Chicago: Northwestern-Newberry, 1970). p. 117.

15. Charles Olson, *Call Me Ishmael: A Study of Melville* (1947; rpt. San Francisco: City Lights Books, n.d.), p. 71.

16. See *Letters,* p. 77 and "Hawthorne and His Mosses" in Norton, *Moby-Dick,* pp. 541-42, Melville's primary enthusiasm was for Shakespeare's dark insights, for "those deep far-away things in him; those occasional flashings-forth of the intuitive Truth in him; those short, quick probings at the very axis of reality" ("Hawthorne and His Mosses," p. 541); however, he certainly also saw and appreciated what Erich Auerbach points out in *Mimesis,* trans. Willard Trask (Garden City, N.Y.: Doubleday, 1957), p. 277, that is, that Shakespeare's "conception of the sublime and tragic is altogether aristocratic."

17. *Melville's Use of the Bible* (Durham: Duke Univ. Press, 1949), p. 23.

18. *The Long Encounter: Self and Experience in the Writings of Herman Melville* (Chicago: Univ. of Chicago Press, 1960), p. 34.

19. *American Renaissance,* p. 437.

20. "The Serious Functions of Melville's Phallic Jokes," *American Literature,* 33 (May 1961), 185.

21. Stanley Geist's *Herman Melville: The Tragic Vision and the Heroic Ideal* brilliantly demonstrates this.

22. These sentiments are echoed by Melville himself in a letter to Hawthorne which expresses an admiration for the "man who, like Russia or the British Empire, declares himself a sovereign nature (in himself) amid the powers of heaven, hell, and earth. He may perish; but so long as he exists he insists upon treating with all Powers upon an equal basis. If any of these other Powers choose to withhold certain secrets, let them; that does not impair my sovereignty in myself; that does not make me tributary" (*Letters,* pp. 124-25). The transition from the third to the first person here reveals Melville's emotional identification with the man he describes.

23. Jay Leyda, *The Melville Log: A Documentary Life of Herman Melville, 1819-1891,* 2 vols. (1951; rpt. with new supplement, New York: Gordian Press, 1969), II, 925.

24. *Clarel,* ed. Walter E. Bezanson (New York: Hendricks House, 1960), pp. 154, 483.

25. Hayford and Sealts, *Billy Budd,* p. 128.

Theron Britt (essay date spring 1995)

SOURCE: Britt, Theron. "The Common Property of the Mob: Democracy and Identity in Poe's 'William Wilson.'" *The Mississippi Quarterly* 48, no. 2 (spring 1995): 197-210.

[*In the following essay, Britt asserts that Poe's tale "William Wilson" reveals Poe's fears of democracy resulting in "mob rule" and his concerns about maintaining individual identity within such a "mob."*]

Thus, not only does democracy make men forget their ancestors, but also clouds their view of their descendants and isolates them from their contemporaries. Each man is forever thrown back on himself alone, and there is danger that he may be shut up in the solitude of his own heart.

Alexis de Tocqueville, *Democracy in America*[1]

In June of 1849 Edgar Allan Poe wrote that "in drawing a line of distinction between a people and a mob, we shall find that a people aroused to action are a mob; and that a mob, trying to think, subside into a people."[2] If Poe's well-known distrust of "the mob" here invokes a fear that even Emerson had of a democratic people's becoming a mob, it also shows the individual in society as doubly marked. More than revealing his pessimism, Poe's dual vision of the role for individuals in society, based on their little-used ability to think before they act as a group, helps us understand the cultural context for the often-noted dualities of his tale "William Wilson" (1839). This tale has often been read as the story of an inner struggle of identity that centers on the failure of its narrator, shut up in the solitude of his own heart, successfully to constitute himself because of his arbitrary will.[3] But such readings tend to dehistoricize the text, and, in response to this sort of a historical reading of Poe's fiction, many recent critics have done excellent work to recover Poe's historical situation.[4] Even these historicized readings, however, all too often show us a great deal about Poe's time without showing how his historical situation connects with the themes and logic of his work.[5]

A genuinely historical reading of this tale begins with Wilson's struggle to maintain himself as a singular identity and recognizes the main focus of the story as a psychological or moral one of "conscience." However, though the struggle with "conscience" remains as a crucial element of the tale, the psychological and moral questions of self-identity it raises cannot exist in an historical vacuum; instead, an historicized reading of the tale acknowledges its psychological themes but relates them to the social tensions of Poe's society. With this in mind, if we look closely at those tensions, we can see that, by figuring its narrator caught between a necessary relation to others and the urge for a radical independence from those others as "the mob," "William Wilson" stages Poe's deep cultural fears about the threat to the individual latent in early nineteenth-century American democracy.[6]

Published in 1839, "William Wilson" appeared at a time of great political and social turmoil during an economic depression and near a low point in American national politics, a fact perhaps linked to Poe's often noted pessimism concerning democracy.[7] In the struggle between a patriarchal aristocracy voiced by the Whigs and the laissez-faire politics of the Democrats during the Presidential election of 1840, Poe had ample confirmation of the authoritarian possibilities latent in democracy. More than previous national elections, however, the election of 1840 turned on the dangers of democracy in relation to an individual self. Poe must have been aware of these dangers, since he helped campaign in Philadelphia for the presidential election of Whig candidate William Harrison.[8] That election was held in the midst of a depression and social unrest brought on by the financial Panic of 1837, and the relatively new Whig Party that Poe apparently supported stood ready to capitalize on the economic woes (supposedly) brought on by Democratic Party laissez-faire policies. Added to this volatile political environment was a new class of voters who, for the first time, entered significantly into national politics. Property and religious qualifications for voting had been recently abolished in most states[9]; and new states joining the Union in general had made their constitutions receptive to the popular will.[10] A key problem for both Whigs and Democrats was how to appeal to the popular will of these voters in the name of the ruling ideology of "democracy." Yet an even more pressing problem was the effect this influx of new voters would have on the place of the individual within American democracy itself.

If their political positions ostensibly were different, Democratic and Whig strategies for managing this emerging situation of American democracy were remarkably similar and hinged on manipulating the individual's fear of being swallowed by the "democratic" body politic. In this struggle the Whigs can be thought in general to represent the business class and conservative interests in the North; under the guidance of Southerner Henry Clay, they stood for tariffs and protectionism and a program of "national development" focused on improving what we would now call infrastructure as an aid to business enterprise (Morrison, p. 574). Despite their "democratic" rhetoric, they did not in practice represent the common man. Instead, they advocated the national government's intervention and protection of business from foreign competition. Their basic stance clearly rested on social interdependence through government action, but of course action for those business and property owners already arrived.[11] In opposition, Jacksonian Democrats then in power claimed to stand for liberty, equality, the common man, and individualism, advocating laissez-faire business practice and the common man's dream of property through westward expansionist "Manifest Destiny," though in practice their spoils system also distributed wealth in a familiar pattern through government action (Howe, p. 5). No matter their rhetoric, Jacksonian Democrats were open to corruption charges by top Whig propagandists such as Calvin Colton, who strove to gain votes by painting the Democrats as antidemocratic and the Whigs as more democratic; in effect the Whigs gained power in 1840 by loudly and repeatedly pointing to the abuse of power in the Jacksonian-era spoils system. More specifically, Colton wanted to show the Democrats as the party of the imposition of one man's arbitrary will—Jackson's—on the whole party and by extension the whole country: for Colton, "General Jackson's will was the law of his party,"[12] and his party's policies were thus based not on democracy but on one man's aristocratic will. Colton's Whig rhetoric went further and linked the anti-democratic will of the Democrats to fear of the mob as figured through the rapidly increasing numbers of Irish and German immigrants (rhetorically, at least, going over to the Democrats). He argued, cynically enough, that they formed a new bloc of manipulable voters who could be used by professional politicians for power and corruption. The Democratic Party, Colton argued, exploited the immigrant mob's ignorance through the "assumption of a false name for itself" (p. 104), duping the poorly educated mob into believing that Democrat meant "democratic"; for the Whigs, the average individual in America's swelling democracy was the easy tool of a strong will and the ultimate origin of a "democratic" tyranny.

By playing on fears of immigrants, Colton of course enacts the demagoguery he condemns. Historian Samuel Morison underlines the contradictions of this Whig approach, noting that "the reason the 1840 campaign became the jolliest—and the most idiotic—presidential contest in our history, is that the Whigs fought the Democrats by their own methods. They adopted no platform, nominated a military hero [William Harrison], ignored real issues, and appealed to the emotions rather than to the brains of the voters" (p. 574). Both parties discounted in advance the power of the individual to make decisions; both seemed to view the individual in a democracy as an opportunity for manipulation. But the Whigs more than the Democrats played on the fear of the mob as the extension of the unbridled will of one man, and so Poe's aristocratic sympathies placed his politics, such as they were, closer to the Whigs' fear of authoritarian tendencies in a democracy, though Whig rhetoric could not have much impressed him either (Elbert, p. 17).

If the sideshow of the 1840 presidential campaign brought to the surface the latent threat of the mob in a democracy, Poe was hardly alone in noticing it. Emerson, writing at this moment in "Self-Reliance" (1839-40), saw that "society everywhere is in conspiracy against the manhood of every one of its members"[13] and further that "now we are a mob" (p. 52) which must be resisted by self-isolation; only after turning inward would one find the strength to resist the mob through true common bonds that "precede true society" (p. 52). Emerson's inward turn of course was a step in his strategy for affirming democracy, but not everyone was as sanguine as Emerson about an inward turn as a cure for democracy's ills. Contra Emerson, conceiving the turn

inward to the self more as a danger to democracy rather than a cure for its ills, Alexis de Tocqueville probably best articulated the Whig fear of democracy's becoming authoritarian through the weak, dull and hence manipulable souls it could produce.[14] American democracy for Tocqueville works through an equality which undermines the sense of self, submerging all into the mob by erasing differences of aristocratic culture that bind each to others in a chain of mutual obligations (Hennis, p. 69). For Tocqueville, American democracy does not, as Emerson would have it, ultimately bring people together but rather isolates them through a radical equality: "Equality puts men side by side without a common link to hold them firm" (p. 510). And thus for Tocqueville, democracy's dangerous equality threatens freedom and encourages a despot's will to dominate and manipulate a disconnected mob of individuals, each shut up in the solitude of his own heart. The irony of Whig politics, of course, which Poe is unlikely to have missed, is that Tocqueville's fear about American democracy is just what Whigs denounced yet counted upon for victory.

In the aftermath of a Whig victory in 1840, Poe's subsequent writings show that he was aware of and deeply concerned about the potential for abuse of the individual latent in American democracy. In "Some Words with a Mummy" (1845), Poe blasts government by the masses as "the most odious and insupportable thing ever heard of upon the face of the Earth"; such a government was ruled by "the usurping tyrant" named "Mob" (p. 1194); the narrator in fact ends this tale by wishing to be embalmed for two hundred years because he is "anxious to know who will be President in 2045" (p. 1195), presumably a time distant enough for things to have changed for the better. Continuing the theme in "Mellonta Tauta" (1849) Poe ironizes his present from an imagined future of 2848 in which Tocqueville's fears of representational democracy have been borne out; looking back, the narrator is flabbergasted that at one time "Americans governed themselves . . . in a sort of every-man-for-himself confederacy" in which "universal suffrage gave opportunity for fraudulent schemes" and thus opened the way for "a fellow of the name of Mob, who took everything into his own hands and set up a despotism" (pp. 1299-1300). While these explicit pronouncements show Poe's later concern, they should also alert us to the possibility of preoccupations with democracy's threat to the self in earlier fictions such as "Wilson" as well.

"Wilson" also gives us a deeper view into the central problem of the subject in a democracy. Given the corruption and abuses on both political sides leading up to the 1840 election, Poe's "William Wilson" can hardly be thought an apology for Whigism, but it does nevertheless confront the key democratic problem of figuring the link of the individual to the group from a similar

Whig position. Nevertheless, most critics have rendered the relation of the individual to the group in "Wilson" in purely psychological or linguistic terms. Kenneth Silverman, for instance, implies only a distant connection to others when he claims the tale recounts "a wound to one's feelings of uniqueness" but is still a "classic psychological thriller."[15] Other critics do, however, pull away somewhat from the purely psychological and acknowledge a social dimension to the tale. David Reynolds, for instance, in *Beneath the American Renaissance* de-emphasizes the psychological and pushes the tale into the social realm of popular fiction, reading it as "a prototypical tale that combines the dark-reform exemplum and the crime narrative"[16] and the narrator as standing for "the ferocity and chaos of popular sensationalism" (p. 235) which Poe labored to contradict. Though Reynolds asserts Poe's hatred of popular literature because it was "directionless, unregulated, amoral," he does not explore why these attributes of the popular should so distress Poe. Reynolds suggestively notes "Wilson's kinship with boisterous mobs" (p. 235) that make the narrator a man of the crowd, but links this only to Poe's distrust of sensationalist fiction. Poe's distrust, however, went much deeper than this. The problem with these and similar readings of "Wilson" is that they fail to link the obvious psychological questions of self-identity posed by the story to anything more than literary history. They need a sense of Poe's society.[17]

We can provide that sense and situate Poe's writing more firmly within his society if we realize that the play of identity in "William Wilson" offers a psychological analogue to contradictions within early American democracy. In "Wilson" the narrator is like a Whig's version of a Jacksonian Democrat who attempts to exert his will over the resistance of his double and everyone else and erase any differences between others and his will; but he fails miserably, demonstrating at the level of psychology the dangerous "mob" tendencies in democracy. Those dangerous tendencies begin in the relation of the narrator's private will to the public contradiction of it by his double. This is of course the focal point of the story, and is the most obvious example of a sort of ambiguous doubling that occurs throughout the tale. Structurally the first bed-chamber confrontation scene in which Wilson really "sees" his double for the first time is doubled in the final unmasking scene; the other scenes of confrontation are paired, or are at the very least repetitions of the same action. Another character, Dr. Bransby, is doubled, with one role as schoolmaster and another as preacher, which presents the narrator with a "gigantic paradox, too utterly monstrous for solution" (p. 429). The narrator's difficult double is the same in age, height, birthday (Poe's own, supposedly) and outward appearance, wears the same clothes, and leaves school the same day. Even the house in which the first unmasking scene occurs is mysteri-ously double in that it has two floors, but these floors never seem to be quite distinct or clear one from the other, blurred together in a way suggestive of the blurred boundaries between the story's many doubles. On almost every level of the story, from overall structure to minor detail, doubling structures the narrative as it does the narrator.

All this doubling begins in the anxiety provoked by the attempt to name the narrator as a singular and private identity, even one with several parts. His trouble with naming himself confronts us from the very first line of the narrative: "Let me call myself, for the present, William Wilson. The fair page now lying before me need not to be sullied with my real appellation" (p. 426). At the outset we are given an effacement of the "true" name of the narrator and his double and receive instead a name explicitly figured as a pose or mask that will suffice "for the present" as a place-holder of identity, and which will also function to repress the "horror" of the narrator's "real appellation," which of course we never learn but must begin to suspect remains somehow elusively outside of his own grasp. Interestingly, his "real appellation" remains hidden because he is an abandoned social "outcast" whose "infamy" accounts for his being expelled from his "race." Though he hints at Wilson's "true" name, through its "infamy" he reminds us it is socially embedded and determined. Thus while Poe posits as his narrator's very beginning point that the "object for the scorn of others—his name—is forever "outcast," this abandoned "outcast of all outcasts" is not so much William Wilson himself, but, as one might more easily assume from the continuity of this opening passage's theme, his name "bruited" about by "indignant winds" of social reputation. His name is doubly marked as provisional, both his and not his, but more than this, it is in the hands of others, a situation the narrator finds intolerable to his autocratic will.

The narrator detests his "real" name in part because something ostensibly private is in fact public. The "horror" for him is that it has been doubled or multiplied in and through the crowd: "mine was one of those everyday appellations which seem, by prescriptive right, to have been, time out of mind, the common property of the mob" (p. 431). Loathe to be a man of the crowd, he wishes for something proper only to himself, or for something which has a proper home outside of influence or control by "the mob." His double so infuriates him not just because he has the same name but "because a stranger bore it . . . whose concerns . . . must inevitably . . . be confounded with my own" (p. 434). Autocratically he wishes, in other words, to free himself from "a stranger" in society who impedes his will, but also to free himself from others as a factor in his identity. In his drive for freedom, however, he ironically enough will produce its opposite for others around him and eventually for himself.

As "common property" Wilson's name is democratized and is literally not proper to him. It is scattered and diffused into the world, given over to the "mob," and thus at the mercy of a chaotic (and—to him—threatening) form of social interaction that is ironically like his favorite card game, ecarte (scattering, isolation). This provisional name, forced on him by his fear of the mob, ironically names the narrator against his will as what he says he is, someone who is "the slave of circumstances beyond human control" (p. 427). Or rather, he is subject to forces in society beyond his singular will. When Emerson wrote of his society in "Self-Reliance" that "now we are a mob," he saw the mob as a danger and offered solitude as a divine or spiritual cure and corrective to "the intruding rabble of men" (p. 51); he figured the mob as an illness of the individual spirit and the ultimate negation of private space by collective action. Like Emerson, Poe's Wilson fears giving his name over to this force because it means giving his self over to the threat of violence and excess and the threat of control by another will.

In contrast to Emerson's self-reliant man, however, Wilson's whole experience can be understood ultimately as a series of disfigured social interactions framed by Whig concerns, and his narration the hopeless search for identity outside of interdependence with others, a fact the narrator will never realize. Looking to his apparent origins, we find his parents merely ciphers rather than guides; Wilson asserts that "At an age when few children have abandoned their leading-strings, I was left to the guidance of my own will, and became, in all but name, the master of my own action" (p. 113). He is master in all but name, or rather, of all but the paradox of his name. And the reason can be found even here in part due to his relation to others. His parents cut him loose from parental authority, and, as almost shadow parents, from the beginning seem to exist not at all; they abandon him to the guidance of his own will, and this again is his "name": Will, I Am Will's Son. As initially a free-agent, he is cut off and drilling with only his own self-generated will as an origin, and as such he begins uncannily to resemble the mob (as an instrument of irrational will) that he fears.[18] Self-created, sprung from his own will, he is an avatar of self-reliance run amok, a sort of Emersonian Everyman gone horribly wrong in his amoral relation to society, prone to the very excesses of the mob that Tocqueville feared and which Whigs painted onto Democrats.

As a sort of self-reliant figure become a sociopath, the narrator does not confront others in society directly, as in "The Man of the Crowd," but rather through the figure of his double, a favorite device for Poe. If, as in most early readings of the tale, the double exists as a necessary part of the process of Wilson's consciousness (traditionally his "conscience"), then he also must figure the main concerns of conscience, that is, the ques-

tion of how we treat others around us in society. We see this in the fact that the double's appearance is quite regular and easily coincides as Wilson's "conscience" since he appears only when the narrator bullies his classmates in school or later attempts to cheat or manipulate (treat as objects of will) those around him. This is to say that the double in this tale does not just "echo" Wilson; he criticizes and confronts Wilson's demeaning arbitrary use of will against others. More important perhaps, the appearance of the double as a dogged oral presence only when the narrator cheats others suggests that "conscience" involves the ultimately social and ethical acts of language, not Emerson's inward turn. These linguistic acts bind up Wilson's consciousness in the process of his self-creation necessarily within a grid of social interaction.

For all this implicit inscription of the social, the story's focus is not, however, directly outward on American society; in fact, the action of the narration barely touches American soil. Though we can never quite lose sight of the social implications of Wilson's will, the story's focus is, as in many of Poe's tales, insistently dreamy and inward. The oddity of his double's "echo" prompts even the narrator to wonder if he has been "living in a dream" (p. 427), for in "William Wilson," as in much of Poe's work, there is an overall sense of dream and of exclusion from consciousness of the external world. Concomitant with this sense is an impression of the engagement of the imagination within an enclosed space; none of the action takes place out of doors; and the story takes place in a series of rooms, the last one locked from the inside and easily metaphorized by early critics as the self locked within the monad of the self-creating will. The first school is set, moreover, "in a misty-looking village of England" which is "a dream-like and spirit-soothing place" (p. 428), often transformed by critics into a setting for the struggle of good and evil or the conscious and the unconscious, since "it was difficult, at any given time, to say with certainty upon which of its two stories one happened to be" (p. 428). Yet as a metaphor of the mind, the two "stories" we confront here do not simply resolve into one story; the dreamscape does not easily divide into consciousness and unconsciousness, nor does the social world evaporate.[19]

Rather, even in Poe's dreamy worlds there is a social function for the oneiric setting and for the double. Both confuse the strict boundary between the public and private, between self and other, and call into question self-reliant individualism. If we turn to the two key unmasking scenes of doubled identity, we can see that both play upon the idea of confusion of boundaries, in spite of the narrator's willful impositions. In the first unmasking scene and elsewhere in the text, the double is faceless; rather, his face is never described, and his face is always dark or in shadow, hidden such that the narrator tells us "the features of his face I could not distinguish" (p. 423). In this first scene the description of the confrontation creates a conspicuous absence. Here as the narrator confronts his double he finds, as if in a dream, only a faceless image, an absent identity. And it is this initial absence which informs the rest of the story. Wilson's double resists naming, resists any final representation that would stabilize and make clear the meaning of this uncanny "other" and thus make clear the difference between Wilson and those around him.

Wilson's task to master his double thus drives the rest of the narrative. In unmasking his double in the doubled second scene and seeing his double's full face, supposedly pinning down his identity once and for all, the narrator opts for the death of his double to put a final stop to the meddling in his schemes. When the narrator confronts his double, unmasks him and stabs and kills him, he confronts a mirror image whose face is his own—a positive identification of sorts (but we have yet to see his face described). As the mirror image of him, the double is momentarily coincident with him. At that stage, the narrator has to kill his double to maintain mastery and control. Without the double as an "other," however, the narrator finds—to his surprise and implicitly as the reason for his narrative confession—that there is no possibility of self-definition, and so the words of the double—that the narrator has killed himself—are true first on the level of consciousness, yet equally true at the social level as a sign of the latent danger in the "democratic" mob Wilson has more and more uncannily come to resemble.[20]

This visual moment of self-reflexive identity is deathly because it is the apparent ultimate moment of mastery by the narrator's will. In sum, the narrator's will denies difference from his double. In the "mirror" of his double, he and the double are intertwined as one in an unheimlich repetition, a self-reflexive moment of specularity, a moment impossible to sustain. There is of course no unification of the two halves. Instead there is the death caused by absolute will, first for the double, and death for Wilson because of his loss of the double. The death of the double we eventually learn is the spark for the narration, for Wilson has lost more than his "conscience." He is literally dying because of his autocratic will. The narrator, "dying a victim," early in the tale tells us "death approaches" (p. 427), and thus turns the narration into a sort of confession, but time and again it is an ironic confession of his horror of subjection to anything outside his own will. His narrative thus becomes the story of the psychological death inherent in the denial of difference Poe saw as the mob's legacy.

In the drive for the private truth of his identity, the narrator's public confession begins not just in the act of writing but in a writing that marks his very fear of the public. The narrator's writing is unfortunately similar to the writing he remembers on the desks at his childhood school.

Interspersed about the room, crossing and recrossing in endless irregularity, were innumerable benches and desks, black, ancient, and time-worn, piled desperately with much bethumbed books, and so beseamed with initial letters, names at full length, grotesque figures, and other multiplied efforts of the knife, as to have entirely lost what little of original form might have been their portion in days long departed. (p. 430)

This writing has lost its original form through the accretion of symbols on top of symbols to the extent that any attempt to maintain a clear and separate name is impossible. The desk marks the deferral, then, of the identity of that child, William Wilson, whose initials one supposes intermingle with the society of "initial letters" and "names at full length" and other "grotesque figures" multiplied by the knives of his peers. Not just a scene of writing and the infinite deferral of identity, the childhood desk crucially enmeshes that writing of one's personal or private identity with others in a horrible or "grotesque" palimpsest of inscription that effaces "what little of original form" these names might have had. Like the mob he fears, his schoolmates here literally cut into his (or anyone's) name, effacing it in the process, or rather, transforming it into something "beseamed" with layer upon layer of inscriptions, initials, names, and figures. The horror of this sort of democratic writing for the narrator is that his name is out of his control since it is "beseamed," crossed and recrossed in "endless irregularity" with the "multiplied efforts" of a public who shape it as much as he does.

Rather than accept these incisions in his identity, Wilson's response to his classmates' knives is a radical isolation within himself, yet his isolation does not, as for Emerson, "precede true society" but attempts to master or to preclude it. Finally, the narrator's folly and ultimate death come from his attempt to hold his name apart from "the common property of the mob." Ironically, the death Wilson ensures for himself comes from his acting like the very "democratic" mob he denies. So when he kills his double in an effort to exclude or master the difference, death comes to him ultimately because through an act of arbitrary will he has halted the constant give and take necessary for identity. Through this unbridled Jacksonian will, Poe shows us, then, the internal consequences of the external social world. He shows us that the dangerous mob impulse in a democracy isolates individuals, throws them back on themselves, and eventually undermines their very identities. And so, thrown back on himself alone, in the solitude of his own heart, Wilson exemplifies Tocqueville's and Poe's worst fears for the American experiment in democracy.

Notes

1. Trans. George Lawrence, ed. J. P. Mayer (New York: Harper and Row, 1969).

2. *Collected Works of Edgar Allan Poe,* 3 vols., ed. Thomas Ollive Mabbott (Cambridge, Massachusetts: Harvard University Press, 1978); XVI, p. 161. Unless otherwise noted, all quotations of Poe's work are from this edition.

3. Useful interpretations of the tale include Ruth Sullivan, "William Wilson's Double," *Studies in Romanticism,* 15 (Spring 1976), 254-262; Leonard Orr, "The 'Other' and 'Bad Faith': The Proto-Existentialism of Poe's 'William Wilson,'" *Studies in the Humanities,* 9 (1981) 33-38; Nicholas Canaday, "Poe's 'William Wilson,'" *Explicator,* 40 (Spring 1982), 28-29; Valentine Hubbs, "The Struggle of Wills in Poe's 'William Wilson,'" *Studies in American Fiction,* 11 (Spring 1983), 73-79; Leonard Engel, "Identity and Enclosure in Poe's 'William Wilson,'" *College Language Association Journal,* 29 (September 1985), 91-99; Tracy Ware, "The Two Stories of 'William Wilson,'" *Studies in Short Fiction,* 26 (Winter 1989), 43-48.

4. A useful and interesting example of the recovery of Poe's historical situation and the material forces at work during his emergence as an "author" is Timothy H. Scherman's "The Authority Effect: Poe and the Politics of Reputation in the Pre-Industry of American Publishing," *Arizona Quarterly,* 49 (1993), 1-19. Scherman is in part responding to Kenneth Dauber's *The Idea of Authorship in America: Democratic Poetics from Franklin to Melville* (Madison: University of Wisconsin, 1990), and in part to Louis Renza's "Poe's Secret Autobiography," in *The American Renaissance Reconsidered: Selected Papers from the English Institute, 1982-83,* ed. Donald E. Pease (Baltimore: Johns Hopkins University Press, 1985), pp. 58-89. Even more helpful is Terence Whalen's "Edgar Allan Poe and the Horrid Laws of Political Economy," *American Quarterly,* 44 (September 1992), 381-417, which links Poe's tales to the conditions of capitalist development in antebellum America.

5. In the review article "Poe and Historicity," (*Emerson Society Quarterly,* 35[3/4 Qtrs. 1989], 273-292), Donald Pease gives a succinct arid telling critical history of Poe's particular transformations in the canon of American literature. Pease outlines three waves of criticism; he begins with F. O. Matthiessen's relegation of Poe in American Renaissance to an eccentric status in the main line of the American symbolic romance, quickly moves through the reconcilement of the New Critical reworking of Poe's "non-Americanist subject matter and formal self-obsession" (p. 274), and finally explores at length the failings of the largely a historical French post-structuralist reworking of Poe's

texts for their "signifying practices" (p. 278) Explicit in Pease's critical history is a sense that Poe's texts have yet to receive an historicized reading.

6. In *Visionary Compacts* Pease works to link Poe's writing to its cultural context, and in a roundabout way to Tocqueville, whom Pease figures as touring America looking for signs of a cultural tradition within the confusion of democracy. See *Visionary Compacts: American Renaissance Writings in Cultural Context* (Madison: University of Wisconsin Press, 1987).

7. Mabbott notes that the precise date of composition is uncertain, but he places the composition as probably late in the year 1839, quoting as source a letter by Poe to Philip Pendleton Cooke dated September 21, 1839. The tale first appeared in print in *The Gift* for 1840.

8. William Bittner, *Poe, A Biography* (London: Elek, 1962), p. 149.

9. Daniel Walker Howe, *The American Whigs: An Anthology* (New York: John Wiley & Sons, 1973), p. 3.

10. Samuel Eliot Morison and Henry Steele Commager, *The Growth of the American Republic,* 2 vols. (New York: Oxford University Press, 1962), I, 575.

11. Poe's Whig sympathies have often been noted, but for a more complex reading of his relation to the problems of Democratic and Whig politics see Monika M. Elbert, "'The Man of the Crowd' and The Man Outside the Crowd: Poe's Narrator and the Democratic Reader" (*Modern Language Studies,* 21 [Fall 1991], 16-30). Elbert summarizes the parties' differences by seeing "Democrats as favoring independence and Whigs favoring interdependence. Whereas Democrats' slogans contained catch phrases like individualism, freedom, and rights, Whig rhetoric espoused community, cohesiveness, and duties" (p. 18). Elbert places Poe somewhere between the Democrats and the Whigs, neither comfortable with Whig community nor Democrat individualism: for Elbert's Poe "the real demon . . . is one's political identification: declaring one's political affiliation and then finding behind the political system nothing which will sustain the individual" (p. 26).

12. Calvin Colton, "Democracy," in *The American Whigs,* p. 98.

13. Ralph Waldo Emerson, "Self-Reliance," in *Emerson's Essays,* ed. Irwin Shaw (New York: Harper and Row, 1926), p. 35.

14. Wilhelm Hennis, "Tocqueville's Perspective; Democracy in America: In search of the 'new science of politics,'" *Interpretation,* 16, no. 1 (1988), 67.

15. Kenneth Silverman, Edgar A. Poe: Mournful and Never-Ending Remembrance (New York: Harper Collins, 1991), p. 149.

16. David S. Reynolds. *Beneath the American Renaissance: The Subversive Imagination in the Age of Emerson and Melville* (Cambridge, Massachusetts: Harvard University Press, 1991), p. 234.

17. Elbert's reading, too, makes few connections between society and the psychological, though she concentrates on society rather than psychology. Robert H. Byer, on the other hand, explores the links between society and self in "Mysteries of the City: A Reading of Poe's "The Man of the Crowd'" (in *Ideology and Classic American Literature,* ed. Sacvan Bercovitch and Myra Jehlen [Cambridge, Massachusetts: Harvard University Press, 1986]). Byer's comments could apply as well to "William Wilson": "Poe's well-known strictures against 'the mob,' in valuing individualism, are, above all, expressions of his awareness of the danger (psychological and erotic, at the same time as social) of the affective bonding requisite to democratic society, of the 'oceanic feeling' that transforms all others into one's intimate doubles" (p. 234).

18. Michael J. S. Williams notes the resemblance of Wilson to the mob as a sort of uncanny double of his will: "in the omnipotence of his will he attempts to make the world conform to his desire—in a sense to make it become a double of himself; yet, ironically, the double of himself takes the form of another will and, in his uncompromising polar view of the world, he can only be either master or slave" (*A World of Words: Language and Displacement in the Fiction of Edgar Allan Poe* [Durham, North Carolina: Duke University Press, 1988], p. 40).

19. See Sigmund Freud, "Repression." (1915), in *Collected Papers,* 5 vols. (London: 1924-50), IV, 84-97. One of Freud's crucial insights was that "the essence of repression lies simply in the function of rejecting and keeping something out of consciousness" (p. 89). We are not constrained in thinking that repression in its functioning must simply stratify the psyche; rather, there is as much reason to believe that repression acts as a dynamic dispersion mechanism with very volatile and dynamic connections to consciousness. "Repression acts, therefore, in a highly specific manner in each instance; every single derivative of the repressed may have its peculiar fate—" (p. 91). See also J. Laplanche and J. B. Pontails, eds. *The Language of Psycho-Analysis,* trans. Donald Nicholson-Smith (New York: Norton, 1973): ". . . repression is described from the outset as a dynamic operation implying the maintenance of an anticathexis, and liable at any moment to be defeated by the strength of the unconscious wish which is striving to return into consciousness and motility" (p. 363).

20. In Lacanian terms there is a mirror stage in the early development of the child's ego in which the child first sees itself as a whole being; what is found by the child is a double, which is necessary for self-definition, but in the mirror is only an illusory integration. Thus the fragmented or uncoordinated image of the self (the body) is not replaced but suspended. In Poe's tale the mirror phase is abruptly ended by the narrator's action, which is itself motivated by a desire for some end to the suspended image of the fragmented body. The irony of an imposter who has usurped his image melts for a moment when the narrator turns back from the door and thinks he sees an unheimlich representation in the mirror. For just a moment there is the illusion of unification with his double.

Emily VanDette (essay date March 2005)

SOURCE: VanDette, Emily. "'It Should Be a Family Thing': Family, Nation, and Republicanism in Catharine Maria Sedgwick's *A New-England Tale* and *The Linwoods.*" *American Transcendental Quarterly* 19, no. 1 (March 2005): 51-74.

[*In the following essay, VanDette discusses how Catherine Maria Sedgwick presents her personal blend of democratic and republican ideological principles in her depiction of family life in* A New-England Tale *and* The Linwoods.]

Trying to bridge her father's federalism and the Jacksonian democracy of her own generation, Catharine Maria Sedgwick disseminated her own brand of republican virtue throughout her prolific career as a writer of domestic advice literature and fiction. A federalist-turned-democrat, and a Calvinist-turned-Unitarian, Sedgwick clearly embodied processes of synthesis and transformation. She sought to bring together the republican values of virtue, selflessness, and patriotism, and the democratic principles of equality, opportunity, and independence. Throughout her career, she grappled with the clash between the restrictive codes of her Calvinist upbringing and the post-Enlightenment appeal to human reason and rationalism that informed the nation's founding.[1] In her fictional depictions of the American family—its values, dynamics, and governance—Sedgwick imagines resolutions to these ideological conflicts.

With her configurations of family life in a *A New-England Tale* (1822), Sedgwick attempts to persuade her readers that a healthy republican nation/family must raise independent-thinking, self-determining citizens/children. More than a decade later, in response to national political embattlement concerning states' rights versus federal authority, Sedgwick's allegorical portrayal of an American family as the American nation in *The Linwoods* (1836) addresses the conflicts that arise when self-determining citizens exercise their independence. In both *A New-England Tale* and *The Linwoods*, Sedgwick explores the style of authority, as well as the political, religious, and social codes that make "good" republican families, nations, and citizens. While both novels advocate a Lockean paradigm for familial/national governance, it is not until *The Linwoods* that Sedgwick attempts to imagine resolutions to the conflicting agendas of rationalist independence and filial obedience/patriotism.

In this article, I map out the philosophical inquiries and literary strategies Sedgwick would later develop more fully in *The Linwoods*. I begin my analysis by examining Sedgwick's earliest attempt to address familial and national governance and authority in her first novel. My overall argument is that while Sedgwick advocated a somewhat simplistic, idealistic policy of self-determination in *A New-England Tale,* she later adopted conventions of historical narrative to depict more compellingly and provocatively the family as a microcosm of the new republican nation, and to interrogate the practicality of rationalist ideology in national governance in *The Linwoods*. Given the shifts in national politics that took place during the years between the publications of *A New-England Tale* and *The Linwoods*, particularly the willingness of factions to put the founding ideology of self-determination to the test and challenge the national government, Sedgwick asks a timely question in her Linwood family allegory: to what extent can republican national/familial unions actually function under a policy of total self-determination? Tracing the literary and ideological shifts in Sedgwick's novels exposes re-acquaints those of us interested in nineteenth-century American Literature and women's intellectual history to the implications of a writer altering her stylistic and political practices in order to address the real concerns of nation and family through her fiction.[2]

A NEW-ENGLAND TALE OF TYRANNICAL FAMILY GOVERNANCE

After leaving the Calvinist church and converting to Unitarianism in 1821, Sedgwick set out to write a religious pamphlet exposing the hypocrisies of the denomination she abandoned. When her attack on Calvinism led to depictions of distinctly New England settings and characters, her project became her first novel, *A New-England Tale; or, Sketches of New-England Character*

and Manners. Because *A New-England Tale* began as a religious tract, its characters are more transparent than in her other works of fiction, and her didactic messages more explicit. For these reasons, *A New-England Tale* reveals the writer's agenda surrounding the inculcation of family values, and, by extension, nationalistic values, for her readers. A close reading of Sedgwick's first novel helps us to understand how she drew upon her personal commitment to republican patriotism and to Christianity in her didactic messages about family values. In *A New-England Tale,* Sedgwick points to a tyrannical mother's dogmatic, anti-rational interpretation of Calvinism as antithetical to the governance of healthy and functional republican families. Within the novel's transparent critique of Calvinism lie the seeds of compelling philosophical questions—questions that Sedgwick will more fully explore in *The Linwoods*: What role does rationalist ideology play in the governance of families and nations? To what extent does the health of the republic actually depend upon the health of its individual families? What exactly are the dangers of tyrannical parenting and governing?

Sedgwick exposes the dangers of "bad parenting" through her delineation of the Wilson family of *A New-England Tale*. For Sedgwick, the worst type of parent is the tyrant, which she represents in the character of Mrs. Wilson, an irredeemably irrational, hypocritical, selfish mother. The widowed head of a middle-class New England family and a professed "saved" Calvinist, Mrs. Wilson wields her power over a household of her own children, as well as Jane Elton (her niece and the heroine of the novel), and her servants. Sedgwick paints the results of the parent's tyranny in no uncertain terms: her children grow up to be disloyal, dishonest, and disreputable—bad children and bad citizens. Jane only escapes their fate because of the lessons of her early childhood and the continued spiritual and moral guidance of her Methodist friend Mary Hull and her Quaker friend (and eventually, husband), Mr. Lloyd. The Wilson children, however, left to the irrational leadership of their mother, learn to deceive and cheat, and grow up to be non-functional members of the American republic. *A New-England Tale* reflects Sedgwick's earliest attempts to represent the family as a microcosm of a nation, with parental/governmental authority directly shaping the characters of children/citizens. Mrs. Wilson's deficient parenting is linked to her strict, hypocritical adherence to Calvinist doctrine, her own moral bankruptcy and neglect of republican virtue, and her failure as a proper republican mother.

The didactic narrator of the novel makes Sedgwick's messages about the obligations of the republican parent explicit for her readers. When Mrs. Wilson discovers that her daughter, Elvira, has deceived her and slipped out of the house to attend a dance, the narrator points out the relationship between the parent's uncontrolled love of power and the child's disloyalty:

> If Mrs. Wilson had not been blinded by self-love, she might have learnt an invaluable lesson from the melancholy results of her own mal-government. But she preferred incurring every evil, to the relinquishment of one of the prerogatives of power. Her children, denied the appropriate pleasures of youth, were driven to sins of a much deeper die, than those which Mrs. Wilson sought to avoid could have been even in her eyes; for surely the very worst effects that ever were attributed to dancing, or to romance-reading, cannot equal the secret dislike of a parent's authority, the risings of the heart against a parent's tyranny, and the falsehood and meanness that weakness always will employ in the evasion of power, and than which nothing will more certainly taint everything that is pure in the character.
>
> (47)

Mrs. Wilson's oppressive family governance leads Elvira from deceptive novel-reading and dancing in her childhood to a much bigger breach of republican virtue in her adulthood, when she defies her mother and flees her home to elope with a stranger. The narrator's linking of tyrannical governance with "self-love" at the beginning of that passage is directly related to the rationalist skepticism of egoism and self-satisfaction.

More specifically, the language the narrator uses to criticize Mrs. Wilson's non-functional parenting echoes the warnings found in a rationalist work that had a profound influence on debates surrounding the education and government of the new nation and its citizens and families, John Locke's *Some Thoughts Concerning Education* (1692). Sedgwick's critique of Mrs. Wilson's parenting particularly draws upon Locke's caution that "imperiousness and severity is but an ill way of treating [young adults], who have reason of their own to guide them; unless you have a mind to make your children, when grown up, weary of you, and secretly to say within themselves, When will you die father?" (40). Martha, the oldest daughter, is also a testament to her mother's failure as a parent, when she grows up to be an alcoholic, abusive wife, and mother. But the most significant product of Mrs. Wilson's poor government is David, who steals his mother's money, seduces and abandons a young girl, and leaves her and her baby to die; by the end of the novel, he is a fugitive from the law after escaping imprisonment for robbery in Philadelphia. As an adult, Mrs. Wilson's son is no longer merely a disobedient son, but a federal criminal, undermining government authority by escaping a federal penitentiary.

Mrs. Wilson, who, as the narrator observes, "seemed now to be visited on every side with the natural and terrible retribution of her maternal sins" (147), refuses her son's desperate plea for her help in hiring a lawyer to escape conviction and life imprisonment. The unrelenting mother uses Calvinist doctrine to justify her decision not to come to her son's aid: "I shall leave David entirely in the hands of Providence" (148). Mrs. Wilson turns to the tenets of Calvinism—where "grace," or predetermined salvation, takes precedence over "works," or moral behavior—repeatedly throughout the novel to validate her careless parenting. Defending her performance as a mother, she claims, "I have planted and I have watered, and if it is the Lord's will to withhold the increase, I must submit" (149). Sedgwick portrays the obviously negative consequences of Mrs. Wilson's dogmatic adherence to Calvinist predetermination to persuade her readers of benefits to raising self-determining children and republican citizens. Through her depiction of the failed, corrupt Wilson family, Sedgwick achieves her most emphatic critique of Calvinism: it is incompatible with republicanism because it yields bad citizens who are incapable of effective self-determination.

Nowhere is Sedgwick's rationalist critique of Calvinist determinism and tyrannical parenting more evident than in David's farewell letter to his mother. In it he points to his mother's oppressive parenting and hypocritical religious practices as the causes of his own demise:

> Mother, mother! oh, that I must call you so!—as I do it, I howl a curse with every breath—you have destroyed me. You, it was, that taught me, when I scarcely knew my right hand from my left, that there was no difference between doing right and doing wrong, in the sight of the God you worship; you taught me, that I have only acted out the nature totally depraved, (your own words), that he gave to me, and I am not to blame for it. I could do nothing to save my own soul; and according to your own doctrine, I stand now a better chance than my moral cousin, Jane. If you have taught me falsely, I was not to blame; the peril be on your own soul. My mind was a blank, and you put your own impressions on it; God (if there be a God) reward you according to your deeds!
>
> (155)

Here again, Sedgwick's critique of dogmatic Calvinism spills over into her value of rationalism, especially when it comes to the governor of republican and nations. Accusing his mother of teaching him that he "only acted out the nature totally depraved," David's character spells out Sedgwick's didactic message about the incompatibility of Calvinism and republicanism. Sedgwick argues that Calvinist doctrine has no place in the raising of republican nations and families, because it precludes the concept of free will, a central tenet of democracy. Effective republican parenting/governance involves teaching children/citizens to become self-determining, a rationalist-inspired value fundamentally at odds with Sedgwick's depiction of Calvinist predetermination.

Furthermore, David's assertion that his "mind was a blank" draws upon the Lockean (tabula rasa) paradigm for education and familial/national government. Jay Fliegelman argues that builders of the new nation were particularly invested in the basic Lockean premise "that education must rest on the teaching of 'precept,' but on the force of 'example,' specifically parental example, for it registers the earliest impressions on the human mind" (13). Fliegelman further explains that "Locke's concern . . . is not with circumscribing parental authority, but with rendering it more effective by making it noncoercive. Parents who too rigorously or irrationally insist upon obedience undermine the cause of their own authority. For such authority to be effective . . . it must be founded on filial 'esteem,' perhaps the most crucial word in the Lockean lexicon" (13). Such lack of esteem was a central flaw of the Wilson family, leading to Elvira's deception and Martha's open defiance, and culminating in David's felony theft and, more significantly for Sedgwick (and Locke), his bitter hatred of his mother. Moreover, Mrs. Wilson's coercive parenting made her children especially poor republican adults because she left them incapable of making reasonable, independent decisions. In this way, Sedgwick's depiction of the failed Wilson family affirms Locke's warning "[h]e that has not a mastery over his inclinations, he that knows not how to resist the importunity of present pleasure of pain, for the sake of what reason tells him is fit to be done, wants the true principle of virtue and industry, and is in danger never to be good for anything" (45). The Wilson children become poor republican citizens precisely because they did not have practice being independently virtuous.

Sedgwick uses the Lockean paradigm not only as a basis for sound republican familial/national governance, but also to expose the shortcomings of Calvinist doctrine. For Sedgwick, the doctrine of predestination is the biggest flaw in Calvinism, especially for its clash with the rationalist founding ideologies of her beloved republic. In *A New-England Tale* Sedgwick imagines a Christianity that harmonizes with the rationalist ideological foundations of the new republic. Negotiating the post-Enlightenment tension between religion and the value for human reason and freedom from tyranny, Sedgwick condemns Calvinism as the antithesis to rationalism (and, by extension, to democracy), and celebrates more flexible, accommodating Christian religious traditions. To that end, in *A New-England Tale* she contrasts Mrs. Wilson's stubborn, narrow-minded adherence to Calvinist doctrine to the basic Christian good will of almost every main character outside of the Wilson family. The characters of *A New-England Tale* represent a spectrum of Christian sects, including Methodism and Quakerism, but their interactions reflect a Christian code of conduct that Sedgwick would like all Christians to emulate. The "good" characters of the novel adhere to the Christian principle for kindness and goodwill to others, a precept that Sedgwick hopes will lead to effective republican communities. In her critique of Calvinism, Sedgwick avoids suggesting another single denomination that should take its place and, instead, promotes a plurality of religions (albeit circumscribed by her Christian bias) and common sense and goodwill in the lifestyles and interactions of Americans. The result is an "American Chemistry" that reflects at once the basic tenets of rationalism and the basic tenets of the Bible.

Sedgwick establishes the importance of humanitarian Christian principles and the danger of sectarianism early in the novel, during the funeral of Jane's mother.

> The clergyman of ———was one of those, who are most zealous for sound doctrine, than benevolent practice; he had chosen on that occasion for his text, "The wages of sin is death," and had preached a long sermon in the vain endeavor of elucidating the doctrine of original sin. Clergymen who lose such opportunities of instructing their people in the operations of providence, and the claims of humanity, ought not to wonder if they grow languid, and selfish, and careless of their most obvious duties.
>
> (13)

The narrator suggests that a better funeral sermon (and certainly one more tasteful in the presence of the twelve-year-old orphan) would have drawn upon scripture that promotes the basic (New Testament) Christian principles of humanitarianism, sympathy, and charity: "'Bear ye one another's burthens'; 'Weep with those who weep,' 'Inasmuch as ye have done it unto one of these, ye have done it unto me';—had his preaching usually been in conformity to the teaching of our Savior, could the scene have followed, which it is our business to relate?" (13). Echoing Locke again, this time in holding up Jesus as an exemplary leader who teaches his disciples by his example, Sedgwick's narrator thus sets up Jane's trials in the context of inadequate religious leadership. She criticizes clergymen who too rigidly promote the doctrines of their own sects, illustrating how such narrow insistence upon precept undermines the development of rationalist, republican communities.

Sedgwick contemporaries recognized her appeal to rationalism over sectarianism, particularly in the raising of American children. The author of a *Southern Literary Messenger* article on Sunday school education, lamenting the increasing number of sectarian texts in the classroom, and proposing the teaching of Locke to school children, praises Sedgwick's latest children's book of stories, *A Love-Token For Children*. After listing some of Sedgwick's literary accomplishments, the writer applauds the impartiality of her Christian messages:

> But the highest praise is yet to be uttered. Although these stories bear the manifest impress of decided Christian piety, they contain not the slightest indication

of the author's particular creed. The truly virtuous of every sect must acknowledge and admire her, as a co-worker for the great end of Religion—human happiness; yet not one of them could claim her exclusively as a sister, in subordinate points of faith. This is well nigh the beau ideal of a book for Sunday school; indeed, I cannot help saying, of a book for any school. It should exhibit not the belief of Calvin, Socinus, or Fenelon; but the maxims of common sense, and the principles of Christianity: just as the speech of a real statesman breathes not the spirit of the party, but the holy dictates of Patriotism and Justice. Such a book ranges within that common-ground, upon which all sects ought to meet.

(225-26)

Assuming an equivalence between religious denominations and political parties, the writer of this article commended a principle that emerges throughout all of Sedgwick's writing, the importance of *rational* Christian behavior to the welfare of the new republic. As illustrated through the Wilson family, strict adherence to religious creed is an ineffective strategy for governing families; by extension, strict adherence to party politics is an ineffective strategy for governing nations—a principle that will play an important role in the family dynamics of *The Linwoods.* In her 1836 novel Sedgwick once again turns to family dramas to promote what she perceived as basic needs of the young republican nation: compromise, neutrality, good will, and, most importantly, rationalism. By the time she wrote *The Linwoods,* though, Sedgwick had reevaluated the role of republican authority and reconsidered the limitations of total self-determination when it comes to governing nations and raising families. The threat of southern secession during the Nullification Crisis led Sedgwick to make exigent qualifications of *A New-England Tale*'s idealistic presentation of the role of self-determination in republican governance.

The Linwoods and/as the New Nation

While *A New-England Tale* exposes the more or less obvious dangers of irrational familial/national governance, *The Linwoods* moves beyond a didactic lesson on how not to raise republican families/nations to consider the challenges of rational governance. *The Linwoods* particularly concerns itself with the extent to which a functional family/government can actually allow its children/citizens to be self-determining. In *The Linwoods,* Sedgwick turns again to family dynamics to reflect upon authority, this time attempting to bridge seemingly conflicting republican values: the rationalist ideals of independence and individuality and the perceived need for filial love/patriotism/obedience of children/citizens. Just as she borrowed language and concepts from Locke to criticize Mrs. Wilson's parenting in the context of the needs of the new nation, Sedgwick draws upon Locke again in *The Linwoods* to imag-

ine how a broken family (and, as I will argue, nation) can be healed by rational, non-coercive governance. *The Linwoods* employs a family/nation allegory to consider how best to govern republican nations and families. Moreover, the novel represents the dynamics that emerge to keep nuclear families (or republican nations) resilient and unified in the face of threats of estrangement (or secession). Finally, while Sedgwick's main objective (the recuperation and preservation of the familial/national union) reflects a conservative political agenda, the circumstances under which she will allow the Linwood family/American nation to reunite reveal that her politics are actually more complicated than previous readings have suggested. Rather than attempting to recast Sedgwick as a liberal-minded republican or to condemn her as a conservative, elitist federalist, my analysis of Sedgwick's most overtly political novel will explore her fraught and nuanced ideas about how the citizens and government of the new nation should interact.

In her introduction to Sedgwick's *The Linwoods, or, "Sixty Years Since" in America,* Maria Karafilis notes the republican values that resonate throughout the 1836 novel and the contemporary response to those values. As Karafilis points out, Sedgwick "depicts for her readers what she considered to be appropriate models of democratic behavior in a post-Revolutionary society, a society whose republican foundation was eroding and whose national self-imagining was thereby threatened" (xv). Truly, the responses of Sedgwick's contemporaries speak to the effectiveness of the novel's republican messages: for at least one reviewer of Sedgwick's day, *The Linwoods* reveals "the marks of a true genius for commencing a literature for the mass of the American people, which shall bring up their moral tone of the spirit of their institutions. Her mind appreciates the peculiar dignity of republicanism, and her heart rejoices in its enacted poetry" (qtd. in *The Linwoods* xii).

It was Sedgwick's willingness to provide literature and literary morality aimed at a distinctly American audience that made her especially valued by nineteenth-century American readers, particularly during the 1830s. The perceived lack of democratic, American literary traditions and the corresponding erosion of republican values concerned many during the era of Jacksonian democracy. For example, in his introduction to the magazine's debut issue, John L. O'Sullivan, the editor of *The United States Magazine* and *Democratic Review,* complains that "Our 'better educated classes' drink in an anti-democratic bit of feeling thinking from the copious . . . fountain of the literature of England; they give the same spirit to our own, in which we have little or nothing that is truly democratic and American. Hence this tone of sentiment of our litera[ture] . . . poisoning at the spring the young mind of our people" (15). Sedgwick's writing answers that widespread plea with its self-consciously republican agenda and its reliance on American rhetorical trends. Readers of *The Linwoods* immediately appreciated the novel's apparent republicanism. Sedgwick achieves such a resonant representation of republican values and controversies through her choice of the Revolutionary War as the historical setting of the novel and, more importantly, her allegorical configuration of the conflicted new nation as a conflicted American family. *The Linwoods* reflects the 1830s struggle between Jacksonian democracy and republican idealism, represented in the dynamics of the title American family as it battles through its private trials and reaches reconciliation during the Revolutionary War.

Indeed, the title and subtitle, *The Linwoods; or, "Sixty Years Since" in America,* enact the very parallel Sedgwick portrays between an American family and the American nation: this novel tells the story of an American family, or, the story of a newly-formed nation. In choosing a family as an allegory for the conflicts of the new nation, Sedgwick tapped into a rhetoric that had been around since long before the Revolution. Nineteenth-century readers were accustomed to the link between nation and family, not only from the revolutionary rhetoric of the abuse of "Mother England" and the rebellion and independence of "her child," but also, more recently for mid-century readers, from the regular references to the republican union as a "family" and the citizens as its "children." The most emphatic political arguments of the day featured appeals for the good of "the republican family." The metaphor for nation as family appears in both sides of the major political battles facing the new nation, including abolition, expansion, sectionalism, states' rights, and, most significantly, national unity. Sedgwick's depiction of the conflicts of the new nation in terms of the conflicts of a loving family, then, was not only captivating to her readers for its tale of a domestic romance, but also recognizable and accessible as a participant in political conversation. In her portrayal of the politics and dynamics of the embattled Revolutionary War-era family and her messages about republican family governance, Sedgwick responds to actual national crises that are worth looking at.

The most important aspect of national politics that Sedgwick addresses in *The Linwoods* is the threat of national disunion presented in the Nullification Crisis.[3] Although this event, as Karafilis notes, "has been overshadowed by other happenings in the political history of the United States" (xxv), it denoted the first serious challenge to the U.S. Constitution. For that reason, it is a significant context for Sedgwick, whose own father, a Revolutionary war hero and U.S. Senator, fought to ratify the Constitution. Furthermore, the Nullification Crisis, which was at its height during the 1835 publication of *The Linwoods,* meant the possible dissolution of the national union—an opportunity for Sedgwick to ponder to what

extent the rationalist right to self-government must be sacrificed for the sake of preserving the national union, as well as to what extent agencies of authority must evolve to accommodate self-government.

Public responses to the Nullification Crisis were emphatic and widely disseminated from the beginning of the conflict to its resolution. Even after the crisis was resolved, Americans grappled with their concepts of the well-being and solidarity of the nation, as they tried to come to terms with the status of states' rights and the extent of the federal government's power. Not surprisingly, the debate over South Carolina's secession frequently featured the popular metaphor of nation as family. During the peak of controversy over nullification in 1830, a writer for *The North American Review,* spelling out what he saw as the potentially catastrophic consequences of a state's secession, expostulates, "God preserve us from the day, when . . . any member of the common family, in war or in peace, shall separate from the Union." The break-up of the national union, to this writer, "would be on the grandest scale in the extremest exasperation, a comprehensive family quarrel, in which a thousand natural bonds of union would be so many causes of unappeasable and remorseless hatred and hostility" ("The Debate in the Senate of the United States," 533). Sedgwick extends the rhetorical trope of using the family as a metaphor for the nation—a trend especially prevalent when the nation's unity is in danger—to allegorize the nation as family, and to reconstruct the disrupted nation/family in *The Linwoods.*

The portrayal of the Linwood family's disunion and reunion allows Sedgwick to imagine the repair of her cherished republic. In the shadow of the first major threat to the national union, Sedgwick offered her readers a resolution to national crisis through the reconciliation of a family torn apart by private and public revolutions. Karafilis sums up the cultural work of *The Linwoods* with the premise that the metaphor of the family as nation achieved Sedgwick's conservative goal of preserving the national union:

> The two competing narratives that emerged from the Nullification Crisis—that of the Nullifiers and that of the Nationalists—clashed and produced a rupture that needed to be sutured by yet a third narrative, such as that of *The Linwoods.* Sedgwick's novel allowed her readers to "intervene in" and reimagine the pending Nullification Crisis, to retell a story of profound discord that eventually results in conciliation. It is "imaginative intervention" that explains in great part why the novel resonated so deeply with its contemporary audience.
>
> (xxvii)

But rescuing the nation from crisis is only one aspect of the novel's cultural work. While Karafilis argues that *The Linwoods* performs the conservative task of preserving the national union by "resisting descent into political divisiveness" (xxx), her argument overlooks the very political divisiveness of the recuperated Linwood family at the end of the novel. Even while finally accepting his children's American patriotism in the final chapter, Mr. Linwood remains a staunch loyalist, mournfully watching the British leave New York. Just as in *A New-England Tale* Sedgwick carefully avoids sectarianism and calls for a sense of Christianity that will tolerate diverse denominations, in *The Linwoods* she imagines a family/nation that will allow diverse political positions. In both novels, Sedgwick's utopian unions feature humanitarian leadership, mutual respect, and goodwill among the various members of families, nations, and communities. In *The Linwoods,* Sedgwick imagines a republican union that accommodates, to some extent, political dissent and self-determination. Though *The Linwoods*reinforces conservative republican standards for virtue, then, it also explores a liberal model of familial/national governance. Sedgwick may have desired the preservation of the union, but only with rational, fair leadership and independent citizenship.

Sedgwick's delineation of the Linwood family patriarch reveals her attitudes and anxieties about familial/national governance. Mr. Linwood's character functions as an allegorical authority figure in two historical contexts: as England in the Revolutionary War (if we choose the setting of the novel), or as the Federal Government during the Nullification Crisis (if we choose the writer's own historical context). In her critique of patriarchal authority in *The Linwoods,* Sedgwick considers the role that affection may play in the recuperation of bonds between authority and subject. Not willing to completely abandon authority that has moved beyond what she sees as it proper democratic boundaries, Sedgwick allows it to revise its role and to reconstruct the union under a more loving, compassionate style of authority. To some extent, Sedgwick's portrayal of an affectionate but authoritative father in *The Linwoods* echoes her portrayal of her own father, who, she says, reprimanded the Sedgwick children with an "awful frown": "It [the frown] was not so dreadful because it portended punishment—it was punishment; it was a token a suspension of the approbation and love that were our life" (*The Power of Her Sympathy* 77). In many ways, her reflections about her own father shape her delineation of Mr. Linwood, the patriarch of the Linwood family.

From the beginning of the novel, Linwood is aligned with England in the context of the American Revolution. In his first appearance in the novel, he is seen sternly checking his thirteen-year-old son Herbert's allegiance to the Whigs: "This matter shall be looked into—here are the seeds of rebellion springing up in their hot young bloods—this may come to something, if it is not seen to in time" (18). This scene takes place "some two or three years before our revolutionary war" (7), when the father figure recognizes the "seeds of rebellion" that will undermine his/England's patriarchal authority. He warns his young son, "I hate a whig as I do a toad, and if my son should prove a traitor to his king and country, By George, I would cut him off forever!" (18). Of course, Mr. Linwood's reaction to his young child playing in a pretend fort to fight the British foreshadows Herbert's involvement with the "real" war and his consequential estrangement from his father and family.

Before Herbert effectively escapes the control of his father to join the American army, Mr. Linwood exercises his paternal power to try to change his son's political convictions and actions. "As soon as Mr. Linwood became aware of his son's whig tendencies, he determined, as far as possible, to counteract them; and instead of sending him, as he had purposed, to Harvard University, into a district which he considered infected with the worst of plagues, he determined to retain him under his own vigilant eye, at the loyal institution in his own city" (22). Unable to talk him out of his allegiance to the country of his birth over the king, Herbert's father resorts to the power of his patriarchal authority to retain his son in New York. When that final attempt to force Herbert's submission failed, Mr. Linwood cuts his son off from his home and family.

The reader learns of the Linwood family crisis through a series of epistolary exchanges between Herbert's sister (and the heroine of the novel), Isabella Linwood, and her friend, Bessie Lee. Isabella's letters underscore the significance of the theme of family to the novel's representation of the American Revolution. Although Isabella will eventually take the side of her brother and country, she sides with England in the beginning of the novel, and in her letter to Bessie about her family's crisis, she laments her brother's rebellion against their king and father. Significantly, she expostulates about the divisive impact of Herbert's politics on her own family, and she adopts the family rhetoric day in her references to the war. She refers to the American cause as a rebellious prejudice that "pervades the country, over her wayward, ungrateful child" (38). Later in the novel, Sedgwick applies that rhetorical trope to the opposite political perspective, in a letter to Isabella from her (American) patriotic aunt, Mrs. Archer, whose patriotism, rationalism, and virtuous republican womanhood are the persuasive combination needed to influence Isabella's transition from a Tory to a Whig. Mrs. Archer uses the family rhetoric to criticize England's abuse of its power and authority: "Our English mother, God bless her, too, should have known better than to trammel, scold, and try to whip her sons into obedience, when they had come to man's estate, and were fit to manage their own household" (158).

The novel's messages about the limitations of patriarchal authority for familial/national governance are often conveyed through Isabella's shifting allegiances and attitudes. In the beginning of the novel, while Isabella's political convictions remain on the side of the "mother country" and her father, she is unable to criticize her father's irrational authoritarian behavior, and, instead, she blames her brother's rebellion for her family's trials. She complains to Bessie that the "stormy miserable week" since she wrote the last letter "has ended in Herbert's leaving us, and dishonouring his father's name by taking a commission in the revel service" (39). Even at this point, though, Isabella acknowledges the role of affection in family dynamics. She continues to express love for her brother and insists that her father's affection for his son will prevail. In closing a letter that fiercely opposes her brother's rebellion, she says, "Ah Herbert!—but I loved him before [this crisis]; and once truly loving, especially if our hearts are knit together by nature, I think the faults of the subject do not diminish our affection, though they turn it from its natural sweet uses to suffering" (39). Moreover, she doubts that her father's authority can overpower his affection for his son: "[Papa] says he has for ever cast Herbert out of his affections. Ah! I am not skilled in metaphysics, but I know that we have no power whatever over our affections" (39).

As with *A New-England Tale,* the Lockean paradigm for childrearing sheds light on Sedgwick's messages about family governance in *The Linwoods.* Mr. Linwood's relationship with his adolescent son exemplifies the pitfalls of coercive parenting that Locke warns his readers about. According to Locke, while strict discipline is appropriate for very young children, parents should gradually loosen the reigns of authority as a child grows into a young adult, replacing strict authority with love and mutual respect: "Fear and awe ought to give you the first power over their minds, and love and friendship in riper years hold it: for the time must come, when they will be past the rod and correction; and then, if love of you make them not obedient and dutiful, if the love of virtue and reputation keep them not in laudable courses, I ask, what hold will you have upon them to turn them to it?" (42). Locke insists (and Sedgwick, apparently, agrees) that the coercive threat of expulsion from the family is not an effective "hold" to wield upon a young adult (particularly a young republican citizen, whose virtuous independent thinking is crucial to the welfare of the nation). "Every man," Locke asserts, "must some time or other be trusted to himself and his own conduct; . . . habits woven into the very principles of his nature, and not a counterfeit carriage, and dissembled outside, put on by fear, only to avoid the present anger of a father who perhaps may disinherit him." Mr. Linwood's harsh criticism, threats, and verbal abuse, and most importantly, his unwillingness to evolve from a strict authoritarian into a loving, toler-

ant friend to his son, result in the breakdown of the Linwood family. Before the father can begin to love his son unconditionally and accept his son's independence, the entire family unit will suffer. Sedgwick emphasizes the need for affection-driven family governance in the scene of the first Linwood family reunion, which ultimately fails, because the father resists his first impulse to act upon his love for his son.

In that scene, Herbert sneaks home and hides in his bedroom, where his discovers his father mourning his loss:

> ". . . what fools we are! We knit the love of our children with our very heart-strings—we tend on them—we blend our lives with theirs, and then we are deserted—forgotten!" "Never, never for one moment!" cried Herbert, who, with one spring was at his father's feet. Mr. Linwood started from him, and then, obeying the impulses of nature, he received his son's embrace, and they wept in each other's arms.
>
> (147)

The father and son are joined by Mrs. Linwood and Isabella, in what seems like a recuperative, nuclear-family reunion, but Mr. Linwood checks his first, affectionate impulses: he "was beginning to recover his self-possession, and to feel as if he had been betrayed into the surrender of a post." Once he has effectively overcome his first impulsive behavior, Mr. Linwood demands Herbert's submission, requiring him to give up the revolutionary cause and join the British army. Mr. Linwood's demand is firm: "I swear to you, Herbert, that on these terms alone will I ever again receive you as my son" (147). Although Herbert is eventually brought back to his sense of duty to the revolutionary cause by his sister, Isabella, he momentarily vacillates, and considers yielding to his father's ultimatum between independence and family.

The conflict Sedgwick portrays between the parent-child bond and the child's need for independence reflects the tension between the affection-based, nuclear-family ideal and the Lockean paradigm in the new nation. As Fliegelman has noted (57-58), the Lockean strategy of raising children to think and act independently, so that they will become healthy, productive adults, conflicts with the emergent emphasis on close, private family life. The Linwood family very closely approximates the affectionate, private, nuclear family ideal. Not only does the family feature the father as head of the family, the submissive mother, and a son and daughter, but also, the Linwood family is insulated from the outside society—every scene of family unity takes place inside the family home, and the family is never shown together outside their home. Moreover, the element of affection in the Linwood family is significant enough to be used as a lure to win back the wayward son. In a desperate attempt to convince Herbert to abandon his role in the revolution and return to the family unit, Mrs. Linwood appeals to her son's love. She pleads, "Oh, my dear, dear son, . . . if you but knew how much we have all suffered for you, and how happy you can now make us, if you only will, you would not hesitate, even if the rebel cause were a good one: you are but as one man to that, and to us you are all the world" (148). Significantly, Herbert's dilemma lies between the comforts and love of his family and home and his own adult independence—a predicament brought on by the conflict between the ideologies of nuclear family and Lockean childrearing. After his mother's pathetic plea, he considers his options: "It was a moment of the most painful vacillation; the forgiveness of father, the ministering, indulgent love of his mother, the presence of his sister, the soft endearments of home, and all its dear, familiar objects, solicited him" (148).

Even more compelling than Sedgwick's willingness to illustrate the friction between independence and affection is how she resolves that conflict. The nuclear-family bond, according to Sedgwick's portrayal of the Linwoods, does not necessarily have to be sacrificed for the sake of a child's independence. Rather, the parent must transfer the guidance and education of his young children to a loving respect and pride in the adult children. The story of the Linwoods imagines the potential compatibility between a Lockean education and an affectionate, private family. Sedgwick points to the love between Mr. Linwood and his children as the chief factor in the reunion and recuperation of the family. Although Mr. Linwood's political allegiances never change, his approach to family governance changes significantly, shifting from unconditional obedience to unconditional love and pride as the sources of family happiness.

Near the end of the novel, at Mrs. Linwood's suggestion that the farewell "should be a family thing" (353), the Linwoods gather to watch the defeated British leave New York. Just as the representatives of the old, patriarchal British authority depart, Mr. Linwood expresses to Isabella his own, newly-awakened sense of his role as a father. He insists that, although he remains as opposed as ever to the patriotic cause, he bears his children's American patriotism because they have been loving, virtuous children:

> "Belle, I'll tell you what it is that's kept the sap running warm and freely in this old, good-for-nothing trunk of mine. My child," the old man's voice faltered, "you have been true and loyal to me through all this dark time of trial and adversity; you have been a perpetual light and blessing to my dwelling, Belle; and Herbert—if a man serves the devil, I'd have him serve him faithfully—Herbert, in temptation and sore trials, has been true to the cause he chose—up to the mark. This it is that's kept me heart-whole. And, Belle, if

> ever you are a parent, which God grant, for you deserve it, you'll know what it is to have your very life rooted in the virtue of your children, and sustained by that—yes, as mine is, sustained and made pretty comfortable, too. . . ."

> (354-55)

Mr. Linwood's new sense of authority features his newly acquired tolerance for diverse political values, a requirement, according to Sedgwick, for republican government. Furthermore, the "virtue" that sustains Mr. Linwood is no longer grounded in obedience and submission but in loyalty, consistency, and love. Isabella's father has come to accept her political independence from him because she has remained loving and faithful to their family. He accepts Herbert's independence because he recognizes his worth as a respectable, loyal adult, and, we should note, a good citizen. The appearance of the term "virtue," especially at this point in the novel, when the British are leaving and the father has accepted his son's independence, should remind us of Sedgwick's own agenda of inculcating republican values in her readers. The characters who allow her to teach "virtue" to her readers are the Linwood children, who are joined under the same rule.

In the context of the family/nation allegory, the Linwood children represent citizens living together under their father's governance. The importance placed on the siblings' virtue parallels the great emphasis given to the citizens' virtue in the period of nation formation; an important facet of that republican civic virtue was patriotism, which translates to filial loyalty in Sedgwick's family/nation allegory. Although they do not always agree with their father, the Linwood children remain loyal, loving, and respectful. The Lockean value for "filial esteem," which was so glaringly and dangerously lacking in the Wilson family of *A New-England Tale*, holds the Linwood family together through political crisis. Even when Herbert seems to be defying his father by joining the American forces, Sedgwick carefully portrays the son's continued respect for his father and his angst over his father's disapproval. In a conversation with his friend, Eliot, Herbert agonizes over his father's "curse" against him: "you really have no conception how miserable my father's displeasure makes me . . . certainly my conscience acquits me, yet I suffer most cruelly for my breach of filial obedience" (105). While Herbert ultimately chooses patriotic duty over "filial obedience," his continued respect for his father and love for his family make him go to extreme lengths to regain his role in the family union. Indeed, reconciliation with his father is only possible when he temporarily abandons his duties to his political cause. Only after sneaking back into New York against Washington's orders, and being held prisoner by the British army, does Herbert eventually regain his relationship with his father and his status in his family.

When Herbert's politics clashed with his father's, he chose the route of involuntary "secession," sacrificing his role in the family union in order to preserve his independence. Isabella, on the other hand, developed an independent position while remaining on good terms with her father and preserving her role in the family. As a female child, Isabella's "filial obedience" was especially crucial in the eyes of republican moralists. A virtuous young republican woman, Isabella stayed by her father's side, nursing him during illness, and entertaining him when he was lonely. Sedgwick keeps Isabella from even uttering her strong patriotic inclinations to her father until the final symbolic scene of the British leaving New York and Mr. Linwood announcing his appreciation for his children's virtue.

More resounding in this novel than the virtue of the individual Linwood children, though, is the unconditional bond between brother and sister. If Sedgwick configures the reconciliation of the nation through the Linwood family, she stresses the importance of cooperation and sympathy among the "compatriots," Herbert and Isabella. In fact, the strength of the brother-sister bond is even more effective in repairing the family union than the father's slowly improving style of authority. In her family/nation allegory, Sedgwick depicts the behavior of the siblings as central to the health of the family, just as the behavior of citizens, according to the nation-building rhetoric, determines the health of the republic. Significantly, Sedgwick underscores the consistency and indestructibility of the bond between brother and sister. For example, although she was still a loyalist at this point in the novel, it was Isabella who recalled Herbert to his patriotic duty when their parents tried to tempt him to switch sides and rejoin the family. "'Herbert,' exclaimed Isabella, and her voice thrilled through his soul, 'is it possible you waver?' He started as if he were electrified: his eye met hers, and the evil spirits of doubt and irresolution were overcome. 'Heaven forgive me!' he said, 'I waver no longer'" (148). Once again, Sedgwick firmly situates the union above politics and the bond between citizens as crucial to the health of the republic.

While their relationship is particularly interesting for its participation in the nation/family allegory, Herbert and Isabella are not the only compelling brother-sister pair in *The Linwoods*. Other brother-sister pairs throughout the novel, include Eliot and Bessie Lee, and the blind twins, Lizzie and Edward Archer, further reveal Sedgwick's intense interest in the opposite-sex sibling relationship. The affectionate sibling theme in *The Linwoods* is strong and explicit. A letter from Eliot to Bessie highlights the sentiments underlying this theme:

> My sweet sister Bessie, nothing has afflicted me so much in leaving home as parting from you. I am inclined to believe there can be no stronger nor tenderer

affection than that of brother and sister; the sense of protection from the one part, and dependance (sic) on the other; the sweet recollections of childhood; the unity of interest; and the communion of memory and hope, blend their hearts together into one existence. So it is with us—is it not, my dear sister?

(63)

Later in that letter, Eliot further insists that no other relationship, including a romantic one, could be more important than the one between a brother and sister.[4]

The brothers and sisters of *The Linwoods* reflect Sedgwick's interest in the role of the opposite-sex sibling relationship plays in the proper rearing of republican families, and, by extension, nations. The strongly affectionate quality of the brother-sister relationship in *The Linwoods* reflects a trend in middle-class republican family values of Sedgwick's day—a trend that was recorded in the contemporary domestic advice literature. Writers of antebellum advice books were particularly persistent about teaching young men to love, serve, and protect their sisters, perhaps in response to a broader vision of social responsibility in the republican nation. One of the most widely published authors of advice books for young adults in the nineteenth century, William Alcott, was so interested in disseminating this sort of instruction to young men, that he gave it special emphasis in both his 1836 book, *The Young Man's Guide,* as well as his 1850 book, *Familiar Letters to Young Men on Various Subjects.* In a section titled "Society of Sisters" in *The Young Man's Guide,* Alcott advised young men that "[t]here is a sort of attention due to the [female] sex which is best attained by practicing at home. Your mother may sometimes require this attention, your sisters still oftener." The type of "attention" Alcott proposed included acting as a protective escort and guide, "when their safety, their comfort, or their respectability require it." Revealing the agenda of the sibling ideology—to teach brothers and sisters to interact as proper republican men and women would be expected to—Alcott urges his readers, "Accustom yourself, then, to wait upon her [your sister]; it will teach you to wait upon others by and by; and in the meantime, it will give a graceful polish to your character."[5] In an 1850 chapter ("letter") titled "Female Society," Alcott notes: "Man, divinely appointed to be a social and not a solitary being, begins his career in the family" (263), and that the opposite-sex sibling relationships is particularly important to a man's social development. Romanticizing the opposite-sex sibling relationship in language typical to the discourse, he asks, "What can be a lovelier sight than of brothers and sisters who truly love one another, and who seek to elevate, adorn, and improve each other?" (266). Moreover, Alcott argues that a brother's protection and devotion to his sister is compensation for her positive influence: "Brothers . . . little know how much they owe to the influence of sisters" (265). In a chapter titled "Brother and Sisters" in one of his family advice manuals, William Aikman states simply an instruction that appears in volumes of advice literature from the day: "A Sister should feel that she has, in her brother, one to whom not only she may look, in time of danger or trouble, for protection, but one whose care over her makes her independent of every one else" (186).

E. Anthony Rotundo's study of nineteenth-century American men's letters reveals that the brother-sister ideology found in advice literature may have even had actual significance in the raising of young American men in the early nineteenth century: "Indeed the relationship was so important that it served an important symbolic function. In the prescriptive literature of the nineteenth century, the brother-sister bond was exalted as a model of purity in an era when sexual control was a cardinal principal of morality. The authors of advice books held up the sibling tie as a shining example of chaste, Christian love between a male and female" (93). Rotundo's analysis of letters between adult brothers and sisters of the day reveals the continuation into adulthood of a strong bond based on confidence and affection. Boys and girls were encouraged to "practice" proper interactions with the opposite sex on their siblings, in order to prepare them for social success outside the family. Rotundo also explains that the affectionate brother-sister bond "served as a bridge between the separate worlds of male and female" (93) and that the opposite-sex sibling relationship was nurtured to be a "trial run at marriage" (96), allowing the young siblings to test their skills and feelings in an intense, affectionate relationship with the opposite sex. Rotundo's observations are consistent with the prescriptive ideology from the advice literature for young adults, which repeatedly suggests that a brother-sister relationship should be practice for and a prediction of their marriages. Aikman's advice for brothers and sisters, for example, insists that "The good sisters make the good wives, and the good brothers make the good husbands of the after time. If you want to know with a fair certainty what each will be in the unalterable relation and solemn responsibilities of married life, you can see it all mirrored in the life that as child and youth they led" (186).

The brother-sister pairs of *The Linwoods* closely adhere to the contemporary expectations for close sibling bonds. Besides being intensely affectionate, each pair is put through some sort of endurance test; that is, each pair faces, at some point in the novel, a threat to their union. Isabella and Herbert prove the strength of their relationship when it is tested by divergent politics and Herbert's exile. The Lee and Archer sibling pairs are also put to the test, and pass. Bessie and Eliot are first separated by war, and then by Bessie's breakdown, and Lizzy and Edward are literally ripped apart by robbers.

In both cases, the sisters end up on the brink of death, and in each situation it is the brother whose love, protection, and attention save her and sustain her. The Lee and Archer siblings particularly reflect the gendered codes for raising American children in Sedgwick's era. Sedgwick's repeated depictions of brother-sister dynamics reinforce the traditional gender codes, most explicitly revealed in Eliot's statement that the brother offers "a sense of protection," and the sister, one of dependence. The portrayals of brotherly protection and sisterly dependence in *The Linwoods* reveal Sedgwick's interest in the social responsibility of the independent republican citizens whose free will she ultimately wants to protect.

The sibling relationships in *The Linwoods* were critical to the continued health and harmony of the family units, a particularly significant assertion when we remember that Sedgwick wanted to repair national fissures and restore the union while protecting rationalist self-determination. For Sedgwick, the functional bond between nuclear-family siblings was as crucial to the health of individual families as was the cooperation of republican citizens crucial to the recuperation of a divided nation. Sedgwick chooses brother-sister bonds to suggest the roles between the enfranchised and disenfranchised compatriots in the republican nation, since their parallel social circumstances make their political distinctions especially apparent. Sharing parents, filial love, racial and class identities, even education in many cases, the brothers and sisters of *The Linwoods* differ significantly only in their gender-determined political agency. The brother-sister depictions in *The Linwoods* allow Sedgwick to strike a compromise between democratic rights and national hierarchies. Sedgwick argues for the preservation of both the union and republican self-determination, by granting the right to think and act independently only to those already enfranchised, and asking them to use that power for the service and protection of their dependent, disenfranchised compatriots. Maintaining the hegemony of white men as the only self-determining, enfranchised republican citizens, Sedgwick asserts that with the freedom to self-determine comes the duty to act righteously for the service and protection of the disfranchised members of the republican nation. While liberal in taking the side of the rebel exercising his right to political independence, then, Sedgwick is nevertheless too conservative to propose the enfranchisement of all Americans. She prefers instead to inculcate young white republican men with a sense of social responsibility to protect those who, like Isabella Linwood, will keep their political dissent to themselves and obey and honor their fathers.

In *A New-England Tale,* Sedgwick endorsed a simple plan of rationalist familial/governance and the raising of self-determining children/citizens. Following the publication of that novel, after a decade rife with political turmoil as American citizens and states test the nation's founding ideology, Sedgwick reconsiders the potential complications of rationalist authority. *The Linwoods* conveys—and responds to—what Sedgwick perceives to be an urgent need to resolve tensions between independence and loyalty, rationalism and patriotism, individualism and civic virtue. Simultaneously tapping into and moving beyond the rhetorical pairing of familial and national health prevalent in her day, Sedgwick's fictional family drama imagines conflicts and resolutions surrounding the raising of nuclear families and the governing of democratic, republican nations. While trapped in the very dilemma she seeks to resolve in her fiction—i.e., trying at once to serve as an exemplary, loyal American as well as an advocate for democratic civil rights—Sedgwick reveals the circumscriptions of her own value system. More importantly, however, she also demonstrates the potential of her fiction to perform meaningful and relevant cultural work.

Notes

1. Several scholars have noted the nationalistic strain running through much of Sedgwick's writing. In her introduction to Sedgwick's short story, "Cacoethes Scribendi" in *Provisions: A Reader from 19th-Century American Women,* Judith Fetterley explains that Sedgwick "grew up in an atmosphere pervaded by politics and informed by a commitment to translating political beliefs into public acts" and that her works "reflect her profound belief in the American democratic experiment and her deep commitment to devoting her talents, as her father did before her, to the service of her country" (41, 44). Mary Kelley further explores the nationalistic agendas in Sedgwick's personal life and writing career in her introduction to Sedgwick's autobiography, *The Power of Her Sympathy,* as well as in her article, "Negotiating a Self: The Autobiography and Journals of Catharine Maria Sedgwick." Also, scholars have paid particular attention to the role of national politics in *Hope Leslie*: See Maria Karafilis, "Catharine Maria Sedgwick's *Hope Leslie*: The Crisis between Political Action and US Literary Nationalism in the New Republic" and Gregory Garvey, "Risking Reprisal: Catharine Sedgwick's *Hope Leslie* and the Legitimation of Public Action by Women." Most recently, in her essay, "The Limits of Authority: Catharine Maria Sedgwick and the Politics of Resistance," in *Catherine Maria Sedgwick: Critical Perspectives,* Susan K. Harris explores five of Sedgwick's most political novels, including the two I look at in this article. While Harris also discusses the theme of democratic authority in Sedgwick's fiction, my work here considers the further reaching contexts of popular domestic advice and contemporaneous alongside close readings of the novels.

Much critical writing on Sedgwick notes her dual interests in domesticity and national politics, but none had adequately considered the intersections of those two agendas. That is, none of the previous studies of Sedgwick's fiction has turned to her compelling representations of family as/and nation to shed light on how she engages in national political issues, particularly the limitations of rationalist governance, by tapping into discourses about family values and the rhetorical trend of using the family as a metaphor for the nation.

2. This article continues and draws upon the work of feminist literary projects that excavate the cultural work of literature by and about women. For the most influential arguments about the potential for nineteenth-century domestic fiction (also referred to as "woman's fiction" or "sentimental fiction") to have political and cultural significance, see Jane Tompkins's *Sensational Designs: The Cultural Work of American Fiction 1790-1860,* especially chapter 5, "Sentimental Power: *Uncle Tom's Cabin* and the Politics of Literary History" (122-47); Nina Baym's *Woman's Fiction: A Guide to Novels by and about Women in America, 1820-1870*; Harris's *19th-Century American Women's Novels: Interpretive Strategies*; and Kelley's *Private Woman, Public Stage: Literary Domesticity in Nineteenth-Century America.*

3. The Nullification Crisis was the result of tension between the power of the federal government and the extent of states' rights. In 1828, just before Andrew Jackson's term as U.S. President began, the federal government passed a tariff, raising the cost of imported goods sold in the United States and sparking the controversial debate about the relationship between the federal government and states' governments. South Carolina responded to the new tariffs by passing the Nullification Act, which declared the federal tariff act null and void and argued that each state government had the right to nullify any federal law that it deemed unconstitutional. South Carolina also threatened to secede from the union if the federal government challenged the state's new law. The Nullification Crisis subsided in 1833, when Congress passed a compromise tariff proposed by Henry Clay (just in time to prevent military conflict, since Congress gave Jackson permission to use federal troops to enforce his tariff). Nevertheless, the five-year-long dispute over the tariff and, more significantly, states' rights versus federal power, left a strong impression on the citizens of the new nation: the union was not invincible.

4. At least to some extent, Sedgwick's portrayal of brothers and sisters in *The Linwoods* reflects her own deeply affectionate relationship with her four

brothers, Theodore, Harry, Robert, and Charles. In her autobiography Sedgwick admits that her older brother, Robert, was especially important to her: "I looked . . . upon my favorite brother as my preserver. He was more than any other my protector and companion. Charles was as near my own age, but he was younger, and a feeling of dependence—of most loving dependence—on Robert began then, which lasted through his life" (*The Power of Her Sympathy* 72). Not only were Sedgwick's brothers protective in the sense prescribed by the domestic advice literature, but they were, according to Sedgwick, loving and supportive, and they directly impacted her literary career. As Kelley notes in her introduction to Sedgwick's *The Power of Her Sympathy,* Sedgwick's brothers "encouraged the initially reluctant author, applauded the novels and stories, and negotiated with the publishers" (29). The close bonds between brothers and sisters in *The Linwoods* echo Sedgwick's own sentiments from her autobiography, where she says, "I can conceive of no truer image of the purity and happiness of the equal loves of Heaven than that which unites brothers and sisters" (89).

5. C. Dallett Hemphill notes how the predominant advice to republican brothers and sisters serves to inculcate preferred dynamics between men and women. She explains that advice literature writers suggested "how men were to begin to cultivate relationships with women: they urged young men to start by cultivating the friendship of their mothers and especially, their sisters. Men were to practice with them the gallantry requisite with all women by escorting them and devoting time to doing them favors. Over and over again the authors claimed that for young men to be their sisters' companions would serve both to protect their sisters and to improve their own manners. Practicing at home would make their gallantry habitual" (195).

Works Cited

Aikman, William. *Life at Home; or, The Family and Its Members.* New York: Wells, 1870.

Alcott, William A. *Familiar Letters to Young Men on Various Subjects* Buffalo: Derby, 1850.

———. *The Young Man's Guide.* 10th ed. Boston: Perkins, 1836.

Baym, Nina. *Woman's Fiction: A Guide to Novels by and about Women in America, 1820-1870.* 2nd ed. Urbana: U of Illinois P, 1993.

"The Debate in the Senate of the United States." *North American Review* Oct. 1830: 462-568.

Fetterley, Judith. Introduction to "Cacoethes Scribendi" in *Provisions: A Reader from 19th-Century American Women.* Bloomington. Indiana UP, 1986. 41-49.

Fliegelman, Jay. *Prodigals and Pilgrims: The American Revolution Against Patriarchal Authority, 1750-1800.* New York: Cambridge UP, 1982.

Garvey, Gregory. "Risking Reprisal: Catharine Sedgwick's *Hope Leslie* and the Legitimation of Public Action by Women." *American Transcendental Quarterly* 8 (Dec. 1994): 287-98.

Harris, Susan K. *19th-Century American Women's Novels: Interpretive Strategies.* New York: Cambridge UP, 1990.

———. "The Limits of Authority: Catharine Maria Sedgwick and the Politics of Resistance." *Catherine Maria Sedgwick: Critical Perspectives.* Ed. Lucinda Damon-Bach and Victoria Clements. Boston: Northeastern UP, 2003.

Hemphill, C. Dallett. *Bowing to Necessities: A History of Manners in America, 1620-1860.* New York: Oxford UP, 1999.

Karafilis, Mary. "Catherine Maria Sedgwick's *Hope Leslie*: The Crisis between Political Action and US Literary Nationalism in the New Republic." *American Transcendental Quarterly* 12 (Dec. 1998): 327-44.

Kelley, Mary. "Negotiating a Self: The Autobiography and Journals of Catherine Maria Sedgwick." *New England Quarterly* 66 (Sept. 1993): 366-98.

———. *Private Woman, Public Stage: Literary Domesticity in Nineteenth-Century America.* New York: Oxford UP, 1984.

Locke, John. *Some Thoughts Concerning Education.* 1692. Ed. John W. Yolton and Jean S. Yolton. Vol. 3. New York: Oxford UP, 1989.

O'Sullivan, John L. "The Democratic Principle." *United States Magazine and Democratic Review* I Oct. 1837:1-15.

Rotundo, E. Anthony. *American Manhood: Transformations in Masculinity from the Revolution to the Modern Era.* New York: Harper, 1993.

Sedgwick, Catharine Maria. *The Linwoods; or, "Sixty Years Since" in America.* 1836. Ed. Maria Karafilis. Hanover: UP of New England, 2002.

———. *A New England Tale; or, Sketches of New-England Character and Manners,* 1822. Ed. Victoria Clements. New York: Oxford UP, 1995.

———. *The Power of Her Sympathy: The Autobiography and Journal of Catharine Maria Sedgwick.* Ed. Mary Kelley. Boston: Massachusetts Historical Society, 1993.

"Thoughts on Sunday Schools." *Southern Literary Messenger* 4.4 (1838): 224-27.

Tompkins, Jane. *Sensational Designs: The Cultural Work of American Fiction 1790-1860.* New York: Oxford UP, 1985.

Philip D. Beidler (essay date spring 2005)

SOURCE: Beidler, Philip D. "Mythopoetic Justice: Democracy and the Death of Edgar Allan Poe." *The Midwest Quarterly* 46, no. 3 (spring 2005): 252-67.

[In the following essay, Beidler considers the anti-democratic sentiment expressed in Edgar Allan Poe's works.]

After more than 150 years, the strange death of Edgar Allan Poe continues to attract the kind of attention worthy of a tale of mystery and imagination by Poe himself. Discovered in the streets of Baltimore on Election Day, October 7, 1849, in a combined state of exhaustion and alcoholic stupor, did he simply meet his end, as asserted by contemporary detractors, as a form of drunken just deserts? Or, as the more charitable were prompt to suggest, was there an underlying physical cause: epilepsy, perhaps, or brain fever? Recent medical readings of the evidence have pointed to diabetic hypoglycemia and even hydrophobia, the consequence of being bitten by a rabid animal. Alternatively, interpreters of a detective bent have postulated extreme physical ill treatment: a series of beatings or some fatal blow to the head. One of these, John Evangelist Walsh, has now gone further to posit a murder scenario where, on a northward journey to complete arrangements for his marriage to Elmira Royster of Richmond, Poe is pursued and waylaid by that lady's brothers, forcibly made to ingest whiskey, and thereby launched on what turns out to be a fatal binge.

One can hardly fault the speculation; indeed one can hardly resist it when the mysterious circumstances in question and the complex of events surrounding them involve the demise of a writer who himself had made a career asserting the essentially mythopoeic character of existence in nineteenth-century America—the essential reciprocity, in a world largely void of the traditional markers of cultural identity, of myth and reality, imagination and experience, art and life. Poe, mourning the death of his beloved Virginia, undertakes a set of increasingly frantic and hallucinatory peregrinations, revisiting the locales of his luckless career. Leaving New York one last time, he sets out for Richmond. Along the way he becomes convinced that he is being pursued by shadowy assassins.

In Baltimore, he reverses course, returning to Philadelphia, where a drunken spree lands him in prison. In a humiliating legal spin on the literary-cultural celebrity he has so long coveted, he is released by a judge who recognizes him as "Poe, the poet" and resumes his southward progress. In Richmond, he alternates between decorous social intercourse and visible binge drinking. Persuaded that he may be able to marry Elmira Royster, a sweetheart torn from him during his

youth, he makes a great show of joining the Sons of Temperance and undertakes a headlong return journey to New York to settle outstanding business and to fetch Virginia's mother back with him for the ceremonies. He never gets there. Possibly again going as far north as Philadelphia this time and then reversing course for Baltimore, he gets off the train in that city, the place of his paternal ancestry. He then disappears for a week before he is discovered in the street outside a tavern doubling as a "crib" for repeat voters. Taken to a hospital, he lives for four days, where his last communications with the world comprise a series of oracular, melancholy utterances, some of them with seemingly literary connections to his own mysterious texts.

The whole business is all almost too Edgar Allan Poe-like to be true. It is Poe's last gothic tale of terror: the great exegete of American existential and aesthetic loneliness vanishes into one of his own nightmare worlds of self-creating and self-annihilating reflexivities. Alternatively, it is his last great tale of detection: afoot in some master final conjuration of plot, simple and odd, the ghost of Poe awaits the Dupin who will accomplish the great unriddling, find the obvious, single thing, there for all the eye to see, that will set everything in place.

As importantly, however, at its obdurate circumstantial core—Poe, discovered dead drunk, or nearly so, in front of a tavern notorious as a collecting point for derelicts herded from polling place to polling place to cast fraudulent multiple votes—it also becomes the realization, I would propose, of a single political nightmare that Poe had been fabulating with increasing obsessiveness in the last decade of his life: the vision of sottish, addled, irrational *homo democraticus* in general and of tumultuous, anarchic nineteenth-century American participatory democracy in particular.

Two of Poe's most visible anti-democratic satires of the period, although omitted now from most anthologies, remain fairly well known. In "The Man That Was Used Up" (1839), the latest backwoods military upstart elevated to the status of popular political demigod is revealed to be a disembodied collection of prostheses. In "The System of Doctor Tarr and Professor Fether" (1842), an American student of dementia visits a French model institution where the inmates have literally taken over the asylum.

Some mention of what might be called the antidemocratic mythopathy in Poe's satires—comparable to that found, for instance, in such acerbic fables of egalitarian excess as Irving's "Legend of Sleepy Hollow" or Hawthorne's "My Kinsman, Major Molineux"—has been made by commentators, most notably Daniel Hoffman. What distinguishes it from the work of contemporaries, however, is the compounded violence *and* virulence of the literary grotesquerie. In the first case, the symbology is that of mutilation and dismemberment. In the second, it is that of madness and incarceration. The composite effect suggests a totality of loathing, a uniform, pathological contempt.

Were one to attempt a current entitling spin on "The Man That Was Used Up," it might be re-styled as *Fear and Loathing on the Campaign Trail, 1839.* In fact, the vernacular title stems from a political slogan trailed through the narrative as a running joke. The narrator, styling himself a kind of roving election correspondent in search of the inside story on the popular military candidate, Brevet Brigadier General John A. B. C. Smith, hero of the Bugaboo and Kickapoo Wars, repeatedly arrives on scenes of conversation about the latter in which one speaker begins promisingly by saying "He's the man . . ." only to have the sentence completed by another's non-sequitur.

Deciding to interview the luminary in person in his chambers, the narrator at length supplies the punch line with a vengeance. The disembodied reification of a violent colloquialism—"I'll use you up!"—that has come down through backwoods generations as a threat of being whipped to flinders, Smith is a man who literally has been flogged to physical nothingness. To wit: having sacrificed his body parts on the altar of the republic in a series of Indian conquests, he himself is revealed only to exist as formless protoplasm reconstructed from the ground up out of artificial body parts—even down to his sonorous vocal apparatus (*Complete Stories,* 356-57). The man of the hour or man of the moment, he is in fact, the man who has been used up.

To be sure, even today it all reads nicely for an age of media candidates all properly concocted by handlers and focus groups, their appearances reduced to slogans and sound bites. While admiring such prescience, however, one too easily misses the bite of the contemporary political humor. As a violent historical creation "Smith" is clearly that stock figure of early American humor, the frontier *miles gloriosus,* Nimrod Wildfire, the Lion of the West, now literally resurrected *and* reconstructed out of political spare parts into the latest canebrake Napoleon.

Further, given the subtitling of the story as "A Tale of the Bugaboo and Kickapoo Wars," the bloodthirsty populist picture could not be more complete. "Smith's" exalted brigadier generalship is a "brevet"—a temporary field promotion, likely a militia rank, in that era most frequently conferred by politicians, on condition of conquering native peoples, in hope of some eventual quid pro quo. His imposing initials confer an equally dubious genealogy, the alphabet as American pedigree.

"Smith" speaks for itself, the great man as democratic everyman. And finally, of course, there is the ground of heroism itself: the various wars of Indian removal and extermination that in the early decades of the century became the launching pads for innumerable political careers. The prototype of the figure was, to be sure, Jackson himself, by no coincidence, in 1836, at the end of his presidency, having completed his martial triumphs of the early decades of the century with the last of the great Indian removals east of the Mississippi.

There was also, however, General Winfield Scott, more recently in the limelight for his campaigns against the Seminoles and his military supervision of the final Creek and Cherokee removals, including the notorious Trail of Tears. And in fact, in the election of 1840, which the story most likely concerns, Scott was at least initially advanced as a prospective presidential candidate.

These are both good guesses. But there are two better. The first was the military hero as Indian fighter who turned out to be the election's actual man-on-horseback nominee. That was William Henry Harrison, a well-born Whig Virginian who, for campaign purposes styling himself a log-cabin populist, must have seemed to Poe a particularly noxious amalgam of class traitor and political sellout. The victor of an Indian battle years earlier at Tippecanoe Creek in Indiana, he managed to resurrect its memory long enough to engineer a rallying cry—"Tippecanoe and Tyler Too"—ingeniously marrying his decades-old martial feat with the name of his running mate. The other was, of course, the Democratic incumbent and Jackson's anointed successor, the oily, diminutive, decidedly un-Jacksonian Martin Van Buren, the Red Fox of Kinderhook, the Little Magician, the ultimate politician as protean midget. The Whigs, it turns out, had some memorable words for him as well. "Van, Van," they went, "He's a used up man" (Lynch, 453).

Thus, in Poe's complex play on contemporary political sloganeering, we arrive at the core of political loathing lodged at the heart of his satire. "Tippecanoe and Tyler Too!" "Van, Van, He's a Used Up Man!" Here is the political flaying not of one politician but two, of the political process at large, of the whole ghoulish, grotesque masquerade of man-making that passes for electoral ritual in participatory American democracy. To be a candidate for office in America, Poe tells us, is to be the man of the hour; and to be the man of the hour is to be, inevitably, a candidate for the title, "The Man Who Was Used Up."

A later story, "The System of Doctor Tarr and Professor Fether" (1842), is displaced to France. The title, however, makes a precise assignment of more localized political geography and practice. The "system" for treating mental illness it describes, as imaged in the phony, inflated titles borne by the American originators it purports to honor, is no system at all. The grand project of "Tarr" and "Fether," and dreamed up, as it turns out, by a rebellious lunatic, is organized insanity, the logic of the smooth-talking leader of the demented mob. So the particular institutional setting is distinctly "American" as well; it is an asylum that has been taken over by the inmates.

Again, the narrator is a somewhat dimwitted roving observer, in this case something of a parody of the friend of Roderick Usher, continually persuading himself that everything is normal despite frequent naggings of unease and suspicion. The inmates, cast into the role of keepers, seem most nervously sane. The keepers, cast by the inmates into the dungeons, constantly protest that it is they who are sane and the others mad. It is altogether a model asylum. The overthrow, it turns out, has been made possible by a permissive treatment of madness, invented by the Americans of the title, called the "system of soothing"—itself a mocking reference to the "moral treatment" asylum method instituted by the English reformer William Tuke and his French counterpart Philippe Pinel—in which lunatics are granted the "apparent freedom" of walking around in normal clothes as if they were in their right mind (*Complete Stories,* 293).

The ringleader, one Maillard, elected head lunatic, treats the narrator to a dinner—an opulent banquet of grandees in ill-fitting borrowed aristocratic dress complete with dissonant orchestra. It is a lavish feast, full of opulence and plenitude, but with "very little taste in the arrangements" (296). Conversation among guests runs to tales of favorite lunatics, who think they are chickens, teapots, and the like.

One, "Bouffon Le Grand," fancies himself with two heads, one of Cicero, the other a composite of Demosthenes and Lord Broughton, in honor of his passion for oratory (298-99). Meanwhile, Maillard extols the new philosophy of "soothing." The product of "a better system of government," he calls it, a "lunatic government" (303). As the narratives continue, the behavior of the guests becomes increasingly erratic.

Apace, Maillard, a vain, voluble popinjay, becomes so boastful of his own schemes that he can't help spilling the story that is really being played out under his orchestration, even as the counterrevolution occurs and the imprisoned storm upward from the dungeons. He is last seen hiding under the buffet.

Meanwhile, the general upheaval brings the final triumph of anarchy, a frenzy of dancing on the tables to the mad playing and singing of "Yankee Doodle" (304). A "perfect army of what I took to be Chimpanzees, Ourang-Outangs, or big black baboons" (304), the narrator tells us, rushes in to restore order. He himself receives a serious beating and is imprisoned for more than a month until things are sorted out. Only then is the full plot revealed. Maillard, as it happens, was actually the keeper of the asylum until he himself went insane, thence conniving with the inmates to overthrow their guards. It has also been those latter, in their own tar and feathers, whom he has mistaken for apes.

As a fable of mob politics, American-style, it is again all beautifully circular and complete. As at Jackson's inauguration, the democratic rabble take over the mansion, a mob breaking furniture and throwing crockery and drunkenly dancing on the tables. Yet when the counterrevolution occurs, it seems mainly a mob of avenging semi-anthropoids, with the innocent narrator among those violently assaulted and imprisoned. It has all been very confusing, he says. Further, he concludes, in his opinion at least, at the particular Maison de Sante in question, the contest of systems remains very much in the balance. "The 'soothing system,' with important modifications," he says, "has been resumed at the chateau; yet I cannot help agreeing with Monsieur Maillard, that his own 'treatment' was a very capital one of its kind. As he justly observed, it was 'simple—neat—and gave no trouble at all—not the least'" (305). A good American to the end, he would seem to cast his vote in a given instance for whatever set of inmates happens at the moment to be running the asylum.

As to Poe's most vicious critiques of democracy, democratic man, and democratic process at large, however, one looks to the far more explicit content of what might be called the mouthpiece or ventriloquist sketches, all clustered in the latter part of the 1840s. Here, the mode is that of Cooper, the bitterness and acerbity of whose anti-democratic politics Poe's most closely resembled. Yet in contrast to the elitist japery of Cooper's traveling bachelor in *Notions of the Americans,* for instance— itself modeled on that in a host of popular works of the era by literary travelers from abroad come to dissect and caricature the follies of the great democratic experiment—what distinguishes the anti-democratic comment in comparable works by Poe such as "Mellonta Tauta" or "Some Words with a Mummy" is their sheer essayistic blatancy. In both cases, Poe's correspondents travel in time; and in both cases such journeys supply the barest pretexts for fulminating expressions of a political contempt so profound that it appears simply apropos of nothing. Transmitted across the ages from future or past, the message to history is virtually identical. Democracy is the dominion of King Mob.

"Mellonta Tauta," published in 1848, is set in the year 2848. (The title, roughly translated, allegedly means "it shall come to pass.") The speaker in the tale is Pundita, with a pundit's views on a variety of matters. Since she is a Poe narrator on a fantastic balloon voyage through time and space, these include metaphysics, astronomy, and celestial navigation. Closer to home, however, she also provides some distinctly time-bound remarks on a political phenomenon of a thousand years earlier, now mercifully consigned to ancient history, called participatory democracy. She is astounded, she tells us, to hear from her husband Pundit "that they ancient Americans *governed themselves!*" (*Complete Stories,* 379). She goes on:

> —did anyone ever hear of such an absurdity?—that they existed in a sort of every man-for-himself confederacy, after the fashion of the "prairie dogs" that we read of in fable. He says that they started with the queerest idea conceivable, viz.: that all men are born free and equal—this in the very teeth of the laws of *gradation* so visibly impressed upon all things both in the moral and physical universe. Everyman 'voted,' as they called it—that is to say, meddled with public affairs—until, at length, it was discovered that what is everybody's business is nobody's, and that the "Republic" (so the absurd thing was called) was without a government at all.
>
> (379)

This notion in turn led to the equally "startling discovery that universal suffrage gave opportunity for fraudulent schemes," called at the time popular elections, "by means of which any desired number of votes might at any time be polled, without the possibility of prevention or even detection, by any party which should be merely villainous enough not to be ashamed of the fraud." Further, "a little reflection upon this discovery sufficed to render evident the consequences, which were that rascality *must* predominate—in a word, that a republican government *could* never be anything but a rascally one" (379).

Reform, however, was balked, when "the matter was put to an abrupt issue by a fellow by the name of *Mob,* who took everything into his own hands and set up a despotism, in comparison with which those of the fabulous Zeros and Hellofagabaluses were respectable and delectable." Rumored of foreign origins, "this Mob," we are told further, "is said to have been the most odious of all men that ever incumbered the heart. He was a giant in stature—insolent, rapacious, filthy; had the gall of a bullock, with the heart of a hyena and the brains of a peacock" (379).

Fortunately, his own chaotic energies insured his eventual self-extinction. Still, the speaker notes from her position of future enlightenment, "he had his uses, as everything has, however vile, and taught mankind a lesson which to this day it is in no danger of forgetting—never to run contrary to the natural analogies." And, "as for the "Republicanism" that spawned him, she concludes, "no analogy could be found for it upon the face of the earth—unless we except the case of the 'prairie dogs,' an exception which seems to demonstrate, if anything, that democracy is a very admirable form of government for dogs" (379).

Compare a similarly extended passage from "Some Words with a Mummy," published in the *American Whig Review* of 1845. The titular character is an ancient Egyptian, Count Allmistakeo. Resurrected by a friend of the narrator, one Dr. Ponnonner, after several millennia of sleep, he discourses on myth, metaphysics, art, and architecture. Finally he turns to the historical folly of a certain form of experimental government tried during his time. "Thirteen Egyptian provinces," he recalls bemusedly, "determined all at once to be free, and to set a magnificent example to the rest of mankind. They assembled their wise men, and concocted the most ingenious constitution it is possible to conceive. For a while they managed remarkably well; only their habit of bragging was prodigious. The thing ended, however, in the consolidation of the thirteen states, with some fifteen or twenty others, in the most odious and insupportable despotism that was ever heard of on the face of the earth."

The narrator goes on:

> "I asked what was the name of the usurping tyrant."
> "As well as the Count could recollect, it was *Mob.*"
>
> (*Complete Stories,* 461)

So it goes with Poe's voyagers throughout history. Whether scathingly uttered by the futuristic Pundita of "Mellonta Tauta," or by the back-from-the-dead titular informant of "Some Words with a Mummy," it is all the same with participatory electoral democracy. In fact, the commentaries are virtually word-for-word in their bitter identicalities of phrasing and sentiment. Pursued throughout time and space by the politics of the age, Poe turns about only to confront near the end of his life a despised democratic present. It was as if he could not find enough venues toward the end to register this vision of political apocalypse. History was indeed for Poe a nightmare from which he could not awake. And the nightmare was the omnipresent specter of nineteenth-century American mobocracy.

Do such texts make Poe anything more than an *occasional* political allegorist or barely-disguised anti-democratic editorialist? Certainly one can point elsewhere to a fascination with images of anarchy and mob violence. In his well-known review of Longstreet's *Georgia Sketches,* Poe put himself on record as a partisan of the Southwestern Whig humorists of the era, themselves well-known and applauded for their grotesque, violent depictions of the backwoods bully, the buffoon, the Jacksonian rabble. In a similar southern-frontier vein, the mutineers launching the travails of the titular character in *The Narrative of Arthur Gordon Pym* include a bloodthirsty Negro and a dim, suggestible half-breed.

Again, the obsessiveness of the content becomes markedly pronounced in works of the 1840s. A political reading of "The Masque of the Red Death" suggests that the plague, the contagion threatening at any moment to break down the doors of the castle, may be the Terror. The western geography suggests so. Likewise does the name of the monarch of the western realm, Prince Prospero. Correlatively, in "The Imp of the Perverse," the condemned murderer madman, one of Poe's frequent hyper-cerebral and aestheticized manipulations of the popular press formula of the likeable criminal, transmogrifies before our eyes into the ultimate man of the crowd. Another of Poe's aristocrats of the intellect, preening, disdainful, smugly arrogant and safe among the throng of lesser mortals with his secret knowledge of the perfect crime, he gradually breaks down, descending back into madness precisely as he recounts at length how he has blurted out the confession of his crime after being hunted down and nearly lynched—by a mob attracted by his odd behavior.

Even in works of a primarily aesthetic orientation, such politically-nourished intellectual elitism had always been the core emotion of Poe's persona. The poetic dreamer of "Sonnet—To Science," complaining of his being awakened from an aesthetic afternoon's nap under the tamarind tree, easily became the dark aphorist of the *Marginalia,* decrying the inevitable link between superior genius and popular misunderstanding. (Entries from 1849, the year of his death, include, "The nose of a mob is its imagination. By this, at any time, it can be quietly led" [193]; and, "In drawing a line of distinction between people and a mob, we find that a people aroused to action are a mob; and that a mob, trying to think, subside into a people" [195].) During two decades before the public eye, Poe, the self-proclaimed apostle of supernal, sublimely non-political and non-utilitarian imagination flaunted his aestheticism in a cash-and-carry democracy, all the while eking out its professional literary artist's pittance against page-filling and meeting editorial deadlines.

In a land where the homely charms of democratic art were supposed to mildly instruct and uplift, Beauty—and its cognate Taste—were part of a signature vocabulary brandished by Edgar Poe against his popularly beloved three-name poet-contemporaries—the Henry Wadsworth Longfellow, William Cullen Bryant, and John Greenleaf Whittier—in all the perverse glee with which Richard Nixon used the trademark double V-for-Victory sign in crowds of anti-war protestors. Beauty in a land where art was supposed to popularly instruct and uplift was a barely disguised term for political contempt.

So too, the formula phrase "the heresy of the didactic," erected a blasphemous religion of art against the popular politics of poetry as a celebration of civic virtue and domestic piety. Finding genuine popular celebrity *as a poet* near the end with "The Raven," he even then made box-office success the occasion for making his audience sit through an insulting tutorial on an aestheticism beyond their lumpish concerns for usable meanings and morals.

"The Philosophy of Composition" promises an inside look at the mysteries of the creative process while simultaneously unwriting and demystifying the poem back down to a collocation of technical cheap tricks—the literary equivalent of prostheses. Like the other lecture of the era, "The Poetic Principle," with which it is virtually interchangeable, or the recycled aesthetico-political harangue—suggestively, probably again, as Daniel Hoffman speculates, by "Pundita"—that begins *Eureka,* it is at once a valedictory stump speech on art and a last bitter hoax on the mob, the tasteless, unreasoning rabble to whom he had been beholden throughout his life for his meager living and reputation. Aesthetic defiance, grounded in profoundly political contempt, conquers history itself, the belief that outside the present age, timeless genius will yet prevail.

"I care not whether my work be read now or by posterity. I can afford to wait a century for readers when God himself has waited six thousand years for an observer. I triumph. I have stolen the golden secret of the Egyptians. I will indulge my sacred fury." So asserts "Pundita" in *Eureka,* writing again from the future, by way of a quote from Kepler, writing from the past (*Selected Prose,* 495). Here, as elsewhere, on the basis of his relentless distancing and projecting of a theory of creative genius into a cosmic aestheticism, Poe is frequently cited among his nineteenth-century American contemporaries as a uniquely apolitical writer. In fact, on the basis of such stratagems, he has been thus characterized by such recent commentators as Jonathan Elmer and Terence Whalen within two major books devoted to his career in relation to mass culture and the popular literary marketplace. And within the context of arguments so framed, the assertion is correct. As with his critical evenhandedness in refusing to kowtow to a text because it was British, or puff one because it was American, Poe, while deeply attuned to the commercial politics of literary production, does *not* in fact seem to have been notably a political partisan, nor political in the sense that, aside from the occasional satirical reference, he addressed major party figures and issues, Whig or Democrat. What he surely did possess, at the deepest springs of his art and his personality, was a profound contempt for democracy as a concept, social or aesthetic. Accordingly, at the topical political level, his works swirl with a pathological anti-egalitarianism. At the very least—in such an Irving-like work as "The Unparalleled Adventures of Hans Pfall," for instance—politics is hot air, flatulence, windy chaos; in "Von Kempeln's Discovery," a sendup of the California Gold Rush, it also comprehends herd behavior and money-lust; most frequently, it promises a Hawthornean descent into a netherworld fueled by rum and riot, mindless mob frenzy.

Accounts of Poe's death now at last give us occasion, I think, to rethink just how much, politically, in life and death alike, he was of that turbulent democratic world, and that world of him. Indeed, in 1851, just two years after the fatal episode in Baltimore, the popular artist George Caleb Bingham would produce one of the best known genre paintings of the era: "The County Election." And if already styled in frontier nostalgia, it also carried a contemporary political bite. The scene is all hubbub and bustle, a small town literally mobbed by voters. One man, corpulent, genial, obviously sated with drink while motioning for more, sits facing us, the tipsy beneficiary of the custom of "treating,"—enjoying a limitless free liquor supply, often provided by political candidates for several weeks in advance of an election (Lender, 54-55). Another, too drunk to stand without help, is being dragged to the polling place. Another, sitting on a bench, drunkenly nurses a broken head. A banner above the door proclaims, "The Will of the People the Supreme Law."

To update the cultural connection, Poe, it also turns out, could easily have explained to me why, as recently as twenty years ago, in my hometown of Tuscaloosa, Alabama, it was illegal to sell beer, wine, or liquor on election day. Nor would the historic interest of the conversation have been diminished by the fact that the town in question, the seat of the state university *and* the state hospital for the insane, had also once, in its days as the old frontier capital, flourished as one of the literary epicenters of Southwestern Humor, including service as the fictional site of some the most celebrated episodes in the career of the rapscallionish hero of Johnson Jones Hooper's 1845 *Adventures of Captain Simon Suggs,* itself a roistering, vicious parody of Jacksonian campaign biography. There, well into the twentieth century, the custom of election-day treating had continued, including the usual Democratic party roundup of drunkards and derelicts as repeat voters. Indeed, even Prohibition had done little to forestall the anarchic ritual of subsidized election-day drunkenness, and only with passage of specific statutes did a righteous legislature attempt to assure the public of its desire to free the ballot box from the dominion of that twin-headed monster Demon Rum and King Mob.

It was the final playing out of a political theater of the absurd that Edgar Poe would have understood. It may have been the final act of the political drama that he saw in his last moments on earth. Comatosely selling his vote repeatedly for the price of a drink on election day in the city of his aristocratic forebears, Poe, the ultimate anti-democratic mythopath, had met with the ultimate form of mythopoeic justice. Alcohol was the fa-

tal agent; and a rough-and-tumble nineteenth-century American election was the fatal occasion. Democracy, in a word, was the death of him.

Bibliography

Elmer, Jonathan. *Reading at the Social Limit: Affect, Mass Culture, and Edgar Allan Poe.* Stanford: Stanford University Press, 1995.

Hawthorne, Nathaniel. *The Snow-Image and Uncollected Tales.* Columbus: Ohio State University Press, 1974.

Irving, Washington. *History, Tales, and Sketches.* New York: Library of America, 1983.

Hoffman, Daniel. *Poe Poe Poe Poe Poe Poe Poe.* New York: Doubleday, 1972.

Lender, Mark Edward, and James Kirby Martin. *Drinking in America: A History.* New York: Free Press, 1982.

Lynch, Denis Tilden. *An Epoch and a Man: Martin Van Buren and His Times.* New York: Liveright, 1929.

Peeples, Scott. "Life Writing/Death Writing: Biographical Versions of Poe's Final Hours." *Biography,* 18/4 (1995), 328-38.

Poe, Edgar Allan. *Complete Stories and Poems of Edgar Allan Poe.* Garden City, New York: Doubleday, 1966.

———. *Edgar Allan Poe: Selected Prose, Poetry, and Eureka.* San Francisco: Rinehart, 1950.

———. *Marginalia.* Charlottesville: University Press of Virginia, 1981.

Walsh, John Evangelist. *Midnight Dreary: The Mysterious Death of Edgar Allan Poe.* New York: St. Martins, 2000.

Whalen, Terence. *Edgar Allan Poe and the Masses.* Princeton: Princeton University Press, 1999.

WALT WHITMAN

Robert Adolph (essay date 1995)

SOURCE: Adolph, Robert. "Whitman, Tocqueville, and the Language of Democracy." In *The Delegated Intellect: Emersonian Essays on Literature, Science, and Art in Honor of Don Gifford,* edited by Donald E. Morse, pp. 65-88. New York: Peter Lang, 1995.

[*In the following essay, Adolph compares Tocqueville and Whitman's views on "the relation . . . between democracy, language, and literature."*]

Alexis de Tocqueville's *Democracy in America,* the great mid-nineteenth century analysis of American democracy in the Age of Jackson by an outsider, naturally invites comparison with the classic celebration of the democracy of roughly the same period by a native, *Leaves of Grass,* the first version of which appeared fifteen years after the publication of the second half of *Democracy in America.* Yet there has not been much written on the two works taken together, probably because their general character—Tocqueville's majestic, detached analysis versus Whitman's passionate, unruly kaleidoscope—is so different. A few critics, some of them eminent, have made comparisons, however. Discussion has centered on Tocqueville's famous prediction of the general character of the genuinely American literature soon to come. Some writers, notably F. O. Matthiessen (532-34) and Richard Chase (82-4), have found in Tocqueville's forecast an inspired prophecy of the entire "American Renaissance"—Emerson, Hawthorne, Thoreau, Melville, and Dickinson as well as Whitman. Everyone, though, beginning with Edward Dowden in 1878, has found Tocqueville's remarks to be most applicable to Whitman's theory and practice of literature; indeed, brief acknowledgement of the relationship has become something of a fixture of Whitman criticism.[1] Let us look, then, first at Tocqueville's theory of democratic literature and then at Whitman's, with some sidelong glances at Whitman's practice in the *Leaves.* We shall find the comparison to be more complex and interesting than previously realized chiefly because Tocqueville is both "right" and "wrong" at the same time. In fact, he is most "right" when he is most "wrong," the kind of paradox to which post-structuralist analysis has made us accustomed.

Let me state at the start that I am not trying to find a direct "influence"; there is only one bit of evidence that Whitman ever even heard of Tocqueville.[2] Nor am I interested here in comparing the two men on the great political issues of the day, such as slavery or "woman's rights," which would be another, and considerable, project. Nor is my concern with the historical accuracy of their understanding of American civilization. Rather, I am attempting to define and compare the relation both saw between democracy, language, and literature.

TOCQUEVILLE ON THE LANGUAGE AND LITERATURE OF DEMOCRACIES

Tocqueville's ideas on language, style, and literature are inseparable, of course, from the rest of *Democracy in America.* In the end the book is a discussion of a value, *égalité,* which Tocqueville sees shaping all American culture and which is embodied in a mode of existence called *démocratie.* Tocqueville went to America for ten months in 1831-32 ostensibly to study the American prison system but in reality to examine the world's most advanced form of *démocratie* in order to understand the future, for recent events in France and elsewhere had convinced him that *démocratie* would carry the day everywhere in the Western world.

What Tocqueville meant by *démocratie* has been debated at length by his commentators, for he was not altogether consistent. The concept, however, served him as the key to unlock all aspects of politics and culture in America. Part One is mostly taken up with the effects of *égalité* on political structures; it is best known for its chapter on the tyranny of the majority. Part Two, which is the more relevant for our purposes, may be the first serious analysis of what we now know as mass culture, which Tocqueville regarded as the inevitable outcome of *égalité.* Throughout *Democracy in America* Tocqueville is engaged in the project, common to a conservative cast of mind found in all periods, of describing, and for the most part lamenting, the passing of a presumed organic, hierarchical order held together by traditional customs, obligations, and the like. A new kind of atomistic or individualistic mass culture is to be its replacement.

Tocqueville divides this culture, the subject of Part Two, into "intellect," "sentiment," and "mores." Language is an aspect of "intellect," and like everything else is affected by the central democratic value of *égalité.* In his theory of language, then, Tocqueville is no Cartesian or Chomskyan, that is, he does not understand language as a self-enclosed system based on innate ideas or "deep structures." Rather, language is more than anything else a creation of cultural and social forces, and can only be understood in relation to them, as in the modern discipline of sociolinguistics. Somewhat paradoxically, however, Tocqueville believes like so many conservatives of his type that language is either Correct or barbarous, that there is a proper or privileged form of language, independent of developments in cultural history, from which we depart at our own risk.

Tocqueville argues that democracy has driven language from Correctness in two principal ways, by introducing *instability,* or variations from the privileged norm, and then, as an inevitable corollary of instability, an excessive amount of ill-defined *abstractions.* In the chapter entitled "How American Democracy has Modified the English Tongue" he traces this instability to the influence of spoken on written language, which he claims is stronger in America than elsewhere. Spoken language, of course, changes much more rapidly. The instability of this democratic language is *lexical*—new terms are constantly being introduced "from the jargon of parties, the mechanical arts, or trade" with a loss of their original significance—and *collocational,* for "the Americans often mix their styles in an odd way, sometimes putting words together which, in the mother tongue, are carefully kept apart" (478). More generally, democracy leads to instability with regard to register, the social aspects of language—its levels of colloquialness ("mode"), subject-matter ("field"), and politeness ("tenor").[3] In a democracy there are quite unexpected and "incorrect" juxtapositions of the colloquial and written, subject-matter from the lower and upper classes, and the vulgar and the polite.

Tocqueville attributes this linguistic instability to the dynamism, openness, and formlessness of Jacksonian America, for "the continual restlessness of a democracy leads to endless change of language as of all else" (478). The specific nature of these democratic additions will be determined by that cardinal product of *égalité,* the tyranny of the majority and its special interests:

> Among such peoples the majority lays down the law about language as about all else. Its prevailing spirit is manifest there as elsewhere. Now, the majority is more interested in business than study, in trade and politics than in philosophic speculation or fine writing. Most of the words coined or adopted for its use will bear the marks of these habits; they will chiefly serve to express the needs of industry, the passions, or politics, or the details of public administration.
>
> (478-479)

With their scorn for the classical past, and ignorance of it, the American democrats "will not be at pains to go back to the classics" except when engaged in the understandable but usually misguided and pretentious project of dignifying the mundane pursuits that preoccupy them. "Thus rope-dancers are turned into acrobats and funambulists" (479). Democracies, in their freedom from traditional forms, invent freely:

> Occasionally they pick up forgotten words and put them back into use, or they will borrow a technical term from some particular group and put it into general currency with some particular meaning. Many phrases originally limited to the trade slang of a craft or group have thus become part of the language.
>
> However, the most common innovation is to give an unwonted meaning to an expression already in use. That method is simple, quick, and easy. No learning is needed to make use of it, and ignorance itself can make it easier.
>
> (479)

For Tocqueville, who follows the Enlightenment cult of clear and distinct ideas designated by well-defined terms certified by public opinion, the result of such enlarging and altering of semantic range represents a dangerous descent into ambiguity:

> Since there is no accepted judge, no permanent court to decide the meaning of a word, the phrase is left to wander free . . . But you cannot have a good language without clear terms.
>
> (480)

Dialectal ambiguity inevitably follows lexical. For example, in aristocratic societies there is an abundance of fixed, separate dialects because the classes are separate; thus we have, in England, non-standard vulgar Cockney in clearly understood contrast to standard refined West End or BBC Queen's English. But in a democracy, by definition, there can be none of the dialectal variations which designate social levels. (Regional dialects are, of course, another matter.) The result, however, is in the direction of chaos, not uniformity.

> The rules of style are almost destroyed. Hardly any expressions seem, by their nature, vulgar, and hardly any seem refined . . . Equality is bound to destroy all that is purely conventional and arbitrary in forms of thought.
>
> (481)

In this way democracy leads to linguistic instability, which in turn accords with the Americans' penchant for unclear and indistinct abstract terms, certified by no authority or *Académie.* In a democracy based on *égalité* people can only trust "the unaided powers of their own minds" (482) and are, therefore, plagued by doubts. In such a dynamic, fluid civilization everything is changing so rapidly that ideas must change, too:

> Democratic citizens, then, will often have vacillating thoughts, and so language must be loose enough to leave them play. As they never know whether what they say today will fit the facts of tomorrow, they have a natural taste for abstract terms. An abstract term is like a box with a false bottom; you may put in what ideas you please and take them out again unobserved.
>
> (482)

Thus democratic peoples "increase the number of words of this type . . . and with the most abstract possible meaning . . . and use them on every conceivable occasion, whether needed or not" (482).

Tocqueville's observations on literature and style are an extension of his views on American culture and language. At present, he notes, America has no literature of its own but tamely follows British models. (Typically, he does not cite examples of American books that he has read.) Tocqueville finds the American soil, dominated by a restless but narrow-minded, materialistic, commercial, and Puritan spirit and, above all, by the conformist tyranny of the majority, to be not a fertile one for the creation of literature at all: "We need seek no other reason for the absence of great writers in America so far; literary genius cannot exist without freedom of the spirit, and there is no freedom of the spirit in America" (256). And again:

> So far America has had only a very small number of noteworthy writers, no great historians, and not a single poet. The inhabitants have a sort of prejudice against anything really worthy of the name of literature, and

there are towns of the third rank in Europe which yearly publish more literary works than all the twenty-four states of the Union put together.

(301)

When, despite these adverse circumstances, it arrives, however, American literature, like the American language, will be marked by great instability. Like everything else in American culture, literature is destabilized by the central paradox that Tocqueville finds in democracies generally: the co-existence of total conformity caused by the tyranny of the majority with, at the same time, undisciplined and unprecedented flights coming from isolated individuals lost in the lonely crowd and cut off from the moderation of tradition or a critical community. This withdrawal from society is what Tocqueville means by "individualism" (506-09) and he sees in it a great danger which could lead to the replacement of democracy by a despotism: "I clearly see two tendencies in equality; one turns each man's attention to new thoughts, while the other would induce him freely to give up thinking at all" (436). Like so many others after him, Tocqueville is both appalled and attracted at the effects of this paradox on the literature of democracies. Mostly, in the end, he is appalled, as the temperamentally conservative neo-classic aristocrat in his complex personality contends—here mostly successfully—with the democrat and Romantic:

> By and large the literature of a democracy will never exhibit the order, regularity, skill and art characteristic of aristocratic literature; formal qualities will be neglected or actually despised. The style will often be strange, incorrect, overburdened, and loose, and almost always strong and bold. Writers will be more anxious to work quickly than to perfect details. Short works will be commoner than long books, wit than erudition, imagination than depth. There will be a rude and untutored vigor of thought with great variety and singular fecundity. Authors will strive to astonish more than please, and to stir passions rather than to charm taste.
>
> (474)

Literature, like everything else manufactured in America, is a mass-produced commodity controlled by the demands of the marketplace. To catch the attention and satisfy the greatest number of readers, writers reject traditional forms and tend towards a "strange, incorrect, overburdened and loose style" and a low-brow suspicion of "formal qualities." In the mass market created by the tyranny of the majority the people, having "give[n] up thinking," "like facile forms of beauty, self-explanatory and immediately enjoyable; above all, they like things unexpected and new. Accustomed to the monotonous struggle of practical life, what they want is vivid, lively emotions, sudden revelations, brilliant truths" (474). The opposite condition in American culture making for instability is the tendency for each American, feeling lost or alienated in the lonely crowd, to indulge in "new thoughts," to distrust all traditional, socially sanctioned "forms," linguistic or otherwise:

> Each citizen of a democracy generally spends his time considering the interests of a very insignificant person, namely, himself. If he ever does raise his eyes higher, he sees nothing but the huge apparition of society or the even larger form of the human race. He has nothing between very limited and clear ideas and very general and very vague conceptions; the space between is empty.
>
> (488)

The empty "space between" is the world of stable, complex social forms, the subject matter of aristocratic literature, of Shakespeare, Sir Walter Scott, and Jane Austen. Democratic literature rejects this social space in favour of unstable colossal abstractions on the one hand, or the minutiae of homely life and the obscure truths of isolated hearts on the other.

Tocqueville's neo-classicism is felt most strongly at the start of the powerful chapter, "On Some Sources of Poetic Inspiration in Democracies," in which he considers the likely subjects and themes of an American literature which rejects the "space between." "For me poetry is the search for and representation of the ideal" (483) he begins, arguing, in the central neo-classical tradition, that the poet traditionally makes things better than they are and thereby "ennobles nature" (483). In pragmatic America, however, "the Imagination is not dead, but its chief function is to conceive what may be useful and to portray what is actual" (483) without making it better than it is. Each isolated American finds only an empty space between him- or herself on the one hand and the unifying abstractions or myths of the nation on the other, rejecting the complex hierarchy of intermediate, traditional, stable forms between them—church, class, nobility—to be found in aristocratic cultures. Writers in a democracy therefore turn away from the institutions and ideas of the past, and are left with far fewer subjects for poetry than in an aristocracy. But writers in a democracy also reject the present, since under *égalité* all people are roughly, and monotonously, the same. Here Tocqueville foreshadows the numerous complaints of nineteenth-century American intellectuals that there was nothing to write about in the United States, "no State, in the European sense . . . no sovereign, no court . . . no Epsom nor Ascot!" in Henry James' famous list of the "items of high civilization" unavailable to the young Hawthorne.

With the institutions of the past rejected and those of the present unsuitable, the modern democrats, beginning in the eighteenth century, turn to "inanimate nature" but "it is about themselves that they are really excited" (484). Nature and Self, we now realize, are the privileged subjects of Romantic art, and what Tocqueville has located here, we can see in retrospect, is an important connection between the ideology of Jacksonian democracy and Romanticism. The American Romantic, however, unlike most of his European counter-parts, rejects the past and present and orients himself toward the future of the United States itself. Thus the American does not write about social institutions, since essentially for him there are none, or at least none that are worthy of serious art, and "none of the single, nearly equal, roughly similar citizens of a democracy will do as a subject for poetry, but the nation itself calls for poetic treatment" (485). The future of the entire American adventure is to be the true subject of art. The American Romantic therefore does not write about "inanimate nature" as his European counterpart does, as a place for contemplation, but rather as the stage and raw material of a magnificent epic of conquest. There is "nothing more petty, insipid, crowded with paltry interests—in one word, antipoetic—than the daily life of an American" (485). The American writer can always turn, however, to the national experience as a whole—with the conquest of physical nature its magnificent backdrop—whose fundamental principle is "to recognize in the actions of each individual a trace of the universal and consistent plan by which God guides mankind" (486). If not insipid daily life, then the idea of the infinite possibilities of the free individual becomes the supreme theme of American art and song. And in the end, not merely the American individual, but "the existence of the entire human race, its vicissitudes and its future, thus becomes a fertile theme for poetry" for the American. Just as Emerson, writing at roughly the same time, is to find as his supreme theme "the infinity of the private man," so Tocqueville finds the All in the one. Tocqueville's understanding, however, is filled with dark, Pascalian overtones:

> There is no need to traverse earth and sky to find a wondrous object full of contrasts of infinite greatness and littleness, of deep gloom and amazing brightness, capable at the same time of arousing piety, wonder, scorn, and terror. I have only to contemplate myself; man comes from nothing, passes through time, and disappears forever in the bosom of God. He is seen but for a moment wandering on the verge of two abysses, and then is lost.
>
> If man were wholly ignorant of himself he would have no poetry in him, for one cannot describe what one does not conceive. If he saw himself clearly, his imagination would remain idle and would have nothing to add to the picture. But the nature of man is sufficiently revealed for him to know something of himself and sufficiently veiled to leave much in impenetrable darkness, a darkness in which he ever gropes, forever in vain, forever trying to understand himself.

(487)

By now the Romantic side of Tocqueville has displaced the neo-classic, and he concludes by paying tribute to the arch-Romantics Byron, Chateaubriand, and Lamartine as the true poets of democracy:

> The writers of our time who have so wonderfully portrayed the features of Childe Harold, Rene, and Jocelyn

have not sought to record the actions of an individual, but by exaggeration to illuminate certain dark corners of the human heart.

> Such are the poems of democracy.
> Equality, then, does not destroy all the subjects of poetry.
> It makes them fewer but more vast.

(487)

WHITMAN AND TOCQUEVILLE ON DEMOCRACY AND ITS DILEMMAS

Whitman, who like his mentor Emerson boasted of his contradictions, was anything but a systematic thinker, and his ideas on language and literature in relation to democracy cannot therefore be summarized in as orderly a fashion as Tocqueville's. On the other hand, Whitman had much more than Tocqueville to say on the subject, both explicitly in his prefaces and other prose works, and implicitly throughout the many editions of *Leaves of Grass*.

Démocratie, for Tocqueville, was a neutral term, an analytical concept by means of which he dissected its foremost contemporary example, American politics and culture. Tocqueville "saw in America more than America" (19). "Democracy," for Whitman, was not merely descriptive, but was, as he said many times, an essentially "religious" notion denoting an ideal value or mode of existence. Like Tocqueville, Whitman saw democracy as fated to conquer the world. But whereas for Tocqueville (most dramatically in his famous "Author's Introduction") the triumph of democracy was an outcome of inexorable forces operating through specific historical events, for Whitman in his poems democracy was more a metaphysical necessity arising out of the human condition itself, especially the universality of sexuality and death which makes everyone equal. Unlike Tocqueville, Whitman, in *Leaves of Grass*, shows little interest in the actual workings and structure of democratic American politics or the great issues of the day. For example, in *Drum-Taps*, the poems drawn from Whitman's experiences as a nurse in the Civil War, there is nothing of the attacks, which we do find in the prose, on the political ineptness and injustices, especially slavery, that led up to the struggle, or even on the evils of the institution of war itself, the sort of thing we find in the war poetry of a Melville or a Wilfred Owen; instead, we find rather optimistic meditations on the meaning for the future of democracy of the suffering of the soldiers. Although there is some fine journalistic writing in *Leaves*, as Carroll Hollis has shown (*Language* 204-32), there was a split in Whitman between the topical journalist of the political prose and the visionary prophet of the poetry and the prose prefaces to it. It is in the prose that he considers specific issues and the general political culture of his own day, and for the most part he is severely critical, especially in pieces like *Democratic Vistas* and the posthumous *The Eighteenth Presidency!*.

For Tocqueville *démocratie* refers to the present state of affairs in the United States; democracy, for Whitman, is an ideal to be realized in the American future, although it is undoubtedly fermenting at all times in the present national psyche. Especially in the *Leaves* it is an exalted mode of existence to be achieved through an erotic and mystic union of individuals with society and the natural world. As with Tocqueville the essence of democracy is equality, but in Whitman equality is mystical (a term which all critics of Whitman sooner or later must confront) as well as political. As in all mysticisms there is a breakdown of hierarchies and distinctions. These include obvious political structures of rank and class (Whitman, alas, pays little attention to the issue of race). Whitman also proclaims the end of equally fundamental (if not as overtly "political") distinctions such as those designating the male superior to the female (there is a strong feminist and even androgynous element in at least the early Whitman), heterosexuality superior to homosexuality (the *Calamus* group), the soul superior to (or even distinct from) the body (the sexual radical of *Song of Myself* and the *Children of Adam* group), the individual set apart from and superior to Nature (the passages of polymorphous union with the earth in *Song of Myself*), language above and distinct from whatever language describes (the organicist and modernist aesthetic of the 1855 preface), the teacher superior to the student ("He most honors my style who learns under it to destroy the teacher . . . I teach straying from me, yet who can stray from me?" [84-85]), and life or sex superior to, or even distinguishable from, death (the great erotic Liebestod sections in *Out of The Cradle Endlessly Rocking* and *When Lilacs Last in the Dooryard Bloom'd*; Whitman, as one recent critic has put it, "makes sex deathly, so too he makes death sexy" [Breitwieser, 124]). With the end of such Blakean mind forg'd manacles there will be an end to inward and external oppression and the beginning of an age of true liberation as the individual becomes one with the mystical democratic body of the infinite in which there are no longer the usual categories of time or space: "It avails not, time nor place—distance avails not / I am with you, you men and women of a generation, or ever so many generations hence," chants Whitman in *Crossing Brooklyn Ferry* (160). His is a mystical vision of a New Jerusalem in which the most universally accepted of the hierarchies governing our ideas of existence and perception are to be dismantled and seen for what they are, as arbitrary, socially defined linguistic categories.

Yet both writers, despite their very different understandings of democracy, saw the same problems at the heart of it, although Tocqueville unlike Whitman did not see any solutions in the long run. The first of these problems turns on the concept of the clash between "the individual" and "society" that characterizes both Enlightenment and Romantic discourse. In Tocqueville, as we have seen, there is the dread of the tyranny of the majority and the "conformity" of modern, materialistic mass culture. Whitman, especially in the political prose, can be just as harsh as Tocqueville on the emptiness, greed, and mindlessness of life in the United States. The contradiction between the possibilities opened up for the individual by democracy and the "mass, or lump character" of democratic conformist culture is in fact for Whitman the supreme problem of American political culture. In *Democratic Vistas* he attempts to reconcile the two:

> First, let us see what we can make out of a brief, general, sentimental consideration of political democracy, and whence it has arisen, with regard to some of its current features, as an aggregate, and as the basic structure of our future literature and authorship. We shall, it is true, quickly and continually find the origin-idea of the singleness of man, individualism, asserting itself, and cropping forth, even from the opposite ideas. But the mass, or lump character, for imperative reasons, is to be ever carefully sought and weighed, borne in mind, and provided for. Only from it, and from its proper regulation and potency, comes the other, comes the chance of individualism. The two are contradictory, but our task is to reconcile them.
>
> (216-17)

The primacy of the reconciliation to the *Leaves* is evident in the "inscription" which Whitman appended to the very beginning of the 1867 edition:

> One's self I sing, a simple separate person,
> Yet utter the word Democratic, the word En-Masse.
>
> (1)

The second menace to democracy for both Tocqueville and Whitman is the danger of democratic societies disintegrating as individual citizens pursue their own selfish interests at the expense of the collectivity. The final chapters of *Democracy in America* are marked by a near-apocalyptic vision of American democracy splintering apart as isolated individuals turn to a despot, just as the French had turned to Napoleon after their revolution.[4] Whitman throughout his career in effect proposed extraordinary ways to avoid disintegration undreamt of by Tocqueville. Where Tocqueville looked to "associations" and his famous "self-interest rightly understood" the sexual mystic Whitman hailed "adhesive love" and "the love of comrades" and, paradoxically, "personalism" or "individualism," or Romantic subjectivity expanding to infinity. "Individualism" as we have seen meant something very different, and much more ominous, to Tocqueville, who in the final analysis did not see a way out of the contradiction between individualism—for Tocqueville a kind of self-centeredness peculiar to democracies—and the need for cohesion. Here

Tocqueville's pessimism puts him closer to the writers of "Romances"—Hawthorne, Melville, Poe—than to Whitman, or at least to Whitman of the *Leaves.*

This is not the place to discuss these concepts in detail. What is relevant to our purpose here is, first, Whitman's most un-Tocquevillian but very Romantic insistence throughout his career that ultimately democracy can be saved from its internal contradictions, but only through the efforts of its artists, especially its poets. This task, in fact, is what he saw himself as inaugurating (he would say "promulging") in both the political prose and the poems. The *Leaves* can be read through its many editions as a large-scale instance of that familiar Romantic genre, The Growth of a Poet's Mind, with the 1855 preface, as so many critics have suggested or argued, Whitman's version of Wordsworth's Preface to the *Lyrical Ballads,* where the claims for a reformed poetry based on the language of common people as the salvation of humanity are almost as extravagant. Whitman has also been seen by Ronald Duerkson (59-60) as an extreme example of another Romantic and equally un-Tocquevillian commonplace, the artist as Unacknowledged Legislator of the World. In Whitman's democratic American variants on the Old Testament, Wordsworth, and Shelley, the artist is a seer issuing Jeremiads on the current political scene in the political prose while proclaiming in the poetry the New Jerusalem to come filled with the dignity of the heretofore marginalized common persons enumerated, in all their chaotic, numberless specificity, in the rolling parallelistic catalogues of the inspired prophet—the stance he is seen taking by virtually all his critics. Tocqueville, too, is rightly praised as a prophet—but surely not the same visionary sort as Whitman.

The Literature of Democracy

To accomplish his extraordinary goals Whitman's ideal American democratic artist-prophet must re-write (in Harold Bloom's sense, "misread") the literature of the past, which is no longer valid for the new order of things. Whitman begins the 1855 preface to the *Leaves*—by far the most important discussion of his aesthetic—with a serene assertion that he has no anxieties about influence: "America does not repel the past or what it has produced under its forms or amid other politics or the idea of castes or the old religions" (711). The implication is clear: ancient "forms" produced "amid other politics" and "old religions" must be welcomed—and completely transformed and "misread." As Tocqueville saw, democracy drives the Americans unwittingly to follow the radical skepticism of a Descartes, and deny tradition and the classical precursors. "This turn of mind soon leads them to a scorn of forms, which they take as useless, hampering veils put between them and truth" (430). Tocqueville's observation might explain Whitman's frequent extreme Romantic or proto-Post-Modernist assertions that his writings are not aesthetic productions at all, and that meaning lies in things themselves which he is presenting unmediated by technique. It could also explain the tendency in Whitman (and so many American authors ever since) to "make it new," to be starting out afresh formally and thematically down an untraveled open road.

The general character of this new democratic literature Tocqueville foresaw well before the event. Tocqueville's predictions seem uncannily accurate, especially for the earlier Whitman. Tocqueville predicts one of the most important personas in *Song of Myself,* the barbaric yawper, defying Correctness by deliberately introducing instability in the form of lexis "from the jargon of parties, the mechanical arts, or trade" (478), startling collocations, and the mixing up of registers by jumbling together the high-falutin' and the colloquial. Another feature of democratic style is its love of vague abstractions, for which Whitman is notorious; often, as Tocqueville says, they "give an unwonted meaning to an expression already in use" (479) (Whitman's "promulge") or consist of preposterous or pretentious half-foreign borrowings ("éclaircise," "exposé" as a verb, "ma femme"). Whitman scorns or misreads the classical past and ignores decorum, mixing up dialects. "The rules of style are almost destroyed. Hardly any expressions seem, by their nature, vulgar, and hardly any seem refined" (481). There is no "order, regularity, skill and art" (474) of the type associated with aristocratic literature. "Formal qualities" are "neglected or actually despised;" as Whitman warns in *A Backward Glance O'er Travelled Roads* (1888), "No one will get at my verses who insists on viewing them as a literary performance, or attempt at such performance, or as aiming mainly toward art or aestheticism" (*Leaves,* 574). Tocqueville warns that "style will often be strange, incorrect, overburdened, and loose, and almost always strong and bold" (474)—adjectives surely applicable to *Song of Myself* and much else in the *Leaves,* at least as it must have struck readers in 1855. Much of Whitman's writing, of course, is carefully wrought. Tocqueville, however, is right as regards the *effect* of Whitman's writing. Tocqueville's "rude and untutored vigor of thought with great variety and singular fecundity," "authors will strive to astonish more than please," and "things unexpected and new . . . vivid, lively emotions, sudden revelations, brilliant truths" (474) could all have come out of the 1855 preface as Whitman's description of his own art, and the democratic art-work of the future. Then there is Tocqueville's observation that American literature oscillates "between very limited and clear ideas and very general and vague conceptions" (488). "The space between"—the world of what Whitman labeled "feudal" authors like Shakespeare, Scott, and Tennyson respected by him but seen as precursors to be rejected by the American Romantic democrat, for whom social hierarchy has no meaning—"is empty." Thus *Leaves of Grass,* and especially *Song of Myself,* oscillates between the so often exquisitely observed particulars of the catalogues, historical vignettes, and journalistic interpolated incidents on the one hand, and metaphysical speculation on the other. In Emerson's famous *mot,* Whitman reads like a "remarkable mixture of the *Bhagvat-Geeta* and the *New York Herald*" (quoted in Matthiessen, 526). What is missing is any complex, sustained social encounter. Finally there is Tocqueville on the sources of inspiration for American poets, and here he is equally prophetic. Whitman's subject matter is indeed Nature and, above all, the Self, rather than the workings of society. It is oriented, as Whitman says so many times, toward the future, and the future of the United States rather than concrete social experiences. "The United States themselves are essentially the greatest poem," Whitman announces near the start (711) of the 1855 preface. As we have seen, this is how, according to Tocqueville, the American artist escapes from the essentially unpoetical quality of actual American society. In a democracy, both the past and the present are rejected in favour of abstractions and an undefined future. In the end, in Tocqueville's prophecy of American themes the individual expands to become identified not only with the future of the nation but with the entire human race, and indeed, the universe, which is what happens to the narrator—or the principal narrator—toward the end of *Song of Myself* as the democratic American muse soars into the infinite. To repeat Tocqueville's summary: "Equality, then, does not destroy all the subjects of poetry. It makes them fewer, but more vast" (487).

There is, of course, more to Whitman than the strident persona which dominates *Song of Myself.* Like most of the significant American writers Whitman apparently fell into moments of self-doubt, alienation and loneliness. "Not only," says Tocqueville, "does democracy make men forget their ancestors, but also clouds their view of their descendents and isolates them from their contemporaries. Each man is forever thrown back on himself alone, and there is a danger that he may be shut up in the solitude of his own heart" (508). Each individual will seem insignificant: "Each citizen of a democracy generally spends his time considering the interests of a very insignificant person, namely, himself" (488) of no consequence against the democratic egalitarian masses, who show little interest in subtle poetry like Whitman's, despite his hope to be read by them. Tocqueville here as always is struck by the sadness underlying the bustling surface of Jacksonian America; he is, as we have seen, the prophet of Riesman's lonely crowd of mass culture. Inevitably the lack of social recognition must lead to self-doubt. This is Whitman the "solitary singer" to be found in some of his greatest poems, such as *Out of the Cradle Endlessly Rocking* and *When Lilacs Last in the Dooryard Bloom'd.* The poignant *loci classici* of such moments are, of course, in the collections entitled *Sea-Drift* and *Whispers of Heav-*

enly Death, in poems which draw upon, or so his biographers conjecture, a personal crisis in the late 1850s. For example, in *As I Ebb'd With the Ocean of Life* the persona could not be more unlike that of the dominant (though by no means the only) one in *Song of Myself*:

> O baffled, balk'd, bent to the very earth,
> Oppress'd with myself that I have dared to open my
> 　mouth,
> Aware now that amid all that blab whose echoes re-
> coil
> 　on me I have not once had the least idea who or
> 　what I am,
> But that before all my arrogant poems the real Me
> 　stands yet untouch'd, untold, altogether unreach'd,
> Withdrawn far, mocking me with mock-congratulatory
> 　signs and bows,
> Because I have dared to open my mouth to sing at all.
>
> 　　　　　　　　　　　　　　　　　　(254)

As with so many major American writers from Benjamin Franklin on, Whitman's defense against the tyranny of the majority may well have been to present an unstable, shifting set of personas; despite Whitman's insistence that his book is identical with himself it is these, rather than the "real" Walt Whitman, if there is such a thing, that we meet in *Leaves of Grass.* In Tocqueville's unforgettable aphorism, "In ages of democracy all things are unstable, but the most unstable of all is the human heart" (582).

Tocqueville is not ordinarily regarded as a literary critic but the depth of his analysis and prophecy put his writings, to my mind, equal to the greatest criticism of both the language and themes of American literature of his time; his only real competition before Whitman's own magnificent preface of 1855 is, the theorizing of Poe apart, Emerson's remarkably similar and even more famous prediction of the themes and styles of forthcoming American literature in, among other places, "Nature," "The American Scholar," and "The Poet" (and Emerson, of course, is Whitman's first sympathetic reader). What makes Tocqueville's achievement all the more remarkable is that, unlike Emerson, he is analyzing tendencies with which he has not much sympathy, for in his literary criticism, the tastes of the neo-classic aristocrat win out, for the most part, over those of the Romantic democrat. What Tocqueville sees as alarming extravagances Whitman (and the rest of the American Renaissance) praise and use.

The Nature of Democratic Language

Tocqueville's uneasiness, however, for all his perception and brilliant prophecy of the surface of Whitman's writing, indicates that he has not grasped what is most fundamental about an art like Whitman's. Tocqueville is "right" and "wrong" at the same time. Since his fundamental asumptions are so different from Whitman's,

Tocqueville's misunderstanding seems, in retrospect, inevitable. At any rate, he can hardly be blamed for misreading literature which did not exist in his own time.

Although they appear to be in agreement about the general *characteristics* of the literature of democracies, their evaluations of them are very different. Perhaps because Whitman's idea of democracy was so different from Tocqueville's, his ideas about language are, too. The result is an art whose greatest effects depend on violations not merely of Decorum, as Tocqueville foresaw and feared, but rational categories of experience itself. To be sure, it is perhaps stretching things to argue that so intuitive a writer as Whitman had a "theory" of language, or of anything else. Nevertheless there are recurring concepts throughout his many writings on the subject of language which are not only of great interest in their own right, but are opposed to Tocqueville's.[5]

We repeatedly find perhaps the most important differences from Tocqueville in the 1855 preface and *Song of Myself*. For the neo-classic Tocqueville literary language is mimetic, that is, it imitates a transcendent hierarchy. But for Whitman, or at least the pre-Civil War Whitman, there is no such order. Not only American society, but the entire universe is democratic, a plenitude of equality or "kosmos," as is Whitman himself. As the earlier quotation from *A Backward Glance* denying that his writings should be seen as aesthetic productions suggests, there can be no such thing as literary, as distinguished from non-literary, language to describe such an exuberant, disorderly world; such a distinction, however, is simply assumed by Tocqueville. Ultimately probably no language can describe whatever Reality, democratic and disorderly or not, there might be Out There. Like many Romantics and all writers with mystic tendencies Whitman frequently laments the insufficiency of language to convey our experience of the world, and especially the instances of our most heightened awareness of it. As a writer Whitman's way out of this conundrum is—apparently following Emerson—to let this world speak for itself.

> All truths inhere in all things,
> They neither hasten their own delivery nor resist it,
> They do not need the obstetric forceps of the surgeon,
> The insignificant is as big to me as any,
> (What is less or more than a touch?)
>
> Logic and sermons never convince,
> The damp of the night drives deeper into my soul.
>
> (58)

For Emerson, as for Coleridge and other Romantics before him, the resulting expression would somehow be unified and "organic." Whitman often echoes organicist theory in the 1855 preface. For example (the most often quoted):

> The rhyme and uniformity of perfect poems show the free growth of metrical laws and bud from them as un-

erringly and loosely as lilacs or roses on a bush, and shed the perfume impalpable to form.

> (716)

Whitman, however, in the same preface and elsewhere goes beyond organicist Romanticism as well as Tocqueville's neo-classicism. Democratic expression, in the end, is random, just like the blooming, buzzing confusion of the United States celebrated in Whitman's catalogues. Nothing is more suitable as a proper subject for literature than anything else, including the notorious "beetles rolling balls of dung" (52) and "the scent of these arm-pits" (53). "Each precise object or condition or combination or process exhibits a beauty," as he puts it in the 1855 preface (723). As can be seen in his subsequent influence on such quintessential Modernists as Ezra Pound, Hart Crane, and Alan Ginsburg, Whitman stands at the boundary between Romanticism and a Modernist or even "Post-Modern" sensibility. What Tocqueville can only perceive as instability and lack of proper taste is really in Whitman a serious attempt to create the basis for a literature suitable for the very same modern world that Tocqueville is predicting.

Whitman also departs from Tocqueville in his progressivism, that is, the rejection of an a priori ahistorical Correctness in favor of the idea that language is constantly evolving, just as America is evolving. (The thought of Whitman, who at times fancied himself a Hegelian, is characteristically nineteenth-century in its evolutionary cast). This point of view is implicit, of course, in the poetry, especially the early *Leaves*. All of Whitman's ideas about language are informed by it. For example, in the writings on language in the notebooks later edited by Horace Traubel in *An American Primer* we find, after an enthusiastic survey of the forthcoming enrichment of English wrought by American democracy:

> These States are rapidly supplying themselves with new words, called for by new occasions, new facts, new politics, new combinations.—Far plentier [!] additions will be needed, and, of course, will be supplied.
>
> (Because it is a truth that) the words continually used among the people are, in numberless cases, not the words used in writing, or recorded in the dictionaries by authority.—There are just as many words in daily use, not inscribed in the dictionary, and seldom or never in any print.—Also, the forms of grammar are never persistently obeyed, and cannot be.
>
> The Real Dictionary will give all words that exist in use, the bad words as well as any.—The Real Grammar will be that which declares itself a nucleus of the spirit of the laws, with liberty to all to carry out the spirit of the laws, even by violating them, if necessary.—The English language is grandly lawless like the race who use it—or, rather, breaks out of the little laws to enter truly the higher ones.
>
> (*An American Primer* 5-6)

Whitman's kind of progressivist understanding of language anticipates that of recent literary theory, much of which also celebrates indeterminacy by exposing hierarchical categories of all sorts, including the ones implicit in such concepts as Correctness, Decorum, The Aesthetic, or The Literary, as well as such heretofore commonsensical distinctions as those between Author, Narrator, Text, and Reader. These topics, as one might expect, have been much discussed in recent Whitman criticism, as if fulfilling, at least for *Leaves of Grass,* Tocqueville's prophetic emphasis on the instability of American life and language.[6]

Like Tocqueville, Whitman saw that democracy required a new kind of expression. American writers and speakers must "make it new." For Whitman the endlessly evolving character of his conception of democracy meant that democratic language, too, would forever be evolving, forever an "experiment" like *Leaves of Grass* itself:

> This subject of language interests me—interests me: I never quite get it out of my mind. I sometimes think the *Leaves* is only a language experiment—that it is an attempt to give the spirit, the body, the man, new words, new potentialities of speech—an American, a cosmopolitan (the best of America is the best cosmopolitanism) range of self-expression. The new world, the new times, the new peoples, the new vista, need a tongue according—yes, what is more, will have such a tongue—will not be satisfied until it is evolved.

> (*An American Primer* viii)

Whitman's implication is that "the new times, the new peoples, the new vista" will never "be satisfied." "Vista"—the impossibility of closure and infinite expansion of consciousness—is in the very nature of democracy itself, as Whitman understands it, and is its greatest attribute. Whitman the Romantic/Democratic Bard sees his writings as the way to arousing Americans to their linguistic potential—and thereby to their potential in general. Without a new sense of language there can be no democracy, and vice versa; at least in certain moods Whitman, as we have seen, thought of democracy and the United States, and ultimately the entire world, post-structuralist fashion, as itself a kind of infinitely significant "text," "essentially the greatest poem." The poet obviously becomes of enormous importance as himself an indeterminate text equivalent to the text of the nation. At the same time, though, Whitman, especially, as we have seen, in his more mystical moments, will not "be satisfied," and insists that language, whether "speech" or "writing," is in the end inadequate to encompass the democratic plenitude of the "kosmos," and that it is wrong to "conceive too much of articulation":

> Speech is the twin of my vision, it is unequal to measure itself,

> It provokes me forever, it says sarcastically,
> *Walt you contain enough, why don't you let it out then?*

> Come now I will not be tantalized, you conceive too much of articulation.

> (55)

Tocqueville, on the other hand, neither valorizes the evolutionary and infinitely expansive tendency of democratic language nor sees "articulation" as in the end impossible, but prefers to have language fixed by a priori canons of Correctness which will presumably suffice to articulate everything. Where Whitman sees in the language of democracy ever-expanding "vista," Tocqueville, as I have argued, sees simply instability and chaos arising from the mixing of classes and the lack of standards deriving from the dismissal or ignorance of Tradition in the conformist culture of the lonely crowd.

> I have no fear that the poetry of democratic peoples will be found timid or that it will stick too close to the earth. I am much more afraid that it will spend its whole time getting lost in the clouds and may finish up describing an entirely fictitious country. I am alarmed at the thought of too many immense, incoherent images, overdrawn descriptions, bizarre effects, and a whole fantastic breed of brain-children who will make one long for the real world.

> (489)

Such a statement could serve as a description, albeit a very unsympathetic one, of Whitman's often fantastic art. Perhaps, however, if Tocqueville could have known about the Stalinist Newspeak, Fascist euphemisms, and one-dimensional obfuscations of the "real world" of today analyzed by the likes of Orwell, Arendt, and Marcuse he would have placed a higher value on the vigorous, infinitely evolving language of the democracy which he so acutely predicted and Whitman celebrated and, at his best, exemplified. On the other hand, if Whitman could have seen the excesses of Romantic democratic permissiveness combined paradoxically with the timid lack of "vista" in today's conformist, commercially driven mass culture foreseen by both himself and Tocqueville he, in his turn, might have moved closer to Tocqueville's less celebratory attitude toward the language of democracy.

Notes

1. For discussions of Tocqueville as literary critic and prophet of democratic American literature, usually with an emphasis on Whitman, see Dowden, Harrison, Cestre, Read, West, and Kummings.

2. Stovall (123-24) notes: "In Bucke's list of Whitman's clippings, No. 6 is a newspaper review of De Tocqueville's *The Old Regime and the Revolu-*

tion, translated by John Bonner (Harper, 1956). Whitman dated the clipping October 1856 and wrote at the head of it, 'Deserves Re-Reading.' In passages quoted by the reviewer, Tocqueville emphasizes the danger of despotism in nations that most love freedom."

3. I am making use here of the sociolinguistic theory and terminology derived chiefly from British scholars such as J. R. Firth, M. A. K. Halliday, and A. McIntosh. For an overview see Gregory and Carroll.

4. For an extended discussion of Tocqueville's apocalyptic pessimism (with some discussion of his prophecies for American literature) see Kaledin, 3-38.

5. For a biography of Whitman's writings on language see Southard.

6. On these topics see Hollis, Pease, Breitweiser, Bauerlein, and Larson.

Works Cited

Bauerlein, Mark. "The Written Orator of Song of Myself." *Walt Whitman Quarterly Review* 3 (1986): 1-14.

Breitwieser, Mitchell Robert. "Who Speaks in Whitman's Poems?" *The American Renaissance Reconsidered*: New Dimensions. Ed. Harry R. Garvin. Lewisburg: Bucknell University Press, 1983. 124.

Cestre, Charles. "*Alexis de Tocqueville, témoin et juge de la civilisation américaine.*" *Revue des cours et des conférences* 35 (1934): 275-88.

Chase, Richard. *Walt Whitman Reconsidered.* New York: William Sloane, 1955.

Dowden, Edward. "The Poet of Democracy: Walt Whitman." *Studies in Literature.* London: Kegan, Paul, 1878, 468-523. Reprinted in part in *Critical Essays on Walt Whitman.* Ed. James Woodress. Boston: G. K. Hall, 1983. 99-108.

Duerkson, Roland. "Shelley's 'Defence' and Whitman's 1855 Preface: A Comparison." *Walt Whitman Review* 10 (1964): 59-60.

Emerson, Ralph Waldo. *The Complete Works of Ralph Waldo Emerson.* Ed. Edward E. Emerson. New York: Houghton Mifflin, 1903-04.

Gregory, Michael, and Susan Carroll. *Language and Situation.* London: Faber, 1978.

Harrison, Katherine. "A French Forecast of American Literature." *South Atlantic Quarterly* 25 (1926): 350-60.

Hollis, Carroll. *Language and Style in "Leaves of Grass".* Baton Rouge: Louisiana University Press, 1983.

————. "Is There a Text in This Class?" *Walt Whitman Quarterly Review* 3 (1986): 15-22.

Kaledin, Arthur. "Tocqueville's Apocalypse: Culture, Politics, and Freedom in *Democracy in America.*" *Tocqueville Review* 7 (1985): 3-38.

Kummings, Donald. "The Poetry of Democracies: Tocqueville's Aristocratic View." *Comparative Literature Studies* 11 (1974): 306-19.

Larson, Kerry. *Whitman's Drama of Consensus.* Chicago: Chicago University Press, 1988.

Matthiessen, F. O. *American Renaissance: Art and Expression in the Age of Emerson and Whitman.* New York: Oxford University Press, 1941.

Pease, Donald. "Blake, Crane, Whitman, and Modernism: A Poetics of Pure Possibility." *PMLA* 96 (1981), 64-85.

Read, Herbert. "De Tocqueville on Art in America." *Adelphi* 23 (1946), 9-13.

Southard, Sherry. "Whitman and Language: An Annotated Bibliography." *Walt Whitman Quarterly Review* 2 1984), 30-49.

Stovall, Floyd. *The Foreground of Leaves of Grass.* Charlottesville: University of Virginia Press, 1974.

Tocqueville, Alexis de. *Democracy in America.* Trans. George Lawrence. Ed. J. P. Mayer. New York: Doubleday, 1969.

Virtanen, R. "Tocqueville on a Democratic Literature." *French Review* 23 (1942), 214-22.

West, Paul. "Literature and Politics II: Tocqueville on the Literature of Democracies." *Essays in Criticism* 12 (1962), 257-72.

Whitman, Walt. *An American Primer.* Minneapolis: Holy Cow! Press, 1987.

————. *Democratic Vistas.* Works, II. New York: Funk and Wagnells, 1968.

————. *The Eighteenth Presidency!* Ed. Edward Grier. Lawrence, KA: The University of Kansas Press, 1956.

————. *Leaves of Grass.* Eds. Sculley Bradley and Harold Blodgett. New York: Norton, 1973.

Taylor Hagood (essay date summer 2003)

SOURCE: Hagood, Taylor. "Hair, Feet, Body, and Connectedness in 'Song of Myself.'" *Walt Whitman Quarterly Review* 21, no. 1 (summer 2003): 25-34.

[*In the following essay, Hagood contends that analyzing Whitman's symbolic representation of the connections between the parts of the human body in "Song of Myself" offers insights into the poet's seemingly paradoxical support for both "individuality and democracy."*]

'I reject nothing,' says Walt.

If that is so, one must be a pipe organ at both ends, so everything runs through.

—D. H. Lawrence[1]

A central paradox in Walt Whitman's "Song of Myself" is its simultaneous championing of individuality and democracy. On one hand, Whitman positions the individual as the predominant vehicle and measuring stick of perception, judgment, and value. At the same time, he promotes fluidity, boundlessness, and connectedness characterized by ideals of democratic social equality. Scholars have long identified this paradox, but its resolution has been elusive: reconciling Whitman's extreme focus on the individual to his equally intense focus on the many requires some difficult imaginative machinations.[2] Yet negotiating this problem is central to the poem's political, social, sexual, racial, and linguistic aspects.

One key to understanding Whitman's complicated presentation of "individuality versus democracy" lies in his depiction and positioning of body in "Song of Myself." Particularly important is his alignment of the human body along horizontal and vertical axes. Whitman portrays the head and the feet as the body's extreme connection points. These points (head and feet) may be the boundaries of a fluid and consolidated entity, or they may represent extremes that serve not to solidify but rather to fragment and disconnect the body and the self. Connectedness and consolidation embody Whitman's democratic ideal and are attainable only when the head and feet successfully make contact with each other and with the earth. This connectedness occurs most obviously in a horizontal orientation of the body, a position that Whitman associates with death and birth, the connection points of the entrance into and the exit out of life. Whitman characterizes the "middle" of the body and of life in the form of the nondemocratic and more individually significant vertical orientation. Connectedness may be achieved in vertical orientation when the remote contact point, the head, connects with the direct contact point, the feet, by means—oddly enough—of hair, which may reach from head to foot.

Whitman uses images of "feet" and "hair" throughout the poem to reconcile the individual-democratic/vertical-horizontal ideals. Connectedness results from a consolidated line of connection both vertically and horizontally. When this connection is inconstant or broken, the individual becomes isolated from the many, and the ideals of simultaneous individuality and democracy—which must exist together in Whitman's figuration—fail to be realized. Whitman drives his point home at the poem's conclusion by positioning himself as the horizontally-oriented point of contact with which the reader must gain connectedness, metaphorically letting

his or her hair down by the "extending" process of reading the poem. In the earth of the poem as well as the literal earth, Whitman awaits the reader's arrival and the historical, political, sexual, and social democratizing that accompanies that arrival.

The first step in understanding Whitman's paradox is understanding his dividing and fragmenting of self. Mark Maslan has accurately identified the importance of division in the poem. Maslan discusses scholars who posit "division" as a problem in Whitman's work because they see division as standing at odds with Whitman's democratic effort and unity. These critics attempt to resolve the problem, but Maslan notes that they fail to understand and apply the fact that "division is a vital principle of Whitman's poetics." Maslan then opens an important door in considering the function of division in Whitman's poetical rhetoric:

> Rethinking division in this manner—as enabling rather than debilitating—would involve re-examining a whole series of relationships in Whitman in which critics have seen union as the organizing principle: the relationship between body and soul, body and text, form and content, man and man, people and government. And, of course, it would involve reassessing Whitman's view of Union itself. This task remains for future studies.[3]

Whitman depicts identity as divided, with *I* standing in opposition to *myself.* This split appears in the very first line, "I celebrate myself."[4] Whitman fills in the division between the objectified *I* and the objectified *myself* with the action of celebration, and, in later versions of the poem, of singing. This depiction of the self anticipates twentieth-century writers who theorize self, especially the crisis of split-identity, such as Jacques Lacan and Jean-Paul Sartre.[5] Mark Bauerlein discusses Whitman's split of self in terms of Lacan's "mirror stage," extending the division of self and othered self to include "the role language plays in frustrating (as opposed to facilitating) self-expression":

> That is, along with the problem of overcoming inherited styles to express a distinctively American self, and the problem of allowing a repressed unconscious identity to emerge in a way that exceeds euphoric by short-lived catharsis, Whitman also faces the dilemma of wielding an intractable, objectifying form—language—to represent a vigorous, transient person—a subject.[6]

Bauerlein explains that the "obvious way to obviate the alienating separation between a subject and the words it uses to manifest itself is to assert a mystical connection between the two," and so "when, in his prose disquisitions, Whitman ascribes an occult bond between self and word, he assigns to language spiritual qualities rather than bringing the self down to rhetorical or empirical levels" (135). This "occult bond" between the self and the word constitutes a rich and ambiguous middle ground of connectedness in which the subject and language intermix.

Although, as Bauerlein argues, "Whitman's body . . . [is] a self-reflexive text whose meaning and value precede linguistic formulation, . . . a corporeal identity in disregard of linguistic difference [that] affords auto-tellic, auto-erotic self-expression" (141), a split identity nevertheless becomes an empirical problem when Whitman transfers the dynamics of the psychological and linguistic split between *I* and *myself* to the material parallel of the body.[7] This figuration presents a consolidated entity existing between the two extremes *feet* and *head*, with *body* as the middle space. These contact points are important, because *feet* are the contact point with earth, with the real, and as humans are positioned vertically the *head* becomes the farthest extreme from contact with the earth. Whitman's rhetoric establishes a Nietzschean opposition between the Apollonian connection point, the head, and the Dionysian connection point, the feet.[8] The Dionysian parallel establishes the connection between democracy, horizontalness, and earth. Although positioned vertically across the earth, everyone is equal when spread horizontally, and the American democratic ideal that Whitman promotes in his preface to the first edition *Leaves of Grass* emerges.

Complete connectedness and democratic equality in "Song of Myself" occur when the connection points of head and feet are equally connected with earth, a position more easily obtainable and more often characterized by horizontal rather than vertical orientation. In horizontal orientation, contact points expand from two to infinity. Fluidity and boundlessness become the rule, and a horizontal center or middle develops.[9] Particularly highlighting this "middleness" is the line "But I do not talk of the beginning or the end" (*LG* 30). The horizontal center unifies, and this unification is exemplified in the following lines: "And that all the men ever born are also my brothers, and the women my sisters and lovers, / And that a kelson of the creation is love" (*LG* 33). In light of the very horizontal image of love's being a "kelson" or spine of creation, the ultimate horizontalness of democracy and the democratic spirit appear in this passage. Contact points exist all along the spine of existence.

Images of centeredness and horizontality particularly appear in Section 6 of the poem. Here, Whitman establishes the importance of horizontalness, middleness, and connectedness with several images. The primary material of boundlessness and democracy and horizontalness is grass. "Sprouting alike in broad zones and narrow zones," grass ignores race, class, and tribe, "[g]rowing among black folks as among white, / Kanuck, Tuckahoe, Congressman, Cuff, I give them the same, I receive them the same." Social equality emerges by means of the horizontal deployment of grass.

At the same time that the horizontal orientation of grass carries democratic significance, its vertical positioning also offers connectedness and consolidation. In the fol-

lowing lines, Whitman equates grass with hair and hair with offspring proceeding from the ultimate horizontal equalizer and one life-connection point: death. As Kuniko Yoshizuki notes, Whitman uses grass "as a motif of life-death-rebirth," an idea also suggested by the geological model of the earth's strata of dead horizontal matter bringing forth vertical elements of life—from blades of grass to human beings—that themselves die and come to rest in a new layer of horizontal strata to begin the process all over again.[10] This use of grass is evidenced in the following lines:

> And now it seems to me the beautiful uncut hair of
> graves.
>
> Tenderly will I use you curling grass,
> It may be you transpire from the breasts of young
> men,
> It may be if I had known them I would have loved
> them;
> It may be you are from old people and from women,
> and from offspring taken soon
> out of their mothers' laps,
> And here you are the mothers' laps.
> . . . . .
>
> I wish I could translate the hints about the dead young
> men and women,
> And the hints about old men and mothers, and the off-
> spring taken soon out of their laps.
>
> What do you think has become of the young and old
> men?
> And what do you think has become of the women and
> children?
>
> They are alive and well somewhere,
> The smallest sprout shows there is really no death,
> And if ever there was it led forward life, and does not
> wait at the end to arrest it,
> And ceas'd the moment life appear'd.
>
> All goes onward and outward, and nothing collapses,
> And to die is different from what any one supposed,
> and luckier.
>
> (*LG* 34-35)

In this passage Whitman presents a symbiotic relationship between vertical and horizontal orientation. Grass, vertically oriented, represents the individual while—since it is horizontally spread—also representing the many. Death, the ultimate and irrevocable horizontal positioning, thus becomes a producer, a signifier of Dionysian vitality. The figure of hair is significant because, as a continuous, non-split strand, it connects with earth, thus connecting the remote extremity to earth, signifying full connection. Furthermore, in this passage, gender equality obtains as both males and females "give birth" to grass. As democracy moves "onward and outward," its strength grows so that none of the framework "collapses." In the circular nature of progression from death to rebirth implied in Whitman's construction and championing of the horizontal, Whitman prefigures the modernist conception of circular time and the theme of death and rebirth derived from Frazer's *The Golden Bough.*[11] Death and birth thus become not merely negative and positive, respectively, but also part of a process in which horizontalness can be extended.

This imagery of hair and horizontality continues in Section 11 of the poem, informing birth, the opposite life-connection point from death. In this section, twenty-eight male bathers occupy a horizontal position as they lie on their backs in the water. In this case, the bodies of the young men floating on their backs are utterly connected with fluidity by association with the medium of water. The young men are completely connected, and as with the grass emanating from the laps of the dead, so the young men become as women with their swollen pregnant bellies capable of giving birth. Stressing the connectedness of the young men, water runs "from their long hair, / Little streams pass'd all over their bodies" and presumably back to the *body* of water from whence the streams came. Whitman extends the democratizing and equalizing effect of cross-gendering the bathers by having the twenty-ninth bather be a woman. In this case, the sexual connectedness clearly emerges alongside the social.

Bodily horizontality and the connection points, feet and hair, occur in an equally conspicuous manner in Section 5. In this scene, the poet loafs in a horizontal position on the grass, a "middle" position in which no one part of the body monopolizes the point of contact of self with the myriad earth. Stressing the democratic equality of the image, Whitman writes that "I believe in you my soul, the other I am must not abase itself to you, / And you must not be abased to the other." "I mind how once we lay such a transparent summer morning," Whitman writes, "How you settled your head athwart my hips and gently turn'd over upon me, / And parted the shirt from my bosom-bone, and plunged your tongue to my bare-stript heart, / And reach'd till you felt my beard, and reach'd till you held my feet." Reaching from one extremity to the other along the lines of horizontalness signifies complete encompassing of the body, and thus complete connectedness.

Read in terms of vertical orientation, this scene carries a different type of connectedness and negotiation of life and death. A metaphorical vertical interpretation of the passage posits the foot as a phallic image and the beard as pubic hair. In this case, the connection points find themselves reversed, with hair characterizing the connecting point of the vertically-oriented member to the body. In such imagery, the vertically-oriented entity becomes the connection point, and the "death" produced from such contact might potentially produce life. Thus, Whitman's argument that "the kelson of creation is love" finds its vertical fulfillment.

Connectedness and consolidation in vertical orientation, however, sometimes prove difficult to attain in "Song of Myself." By its very nature, vertical orientation signifies lack of full connectedness in that it positions one extremity as unconnected and lacking a center from which self may emanate and spread and forgo boundaries and fulfill the carnivalesque commingling that characterizes Whitman's "celebration" of the democratic ideal. Mikhail Bakhtin describes the carnivalesque in *Rabelais and His World,* designating, in strikingly Whitmanesque terms, lower body strata and upper body strata of society and finding their metaphorical counterparts on the human body. These two extremes interact fluidly in carnival, or the moment and space of boundlessness in which "all forms of popular-festive merriment and grotesque realism thrust down, turn over, push headfirst, transfer top to bottom, and bottom to top, both in the literal sense of space, and in the metaphorical meaning of the image."[12] Whitman's depiction of the body falls in the camp of grotesque realism rather than classical idealism, with his relentless stress on carnivalesque corporeality full of barbaric yawps and belched words. This body is the one that can level the two strata and provide a fluid equilibrium and interconnection between them. The problem of reorienting the human from a vertical to horizontal position or at least modifying verticality thus becomes a central mission in the poem. The democratic fluidity and centeredness finds itself replaced by isolated individuality.

An example of vertical orientation isolating the individual from democracy and equality appears in Section 10 in the form of a runaway slave. In this politically and racially charged instance, even the feet cannot connect to the earth. A runaway slave who is "limpsy and weak" appears in the speaker's kitchen. The slave has "bruis'd feet," the metaphorical suggestion of impotence further showing vertical orientation as impaired.[13] When the speaker heals the slave's bruised contact points, strengthening his mobility and the possibility of his escape to freedom, the democratic ideal may be realized. This literal connectedness emerges when the speaker has the slave "sit next me at [the] table." At the same time, the metaphorical healing of the slave's bruised phallus reconfirms his sexual connectedness and introduces the possibility of life in a context of stifled social death.

Whereas hair metaphorically completes connectedness in Section 6, in another vignette in Section 10 hair becomes the literal vehicle of connectedness in vertical orientation by its potential for reaching from head to foot and to earth. In this scene, a Native-American bride has "coarse straight locks descend[ing] upon her voluptuous limbs and reach[ing] to her feet." In this case, the bride's opposite extremity from the contact point of earth, of horizontalness, actually reaches to that contact point, her feet. In Whitman's ideology (and in American ideology, generally), the native girl herself contains a perpetual horizontalness that remains undisturbed by verticalness, symbolized by the length of her hair. And with her connectedness, she and the trapper, whose connectedness appears in his horizontally-oriented lounging and "his luxuriant beard and curls protect[ing] his neck," represent fluid horizontalness and democratization when they join in a union characterized by racial ambiguity (particularly on the trapper's part) and intermixture. Again, horizontalness finds itself modified to achieve connectedness and consolidation.

In Section 9, a different sort of horizontalizing occurs. In this case, dead grass lies horizontally in stacks, and Whitman stretches "atop of the load." He then proceeds to "roll head over heels, and tangle [his] hair full of wisps" (*LG* 36-37). In this fluid inversion of contact points, equalizing and horizontalizing occur, enhancing Whitman's middleness as being completely fluid and boundless. While the red girl and trapper's marriage creates an equalizing situation and the runaway slave's healing represents installment into equality, rolling head over heels modifies the vertical orientation, connecting contact points and opening the potentialities of democratization.

The significance of these images lies in their connecting life and death and connecting them with individuality and democracy. In a poem informed by a historical context of sectional conflict that would ultimately result in civil war, the concept of death creating the exuberance and possibility of life seems a concept not so terribly inaccessible. Eventually, the concern about connecting self to the many would constitute a postbellum crisis of national identity that would inform the local color and regional writing in which individual pockets of the nation would be explored and presented in literature to bolster the unification of the national body.

In light of the importance of feet and hair, the final lines of the poem take on a particularly significant corporeal meaning:

> I depart as air, I shake my white locks at the runaway sun,
> I effuse my flesh in eddies, and drift it in lacy jags.
>
> I bequeath myself to the dirt to grow from the grass I love,
> If you want me again look for me under your boot-soles.
>
> You will hardly know who I am or what I mean,
> But I shall be good health to you nevertheless,
> And filter and fibre your blood.
>
> Failing to fetch me at first keep encouraged,
> Missing me one place search another,
> I stop somewhere waiting for you.
>
> (*LG* 89)

In these final lines, the split, bounded human body of Whitman diffuses into the boundless existence of spirituality, into the air, by shaking his "white locks," an image that informs the manifold images of Whitman as "one of the roughs," with his long hair and defiance of bounds.[14] Indeed, Whitman's very description of himself in one of his reviews of his own work presents him as:

> of American breed, of reckless health, his body perfect, free from taint from top to toe . . . beard short and well mottled with white, hair like hay after it has been mowed in the field and lies tossed and streaked . . . a face that absorbs the sunshine and meets savage or gentleman on equal terms—a face of one who eats and drinks and is a brawny lover and embracer—a face of undying friendship and indulgence toward men and women, and of one who finds the same returned many fold . . . a spirit that mixes cheerfully with the world.[15]

At the same time that this new fluid entity dissolves into air it commits itself into the horizontalized earth and awaits the contact of feet. Again, the Apollonian contact point has been reversed with the Dionysian contact point. And, as the earth produces the uncut hair of graves, so Whitman nourishes his readers who stand vertically over his horizontalness.

In one sense, these lines refer to the body and to the literal earth, but they also include literary significance—they inform the act of reading "Song of Myself." By means of the solitary, individualistic act of reading the "leaves" of the book upon which the poem is written, Whitman offers access to the many, to democratization, to horizontalness.[16] Ultimately, horizontalness perhaps remains unattainable in such an Apollonian and individualistic activity as reading, but the poem's sweeping, horizontally-arranged lines and struggle for common, visceral language characterize an effort to create and perpetuate a peculiar unification of the individual and the many in an America constantly moving "onward and outward."[17]

Notes

1. D. H. Lawrence, *Studies in Classic American Literature* (1923; rpt. New York: Viking, 1961), 165.

2. For a detailed description of these scholars and their works, see Mark Maslan's "Whitman and His Doubles: Division and Union in *Leaves of Grass* and Its Critics," *American Literary History* 6 (Spring 1994), 119-139.

3. Maslan, 136.

4. Whitman, *Leaves of Grass: Comprehensive Reader's Edition*, ed. Harold W. Blodgett and Sculley Bradley (New York: New York University Press, 1965), 28. Abbreviated *LG*. The motif of bodily horizontality and verticality remains a central component of the text throughout the revisions of the poem.

5. Jacques Lacan, "The Mirror Stage as Formative of the Function of the I as Revealed in Psychoanalytical Experience," *Écrits: A Selection,* trans. Alan Sheridan (New York: Norton, 1977), 1-7. Jean-Paul Sartre, *Being and Nothingness: An Essay in Phenomenological Ontology,* trans. By Hazel E. Barnes (Secaucus, NJ: Citadel Press, 1974).

6. Bauerlein, "Whitman's Language of the Self," *American Imago: Studies in Psychoanalysis and Culture* 44 (Summer 1987), 134-135.

7. Discussions of Whitman's use of body include: Harold Aspiz, *Walt Whitman and the Body Beautiful* (Urbana: University of Illinois Press, 1980); M. Jimmie Killingsworth, *Whitman's Poetry of the Body: Sexuality, Politics, and the Text* (Chapel Hill: University of North Carolina Press, 1989); Michael Moon, *Disseminating Whitman: Revision and Corporeality in Leaves of Grass* (Cambridge, Mass.: Harvard University Press, 1991); and Tenney Nathanson, *Whitman's Presence: Body, Voice, and Writing in Leaves of Grass* (New York: New York University Press, 1992).

8. Friedrich Nietzsche, *The Birth of Tragedy* and *The Case of Wagner,* trans. Walter Kaufmann (New York: Vintage, 1967). For an examination of the similarities in thought between Whitman and Nietzsche, see C. N. Stavrou, *Whitman and Nietzsche: A Comparative Study of Their Thought,* University of North Carolina Studies in the Germanic Languages and Literatures, no. 48 (Chapel Hill: University of North Carolina Press, 1964).

9. Here, I mean "fluidity" in the sense that one can transcend the bounds of oneself in the sense that Mikhail Bakhtin identifies in *Rabelais and His World,* trans. Helen Iswolsky (Bloomington: Indiana University Press, 1984). Michael Moon discusses fluidity in Whitman's texts in terms of seminal flow, citing medical treatises warning against masturbation during the nineteenth century.

10. Yoshizaki, "The Theme of Death in *Leaves of Grass,*" *Kyushi American Literature* 22 (May 1981), 43. See Joseph Beaver's *Walt Whitman— Poet of Science* (New York: King's Crown, 1951) and Gay Wilson Allen's *The New Walt Whitman Handbook* (New York: New York University Press, 1975) for Whitman's interest in and knowledge of geology.

11. James George Frazer, *The Golden Bough* (New York: Macmillan, 1940).

12. Bakhtin, 370.

13. The shackles of slavery that bruise the slave's feet and cause the "galls" on his ankles metaphorically attempt to render the African American male impotent by exerting control over the sexual threat he poses. The suggestion of Whitman's restoring the slave's sexual freedom thus represents an especially significant implication of licensed horizontality and connectedness by means of freedom and health for procreation. For discussion of Whitman's treatment of African-Americans see Leadie M. Clark, *Walt Whitman's Concept of the American Common Man* (New York: Philosophical Library, 1955); Ed Folsom, "Lucifer and Ethiopia: Whitman, Race, and Poetics before the Civil War and After," *A Historical Guide to Walt Whitman,* ed. David Reynolds (New York: Oxford University Press, 2000), 45-95; Martin Klammer, *Whitman, Slavery, and the Emergence of Leaves of Grass* (University Park: Pennsylvania State University Press, 1995); and Luke Mancusco, *The Strange Sad War Revolving: Walt Whitman, Reconstruction, and the Emergence of Black Citizenship, 1865-1876* (Columbia: Camden House, 1997).

14. Whitman was one of the most photographed people of his time. Although he did not yet of course have "white locks" in the 1855 edition of the poem, the frontispiece engraving of him portrayed a disheveled, longer-haired, bearded poet violating the bounds of nineteenth-century taste as even the limits of his body in the image—specifically his lower legs and feet—finally fade away. See Folsom's "Whitman and Photographs of the Self" in *Walt Whitman's Native Representations* (New York: Cambridge University Press, 1994), 127-188, for discussion of the significance of photographs of Whitman.

15. Quoted in Aspiz, *Walt Whitman and the Body Beautiful,* 5.

16. Robert F. Fleissner argues that Whitman acquired the concept of pages of poetry as "leaves" of grass from Wordsworth's essay, "The Tables Turned: An Evening Scene on the Same Subject," a work in which William Carlos Williams sees the similar idea of the "common ground [(earth, common people, etc.) being] itself a poetic source," highlighting the fluid democratic context of Whitman's construction of the poem ("Ironic Fertility: 'Defoliating' the Title *Leaves of Grass,*" *Thalia: Studies in Literary Humor* 15 [1995], 77-79). *Leaves of Grass* represents Whitman's attempt to produce a thoroughly organic volume; its title highlights the fact that the physical object of the book replicates nature when its leaves emanate from the spine in the same way leaves of grass sprout horizontally from the vertical earth. Folsom notes that Whitman was conscious of poetry as sprouting from the compost of language—a strik-

ingly vertical/horizontal configuration—in "Whitman and Dictionaries," *Walt Whitman's Native Representations,* 12-26.

17. C. Carroll Hollis's citing of Jakobson's horizontal/vertical axis of metaphor and metonymy in *Language and Style in Leaves of Grass* (Baton Rouge: Louisiana State University Press, 1983) suggests how Whitman's revolutionary long sweeping lines with their relentless horizontality balance the inherent vertical/metaphorical nature of poetry.

ROMANTICISM

Ray B. Browne (essay date March 1963)

SOURCE: Browne, Ray B. "*Billy Budd*: Gospel of Democracy." *Nineteenth-Century Fiction* 17, no. 4 (March 1963): 321-37.

[*In the following essay, Browne addresses Herman Melville's* Billy Budd *as a political allegory of the conflict between autocracy and democracy as exemplified in the works of Edmund Burke and Thomas Paine.*]

That *Billy Budd, Foretopman* must be given on one level a political interpretation is generally recognized. Among other philosophical-political messages, critics see the "doctrine of worldly accommodation" in action,[1] the "sacrifice of self to the historical moment,"[2] exemplification of the "utilitarian principle of social expediency,"[3] and evidence that a "judicious combination of instinct and reason can . . . eventually [produce] a new set of objective conditions which require less repressive forms for man's governance."[4]

Such critics generally agree that in the struggle between Claggart and Budd Captain Vere stands ground between the two, forced by the power of evil to destroy that which he loves, a Lincolnesque figure of great tragic proportions: the spokesman for Melville. Other critics, however, find in Melville's treatment of Vere an irony which turns all forms of "acceptance" into "resistance," and makes of the Captain a caricature of what he appears to be.[5] These readers are, it seems to me, much nearer Melville's meaning. Instead of being the voice of the author, Vere is in fact Melville's antagonist.[6]

On a strictly political level *Billy Budd* is a search for the best form of government—autocratic vs democratic—a question on which Melville worried all of his mature life and on which he had especially agonized during the writing of *Clarel.* On this level, as Noone

has shown, Claggart can be equated with the Hobbesian primitive man and Budd with the Rousseauvian "noble savage," with Vere as a spokesman or apologist for and manipulator of Hobbesian despotism as compromise. But Melville had more immediate political references. As he makes abundantly clear, his concern is with reform and liberalism (as illustrated in the original impulse of the French Revolution, before its excesses) and with its archenemy, status quo and conservatism (as exemplified in the British government). Melville naturally chose as spokesman for these opposing ideologies those authors and their books that were contemporary with the setting of the story: Edmund Burke and his *Reflections on the Revolution in France* (1790); and Thomas Paine and his answer in the *Rights of Man,* Part I (1791) and Part II (1792). For around these authors and works had generally polarized the basic views in the struggle between conservatism and liberalism, political expediency and principle, down to Melville's day. At that time, in fact, the battle was especially violent.

The novel becomes, then, a study in the conflict between these opposing ideologies. In this context the struggle is not between Claggart and Budd, but between Captain Vere as spokesman and apologist for authority (with Claggart serving only as prime mover) and Billy, who is on this level, Melville takes great pains to point out, the common, ordinary sailor. Billy is, in other words, the voice of the people in their insistence on their rights. Vere is the opponent of these rights. He represents Edmund Burke. In his conflict with and ultimate triumph over Vere, Melville uses two voices, that of Billy the common sailor, and his own as author, both of which—or the sum total of which—represent Thomas Paine.

My thesis is, then, that the novel instead of demonstrating the irresistible triumph of political evil, of conservatism, insists on the opposite; that the Veres (and Claggarts) prevail only in the short run, never in the long; that though the Budds seem to lose and are even destroyed personally, they ultimately conquer, not in themselves but in the political philosophy and in the people they represent. In the struggle for power Melville casts his hope with the people. They will outlast all other persons. And they will inevitably inherit the earth.

In this study five aspects of the novel must be considered: 1) the form; 2) the role of Vere; 3) the relationship of this work to Burke and Paine and their political philosophies, and the relevance of this controversy in Melville's time; 4) the role of Billy as common sailor; 5) the use of songs to strengthen the common-man theme. We will correlate these five as we work through the novel.

In *Billy Budd* form is of paramount importance. Though Melville wrote several digressions here, as in his other works, he included no irrelevancies. The Preface is therefore significant: "The year 1797, the year of this narrative belongs to a period which as every thinker now feels, involved a crisis for Christendom not exceeded in its undetermined momentousness at the time by any other era whereof there is record."[7] The key word here is *now*: that is, in Melville's America the conflict between conservatism and liberalism, it was generally agreed, involved a momentous crisis.

The assumption that Melville was anchoring his novel on contemporary political philosophy is not far-fetched. Such a thinker and worrier as he was could hardly have been alive in the time and not be aware of the currents and cross-currents of political upheaval around him. Henry George's *Progress and Poverty,* for example, published in 1879, was creating great agitation among both conservatives and liberals. Edward Bellamy's *Looking Backward,* with its picture of a communistic-socialistic state, came from the press while Melville was working on his novel. Economically and politically the West was rebelling against the East and the rich. Anarchists, foreign and domestic, were terrifying the land with their potential threat.

Thomas Paine was also very much in the air. Two books on him had recently appeared.[8] Elihu B. Washburn, the U.S. Minister to France, had published in 1880 in *Scribner's Magazine* his study of Paine and the French Revolution. The firebrand Robert Ingersoll had recently (1879) brought out his "Vindication of Thomas Paine," and his "Mistakes" had been corrected by James B. McClure (1880). Ingersoll's "atheism," everybody knew, derived from Voltaire and Paine. The biggest bombshell of all had been Theodore Roosevelt's denomination (1887) of Paine as "the filthy little atheist," which words cost him in subsequent years "many moments of explanation and vexation."[9] The 151st anniversary of the birth of Paine was commemorated in Chicago in 1888. The centennial of the publication of Paine's *Rights,* as well as of Burke's *Reflections,* came as Melville was writing his novel.

Burke, too, was on the minds of Americans, and was influential. Increasingly from 1850 to the end of the century he "became the symbol of wise and heroic statesmanship" in America, as well as in England. His love of rhetoric and his pronouncements on the sublime had in the past influenced and still affected American oratory and literature. Men of letters such as Holmes and Emerson, although narrowly read in political classics, never tired of praising Burke.[10] His works had recently been published twice in Boston (1861-1871, 1881).

The Gilded Age was, then, quite conscious of and concerned with the writings and philosophies of Paine and Burke.

Melville, too, was aware of these two antagonists before he discussed them in this particular work. His

"Fragments from a Writing Desk," Sealts says, for example, "imply his youthful familiarity" with Burke. He also apparently owned *The Philosophical Inquiry into the Origin of our Ideas on the Sublime and Beautiful.*[11] But more important evidence is to be found in *Clarel,* Melville's last major work before *Billy Budd,* which he probably meditated on after his return from the Mediterranean in 1857 and began actively to write in 1870. A philosophical poem probing the conflict between "heart" and "head," it also vividly reflects Melville's interest in politics, in the French Revolution, and in Thomas Paine. The doors of the walls around Jerusalem, for example, "as dingy were / As Bastille gates."[12] Are "Mammon and Democracy" inseparably linked? he asks (Part II, canto V). The "holy and right reverend" abbot denounces change and those people who espouse it as being worse than Paine. But the abbot is "stone-blind and old" and longs to retain "that toy, / Dear to the old—authority" (Part III, canto XXIII). Even more revealing is a conversation between Ungar, the part-Indian American, and Derwent and Rolfe, with Vine and Clarel listening in. Ungar, thoroughly disillusioned with materialistic America, writes off the country as a total loss: without the Past, with no regard for its value, the New World will end up in the "Dark Ages of Democracy." Derwent, in answering, bases his hope for America's future on reform:

> Through all methinks I see
> The object clear: belief revised,
> *Men liberated—equalised*
> *In happiness.*
>
> . . . . .
>
> *. . . True reform goes on*
> *By nature; doing, never done.*
> Mark the advance: creeds drop the hate;
> *Events still liberalised the state.*

Even Ungar admits that there was justice initially in the French Revolution:

> The mob,
> The Paris mob of 'Eighty-nine,
> Haggard and bleeding, with a throb
> Burst the long Tuileries. In shrine
> Of chapel there, they saw the Cross
> And Him thereon. Ah, bleeding Man,
> *The people's friend,* thou bled'st for us
> Who here bleed, too!
>
> (Part IV, cantos XX-XXI; emphasis mine)

Though *Clarel* is a series of questions without answers, it vividly reveals Melville's continued interest in the best government for man.

In *Billy Budd* the second sentence carries on Melville's purpose of highlighting the political significance: "The opening proposition made by the Spirit of that Age involved the rectification of the Old World's hereditary wrongs" (p. 131). This "Spirit" is the same as that which motivated the *Rights of Man,* Part I, which had as its main purpose disproving Burke's contention that Englishmen in 1688 had entered into an agreement that bound them and their descendants to a particular form of government "forever." This eternal maintenance of status quo is for Melville the "Old World's hereditary wrongs." He points out that the spirit of rectification "became a wrongdoer" in the French Revolution when under the Directory and Napoleon it became "more oppressive than the king['s]" rule. But the end result of this paroxysm, although temporarily aborted, was good, was "a political advance along nearly the whole line for Europeans," or as a variant version read, "along the whole line for man." Melville further particularized that from the spirit of the Revolution came the successful resistance to "real abuses" in the English navy at Spithead and Nore, and their eventual amelioration.

Melville was not here condemning this "Spirit of that Age." He was against tyranny of either the left or the right. But it was *excesses* he opposed, not change. The Great Mutiny was a "demonstration more menacing to England than the contemporary manifestoes and conquering and proselyting armies of the French Directory" (p. 151). In the Nore Mutiny *"Reasonable* discontent . . . had been ignited into irrational combustion" (p. 151, emphasis mine), which could have been prevented had the English been willing to grant reasonable corrections to the status quo. In other words, Melville saw the alternatives as change or chaos.

Even more unequivocally political was Melville's conclusion about these two mutinies. "Final suppression . . . there was," he said, then added a moment later: "To some extent the Nore Mutiny may be regarded as analogous to the distempering irruption of contagious fever in a frame constitutionally sound, and which anon throws it off" (p. 153). Here is dramatically mirrored one of the great arguments between Burke and Paine. Burke insisted that the English had a constitution tacitly recognized by all—and followed by the king and the lawmakers. But Paine claimed that there was no English Constitution—no inviolable document—unless it could be seen in writing. The French, on the contrary, had a Constitution. This written agreement guaranteed protection of the people. It assured soundness to the body politic. Melville, then, was agreeing with Paine that within the framework of a sound constitution mankind could be assured of progress, but without such a guarantee nothing could be certain.

The political theme of the novel continues in the first chapter, the beginning of the narrative, which is a general statement focusing on the Handsome Sailor. This Handsome Sailor is the universal hero type, the savior. Bastard that he is—and apparently of "noble" parentage—Billy stands with other heroes of uncertain pater-

nity like King Arthur, Roland, Abraham Lincoln,[13] Galahad, Christ, and many others—as well as Mortmain in *Clarel,* and others in Melville's later works. Thus the superhuman Billy and Claggart—who is also a bastard of apparent noble descent—are paired off as antagonists in an elemental struggle. Billy is not therefore in any wise the illegitimate son of Captain Vere, although Melville points out that as far as their ages are concerned he might have been. But there is grim irony in that "might have been." Vere is sterile, incapable of producing anything, even his own kind. A loner in life, unmarried, uninterested in women, he dies with no progeny and no reputation, in fact nameless.

But Billy is also a political figure. He is, as Melville says, primarily the Handsome Sailor "of the military and merchant navies" (p. 133). He is, in other words, the navy man's idealization of the sailor pictured in sea songs, and in navy life as Melville would have remembered it from his own days on the sea. Though this sailor is "some superior figure of their own class," he is *of their own class.* Furthermore he is more than the conventional, white man's Christ. He is every race's savior—black, white and inbetween. In fact the black Handsome Sailor is more remarkable than the white, and more nearly represents mankind of the Revolution, as Melville's mention of Anacharsis Cloots demonstrates: Cloots appeared at the Bar of the French Assembly at the head of thirty-six foreigners of all colors and for this "embassy of the human race"[14] declared that the world insisted on the Rights of Man and of the Citizen.

Billy, like other saviors, stands forth with his disciples, the sailors, clustered around him on the beach—on land, that is. Here we have a joining of the land and sea, which, as we shall see, develops into an important theme in the novel.

Another political point worthy of notice is that Billy is taken from a merchant vessel. Why not some other kind of ship? Or why is he not simply impressed while on shore? Because Melville is here echoing the philosophy of Thomas Paine, who felt that commerce is the proper business between nations: people who trade do not fight; in this commercial intercourse there is great exchange of ideas from which proper alterations in political and social structure will grow.[15]

Not content with having drawn a close parallel with the Burke-Paine controversy, Melville actually labors his point by spending several sentences stating that Captain Graveling named his merchantman *Rights of Man* in honor of Paine, "whose book in rejoinder to Burke's arraignment of the French Revolution had been published for some time and had gone everywhere." This Captain, Melville adds, was in company with "Stephen Girard of Philadelphia, whose sympathies, alike with his native land and its liberal philosophers, he evinced by naming his ships after Voltaire, Diderot, and so forth" (p. 141).

The political aspect of the novel is continued as Billy is selected from the crew of the merchantman to be taken aboard the man-of-war. Billy's fellow sailors, who have known what their rights are and have enjoyed them, all "turned a surprised glance of silent reproach" at him (p. 137) for leaving his ship without resistance. They cannot understand his not fighting for his rights. Furthermore, as Lieutenant Ratcliffe and his crew—with Billy—are leaving the *Rights of Man* and passing under the stern, "officers and oarsmen were nothing—some bitterly and others with a grin—the name emblazoned there" (p. 142). Here is a split reaction to Paine. Some of these sailors have not enjoyed their rights, but they know that they have been deprived of them, and are bitter; others, however, forswear their natural rights easily, and are in fact merely amused by hints—or promises—of them. These people ally themselves with the lieutenant—one of the robots of the King and of Established Authority—who "with difficulty" represses a smile when Billy salutes his former ship. But all is not well with Authority on board the *Indomitable* that the small boat returns to. Though "very little would have suggested to an ordinary observer that the Great Mutiny was a recent event," the key words here are *very little* and *ordinary observer.* Rebellion has not been strangled forever. The common man has not been given his rights. But Democracy will continue to fight for its deserts.

The irony in the portrait of Vere which Melville soon presents proves the author's hostility to him. It also makes the Captain blood brother to Burke. Vere does not owe *all* his advancement to his "influences." Neither did Burke; he was very capable, but his rise resulted from his alliance with the Rockingham Whigs, and throughout life he had to cling to powerful political leaders. Vere and Burke are similar intellectually. Vere's "bias was towards those books to which every serious mind of superior order *occupying any active post of authority in the world,* naturally inclines; books treating *of actual men and events* no matter of what era—history, biography and unconventional writers, who, free from cant and convention, like Montaigne, honestly and in the spirit of common sense *philosophize upon realities*" (emphasis mine). And

> His settled convictions were as a dyke against those invading waters of novel opinion social political and otherwise, which carried away as in a torrent no few minds in those days, minds not by nature inferior to his own.
>
> (p. 164)

Burke's political opinions, even when he was justifying the American Revolution, were always practical, expedient. Like Vere, again, he had grown more and more "intellectual" through the years, profoundly learned and

superb as a reasoner. But as man in authority, or supporting authority, he became more and more politically illiberal. He would entertain only those notions which supported his own point of view, would read only those books which confirmed his feeling that he was correct.

Burke was in Melville's mind when he said the following of Vere:

> While other members of that aristocracy . . . were incensed at the innovators mainly because their theories were inimical to the privileged classes, not alone Captain Vere disinterestedly opposed them because they seemed to him incapable of embodiment in lasting institutions, but at war with the peace of the world and the true welfare of mankind.
>
> (p. 164)

Burke, if narrow and conservative, was the sincerest man alive. He always felt that his views were held only in the best interests of mankind.

There is another strong similarity between Burke and Vere. The former's companions in Commons, like the latter's fellow officers, found him, in Melville's words about Vere, "lacking in companionable quality, a dry and bookish gentleman," rather "pedantic." Again, it could be said of Burke, as it was said of Vere, he was likely to "cite some historic character or incident of antiquity," some "remote allusion" (p. 165) without bothering to remember that most of his auditors were his inferiors in knowledge. So boring did Burke become, in fact, that he was called the "Dinner Bell": when he started to speak many of the members of Commons went to dinner.[16]

More of Melville's political slant is seen in his effort to explain why Billy is completely innocent. He does not know of evil intuitively. But, then, Melville points out, "as a class, sailors are in character a juvenile race. . . . Every sailor, too, is accustomed to obey orders without debating them; *his life* afloat *is externally ruled for him*" (p. 206; emphasis mine). In thus pointing out the universal naivete of sailors Melville is echoing the usual belief[17] of the time, but his real purpose is to contrast sailors with landsmen. The common sailor, he says, is in every way less prepared to combat life than is the common landsman. "The sailor is frankness, the landsman is finesse. Life is not a game with the sailor, demanding the long head" (p. 206), as it is with his counterpart on land. Thus he is easily imposed upon and advantage taken of him. What is the cure for this gullibility? asks Melville: "promiscuous commerce with mankind," which will sophisticate him.

This re-introduction of the comparison of sea men with land men here is extremely important in the development of Melville's political purpose. Both kinds together make up the common man; only when both—*all men*—live together are they complete and prepared to combat evil, especially political evil. The pen is Melville's, but the sentiments are Tom Paine's.[18]

All the above is, of course, background to the drama of the accusation of Billy, the consequences and the *denouement*. In this drama the action is rapid, the air electric. The circumstances surrounding the affair must be remembered.

The climax begins in a supercharged atmosphere. Vere's ship has just encountered a frigate, a sure prize, but the smaller ship has outrun the *Indomitable*. Then "ere the excitement incident thereto had altogether waned away" (p. 213), Claggart, choosing his moment wisely, approaches the Captain with his suspicions of Budd. Vere, "absorbed in his reflections" is caught off guard and off balance; he does not ever regain his equilibrium. Through the next few minutes the tension is intensified. Vere gets more taut, more nervous, less reliable. Claggart, on the contrary, remains always cold and calculating. After Claggart is killed, Vere's mind and nerve crack. He tries to be the strict "military disciplinarian" but cannot. He becomes more and more excited. His actions thereafter are always erratic. Melville spends three paragraphs analyzing the Captain to determine if he is truly mad. The Surgeon surely thinks he is. Melville, speaking in his own person, implies that he is. In this breakup of Vere Melville invalidates the Captain's credentials as a political philosopher. Vere has become, in fact, capable of great evil, of much destructiveness.

In his madness Vere can think only of self-protection. He wants to "guard as much as possible against publicity" by "confining all knowledge [of the event] to the place where the homicide had occurred" (p. 235). Does Melville approve of this action by Vere? Hardly! In being so secretive Vere "may or may not have erred," but surely "there lurked some resemblance" to the tyrannical policies "which have occurred more than once in the capital founded by Peter the Barbarian" (p. 235). In this denial of news to the general public—and its being equated with tyranny—there lie general political overtones and a striking similarity to the efforts of the British Government to strangle the *Rights of Man* by confiscation of the book and prosecution of the author.

The trial scene further highlights the political overtones. Throughout it Vere demonstrates his hatred of democracy. The Captain of the marines was reluctantly appointed to the drumhead court because he was too much a man of "heart" rather than of "head." Furthermore Vere constantly condescends to the court as "men not intellectually mature." But even more important, Melville, speaking in his own person, says, "Similar impatience as to talking is perhaps one reason that deters some minds from addressing any popular assemblies" (p. 243)—in other words, impatience with the speed with which the common people learn, and therefore contempt for their intelligence and for their rights. Vere's real feelings burst forth a few moments later when the junior lieutenant asks if the court might not "convict and yet mitigate the penalty?" Vere answers: "The people (meaning the ship's company [and thus the common man in general]) have native sense." They will "ruminate," will think the clemency "pusillanimous," will believe that Authority is "afraid of them—afraid of practicing a lawful rigor singularly demanded at this juncture. . . . You see then, whither prompted by duty and the law I steadfastly drive" (p. 248). Melville could hardly have drawn a more precise picture of Burke even if he had called the Captain by Burke's name.

With Vere's statement to the sailors about the coming execution of Billy, Melville begins to emphasize the theme which has been present though somewhat subdued all along: the overriding significance of the reaction of the common man. To their Captain's announcement the sailors listened "in a dumbness like that of a seated congregation of believers in hell listening to the clergyman's announcement of his Calvinistic text" ("Jonathan Edwards" was written in the margin of the text.) As Vere ended "A confused murmur went up. It began to wax." It might have grown into mutiny then had it not been quelled by the boatswain's whistle. The importance of the passage lies in the fact that the people were beginning to react strongly to events. Just as most people had earlier found intolerable Edwards' unyielding doctrine of predestination and had forced it to be modified, so most were finding unbearable the iron-bound conservatism—and despotism—of Vere (and Burke) and were beginning to insist that it be altered.

At the actual hanging the people's incipient rebellion begins to run at higher tide. Though they echo Billy's "conventional felon's benediction" ("God bless Captain Vere!"[19]) they do not mean it. At the moment the sailors say these words, "Billy alone must have been in their hearts, even as he was in their eyes" (p. 265).

The absolute silence attending the hanging is followed almost immediately by a murmur which is scarcely audible at the beginning but which gains volume until it clearly emanates from the sailors on the deck. Melville continues, meaningfully: "Being inarticulate, it was dubious in significance further than it seemed to indicate some capricious revulsion of thought or feeling such as mobs ashore are liable to in the present instance possibly implying a sullen revocation on the men's part of their involuntary echoing of Billy's benediction" (p. 269). Melville's political message here is that the masses are inarticulate, and therefore their intentions and actions are often misunderstood, their compliance misread. But he ties together the commoners of the sea and of the land and indicates that this total humanity condemns both the actions of the captains of the world and their own silent allowance of these actions.

The political theme continues as Vere, the "martinet" as the author suggests he is, has the men beat to quarters an hour early to get the decks cleared. "With mankind," Vere felt, "forms, measured forms are everything; and that is the real import couched in the story of Orpheus with his lyre spell-binding the wild denizens of the woods." On which statement Melville editorializes: "And this he once applied to the disruption of forms going on across the Channel and the consequences thereof" (p. 272). To Vere, then, the sailors under his command (and all people) were no more than the wild beasts. Only so unthinking a man as he could equate himself with Orpheus. But he is just mad enough to think that he can control the beasts with forms. Only so blind a man as Vere could insist that the French Revolution was *only* a breaking up of forms.

In ending the novel Melville says that it should terminate with the death of Billy, but "Truth uncompromisingly told will always have its ragged edges" (p. 274), and it is truth he is seeking. He writes three more chapters. The order in which they are presented is important.

In the first Melville switches to France and tells how the ship *St. Louis* was rechristened *Atheiste*. But his words must be carefully noted. He does not condemn the French. Although this renaming apparently indicated a nasty turn from religion to atheism, the new name was the "aptest" that was "ever given to a warship," because it is applicable to all war, and it is war that Melville condemns. In having this French ship destroy the British captain, the author is predicting the fate of all men like Vere (and Burke) and those countries whose political philosophy such men reflect.

Furthermore, Vere's death is no glorious Nelson's demise, and he was no Nelson; he was in fact the exact opposite. Necessarily then his death is ignominious. He is shot by a commoner (a marine no doubt) from the port-hole of the enemy's main cabin. Then, if this is not sufficient ignominy, he is carried below and laid with the wounded commoners. After his ship has prevailed over the Frenchman he is put ashore at Gibraltar. Thus, rock unto rock.

On the rock, when Vere has been denuded of his own character by drugs, when these drugs have allowed the "subtler element in man" to speak, then and only then does he begin to think about Billy, and he calls his name twice. Melville is not precise whether Vere's words indicate remorse. But the Captain's motivation is of no consequence. These words are retold to the Captain of the marines, the man on the drumhead court who was most understanding of and sympathetic toward Billy. He has outlasted Vere. This kind of man, Melville is saying, always outlasts the Vere kind.

The death of Vere is his complete dissolution and dismissal. Throughout the story Melville has shown that Vere and his kind of people are interested only in facts;

they read newspapers, official reports, and men like Montaigne, who "free from cant . . . in the spirit of common sense philosophize upon realities." In the official report of the case, the last chapter but one in the book, Melville gives a "factual" and "true" report. It is, of course, a gross misstatement of truth. It reports that Budd was actually guilty, that Claggart was an honorable and worthy individual. But, most important, Vere is referred to only in the generalized term "the Captain." His personality has been completely lost. In the chronicle of human events, Melville is saying, such a man does not deserve even being named.

The novel ends, as a book with such a message had to end, with the common sailors. These men preserve the chips of the spar on which Billy has hanged. There was something sacred about it. Such is the treatment accorded all heroes and saviors by such people. But even more important is the ballad which concludes the work. Though this song is written in the first person, significantly it was composed by other "tarry hands" "among the shipboard crew" than Billy's (p. 279). The "I" in the song is more the sailor-author than it is Billy personally. The singer, for example, thinks about the "eardrop I gave to Bristol Molly." But Billy was surely as innocent of women as Christ and other heroes were. This is merely a stock statement in sailor songs. In other words, Billy is no longer an individual. He has been universalized. He is Every Sailor. A variant reading of this ballad points this up even more vividly:

> In a queerish dream here I had afore (?)
> A queerish dream of days no more.—
> A general number from every shore
> Countrymen, yes and Moor and Swede,
> Christian Pagan Cannibal breed.
>
> (p. 283, n)

There could be little more thorough mixing of the peoples of the world than here described: black and white and in-between; religious, irreligious and indifferent. The novel has now returned to the Handsome Sailor—the universal savior—of the beginning, this time in a song.

Melville makes his point clear. There are no songs about Vere; none about Claggart. The song is not actually about Billy personally, but about the type of sailor he represents. He is not an unusual sailor. He is not being hanged unjustly. Rather, very much the average sailor under the circumstances, he is hungry and frightened; and once hanged he is slipped under the water in the usual way—the typical sailor of Dibdin's songs. This conclusion should be compared with a statement (made by Derwent) in *Clarel*:

> Suppose an instituted creed
> (Or truth or fable) should indeed
> To ashes fall; the spirit exhales,

But reinfunds in active forms:
Verse, *popular verse,* it charms or warms—
Belies philosophy's flattened sails—
Tinctures the very book, perchance,
Which claims arrest of its advance.

(Part III, canto XXI; emphasis mine)

The political "truth uncompromisingly told" of *Billy Budd*—the real climax—is this ballad, this "popular verse": not the death of Billy, not even the dissolution of Vere. The subject of the novel is the common sailor. Melville has made it clear that this common sailor is inseparably attached to the common landsman—together comprising "the people" throughout the world. The novel demonstrates that "the people" have outlasted all the others and everything else in the book. Here, then, is Melville's reply to the Teddy Roosevelts of his age who cursed Tom Paine. Here is Melville's comment on the Conservative-Liberal controversy of his day and of all times. Here is his resounding affirmation of belief in the ultimate triumph of the Rights of Man and of democracy.

This interpretation is vital to an understanding of Melville's final political philosophy. The anxieties and doubtful hopes—the questions—of *Clarel,* evidenced in the quotes above, have been resolved in new affirmativeness and optimism. His voice in this last work is not much different from what it was when he wrote Hawthorne of his "ruthless democracy," of his asserting "unconditional democracy in all things"[20]; nor from what it was in *White-Jacket* when he thundered against flogging "in the name of immortal manhood." Neither is it far from the sentiment of his motto—"Keep true to the dreams of thy youth"—which was pasted to the inside of the writing box on which he composed *Billy Budd.* But it is far indeed from "acceptance." The Melville who had much earlier come to believe in personal annihilation after death had finally come to this attestation of the power and future of democracy, of hope in "immortal manhood."

Notes

1. Merlin Bowen, *The Long Encounter: Self and Experience in the Writings of Herman Melville* (Chicago, 1960), p. 215.

2. Milton R. Stern, *The Fine Hammered Steel of Herman Melville* (Urbana, 1957), p. 207.

3. Wendell Glick, "Expediency and Absolute Morality in *Billy Budd,*" *PMLA,* LXVIII (1953), 104.

4. John B. Noone, Jr., "*Billy Budd*: Two Concepts of Nature," *American Literature,* XXIX (Nov., 1957), 262. See also Ray B. West, Jr., "Primitivism in Melville," *Prairie Schooner,* XXX (1956), 369-385.

5. Paul Withim, "*Billy Budd*: Testament of Resistance," *Modern Language Quarterly,* XX (1959), 115-127. See this article for a summary of arguments about "acceptance," "resistance," and irony. Though I agree with these findings as far as they go, I think the author stopped far short of their possibilities.

6. A late identification of Vere with Melville is in R. H. Fogle, "*Billy Budd*: The Order of the Fall," *NCF,* XV (Dec., 1960), 189-205. His argument is not convincing.

7. F. Barron Freeman, ed. *Melville's "Billy Budd"* (Cambridge, Mass., 1948), p. 131. Hereafter all quotes are from this text and are given in the body of the paper.

8. John E. Remsburg, *Thomas Paine, The Apostle of Religious and Political Liberty* (Boston, 1880); M. J. Savage, *Thomas Paine: Some Lessons from his Life* (Boston, 1883).

9. Roosevelt's words were in his life of Gouverneur Morris (Nat. Ed. VII, 421-422). Quoted in E. E. Morison, *et al., The Letters of Theodore Roosevelt* (Cambridge, Mass., 1951), II, 1158, with the above comment.

10. Quoted in Naomi Johnson Townsend, "Edmund Burke; Reputation and Bibliography, 1850-1954" (unpublished dissertation, Univ. of Pittsburgh, 1955), p. 55. Melville's attitude toward Holmes was perhaps mixed, but surely he condemned Holmes' touting everything European as being superior to anything American, what Melville thought was Bostonian flunkeyism. See Leon Howard, *Herman Melville, A Biography* (Berkeley and Los Angeles, 1951), p. 158. Though Melville admired some qualities of Emerson, he sorrowed deeply over others, for example, over Emerson's contempt for the masses. William Alger's *The Solitudes of Nature and Man* (1867) quoted Emerson on the subject: "enormous populations, like moving cheese," "the guano-races of mankind," "masses! the calamity is the masses." In his own copy of this book Melville underscored these lines and added, "These expressions attributed to the 'kindly Emerson' are somewhat different from the words of Christ to the multitude on the Mount.— Abhor pride, abhor malignity, but not grief and poverty, and the natural vices these generate." Quoted in F. O. Matthiessen, *American Renaissance* (New York, 1949), pp. 401-402.

11. Merton M. Sealts, Jr., "Melville's Reading," *Harvard Library Bulletin,* II (1948), 147, 390.

12. *Clarel, A Poem and Pilgrimage in the Holy Land* (London, 1924), I, 31 (Part I, canto VII); hereafter

all references are to this edition, given by part and canto in text of paper.

13. In mythology and folklore the hero always has certain characteristics: 1) he has a supernatural bîrth or is illegitimate (Billy is the latter; so is Claggart; but there is something supernatural in their births; 2) he is physically and mentally precocious or outstanding (Billy is the former; Claggart the latter; 3) something about his appearance and behavior is uncommon (Billy is extraordinarily handsome, exceptionally good; Claggart is unusually pale, etc.); 4) often there is highlighted a contest between him and his arch antagonist (occurs in this novel); 5) there is something unusual in his death—convulsions of nature, or some kind of acknowledgement by nature of the hero's passing (so it is in this novel). For the multiple paternity of Lincoln see "The Many-Sired Lincoln," by J. G. de Roulhac Hamilton, *American Mercury* (June, 1925), pp. 129-135 (thirteen men are given as his father).

14. *The Encyclopedia Britannica* (11th ed., New York, 1910), V-VI, 556. He became known as, and called himself, "the orator of the human race."

15. Philip S. Foner, ed. *The Complete Writings of Thomas Paine* (New York, 1945). In *Rights,* Part I (Foner, I, 343) Paine said: "Agriculture, commerce, manufactures . . . by which the prosperity of nations is best promoted, require a different system of government . . . than what might have been required in the former condition of the world." In Part II (Foner, I, 400) he was even more extensive and explicit: "I have been an advocate for commerce, because I am a friend to its effects. It is a pacific system, operating to unite mankind by rendering nations, as well as individuals, useful to each other." "If commerce were permitted to act to the universal extent it is capable of, it would extirpate the system of war, and produce a revolution in the uncivilized state of government."

16. Thomas H. D. Mahoney, *Edmund Burke and Ireland* (Cambridge, Mass., 1960), p. 139.

17. In the search for sources of and parallels to *Billy Budd,* not nearly enough attention has been paid to the numerous sailor songs of the time, especially to those of Charles Dibdin. Melville knew many of them, more than were in the only book containing Dibdin's songs that he is known to have consulted, Charles McKay's *Songs of England.* For example, two of the songs in *White-Jacket*—"True English Sailor" and the one sung to the tune "The King, God Bless Him"—which Melville calls Dibdin's, and which are his, are not in McKay. Melville, therefore, must have known another collection of Dibdin's songs. And Melville drew heavily from these songs for the portraits of Billy and Claggart, and—by inverting Dibdin's extreme Tory sentiments—to develop his final political philosophy in the song which concludes the novel. Concerning the universal naivete of sailors, one of Dibdin's pieces (*Sea Songs,* 3rd ed., London, 1852, p. 102), "The Sailor's Maxim," contains the following lines:

> Of us tars 'tis reported again and again,
> That we sail round the world, yet know nothing of men;
> And, if this assertion is made with the view
> To prove sailors know naught of men's follies, 'tis true.
>
> . . . . .
>
> How should Jack practise treachery, disguise, or foul art,
> In whose honest face you may read his fair heart:
> Of that maxim still ready example to give,
> Better death earn'd with honor than ignobly to live.

See further note 19 below.

18. For example, freedom for man "takes ground on every character and condition that appertains to man, and blends the individual, the nation, and the world." "Whatever the form or constitution of government may be, it ought to have no other object than the *general* [sic] happiness. When, instead of this, it operates to create and increase wretchedness in any of the parts of society, it is on a wrong system, and reformation is necessary" (*Rights,* II, Foner I, 398).

19. Another of Dibdin's songs (*Sea Songs,* 3rd ed., 1852, pp. 157-158) demonstrates further the conventionality of this kind of statement, and the degree to which Melville uses the songs of the common man to develop his political thesis. Entitled "Ben Block" this piece tells of a man sent to sea by his father, leaving behind his sweetheart Kate. A false friend reports that Kate is untrue, and the sailor commits suicide, as the last stanza chronicles:

> Tho sure from this cankerous elf
> The venom accomplish'd its end:
> Ben, all truth and honor itself,
> Suspected no fraud of his friend.
> On the yardarm while suspended in air,
> A loose to his sorrows he gave—
> "Take thy wise," he cried, "false, cruel fair!"
> And plunged in a watery grave.

20. For this famous letter, see *The Letters of Herman Melville,* ed. Merrell R. Davis and William H. Gilman (New Haven, 1960), pp. 126-131.

Clarence Gohdes (essay date 1981)

SOURCE: Gohdes, Clarence. "An American Author as Democrat." In *Literary Romanticism in America,* edited by William L. Andrews, pp. 1-18. Baton Rouge and London: Louisiana State University Press, 1981.

[*In the following essay, Gohdes illustrates the connection between Ralph Waldo Emerson's conception of humanity and democratic ideals.*]

During World War II one of my friends, an anthropologist by profession, served as an officer of our State Department, advising on the essential or nonessential nature of shipments to be made to the west coast of South America. In going over the invoices submitted for his inspection he noticed that there were orders for a surprising amount of florida water, a kind of toilet water, to be shipped from a particular firm in New York City. Certainly, he thought, florida water could be regarded as nonessential with cargo space at a premium. But he noticed that his statements to that effect were completely disregarded by his superiors, who had dwelt long in the area; and the orders went through. When an opportunity for a vacation came along, he indulged himself in anthropological pursuits in a rural and very backward community. The florida water question still bothered him, but upon inquiry he soon found out that the local witch doctors—in plentiful supply—used that particular brand of florida water as an important element in their ceremonies. The victim of a spell or of a demon causing a disease had to be sprinkled with the contents of one of those bottles from New York. No other variety, he was assured, was "strong enough." So far as the natives of that section of Latin America were concerned, the witches at least considered the United States of America a vitally important source of florida water—and very little more.

If one asks in a more general way, What has our country stood for in the eyes of foreign nations? no neat answer readily emerges, for the attitude of the world toward any of its constituent nations varies from time to time and is subject to sudden gusts of emotion. Economics, politics, and even witchcraft, it seems, may condition the reaction. The materials for an answer to such a question abound in the books and articles written by travelers who may have visited our shores for six weeks or six months, who may have seen New York but not Chicago, who may have come with an open mind or with a fixed determination to be displeased. One may illustrate the difficulties best by setting forth some of the aspects of our country and of our people which have from time to time been noted in books of travel.

A hundred years ago we seemed to foreigners, like Charles Dickens, to be especially devoted to the habit of tobacco chewing. More lately we have shifted to gum. Whether the gum chewing has anything to do with it, foreign observers credit us with having better teeth than most peoples—and our dentists with being the best in the world. Visitors from countries with an established church have viewed us as seething in sectarian confusion and as having produced only two religions of our own: Mormonism and Christian Science. We have always appeared as a very busy people, humming with activity. Theodore Roosevelt's phrase for the idea was "the strenuous life." The absence of a leisured class has impressed one writer after the other. One of them once asked an American friend, "Don't you really have any leisured class at all?" and the answer came back, "O, yes, only we call them *tramps.*" A traveling impresario from Italy once picked out as the four most distinctive American products: apples, oysters, white bread, and women. The last of these usually have come in for comment, for both Europeans and Asiatics readily note the unusual respect paid to ladies in this country and sometimes have expressed astonishment at the freedom with which the sexes commingle. In the 1880s one travel-book writer summed up the woman question as follows: "At Cairo," he said, "a woman is an idealized slave"; in Florence, "a cherished article of domestic chattel"; in New York, "an equal, and more often than not, an aggravating, overbearing confederate." Another Italian was particularly impressed by the lack of iron gratings between women employees and their male customers, and still another from a Catholic country found the maidenly habit of flirting to be very characteristic. Boston, he thought, was most notorious in this respect. And he cited as an example a couple whom he saw seated on the grass in the Public Garden, the girl reading aloud from *Harper's Magazine,* the boy shading her with a parasol. Only one change is needed to make that picture of flirting in Boston perfect—the magazine should have been the *Atlantic Monthly.* There was a time when our sexual morality astonished the European travel-book writer; we seemed to be a whole nation of Darbys and Joans. But very recently even the French have been shocked by our novels and the folkways of our young men, and perhaps the old AEF ditty will eventually be revised to read, "The Americans are a naughty race, *parlez-vous.*"

Our people have long been classed as the leading newspaper and magazine readers, and the size of our papers, daily and Sunday, still is a wonder of the New World, like Niagara Falls or Yellowstone Park. Widespread education at state expense seemed, years ago, to be one of our chief accomplishments, but our colleges were only faintly praised as offering very practical training. In architecture we seemed merely to be imitative, until the skyscrapers at length sprang up to give us distinction. In music, also, we lagged, but more recently our symphony orchestras have begun to exact admiration, and our composers are becoming known; though for several decades our specialty has appeared to be dance music. Even in remote villages in the Near East one can hear American "rock," or at least a version of it. We are also recognized as the chief purveyors of the most popular dramatic entertainment ever known to mankind. Not only the movies, but furs, tobacco, cotton, automobiles, airplanes, and even Parker 51 fountain pens have at one time or another seemed to be our most cherished economic products. The procession of our men of daring has run from the Indian fighter and the cowboy to the Chicago gangster. The mixture of races in our melting pot has always been a lively topic for travelers to comment upon—and of course the American Negro has prompted a whole literature by himself. Earlier in our history we had been again and again charged with not paying our debts! Now we are charged with being Uncle Shylock.

Heinrich Heine once observed that in the beginning God created man in his own image, and ever since man has been striving to return the compliment. Certainly men have created a very human image of their fellow-men.

Such aspects of American life as I have used to illustrate—very human as they are—belong to the realm of the superficial, though I should immediately admit that the superficial is of no little importance in the field of international relations. When one looks for something weightier in answer to the question, What has America stood for in the eyes of the world? there are two chief aspects of the answer.

At the time of the establishment of our government, and for many decades thereafter, the United States represented to the intelligence of the world most fundamentally an experiment in democracy. The advanced liberals looked upon us with favor, drank to the health of George Washington, and prophesied all manner of future accomplishment to come from the experiment. The conservatives, a more powerful set in that they usually controlled their own governments, regarded us with disfavor as a nation of plebeians playing with political dynamite that one day would blow up and perhaps injure Europe with the falling wreckage. Late in the nineteenth century, even social-minded John Ruskin, who described himself as a "peculiar Tory," could not forbear twitting American visitors about their "republican experiment." And Matthew Arnold solemnly expressed the opinion that "few stocks could be trusted to grow up properly without having a priesthood and an aristocracy to act as their schoolmasters." We often lay the blame for traditional, old-fashioned isolationism upon the square shoulders of the American people, but an important factor was undoubtedly the hostile attitude of the conservatives of Europe, who despised democracy as a plague and looked upon our future with foreboding. The great test, of course, came at the time of the Civil War, when the broadest intellectual significance of the question was exactly what Abraham Lincoln stated it to be—a test whether this nation, or any nation so conceived and so dedicated, could long endure. The fact that our government did endure was of enormous consequence in shaping foreign opinion, for the dire prophecies of the conservatives were shown by events to have been as false as yesterday's science. The first really important general answer to the question, What has the world thought of us? is to be found in the fact that we have represented an experiment in democracy.

America has also appeared to the world as an example of phenomenal wealth, and of power based upon that wealth. The riches of our country were, of course, a matter of prophecy from the earliest days of exploration. Indeed, exploration was largely motivated by the dreams of wealth. Years after the establishment of the nation, the chief view of our wealth, I think, was that the common man enjoyed a greater prosperity than his European cousin. It was not until after the Civil War, with the astonishing progress of industry, that we came to be identified with riches in spectacular amount. And our reputation in this regard has developed so amazingly in the present century as to make pale the golden vision of America that seemed so enticing in the last decades of the nineteenth.

So far as power is concerned, probably the first overt demonstration that impressed the intellectual world came in 1898 with our war against Spain, when, with one of those ironies occasionally seen in history, the chief American nation turned against the very mother of American colonization and achieved a quick and emphatic victory. This premonitory sign that here was a new element of considerable importance in reckoning the balance of power was soon followed by two wars which proved beyond question that the United States of America represented might. At the present time, it may be said, our country stands as one of the giants of history, holdings in one hand billions of dollars and in the other weapons of indescribable power—the symbols of what the United States stands for in the eyes of the world. Uncle Sam may very well show a look of bewilderment upon his erstwhile provincial face.

It may be interjected that our claims to recognition as an experiment in democracy have been sadly obscured by the vast shadows cast by wealth and power, even though in times of crisis we ourselves assert them with fervor. Change and experiment elsewhere have come so thick and fast that we are now the oldest among the governments of the chief nations of the earth. The word experiment thus seems outmoded, even though we all trust that we shall never cease to experiment.

Considering, now, the opinion that we have stood longest before the eyes of the intellectual world as an experiment in democracy, the question may be asked of the literary historian, How well do the American authors illustrate the chief claim of America upon the world's intelligence? The answer, again, is not easy to derive, for art is art and political and social philosophy are political and social philosophy—despite the efforts of literary critics during the 1930s to make an olio of the three. How American is American literature? . . . How French is French literature? 'Tis hard to say.

Certainly our literary men of past times, with very few exceptions, have been sturdy believers in the democratic experiment. Their political and social views impressed the critics of nineteenth-century England at least as being "radical," in the older European sense of that word. Even the gentle Longfellow, teacher and translator of Dante, refused a decoration offered by the Italian government on the ground that as a citizen of a republic and as an American it would be improper for him to accept it. But do the actual writings of our major authors reflect much of the idea for which we have stood in the eyes of the world? Poe and Henry James we may as well dismiss as belonging to the no-man's-land of art. Though James dealt frequently in his fiction with Americans suffering at the hands of conspiring or hostile Europeans, he told his brother William that he wished to write in such a way that no one could detect his nationality. That, he said, would be "more civilized." Assuredly we should have no objections to James's view, for all that we can wish for our writers is that they be as American as they *unconsciously* can be. Hawthorne, strong as the instincts of the artist were in him, would never have been willing to pass for anyone but an American. In fact, when certain Englishmen, hearing of the very favorable criticism of *The Scarlet Letter* in England, assumed on that account that its author could only be British, he was disgusted instead of flattered.

But what about that author who was capable of elaborating a plot dealing with a pair of Siamese twins, one of whom was a Methodist and a teetotaler, the other a freethinker and a devotee of the bottle? Mark Twain has been read by millions in Germany, Russia, and elsewhere, who have considered him a veritable mirror of the American character. The British critics of the nineteenth century claimed to have found our most original contribution to the world's store of literature in our humorous writing, and surely Mark Twain stands at the head of our vast procession of literary jesters. But, I should say, he has offered to the world primarily a hearty picture of the cheerful irreverence that has been one of the accompaniments of our democratic life—an important picture, to be sure, yet not a central one.

When we consider the work of Whitman and of Emerson, I think we approach a more obvious centrality, for these two men have perhaps come nearest to expressing directly and indirectly what John Dewey called "the metaphysical implications of the idea of democracy." Of the two, Whitman is perhaps more widely read today at home and abroad, but, considering also the days gone by, Emerson is the one whose message has been more widely disseminated. For that reason he is to be preferred as our point of concentration. However, another reason leads one to choose Emerson—and that is the fact that from him Whitman drew ideas and inspiration on a variety of topics, including the metaphysics of democracy. "Master, these shores *you* have found," wrote Whitman in a letter addressed to Emerson and printed in the second edition of *Leaves of Grass.* In a more homely metaphor he remarked, "I was simmering, simmering, simmering. Emerson brought me to a boil."

We might remind ourselves at this point that Emerson has been a potent influence upon a number of American writers. Whitman, Thoreau, Emily Dickinson, Edwin Arlington Robinson—these and more have felt the tonic effect of his ideas. In Europe also the list of those who have acknowledged his catalytic stimulus includes the names of Hermann Grimm, Matthew Arnold, George Eliot, Nietzsche, Tyndall, and Huxley. In centering our thoughts upon him, we are, accordingly, not merely gratifying a patriotic antiquarianism in brushing the dust off the notions of an ex-Unitarian clergyman who lectured on village platforms and later made essays of his lectures—a man full of the chill of his native New England. We deal with one of the most influential thinkers who ever raised his voice in America. Indeed, Emerson's ideas have exerted influence in circles where the name of Thomas Jefferson has never been heard.

When one examines the method of Emerson's thinking and his intellectual climate it may seem astounding that he could have wielded so much influence, for he was not a formal philosopher, he could not argue his points, and his sentences stand as single sentries instead of members of a company bent upon concerted attack or defense. Yet those sentences which stand thus alone are of singular brilliance. Some of them we quote as proverbs without knowing who wrote them: To think is to act; Beauty is its own excuse for being; He builded better than he knew; A foolish consistency is the hobgoblin of little minds; Hitch your wagon to a star. But despite the rhetorical coruscations, Emerson's method of writing strikes us as that of a poetic thinker incapable of coherent and close reasoning.

We may be bothered also by the fact that he pulls his shining thoughts out of the old stream of Neoplatonic idealism—and certainly that seems an old-fashioned place to fish. Moreover, he sometimes retires to a particular pool of mysticism just off the Neoplatonic river. He always returns with a creel full of fine specimens, but most of us can't fish in that pool, for there one uses neither tackle nor bait. The fish just come. For some time T. S. Eliot and his school have nodded in the di-

and mob rule. But Wordsworth was not afraid to use the word, for he was one of the most profound and entire believers in democracy who ever lived and wrote. In 1794, when he was barely 24, he announced boldly, even defiantly, "I am of that odious class of men called democrats, and of that class I shall for ever continue" (EY 119).

When Wordsworth was first bursting upon the literary scene, certainly, the educated society of readers and reviewers of poetry hardly knew what to make of this kind of boldness and defiance. Writing in the journal *Monthly Review* in June 1799 in response to the first publication of the *Lyrical Ballads,* even one of the fairest and most astute of these early reviewers, Dr. Charles Burney, judged those early great poems to be "strange" and "gloomy" but also "unsocial" with "a rhapsody of unintelligible wildness" (204, 210). But he added, nevertheless, that the poetry was obviously produced by "the reflections of no common mind" (210).

It is this final assumption of uniqueness and uncommonness that I believe Wordsworth ironically would have found most objectionable in such a review. For Wordsworth was militantly and enduringly common. One of his most striking and most frequent claims is to be the purveyor of the reflections of a *common* mind in its encounters with *common* things.

"Higher minds," Wordsworth observes near the end of his greatest poem, *The Prelude,* which is his poetic study of his own mind and its education,—"higher minds," he says, possess the ability to "build up greatest things / From least suggestions; ever on the watch, / Willing to work and to be wrought upon, / They need not extraordinary calls / To rouse them" (1850 *Prelude* 14.101-05). Wordsworth himself, although I have said he had a common mind, of course possessed as well one of these higher minds. And Wordsworth himself is also well described by his famous definition of a poet: "He is a man speaking to men: a man, it is true, endowed with more lively sensibility, more enthusiasm and tenderness, who has a greater knowledge of human nature, and a more comprehensive soul, than are supposed to be common among mankind" (1800 Preface to *Lyrical Ballads,* lines 320-324). So then a poet, a Wordsworth, in his own words is a higher mind, with at least a seemingly uncommon sensibility and enthusiasm and knowledge.

And yet even in this context of intellectual superiority, there is in Wordsworth an insistent *commonness* which I find constantly startling in his writings. That insistent rejection of any need for "extraordinary calls" near the end of *The Prelude* is typical of this commonness, and the wording of the Preface to *Lyrical Ballads* about what is "supposed to be common among mankind" suggests a distrust about any negative suppositions on the common.

The insistent ordinariness of Wordsworth, although it has been shown to have familiar roots in a literary tradition which had developed in England by the end of the Eighteenth Century (see Ryskamp and Jordan) has no parallel among the major English poets who preceded him. Much can be seen, I think, in the way poets employ, or avoid, the common. Wordsworth very knowingly threw down a gauntlet of revolutionary poetics and education when he announced that the "principal object" of the *Lyrical Ballads* was "to choose incidents and situations" and language "from common life" (1850 Preface, lines 81-84). He proclaimed himself a champion of the common, and he was the first great poet to offer such a proclamation. It was one of his early convictions, and, in later years, when his attachment to the common perhaps began to lose some of its strength in the period of early manhood, as he tells us near the end of *The Prelude,* his sister Dorothy re-entered his life and helped to reinforce anew in him, as he says, what was always for him a necessary "sense / Of exquisite regard for common things" (*Prelude* 14.261.62).

There is no such expression of exquisite regard for common things in Shakespeare, for example. He expresses a much more traditional view when, in Sonnet 102, he writes that "sweets grown common lose their dear delight" (line 12). And characters in Shakespeare's plays disdain the common. I think of the Prince of Arragon in *The Merchant of Venice,* who proclaims before Portia's caskets: "I will not choose what many men desire, / Because I will not jump with common spirits, / And rank me with the barbarous multitudes" (2.9.31-33). Still less of an admirer of the common is Shakespeare's Coriolanus, who banishes from his presence all his inferiors as he barks, "You common cry of curs, whose breath I hate / As reek a'th'rotten fens" (3.3.120-21). And we recall Prince Hamlet using the very word *common* as one of his verbal daggers when first his mother and then her new husband try to persuade him that "death of fathers" is the "common theme" of Heaven, Nature, Reason (1.2.103-104), a perfectly ordinary fact which "is as common / As any the most vulgar thing to sence" (1.2.98-99); and Hamlet disagreeably agrees: "Ay, madam, it is common" (1.2.74).

Milton, so often Wordsworth's model in important ways, does not even use the word *common* in his poetry in the sense of "ordinary." No one would ever call Milton a poet of the ordinary, which is precisely what I am working toward calling Wordsworth. Milton speaks of such things as our "common Prison" (*Samson,* line 6, also 1161) or our "common Enemy" (*Samson* 1416), but he certainly does not ever reveal any exquisite regard for common things.

So conditioned are we still, and so conditioned was the great number of the reading public in Wordsworth's day, to expecting not inspiration but dulness in commonplace things and situations that Wordsworth found in his efforts to make poetry out of the common a sense of crusade that would stay with him for a lifetime. It was not a mere matter of preference with him, however. He showed a determination not to neglect or lose any source of knowledge or insight, and as a self-proclaimed Prophet of Nature, he found it essential in his role of man speaking to men to omit nothing from his poetry that could benefit and enlighten his readers. "To me the meanest flower that blows can give / Thoughts that do often lie too deep for tears," he writes at the end of the Intimations Ode. That fact being established, it follows that Wordsworth in his poetry must examine with close scrutiny the meanest flower and *all* the flowers and all other common things. He must not miss the deep thoughts they can give. And as a poet he feels the responsibility to convey those thoughts to his readers without loss or omission.

And without false excitement, without spectacular screams for attention. "I have wished to keep the reader in the company of flesh and blood," he announces in the Preface to *Lyrical Ballads* (1850 Preface, lines 198-99), and that intention, as he reminds us there, means an avoidance of the "frantic" and the "sickly" and the "extravagant". He wants always to "counteract" in his readers the "degrading thirst after outrageous stimulation" (1850 Preface, lines 172-76).

I should like, therefore, to explore a bit more this Wordsworthian cultivation of the commonplace—attempting to find out what the common things of earth meant to this uncommon poet, what lessons he learned from the meanest flowers, and what and how he expected us, his readers, to gain from his poetic treatments of the common growth of mother-earth.

The earliest lesson that Wordsworth learned from common things was in some ways the greatest. By observing the things of earth the *child* Wordsworth saw too, or seemed to see, the very face of heaven. The great Ode begins with this memory: "There was a time when meadow, grove, and stream, / The earth, and every common sight / To me did seem / Apparelled in celestial light" (lines 1-4). Nor is this vision splendid a private one. The poet insists that this ability of "every common sight" on earth to convey to children the vision of heaven is universal. "Heaven lies about us in our infancy!" (line 67)—it lies about us *all.*

But of course it does not stay with us, not with our conscious perceptions, and the *loss* of heaven in later years is also universal. There comes a time to every one of us when, thinking of the scenes of heaven, we must admit: "It is not now as it hath been of yore:— / Turn whereso'er I may, / By night or day, / The things which I have seen I now can see no more" (6-9).

Now it is true, the poet tells us, that we retain some indistinct memories of that celestial period of earth life;

there is for him and for us all a sense of "perpetual benediction" (135) in those memories, those "shadowy recollections" (150), despite their blurred vaguenesses.

But this, I fear, begins, despite its poetic beauty—maybe because of all its poetic beauty—to sound like too much poetry, begins to sound like the airy and insubstantial product of a poet's eye, in a fine frenzy rolling, glancing from heaven to earth, from earth to heaven, and having no real contact with the common life of this planet, no solid connection with the common growth of mother-earth to which Wordsworth claims to maintain allegiance.

But no. On the contrary, Wordsworth rarely loses that contact with common reality, and never for very long. The celestial glory of the earth in our childhood is a common reality for him. And just exactly what happens to the celestial light that once has been the apparel of "every common sight"? How does the vague recollection of a light that is gone function still as "the fountain light of all our day" and "a master light of all our seeing"? The answer is pure Wordsworth, and crucial. The light of the heavenly vision does not die, although to the perception of men it *seems* to "die away." It does not fade away either. In modern cinema or television parlance, the technique of "fade-in" produces the gradual coming or bringing into full visibility of an image. Wordsworth uses the same language to describe the same kind of process. The visionary celestial light of heaven on earth, he says, which seems to die away, actually fades "into the light of common day." The celestial light *merges* into and becomes absorbed by that very Wordsworthian-sounding master light of *all* our seeing, the light of common day. This light, common daylight, in one of the poet's favorite images and the very similar phrases he uses to describe it again and again are among his favorite words. As we proceed, I shall point out several more examples, but there are many others that we can all watch for in our reading of him.

Wordsworth's own life and poetic career must be viewed in this heavenly light of common day. And once we shine that light upon him, how revelatory it is of his highest experiences and perceptions, of his education. I think of his description of himself in *The Prelude* as a ten-year-old boy, for example, and his insistent founding of his joys in the commonplace: "The earth / And common face of Nature spake to me / Rememberable things" (1.581-88).

Another example comes out of Wordsworth's poetic description of his years at grammar school in the village of Hawkshead. He describes his youthful excursion to the splendid ruins of Furness Abbey, and another excursion to Bowness and the old White Lion Inn, and a boat race on Lake Windermere out to Lady Holm Isle, and so on—all of these experiences that might inspire poetic gushing. But for Wordsworth it is invariably the ordinary aspects of these potentially exotic places and experiences, *not* the extraordinary, that are of most meaning. He summarizes their effects on him in these words: "Thus were my sympathies enlarged, and thus / Daily the common range of visible things / Grew dear to me: already I began / To love the sun; a boy I loved the sun" (2.175-78). His joys derive from the circulation of common blood through common veins, the breathing of common air in common lungs. It is again and again the light of common day that illuminates the poet's vision.

There is more to all this constant examination of common things by common light than simple admiration, however sublime. For Wordsworth's education was dependent on his association with the common face of earth. I do not mean to detract, as he himself sometimes does, from the unusually good schooling he obtained at Hawkshead and even, despite its problems in the late eighteenth century, at Cambridge. But there is no doubt that he himself believed that, whatever the quality and advantages of his formal schooling, his greatest education lay elsewhere. Academic "glory," he tells us, "was but little sought by me, / And little won" (*Prelude* 3.74-75). At Cambridge particularly he repeatedly had "A feeling that I was not for that hour, / Nor for that place" (3.81-82), a feeling that drove him out alone into the fields outside of Cambridge, where "As if awakened, summoned, roused, constrained, / I looked for universal things; perused / The common countenance of earth and sky" (3.108-10). And he found in that common countenance of earth and sky a lingering celestial light—and an education not offered at Cambridge nor any other university. He sought from common things to learn, and from them he *did* learn—highest truth: "I called on both [heaven and earth] to teach me what they might; / Or turning the mind in upon herself," for that internal landscape for Wordsworth was inseparable from the rest of the common countenance of earth and sky, "Pored, watched, expected, listened, spread my thoughts / And spread them with a wider creeping" (3.115-18).

Not all of his education from earth's commonplaces was so determinedly active or required such pursuit and striving. One of the crucial educational experiences of the poet's life came to him when he was *not* engaged in any conscious effort. It is an account that achieves that perfectly Wordsworthian blend of the personal, the unique, the singling out, but also the very common; it occurred when "vows / Were then made for" him, but typically it occurred amid "the sweetness of a common dawn" (4.334-35, 330). This is surely an extraordinary moment in the life of anyone, including any poet. But even this extraordinary instant of vow-making and dedication, or poetic ordination, does not result from any extraordinary call. No Senate crowned the poet; no

synod annointed him. His companions were "Dews, vapours, and the melody of birds, / And labourers going forth to till the fields"—common labourers, of course, and common birds, appropriate to that common dawn.

To whatever degree contact with common things educates, seeing things in a common light of day, awakening with a common dawn, to a similar degree being cut off from those common contacts can prevent learning, can even in extreme cases, destroy the mind. Thus the young Vaudracour, in one sense representing Wordsworth himself, but also a representative of the "last recess" of human woe, thwarted, utterly frustrated, damned, reaches at last a condition of "shunning even the light of common day" (1805 *Prelude* 9.909, 930). Cut off from that common light of all our seeing, he can be touched or affected or educated by nothing at all, not even "the voice of freedom," nor "public hope, / Or personal memory of his own deep wrongs." Without that common association, having lost the light of common day, Vaudracour, and anyone like him, reverts to mental non-being: "In those gloomy shades, / His days he wasted, an imbecile mind" (9.581-85).

It was out of something of a Vaudracour-like crisis that Dorothy brought her brother back to himself. And, inevitably, her tools were the common things of earth. At a time when the poet's soul had become too severe, too over-stern, too solid and terrible a rock, as he tells her,

> Thou didst plant its crevices with flowers,
> And teach the little birds to build their nests
> And warble in its chambers. At a time
> When Nature, destined to remain so long
> Foremost in my affections, had fallen back
> Into a second place, pleased to become
> A handmaid to a nobler than herself,
> When every day brought with it some new sense
> Of exquisite regard for common things,
> And all the earth was budding with these gifts
> Of more refined humanity, thy breath,
> Dear Sister! was a kind of gentler spring
> That went before my steps.
>
> (14.253-66)

And thus recalled to himself and the truest bases of his knowledge and education and humane concern, Wordsworth could learn his greatest lessons of truth. And the truth that continually mattered most to him was common truth, as he tells us in the Preface to *Lyrical Ballads*—truth "not individual and local, but general and operative" (1850 Preface, lines 379-80).

As *The Prelude* tells the story, the culminating educational experience of Wordsworth's mental development occurred at Mt. Snowdon. Here in his descriptions of this experience, the crucial tension inherent in Wordsworth's theories about the sublime and the commonplace as somehow *one* becomes most apparent. The

Snowdon vision is itself a representation of "the enduring and the transient" (14.100). It is impressive, spectacular, and immensely individual. It is a once-in-a-lifetime event, or rather rarer yet, for Wordsworth compares it to the once-in-all-time Creation of the World. The very rhythms and sounds of the poetry aim at conveying the sharp and sudden impact and uniqueness of this grandest of moments, this extraordinary and highly uncommon event in human history. But even here, Wordsworth insists on the commonplace, for the common, the ordinary, is the soil out of which, for him, inevitably springs the spectacular and the unique. For Wordsworth, the vision of creative power which he witnessed atop Mt. Snowdon would inevitably come "in life's every-day appearances." It is the commonplace object that calls forth both the excellence and best power of the seeing eye.

When Wordsworth wrote in 1794 to William Matthews that he was "of that odious class of men called democrats," he meant it utterly. If the Revolution and its succession of regimes and severed heads offered no lasting hope, "in me," he says, "confidence was unimpaired" (11.7). Wordsworth's democratic faith and philosophy had remarkably little to do with governments and politics. "In the People was my trust," he affirms simply (11.11), but it was an affirmation that few politicians of any brand and none of Wordsworth's political detractors could make so convincingly. And years later, at the time of the Peninsular Wars and the newly hatched tyranny of Napoleon Buonaparte, the poet remained true to his democratic principles. "In despite of the mightiest power which a foreign Invader" or any other source of oppression can bring to bear, he writes in his *Convention of Cintra* tract in 1809, "the cause of the People, in dangers and difficulties issuing from this quarter of oppression, is safe while it remains not only in the bosom but in the hands of the People" (154). But there is little encouragement for office-holders or office-seekers in Wordsworth's writings. In that same 1794 letter to William Matthews, he spoke with disgust of "the infatuation profligacy and extravagance of men in power" (*EY* 119). And it is perhaps lamentably true that political thinkers will never respond very warmly to Wordsworth's apolitical kind of democracy. But central to any understanding of his achievement as poet and thinker is a recognition of his reverence for the common things and common people of earth, that ingredient in his writing which William Hazlitt rightly hailed as the *philosophical* basis of Wordsworth's poetry, that democratizing insistence which claims "kindred only with the commonest" (163).

Works Cited

Burney, Charles. Rev. of *Lyrical Ballads. Monthly Review* 2nd ser. 29 (June 1799): 202-10.

Hazlitt, William. *The Complete Works of William Hazlitt.* Ed. P. P. Howe. 21 vols. New York: AMS, 1967.

Jordan, John E. "The Novelty of the *Lyrical Ballads." Bicentenary Wordsworth Studies in Memory of John Alban Finch.* Ed. Jonathan Wordsworth. Ithaca: Cornell UP, 1970, 340-58.

Milton, John. *John Milton: Complete Poems and Major Prose.* Ed. Merritt Y. Hughes. New York: Odyssey, 1957.

Ryskamp, Charles. "Wordsworth's *Lyrical Ballads* in Their Time." *From Sensibility to Romanticism: Essays Presented to Frederick A. Pottle.* Ed. F. W. Hilles and Harold Bloom. New York: Oxford UP, 1965, 357-72.

Southey, Robert. Rev. of *Lyrical Ballads,* by Wordsworth and Coleridge. *Critical Review* Oct. 1798: 197-204.

Shakespeare, William. *The Riverside Shakespeare.* Ed. G. Blakemore Evans. Boston: Houghton Mifflin, 1974.

Wordsworth, William. *Convention of Cintra.* Ed. Gordon Kent Thomas. Provo: Brigham Young UP, 1983.

———. *The Poetical Works of William Wordsworth.* Ed. Ernest de Selincourt and Helen Darbishire. 5 vols. Oxford: Clarendon, 1952-59.

———. *The Prelude, 1799, 1805, 1850.* Ed. Jonathan Wordsworth, M. H. Abrams, and Stephen Gill. New York: Norton, 1979.

———. *The Prose Works of William Wordsworth.* Ed. W. J. B. Owen and Jane Worthington Smyser. 3 vols. Oxford: Clarendon, 1974.

Wordsworth, William and Dorothy Wordsworth. *The Letters of William and Dorothy Wordsworth.* Vol. 1, The Early Years. Ed. Chester L. Shaver. Cited as EY. Oxford: Clarendon, 1967.

Robert Lawson-Peebles (essay date 1996)

SOURCE: Lawson-Peebles, Robert. "Of Pew Canopies and Pig-Pens: The Transatlantic Travails of James Fenimore Cooper." In *Making America/Making American Literature: Franklin to Cooper,* edited by A. Robert Lee and W. M. Verhoeven, pp. 337-55. Amsterdam and Atlanta, Ga.: Rodopi, 1996.

[*In the following essay, Lawson-Peebles discusses James Fenimore Cooper's navigation of the political and artistic divide between aristocracy and democracy.*]

> [T]he great error of democracy [is that it] fancies truth is to be proved by counting noses; while aristocracy commits the antagonist blunder of believing that excellence is inherited from male to male, and that too in the order of primogeniture! It is not easy to say where one is to look for truth in this life.

These are the words of Mordaunt Littlepage as he opens his narrative in James Fenimore Cooper's 1845 novel, *The Chainbearer,* the second in the Littlepage trilogy. They relate to a dispute over the "New Hampshire Grants," a tract of land later to be part of Vermont. One party to the dispute was Philip Schuyler (1733-1804), described by Littlepage as "a New York gentleman," a talented Revolutionary general but also supercilious and a strict disciplinarian, who supported his state's claims to the land. The other party was described by Littlepage as "the yeomen of New England . . . imbued with all the distinctive notions of their very peculiar state of society"—trying, as it were, to vote themselves farms.[1] Littlepage's words voice Cooper's prejudices and self-esteem, for the author liked to think of himself, too, as a "New York gentleman." But they are also latter-day reflections, firstly on Cooper's longterm and increasingly rueful search for "truth" through the medium of fiction, and secondly on the relation of that search to American history. I want to suggest in this essay that in the course of that search Cooper had to negotiate a path between two differing political and textual systems: those of Europe and the United States. The negotiation was often signaled synecdochally for, as John P. McWilliams has remarked, "Cooper repeatedly saw the largest of issues in the smallest of events."[2] It is a method that has been adopted by a number of twentieth-century writers, including Sherwood Anderson and Ernest Hemingway, and is often used, as Gertrude Stein put it, "to express the rhythm of the visible world."[3] The Cooperian rhythm, I want to suggest, was Anglo-American, often created out of antithesis. For instance, in *The Redskins* (1846), the final novel in the Littlepage trilogy, he embodied the political antinomy of my epigraph by employing two synecdoches: aristocracy is represented by a pew canopy, while the noses of democracy are represented by a pig-pen. I shall return to them towards the end of this essay.

An early published example of Cooper's political and textual negotiation is the review, which appeared in May 1822, of Catharine Maria Sedgwick's first novel, *A New England Tale.* At that point, Cooper had published two novels: *Precaution* (1820), set in Britain, and *The Spy* (1821), set in the United States. James D. Wallace has shown how Cooper mapped the structures of plot and character contained in his "British" novel onto the environment of his "American" novel, "creating a pattern of familial and political conflict . . . which was indisputably American and yet which would be familiar and accessible to an audience accustomed to British fiction."[4] In so doing, as Wallace demonstrates, he created a national audience; but he also used the process of mapping to examine issues which would occupy much of the rest of his career. The review reflects on those issues, in the light of the fictional journey already undertaken on both sides of the Atlantic. Firstly, it sets out his view of an ideal society that is at once stratified and

unified; and secondly, it displays his view of the role of the novelist in helping to create such a society. Because the review is not easily available, I shall examine it at some length.

Cooper begins by noting that American "political institutions, the state of learning among us, and the influence of religion upon the national character, have often been discussed and displayed; but our domestic manners, the social and moral influences, which operate in retirement, and in common intercourse, and the multitude of local peculiarities, which form our distinctive features upon the many peopled earth, have very seldom been happily exhibited in our literature."[5] Cooper's attitude to the importance of "domestic manners" to an extent anticipates the breadth if not (yet) the disdain of Frances Trollope's notorious 1832 *Domestic Manners of the Americans.* Certainly, his view of society, like hers, is hierarchical. To support this he quotes from the *Essay on the Evils of Popular Ignorance,* by the English essayist and Baptist minister John Foster (1770-1843): "'It is of great consequence in a nation, that whatever there is in it of dignity and refinement, of liberalized feeling and deportment, and of intelligence, should have its effect downward through all the gradations of the state, even to the lowest'" (129).[6] But Cooper's vision of a unified society goes further. Talking of "the reciprocal duties of respective stations," he remarks:

> The motive of interest certainly urges the superior orders to cultivate the lower classes in society, for in the course of reaction, the influence of mind upon mind is displayed in the effect produced by the humble on the high, as much, if not more, as in the impressions effected by the latter upon the former.
>
> (129)

Cooper distinguishes between service and servility, identifying the latter with countries "where there are more servants than places." In contrast, in the United States the "general provision for the welfare and improvement of our lower orders does not generate a presumptuous deportment or a selfish conduct in them; and this is proved by the fact, that the best of this class are the most cultivated and intelligent" (128). This was a view of the United States that he would question later on, but it remained a constant element in his model society, to which it was his task to aim as a novelist.

Like Henry Fielding, Cooper believes that the novelist is "a true historian . . . a describer of society as it exists, and men as they are" (98). He particularly admires "the inventive talent which employs itself in the province of daily life, which delineates what we have all felt and observed, which detects the vices that poison domestic peace, and corrupt social virtue, or which displays the opinions and passions that dignify and sweeten, or debase and embitter our earthly existence . . ." (100-01). In this the novelist has an important role to play, for fiction "addresses our love of truth—not the mere love of facts expressed by true names and dates, but the love of that higher truth, the truth of nature and of principles, which is a primitive law of the human mind, and only to be effaced by the most deplorable perversion" (99). Cooper's definition of "truth" here shifts from a representational to a moral one, but in that ambivalence he follows such British writers as Oliver Goldsmith, Maria Edgeworth and Fielding who, he asserts, have rendered "a service to virtue" (101). In comparison with them, the American service to virtue has been small indeed. "National tales" have been lacking, and even now he fears that the few that have so far been written, a tale called "Salem Witchcraft" and Royall Tyler's *The Algerine Captive,* have been lost. It is up to a collector to snatch them "from oblivion, and give them that place among the memorials of other days, which is due to the early and authentic historians of a country" (97-98).

The Sedgwick review encapsulates the negotiation between textual systems which Cooper had so far been undertaking in his fiction. We have known for some time that the immediate inspiration for *Precaution* was Jane Austen.[7] However, behind Austen lay a series of British moral guidebooks, of which Foster's *Essay on the Evils of Popular Ignorance* was a recent example. For instance, Cooper's comments above on "the welfare and improvement of our lower orders" echoes a popular book by the English Anglican priest Thomas Gisborne (1758-1846). Gisborne's *Enquiry into the Duties of Men in the Higher and Middle Classes of Society in Great Britain* was first published in 1794 and by 1824 had reached its seventh edition. Gisborne believed that "[t]o encourage a race of honest, skilful, and industrious tenants, is one of the first duties of a private gentleman; whether he consults his own interest, or the general welfare of the community."[8] British texts, then, provided Cooper with models of virtuous social behavior. The United States provided the ground against which those models could be tested. In writing *The Spy,* Cooper indicated that he was producing, in his well-known phrase to his publisher, "an American novel professedly." The test would be in terms of American history. In looking back to the American Revolution Cooper asserted that "a good portion" of the novel was "true," in both its moral and representational meanings. It follows from this that in the 1821 Preface to *The Spy* Cooper should pour scorn on one of Charles Brockden Brown's less likely coincidences in *Edgar Huntly* (1799), while at the same time following the nationalist intention of his predecessor. Brown had rejected "Gothic castles and chimeras" in favor of the "incidents of Indian hostility, and perils of the western wilderness."

Cooper, likewise, indicated that he would not fill his American scene with "moated castles, drawbridges and a kind of classic nature."[9]

This is not to say that he was declaring literary independence. In exploring the American scene and excavating American history, Cooper sought a model political system that was transatlantic, a complex organism which was hierarchical yet open, honoring rank yet not opposed to change, created in the image of a family in which each member—and servants were members—had a role to play and was respected for it. The system rested on a particularly potent concept of property. In *The American Democrat* (1838), Cooper summed up the concept when he asserted that "[a]s property is the base of all civilization, its existence and security are indispensable to social improvement".[10] Unfortunately for him, by 1838 this was an outmoded view of the function of property. Even before the time that he was writing his first fictions and the Sedgwick review, the concept of property was beginning to undergo significant changes. Morton Horwitz has shown that, in the first decades of the nineteenth century, theories of property rights shifted from the agrarianism associated with Jefferson towards "the utilitarian world of economic efficiency" in which "the ownership of property implies above all the right to develop that property for business purposes."[11]

A related view of social and political change is revealed by a document preceding the Sedgwick review by a few months. In 1821 Cooper's friend William Leete Stone published *Reports of the Proceedings and Debates of the Convention of 1821,* held in Albany to discuss changes to the New York State Constitution. The Report records the speech against adopting manhood suffrage by James Kent (1763-1847), Chancellor of the New York Court of Chancery. Kent was familiar with Cooper for many years. He was the brother of Moss Kent, Cooper's boyhood hero and Judge Cooper's legal secretary; and a member, with Cooper, of the Bread and Cheese Club in New York.[12] In his speech Kent praised the current Constitution, framed forty-four years previously "by those illustrious sages and patriots who adorned the revolution," and which had given the vote to "the farmers of the state." Under this Constitution the population of the State had trebled in size and prospered. But now it was proposed to abolish the property qualification for senatorial office, and Kent anticipated the time when "men of no property, together with the crowds of dependants connected with great manufacturing and commercial establishments, and the motley and undefinable population of crowded ports" would become dominant. Anticipating De Tocqueville, he imagined that a time would come when "the majority [would] tyranize over the minority." It was already apparent that the Republic no longer consisted of the Jeffersonian ideal of "plain and simple republics of farmers." Instead, he remarked, "we are fast becoming a great nation, with great commerce, manufactures, population, wealth, luxuries, and with the vices and miseries that they engender." In his *Commentaries on American Law* (1826-30) Kent would compare American egalitarianism favorably with the British property system, which was dominated by a landed aristocracy, protected by primogeniture. But here, in 1821, Britain posed an altogether different kind of threat. Pointing at its "upwards of five millions of manufacturing and commercial labourers without property," Kent now pictured Britain as the threat of the future rather than the weight of the past. If such people were given the suffrage, they would, he believed, be manipulated by radicals to "sweep away the property, the laws, and the liberties of that island like a deluge." Already New York City seemed to be following the British example. Kent provided figures to show that it is:

> rapidly swelling into the unwieldy population, and with the burdensome pauperism, of an European metropolis. New-York is destined to become the future London of America; and in less than a century, that city, with the operation of universal suffrage, and under skilful direction, will govern this state.

Britain was therefore a dreadful portent of what would happen in the United States.[13]

Kent's argument failed to carry the day. The State Constitution of 1821 increased the suffrage far beyond the select class of freeholders beloved by the declining Federalist Party. The 1846 Constitution went further, making all offices elective and abolishing the remaining residence requirements for suffrage left intact in 1821. The conservative correlation of property and liberty came increasingly under attack from radicals such as Orestes Brownson, who pressed for the abolition of inheritance, and Thomas Skidmore, whose Paine-inspired *The Rights of Man to Property!* (1829) advocated redistribution of land.[14] To Henry Adams, looking back at the beginning of the century from its end, Kent's apocalyptic reaction seemed fully justified. Adams's feelings and metaphors alike were overwhelmed by the view:

> greed for wealth, lust for power, yearning for the blank void of savage freedom such as Indians and wolves delighted in,—these were the fires that flamed under the caldron of American society, in which, as conservatives believed, the old, well-proven, conservative crust of religion, government, family, and even respect for age, education, and experience was rapidly melting away, and was indeed, broken into fragments, swept about by the seething mass of scum ever rising in greater quantities to the surface.[15]

James Kent acted as caterer at the banquet on 29 May 1826, given for Cooper on the eve of his departure for Europe, by the Bread and Cheese Club. In his speech of thanks, Cooper reflected on his career as a novelist. No-

one owed a greater debt to "the Muse of History," he believed; "[n]o writer of our country has invaded her sacred precincts with greater licence or more frequency."[16] The remark about frequency is accurate. Of the six novels he had published by that date, five had examined American history, covering the period 1757-1794. The remark about license is less so. In the course of preparing his novels Cooper read widely in American history.[17] The reading prompted little hope that his model political system would be achieved in America, as a brief review of all the novels he had written by 1826 will show.

The closing chapter of *Precaution* begins with this paragraph:

> The harvest had been gathered, and the beautiful vales of Pendennyss were shooting forth a second crop of verdure. The husbandman was turning his prudent forethought to the promises of the coming year, while the castle itself exhibited to the gaze of the wondering peasant a sight of cheerfulness and animation which had not been seen in it since the days of the good duke. Its numerous windows were opened to the light of the sun, its halls teemed with the faces of its happy inmates. Servants in various liveries were seen gliding through its magnificent apartments and multiplied passages. Horses, grooms, and carriages, with varied costumes and different armorial bearings, crowded its spacious stables and offices. Everything spoke society, splendor, and activity without; everything denoted order, propriety, and happiness within.[18]

At first sight this seems an odd passage to be written by one who believed throughout his life that he was "as good a democrat as there is in America."[19] This passage, and the novel as a whole, have prompted many critics to dismiss *Precaution* as a false start in Cooper's career, a sycophantic and poorly-researched attempt at an English novel, and one which he would not repeat. This is not the case. Strip out the liveries and armorial bearings, replace "the good duke" and his castle with a good landlord and his manor-house, and we are left with an image which would remain Cooper's ideal. The sentences are constructed to convey a network of social groups and to assert a unity of nature and culture which provide the evidence for the closing moral comment. The balanced clauses of that comment recall the famous remark about Donwell Abbey in Jane Austen's *Emma*: "It was just what it ought to be, and it looked what it was."[20]

This image of unity disappears once the shapes of *Precaution* are mapped onto *The Spy*. "At the time of our tale, we were a divided people," remarks the narrative. The novel is riddled with divisions, familial and national, and the result is the devastation of property. The Skinners, the appropriately-named Patriot irregulars, destroy the home of Harvey Birch and then burn down the Locusts, the family home of the Whartons. Its blackened walls are "dreary memorials of the content and security that had so lately reigned within." The carriages with their "armorial bearings" in *Precaution* are now reduced to the single example, tarnished and worn, which carries the broken family away from their home. "'The law of the neutral ground is the law of the strongest.'" cries one of the Skinners as he begins to wreck the Birch home, and the consequence for the United States is bleak indeed.[21]

It could perhaps be argued that the bleakness is an inevitable result of the portrayal of a conflict regarded more as a "civil war" (as Cooper put it in his 1831 Preface to *The Spy*) than a war of liberation.[22] But a review of the other American novels in order of plot chronology reveals no happier a picture. Cooper's survey of American history begins with remarks on "the cold and selfish policy of the distant monarchs of Europe" during the French and Indian War, and portrays a land riven by conflict and deception (*The Last of the Mohicans*, 1826).[23] A colonial novel, perhaps, but *Lionel Lincoln* (1825), too, gives no happier a view of America. As John McWilliams has shown, the novel sits oddly with the other texts commemorating the fiftieth anniversary of Lexington, Concord and Bunker Hill. In place of their triumphalism, Cooper shows the battles which, when not clouded by gunsmoke, reflect the divided loyalties of the time, soaked in blood and punctuated by insanity.[24] Only *The Pilot* (1824) gives some relief from Cooper's social concerns, because of course it is a version of the adventures of John Paul Jones, set around the Northeast coast of England. Even here the English setting now provides no model of a unified society. When Cooper places his characters ashore, he ignores his advice in the 1821 Preface to *The Spy* and indulges in subfusc gothicking somewhere below Scott-land, in a castle replete with gloomy corridors and fluttering heroines. *The Pioneers* (1823) brings us back to America and Cooper's usual worries. His review of American history ends in 1794 with the departure of Natty Bumppo westwards, after refusing the offer of some of "the new-fashioned money that they've been making at Albany, out of paper!" The marginal man is unable to integrate into the modern commercial community of Templeton.[25]

When he left the United States in 1826, Cooper was completing *The Prairie*, bringing his survey of American history almost up to date. It begins by moving westwards, in the footsteps of Natty Bumppo who, in the words of the closing sentence of *The Pioneers*, was "the foremost in that band of pioneers, who are opening the way for the march of the nation across the continent."[26] The date chosen is 1805, allowing Cooper to consider the Louisiana Purchase, which had been completed on 20 December 1803, and which doubled the territory of the United States, thus giving fresh impetus to the questions raised in *The Pioneers*. Indeed, *The*

Prairie can be regarded as a meditation on the meaning of the Purchase; it asks if the nation *should* march across the continent. It is often forgotten now that the Purchase was a controversial act. Many people believed that the land was not worth buying, and that the addition of so much new territory would entice lawless people and might even threaten the integrity of the United States. Zebulon Pike, who led one of the earliest expeditions westward, reported seeing much "barren soil" and used topography to solve the legal and demographic problems:

> These vast plains of the western hemisphere, may become in time equally celebrated as the sandy desarts of Africa . . . But from these immense prairies may arise one great advantage to the United States, viz: The restriction of our population to some certain limits, and thereby a continuation of the union. Our citizens being so prone to rambling and extending themselves, on the frontiers, will, through necessity, be constrained to limit their extent on the west. . . .[27]

The uncultivated areas would thus be left to the Native Americans. Pike's *Account* was one of Cooper's sources for *The Prairie*, and early in the novel Natty repeats Pike's "barrier" theory. Yet, writing in 1826, Cooper knew that Pike's optimistic prediction was not being realized. An expanded Union merely expands the greed of its settlers. In Cooper's most doomladen novel to date, the "bleak and solitary" environment is an appropriate setting for the evil family of squatters.[28]

Cooper's seven-year sojourn in Europe provided him with a wealth of material, including five travel volumes collectively titled *Gleanings in Europe*, published between 1836 and 1838. They were not popular. Indeed, Cooper himself was modest about them, calling them "nothing but the gleanings that are to be had after the harvests gathered by those who have gone before me."[29] Nevertheless, those gleanings allowed him to develop the textual examination of the European political system which previously he had only encountered through the works of others. The result was a richer, more complex, and even more negative view of American society. Living amongst the political unrest of France, he was able to praise American stability: "ours is fast getting to be the oldest political system in Christendom."[30] Yet because he lived in Paris at the moment that the Bourbon Restoration revitalized it as the cultural capital of Europe, he could also see that a monarchy, for which as a good American he had the deepest distaste, could act as a cultural stimulant for which democracy had not yet found an equivalent. Similarly, he now had a more sophisticated view of the class system. With his eye for a synecdoche, he fixed on the visiting card and showed at length how it acts as a social enabler and emollient:

> These things may strike you as of little moment. They are, however, of more concern than one living in the simple society of America may at first suppose. The

etiquette of visiting has of course an influence on the entire associations of a traveller. . . . Ordinary life is altogether coloured by things that, in themselves, may appear trifling, but which can no more be neglected with impunity, than one can neglect the varying fashions in dress.

In contrast, he saw American society as colorless, characterized by "an overwhelming mediocrity," an opinion he shared with Tocqueville's contemporaneous *Democracy in America*. American "ordinary social intercourse," he thought, is "uncomfortable"; and he believed that:

In grace of mind, in a love, and even in a knowledge of the arts, a large portion of the common Italians are as much superior to the Anglo-Saxon race as civilization is superior to barbarism.

As the last comment suggests, he did not exempt Britain from his criticisms. While "[o]ne of the merits of England is the perfect order in which every thing is kept, and the perfect method with which every thing is done"—and to prove it he produced a negative catalogue specifically aimed against France—he believed that Britain was blighted by a rigid class system that was politically and spatially exclusive and gave its society a supercilious tone. Compared with this "dog-in-the-manger propensity," the Native Americans were truly noble. In addition, he provided evidence to demonstrate the truth of James Kent's fears of London. Although London, like Paris, was a cultural center, its traffic-crowded streets made life dangerous for a pedestrian. Industrialisation had created "an excess of pauperism, that hangs like a dead weight on the nation" and which prompted a fearful government into "a crusade against popular rights." And at the bottom of the heap was the female servant, "whose condition I should think less enviable than that of Asiatic slaves." Cooper recounted two instances, one of which affected him deeply. It was of a girl in her early twenties who "had much delicacy of form and expression" but who always kept her eyes downcast and moved with "a sort of drilled trot, as if she had been taught a particular movement to denote assiduity and diligence." Then she lost her job:

I found her weeping in the street. . . . I took the occasion to give her a few shillings as her due for past services, but so complete was her misery in being turned away without a character, that even the sight of money failed to produce the usual effects. I make little doubt she took refuge in gin, the bane of thousands and tens of thousands of her sex, in this huge theatre of misery and vice.

Nothing provided a clearer contrast to his model of a unified familial society, as outlined in the Sedgwick review, where servants played a central role.[31] Even in such later, bitter novels as *The Crater* (1847), Cooper

could not produce such an image of the United States. Servants still had role to play in a society unmarked by what he called the "English system of exclusion."[32] Instead, the more open American system presented other threats to his model society. I shall illustrate this by a discussion of the Littlepage trilogy.

It is, of course, well known that the immediate impulse for the trilogy—*Satanstoe* (1845), *The Chainbearer* (1845) *The Redskins* (1846)—is the Anti-Rent War, a conflict which broke out in New York State in 1839 between landlords and agricultural tenants.[33] The conflict itself is now a footnote in New York history, but Cooper's synecdochal method of thinking prompted him to think that the future of America hung upon its outcome. Writing to some friends shortly after the publication of the trilogy, he asserted:

As to anti-rentism, in my judgment it is to be the test of the institutions. If men find that by making political combinations they can wipe out their indebtedness, adieu to everything like liberty or government. There will be one alternative, and that will be the bayonet.[34]

He seemed here to be recalling the violence that was endemic to the worlds of *The Last of the Mohicans* and *Lionel Lincoln*, and which had shaken many European states. Certainly, so much appeared to be at stake that Cooper reasserted the identity of property and civilization that he had made in *The American Democrat*. One of the older Littlepages in *The Redskins*, Uncle Ro, makes Cooper's point when he clearly sets out the terms of the conflict:

[either] this is a civilized country, or it is not. If it be a civilized country, it will respect the rights of property, and its own laws; if the reverse, it will not respect them.[35]

The trilogy tests this proposition, and the test is signaled by the first sentence of the first novel, when Corny Littlepage remarks: "It is easy to foresee that this country is destined to undergo great and rapid changes."[36] Those changes are set in broad perspective. Working with a historical canvas even larger than that created by his novels of 1821-27, Cooper provides precise historical markers in Ticonderoga, the Revolution, and the Anti-Rent War. Each novel, moreover, is carefully linked to its neighbor by a web of cross-reference, by Cooper's footnotes, and by two dynasties, the Littlepages and the Newcomes.

The Littlepages represent genteel America. They are a close-knit family intensely aware of their genealogy. Each volume opens with a rehearsal of the family history by the narrator. The family is shown growing from a colonial naiveté to a cultural independence finally achieved by foreign travel. The more sophisticated members of the family leaven their patriotism with a healthy critique of their country. Around them, in the form of an extended family, is gathered a collection of friends, yeomen and retainers, most of whom are endowed with good sense if not the grace and linguistic refinement of the gentry. The class structure they uphold is relatively open, because the only qualification for entry into the family is merit. Corny Littlepage marries a lady of greater wealth, thereby establishing the pre-eminence of the family in the locality. Mordaunt and Hugh marry ladies stricken with poverty. The gentility of the family is planted in landed property, and the close relation of ownership and familial morals is neatly summed up by Uncle Ro:

> here is a citizen who has got as much property as he wants, and who wishes to live for other purposes than to accumulate. This property is not only invested to his entire satisfaction, as regards convenience, security, and returns, but also in a way that is connected with some of the best sentiments of his nature. It is property that has descended to him through ancestors for two centuries; property which is historically connected with his name—on which he was born, on which he has lived, and on which he has hoped to die; property, in a word, that is associated with all the higher feelings of humanity.[37]

As the last phrase suggests, property takes on a moral imperative. Indeed, in *The Chainbearer,* Mordaunt Littlepage specifically calls the rights of property "inviolable—that is to say, sacred."[38] It is appropriate, then, that when Hugh Littlepage describes his inheritance, the property recalls the vale of Pendennyss in *Precaution,* but now includes an American wilderness, and a moral assertion capping a strong sense of possession by its owner:

> The whole of the land in sight—the rich bottoms, then waving with grass—the side-hills, the woods, the distant mountains—the orchards, dwellings, barns, and all the other accessories of rural life that appertained to the soil, were mine, and had thus become without a single act of injustice to any human being, so far as I knew and believed.[39]

This, clearly, is not Europe, for here property is not equated with spatial exclusion. And the whole—setting, family, trilogy—is presided over by two representatives of oppressed groups, the Black, Jaap, and the Native American, Susquesus, who perform great services for the family but, unlike the English servant, are not servile; and who, indeed, take on something of the quality of household gods as the trilogy progresses.[40]

Antithetically opposed to the Littlepages is the appropriately named Newcome family, who descend from an émigré Yankee. Cooper merely outlines their history. He need not do more, since they function only as antitypes of the Littlepages. When Corny Littlepage discusses the attitude of their founder to property and gentility, he sums up the whole tribe:

Jason was always a moral enigma, to me; there being an absolute absence, in his mind, so far as the claims and the rights of persons were connected with rank, education, birth, and experience. Rank, in the official sense, once possessed, he understood and respected; but of the claims to entitle one to its enjoyment, he seemed to have no sort of notion. For property he had a profound deference, so far as the deference extended to its importance and influence; but it would have caused him not the slightest qualm . . . to find himself suddenly installed in the mansion of the patroons. . . . The circumstance that he was dwelling under the roof that was erected by another man's ancestors . . . and that others were living who had a better moral right to it, would give him no sort of trouble, so long as any quirk of the law would sustain him in possession. In a word, all that was allied to sentiment, in matters of this nature, was totally lost on Jason Newcome. . . .[41]

Jason is presented as a rising entrepreneur who sees the cash nexus as the basis of property-ownership, and external objects as the mark of rank.

Surrounding the Newcomes is a very different kind of group, people whose attitude to property is devoid of sentiment. Cooper puts the essence of the Anti-Rent arguments into the mouth of the squatter Aaron Thousandacres in *The Chainbearer,* a successor to the Bush family in *The Prairie* and the Skinners in *The Spy:*

> There's two rights to all the land on 'arth, and the whull world over. One of these rights is what I call a king's right, or that which depends on writin's, and laws, and sich like contrivances; and the other depends on possession. It stands to reason, that fact is better than any writin' about it can be.[42]

This view draws a stark opposition between aristocracy and democracy not borne out by Cooper's Anglo-American experience. Further, the link with utilitarianism is made by the Anti-Rent lecturer in *The Redskins:*

> I respect and revere preemption rights, for they fortify and sustain the rights to the elements. Now, I do not condemn squattin' as some does. It's actin' accordin' to natur', and natur' is right. I respect and venerate a squatter's possession; for it's held under the sacred principle of usefulness.[43]

It follows that the violent "neutral ground" of the Revolution in *The Spy* is a feature of both colonial and republican America. The political change simply means a declension in civility, and in *The Redskins* a depleted Littlepage group are shown conducting a last-ditch stand against a community largely subverted by Newcome doctrine.

We can now return to the Littlepage pew canopy. The canopy is the equivalent of the armorial bearings in *Precaution* and *The Spy,* but also endowed with religious as well as familial significance, for it is erected in the church of the upstate New York village of Ravensnest. Furthermore, the trilogy's broad historical sweep allows the Littlepages to develop more complicated views of its significance. The colonial Corny Littlepage defended the canopy as a symbol of rank, against the sneers of Jason that there are no distinctions in Heaven.[44] The younger Littlepages see the canopy's significance in the moral and familial terms of property, rather than in terms of rank. It receives a consequent increment in synecdochal value. If it is not respected, then not only American civilization, but Christendom itself, is in ruins. Its significance is indicated by Hugh Littlepage's warning to the Anti-Renters:

> *Let this attempt on property succeed, ever so indirectly,* AND IT WILL BE FOLLOWED UP BY OTHERS, WHICH WILL INEVITABLY DRIVE US INTO DESPOTISM, AS A REFUGE AGAINST ANARCHY, AS EFFECT SUCCEEDS TO CAUSE.[45]

Littlepage's warning, and Cooper's typography, have no effect. The Newcomes and the people they represent have no regard for the canopy as property, but invest it with enormous importance as a symbol of the rank they want to tear down. The canopy is removed by the mob and becomes a roof for a pig-pen. The Littlepage family make light of the event, but the implication, reiterated by the concluding "Note by the Editor," is clear.[46] The bleakness of America's future is clearly indicated by the destination of the canopy, and can be summed up by two quotations from the King James Version:

> Give not that which is holy unto the dogs, nor cast your pearls before swine, lest haply they trample them under their feet, and turn and rend you.
>
> (Matthew 7:6)

> And the herd rushed down the steep into the sea . . . and they were choked in the sea.
>
> (Mark 5:13)

The Redskins closes with Hugh Littlepage contemplating emigration to Europe.[47] His author, who knew better, decided to stay in America.

Notes

1. James Fenimore Cooper, *The Chainbearer* (Boston: Dana Estes, n.d.), 21.

2. John P. McWilliams, *Political Justice in a Republic: James Fenimore Cooper* (Berkeley: U of California P, 1972), 12.

3. Gertrude Stein, *The Autobiography of Alice B. Toklas* (New York: Harcourt, 1933), 145. See also Tony Tanner, *The Reign of Wonder: Naivety and Reality in American Literature* (Cambridge: Cambridge UP, 1965), 215, 233, 204.

4. James D. Wallace, "Cultivating an Audience: From *Precaution* to *The Spy*," *James Fenimore Cooper:*

New Critical Essays, ed. Robert Clark (London: Vision P, 1985), 50. The argument is developed in Wallace's *Early Cooper and His Audience* (New York: Columbia UP, 1986), particularly chap. 3.

5. Review of Catharine Maria Sedgwick, *A New England Tale,* James Fenimore Cooper, *Early Critical Essays (1820-1822),* ed. James F. Beard, Jr. (Delmar, NY: Scholars' Facsimiles and Reprints, 1977), 97. Further references to this text are given in parentheses in the text. Cooper's review is also discussed in Wallace, *Early Cooper and His Audience,* 119-23.

6. John Foster, *An Essay on the Evils of Popular Ignorance* (London: Holdsworth, 1820).

7. See Harold Scudder, "What Mr. Cooper Read to his Wife," *Sewanee Review* 36 (Apr.-June 1928), 177-94; and George E. Hastings, "How Cooper Became a Novelist," *American Literature* 12.1 (Mar. 1940), 20-51.

8. Gisborne, *An Enquiry into the Duties of Men in the Higher and Middle Classes of Society in Great Britain,* 2nd ed., vol. 2 (London: White, 1795), 384. For further discussions of the influence of such books on Cooper, see Wallace, *Early Cooper and His Audience,* 69-72; and Lawson-Peebles, "Property, Marriage, Women, and Fenimore Cooper's First Fictions," *James Fenimore Cooper: New Historical and Literary Contexts,* ed. W. M. Verhoeven (Amsterdam and Atlanta, GA: Rodopi, 1993), 60-65.

9. Cooper, *The Spy,* ed. J. E. Morpurgo (1821; London: Oxford UP, 1968), 2-4. *The Letters and Journals of James Fenimore Cooper,* ed. James Franklin Beard, 6 vols, vol. 1 (Cambridge, MA: Harvard UP, 1960-68), 49. Brown, *Edgar Huntly; Or, Memoirs of a Sleep-Walker* (1799; London: Penguin, 1988), 3.

10. Cooper, *The American Democrat* (1838; Harmondsworth, UK: Penguin, 1969), 186.

11. Morton J. Horwitz, *The Transformation of American Law, 1780-1860* (Cambridge, MA: Harvard UP, 1977), 32, 37.

12. See *The Letters and Journals of James Fenimore Cooper,* vol. 1, 59.

13. James Kent, 1821 speech, quoted in *Democracy, Liberty, and Property: The State Constitutional Conventions of the 1820's,* ed. Merrill D. Peterson (Indianapolis: Bobbs-Merrill, 1966), 190-97. Kent, *Commentaries on American Law,* quoted in Lawrence M. Friedman, *A History of American Law* (New York: Simon and Schuster, 1973), 210-11.

14. See Arthur M. Schlesinger, *A Pilgrim's Progess: Orestes A. Brownson* (Boston: Little, Brown,

1966), 103, 108; Schlesinger, *The Age of Jackson* (London: Eyre and Spottiswoode, 1946), 184; Arthur A. Ekirch, *The Idea of Progress in America, 1815-1860* (New York: Smith, 1951), chap. 5; Rush Welter, *The Mind of America, 1820-1860* (New York: Columbia UP, 1975), 99-100, 105-12.

15. Henry Adams, *History of the United States,* 9 vols, vol. 1 (New York: Scribner's, 1890-91), 177-78.

16. *The Letters and Journals of James Fenimore Cooper,* vol. 1, 140.

17. *The Last of the Mohicans,* for instance, draws extensively on at least four texts for its account of the massacre at Fort William Henry: Jonathan Carver, *Three Years' Travels Throughout the Interior Parts of North America, in the Years 1766, 1767, and 1768,* 4th Am. ed. (1778; Charlestown, MA: West and Greenleaf, 1802); Timothy Dwight, *Travels in New England and New York,* ed. Barbara Miller Solomon, 4 vols (1822; Cambridge, MA: Harvard UP, 1969); David Humphries, *An Essay on the Life of the Honourable Major General Israel Putnam* (1788; Boston: Samuel Avery, 1810); and Benjamin Trumbull, *A General History of the United States of America,* 3 vols (Boston: Farrand, Mallory, 1810). For relevant discussions, see Ian K. Steele, "Cooper and Clio: The Sources for 'A Narrative of 1757,'" *Canadian Review of American Studies* 20.3 (Winter 1989), 121-35; and Lawson-Peebles, "The Lesson of the Massacre at Fort William Henry," *New Essays on the Last of the Mohicans,* ed. H. Daniel Peck (New York: Cambridge UP, 1992), 117.

18. Cooper, *Precaution* (1820; Grosse Pointe, MI: Scholarly P, 1968), 475.

19. Cooper, *The American Democrat,* 70.

20. Austen, *Emma,* ed. David Lodge (1815; London: Oxford UP, 1971), 323.

21. Cooper, *The Spy,* 147, 261, 264, 176. For good, relevant discussions of the novel, see A. Robert Lee, "Making History, Making Fiction: Cooper's *The Spy,*" and W. M. Verhoeven, "Neutralizing the Land: The Myth of Authority and the Authority of Myth in Fenimore Cooper's *The Spy,*" *James Fenimore Cooper: New Historical and Literary Contexts,* ed. Verhoeven, 31-45 and 71-87.

22. Cooper, *The Spy,* 6.

23. Cooper, *The Last of the Mohicans* (1826; Harmondsworth, UK: Penguin, 1986), 11. See also Lawson-Peebles, "The Lesson of the Massacre at Fort William Henry," *New Essays on the Last of the Mohicans,* ed. Peck, 115-38.

24. John McWilliams, "Revolt in Massachusetts: The Midnight March of Lionel Lincoln," *James Feni-*

more Cooper: New Historical and Literary Contexts, ed. Verhoeven, 99.

25. Cooper, *The Pioneers,* ed. James Franklin Beard (1823; Albany: State U of New York P, 1980), 455. See also Richard Godden, "Pioneer Properties, or 'What's in a Hut?,'" *James Fenimore Cooper: New Critical Essays,* ed. Clark, 121-42.

26. Cooper, *The Pioneers,* 456.

27. Zebulon M. Pike, *An Account of the Expeditions to the Sources of the Mississippi, and through the Western Parts of Louisiana . . .* (Philadelphia: Conrad, 1810), appendix to part 2, 8. On the debate over the Louisiana Purchase, see Lawson-Peebles, *Landscape and Written Expression in Revolutionary America* (Cambridge: Cambridge UP, 1988), 157-64.

28. Cooper, *The Prairie* (1827; Harmondsworth, UK: Penguin, 1987), 24, 11.

29. Cooper, *Gleanings in Europe: Italy* (1838; Albany: State U of New York P, 1981), 51.

30. Cooper, *Gleanings in Europe: The Rhine* (1836; Albany: State U of New York P, 1986), 175.

31. Cooper, *Gleanings in Europe: France* (1837; Albany: State U of New York P, 1983), 137, 145, 139. *Gleanings in Europe: Italy,* 297. *Gleanings in Europe: England* (1837; Albany: State U of New York P, 1986), 210, 19, 89, 68, 146-47, 276-78.

32. *Gleanings in Europe: England,* 177.

33. On the Anti-Rent War, see David M. Ellis, *Landlords and Farmers in the Hudson-Mohawk Region, 1790-1850* (New York: Octogan, 1967); and Ellis, "The Coopers and the New York State Landholding Systems," *James Fenimore Cooper: A Reappraisal,* ed. Mary E. Cunningham (Cooperstown: New York State Historical Association, 1954), 44-54. A good discussion of the novels can be found in McWilliams, *Political Justice in a Republic,* 298-339.

34. *The Letters and Journals of James Fenimore Cooper,* vol. 5, 184.

35. Cooper, *The Redskins* (1846; Boston: Dana Estes, n. d.), 83.

36. Cooper, *Satanstoe* (1845; Boston: Dana Estes, n. d.), 9.

37. *The Redskins,* 34.

38. *The Chainbearer,* 123.

39. *The Redskins,* 139.

40. See Donald A. Ringe, "Cooper's Littlepage Novels: Change and Stability in American Society," *American Literature* 32 (1960), 281-82.

41. *Satanstoe*, 332.

42. *The Chainbearer*, 387.

43. *The Redskins*, 276.

44. *Satanstoe*, 182-83.

45. *The Redskins*, 424.

46. *The Redskins*, 536-38.

47. *The Redskins*, postscript, 506.

HENRY JAMES AND AMERICAN WOMEN

Catherine H. Zuckert (essay date spring-summer 1976)

SOURCE: Zuckert, Catherine H. "American Women and Democratic Morals: *The Bostonians*." *Feminist Studies* 3, nos. 3-4 (spring-summer 1976): 30-50.

[*In the following essay, Zuckert studies* The Bostonians, *and James's expression of his belief "that the development or education of the American woman revealed the possibilities and hidden defects of modern democratic life more clearly than any other social or political phenomenon."*]

Henry James devoted considerable thought to the character of the American woman. It was not merely, as James sometimes said, that the independent woman was a social novelty worthy of detailed observation and description by the student of manners.[1] Rather, James believed that the development or education of the American woman revealed the possibilities and hidden defects of modern democratic life more clearly than any other social or political phenomenon.

> The more we look at American life, the more we see that any social aspect takes its main sense from its democratic connections. . . . It is therefore what her social climate and air have done, and have failed to do, for the American woman that tell us most about her, and we really approach her nearest in studying her . . . as . . . the most confidently "grown" and most fully encouraged plant in our democratic garden.[2]

Thus when James wrote his "American" novel, he focused on the situation of women and the agitation on their behalf. "I wished to write a very *American* tale, a tale very characteristic of our social conditions, and I asked myself what was the most salient and peculiar point in our social life. The answer was: the situation of women, the decline of the sentiment of sex, the agitation on their behalf."[3] Since James described the circle of reformers in Boston critically and ironically, many readers have taken him to be a conservative opponent of the demand for equal rights. But, as some critics have observed, James treated the major male critic of the women as ironically as he did the feminists.[4] In fact, James was very interested in and sympathetic to the problems of American women.

> As for James' interest in feminism in general, what have all his important heroines been to date from Daisy Miller to Isabel Archer but women whose intellects, senses, plans, hopes, are all frustrated simply because they are women. . . . Henry James was consistently sympathetic to the basic claims of the nineteenth century feminist movement; he is, indeed, one of their unsung heroes.[5]

But James did not, apparently, believe that American women would solve their problems through political action. He may, therefore, provide us with a different view of "the woman question"—both the problem of the relation of the sexes in modern democracy and the proposed solutions to the problem. If he is a conservative, he is not the sort of conservative who either expects or desires a return of the aristocratic order. Rather he wishes to explore the possibilities of democratic life. In his own words, his view "both takes the democratic era unreservedly for granted and yet declines to take for granted that it has shown the whole, or anything like the whole, of its hand. Its inexorability and its great scale are thus converted into a more exciting element to reckon with—for the student of manners at least—than anything actually less absolute that might be put in its place.[6] We may thus look to *The Bostonians* not only for an analysis of the situation of women but also for an investigation of the problems in general of American political morality.

Structurally, *The Bostonians* is simple: Olive Chancellor (Book I) and her Southern cousin Basil Ransom (Book II) wage a contest for the affections of Verena Tarrant which Basil finally wins (Book III). The plot resembles a traditional love story: Boy meets girl; they become attracted to one another and they marry. Olive's loss to the force of sexual attraction is conventionally predictable. What is harder to understand is why the young couple does not, according to James, "live happily ever after." Yet in the last sentence of the novel, the narrator states: "It is to be feared that with the union, so far from brilliant into which [Verena] was about to enter, these [tears] were not the last she was destined to shed" (p. 464).[7]

The unhappy ending forces the conscientious reader to reconsider James' apparent damnation of the women's movement and Olive as unnatural and perverse. True, Basil might represent merely a bad choice; the institution of marriage and all it implies might not be at issue. But James informs his readers at the very beginning of the novel that Basil, "is, as representative of his sex, the most important personage in my narrative" (p. 5). If Basil represents American men and the conventional notion of marriage and if this union promises so little happiness, American women would seem to be more than justified in protesting their fate, according to James. But this protest as represented by Olive promises as little happiness, and, it would seem, the American woman has no alternative choice. Thus the plot leads readers to look back in order to discover the reasons why James thinks that "the most confidently 'grown' and most fully developed plant in our democratic graden" finds no promise of happiness or personal fulfillment in America.

James states the problem at the very beginning of the novel: "It proved nothing of any importance with regard to Miss Chancellor, to say that she was morbid; any sufficient account of her would lie very much to the rear of that. *Why was she morbid, and why was her morbidness typical?*" (p. 11, emphasis supplied). In fact, all the characters in *The Bostonians* represent "types"—Basil is "representative of his sex" while Verena personifies "the situation of women," Olive, "the agitation on their behalf," and Mary Prance, "the decline in the sentiment of sex."[8] No one in the novel actually learns from her or his experience or develops; each almost tragically lives out the fate decreed by her or his weakness.[9] Indeed, it turns out that all these characters fail properly to develop as a result of their commitment to egalitarian political principles and to the efficacy of public education in reforming human beings. Once we understand how egalitarian commitments may stultify personal growth, we will be in a position to look at James' critique of American society in terms of the broader issue of the requirements and character of moral education in a liberal democracy.

Verena embodies the freedom of the American girl. She seems able to choose any life she desires—career, fame, love, marriage, family, friendship, wealth, society. Why then, against the wishes of both friends and parents, does she choose an unhappy marriage? Is it that Verena's character makes her unable to choose well, or, is it that all her "opportunities" prove empty? Or both?

All Verena's opportunities involve "unions" of one kind of another. Matthias Pardon offers Verena marriage and notoriety; he would gladly sacrifice any shred of privacy to the public's "right to know." Verena, however, does no seek to exhibit herself so much as to find appreciation of herself. The problem is that she has no real "self" or "identity"; she is only potential, undefined freedom. When Verena comes to Olive, "She[has] no particular feeling about herself; she only [cares], as yet, for outside things . . . she [has] neither a particle of

diffidence nor a particle of vanity" (p. 78). Olive seeks to "take possession" of Verena, literally buying her from her parents. But Olive does not touch the core of the girl. Verena admires Olive's dedication and self-sacrifice, but she cannot really join Olive because she does not share her passion. Nor does she recognize the passion that gradually draws her to Basil. She thinks that she likes him because he sees and loves her as she truly is. "The words he had spoken to her . . . about her genuine vocation, had sunk into her soul and worked and fermented there. She had come at last to believe them. . . . They had kindled a light in which she saw herself afresh and, strange to say, liked herself better. . . ." (p. 396). It is indeed "strange" that she "liked herself better" because the words Basil spoke were:

> You always want to please someone, and now you go to lecturing about the country, . . . in order to please Miss Chancellor, just as you did it before to please your father and mother. It isn't YOU. . . . Ah, Miss Tarrant, if it's a question of pleasing, how much you might please someone else by tipping your preposterous puppet over and standing forth in your freedom as well as in your loveliness!
>
> (p. 346)

Even the Southern conservative appeals to personal freedom. Yet the narrator comments, "I know not whether Ransom was aware of the bearing of this interpretation, which attributed to Miss Tarrant a singular hollowness of character; he contented himself with believing that she was as innocent as she was lovely. . . ." (p. 62).

Neither Basil nor Verena (nor Olive for that matter) seems to appreciate the force of physical attraction. Verena does, however, understand that her preference for Basil Ransom over Henry Burrage with his wealth and social position is rooted in her egalitarian political principles and her respect for dedication and self-sacrifice. She reflects, for example, on her preference for walking through the park with Basil to riding in a cab with Burrage:

> She had to look down so, it made her feel unduly fine. . . . (p. 330) Walking was much more to her taste, . . . It came over her that Mr. Ransom had given up his work to come to her at such an hour; people of his kind, in the morning, were always getting their living, and it was only for Mr. Burrage that it didn't matter. . . . That pressed upon her; she was, as the most good-natured girl in the world, too entirely tender not to feel any sacrifice that was made for her; she had always done everything that people asked.
>
> (p. 331)

As a result of her upbringing Verena is attracted to the champions of unpopular opinions. Despite her disagreement with Basil's opinions, Verena is touched with pity and a feeling of injustice when she hears that his articles have been rejected. "She remembered, though she didn't mention it, how little success her father had when he tried [getting published]" (p. 342). In the end Verena chooses as her mother had before her. At the price of exile from her family, the daughter of the Boston Greenleafs followed a "quack," a past member of a "free love" community to the alter. Though Mrs. Tarrant bemoans her fall in social position and desires "society" for her daughter, she has an even stronger attachment to the people (democracy) and "ideas" (enlightenment) that she bequeathes to her daughter.

The damning difficulty, however, lies in Verena's inability to distinguish one idea, one will, or one passion, from another; and thus she falls prey, in sequence, to her parents, to Olive, and finally to Basil. "She had kept the consummate innocence of the American girl, that innocence which was the greatest of all, for it had survived the abolition of walls and locks (p. 124)". In the company of her parents Verena has seen many of the ugliest aspects of human life. The young girl's accounts of her past life prompt Olive, however, to ask herself whether "the girl was also destitute of the perception of right and wrong" (p. 111).

Ironically, it is Verena's inability of distinguish one cause from another that makes her a true Bostonian. In her innocence, in her boundless generosity, as in her lack of passion and resentment, she is the heir of Miss Birdseye of whom James wrote:

> She belonged to the Short Skirts League, as a matter of course; for she belonged to any and every league that had been founded for almost any purpose whatever. This did not prevent her being a confused, entangled, inconsequent, discursive old woman, whose charity began at home and ended nowhere, whose credulity kept pace with it, and who knew less about her fellow-creatures, if possible after fifty years of humanitary zeal, than on the day she had gone into the field to testify against the iniquity of most arrangements.
>
> (p. 27)

And Miss Birdseye is the heir of the Emerson James described: "He had only one style, one manner, and he had it for everything . . . a kind of universal passive hospitality. . . . It was only because he was so deferential that he could be so detached . . . egotism is the strongest of passions, and he was altogether passionless. It was because he had no personal, just as he had almost no physical wants."[10] The Emersonian moral tradition lacks passion, and lacking passion, it lacks understanding of passion. Its morality, James suggests, consists of a kind of innocence; but an innocence founded upon ignorance must fail when confronted with the facts of human nature. Olive, for example, knows better than to ask Verena to promise that she will never marry, because Olive knows that Verena has not the slightest notion what such a promise might mean. Ver-

ena promises easily and just then as easily breaks those promises. Lacking an ego, Verena lacks understanding of the passions that rage if not rule in other human beings. She had no standards; as Basil tells her, she has merely been parroting speeches given her by her parents and Olive. Verena cannot, therefore, judge and choose among men. Indeed, it seems that rather than Verena choosing Basil, Basil chooses her, and she merely gives in to the strongest will (p. 337). So Verena, completely innocent, ends by completely wronging Olive.

> Nothing was wanting to make the wrong she should do her complete; she had deceived her up to the very last. . . . She knew that Olive would never get over the disappointment. . . . It was a very peculiar thing, their friendship. it had elements which made it probably as complete as any (between women) that had existed. Of course it had been more on Olive's side than on hers; but that, again didn't make any difference . . . She had lent herself, given herself, utterly, and she ought to have known better if she didn't mean to abide by it.
>
> (pp. 398-99)

Whereas Verena is the typical American girl, Olive is the exception. James clearly suggests that she is "abnormal," "atypical," "perverted," "unnatural," (but not, like her sister Adeline Luna, artificial). The problem, indeed the "mystery," of the novel, lies in answering the questions the narrator poses as early as page eleven: "why was she she morbid, and why was her morbidness typical?"

According to the narrator, Olive "was intelligent enough not to have needed to be morbid, even for purposes of self-defense" (p. 156). Something, therefore, hampers the the operation of her intellect. It is her unwillingness or inability to admit any desires on her own part. This unwillingness leads her into fundamental dishonesty even with herself. Olive for example denies herself all personal decoration, yet she lavishes attention on the decor of her long narrow parlor. There she seeks protection from the vulgarity, the push and pull of everyday life. Yet she consistently punishes her dislike of the vulgar by riding in street cars and by associating with reformers in such places as Miss Birdseye's parlor. Why? "By reason of a theory she devotedly nursed, a theory which bade her put off invidious distinctions and mingle in the common life" (p. 23).[11]

Olive sees clearly that there are immense differences among human beings, and she is most repelled by the appalling amount of vulgarity that surrounds her.

> With her immense sympathy for reform, she found herself so often wishing that reformers were a little different. There was something grand about Mrs. Farrinder . . . ; but there was a false note when she spoke to her young friend about the ladies in Beacon Street. Olive

hated to hear that fine avenue talked about as if it were such a remarkable place, and to live there were a proof of worldly glory. All sorts of inferior people lived there. . . . It was, of course, very wretched to be irritated by such mistakes.

(p. 34)

Both Olive and her sister Adeline Luna draw very definite distinctions among people. Those Adeline draws are false, because they are based on an artificially aristocratic notion of society and no understanding of human nature or dignity. Those Olive draws tend to be true, but are formulated with a bad conscience.

> She knew her place in the Boston hierarchy, and . . . there was a want of perspective in talking to her as if she had been a representative of the aristocracy. Nothing could be weaker, she knew very well, than (in the United States) to apply that term too literally; nevertheless, it would represent a reality if one were to say that, by distinction, the Chancellors belonged to the bourgeoisie—the oldest and the best.

(p. 35)

Olive recognizes that there is no aristocracy in America. She does not respect social position or wealth or even public prominence (which, she sees, tends to become notoriety). Instead, she admires moral purity.

> When Miss Birdseye spoke as if one were a "leader of society," Olive could forgive her even that odious expression, because, of course, one never pretended that she, poor dear, had the smallest sense of the real. She was heroic, she was sublime, the whole moral history of Boston was reflected in her displaced spectacles; but it was part of her originality, as it were, that she was deliciously provincial.

(p. 35)

Olive recognizes that human beings in fact differ quite substantially, but she seems to believe that they should, nevertheless, be treated equally; and that requires that one be short-sighted.[12] Thus she praises Miss Birdseye for errors of observation and judgment for which she criticizes Mrs. Farrinder. Olive shares the Bostonian view of morality as selflessness if not self-sacrifice. Her character even more clearly than Verena's reveals the destructive consequences of this notion of morality, however, for in Olive's case, self-sacrifice means primarily the sacrifice of intelligence to "moral principle."

Olive exists in a high state of tension, caught by the conflict of her aristocratic nature with her ardently held democratic opinions, which produces the "tragic shyness" and "emotional convulsions" that so characteristically paralyze her. The only compensation she gains is suffering; and a life consisting only of suffering does not seem very appealing. "It would be far easier to abandon the struggle . . . and, in short, simply expire" (p. 159). But Olive does not want merely to expire.

"The most secret, the most sacred hope of her nature [is] that she might some day . . . be a martyr and die for something" (p. 13). She wants a death with meaning, one in which she would destroy her body and with it the low, while the high, her faith, would remain in the memories of others. Olive thus lives in order to perform a noble deed and at the same time suffers from her ambition to distinguish herself above others.

> Olive had often declared before that her conception of life was as something sublime or as nothing at all. The world was full of evil, but she was glad to have been born before it had been swept away, while it was still there to face, to give one a task and a reward. When the great reforms should be consummated, when the day of justice should have dawned, would not life perhaps be rather poor and pale? She had never pretended to deny that the hope of fame, of the very highest distinction, was one of her strongest incitements; and she held that the most effective way of protesting against the state of bondage of women was for an individual member of the sex to become illustrious.

(pp. 159-60)

Olive wishes to live and die in a crusade to rid the world of evil. Her vision of greatness resembles that of the medieval knight. She has the soul of the nobility of old, with all its pride and rigidity as well as its dedication to high ideals. No wonder Olive envies her brothers' deaths in the Civil War.

But women cannot fight for their country. Moreover, Olive believes, fighting war will not bring justice; fighting produces only more suffering and thus more injustice. Gentle means are required. Women can, indeed, must, lead this new, the only true crusade, for they alone know what it is to suffer.

> In the last resort the whole burden of the human lot came upon them . . . their organism was in itself a challenge to suffering, and men had practiced upon it with an impudence that knew no bounds. As they were weakest most had been wrung from them, and as they were the most generous they had been the most deceived. Olive Chancellor would have rested her case, had it been necessary, on those general facts; and her simple and comprehensive contention was that the peculiar wretchedness which had been the essence of the feminine lot was a monstrous artificial imposition, crying aloud for redress.

(pp. 195-86)

No wonder Olive "would reform the solar system if she could get hold of it" (p. 7). An order in which the weak are persecuted and the strong protected is completely perverse, completely unnatural. "It was the usual things of life that filled her with silent rage; which was natural enough, inasmuch as, to her vision, almost everything that was usual was iniquitous" (p. 12). Not only does the usual lack distinction by the very fact of its being usual, not only is it completely unjust in general, but it represents an order that prevents Olive from expressing and achieving her own distinction. She has a resentful soul. She would rule, because she believes in the superiority of both her moral character and her intelligence, but her democratic principles deny anyone the right to rule; and Olive knows she is unattractive to the people.

Thus instead of seeking rule she seeks revolution. Olive fervently embraces the women's movement because in it she can unite the two warring elements of her nature—her instincts and her principles—into one passion. Thus far men have ruled on the basis of superior physical strength (force) that makes them brutal, insensitive, and vulgar. Olive can prove her superiority by elevating "daintiness to a religion" and in the process give full if not free rein to her fastidious nature. Women are not superior merely because of their physical daintiness or weakness but also because of the knowledge their weakness provides. They know, as men do not, what it is to suffer; and they will, therefore, be the better rulers, because they will be gentle and peaceful. The fact that they would be the best rulers, but do not rule, proves that the present system of male domination is fundamentally unjust and must be overthrown. But her democratic principles and her aristocratic instincts are satisfied. Having achieved final, complete reform (or having sacrificed herself in the effort), Olive can expire happily to let her heiress, Verena, live in the New Eden.

At the heart of the passion of this most unprevaricating representative of the most unprevaricating city there lies a fundamental dishonesty. Olive lives emphatically by principle. She decides, for example, that Adeline and Basil ought to marry.

> Olive considered all this, as it was her effort to consider everything, from a very high point of view, and ended by feeling sure it was not for the sake of any nervous personal security that she desired to see her two relations in New York get mixed up together. If such an event as their marriage would gratify her sense of fitness, it would be simply as an illustration of certain laws. Olive, thanks to the philosophic cast of her mind, was exceedingly fond of illustrations of laws.
>
> (p. 164)

Olive seeks to imitate Emerson in a life of "high thinking" and "moral passion" that entails denial of all personal, if not all material needs and comforts. Yet Olive has very great personal needs indeed. Fundamentally, she wishes to be loved and to love, hence she seeks a friend, not an equal but a complement. She cannot allow herself to love or be loved by a man, because that would to her mind constitute an admission of her inferiority, her lack of independence. Thus to Verena she pleads: "'There is no freedom for you and me save in religiously *not* doing what you will often be asked to do—and I never!'" Miss Chancellor brought out these last words with a proud jerk which was not without it

pathos. 'Don't promise, don't promise!' she went on. 'I would far rather you didn't. But don't fail me—don't fail me, or I shall die!'" (pp. 140-41). By repressing the needs she finds illegitimate, if not degrading, Olive lives in deep personal insecurity, from which she wants not merely peace, but salvation. For her, feminism is more a source of moral rectitude than political right.

> When this young lady, after a struggle with the winds and waves of emotion, emerged into the quiet stream of a certain high reasonableness, she presented her most graceful aspect; she had a tone of softness and sympathy, a gentle dignity, a serenity of wisdom, which sealed the appreciation of those who knew her well enough to like her, and which always impressed Verena as something almost august. Such moods, however, were not often revealed to the public at large; they belonged to Miss Chancellor's very private life.
>
> (p. 140)

Olive admits she can imagine a man she would like very much, but there are none present. Olive's intelligence and her ambition as well as her more personal needs are frustrated in the first instance by the undistinguished character of the American man, but second and more fundamentally, by her adherence to the typically American convictions that all human beings ought to be free and equal and that freedom consists in economic and personal independence.

Basil Ransom has a distinguished appearance. "He was tall and lean and dressed throughout in black . . . , his head had a character of elevation . . . ; it was a head to be seen above the level of a crowd, on some judicial bench or political platform . . . ; the eyes especially with . . . , their smouldering fire, might have indicated that he was to be a great American statesman; or . . . that he came from Carolina or Alabama" (pp. 4-5). In fact, he comes from Mississippi. His Southern origins as well as his economic failure make Basil at first glance a strange "representative of his sex" (p. 5). Would not a "self-made," successful businessman such as James' *The American*, Christopher Newman (literally new man), have been more typical? In the context of American reform movements, James apparently thinks not. Basil's Southern origins associate him with slavery (opposed by the Boston-based abolitionists) and give him aristocratic pretensions, i.e., claims to rule on the basis of differences of birth (in this instance, sexual differences). Some readers have followed Adeline in mistaking Basil for an aristocrat.

> [Adeline Luna] delighted in the dilapidated gentry; her taste was completely different from her sister's who took an interest only in the lower class, as it struggled to rise; what Adeline cared for was the fallen aristocracy . . . ; was not Basil Ransom an example of it? was he like a French *tentilhomme de province* after the Revolution? or an old monarchical emigre from the Langudedoc?
>
> (p. 212)

But James comments: "In reality Olive was distinguished and discriminating, and Adeline was the dupe of confusions in which the worse was apt to be mistaken for the better" (p. 199).

Basil has decidedly Southern manners. "He was addicted with the ladies to the old forms of address and gallantry . . . (p. 197) His accent always came out strongly when he said anything of that sort—and it committed him to nothing in particular" (p. 203). In any matter of importance to him, Basil's "chivalry" does not determine his action. Before he goes to Marmion to pursue Verena, for example, he reviews the extent of his obligations to Olive: "He was not slow to decide that he owed her none. Chivalry had to do with one's relations with people one hated, not with those one loved. He didn't hate poor Miss Olive, . . . and even if he did, any chivalry was all moonshine which should require him to give up the girl he adored in order that his third cousin should see he could be gallant" (pp. 403-404). Like the American South, Basil is more bourgeois than aristocratic; he believes in the importance of economic self-sufficiency and he likes his comfort (pp. 11, 16). Although he cares for the South with "passionate tenderness" (p. 50), after the North wins the war, Basil comes to New York to make money. He will not propose to Verena at first, because he lacks visible means of support.

> His scruples were doubtless begotten of a false pride, a sentiment in which there was a thread of moral tinsel, as there was in the Southern idea of chivalry; but he felt ashamed of his own poverty. . . . This shame was possible to him even while he was conscious of what a mean business it was to practice upon human imbecility, how much better it was even to be seedy and obscure, discouraged about one's self. . . . [In] spite of the years of misery that followed the war [he] could never rid himself of the belief that a gentleman who desired to unite himself to a charming girl couldn't yet ask her to come and live with him in sordid conditions.
>
> (p. 275)

His notions of support seem minimal, however, for he thinks the publication of one article in *The Rational Review* constitutes enough promise to propose marriage.

Basil is neither an aristocrat nor, as some have maintained, James' spokesman.[13] James himself states:

> I shall not attempt a complete description of Ransom's ill-starred views. . . . I shall do them sufficient justice in saying that he was by natural disposition as good deal of a stoic, and that, as a result of a considerable intellectual experience, he was, in social and political matters, a reactionary . . . with a more primitive conception of manhood than our modern temperament appears to require, and a program of human felicity much less varied.
>
> (pp. 194-95)

Where Basil has a set, simple view of manhood and the limits of human happiness, James wants to explore the unknown possibilities of the modern age. He does not share the "narrow notions" he attributes to his "hero." Basil contends, for example, that "the masculine tone is passing out of the world; it's a feminine age, an age of hollow phrases and false delicacy and exaggerated solicitudes and coddled sensibilities, which, if we don't soon look out, will usher in the reign of mediocrity. . . . I don't in the least care what becomes of you ladies" (p. 343). James on the other hand made the "new woman' the center of many of his novels and dwelt on the refinements of "consciousness."

If Basil represents the American man, that man is "narrow" and "primitive" primarily because he has an exceedingly simple and naive view of both the virtues and vices of his fellow human beings (p. 198). Basil prides himself on his insight, but James shows that Basil's view of other people is in fact superficial. For example, he is very proud when he concludes upon seeing Olive that she is "visibly morbid," but the narrator states: "It proved nothing of any importance, with regard to Miss Chancellor, to say that she was morbid; any sufficient account of her would lie very much to the rear of that. Why was she morbid, and why was her morbidness typical? Ransom might have exulted if he had gone back far enough to explain that mystery" (p. 11). Likewise, Basil judges correctly enough that Selah Tarrant represents the worst kind of "carpet-bagger" and that his daughter wants essentially "to please every one who came near her and to be happy that she pleased." He judges correctly because the Tarrants prove to be persons wholly of the surface. When Basil must judge character rather than appearance, he fails abominably, as in his choice of a law partner who proceeds to abscond with the firm's funds. He is, in his own way, as "innocent" as Verena, because he lacks knowledge of good and evil. His "conception of vice was purely as a series of special cases, of explicable accidents" (p. 19).

Basil has a first-rate intelligence, but not much experience (p. 11). Surely the experiences of the Civil War and his trip North should have shown him something about his fellow human beings. The problem lies not so much in what he has or has not seen as in the way he tends to understand his experience. As an example, the narrator presents Basil's reflections after he fails to succeed in law in New York.

> He wondered whether he were stupid and unskilled, and he was finally obliged to confess to himself that he was unpractical. This confession was in itself a proof of the fact, for nothing could be less fruitful than such a speculation, terminated in such a way. He was perfectly aware that he cared a great deal for the theory, and so his visitors must have thought when they found him . . . reading a volume of de Tocqueville. This was the kind of reading he liked; he had thought a great

deal about social and economic questions, forms of government and the happiness of peoples.

(pp. 192-93)

Instead of observing or meditating, Basil loses himself in a book on any occasion (pp. 3, 4, 227); but he does not even remember what he has read (pp. 20, 59, 576). He is neither a careful reader nor a careful observer. He thinks that if he can classify an individual as "impractical" or "morbid" or "pleasing" he has understood him. As a result Basil tends not to learn about human nature from his experience but only to confirm generalizations.

His own views are simple and sweeping: "'The suffering of woman is the suffering of all humanity,' Ransom returned. 'Do you think any movmeent is going to stop that—or all the lectures from now to doomsday? We are born to suffer—and to bear it, like decent people'" (p. 238). Basil's view is fundamentally egalitarian—all people suffer, equally. Men are stronger so they should attempt to protect the weaker women; and women should gratefully "accept the lot which men have made for them" (pp. 197-98). His Southern origins seem to be responsible for his rather passive and fatalistic view of human affairs as much as it is responsible for his Southern "manners." "He had seen in his younger years one of the biggest failures that history commemorates, an immense national fiasco, and it had implanted in his mind a deep aversion to the ineffectual" (p. 17). If Basil is conservative, it is not because he believes life in the past was better. He is rather a "realist" who opposes all dreams of human improvement because these idealistic "illusions" merely give rise to more suffering. Because he does not believe that any fundamental improvement in the human condition is possible, Basil does not believe in the efficacy of political action. He does, however, ironically share the women's belief in the efficacy of education: "He, too, had a private vision of reform, but the first principle of it was to reform the reformers" (p. 20).

Basil's only success is in wooing Verena, and the marriage does not promise to be a happy one. Although his highest ambition is to see his "ideas embodied in national conduct" (p. 193), he does not expect to succeed immediately. During the years of waiting he needs the comfort of a wife who seeks only to please him.[14] And pleasing him is apparently to be her only reward (p. 238). But here Basil's "ideas" work against his own vision of domestic bliss. He cannot, in fact, take much comfort in Verena's preference, because he regards Verena as an essentially inferior being and has no respect for her judgment. Verena's sympathy for Basil rests, moreover, not so much on his strength of will or the content of his ideas as on the unpopularity of his cause and his failure to publish. Even during the apparently casual walk in New York she seems unable to keep off the matter of his failure (p. 341). May not allusions to

his failures (with an implicit contrast to her own success and greater promise) increase when Verena discovers how little Basil really values her.[15]

Basil is not likely to receive either the comfort or the recognition he expects from his wife; and Verena's resentment is apt to grow. But, in an ironic sense, they belong together. He represents the principle of male domination which is, although neither party in the novel seems to see it, merely the other side of the notion that the goodness of women consists in self-sacrifice. Both are inadequate conceptions of human relations because both abstract from particular characteristics of individuals.

Marriage in a liberal democracy is a matter of personal choice, not merely physical attraction or economic advantage. To conceive marriage in political terms of superiority and inferiority or economic terms of possession is to undermine, if not pervert the attachment of wife and husband. But Americans, James observes, seem to know no other relations. In his attempt to "possess" Verena (pp. 327, 351), Basil appears heir to the tradition of the slave-holding South. But Olive, the moral heir of the abolitionist lecturers, also seeks to "possess" Verena (pp. 79, 80, 132, 398), and indeed "buys" her from her parents (pp. 117, 176, 421). Both reflect the general American tendency to conceive of human relations in economic terms that constrict the alternatives to possession, if not exploitation (as represented by Selah Tarrant and Matthias Pardon) or independence.[16] Economic relations based on need and exchange are both impersonal and equalizing (by making all things commensurate in terms of their money value) and thus appealing to democrats; but they easily become relations of domination because the value of any person, according to this understanding, does not inhere in the individual (to be discovered, appreciated, and so developed), but consists only in her or his use of the other persons, her or his service. Olive embodies this understanding in her insistent desire not to owe anything to anyone, particularly not to a man (pp. 23, 146). Basil clearly acts from a desire to escape economic debt when he comes North as well as when he considers marrying Adeline for her money; but his leaving his mother and sisters to farm the plantation alone also represents an attempt to transform more personal, familial obligations into economic terms, if only to evade them entirely. His notion of obligations of human beings to each other is minimal; and these obligations exist between the strong and the weak, not between equals. He is as lonely in his pride or independence as Olive is in hers. We never hear him talk to another man. At the middle of the novel we see him consider returning to Mississippi, that "state of despair," not only because he has failed at both law and publishing, but also because he has no one to talk to (p. 192). It is in this isolation and loneliness that he comes to view Verena as a bright, beckoning light. Yet he no more than Olive seeks merely to remedy loneliness with the love and companionship Verena would gladly give. Both seek domination through "possession," because both tend to see any ties to other human beings as qualifications of their own freedom. In friendship or marriage they both therefore seek to be superior for fear of becoming inferior. The alternative to possession or being possessed would thus appear to be solitary living.

Dr. Mary Prance is particularly important, for in her life and person she achieves all the goals of the feminist revolution. She is as independent as Olive and Basil wish everyone to be; not only does she have a career, indeed a profession, so that she need not depend upon anyone for material support, but she also seems able to do without the comforts of the society of other human beings. Her appearance at Miss Birdseye's has nothing to do with any feeling of need on her part for moral reform or personal freedom. "Ransom could see that she was impatient of the general question and bored with being reminded, even for the sake of her rights, that she was a woman—a detail that she was in the habit of forgetting, having as many rights as she had time for. It was certain that whatever might become of the movement at large, Doctor Prance's own little revolution was a success" (pp. 48-49). She and Basil become "friends" as easily and equally as Verena envisions all women and men will in the future become friends. Unlike Olive, Doctor Prance poses no challenge to Basil's masculinity. "She looked like a boy . . . [although it] was true that if she had been a boy she would have borne some relation to a girl, whereas Doctor Prance appeared to bear none whatever" (p. 41). And she makes no moral or aesthetic demands. All she asks is to be let alone to pursue her studies. She does not practice medicine to alleviate the misery of the poor or to serve humanity, but to learn about human anatomy. Hence she spends her leisure time not on the streets, but in her study with her cadaver.

> "Men and women are all the same to me," Doctor Prance remarked. "I don't see any difference. There is room for improvement in both sexes. . . ." And she went on to declare, further, that she thought they all talked too much. . . . "I don't want any one to teach me what a woman can do! . . . she can find out some things, if she tries. . . . I don't know as I cultivate the sentimental side. . . . There's plenty of sympathy without mine. If they want to have a better time, I suppose it's natural; so do men, too, I suppose. But I don't know as it appeals to me—to make sacrifices for it; it ain't such a wonderful time—the best you *can* have!"
>
> (pp. 42-43)

In Mary Prance we understand what James means by "the decline of the sentiment of sex." He does not envision the disappearance of sex as a means of propagating the species, although Olive's chastity makes this a rel-

evant question, so much as a decay in personal relations that threatens to destroy the very fabric of society. He is concerned with the forces beyond physical need (economics) which draw human beings together into society—particularly into conversation—and which result in the development of character and intelligence.

> All life therefore comes back to the question of our speech, the medium through which we communicate with each other; for all life comes back to the question of our relations with each other. These relations are made possible, . . . are verily constituted by our speech, and are successful . . . in proportion as our speech is worthy of its great human and social function. . . . The more it suggests and expresses the more we live by it—the more it promotes and enhances life. Its quality, its authenticity, its security, are hence supremely important for the general multifold opportunity, for the dignity and integrity, of our existence.[17]

Freedom, morality—all that is distinctively human—inhere in the capacity to speak; and so it is by virtue of her "gift" that Verena is potentially free and Olive confined and tortured in her inability to speak freely. Dr. Prance would substitute action for speech, however; and the action she advocates is study of the body—carried on as well with the dead as with the living. For her, speech is empty; the only realities are the truths of body, matter in motion. Thus she understands women's demands for rights and freedom as a matter of pleasure and pain, "having a better time." And as such, feminism constitutes a false quest, because from a mechanical point of view there is little difference between pleasure and pain; every action brings a reaction, and so there is little to be gained by "sacrificing." All in all, there is no reason to associate with other people beyond need, and for Dr. Prance there is little need. As the good doctor states, she does not "cultivate the sentimental side."

All the characters in the novel misunderstand the demands of the body because each would in her or his own way subordinate nature to the rule of general ideas. Both Basil and Dr. Prance abstract from the particularistic character of the body when they consider physical attraction in terms of laws rather than persons. Olive seeks to deny physical attraction by refusing to recognize its legitimacy or necessity, although she thus implicitly recognizes its existence. And Verena inherits, it appears, her mother's profound ignorance of the strength of physical attraction (p. 74). Although in the end Verena acts, in part, on the basis of physical attraction, it is by no means clear that she recognizes this. Indeed the attachment of all the characters to the moral standard of "innocence" precludes such recognition.

If, as some opponents and proponents have suggested, the goal of the women's movement is to deny the existence of any real difference between the sexes, James has presented this form of the emancipated woman in

Dr. Prance. She is neither particularly feminine nor masculine. She is a professional, economically and socially independent. James does not present her, as he does Olive, as unnatural, perverse, or repulsive, but he does not make her particularly attractive either. No one in the novel seems to admire or even to be very interested in her.

Dr. Prance is but one of the circle of typical American reformers who gather in Miss Birdseye's living room. More specifically, she represents on type of person and set of goals to be found in the cluster of groups formed of and on behalf of women in America in the late nineteenth and early twentieth centuries that I have generally labeled the "women's movement." In depicting the variety and complexity of characters, issues, and motives involved in the agitation on behalf of women, James not only counteracts stereotyping of feminists, if ironically, by using stereoptyes; but he also invites his readers to consider the problematic relation of these different people and their sometimes contradictory opinions. Dr. Prance and Olive appear, for example, to have many things in common. Both are well educated and live solitary, if not lonely lives. Both befriend Miss Birdseye, though neither much respects the elder lady's opinions. Yet neither particularly likes the other. Indeed, they represent almost opposite poles. Where Dr. Prance suggests that any differences between the sexes are irrelevant, if nonexistent, Olive not only reaffirms the essential difference but asserts the superiority of women as well. In presenting this and other contrasts among the women involved in the movement James leads his readers to ask what the significance of the agitation on behalf of women really is.

James pays surprisingly little attention to the historically most effective aspect of the women's movement—the political demand for equal rights. The reason seems to be that the women's movement as represented by Mrs. Farrinder merely constitutes pressure to extend the principles of the existing regime to its constitutents. It does not challenge the notion that independence constitutes the apex of human achievement, the notion that the most important thing is to secure one's right to life, liberty, and property. Instead it becomes just another interest group.

Verena and Olive do not seek merely to help women, however; they seek to help everyone by increasing the influence of women so as to counteract if not destroy the self-interested character of American society. Both the critique they embody and their failure to achieve the reform they seek raise questions not merely about the fate of women in America but about the viability and adequacy of the most fundamental principles of American politics.

James agrees with that focus of the women's movement that suggests that independence constitutes an inadequate moral standard. As represented by Dr. Prance, independence is at best unattractive and uninteresting. More important, it constitutes a misunderstanding of the foundations of society, which include not only pleasure and need but also the desire for mutual improvement of character through education. In the case of Basil the desire to be independent tends to be selfish. In the case of Olive, the idea that the good life is an independent life works against the formation of social relations—Olive is often rude and unjust—because to admit to need the company of others implies a certain inadequacy. What is missing from the independent life is human society. But, James observes, democrats such as Olive are suspicious of "society," because "society" involves distinctions that appear artificial and invidious to people who take seriously their nation's declaration that "all men are created equal." Indeed, as James illustrates in Adeline, external social distinctions are false, because in democracies the differences among individuals are not expressed, if they are to be found at all, in differences of dress and manners. But does the fact that social distinctions are false mean that drawing any distinctions among individuals or preferring the company of some individuals to others is necessarily invidious?

James was not the first to see that the most fundamental problem in modern democracies resides in the tendency for individuals to retire into virtual isolation as a result of their mistaken desire for independence and the further tendency for this indifference to others to degenerate into selfishness. Nor was he the first to view women as the source of a possible check on this tendency. In *Democracy in America,* Alexis de Tocqueville outlined the dangers of what he called "individualism" and categorically stated: "No free communities ever existed without morals, and . . . morals are the work of woman.[18]

Tocqueville's praise of American women has two parts. First, he praised the American girl for her ability to choose her fate intelligently. Unlike her European predecessor, the American girl possessed almost complete freedom before marriage. She had a chance, therefore, to learn the ways of the world through direct experience and exposure; thus if she had to choose a master, she could choose a good one. As for the married woman Tocqueville admitted that her social seclusion was almost without precedent and that it was based on constraint.

> In America the independence of woman is irrevocably lost in the bonds of matrimony. . . . Religious and trading nations entertain peculiarly serious notions of marriage; the former consider the regularity of woman's life as the best pledge and most certain sign of the purity of her morals; the latter regard it as the highest security for the order and prosperity of the household. The Americans are at the same time a puritanical people and a commercial nation. . . . Thus in the United

States the inexorable opinion of the public carefully circumscribes woman within the narrow circle of domestic interests and duties and forbids her to step beyond it.

(II:3:x, 212)

Tocqueville was not one to urge simple obedience to or faith in the wisdom of public opinion.

Tocqueville had a deeper reason for praising the willingness of American women to retire into the immediacy and privacy of the family. The democratic family, which allows natural affections to grow and take hold freely, seemed to Tocqueville to be virtually the only sentimental bond holding individuals together and checking the tendency of individualism to become pure selfishness. The natural "ties" of affection Tocqueville stressed, however, are those between father and son, and brother and brother—not those between husband and wife and mother and daughter—because the family does not constitute a free and natural association for the woman, but rather depends upon a "constant sacrifice of her pleasure to her duties" (II:3:x, 212).

Tocqueville was concerned with women because he was concerned with morals; and he was concerned with morals because he shared the classic understanding that political freedom requires self-control, since if one does not govern oneself someone else or external forces will. He saw that the primary source of self-restraint and social obligation in modern democracies is the calculation of one's own future gain or need, "self-interest, rightly understood" (II:2:vii, 129ff). But he also saw that self-interest does not provide an adequate foundation for all social obligations (II:2:ix, 133). He looked first to religion to extend and support the concern of any person for another; but he also saw that religion had an effect in America only insofar as it agreed with the dominant public opinion (II:1:v, 29). He looked finally, therefore, to the example of moral behavior provided by women and only consistently by women in modern materialistic democracies. According to Tocqueville, women demonstrate true self-restraint when they subordinate their pleasures to their duty in order to preserve the family, the only modern democratic association based on free affection rather than calculated self-interest. Tocqueville explicitly recognized that the strict sexual morals of the nineteenth century incorporated commercial notions and were based on economic interests (II:3:xii, 22ff). But he suggested that the behavior of women in submitting themselves to these codes nevertheless provided an example of a higher morality.

James and his characters in *The Bostonians* take up the idea that women can greatly improve democratic life through their example. But James suggests that if self-control were to be understood as self-sacrifice, it would not constitute an adequate understanding of the moral requirements of a free society. In depicting the fates of his two major characters, he criticizes both the proposition that the American woman chooses her fate knowingly and that the excellence of woman consists in her self-sacrifice. Verena represents not only the freedom but the "consummate innocence of the American girl, that innocence which . . . had survived the abolition of walls and locks." According to James, the American girl is, to be sure, exposed; but she does not learn from her exposure. She does not understand what she sees, in part because she has yet to experience passion and so is as yet unable to perceive the cause of much she views. (When Verena does experience passion, her opinions and actions change dramatically as a result of the bit of self-knowledge she attains.) Again, the young woman fails to understand what she sees because there are no societal standards by which she can determine what is true or false, good or bad. She has neither convention nor nature to guide her. She has, in fact, only her family. But Selah Tarrant has no moral standards; and Mrs. Tarrant in her virtual seclusion has had no opportunity to learn more than the most external marks of social distinction. The young girl cannot learn because of her youth and freedom; and her mother cannot teach her, because her mother's seclusion prevents her from enjoying a sufficient variety of relations with other human beings to learn about their myriad ways.

Olive represents, if in exaggerated form, the notion that the morality of the American woman consists of self-sacrifice. As Tocqueville himself observed, this ideal is not altogether appealing. "I am aware that an education of this kind is not without danger; I am sensible that it tends to invigorate the judgment at the expense of the imagination and to make cold and virtuous women instead of affectionate wives and agreeable companions to man" (II:3:ix, 211). There is, moreover, a further problem with the notion of morality as self-sacrifice that Olive herself recognizes. If women achieve their superior moral status not merely by the fact and knowledge of suffering (everyone suffers to some extent) but by sacrificing themselves—their pleasure and interests—to others (husband and children first but not solely) and accepting this deprivation and suffering silently (thus becoming martyrs), they lose that moral superiority if they protest their lot in public and try to remedy it. If they remain silent, however, they perpetuate a fundamentally unjust system for the sake of their own moral purity. The solution proposed by the women's movement is to put women forward publicly as examples of virtue. Olive, the martyr, appears to follow logically from this moral syllogism—she does sacrifice her "self" or her ego—but the logic is self-defeating. Once unconscious selflessness becomes conscious sacrifice of self, it is no longer attractive. Nor is it understood. It appears to be merely absurd self-righteousness. When forced into public by circumstances at the end of the novel, Olive necessarily sacrifices all her standards by making a direct appeal to an undiscriminating public who, lacking her standards, fails to recognize her sacrifice and before whom, therefore, she looks ridiculous rather than noble. Public exposure—whether of others or of oneself—can produce only shame, or worse, shamelessness; it cannot produce morality any more than innocence can. Indeed, exposure constitutes merely the negative side of the tendency to understand virtue as innocence of all vice.

The source of the popular notion of morality as selflessness is relatively apparent because the selfishness and ugly aspects of American society are so prominent. Further, it is appealing because selflessness threatens no one. That constitutes the first defect of this idea of morality: its makes morality perfectly ineffective. Second, since this innocence constitutes ignorance of the fundamental fact of human nature—that it is passionate—it not only leaves the moral person defenseless against passion, both in her/himself and in others, but it also produces a narrow, blunt view of life that works in the end to cut its adherents off from all other human beings whom she or he must condemn as selfish. This conception of morality thus furthers the isolation of one individual from another which in turn degenerates into a kind of selfishness.

Natural affection cannot effectively check the evils of democratic society, James suggests, because nature will be affected in its operation by all social conditions—including the democratic—although it will not be destroyed. James suggests, for example, that the attraction of the sexes is natural. But that attraction can become distorted and deformed into domination and resentment, as we have every reason to expect it will in the marriage of Basil and Verena, as a result of understanding marriage in economic terms. "Nature" can become misguided if she is not educated.

Americans do need a moral education, according to James; but not the "self-sacrificing" kind the women's movement proposes. They need to learn not only self-control but also the reasons why it is necessary to control both themselves and others in order to really be able to control one's own fate. They need to learn the passion, the pleasures and pains, virtues and vices of which human beings are capable. And they need to learn that social relations are not merely economically based relations of domination or possession, but that the society of others is the only means through which individuals can develop their personal potential.

Public idolization of "innocence" works against this knowledge; so do public "campaigns." As all American political thinkers since the authors of *The Federalist* have observed, the rule of public opinion may become the tyranny of the majority—the worst tyranny in history because it threatens to be more pervasive, more lasting, and more arbitrary than the tyranny of any single man in the past. If the rule of public opinion may be more arbitrary, it would seem that it might also be freer and hence more moral than previous kinds of rule. One need only educate the public; so political programs in America tend to become programs of moral reform. But moral reform as a public program, James suggests, involves a contradiction in terms. In public one must appeal to general principles or the lowest common denominator, to what all people hold in common, their bodily needs. Public opinion is not, therefore, really arbitrary or free; it is rather very much tied to basic needs defined in physical or economic terms to which it will tend to reduce all else. Society may also be a basic need; in Olive, at least, the desire for friendship as well as recognition seems to be the source of her attachment to the women's movement. But democratic people do not recognize the desire for friendship (or any other psychic need) as such; they regard society merely as mutual, if necessary dependence, to be avoided as much as possible. By mounting a public campaign based on "impersonal principles," the women's movement only furthers the basic thrust of American society toward autonomy and sameness; and in its impersonal lack of concern for the individual as an individual, it is as immoral as the society it would reform.

Indeed, James believes, the women's movement would destroy the root of a superior morality in women—their personal concerns. This is precisely what is needed in modern democracies. True, women are often criticized most for precisely this trait, which may produce gossip, but need not do so if the concern is not to expose the defects of others but to develop, learn, and appreciate their individual turns of character. If, in a word, women can keep their interest truly personal and not public. Such a personal concern can, as in the case of Adeline, become too familiar, insinuating and insulting to the integrity of the individual. For this reason as well as her ideological commitment to the equality of all, Olive tries to suppress such a personal interest in herself and others. Unlike Verena, Olive does know how to distinguish among individuals; but as a result she seeks a refuge even more cloister-like than the marriage described by Tocqueville. Because she sees not only the distinctions among individuals, but also the complete lack of public guidance and support for drawing such distinctions in a society characterized by its easy tolerance and democratic creed, Olive becomes afraid precisely where the more ordinary American woman grows, albeit unconsciously, bold.[19] Olive has character because she has pride, which she tries to suppress, however, because her democratic principles tell her all human beings are equal and pride is therefore unjustified. She is afraid to talk to others both because of what the conversation may reveal about her and because the others may not as a result give her the recognition she desires and does, yet does not, deserve. That is the importance of Olive—

why she is morbid and why her morbidity is typical. Of all the characters in *The Bostonians,* she has the finest nature, both morally and intellectually; and that nature is most perverted by her democratic surroundings and education.

All three leading characters in *The Bostonians,* in fact, present us with exceptional natures which are stultified if not perverted in their development as a result of their service to "ideas" rather than attention to individual persons. Basil has a "first-rate intelligence" but his theories prevent him from ever gaining the experience, that is, the knowledge of human nature, he needs to develop it. Verena never learns to distinguish service to one set of ideas from service to another, whereas Olive is psychologically destroyed. None of the characters fails because she or he lacks opportunity in the obvious sense of deprivation of social position or wealth. Nor do they lack education in the formal sense. Rather they suffer from the wrong kind of education; and it is not merely that they learn from books rather than people, but that they read the wrong kind of books. None of the three gives one any reason to think she or he would be an avid, even a casual reader of Henry James, for example. All three would consider such novels frivolous. They read primarily history and philosophy in search of general laws of economic and social behavior whereby they would not merely understand but reform first their compatriots, and finally humanity.

James suggests through practice rather than precept that the novel can provide the kind of moral education Americans need. The novelist can give her or his readers the "experience" Verena and Basil lack by showing them different ways not only of living but also of thinking about living; and she or he can educate readers about the inmost recesses of her or his characters without engaging in journalistic exposure (p. 195). Publicity à la Matthias Pardon, as the phrase goes, "leaves nothing to the imagination"; as a result it destroys all personal integrity, and with integrity the ground of morality. Only through the imagination can one come to know the souls of others and yet protect them from either exposure or shamelessness; through the imagination one can extend oneself to others, moreover, without threat of domination. The novelist not only can supply the knowledge of character social conversation once provided and public preaching cannot, but he can also show the "interest" in the life and thought of the individual who is constantly threatened with extinction by the external sameness of modern industrial life. By portraying the interest, complexity, and beauty of individual consciousness, James performs a very important political function, if in an unpolitical fashion, by giving expression and thus support to the fundamental proposition of American political life—the value of the individual. Tocqueville observed: "The language, the dress, and the daily actions of men in democracies are repugnant to

conceptions of the ideal. . . . This forces the poet constantly to search below the external surface which is palpable to the sense, in order to read the inner soul; and nothing lends itself more to the delineation of the ideal than the scrutiny of the hidden depth in the immaterial nature of man" (II, 80). James' novels, including *The Bostonians,* present criticisms of American intellectual and moral traits, but these criticisms are grounded in a thoroughly liberal commitment to the importance of individual development and fulfillment. By depicting the defects of modern life in terms of the individualistic values of liberal democracy, James reaffirms and refines those values. The moral education his novels provides thus has profound political meaning. Nor was James unaware of the moral character of his art. Rather, he once wrote, "the greater imagination [is] the imagination of the moralist."[20]

Notes

1. Henry James, *The American Scene* (Bloomington: University of Indiana Press, 1968), p. 347. "The woman produced by a women-made society alone has obviously quite a new story. . . . What it came to, evidently, was that she had grown in an air in which a hundred of the 'European' complications and dangers didn't exist, and in which also she had had to take upon herself a certain training for freedom. . . . Thus she arrived, fullblown, on the general scene, the least criticized object, in proportion to her importance, that had ever adorned it. It would take long to say why her situation . . . may affect the inner fibre of the critic himself as one of the most touching on record. . . . For why need she originally, . . . have embraced so confidently, so gleefully, yet so unguardedly, the terms offered her to an end practically so perfidious. Why need she, unless in the interest of her eventual discipline, have turned away with so light a heart after watching the Man, the deep American man, retire into his tent . . . ? Would she not have said, 'No this is too unnatural; there must be a trap in it somewhere—it's addressed really, in the long run, to making a fool of me.'"

2. Henry James, "The Speech of American Women," reprinted in *French Writers and American Women Essays* (Branford, Conn.: The Compass Publishing Co., 1960), p. 33.

3. F. O. Matthiessen and Kenneth B. Murdock, *The Notebooks of Henry James* (New York: Oxford University Press, 1961), p. 47.

4. Charles Thomas Samuels, *The Ambiguity of Henry James* (Urbana: University of Illinois Press, 1973), p. 102; Alfred Habegger, "The Disunity of *The Bostonians,*" *Nineteenth Century Fiction* 24, no. 2

(September 1969): 198; Irving Howe, *Politics and the Novel* (New York: Horizon, 1957), pp. 188, 190.

5. S. Gorley Putt, *Henry James, A Reader's Guide* (Ithaca: Cornell University Press, 1966), p. 184.

6. Henry James, "American Democracy and American Education," in *American Essays*, ed., Leon Edel (New York: Vintage, 1956), p. 243. Cf. his review of E. L. Godkins' *Unforeseen Tendencies of Democracy*: "One feels it to be a pity that, in such a survey, the reference to the social conditions as well should not somehow be interwoven: at so many points are they—whether for contradiction, confirmation, attenuation, or aggravation—but another aspect of the political" (p. 243).

7. Page citations refer to the Modern Library edition of *The Bostonians* [1956].

8. Cf. P. R. Grover, "'The Princess Casimassima' and 'L'Education sentimentale'" *Modern Language Review* 66, no. 4 (October 1971): 760-61, on the superiority of James' analysis of political reality in terms of "types" to more factual literary accounts.

9. According to his notebook, p. 47, James initially contemplated the novel in terms of the struggle that takes place in the mind of Verena Tarrant. Such a tack is truer to the technique of the later James but it is not true to the character. Verena's intelligence is not developed. The absence of a center of consciousness that some critics point out as a fault could lead to deeper insights into James' intention if readers were not so quick to think that they know the "real James." This "fault" in the noel in fact points to one of James' major conclusions: The American regime prevents the development of a fine consciousness. In his other novels, James' heroines or heroes have to go to Europe to develop, and they do so with varying degrees of success.

10. Henry James, in "Emerson," *American Essays*, p. 72.

11. Cf. Richard Chase, *The American Novel and Its Tradition* (Garden City, N.Y.: Doubleday, 1957), pp. 121-30, for an Isabel Archer very like Olive.

12. There seems to be an ironic play on the old lady's name on the notion of a "birdseye view." On James' use of names cf. Joyce Taylor Horrell, "A 'Shade of a Special Sense': Henry James and the Art of Naming," *American Literature* 42 (1970-71): 203-220; Lionel Trilling, "The Bostonians," *The Opposing Self* (New York: Viking, 1955).

Some readers have been tempted to see historical figures such as Elizabeth Peabody in Miss Birdseye and Victoria Woodhull in Verena. James, however, emphatically denied that the characters had any source outside his "moral consciousness." Cf. F. O. Matthiessen, *The James Family* (New York: Knopf, 1947), p. 326.

13. Cf. Louise Bogan, "The Portrait of New England," *Selected Criticism* (New York: Knopf, 1955), pp. 297, 300, 298; Clinton Oliver, "Henry James as Social Critic," *Antioch Review* 7, n. 2 (June 1947): 245; Philip Rahv, "Introduction," *The Bostonians* (New York: Dial, 1945).

14. Basil wants to rule the minds of men. But it seems that the only place he will in fact rule, if at all, is his own hearth. James perhaps refers ironically to Basil's ambition in his first name, from the Greek for king, *Basileus.*

15. Peter Buitenhuis, *The Grasping Imagination* (Toronto: University of Toronto Press, 1970), suggests that Basil "ransoms" Verena's sexuality. James may have used the poem he remembered Emerson delivering at the Music Hall in commemoration of the Emancipation Proclamation ironically, however:

    Pay ransom to the owner
    And fill the bag to the brim.
    Who is the owner? The slave is owner
    and ever was. Pay him!

16. Property is perhaps *the* bourgeois concern, and its extension into the human realm forms a major theme of James' writing, as in *The American, The Spoils of Poynton, The Wings of the Dove,* and *The Golden Bowl.* Cf. Donald L. Mull, *Henry James' "Subtle Economy"* (Middletown, Conn.: Wesleyan University, 1973).

17. "The Question of Our Speech," an address delivered to the graduating class at Bryn Mawr College, Pennsylvania, June 8, 1905, reprinted in Henry James, *French Writers and American Woman Essays*, p. 20.

18. Alexis de Tocqueville, *Democracy in America* (New York: Vintage, 1945), II: 3: ix, 209.

19. Cf. James, *American Scene*, p. 347.

20. James took the outline of the plot of *The Bostonians* from Alphonse Daudet's *L'Evangeliste.* He considered Daudet the "best of all the novelists who have not the greater imagination, the imagination of the moralist" (*French Writers and American Women*, p. 3).

Lynn Wardley (essay date fall 1989)

SOURCE: Wardley, Lynn. "Woman's Voice, Democracy's Body, and *The Bostonians*." *ELH* 56, no. 3 (fall 1989): 639-65.

[*In the following essay, Wardley centers on James's treatment of women's place in democratic society in* The Bostonians.]

Describing what he calls the "perfect human voice," Walt Whitman specifies "celebrated people" in possession of this rare vocal power. The contralto Alboni, the tenor Bettini, Father Taylor, the "old actor Booth," and "in private life, many cases, often women" make his list. Nature has "afforded them all the vocal organ in perfection," by which Whitman means that the quality of their speech is not the product of their education but is instead a native property of their bodies. "To me the grand voice is mainly physiological—(by which I by no means ignore the mental help, but wish to put the emphasis where it belongs.)"[1]

Walt Whitman's perfect human voice is the voice of Henry James's Verena Tarrant, the "New England Corinna" of *The Bostonians*.[2] She reminds her rapt listener Basil Ransom of the "*improvisatrice* of Italy," and where de Stael's novel *Corinne, or, Italy* aligns personal and national identity, Verena is similarly identified with the American democracy, is its "repository of culture," as F. O. Matthiessen says of the Jamesian Girl.[3] Verena represents what James elsewhere calls "our medium of utterance," our "medium of intercourse."[4] But if hers is the voice of a woman in private life, *The Bostonians*' Basil Ransom fears what will take place when Verena enters the public domain; when, performing in public, she ceases to perform the intimate "conversation" within which, Emerson writes in 1855, the American woman reproduces "all our havings."[5]

Of course, the problem with citing the voice as the touchstone and medium of the mutable republic resides in its own mutability. Now embodied, now disembodied, voices carry into public spaces where they are all too easily altered. Punning as they are on "intercourse" and on "conversation," James and Emerson align woman's voice both with domestic privacy and with the reproductive body. But if it is true that woman's speech and her physiology serve as the source of both cultural and biological regeneration in the democracy, it is also the case that voice and the maternal body represent the possibility of unregulated signification and reproduction. In "The Question of Our Speech" and *The Speech and Manners of American Women,* Henry James associates the sound of women in public life with the various aliens, the proliferating newspapers, and the burgeoning urban crowd.[6] Preoccupied with disorderly women, linguistic chaos, and potential cultural revolution, James

yearns in *Speech and Manners* for the "cultivated and consecrated" speech of the gentlewoman who occupies "yet uninvaded" "bowery rural homes" (34). Yet the status of this idyllic model of proper speech does not go unexamined in *The Bostonians*. Verena Tarrant's tone reminds her auditors of "convent-cloisters," but the fact that she is a mesmerist's daughter alerts us at the outset to the possibility that anything like her private or natural or perfect human voice has already been tuned to public life.

The Bostonians examines the problems that an expanding urban society, the modern media, and the Woman Movement pose to a democratic culture understood as regenerated by women in the home and marked there by an organic continuity. Yet unlike his hero Basil Ransom, Henry James does not conclude that women must remain within private life if "civilization itself" is to be saved (50). Instead, James urges domestic women into public performance—now not as fluent mediums but rather as what he calls "closed vessel[s]" of authority (*SM,* 34).[7] While the official seat of cultural transmission shifts from domestic into civic spaces, James in effect urges women to remain the "guardians of civilization and the conservators of the means of culture."[8] But this last description is taken not from Henry James on the peculiar responsibilities of American women but from a contemporary's account of the function of the municipal museum in Boston. Here, the Jamesian "closed vessel" of woman's body and the monumental city museum significantly correspond. I will be arguing that in *The Bostonians* Henry James envisions for women neither that they affiliate entirely with the commercial media, nor that they stay ventriloquized from within their separate sphere. Instead, James suggests that they occupy an interior someplace in between, in the cultural institutions of the decades of American "incorporation," decades in which utopian impulses and ideological proclivities were simultaneously in play.[9] For if such an incorporation seems at first to offer no new birth of freedom, but only a monumental reproduction of a previously silencing privacy, the novel nevertheless identifies the cultural institution as the social platform upon which women and the Woman Movement enter into a "new phase," enter, that is, into the "domain of practical politics" (*B*, 317).

I

Lingering a week in Boston after a public reading of "The Death of Abraham Lincoln" on April 14, 1881, Walt Whitman reports that he "felt pretty well (the mood propitious, my paralysis lull'd)—went around everywhere and saw all that was to be seen, especially human beings." All throughout Boston the poet detected a "subtle something," a something

> indefinable in *the race,* the turn of its development which effuses beyond the whirl of animation, study, business, a happy and joyous public spirit . . . Indeed,

there is something Hellenic in B., and the people are getting handsomer too—padded-out, with freer motions, and with color in their faces. I never saw . . . so many *fine-looking gray-haired women.* At my lecture I caught myself pausing to look at them—plentiful everywhere throughout the audience—healthy and wifely and motherly, and wonderfully charming and beautiful—I think as no such land or time but ours could show.

("The Boston of Today," 901)

The immense material growth of Old Boston into the sprawling metropolis left its impression, but the "best new departures and expansions of Boston, and of all the cities of New England, are in another direction." Somehow able to dissociate Boston's public-spirited padded-out people from the fact of its obvious and "copious capital," Whitman divined democracy's future empire as much in its stock of "healthy and wifely and motherly" women as in its "commerce, finance, commission stores . . . plethora of goods . . . crowded streets and sidewalks" ("A Week's Visit to Boston," 901).

But if the gray-haired ladies who came to hear Walt Whitman occasioned his optimism regarding democracy's best departures, the American girls who met Henry James on his return to America in 1904 left him frightened by the levelling effects of democratic expansion. Crossing the Boston Common in time to hear schoolgirls on recess conversing "at the top of their lungs," listening later to Boston maidens "vociferating over the Boston gutters," and noting the "tongueless slobber, snarl or whine of the emancipated women" in their "full-blown ubiquity," James concludes in *The Speech and Manners of American Women* that these Bostonians present not the prospect of evolutionary excellence but rather a warning to the rest of the race (32, 31). Indifferent to proper vocal tone, woman's voice blurs the refining borders between drawing room and tenement house. Indifferent to New England speech, the "highest type of utterance implanted among us," the Boston girl endangers far more than Boston, for to meet linguistic muddle in the "fountain head of native culture" is to anticipate its transmission nationwide (37, 33). Judging by the state of the language the state of American civilization, Henry James finds America alarmingly unachieved.

When James then journeys south to Pennsylvania and a captive audience of young women, the Bryn Mawr class of 1905, he explains there that the question of our speech is not isolated but is instead the question of our culture itself, and implores American women to become "models," "missionaries," even "martyrs" to proper speech and so to culture's cause (*QS,* 52). Urging each graduate to "embody" as conservative an interest in matters of language as she would in matters of matrimony, the Bryn Mawr address, later published as "The Question of Our Speech," makes suggestive correspon-

dences between women's vocal and sexual propriety. The American idiom is the personal property of the woman of Bryn Mawr, who herself becomes "our medium of utterance" and "our collective medium of intercourse" in the course of James's address (39, 45). Exploiting the ambiguity between cultural and biological reproduction even further, James suggestively warns the Bryn Mawr woman what assaults await her speech upon commencement: the immigrants will attempt to "work their will" upon it, the dominant media will distort it, the common schools and crowds will diminish its distinctions (45).

Echoing Alexis de Tocqueville's observation that the success of the American experiment rests in the superiority of American women, Whitman and James measure in the position of women the progress of liberal democracy. But while Whitman's listeners are the already wifely and motherly ladies of his generation, set self-complacently apart from the whirl of commercial production, James's audience is of rather a more dangerous age and more immediately implicated in the social and material conditions that had newly produced the American woman in public life. No longer "guarding the good idiom" from within established enclosures, young women risk commingling all too indiscriminately with the speech, cultures, and bodies of others (*SM,* 38). Violating those codes of hierarchy and propriety that establish differences in class, gender, and race, women endanger patriarchal prerogatives over the social evolution of American civilization.

For however much she has been handed over to the "forces of betrayal," the American woman is herself the *agent provocateur* of revolution (*QS,* 41). In *Speech and Manners,* Henry James indicts that "innumerable sisterhood," the Woman Movement, for "bristling" with its "proclamation of indifference" to the very institutions that regulate cultural and biological reproduction: proper manners, proper speech, and matrimony (29). Although the voice of the American woman "pleads in a thousand places the cause of culture" (25), it abandons her most precious conquest, domestic life, wherein civilization originates and from which it outwardly unfolds.[10] Leaving the "private garden" for the "pavements of the town," and thus a "large scale of space around them for intercourse," women can scarce do more than "hoot and howl" (32). To enter urban space is to find speech reconstituted within the city's expanding parameters and under such novel forms of production as the advertisement and the daily news. But when James describes billboards as "the *disjecta membra* of murdered Taste, pike-paraded in some September Massacre," and paints a picture of the newspaper's "vast open mouth" as it flings back the "floodgates of vulgarity," the revolutionary potential of the advertisements and the daily press seems to originate within the problem of female sexuality (71, 69). Recording his shock in *Speech and*

Manners at the daily tabloids American girls were "consuming" on a train and the meal they were simultaneously "engulfing," James objects to their "incoherent and indiscriminate" spooning of the "most violently heterogeneous food" (67-68). Aligning speaking, reading, eating, and sexual activity, he focuses on the apertures of the female body, on that body's acts of incorporation and dilation.

It could be argued that in *The Speech and Manners of American Women* the imagined openness of the female body threatens to reduce difference into sameness, although precisely the appeal of that body is that through it, difference is generated and conserved. It is sexual difference, guaranteed, as Tocqueville noted, by woman's internal controls, that protects against indiscriminate mergings in democracies where "members of a community . . . stand so near that they may all at any time be fused into one general mass." Sacrificed specifically into matrimony and so into a discrete domestic space, woman helps generate those distinctions that keep every man "aloof, lest he be carried away against his will in the crowd."[11] If Tocqueville determined that woman's traditional sphere was in fact her natural place, several influential late nineteenth-century biologists and social scientists only fortified his conclusion. The middle- and leisure-class woman's entry into civic life was frequently represented as the disruption of the delicate balance and vital interiority of a society viewed as an evolving human organism writ large.[12]

In the Boston Henry James had dubbed "the fountainhead of native culture," such a disruption was spectacularly staged. Art critic James Jackson Jarves praised the city for its "organic structure," what in 1864 he described as "a heart, head and lungs, as well as extremities," but Boston's body was radically reconstructed in the years of postbellum commercial expansion.[13] The sound of Boston maidens "vociferating over the Boston gutters" (*SM,* 32) suggested to Henry James that modern women had colluded with those modern, material forces at work to upset Boston's established configuration. Yet evident even in James's nostalgic recollection of a lost Bostonian interior and its female guardians is a problematic account of the Bostonian, who, as she functioned to embody a "precious ripe tradition," functioned *merely* as a body (43).

For insofar as James remarks with horror on the ubiquity of mannerless American girls, what frightens him finally in *Speech and Manners* is less that they are suddenly seen and heard in the public domain than that they have entered it untutored and unchaperoned. Acknowledging that the presence of women in American urban life is a *fait accompli,* James does not urge a retreat into domestic scenes of cultural training. Instead, such scenes must be staged in the public domain and such women must serve as culture's "missionaries"

(*QS,* 52). For in woman's nature is the possibility of her becoming the "guardian of the sacred flame of inherited civilization" by so thoroughly internalizing proper speech, manners, customs, and authority that the problem of the body's vulnerability to alien incursions, or, inversely, to its own "slackness," is peculiarly solved (*QS,* 49). Thus the address to the Bryn Mawr women requests that proper habits, organized as instincts, "well-nigh unconscious and automatic," become each woman's "second nature," that she may thereby personally set an unassailable national standard and "tune" (47-52).[14] Here the body, defined by its openness, even by its too-easy assimilation of other bodies, takes that definition to a paradoxical extreme when it becomes second nature to such a body to serve as "model" of or "martyr" to culture's cause.

In fact, the image of biologized influence constructed above neatly accommodates what seems at first to be its alter-image, the cultural museum, which Alan Trachtenberg has called "an infrastructure which monumentalized the presence of culture in society." "As culture came to seem the repository of elevating thoughts and cleansing emotions," he adds, "it seemed as though the rough world of masculine enterprise had called into being its redemptive opposite."[15] Thus invested, the domain of culture, like domesticity, is rendered a functional part of the masculine market, at once its antidote and stay. Yet if culture reposes within a figure like Verena Tarrant—made to "soothe," as she says of herself, the "senseless brutes" "with a word"—Basil Ransom imagines that culture in turn requires its own watch and ward (*B,* 461).

The Bostonians addresses itself to the reconstruction of democracy after domesticity, at times represented as the feminine body of the South, at times as Olive Chancellor's Bostonian chambers, has lost its hold.[16] Basil Ransom's plot to restore democratic social evolution to its proper course involves but is complicated by Verena Tarrant, who possesses both the desirable voice of "convent-cloisters" and the aspect of a "walking advertisement" (*B,* 229, 266). A mesmerist's daughter, Verena Tarrant can "turn herself inside out," and such self-exposure is what Basil Ransom attempts to arrest (392). The novel traces his efforts to keep her from the men of the press, who want to make her "widely popular," and from the feminist movement, represented as internally at odds about how best to market Verena's spectacular oratorical power to "regenerate the world" (405, 204). Verena is adaptable, accommodating, assimilative and absorptive, all as Olive Chancellor describes her, her voice easily "conjoined . . . in emulation" (243). She is markedly susceptible to those who would capitalize on her voice by absorbing it in an organism larger than her own: Basil would marry her to a man, the press would work her "as it were, scientifically" into the papers, and Olive would join her in a "partnership of their two minds" to make an "organic whole" (126, 160). Each seemingly contractual offer is an incorporative gesture. If Olive can counsel Verena to resist matrimony in particular, it is because she can point to its history as a union that claims to abolish dominance only to recuperate dominance in natural terms—Basil Ransom's terms when he courts her.

The sense of urgency communicated in *The Bostonians* that Verena's body must be married, managed, or simply shut as it passes into public space derives in part from the novel's depiction of the other volatile, vulnerable bodies surrounding hers. The city of Boston itself is an alarmingly permeable organism—or so it appears to the Southerner Basil Ransom, who pictures in the dismantling of the private interiors in which his idea of culture is enshrined the violation of feminine, even uterine spaces. From Olive Chancellor's "cushioned feminine nest" to the "*penetralia*" of the daily press and the "*vomitoria*" of the Music Hall, the city's public organs of communication appear to him obscene reproductions of the parts of the private self (17, 106, 442). As private space is entered into and inverted, so too is proper speech; conversation tête-à-tête multiplies into a mixture of voices forced into "ineffectual shrillness" at the Female Convention (243).

It appears that however much Basil Ransom admits to the fact that "North and South were now a single indivisible political organism," when faced with actual social fusion he struggles to erect the discriminations he saw levelled in the war (*B*, 13). A member of a now "dilapidated gentry," Basil seeks to resurrect a democratic body governed by visible distinctions (212). In order to do so he must recover sexual difference, the heart and support of that body. To save his sex from "damnable feminization," and his speech from a "chattering, canting" age of "vulgar mediocrity" he rallies to restore "the masculine character" (343). The tough and technical Doctor Prance, who tells Basil Ransom that men and women are all the same to her, is suspected of dissecting in her back room, as if to prove with her sharpened instruments that there are no essential differences (41). Basil uses other tools to make the opposite case when, as if exercising the right of the stronger, he takes Verena "by muscular force" from her friends (463). Mocking Verena's casual talk of free union, he pursues a more perfect union in an aristocracy of sex. For masculine identity to be recovered, femininity must be restricted, woman's wandering voice placed back within what Verena suggestively calls "the box" (274).

From where or from whom will cultural authority emanate? The question assumes a genuine urgency in a novel that projects what is problematic about the "mysterious democracy" onto the mysterious bodies of women, imagined either as able to generate distinctions or as liable instead to permit fusion into "one general mass," even to serve anatomically as the medium of that fusion (80). "I'm sure we are all solid," Miss Birdseye says of the Bostonians, but Basil Ransom suspects otherwise (57). If Verena's is the voice of democracy, hers is also the voice of a ventriloqual body, and thus potentially indistinguishable from the alien, the crowd, and a femininity "odiously perverted," possibly subversive (243).[17] For if there is a woman behind every great man there are also, Basil remarks, women at the bottom of the wars, women advocates of "our four fearful years of slaughter" (92).

Yet if a vocal female of a dangerous age threatens to wound the democracy, a mature female body is solicited to heal it. While Basil Ransom imagines the disorderly daughters of Walt Whitman's wifely and motherly ladies, his radical Bostonians originate within Whitman's democratic economy, where the nation's political convulsions are only the "endless gestations" of an underlying "Mother of All" ("Pensive on Her Dead Gazing," 605). "Democracy," Whitman writes, "where weapons were everywhere aim'd at your breast. I saw you serenely give birth . . . saw in / dreams your dilating form" ("By Blue Ontario's Shore," 482). The attempted Secession delivers the Union, expressing only the "conflict . . . between the passions and the paradoxes of one and the same identity" or the divisions only natural to one single, indivisible political organism ("Origins of Attempted Secession," 994). On this view, the corpus of a saving maternity naturalizes rebellion and neatly recuperates it. Basil imagines facilitating just such a recuperation when he imagines marrying Verena.

But if Whitman's democracy, much like a mesmerized body, could go peacefully to war with itself, Henry James remains suspicious of assuming any so sanguine a solution to "the situation of women," and "the agitation on their behalf" (*B*, xi). And if in *The Speech and Manners of American Women* he echoes Basil Ransom's opinion of the Bostonians, and laments like him "the decline in the sentiment of sex," he does not condone Basil's impulses. "My interest is my own sex," Basil informs Verena. "That's what I want to save" (*B*, 342). "And I must tell you that I don't in the least care what happens to you ladies while I make the attempt!" (*B*, 343). Tracking a feminine voice into public space, only to still its agitations within the master narrative of "the masculine character," Basil Ransom exposes the politics of his sentimentality to view.

II

Halfway through *The Bostonians,* Basil Ransom hears Verena Tarrant speak before the Wednesday Club and realizes that he is in love with her. This knowledge does nothing to make the "sequel of her discourse more clear to him"; her voice alone continues to move him (275). Basil has "simply felt her presence, tasted her voice," to arrive at the deduction that although her public apostleship is all nonsense, she *is* meant for something "divinely different—for privacy, for him, for love" (275). In a later scene, counterpart to this one, Basil stands outside Olive's rented cottage in Marmion and, hearing only the sounds Verena makes practicing a speech inside, renews his campaign "to press, to press, always to press," as soon he will, rapping "loudly with his walking-stick on the lintel of Miss Chancellor's house-door," although "as usual, on fine days, it stood open" (399, 426).

What is especially striking about Basil Ransom's first, crucial moment of "fusion" with Verena Tarrant is that it is *she* who, through the synesthetic medium of her voice, "tap[s] at" and enters Basil's heart: "and before he could hesitate or challenge, the door had sprung open" (275). Her talk over, he is borne on the current of the crowd to a table spread for supper. Supper at the Wednesday Club

> appeared to be embodied mainly in the glitter of crystal and silver, and the fresh tints of mysterious viands and jellies, which looked desirable in the soft circle projected by lace-fringed lamps. He heard the popping of corks, felt the pressure of elbows, the thickening of the crowd, perceived that he was glowered at, squeezed against the table, by contending gentlemen who observed that he usurped space, was neither feeding himself nor helping others to feed. He had lost sight of Verena; . . . but he found himself thinking—almost paternally—that she must be hungry after so much chatter, and he hoped that someone was getting her something to eat.
>
> (*B*, 275-76)

Basil's wish is immediately granted in the form of Verena, "attached to the arm of a young man" leading her to the table. "She looked beautiful," we are told, and "they were a beautiful couple" (276).

This scene merits citing at some length because it is so strange and central and so like Basil Ransom to stage it. Basil turns Verena's public performance into a private audience; turns her speech about the communion bread and wine of inspiriting women into the voice he more profanely tastes; and turns from that embodied voice to a hypnotic vision of "mysterious viands and jellies" encircled by the light of fringed lamps. This last soft desirable circle seems most like a displaced image of Verena herself—of the body's "mysterious" openings in vocal or sexual orifices—as though the figure being led to the table might then and there herself be sacrificially consumed. Responding as though aroused by this image, Basil feels the perhaps predictable "pressure of elbows," the "popping of corks." But whether the force here exerted derives from within his own body or comes from sources outside of it is unclear. If Verena's voice enables the illusion of fusion with her body it also

serves as a catalyst to propel Basil into the crowd, where it is difficult to tell where his body ends and that of another begins. This is his second such experience at the Burrages. Making a "Mississippian bow" to Mrs. Burrage upon his arrival, Basil is suggestively pressed forward by the guests arriving behind him. "He yielded to the impulsion, and found himself in a great salon . . . where the company was dense, and there were more twinkling, smiling ladies, with uncovered bosoms" (*B*, 275). As if seeking relief from even these moments of indeterminacy between self and others, moments also encoded with gender confusion, Basil sets his eyes on Verena and Henry Burrage. Looking much like the bridal pair at the wedding feast, they reassure and reorient him. The couple restores a familiar hierarchy and teleology; "attached" to Henry Burrage as if by matrimonial bonds, Verena resumes her natural place. Distracted by the public nature of her "intensely personal" performance, Basil believes that marriage, like the food with which he would "almost paternally" feed Verena, will stop her mouth.

In this central scene the novel's thematics of speech, food, interiority, and exposure are given play. Characteristically, Basil Ransom turns from exposure to crowds in which he is touched and almost extinguished to enclosures in which he expands or spaces in which he can stand apart from the crowd. In the home of his Boston cousin, Olive Chancellor, Basil turns his back on her view of the Charles—its factories' "dirty 'works,'" its "brackish expanse of anomalous character"—to an illuminated chamber of objects that "spoke of habits and tastes," and to an abundant table (*B*, 15-16). Olive and Verena turn from Olive's western windows and the "general hard, cold, void of the prospect," "shuddering a little," to their "glittering tea tray" (178-79). The "desolate suburban horizons," "peeled and made bald," are juxtaposed to the feminine rooms of a city-house, the vertical chimneys, "straight, sordid tubes of factories and engineshops" to Olive's "white and muffled" Charles Street parlor (179). If from one perspective the suburbs threaten to enter Olive's home, from another they are safely framed within it, made a feature of its decor. That Basil finds the impoverished landscape picturesque, that Olive takes credit, as Mrs. Luna remarks, for her Back Bay view, peculiarly marks this social geography as the aesthetic property of the room. Yet the novel repeatedly suggests that the house is imperfectly guarded against threats from without, that the house, like the body, is often betrayed from within. The crowd of men at the Burrages "feeding [or] helping others to feed" reminds Basil of the brutal appetites driving even the members of the "best society," of his own stomach "bigger . . . than all the culture of Charles Street could fill" (276, 17).

Basil is duly alarmed, then, when Olive Chancellor seems willing to sacrifice the security her father's patrimony grants her, or to speak indifferently of the advantages of her highly organized privacy. Olive has cultivated, as it were, interiority itself; never had Basil "seen an interior that was so much an interior as this queer corridor-shaped drawing room" of his cousin.

> The general character of the place struck him as Bostonian; this was, in fact, very much what he had supposed Boston to be. He had always heard Boston was a city of culture, and now there was culture in Miss Chancellor's tables and sofas, in the books that were everywhere, on little shelves like brackets (as if a book were a statuette), in the photographs and watercolors that covered the walls, in the curtains that were festooned rather stiffly in the doorway.
>
> (B, 16)

Olive's rooms explicitly form and express "character": her own, her small society's, and eventually Verena Tarrant's. Although she is a "signal old maid," Olive's chamber is the *mise en scène* of the reproduction and transmission of culture. Within it she puts Verena, "nursed in darkened rooms" and "suckled in the midst of manifestations," to school among women with "books from the Athenaeum nursed behind their muff" (B, 84, 180). In a new transplanted environment of "soft influences" Verena proves a quick study.

> Olive had always rated high the native refinement of her countrywomen, their latent "adaptability," their talent for accommodating themselves at a glance to changed conditions; but the way Verena rose with the level of civilization that surrounded her, the way she assimilated all delicacies and absorbed all traditions, left his friendly theory halting behind.
>
> (B, 177)

Lifted out of the "bald bareness of Tarrant's temporary lair," the cottage with its "naked little piazza, which seemed rather to expose than to protect," and into Olive's interior and her accompanying ideas of refinement, the American Girl engages in what is staged as a "civilizing" process. But Olive Chancellor is training Verena up only to sacrifice her to their "real life," the cause, and this helps explain Olive's ambivalence about her own agenda, her perpetual postponements. After "so many ages of wrong," "men must pay!" But only (it is parenthetically added) after Olive and Verena take their European journey (186).

In *The Bostonians,* explicitly feminine interiors exert a biologized influence over their occupants, but women as well as men are guilty of disrupting these operations. Against Olive's "cushioned feminine nest" the novel juxtaposes Miss Birdseye's explicitly barren one, in the back room of which Dr. Mary Prance has set up a little physiological laboratory, "which, if she hadn't been a doctor, might have been her 'chamber,' and perhaps was even with the dissecting, Miss Birdseye didn't

know!" (B, 41). Within Olive herself a small war rages about Miss Birdseye's interior. "[Basil] did not know . . . that she mortally disliked it,"

> and that in a career in which she was constantly exposing herself to offence and laceration, *her most poignant suffering came from the injury of her taste. She had tried to kill that nerve,* to persuade herself that taste was only frivolity in the guise of knowledge, but her susceptibility was always blooming afresh, and making her wonder if the absence of nice arrangements were a necessary part of the enthusiasm of humanity.
>
> (B, 31; my emphasis)

If the exteriorization of what is for Basil Ransom a crucially interior environment is suggested by the vision of Dr. Prance performing anatomies in her maiden-chamber, it was effected in fact by the reorganization of domestic space Henry James identified as a dangerous architectural vogue. The "vagueness of boundary" within Miss Birdseye's house is an example of a custom that "rages like a conspiracy" for "nipping the interior in the bud . . . by wiping out successively each sign by which it may be known from an exterior."

> Thus we have the law fulfilled that every part of every house shall be . . . visible, visitable, penetrable, not only from every other part, but from as many parts of as many other houses as possible, if they only be near enough.[18]

To dismantle the walls between rooms makes private spaces into something like public theaters. Such exposure obstructs the "very play of social relation" itself by inhibiting "conversation." So "merciless a medium" makes the visitor ill at ease:

> [He] finds himself looking around for a background or a limit, some localizing fact or two, in the interest of talk, of that "good" talk that always falters before the complete proscription of privacy. He sees only doorless apertures . . . reminding him that what he says must be said for the house.
>
> (AS, 167, 168).

The experience of James's visitor here in *The American Scene* might well describe the discomfort of Basil Ransom when together he and Olive visit Miss Birdseye's home for a gathering of people interested in ideas. Basil looks around only to note the public qualities of this domestic setting; although friends are assembled there is nothing convivial about the scene: no food, no fire, no conversation. Instead, the guests arranged stiffly in chairs along the sides of the "long bald room" produce "the similitude of an enormous streetcar," and for "good talk," and Basil Ransom's "starved senses," there is chiefly the "strange, sweet, crude, absurd, enchanting improvisation" of Verena Tarrant, talking to a full house, yet as if she were talking in her sleep (B, 29, 31, 61).

A tourist in Boston's South End, Basil envisions as public a vehicle as the streetcar invading Miss Birdseye's private property, and as private a body as that of

Verena Tarrant speaking openly on public display. If he is alarmed by these inversions in Boston, he is intimate with their consequences in New York, where exteriors peculiarly resemble the internal contents of human bodies exposed and at work. In his apartment house a cellarway yawns open like a mouth, exhaling the strong odor of fish, and threatening to swallow those who "gaze too fondly on the savory wares" in the window display (190). A Dutch grocery bulges out of the building's belly-like side; on the pavement, toward the gutters, "dirty panniers" spill onions, carrots, and potatoes. Basil's windows command a view of the "fantastic skeleton" of the Elevated Railway smothering the street with its "immeasurable spinal column and myriad clutching paws" (191). Beer-saloons expose their "shoulders and sides," tenements their bare backs, convulsive streetcars absorb and emit passengers (348). The loose division between the inside and the outside of Basil's apartment house, the horizontal flow of its contents onto the street, is matched on a vertical plane by the confused social order between its walls. A "decayed mansion," imparting an "idle, rural, pastoral air to a scene otherwise expressive of a rank civilization," the house alludes to the Ransoms' Mississippi plantation, or to the South in general, and to his mother and sisters living hand to mouth (189, 190). The New York interior is an "obscure asylum" for cohabitants of both sexes and different races, its basement *table d'hôte* conducted by a "couple of shuffling negresses who mingled in the conversation" (189, 191).

That black women servants might mingle in the conversation of others is meant to suggest the degree to which social hierarchy in this house has fallen. To Basil Ransom, such "mingling" is in itself a degraded and dangerous occupation. Yet on the other side of town in the Burrage mansion, mingling receives a different evaluation, as Verena Tarrant mingles gracefully in the company of New York society and, by so mingling, rises.[19] Unlike Basil's nearly gutted apartment house, the Burrage mansion is a container of thresholds and chambers, the walls of which were "covered with pictures—the very ceiling was painted and framed" (*B,* 254). Exhibiting their own interiority, Mrs. Burrage's gilded rooms resemble the galleries of a museum. But Basil is uneasy about the guests assembled there to hear Verena Tarrant speak; they "pushed each other a little, edged about, advanced and retreated, looking at each other with differing faces—sometimes blandly," sometimes "with a kind of cruelty" (254). This is the setting in which he will sense the elegant company become a contentious group come to feed, if not on Verena, then possibly on Basil, "carried further and further forward" to a room with a little stage, "covered with a red cloth" (254). The scene serves in part to suggest the restraining, uplifting force of women and culture, the force of Verena as she soothes a potentially belligerent group. But the scene also frames Mrs. Burrage and her son Henry as patrons

who take up Verena as if she were an objet d'art. Their rooms are extravagant aesthetic reproductions of Olive Chancellor's organized privacy, and she feels as disturbed and seduced by them as Basil Ransom.

Making their mansion a small museum in which to unveil Verena before the Wednesday Club, the Burrages put their private home, and the privilege of privacy, on display. But in New York not only elite interior but also common exterior spaces are institutionalized as private zones. While the presence of the gigantic Elevated overshadows and, like the company-turned-crowd, threatens to engulf the individual, another public convenience provides him or her the consoling sensation of self-containment. A municipal space plotted as a private garden, Central Park, like the Burrage house, offers its guests a theater of interiority. Described as a narrow enclosure approached by Basil and Verena on the train, the Park possesses a tiny zoo, ornamental water, sequestered benches, nurses and babies, tunnels, grottoes, and the manicured Maze (*B,* 333-35). It is Basil's plan to have Verena "share the noon-day repast with him somehow," to dine in a luxurious restaurant at the top of the park under conditions entirely unlike those of his *table d'hôte*: to wait "until something extremely good, and a little vague, chosen out of a French *carte,* was brought them" (334). Designed by Frederick Law Olmsted to serve as the "tea-table" of Manhattan—Olive's civilized chambers on a civic scale—Central Park is also New York's most maternal habitat.[20]

The maternal body imagined as a walled city, in which the self exists prior to suffering the wounds of any division, appears in the novel as a retreat from the alter-image of that same body aligned with the opened apartments and multiplying crowds that ignore spatial and social boundaries.[21] Central Park, Olive's Bostonian drawing room, and the neighboring campus at Harvard offer Basil Ransom a comforting *point d'appui.* Out walking in Cambridge and passing first with Verena through a "sightless, soundless, interspaced, embryonic region," Basil eventually arrives at the library of Harvard College, its "sanctified spot" (*B,* 240-46). Within it the Olive-like librarian Miss Catching tends to the books in alcoves and the rarer volumes under glass. Verena and Basil pass into Memorial Hall, where the Southerner lingers among the white tablets inscribed with the names of Harvard's Civil War dead. Like the scene in the library, this is a scene of reading. As Memorial Hall provides Basil Ransom a moment's relief, it does so by touching him with "the sentiment of beauty" (248). The monument suggests the power of aesthetic culture to absorb and redeem a violent breach, to show the brutal to be sacred in the manner of Whitman's "Mother of All."

But to see Memorial Hall as a pacifying natural enclosure is to ignore how carefully it has been culturally organized to carry the charge Basil receives. The response

Basil Ransom has to Harvard's library and Memorial Hall resembles the reaction of Henry James himself when, visiting Boston's Public Library in *The American Scene,* he finds himself restored "to emotion" as the Library's inner staircase expands "monumentally, at one of its rests, into admirable commemoration of the Civil War" (*AS,* 250-52). James initially observes that the structure of Boston's Library, like the structure of most buildings in social democracies, appears "unfriendly to the preservation of *penetralia,*" to "some part that should be sufficiently within some other part, sufficiently withdrawn and consecrated, not to constitute a thoroughfare" (*B,* 250, 251). The Library features the "open doors and immediate accesses" more essential to a railway-station than to a place of meditation and study (*AS,* 251). But the painted murals on the Public Library's interior staircase walls prompt James into an immediate charmed perception of the deep court and the inner arcade of the "palace," of the "myriad gold-colored courts of the Vatican" (*AS,* 251). Simultaneously a "masterpiece" and a "bribe," the staircase mural is exposed as the great production of a "wealth of science and taste," a marriage of technology and aesthetics issuing in a war memorial and public art that is also a seductive *trompe l'oeil.*

That James is charmed into the illusion of sumptuous private dimensions in a public library where the "ubiquitous children, *most* irrepressible little democrats of the democracy" pursue the "vain quest" for precisely such "deeper depths," suggests that the social function of the Library is not only to democratize education (*AS,* 251). The Library also potentially accommodates the public's desire for sensations associated here with social hierarchy, with the mysterious interiority of "the palace" and the Vatican, two repositories of aesthetic culture before the advent of public museums. Although the domestic picture of children in the Library, "their little heads bent over their story-books," coexists with James's impression of the Library's resemblance to a "lively distributing house" of commercial fiction, the children pursue an interiority rivaling Basil Ransom's when we first meet him, "already absorbed in a book" in Olive's chambers (*AS,* 252; *B,* 3).

But if in *The American Scene* Henry James detects in a public library the peaceful coexistence of the publishing industry and the domestic story hour, the smooth adjustment to new social imperatives, this is not a discovery he affords Basil Ransom. Basil's project is to combat the culture factories that seem to him to promise only the levelling effects of commodification. We learn that Basil himself is an aspiring writer, even an aspiring politician, but that he seeks to constitute his productions and his persona in opposition to the conditions of consumption and circulation that would make of him what they seem to him to make of Verena, "food for newsboys" (125). To elect the aloof, high culture of the

books under glass at Harvard over and against the speech mechanically reproduced and popularly distributed—to choose to voice his "opinions" and to make his name in the anachronistic *Rational Review* and not through a more modern medium of performance—is to shield himself from a painfully literal public exposure. Basil's "exotic" looks draw attention to him, his head is said to "suggest a topic," and he is asked by Mrs. Farrinder, for one, to tell about the South (255, 50). But Basil refuses any such publicity.

To Basil Ransom, who struggles to keep the voice within the body of Verena Tarrant and to keep the bodies of books ("as if a book were a statuette" [16]) enshrined on shelves between Olive's private walls, publicity appears responsible for the defacement and disintegration of such bodies. What happens structurally to the interior of Miss Birdseye's house happens physiologically to her, after a long career in the public eye. Her pale face

> looked as if it had been soaked, blurred and made vague by exposure to some slow dissolvent. The long practice of philanthropy had not given accent to her features; it had rubbed out their transitions, their meanings.
>
> (*B,* 27)

Because a lifetime of sympathy, of giving herself away, has brought her celebrity, Miss Birdseye appears above as an overexposed photograph of her former self. We see her last in a posthumous appearance, when Basil imagines her in an empty chair on the Music Hall stage on the evening of what is to be Verena's greatest performance. While here Miss Birdseye's absent presence might suggest to us the power of her public image to exist beyond the confines of a private body, it hints to Basil Ransom that the market strategies of the modern advocates have helped to rub Miss Birdseye out.

The scandal of photography, or of any vehicle of publicity, is not that it steals the soul but that it corrupts the body. This is what the barren interior of the reformer Miss Birdseye suggests, and what Basil, hearing that Verena has already been "subjected" to the photographic process, seeks to arrest (*B,* 243). To capitalize on Verena's voice is to capitalize on her body, in Selah Tarrant's plan to betroth her to newsman Matthias Pardon as in Basil's plot to keep her to himself. Indeed, success would not be success to Tarrant unless he could see his daughter's "*physique,* the rumor of her engagement . . . included in the 'Jottings' with the certainty of being extensively copied" (104). Failing to achieve his own publicity by entering the world "bodily," as he says, through the "*penetralia* of the offices of the press," he settles for "going in" by way of Verena, through whom as a mesmerist he has already disseminated his own voice (106). But to engage his daughter to Pardon is to engage her in public performance, to marry her to the mob. Worked, "as it were, scientifically, into the papers" (126), Verena would become for Basil Ransom what in his address at Bryn Mawr Henry James, describing the newspapers but invoking the Medusa, calls a "myriad-faced monster," a "mighty maniac . . . running amuck through the spheres alike of sense and of sound" (*QS,* 43). To secure Verena as the private body of genteel social reproduction is to stem the imagined effects of her monstrous double, affiliated here with the unpredictable People, the "social dusk of that mysterious democracy" (80). Mocked by blurry posters advertising Verena's Music Hall performance on walls all over the city, Basil sets out to take her from the Music Hall stage. In New York, Basil failed to stop her mouth with a "deliberate kiss" or something to eat (139). But having impressed her at Marmion in the space of a boat ride that left her with what James calls a "silent face" (425), Basil senses he is not too late. To finish the job he must make Verena his wife, for to become her husband is to "know a way to strike her dumb" (329).

But if in aligning uncontained female speech and the decline of civilization Basil Ransom seems to speak for Henry James, James does not sanction Basil's solution to the situation of women in the "violently heterogeneous" democracy. To remove Verena's voice from the promiscuity of public space, only to install it within the interiority of the body, is to leave culture's repository to the body's vulnerabilities. Although when Henry James describes the nature of culture in his speech at Bryn Mawr he seems to suggest its essential connection to the bodies of women, he simultaneously calls attention to these bodies as self-conscious constructions, as "models" of culture, even as "walking advertisement[s]." Like the seductive interiority organized at the heart of the Boston Public Library, Verena's performance is at once a "masterpiece" and a "bribe." Seen this way, the heroine of culture is she who artfully professionalizes her relation to it, like the actress who offers herself for public consumption without giving herself away.

When in *The American Scene* Henry James looks to find the "fine old disinterested tradition of Boston least broken," he discovers it in what is a virtual parody of cultivation, the mansion of Isabella Stewart Gardner. A private home turned public museum, Gardner's Fenway Court houses both a conservatory garden and an impressive art collection that brings Boston "consummately to flower" (*AS,* 255). If the image of the house as a museum seems on the one hand to suggest that woman's isolation in a domestic sphere has merely been supplanted by her confinement to an aesthetic one, it serves on the other to enable traffic between private and public space. The Gardner museum becomes a medium of woman's appearance in public life, the stage of her occupation as cultural competitor or manager. When the museum-house appears in *The Bostonians* in the form of the Burrage mansion, James suggests that the pedestal it provides for women can become Verena's platform for her own mobilization, and for the politicization of Verena's audience.

What in fact the Burrages have to offer Verena, Olive, and the movement is an entree not only into the "best society," as Basil calls it, but also into the "domain of practical politics." When Mrs. Burrage speaks to Olive Chancellor about her son's affection for Verena and her own desire to take her in, she frames her proposition in the terms of a royal marriage: to consider Henry's proposal is to form "an alliance with the house of Burrage." And to do so is to equip the movement for each "new phase," for what "we don't see in advance" (*B,* 317). As Verena's promoter, Olive drags her feet, stalled within her sacrificial vision of Miss Birdseye's version of reform, the "heroic age of New England life" (183). "There was a want of bold action," Matthias Pardon observes of Olive's methods. "He didn't see what they were waiting for" (128). To picture Verena at the Burrages, and not in Pardon's hands, or Ransom's, can only appeal to Olive Chancellor, who, listening to Henry Burrage play Schubert and Mendelssohn, surrendering to the gleam of his *bibelots,* is forced to admit to herself that Henry played "with exquisite taste . . . as if the situation were a sort of truce."

> Civilization, under such an influence, in such a setting, appeared to have done its work; harmony ruled the scene; human life ceased to be a battle. She went so far as to ask herself why anyone should have a quarrel with it; the relations between men and women, in that picturesque grouping, had not the air of being internecine.
>
> (*B,* 156)

At the Burrages' the training of the girl from Cambridge would pick up where it had left off in Olive's civilizing house. Under the Burrage wing, Verena could launch bolder, but never "vulgar," public engagements.

But Olive initially rejects Mrs. Burrage's proposition, not because she does not believe her sympathy for the feminist cause to be sincere, but because she does not trust that what the Burrages promise Verena can come to her sex without sacrifice and expiation. Or she thinks perhaps it cannot come at all, and the atmosphere at Mrs. Burrage's has not the air of being internecine enough. "The picturesque grouping" gives away its status as illusion, and Olive has once again found herself susceptible to the "nice arrangements" that mask organized wrongs. What Mrs. Burrage offers Verena is "simply a boundless opportunity," and such an offer can only be "fantastic and false" (*B,* 320).

But in *The Bostonians,* opportunities do exist for women in a public sector that is not the "social swamp" both Olive and Basil imagine, and a commercial market that is not the "disintegral sphere of reproduction" critics of the novel claim it to be (72).[22] The privacy into which Basil would explicitly draw Verena is everywhere linked to poverty, which is linked to mortification and extinction. And the civilization Basil proposes to save by saving Verena's voice from commercialization does not feature women even in its private scenes of production. It is not for women to produce culture, but to remain the somatic mediums, the copyists, and, like Harvard's librarian, Miss Catching, the custodians of the culture produced by men—men like Schubert, Mendelssohn, even Basil Ransom. But Verena's popularity suggests that such an arrangement can change, as Verena produces *herself* in public life. It is Verena, after all, who now offers new models to be copied. Seizing the tools of the modern media and what Philip Fisher has recently called the "high visibility" of the space of modern performance, Verena seizes upon an opportunity to persuade the public, to perform interventions only indirectly available to women in the private sphere.[23] It is not, finally, Basil's suspicion that Verena's voice will be rudely forced "into ineffectual shrillness" that impels him, but that it might prove exceptionally effectual; that Verena's "own little revolution" in her chosen career, like that of the professional Dr. Prance in hers, might be a "success" (248, 249).

Still, critical perspectives on the role of the modern media in *The Bostonians* tend to rephrase only Basil Ransom's perspective on personal integrity and public exposure. Fisher has recently argued that in *The Bostonians* the "full possession of an individual self" is to be had "in the act of disappearing," and that by a "strategy of negation"—the acts of not speaking, of not being entirely visible to another person, and finally, of Verena's stealing away on the night of her great appearance in the Music Hall—"a private self is born and sheltered in the novel." In these illustrations Henry James is "underlining a strategy of self-creation that inverts the strategy of publicity and visibility that are the machinery of celebrity."[24] On this view, to resist the plunge into public performance, whether in newspapers, advertisements, or onstage, is to recuperate a self gradually eroded by what Alan Trachtenberg calls "the forms of reading and looking." In "technologies of communication," Trachtenberg writes, describing the position of the spectator, "vicarious experience began to erode direct physical experience of the world."[25] For Fisher and Trachtenberg, then, to forestall the technology of celebrity is to restore the alienated spirits and the fragmented bodies of Basil as spectator and Verena as player.

But for James in *The Bostonians,* distance from the vulnerable body is to be valued, and it is precisely through such distancing, as it is provided by the representational technology of the stage, that the female body is released from its physical thrall. Nowhere is this clearer in the novel than when Basil abducts Verena from the Music Hall, a scene that Fisher says "invites us to imag-ine a last-minute escape from the life of performance."[26] As Fisher's language confirms, we may only imagine an escape, for when Basil promises Verena that "the dining-table itself shall be our platform, and you shall mount on top of that" (401-2), we see that she will never not be performing. And when Basil abducts Verena from backstage, and Mrs. Burrage's face expresses the "well-bred surprise of a person" asked out to dine, only to witness the "cloth pulled off the table" (463), we understand that her invitation has simply gone out to someone else. Far from rescuing Verena from a life spent as "food" for women and men, the ending surprises us with a more graphic presentiment of just such a life.

III

When at the novel's conclusion Basil Ransom comes to take Verena Tarrant and mark her as his own, we find him in what is by now a familiar pose, standing in (but "aloof" from) the immense and crowded Music Hall. He has passed by the vestibules of the theaters to arrive here, their swinging doors of red leather suggestively "flanked" with the photographs of actresses (*B,* 441). Now the passage of people through the "swinging doors" of the Music Hall reminds him of the "*vomitoria*" of the Colosseum (442). In this projection, food is made waste, interiors exposed, and bodies rendered; it is a place of mob violence and individual sacrifice, and in it Basil feels what a "young man might, who, waiting in a public place, had made up his mind to discharge a pistol at the king or president." No "pistol" goes off in the Hall, but when Basil takes Verena "by muscular force" an act of political dominance is cast in terms of sexual oppression. Feeling what a young man might about Verena is no different from feeling what he might about a king or president—as if Verena is to Basil what Lincoln was to John Wilkes Booth. Verena is to speak, after all, on the Music Hall stage, where Lincoln signed the Emancipation Proclamation to a crowded house.

But even the assassination of a king or president can be seen as having its natural place, as a return to Walt Whitman's speech "The Death of Abraham Lincoln" suggests. When Booth, whom Basil Ransom physically resembles, does "discharge a pistol" (in Whitman's words now), the carnivalesque anarchy that Basil Ransom can only imagine ensues.[27] But within what Whitman calls a theater of "pandemonium," a reordering process is silently engaged, as the President's blood drips slowly down. In "The Death of Abraham Lincoln," Whitman likens Booth's gunshot and the President's fall to the "bursting of a bud or pod in the growth of vegetation," and he implies that this fatal penetration is defloration that leads to a quickening and so to the "parturition and delivery" of "our born-again Republic" (1042-45). "Filtering into the nation and the race," giving "cement to the whole people, subtler, more underlying, than anything in *written* constitution" (1045), Lincoln's blood unifies a divided house. Assassination, then, like civil war—and, we would add, like the sacrifice of women to private life so that "every man" can "keep himself aloof"—is absorbed into democracy's body, as Whitman imagines it.

John Wilkes Booth could not have known how effectively he would put the President into public circulation when he plotted to end Lincoln's life. He would make of Abraham Lincoln, as Michael Paul Rogin suggests, a *corpus mysticum,* securing for him the "sentimental power" of the funeral tour to the martyr's home, and of the popular picture of the slain President's apotheosis, soon to be a *carte de visite* in American parlors.[28] But Basil Ransom knows exactly what will become of Verena Tarrant's career when he marks and martyrs her for private life and for him. "Save your soothing words for me," he tells her. "You will have need of them all, in our coming time" (*B*, 461). Surely he is thinking: "thus to tyrants."

Notes

1. Walt Whitman, "The Perfect Human Voice," in *Walt Whitman: Complete Poetry and Collected Prose* (New York: Literary Classics of the United States, 1982), 1269; all further references to this work will appear parenthetically in the text by title and page number.

2. Henry James, *The Bostonians* (New York: Random House, 1956), 270. All further references to this work (hereafter cited as *B*) will appear parenthetically in the text.

3. Ellen Moers examines what she calls "the myth" of de Stael's *Corinne* and its effect on women writers and feminist advocates; see her chapter 9, "Performing Heroinism: The Myth of Corinne," in *Literary Women: The Great Writers* (New York: Anchor Books, 1977), 263-320. The original "New England Corinne" is, of course, Margaret Fuller.

4. Henry James, "The Question of Our Speech," in *The Question of Our Speech and The Lesson of Balzac: Two Lectures* (1905; reprint, Folcroft, Penn.: The Folcroft Press, 1956), 39, 45. All further references to this work (hereafter cited as *QS*) will appear parenthetically in the text.

5. Ralph Waldo Emerson, *The Works of Ralph Waldo Emerson,* 14 vols. (Cambridge: The Riverside Press, 1883), 11:340. Emerson's alliance of conversation, reproduction, and civilization was brought to my attention by Eric Cheyfitz in his *The Trans-parent: Sexual Politics in the Language of Emerson* (Baltimore: Johns Hopkins Univ. Press, 1981), 42-43.

6. Henry James, *The Speech and Manners of American Women,* ed. J. S. Riggs (Lancaster, Penn.: Lancaster House Press, 1973). This text comprises two series of essays originally appearing in *Harper's Bazaar* in 1906 and 1907. All further references to this work (hereafter cited as *SM*) will appear parenthetically in the text.

7. The "closed vessel of authority" described here is actually the "early Victorian and Mid-Victorian [governess] of English girlhood," "embodying for her companions a precious ripe tradition," and "closed against sloppy leakage" (*SM*, 34).

8. Eugene Benson, "Museums of Art as a Means of Instruction," *Appleton's Journal* 3 (January 15, 1870): 80. Benson is cited by Neil Harris in "The Gilded Age Revisited: Boston and Museum Movement," *American Quarterly* 14 (1962): 561.

9. See Alan Trachtenberg, "The Politics of Culture," in his *The Incorporation of America: Culture and Society in the Gilded Age* (New York: Hill and Wang, 1982), 140-81.

10. I am here paraphrasing Elaine Scarry, who observes that it is "back in the inward and enclosing space of the single room and its domestic content that the outward unfolding (so appropriately called 'the flowering') of civilization originates." See her *The Body in Pain: The Making and Unmaking of the World* (New York: Oxford Univ. Press, 1985), 39. For a different account of the connection between domesticity and "civilization," see Norbert Elias, *The History of Manners: The Civilizing Process* (New York: Pantheon, 1978).

11. Alexis de Tocqueville, *Democracy in America* (New York: Vintage Books, 1945), 2:227.

12. For an analysis of this position, see Aileen S. Kraditor, *The Idea of the Woman's Suffrage Movement, 1890-1920* (New York: Columbia Univ. Press, 1965), 21. Other studies noting the impact of evolutionary theory and the social sciences on feminist and antifeminist ideologies in the late nineteenth century include Carroll Smith-Rosenberg and Charles E. Rosenberg, "The Female Animal: Medical and Biological Views of Women in Nineteenth-Century America," *Journal of American History* 60 (1973): 332-56; Charles E. Rosenberg, *No Other Gods: On Science and American Social Thought* (Baltimore and London: Johns Hopkins Univ. Press, 1976); J. S. Haller and Robin M. Haller, *The Physician and Sexuality in Victorian America* (Urbana: Univ. of Illinois Press, 1974); Rosalind Rosenberg, *Beyond Separate Spheres: Intellectual Roots of Modern Feminism* (New Haven and London: Yale Univ. Press, 1982); William Leach, *True Love and Perfect Union: The*

Feminist Reform of Sex and Society (New York: Basic Books, 1980); and Janet Sayers, *Biological Politics: Feminist and Anti-Feminist Perspectives* (London: Tavistock Publications, 1982).

13. James Jackson Jarves, *The Art-Idea* (New York, 1864), 286-92. See also Sam Bass Warner, *Streetcar Suburbs: The Process of Growth in Boston, 1870-1900* (Cambridge: Harvard Univ. Press, 1962), and Stanley K. Schultz, *The Culture Factory: Boston's Public Schools, 1789-1860* (New York: Oxford Univ. Press, 1973).

14. What James advises women here might well be understood in terms of the neo-Lamarckian doctrine of the inheritance of acquired characteristics, a theory particularly popular in America at the turn of the century. That habits might become both permanent in the life of the individual and transmissible to his or her offspring was an idea popularized in nineteenth-century social thought chiefly by Herbert Spencer, but also accepted and promoted by such figures as Lewis Henry Morgan, John Wesley Powell, and Lester Frank Ward. For a detailed analysis of the prevalence of Lamarckian theory in the United States, see George W. Stocking, "Lamarckianism in American Social Science, 1890-1915," in his *Race Culture and Evolution: Essays in the History of Anthropology* (Chicago: Univ. of Chicago Press, 1982), 234-69. In his address to the women of Bryn Mawr, James underscores the importance of woman's role as the quite literal medium of cultural transmission.

On the role of signs and communication in social evolutionary theories starting with Herbert Spencer, see François Jacob, *The Logic of Life: A History of Heredity,* trans. Betty E. Spillman (New York: Pantheon Books, 1982), 319-21. Jacob writes that as the "mechanisms governing the transfer of information obey certain principles, the transmission of culture through generations can be considered as a kind of second genetic system superimposed on heredity" (320). He adds that "Reproduction . . . lies at the centre of both systems, for codes of culture and societies as for the structure and properties of organisms" (321). See also F. W. Coker, *Organismic Theories of the State: Nineteenth-Century Interpretations of the State as an Organism or a Person, Studies in History, Economics, and Public Law,* 6, 38:2 (New York: Columbia Univ. Press, 1910). The pregnant body as the locus of the founding not only of the series of "little differences-resemblances" that constitute the individual subject but also "civilization" or "social teleology" itself, is described in Julia Kristeva, "Motherhood According to Giovanni Bellini," in *Desire in Language,* ed. Leon S. Roudiez and trans. Thomas Gora, Alice Jardine, and

Leon S. Roudiez (New York: Columbia Univ. Press, 1980), 240-41. "The maternal body," Kristeva writes, "is the module of a bio-social program" (241). The relation between American fiction, self-definition, and "problems of human identity predicated in terms of the body" is provocatively explored in Sharon Cameron, *The Corporeal Self: Allegories of the Body in Melville and Hawthorne* (Baltimore and London: Johns Hopkins Univ. Press, 1981), 6-7 and passim.

15. Trachtenberg (note 9), 144.

16. For Basil's description of his "passionate tenderness" for the South, and his identification of it with a woman, see *B,* 50.

17. For a similar yoking of the imagery of resistant women with that of semiotic chaos, levelling sexuality, and political revolution, see Neil Hertz's "Medusa's Head: Male Hysteria under Political Pressure," and Catherine Gallagher's response to Hertz, "More About 'Medusa's Head,'" in *Representations* 4 (Fall 1983): 27-57. For a careful account of recent theoretical positions on woman's speech as prelinguistic, pre-oedipal, or pre-social, and therefore subversive of dominant patriarchal discourse, and ideology, and for an incisive critique of those positions, see Donna Stanton, "Difference on Trial: A Critique of the Maternal Metaphor in Cixous, Irigaray, and Kristeva," in Nancy K. Miller, ed., *The Poetics of Gender* (New York: Columbia Univ. Press, 1986), 157-82.

18. Henry James, *The American Scene* (Bloomington and London: Indiana Univ. Press, 1968), 167. All further references to this work (hereafter cited as *AS*) will appear parenthetically in the text.

19. That Verena is something of a medium makes her an especially adept "mingler." An important discussion of the social mobility of the female medium in England is in Alex Owen's "The Other Voice: Women, Children and Nineteenth-Century Spiritualism," in Carolyn Steedman, Cathy Urwin and Valerie Walkerdine, eds., *Language, Gender and Childhood* (London: Routledge and Kegan Paul, 1985), 34-73. Owen's essay argues in part that while in England before 1860 spiritualism was chiefly a private affair, the increasing opportunities for mediums to appear in public opened new paths of advancement for women. The working-class girl, for example, could find herself accepted within, even pursued by, middle-class society. Certainly the upper-class Burrages' appreciation of Verena Tarrant, as well as her "adoption" by Olive Chancellor, illustrate that Verena is (successfully) upwardly mobile.

20. S. B. Sutton, ed., *Civilizing American Cities: A Selection of Frederick Law Olmsted's Writings on*

City Landscapes (Cambridge, Mass.: Harvard Univ. Press, 1971), 78-79.

21. For an especially suggestive account of the pregnant body as a place apart, see the "Preface/ Hyperbole" to Susan Stewart's *On Longing: Narratives of the Miniature, the Gigantic, the Souvenir, the Collection* (Baltimore and London: Johns Hopkins Univ. Press, 1984), X.

22. I take this phrase from Richard Godden's provocative argument in his "Some Slight Shifts in the Manner of the Novel of Manners," in Ian F. A. Bell, ed., *Henry James: Fiction as History* (Totowa, N.J.: Barnes and Noble, 1984), 156-83. Godden's discussion of *The Bostonians* takes up John Goode's idea that "character for James preserves its identity through strategies of possession," in an attempt to see less abstractly how these strategies are situated in "a problematic moment in the history of capital" (170). John Goode's essay, "Character and Henry James," is in *New Left Review,* no. 40 (Nov./Dec. 1966): 55-75. Both Godden and Goode pursue lines of inquiry and draw conclusions similar to those of Fisher and Trachtenberg below. I mean to suggest that different conclusions can be drawn when the novel is approached from a feminist perspective.

23. Philip Fisher, "Appearing and Disappearing in Public: Social Space in Late-Nineteenth-Century Literature and Culture," in Sacvan Bercovitch, ed., *Reconstructing American Literary History* (Cambridge: Harvard Univ. Press, 1986), 155-88.

24. Fisher, 179.

25. Trachtenberg, 122.

26. Fisher, 178.

27. See James's description of Basil Ransom (*B,* 4-5), and Walt Whitman's description of John Wilkes Booth (Whitman, 1043).

28. Michael Paul Rogin's comments on a draft of this essay, as well as his reading of popular interpretations of Lincoln's death, has strongly informed this study. See "The King's Two Bodies: Lincoln, Wilson, Nixon, and Presidential Self-Sacrifice," in *Ronald Reagan: The Movie: And Other Episodes in Political Demonology* (Berkeley and Los Angeles: Univ. of California Press, 1986). I borrow the words "sentimental power" from Jane Tompkins' description of the force of Rachel Halliday's rocking chair in "Sentimental Power: *Uncle Tom's Cabin* and the Politics of Literary History," in her *Sensational Designs: The Cultural Work of American Fiction, 1790-1860* (New York: Oxford Univ. Press, 1985), 122-46. The author also thanks Stuart Culver, Eric Sundquist, Sonia Hofkosh, Gillian

Brown, and Walter Benn Michaels for their careful readings of versions of this essay.

Lauren Weiner (essay date 2002)

SOURCE: Weiner, Lauren. "Tocquevillian Americans: Henry James, Daisy Miller, Pandora Day." In *Seers and Judges: American Literature as Political Philosophy,* edited by Christine Dunn Henderson, pp. 33-48. Lanham, Md. and Oxford, England: Lexington Books, 2002.

[*In the following essay, Weiner considers James's portraits of "emancipated women" in his novels and stories, and how these portrayals reflect Tocqueville's observations on American literature.*]

Alexis de Tocqueville's comparisons between how women live in a democracy and how they live under aristocracy reach into every societal realm, including literature. He wrote, in volume two, part three of *Democracy in America*: "In England as in all other countries of Europe, public ill will is constantly exercised over the weaknesses of women. One often hears philosophers and men of state complain that *mores* are not regular enough."[1] In contrast, public opinion in America came down harshly upon a fallen woman, but that was only once she fell. The expectations for women in general were quite otherwise: "In America all books, not excepting novels, assume women to be chaste, and no one tells of amorous adventures in them."[2] Not having to automatically fend off insinuations about one's sexual honor was but one of the things about an American woman's life that Tocqueville found unprecedented, and salutary. In an unmarried state, she was freer to develop herself than her European counterpart, and when she married she was accorded more genuine respect than the European woman enjoyed.

Tocqueville had drawn a national distinction that proved remarkably durable on at least one account: Casanovas and Don Juans are few and far between in classic American literature. Instead of braggarts about sexual conquest we have Cooper's Natty Bumppo, Melville's Ishmael, Twain's Huck Finn, and Lewis's George Babbitt. (What Henry James said of his friend Robert Louis Stevenson, a sort of honorary American, is apt for the actual Americans: "the idea of making believe appeals to him much more than the idea of making love."[3]) Tocqueville found the American literary imagination more wholesome than the European. Others might express it differently, of course, and call American literature more repressed, for while one searches in vain for an American Don Juan, it is also true that Hawthorne's tortured divine, Arthur Dimmesdale, looms large in the canon.

In assuming women to be virtuous until their actions should prove otherwise, American men, as Tocqueville pointed out, put the responsibility for sexual virtue squarely on the women. Self-policing and self-defense were necessities in a society just coming into being. What man had time to scrutinize his wife or daughter's behavior when he was busy clearing the forests for settlement?

> As they could not prevent her virtue from often being in peril, they wanted her to know how to defend it. . . . Far from hiding the corruptions of the world from her, they wanted her to see them right away and to exert herself to flee them; and they would rather safeguard her honesty than respect her innocence too much.[4]

Once married, the American woman scarcely left the domestic circle; she submitted to harsh conditions by her own choice. The voluntary self-sacrifice of this highly independent creature was, Tocqueville believed, the true engine of democratic progress, the principal cause of "the singular prosperity and growing force"[5] of the United States.

Women who proudly put themselves on the moral/sexual straight and narrow—and stay there—could not possibly be novelistically interesting. That view, uttered within Henry James's hearing by a European literary colleague of his, prompted a strong reaction from the New York-born James. Henry James always occupied—by upbringing, by sensibility, and by vocation—a kind of intermediary position between America and Europe, which was his adopted home from the 1870s on. He wished to see his native country advance in culture and civilization without at the same time losing its moral superiority to Europe. In his preface to the 1909 reissuing of "Daisy Miller," "Pandora," and other stories, James replied to his cynical European colleague by saying, in effect, you just aren't imaginative enough. The American woman provides plenty of novelistic material, James said, because "a personal 'adventure' is no a priori, no positive and absolute and inelastic thing, but just a matter of relation and appreciation."[6]

James produced countless stories and novels by taking the American woman, this "most freely encouraged plant in our democratic garden,"[7] and placing her in Europe, where she had to contend with the restrictions of a more traditional way of life. He dramatized this encounter from every conceivable angle. In fact, his intermittent peaks of popularity during his lifetime, and his renown ever after, have rested upon his "quick empathy for the female young,"[8] and upon his keen understanding of the new woman—she who so unconsciously but so "infinitely amused the nations."[9] In the 1909 preface he admitted: "the international young ladies" are "my appointed thematic doom."[10] With a note of wistful regret he went on to discuss his inability to make use of the American material that other American writers found so fruitful—the "great dialectic tracts"[11] of the frontier, the stock market; on the other hand, he believed it his special talent and mission to broaden American fiction and make it more artistic.

In his 1907 book of social criticism, *The American Scene,* James observed that the American woman

> had been grown in an air in which a hundred of the "European" complications and dangers didn't exist, and in which also she had had to take upon herself a certain training for freedom. It was not that she had had, in the vulgar sense, to "look out" for herself, inasmuch as it was of the very essence of her position not to be threatened or waylaid; but that she could develop her audacity on the basis of her security, just as she could develop her "powers" in a medium from which criticism was consistently absent.[12]

So, half a century after Tocqueville made his observations, the American woman—or at least the kind James tends to meet in Europe or during his trips back home to the United States—now lives more or less securely. The lack of criticism at which Tocqueville marveled is still palpable. It is this that gives the American woman room to "develop her 'powers,'" that gives her so much self-assurance as compared to the more submissive women of the Old World. James, though he is the most Tocquevillian of American authors, weighs this factor somewhat differently than the Frenchman did. He goes on, in *The American Scene,* to say:

> Thus she arrived, full-blown, on the general scene, the least criticized object, in proportion to her importance, that had ever adorned it. It would take long to say why her situation, under this retrospect, may affect the inner fibre of the critic himself as one of the most touching on record; he may merely note his perception that she was to have been after all but the sport of fate.[13]

The "sport of fate" aptly sums up some very important women in James's life and his art—not least his most famous creation, Miss Daisy Miller of Schenectady, New York. James adds to the French philosopher's insights by asking, implicitly, what is the cost of that lack of criticism? What is the cost to the woman herself of the relatively free conditions in which she develops?

We who are so used to this high-hearted and forthright form of womanhood must try to recover a sense of surprise that women would dare to assert themselves. Only if we step back in this manner can we play out some of the deeper meanings in James, which involve admiration mixed with qualms. For it made a big impression on men when women behaved in a self-assured way. In fact, it still does. The unwaylayable, unstoppable female is likely to make males jump back just a little bit, as if they've lost the initiative. Tocqueville recorded his own personal reaction this way:

> I was often surprised and almost frightened on seeing the singular dexterity and happy audacity with which these girls of America knew how to conduct their

thoughts and words amid the pitfalls of a playful conversation; a philosopher would have stumbled a hundred times on the narrow path that they traveled without accident and without trouble.[14]

Frederick Forsythe Winterbourne sounds exactly like this when he, a twenty-seven-year-old American living abroad, meets the young tourist, Miss Miller, in Switzerland. He feels "divided between amazement at the rapidity of her induction and amusement at the frankness of her *persiflage*. She seemed to him, in all this, an extraordinary mixture of innocence and crudity."[15]

Daisy Miller, though probably age twenty or so, is in charge of her family's European travels (her father has stayed home in Schenectady), and in full charge of her own destiny. That we end up attributing a moral weight to the character of this coltishly perverse young woman is a great artistic feat on the part of James. He gets us to take her seriously by having us see her through the eyes of Winterbourne, the cultured yet prim American.

The Miller family is nouveau riche and a little uncouth. Daisy, her mother, and her little brother are too familiar with the servants they engage during their travels, and for this and other faux pas they are looked down upon by the more polished American travelers and expatriates who would ordinarily be their social set. Another reason for their isolation, we are given to understand, is that Daisy attracts men and that does not make her popular with women. There seems to be a competitiveness with others of her sex in her boast, to Winterbourne, that "I have always had a great deal of gentlemen's society" (*DM*, 246). Winterbourne, for his part, does not know what to make of comments like this:

> He felt that he had lived at Geneva so long that he had lost a good deal; he had become dishabituated to the American tone. . . . Was she simply a pretty girl from New York State—were they all like that, the pretty girls who had a good deal of gentlemen's society? Or was she also a designing, an audacious, an unscrupulous young person? Winterbourne had lost his instinct in this matter, and his reason could not help him.
>
> (*DM*, 246)

Reason fails him because he is, in spite of his primness, powerfully attracted to the beautiful and forward girl. He is surprised and pleased to find that, aside from the strange "innocence and crudity" of her talk, she is naturally graceful, an elegant and not a showy dresser, and someone who "evidently had a natural talent for performing introductions" (*DM*, 272). Daisy is in these respects another of James's uncultivated American roses. Her grace and style remind one of Isabel Archer's unschooled intellect in *The Portrait of a Lady* and of Verena Tarrant's unchaperoned chastity in *The Bostonians*. These qualities have developed without prompting, even against disadvantageous circumstances, and are presented as a kind of miracle.

Winterbourne only belatedly understands that Daisy's spiritedness is not licentiousness. For in fact she does not lust after men. It is merely that they pay her homage; women don't. Add to this the fact that, during the action of the story, she is far from home and increasingly lonely, and it becomes less surprising that she would allow a handsome and "presumably low-lived foreigner" (*DM*, 273), Giovanelli, to befriend her. Because her mother is so ineffectual—James, like Jane Austen, favors heroines who are orphaned or who have ineffectual parents—Daisy is de facto setter of the family itinerary. She hasn't much of an idea of what to do with her freedom. Chattering away to Winterbourne about her inability to fit in with the high-toned ladies of the American colonies in Geneva and Rome, she sounds somehow both ignorant and witty: "I like a lady to be exclusive; I'm dying to be exclusive myself. Well, we *are* exclusive, mother and I. We don't speak to everyone—or they don't speak to us. I suppose it's about the same thing" (*DM*, 254).

Winterbourne at first responds to Daisy's teasing, I-dare-you manner by getting carried away. He takes her to the castle outside Vevey, Switzerland, knowing full well that the Europeans frown on unmarried people going on such excursions without supervision. He is soon warned away from her by his very snobbish aunt, who tells him, "You had better not meddle with little American girls . . . You have lived too long out of the country. You will be sure to make some great mistake" (*DM*, 252). When Daisy takes up with the handsome Italian, Giovanelli, who is not of their class and who appears to be in search of a rich American wife, she scandalizes the Romans and the Americans.

All of a sudden she must fend off insinuations about her sexual honor—and this she is not willing to do, since it was never necessary at home. James lets us see that there is, at least initially, a certain amount of common sense in taking this position. Winterbourne tells her:

> "Do cease at least to flirt with your friend at the piano; they don't understand that sort of thing here." "I thought they understood nothing else!" exclaimed Daisy. "Not in young unmarried women." "It seems to me much more proper in young unmarried women than in old married ones," Daisy declared.
>
> (*DM*, 281)

Her answer doesn't just amuse us, it implies a willingness on Henry James's part to question whether European rules—or at least those intended to protect the virginity of maidens—need to be quite as strict as they are. Winterbourne warns her, repeatedly but with great courtesy, that that's an American argument. When one is in Rome one must do as the Romans do. Daisy will have none of it. "I have never allowed a gentleman to dictate to me, or to interfere with anything I do" (*DM,* 272), she sniffs. The tense interplay between them continues to perplex and beguile Winterbourne simultaneously, as Daisy "continued to present herself as an inscrutable combination of audacity and innocence" (*DM,* 274).

The key scene of the novella is when a bossy but kind American expatriate, Mrs. Walker, tries to save Daisy from herself. Seeing that Giovanelli's constant and unchaperoned attendance upon Daisy is making a scandal, she enlists Winterbourne's help in trying to whisk the girl away from the Italian in her carriage. The object, says Mrs. Walker, is "to drive her about here for half-an-hour, so that the world may see she is not running absolutely wild, and then to take her safely home" (*DM,* 274). Daisy refuses to come away with them. When that does not work, Mrs. Walker does not give up; rather, she tries to reduce Daisy's supply of men. Winterbourne is willing to fall in with this plan of rehabilitation and promises not to go about with her himself. But Daisy defiantly sabotages this effort by showing up in Mrs. Walker's drawing room with Giovanelli in tow. Perceiving that her well-intentioned worrying over this girl is being answered with insolence, Mrs. Walker turns against Daisy. Now she is down to just one friendly American outside of her family: Winterbourne.

Knowing himself to be "dishabituated to the American tone," Winterbourne does not want to leap to an unfair conclusion—plus, he can't get away from his romantic attraction to her. At times he thinks she does not perceive that her actions endanger her reputation. But "then at other moments he believed that she carried about in her elegant and irresponsible little organism a defiant, passionate, perfectly observant consciousness of the impression she produced" (*DM,* 287). Daisy alternately flirts with Giovanelli to try to entice Winterbourne toward her, and remonstrates with Winterbourne for showing signs that he is about to join the general disapproval. She thinks he should defend her to their countrymen. That he doesn't rescue her from infamy by marrying her himself is pure Jamesian perversity; it is also a very Tocquevillian demonstration of the miscues that can happen when this very special creature is taken out of her native habitat. As we know, the "facts of life" have not been kept from her, and she has been trusted to keep herself pure. What Winterbourne can't tell—since she acts like someone who knows those facts—is whether she *is* pure.

The answer is yes, but he learns too late. Brash and stubborn though Daisy Miller is, she's still an American. As one of the expatriates in an early James story ("Madame de Mauves") puts it: "The silliest American woman is too good for the best foreigner, and the poorest of us have moral needs that the cleverest Frenchman is quite unable to appreciate."[16] She's silly but she has

moral needs. What she needs is guidance, which her mother fails to provide her, which Mrs. Walker unsuccessfully tries to provide her, and which Winterbourne gives up on providing her when he discovers her visiting the Colosseum at night with Giovanelli, in defiance both of propriety and public health warnings (it being the medical wisdom of the day that one caught malaria from the "bad air" at certain sites at certain hours).

By the time Winterbourne discerns her signals—that she never agreed to marry Giovanelli, and that she would have responded favorably to Winterbourne had he offered himself—she is dead. Readers tend to find the rather portentously timed case of *la perniciosa* a bit hokey, and many take Daisy's sudden and premature death as a punishment authorially meted out to her for her misbehavior. They're half right: it is hokey, but it is not a punishment. James uses this melodramatic turn of events to put Daisy beyond rescue so that Winterbourne can have his rueful realization on the last page: that he has "done her injustice" (*DM,* 295). He made a mistake, and ironically, it was not the one his aunt predicted. His mistake was not to entangle himself with a not-quite-reputable American—it was to disentangle himself from an American whose reputation did not accurately represent her. At story's end he sighs, one last time: "I have lived too long in foreign parts" (*DM,* 295). He is conscious of having lost that combination of forthrightness and charity that prompts Americans to help one another regardless of what public opinion may say. He is conscious, on top of that, of having failed to follow his heart.

Daisy is responsible for her errors, particularly in turning down Mrs. Walker's help. Winterbourne is responsible for his errors. Their separate errors combine to make the tragedy. Thus does James take a character who is flighty, sexy, and a little vapid, and endow her with a certain moral heft. This was the fictional work that made him internationally famous because the effect he achieves with its heroine is so subtle and so poignant. Though we are sorely tempted to dismiss Daisy Miller as a coquette, we cannot quite do it. If she were dismissable—either as a woman of sin wholly responsible for her actions, or as a wholly irresponsible victim of the pettiness, malice, and unfairness of those around her—the story would not have the place in our literature that it does.

James was gratified by the renown that came to him in the late 1870s as the author of the popular "Daisy Miller: A Study." It was not long, however, before he sought to challenge and entertain himself, and amuse his readers, by turning the "Daisy Miller" phenomenon on its head. A January 1884 entry in his private notebooks reads: "I don't see why I shouldn't do the 'self-made girl,' whom I noted here last winter, in a way to make her a rival to D[aisy] M[iller]."[17] The end result,

"Pandora," would be published in two installments in the *New York Sun* that same year.

James's plan from the outset was to place this rival creation in America, not in Europe. Interestingly, in tasking himself with this made-to-order artistic exercise, he put himself on course to write something he did not often write: a happy ending for his protagonist. He would depict, as a counterpoint to the tragedy of Daisy (an independent-minded maiden out of her element) the almost comical ease with which the American maiden succeeds when *in* her element. The tale, as I say, is not typical. But it is telling in terms of James's view of the American woman.

In a society as comparatively open as the United States, and as comparatively free of male criticism of the female, what adversity or challenge does James's new heroine face? The challenge of upward social mobility. "The point of the story," he wrote in his work notes, "would naturally be to show the contrast between the humble social background of the heroine, and the position which she has made—or is making for herself and, indirectly, for her family."[18]

While the females of James's international tales—Americans like Charlotte Evans, Euphemia Cleve, Bessie Alden, Miranda Hope, and Isabel Archer—share general traits, James creates some very specific congruities between the story of Daisy Miller and that of Pandora Day. There is a frequent effect, especially early on, of comparison and contrast between the two, with clues so obvious that no contemporary reader could miss the literary inside joke. In 1884's "Pandora," we again have a somewhat uncultivated, nouveau riche family traveling abroad, or in this case returning to the United States from two years spent abroad. The Days are from Utica, New York, derogatorily referred to in the story as "the interior" of the country. One of the people referring to it derogatorily is Pandora Day, for she is the culturally and socially ambitious one in the family. In the manner of her predecessor, she has directed the European itinerary of mother, father, nineteen-year-old brother, and little sister. But unlike the intellectually underachieving Daisy—who considers her nine-year-old brother smarter than she is—Pandora leads with definite a purpose: to raise her prosperous but lusterless family above philistinism.

We meet the counterpart to Winterbourne—in this case not a Europeanized American but an actual European, Count Otto Vogelstein—on the deck of a U.S.-bound ocean liner reading the "Tauchnitz edition" of a certain unnamed popular novel. Vogelstein is studying up on typical American subjects as he begins his first visit to the United States, where he will be a junior member of the German legation in Washington. One source of information for him is a talkative and snobby fellow passenger, Mrs. Dangerfield (who fills the same admonitory function in this work as Winterbourne's aunt did in "Daisy Miller"); another is the "little American story" in his lap; a third, which he compares against the second, is the bustling about, right in front of him, of an energetic young lady who traverses the deck of the ship, tending to her family's every need.

She has taken the initiative and introduced herself to Count Vogelstein, but only because she thinks he might be the one who mistakenly took her parents' deck chair. He compares the living specimen to the American girl in his book: "In a very short time he perceived that Miss Day had nothing in common with the heroine of that work, save a certain local quality and the fact that the male sex was not terrible to her."[19] After he has finished reading his story, this impression has deepened: he "definitely judged that Pandora Day was not at all like the heroine. She was of quite another type; much more serious and preoccupied, and not at all keen, as he had supposed, about making the acquaintance of gentlemen" (*P,* 825).

Thus does Pandora walk on stage, as it were, making an immediate impression as responsible, practical, not a chatterbox, and emphatically not a flirt. So far Vogelstein displays confidence in his conclusions about this "other type" of American female. He also seems confident in gauging Miss Day's intelligence level:

> She told him that they had gone abroad, she and her family, for a little fresh experience. Though he found her very intelligent he suspected she gave this as a reason because he was a German and she had heard that Germans were fond of culture. He wondered what form of culture Mr. and Mrs. Day had brought back from Italy, Greece, and Palestine . . . especially when their daughter said, "I wanted father and mother to see the best things. I kept them three hours on the Acropolis. I guess they won't forget that!" . . . Pandora remarked also that she wanted to show her little sister everything while she was young; remarkable sights made so much more impression when the mind was fresh; she had read something of that sort in Goethe, somewhere.
>
> (*P,* 830)

We can see that she's no genius, but she's certainly a striver. And she wants to train her younger sister to be a striver. (There is no mention of her trying to develop her brother, by the way.)

Despite Vogelstein's confidence during the early stages of his investigation, he will spend the rest of the novella frustrated by his inability to pin down certain important things about this young woman. His perplexity, like Winterbourne's, is intended to be the engine of the story's forward motion. It is the other novella that bears the subtitle, "A Study," but here we have a Pomeranian nobleman-*cum*-intellectual who is relentlessly making a study. Both on the ship and later in Washington, he constantly asks Americans questions about Pandora based on his Continental sense of rigid social strata. He keeps wanting to know: how can a female cut such a swathe through American society when she is the daughter of the drab and unimpressive couple—the two "silent senseless burghers" (*P,* 844)—he saw vegetating in their deck chairs?

The Count's inquiries serve the main point of the story, as announced by James in his work notes. But they also serve to adumbrate the Count's character. They show his curiosity and also his caution: he wants to avoid social contact with any Americans who are not of his exalted class. In this regard, the aptly named Mrs. Dangerfield

> struck a note which resounded in Vogelstein's imagination. She assured him that if he didn't "look out" he would be falling in love with some American girl with an impossible family. In America, when one fell in love with a girl, there was nothing to be done but marry her.
>
> (*P,* 827)

Nothing to be done—why? Because there are no significant impediments, as there would be in Europe, to a blue blood marrying someone of common origins. Tocqueville is the expert on why this is so important: "In aristocratic peoples, birth and fortune often make man and woman such different beings that they can never come to be united to one another. Passions bring them together"[20] but for clandestine affairs only. In contrast, under conditions of equality, a female—one who resists premarital sex, that is—possesses real leverage because "there is no girl who does not believe she can become the wife of the man who prefers her."[21] Thus does democracy offer social mobility not just to men, but to single-minded and chaste women, as well.

James develops this point at length, working off his foil, Count Vogelstein, a man at once avid to learn about a new society and amusingly squeamish about the unique things it contains. He thinks Pandora attractive but not an exceptional beauty, so no danger there—and yet:

> Vogelstein felt the peril, for he could immediately think of a dozen men he knew who had married American girls. There appeared now to be a constant danger of marrying the American girl; it was something one had to reckon with, like the rise in prices, the telephone, the discovery of dynamite, the Chassepot rifle, the socialistic spirit; it was one of the complications of modern life.
>
> (*P,* 828)

Trying to sort everyone out in a classless society nearly trips the visitor up right away. Upon arriving at the docks in New Jersey, he studies the customs house men. These easygoing bureaucrats expect to be treated like old friends of the people whose trunks they must open, not like functionaries; like equals, not subordinates, which Vogelstein realizes just before making a fool of himself by offering a tip. And he's astonished to find that one of them, Mr. Lansing, has a personal connection to the Days, disembarking first-class passengers. The "fish out of water" element of the story is often charming, but when all is said and done, Vogelstein does not really get beyond the cardboard dimensions of the aristocratic elitist, whereas Winterbourne's personality is beautifully and realistically illuminated by his complicated musings about Daisy Miller.

It doesn't help matters that, despite Vogelstein's zeal to figure out Pandora, he learns only at the end that she is engaged to be married and has been since he first met her. This information is artificially held back, it seems, to drive the plot forward and provide a surprise for the hapless foreigner that brings the tale to a dramatic point. It's an implausibility that must be considered a technical weakness of the work. Still and all, one can't help liking Vogelstein some. His proving susceptible in just the way he did not want to be—falling for someone with "an impossible family"—has to speak well of him, to an American view.

In planning the story of Pandora Day, James said in his notebook that he meant his picture of her to be "admiring and appreciative."[22] In the novella itself, however, a kind of ironic fanfare is created around the emergence on the scene of this new model of womanhood, this "self-made girl." Some time having passed after his arrival in America, Vogelstein is integrating himself into diplomatic and social circles in the American capital when he hears that that woman he'd forgotten all about is now the toast of New York City and Washington, D.C. Everyone wants to meet none other than Pandora Day of Utica. Says an excited society hostess, Mrs. Bonnycastle (a character based on Clover Adams): "Why, she's the new type. It has only come up lately. They have had articles about it in the papers" (*P,* 846). His host, Alfred Bonnycastle—based on Henry Adams—calls her "the latest, freshest fruit of our great American evolution" (*P,* 850). Type becomes stereotype as everyone at this social gathering continues to fill him in about the "self-made girl":

> She was possible, doubtless, only in America; American life had smoothed the way for her. She was not fast nor emancipated nor crude nor loud, and there was not in her . . . a grain of the stuff of which the adventuress is made. She was simply very successful, and her success was entirely personal. She had not been born with the silver spoon of social opportunity; she had grasped it by honest exertion . . . you always saw that her parents could never have made her.
>
> (*P,* 851)

Female activity without female notoriety—this is what Pandora Day embodies. She is as sure-footed as Daisy

Miller was blundering. What's more, her sure-footedness is comically exaggerated so as to amaze Vogelstein, the ultratraditionalist European. This "Junker of Junkers" (*P*, 817) practically faints when he discovers his shipboard acquaintance having tea at the Bonnycastles' home, deep in a tête à tête with the President of the United States. James has all along been quite funny about the undistinguished members of the House of Representatives and the only slightly more distinguished Senators with whom the Pomeranian diplomat deals. Vogelstein has met the President several times; the man is willing to shake hands with all comers and thus can't keep straight who everyone is. But Pandora, in contrast, is having an extended visit with the President, and Vogelstein overhears him saying: "Well madam, in that case it's about the fiftieth promise I have given to-day" (*P*, 844). Putting the chief executive in an encounter with a somewhat captivating, somewhat bossy unmarried young lady (who, it turns out, is accomplishing real business during this exchange) constitutes an arch comment by James on the utter openness of the official governing structure in America.

What we are shown in this scene is simply not like a king and one of his female courtiers. In that case there would be undertones or even overtones of the young lady becoming the next mistress of the potentate. This is not *Les Liaisons Dangereuses*. In this story the President takes his leave by saying his wife will wonder why he doesn't come home, and the unmarried woman says, "Why didn't you bring her with you?" (*P*, 845). The scene is imbued with a wholesomeness that James both thinks is comical and admires as an alternative to the corrupt elites he knew of in Europe.

Daisy misstepped because she refused to see the difference between Europe and America. Pandora has taken in the difference, and she explicitly shows us that she guides her own behavior by it. She knows she could not get away with her present activities outside of the United States, and she captivates a roomful of dignitaries (right in front of the flat-footed Vogelstein) by flaunting this knowledge. A judge of the Supreme Court is teasing her, saying she must have been using her chat with the President to get herself appointed U.S. ambassador to England. He adds: "A good position for a lady; they have got a lady at the head, over there" (*P*, 847). A foreign minister joins in:

> "I wish they would send you to my country. . . . . I would immediately get recalled." *"Why, perhaps in your country I wouldn't speak to you! It's only because you are here," the girl returned,* with a gay familiarity which with her was evidently but one of the arts of defence.

> (*P*, 847; emphasis added)

The self-made girl is devilishly attractive. You can't control her, and that makes her exciting. As Vogelstein begins to be smitten, his alarm at what is happening to him grows:

> It was true that a young person who had succeeded so well for herself might be a great help to her husband; but Vogelstein, on the whole, preferred that his success should be his own; it would not be agreeable to him to have the air of being pushed by his wife. Such a wife as that would wish to push him; and he could hardly admit to himself that this was what fate had in reserve for him—to be propelled in his career by a young lady who would perhaps attempt to talk to the Kaiser as he had heard her the other night talk to the President.

> (*P*, 855)

This amusing reaction might well be the reaction a lot of men have to a woman who grabs the initiative. What Vogelstein goes on to say, however, brings something specifically aristocratic—and in fact offensive—into his response to the self-made girl. As Vogelstein toys with the idea of Pandora Countess Vogelstein, he wonders: "Would she consent to relinquish relations with her family?" That her coarse family "was so impossible was to a certain extent an advantage; for if they had been a little better the question of a rupture would have been less easy" (*P*, 855).

It may be easy for Vogelstein to mentally rub Mr. and Mrs. Day out of the picture but it is anathema to loyal Pandora. Pandora and Daisy have this in common: neither conceals moral indignation beneath a ladylike veneer. Just as Daisy reproved Winterbourne for not sticking up for her with the judgmental matrons of the American colony, Pandora reproves Vogelstein for having slighted her loved ones, which injured her pride: "You were not attracted by my family. They are charming people when you know them" (*P*, 858). She is aware of her parents' shortcomings but she believes they are owed respect as modest and good people.[23]

This chastening of the nobleman takes place during his final interaction with Pandora. There is more comeuppance in store for him, however. The test of loyalty faced by the self-made girl as she climbs the ladder of social improvement is twofold. First there is her humble family, and then there is, as Mrs. Bonnycastle belatedly explains to Vogelstein, the fact that "it is never safe to fix your affections upon" the self-made girl "because she has almost always got an impediment somewhere in the background." The impediment is her long-standing promise to marry someone from "her earlier phase," from "the time before she had made herself" (*P*, 860). Mrs. Bonnycastle gives the example—which turns out to be right on point—of "a young man from Utica, say. They usually have to wait; he is probably in a store. It's a long engagement" (*P*, 860). We find out he is "in a store" (in business). And indeed they have had to wait, in Tocquevillian fashion.[24]

Tocqueville emphasizes as quintessentially American and democratic a tendency to be disconnected from the past. Yet we see at this juncture that James is shaping "Pandora" in a way that suggests connections honored, not severed. Even as the heroine rises above her origins (her parents) she clearly intends to keep them with her as she ascends. Pandora doesn't run off to New York City—she gets the whole family to move there from Utica in the interest of their self-improvement (and her self-interest, given her tastes). And now, the allied question: Does Pandora, the forward-looking, self-improving, choice-making American, keep her promise to the fellow from back home—even through a long tour of Europe, even as she becomes the belle of New York and Washington? A coy Vogelstein seeks to know, concealing his own stake in the matter:

> "But with her present, with her future, I suppose it's all over [says Vogelstein]. How do you say it in America? She lets him slide." "We don't say it at all!" Mrs. Bonnycastle cried. "She does nothing of the sort; for what do you take her? She sticks to him; that, at least, is what we expect her to do."
>
> (*P,* 860)

What the self-made girl is expected to do, Pandora Day does. But with a twist: D. F. Bellamy of Utica will be leaving business life, the reader and Vogelstein find out at the last, because the future Mrs. Bellamy has snagged an ambassadorship in Holland for him.

In "Pandora," many of the usual Jamesian concerns take a holiday. The dedicated realist, subtle psychologist, and frequent pessimist Henry James gives us an unusual story in which the choice of a spouse is not fraught with danger; the best laid plans pan out very well, thank you. And life-altering decisions do not—as Tocqueville would have it—erode inherited obligation or human connection. The work shapes up as a kind of fairy tale, as if in undertaking an "un-Daisy" exercise—conjuring up the representatively wholesome and active American girl and outfitting her with the perfect male match—James is prompted to a slightly parodic perfectionism.

While I do believe this work represents James at his most Tocquevillian, this quality seems to have depended on his doing something notably un-Jamesian, namely, having the heroine pick the right mate. "Pandora" is a rare Jamesian demonstration of the consequences, or at least the incipient consequences, of choosing well. What Tocqueville portrayed as typical in America—the marriage tie contracted between two mature, prudent, independent individuals—is blown up by James into something truly exceptional. Instead of the voluntarily chosen drudgery on the frontier that Tocqueville describes, Pandora Day has cut a deal with the President of the United States that puts her, as a married woman, back in Europe, the place she loves. She gains all of the advantages, and avoids all of the disadvantages, of the American marriage—which, as Tocqueville says, normally involves a woman following her husband from rags to riches and back again from riches to rags in "this tumultuous and constantly vexed life which equality gives to men."[25]

And to pull it off, the author suppresses the question of whether it should offend D. F. Bellamy's American manhood—as we know it does offend Vogelstein's Pomeranian manhood—to have his career secured for him by his fiancée. Or perhaps we should say, James answers this question in the negative but cursorily. D. F. Bellamy seems worthy of Pandora's devotion and pleased as punch to have her help, but then again the reader hardly gets to know him at all; that, too, is unusual, and surely deliberate.

To be sure, not all of James's typical concerns take a holiday in "Pandora." Its last line has Vogelstein observing that "there was now ground for a new induction as to the self-made girl" (*P,* 864). Vogelstein has learned much from Pandora. In significant ways, what he learns matches what Winterbourne learned from Daisy. The common thread that runs through these two pieces—and it is James's overriding concern in all of his international tales—is that he would have Americans become more cultivated yet not lose "the value of the Puritan residuum."[26] Jettisoning one's parents would not constitute preserving that residuum. Rather, making a person who is putatively "above" one understand that his arrogance makes him a less than worthy choice of mate—this surely does qualify, for James, as a healthy preservation of the moral instinct. Daisy Miller's protest against the charge of harlotry—a protest whose full import Winterbourne feels only after her death—also resonates with this special American moral quality.

Each of these women conveys this quality because each maintains the combination that James points to incessantly in his fiction. Here he calls it "an extraordinary mixture of innocence and crudity"; there he says "She was not fast nor emancipated, . . . [s]he was simply very successful, and her success was entirely personal." Always what is meant is the idea of being active in the world, yet preserving—preserving in fact, if not in the eyes of conventional opinion—sexual modesty. As for not being emancipated, this is supposed to be understood in both the sexual and the political senses. There is reason to conclude that James is as conservative as Tocqueville on this point. Pandora Day, like the more famous Isabel Archer of *The Portrait of a Lady,* hungers for ideas and knowledge. The two make allusions to enlightened authors like Goethe, but we never hear of their reading, say, Mary Wollstonecraft. In affording American women intellectual and moral equality but maintaining their political inferiority, American men appeared to Tocqueville "to have admirably understood the true notion of democratic progress"[27]; judging from "Pandora" and so many other James works, the American author would subscribe to this formula wholeheartedly.

The self-made girl is satisfied with the moral and intellectual status of women in America and makes no complaint about their political inferiority. She goes out and does what she wants to do, not waiting for such legal trifles as the vote. Female activity without female notoriety was to Tocqueville startling, new, and well suited to the building of democracy in America. For James it was touching, inspiring, amusing, and—absent the magically perfect circumstances of "Pandora"—potentially tragic. There are still American women who "infinitely amuse the nations," and Henry James teaches us how to appreciate them. We can only guess how much more touching, and tragic, the author of "Daisy Miller" and "Pandora" would find the emancipated women now inhabiting what he called "the most organized and most active of Democracies that ever was."[28]

Notes

This article draws in small part from Lauren Weiner, "The American Woman: What Henry James Knew," *The Weekly Standard,* November 13, 2000, 27-30.

1. Alexis de Tocqueville, *Democracy in America,* trans. and ed. Harvey C. Mansfield and Delba Winthrop (Chicago: University of Chicago Press, 2000), 568.

2. Ibid., 568. I have used my own translation of Tocqueville's phrase, "*aventures galantes.*"

3. Cited in Leon Edel, *Henry James: The Middle Years, 1882-1895* (New York: J. B. Lippincott Company, 1962; Avon Books, 1978), 133.

4. Tocqueville, *Democracy,* 564.

5. Ibid., 576.

6. Henry James, *Prefaces to the New York Edition,* in *Literary Criticism: French Writers, Other European Writers, The Prefaces to the New York Edition* (New York: Library of America, 1984), 1285.

7. From "The Speech of American Women," in *Henry James on Culture: Collected Essays on Politics and the American Social Scene,* ed. Pierre A. Walker (Lincoln: University of Nebraska Press, 1999), 59.

8. Leon Edel, *Henry James: The Master, 1901-1916* (New York: J. B. Lippincott Company, 1972; Avon Books, 1978), 85.

9. Henry James, *The American Scene,* in *Collected Travel Writings: Great Britain and America: En-*

glish Hours, The American Scene, Other Travels (New York: Library of America, 1993), 639.

10. James, *Prefaces,* 1277.

11. Ibid., 1280.

12. James, *The American Scene,* 640.

13. Ibid.

14. Tocqueville, *Democracy,* 564.

15. Henry James, "Daisy Miller: A Study," *Complete Stories of Henry James, Volume II: 1874-1884* (New York: Library of America, 1999), 263. All subsequent references to "Daisy Miller" will be parenthetical (as *DM*), with page numbers referring to this collection.

16. Henry James, "Madame de Mauves," *Complete Stories of Henry James, Volume I: 1864-1874* (New York: Library of America, 1999), 832.

17. *The Complete Notebooks of Henry James,* ed. Leon Edel and Lyall H. Powers (New York: Oxford University Press, 1987), 24.

18. Ibid., 25.

19. Henry James, "Pandora," *Complete Stories of Henry James, Volume II: 1874-1884* (New York: Library of America, 1999), 823. All subsequent references to "Pandora" will be parenthetical (as *P*), with page numbers corresponding to this collection.

20. Tocqueville, *Democracy,* 568.

21. Ibid.

22. James, *Complete Notebooks,* 25.

23. The narrator calls them "fat, plain, serious people" (*P,* 824).

24. Tocqueville speaks of the rarity of "precocious unions" in America. *Democracy,* 566.

25. Ibid., 571.

26. James, *The American Scene,* 533.

27. Tocqueville, *Democracy,* 576.

28. James, "The Speech of American Women," 59.

FURTHER READING

Criticism

Bold, Valentina. "'Rude Bard of the North': James Macpherson and the Folklore of Democracy." *Journal of American Folklore* 114, no. 454 (fall 2001): 464-77.

Surveys the influence of the poetry of Scottish author James Macpherson on the emerging American national identity.

Cmiel, Kenneth. "Whitman the Democrat." In *A Historical Guide to Walt Whitman,* edited by David S. Reynolds, pp. 205-33. New York: Oxford University Press, 2000.

Surveys Whitman's democratic political vision.

DeVine, Christine. "Revolution and Democracy in the London *Times* and *The Princess Casamassima.*" *The Henry James Review* 23, no. 1 (winter 2002): 53-71.

Discusses the coverage of political unrest in the London *Times* during the 1880s, when *The Princess Casamassima* was published, and asserts that the endorsement of democracy and revolution are evident in James's novel.

Erkkila, Betsy. "Democracy and (Homo)Sexual Desire." In *Whitman the Political Poet,* pp. 155-89. New York and Oxford, England: Oxford University Press, 1989.

Focuses upon the blending of and conflict between Whitman's personal identity and his role as an advocate of democracy as evidenced in his poetry.

Folker, Brian. "Wordsworth's Visionary Imagination: Democracy and War." *ELH* 69, no. 1 (spring 2002): 167-97.

Argues against the common assertion by critics that William Wordsworth's dedication to his political ideals declined in the early nineteenth century.

Hashemi, Nader. "Islam, Democracy and Alexis de Tocqueville." *Queen's Quarterly* 110, no. 1 (spring 2003): 21-9.

Views democracy in twenty-first-century Islamic nations within the context of Alexis de Tocqueville's writings on early American democracy.

Reeves, Richard. *American Journey: Traveling with Tocqueville in Search of Democracy in America.* New York: Simon & Schuster, 1982, 399 p.

Retraces Tocqueville's travels across America during the nineteenth century, and records his own impressions of American democracy during the 1980s, comparing his findings with those of Tocqueville.

Ruttenburg, Nancy. "An American Aesthetic of Innocence: Domesticating Democratic Personality." In *Democratic Personality: Popular Voice and the Trial of American Authorship,* pp. 290-343. Stanford, Calif.: Stanford University Press, 1998.

Surveys the development of a national identity, or "democratic personality," that occurred as a result of the "transition from a republican to a liberal ethos."

Schaefer, Robert M. "Mark Twain on Democratic Statesmanship: *A Connecticut Yankee in King Arthur's Court.*" In *The Moral of the Story: Literature and Public Ethics,* edited by Henry T. Edmondson, III, pp. 225-35. Lanham, Md. and Oxford, England: Lexington Books, 2000.

Examines Mark Twain's *A Connecticut Yankee in King Arthur's Court* as a cautionary tale urging the careful preservation of democracy.

Homosexuality in Nineteenth-Century Literature

The following entry provides critical commentary from 1993 to 2005 on the treatment of homosexuality in nineteenth-century literature. For further discussion of homosexuality in nineteenth-century literature, see *NCLC,* Volume 56.

INTRODUCTION

The treatment of homosexuality in literature during the nineteenth century primarily reflects Victorian England's conservative sexual mores. Victorian culture permitted little overt discussion of homosexuality outside of the legal and medical fields, but thinly-veiled representations of same-sex desire can be found in a wide variety of Victorian-era prose and poetry. The general silence about sexuality in Victorian culture fostered a hush on the topic in literature; homosexual desire and relationships were covertly depicted in literature and in culture through socially acceptable and heavily disguised forms, such as the romantic friendship. Romantic friendships between women were compatible with Victorian culture in that they affirmed Victorian notions of female asexuality. Historians have disagreed about the extent to which such friendships were actually platonic, some arguing that chaste Victorian women would not have maintained carnal attachments. Others insist that at least some of these relationships—which often lasted a lifetime and involved not only a shared home but also a shared bed—must have included a sexual component. Intimate bonds between men were valorized by many of the century's writers, a number of whom wrote from personal experience. These intimate same-sex relationships filled Victorian literature without ever prompting the charge of homosexuality as writers masked descriptions of physical desire in order to provide the necessary disguise to avoid social and legal condemnation.

Early in the century, when homosexual activity was viewed almost exclusively as a crime, a sin, or both, men who engaged sexually with one another were most often labeled "sodomites." Other terms used to describe homosexuals, such as "inverts" and "Uranians," reflected societal perceptions regarding same-sex activity. Despite heavy persecution of homosexual behavior, homosexual subcultures thrived as they had for centuries. Underground institutions provided space and an economic basis for this subculture, much the way pubs and clubs might service a man's platonic social activities. The most visible subcultural activity occurred among middle- and lower-class men, many of whom were exclusively homosexual, usually passive in sex, occasionally transvestite, and whose social life consisted of participation in this subculture. Some historians contend that these men did not represent the majority of the male population who engaged in homosexual sex, but were simply the most visible. Court documents suggest that most male homosexuals were married men who maintained conventionally masculine manners and families. In general, homosexual men of the upper-middle class and the aristocracy belonged to this less visible milieu, insulated to some degree by wealth and social status. When an explicit subculture emerged later in the century among these men, it contributed to the development of homosexual identity and social rights. Historians attribute this to the influence of two phenomena: the development of a medical definition of homosexuality and the intellectual reevaluation of classical literature. The first, a medical classification of individuals according to their sexual desires, owed its development to the work of neurologists and other scientists throughout Europe, including Richard von Krafft-Ebing and Havelock Ellis. The latter owed its development largely to the efforts of Benjamin Jowett, who reintroduced the teaching of Plato and other classical authors at Oxford University as part of the Oxford Great Works Curriculum. This training allowed homosexual undergraduates to validate their desires as the resurrected spirit of Hellenism: noble, aesthetic, intellectually rigorous, even martial and athletic. Critic Nancy Goslee discusses Percy Bysshe Shelley's attempt to discern, in his essays and notebooks on Greek history, literature, and culture, an egalitarian view of homosexuality in Greek culture, and Abigail F. Keegan explains how Lord Byron used the ideal of Greek love between men and various "visual tropes" to subtly express homoerotic desire in *Lara* (1814). Social condemnation of homosexuality was revived in 1895 in response to the trial, conviction, and imprisonment of Oscar Wilde on charges of "gross indecency between male persons." While the trial brought the discussion of homosexual desire into the open, it also catalyzed the kind of active persecution that had been for some time dormant. Many homosexual men, particularly those of high social status, resettled at least temporarily on the continent, seeking to avoid scandal and prosecution. Even the ambiguous forms of same-sex love that had so far been integral to Victorian culture became suspect, and homoaffectional literature became both more explicit in its sexuality and much less common.

Aside from sexually explicit texts that were a part of a thriving underground Victorian taste for pornography, homosexuality in books, as in real life, was "closeted"—or hidden beneath the trappings of heterosexuality and acceptable same-sex affection. A notable exception to the implicit representation of homosexuality in books was found in certain guidebooks to Paris published near the end of the century, which contained a variety of explicit information on locales frequented by homosexuals in Paris, as well as their activities. Critics have examined the tacit depiction of same-sex desire in nineteenth-century sensation novels, a genre in which authors commonly sought to titillate readers by featuring characters engaged in what were considered immoral activities. Commentator Richard Nemesvari traces the manner in which Mary Elizabeth Braddon hints at Robert Audley's infatuation with George Talboys in her sensation novel *Lady Audley's Secret* (1862). Many critics have discussed the theme of sexual freedom in Kate Chopin's novel *The Awakening* (1899), further noting the consequences women face to attain it. This theme, and protagonist Edna Pontellier's internal conflict regarding her own sexuality, is supported by sensual imagery that acquires symbolic meaning as the story progresses. Edna's conflict is further revealed by her selection of confidantes: Adele Ratignolle, a domesticated, devoted, heterosexual wife, and Madame Reisz, a passionate, antisocial, and unattractive pianist—characteristics associated with lesbianism. Critic Kathryn Lee Seidel asserts that Chopin endorses the acceptance of lesbian relationships through her depiction of the relationship between Edna and Madame Reisz. Other critics, such as Christina G. Bucher, discuss lesbian content in Chopin's short story "The Falling in Love of Fedora."

A number of commentators have observed the conflation of lesbianism and horror, often appearing in the guise of evil women characters in Gothic novels. Critic Ralph J. Poole illustrates the differences between male and female writers' approaches to the subversion of tradition. Poole's delineation of lesbianism and supernatural horror in works by Rose Terry Cooke and Elizabeth Stuart Phelps is contrasted with examples of Edgar Allan Poe's treatment of horror and the unspeakable in his works. Mary Shelley's *Frankenstein* (1818), which has been studied by critics as a feminist text, is also viewed by scholar Frann Michel as a commentary on society's disapproval of lesbianism. This work has been further examined in terms of its treatment of male anxiety surrounding homosexuality. Critic Jin-Ok Kim asserts that Charlotte Brontë, in her early novelettes and in her novel *The Professor* (1857), depicts the detrimental effects that women experience after having been used as a means of strengthening men's homosocial bonds, thus setting up a need for female homosocial relations in Brontë's later works. Henry James's sexual orientation has been the subject of numerous biographical and literary studies; critics such as John R. Bradley contend that examining homosexuality in James's life and works provides unique and valuable insights into the thematic elements of the works, as well as into James's creative abilities. Nathaniel Hawthorne's *The Blithedale Romance* (1852), is analyzed by critic Benjamin Scott Grossberg, who interprets the utopian vision of the novel's narrator, Miles Coverdale, as one that includes homosexuality along with other expressions of erotic desire. The novel is valued not only for its commentary on nineteenth-century utopianism but also for what it reveals, through its autobiographical content, about Hawthorne's personality and artistic stance. Commentator John W. M. Hallock asserts, in a biography of his distant relative, Fitz-Greene Halleck, that Halleck's failure to successfully conceal his homosexuality led to the poet's exclusion from the American literary canon, in spite of the fact that Halleck's poetic skills had earned him the nickname "The American Byron," and that he had been singled out by the usually derisive literary critic Poe as the best poet of the era.

REPRESENTATIVE WORKS

Mary Elizabeth Braddon
Lady Audley's Secret (novel) 1862

Charlotte Brontë
Jane Eyre; an Autobiography [as Currer Bell] (novel) 1847
Villette [as Currer Bell] (novel) 1853
The Professor [as Currer Bell] 1857
Five Novelettes: Passing Events, Julia, Mina Laury, Henry Hastings, Caroline Vernon (novellas) 1971

Lord Byron
Lara (poetry) 1814

Francis Carco
Jésus-la-Caille (novel) 1914

Jean-Martin Charcot
"Inversion du sens genital" [with Valentin Magnan] (essay) 1882; published in the journal *Archives de neurologie*

Kate Chopin
The Awakening (novel) 1899
The Complete Works of Kate Chopin. 2 vols. [edited by Per Syersted] (novels, short stories, and prose) 1969

Ali Coffignon
Paris vivant: la corruption à Paris (nonfiction) 1889

Rose Terry Cooke

"My Visitation" (short story) 1857; published in the
    journal *Harper's Monthly*

Armand Dubarry

L'Hermaphrodite (novel) 1896
Les Femmes eunuques (novel) 1899
Les Déséquilibrés de l'amour: Les Invertis (novel) 1906

Havelock Ellis

*Man and Woman: A Study of Human Secondary Sexual
    Characters* (essays) 1894; revised and enlarged edi-
    tions, 1904, 1914; revised and published as *Man and
    Woman: A Study of Secondary and Tertiary Sexual
    Characters,* 1929
Das konträre Geschlechtsgefühl [*Sexual Inversion*; with
    John Addington Symonds] (essays) 1896
Psychology of Sex: A Manual for Students (psychology)
    1933; also published as *Psychology of Sex: The Biol-
    ogy of Sex; The Sexual Impulse in Youth; Sexual De-
    viation; The Erotic Symbolisms; Homosexuality;
    Marriage; The Art of Love. A Manual for Students*

Gustave Flaubert

Madame Bovary, mours de province. 2 vols. [*Madame
    Bovary: A Tale of Provincial Life*] (novel) 1857

Paul Garnier

*Les Fétichistes. Pervertis et invertis sexuels. Observa-
    tions médico-légales.* (nonfiction) 1896

Fitz-Greene Halleck

Fanny [published anonymously] (poem) 1819
"Young America" (poem) 1864; published in the jour-
    nal *New York Ledger*

Nathaniel Hawthorne

The Blithedale Romance (novel) 1852

Henry James

Roderick Hudson (novel) 1876
The American (novel) 1877
Daisy Miller (novel) 1879
The Portrait of a Lady (novel) 1881
*The Aspern Papers. Louisa Pallant. The Modern Warn-
    ing* (novellas) 1888
"The Lesson of the Master" (short story) 1888; pub-
    lished in the journal *Universal Review*
The Tragic Muse (novel) 1890
The Real Thing, and Other Tales (short stories) 1893
The Ambassadors (novel) 1903
The Novels and Tales of Henry James. 24 vols. (novels,
    novellas, and short stories) 1907-09
"The Jolly Corner" (short story) 1908; first published in
    the journal *The English Review*
Italian Hours (travel essays) 1909
The Middle Years (unfinished autobiography) 1917

Richard von Krafft-Ebing

"Über gewisse Anomalien des Geschlechstriebs und die
    Klinisch-forensische Verwerthung derselben als eines
    wahrscheineich functionellen Degenerationszeichens-
    des centralen Nerven-Systems" (essay) 1877; pub-
    lished in the journal *Archiv für Psychiatrie und Ner-
    venkrankheiten*
*Psychopathia sexualis: mit besonderer Berücksichti-
    gung der conträren Sexualempfindung: eine klinisch-
    forensische Studie* (nonfiction) 1887

Prosper Lucas

*Traité philosophique et physiologique de l'hérédité na-
    turelle dans les états de santé et de maladie du
    système nerveux, avec l'application méthodique des
    lois de la procréation au traitement général des af-
    fections dont elle est la principe, etc.* 2 vols.
    (nonfiction) 1847-50

Bénédict Morel

*Traité des dégénérescences physiques, intellectuelles et
    morales de l'espèce humaine* (nonfiction) 1857

Elizabeth Stuart Phelps

The Gates Ajar (novel) 1868
"Since I Died" (short story) 1873; published in the jour-
    nal *Scribner's Monthly*
An Old Maid's Paradise (novel) 1879
Doctor Zay (novel) 1882

Edgar Allan Poe

Tamerlane and Other Poems. By a Bostonian (poetry)
    1827
Al Aaraaf, Tamerlane, and Minor Poems (poetry) 1829
Poems. By Edgar Allan Poe. Second Edition. (poetry)
    1831
"Ligeia" (short story) 1838; published in the journal
    American Museum
*Tales of the Grotesque and Arabesque. 2 vols. (short
    stories) 1840
†*Tales by Edgar A. Poe* (short stories) 1845
The Raven and Other Poems (poetry) 1846

Mark André Raffalovich

*Uranisme et unisexualité. étude sur différentes manifes-
    tations de l'instinct sexuel* (nonfiction) 1896

Mary Wollstonecraft Shelley

Frankenstein; or, The Modern Prometheus. 3 vols.
    (novel) 1818

Percy Bysshe Shelley

*Essays, Letters from Abroad, Translations, and Frag-
    ments by Percy Bysshe Shelley.* 2 vols. (essays, let-
    ters, translations, and prose) 1840
The Works of Percy Bysshe Shelley (poetry, verse dra-
    mas, and essays) 1847

The Complete Works of Percy Bysshe Shelley. 10 vols. (poetry, verse dramas, essays, and translations) 1924-30

Ambroise Tardieu
Étude médico-légale sur les attentats aux mœurs (nonfiction) 1873

Charles Virmaître
Trottoirs et lupanars (guidebook) 1882
Paris impur (guidebook) 1899

Oscar Wilde
The Picture of Dorian Gray (novel) 1890; first published in the journal *Lippincott's Monthly Magazine*; revised edition, 1891

Émile Zola
La Curée [*In the Whirlpool*] (novel) 1871
Les Quatre Evangiles. Fécondité [*Fruitfulness*] (novel) 1899

*This collection includes, among other stories, "Metzengerstein," "Berenice," "William Wilson," and "The Facts in the Case of M. Valdemar."

†This collection includes, among other stories, "The Purloined Letter," "The Gold-Bug," and "The Man of the Crowd."

DEFINING HOMOSEXUALITY

Vernon A. Rosario (essay date 1997)

SOURCE: Rosario, Vernon A. "Histoires d'inversion: Novelizing Homosexuality at the Fin de Siècle." In *Articulations of Difference: Gender Studies and Writing in French,* edited by Dominique D. Fisher and Lawrence R. Schehr, pp. 100-18. Stanford, Calif.: Stanford University Press, 1997.

[*In the following essay, Rosario assesses the influence of French "belle-lettristes—both medical professionals and scientific dilettantes—" on the medical and social definition of homosexuality at the end of the nineteenth century.*]

Monsieur Emile Zola, Paris

It is to you, Monsieur, who are the greatest novelist of our time and who, with the eye of the savant and the artist, capture and paint so powerfully *all* the failings, all the shame, all the ills that afflict humanity that I send these *human documents* so cherished by the cultivated people of our age.

This confession, which no spiritual advisor has ever learned from my lips, will reveal to you a frightful illness of the soul, a rare case—if not, unfortunately,

unique—which has been studied by learned psychologists, but which till now no novelist has dared to stage in a literary work.

So opens a truly unique "human document" of the late 1880's: a bundle of letters and postcards mailed to Emile Zola by a twenty-three-year-old Italian aristocrat.[1] In florid, raunchy detail, the young man recounts his sexual history from his early cross-dressing experiences and masturbatory addiction through to the feverish evolution of his "frightful illness": *an erotic passion for men.* He notes that Zola had briefly referred to the "horrid vice that dishonors humanity" (Invert 212) in the person of Baptiste the groom-loving valet in *La Curée* (591). But, the Italian complains, that that was a matter of debauchery, not love: "it is a purely material thing, a question of conformation, which doctors have more than once observed and described. All of that is very *common* and terribly *disgusting* and has nothing to do with the confession that I send you, which may perhaps serve you in some way" (212).

The young man's aim is to provide an abundance of authentic documentation so that his unusual "deviation" might be represented more extensively and candidly by Zola, the inventor of the "experimental novel," who had declared: "The dream of the physiologist and the experimental doctor is also that of the novelist who applies [Claude Bernard's] experimental method to the natural and social study of man" ("Roman" 1188). Zola's image as paternal doctor clearly endeared him to the young Italian, for he wrote, "Please forgive my horrible scribble, but I [write] with my heart on my sleeve, as if I were confessing to a doctor or a friend, and I have not paid attention to the form or the spelling" (231).

As it turned out, Zola's mysterious correspondent was indeed confessing to a doctor, in fact, to the whole community of doctors who read the *Archives d'anthropologie criminelle, de criminologie, et de psychologie normale et pathologique* where his letters were first published in 1894-95. What was an erotic confession doing in a medical journal and how did a novelist, Zola, make such a contribution? In addressing these questions, I will show how the construction of "inversion" and "homosexuality" in fin-de-siècle France was a broad literary and cultural affair beyond the professional confines of medical texts and knowledge.

The importance of late nineteenth-century medical science in constructing "homosexuality" has been well documented (Foucault, *Histoire*; Greenberg; Chauncey; Lanteri-Laura). My essay focuses on the significant role of *belle-lettristes*—both medical professionals and scientific dilettantes—in shaping this medical discourse. Some writers, such as Marc-André Raffalovich, were engaged in more or less explicit self-representation and defense of homosexuality. Others, such as Zola and J.-K. Huysmans, were concerned with condemning the epidemic of "perversity." Apologists and censors both argued for the power of fiction in shaping disciplinary knowledges, social stereotypes, and intimate experiences of "inversion." The etiology of "homosexuality"—whether it was a supposed product of biological "degeneration" or of social decay—was of concern to these medical and nonmedical writers who, even as they argued for the congenital "nature" of "inversion of the genital sense," erected new ontological structures out of old materials and new historical experiences.[2] The oldest association was with "sodomy" (any non-phallo-vaginal sex),[3] but French neurologists of the late nineteenth century recharacterized same-sex passion within a new narrative of hysterical gender delusion and fictional excess.

Effeminate Sodomites and Novel Hysterics

Ambroise Tardieu (1818-79) made his fame in forensic medicine with the publication of his *Etude médico-légale sur les attentats aux moeurs* (1857) in which he described how to positively identify both active and passive sodomites by the anatomical peculiarities of their penises and anuses (see also Aron and Kempf 47-52). He was equally preoccupied with the behavioral deviance of pederasts or sodomites (he used the terms interchangeably). Tardieu sketched the following image to illustrate the effeminate façade and psyche of the typical pederast:

> Curled hair, made-up skin, open collar, waist tucked in to highlight the figure; fingers, ears, chest loaded with jewelry, the whole body exuding an odor of the most penetrating perfumes, and in the hand a handkerchief, flowers, or some needlework: such is the strange, revolting, and rightfully suspect physiognomy of the pederast. . . . Hairstyles and dress constitute one of the most constant preoccupations of pederasts.
>
> (216-17)

The physicians who began to describe same-sex erotic attraction in the late 1860's did not equate this *new* phenomenon with the old category of "sodomy" as Tardieu had represented it. For example, the neurologist Wilhelm Griesinger (1817-1869) published his observations under the title "On a *Little Known* Psychopathological State" (emphasis added). Other German writers scrambled for an appellation. The Hanoverian lawyer Karl Heinrich Ulrichs (1826-95), under the pseudonym Numa Numantius, suggested *Urningen* to describe those with a female soul caught in a male body. Dr. Karl Westphal (1833-90), editor of the *Archiv für Psychiatrie und Nervenkrankheiten,* proposed the name *conträre Sexualempfindung* (contrary sexual sensation) in 1869. In a historical review of the condition, Dr. Richard von Krafft-Ebing (1840-1902) was only able to identify seventeen such cases in all the medical literature through 1877. Given the German dominance of the field, it is no wonder that a French medico-moral novel by Armand Dubarry was entitled *Les Invertis (Le vice allemand)* (1896). Journalist and traveler Armand Dubarry published a whole series of novels on the "Déséquilibrés de l'amour," including the volume on *Les Invertis (Le vice allemand).* He eventually succeeded Jules Verne as the science popularizer for the magazine *Le Musée des familles.*

Not to be left out of this hot new research direction, the French entered the arena in 1882 led by two prominent neurologists: Jean-Martin Charcot (1825-93) and Valentin Magnan (1835-1916). They were the first to introduce *inversion sexuelle* into French along with their description of the first French "invert": a man whose imagination since the age of six had been inflamed by the image of naked men. Like the Italian, this French invert had no sensual interest in women but loved women's clothes and wished he were female so he might dress in ladies' garments—which he confessed he did on occasion. Charcot and Magnan exclaimed, "This patient, what is he?" (56).

They founded their answer in the dominant hereditarian, degenerationist theories of the time. These had been initially suggested by Prosper Lucas in his *Traité philosophique et physiologique de l'hérédité naturelle* (1847-50), but gained almost universal currency in France through Bénédict Morel's *Traité des dégénérescences* (1857). Morel argued that all varieties of environmental, biological, and psychological insults (from miasmas to alcohol) could be expressed in offspring through almost any form of pathology. The cumulative weight of these hereditary degenerations would eventually lead to idiocy, sterility, and the termination of family lines.[4] German neurologists such as Westphal and Krafft-Ebing had adopted this hereditary degenerationist model in neuropathology by the 1860's. Charcot and Magnan, therefore, agreed with the Germans that "sexual perversion" was a product of neuropsychopathological degeneration, but they rejected the German notion that inverts suffered from a nosologically distinct gender discordancy between their psyches and their bodies (often called "psychosexual hermaphroditism"). No, Charcot and Magnan argued, inverts were neurodegenerates of the hysterical kind and did not differ much from those with erotic penchants for boots, buttocks, or bonnets—attractions that would later be labeled "erotic fetishes" by Alfred Binet. The invert simply had a delusional attraction to *human* objects of the same sex (Charcot and Magnan 321-22).

Although Charcot and Magnan tried to portray "inversion of the genital sense" as a new nosological entity, the diagnosis was actually a new hybrid of the older medical descriptions of the sodomite and the male hysteric (Rosario in Merrick and Ragan). The construction of the hysterical male in France in the 1870's (the decade when German physicians were uncovering "contrary sexual sensation") is particularly interesting because of the numerous associations made between these patients' symptoms and perverse literary production.

Hysteria in the male (although etymologically an oxymoron) developed as a credible diagnosis in the nineteenth century because hysteria had increasingly been theorized as a neuropsychiatric disorder and not a disease of the uterus (Greek *hystera*) (see Veith; Micale). Nonetheless, hysterics of either sex were portrayed as exhibiting characteristics traditionally associated with "femininity": excessive emotionality, hyperexcitability, and impressionability. Furthermore, male hysterics were regularly found to demonstrate physical stigmata of "*féminisme*" (for example, sparse beard, delicate complexions, fine hair, weak constitutions, and underdeveloped genitals) as well as familial histories of degeneration—in particular, hysterical mothers. For example, Paul Fabre, physician at the Vaucluse Asylum, noted that "the individuals stricken by this neurosis [male hysteria] offer certain psychological and physical analogies that seem to distance them from the sex to which they belong, to direct them to a new sex, so to speak, whose neutrality [i.e., indifference to sex with women] and exaggerated impressionability are the principle attributes" (365). To illustrate this, Fabre described the case of Mr. X———, a "man of letters" whose character "resembles in many ways that of a woman; despite an entirely virile exterior appearance, he cries and laughs easily depending on the circumstances, emotions have the greatest influence on him" (363).

Mr. X———, the hysterical writer, was in good company, since Gustave Flaubert also bore the diagnosis of hysteria. Indeed, Goldstein argues that Flaubert used his hysteria to gain a subversive, androgynous gender position from which to write of women's experiences. While one can interpret hysteria to have been Flaubert's muse, Flaubert instead complained that his hysterical, feminine hypersensitivity—like masturbatory exhaustion—was the cause of his bouts of literary *impotence*: "Each attack . . . was a seminal loss of the picturesque faculty of the brain" (Flaubert to Colet in Dumesnil 430). Flaubert wrote George Sand complaining about his isolation in Croisset: "The sensibility is unduly exalted in such a milieu. I suffer palpitations for no reason, rather understandable, all told, in an old hysteric like myself. For I maintain that men are hysterical like women and that I am one. When I wrote *Salammbô,* I read 'the best authors' on the matter and I recognized all my symptoms. I have the ball [*globus hystericus*] and the nail in the occiput" (January 12-13, 1867; 1980-91, 3:592). He later wrote to Mme. Roger des Genettes, "Dr. Hardy . . . calls me a hysterical old woman. 'Doctor,' I tell him, 'you are perfectly right'" (May 1, 1874; 1926-54, 7:134). To his longtime friend Marie-Sophie Leroyer de

Chantepie, he similarly wrote that he had the *nervous irritability* of a kept woman (March 18, 1857; 1980-91, 2:692).

The diagnosis of hysteria stuck to Flaubert even into the twentieth century; René Dumesnil (editor of the Pléiade edition of Flaubert's works) retrospectively examined Flaubert with the intention of dispelling persistent rumors that the novelist had been epileptic, sexually frigid, and *afraid of women* (88). Dumesnil determined—supposedly in Flaubert's defense—that the novelist's nervous crises were the product of "epileptoid hysteria with a strong neuropathic tendency" (94). Flaubert's superior literary abilities could thus be attributed to his neuro-degeneracy, since "his mania for analysis is pushed to exaggeration, and this is a trait common to all intellectual neuroses and superior mentality" (95). The excessive imaginativeness and hypersensibility of the hystero-epileptic placed Flaubert on the dangerous edge between insanity and literary genius. Fortunately, as the son of the physician-in-chief of the Rouen Hôtel-Dieu, Flaubert was endowed with a medical mentality and steely surgical literary style that prevented him from falling into the abyss (148). Reproducing Third Republic physicians' penchant for degenerationist, hereditary mechanisms of psychopathology, Dumesnil concluded that Flaubert united the ardent imagination and romantic character inherited from his mother with the superior intelligence and scientific spirit of his father the physician (317).

The image of Flaubert as doctor had been popularized since the publication of his first novel, *Madame Bovary* (1856). Inspired perhaps by Sainte-Beuve's comment in *Le Moniteur* (May 4, 1859) that Flaubert "wielded a pen as others a scalpel," A. Lemot's famous caricature in *La Parodie* (December 5-12, 1869) depicted Flaubert as a surgeon conducting an autopsy of Emma Bovary. Baudelaire, in a review of the novel that originally appeared in *l'Artiste* on October 18, 1857, had even declared that Emma was the female incarnation of Flaubert, and inversely that, "despite all his zeal as an actor, [Flaubert] was unable not to infuse virile blood into the veins of his creature, and that Madame Bovary—despite all the energy and ambition she may possess, and also her dreaminess—Madame Bovary remains a man. Like armed Pallas, springing from the brain of Zeus, that bizarre androgyne has kept all the seductions of a virile soul in a charming feminine body" (652). The representational brilliance of hysterical medical novelists to spawn fictional inverts may have struck Baudelaire as the zenith of literary genius, but contemporary physicians were far more wary of the novels of hysterics.

Dr. Ernest Lasègue (1816-83), in an article on "Les hystériques, leur perversité, leurs mensonges" (1881), warned colleagues against the willful malevolence and irresistible deceitfulness of the hysteric's imagination. Hysterics and lunatics both told untrue stories, he noted, but the great danger was that "The latter are unbelievable, whereas *the novels of hysterics* impose themselves by their verisimilitude" (114, my emphasis). The same principle could be applied more broadly, he observed: "Do we not have something analogous in the wide field of human inventions? This is the novelist who, commencing with a premise furnished by the imagination, allows himself to be led by this to the point of believing that everything he creates actually happened" (112). The novels of hysterics and hysterical novelists would seem to collapse into the same category, distinguished by hypersensibility, over-imaginativeness, deceitfulness, and self-delusion. The same characteristics would hold true of the novels and lives of inverts—the literate perverts of the fin de siècle such as the Italian dandy. Echoing Lasègue's warnings concerning hysterics, physicians cautioned against the seductions of inverts' narrative productions and these stories' ability to pervert society.

SCIENCE, INVERTS, AND THE FLAMING TRUTH

> Whenever my nurse sees me, she always tells me that all the women she knows had named me *the little Madonna,* I was so cute and delicate. . . . I still recall the shiver of joy and pleasure that coursed through my little person when I went out in my little puffed-up blue piqué dress with blue bows and my big Italian straw hat.
>
> When I was four, they took away my little dresses to put me in trousers and a little jacket. Once they had dressed me as a boy, I experienced profound shame—I remember it as if it were today—and I quickly ran to my nanny's room to hide and cry; to console me, she had to dress me again as a girl. They still laugh whenever recalling my cries of despair in seeing them take away those little white dresses which were my greatest joy.
>
> It seems as if they took away something that I was always destined to wear.
>
> That was my first great sorrow.
>
> (Invert 215)

Zola was impressed by the Italian invert's confessions of effeminacy and same-sex passion, and felt that the subject was extremely important. "I was struck by the great physiological and social interest [the confession] offered," Zola wrote, "It touched me by its absolute sincerity, because one senses the flame, I would even say the eloquence of truth. . . . It is a total, naïve, spontaneous confession that very few men would dare make, qualities that render it quite precious from many points of view" ("Preface" 1). He hoped that its publication might inspire some pity for these "unfortunates," but he found it impossible to utilize the manuscript in his own writings.

"With each new novel of Zola's," the Italian later wrote, "I hoped to finally discover a character who was the reproduction of myself, but I was always disappointed and I was finally convinced that the writer had lacked the *courage* to stage so terrible a passion" (quoted in Saint-Paul 115). Zola was hardly one to shy away from controversy. Even before the Dreyfus Affair and his famous polemic "J'accuse!" (1895), his naturalist novels had been condemned for their vulgarity, sensuality, and morbidity. Some of Zola's harshest literary critics were those people he claimed as his colleagues—physicians, who nevertheless considered him a "scientific dilettante." Like Flaubert before him, Zola had been deemed a pathological writer and had been "diagnosed" as an epileptoid degenerate, a "superior degenerate," an olfactory fetishist, and a sexual psychopath (Toulouse; Nordau 2:456). Yet Zola had persisted in portraying the great spectrum of physical and moral degenerations: alcoholism, prostitution, monomania, adultery, and homicide. Therefore, Zola's literary impotence on the topic of inversion is quite revealing. He could never have edited the Italian's manuscript, he confessed, because,

> I was then in the roughest hours of my literary battle; critics treated me daily as a criminal capable of all vices and all debaucheries. . . . First of all they would have accused me of entirely *inventing* the story from personal corruption. Then I would have been duly condemned for merely having seen in the affair an occasion for base speculation on the most repugnant instincts. And what a clamor if I had permitted myself to say that no other subject is more serious or more tragic; that it is a far more common and deep wound than pretended and that still the best thing for healing wounds is to study them, to expose them, and to treat them!
>
> ("Preface" 2)

The social taint of "inversion" was clearly too much even for the scientific novelist, despite the dictum "Science, like fire, purifies everything it touches" (regularly cited in the introductions to medical works on sexuality). Privately, Zola confessed to a far more personal impediment: "I can barely overcome the instinctive repulsion I experience in shaking [an invert's] hand" (quoted in Laupts, "Mémoire" 833). And to another correspondent, Marc-André Raffalovich, in a thank-you note (April 16, 1896) for the gift of the former's book, *L'Uranisme et l'unisexualité,* Zola wrote: "If I am full of pity for those whom you call Uranists, I have no sympathy for them, no doubt because I am different" (quoted in Allen 221).

So, after pouring his heart out, the poor Italian never saw himself fictionalized by Zola. *Or did he?* Zola had become increasingly fervent over French natality—a concern most clearly voiced in *Fécondité* (1899), the first volume of his *Quatre Evangiles.* Therefore, he was extremely anxious about all forms of nonprocreative sexuality, and once moaned, "How much seed wasted in one night in Paris—what a shame that all of it does not produce human beings" (quoted in Laupts, "Mémoire" 832, n. 1). This seminal waste was of equal concern to the medical and anthropological communities, particularly after the humiliating defeat in the Franco-Prussian War (1870-71). Therefore, Zola delivered the Italian's confession to his medical friend, Dr. Laupts, who was conducting a survey in 1894 on "sexual inversion" for the prestigious French medicolegal journal *Archives d'anthropologie criminelle*.

Glancing into a bookstore window by chance some years later, the Italian discovered a book entitled *Tares et poisons. Perversions et perversités sexuelles* (1896) in which were republished his own confessions. He immediately wrote to Laupts that he was elated to find himself "printed in *living color,* although I would have much preferred to be reborn in the pages of a novel and not in a medical science treatise" (quoted in Saint-Paul 116). Indeed, the Italian dandy repeatedly suggested that he fancied himself a *belle-lettriste* and envisioned his life as a work of art: "I unloaded my soul somewhat [in my confessions to Zola] and I wrote with a retrospective voluptuousness of the abominable and ardent scenes in which I was the actor. . . . I therefore want to complete the study of my person, whom I often consider favored by nature because she made me a creature that even the most audacious poets have been unable to create" (Invert 231-32). Ironically enough, his "true" confession was printed *verbatim* but under the title, "Le *roman* d'un inverti."

Dr. Laupts, a student of the prominent forensic doctor Alexandre Lacassagne (1843-1924), introduced the "document" in a style more suited to the back cover blurb of a racy "true crime" novella: "It is the true story of a man who bore a great name, a very great name in Italy. As exact as a scientific observation, as interesting as a novel, as sincere as a confession, it is perhaps the most complete and most endearing document of this genre" ("Enquête" 212). Like most of Zola's novels, the confession was published serially, and Laupts had a knack for breaking the action at critical moments of sexual titillation. For example, in the third installment, "Youth—First Acts," we learn of the Italian's first erotic encounter with a handsome young officer during his military service:

> He was half undressed and seated on my legs right up against me. I spoke to him as if enchanted . . . suddenly he leaned over, embraced me in his arms and applied a long kiss to my cheek; at the same time he plunged his hands under the sheets and seized my flesh with both his hands. I thought I would die and an immense joy suddenly seized me. We remained a few seconds like that, resting one head against the other, our fiery cheeks touching, my mouth in his in the warmth of the pillow. I was never so happy!!
>
> The lamp on the floor cast faint rays upon the immense dormitory where, in the distant beds, my companions

were sleeping, and left in the deepest darkness the corner where we were thus ecstatic.

(Invert 737)

Break! Readers had to cool off for two months before the hard-core action continued. But is it science or is it fiction? As Zola feared, some foreign writers were convinced it was entirely his own fabrication—their critiques were related by Laupts ("Mémoire" 837)—and it did not help matters that Laupts labeled it a "novel."

The second half of the title is equally important: "inversion" itself was a novel diagnosis coined just twelve years earlier. Remarkably, the young Italian never applied any label to himself, although he liked comparing himself to Greek heroes. Perhaps he felt the two traditional terms, "pederast" and "sodomite," were inappropriate in his case. Technically he was not a pederast since he was attracted to virile, adult men. "Sodomite" seemed inappropriate because he had only experienced sodomy (anal sex) quite late since he had feared it was too painful. In any case, the Italian dismissed these two designations as old matters of vice and defective genital conformation which had long been examined by doctors. He was quite convinced that his condition was rare and new, and therefore worthy of publication (212).

Physicians of the time clearly agreed, since, as we have seen, the diagnoses of "contrary sexual sensation" and "inversion of the genital sense" which sprang up in the 1870's and 1880's were considered new disease entities. After the publication of Charcot and Magnan's article introducing the terms *inversion du sens génitale* and *perversion sexuelle* into France, French medical journals were pullulating with these queer new creatures. Just three years later, Chevalier published a whole medical thesis on the matter of *Inversion de l'instinct sexuel au point de vue médico-légale* (1885). Chevalier highlighted the dizzying panoply of designations for the illness: "contrary, inverse, perverted, [or] inverted genital sense;—contrary, inverse, [or] perverted sexual attractions, impulsions, [or] sensations;—attraction of same sexes;—crossed sensation of sexual individuality; . . .—perversion, [or] interversion of the sexual instinct, [etc.]" (14). Some order needed to be brought to this field of confusions; therefore, Dr. Laupts had bravely launched a national "Enquête sur l'inversion sexuelle" with a detailed list of questions concerning the heredity, physical and psychological status, and medical and legal history of inverts. The questionnaire was published in the *Archives d'anthropologie criminelle* but was addressed to professors, lawyers, and novelists, as well as doctors (105-6). The first published response was the Italian's manuscript, which was contributed by Zola, who strongly endorsed Laupts's research.

Laupts shared Zola's natality concerns, which were the *raison d'être* of the whole project. In the introduction to his monograph *Tares et poisons,* Laupts argued for the sympathetic treatment of these "patients," but continued:

> These days, no one doubts that the number of degenerations, of cerebral derailings—expressed by the tendencies towards suicide, by phobias, etc.—result in large part from the fact that in our nation the genital functions often are not accomplished as they should be.
>
> Therefore, it is necessary from the point of view of the vitality, of the future of the race, to study the morbid causes, to discern the dangerous and evil elements, amongst which must be ranked for an appreciable part the creature stricken with sexual perversion: the pervert, the feminiform born-invert.
>
> (104-5)

For Laupts, sexual inversion was a terrifying nexus of medical, social, and moral deviations, and the "feminiform born-invert" was the embodiment of almost all fin-de-siècle social ills.

The second published response to Laupts's survey was from Marc-André Raffalovich (1864-1934), who would become the most prolific writer in French on the subject of "unisexuality" (his preferred term) and would eventually accuse Laupts and his colleagues of being far too squeamish and prejudiced to study inversion scientifically. These "fatuous" French scientists, Raffalovich declared in the pages of the *Archives,* discuss inverts "as if they were newly imported savages that had been unknown in Europe" ("Uranisme" 126). Raffalovich was in a privileged position: he kept abreast of the German, French, and English medical literature, and, most significantly, he had insider information—he was an invert. But then, so was Dr. Laupts, literally: "Laupts" was a fiction—the inversion of his real name, St.-Paul. Even better, he was a writer of fiction, under the pseudonym G. Espé de Metz—a name he started using when he discovered to his dismay that bibliographers were cataloguing "Laupts" under German authors (Saint-Paul 5).

Raffalovich was also an impostor of sorts. Although he was entrusted with writing the "Annales de l'unisexualité" within the *Archives d'anthropologie criminelle,* and was the only French writer on homosexuality that British sexologist Havelock Ellis praised, Raffalovich was in fact not a doctor. He had no degree whatsoever—he was an Oxford dropout. Raffalovich came from a wealthy Russian-Jewish family that had emigrated to France. His mother was an intimate friend of Claude Bernard, who had recommended that Marc-André become a doctor. He was shipped off to Oxford but he was too sickly to finish his studies. Instead he became a London dandy, published a few novels and collections of maudlin love poems, and established a literary salon frequented by the notable authors of the day: Henry James, Aubrey Beardsley, Stephan Mallarmé, Pierre Louÿs, and the most coveted of aesthetes, Oscar Wilde.

Raffalovich and Wilde were intimate friends until their vicious falling out in the early 1890's over an indiscreet comment by Wilde. At that time, Raffalovich was enamored of Wilde's companion, a pretty-boy and budding poet named John Henry Gray (1866-1934), whom Raffalovich had met in 1892 through a mutual friend, poet Arthur Symons. *A Portrait of Dorian Gray* was published in 1891 with its secret dedication to John, but the next year Wilde met the younger and more angelic Lord Alfred Douglas. Raffalovich got the suicidal Gray on the rebound and they became lifetime and reportedly Platonic companions (McCormack 151). The Queensbury v. Wilde Affair of 1895 perturbed Raffalovich and Gray as well as other London dandies. Raffalovich converted to Catholicism the following year, and Gray renewed his Catholic faith. In 1898, Raffalovich was admitted to the lay order of Dominicans under the name Brother Sebastian, and Gray began training for the priesthood in Rome thanks to Raffalovich's financial support. After ordination, Gray served as a curate in a poor Edinburgh parish for three years before becoming parish priest of Edinburgh's St. Peter's Church (which was constructed largely with Raffalovich's funds) (McCormack 202-3). Raffalovich moved into a house near St. Peter's in 1905, and the two met every day there for tea. Raffalovich became a great benefactor of the Dominicans, and donated funds for the construction of St. Sebastian's priory in Pendelton, Manchester. His wealth was held in a joint account with Gray. Raffalovich passed away in his sleep on St. Valentine's Day 1934; Canon Gray died four months later (Sewell 33-34, 48; Ellman; McCormack.

Perhaps it was through Arthur Symons, a close friend of John Addington Symonds and Havelock Ellis, that Raffalovich was introduced to the burgeoning scientific study of inversion and to Ellis and Symonds's groundbreaking *Sexual Inversion* (1896). But even before Ellis began to publish his series on *Studies in the Psychology of Sex,* Raffalovich had begun writing a stream of articles on homosexuality for the *Archives,* including a review of the Wilde affair with a spiteful critique of Wilde's pederasty and literary style. Raffalovich inveighed against Wilde's "flaccid" and "unoriginal" writing, which only represented "artificious, superficial, effeminate" homosexuals ("Affaire" 450). These were in the minority, Raffalovich controversially argued. Not all inverts were degenerate sodomites, and he mocked doctors who, in the tradition of Tardieu, "search, almost with desperation, for stigmata of degeneracy" ("Unisexualité" 429). Most unisexuals were virile and law-abiding, but "pseudoscience," caving in to popular prejudice, had pushed these decent homosexuals into the shadows (*Uranisme* 25-26). Given Raffalovich's conservative position condemning flamboyant "effeminates," it is not surprising that he showed even less sympathy than Laupts for the Italian invert and his "novel." "This autobiography resembles those of all effeminate Uranists who have gone public," Raffalovich warned, "This novel of an invert will teach nothing to those with experience in psychiatry. . . . Unbridled vanity and lust are especially demonstrated in the relations between the invert of the novel and the Captain [an older pederast who seduces the hero]. . . . Repugnant or dangerous acts will generally occur between people united by debauchery, vanity, or interest" ("Roman" 333). He cautioned, "It seems to me that one should not dwell on such autobiographies or attach much importance to them" ("Uranisme" 116). Furthermore, Raffalovich made the intriguing literary distinction that "ultra male, male and a half" homosexuals did not write their own *memoirs,* historians wrote their *biographies* ("Roman" 333). It was only the effeminates who penned their conceited, immoral confessions.

Echoing Lasègue on the novels of hysterics, Raffalovich exhorted doctors and the general public alike to beware of the narratives of artifice-loving, effeminate inverts not only because their "true confessions" might be deceitful novels, but, more seriously, because these novels were socially noxious. Raffalovich warned that literature reflected the true, inner moral state of its creator just as the portrait of Dorian Gray (and Wilde's novel itself) reflected the true corrupt and corrupting soul. Appropriating Wilde's dictum that "life imitates art," Raffalovich claimed that literature shaped the moral character of its readers. Artistic representations had long been criticized as dangerous to the malleable brains of women and children, but Raffalovich argued for their salubrious use in the treatment of the imagination. With poetic grandiloquence, he lectured novelists from the bully pulpit of medicine about the connection between fiction and social hygiene:

> I call upon our French novelists. . . . I would tell them: Because your readers, your admirers permit you to say anything, why not deliver them real observations? You have them. Describe then that passion of the strong for the strong, of Hercules for Colossus, of robust flesh, as they say, for robust flesh; show that it is not only the female but also the effeminate who is of no interest to these virile [homosexuals]; draw back the veils of ignorance and of falsehood . . . the clichés must be shattered. . . . We must contemplate the education of our children, of our grandchildren.
>
> ("Unisexualité" 431, n. 1)

The battle over the moral purity of France became even more feverish and nationalistic after Raffalovich drew another French novelist, J. K. Huysmans (1848-1907), into the medical literature by publishing extracts from a letter about the sordid Parisian sodomitic underworld. "It made me think of Hell," Huysmans wrote,

> Imagine this: the man who has this vice willfully *withdraws* from association with the rest of mankind. He eats in restaurants, has his hair done at a coiffeur, lives in a *hôtel* where the patrons are all old sodomites. It is

a life apart, in a narrow corner, a brotherhood recognizing itself by their voice, by a fixed gaze, and that singsong tone they all affect.

> Furthermore, that vice is the *only* one that suppresses the castes, the decent man and the rogue are equal— and speak to each other naturally, animatedly without distinction of education. . . . It is rather strange and disquieting.
>
> (April 19, 1896; Allen 216)

Raffalovich contrasted this "Sodom of Paris" with Dr. Paul Näcke's description of the gatherings of educated, bourgeois homosexuals and lesbians at a meeting of the Scientific and Philanthropic Committee (a homosexual organization started by Magnus Hirschfeld) and at other social venues in Berlin. Näcke was so moved by the narratives of these homosexuals' sufferings and their struggles with their parents, that he wondered, "Why doesn't someone write unisexual novels?" (quoted in Raffalovich, "Groupes" 931). Raffalovich hoped to indict French society for its general immorality, irreligion, and ignorance of the psychology of *healthy* unisexuals. "Heterosexuals, by their example and behavior," Raffalovich complained, "have created many [immoral] inverts" ("Groupes" 935).

Näcke promptly responded to the article complaining that it was totally unbalanced and ill-informed. He imagined that the homosexual worlds of Paris and Berlin were quite similar and that the number of homosexuals given to vice was a small minority in both cities. He estimated that Paris probably had fifty to a hundred thousand homosexuals and that, although pederasty was not the rule amongst homosexuals, he suspected there was a higher incidence of pederasty in Latin cultures than Teutonic ones ("Monde" 184). In a subsequent article in a *German* journal, Näcke further suggested that the French suffered from more degeneration than the Germans ("Einteilung").

Dr. Laupts/Saint-Paul immediately took umbrage at these aspersions against French masculinity. He shot back at both Raffalovich and Näcke that the French were no more degenerate that the Germans (Laupts, "Dégénérescence"). Furthermore, he insisted, "*I know* that homosexuality does not exist save as a *rare* exception in the entirety of continental . . . France. . . . *I know* that the vast majority of my (noncolonial) compatriots experience an undissimulated and *extreme* disgust for homosexuality" ("Lettre" 693, 696; original emphasis). (Laupts was less certain of the sexual normality of France's colonized subjects.) This was in dramatic contrast to the situation in Germany, where notable doctors, such as Westphal, Krafft-Ebing, and Näcke, had taken up the defense of homosexuals and had favored the deletion of antisodomy laws from the Penal Code. Laupts feared that homosexuality was contagious and was spreading in both France and Germany precisely "because it is studied, and spoken, and written about" ("Lettre" 694). The very fact that German doctors had done so much work on the subject was proof of (and presumably cause of) the higher incidence of homosexuality in Germany than in France ("Dégénérescence" 741). In retort to Raffalovich's insult that Laupts's work on homosexuality was in "a literary tradition," Laupts accused Raffalovich of being "a bit too literary, too inclined, in any case, to introduce into a scientific debate considerations of a moral nature which have no place there and are . . . sort of meaningless" ("Lettre" 695-96).

These accusations and counter-accusations that scientific scholarship was merely fictional "literature" continued to be flung across national boundaries thanks to essays by Eugène Wilhelm. A homosexual Alsatian lawyer, Wilhelm had already published several articles in the *Mercure de France* on German sexology and initially joined the debate under the pseudonym "Dr. Numa Praetorius." If Laupts and his French colleagues were practically ignorant of the existence of homosexuality in France, Wilhelm observed, it was because their old prejudices prevented them from broaching the subject with their patients and discovering how many of these, in fact, were homosexual (Praetorius 201). He chastised French men of science for generally neglecting sexual questions and flung Laupts's insult of "literariness" back in the face of French physicians: "They seem to want to leave this terrain to literature and superficial popularizers; one could say that a certain false shame, an ill-placed prudishness prevents them from studying these problems in detail and methodically" (Wilhelm 301). To an extent, Wilhelm was right. Men of letters, heterosexual and homosexual alike, *did* have an especially significant role in shaping the French discourse of homosexuality, but one can hardly accuse the *belle-lettristes* of having perverted science; rather, they informed the very fictions science was dedicated to spinning.

SCIENCE FICTIONS AND INVERSIONS

In his scathing critique of degenerate, fin-de-siècle culture, journalist Dr. Max Nordau (1849-1920) fumed: "Does [Zola] think that his novels are serious documents from which science can borrow facts? What childish folly! Science can have nothing to do with fiction" (2:437). As we have seen, however, the scientific literature on inversion was especially dedicated to fiction: both the fictions it studied and the fictions it sponsored. To label the scientific literature on inversion a "fiction" is not, however, to dismiss it as *untruthful.* Foucault has pointed out that "there is the possibility for fiction to function in truth"; indeed,

> for a fictional discourse to induce effects of truth, and for bringing it about that a true discourse engenders or "manufactures" something that does not as yet exist,

that is, "fictions" it. One "fictions" history on the basis of a political reality that makes it true, one "fictions" a politics not yet in existence on the basis of a historical truth.

(Foucault, *Power* 193)

The novelizing and fictioning of "homosexuality" served to advance the underlying goals of defenders and derogators of homosexuality alike: on the one hand, to reify the notion of a normal, virile homosexual; on the other hand, to fashion a monster of perversity embodying all the degenerations and insecurities that plagued the cultural imagination of fin-de-siècle France.

While perfectly consonant with the latest scientific, biomedical "truths" of the day, the medical debates on the nature of inversion were, nevertheless, also molded by the cultural and political preoccupations of the time. The nationalistic fires of Franco-German rivalries continued to burn on the terrain of science well after France's defeat in the Franco-Prussian War. The construction and counting of inverts was just one among many ideological weapons (just as it is, albeit under different scientific and political conditions, in the United States today).[5] The fictioning of what would later be called "homosexuality"—embellished as it was by associations with effeminacy, hysteria, and deceitfulness—was especially critical in bolstering nationalist myths of strength in which potency was always figured as masculine (see Nye, "Sex" and *Masculinity*).

In the case of the history of inversion, fiction and non-fiction were blurred on a stage bustling with novelists in medical drag, and physicians passing incognito as novelists or inverts. Inverts and homosexuals found their "true" confessions presented as scientific fictions under the fear that these narrative productions shared in the deceitfulness and self-delusion of inverts' sexual natures. Homosexuals also played an active part in the fictioning of their experience—and not just because they wrote anonymously or under pseudonyms. Like the medical researchers of "sexual perversions," homosexual correspondents found it necessary to invent a new history for themselves. Manufactured in the political cause of homosexual emancipation and decriminalization, this *histoire homosexuelle* or historical coming-out narrative advanced seemingly contradictory claims of a long tradition beginning with "the Greek vice" alongside claims of "homosexuality's" historical novelty. Likewise, the scientific *histoires* simultaneously asserted the congenital nature of homosexuality and its acquired, even contagious, nature (Laupts, "Lettre" 695 and 694, respectively).

In the promiscuous intercourse between doctors and novelists over the societal *tares et poisons* of "sexual perversion," science itself served as a potent but ambiguous elixir. As Derrida (in *Dissémination*) points out in his exegesis of the *pharmakon* (poison or elixir) in Plato's *Phaedrus* (274c-275b), symbolic language is unmasked as a dangerous supplement to "true learning": superficially, writing appears to be a technique for remembering, but ultimately it produces forgetfulness.[6] Like the female soul disguised in the male body, the mechanism of poisoning is that of inversion. Physicians and littérateurs played a similarly dangerous game with the *pharmakon* of science, which—like the novels conceived by Zola, Raffalovich, and the Italian invert—had the seductiveness of a social panacea.

We have seen that the Italian invert was delighted to find his confessions represented by science, and, in his letter to Laupts, praised the doctor as a "savant . . . and a kind and indulgent man." The Italian contributed dozens more pages directly to Laupts because "like every sick person who sees in a doctor a friend . . . , I am filled with friendship and gratitude for those who occupy themselves with the odious illness that haunts me, and . . . I seek to render them service by exhibiting that which they painfully seek, and which I, on the contrary, know so well: *by innate science*" (quoted in Saint-Paul 116). Even while attempting to condemn and contain perversity, the scientific fictions of inversion were embraced by the inverts themselves who used science to defend their "naturalness," consolidate an identity, and disseminate their stories of passion and "robust flesh." Where better than in scientific journals could the Italian invert "cry my [joy] from the rooftops" for finally having been sodomized (quoted in Saint-Paul 115)?

In addition to science, there is the *pharmakon* of history itself. Of all the human technologies, none is more inherently dependent on fabricating and forgetting than history. It figured prominently in the fin-de-siècle medical analysis of homosexuality. A patient's individual case history or *anamnesis,* often printed as a confession, was connected to other family histories and anamneses of supposedly related disorders. Doctors and inverts regularly alluded to the "Greek vice" of antiquity; yet, as Raffalovich astutely noted, these historical connections were un-remembered in the convenient science fiction that "inversion" was a new syndrome of organic degeneration and social disintegration. Inverts were thus concocted as a terrible social and cultural poison through the conventions of amnesia and anamnesis: the inversions of forgetting and reminiscence, the masquerade of intolerance as sympathy, the travesty of ignorance as knowledge.

Notes

A different version of this essay appeared as "Inversion's Histories/History's Inversions: Novelizing Fin-de-Siècle Homosexuality," in Rosario, *Science and Homosexualities.* Copyright © Vernon A. Rosario, 1997, for this essay.

1. Invert (212); original emphasis. As I will explain shortly, the Italian's confession (which I cite as "Invert") was published anonymously in a medical journal in 1894-95. Its date of composition is uncertain. Setz in *Der Roman eines Konträrsexuellen* estimates that it was written in 1887 or 1888, based on the Italian's references to historical events (82). Alternatively, the document can be approximately dated to 1889, since the Italian author wrote Dr. Laupts upon encountering the published version of the confession in *Tares et poisons* (1896), and Saint-Paul (*Thèmes psychologique,* 115, n. 2) notes that this was seven years after the original letters were sent to Zola. Unless otherwise noted, all translations are mine.

2. For a discussion of the contemporary stakes of the "essentialism" versus "social constructionism" debate regarding the appropriate historical use of the terms "gay" or "homosexual," see Stein, *Forms of Desire.*

3. The word *sodomy* was used quite loosely in eighteenth- and nineteenth-century France to refer to any variety of "unnatural" sexual acts: anal intercourse (no matter what the sex of the participants), oral sex, and penetration by dildos. *Pederasty* (etymologically, the love of boys) was frequently used interchangeably with *sodomy.* Dr. Fournier Pescay struggled to provide a precise definition in the *Dictionnaire des sciences médicales*: "Sodomy. . . . Under this name is designated the infamous coitus, for the accomplishment of which, the depraved man prefers, instead of the organ destined by nature to receive the fecundating liqueur of the male, that neighboring organ where the most disgusting excretion of the human body occurs. Theologians, as well as legists, define this vile action: *Sodomia, turpitudo masculum facta.* This definition is incomplete and applies only to pederasty. Sodomy is equally well exerted between a man and a person of the other sex as between two men: when it takes place between a man and a child, and even between two men, it is distinguished under the name of pederasty" (441).

4. For more on the extensive social impact of the theory of degeneration, see Pick, *Faces of Degeneration.*

5. In the United States—particularly since the wave of "gay liberation" and public visibility sparked by the Stonewall Riot in 1969—fictions of homosexuality have served the nationalist cause. During the Gulf War (1990-91), Iraq's President Saddam Hussein was portrayed as a transvestite sadistic pederast (*National Examiner,* March 12, 1991). T-shirts sporting an image of a camel with Hussein's face for an anus declared patriotically, "America Will Not be Saddam-ized" (see Gold-

berg, *Sodometries* 1-5). Homosexualizing the enemy and protecting the U.S. nation from homosexual invasion were a unified strategy of defense. The U.S. military, quite literally, feared a homosexual invasion in 1993 when threatened by President Bill Clinton with the open admission of gays into the armed services. U.S. television viewers were treated to grainy footage of enlisted men in the showers as soldiers confessed their fears of being cruised by the impending hordes of queers clamoring to enter the services. These soldiers' anxieties (or fantasies) of homosexual objectification and scopophilic feminization clearly outweighed their concerns of flashing on millions of television screens. Given the incessant mention of AIDS throughout the debate, one imagines that these showering soldiers feared a double contagion: both AIDS and homosexuality. Their generals' paranoid fabrications of the homosexual menace strangely mirror the very neuropsychiatric unfitness for which homosexuals were originally screened out by the Selective Service in 1940 ("Medical Circular"; also see Bérubé, *Coming Out Under Fire*, 11-15).

6. In this Platonic dialogue, Socrates tells Phaedrus the following story. Theut (the god of numbers, geometry, letters, and games) offers Thamus, King of Egypt, letters (*grammata*) as a means of making Egyptians wiser and of improving their memory: it will be an elixir (*pharmakon*) of memory and wisdom, Theut promises. Thamus rejects letters, predicting that they will produce forgetfulness since people will come to rely on alien marks rather than their own memory. "You have discovered an elixir not of memory," Thamus declares, "but of reminding" (275a). Writing merely produces an appearance of learning rather than true learning. Instead of a cure for forgetfulness, the *pharmakon* of writing (*logos*) is rejected as an artifice of learning: it is rather a poison of memory and knowledge.

Works Cited

Aron, J.-P. and R. Kempf. *La Bourgeoisie, le sexe et l'honneur.* Brussels: Editions Complexes, 1984.

———. *Le Pénis et la démoralisation de l'occident.* Paris: Grasset, 1978.

Assouline, Pierre. "Du côté des femmes . . ." *Lire* 206 (November 1992): 26-30.

de Balzac, Honoré. *La Comédie humaine.* Ed. Pierre-Georges Castex. Paris: Gallimard, 1976-81. 12 vols.

Barthes, Roland. *Fragments d'un discours amoureux.* Paris: Seuil, 1977.

———. *Incidents,* Paris: Seuil, 1987.

———. *Michelet par lui-même.* Paris: Seuil, 1954.

———. *Le Plaisir du texte.* Paris: Seuil, 1973.

———. *Sade, Fourier, Loyola.* Paris: Seuil, 1971.

———. "Sur André Gide et son *Journal.*" *Magazine littéraire* 97 (February 1975): 23-28.

———. *S/Z.* Paris: Seuil, 1970.

Bataille, Georges. *L'Erotisme.* Paris: Minuit, 1957.

Baudelaire, Charles. *The Flowers of Evil.* Trans. James McGowan. Intro. Jonathan Culler. Oxford: Oxford University Press, 1993.

———. *Oeuvres complètes.* Paris: Gallimard (Pléiade), 1975. 2 vols.

———. *Correspondance.* Paris: Gallimard (Pléiade), 1973.

Bérubé, Allan. *Coming Out Under Fire: The History of Gay Men and Women in World War Two.* New York: Free Press, 1990.

Binet, Alfred. "Le fétichisme dans l'amour." *Revue philosophique* 24 (1887): 143-67; 252-74.

Charcot, Jean-Martin, and Valentin Magnan. "Inversion du sens genital." *Archives de neurologie* 3 (1882): 53-60, 296-322.

Chevalier, Julien. *De l'inversion de l'instinct sexuel au point de vue médico-légale.* Paris: Octave Doin, 1885.

Dubarry, Armand. *Les Invertis (Le vice allemand).* Paris: Chamuel, 1895.

Ellis, Havelock, and John Addington Symonds. *Das konträre Geschlechstgefühl.* Trans. Hans Kurella. Leipzig: George H. Wiegand, 1896. Published in English as *Sexual Inversion.* London: University Press, 1897.

Fabre, Paul. "De l'hystérie chez l'homme." *Annales médico-psychologiques* 5th ser. 13 (1875): 354-73.

Flaubert, Gustave. *Correspondance.* 13 vols. Paris: Editions Louis Conard, 1926-54.

———. *Correspondance.* 3 vols. In *Oeuvres complètes.* Paris: Pléiade, 1980-91.

———. "La Légende de Saint Julien l'Hospitalier." In *Oeuvres.* Paris: Gallimard [Pléiade], 1952 [1877]. 2: 623-48.

Goldberg, Jonathan. *Sodometries: Renaissance Texts, Modern Sexualities.* Stanford: Stanford University Press, 1992.

Goldstein, Jan. "The Uses of Male Hysteria: Medical and Literary Discourse in Nineteenth-Century France." *Representations* 34 (1991): 134-65.

Griesinger, Wilhelm. "Über einen wenig bekannten psychopathischen Zustand." *Archiv für Psychiatrie und Nervenkrankheiten* 1 (1868-69): 626-35.

[Invert]. [Letters to Emile Zola published anonymously as] "Le roman d'un inverti." Ed. Dr. Laupts (Georges Saint-Paul). *Archives d'anthropologie criminelle* 9 (1894): 212-15, 367-73, 729-37; 10 (1895): 131-38, 228-41, 320-25.

Krafft-Ebing, Richard von. "Über gewisse Anomalien des Geschlechtstriebs und die klinisch-forensische Verwerthung derselben als eines wahrscheinlich functionellen Degenerationszeichens des centralen Nerven-Systems." *Archiv für Psychiatrie und Nervenkrankheiten* 7 (1877): 291-312.

Lasègue, Ernest. "Les hystériques, leur perversité, leurs mensonges." *Annales médico-psychologiques* 6th ser. 6 (1881): 111-18.

Laughlin, Henry P. *The Ego and Its Defenses.* New York: Appleton-Century-Crofts, 1970.

Dr. Laupts (Georges Saint-Paul). "Dégénérescence ou pléthore?" *Archives d'anthropologie criminelle* 23 (1908): 731-49.

———. "Enquête sur l'inversion sexuelle (Réponses)," [and editorial remarks to "Le roman d'un inverti."] *Archives d'anthropologie criminelle* 9 (1894): 105-8; 211-15; 367-73; 729-37; 10 (1895): 131-38; 228-41; 320-25.

———. "Lettre au Professeur Lacassagne en réponse au lettre de M. Raffalovich." *Archives d'anthropologie criminelle* 24 (1909): 693-96.

———. "A la mémoire d'Emile Zola." *Archives d'anthropologie criminelle* 22 (1907): 825-41.

———. *Tares et poisons. Perversions et perversités sexuelles. Une enquête sur l'inversion. Notes et documents. Le roman d'un inverti né. Le procès Wilde. La guérison et la prophylaxie de l'inversion.* Paris: George Carré, 1896.

Lucas, Prosper. *Traité philosophique et physiologique de l'hérédité naturelle.* Paris: Baillière, 1847-50.

McCormack, Jerusha H. *John Gray: Poet, Dandy, and Priest.* Hanover, N.H.: Brandeis University Press, 1991.

Merrick, Jeffrey, and Bryant Ragan, Jr. *Homosexuality in Modern France.* New York: Oxford University Press, 1995.

Micale, Mark S. *Approaching Hysteria: Disease and its Interpretations.* Princeton: Princeton University Press, 1995.

Morel, Bénédict. *Traité des dégénérescences physiques, intellectuelles et morales de l'espèce humaine et des causes qui produisent ces variétés maladives.* Paris: Baillière, 1857.

Näcke, Paul Adolf. "Einteilung der Homosexuellen." *Allgemeine Zeitschrift für Psychiatrie* 65 (1908): 109-28.

———. "Le monde homosexuelle de Paris." *Archives d'anthropologie criminelle* 20 (1905): 182-85; 411-14.

Nordau, Max Simon. *Dégénérescence.* 2 vols. Trans. August Dietrich. Paris: Félix Alcan, 1894-95. Originally published as *Entartung.* Berlin: Carl Dunder, 1893.

Nye, Robert. *Masculinity and Male Codes of Honor in Modern France.* New York: Oxford University Press, 1993.

———. "Sex Difference and Male Homosexuality in French Medical Discourse, 1830-1930." *Studies in Homosexuality, vol.* 9: Homosexuality and Medicine, Health and Science. Ed. Wayne R. Dynes and Stephen Donaldson. New York and London: Garland Publishing, 1992. 168-87.

Pick, Daniel. *Faces of Degeneration, A European Disorder, c.1848-c.1918.* Cambridge: Cambridge University Press, 1989.

Raffalovich, Marc-André. "L'affaire Oscar Wilde." *Archives d'anthropologie criminelle* 10 (1895): 445-77.

———. "Les groupes d'uranistes à Paris et à Berlin." *Archives d'anthropologie criminelle* 19 (1904): 926-36.

———. "A propos du roman d'un inverti et quelques travaux récents sur l'inversion sexuelle." *Archives d'anthropologie criminelle* 10 (1895): 333-36.

———. "Unisexualité anglaise." *Archives d'anthropologie criminelle* 11 (1896): 429-31.

———. "L'Uranisme. Inversion sexuelle congénitale." *Archives d'anthropologie criminelle* 10 (1895): 99-127.

———. *Uranisme et unisexualité. Étude sur différentes manifestations de l'instinct sexuel.* Paris: Masson, 1896.

Saint-Paul, Georges. *Thèmes psychologiques. Invertis et homosexuels.* Paris: Vigot, 1930.

Setz, Wolfram, ed. *Der Roman eines Konträrsexuellen.* Berlin: Verlag Rosa Winkel, 1991. German translation of Invert (1894-95).

Stein, Edward, ed. *Forms of Desire: Sexual Orientation and the Social Constructionist Controversy.* New York: Routledge, 1992.

Stendhal. *De l'amour.* Paris: Garnier-Flammarion, 1965.

———. *Lucien Leuwen.* Paris: Gallimard, 1952. In *Romans et nouvelles.* Ed. Henri Martineau. 1:733-1414.

Tardieu, Ambroise. *Étude médico-légale sur les attentats aux moeurs.* 7th ed. Paris: J.-B. Baillière, 1878 [1857].

———. *La Pédérastie.* 1857. In Fernandez.

Toulouse, Edouard. *Emile Zola.* Paris: Société des Editions Scientifiques, 1896.

Ulrichs, Karl Heinrich. *Forschungen über das Räthsel der mannmännlichen Liebe.* 4 vols. Ed. Hubert Kennedy. Berlin: Verlag Rosa Winkel. 1994 [1864-79].

Veith, Ilza. *Hysteria: The History of a Disease.* Chicago: University of Chicago Press, 1965.

Westphal, Karl Freidrich. "Die conträre Sexualempfindung: Symptom eines neuropathischen (psychopathischen) Zustandes." *Archiv für Psychiatrie und Nervenkrankheiten* 2 (1869): 73-108.

Wilhelm, Eugène. "Publications allemandes sur les questions sexuelles." *Archives d'anthropologie criminelle* 27 (1912): 301-9.

Zola, Émile. *La Curée.* In *Les Rougon-Macquart,* vol. I. Paris: Pléiade, 1963 [1871].

———. *Fécondité.* Paris: E. Fasquelle, 1899.

———. Preface. *Tares et poisons. Perversions et perversités sexuelles.* By Dr. Laupts (Georges Saint-Paul). Paris: George Carré, 1896. 1-4.

———. "Le Roman expérimental." *Oeuvres complètes.* Ed. Henri Mitterand. Lausanne: Cercle du Livre Précieux, 1968 [1880]. 1145-1203.

Michael L. Wilson (essay date 1998)

SOURCE: Wilson, Michael L. "Swishing on the Boulevards Extérieurs: Representations of Male Same-Sex Desire in *Fin-de-Siècle* Popular Culture." *Proceedings of the Western Society for French History* 26 (1998): 112-21.

[*In the following essay, Wilson concentrates on images of homosexuality in literature that was mass-produced in France at the end of the nineteenth century.*]

Twenty-two years after the publication of the introductory volume of Michel Foucault's *History of Sexuality,* we no longer think about the late nineteenth-century "invention" of homosexuality in quite the same way. An impressive body of scholarly literature has greatly enlarged and clarified our understanding of male same-sex sexuality in this period by focusing on medical discourse, the legal-juridical system, and canonical French literature.[1] Though careful to stress continuity across the entire nineteenth century in both the perception and practice of same-sex sexuality, these scholars identify the latter half of the century as producing strikingly novel moments of emergence, crystalization, consolidation or counter-discursivity. But would this now familiar narrative be confirmed if we alter the evidentiary base, if we move away from an examination of the

more accessible, better preserved official and elite records, to investigate more ephemeral, less complex and ambitious, less self-conscious and self-confident cultural productions? If we were to look at the venues through which the majority of the literate public would most commonly encounter and understand same-sex sexuality, how would this alter our construction of this Belle Epoque in the history of sexuality? Two caveats: first, I am at a preliminary stage of my research and lack sufficient evidence to make large claims. Second, I use "popular culture" in only one of its possible senses: those cultural artifacts mass-produced for a general audience of consumers.

I begin my limited excursion through *fin-de-siècle* popular culture with guidebooks to Paris. Guidebooks condense several characteristic aspects of nineteenth-century popular publishing: the identification of Paris as the center of French life, the almost compulsive transformation of the quotidian details of urban life into prescriptive written texts, and the desire to categorize and explain to the French themselves the nature of their society. For my purposes, the guides to touristic Paris are of little use. Though starting in the 1890s they increasingly include mention of the institutions of the lesbian subculture; even those volumes explicitly promising to reveal the hidden erotic delights of Paris-Babylon omit mention of male same-sex activities.

Instead, we turn to what might be termed works of popular sociology focusing on the urban underworld, popular guides to the Parisian "lower depths." The three representative and well-known titles I use here are: Charles Virmaître's *Streets and Brothels* (1882) and *Impure Paris* (1900), and Ali Coffignon's *Corruption in Paris* (1889).[2] These texts have several antecedents, including the early nineteenth century physiologies, those early descriptions of urban life with which Walter Benjamin was much concerned; the full range of social and moral reform tracts; and the products of literary naturalism. (Coffignon's book, for instance, is only one title in a Zolaesque series including *The Stomach of Paris, The Streets of Paris,* and *Behind the Scenes in Fashion*).

These three works have as their major focus the revelation to a supposedly ignorant audience of "the places of debauchery in the capital" and the burgeoning world of prostitution.[3] Prostitution was accorded great prominence in the imagination and social relations of nineteenth-century Paris, and was the focus of a variety of official, medical, legal and artistic discourses.[4] It is hardly surprising, then, that it is under the sign of prostitution—a potent symbol of the vagaries of sexuality, commerce and modernity—we find extensive investigation of another marginal but highly charged form of sexual commerce, "pederasty." The association of same-sex sexuality with crime or criminality is, of course, very ancient; the association with prostitution seemingly more recent but by this point well established. The basic outlines of the identification between prostitution and pederasty were formally established in two memoirs written by former officials of the Paris police, Louis Canler and François Carlier.[5] In both memoirs, pederasty is identified as a major social problem and the two texts are marked by a consistent effort to explain the phenomenon of pederasty as the inverted double of prostitution.[6]

The influence of Canler and Carlier on the guides to the underworld is quite direct. Not only do the authors acknowledge their debt to the writings of the police officials, but they aspire to a similar level of expertise and "insider" knowledge. They list the many terms used to indicate pederasts in slang: *pédé, bique, bouc, coquine, pédéro, tante, tapette, corvette, grégate, rivette, gosselin, emproseur,* Emile.[7] The writers detail the settings in which pederasts may be found; Virmaître is more concerned with their presence in popular music halls and balls, Coffignon with their secret meeting places and public cruising spots. Each offers suggestions on how to spot a pederast and in which professions they are most commonly to be found (both feel that the willingness of pederasts to serve leads them to work as waiters, valets and clerks).[8] Virmaître even provides his estimate of the number of male prostitutes working in Paris in 1900: 4,500.[9] Both writers are adamant in their identification of pederasty as a source of intense social disruption, overturning the most fundamental social hierarchies:

> It is no exaggeration to say that pederasts of all nations form a sort of freemasonry . . . The common vice effaces all social differences. The master and the manservant are on the same footing; the millionaire and the barefoot fraternize; the functionary and the repeat offender exchange their ignoble caresses.[10]

Coffignon goes even further in his emulation of his predecessors by formulating a taxonomy of pederasts to replace those conceived by Canler and Carlier. Like theirs, Coffignon's taxonomy has as its first principle that pederasty must echo normative heterosexuality in being divided into two "sexes"; pederasts are either active and passive—according to one's tastes, "a man or a woman."[11] In this sense, he warns, pederasty is unlike sapphism: its roles are very much entrenched. To stress this point, Coffignon details mock marriages, complete with ceremony and wedding banquet, carried on by pederasts in the neighborhood of Les Halles.[12]

Coffignon divides each of the two primary classes of pederasts into three subdivisions: active pederasts are either *amateurs, entreteneurs* or *souteneurs*; passive pederasts are divided into the *petit-jésus,* the *jésus* (of which there are three varieties) and the *tante.* These nine categories far exceed the four basic "types" detailed by Canler and even the six "types" identified by Carlier. To explicate briefly Coffignon's taxonomy: *ama-teurs* are older, more affluent and established men who are ashamed of their proclivities and engage in same-sex relations as part of a double life. *Entreteneurs* are "hardened" pederasts for whom the dangers of this life are part of its appeal; unlike the amateurs they are seen in public at all times of day with other pederasts. A *souteneur* is a habitual offender who has acquired the taste for pederasty in prison and who lives in common with a younger man, a *petit-jésus* or *jésus,* whose pimp he is. A *petit-jésus* is an adolescent or young man who happens into debauchery by chance but is rapidly introduced into prostitution, either as a street-walker or a kept boy. When a *petit-jésus* has lost his freshness—usually by age 20 but as late as 25—he becomes a *jésus*; a *jésus* may still work as a street-walker or be kept but often takes a job as a house-boy for other pederasts. Finally, the *tante* is the pimp of a female prostitute whose business dealings bring him into contact with pederasts, with whom he will have sex for money.[13]

What is most striking about Coffignon's delineation of sexual roles and identities is that they are not derived from ascribed gender—that is, activity or passivity—alone. Age, class, and financial need form important vectors, as do innate orientation and acquired taste. We notice easily the internal incoherence of this panorama of pederastic life that derives not only from the competing claims of what Eve Sedgwick has called universalizing and minoritizing views of homosexuality,[14] but from the uneasy mapping of male same-sex behavior onto the presumed roles of prostitute, pimp and customer. In assigning sexual roles putatively analogous to the positions taken in a commercial transaction, Coffignon dislodges the basic gender binarism that is supposed to undergird the taxonomy. Indeed, Coffignon seems to recognize that this system lacks coherence. In trying to account for what unites the spectrum of pederasts, he abandons his previous classification criteria and has recourse to an affective state, ferocity, by which he seems to mean an excess of emotion, irrationality in private relations, and a lack of personal control.[15] In this context, ferocity can be deployed to describe behavior across gender role, age, experience and class.

This stress on ferocity signals something of the interest of these authors in the exemplary or symptomatic dimension of pederasty, in its amenability to narrative inscription. Despite their sociological ambitions, these texts devote surprisingly little space to the "factual" description of male same-sex activity. Instead, they tell stories about it, inevitably cautionary tales centering on criminal activity. The most common form of criminality mentioned is blackmail; for these authors it is the most basic fact of a pederast's life and "the anonymous letter the grand weapon of combat."[16] Virmaître details several stories of blackmail, the most extended of which recounts the exploits of the "celebrated pederast Saurin" and his gang of *jésus.* One young man would lure a potential victim into a public urinal or other isolated spot at which point accomplices masquerading as the vice squad would "arrest" both men; en route to the police station, one of the "officers" would suggest a bribe, which would be invariably paid.[17] Each author suggests that the constant threat of blackmail also seems to encourage more serious crimes because the victim is unlikely to report them. For Coffignon, the ferocity of pederasty combined with the constant exposure to criminality can escalate to murder.

In order to make clear the "passion," "rage," and moral state of pederasts, Coffignon devotes an entire chapter to one such exemplary, "Pederasts' Love Drama."[18] The tale begins with the robbery of a grocery, the main suspects for which crime are the Simon brothers who, it is discovered, are actually not brothers but a male couple. In order to clear their names, the "husband" Simon leads the police on a tour of cafés. At one café, a police officer observes a frightened young man—whom Simon unconvincingly denies knowing—throwing away a wad of paper. Retrieved, it is found to be a letter written by someone named Blum from Mazas prison. When summoned by the authorities, the prisoner Blum, who has just been sentenced to eight years of hard labor, refuses to discuss either the robbery or what the police now believe to be a conspiracy of pederasts. By chance, as Blum is being interrogated, one of the officers notices that the man who had thrown away Blum's letter has just arrived at the prison, arrested for swindling. Brought together in the same room, the two men "fell into one another's arms and embraced with effusion."[19] When the police separate them again, Blum continues to refuse to speak but his partner, Thomas, confesses not only to the robbery of the grocery but to forty-seven additional robberies and to the murder ten years earlier of a furniture-store owner. Thomas confesses, it turns out, because he cannot bear to be separated again from his "wife," Blum, and hopes that by implicating them both in this series of crimes they will be sent together to New Caledonia. For Coffignon the final irony is that, though the men are indeed spared the scaffold and sent to the South Pacific, they have by that point broken up.

This "love drama" recapitulates all the sociological themes raised by Coffignon in his explication of pederasty: the pervasive but barely visible social ties between pederasts, the strict division of roles in same-sex couples, the ferocity yet ephemerality of affective ties between men, the lack of emotional control displayed by pederasts, and the identification of sexual dissidence with criminality (albeit crimes of violence rather than prostitution). These themes are realized, though, through a highly stylized narrative replete with all the thwarted investigations, false identities, secret alliances, and unexpected coincidences of a mid-century popular novel. But, similar as this and the other stories narrated by

Virmaître and Coffignon are to the genre of the crime novel, they are tied formally much more closely to the *faits divers*. Indeed, I suspect that subsequent research would be able to trace these specific "dramas" back to their origin as *faits divers*.

We are only beginning to explore the importance of the *faits divers* as one of the crucial means deployed to shape and satisfy what Vanessa Schwartz has identified as "the public taste for reality" in late nineteenth-century France.[20] The *faits divers* represented in concise, dramatic form [are] titillating and abject incidents from modern urban life. They stress the contrasts between different social milieux, the contingency and unpredictability of everyday life, the chaos underlying the seeming order of metropolitan routines, and the violence that could suddenly erupt in the city, especially among the poor and disenfranchised. The *faits divers* had paradoxical effects, offering readers a comfortable distance from the socially marginal yet creating a sense of impending social disruption.

The *faits divers* thus merit, but have not yet received, systematic examination to establish their representation of male same-sex desire. We do have, though, a survey made of *Le Journal* by a contemporary German writer who discovered twenty-seven *faits divers* concerned with male same-sex behavior between 1900 and 1913.[21] The majority of these items report the arrest of men engaged in sexual conduct of some sort; most of those arrested were having sex with partners of significantly disparate age or social status. Most articles concern either soldiers or sailors or men of social standing, such as a lawyer, judge, or teacher. Prostitution is mentioned explicitly only four times, and blackmail, robbery, suicide and murder are each a subject once. Though these short articles do not attempt to reconstruct a larger social milieu in the manner of Virmaître and Coffignon— *faits divers* are less explanatory than descriptive in character—they reiterate the thematics of pederastic criminality. The journalists who wrote the *faits divers* thus seem to reproduce even more directly the view of male same-sex desire formulated by the penal system: pederasty drives men to the crime of public sexual expression, with that expression itself providing an opportunity for an escalation of criminal behavior, either as victim or perpetrator. That pederasty is a crime against the social order is confirmed further by the inappropriate and socially asymmetrical couplings uncovered by arrest. Such a confluence of attitudes between the police and journalists is hardly surprising, given that the former were a primary source of information for the latter. Our reading of the larger social meanings of the *faits divers* will be found by placing these articles within the fragmented and discontinuous text of the newspaper itself. In their original setting, the *faits divers* are juxtaposed to—and may become alarming instantiations of—contemporary social and political issues such as the depopulation crisis, fears of national degeneration, and revanchiste tensions between France and Germany.

However, lest the condemnatory conflation of male same-sex desire with criminality and social disorder seem utterly over-determined, let us consider one last example of popular culture, a text in which the thematics being discussed are manifested in a rather different manner. In 1914, Francis Carco published his first work of popular fiction, *Jésus-la-Caille*.[22] The novel established Carco's reputation as a chronicler of "the milieu," the underworld of petty criminals and social marginals inhabiting lower Montmartre. In this world the slogan is: "Death to snitches and death to aunties!"[23] While not the first French novel to feature a "pederast" or "invert" as protagonist, it is the first to feature a male prostitute as a main character. At the beginning of the novel, Jésus's lover, Bambou, has just been arrested by the vice squad in a trap set by Dominique-le-Corse, a powerful pimp. Jésus's peregrinations of Montmartre in search of news of Bambou allows Carco to sketch the major features of the sexual underworld. As his nickname would suggest, Jésus is characterized as young, effeminate and timid, with "the pretty face of a girl, hardly made up."[24] He thinks of confronting le Corse about Bambou, but knows he would be "weak as a girl, cowardly and trembling like a girl before him."[25] He also knows he is without allies. Most people he knows are terrified of le Corse, and he's aware that in his friends from the bars, a trio of drag queens who haunt the narrative, he would meet nothing but "egotism and fright": "He knew them to be, among themselves, jealous and vile . . . He himself, in their circumstances, would be the same."[26]

Jésus, though, develops an unexpected alliance with Fernande, le Corse's lover. Fernande is intrigued by Jésus, attracted by his effeminancy, drawn to "this delicious and tempting equivocater, this little kid, this spoiled and sentimental doll."[27] The most detailed descriptions we have of Jésus are drawn from Fernande's ruminations on his delicate but powerful appeal: "His vice, which he displayed openly, threw her into extreme confusion and seduced her."[28] Though Fernande is unsure of what their relationship could be—"He was too much a woman for a woman"—she and Jésus become sexually involved. Unbeknown to both, le Corse is himself arrested as Fernande and Jésus spend their first night together.

The relationship between the two is doomed to failure, not least because Jésus spends a good deal of his time when in Fernande's company daydreaming about his romance with Bambou. Moreover, their coupling begins to take on the character of all her previous liaisons: Fernande supports Jésus though he grows less interested in her except when exerting his authority over her:

> Then, suddenly, he demanded money from her, took her in his arms and said 'Kiss me, little woman!'[29]

This almost parodic enactment of masculine dominance escalates to Jésus regularly battering Fernande, who finds herself unable to leave Jésus. Only the reappearance of Pépé-la-Vache, a rival thug who helped put le Corse in jail, enables Fernande to end the relationship with Jésus. She and la Vache begin a romance and Jésus, in turn, starts to live with the petit-Jésus la Puce, who is the brother of his jailed lover, Bambou.

The final third of the novel is concerned with describing these parallel romances, the more enduring of which, surprisingly, is that of Jésus and la Puce. Fernande leaves la Vache when she learns that not only is he a police informer but he's the one who helped send le Corse, whom she now realizes is the man she really loves, to jail. In the novel's tragic ending, le Corse returns from prison only to kill la Vache, a crime for which Fernande, in a desperate act of loyalty, takes the blame.

For our purposes, Carco's uneasy melange of naturalism, *chansons réalistes* and journalistic accounts of *les apaches* revises earlier popular texts identifying crime and pederasty in two significant ways. Though Jésus in most ways conforms to the stereotype of the youthful pederast, his affairs, first with Fernande and then with la Puce, break down the generalizations and typologies underlying most popular texts. His moving between same- and opposite-sex couplings and between passive and active roles does not admit of any conventional developmental narrative. The fluidity of Jésus's sexual behavior, moreover, is motivated by his shifting emotional needs, not economic necessity, advancing age or debauched sensibilities. The book's narrative also describes at length, in free, indirect voice, the physical and affective dimensions of Jésus's same-sex relationships. These passages are remarkably frank in their recounting of sexual desire, particularly Jésus's attraction for Bambou, a former circus acrobat, but link sexuality with the habits of domesticity and emotional intimacy. The character of Jésus thus possesses an interiority, a represented subjectivity, explicitly positioned as equivalent to that of Fernande. The thematic doubling of Jésus and Fernande is itself an ambivalent move, stressing the emotional lability and social marginality of both characters and reiterating the trope of gender inversion; but, hemmed in by what Carco calls the "instinctual hatred" of "Bambou, la Caille and those of their species,"[30] the novel expresses considerably more identification with and sympathy for such men than the other popular sources can generate.

To conclude, I'd like to hazard a few preliminary observations. Even in so limited a selection of popular texts, we can see the repetition of some familiar tropes in the representation of male same-sex sexuality: the description of same-sex relations as perversely imitative of normative heterosexuality; the strong association of pederasty with urban criminality, particularly prostitution; and the stress on the socially disruptive consequences of such sexual practices and identities. However, we might also note a few surprises. First I would point out how consistently the popular discourses take up the construction of male same-sex sexuality promulgated by the police and the penal system and how these texts are untouched by, even resistant to, the influence of the emerging scientific or medical discourse. The writers betray virtually no interest in investigating the origins or etiology of pederasty. Only Coffignon raises the matter—briefly—and he offers a bewildering and inconsistent set of explanations for sexual behavior between men: "physical deformity," childhood exposure, adult acquisition in schools and prisons, over-indulgence in heterosexuality, and sexual boredom.[31]

This points to a second observation: how incompletely and inconsistently these popular texts characterize male same-sex sexuality. The texts are marked by the very difficulty their authors faced in trying to make sense of their subjects. Indeed, the greatest anxiety in these texts centers not around those men who are recognizably pederasts but those who are not. The sometimes contradictory assumptions about pederasts that animate these texts—the shifting attention paid to the contingency of sexual acts, the persistence of affective orientations, and the vagaries of gender emulation—suggest that there did not yet exist a coherent, popularly-accepted model of sexual identity. The absence of such clarity may also in part explain the regularity with which representations of same-sex sexuality take the form of narratives, particularly highly convention-laden genres of narrative such as the *faits divers,* the crime story, the moral fable, and (however ironically) the love story. The narrative conventions may have worked to render male same-sex sexuality much more comprehensible to both their producers and consumers by depicting it in the terms of established social typologies and their attendant values. (The ability of the arrest—and, at a higher social level, the scandal—to force male same-sex sexuality into an otherwise elusive visibility and, further, to cast that visibility in the moral terms of judgment and punishment may also account for the pervasiveness of legal-juridical discourses in popular texts.) Finally, I would like to stress the degree to which in these texts pederasty is "discovered" as a phenomenon of urban modernity. Same-sex sexuality is located, described and judged as yet another of the pleasures and dangers of the crowded metropolis, a symbol of social confusion, illicit sensation and unimaginable possibilities. In particular, the Paris that emerges in these texts is an unpredictable social arena in which appearances are surprisingly, sometimes dangerously deceiving, relationships are intense but ephemeral and untrustworthy, Thus, these representations are freighted not only with the moral disapprobation that has historically been visited on sexual dissidence, but with the allure of forbidden knowledge and vicarious sensation, and the anxieties of people struggling with the forms and customs of modern civil society. Such a burden of cultural representation may seem too great to be carried by so slender a cultural figure as Jésus-la-Caille as he swishes down the *boulevards extérieures,* but that is precisely what I suspect he's doing.

Notes

1. Robert A. Nye, *Masculinity and Male Codes of Honor in Modern France* (New York: Oxford University Press, 1993); and his "Sex Difference and Male Homosexuality in French Medical Discourse, 1830-1930," *Bulletin of the History of Medicine* 63: 1 (Spring 1989): 32-51; Vernon Rosario, *The Erotic Imagination: French Histories of Perversity* (New York: Oxford University Press, 1997), esp. ch. three; Pierre Hahn, *Nos Ancêtres, les pervers* (Paris: Olivier Orban, 1979); Antony Copley, *Sexual Moralities in France, 1780-1980: New Ideas on the Family, Divorce and Homosexuality* (New York: Routledge, 1989); William Peniston, "Pederasts and Others": *A Social History of Male Homosexuals in the Early Years of the French Third Republic* (Ph.D. diss., University of Rochester, 1997); Paul Schmidt, "Visions of Violence: Rimbaud and Verlaine," *Homosexualities and French Literature: Cultural Contexts/Critical Texts,* ed. G. Stamboulian and E. Marks (Ithaca: Cornell University Press, 1979); Patrick Pollard, *André Gide, Homosexual Moralist* (New Haven: Yale University Press, 1991); J. E. Rivers, *Proust and the Art of Love* (New York: Columbia University Press, 1980); Eve Kosofsky Sedgwick, *Epistemology of the Closet* (Berkeley: University of California Press, 1990).

2. Charles Virmaître, *Trottoirs et lupanars* (Paris: Henri Perrot, 1882); and his *Paris Impur* (Paris: A. Charles, 1900); Ali Coffignon, *Paris vivant: La Corruption à Paris* (Paris: Kolb/Henry du Parc, 1889).

3. Coffignon, *Paris vivant,* 8.

4. Alain Corbin, "Commercial Sexuality in Nineteenth Century France: A System of Images and Regulations," *Representations* 14 (1986): 209-219.

5. Louis Canler, *Mémoires de Canler, Ancien Chef du Service de Sûreté* (Bruxelles: A. La Croix, 1862); François Carlier, *Etudes de pathologie sociale: les deux prostitutions, 1860-1870* (Paris: Dentu, 1887).

6. See Peniston, "Pederasts and Others," 53-64.

7. Virmaître, *Paris impur,* 234; see also his *Trottoirs et lupanars,* 155.

8. See, for instance, Virmaître, *Paris Impur,* 236.

9. Virmaitre, *Trottoirs et lupanars,* 155.

10. Coffignon, *Paris vivant,* 328, 330.

11. Ibid., 333, emphasis in original.

12. Ibid.

13. Ibid., 332-336.

14. Sedgwick, *Epistemology of the Closet,* 82-86.

15. Coffignon, *Paris Vivant,* 336.

16. Ibid., 335.

17. Virmaître, *Paris impur,* 232-235.

18. Coffignon, *Paris vivant,* 355-366.

19. Ibid., 360.

20. Vanessa R. Schwartz, *Spectacular Realities: Early Mass Culture in Fin-de-Siècle France* (Berkeley: University of California Press, 1998), esp. ch. two.

21. Numa Praetorius, "Homosexuelle Ereignisse in Frankreich," *Jahrbuch für sexuelle Zwischenstufen,* cited in Pollard, *André Gide, Homosexual Moralist,* 131-132.

22. Francis Carco, *Jésus-la-Caille* [1914] (Paris: Albin Michel, 1953).

23. Ibid., 13.

24. Ibid., 12.

25. Ibid., 23.

26. Ibid., 24

27. Ibid., 42.

28. Ibid., 34.

29. Ibid., 131.

30. Ibid., 12-13.

31. Coffignon, *Paris vivant,* 330-331.

Richard Nemesvari (essay date 2000)

SOURCE: Nemesvari, Richard. "Robert Audley's Secret: Male Homosocial Desire and 'Going Straight' in *Lady Audley's Secret.*" In *Straight with a Twist: Queer Theory and the Subject of Heterosexuality,* edited by Calvin Thomas, pp. 109-21. Urbana and Chicago: University of Illinois Press, 2000.

[In the following essay, Nemesvari studies Mary Elizabeth Braddon's presentation of "sexual identity [as] not fixed but fluid" in Lady Audley's Secret.*]*

Elaine Showalter has characterized Victorian sensation novels of the 1860s as "a genre in which everything that was not forbidden was compulsory."[1] Thus, much to the chagrin of many contemporary reviewers, these works focused on murder, attempted murder, bigamy, adultery, and a series of "lesser" transgressions that shocked and titillated their audience. Sensation fiction also tended to present sexual irregularities as being behind the crimes that drove its plots, something that played no small role in reinforcing its popularity.

There was, however, one "forbidden" sexual topic that could not be addressed directly, even within the risqué confines of these novels, and that was homosexuality. Nonetheless, the origins and themes of sensation novels allowed them to explore this taboo subject in ways unavailable to most other forms of "mainstream" mid-nineteenth-century literature. In *The History of Sexuality,* Foucault asserts that, as far as the categorization of homosexuality is concerned, "Westphal's famous article of 1870 on 'contrary sexual sensations' can stand as its date of birth."[2] The concept of "homosexual" as it has come to be understood in the twentieth century was therefore being formulated at almost the exact historical moment sensation fiction first achieved notoriety. As queer theorists have pointed out, however, the creation of this newly formulated "category" gave rise to an equally unprecedented sexual identification: that of the "heterosexual." It is perhaps not surprising that sensation authors found ways to explore the tensions produced by these provocative new distinctions in their texts—which, after all, were intended to startle, if not appall, their audience.

Thus, in *Lady Audley's Secret* (1862), one of the earliest and most successful examples of sensation fiction, Mary Elizabeth Braddon explores the anxieties produced in Victorian men by the development of male homosocial bonds. Eve Kosofsky Sedgwick's hypothesis of "the potential unbrokenness of a continuum between homosocial and homosexual—a continuum whose visibility, for men, in our society, is radically disrupted"[3]— becomes particularly evocative for this novel. By portraying her putative hero, Robert Audley, as driven by repressed homoerotic desires, Braddon exposes the denial that underlies Victorian society. The subtextual revelation of the unspeakable secret of male homosocial desire is essential to the text as, through his conflict with, and destruction of, Lady Audley, Robert determines his "proper" place on the sexual continuum and therefore learns to "go straight."

It has become something of a critical commonplace to describe sensation novels as "domesticated Gothic," since one of their most effective devices is the transferal of Gothic events and emotions from exotic and romantic locales into the heart of respectable, nineteenth-century Britain. In discussing Gothic fiction, Sedgwick makes the following observations:

> The ties of the Gothic novel to an emergent female authorship and readership have been a constant for two centuries, and there has been a history of useful critical attempts to look to the Gothic for explorations of the position of women in relation to the changing shapes of patriarchal domination. A less obvious point has to do with the reputation for "decadence": the Gothic was the first novelistic form in England to have close, relatively visible links to male homosexuality.

(*Between Men* 91)

The critical furore that surrounded the Victorian manifestation of this older genre and that led it to be judged as "more pernicious than its gothic and romantic ancestors"[4] was generated by sensation fiction's insistence that even the sanctified realm of Victorian domesticity provided no real barrier to the "deviant" criminal/sexual urges that seemed waiting to overwhelm it. By tapping directly into a series of Victorian uncertainties about gender roles and sexual identification, uncertainties that became increasingly difficult to repress as the century proceeded, these novels provided an expression of the "desperation and dissent" (Hughes, *Maniac* 36) underlying middle-class assumptions and values. For a writer like Braddon, then, this neo-Gothic form holds obvious attractions: as part of its literary inheritance, it already possesses the potentially subversive elements outlined by Sedgwick, while at the same time it provides an opportunity to bring them, both literally and figuratively, "home."

The disruptive threat posed by the novel's main female character, Lady Audley, is founded on her physical appearance and assumed personality, which so closely match the Victorian ideal of the "angel in the house" that they effectively cloak a willful character ready to dare bigamy and attempted murder to get what she wants. Along with a seemingly "amiable and gentle nature always . . . light-hearted, happy, and contented under any circumstances,"[5] she possesses "soft blue eyes" (6) and "the most wonderful curls in the world—soft and feathery, always floating away from her face, and making a pale halo round her head when the sunlight shone through them" (8). Braddon undercuts gender stereotypes by demonstrating that "the dangerous woman is not the rebel or the intellectual, but the pretty little girl whose indoctrination in the feminine role has taught her deceitfulness almost as a secondary sex characteristic."[6] Interestingly enough, however, the voluntary adoption and manipulation of this rigid cultural ideal by "Lucy Graham" illustrates a perhaps even more threatening characteristic: her elastic ability to define and redefine herself.

The string of names by which Braddon's female lead is identified throughout the text indicates a protean talent for escaping the constraints of a society that attempts to restrict women's social movement and definition. As Helen Maldon, daughter of an impoverished, half-pay naval officer, she quickly learns that if her situation is to improve, she must use her looks to achieve an advantageous marriage. When, as Helen Talboys, her new husband has his income cut off by his disapproving father and then abandons her for the goldfields of Australia, she reinvents herself as the governess Lucy Graham and takes the post that brings her into contact with Sir Michael. When he proposes to her, she hesitates only momentarily at the prospect of bigamy and then accepts him and her next identity as Lucy, Lady Audley. When word reaches her that her first husband has returned, she fakes the death of "Helen Talboys" to prevent the discovery of her crime and ensure the security of her new status; and when that first husband confronts her after accidentally discovering her fraud, she tries to kill him by pushing him down a well. Her final "incarnation," as Madame Taylor, is imposed on her by Robert Audley after he exposes her and expels her from England, locking her into an identity just as he locks her into a French *maison de santé*. This act thus symbolizes both his victory over her and his neutralization of the dangerous potential for unrestrained female autonomy she represents.

Lady Audley's refusal to accept the limited roles of impoverished daughter, deserted wife, and toiling governess acts as a covert critique of the narrow, unfulfilling roles available to women in general. More significantly, however, Lady Audley's fluid identity, her masculine insistence on self-determination, threatens a class hierarchy dependent on the assurance that women remain *passive* objects of exchange through which men determine and create their own status. By aggressively attempting to advance her own social standing—and, indeed, succeeding in that attempt—Lady Audley challenges her society's assumption that "the power relationships between men and women [are] dependent on the power relationships between men and men" (Sedgwick, *Between Men* 25). It is Robert Audley's task to meet and beat back the threat posed by Lady Audley by reestablishing the homosocial bonds she has disrupted. In doing so, however, Braddon has him reveal more about himself and the society he represents than he is willing to recognize.

When the reader is first introduced to Robert, he seems an unlikely candidate for the role of social guardian. Braddon goes out of her way to provide a description that would have been problematic to a Victorian audience—and problematic in some very specific ways:

> Robert Audley was supposed to be a barrister. . . . But he had never either had a brief, or tried to get a brief, or even wished to have a brief in all those five years, during which his name had been painted upon one of the doors in Fig-tree Court. He was a handsome, lazy, care-for-nothing fellow, of about seven-and-twenty; the only son of a younger brother of Sir Michael Audley. . . . Sometimes, when the weather was very hot,

and he had exhausted himself with the exertion of smoking his German pipe, and reading French novels, he would stroll into the Temple Gardens, and lying in some shady spot, pale and cool, with his shirt collar turned down and a blue silk handkerchief tied loosely about his neck, would tell grave benchers that he had knocked himself up with overwork.

(32)

Clearly, Robert has no real reason to work for his living, and his aristocratic background, even if he is not in its direct lineage, allows him to indulge in a leisured existence. Nonetheless, as a barrister, he is an official caretaker and defender of his society's laws. His social/sexual "development" throughout the text will be measured by a growing awareness of his responsibility to ensure that their authority is maintained, but his position before that realization takes hold is more interesting. David Skilton suggests that in *Lady Audley's Secret* "the use of French fiction is suggestive of a certain moral and intellectual atmosphere. . . . Audley's failing according to Victorian standards is a quite 'Continental' lack of moral concern and energy in relation to the serious issues of life. . . . But this lack of English moral fibre is vague and his amoral outlook quite unfocussed."[7] Thus, on one level, Braddon begins her text by providing a hero who is apparently in need of some kind of moral reform. However, the question of just how much his "English fibre" has been shaped by "Continental" influences needs to be explored further.

While Skilton is right to note that Robert's "amorality" never finds an explicit expression within the text, I think he has missed the implied significance of Robert's style of dress, his mannerisms, and his attachment not only to French fiction and German pipes but also, as Braddon later writes, to "Turkish tobacco" (113). Robert's tendency toward a laconic, drawling irony in his speech and his complete lack of skill and interest in fox hunting on his uncle's estate provide a foreshadowing of Wilde's quip about the unspeakable in full pursuit of the uneatable, and this anachronistic connection between the two is not completely strained. At the very least, a Victorian audience would have associated Robert's habits with the kind of Romantic decadence against which the period defined itself. But by the time Braddon comes to write her novel, the very word "decadence" has taken on a more specific connotation, as Sedgwick's previously quoted statement about Gothic fiction indicates. In outlining her exploration of potential reader responses to evocations of homosexuality, Sedgwick is careful to make clear how tentative any conclusions drawn from such generalizations must be, and I can only echo her cautions here. Still, her observations are helpful in this context:

With respect to homosocial/homosexual style, it seems to be possible to divide Victorian men among three rough categories according to class. The first includes aristocratic men and small groups of their friends and dependents, including bohemians and prostitutes; for these people, by 1865, a distinct homosexual role and culture seem already to have been in existence in England. . . . It seems to have constituted a genuine subculture, facilitated in the face of an ideologically hostile dominant culture by money, privilege, internationalism, and for the most part, the ability to command secrecy. . . . This role is closely related to—is in fact, through Oscar Wilde, the antecedent of—the particular stereotype that at least until recently has characterized American middle-class gay homosexuality; its strongest associations, as we have noted, are with effeminacy, transvestitism, promiscuity, prostitution, continental European culture, and the arts.

(*Between Men* 172-73)

Clearly, Robert does not fit all the characteristics presented here, or even perhaps most of them, but then I am not arguing anything so simplistic as that he "is" homosexual. Rather, Braddon has associated him with a recognizable aristocratic type possessed of, by this historical moment, clear homosocial/homosexual overtones. His equivocal social status—as a member of an aristocratic family fulfilling the middle-class role of a barrister—makes that association even more provocative in that it hints at the possible transference of this "style" from one class to another. From Robert Audley's first introduction in the text, therefore, Braddon subtly implies that her hero's most intense bonds will be between himself and other men, something that the novel's events bear out.

In particular, this view of Robert helps explain his reaction to the plot development that initiates the conflict in the text: George Talboys's return to England from Australia. When the two accidentally encounter each other, Robert is momentarily startled out of his air of supercilious detachment:

"Be so good as to look where you're going, my friend!" Robert remonstrated, mildly, to the impetuous passenger; "you might give a man warning before you throw him down and trample upon him."

The stranger stopped suddenly, looked very hard at the speaker, and then gasped for breath.

"Bob!" he cried, in a tone expressive of the most intense astonishment; "I only touched British ground after dark last night, and to think that I should meet you this morning!"

"I've seen you somewhere before, my bearded friend," said Mr. Audley, calmly scrutinising the animated face of the other, "but I'll be hanged if I can remember when or where."

"What!" exclaimed the stranger, reproachfully, "you don't mean to say that you've forgotten George Talboys?"

"No I have not!" said Robert, with an emphasis by no means usual to him; and then hooking his arm into that

of his friend, he led him into the shady court, saying with his old indifference, "and now, George, tell us all about it."

(34-35)

That Robert reacts "with an emphasis by no means usual to him," before his affected persona reasserts itself, demonstrates an attachment to George that has been elicited by no other character thus far in the book. The description that follows, however, is equally significant:

Robert Audley was for starting off immediately for the Crown and Sceptre, or the Castle, Richmond, where they could have a bit of dinner, and talk over those good old times when they were together at Eton. But George told his friend that before he went anywhere, before he shaved, or broke his fast, or in any way refreshed himself after a night journey from Liverpool by express train, he must call at a certain coffee-house in Bridge Street, Westminster, where he expected to find a letter from his wife.

(35)

This is the first time—but certainly not the last—in which George's wife is going to come between Robert and his friend, and his response to the information that George is married is more than a little revealing: "'The idea of you having a wife, George; what a preposterous joke'" (35). The text's passing reference to Eton provides the clue to Robert's reaction, for the attachments formed there were often more than platonic, and "candid accounts agree that in most of the public schools, the whirlwinds of the soul were often acted out in the flesh" (Sedgwick, *Between Men* 176).

It is hardly surprising, therefore, that when George receives the devastating news that his wife is dead and misses the boat that would have returned him to Australia, he "once more threw himself upon Robert Audley's hospitality," and "the barrister received him with open arms" (46). The potential disruption posed by George's "preposterous" wife is momentarily nullified, and the homosocial relationship Robert so clearly craves is reestablished when the two end up sharing his rooms. However, with George's mysterious disappearance, Robert is forced into the role of reluctant detective and into a confrontation not only with Lady Audley but with his own suppressed feelings. Throughout much of the rest of the novel, until the mystery is seemingly (re)solved, Robert finds himself both wanting and not wanting to pursue the various clues that present themselves. This ambivalence is paradigmatic of sensation fiction, for it "is a characteristic of Robert Audley's hunt . . . as of Walter Hartright's in *The Woman in White* and Pip's in *Great Expectations,* that revelation of truth will overwhelm the world of the hunter and of those he loves" (Skilton, "Introduction" xxi). But in *Lady Audley's Secret,* the protagonist's reevaluation of self is more potentially threatening than in the novels by Collins and Dickens because it entails questions of sexual identity. Braddon describes Robert's reaction to George's disappearance in the following passage:

If any one had ventured to tell Mr. Robert Audley that he could possibly feel a strong attachment to any creature breathing, that cynical gentleman would have elevated his eyebrows in supreme contempt at the preposterous notion. Yet here he was, flurried and anxious, bewildering his brain by all manner of conjectures about his missing friend, and, false to every attribute of his nature, walking fast.

"I haven't walked fast since I was at Eton," he murmured, as he hurried across one of Sir Michael's meadows in the direction of the village; "and the worst of it is that I haven't the most remote idea of where I am going."

(82)

This second reference to Eton again hints at the reason for Robert's intensity of response, and his perplexity about why he is acting this way and about "where [he is] going" suggests that on some level he does not *want* to analyze too closely the motives that are driving him. If it is in Robert's own interest to avoid the kind of sexual self-knowledge that seems poised to overwhelm him, however, at least one character in the novel possesses enough insight to make the most overt statement on this topic in the entire text. Alicia Audley, Robert's cousin, holds the distinction, along with her dog, of being the only character to dislike and distrust Lady Audley from the beginning. Her description of her new stepmother as a "wax-doll" (56) indicates an awareness of Lady Audley's calculated artificiality as well as a rejection of the angel-in-the-house stereotype that she wields so effectively. More significantly, Alicia's unrequited love for Robert apparently gives her a deeper perception of his passions than even he possesses.

As Robert's uneasiness about George increases, and as he becomes more and more fixated on his friend's unexplained departure, Alicia sarcastically exclaims: "'What a dreadful catastrophe! . . . since Pythias, in the person of Mr. Robert Audley, cannot exist for half an hour without Damon, commonly known as George Talboys'" (84). An illustration from Cicero's *De Officiis,* the story of Damon and Pythias—in which Damon stands as a hostage for Pythias, with his life forfeit if his companion does not return in time for his own execution—was for the Victorians representative of trust, devotion, and perfect friendship. Yet given the original setting of the tale, the Greek court and culture of Dionysius I of Syracuse, the association of Robert and George with Pythias and Damon has additional implications. An interesting parallel reference occurs in a letter that Arthur Henry Hallam sent to fellow "Apostle" Richard Milnes in 1831:

Whether it may not be better for you to take me on these terms, and to give up cheerfully the theory to which you have been visibly labouring to accommodate me, and which depends on the pleasant postulate that Arthur Hallam was once an enthusiast, and worthy to be the Pythias of that new Damon, Richard Milnes, but that all of a sudden the said AH became a reprobate, and is now grovelling on some "Alcian field," afar from everything ideal, beautiful and true, and consequently from the aforesaid Richard, this I leave you to consider.[8]

Richard Dellamora interprets this passage as Hallam taking "the opportunity to deny for the record that his earlier confidences may have included the fact that he 'was once an enthusiast': a term that Shelley, Hallam's father, and later Pater use to denote a male committed to sexual and emotional relations with other males" and further suggests that "in referring to Damon and Pythias, two heroic Greek lovers . . . Hallam specifies the context of Milnes's investments in male relationships" (*Masculine Desire* 27).

By alluding to a historical moment in which the homosocial bond between men was often initiated and confirmed by sexual relations and then directly connecting this allusion to her central male characters, Braddon briefly exposes the foundational "secret" of masculine desire that both Robert and his society attempt to elide. Alicia's accurate evaluation of Lady Audley lends credence to her "revelation" about Robert, and although the primary text never explicitly confirms her apparently passing remark, subsequent events in the plot certainly suggest its subtextual aptness. What Alicia has perceived, quite rightly, is that George is her *rival,* and eventually she will indeed lose Robert to "him," although in a way that leaves the homoerotic nature of their relationship safely unspoken.

The further Robert proceeds in his investigation of George's disappearance, the more agitated he becomes. He experiences a series of disturbing dreams and is much given to the kind of self-questioning that might lead him to give up his role as detective: "'Why do I go on with this,' he said, 'when I know that it is leading me, step by step, day by day, hour by hour, nearer to that conclusion which of all others I should avoid? Am I tied to a wheel, and must I go with its every revolution, let it take me where it will?'" (157). Although Robert tends to couch his reluctance in terms of the effect his disclosures may have on his uncle, it is not difficult to see in quotations such as this a personal fear of self-exposure. In *Epistemology of the Closet,* Sedgwick notes that "because the paths of male entitlement, especially in the nineteenth century, required certain intense bonds that were not readily distinguishable from the most reprobated bonds, an endemic and ineradicable state of what I am calling homosexual panic became the normal condition of male heterosexual entitlement."[9] This nicely describes the situation Robert finds himself in, for the further he proceeds, the more panicked he becomes about what he may uncover. Braddon's text

therefore reveals the way in which a growing awareness of the homosocial may incite homophobia, as Robert desperately, and at times angrily, struggles to deny the significance of his reactions. Finally, having reached such a psychological impasse that he is ready to abandon his search for the "truth," he decides that he will approach George's family for guidance. And it is here that he finds the resolution to his dilemma in the figure of George's sister, Clara.

Robert's interview with Mr. Talboys does not go very well, for George's father sees his son's disappearance as a ploy to create alarm and worry, thus forcing an eventual reconciliation with his rich and estranged parent. Further, George's sister remains silent during the exchange between Robert and Mr. Talboys and therefore seems to accept her father's cold response to the suggestion that her brother has been murdered. Robert takes their supposed indifference as a warrant for dropping his role as detective:

> "Thank God!" thought Robert Audley—"thank God! it is over . . . I shall not be the means of bringing disgrace upon those I love. It will come, perhaps, sooner or later, but it will not come through me. The crisis is past, and I am free."
>
> He felt an unutterable relief in this thought. His generous nature revolted at the office into which he had found himself drawn—the office of spy, the collector of damning facts that led on to horrible deductions.
>
> He drew a long breath—a sigh of relief at his release. It was all over now.
>
> (196)

Once again, the extremity of Robert's reaction suggests that the "disgrace" he has been saved from deducing is more personal than he might like to admit; but, as it turns out, he is given the opportunity to pursue the external element of his search while leaving its internal motives securely unexamined. Clara Talboys, following Robert's departure, runs after his carriage: "'Oh, let me speak to you,' she cried—'let me speak to you, or I shall go mad. I heard it all. I believe what you believe; and I shall go mad unless I can do something—something towards avenging his death'" (197). From this point on, it is Clara whom Robert will perceive as the driving force behind his investigation; she all but literally becomes the hand of fate "beckon[ing] him onwards to her brother's unknown grave" (253). The key point for my purposes, however, is Robert's perception, and the text's constant declaration, that Clara is exactly like her brother.

Robert's first perception of Clara is "that she was young, and that she was like George Talboys" (187). After this opening statement, we are told "she is like George" (189), that she has "brown eyes, like George's" (197), that "she was so like the friend whom he had loved and lost, that it was impossible for him to think of her as a stranger" (202), that her handwriting possesses a "feminine resemblance to poor George's hand; neater than his, and more decided than his, but very like, very like" (209), and that she has his "lost friend's face" (258). Clara provides Robert with the perfect object of transference and offers him the opportunity to turn his illicit homosocial desire for George in a socially acceptable direction. Indeed, Braddon goes out of her way to portray almost the exact moment of that transference; sitting alone in his rooms, Robert ponders his situation: "'It's comfortable, but it seems so d———d lonely tonight. If poor George were sitting opposite to me, or—or even George's sister—she's very like him—existence might be a little more endurable" (208). From here on, Robert's pursuit of Lady Audley receives an increased impetus, because the possibility of being forced to confront his own homoerotic responses is safely evaded. He is on the way to being "straightened out" as, through his detections, he relievedly (dis)covers his "true" sexual orientation.

Nonetheless, given the tensions the novel has been exploring, it is hardly surprising that Robert's eventual (and inevitable) proposal to Clara is more than a little conflicted. Having banished Lady Audley to France and having discovered that her attempt to murder George failed, Robert offers to search for him in Australia:

> "You are very good and generous, Mr. Audley," [Clara] said, at last, "and I feel this offer too much to be able to thank you for it. But—what you speak of could never be. By what right could I accept such a sacrifice?"
>
> "By the right which makes me your bounden slave for ever and ever, whether you will or no. By the right of the love I bear you, Clara," cried Mr. Audley, dropping on his knees—rather awkwardly it must be confessed—and covering a soft little hand he had found half-hidden among the folds of a silken dress, with passionate kisses.
>
> "I love you, Clara," he said, "I love you . . . and I shall love you for ever and ever, whether you will or no. . . . Clara, Clara!" he murmured, in a low pleading voice, "shall I go to Australia to look for your brother? . . . Shall we both go, dearest? Shall we go as man and wife? Shall we go together, my dear love, and bring our brother back between us?"
>
> (440-41)

The conflation here of Clara with George, of marrying the sister with searching for the brother, might leave even the most conventionally romantic of readers feeling a little uncomfortable. And Braddon drives home her point by never showing Clara actually consenting to Robert's proposal—or, indeed, saying another word for what remains of the novel. Instead, there is a break in the text, followed by an interview between Robert and Mr. Talboys that concludes with this statement by George's father: "'You are going to look for my

son. . . . Bring me back my boy, and I will freely forgive you for having robbed me of my daughter'" (441). With Lady Audley gone, women are securely back in their place as passive and silent objects of exchange, while the men are free to work out the (at this point safely heterosexualized) homosocial relationships that determine society's structures.

The final chapter of *Lady Audley's Secret*, which describes events two years after the main action, is so overdetermined that it can only be read as an ironic statement on what the novel has "revealed." George—who, as it turns out, went to New York instead of Australia after surviving Lady Audley's murderous attack—returns in time to prevent Robert and Clara from setting out on what would have been a fruitless search. Robert, a "rising man on the home circuit" (445), has established a "fairy cottage . . . between Teddington Lock and Hampton Bridge" (445) for his new family, which now includes a baby, and George "lives there with his sister and his sister's husband" (445). "Madame Taylor" dies of a *"maladie de langueur"* (446), and Audley Court, the scene of Lady Audley's sphere of influence, is shut up. The other main characters, while proceeding with their lives, are apparently centered on the blissful domesticity established by Robert, in which "the gentlemen sit and smoke in the summer evenings . . . [until] they are summoned by Clara and Alicia to drink tea, and eat strawberries and cream upon the lawn" (446). But this idyllic scene is undercut by the subtextual secrets that remain unaddressed. The nature of Robert's detections, which uncover just enough to banish the threatening female presence while concealing the male desire that cannot be named, has been "outed" sufficiently that the novel destabilizes the heterosexual norm of its closure. Robert has learned his lesson and been rewarded for it, but the text reveals the way in which homo- and heterosexual slide into each other and therefore subverts the rigid distinctions on which this type of categorization depends.

Victorian sensation fiction became popular at a time when there was a growing perception "that knowledge meant sexual knowledge and secrets sexual secrets, [and when] there had in fact developed one particular sexuality that was distinctively constituted as secrecy" (Sedgwick, *Epistemology* 73). Thus, *both* of the main characters in *Lady Audley's Secret* have guilty secrets that are revealed; but, within the text, only the one is called on to pay for her transgressions. Because Lady Audley's criminal activities of bigamy and attempted murder embody challenges to a male-constructed social order, she cannot be allowed to "go straight" and survive. Robert Audley, on the other hand, successfully negotiates the movement from "queer" to "straight" that his society demands be made by successful men. Braddon, by revealing this *as* a "negotiation," undercuts the kind of essentialist paradigm being generated at this particular historical/cultural moment and opens the disturbingly sensational possibility that sexual identity is not fixed but fluid. *Lady Audley's Secret* thus manages to be both feminist and queer at the same time, a combination that could be counted on to provoke some of the most basic anxieties and resistances of its mid-Victorian audience.

Notes

An earlier version of this essay appeared as "Robert Audley's Secret: Male Homosocial Desire in *Lady Audley's Secret*," *Studies in the Novel* 27:4 (Winter 1995): 515-28, and is used here by permission of the University of North Texas.

1. Elaine Showalter, *A Literature of Their Own: British Women Novelists from Brontë to Lessing* (Princeton, N.J.: Princeton University Press, 1977), 158.

2. Michel Foucault, *The History of Sexuality,* vol. 1: *An Introduction,* trans. Robert Hurley (New York: Random House, 1980), 43.

3. Eve Kosofsky Sedgwick, *Between Men: English Literature and Male Homosocial Desire* (New York: Columbia University Press, 1985), 1-2. Subsequent references to this work will be included parenthetically in the text.

4. Winifred Hughes, *The Maniac in the Cellar: Sensation Novels of the 1860s* (Princeton, N.J.: Princeton University Press, 1980), 5. Subsequent references to this work will be included parenthetically in the text.

5. Mary Elizabeth Braddon, *Lady Audley's Secret* (Oxford: Oxford University Press, 1987), 5. Subsequent references to this work will be included parenthetically in the text.

6. Elaine Showalter, "Desperate Remedies: Sensation Novels of the 1860s," *Victorian Newsletter* 49 (Spring 1976): 3.

7. David Skilton, "Introduction," in *Lady Audley's Secret,* Braddon, xiii-xiv. Subsequent references to this work will be included parenthetically in the text.

8. Quoted in Richard Dellamora, *Masculine Desire: The Sexual Politics of Victorian Aestheticism* (Chapel Hill: University of North Carolina Press, 1990), 26-27. Subsequent references to this work will be included parenthetically in the text.

9. Eve Kosofsky Sedgwick, *Epistemology of the Closet* (Berkeley: University of California Press, 1990), 185. Subsequent references to this work will be included parenthetically in the text.

Abigail F. Keegan (essay date 2003)

SOURCE: Keegan, Abigail F. "Coming to Terms: *Lara,* the Effeminate Page, and Queer Reading." In *Byron's Othered Self and Voice: Contextualizing the Homographic Signature,* pp. 129-43. New York: Peter Lang, 2003.

[*In the following essay, Keegan centers on Byron's connection between Greek homosexual love and the Victorian "effeminate" male homosexual in his poem* Lara.]

The eighteenth- and early nineteenth-century sense of dis-ease with homosexuality included a number of changed definitions of sodomy. The historian Randolph Trumbach, who locates the beginnings of the modern homosexual in the early eighteenth century, suggests that along with new denominations of the sodomite came changes in sexual practices. He argues that prior to 1700, men married women and had sexual relations with adolescent boys. After the development of the molly houses, the name sodomite was ascribed to men, married or not, who formed intimate relationships or engaged in sexual relations not only with boys but also with other adult men. Significantly, sodomites began to be described as men exclusively interested "in [their] own gender and inveterately effeminate and passive" ("Sodomitical" 119). Men also became increasingly subject to public scandal and the fear of being charged with being sodomites. Flamboyant clothing, gestures ascribed to female behavior, or excessive gesturing and cross-dressing were a few of the behaviors ascribed to the effeminacy of the subject.[1] Connections between sodomy and effeminacy underwent a translation into a metaphoric essential of equivalence; that is, sodomy equals effeminacy. This occurred, Lee Edelman argues, as sexuality went through a transition into a "metaphoric category of essence, into a fixed and exclusive identity" (*Homographesis* 11). Accompanying this shift, Trumbach suggests, was the denomination of the effeminate sodomite as of "another" gender, a "third sex," neither exclusively male nor exclusively female ("Sodomy Transformed" 106). This third sex was frequently made the object of derision and satire, and the term *effeminate* came increasingly to be a derogatory term; even now it remains as such, derogatory to both women and the men the term attempts to categorize. This cultural phenomenon suggests a certain readability of the body; its use or appearance signifies desire. It also implies a fluid boundary between the inside and outside of the individual subject.

This term, "effeminacy," held sway over the lives of men. Sexuality, closely bound up with the ideology of gendered binarism that produced effeminacy as a means of disciplining sexuality, produced many possibilities for (mis)reading hetero/homosexual identity. Identification of effeminate sexual difference made it imperative to recognize and expose the signs of homosexual difference. Unlike gender difference, homosexual difference threatened to remain undetected if not demarcated by the terms of effeminacy. Such markings, however, became more than just an excess of dress or gesture as effeminacy was linked to sexual practice. It also became associated with an excess of emotional expression of one man for another. In the early nineteenth-century, the Reverend John Church was one of the first Englishmen to perform marriages of sodomites in chapels and molly houses. He himself, several times accused but not convicted of sodomy, was moved from one church position to another. Finally he was positioned as a conventicle preacher at Obelisk Chapel, St. George Fields. While serving as chaplain to the Vere Street molly house, he fell in love with one of the men. A surviving letter of 3 March, 1809, to Ned B. (the last name was expunged from court records) points to the anxiety that surrounds the term effeminacy and homosexual affection and desire:

> I can only say I wish you was as much captivated with sincere friendship as I am. . . . Friendship those best of names, affection those sweetest powers like some powerful charm that overcomes the mind—I could write much on this subject but I dare not trust you—you would consider it unmanly and quite effeminate, having proved already what human nature is I must conceal those emotions of love which I feel.
>
> (qtd. in Norton *Mother Claps* 203)

Despite his desire to conceal his emotions, Church goes on to talk about his love for Ned, and his fears proved to be warranted. People who had been trying to find evidence to stop Church from performing illegitimate marriages for sodomites persuaded Ned to turn informer and use the letter as evidence against Church. The group tried to oust him through blackmail. However, some unknown person paid the blackmail fee, so Church was not convicted. What most interests me here is that the fear of being unmanly and effeminate is associated with a desire to express his affection and with the hope of altering the terms of his relationship to another man. The overdetermined significance of effeminacy suggests that the repetitious, discursive denigration of the term served not only to make abject figures of sodomites and thereby to delimit sexual practice, but effeminacy served also to develop psychological determinants for masculinity. Excesses of dress and gesture, associated with sexual practices of Sodom, are translated to fears about excesses of feeling and emotive expression between men. What has been a matter of social custom is internalized as psychological discipline. Stallybrass and White's outlining of the development of a refined, public body serves analogically to illuminate the effects of the development of the effeminate sodomite on male sexuality:

> The formation of a refined, cosmopolitan public, internally disciplined, was something which took place gradually over decades and even centuries; it was an almost geological shift in the cultural threshold of shame and embarrassment which regulates the body in public.
>
> (85)

They demonstrate the ways discursive denigration of bodily practices served to develop psychological structures that kept individuals from performing "unacceptable" public practices. Church's letter suggests that sexual practices and acceptable speech about sexuality and desire were affected by the derision of effeminacy. The fact that effeminacy was associated with dress, gesture, and forms of speech marked and disciplined not only the practices of the body, but men's very sense of themselves as sexual subjects. The repeated production of the degenerate, effeminate sodomite in public discourse served to regulate and discipline masculinity and sexuality. The anonymous author of the now frequently reprinted *Satan's Harvest Home* (1794), which offers its "Reasons for the Growth of Sodomy," suggests: "Master *Molly* [has] nothing to do but slip on his *head clothes* and he is an errant woman . . . as much in vogue as the ladies in France" (139). Such transformations produce "the height of aversion" in the author. But the most "hateful . . . pernicious" form of effeminacy is that of "men's kissing each other. The fashion was brought over from Italy (the Mother Nurse of Sodomy; where the master is oftener intriguing with his *page,* than a *fair lady*" (138-39). Such aversions and citations of aversions in response to the effeminate, "another sex," or a "third sex," and the paranoia that surrounds effeminacy mark the final inscriptions of Byron's own homographesis in the last poem of his series.

In the poem *Lara* (1814), Byron conjoins his own homoerotic desires for Greek heroic love between men with the figure of the effeminate third sex of his own era. Byron gives particular attention to visual elements of the poem, for within British society, the figure of the effeminate man suggests that how men look at one another has become extremely important. Byron destabilizes the verbally unrepresentable homosexual subject by the attention he gives to the visual. Further, he uses the effeminate, foreign page as a double entendre to bring into focus the connections between his own homosexual desire and his written page. The boundaries between the viewing subject and object are inverted several times within the poem as Byron analogically represents the unstable barriers between homosocial and homosexual identifications within the text. Male homosexuality, the poem suggests, shifts perspectives and as well affects how voices are heard in the poem, as he plays with the use of words and the use of auditory tropes to suggest the process of inside-outside identifications of the homosexual subject. Byron's use of visual tropes anticipates Oscar Wilde's writing in *Dorian Gray,* where, as Dennis W Allen suggests, Basil's portrait of Dorian and all the attention on scopic interactions in the novel allow for the expression of the "homoerotic desire traditionally excluded from verbal representation" (118). Byron examines the effects of homophobia on the relations between men and on their relation to a sense of self; he points to the confusion between identifying with another man and desire for another man in a climate of prohibitions. Finally, the poem submits to the discursive laws that insist on homosexual silence, but not without suggesting possibilities for subversive reading of sexuality. His attempt at inscribing the significance of the homoerotic to his own sense of self and to his writing within the frame of discursive prohibitions that denigrate effeminacy and homoeroticism reveals the brutal erotics of social regulation. Through a comparison of homoerotic with homosocial relations, the poem also exposes homosexuality as the constitutive necessity for a disciplined, heterosexual masculinity. Within inscriptions of silences and paranoia, social forms of men's relationships are contrasted with the homoerotic relationship of the protagonist, Lara, to his foreign page, Kaled.

Byron's poem is displaced in time to a medieval world rather than another culture. He keeps the doubled heroes of *The Corsair*, but this time he makes them collaborative equals. Lara returns from his journey to the East disaffected with his own country. He embodies Byron's sense of alienation, and Lara is perhaps a figure who exposes the British society's fear that men traveling to foreign places will find themselves changed. Byron himself came home and married Annabella Milbanke, who he hoped would reform him. One year after their marriage, they divorced and he, like Beckford before him, was forced to flee England amidst rumors and accusations of incest and sodomy.[2]

Despite the necessary displacements of the poem, it seems to resolve Byron's grief, but it is also a testament to his recognition of the significance of his personal and public experience of homosexuality to the formation of his writing. He was quoted by his wife as saying, "There's more in that [poem] than in any of them" and that it was the most "metaphysical of his works" (HVSV: 112). I suggest that the "metaphysical" is Byron's sense of his own moving beyond grief and at least provisionally beyond the prohibition of speech about homosexuality. Partly he finds a resolution to the grief that has not been allowed the significant acknowledgement of ritual and social support the death of lovers affords to legitimate relationships. In addition, he comes to terms with his own sense of his effeminate silences in the embrace of the page, Kaled. *Lara* is a complex work moving between and accepting and overwriting the negotiations of silence that Byron of necessity performed in regard to aspects of his own homosexual identity. As I have argued throughout, this is not an exclusive sense of identity, but an identity constituted in

relationship to a self posited within a sense of being a British male subject, a public figure, and a poet. Yet this poem suggests that Byron's homosexuality was a consistent aspect of his emergence and creation of himself as an author. He uses tropological signs of foreignness, effeminacy, and a page, combined with an emphasis on visual and verbal interactions between men, to bring his homosexuality into the realm of representation. But the poem also stresses the difficulty of making his homographesis recognizable in an oppressive climate.

The stripping away of the oriental material, with the exception of a foreign page, to invoke the world of the Gothic has its precedent in Matthew Lewis's *The Monk*, where cross-dressed Rosario allows Lewis the expression of homoerotic desire between Rosario and Ambrosio in the cloister. Cross-dressing serves as a means of concealing and revealing the homoerotic. And this use of illusion adds to Byron's representation of homosexual-homosocial paranoia, which Eve Kosofsky Sedgwick has argued is a significant aspect of many gothic novels.[3]

Lara, the protagonist, returns from the East to some secret past in a European setting, and to an all male world of no particular country. He resumes residence in his ancestral estate. He has brought with him a page from another country. Lara is a writer trying to cover over his past:

> Not much he loved long questions of the past,
> Nor told of wondrous wilds, and deserts vast,
> In those far lands where he had wander'd lone,
> And—as himself would have it seem—unknown[.]
>
> (1: 85-88)

He is also doubtful about his connections to the world to which he has returned. In his estate, he spends "night's long hours" walking through the "dark gallery, where his fathers frown'd" from the "antique portraiture" (1:136-38). He is separated from his personal past as well as from the tradition of frowning patriarchs. As Lara looks at other paintings in his hall,

> He turned within his solitary hall,
> And his high shadow shot along the wall:
> There were painted forms of other times,
> 'Twas all they left of virtues or of crimes,
> Save vague tradition; and the gloomy vaults
> That hid their dust, their foibles, and their faults[.]
>
> (1: 181-86)

The portraits' painted forms, crimes and vague tradition of dust and foibles, impose on the poem an idea that looking, identifications, and misidentifications will be a central concern for Lara. The solitary hall, suggestive of his own unconscious, also gives hints of a repressed history of crimes and faults, but it is a repressed social and personal history. Such a history, coming just after the frowning tradition of the fathers, reveals a character who is as distant and disassociated from his own past as he is from the tradition of the fathers and their patrimony. The narrator says that this sense of history, this seemingly disconnected and vague tradition, is recorded in "specious tales from age to age; / Where history's pen its praise or blame supplies / And lies like truth, and still most truly lies" (1:188-90). The specious tales of different ages suggest Byron's own use of the previous tales; personal history in these narrative tales reflects the buried crimes and lies that serve to constitute public and private history. Lara's face is reflected into windows, and the reflection gives "[h]is aspect all that terror gives the grave" (1: 200). The writer's image is marked by refracted images of a self and, as in the other poems, the self is intimately associated with fear and the grave. The history, the secret of crime, has left its impression on the hand of the writer, a "shaken plume" substitutes for the severed, shaking hands of the previous poems; tales that have "lied like truth," continue, because of patrimonial structures, to be made of lies and indirections. The dim shadowy self finds its way to its own terrors in the act of writing of things it is forced to conceal.

In contrast to his isolation in the halls of his fathers, Lara's relationship to his foreign page affords solace and articulation of things not quite speakable, or perhaps not quite imaginable within the halls of the fathers. With Lara, Kaled presents possibilities of intimacy in men's relationships:

> If aught he loved, 'twas Lara; but was shown
> His faith in reverence and in deeds alone;
> In mute attention; and his care, which guess'd
> Each wish, fulfill'd it ere the tongue expressed.
>
> (1: 554-57)

Lara evokes feeling in Kaled, even if it is indirectly expressed. Kaled is the ideal lover, a second self who anticipates and allows for Lara's language. Kaled's ability to read Lara in "mute attention" creates his care and his wish to fulfill Lara's desires. And yet, Kaled's posture expresses a certain "haughtiness . . . his air commands; / As if 'twas Lara's less than *his* desire / That thus he served, but surely not for hire" (1: 558-63). The poet's emphasis on *his* suggests that the sex of Kaled is of a primary concern here. The boundaries between these two are not absolute but fluid and, as the poem goes on, transitive. The boy page is submissive, but he is a "haughty male," capable of entering into combat as the tale progresses.

Kaled achieves a kind of intimacy with Lara that no other characters share in the tales. When Lara wakes, startled by a dream in the night, he faints, and Kaled goes to his side, bending over him and comforting him

in a language no one else understands: "And Lara heeds those tones that gently seem / To soothe away the horrors of his dream" (1: 243-44). Their shared language allows Kaled to understand him without speaking. The erotic boy bending by his master and the page intersect in a homoerotic dream that relieves the nightmare, the secret terror of the darks halls in which Lara often finds himself. The emphasis on Kaled's tones that soothe horrors suggests that the figure of the page allows Byron homoerotically to enact a relationship in writing that soothes the tones of grief and horror that have been repeatedly reinscribed in the earlier poems. The page Kaled's relationship to language and tone reveals Kaled as a doubled figure, one that embodies Byron's ideal homosexual relationship and simultaneously links his language to the homoerotic. The page both expresses and veils the homoerotic desire that animates Byron's written page here and in the previous poems.

Within a land of "many a malcontent," a "soil full" of "many a wringing despot . . . / Who work'd his wantonness in form of law" (2: 157-60), Lara and Kaled's relationship stands in contrast to the relationships Lara has with other men. The wanton law inverts the focus of wantonness from the homoerotic to the law which would judge it. In Kaled's mind, the shared secrets and silent communications between him and Lara resemble a kind of marriage, one which defies the wanton, despotic laws of gendered and heterosexual imperatives that dominated the previous tales. Kaled vows to Lara, "We will not part! / Thy band may perish, or thy friends may flee, / Farewell to life but not adieu to thee!" (2: 357-59). Like Byron's repeated reinscriptions of the loss of homosexual love, Kaled's vows promise fidelity more permanent than the vows "until death do us part" (Giuliano 798).

When Lara looks on Kaled, what he describes is a figure not unlike an effeminate sodomite, the figure of another sex, whose color is not dissimilar to a printed page. The narrator says of Lara that he first looks at Lara's hand and then he continues the admiring gaze on Kaled:

> So femininely white it might bespeak
> Another sex, when match'd with that smooth cheek,
> But for his garb, and something in his gaze,
> More wild and high than woman's eye betrays;
> A latent fierceness that far more became
> His fiery climate than his tender frame:
> True, in his words it broke not from his breast,
> But from his aspect might be more than guess'd
> Kaled his name, though rumour said he bore
> Another ere he left his mountain-shore[.]
>
> (1: 576-85)

That third sex, that name not quite speakable, that glance between two male lovers misinterpreted by Jeffrey's comments about the Thryza lyrics, and the latent fierceness of a desire more wild than a desire for a woman is connected to the hand that writes the page. A number of scholars have commented on the homoerotic quality of the gaze between Kaled and Lara. The comments seem quite brief but most agree that this is Byron's means of providing a homosexual moment in a repressive society. Nigel Leask argues that this discomforting homosexual gaze may be a sign of Byron's anxieties about transgressively "orientalizing classical forms" (56).[4] The connection between these male lovers does not last; finally Kaled will be returned to the wanton laws of the land and revealed to be a female. However, before that happens, Byron has made the reader complicit in the secret glances of homoerotic subject and his object of desire, the effeminate male page.

Even the final revelation cannot arrest the unsettling experience of being in a world of guessing and suspicions, of gazes not quite certain.[5] Byron plays further on the fluid boundaries of homoerotic pages. Kaled and Lara's relationship is placed in relief against the social sphere of lords and manor houses, a festival and another kind of gaze. As the poem develops, the wanton laws of the land corrupt men's gazes into spectacles of surveillance. Looking, seeing, revealing, and reading men's signs dominate the twists and turns of the poem as Byron foregrounds and betrays his view of the relations of men. Lara attends a festival at the neighboring manor house of Sir Otho. In a pose we might now identify as cruising, Lara looks across a crowded room: "his glance follow'd fast each fluttering fair, / Whose steps of lightness woke no echo there" (1:399-400). The fluttering and lightness of fair steps are unattached to pronouns, but suggestive of feminine or effeminate excess. Yet there is no echo there; the not-quite-rightness of the gaze only makes him continue looking for something. Soon the looking for an echoing gaze will, like the letter of John Church, turn to a scene of betrayal:

> He lean'd against the lofty pillar nigh
> With his folded arms and long attentive eye, . . .
> At length he caught it, 'tis a face unknown,
> But seems as searching his, and his alone;
> Prying and dark, a stranger's by his mien,
> Who still till now had gazed on him unseen:
> At length encountering meets the mutual gaze
> Of keen enquiry, and of mute amaze;
> On Lara's glance emotion gathering grew,
> As if distrusting that the stranger threw;
> Along the stranger's aspect, fixed and stern
> Flash'd more than thence the vulgar eye could learn.
>
> (1: 401-2; 405-15)

The frisson of the gaze promises the lure of the erotic. But the lines after "emotion grows" begin to disturb what seemed to build toward a sexual encounter. The allure of the stranger turns to a stern look. Byron's tales are repetitive to a fault; age after age, they "lie like truth and still most truly lie" (1: 190). More than "the

vulgar eye could learn" turns the focus of the poem all the way back to *Childe Harold* and the vulgar eyes of the crowd that watched the killing of the bull, and to the vulgar eye that misperceived the secret glances between Byron and Edleston in the Thryza poems, as Byron begins to tie his vision of the earlier poems to the fears that kept the homoerotic unseen. The gaze between Lara and Sir Ezzelin leads to accusations, to violence between men, and to disturbing memories. The possibilities of reading gazes between men in this social structure appear to be perilously limited. The choices are identification with the "vulgar eye" of an "alien stranger's aspect" or the enticement of a gaze that too easily turns to surveillance and accusation. In this narrative of men's relations, surveillance leads to death. Sir Ezzelin ruptures Lara's desire for a mutual gaze:

> 'Tis he!' the stranger cried, and those that heard
> Re-echoed fast and far the whisper'd word.
> 'Tis he!—Tis who?' they question far and near,
> Till louder accents rung on Lara's ear;
> . . . though still the stranger gazed;
> And drawing nigh, exclaim'd with haughty sneer,
> 'Tis he!—how came he thence?—What doth he here?'
>
> (1: 415-18, 424-26)

The echoes of alienation repeat the sense of displacement Lara felt earlier in the poem and that the tales have repeated throughout. Recrimination and reproach and fear of being identified for an unnameable crime committed in the past resound in Sir Ezzelin's words as he accuses: "Art thou not he? whose deeds—" (1: 455). The unnameable crime might be anything; the more unnameable, the more powerful the anxieties it produces. Byron has learned how to manipulate the horror that surrounds the silence of unnameable crimes. To the insidious but unspecified accusations Lara responds: "What'er I be, / Words wild as these, accusers like to thee / I list no further; those with whom they weigh / may hear the rest" (1: 455-58). Within the "wordy war" (1: 466), attack, scandal, social displacement can all ruin a man's reputation; it is the way of public life.

Lara's desires to be seen in public, and his desires to find the sympathetic, mutual and erotic gaze of another man leave him open to questions about his identity, his past memories, his secrets. The ideal relationship of companionship and bonding Lara shares with his page is contrasted with his public engagement with Sir Ezzelin. What is erotic, homosexual, and narcissistically healing of the wounds of Lara's past in relation to Kaled is contrasted with the accusation and social climate of fear in the doubled gaze and voice of Sir Ezzelin echoed in the crowd: "Tis he—Tis who?" The confusion about who Lara is, what he is guilty of, creates an environment ripe for misunderstood and misdirected recriminations between men. It creates a mood of repression through echoing tones of accusation.

This dramatization develops into a rupture of Lara's identity. The voices outside of Lara move inside. Accusations are directed toward memory. To the Lara barely recognized, Sir Ezzelin triggers memory: "Gaze again" says Ezzelin. (The syllables of "Ezzelin" and "Edleston" do not sound altogether dissimilar; it could almost be a slip of the tongue, floating in the air like Zuleika's name and ringing on the ear). Whatever this unmentionable crime is, "'Eternity forbids thee to forget.'" (1: 442). The public voice rings "louder" upon Lara's ear, the private ear of the self. And despite his disavowal of the claims Ezzelin makes he must accept the duel to which Ezzelin challenges him. No court need preside; the challenges of social structures are relocated within the self and within relations between men. To Ezzelin's challenge, Lara stands silent and "heedless of all around," his thoughts, drifting far away, "[b]espoke remembrance only too profound" (1: 489). In the face of threat, this memory cannot be spoken directly; silences allow men to be controlled in memory and body.

Only one stanza later, Kaled, with Lara, is able to recall: "Friends,' kindreds,' parents,' wonted voice recall, / Now lost, abjured, for one—his friend, his all" (1: 525-26). Significantly, in what I would mark as the climax of the poem, the subject-object position of Kaled and Lara is reversed. Lara, who is usually mirrored by the page Kaled, "awakes" something in Kaled's ear with his voice. Lara's "lips breathed into life" the page's memory. The writer's voice gives a gift to the page, a gift that honors the one abjured, the ones lost, the ones who would otherwise be unremembered or only remembered in disgrace. The "clear tones" of the voice echo like a choir boy's. In the violent world of dueling men, such intimacy is possible only in coded memories and in death. Such is the heart of Byronic irony.[6]

Sir Ezzelin mysteriously disappears in the night. Some critics have suggested he was killed by the page Kaled, but the poem is unclear.[7] Within the social structure of secrets and accusations that the poem represents, the circumstances of men's deaths might well remain secret.[8] However, Lara is suspected by Sir Otho and, as the narrator says, Lara "must answer for the absent head / Of one that haunts him still, alive or dead" (2: 155-56). The poem builds on the tension of things unknown, things like death and the disappearance of men. Although it is not yet clear at this point in the plot whether Ezzelin has died or merely disappeared, Sir Otho, the owner of the manor house where the festival was held, decides he must defend Sir Ezzelin's honor against Lara. "Otho's frenzy would not be opposed" (2: 64). The climate of fear and accusation produces frenzied ideas of honor in irrational men whose insults turn to weapons (1:165). Few actions prove heroic in a climate such as this, and no man can have the "confidence" to "trust mortal look or speech" of another man (1: 506-7). Within such an environment, individual men

like Lara live in "guilt grown old in desperate hardihood" (1: 505). The effects of accusation, guilt, fear, and the frenzy of honor, move almost palpably inside and outside the voices of these men. Determining who is guilty for the death of another man weighs on the eternity of the times. This is the homeland to which Lara returned. The encounters with Ezzelin and Otho leave Lara only with his foreign page.

There are two battles between Sir Otho and Lara. In the first Otho is wounded, but he later returns to do battle again. And though it is Otho who wants a repeat battle, it is Lara, the writer, once publicly humiliated by accusations, who waits for "[t]he deep reversion of delay'd revenge" (2: 206). The tone of revenge is only part of what motivates the desire of the narrative. Within this historical frame, Byron is able to alter the terms of death from punishment for some past crime to scenes of battle. Lara, while waiting for the ensuing fight, has been engaged in freeing serfs for whom his "soul knew" compassion. The serfs to whom Byron refers I would believe to be his subjected readers. The extreme popularity of Byron's writings with men and women perhaps suggests the paradox that a powerful sexual myth is evoked within his writings. Fears for sexual, domestic, and national security and restrictions and failures of ideals both created and provoked identifications. The erotic charges of enslavement and the struggle for individual freedom of the hero and heroines of the tales and sexual role-reversals must have allowed for identifications and disavowals the emerging bourgeois reader sought.[9] Now, because of Lara's "well-won charms of success," "[a]ll now was ripe, he waits but to proclaim / That slavery nothing which was still a name" (2: 210-11). The deep reversion points back to the slavery of things unable to be named, things like "another sex" and social displacement. Lara's success provides him with at least a modicum of the freedom of revenge.

Lara is killed in his duel with Sir Otho, which might suggest that revenge was not achieved. However, in the death scene, the revenge sought becomes clearer and the series of poems turns the reversion all the way back to Byron's *Hours of Idleness*. Lara dies in manly combat with his young page fighting at his side. Kaled and Lara are united in a way that others watching the death "understood not, if they distinctly heard." Lara turns to Kaled, for "[h]is dying tones are in that other tongue." The words bear the tone of elegy that has marked these works throughout:

> His dying tones are in that other tongue
> To which some strange remembrance wildly clung.
> They spake of other scenes, but what—is known
> To Kaled, whom their meaning reach'd alone;
> And he replied, though faintly, to their sound,
> While gazed the rest in dumb amazement round:
> They seem'd even then—that twain—unto the last
> To half forget the present in the past;

To share between themselves some separate fate,
Whose darkness none beside should penetrate.

(2: 444-53)

The splitting in twain of the turban is rejoined here in an act of revenge against "dumb amazement" that gathers round this language without understanding what has been repeated again and again in the previous tales. The dark which none should penetrate seems the other side of silence, and the "should" perhaps a warning and a challenge, a desire to be read and to remain silent. Byron invites a reading, a penetrating, of this homosexuality and yet commands that it remain a secret.

Lara's life does not end with this tone of revenge. As Lara dies, Nisus once again lays his breast upon Euryalis in a scene of overdetermined meanings. The effeminate page becomes the heroic lover as Lara, the writer, who has fought for his life with the eternity of another's memory in mind, lays his head upon Kaled's breast:

His limbs stretch'd fluttering, and his head dropp'd o'er
The weak yet still untiring knee that bore;
He press'd the hand he held upon his heart . . .

(2: 492-94)

When Lara is finally dead, the narrator says that Kaled

. . . saw the head his breast would still sustain,
Roll down like earth to earth upon the plain.

(2: 506-7)

Many silences are overwritten with this scene. The lost bodies of the homosexuals, the names not quite speakable, are written and visualized as heroes joined. The borders of the manly and unmanly are blurred as Byron joins the two men. The hand of the writer is placed against the body of the lover, the homoerotic page. For Byron, at last a plain and a public burial takes place as the lover's body is laid to rest upon the earth. But Byron's Greek homosexual ideal proves to be a dream deferred. Like the song of Keats' nightingale, homosexuality is that which cannot last, that which is trodden down by death and a history of disparaged bodies, but to speak what is not quite speakable or knowable is the impulse of Byron's voice. The homosexual is never completely realizable or graspable within the public world in which Byron's poetry was written.

Gender and heterosexual imperatives reinhabit the poem. After Lara dies, Kaled reveals her sex to be female. The sign of the not-quite-right, effeminate sex is effaced by a woman. As Byron resolves his own inner divisions, ironically he evokes the annihilation of his male page.[10] This annihilation may signal Byron's death into an effeminized self. At the same time, Kaled as a cross-dressed woman has deceived Lara, even as Byron

deceived the reader. Kaled's revelation of her transvestitism reminds readers that the discourse of heterosexuality depends upon the violent enforcement of the fictions of gender difference.[11] Sex must be confessed in its proper forms:

In baring to revive that lifeless breast,
Its grief seem'd ended, but the sex confess'd;
And life return'd, and Kaled felt no shame—
What now to her was Womanhood or Fame?

(2: 516-19)

The capitalizing of Womanhood seems an excess of emphasis, like an excess associated with cross-dressers. Separation from grief is short-lived: "Her tears were few, her wailing never loud; / But furious would you tear her from the spot / Where yet she scarce believed that he was not" (2: 603-5). She is still wild and fierce in grief. Kaled suggests that Byron remembers homosexual loss by reinscribing it, trans-sexing and cross-culturing it. Kaled takes over the grieving voice of previous poems in her foreign tongue. But the forced notion of sexual difference in her voice becomes a kind of insanity. She shaves off her raven hair and "She talk'd all idly unto shapes of air" (2: 609). Like the tongued air of Zuleika, she is whispering idly of a man's name.

Kaled "trace[s] strange characters along the sand" (2: 625), and her mad articulations in a strange tongue suggest that hers is a voice that crosses over sexes and the rigid structures of signs. Kaled is a figure who can only be read on the edges, the margins of a man's writings, like the scribblings in Bentham's margins or Hobhouse's notes in Byron's biography. She madly insists that there are signs of sex here to be interpreted, even for those who stand in "dumb amazement" wondering whether Kaled's and Lara's relationship was sexual or not. Byron's narrator says, "This could not last—she lies by him she lov'd; / Her tale untold—her truth too dearly prov'd" (2: 626-27). As Giuliano points out in her discussion of Kaled, the ambiguous dangling clause in the last line of the poem refers to Kaled's imperceptible scrawling and her very tentative hold on life (804). Yet the narrator's intrigue of the line seems to insist on interpretation: to read Kaled's page is to read the mutability of (homo)sexuality into our fictions of history. Kaled's dangling grief and untold tale invite us to read past the shrouds of misrecognition that silence empowers. The cryptic figures in sand imply that the solid ground of the sexual subject is a fiction that can be loosed from the stranglehold of silence, reinscribed, effaced, but not finalized. The movement of language bears "imagined spectre[s] in pursuit" (2: 622). Our ability to read these lines might also mean that the racialized and gendered discourses that the oriental tales often invoked and covered-over in silence might inevitably lead to their own death. Kaled too dies; she will not be productive; she claims no country. The cultural ideologies that have commanded sex to have social meaning, definition and the certainty of regulation fade in her strange characters of sand.

The transitive nature of Kaled's sexuality, "the untold tale" "too dearly proved," asks for rereadings of what sexuality might mean. The page's ending, like the poems themselves, prohibits a final knowing, a final understanding of the sexual subject.

Notes

1. See King on the semiotics of the effeminate body in the eighteenth century. King distinguishes specific dress and gestures that were used to identify sodomites and to separate the bourgeois values from the slothful effeminate gestures and dress of the aristocracy, 23-50. Davenport-Hines also identifies the features of the effeminate sodomite that had become standardized by the time of Tobias Smollett's inscription of him in *Roderick Random*, 88-90. See Cady's discussion of distinctions made between a homoerotic "masculine love," such as Francis Bacon's homoerotic attractions to other men, which envisioned peer relationships, and the homoerotic love that involved the love of boys, 14-33. I note all of this to suggest that, as Trumbach, King and Davenport-Hines suggest, effeminacy in male-male relations was viewed differently in the Renaissance than in the eighteenth century. Eighteenth century inscriptions of effeminacy were repeatedly associated with an abject subject, a debased social position. Woods says that the effeminate boy in Marlowe's poetry is a figure invested with signs of power. Effeminate ornamentation augmented and assisted a boy's entry into manhood. Effeminate boys were also perceived as a threat to the state because desirous men might be distracted from public affairs, 69-84.

2. Crompton offers an important discussion of Byron's marriage, divorce, and ensuing scandals as well as Byron's exile in Italy in his chapter "Fame and Exile" 196-235

3. Sedgwick's *Between Men* is a study of the ways gothic novels are marked by the savage "patriarchal oppressions of homosexuals," 3. I am sympathetic to and rely upon her readings of homosexual oppression and the ways the construction of homosexuality haunts heterosexual romantic triangles to reveal homosexual panic and homosocial paranoia. The gothic, with its attention to psychological and social structures, does afford the possibilities of revealing the social paranoia and psychological conflicts homosexual writers faced.

   I also believe that the tradition of patriarchy has a dominant role in these social structures, and By-

ron's own inscription of the force of patriarchy in providing portraits for what a man should be marks the beginning of this poem. However, the development of the domestic life, which women were both subjected to and participants in is a factor Sedgwick ignores.

4. See also Crompton 206-209; Hammond 119.

5. See Hammond's discussion of the unsettling homoerotic gaze 120.

6. On the representation of violence between men, see Cottom's study of Sir Walter Scott's Waverly novels and his discussion of distinguishing civilization from decadence in relation to the law. "Codes of behavior required by society make it so difficult for men to have sure understanding of each other that a pressure develops for violence that would penetrate social forms," 175. Similarly, within this poem, violence is the only possible outcome. See also Franklin's brief notes on Scott's romance poetry. Although it is a different genre, she says that his heroines "exhibit puritanical preoccupations." In addition, restrictions on sexual passion are mixed in Scott with an idealization of a "pre-sexual childhood innocence," 28, and in his letters, a dread of the onset of puberty, 28. Consideration of forms of male violence and sexuality might yield much if studied in relation to the social regulation of sodomy in readings of Scott's works.

7. On the metaphysical and metaphorical level I would like to believe the page killed Sir Ezzelin's accusation. But within the structures of theory and interpretation, such wishful thinking is subjectively romantic.

8. Within the discursive world that the poem never fully represents, in addition to hangings, blackmail and secret deaths of sodomites or people who were threats to powerful sodomites were not uncommon. Norton records a number of murders and blackmail intrigues which followed the discovery of aristocrats' homosexual relationships, *Mother Clap's* 212-231, and Crompton's biography of Byron points to several such incidents. William Beckford kept a scrapbook of persecutions of sodomites and suspicious incidents, a scrapbook of what he called "shocking human sacrifices," qtd in Norton *Mother Clap's* 230. Beckford's collections of materials are now held in the British Library.

9. See Franklin's discussion of women and working class readers of Byron, 1-71.

10. Rapf has written that "Byron's poetry represents a struggle to annihilate self by becoming one with another and to assert that self against that other,"

"Byronic Heroine" 642. I would suggest that annihilation is the force within and the force outside of Byron to which he submits and against which he struggles.

11. Wolfson's study of cross-dressings in *Don Juan* reveals Byron's continued "experiments with codes of Gender," and suggests their radical implications for potential chaos in social and psychological consequences, "Their She Condition" 594. She also reads Byron's destabilizing of gender in *Sardanapulus,* "A Problem."

Works Cited

Allen, Dennis. *Sexuality in Victorian Fiction.* Norman: U of Oklahoma P, 1993.

Beckford, William. *Vathek.* 1782. Ed. with Intro. Roger Lonsdale. New York: Oxford UP, 1983.

Byron, George Gordon, Lord. *Byron's Letters and Journals.* Ed. Leslie Marchland. 12 Vol. Cambridge: Harvard UP, 1973-81. (BLJ)

———. *His Very Self and Voice: Collected Conversations of Lord Byron.* Ed. Ernest J. Jovell Jr. New York: Macmillan, 1954. (HVSV)

———. *The Complete Poetical Works.* Ed. Jerome McGann. Vol. 1-3. Oxford: Clarendon, 1980-81. (CPW)

Cady, Joseph. "'Masculine Love,' Renaissance Writing and the 'New Invention' of Homosexuality." *Homosexuality in Renaissance and Enlightenment England: Literary Representations in Historical Context.* Ed. Claude J. Summers. New York: Harrington Park, 1992. 9-40.

Cottom, Daniel. *The Civilized Imagination: A Study of Ann Radcliffe, Jane Austen, and Sir Walter Scott.* Cambridge: Cambridge UP, 1985.

Crompton, Louis, *Byron and Greek Love: Homophobia in 19th-Century England.* Berkeley: U of California P, 1985.

Davenport-Hines, Richard. *Sex, Death and Punishment.* London: Collins, 1990.

Edelman, Lee. *Homographesis: Essays in Gay Literary and Cultural Theory.* New York: Routledge, 1994.

———. "Seeing Things: Representation, the Scene of Surveillance, and the Spectacle of Gay Male Sex." *Inside/Out: Lesbian Theories, Gay Theories.* New York: Routledge, 1991. 93-116.

Franklin, Caroline. *Byron's Heroines.* New York: Oxford, 1992.

Giuliano, Cheryl Fallon. "Gulnare/Kaled's 'Untold' Feminization of Byron's Oriental Tales." *Studies in English Literature* 33(1993): 785-806.

Hammond, Paul. *Love Between Men in English Literature.* New York: St. Martin's, 1996.

King, Thomas A. "Performing Akimbo: Queer Pride and Epistemological Prejudice." *The Politics and Poetics of Camp.* Ed. Moe Meyers. New York: Routledge, 1994. 23-50.

Leask, Nigel. *British Romantic Writers and the East.* New York: Cambridge UP, 1992.

———. "Wandering through Eblis: Absorption and Containment in Romantic Exoticism." *Romanticism and Colonialism.* Ed. Tim Fulford and Peter J. Kitson. Cambridge: Cambridge UP, 1998: 165-88.

Lewis, Matthew G. *The Monk.* New York: Grove, 1993.

Norton, Rictor. *The Myth of the Modern Homosexual: Queer History and the Search for Cultural Unity.* Washington: Cassell, 1997.

———. *Mother Clap's Molly House: The Gay Subculture in England 1700-1830.* London: GMP Publishers, 1992.

Rapf, Joanna. "The Byronic Heroine: Incest and the Creative Process." *Studies in English Literature* 21 (1981): 637-45.

———. "Poetic Performance: Byron and the Concept of the Male Muse." *Approaches to Teaching Byron's Poetry.* Ed. Frederick Shilstone. New York: MLA, 1991.

Sedgwick, Eve Kosofsky. *Between Men: English Literature and Male Homosocial Desire.* New York: Columbia UP, 1985.

Smollett, Tobias. *The Adventures of Roderick Random.* 1748. Ed. Paul-Gabriel Bouce. New York: Oxford UP, 1979.

Trumbach, Randolph. "Sex, Gender and Sexual Identity in Modern Culture: Male Sodomy and Female Prostitution in Enlightenment London." *Forbidden History: The State, Society and the Regulation of Sexuality in Modern Europe.* Ed. John Fout. Chicago: U of Chicago P, 1992. 89-102.

———. "Sodomitical Subcultures, Sodomitical Roles, and the Gender Revolution of the Eighteenth Century: The Recent Historiography." *'Tis Nature's Fault: Unauthorized Sexuality During the Enlightenment.* Ed. Robert Purks MacCubbin. Cambridge: Cambridge UP, 1987. 109-21.

———. "Sodomy Transformed: Aristocratic Libertinage, Public Reputation, and the Gender Revolution of the 18th Century." *Journal of Homosexuality* 19: 2 (1990): 105-24.

Wolfson, Susan J. "A Problem Few Dare to Imitate: Sardanapulus and Effeminate Character." *ELH* 58 (1991): 867-902.

————. "'Their She Condition': Cross-dressing and the Politics of Gender." *ELH* 54 (1987): 585-617.

Wolfson, Susan J. and Peter J. Manning, ed. and notes. *Lord Byron, Selected Poems.* New York: Penguin, 1996.

Woods, Gregory. "Body, Costume, and Desire in Christopher Marlowe." *Homosexuality in Renaissance and Enlightenment England: Literary Representations in Historical Context.* Ed. Claude J. Summers. New York: Harrington Park, 1992. 85-102.

Nancy Goslee (essay date winter 2005)

SOURCE: Goslee, Nancy. "Shelley's Cosmopolitan 'Discourse': Ancient Greek Manners and Modern Liberty." *Wordsworth Circle* 36, no. 1 (winter 2005): 2-5.

[*In the following essay, Goslee outlines Percy Bysshe Shelley's "Discourse on the Manners of the Antient Greeks Relative to the Subject of Love," in which Shelley attempts to discern an egalitarian ideal of love that includes both homosexuality and heterosexuality.*]

When he headed for Italy in the spring, 1818, Percy Shelley left behind at Marlow the life-sized plaster casts of the Belvedere Apollo and the Medici Venus which had presided over his reading of Plato and his writing of *Laon and Cythna* (MWS *Letters* 1: 38, 38n and White 1.505). Reading A. W. Von Schlegel's *Lectures on Dramatic Art and Literature* on the way to Italy, a work that describes Greek classical drama as fundamentally analogous to sculpture, he anticipated a less bookish, more direct encounter with the sculpture and architecture of classical civilizations (MWS J 16-21, march 1818). Like his modern Greek protagonists in *Laon and Cythna,* he sought to regenerate from Mediterranean culture the material ruins of a classical Greek ideal of civic liberty. Halting for the summer in the cool retreat of Bagni di Lucca, however, Shelley continued to analyze Greek culture through its texts-first working on a translation of Plato's *Symposium* and then, in late July, drafting his second try at an introduction to the dialogue (Weinberg 21; Jones, xiii). This essay, which he titled "Discourse on the Manners of the Antient Greeks," opens a cosmopolitan defense of classical Athenian "manners" in love-that is, of their practice of homoeroticism. Homophobia had blocked modern British readers from accepting Plato's portrayal of love between men as a desire for "ideal beauty & truth" equal to that in Phidias' and Praxiteles' sculpture. In this essay, then, Shelley attempts a sympathetic explanation of that difference in sexual orientation; and he mediates that explanation through an appeal to the beautiful forms of the sculpted human figure. Yet, as he works through drafts of the essay in two different notebooks, his argument becomes a different sort of cosmopolitanism, one that would in his view be more inclusive and egalitarian. For Greek homoeroticism, he argues, mars the otherwise perfect society of ancient Greece because it excludes a heterosexuality based upon the intellectual and civic liberty of women.[1]

The mediating, persuasive form of his argument is the "loveliness"—the desirable beauty—of the human form. Shelley begins drafting this preface in a small notebook (Bod. MS. Shelley adds. e. 11) just after the fragment "On Love." In that essay, which Donald Reiman and Steven Jones suggest was his first try at writing an introduction to the *Symposium* translation (Jones xiv, xx n. 8; Reiman, SC VI, 638-47), he analyzes the idea of the "epipsyche" or mental projection of an ideal version of the self as an object of desire. Having explored the consequences of pursuing such an ambiguous ideal in *Alasto,* his reading of the *Phaedrus* on August 4-5 would have grounded this concept more firmly in Athenian culture (MWS *Journal* 217-18; Halperin, "Diotima" 269, citing *Phaedrus* 255c-e). Following "On Love" in the notebook, the "Discourse" also associates "loveliness" with an idealizing image-making by the lover.

Though the pages of these drafts include scarcely any of his characteristic visual sketches, his verbal text immediately evokes this visuality, first, with the graphically expressive title, written with a flourish, and then with the content. Shelley opens his "Discourse" by asking, "What was the combination of moral & political circumstances which produced so [unc] unparalleled a progress . . . in literature & the arts" and why it "so soon recieved a check" are "problems left to . . . posterity" to wonder over, as "the ruins of a fine statue obscurely suggest to us the grandeur & perfection of the whole" (17-18). This powerful simile of sculpture as bridging time even in its ruined state leads into a consideration of the original and interdependent grandeur of all the arts practiced in classical Greece. Though little evidence of their painting remains except for verbal description. "Their sculptures are such as we in our presumption assume to be the models of ideal truth & beauty & ^to which with all no artist of modern times can produce anything com forms in any degree comparable" (18). All of the arts in that culture "assumed a more harmonious & perfect form" than they would have in another era, for they possess a "sympathetic connection between each other, being no more than the various expressions of one internal power, modified [b]by the different circumstances either of the [an] individual or of the society" (23, 19).

This model of a varied yet "sympathetic" expressivity from a common, possibly transcendent source postulates a continuity of meaning from source through artist to artifacts to audience. Thus it resembles in a more positive mode de Man's critical use of "monumental-ity" in "Shelley Disfigured" (*Deconstruction and Criticism*, 67-8). As in the magnetic or maenadic inspiration of Plato's *Ion* or the complex mediations of beauty in his *Phaedrus,* this continuity moves through the inspired artist-prophet but also conveys and creates a broader, harmonious cultural ideal. Speculating that "there seems to be a principle in modern nations the modern world" that in "analogous . . . circumstances" might renew such interlinked forms of creativity, he first laments, "yet this principle has never been called into action, and requires indeed a universal & almost apalling change in . . . the system of existing things. What the Greeks were was a reality not a promise. And what we are & hope to be is [derived] is as it were from the influence & inspiration of these glorious generations.[?]" (27-28).

Though he had probably not yet read Winckelmann's *History of Ancient Art* (the first references appear as he tours Naples and Pompeii late in 1818 MWS J 246-7; December 24-31, 1818, January 2, 4 1819), he anticipates its arguments that Athenian liberty is a spirit that infuses all of that culture's arts. In Winckelmann, David Ferris has recently argued, an organic model of the growth and decay of liberty in classical Greece limits modern emulation to a recognition of tragic loss (*Silent Urns,* 23-35 and ch. 3). Yet first Schiller and then Schlegel respond to Winckelmann by making recognition a part of a "romantic" or sentimental consciousness that is progressive, developmental, and shaped decisively by Christianity and chivalry.[2] In his "Discourse," I argue, Shelley's reading of Schlegel will help him discover a way to emulate a lost Greek culture and to activate that "principle" of a central spirit of liberty in modern culture. To do so, to open up that closed model of classical perfection and to call his "principle" into action in the modern world, he cautiously turns to a complex analysis of difference.

First, he begins to redefine "perfection," still somewhat obliquely: "When we discover that the most how for the most admirable society men who [ever] [lived] community ever [formed] was removed from perfection that perfection which to which human society is impelled by some active power within each bosom, to aspire, how great ought to be our hopes, how resolute our struggles" (29-30). This "active power," temporarily undefined, echoes the definition of love developed in his just-abandoned essay "On Love" at the beginning of the draft notebook (and I quote from the earlier essay): "There is something within us which from the instant that we live & move thirsts after its likeness . . . We feel within our hearts see dimly see within our intellectual nature a the miniature as it were of our our entire self. . . . The ideal prototype of . . . every thing excellent or lovely that we are capable of concieving as belonging to the nature of man." Desire searches for the "antitype" of its internal self, this "soul within our soul"

(4-5). In the context of the new essay, this "active power" also carries a more communal sense of progressive development toward "every thing excellent & lovely." Further, although the search for an antitype or epipsyche based upon a union of erotic and aesthetic "loveliness" will be the basis of his defense of homoeroticism, at this point the "Discourse" turns from a narcissistic mirroring "likeness" to difference as precisely the form of "that perfection" that Greek culture lacked.

Recognizing and respecting difference is both intellectually and ethically important, he argues. Those who lack knowledge of the Greek language, for whom his translation of *The Symposium* is intended, nevertheless "ought . . . to posess an exact & comprehensive conception of the history of man," since that knowledge leads to greater tolerance and, in a cancelled phrase, greater ability to understand and evaluate "the past the present & the future." Yet his rhetoric occasionally slips into accusation and even satire. Accounts thus far, he writes, have not shown "the Greeks precisely as they were," but "seem all written for children," censoring any "practise or sentiment highly inconsistent with our present manners . . . lest those manners should recieve outrage & violation." Modern "manners," in this figure, become bodies subject to a form of psychological rape (30-31).

Though he speculates that one cause of this difference in "manners"—that is, sexual practice—might be a "difference of physical nature existing in the Celt" or the northern European (32), he proposes two others that are more important to his argument: Christ's doctrine of "the absolute & unconditional equality of human beings" and the medieval chivalric elevation of women, both of these ideas drawn at least in part from Schlegel's theory of a "romantic" culture contrasting to the classical one. Because Greek women were treated as slaves, they had none of that "intellectual harmony loveliness with which the boundless acquisition of knowledge, & the cultivation of sentiment animates, . . . as with a life of overpowering grace, lineaments which neither the . . . lineaments & the gestures of the every form which it . . . inhabits" (33-4). By replacing "intellectual harmony" with "intellectual loveliness," Shelley's description of modern, educated and hence more liberated women attempts to praise both their subjectivity and their physical beauty as object for the male gaze. Yet, as in his preceding draft of "On Love," the gazing he proposes is reciprocal: "Their eyes [the eyes of uneducated Greek women] could not have been deep & intricate from the workings of the mind spirit, & could have entangled no heart in soul-enwoven labyrinths" (35). Because the yearning for "sentimental love," "this passion," for a perfect image or antitype of the mind's internal ideal, is a "universal thirst for a communion not merely of the senses but of our whole nature; intellectual, imaginative & sensitive" (35) Greek men found these feelings ". . . deprived of their natural object, [and] sought a compensation & a substitute. The men of Greece were corresponded in external form to the models which they have left as specimens of what they were"—that is, they resembled their sculpture with its "delicatefirm [yet] & [?] flowing proportions of their forms." They possessed, in addition, charm, eloquence, and the capacity for "governing themselves & others"; and this union of objective and subjective merit led to the word "beautiful" being applied to them more than to women (39-40). With this sense of "the youth of Greece" as animated, desirable, statues fulfilling the projections of the epipsyche as described in the preceding draft of "On Love," the part of the essay in "adds. e. 11" breaks off.

Though the pages that follow were probably still blank, he turned to another notebook to work on the draft. This new, larger notebook (now known as Bod. MS. Shelley adds. E. 6) was dedicated to completing the essay, for Shelley labels its spine "continuation of discourse on Ancient Greeks." He probably planned to copy the first part of the draft into its larger pages, since he began the new section on p. 45, leaving the earlier pages blank. "Adds. E. 6" was laid aside, Carlene Adamson argues, in the furor of the Shelleys' travels in the fall of 1818 (BSM V, xxxi). Their hot, hasty journey to Venice to negotiate with Byron over his and Claire's daughter Allegra "ended tragically," Steven Jones writes, "with the death of his own daughter" (BSM 15, xiii). From Venice they travelled south to live first in Naples and then in Rome. Not until late 1819 or spring 1820 did Shelley rediscover the larger notebook with its abandoned draft of the "Discourse" and begin using it again (Adamson, introduction to adds. E. 6, xxxi). On the other hand, "adds. E. 11," with the first part of the "Discourse" draft, was at hand in Venice, where Shelley used it to begin *Julian and Maddalo* (Jones, BSM XV, 176; Reiman, SC VI.854-65). One wonders whether during their long conversations in Venice, Byron saw or heard the first part of the "Discourse" as Shelley heard the first canto of *Don Juan.*

I speculate about this possibility because the section of the "Discourse" in "adds. E. 6" begins with an attack on libertinism and merely physical sex of whatever orientation—an attack possibly prompted either by the accounts of Byron's licentious but at that point heterosexual living arrangements in Venice that led to Shelley's concerns for Allegra—or from direct observation once in Venice. This critique of an eroticism that is merely physical leads him to develop three criteria which all love relationships should meet, and arising from those criteria a more detailed account of homoerotic practices in ancient Athens. His relative frankness in this section of the draft and what I will describe as his resolute attempt to portray these practices sympa-

thetically led Mary Shelley to omit this portion of the essay and to publish only the first portion, with considerable trepidation, in 1840 (Jones BSM XV, 171; Adamson, BSM V). I say "resolute," for his heterosexual bias and his mediating aesthetic of the beautiful sculpted form lead him into a rhetoric of denial, if perhaps a strategic one.

His first "maxim" adds to the aesthetics of the beautiful sculptural object an ethical subjectivity: "the subject of this gratification should be as perfect & beautiful as possible, both in body & mind," to prepare "moments of abandonment" through "consent of all the conscious portions of our nature being" (p. 49). This intellectual discipline of "the instinctive sense" leads to his second, and anti-Byronic, criterion, "Temperance in pleasure." Third, and presenting most difficulties to his argument for tolerance, "This act ought to be indulged according to *nature*"; and he underlines "nature."

Although he concedes that the "habitual passion" of the Greek "poets & philosophers . . . seemd inconsistent with this . . . maxim," Shelley returns to his first proposition and to his theory of the epipsyche to offer a defense for a modified form of homoeroticism. "[W]hat th[is]e action was by which the Greeks expressed this passion," he argues, ". . . was *tot*ally different from the . . . ridiculous & vulgar disgusting <co>ceptions of the which vulgar on the subject have formed on the subject. It is impossible," he writes on page 51, "that a lover could often ever . . . have subjected the object of his attachment to so detestable a violation, or have consented to associate his image own remembrance in the beloved mind with imageries of pain & horror." He then proposes his alternate theory of a "reverie," of "certain phenomena connected with sleep at . . . puberty [which] associate themselves with those images which are the objects of our waking desires." Such a "state of abandonment in the society of a person of surpassing attractions, . . . when the sexual connexion cannot exist, . . . [is] such as to preclude the necessity of so operose & diabolical a machination, as that usually concieved described. This is the result apparently alluded to by Plato"—and he writes above the line, "Phaedrus" (52). Shelley is probably interpreting as parallel masturbation in "reverie" the practice of "intercrural" [between the thighs] intercourse, in which, according to Kenneth Dover's analyses of vase paintings, the *erastes* or older lover faced the *eromenos,* the passive youth (97-8), bending over him as if in reverie. Yet the way in which Shelley distinguishes these practices from the "vulgar" or "disgusting" practice of anal intercourse, which was also widely accepted in Athenian as well as other classical Greek cultures (Dover 99), leads his essay, not surprisingly, into difficulties and surely contributes to his inability to finish it.[3]

For when he attempts to separate classical Greek homosexual practices from those of the "licentious Romans" or British Restoration writers—or even the evidence offered by Aristophanes—on the "vulgar" act of penetration, his aesthetic criterion of "intellectual loveliness" risks losing the universality he has claimed for it. Whether this imputation of vulgarity emerges from genuine horror on Shelley's part, perhaps a horror inspired by experiences as a schoolboy (Bonca 60-2, 144, 247n. 25), or whether it is a more mixed attitude, partly a calculated rhetorical appeal to a British audience suffering from prudery and anxiously-professed homophobia, its link to a rank- or class-based criterion undermines his two foundational claims for equality and hence for cultural liberty. First, it implies that the universal human impulse to desire a "loveliness" of both body and mind requires both a self-image and an image of the other that "vulgar" practices —and by implication "vulgar" classes—violate. The lover's impulse toward the beautiful seems now only minimally innate or "natural," and to require a *paideia* of aesthetic education that initiates the *beloved,* beautiful object into the status of a ruling class male represented by the older lover—whether of ancient Greece or of modern Europe—a point made by Jennifer Wallace (106).

Ironically, that classical *paideia* was based upon a difference in age and status, if not on what we would now term class, and cultivated an asymmetrical erotic relationship: erotic pleasure for the dominant lover and education and a brotherly "love in return" [*antiphilein*] for the passive beloved (Dover 53, citing *Phaedrus* 255d-256a, *Symposium* 217a, 218c), thus recapitulating within the relationship a larger social hierarchy and only a sort of diachronic equality of status. As Foucault argues, the classical Greeks also distinguished in their homosexual practices between vulgar or licentious behavior and the *sophrosyne* or moderate, appropriate behavior leading to mastery of the self and thus to civic participation on a high level (196-7, 208-9). Moreover, a part of that *paideia,* that growth toward self-mastery, for the boy was to move in a few years from passive object to active subject—a complexity that Foucault labels the "antinomy of the boy" (221). Thus two levels of distinguishing the subordinate from the dominant or ruling class come into play, but neither repudiates—as Shelley seems to—a particular sexual practice such as intercrural or anal intercourse, but only regulates, in Foucault's terminology, its use. David Halperin argues that Plato's Diotima in the *Symposium* proposes a more mutual, reciprocal relationship between man and youth than the usual pattern, a relationship based as he speculates upon a woman's ability to both give and receive pleasure even in a subordinate social and sexual position. Yet even this particular Platonic spin still remains class—limited and to some extent status—differentiated (Halperin 270, 276, 285).

Even if Shelley insists, then, that mutual erotic and intellectual relationships are made more perfect in the modern world by including women as partners, only some women and some men will have the intellectual capacity to realize a mutual love of the beautiful that includes the physical, the civic, and the transcendent. Thus he has greatly complicated his argument for the interdependence of a heterosexuality based on the equality of women and a civic liberty enlarged, from its Athenian model, by including heterosexuality, the argument that allows him to challenge the "perfection" of Greek culture with the possibility of a "more perfect" modern one. Nevertheless, his feminism, fusing Wollstonecraft's Enlightenment with Schlegel's Romanticism, anticipates a possible escape route from the organic determinism of Winckelmann's view of Greek culture, a determinism that necessitates the "death" of that culture, by including women as equal partners in "the beautiful order of social life." And he argues for more tolerance of Greek "manners" in love, arguments based upon a universal aesthetic impulse toward erotic mutuality and thus political equality. Yet this ideal of perfection seems limited both by class privilege and by a lingering criterion of "natural" heterosexuality.

Notes

1. Nathaniel Brown noted this championing of feminism as early as 1979, but he does not evaluate in detail its connection to the relationship between homoeroticism and aesthetics that I pursue here.

2. Robert Aldrich reviews classical Athenian homosexuality before turning to a chapter on the link between Winckelmann's homosexuality and his "erotic aesthetics." For further discussion of Schlegel's aesthetic analogies for historical development, see my *Uriel's Eye,* pp. 25, 70-2, 136, 140-4, 191-3.

3. Jennifer Wallace points out, as well, that even his translation of *The Symposium* shows "elements of aesthetic censorship and bowdlerization" in its treatment of passages that describe sexual practices (106).

Works Cited

Aldrich, Robert. *The Seduction of the Mediterranean: Writing, Art, and Homosexual Fantasy.* 1993; Bonca, Teddi Chichester. *Shelley's Mirrors of Love: Narcissism, Sacrifice, and Sorority.* 1999; Brown, Nathaniel. *Sexuality and Feminism in Shelley.* 1979; De Man, Paul. "Shelley Disfigured." In *Deconstruction and Criticism.* 1979; Dover, K. J. *Greek Homosexuality.* 1978; Ferris, David. *Silent Urns: Romanticism, Hellenism, Modernity.* 2000; Foucault, Michel. *The Use of Pleasure. Volume II of The History of Sexuality,* tr. Robert Hurley. 1985; Goslee, Nancy Moore. *Uriel's Eye: Miltonic Stationing and Statuary in Blake, Keats, and Shelley.* 1985; Halperin, David M. "Why is Diotima a Woman? Platonic Eros and the Figuration of Gender." In *Before Sexuality: The Construction of Erotic Experience in the Ancient Greek World,* ed. Halperin, et.al. 1990. 257-308; Reiman, Donald H. Ed. *Shelley and his Circle* VI. 1973. 638-47, 854-65; Schlegel, A. W. von. *A Course of Lectures on Dramatic Art and Literature,* tr. J. Black. 1815; Shelley, Mary Wollstonecraft. *The Journals of Mary Shelley,* ed. Paula R. Feldman and Diana Scott-Kilvert. rpt. 1995; Shelley, Percy B. *Bodleian Shelley Manuscripts V: The 'Witch of Atlas' Notebook: Bodleian MS. Shelley adds. E. 6,* Ed. Carlene Adamson. 1997; ———. *Bodleian Shelley Manuscripts XV: Bodleian MS. Shelley adds. E. 11,* Ed. Steven E. Jones. 1990; ———. *Letters, Volume II: Shelley in Italy.* Ed. Frederick L. Jones. 1964; Wallace, Jennifer. *Shelley and Greece: Rethinking Romantic Hellenism.* 1997; Weinberg, Alan M. *Shelley's Italian Experience.* 1991; White, Newman Ivey. *Shelley.* 2 vols. 1940. rpt. 1972; Winckelmann, Johann Joachim. *Histoire de l'Art chez les anciens, traduit de la'allemagne par Huber et revue par Jansen.* 1802.

TREATMENT BY WOMEN WRITERS

Kathryn Lee Seidel (essay date spring 1993)

SOURCE: Seidel, Kathryn Lee. "Art Is an Unnatural Act: Mademoiselle Reisz in *The Awakening.*" *The Mississippi Quarterly* 46, no. 2 (spring 1993): 199-214.

[*In the following essay, Seidel declares that Chopin's affirmation of the lesbian character Mademoiselle Reisz in* The Awakening *is an endorsement of lesbianism as an acceptable expression of love.*]

Kate Chopin's *The Awakening* has become a classic feminist text, most often read for its devastating portrait of Victorian marriage and the discovery of the protagonist, Edna Pontellier, of her talent, her sexuality, and her sense of self. From this perspective, the novel ostensibly focuses on Edna's relationships with her husband, a would-be lover, Robert, and her actual lover, Alcee Arobin. Yet Edna's relationships with her women friends are as various, subtle and more comprehensive than those with men. In fact, in the middle of Alcee Arobin's seduction, Edna Pontellier mentions her friend Mademoiselle Reisz. Her comment derails Arobin's skilled and up to that point effective arousal of Edna's sexual desires. He and Edna begin to quarrel about Mademoiselle, and he complains, "why have you introduced her at a moment when I desired to talk to you?"[1]

Critics have noted Mademoiselle's close relationship with Edna; they have commented on her appearance, her role as an artist figure, and her attraction to Edna,

but they have stopped short of considering the sources of that attraction. Elaine Showalter notes that Mademoiselle's "attraction to Edna suggests something perverse,"[2] but she does not name it. Cristina Giorcelli views Mademoiselle as "a conjurer and a facile," a Medusa-like female artist who "stands for the spiritual urged perverted by an excessive turning on itself."[3] These two critics echo the contemporary reviews of the novel, one of which calls Mademoiselle a "witch."[4] Anne Goodwyn Jones notes more neutrally that Mademoiselle "embodies several of the significant masculine values in the world"[5] and remarks on Mademoiselle's attempts to influence Edna. Although most critics notice Mademoiselle's rejection of conventional feminine behavior, they make the assumption that such behavior is abnormal.

Not only an eccentric spinster, not merely an isolated artist, Mademoiselle Reisz embodies the traits of the female artist as lesbian, at least as the late nineteenth century understood this concept. Chopin uses metaphors of homoeroticism and of witchcraft, the traditional enterprise associated with the female artist, to develop Mademoiselle Reisz's characterization; moreover, Edna's exploration of female sexuality was inclusive of a broad range of behavior, not only heterosexual liaisons but also autoerotic fantasies, warm female friendships, and homoerotic possibilities. Chopin's knowledge of the emerging stereotypes of lesbianism enables her to provide in the relationship between Mademoiselle and Edna a provocative contrast to the stereotypical love plots of Edna's marriage and of Edna's longing for Robert, and to the seduction plot involving Arobin.

Most scholars are in agreement that the 1880s and 1890s were a pivotal point, perhaps the pivotal point in modern history in devising the contemporary definition of homosexuality. Eve Kosofsky Sedgwick's study *Epistemology of the Closet*[6] asserts that while behavior currently called "homosexual" has a three-thousand-year recorded history, it was in the last third of the nineteenth century that every person, heretofore "assignable to male or female gender, was now considered necessarily assignable as well to a homo to a heterosexuality" (p. 2). Moreover, this either-or identity came to have vast "implications, however confusing, for even the ostensibly least sexual aspects of personal existence. It was this new development that left no space in the culture exempt from the potent incoherences of the homo/heterosexual definition" (p. 2). Sedgwick summarizes the reasons for this change as a coming together of medical and psychological theory as well as sociocultural circumstances which brought into public light the famous case of Oscar Wilde, whose fortunes encapsulated trends in the culture only partially articulated until his trial. In the first instance, the budding psychomedical establishment came to accept the opinions of Richard Krafft-Ebing and Havelock Ellis, whose work was grounded in the premise that some behavior was healthy and some was diseased. As David Halperin notes in *One Hundred Years of Homosexuality,*[7] at the turn of the century, people who may have represented a broad range of behavior in their dress, their manner, and their conversation, their choice of friends, and their preferred sex acts were now all "classed alike and placed under the same heading" (p. 16). Both Sedgwick and Halperin refer separately but not coincidentally to the emergence of a type of "binary thinking" in the late nineteenth century. It is this thinking that caused a cultural generalization in famous criminal cases involving lesbians in the United States, as Lillian Faderman records,[8] and of the case of Oscar Wilde in England. As Sedgwick notes, homosexual behavior, which early in the 1870s and 80s denoted the revolt from Victorian sentimentality and the preference for the elite and selective, came to denote abnormality, criminality and disease (Chapter 3, passim).

When we apply these insights to *The Awakening,* we can see that these issues were not yet settled. On the contrary, the novel reveals the sea of ideas regarding such areas as male-female friendship, male-female love, male-female sexual behavior, as well as female-female friendship, love, and sexual behavior. As Laurie George has noted, Edna's dear and affectionate friend Adele Ratignolle is the conventional, healthy, married companion whom Edna admires, loves, and even finds physically appealing.[9] Yet the unconventional, cranky, sickly, single, artistic Mademoiselle Reisz moves Edna, inspires Edna, touches Edna, and causes in her feelings so powerful that they undermine the calm, domesticated underpinnings of society.

After two decades of relentlessly heterosexual criticism, considering *The Awakening* from a lesbian perspective reveals characterizations, conventions, and narrative techniques found in 1890's fiction which treats same-sex love, a ubiquitous topic of the 1890s, as Bonnie Zimmerman notes.[10] Early in the 1890s what may have been regarded as a physically affectionate, even erotic if non-orgasmic friendship, by 1899 was widely regarded as a medical anomaly and a moral excess. Perhaps this is one reason Chopin's narrator explains that Edna's Creole friend Adele Ratignolle was of a group which encouraged physical affection among women friends of the sort described in detail by Carroll Smith-Rosenberg in "The Female World of Love and Ritual."[11] Edna herself, reared as a Calvinist, not a Creole, regards touching with suspicion. Laurie George (p. 58) links Edna's relationship with Adele to Adrienne Rich's contention that the lesbian reality is "a primary intensity between women," not merely and only a sexual bond.[12] George discusses the homoerotic elements of Edna's relationship with Adele. While Edna is obviously drawn to Adele, their friendship ultimately qualifies as one of increasing warmth and trust, an affectionate relationship

typical of Creole women and, even more, typical of women's friendships in the nineteenth century. Edna's initial aversion to being touched by Adele not only signifies her Calvinistic, Kentuckian unease with this form of friendship but also reflects Chopin's feeling that she needed to explain that women commonly touched one another. The shift toward viewing such behavior as evidence of lesbianism was occurring gradually in the late nineteenth century, according to John D'Emilio and Estelle B. Freedman, who chronicle a shift in sensibility.[13]

A number of well-documented criminal cases in the early 1890s involving jealousy and murder among female lovers led to a public questioning of close female friendships (Smith-Rosenberg, pp. 273-274). But most crucial for Chopin, because she was an artist, may have been the events of 1895, among them the notorious trial of Oscar Wilde, whose fame and downfall occurred as Chopin was writing many of her major works. Richard Ellmann's fine biography of Wilde fully describes the transformation of homosexuality from a curiosity associated with artistic creativity to a perversion associated with criminals. Chopin could have known of Wilde perhaps as early as his 1882 lecture tour when he lectured in St. Louis and New Orleans about the role of the artist.[14] By the 1890s she knew of his plays and fiction, as Emily Toth notes.[15] Believing that art was by its nature the destroyer of convention, Wilde covertly urged that the life of the artist need not include categories such as moral and immoral (Ellmann, p. 322), so that just as art should be judged on its beauty alone, so too should an artist strive to make his, or her, world a world of art without regard to morality.

The echoes of Wilde's beliefs reverberate in Mademoiselle Reisz's advice to Edna that the artist "dares and defies" (p. 63). Some critics assume that Mademoiselle refers to Edna's need to defy conventional definitions of marriage or at least to control her destiny,[16] but the comments are far more provocative when one considers the role of the female artist in the 1890s. Anne Goodwyn Jones points out in *Tomorrow is Another Day* that nineteenth-century women writers adopted a mask of conventionality to assure readers that writers did not openly defy the conceit of woman as domestic angel. Elaine Showalter, in "Tradition and the Female Talent," indicates the extent to which Chopin violated conventional expectations that female writers would avoid hard-hitting realism and uphold Victorian domestic values. Lillian Faderman's comprehensive study of women artists contends that some did not see fit to create an acceptable persona; in this regard Mademoiselle Reisz is indeed an artist with very little of the domesticated persona. Mademoiselle's sexual preferences and her artistic theories are part of the chronicle of lesbianism, which came to be differentiated from affectionate female friendships and which was increasingly associated with female creativity. In candidly portraying Mademoiselle Reisz, Chopin both recognizes the emerging stereotype yet understands and still regards positively the range of behavior Mademoiselle exhibits.

Lillian Faderman studied several aspects of the late nineteenth-century conventional representations of lesbians by writers such as George Sand, Zola, de Maupassant, and O. Henry, all of whose works were well known to Chopin, as Per Seyersted reports.[17] Very often, the lesbian figure was physically deformed, an emblem of her emotional "unnaturalness" (Faderman, pp. 283, 289). A second trait conventionally associated with lesbians was hostility to men, children, and all domestic pursuits (Faderman, pp. 275-280). Hence the lesbian was not merely a curiosity; she was a danger to the family. In *The Awakening,* these qualities are part of Mademoiselle Reisz's personality. She is not merely the stereotyped "spinster"; her impatience with children excludes her from this category, because the unmarried woman whose sexual preference was beyond reproach was conventionally portrayed as having a sentimental love of children and usually living with a family, not in a solitary garret.

The most telling aspect of lesbianism Chopin's audience might recognize was that in literature the profession of such women, if not prostitution, was frequently that of the artist. Authors such as Swinburne and de Maupassant who were openly hostile to lesbians and portrayed them as artists or poets were well known to Chopin. Her work had already dealt with the theme of the woman artist who must separate herself from domestic life; her first published story, "Wiser than a God," looked at the dilemma of a pianist who foregoes marriage in order to be an artist. Thus Chopin, writing in the *St. Louis Post-Dispatch* in her own defense, compared writing to a domestic task that she would casually indulge in "if the temptation to try a new furniture polish on an old table leg is not too powerful."[18] As Anne Goodwyn Jones points out, such statements reassured readers that Chopin was not a "masculine" woman (p. 145); even more crucial, however, is that Chopin felt she must prove herself to be a domestic female, for the opposite was the independent, "unnatural" artist. Some critics such as Carole Stone have asserted that Mademoiselle is a "true artist" who offers Edna a chance to explore the independent life available to the female artist[19]; this perspective, however, belongs to our age, not Chopin's. While we may be tempted to applaud Edna's attempts to become a painter, the fact that her painting does not enhance her roles as wife and mother but causes her to remove herself from her family made it a suspect activity, as indicated by the hostile reviews of *The Awakening* after its publication. Moreover, Mademoiselle's talent is more socially acceptable than Edna's; Mademoiselle can play the piano to earn money and to entertain other people whereas Edna chooses, far more radically, to paint for herself.

The closest evidence that Chopin knew about female homosexuality has three sources; she probably knew of the work of the medical sexologists Richard Von Krafft-Ebing and Havelock Ellis because her friend William Ready, editor of the *St. Louis Mirror,* published articles on Ellis which Chopin would certainly have read, according to Emily Toth. Toth's biography of Chopin, moreover, chronicles Chopin's own close friendship with her schoolmate, Helen, and, of course, reveals Chopin's penchant for rebellious behavior, especially when she was in residence in Cloutierville.

Moreover, Chopin published a short story in 1887 with direct homosexual content. "The Falling in Love of Fedora" presents a grim thirty-year-old spinster who to her own surprise falls in love with a young man. Always intrigued by the surprise plot, Chopin creates a twist: at the story's end, Fedora meets the young man's sister, who physically resembles her brother; at this point Fedora "bent down and pressed a long, penetrating kiss upon her mouth." While the sister was "astonished, and not too well pleased," Chopin offers no explanation for Fedora's behavior, and the story ends with Fedora calmly proceeding on her way. Emily Toth suggests that the lesbian overtones of this story fit well into the context of the erotic friendships of nineteenth-century women (Toth, p. 438 n.) but is unable to locate a living prototype for Fedora (p. 289). With all these influences, it is no wonder that the portrait of Mademoiselle is so complex and perplexing.

Mademoiselle Reisz is present at crucial points in Edna Pontellier's life, and Edna recalls her advice at other critical moments such as when she is alone with Arobin and at the novel's end when she walks into the Gulf. Reisz's advice ranges from the correct stance of the artist to the sort of man to love. Chopin portrays Mademoiselle Reisz as physically and emotionally abnormal. She is disagreeable, eccentric, small, and unattractive; her ever-present sprig of artificial violets is a parody of feminine charm. She often sits in postures that make her appear physically deformed. Her room under the eaves in the bohemian section of town where blacks and whites live side by side represents the dwelling of an American madwoman in the attic, in Sandra M. Gilbert and Susan Gubar's terms; thus she represents an unstated alternative for Edna. The metaphors which Chopin uses regarding Mademoiselle's relation to Edna are those of magic, witchcraft, and enchantment. She is "grotesque," plays music that is "strange and fantastic," and even owns a small cauldron. Chopin extends these metaphors to establish an alternate female linguistic code which contrasts with the patriarchal language which Edna hears from her father and husband but rejects. In "Sexual Linguistics: Gender, Language, Sexuality," Gilbert and Gubar observe that many women writers use terms associated with female sorcery as a vision of female verbal power which stands apart from the sentences of patriarchy.[20] Thus Mademoiselle comes to represent to Edna not a masculine alternative, as some critics have assumed, but another way of being female.

Early in the novel, their special relationship has already begun. Far from feeling anxious and withdrawn, Edna has a special warmth with Mademoiselle. She even allows Mademoiselle to touch her, an action which she found uncomfortable when Addle Ratignolle attempted it. When Mademoiselle will play only to please Edna, Robert entreats her to play by saying to Edna, "I'll tell her that you want to hear her. She likes you. She will come" (p. 45). Robert has noted Mademoiselle's special preference for Edna; indeed, irascible though she is, Reisz asks Edna what selections she prefers. The music Mademoiselle chooses sends "a keen tremor down [Edna's] spine." Their relationship is already such that Edna is emotionally transported by Mademoiselle's music; for her part, Mademoiselle is deferential to and affectionate with Edna. She pats Edna on the shoulder, and Edna, choked with emotion, answers by squeezing Mademoiselle's hand.

Perhaps Edna allows Mademoiselle's affection not in spite of but because she is so peculiar; her "shuffling and sidling" (p. 45) walk differs from Adele's madonna-like gracefulness, which for Edna, reared with austere Calvinistic stoicism, may seem cloying and overwhelming. Edna prefers to be touched by Mademoiselle's music; this inward mode of communication has a greater significance for her. Already in an aroused emotional state, she responds boldly to Robert's suggestion that they go for a midnight swim. Chopin is careful to extend the mood established by Mademoiselle's music into the setting: the moon that night is a "mystic moon"; there are rare and strange odors of perfumed flowers; the waves break on the beach like "slow, white serpents' (p. 47).

The mood is one of magic with Mademoiselle as the magician who created it. Thus, when Edna takes her first swim, she is, of course, awakening to the exhilaration of controlling her body, and to the excitement of sensuality, but as she tells Robert: "I wonder if I shall ever be stirred again as Mademoiselle Reisz's playing moved me tonight. . . . It is like a night in a dream. The people about me are like some uncanny, half-human beings" (p. 49). Edna is moved by the unreality and strangeness of the night. Robert responds with a story that on August 23, that very night, a spirit rises from the Gulf seeking a worthy mortal as a companion. A clever story which he doubtless improvises, it encapsulates Edna's desire for a spiritual and magical companion, one different from the placid Adele, the obsequious Robert, and her husband, who understands none of this.

At their next meeting Mademoiselle attempts to further her relationship with Edna. While Edna swims, Mademoiselle lingers on the shore to watch her. She herself has an aversion to water, a quality popularly associated with witches. She is eating chocolates, her treat which she eats habitually. She tells Edna that she is sympathetic to Robert, but she warns that the Mexican woman Mariequita, a former amour of Robert's brother, is a "sly one and a bad one" (p. 81). The conversation shows that Mademoiselle can arouse jealousy in Edna by questioning the motives of Robert. Having called into question his chastity, she then substitutes her own praise. She raves over Edna's appearance in a bathing suit, and gives her her address in New Orleans. The physicality of Mademoiselle's appetite is the scene's focus; she loves to eat chocolate, she loves to watch Edna in her bathing costume. Chopin is showing that women have physical desires and that women can be attracted by the physicality of other women.

In that hazy land between friendship and erotic attraction, Mademoiselle's attraction to Edna is the novel's first indication that the relationships between women are ambiguous and complex in *fin-de-siecle* Louisiana. While the novel focuses on male-female relationships, Chopin is also interested in the subtle tones of female relationships.

After this initial meeting, the relationship between Mademoiselle and Edna is extended with Edna's three visits to Mademoiselle's apartment. The dingy, smoke-filled room, so unlike the ordered domestic household of a married woman, represents her unconventional life. She lives alone in a room in which the only accoutrements are her piano and a bust of Beethoven. Chopin selects details that establish Mademoiselle as a female outcast, a grotesque figure who resembles a witch both in her appearance and in her "unnatural" desires. Early in the scene, Mademoiselle's smile is described as a "contortion of the face and all the muscles of the body" (p. 62). Her first words to Edna are conventional words of flattery: she remarks on how "handsome," healthy, and "content" Edna looks. Softened by the compliments, Edna allows Mademoiselle to take her hand, for her a sign that she is beginning to respond to close female friendship. With Edna now receptive and calm, Mademoiselle tells of having received a letter from Robert that Edna may not see. This dialogue continues until Edna is agitated and distraught. The teasing establishes that Mademoiselle occupies a superior position to Edna; she controls Edna's access to messages from Robert and she manipulates Edna's reactions to the letters.

It is at this point that Mademoiselle delivers the important but ambiguous speech about the requirements for the artist, who must possess the courageous soul, the "soul that dares and defies" (p. 63). Mademoiselle's definition of the artist differs severely from one offered by Edna's husband in the scene preceding this one, when Leonce points out that Adele Ratignolle is able to keep her household from descending into "chaos" (p. 57) and still be a "musician"; Edna replies, "She isn't a musician and I'm not a painter. It isn't on account of painting that I let things go" (p. 57). Edna, like Mademoiselle, defies the Victorian imperative to tend house, husband, and children, but she also denies the conventional explanation that artistic ability is the cause of the aberration. Mademoiselle might be more clearly identifiable as an artist figure and unnatural woman if Chopin had made her a composer, but she would be unable to support herself. Who would buy her pieces? Would she be invited to entertain after dinner? Probably not. Mademoiselle is not the daring artist she might be; she much be careful; she must be discreet.

At the end of the scene in her flat, Mademoiselle abandons words as an interpretation of Robert's letter and translates the written words into another medium, music. As Margaret Homans shows, the function of woman as translator of one code into another medium is ubiquitous in nineteenth-century fiction.[21] The Chopin *Impromptu* seems to Edna to be "strange" and "fantastic"; it moves her to tears. Mademoiselle's music has the effect of "conjuring" a mood in Edna, as the narrator reports, one which resembles the loss of self Edna feels when she swims and will later feel in the sex act: "The music grew strange and fantastic—turbulent, insistent, plaintive and soft with entreaty" (p. 80). Edna sobs in response and is extremely agitated. The sexually charged description is reminiscent of similar scenes in lesbian fiction; Catharine R. Stimpson discusses the convention in early twentieth-century lesbian fiction, in which there is a "metonymic encoding" of eroticism, often with a wildly passionate kiss representing the sexual desires of the characters.[22] The rapture Edna feels and Mademoiselle's willingness to engender it suggest a passionate connection, unfulfilled in a literal sense, but present and alive symbolically.

Edna's second visit to Mademoiselle Reisz occurs on a cold misty day; Mademoiselle is again described as a grotesque, having to hold her head to the side as a result of a stiff neck. On this visit Edna tells Mademoiselle that she has decided to move into her own little house. Immediately after Edna makes this announcement, Chopin describes the little stove in the flat as "roaring, it was redhot" (p. 80), and the chocolate on the stove "sizzled and sputtered." The chocolate's sweetness and heat may again be a metonymic emblem both of Mademoiselle's desire for Edna and Edna's own turbulent emotions. This image of a small but hot cauldron extends the metaphor of Mademoiselle as a witch, albeit a lesser one than those in Macbeth; and indeed at this moment she reaches under the bust of Beethoven and like a magician produces yet another letter from Robert. Again she withholds the letter but imposes an interpretation of it by asserting that Robert loves Edna and is trying to forget her. When Edna asks why Mademoiselle refuses to let her see the letters, she replies, "Haven't you begged for them? Can I refuse you anything?" (p. 80). Robin Lakoff has pointed out that exaggerated deference can be an indirect attempt to control another individual.[23] Mademoiselle frequently uses the word captivate (p. 63) to describe how she feels in relationship to Edna. Anne Goodwyn Jones has commented that this is a metaphor for slavery (p. 176).

In playing the piano as Edna reads, Mademoiselle translates, in Margaret Homans' terms, the contents of the letter into the feelings it arouses in Edna: the "music penetrated her whole being like an effulgence, warming and brightening the dark places of her soul. It prepared her for joy and exultation" (p. 80). The use of penetrated, which prepares her for "joy," suggests the ecstatic sexual union with Robert that Edna desires. Because this feeling is elicited through the medium of Mademoiselle Reisz, Mademoiselle participates in a vicarious way in Edna's ecstasy. While James Justus calls Edna's passionate reaction an emotion with no referent in Romantic (or any other) imagery,"[24] the referent he seeks is the imagery of lesbianism. It is a sensual scene which functions visually like the erotic art of the time: two women are alone in a room, one playing music which arouses the other. Moreover, Mademoiselle attempts to supply a code to allow Edna to interpret her feelings. Mademoiselle asserts that she would only love a man with lofty aims, never a man of "ordinary caliber." The metaphor of a man as a bullet, a masculine object which penetrates the body, extends the sexual overtones of the scene. Mademoiselle's comment metaphorically juxtaposes female love as music, which penetrates and renews, with male love as a bullet fired by unworthy men who destroy. This speech forces Edna to defend both Robert and her reasons for loving such an ordinary man, and, indeed, any man. In the text, Edna is unable to produce specific reasons for loving Robert; however, in an earlier version of the manuscript Edna described Robert's physical features in great detail (Toth, p. 310). Thus, Chopin changed this section by leaving Edna's motives for loving Robert vague, perhaps to enhance Mademoiselle's argument that there is no sufficient reason for Edna's loving him. Mademoiselle's influence is emphasized by her physical position during the scene; she delivers the speech as she sits on a high piano stool and looks down at Edna, so that Edna must literally look up to her. Mademoiselle imposes further interpretations on Edna by asking if Edna loves Robert and what she plans to do when Robert comes back. Edna had not been planning to do anything, but the question implies that some action is called for.

By showing Edna these letters, and by withholding and interpreting them, Mademoiselle has complicated Edna's emotional reactions to Robert. She has kept Robert in the forefront of Edna's thoughts, she has provided the interpretation that Robert loves her, and she has aroused sexual feelings in Edna by playing music as a substitute for Robert. Mademoiselle has further impugned Robert's fidelity and his worthiness, only to have Edna respond by defending him all the more vigorously. While Edna accuses her of not understanding love, in fact Mademoiselle understands very well that feelings of love are too often based on uncertainty, jealousy, and lust, and she has effectively catered to these feelings in Edna. The scene may be one in which Mademoiselle is testing Edna's allegiances, but a contemporary such as Havelock Ellis might assert that several of the conventional traits of the lesbian as seducer are present.[25] Mademoiselle is an older woman, Edna younger. Edna is disappointed in love, is now living alone, and is interested in becoming an artist. To Ellis, she would seem to be ripe for inversion.

Always careful of her novel's structure, Chopin selects as the next scene in the novel the heterosexual scene in which Arobin and Edna mutually seduce one another. While this is a sly and amusing scene, of great interest is that in the middle of it, Edna mentions the seemingly irrelevant topic of Mademoiselle Reisz. The context of the scene is an anatomy of seduction. Arobin's technique is a primer for roues; he begins with touching Edna on the hair and working his way down. Edna is no naif in this situation; she asserts that he will soon tell her that she is "adorable . . . and captivating" (p. 82). Her comment shows that she expects Arobin, a male seducer, to use flattery and the pretense of being her slave as techniques in his quest for power over her. Her experience must be compared with what happened in the previous scene, when she was alone with Mademoiselle Reisz, who also provided ample compliments. Arobin, smooth operator that he is, cleverly denies that he would resort to mere flattery, though he says, "I shouldn't be lying if I did." It is at this moment that Edna asks if he knows Mademoiselle. Arobin's reaction seems extreme; he calls Mademoiselle "partially demented," "disagreeable," and "unpleasant." Then he and Edna begin to argue about Mademoiselle, and Edna reveals another detail of her earlier visit to Mademoiselle, that Mademoiselle had put her arms around her and felt her shoulder blades to see if her wings were strong enough to "soar above the level of plain of tradition and prejudice" (p. 82). Her recollection of this conversation in this context may confirm the sexual undertones of this advice; perhaps Mademoiselle was daring Edna to prove by some unnamed action that she is not a weakling. Arobin, exasperated by this turn in the conversation, asks, "Why have you introduced her at a moment when I desire to talk to you?" Edna puts the seduction back on course by performing a chest thrust, that is, putting her hands in back of her head, a typical gesture of sexual openness, and then telling him he can once again talk about her.

Arobin is annoyed that the topic of Mademoiselle Reisz has derailed his efficient seduction because Mademoiselle is a woman who refuses to be defined by a man. Arobin also perceives that Mademoiselle has power over Edna that interferes with his desires. Like Arobin, Mademoiselle touches Edna literally and figuratively; Mademoiselle makes Edna think, and thinking is antithetical to the feelings Arobin is trying to arouse. He admits that he is jealous of Edna's thoughts, but in fact he is jealous of the possibility that Mademoiselle has the sort of influence he would like to have over Edna. In this scene Chopin contrasts Arobin, the hyperheterosexual, with Mademoiselle Reisz, who also touches Edna, flatters her, and has power over her. The rivalry for Edna's attentions places Arobin and Mademoiselle on a continuum of heterosexuality and homosexuality. Thus Edna's reference to Mademoiselle in the middle of Arobin's seduction shows that she recognizes that she has experienced a similar scene with Mademoiselle.

Edna attempts to visit Mademoiselle again but instead of seeing her translator, she meets the text himself, Robert. This scene draws much of its impact from the setting, since Mademoiselle's dingy flat is now charged with remembrances of the music that transported Edna, and with her torment of longing when Mademoiselle withheld Robert's letters. Seeking a more private place, they move to Edna's house, but even there Mademoiselle's influence interprets events. Robert pulls out an embroidered tobacco pouch, sewn, Edna surmises, by Mariequita, the "sly and bad one" of whom Mademoiselle had spoken. Edna's jealousy adds to her longing for Robert, so that she interprets Robert's reserve as love. In this room, Edna now "soars" above tradition: she acts; she confesses her love to Robert and kisses him. Aroused but confused and frightened, Robert is a conventional man in the end; he writes her one more letter. This is the only one of the letters which Edna reads without Mademoiselle Reisz to convey the message or interpret it; the note reads, "Good-by—because I love you" (p. 111).

Mademoiselle Reisz's role in the novel has been important. She provides Edna with an interpretation of Robert's letters by furnishing the code to explain the signs which the letters represent. Edna is susceptible to her suggestions because Mademoiselle uses the language of seduction and presents herself as an authority figure over Edna, though not the sort that Edna readily recognizes. Edna is used to male authority; her stern Calvinistic father and her husband, who thinks of her as a prized possession, embody codes that she comes to notice, understand, and reject in the course of the novel. Nor is Mademoiselle's authority that of a female parent, a role which to some extent Adele Ratignolle plays in the novel.

Mademoiselle's authority is that of the non-heterosexual, artist-outsider, who is not bound by sentimental conventions. She is presented as a witchlike figure with the ability to transport Edna to new levels of reality. She controls the important letters from Robert. She challenges Edna to defy convention and implies that Edna will be a coward if she does not do so. She is adept at using female linguistic codes of translation and mediation, but she can also use male linguistic codes of power and seduction. Thus, Chopin did not reject beliefs such as Havelock Ellis's that lesbians were interested in the seduction of women (p. 322). Nevertheless, Chopin is also accepting of Mademoiselle's positive qualities. This is apparent when Edna walks into the sea at the novel's end in part because she has despaired of understanding her experiences. Her last thought of Mademoiselle is of someone who would laugh derisively at her "pretensions" (p. 114), but who might have understood. Within the context of the 1890s, Mademoiselle Reisz is sympathetically portrayed.

An elusive but pertinent question is the extent to which Edna responds to Mademoiselle. One can see in abundance Edna's awakening to heterosexual desire and behavior, but Chopin does not limit her exploration of female sexuality. Edna's desire to be an artist; her leaving house and husband and pursuing art were activities associated with lesbians. The fact that her children are ages eight and six raises the question of where are her four-and two-and one-month old children; like Adele, she would be pregnant biannually if she and Leonce were sexually active. We understand from his comments to Dr. Mandelet that their sex life has ceased. Indeed, the early scene in the novel when Leonce returns late, awakens Edna, and starts an argument sums up the reasons there are no more babies. The lack of a satisfying sexual life, to Krafft-Ebing, was a possible source of "inversion."[26] Havelock Ellis would add that Edna's disappointment in all her relationships with men makes her susceptible to lesbian seduction; in fact, since Mademoiselle takes every opportunity to point out the failings of men in general and Robert in particular, she seems to be attempting to present herself or at least women as more suitable friends and lovers.

Edna also displays a tendency which Krafft-Ebing believed was an inevitable precursor of lesbianism (p. 397). Early in the novel as Edna rests in Madame Antoine's cottage, she removes her clothes, stretches out in bed, caresses her hair, and "looked at her round arms . . . and rubbed them one after the other observing closely, as if it were something she saw for the first time, the fine, firm quality and texture of her flesh" (p. 37). The autoerotic behavior which Cynthia Griffin Wolff identifies as essentially narcissistic (p. 214) is also a sign of Edna's willingness to give herself pleasure. She is awakening to all aspects of her physical being. She desires to be with Mademoiselle Reisz, to share her most private, intimate thoughts with her, and to be physically aroused by her. Edna does not return the physical advances of Mademoiselle but neither does she shrink away from them. Ultimately Edna manifests her sexuality heterosexually, but only after the marriage plot, the adultery love plot, and the seduction plot have been undermined by her relationship with Mademoiselle.

Edna's sexuality demonstrates the rich and diverse choices available for the expression of human passion. She is not the sacred object of heterosexual criticism; she and Mademoiselle Reisz pushed against the limit of their milieu's conventional expectations of women's sexual behavior, even at a time when these conventions were rapidly changing. Cloaked in the codes of lesbianism ubiquitous in the nineteenth century, Chopin's novel nonetheless daringly presents lesbianism as a reality to be faced, perhaps even embraced, not condemned.

Notes

1. Kate Chopin, *The Awakening: An Authoritative Text, Contexts, Criticism,* ed. Margaret Culley (New York: Norton, 1969), p. 83.

2. Elaine Showalter, "Tradition and the Female Talent," in *New Essays on "The Awakening,"* ed. Wendy Martin (Cambridge: Cambridge University Press, 1988), p. 46.

3. Cristina Giorcelli, "Edna's Wisdom: A Transitional and Numinous Merging," in *New Essays on "The Awakening,"* ed. Wendy Martin (Cambridge: Cambridge University Press, 1988), p. 137.

4. C. L. Deyo, St. Louis Post-Dispatch (May 20, 1899); quoted in *The Awakening,* ed. Margaret Culley (New York: Norton, 1976), p. 143.

5. Anne Goodwyn Jones, *Tomorrow is Another Day: The Woman Writer in the South,* 1859-1936 (Baton Rouge: Louisiana State University Press, 1981), p. 143.

6. (Berkeley: University of California Press, 1990).

7. David M. Halperin, *One Hundred Years of Homosexuality: Essays on Greek Love* (New York: Routledge, 1990).

8. Lillian Faderman, *Suppressing the Love of Men: Romantic Friendship and Love between Women from the Renaissance to the Present* (New York: William Morrow, 1981).

9. Laurie E. George, "Women's Language in *The Awakening,*" in *Approches to Teaching Kate Chopin's "The Awakening,"* ed. Bernard Koloski (New York: Modern Language Association, 1988).

10. Bonnie Zimmerman, "What Has Never Been: An Overview of Lesbian Feminist Criticism," in *The

New Feminist Criticism: Essays on Woman, Literature and Theory, ed. Elaine Showalter (New York: Pantheon, 1985), p. 208.

11. Carroll Smith-Rosenberg, *Disorderly Conduct: Visions of Gender in Victorian America* (New York: Knopf, 1985), pp. 53-77. "The Female World of Love and Ritual" first appeared in *Signs* in 1978.

12. Adrienne Rich, *On Lies, Secrets and Silence: Selected Prose: 1966-1978* (New York; Norton, 1979).

13. *Intimate Matters: A History of Sexuality in America* (New York: Harper & Row, 1988), pp. 121-129.

14. Richard Ellmann, *Oscar Wilde* (New York: Alfred A. Knopf, 1988), pp. 188-190.

15. Emily Toth, *Kate Chopin* (New York: William Morrow, 1990), pp. 278, 296.

16. Culley, p. 22; see also Cynthia Griffin Wolff, "Thanatos and Eros: Kate Chopin's *The Awakening,*" *American Quarterly,* 25 (October 1973), 449-472.

17. *Kate Chopin: A Critical Biography* (Baton Rouge: Louisiana State University Press, 1969), pp. 289-292.

18. *The Complete Works of Kate Chopin,* ed. Per Seyersted (Baton Rouge: Louisiana State University Press, 1969), II, 721-722.

19. Carole Stone, "The Female Artist in Kate Chopin's *The Awakening.* Birth and Creativity," *Women's Studies,* 13, nos. 1-2 (1986), 28.

20. Sandra M. Gilbert and Susan Gubar, "Sexual Linguistics; Gender, Language, and Sexuality," *New Literary History,* 16 (Spring 1985), 529.

21. See Margaret Homans, *Bearing the Word: Language and Female Experience Nineteenth Century Women's Writing* (Chicago: University of Chicago Press, 1986).

22. Catherine R. Stimpson, "Zero Degree Deviancy: The Lesbian Novel in English," in *Writing and Sexual Difference,* ed. Elizabeth Abel (Chicago: University of Chicago Press, 1982), p. 246.

23. Robin Lakoff, "Stylistic Strategies within a Grammar Style," in *Language, Sex, and Gender,* ed. Judith Orasamu, Miriam K. Slater, and Leonore Loeb Adler (New York: New York Academy of Sciences, 1979), p. 66.

24. James H. Justus, "The Unawakening of Edna Pontellier," *Southern Literary Journal,* 10 (Spring 1978),116.

25. Havelock Ellis, *Studies in the Psychology of Sex, Sexual Inversion* (1897; rpt. Modern Library, 1940), p. 322.

26. Richard von Krafft-Ebing, *Psychopathia Sexualis* (1882; rpt. New York: Physicians and Surgeons Book Co., 1922), p. 397.

Ralph J. Poole (essay date 1999)

SOURCE: Poole, Ralph J. "Body/Rituals: The (Homo)Erotics of Death in Elizabeth Stuart Phelps, Rose Terry Cooke, and Edgar Allan Poe." In *Soft Canons: American Women Writers and Masculine Tradition,* edited by Karen L. Kilcup, pp. 239-61. Iowa City: University of Iowa Press, 1999.

[*In the following essay, Poole explores the connection between lesbianism and supernatural horror in works by Rose Terry Cooke and Elizabeth Stuart Phelps, and uses examples of Edgar Allan Poe's treatment of horror and the unspeakable to illustrate the differences between male and female writers' approaches to the subversion of tradition.*]

> We are not free, nor will we be, until this silence at last is ended and we are invisible no more.
>
> —Paula Bennett

In his (in)famous, obsessively quoted statement that the death of a beautiful woman is "unquestionably" the most poetical topic in the world, Edgar Allan Poe also contemplates the adequate narrator of this topic, declaring that "equally it is beyond doubt that the lips best suited for such a topic are those of a bereaved lover."[1] Clearly, what Poe has in mind are the lips of a *male* lover telling the story of the death of his *female* beloved. What if this polarized heterosexual setting were disrupted, if both the lover and the beloved were female? Does Poe's erotics of death or deathly eroticism apply equally to homoerotically charged narratives, or do these tales tell different stories altogether? In the context of such questions, it is appropriate to invoke Bonnie Zimmerman's call for a lesbian "resisting reader" who creates new possibilities and transforms old realities by resisting "heterotexts," rewriting and appropriating them as lesbian texts instead. This is not to say that the lesbian resisting reader is "merely demanding a plot or character study that the writer has not chosen to create. She is picking up on hints and possibilities that the author, consciously or not, has strewn in the text."[2] Such a reading may reveal subtexts of women's bonding and female friendship that lead "to the rewriting of cultural stereotypes and literary conventions by reversing the values attached to the idea of lesbianism" (142). It may also complicate our understanding of such terms as "masculine literary tradition" and "feminine literary tradition."

Pioneering studies by Lillian Faderman and Carroll Smith-Rosenberg argue persuasively that although there was no name for lesbian love in the nineteenth century, there existed an affirmative tradition of romantic friend-ship between women.[3] Until the end of the century in America, women loving women were not thought to be perverse inverts, a sexological term later attributed to them. While it may be difficult—not to say impos-sible—to apply current notions of lesbianism to nineteenth-century society and, accordingly, to its liter-ary texts, we must acknowledge the abundance of sources that indicate the existence and, indeed, the com-mon practice of love between women in the presexolo-gist era. As Smith-Rosenberg observes, "The question of female friendships is peculiarly elusive; we know so little or perhaps have forgotten so much. An intriguing and almost alien form of human relationship, they flour-ished in a different social structure and amidst different sexual norms" (313). However difficult it might seem to grasp the nature of these romantic friendships, the focus of discussion should not be limited to the question of genital contact as the dividing line between hetero-sexual and homosexual: "whether or not these women expressed themselves genitally there is no doubt that physical excitement and eroticism played an important part in their love."[4] What is at stake here is a question-ing of the hetero/homo binary. The opposition between "heterosexual" and "homosexual," like so many other binary constructions, has always been constructed on the foundations of the related oppositional pair "inside" and "outside." As Diana Fuss observes, "Many of the current efforts in lesbian and gay theory have begun the difficult but urgent textual work necessary to call into question the stability and ineradicability of the hetero/homo hierarchy, suggesting that new (and old) sexual possibilities are no longer thinkable in terms of a simple inside/outside dialectic."[5]

Borders are notoriously unstable,[6] and sexual identity may not be so secure after all. Using a vocabulary evok-ing the male literary tradition of ghost stories (and the female counterparts that I want to look at here), Fuss claims that for heterosexuality there always remains the psychic proximity of its terrifying (homo)sexual other; and, vice versa, homosexuality can never fully escape the insistent social pressures of (hetero)sexual confor-mity: "Each is *haunted* by the other, but here again it is the other who comes to stand in metonymically for the very occurrence of *haunting* and *ghostly* visitations" (3, emphasis added). The other, in this discourse, is the fig-ure of the homosexual as abject, undead, and—we might add—ghost. Fuss goes as far as to call the emergence of homosexual production a kind of ghostwriting itself: "Paradoxically, the 'ghosting' of homosexuality coin-cides with its 'birth,' for the historical moment of the first appearance of the homosexual as a 'species' rather than a 'temporary aberration' also marks the moment of the homosexual's disappearance—into the closet" (4). However tempting the implied idea of a homo-writing as ghost-writing might seem for my concern, I will try not to swallow this alluring bait—at least not right away.

Instead of inscribing the concept of homophobic closet-writing that Eve Sedgwick so perfectly applies to male writers[7] onto the female-authored ghost stories with which I am concerned (and thus creating another inside/out dichotomy), I shall ponder the idea that every out-side is also an alongside, that there may also be some-thing like a borderline writing that collapses fixed boundaries of both gender and sexuality.

Ghost stories are the perfect medium for such a project. They breathe the air of the forbidden and intimate the unspeakable. This is true of most nineteenth-century ghost writings, and especially of Poe's ritualized erotic death scenes celebrated in such famous stories as "Ligeia," "Berenice," "Morella," and "Eleonora."[8] The "unspeakable," however, means different things for dif-ferent authors. According to David S. Reynolds, Poe "redirects" the vulgarity and inhumanity of the (often female) sensationalists' literature of his time, which, in turn, accounts for a depoliticization and loss of often explosive social implications. Reynolds also speaks of Poe's containment, which produces a moment of con-trol especially obvious in his first-person narrators. Thus, a typical Poe narrator serves as controlling de-vice, for he translates a sensational plot into the overac-tive workings of his fancy, depriving the story of its subversive potential: "His horror tales feature violence without repulsive gore, criminality without political im-port, women without sexuality, nightmares without revolutionary suggestions."[9] According to J. Gerald Kennedy—and quite contrary to Reynolds.—the narra-tor of Poe's stories depicting the death of a woman ex-hibits a perverse impatience. In stories like "Morella" and "Ligeia," death is portrayed as an ambiguous, tem-porary parting: "In a monstrous parody of the death of the Other, Poe represents the return of the beloved not in spiritual terms but as a ghastly reincarnation tinged with vampirism. Through such supernaturalism, he im-plies that death is neither an extinction of the self nor admission to a heavenly social club. Rather, it is a con-dition of spiritual confinement and unrest, a dream world where one acts out the desires and hostilities of an earlier existence."[10]

One easily forgets that Poe's ghostly death scenarios are not always arranged around a strictly heterosexual male-female setting. His three stories from 1844-1845 on the topic of mesmerism, "Mesmeric Revelation," "A Tale of the Ragged Mountains," and especially "The Facts in the Case of M. Valdemar," evolve around a male first-person narrator and a second, mesmerized male in various states of dying. The scandal here hardly lies in any erotic—not even to mention *homo*erotic—implications, but in the articulated assertion of one's own death in utterances such as "I struggled—I gasped—I died" or "Yes;—no; I *have been* sleeping—and now—now—*I am dead*."[11] In the textual analysis performed by Roland Barthes, this utterance is a scandal in more than one sense. By turning this sentence from the metaphoric back into the literal, it is a scandal (of the structure) of language since "the coupling of the first person (I) and the attribute 'dead' is precisely what is radically impossible: it is the empty point, the blind spot of language structure which the tale will occupy very exactly."[12] The semantic scandal rests in the assertion of two contraries at the same time (Life, Death): "the signifier expresses a signified (Death) which contradicts its utterance." The psychoanalytic scandal, finally, is produced by the effect "that Death, as primordial repressed, erupts directly into language," resulting in a radically traumatic experience of return, an "exploded taboo." Enter psychosis: it is the scandalous return of the literal that leaves the symbolic (as field of neurosis) and opens the space of psychosis where "every symbol ceases, as does every neurosis" (10). Thus, the cause for trouble is not so much the unbelievability of the utterance but the more radical impossibility, its madness. In Poe's "The Facts," the violation of the taboo is sanctioned at the end. M. Valdemar's return does not end happily: he shrinks and rots, leaving but a "nearly liquid mass of loathsome—of detestable putrescence" (103).

In a Barthesian rereading of Poe's story, Tracy Ware deemphasizes Valdemar's utterance, leading her to a different conclusion: "Poe's readers may feel that there are greater horrors than the transgression of a paradigmatic opposition."[13] Poe's combination of humor and horror is most apparent in the story's ending; two "monstrous" puns in the narrator's account appear before waking the mesmerized Valdemar: even though it seemed clear to the narrator that to awaken him would insure "at least his speedy dissolution," he nevertheless "made an endeavor to recompose the patient" (102-103). While "re-compose" may be read as a pun anticipating Valdemar's imminent decomposition, "dissolution" can refer to decomposition as well as to death. The ambiguity of the situation between rebirth and final death is heightened by the narrator's clinging to a blind confidence in his scientific powers: "In this attempt I soon saw that I should be successful—or at least I soon fancied that my success would be complete" (103). Is it a "success" that a person being mesmerized for seven long months awakens only to "absolutely [rot] away beneath my hands"? In "The Philosophy of Composition," Poe claims to always have the ending in mind while writing: "Nothing is more clear than that every plot, worth the name, must be elaborated to its *dénouement* before any thing be attempted with the pen. It is only with the *dénouement* constantly in view that we can give a plot its indispensable air of consequence, or causation, by making the incidents, and especially the tone at all points, tend to the development of the intention" (31).

What did Poe have constantly in view when he let the narrator put Valdemar through the horrors of mesmerizing his already decaying body under the guise of scientific experimentation? Valdemar is a hybrid character. Not only does he seem to come from Eastern Europe, presumably Poland, thus marking him as foreign and strange, he also looks and acts queerly: the effect of a "violent contrast" between his white whiskers and his black hair is paralleled by the dissimilarity between "the extreme spareness of his person," his "markedly nervous" temperament, and an odd calmness concerning his near death: "his physicians had declared him in a confirmed phthisis. It was his custom, indeed, to speak calmly of his approaching dissolution, as of a matter neither to be avoided nor regretted" (96-97). To what end does the narrator's interest in Valdemar's "peculiar constitution" lead? No (homo)erotics of death appears in the final scene—indeed, if anything, we could call the deathbed scenario between the two men a homophobic disclosure of a possible emotional attachment. In the seven months' state of suspension, Valdemar's cadaverous body is reduced to the "vibratory movement of the tongue" that "rolled violently in the mouth" until finally emitting the scandalous words while the narrator "makes passes" at the victim that he calls mesmeric: "I rapidly made the mesmeric passes, amid ejaculations of 'dead! dead!' absolutely *bursting* from the tongue and not from the lips of the sufferer" (103). A second later, the sufferer suffers no more. Surely, he will not return, as do the numerous female corpses in Poe's texts.[14]

How significantly different are the endings of the stories I want to examine now. In her evaluation of the nineteenth-century female ghost story, Barbara Patrick claims that the disparity between women's works and those of their male counterparts lies in the experiencing of reality. While male writers' ghost stories are more about "what we cannot know (epistemological doubt) or the fact that people frighten themselves with chimeras (psycho-drama)," women's supernatural tales "address a world in which things *are* frightening—not least of which are the silencing and marginalization of women."[15] The women's works expose "the true horror of reality" by exploring social evils through the veil of the supernatural. "Just as ghosts speak from a world beyond to the world we know," according to Patrick, "these writers speak from the world of the text to the world of the reader" (74). There is a sharp discrepancy between the evocation of a ghost as a highly antirealistic device and the otherwise often strikingly realistic settings of the stories. As Patrick points out, the presence of a ghost in these tales "drew attention to the horrors of living in patriarchal culture, particularly the oppression of women through domestication, the withholding of power and knowledge from women, and the discounting of women and women's perceptions" (82).

Both Poe's and the women writers' narratives that I discuss here conjure the unsayable. In a tale such as "Valdemar," language, logic, and cultural taboo are broken, allowing the unspeakable to speak and the unbearable sight to be seen; its supernaturalism "intrudes upon the world of reason and experience to deliver the message of mortality" (Kennedy, 63). However, while Poe invokes the haunting fact of mortality, the women writers seek to challenge death, which functions not as a device of horror, but as a means of transcendence and communication. Ghost stories like Rose Terry Cooke's "My Visitation" (1858) and Elizabeth Stuart Phelps's "Since I Died" (1873) explore the taboo region of "the unspeakable," but this region is configured differently than in Poe's work. At the center of both stories is the love of one woman for another; both are tales of love and loss, mystery and death, in which the understanding of supernatural events was left to the imagination of the reader. According to Susan Koppelman, this kind of elision "gave writers the opportunity to allude to the unsayable, or, perhaps, the unpublishable." We can find coded narratives dealing with such matters as incest, infidelity, addiction, and rape. Koppelman adds: "In this same category of stories female characters rebel against the patriarchy, pursue their personal ambitions, achieve success where they are forbidden to even enter, and love women more than they love men."[16]

Popular and successful writers in the New England local color tradition,[17] neither Rose Terry Cooke (1827-1892) nor Elizabeth Stuart Phelps (1844-1911) is generally regarded as a "lesbian (ghost) writer." Cooke's stories are known for their criticism of many married women's experiences; as Emily Toth has observed, "No other New England local colorist felt so vehemently, or observed in print so acutely, the sufferings of women . . . in bad marriages."[18] These tales highlight the domestic violence within a repressive Calvinist society situated in rural, white, predominantly middle-class New England.[19] While a generation younger, Phelps nevertheless belongs to the same tradition of local colorists as Cooke. Her literary career lasted nearly fifty years, from her first published story in 1864 to her death. She published fifty-seven books, including twenty novels and five collections of short stories. During these years, Phelps underwent an astonishing transformation in her attitude toward the possibilities and limits in women's lives. Her early, almost utopian optimism about women's strengths and abilities, much like that of Harriet Beecher Stowe, changed into a thoroughly pessimistic view that Cooke had often expressed and that would later find ambivalent expression in the works of Mary Wilkins Freeman and Edith Wharton. Even more puzzling is the fact that, as Josephine Donovan points out, "Phelps' alteration may be seen as a transition from a fundamentally female-identified position to one that is male-identified. That is, she moved—both personally and in her works—from an attitude where her emotional and ideological identification was primarily with women to one in which that identification was with men. In this sense she may be said to have abandoned women's literary realism . . . in her late works."[20]

Phelps's stories and novels from the mid-1860s to the early 1880s feature strong female friendships across the borders of age, race, and class. For example, in *An Old Maid's Paradise* (1879), a novel that Donovan calls nearly autobiographical, Puella, an independent rural woman, says: "A—MAN!!! . . . What . . . two full-grown women—should want of *a* man."[21] And in *Dr. Zay* (1882), a novel about a woman physician that Donovan claims as "the high-water mark of Phelps's female-identified commitment" (89), an observer comments on the doctor's independence: "Now then! There are women that love women . . . care for 'em, grieve over 'em, worry about 'em, feel a fellow feeling and a kind of duty to 'em, and never forget they're one of 'em, misery and all."[22] In this period Phelps wrote her proleptic "Since I Died" (1873),[23] one of her numerous stories that present erotic or romantic relationships between women that often have gone unnoticed. Here, however, Phelps turns to the tradition of the ghost story and its implicit death scenario: a woman recently dead narrates her experience as she gradually realizes her transformation. In her undead condition she struggles to communicate with her beloved, whom she has left behind sitting at her bedside. Koppelman notes: "The fact that her beloved is a woman almost, but not quite, escapes notice in the reader's fascination with the mystery of this voice from beyond" (45). Phelps's description of the rising consciousness of a newly dead person may be compared with strikingly similar popular contemporary descriptions of "near-death" or "out-of-body" experiences. However, I find much more interesting Koppelman's remark on "the tension between the narrator's desire to experience 'the immensity' that opens before her once she leaves her body and the pull of her beloved's eyes." She also notes that for us it might seem surprising that the editor of Phelps's story, who had turned down Walt Whitman because he considered the poet a threat to the "religious and upright moral tone" of his magazine, had no objection to this story: "He found nothing immoral or irreligious in a story about a recently dead woman torn between her earthly love for another woman and the beckoning deity" (46).

We might ask, is this love so "earthly" after all? The first-person narrator—never explicitly marked as female—addresses a "you" who later is clearly defined as female, in an affirmative rewriting of Poe's deathly homoerotic narratives. The story starts out with the statement "How very still you sit!" directed at the other woman. Sixteen unfinished "if" clauses follow, linguistically marking the unfulfilled and/or unfulfillable desire of the speaker, who waits for a sign of acknowledgment and perhaps of love:

If the shadow of an eyelash stirred upon your cheek
. . . if you should turn and look behind your chair, or
lift your face, half lingering and half longing, half loving and half loth, to ponder on the annoyed and
thwarted cry which the wind is making, where I stand
between it and yourself, against the half-closed window.

. . . [I]f you named my name; if you held your breath
with terror, or sobbed aloud for love, or sprang, or
cried—.

But you only lift your head and look me in the eye.[24]

Horrified that there might be no sign whatsoever, the
speaker imagines the impossible: "If I dared step near,
or nearer . . . if I dropped an arm as lightly as a snow-
flake round your shoulder. . . ." Again she breaks off,
suggesting that the enigmas of desire manifest a border-
land between the person dead but desiring and the other
person alive but fixed: "The *fear* which no heart has
fathomed, the *fate* which no fancy has faced, the *riddle*
which no soul has read, steps between your substance
and my soul." The speaker writhes with the effort to
speak: "Speech and language *struggle* over me. *Mute
articulations* fill the air. . . . Is there an alphabet between us?" (47, emphasis added). What she seeks is to
speak the unspeakable, passionate love to which death
alone can give voice.

The speaker remembers former times when there was
communication. But a closer look reveals that she has
been passive all along to the point of numbness: she did
not see her own tears, she did not actually articulate her
own thoughts. After death, however, she has become
strangely active: "Now that I hold your eyes in mine,
and you see me not; now when I stretch my hand and
you touch me not; now that I cry your name, and you
hear it not,—I comprehend you, tender one! A wisdom
not of earth was in your words. 'To live, is dying; I will
die. To die is life, and you shall live'" (47). While the
speaker was still alive, she remained passive and receptive; now that she is dead, she has passed into a realm
of action, has gained life. But now she has no one to
act upon, although she has entered a new spatial ground,
where "I could show you the fairest sight and sweetest
that ever blessed your eyes." She finds death, now that
she is experiencing it, no "source of distress," a fact,
however, that perplexes her: "I am often bewildered
here. . . . Here is a mystery" (48). This mystery relates
to her paradoxical agency and ability to speak that
marks the story's inverse structure as a whole. In contrast to the "de-composition" that we see in Poe,
Phelps's narrator acquires in dying a language she
lacked in life.

As the narrative concludes, the speaker struggles to retain her connection with the beloved. Addressing her
for a last time, a series of questions desperately asks for
reassurance: "Would you not know how it has been

with me since your perishable eyes beheld my perished
face?" (51). Being left with "a matchless, solitary fear,"
the addressed "you" gains distance and becomes "she":
"I slip from her. . . . I lose her." There is only one moment left to tell her the "guarded thing," the "treasured
word" that renders all that has been said a lie: "*Death is
dumb, for Life is deaf!*" (52). This recognition brings us
back to the narrative's beginning. When exactly is it
told? Not at the moment of her death, because we know
this moment occurred sometime earlier. It must be a
state of being that follows the treacherous present tense
of the first paragraphs. The speaker uses the "moment
to tell her" the agonies of love as camouflage to tell us
a quite different story: the mutual understanding between the two women—that living is dying and dying
means living—is precisely the paradox that it seems to
be. This clever construction of an ambivalent state of
being is wrong: as long as life is deaf, death remains
dumb. Is this meant to be a pessimistic outlook on romantic friendship? Or, rather, a fierce appeal for a balanced emotional and physical exchange between lovers?

One of the first women in nineteenth-century America
who, like Poe, dared to examine the mind's nighttime,
Phelps probed the recesses of the unconscious, the supernatural, the other. Her enormously popular novel,
The Gates Ajar (1868), served the growing interest of a
largely female mass audience by treating the unconscious in a comfortable fashion. Phelps's unconscious is
spatial, it "consists of intimations of a superior world in
the promptings of God and friendly spirits; it is 'other,'
but just a step away, 'over there.' Above all, the unconscious is understood as a definite place in which, mostly
unknown to consciousness, spiritual activity is continuous."[25] In this formulation, the unconscious is understood as a gate through which spiritual visitors pass.
Dreams, memories, prophecies, divinations are thought
to visit the space of the unconscious, all of them ghosts
calling upon the self-haunted self.

The coexistence of heaven and earth, marked in the
spatial metaphors of the unconscious, is clearly discernible in "Since I Died," where the speaker enters a space
located between the earthliness of her beloved, whom
she is leaving behind, and the heavenliness of the "Presence" coming for her. Seen in this context, the moment
of which she speaks at the end, which marks the exact
time of her narrative, may be understood as a ritualistic
effort to maintain a connection between two lovers parting. It is an unfixed, unstable moment in which death
can speak and life can hear, before all has changed and
communication no longer will be possible. This single
moment tells the story of their love, which establishes
the story we read. Thus, there is a circular as well as a
linear movement in this story: circular in its mingling
of beginning and end that marks the eternity of love;
linear in its closure, since the end of the story coincides

with the end of their chance for communication. There-fore, even while there is a melancholic undercurrent, the overall message is a positive one: there is time enough to tell the guarded thing, indeed, "Time to whis-per a treasured word!" (52).

At first glance, Rose Terry Cooke's early story "My Visitation" seems much more conventionally structured, closer to the Romantic and Gothic tradition than her later "grimly authentic realism" (Donovan, 68). "My Visitation" shares Poe's fascination with darkness, death, ghosts, and vampires, and his concept of death as transformation as he articulates it, for example, in "Mes-meric Revelation": "There are two bodies—the rudi-mental and the complete, corresponding with the two conditions of the worm and the butterfly. What we call 'death,' is but the painful metamorphosis. Our present incarnation is progressive, preparatory, temporary. Our future is perfected, ultimate, immortal. The ultimate life is the full design."[26] Like Poe's narrators, who are often regarded as unreliable and disturbed,[27] Cooke's narrator, who supposedly tells the story of her passion she feels for another woman, Eleanor, is, according to Elizabeth Ammons, "disturbed." Ammons sees in the story both a "painful journey . . . away from this passionate same-sex attachment to union with a man" and a horror story—"a kind of living nightmare that tips the narrator into madness." For Ammons, the narrative reveals the danger and damage of such an enforced journey into heterosexuality: "Cooke's heroine must renounce her feelings for Eleanor; she must come to see her beloved as a monster and her own passionate love for her as de-ranged."[28] This interpretation suggests that we should dismiss "My Visitation" as a failed attempt to resist men's power over women in patriarchal culture.

But there is another way to read this story: as a parable of one woman's (Eleanor's) unspeakable betrayal of an-other woman. The obviously Poe-like narrator presents herself as unreliable from the beginning: "If this story is incoherent—arranged rather for the writer's thought than for the reader's eye—it is because the brain which dictated it reeled with the sharp assaults of memory."[29] It is the story of a visitation: the ghostly visitor is the woman she once loved, as we finally learn. The setting for the first visit is characterized as a melancholic fore-shadowing of death. The narrator is ill—like many women of the time, it seems—and the sadness of au-tumn's solitude bothers her: "I can endure any silence better than this hush of decay, it fills me with preter-natural horror; it is as if a tomb opened and breathed out its dank, morbid breath across the murmur of life, to paralyze and to chill" (15). Yet this atmosphere en-genders the speakable truth of love between women.

While savoring the fictional world of Charlotte Brontë ("I was deep in *Shirley*; it excited, it affected me; it was always to me like a brief and voluntary brain-fever to

read that book"), the narrator senses a presence of "something else I could not see" (15). She then inter-rupts her narrative (the first of several interruptions) to return to her youth, when she first met Eleanor, falling passionately in love with her at once: "I speak advis-edly in the use of that term; no other phrase expresses the blind, irrational, all-enduring devotion I gave to her; no less vivid word belongs to that madness" (16). The love that she calls madness is addressed toward a young girl described as a marble deity, a "Pallas Athena." She sketches their friendship in almost sadomasochistic terms: "If she was kind in speech or act—if she spoke to me caressingly—if she put her warm lips upon my cheek—I was thrilled with joy; . . . and when she fell into some passion, and burned me with bitter words, stinging me into retort by their injustice, their hard cru-elty, it was I who repented—I who humiliated myself—I who, with abundant tears, asked her pardon, worked, plead, prayed to obtain it; . . . I was glad to be clay as long as she was queen and deity" (17). The speaker's "worship" earned her the "masculine contempt for span-iels," the contempt of her beloved, who "despised a creature that would endure a blow, mental or physical, without revenging itself; and from her I endured almost any repulse, and forgot it" (18). How very remote this description of friendship and love is from what we know of the romantic friendships described by Carroll Smith-Rosenberg and Lillian Faderman.

The discrepancy becomes even more evident when a man enters the female sphere in Cooke's story, engen-dering a precarious ménage à trois that seems to signify the narrator's rejection of a lesbian connection. Herman first loves Eleanor before turning his affection toward the speaker, who finally marries him. The speaker, we learn, is not interested in men; she mentions only a brief engagement that she accounts for by her total in-experience. The incident causes a nervous breakdown, however, and at the same time inspires the recognition that "I had loved Eleanor too well. I had always loved her more than that man; and when the episode was over, I discovered in myself that I never could have loved any man as I did her . . . that so long as she lived for me I should neither die nor craze" (19). It is in this period of feebleness that she again meets Herman, whose health is equally weak. Ironically, quite contrary to the ups and downs that characterize the homosocial friendship of the two women, this heterosocial relation-ship is perfectly balanced and complementary. Where Eleanor's gender was inclined toward the masculine, Herman's tilts toward the feminine. Their similarity is based on the exclusion of Eleanor: "We talked together as few men talk—perhaps no women—. . . but we never spoke of Eleanor" (22). Herman is so unmanly, so desex(ualiz)ed that, accordingly, the narrator is sur-prised when he asks to marry her. Because of the nar-cissistic origins of their relationship, she has to admit that "I had but the lesser part of heart to give any man.

I loved a woman too well to love or to marry" (22). She does not tell him that besides Eleanor's being the "one present and all-absorbing passion of my soul," she has yet another reason for declining his offer: "I shuddered at the possibility of loving a man so utterly, and then placing myself at his mercy for life. I felt that my safety lay in my freedom from any such tie to Eleanor" (23). This single moment aligns Cooke's story with her other stories highlighting the sufferings of women in bad marriages. Here, however, this hint against wedlock is almost an aside, too unimportant to be pursued.

Instead, a strange incident occurs at this point: upon her return home, the narrator learns of Eleanor's putative deceit, yet we never discover what happened to divide them: "And here must I leave a blank. The forgiveness which stirs me to this record refuses to define for alien eyes what that trouble was" (23). We must suspect, of course, that she feels betrayed because Eleanor loves somebody else. Why else should the narrator speak of "the loss of all that bound to life a lonely, morbid, intense, and excitable woman" (24)? So far, she has believed "that men are liars in spite of education or policy; what was it, then to know this of my ideal—Eleanor?" (24). Painfully, the narrator learns that in her absence Eleanor has married. Although we are to believe that Eleanor's corporeal removal, rather than the marriage itself, brings about the narrator's disturbance, we are left with the latter's unaccountable refusal to forgive her beloved.

What is striking, however, is that shortly after this discovery of Eleanor's marriage the "visitations" begin, as the narrator returns to her story's beginning. The stages of the visitation, which lasts for weeks, move from "a sense of alien life," from hearing "cries from half-free souls," to feeling that "something yearning, restless, pained, and sad regarded me." First asking herself whether this was death, she resolves to "pity a soul that had cast off life yet could not die to life." Gradually, she begins to perceive a shadow, "a shapeless shape," when once again she interrupts her narrative to return to a description of Herman's virtues. Compared to Cooke's other portraits of manly (mis)behavior, it is astonishing that the narrator here speaks of a "beauty indefinable, fired by the sweet vivid smile of the irradiate soul within," of a "most delicate and careful tenderness," of her sense that "what began in gratitude ended in love. . . . Truly, so far as man can do it, he saved my soul alive!" (28-29). Significantly, the narrator depicts a relationship remote from sexuality and passion; their souls, not their bodies, mingle: "In all this I was drawn toward Herman by the strongest tie that can bind one heart to another—a tie that overarches and outlasts all the fleeting passions of time, for it is the academic link of eternity; . . . there was a relation between us, undying and sure, . . . where there is neither marrying nor giving in marriage" (28). Far from representing a coer-cive movement toward heterosexuality, this passage underscores the narrator's movement away from erotic connection entirely.

The story climaxes on Christmas Eve. While the narrator and Herman are having a conversation that she conceals from us, she receives notice of Eleanor's death three months earlier, and the final visitation that night reveals the expected: they have been Eleanor's visits all along. This last time, finally, Eleanor, with "an expression of intense longing," pleads "Forgive! forgive!" (30-31). In this melodramatically tinged ending, the narrator forgives her "darling" Eleanor, giving her the freedom to leave her undead state: "I closed my eyes to crush inward the painful tears, and a touch of lips sealed them with sacred and unearthly repose. I look again; *It* had gone forever" (31). Yet she continues to address Eleanor in "that mystic country."

Reaffirming her forgiveness and love "with a truth and faith eternal!" the narrator offers an ambiguous final sentence: "Thee, forever loved, but, ah! not now forever lost?" This could be a plea that Eleanor's soul should be freed from its ghostly wanderings; in this case, the salvation of Eleanor's soul would not mean a parting forever and could instead provide the possibility for their reunification after death. The end could also signify a symbolic merging of Eleanor's physical presence with Herman's spiritual qualities, with Herman providing the realistic and, above all, speakable possibility for unification. Finally, this closing question may represent an appeal for Eleanor's continued presence. Earlier, hearing that Eleanor's last cry was for her, she had said: "If Death is the Spoiler, so is he the Restorer. . . . I remembered only love" (29). The restoration of the love between the two women may transcend the gap between life and death. In all these readings, I believe this story to center on the love between two women. Herman figures as camouflage in this homoerotic setting, providing a safe place from which the narrative can evolve. This returns us to Ammons's argument. The narrator may not be so unreliable after all. What is told is not the narrator's horrific journey into heterosexuality, it is the untold story of Eleanor's unspeakable betrayal and her unexplained death—perhaps, we might consider, *because* of her betrayal.

However great the mysteries surrounding Eleanor's death and her ghostly visitations, as well as the supernatural wanderings of Phelps's (un)dead narrator, death as such is not depicted as horrifying, which returns me to Poe's own death performances. Philippe Ariès claims: "Since death is not the end of the loved one, however bitter the grief of the survivor, death is neither ugly nor fearful. On the contrary, death is beautiful, as the dead body is beautiful."[30] Elisabeth Bronfen reflects extensively on Poe's dictum on the alliance between melancholy, death, poetics, and beauty, and she speaks of a dangerously fluid boundary between the two registers of a body's being perceived or culturally constructed as an animate natural material, on the one hand, and an inanimate aesthetic form, on the other hand: "The equation between femininity and death is such that while in cultural narratives the feminine corpse is treated like an artwork, or the beautiful woman is killed to produce an artwork, conversely, artworks emerge only at the expense of a beautiful woman's death and are treated like feminine corpses."[31] Extrapolating to the homoerotic stories of Cooke and Phelps, I question Bronfen's generalization that "a colloquial understanding of the corpse is that it is not gendered, that it is an anonymous, inanimate body, pure materiality without soul or personality" (64-65).

Moreover, we might ask: Is there melancholy involved in these poetics of death? According to Freud, melancholia is failed mourning, a denial of loss; the inability to accept the beloved's death produces a perpetual rearticulation of the repression. Only with a masculine mourner do we have the specific structural analogy between mourning and art that Bronfen discovers in Poe. Following Sarah Kofman, Bronfen argues that an ambiguous attitude toward loss is inherent in effective art as the work of melancholy. Art mourns beauty, which in turn creates a self-reflexive moment causing art to mourn itself: "The creation of beauty allows us to escape from the elusiveness of the material world into an illusion of eternity (a denial of loss), even as it imposes on us the realisation that beauty is itself elusive, intangible, receding" (64). In his ghost stories, Poe has represented the death of a female body as the ultimate moment of self-reflexivity. The self-reflexivity of Cooke's and Phelps's texts are undeniable. However, do we encounter in their stories an "illusion of eternity," i.e., "a denial of loss"? Does the death of a beautiful woman serve as motive for the creation of art in their work as it did in Poe's? What about Phelps's speaker, who is the dead woman telling her own story? Is there an autoerotic motive at work here that very well might be analogous to Poe's death rituals? This reading would shed a totally different light on "the moment of self-reflexivity, where the text seems to comment on itself and its own process of composition, and so decomposes itself" (71).

Poe's narrators in poems like "Ulalume" and "Annabel Lee" and stories like "Morella," "Berenice," and "Ligeia" seek a continued bond with a departed lover, holding onto an intermediary position that is balanced between a denial or repression and an embrace of death. The speaker acknowledges death as a mystery penetrating the world of the living and uses his poetic inscription to come to terms with the inflicted loss. Like vampires, the beloved ones seek power over their former lovers from the realm of the (un)dead. Poe's male narrators are torn between a longing for death and a will to live, producing a psychic impasse that marks an unfulfilled desire; their longing is either pathologically repeated or poetically sublimated. Viewed from this perspective, Poe's work suggests a gap between the stories of Cooke and Phelps: while Cooke uses this narrative pattern to tell a different story, Phelps transforms the pattern by exchanging the roles of living speaker and dead beloved. Here, the speaker recounts the experience of her own death, and the melancholic cycle is disrupted.

We might still ask, however, why are the women who love women in these texts bodiless ghosts wandering about the margins of worldly existence? Is this ghostly lesbian, if we want to call her that, a vampire, a monster? Marilyn Farwell argues that "Western tradition codes the female body as negative and threatening, a body so excessive in its functions and sexuality that it must be controlled. The lesbian body . . . is an extension of the excessive female body and therefore the ultimate threat to the dominant order."[32] Farwell argues that the lesbian narrative is not necessarily a story by a lesbian about lesbians but "rather a plot that affirms a place for lesbian subjectivity, that narrative space where both lesbian characters and other female characters can be active, desiring agents." Thus, according to its solution, Cooke's story could indeed be called lesbian, since "*Lesbian* is then a place or narrative space that partakes of old definitions of gender and realigns them" (157, emphasis added).

The narrators in both Cooke's and Phelps's stories exhibit a mobility through and across boundaries that in the traditional ghost narrative is clearly marked as male. Unlike Poe's many narrators, in Cooke and Phelps they perform a gender inversion; Poe's dichotomy—lover = subject = I, beloved = object = you—is radically transformed in the erotics of the lesbian ghost story. In Poe's gender system, only males have agency and subjectivity, and thus, the ability to conquer and manipulate the constructed, female opposite. Important in this ideology is the maintenance of the boundaries that define binaries. The "lesbian," however, fits into Julia Kristeva's concept of the abject as that which "disturbs identity, system, order."[33] In Kristeva's theory, the abject is a body that exceeds limits. Similarly, Mikhail Bakhtin's grotesque body is "not a closed, completed unit; it is unfinished, outgrows itself, transgresses its own limits."[34] Farwell asserts that "not only [must] the lesbian hero . . . be the monster but also . . . the monstrous female must be read as lesbian. The lesbian narrative, then, can be defined as a disruptive story in which the female is given subjectivity, not as a substitute man, but as an oversized, monstrous woman—as a lesbian" (166-167). While such a statement may sound excessive, when applied to the erotics of death in the lesbian ghost story, it makes sense. Importantly, not only character images but the narrative system as such becomes the site of transgression. If an author questions the cultural construction of femininity, as Cooke and Phelps do, the narrative in which these transgressive bodies are positioned itself undergoes transformation: "The gender boundaries are rearranged; the narrative positioning of gendered subjects and objects is altered" (167).

Poe's scenario of reincarnation is that of a completed curse. The return of the other dramatizes a loss that haunts the living and destroys the narrator's sense of reason. While estranging him from himself, "[the] ultimate implication of the separation model becomes clear: death makes us strangers to each other" (Kennedy, 57). According to Kennedy, whenever supernaturalism intrudes upon the world of reason in Poe's texts, it is to deliver the message of mortality. Yet we might question this assumption's application to Cooke's and Phelps's texts, where I would claim that supernaturalism as the return of the dead (Cooke) or as life beyond death (Phelps) discloses the precise opposite: a manifestation of immortality. While in Poe, the uncanny "shatters the illusion of one's control over the flow of existence" (Kennedy, 63), here it does not produce a disruption. Instead, in Cooke and Phelps, the disruption has taken place somewhere in the past, and it is the experience of death that initiates an end to the threat of dissolution. Thus, whereas the female bodies in Poe dissolve into vampirically coded ghosts haunting the autoerotically prone narrator from beyond, the abjected lesbian body articulates the homoerotics of her longing by resorting to channels of communication that are silent, invisible, yet strangely—"ghostly"—coded prophesies of future fulfillment.

Notes

1. Edgar Allan Poe, "Philosophy of Composition," in *The Works of Edgar Allan Poe,* ed. Edmund C. Stedman and George E. Woodberry (New York: Colonial, 1903), 6:39. All second and subsequent references to this and other sources are cited in the text.

2. Bonnie Zimmerman, "Perverse Reading: The Lesbian Appropriation of Literature," in *Sexual Practice, Textual Theory: Lesbian Cultural Criticism,* ed. Susan J. Wolfe and Julia Penelope (Cambridge, England: Blackwell, 1993), 144.

3. Lillian Faderman, *Surpassing the Love of Men: Romantic Friendship and Love between Women from the Renaissance to the Present* (1981; reprint, London: Women's Press, 1991); see especially chapter 2, "The Nineteenth Century," 145-294. Carroll Smith-Rosenberg, "The Female World of Love and Ritual: Relations between Women in Nineteenth-Century America," in *A Heritage of Her Own: Toward a New Social History of Ameri-*

can Women, ed. Nancy F. Cott and Elizabeth H. Pleck (New York: Simon and Schuster, 1979), 311-342.

4. Sheila Jeffreys, *The Spinster and Her Enemies: Feminism and Sexuality 1880-1930* (London: Pandora, 1985), 104.

5. Diana Fuss, "inside/out," in *Inside/Out: Lesbian Theories, Gay Theories,* ed. Diana Fuss (New York: Routledge, 1991), 1. See also Marjorie Garber, *Vice Versa: Bisexuality and the Eroticism of Everyday Life* (New York: Simon and Schuster, 1995).

6. See Gloria Anzaldúa, *Borderlands/La Frontera: The New Mestiza* (San Francisco: Aunt Lute, 1987).

7. See Eve Kosofsky Sedgwick's *Between Men: English Literature and Male Homosocial Desire* (New York: Columbia University Press, 1985) and *Epistemology of the Closet* (Berkeley: University of California Press, 1990).

8. For discussions of Poe's erotic ghost stories, see, for example, Grace McEntee, "Remembering Ligeia," *Studies in American Fiction* 20.1 (1992): 75-83; Yaohua Shi, "The Enigmatic Ligeia/ 'Ligeia,'" *Studies in Short Fiction* 28.4 (1991): 485-496; Joseph Andriano, "Archetypal Projection in 'Ligeia': A Post-Jungian Reading," *Poe Studies* 19.2 (1986): 27-31; Terence J. Matheson, "The Multiple Murders in 'Ligeia': A New Look at Poe's Narrator," *Canadian Review of American Studies* 13.3 (1982): 279-289; Maurice J. Bennett, "'The Madness of Art': Poe's 'Ligeia' as Metafiction," *Poe Studies* 14.1 (1981): 1-6; Jacqueline Doyle, "(Dis)Figuring Woman: Edgar Allan Poe's 'Berenice,'" *Poe Studies* 26.1-2 (1993): 13-21; Jules Zanger, "Poe's 'Berenice': Philosophical Fantasy and Its Pitfalls," in *The Scope of the Fantastic: Theory, Technique, Major Authors,* ed. Robert A. Collins and Howard D. Pearce (Westport, Conn.: Greenwood, 1985), 135-142; Hal Blythe and Charlie Sweet, "Poe's Satiric Use of Vampirism in 'Berenice,'" *Poe Studies* 14.2 (1981): 23-24; Curtis Fukuchi, "Repression and Guilt in Poe's 'Morella,'" *Studies in Short Fiction* 24.2 (1987): 149-154; Benjamin Franklin Fisher IV, "'Eleonora': Poe and Madness," in *Poe and His Times: The Artist and His Milieu,* ed. Benjamin Franklin Fisher IV (Baltimore: Edgar Allan Poe Society, 1990), 178-188.

9. David S. Reynolds, *Beneath the American Renaissance: The Subversive Imagination in the Age of Emerson and Melville* (New York: Knopf, 1988), 230.

10. J. Gerald Kennedy, "Phantasms of Death in Poe's Fiction," in *The Haunted Dusk: American Super-*

natural Fiction, 1820-1920, ed. Howard Kerr et al. (Athens: University of Georgia Press, 1983), 54. See also Steven E. Kagle, "The Corpse Within Us," in Fisher, 103-112; E. F. Bleiler, "Edgar Allan Poe," in Supernatural Fiction Writers: Fantasy and Horror, vol. 2, ed. E. F. Bleiler (New York: Scribner's, 1985), 697-705.

11. Edgar Allan Poe, "A Tale of the Ragged Mountains," in Complete Tales and Poems (New York: Vintage, 1975), 684, 101; original emphasis.

12. Roland Barthes, "Textual Analysis of a Tale by Edgar Poe," Poe Studies 10 (1977): 10.

13. Tracy Ware, "The 'Salutary Discomfort' in the Case of M. Valdemar," Studies in Short Fiction 31.3 (1994): 478.

14. For biographical contexts for "Valdemar," see Richard Kopley, "Poe's Pym-esque 'A Tale of the Ragged Mountains,'" in Fisher, 167-177; Clive Bloom, "The 'Humunculus': Marie Bonaparte's, The Life and Work of Edgar Allan Poe and Poe's 'The Facts in the Case of M. Valdemar,'" in The 'Occult' Experience and the New Criticism: Daemonism, Sexuality and the Hidden in Literature (Sussex: Harvester, 1986), 27-55.

15. Barbara Patrick, "Lady Terrorists: Nineteenth-Century American Women Writers and the Ghost Story," in American Women Short Story Writers, ed. Julie Brown (New York: Garland, 1995), 74.

16. Susan Koppelman, introduction to Two Friends, and Other Nineteenth-Century Lesbian Stories by American Women Writers (New York: Meridian, 1994), 9, 10. See also David G. Hartwell, "Notes on the Evolution of Horror Literature," New York Review of Science Fiction 39 (1991): 1, 10-13; Alfred Bendixen, introduction to Haunted Women: The Best Supernatural Tales by American Women Writers (New York: Ungar, 1987), 1-2.

17. For a revaluation of Cooke, see Susan Allen Toth, "'The Rarest and Most Peculiar Grape': Versions of the New England Woman in Nineteenth-Century Local Color Literature," in Regionalism and the Female Imagination, ed. Emily Toth (New York: Human Sciences Press, 1985), 15-28; Susan Allen Toth, "Rose Terry Cooke," American Literary Realism 4 (1971): 170-176; Cheryl Walker, "Legacy Profile: Rose Terry Cooke," Legacy 9.2 (1992): 143-150; Cheryl Walker, "American Women Poets Revisited," in Nineteenth-Century American Women Writers: A Critical Reader, ed. Karen L. Kilcup (Malden, Mass.: Blackwell, 1998), 231-244. For a discussion of Phelps, see Lori Duin Kelly, The Life and Works of Elizabeth Stuart Phelps, Victorian Feminist Writer (Troy: Whitston, 1983); Carol Farley Kessler, Elizabeth

Stuart Phelps (Boston: Twayne, 1982), and "The Heavenly Utopia of Elizabeth Stuart Phelps," in Women and Utopia, ed. Marleen Barr and Nicholas D. Smith (Lanham, Maryland: University Press of America, 1983), 85-95. For an interpretation of mutual influences between female regionalists such as Cooke, Phelps, and Rebecca Harding Davis, see Sharon M. Harris, Rebecca Harding Davis and American Realism (Philadelphia: University of Pennsylvania Press, 1991). For a more general discussion of regionalism, see Judith Fetterley and Marjorie Pryse, introduction to American Women Regionalists, 1850-1910 (New York: Norton, 1992); for a discussion of women writers at the end of the century, see Elizabeth Ammons, Conflicting Stories: American Women Writers at the Turn into the Twentieth Century (New York: Oxford University Press, 1991).

18. Toth, "'The Rarest and Most Peculiar Grape,'" 22. Van Wyck Brooks provides an early critique of Cooke in New England: Indian Summer (New York: Dutton, 1950), 89-90.

19. See Sherry Lee Linkon, "Fiction as Political Discourse: Rose Terry Cooke's Antisuffrage Short Stories," in American Women Short Story Writers, ed. Julie Brown (New York: Garland, 1995), 17-31; Katherine Kleitz, "Essence of New England: The Portraits of Rose Terry Cooke," American Transcendental Quarterly 47-48 (1980): 129-139.

20. Josephine Donovan, New England Local Color Literature: A Women's Tradition (New York: Frederick Ungar, 1983), 82.

21. Phelps, An Old Maid's Paradise (Boston: Houghton Mifflin, 1885), 85; cited in Donovan, 88.

22. Phelps, Dr. Zay (Boston: Houghton Mifflin, 1882), 88; cited in Donovan, 89. For a further discussion, see also Rosemary Garland Thomson, "Benevolent Maternalism and Physically Disabled Figures: Dilemmas of Female Embodiment in Stowe, Davis, and Phelps," American Literature 68.3 (1996): 555-582; Susan Albertine, "Breaking the Silent Partnership: Businesswomen in Popular Fiction," American Literature 62.2 (1990): 238-261.

23. "Since I Died" was first published in Scribner's Monthly Magazine in February 1873 and later collected in Phelps's fifth and last volume of short stories, Sealed Orders (1879).

24. Elizabeth Stuart Phelps, "Since I Died," in Two Friends: And Other Nineteenth-Century Lesbian Stories by American Women Writers, ed. Susan Koppelman (New York: Meridian, 1994), 46.

25. Jay Martin, "Ghostly Rentals, Ghostly Purchases: Haunted Imaginations in James, Twain, and Bel-

lamy," in *The Haunted Dusk: American Super-natural Fiction, 1820-1920,* ed. Howard Kerr et al. (Athens: University of Georgia Press, 1983), 125.

26. Poe, "Mesmeric Revelation," in *Complete Tales and Poems* (New York: Vintage, 1975), 93. See, however, Kennedy, who claims that Poe's vision-ary texts "project a false transcendence, a phantas-mic existence after death, conceptually embedded in a cosmos of matter and energy, a system that culminates in irreversible dissolution: entropy" ("Phantasms of Death in Poe's Fiction," 60).

27. See David Punter, *The Literature of Terror: A His-tory of Gothic Fictions from 1765 to the Present Day* (London: Longman, 1980), 203.

28. Elizabeth Ammons, introduction to *How Celia Changed Her Mind and Selected Stories,* by Rose Terry Cooke (New Brunswick, N.J.: Rutgers Uni-versity Press, 1986), xxviii-xxix. Besides Am-mons, who perceives Cooke as coming out of "the same mid-century fascination with evil and dark-ness which produced Poe, Melville, Spofford, and Stowe" (xxvi), Fred Lewis Pattee, in *The Devel-opment of the American Short Story* (New York: Harper & Brothers, 1923), acknowledges that Cooke took up the "short-story technique, as Poe had set it forth" (176).

29. Rose Terry Cooke, "My Visitation," in Ammons, 14. "My Visitation" was first published in *Harp-er's* 17 (July 1858) but was not reprinted by Cooke in any of her four collections.

30. Philippe Ariès, *The Hour of Our Death* (New York: Knopf, 1981), 43.

31. Elisabeth Bronfen, *Over Her Dead Body: Death, Femininity and the Aesthetic* (Manchester: Manchester University Press, 1992), 72-73. For a further gender-oriented discussion of Poe, see Joan Dayan, "Poe's Women: A Feminist Poe?" *Poe Studies* 26.1-2 (1993): 1-12; Leland S. Person, Jr., "Poe's Fiction: Women and the Subversion of Masculine Form," in *Aesthetic Headaches: Women and a Masculine Poetics in Poe, Melville, and Hawthorne* (Athens: University of Georgia Press, 1988), 19-47.

32. Marilyn R. Farwell, "The Lesbian Narrative: The Pursuit of the Inedible by the Unspeakable," in *Professions of Desire: Lesbian and Gay Studies in Literature,* ed. George E. Haggarty and Bonnie Zimmerman (New York: MLA, 1995), 157-158.

33. Julia Kristeva, *Powers of Horror: An Essay on Abjection* (New York: Columbia University Press, 1982), 4.

34. Mikhail Bakhtin, *Rabelais and His World* (Cambridge: MIT Press, 1968), 26.

Frann Michel (essay date 2000)

SOURCE: Michel, Frann. "Lesbian Panic and Mary Shelley's *Frankenstein.*" In *Frankenstein: Complete, Authoritative Text with Biographical, Historical, and Cultural Contexts, Critical History, and Essays from Contemporary Critical Perspectives,* edited by Johanna M. Smith, pp. 349-67. Boston and New York: Bedford/ St. Martin's, 2000.

[*In the following essay, Michel offers a reading of* Fran-kenstein *as a commentary on the condemnation of erotic desire between women.*]

When is a lesbian fiction not a lesbian fiction? Fairly often, one might gather from the variety of approaches to defining the territory of a lesbian criticism: much de-pends on who is reading, and how. On the one hand, there is the failure—sometimes the refusal—of straight readings to recognize lesbian elements of a text. On the other, there are the efforts to construct lesbian readings of apparently straight texts by seeking subtextual and coded representations. Thus Barbara Smith has sug-gested that a lesbian novel is one that takes a "critical stance toward the heterosexual institutions of male/ female relationships, marriage and the family." Addi-tionally, Smith sees as essential to the lesbian novel women's being "central figures . . . positively por-trayed and hav[ing] pivotal relationships with one an-other" (9). Building on this analysis, Marilyn Farwell has argued that "lesbian narrative space" is "a disrup-tive space of sameness" because "only in the space of sameness can [lesbian] desire emerge" (93, 97).

Yet relations of sameness or identification between women do not necessarily constitute specifically lesbian relations. Teresa de Lauretis comments that "the sweep-ing of lesbian sexuality and desire under the rug of sis-terhood, female friendship, and the now popular theme of the 'mother-daughter bond'" implies that women's sexual relations with each other are somehow less im-portant, less powerful, less conflicted than those other bonds (258). "In all three parts of the rug," de Lauretis observes, "what is in question is not desire but identifi-cation," where "desire" is defined as a sexual "wanting to have (the object)" and "identification" as a desexual-ized "wanting to be or to be like or seeing oneself as (the object)" (258, 260). Though desire and identifica-tion are intimately related, they are not identical. Thus while Smith's definition of the lesbian novel is useful for raising the questions of desire between women, it also replicates the elision of the *specificity* of that desire in cultural discourse. Furthermore, it cannot apprehend women's phobic responses to such desire.

Indeed, that phobic reaction to sexual desire between women delineates the erotic as an arena significantly distinct from the more simply affective. The precise exemplification of the erotic is, of course, historically and culturally variable, and not necessarily coherent. But a number of late-eighteenth- and early-nineteenth-century texts suggest a discourse in which sexual desire is signified not only by the primacy of bonds between women, but also by socially resonant *differences* between women (of race, class, gender style).[1] The possibility of reading Mary Shelley's *Frankenstein* in relation to such a discourse, however, has been occluded by readers' tendency to subsume erotic relations between women under the rubric of identification, and thus to avoid the possibility of discovering in the novel a lesbian subtext.

Admittedly, *Frankenstein* seems at first sight an unlikely book to discuss in terms of erotic relations between women, since it is so much a novel about men. But the novel's complexity reveals multiple influences, and leaves it open to multiple readings. *Frankenstein*'s monster has been read as the embodiment of scientific hubris, of the enraged working class, of maternal and neonatal monstrosity, and of male homosexual panic.[2] In particular, among the most persuasive readings have been those straight (and largely psychoanalytic) feminist studies of the novel in terms of the monstrous maternity of female authorship, together with gay male-oriented studies that see it as an example of the paranoid Gothic. Visible between these (sometimes mutually repellent) readings are moments in the novel at which representations of *identification* between women almost, but not quite, slide over into representations of *desire* between women; visible, too, is the penumbra of moments surrounding the novel in which legibly sapphic engagements elicit varying degrees of horror, dismay, and embarrassment. In context of the cultural discourse of sapphic monstrosity contemporary to the novel, *Frankenstein*'s creature can also be read as the embodiment of this lesbian panic. The proscription of nonidentificatory bonds between women in the novel can best be understood in the wider context of cultural representations of horror associated with the late-eighteenth- and early-nineteenth century's newly constructed role of the sapphist.

Sapphic Monstrosity

Beginning in the eighteenth century in Britain, women who pursued and engaged in sexual relations with other women came to be known as sapphists. Unlike women who had erotic relations with other women in earlier periods, they were no longer seen as hermaphrodites (having a different gender than women), nor as engaging in a sin to which any woman might succumb through libertinism. Instead, sapphists occupied a new social role, as a minority "whose minds had been corrupted from the normal desires of their female bodies" (Trumbach 121). In this essay, I use the term "sapphist" to call attention to the understanding of women's same-

sex eroticism current in Shelley's day. But I also use the term "lesbian" to suggest the historical continuities (real or retrospective) of women's erotic relations with each other. By "lesbian panic" I mean a phobic reaction to sexual desire between women, characteristically represented through the reaction of a third person, whose triangulating gaze disrupts the bond between two women, and renders visible the differences between them.

At least one possible example of horror at sapphic sexuality was known to Mary Shelley. A few days after the beginning of the ghost story contest in which *Frankenstein* originated,

> Byron was reciting some lines from Coleridge's "Christabel" about Geraldine, who is, like the demon, a composite body, half young and beautiful, and half (in the version Byron recited) "hideous, deformed, and pale of hue." Percy, "suddenly shrieking and putting his hands to his head, ran out of the room with a candle." Brought to his senses, he told Byron and Polidori that "he was looking at Mrs. Shelley" while Byron was repeating Coleridge's lines, "and suddenly thought of a woman he had heard of who had eyes instead of nipples."
>
> (Homans 109, quoting Polidori's diary)

Like the complex structure of indirection that presents *Frankenstein*'s monster to us (through Walton's narrative of Victor's narrative of the creature's narrative of others' responses to his hideousness), this moment encodes a network of sexual and affectional terrors and bonds—a network merely indexed by Percy Shelley's notable presence of mind in grabbing his candle before fleeing. More specifically, of course, "Christabel" has been widely read as representing lesbian sexuality.[3] Christabel finds the mysterious Geraldine in a wood and takes her home to bed; there Geraldine, holding Christabel in her arms, works "harms" and has her "will" (ll. 298, 306). Christabel wakes the next morning, sees Geraldine's "heaving breasts," and thinks, "'Sure I have sinn'd!'" (380, 381). Later in the poem, a dream images their relationship as that of a snake coiled about a dove, and Christabel, for a moment, sees Geraldine as having "shrunken serpent eyes" (602). Percy's vision of the repulsive embodiment of a collection of mismatched body parts thus seems inspired by a figure of sapphic agency: "Mrs. Shelley" appears monstrous by her association with Geraldine the satanic sapphist.

Percy's visionary leap from sapphic monstrosity to Mary-as-monster seems propelled by the monstrous maternal agency of the breasts-with-eyes. Monstrous maternity is, clearly, one way of understanding Victor's animation of the repulsive body composed of collected body parts. But the route from sapphic monstrosity to Mary's monstrosity may lie by way of horror not just at maternal sexuality in general, but at the sexuality of

Mary's mother in particular. The use of the serpent as an image for Geraldine resonates against the use that Mary's father, William Godwin, made of the rejuvenating serpent as an image for Mary Wollstonecraft, her mother (Todd xx). Moreover, while Godwin saw Wollstonecraft's friend Fanny Blood as no worse than unworthy of his wife, and Wollstonecraft later saw the friendship nostalgically, her early writings suggest that the relationship with Blood may once have been erotically problematic.

Both Shelleys were familiar with Wollstonecraft's works, including the somewhat autobiographical early novel, *Mary*. The protagonist of that eponymous text "loved Ann better than anyone in the world . . . To have this friend constantly with her . . . would it not be superlative bliss?" (15). So far, so sentimental. But when the two women go abroad together, Ann falls ill, and Mary tells her fellow lodgers,

> "I cannot live without her!—I have no other friend; if I lose her, what a desart [sic] will the world be to me." "No other friend," re-echoed they, "have you not a husband?" Mary shrunk back, and was alternately pale and red. A delicate sense of propriety prevented her replying; and recalled her bewildered reason.
>
> (23)

As with Percy's monstrous vision, the impropriety of the character Mary's position is available to her only through the responses of others. Embarrassment effects a physical withdrawal, a shrinking back, and the passion of Wollstonecraft's heroine for another woman is framed as unspeakable and unreasonable.

Neither Coleridge's poem nor Percy's vision need reflect Mary Shelley's view, of course. But both poem and vision help constitute a discourse of sapphic monstrosity as part of the cultural context in which the novel was produced. If "Christabel" provides a context for *Frankenstein*, however, it is one that is visible only obliquely, through the gaps and silences in the novel, evaded not just by Percy but also by *Frankenstein*'s text itself. Geraldine does not seem to be simply half-beautiful, half-hideous, like Milton's Sin or Spenser's Errour. Rather, Christabel has moments of "vision" in which she sees "that bosom old . . . that bosom cold" (453, 457-58) or in which Geraldine's "look askance" reveals "those shrunken serpent eyes" (608, 602). Geraldine's hideousness, in other words, appears to be revealed only by an optical shift, a difference in view. Bringing into view the horror of sapphic agency that constitutes a background to *Frankenstein*, visible only from an oblique angle, reenacts the optical shift necessary to perceive even the (foreclosed) possibility of erotic relations between the novel's women.

READING MOTHERS AND LOVERS

In designating this erotic desire between women as "lesbian," of course, I risk anachronism and impreci-

sion. Adrienne Rich has placed all women's supportive bonds with each other—including friendship, sisterhood, and mother-daughter relations—on a "lesbian continuum," of which specifically sexual "lesbian existence" is only one pole. But others have stressed that such usage not only implies an unbroken continuity between affective and erotic relations, but also obscures the different experiences of women-loving-women in other times and places. Historians of sexuality have suggested that not only the terms by which we designate sexualities, but also the concepts those terms represent—the concepts through which we understand and experience sexuality—have changed across time and cultures. Thus the boundaries of lesbian history are as vexed as the boundaries of the lesbian novel: though there have always been women who loved other women, they have not always identified as lesbian. Taking a more historical approach than Rich, Lillian Faderman finds precursors to modern lesbian relationships in women's "romantic friendships," passionate relations that were not necessarily genitally sexual, and not stigmatized until the late nineteenth century. The work of Rich and Faderman offers a useful counterweight to popular misconceptions about lesbians. It emphasizes that modern lesbian identity is about more than just genital sexuality, and it challenges the model promoted by late-nineteenth-century sexologists, who viewed women-who-love-women as mannish, or even as men trapped in women's bodies. But in accentuating affective bonds, both the "lesbian continuum" and the notion of "romantic friendship" may neglect what is specific to women's erotic bonds.

My point here is not that a lesbian subtext is "really there" or that *Frankenstein* is a "lesbian novel." It is, rather, the converse: the *absence* of erotic bonds between women is constitutive both of Mary Shelley's text and of straight feminist readings of the novel. Such bonds are, in other words, marginalized by the homophobic and heterosexist paradigms both critiqued and constructed by the novel and by the critical perspectives that replicate or exacerbate those patterns. Many such readings have interpreted the creature as coded female, and in doing so have elided male homosocial relations in the novel, or even reinscribed homophobic paradigms. Reading the novel as a critique of male homosexual panic, however, helps reveal the ways in which that critique depends on the absence of erotic relations between women. Thus both *Frankenstein* and straight feminist readings of the novel emphasize relations of identification between women, while proscribing relations of desire between women. Moreover, critics enforce this proscription by construing desire between women in terms of identification, while ignoring differences that might open a space for erotic desire.

Most of the now-canonical feminist studies of the novel have pursued arguments primarily concerned with maternity, often seeing Victor as "usurping the female" (Mellor 115).[4] Ever since Ellen Moers's study of *Frankenstein* as a birth myth, for instance, the novel has been persuasively read as a text of maternal anxiety (79). *Frankenstein* was written in the midst of a series of well-known maternal horrors in Shelley's life—her mother had died from a postpartum hemorrhage after giving birth to her, two of her own daughters died in infancy, her son William died at age three and a half, and during the writing of *Frankenstein* Mary's half-sister Fanny Imlay killed herself on discovering she was illegitimate; further, Percy's first wife Harriet committed suicide while pregnant by another man. Those biographical circumstances are, according to these readings, reflected in the text itself: *Frankenstein* is a story about a man giving birth to a creature that destroys his life and family, a story in which all the mothers and maternal figures die or have died, a story that is itself the author's "hideous progeny" (p. 25).

In addition to seeing Victor as a kind of male mother, a number of readers have also seen the (male) creature as a representation of femaleness or femininity.[5] Particularly since Sandra Gilbert and Susan Gubar's reading of *Frankenstein,* in which they see the novel as a rewriting of *Paradise Lost,* feminist critics have tended to interpret the creature as both female and maternal. Nameless, homeless, repellently embodied, the creature further shares with Milton's Eve a watery self-recognition and a capacity for bringing death into the human world (see Gilbert and Gubar 241-42, 247). The doubling of Victor and his creature becomes an analogue for the relations of mirroring or doubling between women in the novel—mother-daughter or surrogate mother-daughter relations between Caroline and Elizabeth, Caroline and Justine Moritz, Madame Moritz and Justine, Safie and her mother; and relations of surrogate sisterhood between Agatha and Safie and between Elizabeth and Justine. Both Victor and the creature have been seen as figuratively women, but the relation of desire between them has been discussed in terms of heteroeroticism or of male homoeroticism, never in terms of female homoeroticism.

Margaret Homans's syncretic psychoanalytic feminist reading of *Frankenstein* is exemplary of this line of study. Homans delineates what she sees as a dominant, androcentric myth of language in which the infant's acquisition of language depends on the mother's absence, and the preservation of language requires the absence—mythically, the murder—of the mother. This myth of the death and obviation of the mother for whom an infinite chain of figures comes to stand has obvious resonance with *Frankenstein* in the deaths of Caroline, Justine, and Elizabeth, as well as in the dead or unmentioned and presumably dead mothers of Caroline,

Safie, Felix and Agatha De Lacey, and Henry Clerval, and in the many substitutions of one woman for another (Caroline's replacement of Elizabeth in Victor's dream, or the resemblance Elizabeth and the creature note between Caroline and Justine). Homans thus argues that "[t]he horror of the demon that Frankenstein creates is that it is its creator's desire for an object, a desire that never really seeks its own fulfillment" (106). Seeing this as evidence that the creature is a figure of what it feels like to be the "feminine object of [male] desire" (100-01), Homans assimilates erotic relations in the novel to heterosexuality, and assimilates relations between women in the novel to relations of identification.

Thus although one might expect feminist criticism to address a fiction's representations of all kinds of relations between women, straight feminist criticism of *Frankenstein* has instead typically repeated the novel's evasions. As even Smith implicitly assumes a continuum of relationships between women without a point of division between erotic and nonerotic relations, Homans too presents women's relation to female same-sex relationships as uncomplicated by an intervening break—in this case by the division implied in the triangular structure of the Lacanian Symbolic instigated by the intervention of the phallus. Whereas Homans alludes to male homoeroticism through her discussions of "narcissism" and "solipsism" (106, 104), she more directly addresses, and in doing so more fully displaces, questions of female homoeroticism, in part by assimilating female same-sex desire to identification:

> Because of her likeness to and identification with her mother, the daughter does not need a copula [a link, hyphen, or coupler] such as the phallus to make the connection, as the son does. She also does not need a phallus, paradoxically, because she is never told she may not use it: in a culture already heterosexual, the father would be unlikely to suspect threats to his sexual terrain from that quarter. . . . [A] daughter is never encouraged to abandon her mother in the way that a son is, never needs to replace the lost phallus . . . with other hyphens.
>
> (11-12)

Homans here equates affective and erotic connections. But the daughter needs the hyphen or copula precisely to the extent that her bond with the mother is not simply affective but also erotic. Although, as Homans notes, father-daughter incest is authorized by the Law of the Father, mother-daughter incest is not: for the son, the Law of the Father is a taboo on some women; for the daughter, as Gayle Rubin has noted, "it is a taboo on all women" (95). The psychoanalytic text thus codifies the girl's oedipal moment as the paradigmatic instance of lesbian panic: according to psychoanalytic theory, the daughter turns away from her mother because of the presence of the father—his triangulating gaze disrupts their bond, and precipitates the daughter's phobic recoil from the possibility of desire between women. Homans argues that "the impossibility of Frankenstein giving [the creature] a female demon, an object of its own desire, aligns the demon with women, who are forbidden to have their own desires" (106). And if the creature is like a woman here, he is specifically like a woman denied a female object of desire.

DIFFERENCE AND DESIRE

In making this argument about *Frankenstein,* of course, one must remember that the categories of the affective and the erotic are culturally constructed and variable. According to Lillian Faderman, for instance, romantic friendship or passionate same-sex love was approved between similarly situated middle- and upper-class European and North American women until the later nineteenth century. Such relationships were considered spiritual and pure, while sex was seen as impure (33). But women whose relations with other women were perceived as sexual were indeed stigmatized, so that we cannot say that women's relations with other women were characterized by a seamless "lesbian continuum": the introduction of what was understood as sexual behavior did open a breach in the range of possible relations. In the late eighteenth century, for example, Ann Seymour Damer suffered partial social ostracism because she was known for pursuing other women sexually and having female lovers; and somewhat later, Ann Lister pursued her love affairs in secret to avoid scandal. Moreover, given the emphasis on similarities between romantic friends, sexual or erotic connection might be signaled by social differences (of class, race, gender style) between intimates. In 1790 Eleanor Butler and Sarah Ponsonby, the "Ladies of Llangollyn," who lived together into the nineteenth century, contemplated a libel suit when a London newspaper described Butler as "masculine" and Ponsonby as "effeminate"—the ascribed gender difference evidently indicating that their relationship was not just romantic but sexual (see Trumbach 125-35). In Wollstonecraft's *Mary,* the impropriety of the affluent Mary's giving primacy to a relation with a poor woman rather than to marriage is registered by the lodgers' responses to the women's bond. As these examples show, both the primacy of relations between women and the differences between the women involved can signal an improperly erotic bond.

A synecdoche for the evasion of these improper bonds between women in *Frankenstein* lies in an incident near the center of the book: one woman's abandonment of another in the face of that monstrosity. The only women to survive the sight of the creature—indeed, virtually the only female characters to survive the novel at all—are Agatha De Lacey and Safie, two of the cottagers whom the monster sees as his protectors. The creature seeks refuge with the blind father of the De Lacey family, but the other cottagers' early return forecloses the

possibility of sanctuary. "'Who can describe their horror and consternation on beholding me?'" says the creature. The inarticulate and inarticulable response to monstrosity is all that makes it visible. "Agatha fainted; and Safie, unable to attend to her friend, rushed out of the cottage" (121). If sapphic sexuality cannot be seen by the patriarch, it threatens to be all too visible to his children. The women who avert their eyes—who faint or rush out—and who do not attend to each other are those who survive. Those who are touched by the monster, and who stand by each other—Justine and Elizabeth—die.

Though straight feminist readings of *Frankenstein* have delineated relations of identification—of mirroring or doubling—between women, the novel also reveals a triangulated and mediated relationship—a relation of differences and, potentially, of desire—among Justine, Elizabeth, and Caroline. Justine and Agatha are the only women characters in the novel who are not inserted into heterosexual relations. While Agatha's primary bonds are heterosocial ties to her father and brother, however, Justine's primary attachments are to other women. Working-class and unattached to any man, Justine is thus the most problematic figure in terms of her potential for erotically tinged relations with other women. The relation between Justine and Elizabeth adumbrates the limits of women's friendship in *Frankenstein.* Elizabeth describes Justine as "very clever and gentle, and extremely pretty" (p. 68), and as she "whom I loved and esteemed as my sister . . . my play-fellow, my companion, my sister" (pp. 83-84); she tells Justine, "I wish . . . that I were to die with you; I cannot live in this world of misery" (p. 85). Justine, falsely convicted of William's murder, "embraced Elizabeth," and speaks her final words: "Farewell, sweet lady, dearest Elizabeth, my beloved and only friend; may Heaven, in its bounty, bless and preserve you" (p. 85).

Despite these avowals, the relationship between Justine and Elizabeth does not constitute an instance of romantic friendship as discussed by Faderman: the women do not express jealousy, display anxiety about the beloved's reciprocation of the lover's feeling, or hope to spend their lives together. Their declarations of feeling are immediately motivated by Justine's impending execution, of course, and Elizabeth's position is circumscribed by her engagement to Victor. The book thus minimizes the romantic aspects of their friendship, since the class difference between them might have blurred romantic into erotic connection. Justine's considerably more impassioned statements come not only from a woman scheduled to die the next day, but also from a woman of a class different from that of her "beloved and only friend." In a passage written by Percy Shelley, Elizabeth reminds Victor that in Geneva "there is less distinction between the several classes of . . . inhabitants; and the lower orders, being neither so poor nor so despised, their manners are more refined and moral. A servant in Geneva does not mean the same thing as a servant in France and England" (p. 66; Rieger 61n). Nonetheless, Justine "learned the duties of a servant" (p. 66), and romantic friendship appears to have occurred chiefly if not exclusively between women of similar class positions—usually, in extant representations, between middle-, or upper-class women.

Eighteenth- and early-nineteenth-century representations of sexual or erotic relationships between women, in contrast, tend to involve hierarchical relationships and/or women of the decadent aristocratic or working classes (particularly actresses and prostitutes). Wollstonecraft's relation with Fanny Blood, for instance, may have been, as *Mary* suggests, socially risky, in part because the Bloods were poorer than Fanny's lover. Percy's interpolation in *Frankenstein* about Genevan servants thus may have functioned not only to critique the English class structure but also to deflect a possible reading of sapphic desire. So, too, the relation between the French Agatha and the Turkish Safie might have had a particularly sapphic charge had Safie not found herself "unable to attend to her friend" when they encountered the monster. Social-structural differences between women, differences of class or race, may themselves have come to signify a genitally sexual, as opposed to a purely romantic, relationship.[6] The sisterly bond between Elizabeth and Justine is thus doubly constrained. Expressions of mutual devotion between women of different classes might not have clearly signified romantic friendship, and in any case, either sexual or romantic intimacy between Elizabeth and Justine would have compromised Elizabeth's position as innocent victim dependent on her relationship to Victor.

Justine and Elizabeth are initially both adopted daughters of Caroline, and both subsequently become replacements for her; their apparent interchangeability would seem to emphasize their similarities rather than differences. But the relationship between Elizabeth and Justine does betray the need and danger of the hyphen or copula that Homans discusses. Homans argues that sons seek to represent their lost attachments to their mothers through heterosexual desire or figurative language, while daughters seek to reproduce or repeat their preoedipal relations to their mothers through childbirth or literal language. But what circulates between Elizabeth and Justine, and is Justine's legal undoing, is a figurative representation, a signifier: not, as Homans would have it, the reproduction of the mother's body, but the *representation* of the mother in the painted miniature of Caroline Beaufort, which Elizabeth gives to William and the creature plants on Justine after the murder. Elizabeth's testimony that she would willingly have given the portrait to Justine is taken by the court not as evidence that Justine had no reason to kill William to get it, but as evidence of Justine's "blackest ingrati-

tude" (p. 82). The sign of the (surrogate) mother connecting the two women is read as demonstrating Justine's failure to act "like a most affectionate mother," her failure to reproduce the mother as herself (p. 82).

Justine has imitated and come to resemble Caroline, but in the process of doing so, Elizabeth observes, "you could see by her eyes that she almost adored her protectress. . . . [S]he paid the greatest attention to every gesture of my aunt. She thought her the model of all excellence" (p. 67). If Justine's resemblance to Caroline reduces the difference between them, then her adoration, her minute attention to Caroline's bodily movement, highlights that difference. Like the "watery, clouded eyes of the monster" (p. 157), or like Percy's vision of disembodied eyes in place of nipples, Justine's distinctly articulated eyes express and encode a vital agency. Moreover, that agency, like Mary's passion for Ann in Wollstonecraft's novel, is visible to others: it is triangulated first through Elizabeth's gaze, then through the censure of the court.

Thus the crime of which Justine is convicted seems to be her raising the possibility of a relation between women that is not constituted by identification. While many readings of *Frankenstein* have suggested the importance of women's identifications with each other, then, the novel also suggests that monstrosity lies in women's differences from each other. In Victor's dream following the animation of the creature, he finds himself embracing Elizabeth, who turns into the corpse of Caroline, and he then finds, upon awaking, that he is facing the creature, "[a] mummy again endued with animation" (p. 61). While this episode encodes the possibility of exchanging one woman for another, it also encapsulates the horror of the exchange. The difference between mother and daughter lies in the mother's repulsiveness (perhaps an echo of Wollstonecraft's potentially improper relation with Fanny Blood). But the difference between women is also itself monstrous: it is what helps make possible an erotic relation between them.

MEN AND MARRIAGE

Clearly, then, identifications of women with each other do not necessarily promote the "critical stance toward . . . heterosexual institutions" Smith looks for in a lesbian text. Indeed, such identifications may do just the reverse. Foregrounding women's sameness occludes the differences that can signal an erotic challenge to the patriarchal structures of marriage and the family. The critical emphasis on women's interchangeability highlights their connections to men, and thus predicates its defense of women on their right to access those connections. Interpreting the creature as female leads Homans to a reading that sees in Victor's actions the rejection of women and, concomitantly and implicitly, of heterosexuality. The particular feminism of this reading thus depends upon feminist allegiance to heterosexuality. Homans repeatedly characterizes Victor's sexuality as not "normal" and his desires as narcissistic and solipsistic. She observes that "the demon's creation amounts to an elaborate circumvention of *normal* heterosexual procreation," and emphasizes that to "bring a composite corpse to life is to circumvent the *normal* channels of procreation; the demon's 'birth' violates the *normal* relations of family, especially the *normal* sexual relation of husband and wife" (101, 103, emphasis added). As Sedgwick has noted, *Frankenstein* embodies "strongly homophobic mechanisms" (*Between* 92); it seems also to elicit them.

Conversely, as Sedgwick also notes, it is "not always easy (sometimes barely possible) to distinguish ['homosexuality' and 'homophobia'] from each other" (*Between* 20). Thus *Frankenstein* can be seen as both enacting and critiquing male homophobia. The most fully represented emotional bonds in the novel occur between men, as do the major episodes of face-to-face narration. Walton writes to his sister that he longs for a friend: "I desire the company of a man who could sympathise with me; whose eyes would reply to mine" (p. 31). Victor agrees with Walton that "we are unfashioned creatures, but half made up, if one wiser, better, dearer than ourselves—such a friend ought to be—do not lend his aid to perfectionate our weak and faulty natures," and calls his friend Henry Clerval "the most noble of human creatures" (p. 37). Given this emphasis throughout the novel on the values of male friendship, it becomes striking that none of the characters ever considers why Victor is to produce for the creature a female mate, rather than a male friend (who would, at least, not pose the danger of "children . . . a race of devils . . . propagated upon the earth" [p. 144]).

But this omission becomes more comprehensible when we look at the shape of male homophobia in Shelley's day, and specifically at the belief that male homosexuality encouraged neglect of women. Louis Crompton, in his *Byron and Greek Love,* notes that the idea that male homosexuality "produced indifference to women and thereby robbed them of their rights" had "a great vogue in the eighteenth century when it appears in a remarkably wide range of contexts, from philosophy to pornography" (50). It appears, for instance, in Percy Shelley's essay "A Discourse on the Manners of the Ancient Greeks Relative to the Subject of Love," written the same year *Frankenstein* was published. In that work, Percy Shelley argues both that sexual love between men causes neglect of women and that it was itself caused, in ancient Greece, by women's unworthiness of attention. Women's equality with men is thus doubly incompatible with male homosexuality. In refuting objections to male homosexuality, Jeremy Bentham in 1785 and 1814 gave most attention to this idea of the neglect of women, emphasizing that he did not think male homosexuality "discourages men from marrying. Only matrimony can gratify the desire for children, for family alliances" (qtd. in Crompton 51). If a male same-sex relation took the place not of marriage but of pre- or extramarital affairs, it would not rob women of their "rights" to marry and procreate.

The "neglect of women" argument would, of course, carry little weight if women did not mind being neglected. Wollstonecraft, for example, did not mind; she early declared herself averse to marriage and, with Fanny Blood and her sisters, set up a school, for a time living independently with them. As Sedgwick points out, then, we cannot say that "homophobia is a *necessary* consequence of such patriarchal institutions as heterosexual marriage" (*Between* 3). Yet perceived shifts in such institutions can contribute to heightened terror about sexual practices that fall outside their parameters. In this way the argument that "male homosexuality is an epitome, a personification, an effect, or perhaps a primary cause of woman hating" intersects with women's investment in and perception of threats to institutions of heterosexuality (*Between* 19-20).

But while some of Shelley's contemporaries viewed male homosexuality as leading to an unfair "neglect of women" (Crompton 51), in *Frankenstein* the real harms to women come not from this male desire but from the view of it as monstrous, from the failure to acknowledge it, and from the persistent attempt to achieve its sublimation through the subordination of women. When Elizabeth offers to release Victor from their engagement, asking, "Do you not love another?" (p. 161), she has, as Homans notes, hit upon the real source of division between her and Victor: there is someone else. But if Elizabeth had not married Victor, the creature would not have killed her; just so, if Victor had not turned away from his desire for the creature, it would not have killed William or framed Justine for the murder.

The "neglect of women" argument against male homosexuality, then, seems to presume women's heterosexuality. But the "harms to women" argument against male homophobia seems also to have left in place women's presumptive heterosexuality. The repression of homosexual desire in men evidently heterosexual redounds upon women: as conduits or objects of exchange between men whose desire for each other is repressed, women become not merely objects, but objects of hostility. (Victor's rather ludicrous inability to comprehend the monster's obvious threats against Elizabeth is entirely legible as evidence of Victor's hostility toward her.) As Terry Castle notes, bonds between women would disrupt this structure of exchange between men (132). And as Sedgwick argues, "homophobia directed by men against men is misogynistic . . . [that is,] oppressive of women" (*Between* 20). While the homophobic link between homosexuality and "neglect of women" has relied on women's investments in heterosexual institutions, *Frankenstein*'s critique of the dangers of male homophobia to women itself relies upon a suspension of erotic connections between women in the novel.

The idea that male homosexuality is linked to misogyny is thus in part a function of embeddedness in what we would now call the institution of heterosexuality. Bentham's response to the "neglect of women" argument indicates the wider cultural context at the time of his writing, when he points to the material anxieties at work in pitting women against homosexual men. The marriage market in Georgian England was apparently a difficult one for women.[7] Insofar as homosexuality was beginning to be perceived as an identity, it was apparently beginning to be thought of as a potential life choice that would exclude marriage. Women's economic and social dependence on the institution of marriage would, understandably, put them at odds with perceived threats to that central female livelihood, as well as threats of harm from within it.

Writing in 1985, Louis Crompton suggests that the "neglect of women" argument "seems strange to us. Nowadays, women and homosexuals tend to make common cause politically on the ground that both suffer from invidious sex-role stereotyping" (50). But of course Homans's reading of *Frankenstein* turns on a variant of that seemingly strange argument: it is not that male homosexuality leads to a neglect of women, but, conversely, that the wish for the deferral of the desire for the mother leads to a view of actual women's bodies as repellent, and thus to an avoidance of women and to an abnormal, narcissistic sexuality.

Invisible as the monster is to the reader, he inspires in those who see him a reaction that is quite visible to others, and that provides, indeed, a fulcrum for the narrative. So, too, the deferred possibility of sapphic sexuality in the novel, invisible as it apparently is to the characters as well as to most readers, can nonetheless be indirectly discerned through the sapphic intertexts for terrified responses to the creature. Potentially erotic relations of difference between women can be a source of horror in Shelley's text, elided or recast as relations of identification. That elision, paradoxically, provides the linchpin of such critique of male homosexual panic as the novel offers, and has provided the crux of the canonical straight feminist readings of the novel as well.

Western culture's "chronic, now endemic crisis of homo/heterosexual definition" may be, as Sedgwick suggests, "indicatively male," but it is hardly exclusively so (*Epistemology* 1). Lesbian-baiting has an infamous, lengthy, and still evolving history. Moreover, the oedipal configurations that crystallized with male ho-

mosexual panic are equally, albeit differently, inextricable from lesbian panic. Where the paranoid Gothic constitutes male homosexual panic as a dyadic structure in which one man is persecuted by another, the female-authored paranoid Gothic also constitutes lesbian panic as the effect of a triangulated structure in which one woman's relation to another is seen by a third party as monstrous, improper, or monstrously improper. Rather than functioning as a pervasive theme, lesbian panic emerges briefly, obliquely, or tangentially, and its deferral undergirds the narrative.[8]

Study of the textual relationships and intertextual references within *Frankenstein* thus reveals that speculative questions about relations between women in the novel turn out to be specular questions about how those relations are and are not to be seen, and how they are (not) seen by critics. Such omissions in straight feminist readings of the novel seem the product of critical anxiety about a potential lesbian subtext. One now-standard mode of dealing with that anxiety is to present erotic desire between women as simply one expression of affectional relation, and thus to elide what is specifically erotic about such desire. When that desire cannot be assimilated to affectional relations or relations of identification, it becomes a source of horror. The fit between the deferral of lesbian panic and the embodiment of mechanisms of male homophobia in *Frankenstein* and in critical responses to the novel reveals not a lesbian continuum, but the beginnings of the discontinuities by which women's differences even now become divisions.

Notes

This is a revised version of the essay that appeared in *GLQ: A Journal of Lesbian and Gay Studies,* OPA (Overseas Publishers Association), 1995.

1. Terry Castle has made a congruent argument about the structural importance of homosocial bonds between women in twentieth-century lesbian fiction.

2. For descriptions and examples of readings of the novel through scientific issues, Marxist criticism, and hetero-maternalist feminist criticism, see the essays in Levine and Knoepflmacher. On male homosexual panic, see Sedgwick, *Between* 91, 115, 151.

3. Faderman suggests that contemporaries probably thought the poem was obscene not because it represented sex between women but because Geraldine was thought to be a man in disguise. But the figure of the sapphist or "tommy" was familiar by the late eighteenth century (Trumbach 129), and Faderman acknowledges that the poem may indeed have been understood as being about the evils of lesbian sex (277, 463). Sandra Gilbert and Susan Gubar mention "Christabel" as a possible

influence on the novel, but focus on Geraldine's anxiety about Christabel's dead mother; they do not suggest that the absence of the mother may enable sexual connection between the women (245).

4. These accounts, written in the late 1970s and early 1980s, have acquired a canonical status through their continuing presentation to undergraduate readers in volumes such as that edited by Levine and Knoepflmacher.

5. Among those who have seen the creature as figuratively female are Sandra Gilbert and Susan Gubar, Barbara Johnson, Anne Mellor, Mary Poovey, and Margaret Homans.

6. Ruby Rich takes up this point in the discussion following de Lauretis (274-75).

7. "The disproportionate number of socially and economically suitable bachelors . . . meant that a woman had less choice as to her future husband; the complaisance of male suitors, who took their success for granted, is a commonplace of eighteenth-century novels, as is the sad circumstance of uncourted daughters" (Poovey 13).

8. My description of male homosexual panic in the "paranoid Gothic" here relies on Sedgwick's accounts in *Between Men* (especially 91) and *Epistemology of the Closet* (especially 187).

In Ann Radcliffe's *The Italian* (1797), the captive Ellena's relationship with the kind Olivia must be hidden from the other nuns in the convent. An epigraph to an earlier chapter in the novel, drawn from the love scene between Shakespeare's Olivia and Viola in *Twelfth Night* in which Olivia falls in love with the disguised Viola (I. 5.268-77), provides a potentially sapphic intertext shaping our readings of the scenes between Radcliffe's Olivia and Ellena. Ellena is "fascinated by this interesting nun," and her first comment about Olivia is, "She is very handsome" (87). Vivaldi's anxiety about the possible primacy of the bond between the women is revealed in his comment, "Ah, Ellena! . . . do I then hold only the second place in your heart?", to which Ellena replies only with "a smile more eloquent than words" (135). The potential eros of the interactions between the two women is recuperated as identification and inscribed within the oedipal family by the discovery not only that the agent of Ellena's captivity is the man she believes to be her father but also that Olivia is her mother.

Works Cited

Castle, Terry. "Sylvia Townsend Warner and the Counterplot of Lesbian Fiction." *Sexual Sameness. Textual*

Difference in Lesbian and Gay Writing. Ed. Joseph Bristow. New York: Routledge, 1992. 128-47.

Coleridge, Samuel Taylor. "Christabel." *Selected Poetry and Prose of Coleridge.* Ed. Donald Stauffer. New York: Modern Library, 1951. 25-43.

Crompton, Louis. *Byron and Greek Love: Homophobia in Nineteenth-Century England.* Berkeley: U of California P, 1985.

de Lauretis, Teresa. "Film and the Visible." *How Do I Look? Queer Film and Video.* Ed. Bad Object-Choices. Seattle: Bay, 1991. 223-64.

Faderman, Lillian. *Surpassing the Love of Men: Romantic Friendship and Love between Women from the Renaissance to the Present.* New York: Morrow, 1981.

Farwell, Marilyn R. "Heterosexual Plots and Lesbian Subtexts: Toward a Theory of Lesbian Narrative Space." *Lesbian Texts and Contexts: Radical Revisions.* Ed. Karla Jay and Joanne Glasgow. New York: New York UP, 1990. 91-103.

Gilbert, Sandra, and Susan Gubar. *The Madwoman in the Attic: The Woman Writer and the Nineteenth-Century Literary Imagination.* New Haven: Yale UP, 1979.

Homans, Margaret. *Bearing the Word: Language and Female Experience in Nineteenth-Century Women's Writing.* Chicago: U of Chicago P, 1986.

Johnson, Barbara. "My Monster/My Self." *Diacritics* 12 (1982): 2-10.

Mellor, Anne K. *Mary Shelley: Her Life, Her Fiction, Her Monsters.* New York: Routledge, 1989.

Moers, Ellen. "Female Gothic." *The Endurance of "Frankenstein": Essays on Mary Shelley's Novel.* Ed. George Levine and U. C. Knoepflmacher. Berkeley: U of California P, 1979. 77-87.

Poovey, Mary. *The Proper Lady and the Woman Writer: Ideology as Style in the Works of Mary Wollstonecraft, Mary Shelley, and Jane Austen.* Chicago: U of Chicago P, 1984.

Radcliffe, Ann. *The Italian; or, The Confessional of the Black Penitents: A Romance.* 1797. London: Oxford UP, 1968.

Rich, Adrienne. "Compulsory Heterosexuality and Lesbian Existence." *The Signs Reader: Women, Gender and Scholarship.* Ed. Elizabeth Abel and Emily K. Abel. Chicago: U of Chicago P, 1983. 139-68.

Rieger, James, ed. *Frankenstein; or, The Modern Prometheus: The 1818 Text.* Chicago: U of Chicago P, 1974.

Rubin, Gayle. "The Traffic in Women: Notes on the 'Political Economy' of Sex." *Women, Class, and the*

Feminist Imagination: A Socialist-Feminist Reader. Ed. Karen V. Hansen and Ilene J. Philipson. Philadelphia: Temple UP, 1990. 74-113.

Sedgwick, Eve Kosofsky. *Between Men: English Literature and Male Homosocial Desire*. New York: Columbia UP, 1985.

———. *Epistemology of the Closet*. Berkeley: U of California P, 1990.

Smith, Barbara. "Toward a Black Feminist Criticism." *Feminist Criticism and Social Change: Sex, Class and Race in Literature and Culture*. Ed. Judith Newton and Deborah Rosenfelt. New York: Methuen, 1985. 3-18.

Todd, Janet. Introduction. *Mary, Maria and Matilda*. Ed. Janet Todd. New York: New York UP, 1992. vii-xxviii.

Trumbach, Randolph. "London's Sapphists: From Three Sexes to Four Genders in the Making of Modern Culture." *Body Guards: The Cultural Politics of Gender Ambiguity*. Ed. Julia Epstein and Kristina Straub. New York: Routledge, 1991. 112-41.

Wollstonecraft, Mary. *Mary*. Todd 1-53.

Christina G. Bucher (essay date summer 2003)

SOURCE: Bucher, Christina G. "Perversely Reading Kate Chopin's 'Fedora.'" *The Mississippi Quarterly* 56, no. 3 (summer 2003): 373-88.

[*In the following essay, Bucher offers an alternate, "lesbian reading strategy" of Chopin's "The Falling in Love of Fedora," declaring that such a reading reveals the story as part of Chopin's wider exploration of desire and sexuality.*]

Kate Chopin's "Fedora" is surely one of her most interesting and ambiguous stories. Published in 1895, under the pen name "La Tour" and the title "The Falling in Love of Fedora." "Fedora" is a very brief story recounting the experience of its thirty-year-old title character, a rather stern, unmarried woman who is suddenly smitten with a twenty-three-year-old man, Young Malthers. She does not act on this passion but resorts to touching his hat or burying her face in the folds of his coat. When Young Malther's sister is set to arrive for a visit, Fedora insists on driving to the station to meet her. She is delighted with the young woman, who bears a close resemblance to her brother, and after helping her into the carriage, Fedora puts her arm around Miss Malthers, bends down, and presses a "long penetrating kiss upon her mouth."[1] She then quietly picks up the reins and drives her astonished guest home.

A traditional reading of the story has seen Fedora as a repressed old maid whose passion is awakened by a tall, good-looking young man. Unaware of what to do

with such passion, she momentarily displaces it onto the sister and then, treating it like the "restive brute" she is driving, firmly takes it back in hand. She will hereafter continue to repress this new-found sensuality. Certainly, this is a possible reading. Chopin does describe Fedora as a woman who is "tall and slim, and carried her head loftily, and wore eyeglasses and a severe expression" (p. 467). Most of the young people "felt as if she were a hundred years old" (p. 467). Conversely, Fedora is uninterested in the young people and their merry-making. She is thus painted in stereotypical spinsterly terms. Her repression is also evident. One day Fedora looks up at Young Malthers and realizes suddenly "that he was a man—in voice, in attitude, in bearing, in every sense—a man" (p. 468); "from that moment on he began to exist for her" (p. 468). Fedora begins experiencing conflicting emotions: "uneasiness, restlessness, expectation" and "inward revolt, astonishment, rapture" (p. 468). Clearly, her reaction to this young man has upset her otherwise uneventful life. At this point she begins to fondle his clothing and insists on going for his sister at the station. When she sees the young woman, who looks so much like the young man, her passion for him rises. Because Miss Malthers resembles her brother so closely and because Fedora's avenues for acting on her desires for the young man are limited in the time in which she lives, the young woman is the recipient of Fedora's outburst of passion. In "The Restive Brute: The Symbolic Presentation of Repression and Sublimation in Kate Chopin's 'Fedora,'" the primary piece of criticism on the story to date, Joyce Dyer suggests that such outbursts will be the extent of Fedora's expression of her sexuality: "[Fedora] may try to caress the clothing of Young Malthers (or of other men) and to press desperate kisses on the mouths of unacceptable surrogates, but in public she will forever stare straightly ahead—'unruffled.'"[2] Dyer goes on to characterize Fedora as a "perverse, pathetic, desperate woman" (p. 265).

While Dyer ultimately sees Fedora as the classic repressed spinster, she and other critics have recognized what early critic Robert Arner calls the "homosexual overtones of Fedora's actions."[3] All view these "overtones" negatively. For example, Arner calls "The Falling in Love of Fedora" "a tale with strong overtones of sexual decadence manifest in the reticent lesbianism of Fedora" (p. 118), and Richard Arthur Martin, another early critic, deems the story an example of "the twisted paths sexuality can take."[4] More recently, Barbara Ewell, though sympathetic to the story's critique of repression, speaks of Fedora's "immature efforts at desexualization" and sees the kiss merely as an "uncontrollable outbreak of repressed passion,"[5] presumably for Young Malthers. Dyer's assessment, however, is the most troubling. She writes:

> [T]here are suggestions of Fedora's Sapphic tendencies in addition to the kiss; her clothes fetish might make

some readers wonder if what she really desires is to become male and assume a man's sexual role; Fedora's obsession with her whip hints at the sexual dominance conventionally attributed to the male in a heterosexual relationship; even her unusual name itself, a word that commonly refers to a man's soft, felt hat, might be meant to provide an indication of her male proclivities.

(p. 264)[6]

The phrase "Sapphic tendencies" trivializes Fedora's potential lesbian desire, and Dyer's conflation of lesbian desire with the desire to be a male traffics in a traditional negative and usually untrue stereotype. More importantly, once Dyer raises the possibility of Fedora's lesbian desire, she erases it:

> However, as I've attempted to show, there seems to be perhaps even more substantial evidence to suggest that Fedora is transferring her emotion for Young Malthers to Miss Malthers—an inappropriate displacement, certainly, but nevertheless, a transference that Fedora, in all her rigidity and repression, can find socially acceptable. Chopin works hard and carefully to stress Fedora's intense attraction to Young Malthers' masculinity—his voice, his attitude, his bearing, his face and form. And she works with equal intensity to help us understand that it is Miss Malthers' physical similarity to Young Malthers that attracts Fedora, not the girl herself.

(p. 264)

My belief is that both a reading of the story that sees Fedora merely as a repressed spinster and Dyer's with its negative dismissals of the kiss suffer from a sort of heterosexual tunnel vision; they do not adequately explore the lesbian element of the text. I would like to propose that adopting a lesbian reading strategy allows us to read Fedora and the kiss more complexly; it also allows us to see the story as yet another instance of Chopin's expression of the varieties of desire and sexualities in her works.

Such a reading strategy has been described as "perverse reading" by Bonnie Zimmerman. Drawing on Judith Fetterley's seminal theory of the "resisting reader," Zimmerman suggests that lesbian readers often find their own way through ostensibly heterosexual texts, "resisting" the heterosexual prescription and constructing alternate meanings out of textual hints and clues. She writes, "There is a certain point in a plot or character development—the 'what if' moment—when a lesbian reader refuses to assent anymore to the heterosexual imperative; a point in the narrative labyrinth where she simply cuts a hole and follows her own path."[7] The lesbian reader, she says, will pay particular attention to the ways women relate to each other in texts, often "see[ing] and emphasiz[ing] the sexual, romantic, and/or passionate elements of this relation" (p. 138), as well as noting and investing with meaning communities of women within texts.[8] Zimmerman

chooses to name such readings "perverse" to rob the word of its traditional negative meaning, especially as it has been applied to lesbian sexuality; she instead wishes "to reclaim a word defined by the dictionary as 'willfully determined not to do what is expected or desired'" (p. 139).

Zimmerman makes two crucial points designed to ward off the protests of those who might decry such a reading practice as textually destructive and grossly limited in its usefulness. The first is her assertion that *applying* a perverse reading is not the same as *imposing* one:

> Let me emphasize that the lesbian resisting reader, reading perversely, is not merely demanding a plot or character study that the writer has not chosen to create. She is picking up on hints and possibilities that the author, consciously or not, has strewn in the text. A text that manifests certain symbolic elements—perhaps the absence of men, of women's attention to men, or of marked femininity; perhaps the presence of female bonding, or of strong and independent female characters—may trigger the act of lesbian reading. The reader is simply bringing to the text an understanding of the world as *she* has learned to read and thus to know it.

(p. 144)

In other words, a perverse reading does not do violence to a text by demanding elements that are not already inscribed to some degree. And while Zimmerman acknowledges that part of the value of perverse reading is that it makes texts "more personally meaningful to lesbian readers" (p. 142), a goal many scholars would see as theoretically weak and outdated, she also points out that its meaning for the larger critical arena is undeniable. "Perverse reading," Zimmerman says, "reveals subtexts of female friendship previously unrevealed; it also leads to the rewriting of cultural stereotypes and literary conventions by reversing the values attached to the idea of lesbianism" (p. 142), a project she believes should appeal to "literary critics who understand that no single interpretation of a text is complete without reference to many others" (p. 146). Moreover, reconsidering cultural stereotypes and the biases that helped create them can not only lead to a destruction of such stereotypes but can also help us "see new complexity in women's past and contemporary lives" (p. 142).[9]

Before proceeding with my own perverse reading of "Fedora," it may be necessary to note the potential tension between my primary desire to apply a reader-response theory in which historical context does not matter very much at all and a secondary desire to show that applying such a theory, in this case, is not necessarily at odds with the story's historical context. What I mean is that Zimmerman's practice of perverse reading is based on appropriating texts so they are in accordance with the reader's view of the world; in such a reading, it matters little if the term "lesbian" is historically accurate. For example, a perverse reader might deem the poems eighteenth-century writer Anna Seward wrote to Honora Sneyd as frankly lesbian, even though the term does not begin to be used widely until the late nineteenth century.[10] Similarly, the reading I want to propose of "Fedora" is valid and valuable, according to Zimmerman's theory, regardless of the period in which the story was produced. However, I also want to show that because Chopin was writing in the 1890s, a time in which, as we will see later, much medical and psychological discussion about sexual identity was beginning to take place, a perverse reading is not only a valid reader-response approach to the story but also a historically appropriate one.

Instead of seeing Fedora as a classic repressed spinster, the perverse reader is more likely to see her as having qualities of, in twentieth-century parlance, a classic "butch."[11] As Zimmerman notes, the lack of "marked femininity" is one detail that may trigger the act of perverse reading. Fedora's physical description—tall, angular, "severe"—and characterization as an avid and skilled horsewoman are clues that mark her as standing outside conventional notions of femininity, especially in the late-nineteenth-century South.[12] The lesbian reader will note such clues and rather than reading them negatively, she will see Fedora as a strong, athletic, determined woman, one who resists the traditional gender dictates in her society. Dyer's brief characterization of Fedora as a sort of dangerous, whip-wielding dominatrix, intended to be negative, might in fact please the perverse reader. As such, Fedora is an even more transgressive figure, and while Dyer sees Fedora as wanting to "become" a man, the lesbian reader will be aware that "performing" or "playing" male roles does not necessarily mean one wishes to relinquish being a woman.[13] Of course, suggesting that Fedora is some nineteenth-century version of a leather-clad, queer theory-declamating lesbian is untenable; what is valid is that Fedora is portrayed in a way that, even by nineteenth-century standards, allows us to see her as a woman marked by gender difference and to read that difference sympathetically.

If Fedora violates her culture's notions of feminine physical appearance, she also has violated its notions of how women should respond to men. They should, of course, desire and seek male attention. That Fedora is unmarried at thirty is another clue the perverse reader will note and invest with meaning. We are told that Fedora "too early in life formed an ideal and treasured it. By this ideal she had measured such male beings as had hitherto challenged her attention and needless to say she found them wanting" (p. 476). Even when she becomes attracted to Young Malthers, she does not seek his attention or approval, though she notices him more often and wants to spend time with him. Perhaps even he does not measure up to her ideal. We, in turn, might

have questions about what exactly that ideal is. In this regard, Fedora resembles Mademoiselle Reisz in *The Awakening,* another of Chopin's "butch" women and one who has been read as a lesbian.[14] In the conversation Edna has with Mlle. Reisz about men, Reisz asserts that she could only be in love with a man if he were some "*grand esprit*" (p. 964); a "man of ordinary caliber" would never be "worthy of [her] devotion" (p. 964). As far as we know, no man has ever met those standards for Mademoiselle Reisz, though her interest in Edna is quite apparent. So while we may have no concrete evidence that Fedora harbors desire for women prior to the kiss, the lesbian reader, already inclined to see Fedora as bending conventional gender roles, is thus more apt to read such gaps in the text as evidence of lesbian desire, or even identity.

But what of Young Malthers? If we are to see Fedora as having lesbian desire or identity, is not her attraction to the young man contradictory and problematic? Without a doubt, she begins to desire him, but we should look carefully at that desire, how it is characterized, and the possible reasons for it. Dyer says that Chopin "works hard" to stress Fedora's attraction to Young Malthers' masculinity (p. 264). While Fedora does have a "sudden realization" that he is a man (p. 468), his physical description is not overly masculine. He has "earnest" blue eyes; his face is "brown from the sun, smooth, with no suggestion of ruddiness, except in the lips, that were strong, firm, and clean" (p. 468). Certainly his brownness marks his masculinity since it speaks to not having to shield his skin from the sun as women were expected to do, and the adjectives "strong" and "firm" have traditional masculine associations. However, the smooth skin, the rosy lips, and the fact that there is no mention of a beard or mustache can just as easily suggest androgyny rather masculinity.[15] These qualities are what Fedora finds attractive. We should also look at the conflicting emotions Fedora feels for the young man:

> She wanted him by her, though his nearness troubled her. There was uneasiness, restlessness, expectation when he was not within sight and sound. There was redoubled uneasiness, when he was by—there was inward revolt, astonishment, rapture, self-contumely; a fierce swift encounter between thought and feeling.
>
> (p. 468)

While these conflicting feelings may be attributed to Fedora's discomfort and confusion over this new passion for Young Malthers, especially since she has prided herself on her sternness and control, they might also be explained by her uncertainty about those feelings in themselves. When he is near there is "redoubled uneasiness," an indication that his closeness disturbs her as well as excites her, and while she is attracted to him, she never acts on her feelings. Dyer believes that "Fedora's fear of social disapproval and her own impulses" are responsible for this inability to act (p. 262). But perhaps Fedora simply does not wish to express her passion for him any further. In a perverse reading of the story, the "fierce encounter between thought and feeling" she experiences might indeed indicate a conflict between what she truly desires, women, and what society says she must desire, men. Thus, a possible reason for Fedora's "sudden" passion for Young Malthers is that she succumbs, at least momentarily, to finding an acceptable object of desire in the heterosexual world in which she lives, but one androgynous enough to meet her tastes.[16] Moreover, one does not have to discount Fedora's desire for young Malthers in order to validate her desire for his sister, especially for an understanding of Chopin's views of desire. By the evidence we are given in the story, Fedora does indeed seem to be undergoing her first experience with sexual desire; it is not unusual for such an experience to be marked by a sort of fluidity or bisexual imperative. In a recent article drawing on French feminist theory, Karen Day offers brief commentary on "Fedora," arguing just this point. She believes the story might be read as "signifying a continuum of sexuality and desire, not bound by social constructions."[17] One need only recall Chopin's portrayal of Edna Pontellier's sexual awakening and the role that Adèle Ratignolle and Mlle. Reisz arguably play in it to see that she has some level of awareness of such multiple desires.[18] Consequently, Fedora's attraction to the young man, for whatever reasons, does not discount the possibility of her lesbianism.

Fedora's encounter with Miss Malthers is primary, of course, in considering this lesbianism; the kiss is the prime trigger for perverse reading. Dyer says that Chopin is careful to show that it is Miss Malthers' resemblance to her brother and not the girl herself which attracts Fedora (p. 262) and results in the "long, penetrating kiss" (Chopin, p. 469). But, if we again recall Young Malthers' androgynous features, it is no surprise that Miss Malthers seems equally attractive to Fedora. The fact that the sister, like the brother, has "blue, earnest eyes," the same "firm, full curve of the lips" (p. 469) emphasizes the androgyny of both figures and stresses again that these qualities are the ones that attract Fedora.[19] We are also told that Fedora "could hardly explain to her own satisfaction why she wanted to go herself to the station for Young Malthers' sister. She felt a desire to see the girl, to be near her" (p. 468). Fedora is obviously more comfortable with the idea of being near Miss Malthers than she is being near the brother. She is also, for some reason, motivated to act where the sister is concerned—something she is not willing to do with Young Malthers; the fact remains that it is Miss Malthers whom Fedora passionately kisses. The perverse reader might note, too, that the kiss is one of the easier, more "natural" of Fedora's actions in the story; she gives the kiss very calmly and gracefully, as if it suits her. Even the pastoral setting, a "long, quiet, leafy

road into which the twilight was just beginning to creep" (p. 469), adds to its naturalness. The scene also marks the only time Fedora speaks in the text. Addressing the young woman as "dear child" she says, "Come to me freely and without reserve—with all your wants: with any complaints. I feel that I shall be quite fond of you" (p. 469). The words here are a curious mix of the parental and the romantic, which might indicate Fedora's own confusion and anxiety over the soon-to-follow outburst of desire. Most important, however, is that the young woman is the impetus for both speech and action on Fedora's part. To the perverse reader, the kiss may seem a momentary release of Fedora's true desire.

Traditional readings have not seen the kiss in this way but rather as a "twisted" (Arner, p. 118) displacement of Fedora's heterosexual desire for Young Malthers. Such readings, as I acknowledged earlier, are possible, but they might also be questioned. For example, Joyce Dyer asserts that the sister "somehow" (p. 263) provides "a socially acceptable release of Fedora's passion" (pp. 263-264), but the assertion is unsupported. Certainly, Dyer may be thinking of the tradition of romantic friendships and of "the female world of love and ritual," detailed by Caroll Smith-Rosenberg, in which intense professions of love and physical expressions of it were common among women during the nineteenth century.[20] Such relationships, as Smith-Rosenberg, Lillian Faderman,[21] and others have shown, were not only common but also socially condoned. However, while it may be more acceptable for Fedora to express herself physically with women rather than men at this time, such a passionate kiss on the lips of a woman one has just met seems rather different than the developed relationships that were at the heart of romantic friendships. Miss Malthers' shock and displeasure at Fedora's kiss is a testament that her behavior is unusual. One should also remember that Chopin penned the story in 1895. Richard Von Krafft-Ebing's *Psychopathia Sexualis* appeared in 1886, and Havelock Ellis's *Studies in the Psychology of Sex, Sexual Inversion* in 1897, though his ideas were beginning to appear in print before then. These men, the most famous of the sexologists that emerged during the last decade of the nineteenth century, began carving out a theory of homosexuality, studying men and women whose gender characteristics were often untraditional and who professed desire for same-sex relationships. Ellis, drawing on the earlier work of German psychiatrist Carl von Westphal, famously designated such people sexual "inverts," and though he was not unsympathetic, his theories did mark these "inverts" as abnormal.[22] One result of these two men's views was that the once-accepted romantic friendships began to be scrutinized in a new way, a way that began to invest them with sexual meaning.[23] Chopin biographer Per Seyersted notes that William Reedy, the editor of the St. Louis *Times Mirror* and a friend of Chopin's, devoted space in his newspaper to Krafft-

Ebing and Ellis;[24] thus, it is quite possible that Chopin knew of their work. She may indeed have been aware that the kiss between Fedora and Miss Malthers would now be regarded as a sexual act, not merely the "harmless" expression of emotion in a world that condoned women's romantic friendships. Emily Toth, Chopin's most recent biographer, does not believe that Chopin was trying to conceal her authorship by choosing to publish the story under the pen name La Tour, but she does believe that the story's ending made it hard to publish (p. 289). Thus, simply to say that Miss Malthers presents a more acceptable recipient of Fedora's desire is historically arguable, and the kiss itself remains delightfully ambiguous.

Finally, we should look at the image of Fedora with which we are left. After the kiss, Fedora, "with seemingly unruffled composure, gathered the reins, and for the rest of the way home stared steadily ahead of her between the horse's ears" (p. 469). This image is usually connected to the symbolism of the "restive brute." At the beginning of the story we are told that Fedora determined to go to the station herself because "the brute was restive" (p. 467). Most critics see the horse as a metaphor for Fedora's awakening passion, her heterosexual passion. For someone of Fedora's disposition—severe, stern, repressed—such passion, like the spirited horse, must be kept carefully in check. In a perverse reading, the "restive brute" remains a symbol of her passion, but it is a passion particularly regarded as "brute," as something unruly and ugly, by a society which does not understand or accept it. Consequently, it must be kept under tight rein, under complete control. If the story is to be read as one of sexual repression, then it is an understandable repression. Fedora will continue to squelch her desires because she must; there is no place for them in the world in which she lives. In this regard, one may then question whether Dyer's characterization of Fedora as "a perverse, pathetic, desperate woman" is entirely accurate or just.

I might also suggest, however, that this final image of Fedora does not have to be limited to a further indication of her repression. To be sure, the story offers ample evidence that Fedora has learned to control her emotions; for example, even in the midst of the sensuous wonderland of the station's nook when we're told that "Fedora loved it all—sky and woods and sunlight; sounds and smells," her "bearing—elegant, composed, reserved—betrayed nothing emotional" (p. 468). Thus, Chopin's choice to have Fedora take up the reins again with "seemingly unruffled composure" and to stare between the horse's ears the rest of the way home can be seen to fit with the stern, controlled characterization of Fedora she has created earlier in the story. But the image might also be seen as much more open-ended, one that invites the reader to wonder about Fedora's thoughts as she stares so intently between the horse's

ears. That Chopin chose to say Fedora is "*seemingly* unruffled" (emphasis mine) is quite possibly an indication that she is not. Of what or whom is she thinking? Young Malthers? The young woman and the long, penetrating kiss she just delivered in the lush setting of the country road? Both? Is she contemplating the difficulty of her situation, what to do with this new-found desire, whatever its nature? Is she feeling free after having kissed Miss Malthers? A perverse reading invites us to see this closing image of Fedora as one that is just as ambiguous as the kiss itself; it also allows for a more hopeful, less "pathological" ending to the story. Perhaps Fedora will find a way to be who she is and to fulfill her desires.

For lesbian readers, the spinster/old maid has often been a figure of identification. Unmarried and often independent, seeking out the company of women or living in a community of women, the spinster is a woman in whom the lesbian reader can recognize herself. Unfortunately, the positive qualities of the spinster are usually overshadowed by the negative. Writers and critics are quick to emphasize the sexual repression, the comic neuroses, and the frightful undesirability of the old maid. The lesbian reader often reads "against the grain" of these qualities to try to salvage a dignified, desiring portrait of the unmarried woman. This is precisely what a perverse reading of "Fedora" seeks to do—in Zimmerman's words to "rewrite a cultural stereotype." I am not suggesting that Fedora be championed as a sort of super-lesbian of the late-nineteenth century, utterly admirable and well-adjusted; to do so would indeed do damage to the text. But she can be read more positively and more complexly than she has been in the past.

It is also worth considering that a strategy of perverse reading is not limited to "Fedora"; along with *The Awakening,* other Chopin stories could usefully be read through this lens. Certainly "Charlie," with its cross-dressing, gun-toting heroine who decides to try conventional femininity and heterosexuality on for size only to reject them and re-assume her "butch" persona at the end of the story is a potential goldmine for the perverse reader, especially since, as Emily Toth speculates in her biography of Chopin, there was a real-life inspiration for Charlie—Ellis Glenn, a dashing young "man" engaged to a young woman who was himself revealed to be a young woman three days before the wedding (p. 376). Even more ripe, and worth brief examination, is "Lilacs." The story of *chanteuse* Adrienne Farival's yearly return to the convent where she was once a student and her subsequent banishment from that convent once the Mother Superior discovers her "immoral" life in Paris becomes, when perversely read, not only a parable about the clash between the physical and spiritual life but also a sorrowful lesbian love story. Chopin emphasizes, from the first paragraph of the story, the bond between Adrienne and a particular nun at the convent,

Sister Agathe. Sister Agathe, described as "more daring and impulsive than all" (p. 355) the other nuns, lives for Adrienne's visits. "If you should once fail to come," she says, "it would be like the spring coming without the sunshine or the song of birds" (p. 358). The two women greet each other with fervent passion and spend their days together strolling the grounds of the convent, revelling in the sensuous pleasures that the natural world offers. After Adrienne returns one spring to find the lovely gifts she had given the convent over the years thrust through the front door to her and that door then shut against her, Chopin closes the story with two images: the final symbolic image of a lay sister sweeping away the lilac petals that Adrienne had let fall upon the front steps and the heartbreaking image of Sister Agathe kneeling upon the bed in which Adrienne had slept, "her face . . . pressed deep in the pillow in her efforts to smother the sobs that convulsed her frame" (p. 365). For the perverse reader, the story is very much about the love between these two women and the severing of the passionate bond between them, and while ostensibly the reason Adrienne is banished from the convent is that the Mother Superior, presented as the voice of a rigid, flesh-hating, patriarchal religion, has learned of her dalliances with male lovers in Paris, the perverse reader wonders whether the real reason is the even more dangerous liaison she has with Sister Agathe.[25]

That stories like "Lilacs," "Charlie," and "Fedora" lend themselves so readily to the strategy of perverse reading provides additional evidence that Kate Chopin was aware of, and inscribed in her writings, a wide spectrum of gender and sexuality; conversely, our understanding of her work and her views of gender and sexuality can only be enhanced by perversely reading them. Bonnie Zimmerman finally suggests that the worth of perverse reading lies in the way it adds to our understanding of literary texts. In seeking an analogy for the way her reading strategy can work, she recalls an encyclopedia section that was one of her favorites as a child, the section on anatomy in which transparencies were used to illustrate each system of the body: "Each system could be viewed separately with complete attention to its use and meaning in the body. But viewed together, one through the other, the transparencies created a three-dimensional image of the body as a whole" (p. 148). Like one of the transparencies, she concludes, perverse reading can add richness to our interpretation of texts. It is not meant to replace other readings, or assert its superiority over other readings; it can, however, along with those other readings, give us a fuller, more complete view of the whole.

Notes

1. Kate Chopin, "Fedora," in *The Complete Works of Kate Chopin,* ed. Per Seyersted (Baton Rouge: Louisiana State University Press, 1969), p. 469. All quotations from Chopin's work are from this edition.

2. *Studies in Short Fiction,* 15 (Fall 1981), 265. Also reprinted in *Critical Essays on Kate Chopin,* ed. Alice Hall Petry (New York: G. K. Hall, 1996).

3. *Music From a Farther Room: A Study in the Fiction of Kate Chopin* (Diss., Pennsylvania State University, 1970), p. 48.

4. *The Fictive World of Kate Chopin* (Diss., Northwestern University Press, 1971), p. 116.

5. *Kate Chopin* (New York: Ungar, 1988), p. 115.

6. One may want to take into consideration that Dyer's piece was published in 1981, a time in which there was less discussion and acceptance of gay and lesbian issues, and certainly gay and lesbian studies were in their infancy. However, the inclusion of "The Restive Brute" in Alice Hall Petry's 1996 anthology *Critical Essays on Kate Chopin* is an indication that it is still regarded as the seminal piece of criticism on the story.

7. "Perverse Reading: The Lesbian Appropriation of Literature," in *Sexual Practice, Textual Theory: Lesbian Cultural Criticism,* ed. Susan J. Wolfe and Julia Penelope (Cambridge, Massachusetts: Blackwell, 1993), p. 139.

8. Here Zimmerman builds upon her early groundbreaking essay "What Has Never Been: An Overview of Lesbian Feminist Literary Criticism," in *The New Feminist Criticism,* ed. Elaine Showalter (New York: Pantheon Books, 1985), pp. 200-224, in which she speaks of a reading strategy that "involves peering into shadows, into the spaces between words, into what has been unspoken and barely imagined. It is a perilous critical adventure with results that may violate accepted norms of traditional criticism, but that may also transform our notions of literary possibility" (p. 208). For other work on lesbian reading strategies see Marilyn Farwell's "Heterosexual Plots and Lesbian Subtexts: Toward a Theory of Lesbian Narrative Space," in *Lesbian Texts and Contexts: Radical Revisions,* ed. Karla Jay and Joanne Glasgow (New York: New York University Press, 1990), pp. 91-103; Jean E. Kennard's "Ourself Behind Ourself: A Theory for Lesbian Readers," in *Gender and Reading: Essays on Readers, Texts, and Contexts,* ed. Elizabeth Flynn and Patrocino P. Schweickert (Baltimore: Johns Hopkins University Press, 1986), pp. 63-80; and Paula Bennett's "Gender as Performance: Shakespearean Ambiguity and the Lesbian Reader," in *Sexual Practice, Textual Theory: Lesbian Cultural Criticism,* pp. 94-109.

9. Nor does one have to be a lesbian to apply this kind of reading strategy. In their introductory essay to *Lesbian Texts and Contexts,* Joanne Glasgow and Karla Jay draw on reader-response theory to confront the difficult questions of what is a lesbian text, who is a lesbian writer, and who is—or can be—a lesbian reader. Borrowing from Jonathan Culler, Glasgow and Jay suggest that anyone can adopt the strategy of "reading as a lesbian." In "Reading As a Woman," in *On Deconstruction: Theory and Criticism After Structuralism* (Ithaca: Cornell University Press, 1982), Culler argues that since for years women have been taught to read texts "as men," often having to identify against themselves in the process, men could and should be trained to read "as women." In doing so, they would "avoid reading as a man" and seek "to identify the specific defenses and distortions of male readings and provide corrections" (p. 54). Similarly, Glasgow and Jay suggest that straight people be trained to read "as lesbians," a strategy that would allow one to recognize the "defenses and distortions" of heterosexual readings and open up other possible interpretations. Echoing Zimmerman's reasons for the value of such a reading strategy, they write, "Reading with a lesbian consciousness can make us alert to 'coded' texts and enable us to read them in radically altered ways . . . [and] can also enable us to deconstruct the heterosexual surfaces of seemingly 'straight' forward texts" (p. 5).

10. The *Oxford English Dictionary Online* notes the earliest use of "lesbian" to describe a female homosexual in 1890 from a medical dictionary; the earliest use of "lesbianism" to describe female homosexuality is slightly earlier, 1870. Interestingly, though most scholars hold to this timeline for the use of the term "lesbian," Emma Donoghue, in *Passions Between Women: British Lesbian Culture 1668-1801* (New York: HarperCollins, 1993), notes a 1732 reference in a mock-epic by William King to sexual relationships between women as "Lesbian Loves" and, in a later 1736 edition of the text, a reference to these women as "Tribades or Lesbians" (p. 3).

11. Obviously, the application of the term "butch" here is anachronistic, as the use of the term to refer to a type of lesbian originates in the mid-twentieth century. My choice to use it reflects the reader-response foundation of perverse reading. It is worth noting, however, that there was an equivalent eighteenth- and nineteenth-century term to describe a "mannish" woman who sought sexual companionship with other women. Donoghue points out that as early as 1773, "Tommy" was a "home-grown slang word for a woman who had sex with other women" (p. 5). She notes the term's

derivations from "'tom boy,' 'tom lad,' or 'tom rig,' all names for boyish uncontrollable girls, or indeed from other phrases in which 'tom' suggested masculinity" (p. 5); it continued to be used throughout the nineteenth century (p. 5). In *Gay American History* (New York: Avon, 1976), Jonathan Katz includes an 1892 medical report about Alice Mitchell, who stood trial for murdering her female lover in Memphis, Tennessee. In the report, Dr. F. L. Sim links Mitchell's "masculine" characteristics with her lesbianism when he recounts her penchant for boyish things and notes, "To the family she seemed a regular tomboy" (p. 83).

12. One might question whether being an avid horse-woman marks one as transgressing gender dictates. While admittedly many women took part in equestrian activities, often a particular interest in riding, driving, or racing horses suggested a woman's nonconformity. Certainly, Chopin uses equestrian interests to designate rebellious women; one need only think of Edna Pontellier's knowing race-horses better than nearly any man at the track and of the "trouserlet"-clad Charlie Laborde's wild galloping astride her big black horse in "Charlie." Chopin biographer Emily Toth, in *Kate Chopin* (New York: William Morrow, 1990), also connects Chopin's own horseback riding with her nonconformity (p. 141). My suggestion here is not that being a skilled horsewoman means one is a lesbian, but that those skills might be a "clue" that helps propel a perverse reading.

13. Judith Butler, in *Gender Trouble: Feminism and the Subversion of Identity* (New York: Routledge, 1990), refutes the notion that lesbian butch-femme identities are merely a replication of heterosexual roles. She argues that because gender itself is an unstable, socially constructed category, to say that butch-femme roles are "'replicas' or 'copies' of heterosexual exchange underestimates the erotic significance of these identities as internally dissonant and complex in their resignification of the hegemonic categories by which they are enabled" (p. 123). See also Judith Halberstam, *Female Masculinity* (Durham: Duke University Press, 1998). Less academic but still useful analyses of butch roles appear in Joan Nestle's *The Persistent Desire: A Femme-Butch Reader* (Los Angeles: Alyson, 1992) and Joann Loulan's *The Lesbian Erotic Dance: Butch, Femme, Androgyny and Other Rhythms* (Duluth, Minnesota: Spinster's Ink, 1990).

14. See Kathryn Seidel, "Art Is an Unnatural Act: Mademoiselle Reisz in *The Awakening,*" *Mississippi Quarterly,* 46 (Spring 1993), 199-214, and Christina Bucher, *Transgressive Triangles: Desire,*

Gender, and the Text in Five American Novels 1852-1905 (Diss., University of Tennessee Press, 1994), pp. 86-129.

15. Robert's physical appearance in *The Awakening* is worth recalling for comparison. His androgyny, especially compared to Léonce Pontellier's more traditional masculine appearance, is emphasized, as are his similarities to Edna: "In coloring he was not unlike his companion. A clean-shaved face made the resemblance more pronounced than it would otherwise have been" (p. 883)

16. Peggy Skaggs, in *Kate Chopin* (Boston: Twayne, 1985), recognizes Chopin's emphasis on Fedora's attempt to reconcile "the spinster's conflicting needs for a place where she feels that she belongs and for sexual love" (p. 48), but she still sees heterosexual desire at the heart of the story, criticizing Arner for not giving enough attention to Fedora's lust for Young Malthers. Skaggs notes that "[Fedora's] attitude toward the small girl who looks like the man for whom she yearns seems to be an attempt to recognize these conflicting forces" (p. 48). My own argument is that Fedora's supposed desire for Young Malthers might just as easily be seen as an attempt to reconcile those two conflicting forces.

17. Karen Day, "The 'Elsewhere' of Female Sexuality and Desire in Kate Chopin's *A Vocation and a Voice*," *Louisiana Literature,* 11 (1994), 116.

18. See Kathleen Margaret Lant, "The Siren of Grand Isle: Adèle's Role in the Awakening," *Southern Studies,* 23 (Summer 1984), 167-175; Kathryn Lee Seidel, "Art As an Unnatural Act: Mademoiselle Reisz in *The Awakening*"; and Elizabeth LeBlanc, "The Metaphorical Lesbian: Edna Pontellier in *The Awakening*," *Tulsa Studies in Women's Literature,* 15 (Fall 1996), 289-307. Bonnie Zimmerman also uses *The Awakening* as an example of a text ripe for perverse reading in the article which is the foundation of my argument.

19. We might consider again how Chopin's emphasis on androgyny here matches that in her characterization of both Edna and Robert in *The Awakening*. Edna, unlike Adèle, is not voluptuous and feminine but is rather described as handsome and angular. She also sprawls on a hammock, drinks brandy from a glass "as a man would have done" (p. 962), and knows horses and horse-racing better than any man at the track. Robert, too, blurs rigid gender lines. He is clean-shaven, smokes cigarettes rather than cigars, prefers the company of women, and is described as resembling Edna in height, hair color, and skin tone. Chopin suggests that each finds these androgynous features attractive in the other. While the suggestion can lead to a discussion of narcissism, it can just as easily lead to a discussion of same-sex desire.

20. Carroll Smith-Rosenberg, "The Female World of Love and Ritual," *Signs,* 1 (1975), 1-29.

21. *Surpassing the Love of Men* (New York: William Morrow, 1981).

22. "Sexual Inversion," *Studies in the Psychology of Sex Vol. I* (New York: Random House, 1941).

23. For a thorough discussion of the influence of Krafft-Ebing and Ellis on attitudes towards romantic friendships, see Faderman, pp. 239-253.

24. Per Seyersted, *Kate Chopin: A Critical Biography* (Baton Rouge: Louisiana State University Press, 1969), p. 102.

25. Thomas Bonner in an early article, "Kate Chopin's European Consciousness," *American Literary Realism 1870-1910,* 8 (Summer 1975), 283, notes the possibility of a "growing carnality in [the] affections" between Adrienne and Sister Agathe and suggests that the Mother Superior was really motivated to reject Adrienne because of the changes she has wrought in Sister Agathe. Little had been made of this possible interpretation until 1994 when Jacqueline Olson Padgett discussed the story in "Kate Chopin and the Literature of Annunciation, with a Reading of 'Lilacs,'" *Louisiana Literature,* 11 (Spring 1994), 97-107. Padgett speaks of the "emerging sensuality" and "passion in the two women and their relationship with each other" (p. 102), though her focus seems to be more on showing how the bonds of "sisterhood" are disrupted in the course of the story, which in turn prevents women from achieving "wholeness and well-being, redemption and salvation" (p. 106).

Jin-Ok Kim (essay date 2003)

SOURCE: Kim, Jin-Ok. "Novelettes and *The Professor*: Identity and Sexuality." In *Charlotte Brontë and Female Desire,* pp. 25-44. New York: Peter Lang, 2003.

[In the following essay, Kim argues that Brontë reveals her interest in same-sex desire through her use of male narrators and expression of the detrimental effects of male homosocial bonds on women in her novelettes and in The Professor.*]*

In Charlotte Brontë's early works, men dominate women, causing women to search for the fulfillment of their own identity and sexuality. In her early novelettes, Brontë carefully depicts the ways in which women are marginalized by men. The marginalization of women by men and the desire for fulfillment of women's ambitions are impetuses that lead Brontë to emphasize the need for female homosocial relations in her later novels.

Most of Brontë's novelettes, with the exception of "Caroline Vernon," describe a world in which women function only as the objects of exchange between men who employ them to create homosocial bonds. Women can become pawns in power struggles between men. For example, Zamorna marries Mary Percy to secure the continuance of his sadistic relationship with her father, Alexander Percy. Sally Shuttleworth asserts that "through the early tales, Zamorna steals Percy's women, and attempts to make him suffer through his mistreatment of them. Sexual desire itself seems to play little role in these exchanges; women are the insignificant conduit of the males' mutual absorption."[1] Zamorna, Percy, and most of the male characters in Brontë's novelettes have many affairs with women to approach the men whom the women are connected with. Within the world of Angria, there are countless triangles of desire which place the woman as the mediating object between two male rivals. For example, Mina Laury and Caroline are used to cement the male homosocial bond between Zamorna and Percy Alexander. In the same manner, Frances in *The Professor* is employed to strengthen the bond between Crimsworth and Hunsden.

Eve Kosofsky Sedgwick illuminates the triangular paradigm between men in which women are victimized. She depicts homosocial desire with triangular heterosexual desire, "a male traffic in women" paradigm. She maintains that the European canon as it exists is already homosocial in a heterosexual context, demonstrating the male homosocial spectrum as a means for the transmission of unequally distributed power. Sedgwick argues that the different shapes of female and male homosociality are articulations and mechanisms of the enduring inequality of power between men and women.[2] Brontë depicts women's victimized situation in a world in which the bond between males becomes strong. Brontë seems to assert that males are strongly allied for a political purpose and women are mainly used to forge this alliance. She describes the psychological pain that women suffer from the conflict between two men, in the same vein as Sedgwick.

The suffering and pain that women experience in a masculine-dominated world is fully explored in "Mina Laury." Mina Laury is emotionally torn between Northangerland and Zamorna. Lord Hartford, the commander of Northangerland, loves Mina passionately and he wants to fight with Zamorna to win Mina. Mina refuses Lord Hartford in favor of Zamorna's love. Although Mina Laury recognize Zamorna's infidelity and his neglect of her, she still loves him deeply. She expresses strong feelings for Zamorna:

> I will tell you what feelings I had for him?—no tongue could express them—they were so fervid and glowing in colour that they effaced everything else—I lost the power of discerning the difference between right and wrong. Zamorna was sometimes more to me than a human being.

> (*FN* 147)

Mina's sensual love for Zamorna represents the denial of all convention. In a sense, this novelette foreshadows Brontë's mature studies of women's passion and desire and its repression as it emerges in *Jane Eyre* and *Villette*. Here, Brontë struggles with the issue of desire, indicating the danger of not being able to contain or control female desire. Brontë also implies in this triangular dynamic that male homosocial bonds occur at the expense of women. It seems likely that the victimization and polarity that she depicts women as experiencing (owing to the influence of the men in her protagonists' lives) will lead Brontë in her future works to explore directions in which women can find empowerment and identity within their own community.

It is in "Passing Events" that Brontë persuasively depicts the victimization of a woman who is unwittingly caught in a triangular love relationship and subsequently manipulated by two men. Mary Percy was married to Zamorna by her father to cement the alliance between her father and Zamorna. Mary finds her loyalties divided between the two:

> [Zamornora] would not mention my name, I am nothing to him. I am utterly compr[om]ised by my father's actions. Oh, I used to be so sinfully proud of such a father & I am so still, but, my pride is eating away my happiness like rust. . . . He would think of me more as a woman I am sure & less as a bodiless link between himself & my terrible father if I were near at hand.

> (*FN* 58)

When political quarrels erupt between her husband and father, Mary suffers a perplexity of emotions. She longs for the time prior to her marriage when her father's relation with her was strong. Yet, Mary Percy is pulled by an equally strong passion and a sense of obligation to her husband. It is precisely because Mary Percy knows that she serves to cement the bond between her husband and her father that she finds herself in an inescapable predicament. Her husband, Zamorna, views her as a sexual object as well as a political liability now; it is not surprising that he becomes unfaithful to her. Thus, Brontë shows how women suffer psychologically in a masculine homosocial world. She becomes highly objectified as a result of the homosocial bond and also suffers from the fall-out of the relationship between the men—she is not given the opportunity to develop a sense of identity. Similarly, in "Captain Henry Hastings," Brontë depicts a woman's psychological suffering and pain due to a masculine-dominated society. Here, as in "Passing Events," a triangular love relationship emerges with the appearance of a suitor to Elizabeth, Sir William Percy. Elizabeth passionately loves Sir William Percy, but she controls her desire for him since he is her brother's opponent. Elizabeth, like Mary Percy, suffers from the conflict of passion between her brother and her lover. Among other novelettes, Brontë wrote this work at a more mature age, which may explain why she expresses desire for women's independence more explicitly than in her early novelettes. Unlike the passive Mary Percy, Elizabeth exits from a triangular homosocial bond between her brother and Sir William Percy by declaring her independence from both. Although Elizabeth suffers because she still desires Sir William Percy, Brontë has her elect to be independent and self-assertive.

Like Mina Laury and Mary Percy, Elizabeth Hastings is presented as a person with strong potential for passion and very strong repression. We know that Elizabeth has restraint as well as passion from our first acquaintance with her. Elizabeth is capable of departing from the conventions of the male homosocial Angrian world. Aware of the power of passion, Elizabeth nevertheless maintains an independent position. She seems to recognize that independence is power when she says to Sir William Percy that "I'll not be your mistress" (*FN* 256). The narrator reveals that Sir William Percy is very impressed by Elizabeth's "intense emotions" and her strong passion (*FN* 251). Thus, Brontë suggests that Elizabeth has agency and is capable of exercising control over her emotions. Elizabeth Hastings may be the prototype for Jane Eyre, whom Brontë skillfully depicts as embattled between her passion for Rochester and her need for independence and self-assertion. The character of Elizabeth also bears similarities to Lucy Snowe in *Villette*. Like Lucy Snowe, Elizabeth comes to own her own school, and is "dependent on nobody—responsible to nobody" (*FN* 243). The sense of agency that Elizabeth exerts seems to be attributed to her personality. Brontë, however, does indicate that she is a lady companion to Jane Moore and this may be a hint of an incipient female homosocial bond that Elizabeth has formed.

Although Brontë depicts here a forceful view of women's independence, most of her emphasis in these early narratives is on depicting the ways in which women suffer from their oppressed situations in a patriarchal society. Brontë here depicts the strong power of a male homosocial world: the depiction of the oppressive power of a male homosocial world in her early works allows Brontë to open up space for women's homosocial bond, which will be presented in her later works.[3] In Brontë's early works, women are depicted as passive figures in a male homosocial world, for the most part isolated from other women.

However, Brontë later reverses this pattern: in *Jane Eyre, Shirley* and *Villette,* each heroine develops an emotional bond with other women. Brontë suggests that women are thus able to find their own identity and subjectivity within this female community. Brontë's cognizance of masculine homosocial bonds may have been the impetus for her exploration of the emotional and physical bonds between women portrayed in *Jane Eyre, Shirley,* and *Villette.* The status quo of male homosocial bonds and the subsequent sense of isolation that women experienced may have led women to the search for a sense of their own community that Brontë addresses.

Unlike in her later novels, which use female narrators, Brontë employs a male narrator in both early mature novelettes and *The Professor*—Charles Townshend and William Crimsworth respectively. Brontë adopts the persona of a male narrator to say what she cannot otherwise express in her own voice. Conscious of the limitations society imposes on a woman, Brontë deliberately creates a man as the central character, to avoid the limitations that a female protagonist would impose on the novel. Brontë seems to enjoy masquerading as a man—as in the long correspondence with her publishers as "Currer Bell." On the other hand, Brontë might have thought that she could better depict the power of the male homosocial bond by adopting the persona of a male narrator, and thus subtly convey the ways in which a woman's life is victimized by the relationships between two men.

Critics have various attitudes toward Brontë's use of the male narrator. Helen Moglen argues that since Brontë never "encountered a heroine in her personal, cultural or political experience—or, for that matter, in literature—it was difficult for her to conceive of any woman as the focus of a work of fiction."[4] Winifred Gérin views the male narrators as a demerit in the work: Charlotte Brontë as Crimsworth lacks the confessional feelings of Charlotte Brontë as Jane Eyre or Charlotte Brontë as Lucy Snowe.[5] Instead of attributing the narrator to a "clumsy mistake by a young writer," Sandra Gilbert and Susan Gubar account for the masculine voice, explaining that "many women working in a male-dominated literary tradition at first attempt to resolve the ambiguities of their situation not merely by male mimicry but by some kind of metaphorical male impersonation."[6] In other words, Brontë can better talk about what society allows her to do or not to do by pretending to be a male. Clearly, Brontë was aware of her society's attitude toward herself as an author. Southey wrote to her bluntly: "Literature cannot be the business of a woman's life, and it ought not to be."[7] Brontë knew that Southey's response was a reflection of her society's view of female writers, and it explained why Brontë elected to use a male name.

Gilbert and Gubar's view, that Brontë uses a male persona as a mask to express symbolically the oppressed situation of women, seems accurate. However, Brontë moves beyond the representational value of a male narrator. The male narrator becomes an enabling tool for depicting the negative impact of the male homosocial bond for women in the novel. Brontë must have thought that she could better depict the power of the male homosocial bond by adopting the persona of a male narrator and also subtly convey the ways in which Frances' life is circumscribed by the relationships between the male narrator and Hunsden.

The relationship between Crimsworth and Hunsden is deliberately depicted as stronger and more intense than that which Crimsworth and Frances share. The conflicts that characterize the relationship between the men are never resolved in the story. As odd as their friendship may seem, there is a mutual attraction-repulsion between Crimsworth and Hunsden. Despite his genuine gratitude to Hunsden for liberating him from Edward's employ, Crimsworth will not thank his friend and rudely tells him to "look for [gratitude] in a better world, as he [is] not likely to meet with it here." Hunsden replies by calling Crimsworth "a dry-hearted aristocratic scamp," and a heated argument ensues (*P* 43-4). Brontë suggests the simple point that the present hostility in their relationship is actually an indication of the respect and affection that these men feel for one another.

Hunsden acts for Crimsworth's good throughout *The Professor*. Hunsden shows more affection toward Crimsworth than Crimsworth returns. Hunsden seems to almost enact a sexual role as the dominating male. He invites Crimsworth in for an evening's talk with the comment that he seems hurrying on as "Lot from Sodom" (*P* 27). He also compares Crimsworth to a female alternative: "instead of Rebecca on a camel's hump, with bracelets on her arms and a ring in her nose, Fate sends me only a counting-house clerk, in a grey tweed wrapper" (*P* 27). This scene, in which Hunsden is compared to Lot, and Crimsworth to Rebecca, is cast in the language of sexual roles. The male bonding in *The Professor* is more overtly sexual than in most of Sedgwick's cases; Sedgwick sees the male homosocial bonding as the site which represses homoerotic feeling and homosexual desire.

As Hunsden emerges as an androgynous figure, the homoerotic overtone becomes more evident. Crimsworth says that Hunsden is a handsome, "feminine" man: As his masculine and feminine selves flicker successively across his countenance, he has sometimes "the mien of a morose bull" and sometimes that of "an arch and mischievous girl; more frequently, the two semblances were blent" (*P* 30). Crimsworth feels strangely attracted to Hunsden's androgyny or the character of "a foreigner" (*P* 24). When Hunsden blames Crimsworth for his passive behavior, Crimsworth accepts this criticism because it comes from the man who is his alter-ego:

> "What are you then? You sit at that desk in Crimsworth's counting-house day by day and week by week, scraping with a pen on paper, just like an automaton; you never get up; you never say you are tired; you never ask for a holiday; you never take change or relaxation; you give way to no excess of an evening; you neither keep wild company, nor indulge in strong drink. . . . When a man endures patiently what ought to be unendurable, he is a fossil."
>
> (*P* 30)

Although Crimsworth is perplexed by Hunsden's advice, he feels himself emotionally tied to Hunsden. Hunsden is the only person who is willing to get Crimsworth out of trouble. Hunsden further tells Crimsworth to free himself from his brother's oppressive hands and "go on to the Continent" to make his own money (*P* 46). Gilbert and Gubar argue that "Hunsden acts as Crimsworth's agent."[8] With Hunsden's help, Crimsworth begins to define his identity, which eventually leads him to master Hunsden.

Before achieving his masculine identity, Crimsworth comes under Hunsden's mastery. At first, Crimsworth's relationship to Hunsden appears to be another relationship in which "Crimsworth plays the role of the feminine object and Hunsden the dominating male subject."[9] Crimsworth's wish for liberty is compared to Jane Eyre's meditations on that subject. Although Crimsworth has social and psychological advantages over Jane Eyre or Lucy Snowe, he allows himself to be exploited by another male. By allowing himself to be treated like a slave, "kept down like some desolate tutor or governess" (*P* 19), Crimsworth obeys a feminine code of passivity, which Hunsden mocks.

Brontë uses Crimsworth as a lens to filter the narrow world of the pensionnat in which Brontë herself was shut in for two painful years. Crimsworth is treated as a desolate tutor or governess (a story from Brontë's own experience). Hunsden remarks that "Any woman, sinking her shaft deep enough, will at last reach a fathomless spring of sensibility in thy breast, Crimsworth" (*P* 84). While Hunsden appears as an active master, Crimsworth is constantly compared to a passive feminine figure who is disinherited and orphaned: Crimsworth becomes "wrecked and stranded on the shores of commerce" (*P* 32). His condition is compared to female powerlessness with feelings of enclosure and imprisonment.

The homosocial relationship that Brontë depicts here is what allows Crimsworth and Hunsden to explore different gender roles before they embrace their heterosexual identities. What Brontë thus suggests is that homosocial relationships here have heterosexual dynamics. Crimsworth eventually learns to achieve masculine identity from another masculine figure, Hunsden. Crimsworth obtains mastery over women at the end of the novel.

Crimsworth's practice in the male community and his mastery over women allows him to work out a heterosexual relationship with Frances. The gender reversals of a masculinized and a feminized male in both male characters and the alternation of both characters in each role allows the male characters to work out their masculine identities for future heterosexual relationships.

Frances functions as a promise of a future potential heterosexual relationship for Crimsworth once he comes to terms with owning his true gender identity. Frances is thus on the periphery of the relationship between Crimsworth and Hunsden: She is incidental in so far as she makes Crimsworth's movement towards heterosexuality complete. In order for the men to work out the dynamics of a heterosexual relationship and their feelings toward each other, Frances needs to remain in the background. Thus, Frances occupies a marginalized position in relation to these men—she is not the immediate focus. Women function in this novel to legitimize otherwise unacceptable male homosocial bonds and are used as such by the two men as a way of opening the discussion of how these men feel towards one another. Brontë's point, here, may be that women function to reinforce male homosocial bonds rather than achieving an identity of their own. Brontë seems to say that women in *The Professor* continue to have value only insofar as they are the mediating objects between two masculine subjects, very much in keeping with her other early novelettes.

In this novel, Frances, Zoraïde, and Crimsworth's mother are mediated in their connections to this male society. Women function as the mediums of exchange between Hunsden and Crimsworth. For example, in Hunsden's letter to Crimsworth after the long separation, Hunsden first tries to make a connection with him by referring to Crimsworth's lover: "a pursy little Belgian schoolmistress—a Mdlle Zénobie, or some such name . . . if she pleases my taste, or if I think it worth while in a pecuniary point of view, I'll pounce on your prize and bear her away triumphant in spite of your teeth"(*P* 178-9). After his long separation from Crimsworth, Hunsden attempts to resume his relationship with Crimsworth by referring to a woman, Zenobie (obviously Zoraïde). Crimsworth also seems aware that if Hunsden hears of his happy marriage, he will envy him. In his response to Hunsden's letter, Crimsworth writes, if [Crimsworth] marries "a pretty, wealthy wife, [Hunsden] would have hated" Crimsworth himself (*P* 187). As Crimsworth suggests, Hunsden does intervene in the relationship between Crimsworth and his female partner. Hunsden positions himself as the strong man who desires the feminine Crimsworth. Hunsden sets himself up as the masculine subject who determines whether Crimsworth's wife is truly worthy of contention or not. As Crimsworth's response to Hunsden's letter suggests, Crimsworth acknowledges Hunsden's position as masculine rival for his chosen object of desire. Thereby, Crimsworth confirms the triangular paradigm.

The close relationship between Hunsden and Crimsworth involves mutual hatred: Crimsworth and Hunsden would not hate each other if they did not love each other. Hunsden and Crimsworth try to break up their relationship, but they cannot do so because both of them regard Frances as the object of desire. What is really being invoked is a triangulation of desire: under the guise of desiring Frances, they explore their desire for each other. Hunsden's verbal duels with Frances take place under Crimsworth's eye, though they are plainly exhilarating to both protagonists and, to the novelist herself. They try to master each other and this desire for mastery, Brontë seems to suggest, comes from a sado-masochistic love relationship. To assume his masculine position, Crimsworth must now escape Hunsden's gaze, for Hunsden's gaze has discovered and uncovered Crimsworth's feminization. When Hunsden tyrannizes Crimsworth, Crimsworth growls, "Were he the devil himself, instead of being merely very like him, I'd not condescend to get out of his way, or to forge a smile or a cheerful word wherewith to avert his sarcasm"(*P* 179). However, Crimsworth is unable to close his relationship with Hunsden because Hunsden stands as Crimsworth's own paternal adviser.

Hunsden also determines to break with Crimsworth. However, after an encounter between Frances and Hunsden (in which Frances makes a good show of herself on behalf of Crimsworth), Hunsden again views Crimsworth as his worthy rival for Frances. Yet, it must be remembered that Frances functions as a fictive goal to both of them. Hunsden's recognition of Frances' intellect in his conversation with her energizes the relationship between Crimsworth and Hunsden. Hunsden teases her, saying that Switzerland is the country of "servility," and her resistance to this is fierce: "Do you abuse Switzerland to me, Mr. Hunsden?" (*P* 220). In his conversation with her, he finds her worthy of being an object of jealousy between Crimsworth and Hunsden: "[Hunsden] liked something strong, whether in man or woman; he liked whatever dared to clear conventional limits" (*P* 219). Through Frances, Crimsworth becomes Hunsden's combative equal.

In the power struggle between men, Frances stimulates the alternative feelings of love and hate between Crimsworth and Hunsden. Hunsden continues to exert his power over Crimsworth: "Don't be vainglorious. Your lace-mender is too good for you, but not good enough for me; neither physically nor morally does she come up to my ideal of a woman" (*P* 225). Despite Hunsden's teasing, Hunsden himself is clearly attracted to Frances. Hunsden's attraction for Frances occurs because of Crimsworth's interest in Frances, and is therefore mimetic. Here, Frances' function is to enable the circulation of homosocial desire and to signify masculine empowerment. She exists as a symbolic object that males fight over when in fact they are desirous of each other. It is only after Crimsworth is assured that Hunsden finds Frances worthy of obtaining, that Crimsworth becomes truly satisfied in having chosen Frances for a wife. For it is only at this point that Crimsworth's desire for her is validated by the other masculine subject's desire for her.

Unlike Frances, Zoraïde seems to function as a subject, the one who controls and deceives Crimsworth. However, Zoraïde is reduced to being a victim like Frances, and comes to also occupy a position as an object for men to obtain. Zoraïde gazes at Crimsworth, and simultaneously she is watched by Crimsworth:

> I watched her as keenly as she watched me; I perceived soon that she was feeling after my real character; she was searching for salient points, and weak points, and eccentric points. . . .
>
> (*P* 118-9)

Here, the way Zoraïde and Crimsworth watch each other has a sexual overtone. The gaze can be read as a combination of control and erotic attraction. Zoraïde tries to exert power over Crimsworth, but her role as a controlling subject turns to the position of an object since her surveillance creates Crimsworth's desire for Frances. In denying Crimsworth access to Frances, Zoraïde unleashes Crimsworth's desire for Frances. In this aspect, Zoraïde plays the role of a mediator—one who creates desire between Crimsworth and Frances. This novel demonstrates that desire is not created alone, but is produced by another's mediation. René Girard argues that desire is mediated by the presence of a third person. He has pointed out that we speak of our desire for an object as "a simple straight line which joins subject and object.[10] However, desire, according to him, is triangular as opposed to linear. Zoraïde the mediator allows Crimsworth to express his desire for Frances. In other words, Crimsworth does not realize his desire for Frances until Zoraïde casts Frances in the role of the missing object, the role that Zoraïde now wants to assume in her relationship with Crimsworth.

When Crimsworth overhears M. Pelet and Zoraïde's conversation in the garden, he does not want to suffer from his desire for Zoraïde. Crimsworth is now confident in his mastery and can turn the tables on Zoraïde easily. As soon as Crimsworth strongly places himself in the role of the masculine subject, Zoraïde becomes his slave; she lets Crimsworth feel "gratification in receiving the incense from an attractive and still young worshipper" (*P* 109). Crimsworth now takes a kind of conqueror's pleasure in his power over Zoraïde. Although he fears his sexual desire for Zoraïde, he looks toward Frances as one whom he can master.

Like Frances', Zoraïde's function is to energize the homoerotic relationship between Crimsworth and Hunsden: at the end of the novel, Hunsden again wants to know whether Crimsworth's desire for Zoraïde still remains in his mind. Hunsden tells Crimsworth "to see your first flame, Zoraïde" (*P* 247). Hunsden still has jealousy toward Crimsworth's love for Zoraïde, and here, Hunsden's jealousy suggests his homoerotic desire for Crimsworth. In this view, Zoraïde is the object that Hunsden employs to demonstrate his desire for Crimsworth. Whether Zoraïde's role is passive or active, she is reduced into only a mediator who connects Crimsworth and Frances.

Like Frances and Zoraïde, Crimsworth's mother also becomes a symbolic object between Crimsworth and Hunsden. Hunsden knows that Crimsworth values his own mother in his life, and Hunsden therefore purchases Crimsworth's mother's picture from Edward (Hunsden purchases it at Edward's bankruptcy sale) in order to present it to Crimsworth. In a sense Hunsden appropriates what is dear to Crimsworth (the picture of Crimsworth's mother) and in doing so Hunsden shows his affection for Crimsworth. After the long separation, Hunsden writes to Crimsworth, "In giving William Crimsworth his mother's picture, I give him sweets, bells, and bone all in one" (*P* 194-5). In this way, Hunsden attempts to fulfill Crimsworth's emotional and psychological needs which might be created by the loss of Crimsworth's own mother. Hunsden himself attempts to fill up the feelings of loss that Crimsworth experiences. Hunsden uses this mother figure to approach Crimsworth, and in this situation the mother's role is to cement the bond between Hunsden and Crimsworth. It is the portrait of Crimsworth's mother which confirms Crimsworth's relationship with Hunsden, the significant other masculine subject in the novel. It is while gazing at the portrait of Crimsworth's mother that Crimsworth and Hunsden have their first significant encounter.

The mother figure also functions as a catalyst in the process of Crimsworth's identity-formation; he learns to transfer his homosocial relationship into a heterosexual one via his mother. Crimsworth's desire to be in his mother's company is what eventually leads him to experience sexual desire for Zoraïde and Frances. This leads him to experience sexual desire for Zoraïde and Frances from his desire to be in his mother's company. Thus, he learns from his mother that he wants to experience a desire to be with women in a general sense. Crimsworth's encounter with his mother tests his own sexuality, which has been repressed for a long time, and allows him to express his desire to be heterosexual. Brontë, a stand-in for Crimsworth, emphasizes the maternal figure who plays an important role in his life. More importantly, Crimsworth identifies with his mother and feels the kinship between them. Crimsworth identifies on some level with his mother in his physical features and in his emotional makeup. Before he possesses his mother's picture, Crimsworth's desire for his mother throughout his life is already quite explicitly manifested: "[he] gazed long, earnestly; [his] heart grew to the image"(*P* 20). The desire for an absent mother intrinsic to the process of identity is resolved for Crimsworth upon viewing the image:

> "Mother!" I might have said more—but with me, the first word uttered aloud in soliloquy rouses consciousness; it reminds me that only crazy people talk to themselves, and then I think out my monologue, instead of speaking it. I had thought a long while, and a long while had contemplated the intelligence, the sweetness, and—alas!
>
> (*P* 194)

Seeing the image of his absent mother recalls him to her and provides him with a feeling of emotional fulfillment. Brontë evokes the feeling of identity between Crimsworth and his mother (since Crimsworth is Brontë herself), and the importance of a maternal influence in his life. This identity may reflect Brontë's own experience in her relationship with her mother as it remained in her memory. In any case, the novel indicates the importance of the nurturing, maternal role as an important component of the identity formation process.

In this novel as in Brontë's other novels, hypochondria seems to be linked to feelings of isolation and loneliness that Brontë's protagonists experience, owing to the loss of their mothers. Crimsworth suffers from the loss of connection with his mother: he says "my boyhood was lonely, parentless; uncheered by brother or sister" (*P* 211). Crimsworth suffers from attacks of hypochondria which are personified as a female figure who entices him to enter his secret chamber, subsequent to establishing himself as a professor, and following Frances' agreement to be his wife: "I had entertained her [hypochondria] at bed and board for a year; for that space of time I had her to myself in secret; she lay with me, she ate with me, she walked out with me" (*P* 211). The loneliness Crimsworth as an orphan experiences is so deeply intense that it leads him to personify it—an indication of the depths to which he experiences this sense of isolation.

The psychoanalytic approach to reading Crimsworth's bouts with hypochondria is to see them as unresolved conflicts he has with his mother's absence in his boyhood. Throughout this novel, Crimsworth, as many critics argue, suffers from emotional outbursts brought on by his intense longing for his mother and his sexual stimulation in his relationship to Zoraïde and Frances. John Maynard suggests that "[t]here are also indications that Crimsworth finds himself, when brought this close to an adult sexual commitment, attracted backwards by the undertow of guilt for unresolved boyhood desires

for his mother." Maynard points out that Crimsworth's suffering comes from the childhood problem: he has a severe depression over guilt to "possess the mother figure symbolically in Frances." Here, Maynard emphasizes Crimsworth's Oedipal context: Crimsworth competes with his brother-father figure, Hunsden and has anxiety and guilt due to his love for Frances, a mother figure. Hunsden, a father figure, comes to possess Crimsworth's mother (Hunsden comes to own the picture of Crimsworth's mother) and "Crimsworth finds, like Oedipus, that his competition has not only been weakened, but eliminated."[11] It is important to note that Crimsworth's longing for his mother and his sexual stimulation in his relationship to Zoraïde and Frances are not interrupted by his strong relationship with Hunsden. Like a girl in Chodorow's paradigm, Crimsworth does not desert his mother in order to have his father. Crimsworth's desire for his mother is clearly manifested throughout this novel. Crismsworth is not only attracted to Hunsden (in this case, the role of female figures is to cement the bond between Hunsden and Crimsworth), but he also has sexual desire for Zoraïde and Frances. In his various relationships with others, Crimsworth learns to have both homosocial and heterosexual relationships.

The sickness which Crimsworth has for two weeks is similar to the pain later experienced by the motherless Jane Eyre, Caroline Helstone, and Lucy Snowe. By referring to each protagonist's strong desire for her/his mother, Brontë's novel emphasizes the role of a mother in the child's ego development and the subsequent sense of loss that these protagonists experience with the absence of their mothers. Moreover, this novel suggests that part of the natural development of an individual is to find others to fill this sense of loss, to nurture them and thus fulfill their most basic needs and desires.

In *The Professor,* Brontë depicts a triangular relationship between males: Crimsworth, who plays a feminine role (personified as Brontë), becomes the object that strengthens this bond between Hunsden and Edward Crimsworth. Crimsworth has become feminized, and his feminization reveals the fact that he serves as the mediating object of desire whom the two men (Hunsden and Edward) engage in war. However, Crimsworth's role as an object in male homosocial bonding is temporary. Unlike Frances, who remains unable to escape from men's mastery, Crimsworth succeeds in escaping from the role of a servant. After testing his sexual desire in his relationship with women and achieving control of his mother's picture from his brother Edward, Crimsworth comes to possess mastery. When Crimsworth ultimately takes possession of his mother's portrait, he undoubtedly values his prize, but Crimsworth values it because he has also taken it away from his brother, Edward Crimsworth. The attainment of the portrait signifies his victory over his brother. It is his acknowledgment of his masculine sexual desire that enables Crimsworth to gain mastery over it. When he tests his sexual desire for women and is finally disillusioned with sexual fantasy, Crimsworth finally comes to possess mastery. As Gilbert and Gubar put it, "escaping an oppressively female role," Crimsworth "is on the brink of metamorphosis into a more powerful creature," into masculine sexuality.[12] Crimsworth sees three girls' charms in Zoraïde's school. Even though he realizes their sensual charms, he suggests that their sensual beauty, as Maynard indicates, "is more threatening to him than he can admit."[13] Crimsworth becomes gradually disillusioned by women: he is kept awake by the confession of love between Pelet and Zoraïde. He overhears the fact that Zoraïde plans to marry Pelet, assuring Pelet that she has no interest in Crimsworth. Crimsworth now feels driven to treat her with special coldness. However, Crimsworth cannot resist his desire for Zoraïde: after Crimsworth pays attention to his future wife, Frances, his physical attraction to Zoraïde seems to grow. He says that "When [Zoraïde] stole about me with the soft step of a slave, I felt at once barbarous and sensual as a pasha" (*P* 171). Crimsworth decides ultimately not to act on his sexual desire for Zoraïde and in doing so gains mastery over these feelings.

In his own conflict between reason and desire, Crimsworth chooses reason: after having difficulties in asserting independence (since he plays the feminine, passive role), he finally obtains masculine mastery in a love triangle relationship (he is a master of Frances, he thinks). Unlike Crimsworth at the beginning of the novel, Crimsworth now ends the conversation with a paean to victory and triumph in their married life; he says "we have realized an independency"(*P* 236). Crimsworth implies that in marriage neither he nor his wife have the upper hand: in fact, both are masters of their own destiny. However, Brontë is careful to reveal that from Frances' point of view, Crimsworth still occupies the position of a master in the relationship.

The consequence of homosocial relations in this novel is that it forces Frances to exercise her ability to express herself. Realizing her limited space, Frances begins to assert her own independence in the later part of the novel. Maynard addresses this issue of Frances' incipient self-assertiveness: "[t]his major issue of female independence of 'Captain Henry Hastings' of the later novels finds a surprisingly easy solution here."[14] Near the end of the novel, Frances begins to claim the self-confidence and emotional independence Brontë as both a woman and writer must have sought. Brontë allows Frances to speak as the narrative continues: Brontë works for Frances "behind" Crimsworth's narrative voice. Frances is not like the heroines in the early novelettes. Although Crimsworth and Hunsden use Frances to strengthen their relations, she remains unwilling and insistent on not submitting herself totally to the strong bond of male homoeroticism. Unlike Mary Percy and Mina Laury in Brontë's early novelettes, Frances *will not* sacrifice herself to the male homosocial world.

At the close of this novel, Brontë comes to focus upon the figure of Frances as one who rails against her socio-economic situation in her married life. Here, Brontë decidedly shows sympathy toward Frances' difficulty and suffering, and suggests a feeling of identity and sameness with Frances. The author Brontë seems to become further embedded in her own work as the narrative continues. Carol Bock asserts that "Brontë did not clearly understand her relationship to her narrator when she wrote *The Professor*" in the way that she did in her later novels.[15] Brontë may have thought that there was a limitation in using Crimsworth as her mouthpiece. Although she uses a male narrator, Brontë seems to intrude into the voice of the existing narrator. The novel shows a more sympathetic attitude toward Frances, who cries repeatedly before the wedding and complains about her unequal treatment by society.

Although the narrator is Crimsworth, we hear more from Frances than from Crimsworth. The later part of this novel seems to be narrated by Frances, who rebels against the patriarchal social system:

> 'I am not satisfied,' returned she: 'you are now earning eight thousand francs a year' (it was true; my efforts, punctuality, the fame of my pupil's progress, the publicity of my station, had so far helped me on), 'while I am still at my miserable twelve hundred francs. I *can* do better, and I *will*.'
>
> (*P* 228)

Unlike the earlier part of this novel which identifies Brontë as merged with Crimsworth, the later part seems to produce a different kind of narrative in which Brontë seems to merge into Frances. On a metatextual level, Brontë might seem to be attracted to Frances who, as a character, takes shape and becomes increasingly independent. Here, Brontë foreshadows the psychological bond which is shared between females, to be revealed in her later works. Frances' narrative leaves Crimsworth with a number of questions about how he understands the complexity of human life. For example, when Crimsworth tells Frances to quit her teaching position and stay at home, she cries out against him:

> "How rich you are, Monsieur!" and then she stirred uneasily in my arms. "Three thousand francs!" she murmured, "while I get only twelve hundred!" She went on faster . . , "Think of my marrying you to be kept by you, Monsieur! I could not do it—and how dull my days would be! You would be away teaching in close, noisy schoolrooms from morning till evening, and I should be lingering at home unemployed and solitary; I should get depressed and sullen, and you would soon tire of me."
>
> (*P* 209)

Frances' angry tone indicates that Crimsworth does not understand the limitations placed on her life. It is clear that Frances' view of the marriage has realistic complications that Crimsworth has no awareness of. Frances complains about the inequality of her social situation compared to her husband's. Frances describes a woman's lot in the personal terms which she faces in her marriage:

> Monsieur, if a wife's nature loathes that of the man she is wedded to, marriage must be slavery. Against slavery all right thinkers revolt, and though torture be the price of resistance torture must be dared: though the only road to freedom lie through the gates of death, those gates must be passed; for freedom is indispensable. Then, monsieur, I would resist as far as my strength permitted; when that strength failed I should be sure of refuge. Death would certainly screen me both from bad laws and their consequences.
>
> (*P* 235-6)

Frances does not have an idealistic view—she does not regard marriage as an entirely happy experience. She is the prototype of Mrs. Pryor who abandons her daughter because of her shattering marriage in *Shirley*.

Crimsworth does not understand Frances' complex view of human life; from his viewpoint, she is a contradictory person. Crimsworth says that she leads a bifurcated life: "So different was she under different circumstances, I seemed to possess two wives" (*P* 230). He does not want to view her as an integral whole being. The masculine Frances, for him, is all "firmness, activity, and enterprise" (*P* 230). This Frances takes care of business: "In the daytime my house and establishment were conducted by Madame the Directress, a stately and elegant woman, bearing much anxious thought on her large brow . . . silence, industry, observance, attending on her presence" (*P* 231). The second Frances is the womanly, feminine Frances, "his" Frances, who is "fresh and fair," inwardly full of "poetic feeling, and fervour" (*P* 230). Crimsworth grants that Frances has some measure of power as far as he remains a master:

> Duties she must have to fulfill, and important duties; work to do—and exciting, absorbing, profitable work . . . mine was not the hand ever to starve or cramp them; no, I delighted in offering them sustenance, and in clearing them a wider space for action.
>
> (*P* 229)

Crimsworth grants Frances her empowerment, but she is still the slave whose power is wholly dependent on her master's generosity. Crimsworth expects her to play two roles which cannot be integrated: as Madame, the directress, Frances is "a stately and elegant woman," dignified, vigilant. But at six o'clock "the lady-directress vanished before my eyes, and Frances Henri, my own little lace-mender, was magically restored to

my arms" (*P* 232). Although Crimsworth does not see Frances as an independent whole being, she argues for her independence and individuality. Frances refuses to remain his pupil: she attempts to "retain her employment of teaching" after her marriage (*P* 208). Crimsworth's attempt to bifurcate and marginalize Frances is a consequence of the homosocial relation Crimsworth experiences with Hunsden. In other words, the close bond between Crimsworth and Hunsden (with two aspects of the patriarchy) leads Crimsworth to have his egoistic view in his married life: Crimsworth reads Frances as he wants to do—as both a Madame during the day and as a lace-mender at night.

However, the result of bifurcation and marginalization of Frances by Crimsworth does not let her remain in a marginal space; it gradually leads her to find a voice. The relationship between a master and a pupil (Crimsworth and Frances respectively) is subject to change. Brontë foreshadows that Frances will have influence over Crimsworth, albeit a limited one, in the passage quoted below:

> . . . we met as we had always met, as Master and pupil, nothing more. I proceed to handle the papers, Frances, observant and serviceable, stept into an inner room brought a candle, lit it, placed it by me; then drew the curtain over the lattice, and having added a little fresh fuel to the already bright fire, she drew a second chair to the table and sat down at my right hand, a little removed. The paper on the top was a translation of some grave French author into English, but underneath lay a sheet with stanzas; on this I laid hand. Frances half rose, made a movement to recover the captured spoil, saying that was nothing; a mere copy of verses. I put by resistance with the decision I knew she never long opposed, but on this occasion her fingers had fastened on the paper; I had quietly to unloose them; their hold dissolved to my touch; her hand shrunk away; my own would fain have followed it, but for the present I forbade such impulse.
>
> (*P* 201)

Critic Janet Gezari comments that the passage describes "a much more intimate relation than that of master and pupil; the setting is as different as possible from the classroom because of its privacy, its informality, and the comforting domesticity of candle, bright fire, and closed curtain."[16] The scene describes the intimacy essential to the relation of master and pupil as Brontë idealizes it. Here, Brontë undercuts this hierarchical arrangement of society with its emphasis on gender and subsequent class distinctions—women as slaves, men as masters.

This novel's ending is ambiguous, in spite of Brontë's emphasis on the identity formation of both Crimsworth and Frances. The unconnected images of insecurity and violence manifest themselves. Crimsworth struggles against his own demons: he shoots his son's dog without warning because of fear that the dog may be rabid. As a result, Crimsworth sends his son to dad's old and unreformed school, although Victor's mother does not want to send her son there. Unlike her, Crimsworth has a tyrannical arrogance like his brother Edward Crimsworth. Like the unanswered letter of the opening chapter, these final images are more integrally related to the rest of the novel than they seem at first. They articulate a disquieting sense—a sense of something violent, which threatens to disrupt security. Beneath the surface of Crimsworth's tale of successful self-help lies another world, the world of insecurity. Crimsworth appears to be either frustrated with his choice of marriage partner, or hostile toward his son, or both.

Despite the pessimistic ending to the novel, Brontë also offers a positive ending by emphasizing the strength of Frances' maternal love. While Crimsworth turns away from Victor's grief, it is Frances who comforts their distraught child. Her warm love for Victor is reminiscent of Crimsworth's love for his mother:

> . . . though Frances will not make a milksop of her son, she will accustom him to a style of treatment, a forbearance, a congenial tenderness, he will meet with from none else. She sees, as I also see—a something in Victor's temper, a kind of electrical ardour and power, which emits, now and then, ominous sparks—Hunsden calls it his spirit and says it should not be curbed—I call it the leaven of the offending Adam, and consider that it should be, if not *whipped* out of him, at least soundly disciplined.
>
> (*P* 245)

Unlike the male figures, who contemplate Victor's suffering with chilling complacency, Frances maintains an independent relationship with Victor that is not influenced by Crimsworth's view of him. Frances emerges with a wider vision at the end of the novel, after her ten-year marriage:

> The faculties of her nature, already disclosed when I married her, remained fresh and fair; but other faculties shot up strong, branched out broad, and quite altered the external character of the plant. Firmness, activity, and enterprise, covered with grave foliage, poetic feeling, and fervour; but these flowers were still there, preserved pure and dewy under the umbrage of later growth and hardier nature.
>
> (*P* 230)

Brontë compares Frances' constructive role in her family to her nurturing image. At the end of the novel, Frances' maternal love also extends outward. This maternal figure cares for her female students' private lives. Here, the relationship between a teacher and students can be defined as mutual respect and affection:

> . . . some of Frances' pupils in time learnt to love her sincerely, all of them beheld her respect; her general demeanour towards them was serious . . . As to Julia

Georgiana G—daughters of an English baronet—as to Mdle. Mathilde de—heiress of a Belgian Count, and sundry other children of patrician race, the Directress was careful of them as of the others, anxious for their progress, as for that of the rest—but it never seemed to enter her head to distinguish them by a mark of preference—one girl of noble blood she loved dearly, a young Irish baroness, Lady Catherine—, but it was for her enthusiastic heart and clever head—for her generosity and her genius—the title and rank went for nothing.

> (*P* 231-2)

The relationship between a master and pupils, here, is depicted in the terms of identity and sameness of females. They are in equal relation: Frances loves her students equally and exchanges friendly greetings with them. In Frances we anticipate a character like Miss Temple in *Jane Eyre,* who plays a maternal role and simultaneously functions as a teacher to Jane. Brontë gives her readers an opportunity to see the emotional power in the female community that will be clearly explored in her later works.

The male homosocial world of *The Professor* leads Frances to exercise her ability to express herself and to find her own identity. This depiction of the male homosocial world creates the poles that she moves between, causing Frances to explore her own connections with her female students at the end of the novel. In both early mature novelettes and *The Professor,* the domination of male homosocial relations creates a need and a subsequent search for connections between women. It is in her later novels that Brontë will more deeply explore the ways in which women nurture each other.

Notes

1. Sally Shuttleworth, *Charlotte Brontë and Victorian Psychology* (Cambridge: Cambridge University Press, 1996), p. 120.

2. Eve Kosofsky Sedgwick asserts that homosociality has been related to women in European history: women are used as symbolic property primarily for the purpose of cementing the bonds between men. See *Between Men: English Literature and Male Homosocial Desire,* pp. 1-27 for details.

3. Sedgwick in *Between Men* indicates that "homosocial" operates in the ways unknown to the males involved to produce "intense homophobia, fear and hatred of homosexuality" (p. 1). Sedgwick sees "the homosocial" as a hidden continuum of "desire,"—even subtitling her book "homosocial desire." She views it as the place where male bonding oppresses women and creates patriarchy; it is created at the site of homosexual repression. As such, Sedgwick's paradigm fits my

discussion of *The Professor.* As I note elsewhere, I do not find any antithesis in the bonding between women, which does not require full repression of homoerotic desire as it does in men. For this different psychic structure, I use the term "homosocial-erotic," as opposed to "homosocial" which I use as Sedgwick does in her application of it to men.

4. Helen Moglen, *Charlotte Brontë: the Self Conceived* (Wisconsin: University of Wisconsin Press, 1984), p. 88.

5. Winifred Gérin, *Charlotte Brontë: the Evolution of Genius* (Oxford: Oxford University Press, 1967), pp. 311-8.

6. Sandra Gilbert and Susan Gubar, *The Madwoman in the Attic: the Woman Writer and the Nineteenth-Century Literary Tradition* (New Haven: Yale University Press, 1979), p. 316.

7. See Gaskell, p. 105.

8. Gilbert and Gubar, p. 333.

9. See Linda Lee Gill, "Charlotte Brontë and the Possibility of Female Desire," diss., University of California, Riverside, 1992, p. 68. Gill shows how women in Brontë's works are the eternal objects of desire and exchange between men.

10. See René Girard, *Deceit, Desire, and the Novel: Self and Other in Literary Structure,* trans. Yvonne Freccero (Baltimore and London: John Hopkins University Press, 1965), p. 2. Like Sedgwick, Girard takes Freud's paradigm that the triangles involve bonds of rivalry between "males" over "a woman," and extends Freud's view: any rivalry is structured by the same play of emulation and identification, regardless of the type of characters. Sedgwick complains that both Girard and Freud treat the erotic triangle as symmetrical, in the sense that its structure is unaffected by the power difference that would be brought by a change in the gender of one of the characters. Sedgwick's complaint seems fair, yet her complaint does not discount the application of Girard's theory in this chapter, that desire is mediated by the other, and is mimetic. According to his theory, Crimsworth's desire for Frances is postponed until Zoraïde expresses her desire for Crimsworth. In this manner, Frances' desire for Crimsworth also imitates Zoraïde's love for Crimsworth.

11. Maynard, p. 88-9.

12. Gilbert and Gubar, p. 320.

13. Maynard, p. 85.

14. Maynard, p. 88.

15. Carol Bock, *Charlotte Brontë and the Storyteller's Audience* (Iowa: University of Iowa Press, 1992), p. 56.

16. Janet Gezari, *Charlotte Brontë and Defensive Conduct: The Author and the Body at Risk* (Philadelphia: University of Pennsylvania, 1992), p. 54.

Abbreviations

FN *Charlotte Brontë: Five Novelettes.* Ed. Winifred Gérin. London: The Folio Press, 1971.

JE *Jane Eyre.* Ed. Margaret Smith. Oxford and New York: Oxford University Press, 1993.

LCB *The Letters of Charlotte Brontë.* Vol. One. 1829-1847. Ed. Margaret Smith. Oxford: Clarendon Press, 1995.

P *The Professor.* Ed. Margaret Smith and Herbert Rosengarten. Oxford and New York: Oxford University Press, 1991.

S *Shirley.* Ed. Herbert Rosengarten and Margaret Smith. Oxford and New York: Oxford University Press, 1981.

V *Villette.* Ed. Margaret Smith and Herbert Rosengarten. Oxford and New York: Oxford University Press, 1990.

TREATMENT IN WORKS BY HENRY JAMES, NATHANIEL HAWTHORNE, AND FITZ-GREENE HALLECK

John R. Bradley (essay date October 1997)

SOURCE: Bradley, John R. "Henry James's Permanent Adolescence." *Essays in Criticism* 47, no. 4 (October 1997): 287-314.

[*In the following essay, Bradley contends that studying the significance of homosexuality in James's life and works illuminates unique facets of the narratives and James's skill as a writer.*]

One evening around the turn of the century in the garden of his home, Lamb House, Henry James revealed to one of his closest friends, Edmund Gosse, what the latter assumed to be one of the novelist's most intimate secrets. 'As twilight deepened and we walked together,' Gosse was later to recall,

> I suddenly found that in profuse and enigmatic language [James] was recounting for me an experience, something that had happened, not something repeated

or imagined. He spoke of standing on a pavement of a city, in the dusk, and of gazing upwards across the misty street, watching, watching for the lighting of a lamp in the window on the third storey. And the lamp blazed out, and through bursting tears he strained to see what was behind it, the unapproachable face. And for hours he stood there, wet with the rain, brushed by the phantom hurrying figures of the scene, and never from behind the lamp for one moment was visible the face. The mysterious and poignant revelation closed, and one could make no comment, ask no question, being throttled oneself by an overpowering emotion. And for a long time Henry shuffled beside me in the darkness, shaking the dew off the laurels, and still there was no sound at all in the garden but what our heels made crunching the gravel, nor was the silence broken when suddenly we entered the house and he disappeared for an hour.[1]

Hugh Walpole, the recipient of a number of intense, indulgent letters from James, was also confided in some twelve years later when James fleetingly explained that sexually he had 'suffered some frustration. What that frustration was I never knew, but I remember him telling me how he had once in his youth in a foreign town watched a whole night in pouring rain for a figure at a window. "That was the end," he said, and broke off . . .'[2]

Walpole was, perhaps, being a little disingenuous here. James characteristically treated himself as though he was one of his later protagonists, seemingly offering a meaningful account of an event of significance but breaking off teasingly before explaining the crucial details (and ambiguously failing to specify the figure's gender). Teasing may also be what Walpole himself was up to, since what he did or did not know about James's 'sexual frustration' is open to debate. Stephen Spender told Leon Edel that Walpole had confessed to him that when on another evening at Rye he had offered himself to James he was refused with the words: 'I can't! I can't!'.[3] According to Miranda Seymour in *A Ring of Conspirators* (1988), James and his friends 'could, and did, discuss each other's grand passions with a frank and avid interest which had much to do with the possessive adulation of the older men for the younger men of their circles'. She quotes as one of many examples A. C. Benson's recollection of talking to Gaillard Lapsley in the spring of 1913 on the subject of an emotional scene the latter had experienced with James: 'Lapsley said, "If I had caught him in my arms, kissed his cheeks, as I have often done, it would be all right"—this power of receiving caresses is a new light to me on H. J.—he lives in an atmosphere of constant hugging—that is probably the secret of Hugh Walpole's success, the kisses of youth' (p. 188).

What is extraordinary is not only that these revelations presented for an old friend of James like Benson a new angle on James's character, but that they continue to do

so now. So sexually guarded was James during his lifetime that more than eighty years after his death the calling into question of his long-presumed asexuality still causes resentment. But with the publication of Fred Kaplan's *Henry James: The Imagination of Genius* (1991), and the more recent appearance in the United States of the first volume of Sheldon M. Novick's biography *Henry James: The Young Master* (1996), there is now undoubtedly enough evidence to entertain the idea that James's response to homosexuality was more than the objective and aloof observation of it in others.

Two of James's encounters with boys reveal in detail the sort of psychological narcissism hinted at to Gosse and Walpole which defines many of his fictional male characters. They present James in situations with which those characters themselves frequently have to deal: enjoying being in close physical proximity to, while having to remain emotionally and socially ambiguously distanced from, attractive younger males. Like those troubled male characters in his fiction, James is both the observer and the consciousness being observed. One of the events was relayed by James himself in a travel essay written during a trip to Italy in 1873, reprinted in *Italian Hours* (1909); the other, reported by Mrs Humphry Ward in her *Recollections of Writers* (1916), concerns a visit James made with her in the same country in 1899. The incidents are distant enough chronologically, while being close enough in tone and content, to define aspects of James's sensual, if not explicitly sexual, curiosity about younger members of his own sex.

In 1873 James, writing about a group of boys he had come across while out walking in Venice, remarked of one of the lads that 'he was the most expressively beautiful creature I had ever looked upon':

> He had a smile to make Correggio sigh in his grave. . . . Verily nature is still at odds with propriety. . . . I think I shall always remember, with infinite conjecture, as the years roll by, this little unlettered Eros of the Adriatic strand.
>
> (*Italian Hours*, p. 56)

Mrs Ward recalled a visit with James to Lake Nemi more than a quarter of a century later:

> On descending from Genzano to the strawberry farm that now holds the sight of the famous temple of Diana Memorensis, we found a beautiful youth at the *fattoria*, who for a few pence undertook to show us the fragments that remain. Mr. James asked his name. 'Aristodemo,' said the boy, looking as he spoke the Greek name, 'like to a God in form and stature.' Mr. James's face lit up; and he walked over the historic ground beside the lad, Aristodemo picking up for him fragments of terracotta from the furrows through which the plough had just passed, bits of the innumerable small *figurines* that used to crowd the temple walls as

ex-votos. . . . I presently came up with Mr. James and Aristodemo, who led us on serenely, a young Hermes in the transfiguring light. One almost looked for the winged feet and helmet of the messenger God! Mr. James paused—his eyes first on the boy, then on the surrounding scene. 'Aristodemo!', he murmured smiling, more to himself than me, his voice caressing the word.

(*Recollections of Writers*, pp. 328-9)

In the first extract, James's own casually remarked-upon but obviously intense involvement is qualified by a universalising reference to art, as the boy undergoes an apotheosis into Eros. Mrs Ward's reference to Hermes similarly creates a refined, classical context—they were after all strolling among Roman ruins—and the fact that she and James 'found' the boy further makes it appear that he was a relic from another age. The boy is also said to be, this time in a more obviously homo-erotic classical sense, 'like to a God in form and stature'. Mrs Ward indicates a movement from the sensory to the imaginative: from the boy to his name, and to James's withdrawn, verbal manifestation of his enchantment. James's association with any kind of sexuality, whether in his fiction or in his life, always appeared, to others as much as to himself, to be unavoidably otherworldly in this way, presenting opportunities for private reflection and regret rather than for indulgence, or at the very most for private, secret indulgence. It is significant that Mrs Ward, a notoriously moral person, wasn't offended by anything she witnessed. In these incidents, as with those recorded by Gosse and Walpole, there is an overwhelming sense, not of the sexual, but the narcissistic and nostalgic. James talks of forever remembering the Italian boy, as he was to talk to Gosse and Walpole about forever remembering the defining incident on that rainy evening during his youth. Mrs Ward's comment, that James repeated Aristodemo's name as though 'caressing' it, strikes one more as an act of loving remembrance than the contemplation of what might actually happen—though when James began to repeat the lad's name, its bearer had yet to depart. Later, in a letter to Mrs Ward, James referred to his fond memories of 'the Nemi Lake, and the walk down and up (the latter perhaps most), and the strawberries and Aristodemo were the cream. . . . I am clear about that'.[4]

However verbally flirtatious and prone to embracing James may have become, his sexual inhibitions prevented him from forming openly sexual relationships, and he became more evasive and self-protective about the subject as he grew older. James's homosexual propensity was to a significant degree sublimated into his fiction, much as his contemplation of these Italian boys was transfigured into a contemplation of classical myth and art. The crucial event during James's youth led to the lonely, intense realisation that sexual bonding would never, in any normal social way, form a part of his non-literary existence.

James remained the sort of man Freud characterised as hopelessly introspective, focused on adolescent boys and young men, and on his own adolescence and early manhood, in an attempt to recapture the lost sense of a real, defining self, first encountered and indulged during sexual awakening.[5] In *The Middle Years* (1917), James explained his understanding of what Cyril Connolly would later call, in *Enemies of Promise* in a specifically homosexual context, 'Permanent Adolescence', by noting how some men remain forever young:

We are never old, that is we never cease easily to be young, for *all* life at the same time: youth is an army, the whole battalion of our faculties and our freshness, our passions and our illusions, on a considerably reluctant march into the enemy's country, the country of the general lost freshness; and I think it throws at least as many stragglers behind as skirmishers ahead—stragglers who often catch up but belatedly with the main body, and even in many a case never catch up at all.[6]

Fictional examples of this kind of psychological situation abound in James's *oeuvre,* and it is occasionally given specific attention, as in 'The Diary of a Man of Fifty' (1879), in which a man contemplates a life of lost opportunities and in particular his decision not to accept the offer of marriage from a girl when he was younger because of a strange lack of romantic spontaneity:

I suppose that, whatever serious step one might have taken at twenty-five, after a struggle, and with a violent effort, and however one's conduct might appear to be justified by events, there would always remain a certain element of regret; a certain sense of loss lurking in the sense of gain; a tendency to wonder, rather wishfully, what *might* have been. What might have been . . .

In 'The Great Good Place' (1890), the sole companion for the protagonist is the younger Brother, a mirror image of himself, and James locates their paradise in a sort of Oxford-cum-Athenaeum all-male environment, where physical intimacy and knowing glances define the special bonds formed between the exclusive members, who are drawn to one another because of their shared yearning for something unnameable and subjective. 'The Middle Years' (1893) presents a highly autobiographical novelist, arriving at middle age, who longs for a young man who loves him and in whose gaze there are 'wedding bells'—but the novelist realises, just as James explained he himself realised, that there are no second chances, and he expires ecstatically in the young man's arms. In 'The Jolly Corner' (1904) the protagonist seeks his *doppelgänger,* a projection of what James thought he might have become if he had stayed in New York, and the narrator faints in fright when he finally encounters an unappealing, disfigured ghost. In these stories what is explored is an older man's seeking his own younger self, or for a young man who resembles that younger self. The result is a turning inward, a realisation of the limitations of the real world and a consequent recognition of the need to draw on the world of the imagination.

Novick has charted the physical solitariness and emotional sense of detachment James himself experienced during his early adolescence, remarking that 'almost from the moment he began to construct his secure, private little self, he felt the pain of loneliness' (*Young Master,* p. 36). He points to a series of crucial remembrances by James in the late autobiographies of certain attachments and images, all experienced before that time a little later when it appears—if we are to accept the stories of Gosse and Walpole—that James abandoned the idea of forming openly sexual relationships for good.[7] James's early friendship with Gus Barker, whom he met when Gus was studying as a military cadet, points to the nature of the cautious, distant friendships James would form throughout his life with young men. Gus was by all accounts an exceptionally beautiful little twelve-year-old boy: blond, strong, clever, mature for his years. James called on his older brother William and John La Farge in the studio they were sharing and found that they had placed Gus naked on a pedestal. James could have stayed, since he was practising painting at the time; but he turned away and walked out, confused and overwhelmed. When he saw Gus later at Harvard, he was again struck by his elegance, but couldn't bring himself to greet him. A few months afterwards, the boy was killed in the American Civil War.

Novick, however, explains his belief that James did have a sexual relationship, however brief, while a young man still at Cambridge, by quoting another late reminiscence:

> How I can speak of Cambridge at all. . . . The point for me (for fatal, for impossible, expansion) is that I knew there, *had* there, in the ghostly old C. that I sit and write of here by the strange Pacific on the other side of the continent, *l'initiation première* (the divine, the unique), there and in Ashburton Place . . . Ah, the 'epoch-making' weeks of the spring of 1865.[8]

In a footnote, Novick claims that 'This passage seems impossible to misunderstand'. Whether his confidence that it signifies the loss of James's virginity is justified is less interesting, for me, than the fact that James should recall such an early, defining experience so many years after the event with the sort of retrospective obsessiveness—the constant drawing on the past for meaning in the present—that so thoroughly characterised his personality. Novick, however, writes about James's assumed sexual activity alongside his discussion of James's intense nostalgia about his vanished 'golden years', and sees no contradiction between the two.

Jamesians have reacted to Novick's speculation with characteristic guardedness. Millicent Bell's hostile review of the biography in the *Times Literary Supplement* (20 December 1996) argued (as Edel had done) that the experience recalled by James was literary. Her implication was not only that Novick's scholarship was bad but also that James was somehow contaminated by his insistence on a homosexual meaning. In his reply (27 December), Novick noted that Bell 'acts as if she were the defence council for Henry James, insisting that every particular of an indictment of sexual misconduct be proven beyond a reasonable doubt, and darkly hinting at the prosecutor's malfeasance' (Novick is himself a lawyer). He also remarked that James's sexual orientation has been 'an open secret' for at least a hundred years, and that to call him gay, in any case, is not in itself an insult. Moreover, if the reference (perhaps significantly in French) was, as Bell and others claim, about a book or article contract James had received, why would it have been, some fifty years later, 'fatal', 'impossible' to reveal? Novick is relying on what he calls 'common sense' and to my mind his is a plausible interpretation of this passage. That is not to say that it is indisputable. Novick may be reading too much into the stylistic circularity and self-indulgence so typical of late James.

The criticism of Novick's biographical speculation by other interested parties is symptomatic of their defensive manoeuvring when presented with work by critics intent on exploring the gay side of James's fiction. Philip Horne, the author of the impressive *Henry James and Revision: The New York Edition* (1991), attacked 'queer theorists' (particularly Eve Kosofsky Sedgwick) for what he takes to be their typical approach to the subject of James and homosexuality, which he summarises as follows: '(1) James writes about the unnameable; (2) homosexuality has often been spoken of as unnameable; (3) James therefore means homosexuality when he refers to something unnameable'.[9] In Sedgwick and her imitators, Horne has selected a rather extreme example of what gay criticism has to offer James studies, perhaps partly because by doing so he was able to develop his argument without having to deal with anything that really challenged it. The best essay on James from a gay perspective—one that would certainly be more difficult to refute—is by the late Richard Ellmann, 'James Among the Aesthetes', in his collection of essays *A long the riverrun* (1988).

Critics who want to prove that homosexuality is important to James's fiction could raise the same objections Horne himself raises and still convincingly argue that gay readings of certain of James's novels and stories are valuable. They can do this without relying on either what Horne refers to as 'the abuse of speculation' or Novick's 'common sense'. Neither James critics 'defending' James from gay readings, nor gay critics 'claiming' James as a gay novelist, are to the point: to unearth a concern with homosexuality in much of his fiction is not to invalidate all previous interpretations, but rather to provide a variation on them which sits alongside or merges with them. Resisting all attempts to explore James from a gay point of view, as Horne and Bell in effect do, leaves them vulnerable to charges of adopting double standards, and of homophobia. In her review, Bell wrote in passing that Minny Temple was someone 'with whom all the young men [of James's circle] were a little in love', but if this had been said of a man or boy, objections would have been instantaneous. In his book on the New York Edition, Horne similarly discusses Minny Temple, writing at one point that 'The "single character" in [*The Portrait of a Lady*] is Isabel Archer; but James's "grasp", his sense of "complete possession" as he calls it, was derived from his knowledge of the remarkable girl dead a decade before' (p. 184).

If it is conceded that there is a connection of this kind, one cannot logically object to the idea that, say, James's story 'The Author of "Beltraffio"' (1884) was based on the knowledge he had acquired about the homosexual life and writings of John Addington Symonds. Such biographical evidence—which is extensive—equally well results in a useful discussion of the story and is not therefore 'the abuse of speculation'. James, in fact, characteristically tried to discuss an event of significance which ultimately had to remain mysterious in a letter written to Gosse in 1884 about Symonds's homosexuality:

> Perhaps I have divined the innermost cause of J. A. S.'s discomfort—but I don't think I seize, on p. 571, exactly the allusion you refer to. I am therefore devoured with curiosity as to the further revelation. Even a postcard (in covert words) would relieve the suspense of the perhaps already-too-indiscreet.[10]

James wrote to Symonds a number of times, but only one of his letters survives. 'I sent you the *Century* more than a year ago with my paper on Venice,' he reminded Symonds, and that

> I sent it to you because it was a constructive way of expressing the good will I felt towards you in consequence of what you had written about the land of Italy—and of intimating to you, somewhat dumbly, that I am an attentive and sympathetic reader. I nourish for the said Italy an unspeakably tender passion, and your pages always seemed to say to me that you were one of the small number of people who love it as much as I do—in addition to your knowing it immeasurably better, I want to recognise this (to your knowledge); for it seemed to me the victims of a common passion should exchange a look.[11]

The piece published in the *Century* James sent to Symonds contained the reference, already quoted, to 'the little unlettered Eros of the Adriatic strand' and the group of young, nearly-naked boys. It might be argued that this letter has nothing to do with homosexuality, but if so why does James write in such a coded way? Why is the information he is offering for Symonds's 'knowledge' only? Why should the 'passion' for Italy be described as 'unspeakable'? And why should that same 'passion' later be referred to in the context of a flirtatious reference to a small number of 'victims' looking out for, or 'glancing', at one another? To most homosexuals, then as now, such coterie expressions would be recognisable in any other context as playing in words on the physical activities of gay men, whether on the streets of London or in Venice (where, incidentally, Symonds had a gondolier lover). In this letter, as with the other about Symonds to Gosse, James is once again divulging his need both to reveal and conceal his interest, and the word 'outpourings' has been used twice with a relaxed confidence, as though James instinctively grasped the importance writing had for the married Symonds in his attempts to deal with his homosexuality.

James was certainly aware that Symonds *was* homosexual, and his response to this 'knowledge' was ambivalent (perhaps the reason he chose to call the character based on Symonds 'Ambient'). When Gosse sent James Symonds's defence of pederasty, *A Problem of Modern Ethics* (1891), James thanked him for having forwarded the marvellous (again) 'outpourings', but after Symonds died James refused to write an appreciation because of 'his strangely morbid and hysterical side'. To do so, James wrote, with a revealing capital P, 'would be a Problem—a problem beyond me'. During Oscar Wilde's trial, James even returned his copy of *Modern Ethics* in a registered envelope, on the extraordinarily self-conscious grounds that 'These are days in which one's modesty is, in every direction, much exposed, and one should be thankful for every veil that one can hastily snatch up or that a friendly hand precipitately muffles one withal'.[12]

When James explored Symonds's predicament in 'The Author of "Beltraffio"', it is hardly surprising, given this context, that the homosexual part of Symonds's life was presented in a 'veiled' manner. James knew that Symonds's wife had reacted negatively to the homosexual content of his books. In the story, Ambient's wife disapproves of her husband's 'insufficiently Christian' outpourings, and she is most anxious to keep them away from their indescribably beautiful little boy. The interest Ambient's young male admirer has in the writer is, as on other occasions in James's fiction, strikingly passionate, and quite out of keeping with what one would usually expect in this sort of relationship. However, 'The Author of "Beltraffio"' is one of many instances where James's inability, for whatever reason, to deal openly with the homosexuality it hints at had creative literary consequences: it is presented as part of a more general debate about 'religious' qualities versus 'aesthetic' ones, thus placing homosexuality—and Symonds—in the context of broader social, spiritual and literary Victorian preoccupations. But that it was essentially to do with homosexuality is demonstrated by the title, since the historical Beltraffio (or 'Boltraffio', as he is more commonly referred to) idealised his male subjects to the point of causing minor scandals. In the famous *Portrait of a Young Man,* for example, 'the ambiguous beauty that Boltraffio gave to the sitter . . . led to the suggestion that the portrait is that of a woman'.[13]

Despite the defensive ranks formed by the army of James critics in America and Britain, there has in fact been little critical—as opposed to popular biographical—discussion of James's homosexuality. Unrelated essays have begun to appear, particularly since the publication of Sedgwick's essay on 'Henry James and Homosexual Panic';[14] but Sedgwick herself discussed only one short story, 'The Beast in the Jungle', and other critics similarly have focused on single or a small selection of novels and stories, and are likewise prone to adopt theoretical jargon at the expense of practical criticism. Homosexuality manifests itself in James's fiction from its beginnings in the 1860s to its culmination after the turn of the century and in various ways, but most consistently as a pederastic yearning of an older man for a younger man or boy. The novels and stories are populated with men for whom successful, open sexual relationships in adulthood have proved, as in his own life, impossible. Where male characters demonstrate an active interest in, if not necessarily a passion for, beautiful women, they are usually inept, self-conscious and seemingly crippled by the prospect—like the suggestively named Winterbourne in 'Daisy Miller' (1869), who analyses, categorises and objectifies, but never acts. In *The American* (1877), Mrs Tristram especially wishes to know if Christopher Newman 'had ever been in love—seriously, passionately—and, failing to gather any satisfaction from his allusions, she at last directly inquired. He hesitated awhile, and at last he said: "No!" She declared that she was delighted to hear it, as it confirmed her private conviction that he was a man of no feeling'. Nick Dormer in *The Tragic Muse* (1890) is similarly unconvincing as a prospective lover for Julia, and she recognises his insincerity without difficulty. After he postpones a proposal of marriage, it is said that Nick had the sense of 'having escaped a great and ugly mistake'. Nick later explains that '"The difficulty is that I'm two men; it's the strangest thing that ever was"'. His mother protests: '"Oh Nick, don't spoil your victory by your perversity"'. The novel is deeply concerned with Nick's hovering between his 'two sides': either he is to accept the part of himself drawn to the Wildean high-aesthete Gabriel Nash (symbolised by Nick's otherwise unconvincing portrayal as an artist) or stick to the conventional world of heterosexual family and public life (symbolised by his otherwise equally unconvincing role as a politician). Like James, André

Gide was influenced by his various meetings with Oscar Wilde, and he charted his maturation, both as a homosexual and an intellectual, in his various responses to Wilde's aesthetic-decadent pronouncements. Wilde appeared, faintly disguised, as 'Menalqué' in *Les Nourritures terrestres* (1897) and *L'Immoraliste* (1923). The characters have the same role in drawing out the protagonists of these novels that Gabriel Nash is given in *The Tragic Muse.* While it would be sadly reductive to argue that the novel balances only on this specific point, that it is 'about' Nick's homosexuality, it cannot be made sense of unless the homosexual dilemma is taken into account.

Lambert Strether in *The Ambassadors* (1903) is another essentially passive and distanced male protagonist. At the beginning of the novel the daughter of the woman with whom Strether is supposed to be in some way romantically involved is said to have (just as Mrs Tristram was said to have of Newman) 'at best' a 'scant faith in [Strether's] ability to find women'. 'It wasn't even,' the narrator continues, 'as if he had found her mother—so much more, to her discrimination, had her mother performed the finding.' Despite his aesthetic admiration for Madame de Vionnet, Strether expresses much less physical interest in women than he does in Little Bilham and Chad, and remarks on the latter's 'massive young manhood' and 'Pagan' side. Chad's first appearance at the theatre is a moment of profound contemplation for Strether and authorial indulgence for James—as meticulously arranged and theatrically prepared for as the appearance of Saint-Loup in Proust's novel.

Other male protagonists in James's fiction are more specifically interested only in younger men or boys. In *Roderick Hudson* (1875), the tension, as Tony Tanner has acknowledged in his introduction to the World's Classics edition, is between Rowland Mallet and Christina Light as they compete for the affection of beautiful young Roderick. The novel's central question is put by the painter Sam Singleton: '"[Roderick] is the handsomest fellow in Rome . . . he has the most genius, and as a matter of course the most beautiful girl in the world comes along and offers to be his model. If that is not completeness, where shall we find it?"' Rowland's increasing frustration at the inevitability of this process, his inability to articulate his affection for Roderick in socially acceptable terms, is his defining characteristic, and the sort of agitation found in sentences like the following is incomprehensible if he is seen solely as performing the role of objective patron: 'I am pestered to death; I go about with a chronic heartache; there are moments when I could shed salt tears'. Mary Garland herself manifests what many readers have felt by saying to Rowland that '"I never suspected, I confess, that [the world] contained persons of such liberality as yours. . . . [I]t is like something in a fairy tale . . .

you coming here all unknown, so rich and polite, and carrying off my cousin in a golden cloud"'. When Rowland finally discovers Roderick's engagement to Mary, he listens 'with a feeling that fortune had played him an elaborately-devised trick. It had lured him out into mid-ocean and smoothed the sea and stilled the winds and given him a singularly sympathetic comrade, and then it had turned and delivered him a thumping blow in mid-chest'. The emphasis in this passage is on Rowland's loss of his 'sympathetic comrade' Roderick, rather than on his lost intimacy with Mary Garland, with whom Rowland is superficially supposed to be in love. Rowland's interest in Mary is important for the plot of *Roderick Hudson,* particularly in the opening chapters, but is in no way explored with any feeling or passion, so the novel would have to be seen as being unsuccessful unless the homosexual subtext is recognised.

The friendship between Pemberton and Morgan in 'The Pupil' is likewise so intense that it invites a reading which sees it as pederastic. Its context is the socially sanctioned intimacy of teacher and pupil, and it is defined by Pemberton's attraction to Morgan's adolescent qualities. Morgan is eleven when Pemberton meets him, and has turned sixteen at the close of the story: the time-span in 'The Pupil' therefore parallels the boy's sexual maturation—the sort of patterning that Gide adopted in *L'Immoraliste,* where Michel, the protagonist, is appalled when a young farm hand he had been in love with later returns with adult whiskers. As the termination of the teacher-pupil relationship beckons in 'The Pupil', Pemberton distances himself from what he knows would be unavoidable complications, and is overtaken by his anxiety about 'what will become' of the boy after they have separated. He is reluctant sympathetically to dwell on Morgan's persistently expressed desire that they should move together to Oxford, where Pemberton himself had been educated, once he comes of age and can therefore earn a living. '"You can talk about it as much as you like,"' he tells the boy, '"but don't think you can attempt to live with me."' The narrator dryly comments that 'It was all very well for Morgan to consider that he would make up for all the inconvenience by settling himself upon him permanently. There was an irritating flaw in such a view. . . . [T]he poor friend didn't desire the gift—what could he do with Morgan's life?' This is the same sort of 'irritating flaw' Singleton had made Mallet aware of in *Roderick Hudson:* there isn't any possibility that the sort of relationship being explored can develop. The patron-artist relationship had provided a cover for Rowland and Roderick, as the tutor-pupil had for Pemberton and Morgan, but in both instances society eventually closes in. The deaths of Roderick and Morgan at the end of both novel and story are symbolic, and contrast with the

conventionally happy ending of James's first novel *Watch and Ward* (1871) in which a man adopts not a boy but a young girl, whom he eventually will marry.

There is a hitherto unexplored link between James's vague, American, taken-for-granted experience of a sentimental, ill-defined sort of adolescent homosexuality, his focused distress at the emergence of a social, negatively defined concept of 'the homosexual' witnessed later in England, and the stylistic treatment of the theme of what is never more than a nostalgic pederasty in the fiction. The idea that a modern concept of homosexuality emerged in the late nineteenth century, during the years in which James made his home in England, was first put forward by Jeffrey Weeks in his study *Homosexual Politics in Britain, from the nineteenth century to the present* (1977):

> From the nineteenth century the medical profession began to break down the formerly universal execrated forms of non-procreative sex into a number of 'perversions and deviations', so that, for the succeeding generations, the prime task of theory seemed to be the classification of new forms, the listing of their manifestations, the discussion of their causes . . . In this process homosexuality gradually emerges as a specific category.
>
> (p. 25)

More recently, historians have been tracing this shift away from a generalised emphasis on 'perversion' to a more specific idea of 'the homosexual' in literary and polemical publications. In *Masculine Desire: The Sexual Politics of Victorian Aestheticism* (1991), Richard Dellamora documented the response of a range of literary Victorian figures to the growing discussion of homosexuality, from Tennyson, Pater and the leading members of the Oxford Movement like Newman and Keble, to Wilde, Hopkins and Hardy. He argues that historical moments can be shown retrospectively to represent changes in perceptions of homosexuality by society and, crucially, by homosexuals themselves—particularly those who formed part of the educated élite in Oxford and Cambridge, who saw themselves as the new arbiters of taste. The major events, according to Dellamora, were Walt Whitman's initial publication of *Leaves of Grass* in 1855; the passage of the Criminal Law Amendment Act in 1855, which extended legal prohibition of the act of sodomy to virtually all male homosexual activity or speech whether in public or private; the Cleveland Street scandal of 1889-90; and the trials of Wilde in 1895. To these can be added the work of Dr Casper, who developed the distinction between 'innate' and 'acquired' homosexuality which, according to Weeks, 'were to be the poles of the debate for generations'; the publication of Pater's *The Renaissance* in 1873; the appearance, in private editions, of John Addington Symonds's two studies of Greek pederasty, *A Problem of Greek Ethics* (1883) and *A Problem of Modern Ethics*

(1891); the huge demonstration in Hyde Park, London, in 1885 at which speakers remonstrated against homosexuality and prostitution; the Vagrancy Act of 1898, which made even homosexual soliciting illegal; and the profusion of medical books on homosexuality which according to the leading homosexual campaigner Magnus Hirschfeld totalled more than one thousand published volumes between the years 1898 and 1908.

It is in this specific historical context that Henry James and his own painfully private reactions to homosexuality should be placed. Such an approach would allow for a new interpretation of that aspect of his career which has hitherto received more attention than any other: the movement in the fiction between American and European culture and values, and James's own literal move from America to (eventually) London and Rye, where he chose, shortly before he died, to adopt British citizenship. A development of the international scene, setting James off against English social and cultural events and movements, has been attempted by Jonathan Freedman, whose *Professions of Taste: Henry James, British Aestheticism, and Commodity Culture* (1990) traces James's career-long encounter with British aestheticism, but Freedman has almost nothing to say about James and homosexuality. This is puzzling, since his study appeared over a decade after Ellmann's summary of the interrelationship between James, aestheticism and homosexuality, to which Freedman makes passing reference. Freedman presents his main observation in a footnote:

> [James's] idealised, if not necessarily chaste, eroticising of the adolescent male is precisely the form taken by upper- and upper-middle-class British homosexual discourse of the late nineteenth century, for a complex chain of reasons that historians are only beginning to investigate. The question of James's sexual inclination, it therefore appears, needs to be approached by an analysis that places sexuality in the context of class and social setting.
>
> (pp. 256-7)

James remained interested in homosexuality throughout his life, but the social context in which that interest developed became increasingly restrictive and threatening. His discovery of Pater's *The Renaissance* in a book shop in Paris in 1873 had a direct influence, according to Ellmann, on his first 'real novel' *Roderick Hudson.* He received, as has already been noted, a copy of Symonds's *A Problem in Modern Ethics* and met the author in 1876, and according to Edel James had nearly all of Symonds's books in his library.[15] He met Wilde at literary gatherings in America, France and England, and commented that he was 'an unclean beast' at the time of his trials in 1895. He refused to sign a petition on Wilde's behalf, but privately expressed his sympathy in a letter to Gosse. After he moved to Rye two years later, James moved in social circles in which homo-

sexuality was part of the natural run of things, and became devoted to a series of young men, including A. C. Benson, Morton Fullerton, Hugh Walpole and Jocelyn Persse. Despite all this, James refused ever publicly to be associated with homosexuality, and remained to the outside world not only prudent but prudish. As late as 1905, for example, he cut off all correspondence with the Irish novelist Forrest Reid after the latter dedicated his openly homo-erotic but not sexually explicit novel of that year, *The Garden God,* to James 'as a slight token of respect and admiration'. James also insisted the dedication be removed.

An understanding of the influence of homosexuality on James's fiction has, of course, to accommodate other literary and social contexts. Then as now homosexuals lived as part of the larger social world, and gay novelists published first and foremost as authors, not gay men. Allon White's *The Uses of Obscurity: The Fiction of Early Modernism* (1981), examining the way James's fiction became more obscure as his career progressed, pointed to trends in publishing, psychology and education which, White argued, largely accounted for his stylistic movement towards Modernism. His study can be extended to accommodate the homosexual aspects of James's life and writing, since it analysed the fiction as being in equivocal relation to various social and publishing transformations, the most important of which was the emergence of an élite readership which set itself against the new mass literary market:

> There is evidence to show that, by the late 1880s, the fiction-reading public had begun to split into two different groups. . . . With the end of the three-decker the market for the 'respectable' novel seems to have split internally into an 'élite' or reviewers' public. Again and again . . . we meet the same distinction between an élite and popular audience.
>
> (pp. 31-2)

According to White, the change in reading habits towards seeing novels not as autonomous entities but as representations of their author's psychology was the result of a new thesis that insisted artistic ability should closely be related to various forms of abnormality:

> Within a few years in the 1880s, under the influence of proto-psychology, literary texts were transformed into primary evidence of the inner private fantasies of the author. The sincerity of the relationship between author and middle-class reader . . . their mutual interest in the honest transcription of the emotional life, was supplemented by a new kind of relationship which made the old contract extremely difficult to keep. The author was suddenly placed at a disadvantage by the sophistication in reader response, he became vulnerable to a certain kind of knowing smile which found in his words the insufficiently disguised evidence of his most intimate preoccupations. As more and more intellectual readers began to regard fiction as a transformation of

fantasy by various quasi-defensive devices, the notion of the 'truth' of the text, and the relations between text, author and reader, swiftly changed.

(pp. 45-6)

This change was as consciously observed by James as it was by his readers, or potential readers, and is reflected in a number of his stories of the 80s and 90s—notably 'The Lesson of the Master' (1888) and 'The Figure in the Carpet' (1896)—which deal with the relationship between a well-known but obscure male author and his prying, persistent younger male critic. In 'The Aspern Papers' (1888), the widow of the eponymous author is said to have escaped the intrusiveness of her dead husband's obsessive critics, and the surprise is that 'self-effacement on such a scale had been possible in the latter half of the nineteenth century—the age of newspapers and telegrams and photographers and interviewers'.

James suffered a real-life battle with readers who conversely found in his plays and novels little to appreciate. After the unsuccessful first night of his play *Guy Domville* (1895) the embarrassed James remarked that, though at least *some* of the audience clapped, they were less expressive than those who let out 'hoots and jeers and catcalls', whose roars were 'like those of a cage of beasts at some infernal zoo', and who, for James, represented 'the forces of civilisation'. A few days afterwards, he reflected that

> I have fallen upon evil days—every sign and symbol of one's being in the least wanted, anywhere or by anyone, having so utterly failed. A new generation that I know not, and mainly prize not, has taken universal possession. The sense of being utterly out of it weighed me down, and I asked myself what the future would be.[16]

The conclusion James arrived at was that the way out of this quagmire was 'to *be* one of the few'. He would renounce, he said, 'the childishness of publics', and no longer seek to win over a large audience. Henceforth he would not care if 'scarce a human being will understand a word, or an intention, or an artistic element of any sort' in what he wrote. Michael Anesko, in his admirable *'Friction with the Market': Henry James and the Profession of Authorship* (1986), observed of this period that 'James shrewdly sensed that being *un*popular, unsalable at any price, had a cachet of its own—one that publishers, curiously, might bid for' (p. 143).

James's short story 'The Death of the Lion' (1894) was published in the first issue of *The Yellow Book,* and while not 'decadent' like much of what else appeared there, it was concerned with questions of gender and 'notorious' authorship. The protagonist, a young re-porter, remarks that 'in the age we live in one gets lost among the genders and the pronouns', and asks a question similar to that posed in 'The Aspern Papers': isn't 'an immediate exposure of everything just what the public wants?'. 'The Coxon Fund' (1894) and 'The Next Time' (1895) also subsequently appeared in *The Yellow Book*'s pages. The English decadents associated with *The Yellow Book* were, as Elaine Showalter has put it in *Sexual Anarchy: Gender and Culture at the Fin de Siècle* (1991), the 'most dramatic casualties of the crisis in masculinity at the *fin de siècle*' (p. 170). A more recent article on James's 'aesthetic' tales of the 90s argues that they explore 'the relation between male authors and their audience', and that James 'consistently imagines enabling and empowering male readers, who enjoy an intimate, closeted relationship with the Master writers whose work they admire'.[17]

One way, then, that James created for himself this new, intimate bond with more sophisticated readers than those who had previously enjoyed such stories and novels as 'Daisy Miller' and *The Portrait of a Lady* (1881) was to write tales which, while not explicitly or exclusively homosexual, would be recognised as dealing with the theme by the initiated. He would, to use his own words, set himself up as 'one of the few'. Henry Harland, the editor of *The Yellow Book,* idolised James, as Katherine Mix explains in her *A Study in Yellow: The Yellow Book and its Contributors* (1960), to the point of appearing absurd (p. 169). He at least recognised the subtexts. But James would never have allowed himself to be viewed as so exclusive or decadent as to provoke the wrath of the mainstream critics who had condemned Wilde's *The Picture of Dorian Gray* (1891) for its homosexual insinuations and ambience. He can, I think, be forgiven for having been so cautious. Even if he was as sexually active as Novick asserts, he was not obliged to align himself with such pederastic enthusiasts as John Addington Symonds. James was too interested in the real-life restrictions on freedom and expression, and how these limitations affected fictional form, to be taken over by gay liberation ideals that had no chance of success. Moreover, a number of American magazines commented negatively, even without any biographical evidence of James's homosexuality, on his appearance in *The Yellow Book*. A writer in *Munsey's* of 13 June 1895 stated that 'of late . . . Mr. James has been in bad company. . . . He has become one of the *Yellow Book* clique', and called on James to return home to the comfortable moral certainties of America (p. 310). No 79 of *The Atlantic* (January, 1897) noted that a 'super-subtlety of theme, for which no form of expression can be too carefully wrought . . . place[s] Mr. James inextricably in the decadent ranks' (p. 169). If we read 'decadent' for 'homosexual', as many Victorians did after Wilde,[18] and relate this to the new emphasis on seeing texts as representations of their author's private world, we can see how the publishing context White explored in *The Uses of Fiction* can be made to relate specifically to a more general emergence of the concept of the homosexual.

However, it is equally clear that despite James's desire to discover a new audience and his readiness to become associated if only in a vague way with what was considered *risqué,* he never entirely gave up the ideal of earning a decent living from his writing, even as late as his definitive New York Edition of 1907-9. These tensions—between wanting to be a part of the mainstream and realising that his only chance of finding a loyal, sustaining readership was by becoming more exclusive; between needing to write stories and novels that covertly expressed homosexuality, while remaining himself publicly and professionally distanced from all obvious manifestations of it—are illuminated in a letter James sent to his brother William about the appearance of 'The Death of the Lion' in *The Yellow Book*'s inaugural issue:

> I haven't sent you 'The Yellow Book'—on purpose; and indeed I have been weeks and weeks receiving a copy of it myself. I say on purpose because although my little tale which ushers it in ('The Death of the Lion') appears to have had, for a thing of mine, an unusual success, I hate too much the horrid aspect of the whole publication. And yet I am again to be intimately—conspicuously—associated with the second number.

There is an intriguing movement towards revelation and then finally back again to teasing concealment; of an unavoidable desire intimately to be involved with that which he is so eager to distance himself from. The story, he can't help but note, is 'an unusual success', and yet he finds unacceptable the notoriety that comes from an association with a publication that had such a particular kind of circulation. He claims to 'hate too much' publishing there, but in the same breath reveals that he is once again—'intimately, conspicuously'—to publish in its pages, suggesting that, far from hating it all too much, he could not actually bring himself to hate appearing there nearly as much as the public, self-protective side of his personality would have preferred.

The treatment of homosexuality in James's fiction, when considered in this personal and publishing context, helps to explain the much-discussed stylistic movement from the early fables through middle realism to Modernism. Camaraderie and sexual tension could be dealt with openly in such early works as 'A Light Man' (1869) and *Roderick Hudson* because when they were written James had still to feel threatened by hostile English public opinion. They allude to classical examples of homosexuality, are ironic about the homosexual situations presented, and draw parallels between them and alternative socially acceptable heterosexual scenarios. 'A Light Man' presents a gay reworking of Browning's 'A Light Woman'. The narrator, Max, accepts his friend Theodore's invitation to visit him at the secluded mansion of his patron, the elderly and infirm Mr Sloane, 'worth about a million', who is in search of an heir. Sloane is James's least authorially protected gay character, and the two young men compete to win his affection and so inherit his wealth. Max draws a Hogarthian analogy between his own sexually charged relationship with Sloane and other young men in comparable situations with females: 'What better legend could I scrawl beneath [a] picture of So-and-So's progress to a mercenary marriage?' he asks himself. If only, he sighs, the old man were female: '[M]y only complaint is that, instead of an old widower, he's not an old widow (or a young maid), so that I might marry him, and dwell forever in his rich and mellow home'. This sort of displacement, which also characterised the comments on Italian boys by James and Mrs Ward which end up in universalising references to art and artists, is again found in *Roderick Hudson*. When Roderick's cousin Cecilia introduces Rowland to his charge by showing him a statue Roderick has created, she comments: '"If I refused last night to show you a pretty girl, I can at least show you a pretty boy"'. The figure, the narrator elaborates, 'might have been some beautiful youth of ancient fable—Hylas or Narcissus, Paris or Endymion'. Robert K. Martin, an intelligent critic who convincingly dealt with James and homosexuality long before the current controversies made such essays fashionable, summarised the significance of these references in *Roderick Hudson* by explaining that 'each of the figures named is an indication of Roderick's role in the story':

> Endymion evokes Keats's poem, of course, and its story of the quest for ideal beauty; it foreshadows Roderick's infatuation for Christina Light, who plays moon-goddess to Roderick's shepherd. Paris evokes fatal love and beauty, since Paris abandons his first lover, the nymph Oenone, elopes with Helen, and is killed in the Trojan war; it foreshadows Roderick's abandonment of Mary, his love for Christina, and his death. Narcissus evokes the fatal love of self, with which Roderick is certainly imbued, and suggests the metaphor of drowning which runs throughout the novel. Hylas is the least obvious and perhaps most significant of these allusions. Hylas was the beloved of Hercules and his companion on the 'Argo'; it is Hylas's death by drowning which causes Hercules to abandon the expedition. His mention here has no other function than to make the reader aware of a homosexual (or homoerotic) relationship between the two men.[19]

This sort of explicitness and direct allusion disappears from the novels and stories of the middle period, such as *The Tragic Muse* and 'The Pupil'. As has been shown, they present a more self-conscious exploration of the threatening social consequences should the characters decide to accept and act openly on their homosexual instincts. When James was writing and publishing both the novel and story, the Cleveland Street Scandal of 1889, which involved a boy-brothel and its gentleman clientele, was on the front page of the public prints; Wilde's *The Picture of Dorian Gray* was being published; and James was sent that same year his copy of Symonds's *Modern Ethics,* which championed what had become for the general public a disturbingly subversive lifestyle associated with 'decadent aesthetes'. 'Homosexuality' had arrived in the public consciousness, and James was involved in his literary capacity with leading gay rights advocates, as well as quietly homosexual people. It is inconceivable, to my mind, that he could have been unaware of homosexuality, as his devotees still sometimes claim, when he was writing these works—even those which superficially are not concerned with relations between men.

In the Cage (1898), for instance, has its emphasis on scandal, blackmail, telegrams and unnameable sexual 'crimes', and an observer who leads a 'double life' in relation to it all inside and outside of a cage, and is primarily concerned with heterosexual infidelity and the general question of gaining knowledge about other people's lives through inference and suggestion. It could, though, be seen as creating a heterosexual world which usefully for James paralleled the world of homosexual scandal—its telegraph boys, secret rendezvous, extramarital affairs and so on—which James was so intrigued by. It might be exploring the obsessiveness of men who like James were cautious about being associated with that homosexual world but who nevertheless self-consciously took it all in from the shadows. In the story, Mr Mudge's comment about not understanding 'people's hating what they liked or liking what they hated' accurately articulates what many readers have felt about James's own treatment of his and others' homosexuality. The Catholic poet Marc André Raffalovich related that 'I remember teasing [James] with a friend to know what the Olympian young man in *In the Cage* had done wrong. He swore he did not know, he would rather not know'[20]—as he would insist on knowing and yet not knowing about Symonds's homosexuality or about homosexuality in society more generally. This is not to claim *In the Cage* for the gay fiction canon, but to suggest that, by placing it in this specific social context, a new reading is made possible, thus making the story even more diverse and accomplished than has already been acknowledged.

In her *TLS* review of the Novick biography, Millicent Bell posed the absorbing question 'how Novick will deal with a late James who avoided direct self-representation yet wrote from the depths of his being'. We should, I think, be glad for James's holding back, should resist from making him explicit. His moral and sexual ambiguity is the source of much of his elusiveness and complexity, particularly during the late phase,

and so to bully him into being polemical would be to ignore the absorbing qualities of his art. James invested so much of himself in so many ways into so many of his characters and their situations that he is best compared to Shakespeare and Proust, both of whom dealt with homosexual love and much more besides. However, specifically gay interpretations of James should be sensitively insisted upon, despite the apparent hostility of influential Jameseans, not in order to claim James as a 'gay novelist' but to add to our general appreciation of his diverse fictional worlds.

Notes

1. Edmund Gosse, 'Henry James', *The London Mercury,* (No. 7, 1920), p. 33.

2. Hugh Walpole, 'Henry James: A Reminiscence', *Horizon,* (Vol. 1, No. 2, 1940), p. 76.

3. See Leon Edel, *Henry James: A Life,* (1985), p. 652.

4. This remark by James, in a letter to Mrs Ward, is quoted in Leon Edel, *The Treacherous Years: 1895-1901,* (1969), pp. 297-98.

5. See Sigmund Freud, *The Standard Works of the Complete Psychological Works of Sigmund Freud,* trans. James Strachey, (1973-4), 24 Vols., Vol. 14, p. 88.

6. Henry James, *The Middle Years,* (1916), pp. 1-2.

7. That is not to say, according to Novick, that James abandoned the idea of private sexual relationships. He will quote a number of unpublished letters in the second volume of his biography to support his theory that James was throughout his life sexually active, particularly with the young men who regularly stayed at Lamb House after James became its Master. (I am summarising Novick, with permission, from our private correspondence.)

8. See Leon Edel and Lyall H. Powers (ed.), *The Complete Notebooks of Henry James,* (Oxford, 1987), p. 238.

9. Philip Horne, 'Henry James: the master and the "queer affair" in "The Pupil"'. Collected in N. H. Reeve (ed.), *Henry James: The Shorter Fiction: Reassessments,* (1996).

10. Rayburn S. Moore (ed.), *Selected Letters of Henry James to Edmund Gosse 1882-1915: A Literary Friendship,* (Louisiana, 1988), p. 32.

11. Leon Edel (ed.), *Henry James Letters,* (Cambridge, Mass. 1984), Vol. III, pp. 29-30.

12. See Leon Edel, *Letters,* op. cit., Vol. IV, p. 12.

13. This quotation is taken from Jane Turner (ed.), *The Dictionary of Art,* (1996), 35 Vols., Vol. 4, p. 284.

14. *Henry James and Homo-Erotic Desire,* a collection of essays edited by John R. Bradley with an introductory essay by Sheldon M. Novick, will appear in 1998.

15. See Leon Edel, *Letters,* op. cit., Vol. III, p. 31.

16. See Leon Edel (ed.), *The Complete Plays of Henry James,* (1962), p. 162 ff.

17. Leland S. Person, Jr.: 'James's Homo-Aesthetics: Deploying Desire in the Tales of Writers and Artists', in *The Henry James Review,* (No. 14, 1993), p. 187.

18. See Elaine Showalter's *Sexual Anarchy,* (1991) for a discussion of how decadence came to be seen as 'a *fin-de siècle* euphemism for homosexuality' long before this remark in *The Atlantic* was published, p. 171.

19. Robert K. Martin: 'The High Felicity of Comradeship', in *American Literary Realism,* (No. 11, 1977), pp. 102-3.

20. See Forrest Reid, *Private Road,* (1940), p. 70.

Benjamin Scott Grossberg (essay date spring 2000)

SOURCE: Grossberg, Benjamin Scott. "'The Tender Passion Was Very Rife among Us': Coverdale's Queer Utopia and *The Blithedale Romance.*" *Studies in American Fiction* 28, no. 1 (spring 2000): 3-25.

[*In the following essay, Grossberg focuses upon Miles Coverdale's vision of Blithedale as "a utopia of sexual desire" as it relates to the ultimate failure of utopian community in Nathaniel Hawthorne's novel* The Blithedale Romance.]

To what can we attribute the failure of the Blithedale experiment? In one way or another, most readers of Hawthorne's *The Blithedale Romance* approach this question. As John Hirsh observes, the fate of the Blithedalers' social experiment is at least as important as their inter-personal dynamics—is, in fact, inseparable from them: "The dichotomy between political and personal motivation . . . is not Hawthorne's, who was well aware of how the two impinged on each other."[1] Hirsh sees the experiment as an initial success (in its rehabilitation of Coverdale and Priscilla) and insists that readers acknowledge the community's political fortune, success and then failure. Critics often bear out the truth of Hirsh's point. Most discussions of the novel, whether in terms of character, allegory or plot, do eventually confront the same question: why does this political community fail?

There seems to be less agreement on the cause. Quite a few readers have located responsibility for the failure in Hollingsworth. This approach focuses on Hollingsworth's vision, the extent to which it is incompatible with the utopian vision of Blithedale, and his character, which lacks the social flexibility necessary to work with others toward a common goal. Such a reading might find support in the exclusive nature of Hollingsworth's demands. It isn't just that he has his own utopian vision, but that his vision is contingent upon the failure of Blithedale; it requires the very same real estate. It isn't just that he wants Coverdale to work with him, but that he wants his person to the exclusion of all Coverdale's other attachments, a life-long commitment. Hollingsworth, then, becomes the worm that eats the apple, the essential undermining force. But this approach is not completely convincing. Are we to understand that Blithedale (or whatever it represents) would have succeeded without Hollingsworth, that he is the only destabilizing force? While it is important to note the idiosyncrasy of his vision, I suggest that the other principle Blithedalers possess a vision no less idiosyncratic or dissonant.

Other critics spread the cause of Blithedale's failure more generally among the characters, even finding it intrinsic to the utopian project itself. This argument is based on individuality, the idea that the novel takes a strong stance against communal utopian thinking by suggesting that such thinking entails a critical, costly loss of self and individual vision. Those who favor this approach might focus on the loss of individuality involved in becoming a member of the Blithedale community, for example the blurring of Zenobia's ideals in her love for Hollingsworth. The Blithedale experiment might then be understood as the expression of a strongly anti-romantic impulse: the desire to take refuge from the self. Hawthorne sets up the community only to demonstrate its failure, with the implication that this failure is both good and necessary.[2]

I risk the generalization, then: in the simplest terms, there may be a loose consensus among critics. Blithedale fails because of an incompatibility of vision, whether Hollingsworth alone be the cause, or whether such incompatibility be endemic to utopian thinking. Coverdale himself sketches the problem for us a third of the way through *Blithedale*:

> Our bond, it seems to me, was not affirmative, but negative. We had individually found one thing or another to quarrel with in our past life, and were pretty well agreed as to the inexpediency of lumbering along with the old system any further. As to what should be substituted, there was much less unanimity.[3]

Coverdale notices this tension throughout the novel, both directly, as here, and indirectly, through the tensions he observes between characters, for example during the debate at Eliot's pulpit. The problem in forging utopia is not finding willing participants; as Coverdale notes, the participants are both diverse and tolerant. The problem is that "persons of marked individuality—crooked sticks, as some of us might be called—are not exactly the easiest to bind up into a fagot" (89).

Hollingsworth's utopian vision has received much critical attention, especially from Hirsh. Zenobia's vision has also been well discussed, though perhaps not as fully. One critic who encounters Zenobia's utopian vision, albeit indirectly, is Gustaaf Van Cromphout, who compares her ideas with those of Margaret Fuller.[4] Zenobia's utopia is not difficult to sketch, at least in terms of its general contours. Zenobia strives for equality of the sexes. Like Hollingsworth, she explicitly is a reformer. Both give public talks, and she also writes—though, as Emerson said of Fuller, her written work does not reflect the power of her oratory. Zenobia repeatedly demonstrates her utopian plan for Blithedale, especially before she becomes enmeshed in Hollingsworth. For example, at the community's first dinner, she makes clear that she hopes men and women in this new society will choose their vocations by ability, not gender roles:

> To bake, to boil, to roast, to fry, to stew,—to wash, and iron, and scrub, and sweep,—and at our idler intervals, to repose ourselves on knitting and sewing,—these, I suppose, must be feminine occupations, for the present. By and by, perhaps, when our individual adaptions begin to develop themselves, it may be that some of us who wear the petticoat will go a-field, and leave the weaker brethren to take our place in the kitchen.
>
> (38)

No doubt Zenobia's ideal seems as incongruous to some of the Blithedalers as we know Hollingsworth's does to others. There is certainly no mention of her idea coming to fruition. When Coverdale states his intention to return to Boston three months later, Silas Foster observes "he can do a day's work, if he likes, with any man or ox on the farm" (170). The suggestion seems to be that the fields are still the domain of men and oxen only, no women. Zenobia's speeches on Eliot's pulpit further define her utopian vision, and Hollingsworth's reaction—and Priscilla's—further show the extent to which that vision might seem incongruous.

But what seems to me to be neither as obvious as Hollingsworth's and Zenobia's visions nor as fully explored by readers of this novel is the nature of Coverdale's utopian vision. Unlike Hollingsworth and Zenobia, Coverdale (like Priscilla) can strike readers as essentially passive and visionless. But in reality he has a very specific paradigm, and in fact, all events of the narrative are inflected through it. Coverdale's vision is the one we get most intensely because we can only judge the other two paradigms through his. It is the lens through which we view all events at Blithedale, imposed on us implicitly. Nina Baym states, "What Blithedale 'is' is inseparable from what it is to Cover-

dale, for nothing is known in the book but what is known by him."[5] Baym's reading is—in her own words—radical. She posits the possibility that none of the events actually happen outside the narrator's mind. But her point is well taken. The novel is unabashedly from Coverdale's point of view; he even takes pains to remind us that he is actively controlling its parameters, manipulating and shaping narrative meaning.

The presence of Coverdale's narrative hand is unavoidable, especially on a second reading. Coverdale almost makes us groan with his too-accurate foreshadowings, such as his coy sick-bed delusion that Zenobia is "sister of the Veiled Lady" (69). Such moments of narrative manipulation remind us that we are being told a story by someone only posing ignorance of events to come. His writing is like our rereading: heavily self-conscious, aware of the process of constructing a narrative from fragmented events. The result is that we become sensitive to the narrative as a surface distinct from events, an interpretation. And this sense of dissonance forces us to distinguish Coverdale's vision of Blithedale from the community itself, his ambition for the thing as opposed to what it actually seems to be.

Coverdale both explicitly and implicitly characterizes Blithedale as a utopia of sexual desire.[6] For example, in the first two chapters, Blithedale is repeatedly contrasted with his "bachelor apartments" (25) and his "bachelor-rooms" (31). The effect is to align location with desire: he will evacuate his "bachelor-rooms" in order to occupy what clearly must *not* be bachelor rooms, that is, a location associated with fulfilled desire, a kind of marriage. Later we have it on his authority and his authority alone that Blithedale "seemed to authorize any individual, of either sex, to fall in love with any other, regardless of what would elsewhere be judged suitable or prudent" (99). Whether this is utopia as constructed by other Blithedalers is questionable; aside from those relationships in which he is involved, no other indications of aberrant desire intrude on Coverdale's narrative. Toward the end of the novel, Coverdale explains, "it was impossible, situated as we were, not to imbibe the idea that everything in nature and human existence was fluid, or fast becoming so" (174). If we understand "nature and human existence" in the context of sexuality, this statement may serve as the thesis for Coverdale's paradigm: a space for sexual desire and gender definition that is similarly "fluid."[7]

In order to get a full sense of the resonance of Coverdale's vision, it may be useful to recall the evolution of nineteenth-century sexuality, understanding "sexuality" as those structures and definitions we construct in order to understand and relate to ourselves as sexual beings. Definitions of sexuality changed dramatically in the decades between 1850 and 1900. Foucault explains this as sex rapidly coming into discourse, forming a space of juridical-discursive power; in other words, the latter nineteenth century saw a culmination of centuries of increasing talk about sex—and this increased talk, and the ever more rigid and specific definitions it entailed, eventually opened up spaces of power through which behavior might be manipulated.[8] Sexuality becomes a tool potentially anyone can wield, a means to validate or invalidate. As part of this increasing specificity, definitions of homosexuality (and therefore also heterosexuality) were just becoming fixed in the period during which Hawthorne wrote. Eve Sedgwick suggests that as a result of this process, the nineteenth century was "suffus[ed with] the stain of homo/heterosexual crisis."[9] Some cultural critics theorize that before this period there was no such thing as a homosexual identity; David Halperin notes that the term "homosexuality" was not coined until 1892, and contends that the concept that sex acts might constitute an identity based on object choice did not crystallize until about then.[10]

In this light, Coverdale's focus on desire may be seen as something other than a trivial distraction from the bona fide utopian thinking at Blithedale (that is, Hollingsworth's and Zenobia's), and also as something more than an outgrowth of his physical and emotional need. Coverdale's vision may be read as an attempt to cope with a society whose sexual definitions are crystallizing, a reaction to "the suffusing stain of homo/heterosexual crisis." Rather than succumb to the new identities "homosexual" and "heterosexual"—rather than see himself as one of these odd, new, discrete animals—Coverdale attempts to make Blithedale a community apart from them. Coverdale's Blithedale is a place of queer desire and queer gender, a place where the discrete categories of man, woman, heterosexual and homosexual are set up to be undermined. But because Coverdale is the narrator, because our first impulse is to accept his narrative as transparent, the parameters and extent of his vision can be elusive.

Coverdale begins disrupting stable categories as one must—by constructing them. He sets up stable gender categories through his introductions of Hollingsworth and Zenobia. It is impossible to know what these characters are actually like, but Coverdale presents them as almost the prototypically masculine man and prototypically feminine woman. Zenobia is woman enough actually to remind Coverdale of the biblical prototype: "One felt an influence breathing out of her such as we might suppose to come from Eve, when she was just made, and her Creator brought her to Adam, Saying, 'Behold! here is a woman!'" (39). She is more woman than other women, having "a certain warmth and rich characteristic, which seems, for the most part, to have been refined away out of the feminine system" (40). Zenobia is not only "remarkably beautiful" (37), she is a woman who identifies with women in her feminist vision. Coverdale similarly presents Hollingsworth as the extreme of mas-culinity, "a polar bear" (49), "a tolerably educated bear" (52) with a "dark, shaggy face" (53) and "a chest as capacious as a barrel" (49). Furthermore, like Zenobia whose vision identifies with women, Hollingsworth's vision identifies with men: he will reform (presumably male) criminals. Rather than fantasize about a heterosexual family, Hollingsworth fantasizes about his criminal institute. Coverdale remarks:

> I have seen him, a hundred times, with a pencil and sheet of paper, sketching the facade, the sideview, or the rear of the structure, or planning the internal arrangements, as lovingly as another man might plan those of the projected home where he meant to be happy with his wife and children.
>
> (82)

The simile is Coverdale's. What Hollingsworth thinks about the relative importance of family and his institute may or may not finally be discernible through the text. But note that Coverdale sets up his institution in distinction to heterosexual marriage: masculine Hollingsworth will not be effeminized by marrying a woman. He will live with criminals in place of such a union.

But no sooner does Coverdale set up these ideals than he muddies them. Unlike Zenobia, who argues for fluidity in gender roles, Coverdale argues for fluidity in gender itself. She attempts to blur the distinction between men's and women's spheres; he blurs the correspondence between masculinity and femininity, and gender. His further descriptions of Zenobia and Hollingsworth make masculinity equally defining for the ideal woman, and femininity inseparable from the ideal man, thereby dissociating gender from gender-identity. Zenobia, then, has hands "larger than most women would like to have, or than they could afford to have" (37). Her laugh is "not in the least like an ordinary woman's laugh" (38). And Coverdale later observes, "It was one peculiarity, distinguishing Zenobia from most of her sex, that she needed for her moral well-being, and never would forgo, a large amount of physical exercise" (190). Furthermore there is Zenobia's verbal slip: she has been "an auditor—auditress, I mean—" (44) of Hollingsworth's lectures. Unless we are to grant Coverdale perfect recall—and he himself reminds us that he reconstructs dialogue—it seems very unlikely that this is the only verbal slip made in the course of the romance. What says as much about Coverdale's perception as Zenobia's is that this is the only slip he remembers and chooses to record. We are thus invited to think about Zenobia both as an ideal woman and as too masculine.

Hollingsworth's case is more clear-cut. Coverdale queers Hollingsworth when the latter becomes a nurse. Rather than paint the nurturing in a masculine context, Coverdale announces, "there was something of the woman moulded into the great, stalwart frame of Hollingsworth; nor was he ashamed of it" (66). The extent to which this interpretation is Coverdale's becomes clear in the interchange that follows. Coverdale tells Hollingsworth that he thinks him tender. Hollingsworth is taken back. "And you call me tender!" He replies, "I should rather say that the most marked trait in my character is an inflexible severity of purpose" (67). Hollingsworth, supposed by Coverdale to be unashamed of his feminine characteristics, fails even to acknowledge their possibility; in fact, he counters by suggesting that he is better characterized by a masculine rigidity—the truth of which the novel will bear out. Coverdale's lens is primarily responsible here, both for making these characters gender extremes and then for attempting to muddy those extremes. Hollingsworth's reaction suggests what will be true, not only for Coverdale's utopian vision, but for all the characters' visions. They do not fit the reality of Blithedale; "crooked sticks, as some of us might be called—are not exactly the easiest to bind up into a fagot."

Coverdale's narrative also takes the reverse tactic in queering gender. He presents two almost genderless characters, himself and Priscilla, and shows that they evolve into traditionally gender identified types. In this way, masculinity and femininity are further characterized as acquired and acquirable, learned roles, rather than essentially tied to gender. Coverdale becomes masculine, eventually earning terms equal to Hollingsworth's; and Priscilla, in "The Hotel," overtakes Zenobia as the most "bewitching" female in *The Blithedale Romance*. Coverdale effects his change through illness. He defines his illness as a process of death and rebirth, one that separates his effeminate city self from his masculine Blithedale self. For example, he decides that it is "nonsense and effeminacy" (85) to keep himself in bed on Mayday. He emerges, "in literal and figurative truth . . . quite another man," having thrown off the weakness of city life. "The very substance upon my bones had not been fit to live with in any better, truer, or more energetic mode" (87). Coverdale similarly reports Foster's appraisal of him in "Leave-Takings": "His shoulders have broadened a matter of six inches, since he came among us; he can do his day's work, if he likes, with any man or ox on the farm . . ." And a few lines later, "Your lungs have the play of a pair of blacksmith's bellows already" (171). Such a literal transformation is just not possible in the space of three months. But the narrative as Coverdale presents it, the words as he has chosen to remember and record them, suggests that he can end the novel on a par with Hollingsworth—who literally was once a blacksmith, and who similarly earns comparisons with animals (bears rather than oxen).

Priscilla also becomes increasingly feminine. At the beginning of the romance, Zenobia sums up Coverdale's assessment: "as she has hardly any physique, a poet, like Mr. Miles Coverdale, may be allowed to think her spiritual" (57). But one hundred pages later, Coverdale's reaction indicates Priscilla's increasing and increasingly feminine physicality. Her dismissal of Coverdale as the four return from Eliot's pulpit is "the most bewitching thing that Priscilla had ever done" (159). And at the end of the novel—a mere three months later—Priscilla displaces Zenobia as the focus of Coverdale's narrative gaze. In Zenobia's hotel, Coverdale tells Priscilla she seems like a dream:

> "Oh there is substance in these fingers of mine," she answered, giving my hand the faintest possible pressure, and then taking away her own. "Why do you call me a dream? Zenobia is much more like one than I; she is so very, very beautiful! And, I suppose," added Priscilla, as if thinking aloud, "everybody sees it, as I do." But for my part, it was Priscilla's beauty, not Zenobia's, of which I was thinking at the moment.
>
> (204)

Priscilla invokes the comparison to Zenobia, and Coverdale offers a surprising reaction: Priscilla herself commands attention here. Priscilla has demonstrated the possibility that feminine beauty, feminine "bewitching" charms, can be learned or evolved in a matter of months. Nina Baym attributes the culmination of Priscilla's beauty to the new setting: "Priscilla is the true artificial flower of the book, the flower that appears natural in the city, the domain of repression and artificial pleasures."[11] And Zenobia, Baym further argues, is at her most natural in the country, and therefore pales in this scene. But surely the increase in Priscilla's charms owes at least as much to her withdrawal from the city as to her return. Priscilla may eventually become fully feminine in the city, but the city also made her what she was two hundred pages earlier, essentially genderless: "hardly any physique." The only completely convincing explanation for her culminating beauty is in our narrator's eye. He sees the change in her and therefore makes it real to us. Coverdale's presentation of the four characters suggests that there is no essential relationship between gender and gender identity. The masculine become feminine; the feminine become masculine; and the essentially genderless acquire convincing masculinity and femininity—all in three short months.

Within this space of fluctuating gender, Coverdale also inflects erotic relationships through a queer paradigm. He characterizes desire outside the parameters of newly-evolving nineteenth-century definitions. Coverdale presents his relationships with all three characters, Zenobia, Hollingsworth, and Priscilla, in terms of sexual desire—which makes it impossible to contain and stabilize him as a desiring subject without ignoring or committing interpretive violence on some aspect of his interaction. He makes it clear that his desire for each is in no way discrete from his desire for any other; in this way, terms such as monogamy, homosexuality, and heterosexuality have no place in qualifying his erotic impulses. Furthermore, Coverdale offers us an image—and an interpretation of that image—in order to unify and understand his utopian paradigm: the hermitage. This image, like the desire it represents, centers on the impossibility of distinction.

Baym insists that we cannot read Coverdale as an artist simply because he narrates *The Blithedale Romance*. She writes, "To say that he is an artist because he has written *The Blithedale Romance* is to beg the question, since all first-person narrators thereby become artists."[12] And yet Coverdale is more actively and self-consciously engaged in making meaning than other first-person narrators. Throughout the narrative, he directs us to read concrete objects as metaphors—thus controlling our reading by directing interpretation. An example of this narrative strategy occurs when Priscilla begins to craft a silk purse during her first evening at Blithedale. Coverdale self-consciously makes the purse an emblem for Priscilla, one that directs us to his understanding of her:

> [The purses'] particular excellence, besides the great delicacy and beauty of the manufacture, lay in the almost impossibility that any uninitiated person should discovery the aperture; although, to a practiced touch, they would open as wide as charity or prodigality might wish. I wondered if it were not a symbol of Priscilla's own mystery.
>
> (58)

Even before he overtly suggests symbolism, Coverdale's description of the purse echoes his impression of Priscilla, or at least what she will evolve into, something delicate and beautiful. The image begins to prepare us for Priscilla's eventual status as desirable object, which comes to fruition in the romance's final line. Furthermore, the image contains the same mixture of curiosity and prurience that characterizes Coverdale's interactions with all characters in this text. His desire to sound "Priscilla's own mystery" resonates sexually: a "practiced touch" that could render her mystery "as wide as charity or prodigality might wish." It also echoes his desire a few chapters later to understand Zenobia's mystery—which is explicitly a question of her virginity. The image is therefore both idiosyncratic and authorial. Coverdale uses it to characterize himself and his feelings for Priscilla, on the one hand, and—by prefiguring Priscilla's transformation and her mystery, and also, in part, the mystery of the entire romance—his authorial knowledge, on the other. Once we, as readers, develop "a practiced touch," events at Blithedale will similarly unfold for our understanding. Similar tensions may be found in Coverdale's use of the image of pigs in the chapter "Leave-Takings" and the dove in "The Hotel." Each of these reveals Coverdale's dual role in the text, as both ignorant participant and narrative shaper.

The most significant image for Coverdale's eroticism is his hermitage. Not only does this image function as a template for his utopian vision of queer desire, it also suggests the extent to which he is ambivalent about that vision. Through the hermitage, Coverdale both represents and critiques his own desire. Just as with his image of Priscilla, his voice is idiosyncratic and authorial, both what he wants for Blithedale and how narrative events will unfold. Coverdale describes the hermitage as formed by a wild vine that had

> twined and twisted itself up into the tree, and, after wreathing the entanglement of its tendrils almost around every bough, had caught hold of three of four neighboring trees, and married the whole clump with a perfectly inextricable knot of polygamy.
>
> (128)

The grape vine, the "knot," binds four trees, just as the Blithedale "knot of dreamers" binds four characters: Coverdale, Hollingsworth, Zenobia and Priscilla. The language is explicit in its erotic connection: "married"; "inextricable knot of polygamy." Throughout the novel, Coverdale uses the word "knot" to describe the situation at Blithedale; after this image, the word always resonates romantically. Coverdale's desire is not just for "polygamy" but for "inextricable . . . polygamy." What defines the hermitage also defines Coverdale's utopia: "entanglement." Just like vines knotting between trees, Coverdale's vision of the Blithedale connection is messy, defined by a lack of order.

Coverdale's further description of the hermitage reveals his ambivalence—his authorial knowledge that this particular "knot" will prove as restrictive and dangerous as it is utopian. He describes the way in which the vines form a hollow:

> A hollow chamber of rare seclusion had been formed by the decay of some of the pine branches, which the vine had lovingly strangled with its embrace, burying them from the light of day in an aerial sepulchre of its own leaves.
>
> (128)

This "loving . . . embrace" in which Coverdale envisions spending his honeymoon is also potentially deadly, "strangl[ing]." Just in case we do not connect the image to Zenobia's death at the end of the novel, Coverdale reports Zenobia's use of the same language a handful of pages later, in a conversation that he acknowledges he had to reconstruct. Zenobia and Westervelt are discussing the appearance of Priscilla:

> "With what kind of a being am I linked?" cried she. "If my Creator cares aught for my soul, let him release me from this miserable bond!"
>
> "I did not think it weighed so heavily," said her companion.

"Nevertheless," answered Zenobia, "It will strangle me at last."

(135)

Zenobia feels this relationship as a "link" and a "bond," just as the vines link between the trees. She fears she will be "strangle[d]"; her diction echoes Coverdale's description of the dead branch exactly.

The hermitage also reflects Coverdale's ambivalence over his independence (or isolation) within the queer utopia he envisions. This "knot of polygamy" also "symbolized my individuality, and aided me in keeping it inviolate" (129). His ambivalence comes across most clearly in the way Coverdale uses his hermitage. He goes there to be alone, to "make verses . . . or to meditate an essay" (129). In this sense, it suggests a desire for independence. But the afternoon he narrates in his hermitage is not spent independently. Instead, it is spent gazing at and meditating on his three lovers. The height allows him to see all three at once, collect them from all over the farm into a single gaze. At the same time, he can keep his own presence hidden. So he watches Hollingsworth order the oxen, Priscilla sitting at Zenobia's window, and half hears Zenobia walking below, all within a single moment—while interacting with no one. His hermitage, then, anticipates his position in the latter half of the romance, after "Leave Takings." Though still bound up in the "knot," he is largely reduced to auditor: that is, to isolation, not independence. Indeed, his physical stance in the tree prefigures him at the boarding house window.

Coverdale also more directly suggests queer desire. Perhaps the most direct way he manages this is by enacting such desire, by refusing to limit his own erotic interest to any single character or gender. Many critics have noted the extent to which his relationships with some one or two of the principle Blithedalers are eroticized. There are many examples of this eroticism, such as the "great piece of good fortune" (37) that Coverdale should see Zenobia's shoulder, Priscilla's ability to become ever more "bewitching," and the erotic language in which he frames his most emotional discussions with Hollingsworth. David Leverenz notes that some of the discussions with Hollingsworth employ images of potential penetration, perhaps rape.[13]

Rather than dwell on his individual fascinations—they have been well documented—I want to suggest that Coverdale's erotic desire also invests the characters as a group, an "inextricable knot." He does not just want each individually; he wants them all together. This becomes especially apparent after Coverdale leaves Blithedale. He mourns his inability to forget his associates in terms that might suggest a kind of polygamy, even to the point of repeating their three names together in a single breath, like one lover's name:

Hollingsworth, Zenobia, Priscilla! . . . The three had absorbed my life into themselves. Together with an inexpressible longing to know their fortunes, there was likewise a morbid resentment of my own pain, and a stubborn reluctance to come again within their sphere.

(231)

The three Blithedalers have a single "sphere"; Coverdale feels "inexpressible longing" to know of them. His ache echoes that of a jilted lover. The same note is struck a few chapters earlier in "Leave-Takings." After his break with Hollingsworth, Coverdale experiences or imagines a break with his entire set:

Your understanding, possibly, may put faith in denial. But your heart will not so easily rest satisfied. It incessantly remonstrates, though, most of the time, in a bass-note, which you do not separately distinguish; but, now and then, with a sharp cry, importunate to be heard, and resolute to claim belief. "Things are not as they were!" it keeps saying.

(172)

Again, Coverdale frames his break with all three of his friends in terms that echo a split with a single lover: the "[dis]satisfied" heart cries out, "importunate to be heard."

Coverdale further suggests queer desire in his boarding-house dream, which dramatizes a strange sexual criss-crossing that can only be described as queer:

In those [dreams] of the last night, Hollingsworth and Zenobia, standing on either side of my bed, had bent across it to exchange a kiss of passion. Priscilla, beholding this,—for she seemed to be peeping in at the chamber-window,—had melted gradually away, and left only the sadness of her expression in my heart.

(187)

Hollingsworth and Zenobia share a stable, identifiably heterosexual "kiss of passion," but this kiss is complicated as Coverdale envisions them "bent across" his bed. Discrete heterosexual monogamy is therefore confused with homoeroticism on Hollingsworth's side and voyeurism all around. The knot is even further complicated by Priscilla, whose gaze seems as important to the passionate kiss—it may be at least partially for her benefit—as it is to Coverdale's experience. Coverdale's desire is most diffused. The imagery suggests erotic participation as he is caught physically between the kissing lovers, but his primarily pleasure may lie with watching and identifying with all participants, both the melting sadness and the passion. Coverdale's pleasure is not just seeing, but also naming (and therefore experiencing) every sensation. What makes this desire specifically queer is that it is impossible to qualify without reductive terms. It stubbornly resists attempts at categorization.

Another way in which Coverdale suggests queer desire is in his destabilization of monogamous couplings among any two of the four central characters. He works to keep eroticism diffuse by discouraging any restricting intimacies. His own relationship with Hollingsworth dramatizes the point. Coverdale desires erotic intimacy with Hollingsworth, but not exclusivity. When Coverdale first broaches the question, he poses it in these terms:

> It would be so great a happiness to find myself treading the same path with you. But I am afraid there is not stuff in me stern enough for a philanthropist,—or not in this peculiar direction,—or, at all events, *not solely in this.* Can you bear with me, if such should prove to be the case?
>
> (82, emphasis added)

As many readers have noted, Coverdale's language resonates romantically. Participation in Hollingsworth's scheme becomes amorous participation: it is to "tread the same path" with him, a kind of marriage. Coverdale's objection, then, is telling. He says it may be his lack of sternness; or it may be Hollingsworth's particular plot; but if it is not those two, then, "at all events," it is the question of exclusivity: *"not solely in this."* In this way, Hollingsworth's vision (so far as it includes Coverdale) clashes with Coverdale's: Hollingsworth demands exclusivity.

This tension between exclusivity and openness also animates the climactic fight between Hollingsworth and Coverdale in "A Crisis." Hollingsworth wants single devotion: "there is not the man in this wide world whom I can love as I could you." But Coverdale's vision cannot exclude the others. He therefore asks: "Is Zenobia to take a part in your enterprise?" (167). There is no explicit connection between this interview and Zenobia's fate. Coverdale's question suggests only a desire to know the exact parameters of Hollingsworth's proposal, whom it does and does not include. After Hollingsworth responds to this question, Coverdale presses on, "What is to become of Priscilla?"

> Hollingsworth looked at me fiercely, and with glowing eyes. He could not have shown any other kind of expression than that, had he meant to strike me with a sword.
>
> "Why do you bring in the names of these women?" said he, after a moment of pregnant silence. "What have they to do with the proposal which I make you? I must have your answer! Will you devote yourself, and sacrifice all to this great end, and be my friend of friends forever?"
>
> (167)

This dialogue may be the most electric in *Blithedale*. Hollingsworth's ferocity resolves if the discussion is considered in terms of romantic exclusivity. In this context, it becomes clear why Coverdale's questions about Priscilla and Zenobia are so inappropriate, why Hollingsworth demands, "Why do you bring in the names of these women?" Hollingsworth's tone is especially derisive, suggesting the misogyny he will reveal more fully at Eliot's pulpit. Hollingsworth's homosexual desire, finally, is incompatible with Coverdale's queer vision because it requires a no less discrete, stable sexual identity than heterosexuality would. The way Hollingsworth offers his "proposal" makes the exclusivity paramount: "this great end" that requires "sacrific[ing] all" is easy to elide with being the "friend of friends." Is the proposal to *work* exclusively with Hollingsworth or to *be* exclusively with Hollingsworth? Coverdale's desire is accurately called a "third choice" (168). He does want Hollingsworth, but he wants all the participants.

Coverdale also works to destabilize discrete, monogamous desire in Zenobia and Priscilla. He destabilizes their desire by reminding each at key points in the romance that their erotic interest in Hollingsworth is balanced by the other (and, though he does not mention it, presumably by his own). Coverdale reminds Priscilla of the relationship between Zenobia and Hollingsworth after the discussion of women's rights at Eliot's pulpit, which ends with Priscilla and Hollingsworth in concert about the role of women. As if to destabilize the growing sympathy between them—and therefore the possibility that it might lead to exclusivity—Coverdale accosts Priscilla on the path back to the farm house. He taunts, "But observe how pleasantly and happily Zenobia and Hollingsworth are walking together. I call it a delightful spectacle. It truly rejoices me that Hollingsworth has found so fit and affectionate a friend" (158). As this chapter immediately precedes "A Crisis," I am inclined to believe Coverdale's rejoicing. The possibility that Hollingsworth may nurture erotic relationships (in addition to the one between them) fits Coverdale's vision because it keeps romantic energy diffuse among the four. Although Coverdale himself sees his goading of Priscilla as "foolish bitterness of heart," it may be no more than the half-conscious pursuit of his utopia. The more Coverdale can destabilize Priscilla's desire, the less Priscilla will imagine an exclusive coupling. The pursuit of vision in *The Blithedale Romance* tends to be selfish because it involves imposing that vision on unwilling participants, in this case Priscilla. But that does not necessarily make it "foolish bitterness." Coverdale maneuvers similarly with Zenobia late in the romance, when he visits her hotel. Observing Priscilla at her most beautiful, he asks Zenobia, "By the by, has Hollingsworth ever seen her in this dress?" (205). In this way, he keeps the "knot of polygamy," the inextricable instability, alive for as long as possible.

All the utopian visions at Blithedale fail, most often undermined by those who posit them no less than by those who do not. Zenobia's feminist vision fails first through her own inability to resist Hollingsworth, and then through her suicide after he chooses Priscilla and her fortune. Perhaps the fulcrum of Zenobia's self-betrayal is her failure to respond to Hollingsworth's misogynist rant at Eliot's pulpit. Hollingsworth imagines using "physical force" to "scourge [women] back within their proper bounds" (154). Zenobia—feminist, pamphleteer, orator—replies: "Well, be it so. . . . I, at least, have deep cause to think you right. Let man be but manly and god-like, and woman is only too ready to become to him what you say!" (155). Baym reads Zenobia's caveat as consistent with feminist ideals, provided we understand that "her qualification is vital. Except as man takes woman as a free spirit, equal to his own and with the same rights, he is not manly or god-like."[14] But while I share Baym's impulse to defend Zenobia, this qualification belongs to Baym, not Zenobia. Zenobia's definition of "manly and god-like" is never laid out. Furthermore, Zenobia replies in a spirit of defeat. Coverdale observes "tears sparkl[ing] in her eyes . . . wholly of grief, not anger" (155). The suggestion is not that Zenobia's message is secretly feminist, but that she is caught between her ideals and her desire for Hollingsworth—and that her desire is finally stronger. Hollingsworth undermines his vision similarly, by giving up his ideals. In his case, he surrenders to his own "criminality," guilt over Zenobia's death, and lets himself by supported by Priscilla, just as he once sought to support criminals.

The failure of Coverdale's vision is similarly complicated, effected both from within and without. Because we have the benefit of Coverdale's first-person voice, we are intimate with the extent to which he, like Zenobia, is conflicted about his vision of Blithedale. For her, the conflict is between love and ideology. For Coverdale, it is intrinsic to his voice, his personality. As the image of his hermitage suggests—and even the fact that he can feel comfortably "married" in a hermitage—Coverdale's willingness and ability to commit himself to any community, any utopia (even his own) is uncertain. As Hollingsworth remarks and other characters echo, "Miles Coverdale is not in earnest, either as a poet or a laborer" (95). Hollingsworth might have added, or as a visionary. Coverdale has an intellectual's detachment from and ambivalence about his every project—whether going to Blithedale, being there, or leaving. He both pursues his vision and castigates himself for steps in its pursuit, for example his regret after rejecting Hollingsworth's exclusive proposal and his guilt over destabilizing Priscilla's desire in "Eliot's Pulpit." He lacks Hollingsworth's "inflexible severity of purpose" (67).

Coverdale's vision is also successfully resisted from without, by both Hollingsworth and Zenobia. Hollingsworth resists Coverdale's vision consistently throughout the novel. Their discussion of Fourier is one example. Although Fourier's utopia may be somewhat less radical than Coverdale's—Fourier's stands against monogamy, but he retains gender stability and discrete desire—Coverdale uses Fourier as a tentative way to bring his paradigm to Hollingsworth. Coverdale too may be looking for proselytes, just like Zenobia at the first Blithedale dinner and Hollingsworth at Eliot's pulpit. But unlike the latter two, Coverdale's ambivalence is evident even in his attempt to make converts. The very narration suggests ambivalence by the extent to which it is occluded. Rather than directly recording the discussion, Coverdale gives us only Fourier's name, a subtext, and a few reactions. Lauren Berlant attempts to reconstruct how and why Coverdale uses Fourier:

> Coverdale instinctively understands that a literal extension of the Fourierist plan to harness the passions to improve both love and play, an achievement made by breaking down the traditional philosophical primacy of reason and of conventional juridical and moral law would be to provide not only a "social" minimum for the members of the phalanx, but also a "sexual minimum." The utopian state's commitment to the production of pleasure would liberate both women and men from monogamy.[15]

Berlant must rely on Coverdale's "instinctive" understanding because the narrative never provides a more explicit understanding. But Fourier's name becomes a testing ground, a way for Coverdale to sound Hollingsworth and learn who will make a proselyte of whom.

Hollingsworth's vehement rejection of Fourier suggests that he understands Coverdale's intimation. "'Let me hear no more of it!' cried he, in utter disgust. 'I never will forgive this fellow! He has committed the unpardonable sin; for what more monstrous iniquity could the devil himself contrive than to choose the selfish principle,—the principle of all human wrong, the very blackness of man's heart'" (79). Hollingsworth's language betrays disgust at an unfettered sexuality—not just a dissolution of monogamy, but possibly a wholesale dissolution of stable sexual categories. He calls Fourier's ideas "the unpardonable sin" and "monstrous iniquity," terms that call to mind sexual transgressions such as sodomy, one of those crimes that James I famously decided a king is conscience-bound never to forgive. Hollingsworth later talks with disgust of Fourier's "consummated Paradise" (79), further indicating through his sarcasm an unnatural (fallen) sexuality.

The ferocity of Hollingsworth's displeasure also foreshadows his anger at Coverdale's insistence on the fate of Zenobia and Priscilla during "A Crisis." He is similarly reacting there against a less stable sexuality than his own. In this way, both discussions cover the same territory of exclusivity and openness. The scenes also echo each other in that Hollingsworth's final rejection, "Take the book out of my sight" (80) is equivalent to

Coverdale's dramatic, "No!" (168). And Coverdale accepts rejection no more gracefully than does Hollingsworth. The rest of the chapter is a prolonged reflection on Hollingsworth's faults, such as his obsessive nature and lack of education. Coverdale states, "It is my private opinion that, at this period of his life, Hollingsworth was fast going mad; and, as with other crazy people . . . it required all the constancy of friendship to restrain his associates from pronouncing him an intolerable bore" (81). Coverdale's anger is revealed through his spite; there is no other way to read his harangue at this instant, as the question of Hollingsworth's sanity never resurfaces.

Another example of Hollingsworth resisting Coverdale's vision occurs at the end of the novel, over the question of Zenobia's burial plot. Coverdale wants to bury Zenobia at Eliot's pulpit, which would foreground the connection between the four Blithedalers. Zenobia's burial site would thus honor the "knot of Polygamy" by elevating the place where all four gathered on Sundays. He also desires that her tomb, the rock itself, should bear "the name by which we familiarly knew her,— Zenobia,—and not another word" (278). Again, Coverdale privileges the diffuse ties of Blithedale over those that would be concretely determined by full names, those of father and sister. Indeed, it is interesting to note that Coverdale never reveals Zenobia's full name, only that title by which her friends knew her. We are hard put to identify a Zenobia outside the sphere of his utopian vision. Hollingsworth's feelings about Zenobia's burial are more complicated. He "requested that her grave be dug on the gently sloping hillside, where, as we once supposed, Zenobia and he had planned to build their cottage" (278). He desires a plot associated with stable heterosexual coupling. Hollingsworth's choice may be motivated by his conservative view of marriage, or perhaps by an impulse to express his guilt over Zenobia's suicide. In any case, the contrast with Coverdale's preference remains marked: the commemoration of an "inextricable . . . knot" versus a location tied to discrete monogamy.

Zenobia resists Coverdale's vision very much as she resists her own, through her devotion to Hollingsworth and therefore to stable, monogamous desire. The relationship between Coverdale and Zenobia is hard to define throughout the book, always eroticized, always denied. Zenobia occasionally speculates on Coverdale's sexual mystery, while he obsesses over hers. In Coverdale's sick room, Zenobia first takes note of his fascination with her. In response to his "watching her" as she serves gruel, she says, "I seem to interest you very much; and yet—or else a woman's instinct is for once deceived—I cannot reckon you as an admirer" (72). Zenobia's speculation both raises and denies the specter of erotic attachment—with a reservation: the nature of Coverdale's interest may be beyond even her usually trustworthy "woman's instinct." Coverdale's interior response similarly raises and denies possibility. First he admits and blandly generalizes away his sexual jealousy: "A bachelor always feels himself defrauded, when he knows, or suspects, that any woman of his acquaintance has given herself away" (72). Then he ardently denies erotic tension between them: "I should not, under any circumstances, have fallen in love with Zenobia" (73). The effect of his denials is only to reinforce our sense of his desire; he protests too much. This pattern also manifests itself in their last meeting before Zenobia's suicide. Zenobia, again moved by Coverdale's gaze, raises the issue of erotic attachment: "'It is an endless pity,' said she, 'that I had not be thought myself of winning your heart, Mr. Coverdale, instead of Hollingsworth's. I think I should have succeeded'" (265). Zenobia both sees and does not see romantic possibility; she half-recognizes the depth of Coverdale's desire.

But most resonant is the nature of their interaction in the moments between these two encounters, between Coverdale's sickbed stay and their last interview. When Zenobia is most taken with Hollingsworth—that is, for most of the romance—she fully denies the erotic tension between herself and Coverdale. She limits her focus to Hollingsworth and undermines what she at least half-recognizes both before and after, that Coverdale's affection is significant, intense, erotic, and difficult to qualify. During the height of her involvement with Hollingsworth, she reduces Coverdale's motives to mere "bigotry; self-conceit; an insolent curiosity; a meddlesome temper; a cold-blooded criticism" (205). It is only after the affair with Hollingsworth is over, after that romantic possibility is completely diffused, that she again acknowledges the complication of Coverdale's stance. Zenobia's rejection of Coverdale's vision is actually enacted in her rejection of Coverdale through the bulk of *Blithedale*: she rejects queer desire by closing herself off to a more complicated model of sexuality, one that might recognize an undefined erotic attachment to two men.

Gustaaf Van Cromphout indicates a way in which Zenobia's utopian ideals may not be incompatible with Coverdale's.[16] He suggests that Zenobia embodies the ideals of Margaret Fuller, including her wished-for dissolution of gender and portrayal of the androgyne as an ideal figure—ideals that overlap with the queer utopia I have been sketching for Coverdale. Van Cromphout finds support for this assertion, not in Zenobia's actions, but in how the text describes her, arguing that Hawthorne purposefully confuses Zenobia's gender in an attempt to locate her within Fuller's system of belief. But it is Coverdale working to confuse Zenobia's gender, not Hawthorne. Coverdale attempts the same queering of all the principle Blithedalers. The impulse is specific to his character; it therefore reveals Coverdale's vision rather than Zenobia's.[17]

At the end of the novel, a dozen years after Blithedale, Coverdale describes himself as "a bachelor, with no very decided purpose of ever being otherwise" (286). Given the dichotomy established between Blithedale and bachelorhood early on in the novel, his acknowledgement of bachelor status is not surprising. The failure of Blithedale equals his failure to realize sustainable romantic interaction. But the final pages of *Blithedale* do provide readers with a few questions. How do we accept Coverdale's confession of love for Priscilla, and how do we explain his indolence? The answers to both questions may be tied to the fact of Coverdale's continuing bachelorhood—that is, to the failure of his queer vision. Coverdale's listlessness recalls the fate of Theodore in Zenobia's legend: "to pine for ever and ever for another sight of that dim, mournful face,—which might have been his life-long household fireside joy,—to desire, and waste life in a feverish quest, and never meet it more" (145). Theodore's fate suggests that the focus of Coverdale's "waste[d] life" is also regret over a veiled lady, which resonates with his confession of love for Priscilla. This reading seems partially right, but only partially. As David Leverenz dramatically notes, Coverdale's confession "hangs like a guillotine over each rereading."[18] The paradigm of Coverdale-as-Theodore does provide an answer to Coverdale's fate, perhaps the interpretation toward which Coverdale directs us. But it is neither satisfying nor convincing. I suggest that the comparison to Theodore and the last line may instead resonate with Coverdale's failed desire more generally. Coverdale is like Theodore, but not in desiring a single subject. He is like Theodore simply in that he, too, is undone by a masked or veiled desire, a desire obscured by its own utopian nature. The novel's last line has usually been understood as a focusing of Coverdale's desire, but it may also be read as an acknowledgement of its expansiveness. Coverdale may not simply be saying, I was in love with Priscilla, but rather, I was in love with Priscilla, *too.* Coverdale's love for Hollingsworth and Zenobia is manifest; no confession is necessary in these cases. And there is no reason why love for Priscilla would mitigate the love he has expressed and dramatized throughout the romance.

The Blithedale Romance, finally, presents a dark vision of utopian thinking. The problem with the community is not the failure of its vision, but the failure of its members to agree on a unified vision. Just as Blithedalers find fault with each suggestion of a name for the community during their first night together (60-61), they implicitly find fault with the vision each brings to make their utopia a reality. Along with the characters' inability to find concert with each other, Hawthorne's characters further cannot find concert within themselves. Even Coverdale's final confession suggests this ambivalence. It is a confession, but a startlingly incomplete one. Loving Priscilla is simultaneously a revelation of queer desire and an escape to conventional desire, as Priscilla fits nineteenth-century expectations of a desirable woman.[19] In a single breath, Coverdale affirms and denies the disappointment that keeps him lifeless.

Notes

My thanks to Dr. Roberta Welden for her help with this argument.

1. John C. Hirsh, "The Politics of Blithedale; The Dilemma of the Self," *Studies in Romanticism* 11 (1972), 139.

2. Hirsh is one example of a reader who faults Hollingsworth for the failure of Blithedale, both personally and in terms of his political views. Despite her other differences with Hirsh, Nina Baym similarly blames Hollingsworth in "*The Blithedale Romance*: A Radical Reading," *Journal of English and Germanic Philology* 67 (1968), 545-69. Baym views the text in the tradition of "Tintern Abbey," a Romantic journey inside the self, rather than an externally real political endeavor. In this reading, all characters become aspects of Coverdale, which he encounters in an attempt to reinvigorate himself and his poetry. Zenobia becomes life force; Hollingsworth becomes that aspect of the Romantic traveler (Coverdale) which judges, the "spirit of authoritarian domination" (558). Baym eventually finds that the community fails, that Coverdale does not find a spirit or genius, because the Hollingsworth in him banishes the Zenobia: social inhibition overcomes his life force. The failure of Blithedale, then, is not due to too much passion, but to too little. Harvey Gable, Jr., among other readers, distributes the cause of failure more generally. In "Inappeasable Longings; Hawthorne, Romance, and the Disintegration of Coverdale's Self in *The Blithedale Romance*," *New England Quarterly* 67 (1994), 257-78, Gable finds that the problem with Blithedale is not simply that Hollingsworth's vision is incompatible, but that all the characters' visions are. Gable reads the novel as a lesson in the necessity of surrendering one's individual vision in order to join a group—a surrender that Gable claims Hawthorne finds neither desirable nor possible.

3. Nathaniel Hawthorne, *The Blithedale Romance* (New York: Dell, 1971), 88. Hereafter cited parenthetically.

4. Gustaaf Van Cromphout, "*Blithedale* and the Androgyne Myth: Another Look at Zenobia," *ESQ: A Journal of the American Renaissance* 18 (1872), 141-45.

5. Baym, 547.

6. My argument is related to Berlant's in "Fantasies of Utopia in *The Blithedale Romance*," *American*

Literary History 1 (1989), 30-62, in that we both focus on the central role of love and sexuality in Coverdale's discourse. Berlant also anticipates my argument by recognizing Coverdale as a subject desiring both men and women. But rather than see liberated desire as an independent utopian goal related to a general release from the nineteenth-century sex-gender system, Berlant focuses her study on the tension between "tragic" and "utopian" modes of thinking (31), which she sees articulated in Coverdale and Hollingsworth respectively.

7. Critics have generally made Coverdale's sexual desire both stable and discrete in terms of sexual orientation. Some focus on Coverdale's fascination with Zenobia, most notably Donald Ross Jr. in "Dreams and Sexual Repression in *The Blithedale Romance*," *PMLA* 86 (1971), 1014-17; others, such as David Leverenz and Edwin Haviland Miller, focus on his desire for Hollingsworth. See Edwin Haviland Miller, *Salem Is My Dwelling Place: A Life of Nathaniel Hawthorne* (Iowa City: Univ. of Iowa Press, 1991), 357-58, 366-76. But such attempts to contain Coverdale's erotic desire lead to strange contortions of the text. Leverenz, for example, in *Manhood and the American Renaissance* (Ithaca: Cornell Univ. Press, 1989) makes Coverdale into a kind of power-hungry monster, the point of which, he says, is to implicate the reader for prying—for becoming exactly the same kind of monster in an effort to apprehend the text. Leverenz further explains Coverdale's confessions of desire, all of them, as devious ways to love Hollingsworth without the potential power compromise implicit in loving another man. I, at least, find nothing in Coverdale extreme enough to overcome the conventional identification with a first-person narrator, and suggest that Leverenz is forced to make Coverdale a monster because he insists on focusing Coverdale's sexual desire in a way that Coverdale clearly does not. If we insist he loves only Hollingsworth, his desire for Priscilla and Zenobia may become a strategy to power. But Coverdale's actions and affections are best understood through his own lens, one that staunchly refuses to limit desire or gender to stable, discrete categories.

8. Michel Foucault, *The History of Sexuality,* vol. I (New York: Vintage Books, 1990).

9. Eve Kosofsky Sedgwick, *The Epistemology of the Closet* (Berkeley: Univ. of California Press, 1990), 71.

10. David Halperin, *100 Years of Homosexuality* (New York: Routledge, 1990), 15-16.

11. Baym, 560.

12. Baym, 549n.

13. Leverenz, 247-48.

14. Baym, 564.

15. Berlant, 40.

16. Van Cromphout, 141-45.

17. For a refutation of readings aligning Zenobia with Fuller, see Baym, 563n.

18. Leverenz, 251.

19. See Baym, 562-63.

John W. M. Hallock (essay date 2000)

SOURCE: Hallock, John W. M. Introduction to *The American Byron: Homosexuality and the Fall of Fitz-Greene Halleck,* pp. 3-16. Madison: University of Wisconsin Press, 2000.

[*In the following essay, Hallock chronicles the significance of homosexuality in Halleck's life and works and in his exclusion from the American literary canon.*]

> And when the death-note of my bugle has sounded,
> And memorial tears are embalming my name,
> By young hearts like his may the grave be surrounded
> Where I sleep my last sleep in the sunbeams of fame.
>
> Fitz-Greene Halleck, "Young America"

The sun beamed brightly at three o'clock on Tuesday afternoon, May 15, 1877, as William Cullen Bryant introduced the president of the United States to an audience of fifty thousand men, women, and children.[1] At a private luncheon before the ceremony, President and Mrs. Hayes had been presented with a miniature of the twelve-thousand-dollar monument that was about to be unveiled in New York's Central Park. President Jackson had dined twice with the man honored on this day, President Lincoln had complimented him, and John Quincy Adams had alluded to one of his poems in a speech delivered to the House of Representatives in 1836. In addition to nurturing political relationships in the United States with the likes of Daniel Webster, Henry Clay, and John C. Calhoun, the venerated poet had been a personal friend of such foreign dignitaries as Joseph Bonaparte and British government minister Charles Richard Vaughan, who had thrown a grand dinner just to honor him. The poet had also impressed other major authors of his time who almost unanimously ranked him their superior. He was a favorite of Charles Dickens and William Thackeray as well as of the American literary giants, Bryant, James Fenimore Cooper, Washington Irving, and Edgar Allan Poe. As military bands played on the day of the unveiling, artists and politicians rubbed elbows with polished etiquette.

The illustrious poet had once joked about being carved in stone along with the green umbrella that had become his trademark accessory. In fact, he had told a friend who had helped to plan the statue that "the likeness would not strike" without the umbrella and that he hoped another admirer of his work had obtained "a sculptor cunning enough in carving stone umbrellas."[2] But it was without an umbrella that his figure would have to withstand the torrents of praise showered upon him that day. Even so, the fine weather and smooth collaboration of the elite could not prevent controversy from overshadowing the auspicious occasion commemorating America's earliest homosexual poet, Fitz-Greene Halleck.

President Hayes, who had taken office only two months earlier, unknowingly sparked the controversy when he yanked a sheet painted with the national colors off of the stone figure of the man he called "the favored of all the early American poets."[3] While favorable portraits of Halleck had been painted by America's leading artists (including Brown, Elliott, Hicks, Inman, Jarvis, Morse, Rogers, and Waldo), the statue by J. Wilson MacDonald, who had recently created Irving's memorial bust, was sharply criticized. *Harper's Weekly* declared it "a very poor work of art,"[4] and Bayard Taylor complained:

> It is not a fortunate specimen of our native art. The posture is ungraceful, the face over-conscious to the verge of ostentation, and the general character of the figure is so theatrical that few of those who knew the poet will immediately recognize him.[5]

Taylor denounced the effeminate depiction of his friend and had commented elsewhere on Halleck's unease with his looks and age. William Allen Butler, another poet, also commented on Halleck's "habitual self-depreciation."[6] Indeed, Halleck joked that no paintings of himself had caused him or "any one else to violate the second commandment" and complained that he was the ugliest of the numerous men in the famed group portrait of Washington Irving and his literary friends.[7] He declined to be photographed for *Putnam's Magazine,* asking instead to be illustrated "not as I am but as I ought to be"—words echoed in his initial refusal to be photographed by M. B. Brady: "I much prefer that you should remember me as I have been, not as I am."[8] Often relieved when admirers managed to get outdated pictures of him rather than images that conveyed the ravages of time, Halleck displayed a self-conscious neurosis about his appearance that proved utterly modern. He would have been pleased to see that the statue depicted a youthful Halleck, in spite of its flamboyant pose.

In addition to the alleged misrepresentation of Halleck's person, the occasion was dampened by the absence of certain key figures. Ralph Waldo Emerson, Henry Wadsworth Longfellow, and former president Ulysses S. Grant had sent notes expressing their regrets.[9] Even worse, John Greenleaf Whittier, who had written a fourteen-stanza poem for the ceremony, was too ill to attend. General James Grant Wilson, Halleck's literary executor and first biographer, read Whittier's elegy.

The statue was placed in the "Poet's Corner of America," strangely nicknamed since it had previously included only the English and Scottish figures of William Shakespeare, Robert Burns, and Sir Walter Scott. Halleck remains the only American among the writers honored on what is now referred to as Literary Walk. Though New York City mayor Smith Ely graciously responded to remarks by the country's president, he was clearly annoyed by the trampling of the mall, which motivated him to create an ordinance prohibiting future parades in Central Park.[10]

With much pomp, a Rhode Island granite monument had already been dedicated to Halleck in 1869 near his birthplace and grave site in Guilford, Connecticut. Several thousand people had arrived by special trains from New Haven on the anniversary of his birthday.[11] A two-thousand-dollar, eighteen-foot obelisk, surrounded by clippings of the Melrose Abbey ivy given to Washington Irving by Sir Walter Scott, had been dedicated in the oval center of Alderbrook Cemetery. The event had featured military bands and a keynote speech by Bayard Taylor. Oliver Wendell Holmes had planned to participate, but Wilson had delivered Holmes's elegiac lines in the ailing poet's absence.

Both the monument and the statue were forged to immortalize Halleck, who had the dual distinction of being "the first American poet to whom a public monument was ever erected in this country, and the first to have a full bronze statue in the New World."[12] Both representations indubitably failed their purpose. In 1980, the *New York Times* complained that more famous authors (such as Irving and Cooper) are not represented on the Mall and deprecatingly described Halleck's statue: "Halleck's teacup fingers, pursed lips and negligently strewn books suggest a literary prig . . . now forgotten."[13] In 1993, a centerfold of the statue and famous walk appeared in the May *National Geographic,* which only identified Halleck in a caption. A 1997 photograph and explanation of the statue's presence appeared in the *New York Times Magazine,* which accused Halleck of "schmoozing" his way into stone.[14] But friends and admirers at the time were vocal about Halleck's asocial propensity and horror of being publicly "called out," and despite recent appearances in popular magazines, he remains thoroughly unsung. Further, the reasons for his anonymity today are themselves obscure.

Nineteenth-century American readers would be perplexed by the current neglect of Halleck. Poe, whose reviews were so notoriously harsh that he was nick-named the Tomahawk Critic, wrote that a passage of "Alnwick Castle" was "the noblest to be found in Halleck, and I would be at a loss to discover its parallel in all American poetry."[15] While the *National Magazine* noted that this critique was a rare example of "when Poe *did* praise anything," by 1843 Poe had concluded, "No name in the American poetical world is more firmly established than that of Fitz-Greene Halleck."[16] Twenty-six years later, Bryant held that Halleck "furnishes a standing and ever-ready allusion to all who would speak of American literature, and is familiar in the mouths of hundreds who would be seriously puzzled if asked to name any other American poet."[17] Edith Wharton certainly felt that Halleck's name needed no explanation in *The Age of Innocence* (chapter 12) and ranked his notoriety alongside that of Irving in her 1917 novel, *Summer.*

Although Halleck was endorsed as the national poet of America by the *New York Times* on January 30, 1864, this reputation was lost by 1930, when a *New York Times* critic realized that "few outside a very small circle of close students of literary history in this country could identify off-hand the name of Fitz-Greene Halleck."[18] His radical fall from fame demonstrates the politics of decanonization, just as his decanonization negates his significant contributions to American verse and sexual ideology. Halleck's love for another man contributed to the dismantling of the platonic framework of Romantic idealism.

Fitz-Greene Halleck was born in 1790 and remained in rural Connecticut throughout his adolescence, when he began writing verse with same-sex love themes. He was alienated by the puritanical community's tenacious repression of aesthetic and romantic impulses. His poetry increasingly empathized with the plight of Native Americans, slaves, women, and heretics as he came to perceive his own position as an outcast. When business took him to New York City at age eighteen, he determined to reside there, and he would call Greenwich Village home for the next forty years.

Nourished by New York's urban sophistication, Halleck rose rapidly. He was elected poet laureate of the Ugly Club, a fraternity of the city's best-looking men, and joined the Bread and Cheese Lunch (ca. 1824-1830) along with James K. Paulding, Gulian C. Verplank, Richard H. Dana, Bryant, and Cooper. Halleck was increasingly courted by New York's most elite social circles. Privately, he had begun a series of erratic romances with foreign men, but these did not eclipse his persistent doubt that he would ever find his ideal partner.

Halleck's search for a soul mate was delayed by the War of 1812 when he served in the Iron Grays, a metropolitan military unit consisting of wealthy boys. By his mid-twenties, his muse finally materialized in the figure of Joseph Rodman Drake, a young doctor and the most desirable man in town. Halleck was physically and emotionally drawn to Drake, but the powerful attraction was not completely mutual. The two men did collaborate, however, on a series of comic social commentaries. An overnight sensation, their Croaker poems initiated a form of social dialogue unprecedented in American periodicals. In the spring of 1819, more than thirty-five of these satirical Pindaric odes appeared anonymously in the *New York Evening Post* and later in the *National Advocate.* This venture of "Croaker" (Drake) and "Croaker Jr." (Halleck) awoke Halleck's poetic strength and permanently linked him with Drake.

Within three months, the Croakers catapulted Halleck to fame. Halleck's enormously popular *Fanny* (1819) followed and was the first noteworthy American mock-epic. The unmarried woman satirized in the poem was modeled on Drake. This profitable work elevated Halleck to the status of the only other American writer Irving's publisher would print, and first editions quickly became exceedingly valuable.[19] *Fanny* railed against wedlock just as ardently as Halleck had protested Drake's sudden 1816 marriage to a wealthy socialite. Halleck grew despondent in this competition for Drake's affection and pulled away. But Drake's effort to include Halleck as a family member and his poems written to Halleck (during the Drakes' honeymoon) proved irresistible bait and rekindled the friendship. The contest between Halleck and Drake's wife did not last long, for the physician could not cure himself of consumption; Drake died in 1820. Situated in what became Joseph Rodman Drake Park, his stone is engraved with Halleck's quatrain beginning, "Green be the turf above thee," which opens what became a classic American elegy still recited on the radio as late as the 1950s.[20] The poem protests Halleck's diminished role at the funeral and reiterates his belief that marriage had consumed Drake's spirit. Halleck lived a long life, but never loved again.

Halleck attempted to eulogize Drake in a series of sporadic poems and translations. Although none of the attempts seemed adequate, he did develop several strategies for expressing his homosexual longings and grief. Metaphorical crime, antinationalism, and silence came to represent his misunderstood feelings for Drake, who was nicknamed the American Keats. (Indeed, Drake and Keats had their birth year, age of death, study of medicine, and fatal consumption in common.) Soon after the burial, Halleck's spoofs on marriage and his political antagonism increasingly undermined federalist conventions of love and freedom, and his themes and satires grew so irreverent that he became known as the American Byron.

Halleck was contracted to edit anonymously the first complete edition of Lord Byron's works and letters; it appeared in 1832. Halleck's text contained many suppressed letters and boldly incorporated bisexual aspects of Byron's life. As in the case of his coauthorship with Drake, Halleck's allegiance to Byron was simultaneously artistic and erotic. Although Halleck and Byron never met, Halleck burst into tears upon the news of Byron's death in an uncharacteristic display of emotion that startled friends.

Halleck objected to cultural conformity and defended his eccentric friends with renewed fervor following the deaths of Drake and Byron. He also defied the social expectations of marriage and fatherhood. Instead, he revised national history in the countercultural lines of "Connecticut" (a deconstruction of Puritan tyranny), "Red Jacket" (a sarcastic tribute to the Native American), and "Wyoming" (a satire of Thomas Campbell's "Gertrude"). His 1822 European tour was patterned on Drake's honeymoon trip and seemed cathartic. Halleck returned a serious poet. International topics wooed a larger audience. "Alnwick Castle," "Burns," and "Marco Bozzaris" were written on the heels of this literal and psychological journey. These and other poems were included in a collection of Halleck's poetry published in 1827. "Marco Bozzaris" defended Greek liberation and became known as America's eminent lyric poem, frequently recited at academic graduations and political conventions.

Halleck was astounded by the success of his poetry and wore the role of national poet uncomfortably. Perhaps in an effort to shun this burden, he published "The Field of the Grounded Arms" in 1828. Devoid of rhyme, its innovative form was a daring attack on convention that would not be launched again until Whitman's experimental *Leaves of Grass* decades later. Halleck's entirely unrhymed poem "greatly puzzled the reviewers,"[21] and a critical debate ensued in which his personal character came under attack. Halleck found his inheritance of the Byronic myth too invasive and retreated from society.

Pursued by aristocratic women, professionally solicited by men of letters, and often the center of the most prominent sphere in New York, Halleck found refuge in the fast-paced world of New York's wealthiest entrepreneur, John Jacob Astor. In 1832, Halleck was installed as Astor's right-hand man. Astor named him an original trustee of the Astor Library, but Halleck was cheated of a large pension at the time of the millionaire's death in 1842, in spite of Samuel F. B. Morse's canvas of Halleck that still decks the portrait room's east wall of the New York Public Library. Halleck was forced by finances to retire to Guilford, where his verse became an affront to the conservatism brought on by an ensuing national crisis.

Convinced that civil war would blur the democratic vision he had glimpsed in urban New York, Halleck grew debilitated. Homophobic criticism began to insinuate that his verse was unhealthy. While Poe commented that *bonhomie* was the leading feature of Halleck's poetry "and, indeed, of his whole moral nature,"[22] an incendiary article of the *Southern Literary Messenger*'s Moral and Mental Portrait Series (1842) further isolated the already reclusive poet with its sexually suspicious terminology. The reviewer, who had previously had hostile dealings with Halleck, accused his subject of "unnatural transition" and "unnatural similes," adding, "the alliteration and antithesis, if effective, are unnatural."[23] Naturally, Halleck took cover.

A decade of virtual poetic silence followed. Back in Guilford, drinking heavily, Halleck finally produced an addition to "Connecticut" in 1852. A bitter denunciation of American Puritanism, the poem provided a sharp contrast to the pleasant transcendental meandering of its 1826 version. The inherent irony of civil war was not lost on Halleck, whose "Connecticut" blasted the American forefathers' legacy of intolerance and hypocrisy. Civil war is an oxymoron, and the idea of one nation divided against itself particularly reinforced Halleck's view that the American government threatened the very rights that it had guaranteed. What some read as his "disgust for things modern and American"[24] was not antiquarianism at all, rather his fear that national evolution was proving retrogressive. Halleck took a sarcastic political stance declaring himself a Loyalist and refusing to write about a failed democracy that pitted brother against brother. His verse mingled democracy and anarchy as his sexual imagery continued to blur love and crime.

From the outset, Halleck refused invitations to write on the national conflict, asking instead, "Is this Southern, this sin-born war of ours, worthy of a poet's consecration?"[25] At the end of the Civil War, he emerged from his self-imposed literary exile. In a letter written that year, N. P. Willis asked the rhetorical question, "How is it that Fitz-Greene Halleck has never let himself be known to audiences?"[26] Halleck answered the inquiry with his last major poem, "Young America" (1864). Produced at the age of seventy-four, "Young America" appeared in the *New York Ledger,* ending the literary silence that had left his readership mystified. The poem was at once a jaded critique of marriage and a pederastic boy-worship reminiscent of classical homosexuality. It joined the rest of Halleck's work which "violates many of the fundamental rules of taste and art."[27] It also coincided with the new sexual literacy of medical, psychological, and social sciences that left "inverts" or "the third sex" standing naked before the unblinking eye of a modern society. Halleck had succeeded in a fiercely heterosexist market only because it had been sexually blind. Already by the middle of the nineteenth century, the techniques that he had employed were no longer viable. Silent signifiers replaced the Byronic "negative" Romanticism and overt protestation of earlier works.

Silence as a practice and as a metaphor came easily to Halleck who had suffered from partial deafness since the age of two. The hearing loss was traceable to a prank two drunken soldiers had played on Halleck. Planning to startle the toddler, the men discharged their guns near his left ear. The assault resulted in a number of public embarrassments and ultimately an almost total loss of hearing in the years following an unsuccessful and excruciating remedy Halleck underwent when he was thirty years old. In addition to corresponding to his physical disability, soundless symbols were perfectly suited to the suppressed existence of American homosexuals driven underground. The resulting nuance of poetry which no longer spoke but which only gestured to the reader produced content rich in irony that both disgusted and delighted his audience. The muted emotion of Halleck's work became an international landmark of gay representation. Dropping his mask for a moment in 1861, he scolded a crony who failed to decode his last letter by quoting the motto: "one true use of language is, not to express, but to conceal our thoughts."[28]

In 1859, Halleck replied to a potential biographer with characteristic modesty and comic guardedness:

> I have published very little, and that little almost always anonymously, and have ever been but an amateur in the literary orchestra, playing only upon a pocket flute, and never aspiring, even in a dream, to the dignity of the bâton, the double bass, or the oboe. My every-day pursuits in life have been quite opposite to those of authors; and if, among them, there is one who deems me worthy of a biography from his pen and a place in the future, he must be a very clever fellow himself to make out of my "Life and Adventures" any other than an exceedingly dull and unsalable book![29]

If bravado can compensate for one's inadequacies, then Halleck's humility can be said to hide his accomplishments. This pocket flute player resounded in Whitman's unrhymed emancipation of the poetic body from its previous constraints. Equally significant, Halleck's love for Drake inspired Bayard Taylor to challenge the conventional heterosexual novel with his homosexual romance *Joseph and His Friend,* published shortly after Halleck's death. A ghostly figure in his last years, the white-bearded Halleck haunted New York's streets through 1867 and revitalized his interest in the next generation of young male poets who paused to flatter him.

As a central influence in the Americanization of poetic form and as a founding father of a subculture in panic, Halleck occupies a complicated position in cultural history. Although no poet had received such tribute in American history, in the second half of his life Halleck's voice became a hollow song devoid of democratic hope. He dwelled alone as Drake's survivor and felt increasingly frightened as the veil of homosexual allusion was lifted from his lines.

Halleck escaped the exiles suffered by Byron and Oscar Wilde and avoided the desperate denial of homosexuality such as that Whitman made to John Addington Symonds in 1890 when he claimed six illegitimate children. Rather, Halleck had recognized that the physical desire for male companionship had to be balanced with a prudent respect for the social limits of homoerotic expression. Perhaps less self-aware (or more careful) than his contemporaries, he still faced serious opposition. In the patriotic atmosphere of Reconstruction, he was accused of converting to Catholicism, displaying excessive wealth, and indulging in sloth and decadence. All of these accusations had sodomitical implications for his hometown detractors.

Poetry and love, like nation and self, formed a complex relationship for Halleck, whose determination to free his culture was only matched by its ultimate mastery of his singular form and content. Absorbed in Halleck's literary experimentation, an enthusiastic readership had unknowingly suffered the infusion of same-sex passions into the poetics of American Romance. Biography can readily be reconstructed by modern scholars to out Halleck by reexamining his sexual identity in light of postmodern precepts. The more valuable study, however, lies in unraveling the frustration apparent in his prose and verse. As a man living in an era lacking homosexual constructs, he vacillated between embracing heterosexual paradigms and confessing his lack of emotional identification with them. The central struggle decipherable in his poetry is remarkably modern. Gay writers today still struggle to define their place in American society and in so doing reveal an irreconcilable tension: they simultaneously aspire to emulate and to resist the heterosexual institutions that legitimize relationships in the culture.

Halleck's previous popularity was enhanced by his condemnation of the emerging political machinery of the federalist period and by his elevation of same-sex friendship. He was often "proclaimed as the literary savior of America" by reason of his radical break from past form and his controversial lampoons.[30] As such, he remains a significant figure in the development of American verse as a prophet of the poetic and sexual revolution of which Walt Whitman was the messiah.

Mortified by titles like Gary Schmidgall's *Walt Whitman: A Gay Life,* the dominant camp of gay studies, social constructionists, believes that early nineteenth-century homosexuality is an impossible category since homosexuality did not become formally conceptualized until late in the century. Given this historical framework, then, one must ask: What's a gay man like Halleck doing in the nineteenth century? The rhetorical question is threefold.

As a colloquial expression, the question ponders the psychosocial presence of a homosexual figure in pre-Stonewall America. It appears that Fitz-Greene Halleck's sexuality was developing during the 1790s when "gay," "queer," and "friend of Christopher Marlowe" did not allude to homosexual orientation. In fact, no words at that time clearly communicated homosexual love. "Sodomy," "buggery," and "pederasty" were not only criminal acts but terms of coercive sex which also included heterosexual behaviors. Therefore, Halleck would not have seen himself as a "sodomite," that is, as a rapist. Nonsexual terms such as "friend," "bachelor," and "comrade" were generally not employed as codes for homosexual men by the general public. Literary allusions to Jonathan and David, Arabian Tales, or Turkish baths were more often innocent historical or literary references than homosexual signs laden with double meaning. Yet in the midst of this apparently neutral language, there are symbols of deliberate same-sex romance—such as the mythological Calamus or the color green, then red, then eventually lavender.

Rictor Norton's *The Myth of the Modern Homosexual* argues that "the American experience is largely irrelevant" in examining the birth of homosexual culture, providing an essentialist counterattack to constructionist essays like Jonathan Katz's "The Early-Nineteenth-Century Organization of Love." Social constructionist essays, for example, David M. Halperin's "Sex before Sexuality," and essentialist counterarguments, such as John Boswell's "Revolutions, Universals, and Sexual Categories," can only agree that it is unproductive to speculate about the physical sex acts of an earlier subject. Given the general divisiveness, the very use of the word "homosexual" in this cultural biography may be convenient but illegitimate. How, then, can one answer the critical question: Was there any such creature as a gay man cruising nineteenth-century America?

According to radical social constructionists, who rely heavily upon Foucault's demonstration of evolutionary sexual identifications, the answer is no. Constructionists do not deny that homosexuality is omnipresent but insist that interpretations of this behavior (i.e., as initiation/fertility rite or spiritual transportation) constitute a social rather than individual function. True constructionists argue that there was no such thing as homosexuality in early America and, accordingly, no such thing as homophobia. That would be a hard sell to those colonists executed for bedding other men.

At the other theoretical extreme, pure essentialists affirm that the self-defined homosexual person has and will exist in any time and place, whether or not the language and society acknowledge that presence. This predetermined state might include universally inherent traits such as crossgender tendencies or aesthetic capabilities. The rift of public opinion is evident in *Newsweek*'s front-page question for August 1998, "Gay for Life?" In admittedly oversimplified terms, the new theoretical debate is an abstraction and a complication of the older scientific discussion on homosexuality: chromosomes or choice, innate or learned, nature or nurture. Between these extremes, and more complex than either, I propose a con-sential or consensual theory of homosexuality. Of course, consensual homosexuality excludes male rape and conditional cases of male-male contact, as in prison. However, con-sential (constructed + essential) sexuality represents a larger paradigm that incorporates the extremes of purely biological sexual orientation and external sexual composition.

Con-sential homosexuality suggests that a mutual agreement, either conscious or subconscious, positive or negative, emerges between an individual outside of the sexual norm and his culture. A space, jointly created by the self and other, takes shape in which an essentially homosexual person agrees (consents) to express this difference by conforming to the arbitrary social boundaries established to define him. Not limited to sexual identity, con-sential dynamics also take place regarding race, gender, and other social distinctions. This interpersonal relationship explains both the varieties of gay subcultures, often binary poles where two cultures clash, as well as the common tension between expression and repression, individual protest and public policing. Self-recognition and/or cultural regulation of the homosexual individual may result in a celebrated, elevated position (usually in Eastern and aboriginal communities) or in criminal or fatal catastrophe (as often seen in Western and Christian societies). Homosexuality is the metaphorical seed (essentialism), culture the rich or poor soil (social climate), and expression of sexuality in a given time and place is the resulting plant that may be thwarted and thorny, lush and blooming, or pruned somewhere in between. This dynamic is also reciprocal: a hearty seed can loosen the hardest soil. Thus, essentially gay members can shape themselves to social confines or cultivate new forms that the existing culture may tolerate. For instance, Halleck did not find himself in puritanical models of nonconsensual sodomy, and yet he consented to utilize the criminal motif as the central symbol in writing about his love for another man—which in turn promoted a homosexual literary tradition accepted by the mainstream. Although this book generally applies "sodomite," "homosexual," and "gay" with regard to the era under discussion, the employment of these terms is potentially misleading since the reader cannot fully disregard the connotation bound to each word.

Second, the question, "What's a gay man like Halleck doing in the nineteenth century?" functions at a sexual level which is quite literal. What were homosexual men doing with one another in the nineteenth century? Fellatio, anal intercourse, and mutual masturbation between men represent the majority of applications of sodomy law in early American texts predating the term "homosexual," which did not appear in any American document before 1890 and was not in common use until more than thirty years after that.[31] In 1850, Melville wrote that Hawthorne had "dropped germinous seeds into my soul" and had "shot his strong New England roots into the hot soil of my soul." Was his review expressing genteel love or did he just want to get plowed? Did he even know himself? Similarly, Halleck chose to clothe his sentiments for Drake in sexually charged metaphors as well as modified marriage (same-sex holy union). Melville's scatological figurativeness has more in common with the homosexual pattern of an earlier American period than his own.

Colonial literature suggests that anal intercourse was the preferred application of male sodomy, whereas letters of American Romanticism suggest that fellatio and mutual masturbation had become the homosexual experiences of choice. Since most of the recorded male-male acts of colonial America and early Federalism are court cases for nonconsensual sodomy or male rape between men of significant economic or age differences, it is not surprising that anal intercourse, also known as Greek sex, prevailed in these violent power struggles. Masturbation and fellatio would be harder to force. Ideology may have reinforced the physical preference for anal intercourse in that classical culture, which depicted anal rather than oral pederasty, was more influential in earlier American literature.

Fellatio, like mutual masturbation, implies consent. Curiously, fellatio and mutual masturbation appear in American documents more commonly from the advent of the new democracy. Both acts suggest an egalitarian model of homosexuality; evidently, same-sex relations of the nineteenth century were increasingly held between men of common age, class, and education. Halleck himself moved from adolescent associations with foreign men beneath his social status to his adult infatuations with co-workers and particularly with Drake, who almost perfectly matched Halleck's age, income, and professional standing.

Just as one does not consciously consider one's parents as sexual beings, our culture is notably squeamish about the sex lives of our collective forefathers. The psychological need to desexualize the past does not diminish the intellectual probability that sexual relations in earlier American history were ardently pursued in all known and sundry varieties. Our comfort level with nineteenth-century homoeroticism is high because the term effectively (and ironically) negates homosexual activity and actuality. The visualization of sucking and fucking by nineteenth-century men strikes most Americans as incongruous with the age. But the recent scholarship of Patricia Cline Cohen on a New York prostitute murdered in 1836 and Janet Farrell Brodie on abortion in nineteenth-century America clearly demonstrate that Halleck's heterosexual neighbors were sexually active and knowledgeable. There is reason to believe that homosexual activity was equally lurid and present. While a soldier was executed for engaging in same-sex activity in 1660s New Amsterdam, same-sex unions in the homosocial New York of the 1840s and 1850s "might well have been taken as an extension of existing norms rather than a flagrant transgression of them."[32] While constructionists may argue that moderns invented sexual orientation, they certainly did not invent sex.

The third layer of rhetoric in the question, What's a gay man like Halleck doing in the nineteenth century? ponders the value of visiting past sexualities. For one thing, this study of Halleck provides a measure of our present progress (or lack thereof) regarding American masculinities. For example, the masculine types of the past (dandies, fops, rakes, aesthetics, athletes, and actors) have respective modern equivalents that additionally define sexuality (queens, fags, jocks, bottoms, butches, and actors). Such rigid sexual categories suggest that Americans have grown less comfortable with the ambiguity of male sexual genres. The reader may experience some small sense of Halleck's psychological discomfort in an era lacking the extraordinary labels and dichotomies that, however artificially, soothe the modern sensibility.

Gay academics appear equally distressed outside of absolute ideas. This angst can lead to premature interpretations of the past based upon insufficient data. With every new leaf of archival material rediscovered, I am more convinced that we have failed to excavate enough material on past consensual homosexuality to espouse many theories about it. Nineteenth-century scholars have particularly narrowed their focus on Whitman, as though he is a fair representation of an immensely complex and varied American society. In fact, Whitman's pederastic gaze was conspicuously aimed at boys who were almost exclusively blue-collar youths of inferior education (preferably illiterate). Whitman, unlike his predecessor Halleck who sought an egalitarian and committed connection, represents a gay throwback to the ancient Greek model.

The past is crucial for understanding our current mistakes in framing sexuality and its history. As African Americans and feminists know, public voices and private silences have perpetuated American myths for centuries. Panting beneath heterosexual and homosexual sex, there is often love, but—as critics, scholars, and theorists—we never seem to know what to make of it. Most academics argue their way through the genderfied purgatory of nineteenth-century American sexuality, while only a few invoke its emotional content. Halleck's internal turmoil was not cerebral. He openly expressed physical disdain for women; his "central emotional direction"[33] was toward men, to whom he was intensely attracted. Alongside these fundamental observations regarding his feelings of love, Halleck simultaneously denied that he could be "in" love with a man.

Though shrouded by a century of neglect, Halleck's writing reveals more than an anomaly that contradicts historical assumptions about sex and art in nineteenth-century America. Just as the statue suggests that his poetry was of special significance in his time, his decanonization tells us a great deal about America since the *New York Tribune*'s assessment a decade after Halleck's death:

> To-day, for the first time, an American author will receive the honor of a commemorative statue. Busts, shafts, or tablets have been erected to others of the guild of letters, but Fitz-Greene Halleck is the first to be monumentally treated as the equal of statesmen, divines, and inventors. . . . no reader of to-day can fairly estimate the service he rendered, without intimate knowledge of that earlier day when each of his poems was at once a surprise and a prophecy.[34]

Halleck's lines contained emotional contradictions and communal conflicts that have yet to be fully appreciated.

The discrepancy between Halleck's cultural autonomy and professed nationalism was related to his disruption of conventional romance. Unable to conform to the American dream, he favored the amorphous metaphor. Perhaps a complete disclosure of earlier homosexual aesthetics is not possible, but Halleck's expression of his love for a dashing young doctor was not entirely turned to stone with him.

Notes

1. *Memorial* 43; Wilson, "Recollections" 175; Anderson, "From These Roots." The *New York Tribune* estimated only thirty thousand in attendance ("Halleck Statue" 17).

2. In Wilson, *Letters* 494-96; in Adkins 408.

3. In "Halleck Statue," *Harper's Weekly* 425.

4. Curtis 422.

5. Taylor, "Fitz-Greene Hallock," *North American Review* 60.

6. In *Memorial* 51.

7. In Duyckinck, "Fitz-Greene Halleck" 238; in Adkins 337.

8. In Adkins 354; in Wilson, *Letters* 558.

9. These and numerous other regrets are reproduced in *Memorial* 39, 40, 35, respectively.

10. Lee, "150 Years" 1.

11. "Halleck Monument," *New Haven Palladium* 19; *Memorial* 13.

12. Rutherford 153.

13. Dunning C19. Lee's "Famed Local Poet Snubbed" was a rebuttal to the *Times*'s minimizing Halleck's fame.

14. Tierney 18. Warren Reiss's letter refuted Tierney and asserted Halleck's significance (8).

15. See Poe's reputation in Parks 4; Moss 55. Poe, "The Literati" 14.

16. Stevens 484, emphasis in original; Poe, "Fitz-Greene Halleck" 160.

17. Bryant, "Fitz-Greene Halleck" 520.

18. "American Poetry," *New York Times* 5, col 1; Hutchinson 6.

19. "Poetry of Fitz-Greene Halleck" 553-54; Lathrop 721. Halleck's second edition of *Fanny,* expanded by fifty stanzas, was published in 1821.

20. A. Quinn 261.

21. Adkins 231.

22. Poe, "The Literati" 14.

23. Lawson 348.

24. Lathrop 726.

25. In Adkins 339.

26. In Wilson, *Letters* 536.

27. Stevens 484.

28. In Wilson, *Letters* 525.

29. Ibid. 5-6.

30. Adkins 219.

31. Katz, *Almanac* 45; Halperin, *Hundred Years* 17.

32. Burrows and Wallace 58-59, 797.

33. R. K. Martin, *Tradition* 91. Martin defines Halleck and other premodern homosexual poets with this phrase.

34. Taylor in *Memorial* 60.

Bibliography

Adkins, Nelson Frederick. *Fitz-Greene Halleck: An Early Knickerbocker Wit and Poet.* New Haven, Conn.: Yale University Press, 1930.

Anderson, Beverly. "From These Roots." *Shore Line Times* [Guilford, Conn.] November 16, 1980.

Boswell, John. "Revolutions, Universals, and Sexual Categories." Duberman, Vicinus, and Chauncey 17-36.

Bryant, William Cullen, and George Palmer Putnam. *Memorial of James Fenimore Cooper.* New York: G. P. Putnam, 1852.

Burrows, Edwin G., and Mike Wallace. *Gotham: A History of New York City to 1898.* New York: Oxford University Press, 1999.

Curtis, George William. "Halleck Commemoration." *Harper's Weekly* June 2, 1877: 422.

Drake, Joseph Rodman. *The Culprit Fay and Other Works.* 1835. Ed. Janet DeKay. New York: G. Dearborn, 1859.

———. Miscellaneous Papers. New York: New York Public Library Rare Manuscripts Department.

———. "To Fitz-Greene Halleck." *New York Mirror* March 4, 1832: 1.

"Drake." *New York Daily Tribune* January 6, 1881: 4-6.

"Drake's Poems." *American Monthly* September 1835: 65-78.

"Drake's Poems." *New York Mirror* November 21, 1835: 164-65.

Dunning, Jennifer. "A Central Park Tour: Who's Who in Stone." *New York Times* November 21, 1980: C1+.

Duyckinck, Evert A. "Fitz-Greene Halleck: With a Portrait by Horatio Greenough." *Putnam's* February 1868: 231-47.

"Gay for Life? Going Straight: The Uproar over Sexual 'Conversion'" *Newsweek* August 17, 1998.

Halleck, Fitz-Greene. *Alnwick Castle and Other Poems.* New York: G. and C. Carvill, 1827. 2d ed. New York: George Dearborn, 1836. 3d ed. New York: Harper and Brothers, 1845.

———. *Fanny.* New York: C. Wiley, 1819. 2d ed. New York: Wiley and Halstead, 1821; New York: W. L. Andrews, 1866.

———. *Fanny and Other Poems.* New York: Harper and Brothers, 1839.

———. Folder 1, Halleck Papers. New York Public Library Rare Manuscripts Department.

———. "The Indian Warrior." *Holt's Columbian* [New York] August 22, 1810.

———. "Joel Lewis Griffing, Esq'r." Letter printed for Charles F. Heartman. New York: Rutland, 1921. New-York Historical Society Manuscripts Room.

———. "Lines." *Holt's Columbian* [New York] July 22, 1814.

———. "Lines on the Late Doctor Joseph R. Drake; by a Friend." *Literary Gazette* February 24, 1821: 115.

———. *Lines to the Recorder.* New York: W. L. Andrews, 1866.

———. "Marco Botzares" ["Marco Bozzaris"]. Trans. George D. Canale. Cambridge, Mass.: Welch, Bigelow, 1859.

———. "Memory." *New York Times* February 2, 1868: 2.

———. *Poems by Fitz-Greene Halleck.* New York: Harper and Brothers, 1839.

———. *Poetical Works of Fitz-Greene Halleck.* New York: D. Appleton, 1847.

———. *Poetical Writings of Fitz-Greene Halleck: With Abstracts of Those from Joseph Rodman Drake.* 1852. Ed. James Grant Wilson. New York: D. Appleton, 1869; New York: Greenwood Press, 1969.

———. Special Collections. Columbia University Rare Books and Manuscripts Library, New York.

———. "Strong as That Power. . . ." *New York Times* February 2, 1868.

———. Untitled lines on the Ugly Club. *Holt's Columbian* [New York] January 19, 1815.

———. *Young America.* New York: D. Appleton, 1865.

———, ed. *Selections from the British Poets.* 2 vols. New York: Harper and Brothers, 1840.

———, ed. *Works of Lord Byron: In Verse and Prose, Including His Letters, Journals, etc., with a Sketch of His Life.* 1834. 2d ed. New York: George Dearborn, 1836.

———, and Joseph Rodman Drake. *Croakers.* 1819. New York: Bradford Club, 1860.

Halleck, Reuben Post. *History of American Literature.* New York: American, 1911.

"Halleck and Bryant." *Literary Gazette* July 25, 1819: 483.

"Halleck Monument." Folder 1, Halleck Papers. New York Public Library Rare Manuscripts Department.

"Halleck Monument." *New Haven Palladium* July 9, 1869: 19-20.

"Halleck Monument." *New York Evening Post.* n.d. Folder 1, Halleck Papers. New York Public Library Rare Manuscripts Department.

"Halleck Monument." *New York Times* July 9, 1869: 5.

"Halleck's Monument." *Harper's Weekly* September 26, 1868.

"Halleck Statue." *Harper's Weekly* June 2, 1877: 425.

"Halleck Statue." *New York Tribune* May 16, 1877: 17.

Halperin, David M. *"One Hundred Years of Homosexuality" and Other Essays on Greek Love.* New York: Routledge, 1990.

———. *Saint Foucault: Towards a Gay Hagiography.* New York: Oxford University Press, 1995.

———. "Sex before Sexuality: Pederasty, Politics, and Power in Classical Athens." Duberman, Vicinus, and Chauncey 37-53.

Katz, Jonathan. "The Early Nineteenth-Century Organization of Love." *The Invention of Heterosexuality.* New York: Dutton-Penguin, 1995. 40-47.

———. *Gay American History: Lesbians and Gay Men in the U.S.A.* New York: Harper and Row, 1985.

———. *Gay/Lesbian Almanac.* New York: Harper and Row, 1983.

Lathrop, George Parsons. "Fitz-Greene Halleck." *Atlantic Monthly* June 1877: 718-29.

Lawson, James. "Fitz-Greene Halleck: Moral and Mental Portrait Series." *Southern Literary Messenger* April 1842: 341-49. Reprinted in *New World* November 25, 1843: 718-29.

Lee, Kenneth R. "Famed Local Poet Snubbed." *Shore Line Times* [Guilford, Conn.] November 16, 1988.

———. Letter. *Shore Line Times* [Guilford, Conn.] December 4, 1980.

———. "150 Years Ago—Fitz-Greene Halleck." *Shore Line Times* [Guilford, Conn.] November 8, 1977: 1-3.

Martin, Robert K. *The Homosexual Tradition in American Poetry.* Austin: University of Texas Press, 1979.

Moss, Sidney P. *Poe's Literary Battles: The Critic in the Context of His Literary Milieu.* Durham, N.C.: Duke University Press, 1963.

Norton, Rictor. *The Myth of the Modern Homosexual: Queer History and the Search for Cultural Unity.* Washington, D.C.: Cassell, 1997.

Parks, Edd Winfield. *Edgar Allan Poe as Literary Critic.* Athens: University of Georgia Press, 1964.

Poe, Edgar Allan. "Critical Notices, Drake-Halleck." *Southern Literary Messenger* April 1836: 326-36. Reprinted in *Southern Literary Messenger* June 2, 1877.

———. "Fitz-Greene Halleck: With a Portrait by Henry Inman." *Graham's* September 1843: 160-63.

———. "The Literati of New York City—No. III: Some Honest Opinions at Random Respecting Their Auctorial Merits, with Occasional Words of Personality. Fitz-Greene Halleck." *Godey's Magazine and Lady's Book* July 1846: 13-15.

———. *The Poets and Poetry of America; a Satire.* 1847. New York: Benjamin and Bell, 1887.

Quinn, Arthur Hobson, ed. *The Literature of the American People: An Historical and Critical Survey.* New York: Appleton-Century-Crofts, 1951.

Reiss, Warren P. "An Ode to Fitz." Letter to the editor. *New York Times Magazine* July 13, 1997: 8.

Rutherford, Mildred. *American Authors.* Atlanta: Franklin Press, 1894.

Stevens, Abel, ed. "Fitz-Greene Halleck." *National Magazine* December 1852: 481-87.

Taylor, Bayard. "Fitz-Greene Halleck." *New York Tribune* May 15, 1877: 20-21.

———. "Fitz-Greene Halleck." *North American Review* July 1877: 60-67.

———. *Joseph and His Friend: A Story of Pennsylvania.* New York: Putnam, 1903.

———. *The Lands of the Saracens: Or, Pictures of Palestine, Asia Minor, Sicily and Spain.* 1855. New York: Putnam's Sons, 1881.

Tierney, John. "An Ode to Fitz." *New York Times Magazine* June 22, 1997.

Wharton, Edith. *Summer.* Introd. Marilyn French. New York: Macmillan, 1981.

Whitman, Walt. *Leaves of Grass.* Eds. Sculley Bradley and Harold W. Blodgett. New York: Norton, 1973.

Wilson, James Grant. *Bryant and His Friends: Some Reminiscences of the Knickerbocker Writers.* New York: Fords, Howard and Hulbert, 1886.

———. "Fitz-Greene Halleck." *New York Ledger* January 25, 1868.

———. "Halleck and His Theatrical Friends." *Potter's American Monthly* March 1875: 217-22.

———. "Halleckiana." *Independent* February 1872.

———. "Joseph Rodman Drake." *Harper's New Monthly* June 1874: 65-71.

———. *Life and Letters of Fitz-Greene Halleck.* New York: D. Appleton, 1869.

———. "Poet Halleck." *Littell's Living Age* December 12, 1868: 701-3.

———. "Recollections of American Authors, No. 5. Fitz-Greene Halleck." *Book News Monthly* November 1911: 170-76.

———, and John Fiske. *Appleton's Cyclopaedia of American Biography.* Vol. 3. New York: D. Appleton, 1888.

FURTHER READING

Criticism

Cocks, H. G. "Reading the Sodomite." In *Nameless Offences: Homosexual Desire in the Nineteenth Century.* London: Tauris, 2003, 258 p.

Provides an overview of the vocabulary and conceptual framework used to define homosexuality during the nineteenth century.

Cooke, Mervyn. "Homosexuality in *Billy Budd.*" In *Melville's Short Novels: Authoritative Texts, Contexts, Criticism,* edited by Dan McCall, pp. 359-61. New York: W. W. Norton, 2002.

Argues for the central importance of homosexual desire in *Billy Budd.*

Dellamora, Richard. "Stupid Trollope." *Victorian Newsletter* 100 (fall 2001): 22-6.

Traces Anthony Trollope's sociocultural and political ideals to the author's desire for "a respectable male homosocial conviviality."

Eells, Emily. *Proust's Cup of Tea: Homoeroticism and Victorian Culture.* Aldershot, England: Ashgate, 2002, 220 p.

Asserts "that in addition to significant other cultural references . . . Proust used Victorian culture as one of the sustained referents in his construction of the aesthetics of homosexuality."

Emery, Kim. "Steers, Queers, and Manifest Destiny: Representing the Lesbian Subject in Turn-of-the-Century Texas." *Journal of the History of Sexuality* 5, no. 1 (July 1994): 26-57.

Traces the efforts of John Carhart to define "lesbian identity within the context of turn-of the-century U.S. culture" in his novel *Norma Trist; or, Pure Carbon: A Story of the Inversion of the Sexes,* and asserts that Carhart's goal determines his narrative strategy.

Gold, Barri J. "The Domination of Dorian Gray." *Victorian Newsletter* 91 (spring 1997): 27-30.

Explores the representation of the desire for domination alongside homosexual and heterosexual desire in *The Picture of Dorian Gray.*

Kolb, Jack. "Hallam, Tennyson, Homosexuality and the Critics." *Philological Quarterly* 79, no. 3 (summer 2000): 365-96.

Surveys critical debate over the nature of the relationship between Arthur Henry Hallam and Alfred, Lord Tennyson, and questions the validity of the interpretation of biographical and historical details by recent critics.

Markley, A. A. "Tainted Wethers of the Flock: Homosexuality and Homosocial Desire in Mary Shelley's Novels." *Keats-Shelley Review* 13 (1999): 115-33.

Considers what Mary Shelley's treatment of male-male relations in her novels reveals about the author's attitudes toward homosexuality.

McColley, Kathleen. "Claiming Center Stage: Speaking Out for Homoerotic Empowerment in *The Bostonians.*" *Henry James Review* 21, no. 2 (spring 2000): 151-69.

Maintains that James uses the lesbian relationship depicted in *The Bostonians* to explore new alternatives to traditional ideology and patriarchal culture.

McGavran, James Holt. "'Insurmountable Barriers to Our Union': Homosocial Male Bonding, Homosexual Panic, and Death on the Ice in *Frankenstein.*" *European Romantic Review* 11, no. 1 (winter 2000): 46-67.

Approaches *Frankenstein* from a feminist and queer theory perspective, contending that Shelley uses the relationship between Victor and his monster to illustrate the destructive qualities of overwhelming male homoerotic desire and homophobia.

Morgan, Thaïs E. "Male Lesbian Bodies: The Construction of Alternative Masculinities in Courbet, Baudelaire, and Swinburne." *Genders* 15 (winter 1992): 37-57.

Examines the varied goals of nineteenth-century male French authors' and artists' depictions of lesbians in their works.

Schor, Naomi. "Male Lesbianism." *GLQ: A Journal of Lesbian and Gay Studies* 7, no. 3 (2001): 391-99.

Considers male authors' and artists' appropriation of lesbian subjects as a means of escaping the demands of masculinity in turn-of-the-century France.

How to Use This Index

The main references

> **Calvino, Italo**
>   1923-1985 .... CLC **5, 8, 11, 22, 33, 39,**
>   **73; SSC 3, 48**

list all author entries in the following Thomson Gale Literary Criticism series:

AAL = Asian American Literature
BG = The Beat Generation: A Gale Critical Companion
BLC = Black Literature Criticism
BLCS = Black Literature Criticism Supplement
CLC = Contemporary Literary Criticism
CLR = Children's Literature Review
CMLC = Classical and Medieval Literature Criticism
DC = Drama Criticism
FL = Feminism in Literature: A Gale Critical Companion
GL = Gothic Literature: A Gale Critical Companion
HLC = Hispanic Literature Criticism
HLCS = Hispanic Literature Criticism Supplement
HR = Harlem Renaissance: A Gale Critical Companion
LC = Literature Criticism from 1400 to 1800
NCLC = Nineteenth-Century Literature Criticism
NNAL = Native North American Literature
PC = Poetry Criticism
SSC = Short Story Criticism
TCLC = Twentieth-Century Literary Criticism
WLC = World Literature Criticism, 1500 to the Present
WLCS = World Literature Criticism Supplement

The cross-references

> See also CA 85-88, 116; CANR 23, 61;
> DAM NOV; DLB 196; EW 13; MTCW 1, 2;
> RGSF 2; RGWL 2; SFW 4; SSFS 12

list all author entries in the following Thomson Gale biographical and literary sources:

AAYA = Authors & Artists for Young Adults
AFAW = African American Writers
AFW = African Writers
AITN = Authors in the News
AMW = American Writers
AMWR = American Writers Retrospective Supplement
AMWS = American Writers Supplement
ANW = American Nature Writers
AW = Ancient Writers
BEST = Bestsellers
BPFB = Beacham's Encyclopedia of Popular Fiction: Biography and Resources
BRW = British Writers
BRWS = British Writers Supplement
BW = Black Writers
BYA = Beacham's Guide to Literature for Young Adults
CA = Contemporary Authors
CAAS = Contemporary Authors Autobiography Series
CABS = Contemporary Authors Bibliographical Series
CAD = Contemporary American Dramatists
CANR = Contemporary Authors New Revision Series
CAP = Contemporary Authors Permanent Series
CBD = Contemporary British Dramatists
CCA = Contemporary Canadian Authors
CD = Contemporary Dramatists
CDALB = Concise Dictionary of American Literary Biography

CDALBS = *Concise Dictionary of American Literary Biography Supplement*
CDBLB = *Concise Dictionary of British Literary Biography*
CMW = *St. James Guide to Crime & Mystery Writers*
CN = *Contemporary Novelists*
CP = *Contemporary Poets*
CPW = *Contemporary Popular Writers*
CSW = *Contemporary Southern Writers*
CWD = *Contemporary Women Dramatists*
CWP = *Contemporary Women Poets*
CWRI = *St. James Guide to Children's Writers*
CWW = *Contemporary World Writers*
DA = *DISCovering Authors*
DA3 = *DISCovering Authors 3.0*
DAB = *DISCovering Authors: British Edition*
DAC = *DISCovering Authors: Canadian Edition*
DAM = *DISCovering Authors: Modules*
   DRAM: *Dramatists Module;* **MST:** *Most-studied Authors Module;*
   MULT: *Multicultural Authors Module;* **NOV:** *Novelists Module;*
   POET: *Poets Module;* **POP:** *Popular Fiction and Genre Authors Module*
DFS = *Drama for Students*
DLB = *Dictionary of Literary Biography*
DLBD = *Dictionary of Literary Biography Documentary Series*
DLBY = *Dictionary of Literary Biography Yearbook*
DNFS = *Literature of Developing Nations for Students*
EFS = *Epics for Students*
EXPN = *Exploring Novels*
EXPP = *Exploring Poetry*
EXPS = *Exploring Short Stories*
EW = *European Writers*
FANT = *St. James Guide to Fantasy Writers*
FW = *Feminist Writers*
GFL = *Guide to French Literature,* Beginnings to 1789, 1798 to the Present
GLL = *Gay and Lesbian Literature*
HGG = *St. James Guide to Horror, Ghost & Gothic Writers*
HW = *Hispanic Writers*
IDFW = *International Dictionary of Films and Filmmakers: Writers and Production Artists*
IDTP = *International Dictionary of Theatre: Playwrights*
LAIT = *Literature and Its Times*
LAW = *Latin American Writers*
JRDA = *Junior DISCovering Authors*
MAICYA = *Major Authors and Illustrators for Children and Young Adults*
MAICYAS = *Major Authors and Illustrators for Children and Young Adults Supplement*
MAWW = *Modern American Women Writers*
MJW = *Modern Japanese Writers*
MTCW = *Major 20th-Century Writers*
NCFS = *Nonfiction Classics for Students*
NFS = *Novels for Students*
PAB = *Poets: American and British*
PFS = *Poetry for Students*
RGAL = *Reference Guide to American Literature*
RGEL = *Reference Guide to English Literature*
RGSF = *Reference Guide to Short Fiction*
RGWL = *Reference Guide to World Literature*
RHW = *Twentieth-Century Romance and Historical Writers*
SAAS = *Something about the Author Autobiography Series*
SATA = *Something about the Author*
SFW = *St. James Guide to Science Fiction Writers*
SSFS = *Short Stories for Students*
TCWW = *Twentieth-Century Western Writers*
WLIT = *World Literature and Its Times*
WP = *World Poets*
YABC = *Yesterday's Authors of Books for Children*
YAW = *St. James Guide to Young Adult Writers*

Literary Criticism Series
Cumulative Author Index

Alexander, Lloyd (Chudley) 1924- ... **CLC 35**
    See also AAYA 1, 27; BPFB 1; BYA 5, 6,
    7, 9, 10, 11; CA 1-4R; CANR 1, 24, 38,
    55, 113; CLR 1, 5, 48; CWRI 5; DLB 52;
    FANT; JRDA; MAICYA 1, 2; MAICYAS
    1; MTCW 1; SAAS 19; SATA 3, 49, 81,
    129, 135; SUFW; TUS; WYA; YAW
Alexander, Meena 1951- .... **CLC 121**
    See also CA 115; CANR 38, 70, 146; CP 5,
    6, 7; CWP; DLB 323; FW
Alexander, Samuel 1859-1938 .... **TCLC 77**
Alexeiev, Konstantin
    See Stanislavsky, Constantin
Alexeyev, Constantin Sergeivich
    See Stanislavsky, Constantin
Alexeyev, Konstantin Sergeyevich
    See Stanislavsky, Constantin
Alexie, Sherman 1966- .... **CLC 96, 154;**
    NNAL; PC 53
    See also AAYA 28; BYA 15; CA 138;
    CANR 65, 95, 133; CN 7; DA3; DAM
    MULT; DLB 175, 206, 278; LATS 1:2;
    MTCW 2; MTFW 2005; NFS 17; SSFS
    18
al-Farabi 870(?)-950 .... **CMLC 58**
    See also DLB 115
Alfau, Felipe 1902-1999 .... **CLC 66**
    See also CA 137
Alfieri, Vittorio 1749-1803 .... **NCLC 101**
    See also EW 4; RGWL 2, 3; WLIT 7
Alfonso X 1221-1284 .... **CMLC 78**
Alfred, Jean Gaston
    See Ponge, Francis
Alger, Horatio, Jr. 1832-1899 .... **NCLC 8, 83**
    See also CLR 87; DLB 42; LAIT 2; RGAL
    4; SATA 16; TUS
Al-Ghazali, Muhammad ibn Muhammad
    1058-1111 .... **CMLC 50**
    See also DLB 115
Algren, Nelson 1909-1981 ..... **CLC 4, 10, 33;**
    SSC 33
    See also AMWS 9; BPFB 1; CA 13-16R;
    CAAS 103; CANR 20, 61; CDALB 1941-
    1968; CN 1, 2; DLB 9; DLBY 1981,
    1982, 2000; EWL 3; MAL 5; MTCW 1,
    2; MTFW 2005; RGAL 4; RGSF 2
al-Hariri, al-Qasim ibn 'Ali Abu
    Muhammad al-Basri
    1054-1122 .... **CMLC 63**
    See also RGWL 3
Ali, Ahmed 1908-1998 .... **CLC 69**
    See also CA 25-28R; CANR 15, 34; CN 1,
    2, 3, 4, 5; DLB 323; EWL 3
Ali, Tariq 1943- .... **CLC 173**
    See also CA 25-28R; CANR 10, 99
Alighieri, Dante
    See Dante
    See also WLIT 7
al-Kindi, Abu Yusuf Ya'qub ibn Ishaq c.
    801-c. 873 .... **CMLC 80**
Allan, John B.
    See Westlake, Donald E.
Allan, Sidney
    See Hartmann, Sadakichi
Allan, Sydney
    See Hartmann, Sadakichi
Allard, Janet .... **CLC 59**
Allen, Edward 1948- .... **CLC 59**
Allen, Fred 1894-1956 .... **TCLC 87**
Allen, Paula Gunn 1939- .... **CLC 84, 202;**
    NNAL
    See also AMWS 4; CA 143; CAAE 112;
    CANR 63, 130; CWP; DA3; DAM
    MULT; DLB 175; FW; MTCW 2; MTFW
    2005; RGAL 4; TCWW 2
Allen, Roland
    See Ayckbourn, Alan
Allen, Sarah A.
    See Hopkins, Pauline Elizabeth

Allen, Sidney H.
    See Hartmann, Sadakichi
Allen, Woody 1935- .... **CLC 16, 52, 195**
    See also AAYA 10, 51; AMWS 15; CA 33-
    36R; CANR 27, 38, 63, 128; DAM POP;
    DLB 44; MTCW 1; SSFS 21
Allende, Isabel 1942- ... **CLC 39, 57, 97, 170;**
    HLC 1; SSC 65; WLCS
    See also AAYA 18, 70; CA 130; CAAE 125;
    CANR 51, 74, 129; CDWLB 3; CLR 99;
    CWW 2; DA3; DAM MULT, NOV; DLB
    145; DNFS 1; EWL 3; FL 1:5; FW; HW
    1, 2; INT CA-130; LAIT 5; LAWS 1;
    LMFS 2; MTCW 1, 2; MTFW 2005;
    NCFS 1; NFS 6, 18; RGSF 2; RGWL 3;
    SATA 163; SSFS 11, 16; WLIT 1
Alleyn, Ellen
    See Rossetti, Christina
Alleyne, Carla D. .... **CLC 65**
Allingham, Margery (Louise)
    1904-1966 .... **CLC 19**
    See also CA 5-8R; CAAS 25-28R; CANR
    4, 58; CMW 4; DLB 77; MSW; MTCW
    1, 2
Allingham, William 1824-1889 ...... **NCLC 25**
    See also DLB 35; RGEL 2
Allison, Dorothy E. 1949- .... **CLC 78, 153**
    See also AAYA 53; CA 140; CANR 66, 107;
    CN 7; CSW; DA3; FW; MTCW 2; MTFW
    2005; NFS 11; RGAL 4
Alloula, Malek .... **CLC 65**
Allston, Washington 1779-1843 .... **NCLC 2**
    See also DLB 1, 235
Almedingen, E. M. .... **CLC 12**
    See Almedingen, Martha Edith von
    See also SATA 3
Almedingen, Martha Edith von 1898-1971
    See Almedingen, E. M.
    See also CA 1-4R; CANR 1
Almodovar, Pedro 1949(?)- .... **CLC 114, 229;**
    HLCS 1
    See also CA 133; CANR 72, 151; HW 2
Almqvist, Carl Jonas Love
    1793-1866 .... **NCLC 42**
al-Mutanabbi, Ahmad ibn al-Husayn Abu
    al-Tayyib al-Jufi al-Kindi
    915-965 .... **CMLC 66**
    See Mutanabbi, Al-
    See also RGWL 3
Alonso, Damaso 1898-1990 .... **CLC 14**
    See also CA 131; CAAE 110; CAAS 130;
    CANR 72; DLB 108; EWL 3; HW 1, 2
Alov
    See Gogol, Nikolai (Vasilyevich)
al'Sadaawi, Nawal
    See El Saadawi, Nawal
    See also FW
al-Shaykh, Hanan 1945- .... **CLC 218**
    See Shaykh, al- Hanan
    See also CA 135; CANR 111; WLIT 6
Al Siddik
    See Rolfe, Frederick (William Serafino Aus-
    tin Lewis Mary)
    See also GLL 1; RGEL 2
Alta 1942- .... **CLC 19**
    See also CA 57-60
Alter, Robert B. 1935- .... **CLC 34**
    See also CA 49-52; CANR 1, 47, 100, 160
Alter, Robert Bernard
    See Alter, Robert B.
Alther, Lisa 1944- .... **CLC 7, 41**
    See also BPFB 1; CA 65-68; 30; CANR 12,
    30, 51; CN 4, 5, 6, 7; CSW; GLL 2;
    MTCW 1
Althusser, L.
    See Althusser, Louis
Althusser, Louis 1918-1990 .... **CLC 106**
    See also CA 131; CAAS 132; CANR 102;
    DLB 242

Altman, Robert 1925-2006 .... **CLC 16, 116**
    See also CA 73-76; CAAS 254; CANR 43
Alurista .... **HLCS 1; PC 34**
    See Urista (Heredia), Alberto (Baltazar)
    See also CA 45-48R; DLB 82; LLW
Alvarez, A. 1929- .... **CLC 5, 13**
    See also CA 1-4R; CANR 3, 33, 63, 101,
    134; CN 3, 4, 5, 6; CP 1, 2, 3, 4, 5, 6, 7;
    DLB 14, 40; MTFW 2005
Alvarez, Alejandro Rodriguez 1903-1965
    See Casona, Alejandro
    See also CA 131; CAAS 93-96; HW 1
Alvarez, Julia 1950- .... **CLC 93; HLCS 1**
    See also AAYA 25; AMWS 7; CA 147;
    CANR 69, 101, 133; DA3; DLB 282;
    LATS 1:2; LLW; MTCW 2; MTFW 2005;
    NFS 5, 9; SATA 129; WLIT 1
Alvaro, Corrado 1896-1956 .... **TCLC 60**
    See also CA 163; DLB 264; EWL 3
Amado, Jorge 1912-2001 ... **CLC 13, 40, 106,**
    232; HLC 1
    See also CA 77-80; CAAS 201; CANR 35,
    74, 135; CWW 2; DAM MULT, NOV;
    DLB 113, 307; EWL 3; HW 2; LAW;
    LAWS 1; MTCW 1, 2; MTFW 2005;
    RGWL 2, 3; TWA; WLIT 1
Ambler, Eric 1909-1998 .... **CLC 4, 6, 9**
    See also BRWS 4; CA 9-12R; CAAS 171;
    CANR 7, 38, 74; CMW 4; CN 1, 2, 3, 4,
    5, 6; DLB 77; MSW; MTCW 1, 2; TEA
Ambrose, Stephen E. 1936-2002 .... **CLC 145**
    See also AAYA 44; CA 1-4R; CAAS 209;
    CANR 3, 43, 57, 83, 105; MTFW 2005;
    NCFS 2; SATA 40, 138
Amichai, Yehuda 1924-2000 .. **CLC 9, 22, 57,**
    116; PC 38
    See also CA 85-88; CAAS 189; CANR 46,
    60, 99, 132; CWW 2; EWL 3; MTCW 1,
    2; MTFW 2005; PFS 24; RGHL; WLIT 6
Amichai, Yehudah
    See Amichai, Yehuda
Amiel, Henri Frederic 1821-1881 .... **NCLC 4**
    See also DLB 217
Amis, Kingsley 1922-1995 . **CLC 1, 2, 3, 5, 8,**
    13, 40, 44, 129
    See also AITN 2; BPFB 1; BRWS 2; CA
    9-12R; CAAS 150; CANR 8, 28, 54; CD-
    BLB 1945-1960; CN 1, 2, 3, 4, 5, 6; CP
    1, 2, 3, 4; DA; DA3; DAB; DAC; DAM
    MST, NOV; DLB 15, 27, 100, 139, 326;
    DLBY 1996; EWL 3; HGG; INT
    CANR-8; MTCW 1, 2; MTFW 2005;
    RGAL 2; RGSF 2; SFW 4
Amis, Martin 1949- ... **CLC 4, 9, 38, 62, 101,**
    213
    See also BEST 90:3; BRWS 4; CA 65-68;
    CANR 8, 27, 54, 73, 95, 132; CN 5, 6, 7;
    DA3; DLB 14, 194; EWL 3; INT CANR-
    27; MTCW 2; MTFW 2005
Ammianus Marcellinus c. 330-c.
    395 .... **CMLC 60**
    See also AW 2; DLB 211
Ammons, A.R. 1926-2001 .. **CLC 2, 3, 5, 8, 9,**
    25, 57, 108; PC 16
    See also AITN 1; AMWS 7; CA 9-12R;
    CAAS 193; CANR 6, 36, 51, 73, 107,
    156; CP 1, 2, 3, 4, 5, 6, 7; CSW; DAM
    POET; DLB 5, 165; EWL 3; MAL 5;
    MTCW 1, 2; PFS 19; RGAL 4; TCLE 1:1
Ammons, Archie Randolph
    See Ammons, A.R.
Amo, Tauraatua i
    See Adams, Henry (Brooks)
Amory, Thomas 1691(?)-1788 .... **LC 48**
    See also DLB 39
Anand, Mulk Raj 1905-2004 ...... **CLC 23, 93**
    See also CA 65-68; CAAS 231; CANR 32,
    64; CN 1, 2, 3, 4, 5, 6, 7; DAM NOV;
    DLB 323; EWL 3; MTCW 1, 2; MTFW
    2005; RGSF 2

Aragon, Louis 1897-1982 .... **CLC 3, 22; TCLC 123**
See also CA 69-72; CAAS 108; CANR 28, 71; DAM NOV, POET; DLB 72, 258; EW 11; EWL 3; GFL 1789 to the Present; GLL 2; LMFS 2; MTCW 1, 2; RGWL 2, 3

Arany, Janos 1817-1882 .... **NCLC 34**

Aranyos, Kakay 1847-1910
See Mikszath, Kalman

Aratus of Soli c. 315B.C.-c. 240B.C. .... **CMLC 64**
See also DLB 176

Arbuthnot, John 1667-1735 .... **LC 1**
See also DLB 101

Archer, Herbert Winslow
See Mencken, H(enry) L(ouis)

Archer, Jeffrey 1940- .... **CLC 28**
See also AAYA 16; BEST 89:3; BPFB 1; CA 77-80; CANR 22, 52, 95, 136; CPW; DA3; DAM POP; INT CANR-22; MTFW 2005

Archer, Jeffrey Howard
See Archer, Jeffrey

Archer, Jules 1915- .... **CLC 12**
See also CA 9-12R; CANR 6, 69; SAAS 5; SATA 4, 85

Archer, Lee
See Ellison, Harlan

Archilochus c. 7th cent. B.C.- .... **CMLC 44**
See also DLB 176

Arden, John 1930- .... **CLC 6, 13, 15**
See also BRWS 2; CA 13-16R; 4; CANR 31, 65, 67, 124; CBD; CD 5, 6; DAM DRAM; DFS 9; DLB 13, 245; EWL 3; MTCW 1

Arenas, Reinaldo 1943-1990 .. **CLC 41; HLC 1**
See also CA 128; CAAE 124; CAAS 133; CANR 73, 106; DAM MULT; DLB 145; EWL 3; GLL 2; HW 1; LAW; LAWS 1; MTCW 2; MTFW 2005; RGSF 2; RGWL 3; WLIT 1

Arendt, Hannah 1906-1975 .... **CLC 66, 98**
See also CA 17-20R; CAAS 61-64; CANR 26, 60; DLB 242; MTCW 1, 2

Aretino, Pietro 1492-1556 .... **LC 12**
See also RGWL 2, 3

Arghezi, Tudor .... **CLC 80**
See Theodorescu, Ion N.
See also CA 167; CDWLB 4; DLB 220; EWL 3

Arguedas, Jose Maria 1911-1969 .... **CLC 10, 18; HLCS 1; TCLC 147**
See also CA 89-92; CANR 73; DLB 113; EWL 3; HW 1; LAW; RGWL 2, 3; WLIT 1

Argueta, Manlio 1936- .... **CLC 31**
See also CA 131; CANR 73; CWW 2; DLB 145; EWL 3; HW 1; RGWL 3

Arias, Ron 1941- .... **HLC 1**
See also CA 131; CANR 81, 136; DAM MULT; DLB 82; HW 1, 2; MTCW 2; MTFW 2005

Ariosto, Lodovico
See Ariosto, Ludovico
See also WLIT 7

Ariosto, Ludovico 1474-1533 ... **LC 6, 87; PC 42**
See Ariosto, Lodovico
See also EW 2; RGWL 2, 3

Aristides
See Epstein, Joseph

Aristophanes 450B.C.-385B.C. .... **CMLC 4, 51; DC 2; WLCS**
See also AW 1; CDWLB 1; DA; DA3; DAB; DAC; DAM DRAM, MST; DFS 10; DLB 176; LMFS 1; RGWL 2, 3; TWA; WLIT 8

Aristotle 384B.C.-322B.C. .... **CMLC 31; WLCS**
See also AW 1; CDWLB 1; DA; DA3; DAB; DAC; DAM MST; DLB 176; RGWL 2, 3; TWA; WLIT 8

Arlt, Roberto (Godofredo Christophersen) 1900-1942 .... **HLC 1; TCLC 29**
See also CA 131; CAAE 123; CANR 67; DAM MULT; DLB 305; EWL 3; HW 1, 2; IDTP; LAW

Armah, Ayi Kwei 1939- . **BLC 1; CLC 5, 33, 136**
See also AFW; BRWS 10; BW 1; CA 61-64; CANR 21, 64; CDWLB 3; CN 1, 2, 3, 4, 5, 6, 7; DAM MULT, POET; DLB 117; EWL 3; MTCW 1; WLIT 2

Armatrading, Joan 1950- .... **CLC 17**
See also CA 186; CAAE 114

Armin, Robert 1568(?)-1615(?) .... **LC 120**

Armitage, Frank
See Carpenter, John (Howard)

Armstrong, Jeannette (C.) 1948- .... **NNAL**
See also CA 149; CCA 1; CN 6, 7; DAC; SATA 102

Arnette, Robert
See Silverberg, Robert

Arnim, Achim von (Ludwig Joachim von Arnim) 1781-1831 .. **NCLC 5, 159; SSC 29**
See also DLB 90

Arnim, Bettina von 1785-1859 ...... **NCLC 38, 123**
See also DLB 90; RGWL 2, 3

Arnold, Matthew 1822-1888 ..... **NCLC 6, 29, 89, 126; PC 5; WLC 1**
See also BRW 5; CDBLB 1832-1890; DA; DAB; DAC; DAM MST, POET; DLB 32, 57; EXPP; PAB; PFS 2; TEA; WP

Arnold, Thomas 1795-1842 .... **NCLC 18**
See also DLB 55

Arnow, Harriette (Louisa) Simpson 1908-1986 .... **CLC 2, 7, 18**
See also BPFB 1; CA 9-12R; CAAS 118; CANR 14; CN 2, 3, 4; DLB 6; FW; MTCW 1, 2; RHW; SATA 42; SATA-Obit 47

Arouet, Francois-Marie
See Voltaire

Arp, Hans
See Arp, Jean

Arp, Jean 1887-1966 .... **CLC 5; TCLC 115**
See also CA 81-84; CAAS 25-28R; CANR 42, 77; EW 10

Arrabal
See Arrabal, Fernando

Arrabal (Teran), Fernando
See Arrabal, Fernando
See also CWW 2

Arrabal, Fernando 1932- ... **CLC 2, 9, 18, 58**
See Arrabal (Teran), Fernando
See also CA 9-12R; CANR 15; DLB 321; EWL 3; LMFS 2

Arreola, Juan Jose 1918-2001 .... **CLC 147; HLC 1; SSC 38**
See also CA 131; CAAE 113; CAAS 200; CANR 81; CWW 2; DAM MULT; DLB 113; DNFS 2; EWL 3; HW 1, 2; LAW; RGSF 2

Arrian c. 89(?)-c. 155(?) .... **CMLC 43**
See also DLB 176

Arrick, Fran .... **CLC 30**
See Gaberman, Judie Angell
See also BYA 6

Arrley, Richmond
See Delany, Samuel R., Jr.

Artaud, Antonin (Marie Joseph) 1896-1948 .... **DC 14; TCLC 3, 36**
See also CA 149; CAAE 104; DA3; DAM DRAM; DFS 22; DLB 258, 321; EW 11; EWL 3; GFL 1789 to the Present; MTCW 2; MTFW 2005; RGWL 2, 3

Arthur, Ruth M(abel) 1905-1979 ..... **CLC 12**
See also CA 9-12R; CAAS 85-88; CANR 4; CWRI 5; SATA 7, 26

Artsybashev, Mikhail (Petrovich) 1878-1927 .... **TCLC 31**
See also CA 170; DLB 295

Arundel, Honor (Morfydd) 1919-1973 .... **CLC 17**
See also CA 21-22; CAAS 41-44R; CAP 2; CLR 35; CWRI 5; SATA 4; SATA-Obit 24

Arzner, Dorothy 1900-1979 .... **CLC 98**

Asch, Sholem 1880-1957 .... **TCLC 3**
See also CAAE 105; DLB 333; EWL 3; GLL 2; RGHL

Ascham, Roger 1516(?)-1568 .... **LC 101**
See also DLB 236

Ash, Shalom
See Asch, Sholem

Ashbery, John 1927- ... **CLC 2, 3, 4, 6, 9, 13, 15, 25, 41, 77, 125, 221; PC 26**
See Berry, Jonas
See also AMWS 3; CA 5-8R; CANR 9, 37, 66, 102, 132; CP 1, 2, 3, 4, 5, 6, 7; DA3; DAM POET; DLB 5, 165; DLBY 1981; EWL 3; INT CANR-9; MAL 5; MTCW 1, 2; MTFW 2005; PAB; PFS 11; RGAL 4; TCLE 1:1; WP

Ashdown, Clifford
See Freeman, R(ichard) Austin

Ashe, Gordon
See Creasey, John

Ashton-Warner, Sylvia (Constance) 1908-1984 .... **CLC 19**
See also CA 69-72; CAAS 112; CANR 29; CN 1, 2, 3; MTCW 1, 2

Asimov, Isaac 1920-1992 ..... **CLC 1, 3, 9, 19, 26, 76, 92**
See also AAYA 13; BEST 90:2; BPFB 1; BYA 4, 6, 7, 9; CA 1-4R; CAAS 137; CANR 2, 19, 36, 60, 125; CLR 12, 79; CMW 4; CN 1, 2, 3, 4, 5; CPW; DA3; DAM POP; DLB 8; DLBY 1992; INT CANR-19; JRDA; LAIT 5; LMFS 2; MAICYA 1, 2; MAL 5; MTCW 1, 2; MTFW 2005; RGAL 4; SATA 1, 26, 74; SCFW 1, 2; SFW 4; SSFS 17; TUS; YAW

Askew, Anne 1521(?)-1546 .... **LC 81**
See also DLB 136

Assis, Joaquim Maria Machado de
See Machado de Assis, Joaquim Maria

Astell, Mary 1666-1731 .... **LC 68**
See also DLB 252; FW

Astley, Thea (Beatrice May) 1925-2004 .... **CLC 41**
See also CA 65-68; CAAS 229; CANR 11, 43, 78; CN 1, 2, 3, 4, 5, 6, 7; DLB 289; EWL 3

Astley, William 1855-1911
See Warung, Price

Aston, James
See White, T(erence) H(anbury)

Asturias, Miguel Angel 1899-1974 .... **CLC 3, 8, 13; HLC 1; TCLC 184**
See also CA 25-28; CAAS 49-52; CANR 32; CAP 2; CDWLB 3; DA3; DAM MULT, NOV; DLB 113, 290, 329; EWL 3; HW 1; LAW; LMFS 2; MTCW 1, 2; RGWL 2, 3; WLIT 1

Atares, Carlos Saura
See Saura (Atares), Carlos

Athanasius c. 295-c. 373 .... **CMLC 48**

Barnes, Peter 1931-2004 .... **CLC 5, 56**
See also CA 65-68; 12; CAAS 230; CANR
33, 34, 64, 113; CBD; CD 5, 6; DFS 6;
DLB 13, 233; MTCW 1

Barnes, William 1801-1886 .... **NCLC 75**
See also DLB 32

Baroja, Pio 1872-1956 .... **HLC 1; TCLC 8**
See also CA 247; CAAE 104; EW 9

Baroja y Nessi, Pio
See Baroja, Pio

Baron, David
See Pinter, Harold

Baron Corvo
See Rolfe, Frederick (William Serafino Austin Lewis Mary)

Barondess, Sue K(aufman)
1926-1977 .... **CLC 8**
See Kaufman, Sue
See also CA 1-4R; CAAS 69-72; CANR 1

Baron de Teive
See Pessoa, Fernando (Antonio Nogueira)

Baroness Von S.
See Zangwill, Israel

Barres, (Auguste-)Maurice
1862-1923 .... **TCLC 47**
See also CA 164; DLB 123; GFL 1789 to
the Present

Barreto, Afonso Henrique de Lima
See Lima Barreto, Afonso Henrique de

Barrett, Andrea 1954- .... **CLC 150**
See also CA 156; CANR 92; CN 7; SSFS
24

Barrett, Michele .... **CLC 65**

Barrett, (Roger) Syd 1946-2006 .... **CLC 35**

Barrett, William (Christopher)
1913-1992 .... **CLC 27**
See also CA 13-16R; CAAS 139; CANR
11, 67; INT CANR-11

Barrett Browning, Elizabeth
1806-1861 ...... **NCLC 1, 16, 61, 66, 170;**
PC 6, 62; WLC 1
See also AAYA 63; BRW 4; CDBLB 1832-
1890; DA; DA3; DAB; DAC; DAM MST,
POET; DLB 32, 199; EXPP; FL 1:2; PAB;
PFS 2, 16, 23; TEA; WLIT 4; WP

Barrie, J(ames) M(atthew)
1860-1937 .... **TCLC 2, 164**
See also BRWS 3; BYA 4, 5; CA 136;
CAAE 104; CANR 77; CDBLB 1890-
1914; CLR 16; CWRI 5; DA3; DAB;
DAM DRAM; DFS 7; DLB 10, 141, 156;
EWL 3; FANT; MAICYA 1, 2; MTCW 2;
MTFW 2005; SATA 100; SUFW; WCH;
WLIT 4; YABC 1

Barrington, Michael
See Moorcock, Michael

Barrol, Grady
See Bograd, Larry

Barry, Mike
See Malzberg, Barry N(athaniel)

Barry, Philip 1896-1949 .... **TCLC 11**
See also CA 199; CAAE 109; DFS 9; DLB
7, 228; MAL 5; RGAL 4

Bart, Andre Schwarz
See Schwarz-Bart, Andre

Barth, John (Simmons) 1930- ... **CLC 1, 2, 3,**
5, 7, 9, 10, 14, 27, 51, 89, 214; SSC 10,
89
See also AITN 1, 2; AMW; BPFB 1; CA
1-4R; CABS 1; CANR 5, 23, 49, 64, 113;
CN 1, 2, 3, 4, 5, 6, 7; DAM NOV; DLB
2, 227; EWL 3; FANT; MAL 5; MTCW
1; RGAL 4; RGSF 2; RHW; SSFS 6; TUS

Barthelme, Donald 1931-1989 ... **CLC 1, 2, 3,**
5, 6, 8, 13, 23, 46, 59, 115; SSC 2, 55
See also AMWS 4; BPFB 1; CA 21-24R;
CAAS 129; CANR 20, 58; CN 1, 2, 3, 4;
DA3; DAM NOV; DLB 2, 234; DLBY

1980, 1989; EWL 3; FANT; LMFS 2;
MAL 5; MTCW 1, 2; MTFW 2005;
RGAL 4; RGSF 2; SATA 7; SATA-Obit
62; SSFS 17

Barthelme, Frederick 1943- ...... **CLC 36, 117**
See also AMWS 11; CA 122; CAAE 114;
CANR 77; CN 4, 5, 6, 7; CSW; DLB 244;
DLBY 1985; EWL 3; INT CA-122

Barthes, Roland (Gerard)
1915-1980 .... **CLC 24, 83; TCLC 135**
See also CA 130; CAAS 97-100; CANR
66; DLB 296; EW 13; EWL 3; GFL 1789
to the Present; MTCW 1, 2; TWA

Bartram, William 1739-1823 .... **NCLC 145**
See also ANW; DLB 37

Barzun, Jacques (Martin) 1907- ..... **CLC 51,**
145
See also CA 61-64; CANR 22, 95

Bashevis, Isaac
See Singer, Isaac Bashevis

Bashevis, Yitskhok
See Singer, Isaac Bashevis

Bashkirtseff, Marie 1859-1884 .... **NCLC 27**

Basho, Matsuo
See Matsuo Basho
See also RGWL 2, 3; WP

Basil of Caesaria c. 330-379 .... **CMLC 35**

Basket, Raney
See Edgerton, Clyde (Carlyle)

Bass, Kingsley B., Jr.
See Bullins, Ed

Bass, Rick 1958- .... **CLC 79, 143; SSC 60**
See also AMWS 16; ANW; CA 126; CANR
53, 93, 145; CSW; DLB 212, 275

Bassani, Giorgio 1916-2000 .... **CLC 9**
See also CA 65-68; CAAS 190; CANR 33;
CWW 2; DLB 128, 177, 299; EWL 3;
MTCW 1; RGHL; RGWL 2, 3

Bastian, Ann .... **CLC 70**

Bastos, Augusto Roa
See Roa Bastos, Augusto

Bataille, Georges 1897-1962 .... **CLC 29;**
TCLC 155
See also CA 101; CAAS 89-92; EWL 3

Bates, H(erbert) E(rnest)
1905-1974 .... **CLC 46; SSC 10**
See also CA 93-96; CAAS 45-48; CANR
34; CN 1; DA3; DAB; DAM POP; DLB
162, 191; EWL 3; EXPS; MTCW 1, 2;
RGSF 2; SSFS 7

Bauchart
See Camus, Albert

Baudelaire, Charles 1821-1867 . **NCLC 6, 29,**
55, 155; PC 1; SSC 18; WLC 1
See also DA; DA3; DAB; DAC; DAM
MST, POET; DLB 217; EW 7; GFL 1789
to the Present; LMFS 2; PFS 21; RGWL
2, 3; TWA

Baudouin, Marcel
See Peguy, Charles (Pierre)

Baudouin, Pierre
See Peguy, Charles (Pierre)

Baudrillard, Jean 1929- .... **CLC 60**
See also CA 252; DLB 296

Baum, L(yman) Frank 1856-1919 .. **TCLC 7,**
132
See also AAYA 46; BYA 16; CA 133;
CAAE 108; CLR 15, 107; CWRI 5; DLB
22; FANT; JRDA; MAICYA 1, 2; MTCW
1, 2; NFS 13; RGAL 4; SATA 18, 100;
WCH

Baum, Louis F.
See Baum, L(yman) Frank

Baumbach, Jonathan 1933- .... **CLC 6, 23**
See also CA 13-16R; 5; CANR 12, 66, 140;
CN 3, 4, 5, 6, 7; DLBY 1980; INT CANR-
12; MTCW 1

Bausch, Richard (Carl) 1945- .... **CLC 51**
See also AMWS 7; CA 101; 14; CANR 43,
61, 87; CN 7; CSW; DLB 130; MAL 5

Baxter, Charles 1947- .... **CLC 45, 78**
See also CA 57-60; CANR 40, 64, 104, 133;
CPW; DAM POP; DLB 130; MAL 5;
MTCW 2; MTFW 2005; TCLE 1:1

Baxter, George Owen
See Faust, Frederick (Schiller)

Baxter, James K(eir) 1926-1972 .... **CLC 14**
See also CA 77-80; CP 1; EWL 3

Baxter, John
See Hunt, E. Howard

Bayer, Sylvia
See Glassco, John

Bayle, Pierre 1647-1706 .... **LC 126**
See also DLB 268, 313; GFL Beginnings to
1789

Baynton, Barbara 1857-1929 .... **TCLC 57**
See also DLB 230; RGSF 2

Beagle, Peter S. 1939- .... **CLC 7, 104**
See also AAYA 47; BPFB 1; BYA 9, 10,
16; CA 9-12R; CANR 4, 51, 73, 110;
DA3; DLBY 1980; FANT; INT CANR-4;
MTCW 2; MTFW 2005; SATA 60, 130;
SUFW 1, 2; YAW

Beagle, Peter Soyer
See Beagle, Peter S.

Bean, Normal
See Burroughs, Edgar Rice

Beard, Charles A(ustin)
1874-1948 .... **TCLC 15**
See also CA 189; CAAE 115; DLB 17;
SATA 18

Beardsley, Aubrey 1872-1898 .... **NCLC 6**

Beattie, Ann 1947- ..... **CLC 8, 13, 18, 40, 63,**
146; SSC 11
See also AMWS 5; BEST 90:2; BPFB 1;
CA 81-84; CANR 53, 73, 128; CN 4, 5,
6, 7; CPW; DA3; DAM NOV, POP; DLB
218, 278; DLBY 1982; EWL 3; MAL 5;
MTCW 1, 2; MTFW 2005; RGAL 4;
RGSF 2; SSFS 9; TUS

Beattie, James 1735-1803 .... **NCLC 25**
See also DLB 109

Beauchamp, Kathleen Mansfield 1888-1923
See Mansfield, Katherine
See also CA 134; CAAE 104; DA; DA3;
DAC; DAM MST; MTCW 2; TEA

Beaumarchais, Pierre-Augustin Caron de
1732-1799 .... **DC 4; LC 61**
See also DAM DRAM; DFS 14, 16; DLB
313; EW 4; GFL Beginnings to 1789;
RGWL 2, 3

Beaumont, Francis 1584(?)-1616 .. **DC 6; LC**
33
See also BRW 2; CDBLB Before 1660;
DLB 58; TEA

Beauvoir, Simone de 1908-1986 .... **CLC 1, 2,**
4, 8, 14, 31, 44, 50, 71, 124; SSC 35;
WLC 1
See also BPFB 1; CA 9-12R; CAAS 118;
CANR 28, 61; DA; DA3; DAC;
DAM MST, NOV; DLB 72; DLBY 1986;
EW 12; EWL 3; FL 1:5; FW; GFL 1789
to the Present; LMFS 2; MTCW 1, 2;
MTFW 2005; RGSF 2; RGWL 2, 3; TWA

Beauvoir, Simone Lucie Ernestine Marie
Bertrand de
See Beauvoir, Simone de

Becker, Carl (Lotus) 1873-1945 ..... **TCLC 63**
See also CA 157; DLB 17

Becker, Jurek 1937-1997 .... **CLC 7, 19**
See also CA 85-88; CAAS 157; CANR 60,
117; CWW 2; DLB 75, 299; EWL 3;
RGHL

Becker, Walter 1950- .... **CLC 26**

Becket, Thomas a 1118(?)-1170 .... **CMLC 83**

Beckett, Samuel 1906-1989 ... **CLC 1, 2, 3, 4, 6, 9, 10, 11, 14, 18, 29, 57, 59, 83; DC 22; SSC 16, 74; TCLC 145; WLC 1**
See also BRWC 2; BRWR 1; BRWS 1; CA 5-8R; CAAS 130; CANR 33, 61; CBD; CDBLB 1945-1960; CN 1, 2, 3, 4; CP 1, 2, 3, 4; DA; DA3; DAB; DAC; DAM DRAM, MST, NOV; DFS 2, 7, 18; DLB 13, 15, 233, 319, 321, 329; DLBY 1990; EWL 3; GFL 1789 to the Present; LATS 1:2; LMFS 2; MTCW 1, 2; MTFW 2005; RGSF 2; RGWL 2, 3; SSFS 15; TEA; WLIT 4

Beckford, William 1760-1844 .... **NCLC 16**
See also BRW 3; DLB 39, 213; GL 2; HGG; LMFS 1; SUFW

Beckham, Barry (Earl) 1944- .... **BLC 1**
See also BW 1; CA 29-32R; CANR 26, 62; CN 1, 2, 3, 4, 5, 6; DAM MULT; DLB 33

Beckman, Gunnel 1910- .... **CLC 26**
See also CA 33-36R; CANR 15, 114; CLR 25; MAICYA 1, 2; SAAS 9; SATA 6

Becque, Henri 1837-1899 .... **DC 21; NCLC 3**
See also DLB 192; GFL 1789 to the Present

Becquer, Gustavo Adolfo
1836-1870 .... **HLCS 1; NCLC 106**
See also DAM MULT

Beddoes, Thomas Lovell 1803-1849 .. **DC 15; NCLC 3, 154**
See also BRWS 11; DLB 96

Bede c. 673-735 .... **CMLC 20**
See also DLB 146; TEA

Bedford, Denton R. 1907-(?) .... **NNAL**

Bedford, Donald F.
See Fearing, Kenneth (Flexner)

Beecher, Catharine Esther
1800-1878 .... **NCLC 30**
See also DLB 1, 243

Beecher, John 1904-1980 .... **CLC 6**
See also AITN 1; CA 5-8R; CAAS 105; CANR 8; CP 1, 2, 3

Beer, Johann 1655-1700 .... **LC 5**
See also DLB 168

Beer, Patricia 1924- .... **CLC 58**
See also CA 61-64; CAAS 183; CANR 13, 46; CP 1, 2, 3, 4, 5, 6; CWP; DLB 40; FW

Beerbohm, Max
See Beerbohm, (Henry) Max(imilian)

Beerbohm, (Henry) Max(imilian)
1872-1956 .... **TCLC 1, 24**
See also BRWS 2; CA 154; CAAE 104; CANR 79; DLB 34, 100; FANT; MTCW 2

Beer-Hofmann, Richard
1866-1945 .... **TCLC 60**
See also CA 160; DLB 81

Beg, Shemus
See Stephens, James

Begiebing, Robert J(ohn) 1946- .... **CLC 70**
See also CA 122; CANR 40, 88

Begley, Louis 1933- .... **CLC 197**
See also CA 140; CANR 98; DLB 299; RGHL; TCLE 1:1

Behan, Brendan (Francis)
1923-1964 .... **CLC 1, 8, 11, 15, 79**
See also BRWS 2; CA 73-76; CANR 33, 121; CBD; CDBLB 1945-1960; DAM DRAM; DFS 7; DLB 13, 233; EWL 3; MTCW 1, 2

Behn, Aphra 1640(?)-1689 .. **DC 4; LC 1, 30, 42, 135; PC 13; WLC 1**
See also BRWS 3; DA; DA3; DAB; DAC; DAM DRAM, MST, NOV, POET; DFS 16; DLB 39, 80, 131; FW; TEA; WLIT 3

Behrman, S(amuel) N(athaniel)
1893-1973 .... **CLC 40**
See also CA 13-16; CAAS 45-48; CAD; CAP 1; DLB 7, 44; IDFW 3; MAL 5; RGAL 4

Bekederemo, J. P. Clark
See Clark Bekederemo, J.P.
See also CD 6

Belasco, David 1853-1931 .... **TCLC 3**
See also CA 168; CAAE 104; DLB 7; MAL 5; RGAL 4

Belcheva, Elisaveta Lyubomirova
1893-1991 .... **CLC 10**
See Bagryana, Elisaveta

Beldone, Phil "Cheech"
See Ellison, Harlan

Beleno
See Azuela, Mariano

Belinski, Vissarion Grigoryevich
1811-1848 .... **NCLC 5**
See also DLB 198

Belitt, Ben 1911- .... **CLC 22**
See also CA 13-16R; 4; CANR 7, 77; CP 1, 2, 3, 4, 5, 6; DLB 5

Belknap, Jeremy 1744-1798 .... **LC 115**
See also DLB 30, 37

Bell, Gertrude (Margaret Lowthian)
1868-1926 .... **TCLC 67**
See also CA 167; CANR 110; DLB 174

Bell, J. Freeman
See Zangwill, Israel

Bell, James Madison 1826-1902 .... **BLC 1; TCLC 43**
See also BW 1; CA 124; CAAE 122; DAM MULT; DLB 50

Bell, Madison Smartt 1957- ..... **CLC 41, 102, 223**
See also AMWS 10; BPFB 1; CA 183; 111, 183; CANR 28, 54, 73, 134; CN 5, 6, 7; CSW; DLB 218, 278; MTCW 2; MTFW 2005

Bell, Marvin (Hartley) 1937- .... **CLC 8, 31**
See also CA 21-24R; 14; CANR 59, 102; CP 1, 2, 3, 4, 5, 6, 7; DAM POET; DLB 5; MAL 5; MTCW 1; PFS 25

Bell, W. L. D.
See Mencken, H(enry) L(ouis)

Bellamy, Atwood C.
See Mencken, H(enry) L(ouis)

Bellamy, Edward 1850-1898 ..... **NCLC 4, 86, 147**
See also DLB 12; NFS 15; RGAL 4; SFW 4

Belli, Gioconda 1948- .... **HLCS 1**
See also CA 152; CANR 143; CWW 2; DLB 290; EWL 3; RGWL 3

Bellin, Edward J.
See Kuttner, Henry

Bello, Andres 1781-1865 .... **NCLC 131**
See also LAW

Belloc, (Joseph) Hilaire (Pierre Sebastien Rene Swanton) 1870-1953 .... **PC 24; TCLC 7, 18**
See also CA 152; CAAE 106; CLR 102; CWRI 5; DAM POET; DLB 19, 100, 141, 174; EWL 3; MTCW 1; MTFW 2005; SATA 112; WCH; YABC 1

Belloc, Joseph Peter Rene Hilaire
See Belloc, (Joseph) Hilaire (Pierre Sebastien Rene Swanton)

Belloc, Joseph Pierre Hilaire
See Belloc, (Joseph) Hilaire (Pierre Sebastien Rene Swanton)

Belloc, M. A.
See Lowndes, Marie Adelaide (Belloc)

Belloc-Lowndes, Mrs.
See Lowndes, Marie Adelaide (Belloc)

Bellow, Saul 1915-2005 ...... **CLC 1, 2, 3, 6, 8, 10, 13, 15, 25, 33, 34, 63, 79, 190, 200; SSC 14; WLC 1**
See also AITN 2; AMW; AMWC 2; AMWR 2; BEST 89:3; BPFB 1; CA 5-8R; CAAS 238; CABS 1; CANR 29, 53, 95, 132; CDALB 1941-1968; CN 1, 2, 3, 4, 5, 6, 7; DA; DA3; DAB; DAC; DAM MST, NOV, POP; DLB 2, 28, 299, 329; DLBD 3; DLBY 1982; EWL 3; MAL 5; MTCW 1, 2; MTFW 2005; NFS 4, 14; RGAL 4; RGHL; RGSF 2; SSFS 12, 22; TUS

Belser, Reimond Karel Maria de 1929-
See Ruyslinck, Ward
See also CA 152

Bely, Andrey .... **PC 11; TCLC 7**
See Bugayev, Boris Nikolayevich
See also DLB 295; EW 9; EWL 3

Belyi, Andrei
See Bugayev, Boris Nikolayevich
See also RGWL 2, 3

Bembo, Pietro 1470-1547 .... **LC 79**
See also RGWL 2, 3

Benary, Margot
See Benary-Isbert, Margot

Benary-Isbert, Margot 1889-1979 .... **CLC 12**
See also CA 5-8R; CAAS 89-92; CANR 4, 72; CLR 12; MAICYA 1, 2; SATA 2; SATA-Obit 21

Benavente (y Martinez), Jacinto
1866-1954 .... **DC 26; HLCS 1; TCLC 3**
See also CA 131; CAAE 106; CANR 81; DAM DRAM, MULT; DLB 329; EWL 3; GLL 2; HW 1, 2; MTCW 1, 2

Benchley, Peter 1940-2006 .... **CLC 4, 8**
See also AAYA 14; AITN 2; BPFB 1; CA 17-20R; CAAS 248; CANR 12, 35, 66, 115; CPW; DAM NOV, POP; HGG; MTCW 1, 2; MTFW 2005; SATA 3, 89, 164

Benchley, Peter Bradford
See Benchley, Peter

Benchley, Robert (Charles)
1889-1945 .... **TCLC 1, 55**
See also CA 153; CAAE 105; DLB 11; MAL 5; RGAL 4

Benda, Julien 1867-1956 .... **TCLC 60**
See also CA 154; CAAE 120; GFL 1789 to the Present

Benedict, Ruth 1887-1948 .... **TCLC 60**
See also CA 158; CANR 146; DLB 246

Benedict, Ruth Fulton
See Benedict, Ruth

Benedikt, Michael 1935- .... **CLC 4, 14**
See also CA 13-16R; CANR 7; CP 1, 2, 3, 4, 5, 6, 7; DLB 5

Benet, Juan 1927-1993 .... **CLC 28**
See also CA 143; EWL 3

Benet, Stephen Vincent 1898-1943 ..... **PC 64; SSC 10, 86; TCLC 7**
See also AMWS 11; CA 152; CAAE 104; DA3; DAM POET; DLB 4, 48, 102, 249, 284; DLBY 1997; EWL 3; HGG; MAL 5; MTCW 2; MTFW 2005; RGAL 4; RGSF 2; SSFS 22; SUFW; WP; YABC 1

Benet, William Rose 1886-1950 ..... **TCLC 28**
See also CA 152; CAAE 118; DAM POET; DLB 45; RGAL 4

Benford, Gregory (Albert) 1941- ..... **CLC 52**
See also BPFB 1; CA 175; 69-72, 175; 27; CANR 12, 24, 49, 95, 134; CN 7; CSW; DLBY 1982; MTFW 2005; SCFW 2; SFW 4

Bengtsson, Frans (Gunnar)
1894-1954 .... **TCLC 48**
See also CA 170; EWL 3

Benjamin, David
See Slavitt, David R(ytman)

Benjamin, Lois
See Gould, Lois

Benjamin, Walter 1892-1940 .... TCLC 39
See also CA 164; DLB 242; EW 11; EWL
3

Ben Jelloun, Tahar 1944-
See Jelloun, Tahar ben
See also CA 135; CWW 2; EWL 3; RGWL
3; WLIT 2

Benn, Gottfried 1886-1956 .. PC 35; TCLC 3
See also CA 153; CAAE 106; DLB 56;
EWL 3; RGWL 2, 3

Bennett, Alan 1934- .... CLC 45, 77
See also BRWS 8; CA 103; CANR 35, 55,
106, 157; CBD; CD 5, 6; DAB; DAM
MST; DLB 310; MTCW 1, 2; MTFW
2005

Bennett, (Enoch) Arnold
1867-1931 .... TCLC 5, 20
See also BRW 6; CA 155; CAAE 106; CD-
BLB 1890-1914; DLB 10, 34, 98, 135;
EWL 3; MTCW 2

Bennett, Elizabeth
See Mitchell, Margaret (Munnerlyn)

Bennett, George Harold 1930-
See Bennett, Hal
See also BW 1; CA 97-100; CANR 87

Bennett, Gwendolyn B. 1902-1981 .... HR 1:2
See also BW 1; CA 125; DLB 51; WP

Bennett, Hal .... CLC 5
See Bennett, George Harold
See also CA 13; DLB 33

Bennett, Jay 1912- .... CLC 35
See also AAYA 10, 73; CA 69-72; CANR
11, 42, 79; JRDA; SAAS 4; SATA 41, 87;
SATA-Brief 27; WYA; YAW

Bennett, Louise 1919-2006 .. BLC 1; CLC 28
See also BW 2, 3; CA 151; CAAS 252; CD-
WLB 3; CP 1, 2, 3, 4, 5, 6, 7; DAM
MULT; DLB 117; EWL 3

Bennett, Louise Simone
See Bennett, Louise

Bennett-Coverley, Louise
See Bennett, Louise

Benson, A. C. 1862-1925 .... TCLC 123
See also DLB 98

Benson, E(dward) F(rederic)
1867-1940 .... TCLC 27
See also CA 157; CAAE 114; DLB 135,
153; HGG; SUFW 1

Benson, Jackson J. 1930- .... CLC 34
See also CA 25-28R; DLB 111

Benson, Sally 1900-1972 .... CLC 17
See also CA 19-20; CAAS 37-40R; CAP 1;
SATA 1, 35; SATA-Obit 27

Benson, Stella 1892-1933 .... TCLC 17
See also CA 154, 155; CAAE 117; DLB
36, 162; FANT; TEA

Bentham, Jeremy 1748-1832 .... NCLC 38
See also DLB 107, 158, 252

Bentley, E(dmund) C(lerihew)
1875-1956 .... TCLC 12
See also CA 232; CAAE 108; DLB 70;
MSW

Bentley, Eric 1916- .... CLC 24
See also CA 5-8R; CAD; CANR 6, 67;
CBD; CD 5, 6; INT CANR-6

Bentley, Eric Russell
See Bentley, Eric

ben Uzair, Salem
See Horne, Richard Henry Hengist

Beranger, Pierre Jean de
1780-1857 .... NCLC 34

Berdyaev, Nicolas
See Berdyaev, Nikolai (Aleksandrovich)

Berdyaev, Nikolai (Aleksandrovich)
1874-1948 .... TCLC 67
See also CA 157; CAAE 120

Berdyayev, Nikolai (Aleksandrovich)
See Berdyaev, Nikolai (Aleksandrovich)

Berendt, John 1939- .... CLC 86
See also CA 146; CANR 75, 83, 151

Berendt, John Lawrence
See Berendt, John

Beresford, J(ohn) D(avys)
1873-1947 .... TCLC 81
See also CA 155; CAAE 112; DLB 162,
178, 197; SFW 4; SUFW 1

Bergelson, David (Rafailovich)
1884-1952 .... TCLC 81
See Bergelson, Dovid
See also CA 220; DLB 333

Bergelson, Dovid
See Bergelson, David (Rafailovich)
See also EWL 3

Berger, Colonel
See Malraux, (Georges-)Andre

Berger, John (Peter) 1926- .... CLC 2, 19
See also BRWS 4; CA 81-84; CANR 51,
78, 117; CN 1, 2, 3, 4, 5, 6, 7; DLB 14,
207, 319, 326

Berger, Melvin H. 1927- .... CLC 12
See also CA 5-8R; CANR 4, 142; CLR 32;
SAAS 2; SATA 5, 88, 158; SATA-Essay
124

Berger, Thomas 1924- .... CLC 3, 5, 8, 11, 18,
38
See also BPFB 1; CA 1-4R; CANR 5, 28,
51, 128; CN 1, 2, 3, 4, 5, 6, 7; DAM
NOV; DLB 2; DLBY 1980; EWL 3;
FANT; INT CANR-28; MAL 5; MTCW
1, 2; MTFW 2005; RHW; TCLE 1:1;
TCWW 1, 2

Bergman, (Ernst) Ingmar 1918- ...... CLC 16,
72, 210
See also AAYA 61; CA 81-84; CANR 33,
70; CWW 2; DLB 257; MTCW 2; MTFW
2005

Bergson, Henri(-Louis) 1859-1941 . TCLC 32
See also CA 164; DLB 329; EW 8; EWL 3;
GFL 1789 to the Present

Bergstein, Eleanor 1938- .... CLC 4
See also CA 53-56; CANR 5

Berkeley, George 1685-1753 .... LC 65
See also DLB 31, 101, 252

Berkoff, Steven 1937- .... CLC 56
See also CA 104; CANR 72; CBD; CD 5, 6

Berlin, Isaiah 1909-1997 .... TCLC 105
See also CA 85-88; CAAS 162

Bermant, Chaim (Icyk) 1929-1998 ... CLC 40
See also CA 57-60; CANR 6, 31, 57, 105;
CN 2, 3, 4, 5, 6

Bern, Victoria
See Fisher, M(ary) F(rances) K(ennedy)

Bernanos, (Paul Louis) Georges
1888-1948 .... TCLC 3
See also CA 130; CAAE 104; CANR 94;
DLB 72; EWL 3; GFL 1789 to the
Present; RGWL 2, 3

Bernard, April 1956- .... CLC 59
See also CA 131; CANR 144

Bernard, Mary Ann
See Soderbergh, Steven

Bernard of Clairvaux 1090-1153 .. CMLC 71
See also DLB 208

Bernard Silvestris fl. c. 1130-fl. c.
1160 .... CMLC 87
See also DLB 208

Berne, Victoria
See Fisher, M(ary) F(rances) K(ennedy)

Bernhard, Thomas 1931-1989 ..... CLC 3, 32,
61; DC 14; TCLC 165
See also CA 85-88; CAAS 127; CANR 32,
57; CDWLB 2; DLB 85, 124; EWL 3;
MTCW 1; RGHL; RGWL 2, 3

Bernhardt, Sarah (Henriette Rosine)
1844-1923 .... TCLC 75
See also CA 157

Bernstein, Charles 1950- .... CLC 142
See also CA 129; 24; CANR 90; CP 4, 5, 6,
7; DLB 169

Bernstein, Ingrid
See Kirsch, Sarah

Beroul fl. c. 12th cent. - .... CMLC 75

Berriault, Gina 1926-1999 .... CLC 54, 109;
SSC 30
See also CA 129; CAAE 116; CAAS 185;
CANR 66; DLB 130; SSFS 7,11

Berrigan, Daniel 1921- .... CLC 4
See also CA 187; 33-36R, 187; 1; CANR
11, 43, 78; CP 1, 2, 3, 4, 5, 6, 7; DLB 5

Berrigan, Edmund Joseph Michael, Jr.
1934-1983
See Berrigan, Ted
See also CA 61-64; CAAS 110; CANR 14,
102

Berrigan, Ted .... CLC 37
See Berrigan, Edmund Joseph Michael, Jr.
See also CP 1, 2, 3; DLB 5, 169; WP

Berry, Charles Edward Anderson 1931-
See Berry, Chuck
See also CA 115

Berry, Chuck .... CLC 17
See Berry, Charles Edward Anderson

Berry, Jonas
See Ashbery, John
See also GLL 1

Berry, Wendell 1934- .... CLC 4, 6, 8, 27, 46;
PC 28
See also AITN 1; AMWS 10; ANW; CA
73-76; CANR 50, 73, 101, 132; CP 1, 2,
3, 4, 5, 6, 7; CSW; DAM POET; DLB 5,
6, 234, 275; MTCW 2; MTFW 2005;
TCLE 1:1

Berryman, John 1914-1972 ... CLC 1, 2, 3, 4,
6, 8, 10, 13, 25, 62; PC 64
See also AMW; CA 13-16; CAAS 33-36R;
CABS 2; CANR 35; CAP 1; CDALB
1941-1968; CP 1; DAM POET; DLB 48;
EWL 3; MAL 5; MTCW 1, 2; MTFW
2005; PAB; RGAL 4; WP

Bertolucci, Bernardo 1940- ...... CLC 16, 157
See also CA 106; CANR 125

Berton, Pierre (Francis de Marigny)
1920-2004 .... CLC 104
See also CA 1-4R; CAAS 233; CANR 2,
56, 144; CPW; DLB 68; SATA 99; SATA-
Obit 158

Bertrand, Aloysius 1807-1841 .... NCLC 31
See Bertrand, Louis oAloysiusc

Bertrand, Louis oAloysiusc
See Bertrand, Aloysius
See also DLB 217

Bertran de Born c. 1140-1215 .... CMLC 5

Besant, Annie (Wood) 1847-1933 ..... TCLC 9
See also CA 185; CAAE 105

Bessie, Alvah 1904-1985 .... CLC 23
See also CA 5-8R; CAAS 116; CANR 2,
80; DLB 26

Bestuzhev, Aleksandr Aleksandrovich
1797-1837 .... NCLC 131
See also DLB 198

Bethlen, T. D.
See Silverberg, Robert

Beti, Mongo .... BLC 1; CLC 27
See Biyidi, Alexandre
See also AFW; CANR 79; DAM MULT;
EWL 3; WLIT 2

Betjeman, John 1906-1984 ...... CLC 2, 6, 10,
34, 43; PC 75
See also BRW 7; CA 9-12R; CAAS 112;
CANR 33, 56; CDBLB 1945-1960; CP 1,
2, 3; DA3; DAB; DAM MST, POET;
DLB 20; DLBY 1984; EWL 3; MTCW 1,
2

Brown, Alan 1950- .... **CLC 99**
See also CA 156

Brown, Charles Brockden
1771-1810 .... **NCLC 22, 74, 122**
See also AMWS 1; CDALB 1640-1865;
DLB 37, 59, 73; FW; GL 2; HGG; LMFS
1; RGAL 4; TUS

Brown, Christy 1932-1981 .... **CLC 63**
See also BYA 13; CA 105; CAAS 104;
CANR 72; DLB 14

Brown, Claude 1937-2002 ...... **BLC 1; CLC 30**
See also AAYA 7; BW 1, 3; CA 73-76;
CAAS 205; CANR 81; DAM MULT

Brown, Dan 1964- .... **CLC 209**
See also AAYA 55; CA 217; MTFW 2005

Brown, Dee 1908-2002 .... **CLC 18, 47**
See also AAYA 30; CA 13-16R; 6; CAAS
212; CANR 11, 45, 60, 150; CPW; CSW;
DA3; DAM POP; DLBY 1980; LAIT 2;
MTCW 1, 2; MTFW 2005; NCFS 5;
SATA 5, 110; SATA-Obit 141; TCWW 1,
2

Brown, Dee Alexander
See Brown, Dee

Brown, George
See Wertmueller, Lina

Brown, George Douglas
1869-1902 .... **TCLC 28**
See Douglas, George
See also CA 162

Brown, George Mackay 1921-1996 ... **CLC 5,
48, 100**
See also BRWS 6; CA 21-24R; 6; CAAS
151; CANR 12, 37, 67; CN 1, 2, 3, 4, 5,
6; CP 1, 2, 3, 4, 5, 6; DLB 14, 27, 139,
271; MTCW 1; RGSF 2; SATA 35

Brown, Larry 1951-2004 .... **CLC 73**
See also CA 134; CAAE 130; CAAS 233;
CANR 117, 145; CSW; DLB 234; INT
CA-134

Brown, Moses
See Barrett, William (Christopher)

Brown, Rita Mae 1944- .... **CLC 18, 43, 79**
See also BPFB 1; CA 45-48; CANR 2, 11,
35, 62, 95, 138; CN 5, 6, 7; CPW; CSW;
DA3; DAM NOV, POP; FW; INT CANR-
11; MAL 5; MTCW 1, 2; MTFW 2005;
NFS 9; RGAL 4; TUS

Brown, Roderick (Langmere) Haig-
See Haig-Brown, Roderick (Langmere)

Brown, Rosellen 1939- .... **CLC 32, 170**
See also CA 77-80; 10; CANR 14, 44, 98;
CN 6, 7

Brown, Sterling Allen 1901-1989 ...... **BLC 1;
CLC 1, 23, 59; HR 1:2; PC 55**
See also AFAW 1, 2; BW 1, 3; CA 85-88;
CAAS 127; CANR 26; CP 3, 4; DA3;
DAM MULT, POET; DLB 48, 51, 63;
MAL 5; MTCW 1, 2; MTFW 2005;
RGAL 4; WP

Brown, Will
See Ainsworth, William Harrison

Brown, William Hill 1765-1793 .... **LC 93**
See also DLB 37

Brown, William Larry
See Brown, Larry

Brown, William Wells 1815-1884 ...... **BLC 1;
DC 1; NCLC 2, 89**
See also DAM MULT; DLB 3, 50, 183,
248; RGAL 4

Browne, (Clyde) Jackson 1948(?)- ... **CLC 21**
See also CA 120

Browne, Sir Thomas 1605-1682 .... **LC 111**
See also BRW 2; DLB 151

Browning, Robert 1812-1889 . **NCLC 19, 79;
PC 2, 61; WLCS**
See also BRW 4; BRWC 2; BRWR 2; CD-
BLB 1832-1890; CLR 97; DA; DA3;
DAB; DAC; DAM MST, POET; DLB 32,
163; EXPP; LATS 1:1; PAB; PFS 1, 15;
RGEL 2; TEA; WLIT 4; WP; YABC 1

Browning, Tod 1882-1962 .... **CLC 16**
See also CA 141; CAAS 117

Brownmiller, Susan 1935- .... **CLC 159**
See also CA 103; CANR 35, 75, 137; DAM
NOV; FW; MTCW 1, 2; MTFW 2005

Brownson, Orestes Augustus
1803-1876 .... **NCLC 50**
See also DLB 1, 59, 73, 243

Bruccoli, Matthew J(oseph) 1931- ... **CLC 34**
See also CA 9-12R; CANR 7, 87; DLB 103

Bruce, Lenny .... **CLC 21**
See Schneider, Leonard Alfred

Bruchac, Joseph 1942- .... **NNAL**
See also AAYA 19; CA 33-36R; CANR 13,
47, 75, 94, 137; CLR 46; CWRI 5; DAM
MULT; JRDA; MAICYA 2; MAICYAS 1;
MTCW 2; MTFW 2005; SATA 42, 89,
131, 176; SATA-Essay 176

Bruin, John
See Brutus, Dennis

Brulard, Henri
See Stendhal

Brulls, Christian
See Simenon, Georges (Jacques Christian)

Brunetto Latini c. 1220-1294 .... **CMLC 73**

Brunner, John (Kilian Houston)
1934-1995 .... **CLC 8, 10**
See also CA 1-4R; 8; CAAS 149; CANR 2,
37; CPW; DAM POP; DLB 261; MTCW
1, 2; SCFW 1, 2; SFW 4

Bruno, Giordano 1548-1600 .... **LC 27**
See also RGWL 2, 3

Brutus, Dennis 1924- ... **BLC 1; CLC 43; PC
24**
See also AFW; BW 2, 3; CA 49-52; 14;
CANR 2, 27, 42, 81; CDWLB 3; CP 1, 2,
3, 4, 5, 6, 7; DAM MULT, POET; DLB
117, 225; EWL 3

Bryan, C(ourtlandt) D(ixon) B(arnes)
1936- .... **CLC 29**
See also CA 73-76; CANR 13, 68; DLB
185; INT CANR-13

Bryan, Michael
See Moore, Brian
See also CCA 1

Bryan, William Jennings
1860-1925 .... **TCLC 99**
See also DLB 303

Bryant, William Cullen 1794-1878 . **NCLC 6,
46; PC 20**
See also AMWS 1; CDALB 1640-1865;
DA; DAB; DAC; DAM MST, POET;
DLB 3, 43, 59, 189, 250; EXPP; PAB;
RGAL 4; TUS

Bryusov, Valery Yakovlevich
1873-1924 .... **TCLC 10**
See also CA 155; CAAE 107; EWL 3; SFW
4

Buchan, John 1875-1940 .... **TCLC 41**
See also CA 145; CAAE 108; CMW 4;
DAB; DAM POP; DLB 34, 70, 156;
HGG; MSW; MTCW 2; RGEL 2; RHW;
YABC 2

Buchanan, George 1506-1582 .... **LC 4**
See also DLB 132

Buchanan, Robert 1841-1901 .... **TCLC 107**
See also CA 179; DLB 18, 35

Buchheim, Lothar-Guenther
1918-2007 .... **CLC 6**
See also CA 85-88

Buchner, (Karl) Georg
1813-1837 .... **NCLC 26, 146**
See also CDWLB 2; DLB 133; EW 6;
RGSF 2; RGWL 2, 3; TWA

Buchwald, Art 1925-2007 .... **CLC 33**
See also AITN 1; CA 5-8R; CANR 21, 67,
107; MTCW 1, 2; SATA 10

Buchwald, Arthur
See Buchwald, Art

Buck, Pearl S(ydenstricker)
1892-1973 .... **CLC 7, 11, 18, 127**
See also AAYA 42; AITN 1; AMWS 2;
BPFB 1; CA 1-4R; CAAS 41-44R; CANR
1, 34; CDALBS; CN 1; DA; DA3; DAB;
DAC; DAM MST, NOV; DLB 9, 102,
329; EWL 3; LAIT 3; MAL 5; MTCW 1,
2; MTFW 2005; RGAL 4; RHW; SATA
1, 25; TUS

Buckler, Ernest 1908-1984 .... **CLC 13**
See also CA 11-12; CAAS 114; CAP 1;
CCA 1; CN 1, 2, 3; DAC; DAM MST;
DLB 68; SATA 47

Buckley, Christopher 1952- .... **CLC 165**
See also CA 139; CANR 119

Buckley, Christopher Taylor
See Buckley, Christopher

Buckley, Vincent (Thomas)
1925-1988 .... **CLC 57**
See also CA 101; CP 1, 2, 3, 4; DLB 289

Buckley, William F., Jr. 1925- ..... **CLC 7, 18,
37**
See also AITN 1; BPFB 1; CA 1-4R; CANR
1, 24, 53, 93, 133; CMW 4; CPW; DA3;
DAM POP; DLB 137; DLBY 1980; INT
CANR-24; MTCW 1, 2; MTFW 2005;
TUS

Buechner, Frederick 1926- ..... **CLC 2, 4, 6, 9**
See also AMWS 12; BPFB 1; CA 13-16R;
CANR 11, 39, 64, 114, 138; CN 1, 2, 3,
4, 5, 6, 7; DAM NOV; DLBY 1980; INT
CANR-11; MAL 5; MTCW 1, 2; MTFW
2005; TCLE 1:1

Buell, John (Edward) 1927- .... **CLC 10**
See also CA 1-4R; CANR 71; DLB 53

Buero Vallejo, Antonio 1916-2000 ... **CLC 15,
46, 139, 226; DC 18**
See also CA 106; CAAS 189; CANR 24,
49, 75; CWW 2; DFS 11; EWL 3; HW 1;
MTCW 1, 2

Bufalino, Gesualdo 1920-1996 .... **CLC 74**
See also CA 209; CWW 2; DLB 196

Bugayev, Boris Nikolayevich
1880-1934 .... **PC 11; TCLC 7**
See Bely, Andrey; Belyi, Andrei
See also CA 165; CAAE 104; MTCW 2;
MTFW 2005

Bukowski, Charles 1920-1994 ... **CLC 2, 5, 9,
41, 82, 108; PC 18; SSC 45**
See also CA 17-20R; CAAS 144; CANR
40, 62, 105; CN 4, 5; CP 1, 2, 3, 4, 5;
CPW; DA3; DAM NOV, POET; DLB 5,
130, 169; EWL 3; MAL 5; MTCW 1, 2;
MTFW 2005

Bulgakov, Mikhail 1891-1940 .... **SSC 18;
TCLC 2, 16, 159**
See also AAYA 74; BPFB 1; CA 152;
CAAE 105; DAM DRAM, NOV; DLB
272; EWL 3; MTCW 2; MTFW 2005;
NFS 8; RGSF 2; RGWL 2, 3; SFW 4;
TWA

Bulgakov, Mikhail Afanasevich
See Bulgakov, Mikhail

Bulgya, Alexander Alexandrovich
1901-1956 .... **TCLC 53**
See Fadeev, Aleksandr Aleksandrovich;
Fadeev, Alexandr Alexandrovich; Fadeyev,
Alexander
See also CA 181; CAAE 117

Bullins, Ed 1935- ... **BLC 1; CLC 1, 5, 7; DC
6**
See also BW 2, 3; CA 49-52; 16; CAD;
CANR 24, 46, 73, 134; CD 5, 6; DAM
DRAM, MULT; DLB 7, 38, 249; EWL 3;
MAL 5; MTCW 1, 2; MTFW 2005;
RGAL 4

Bulosan, Carlos 1911-1956 .... **AAL**
See also CA 216; DLB 312; RGAL 4

Bulwer-Lytton, Edward (George Earle Lytton) 1803-1873 .... **NCLC 1, 45**
See also DLB 21; RGEL 2; SFW 4; SUFW 1; TEA

Bunin, Ivan
See Bunin, Ivan Alexeyevich

Bunin, Ivan Alekseevich
See Bunin, Ivan Alexeyevich

Bunin, Ivan Alexeyevich 1870-1953 ... **SSC 5; TCLC 6**
See also CAAE 104; DLB 317, 329; EWL 3; RGSF 2; RGWL 2, 3; TWA

Bunting, Basil 1900-1985 ...... **CLC 10, 39, 47**
See also BRWS 7; CA 53-56; CAAS 115; CANR 7; CP 1, 2, 3, 4; DAM POET; DLB 20; EWL 3; RGEL 2

Bunuel, Luis 1900-1983 ... **CLC 16, 80; HLC 1**
See also CA 101; CAAS 110; CANR 32, 77; DAM MULT; HW 1

Bunyan, John 1628-1688 .. **LC 4, 69; WLC 1**
See also BRW 2; BYA 5; CDBLB 1660-1789; DA; DAB; DAC; DAM MST; DLB 39; RGEL 2; TEA; WCH; WLIT 3

Buravsky, Alexandr .... **CLC 59**

Burckhardt, Jacob (Christoph) 1818-1897 .... **NCLC 49**
See also EW 6

Burford, Eleanor
See Hibbert, Eleanor Alice Burford

Burgess, Anthony . **CLC 1, 2, 4, 5, 8, 10, 13, 15, 22, 40, 62, 81, 94**
See Wilson, John (Anthony) Burgess
See also AAYA 25; AITN 1; BRWS 1; CDBLB 1960 to Present; CN 1, 2, 3, 4, 5; DAB; DLB 14, 194, 261; DLBY 1998; EWL 3; RGEL 2; RHW; SFW 4; YAW

Burke, Edmund 1729(?)-1797 .... **LC 7, 36; WLC 1**
See also BRW 3; DA; DA3; DAB; DAC; DAM MST; DLB 104, 252; RGEL 2; TEA

Burke, Kenneth (Duva) 1897-1993 ... **CLC 2, 24**
See also AMW; CA 5-8R; CAAS 143; CANR 39, 74, 136; CN 1, 2; CP 1, 2, 3, 4; DLB 45, 63; EWL 3; MAL 5; MTCW 1, 2; MTFW 2005; RGAL 4

Burke, Leda
See Garnett, David

Burke, Ralph
See Silverberg, Robert

Burke, Thomas 1886-1945 .... **TCLC 63**
See also CA 155; CAAE 113; CMW 4; DLB 197

Burney, Fanny 1752-1840 .... **NCLC 12, 54, 107**
See also BRWS 3; DLB 39; FL 1:2; NFS 16; RGEL 2; TEA

Burney, Frances
See Burney, Fanny

Burns, Robert 1759-1796 ... **LC 3, 29, 40; PC 6; WLC 1**
See also AAYA 51; BRW 3; CDBLB 1789-1832; DA; DA3; DAB; DAC; DAM MST, POET; DLB 109; EXPP; PAB; RGEL 2; TEA; WP

Burns, Tex
See L'Amour, Louis

Burnshaw, Stanley 1906-2005 ..... **CLC 3, 13, 44**
See also CA 9-12R; CAAS 243; CP 1, 2, 3, 4, 5, 6, 7; DLB 48; DLBY 1997

Burr, Anne 1937- .... **CLC 6**
See also CA 25-28R

Burroughs, Edgar Rice 1875-1950 . **TCLC 2, 32**
See also AAYA 11; BPFB 1; BYA 4, 9; CA 132; CAAE 104; CANR 131; DA3; DAM NOV; DLB 8; FANT; MTCW 1, 2; MTFW 2005; RGAL 4; SATA 41; SCFW 1, 2; SFW 4; TCWW 1, 2; TUS; YAW

Burroughs, William S. 1914-1997 . **CLC 1, 2, 5, 15, 22, 42, 75, 109; TCLC 121; WLC 1**
See Lee, William; Lee, Willy
See also AAYA 60; AITN 2; AMWS 3; BG 1:2; BPFB 1; CA 9-12R; CAAS 160; CANR 20, 52, 104; CN 1, 2, 3, 4, 5, 6; CPW; DA; DA3; DAB; DAC; DAM MST, NOV, POP; DLB 2, 8, 16, 152, 237; DLBY 1981, 1997; EWL 3; HGG; LMFS 2; MAL 5; MTCW 1, 2; MTFW 2005; RGAL 4; SFW 4

Burroughs, William Seward
See Burroughs, William S.

Burton, Sir Richard F(rancis) 1821-1890 .... **NCLC 42**
See also DLB 55, 166, 184; SSFS 21

Burton, Robert 1577-1640 .... **LC 74**
See also DLB 151; RGEL 2

Buruma, Ian 1951- .... **CLC 163**
See also CA 128; CANR 65, 141

Busch, Frederick 1941-2006 .. **CLC 7, 10, 18, 47, 166**
See also CA 33-36R; 1; CAAS 248; CANR 45, 73, 92, 157; CN 1, 2, 3, 4, 5, 6, 7; DLB 6, 218

Busch, Frederick Matthew
See Busch, Frederick

Bush, Barney (Furman) 1946- .... **NNAL**
See also CA 145

Bush, Ronald 1946- .... **CLC 34**
See also CA 136

Bustos, F(rancisco)
See Borges, Jorge Luis

Bustos Domecq, H(onorio)
See Bioy Casares, Adolfo; Borges, Jorge Luis

Butler, Octavia E. 1947-2006 .... **BLCS; CLC 38, 121, 230**
See also AAYA 18, 48; AFAW 2; AMWS 13; BPFB 1; BW 2, 3; CA 73-76; CAAS 248; CANR 12, 24, 38, 73, 145; CLR 65; CN 7; CPW; DA3; DAM MULT, POP; DLB 33; LATS 1:2; MTCW 1, 2; MTFW 2005; NFS 8, 21; SATA 84; SCFW 2; SFW 4; SSFS 6; TCLE 1:1; YAW

Butler, Octavia Estelle
See Butler, Octavia E.

Butler, Robert Olen, (Jr.) 1945- ...... **CLC 81, 162**
See also AMWS 12; BPFB 1; CA 112; CANR 66, 138; CN 7; CSW; DAM POP; DLB 173; INT CA-112; MAL 5; MTCW 2; MTFW 2005; SSFS 11, 22

Butler, Samuel 1612-1680 .... **LC 16, 43**
See also DLB 101, 126; RGEL 2

Butler, Samuel 1835-1902 .... **TCLC 1, 33; WLC 1**
See also BRWS 2; CA 143; CDBLB 1890-1914; DA; DA3; DAB; DAC; DAM MST, NOV; DLB 18, 57, 174; RGEL 2; SFW 4; TEA

Butler, Walter C.
See Faust, Frederick (Schiller)

Butor, Michel (Marie Francois) 1926- .... **CLC 1, 3, 8, 11, 15, 161**
See also CA 9-12R; CANR 33, 66; CWW 2; DLB 83; EW 13; EWL 3; GFL 1789 to the Present; MTCW 1, 2; MTFW 2005

Butts, Mary 1890(?)-1937 .... **TCLC 77**
See also CA 148; DLB 240

Buxton, Ralph
See Silverstein, Alvin; Silverstein, Virginia B(arbara Opshelor)

Buzo, Alex
See Buzo, Alexander (John)
See also DLB 289

Buzo, Alexander (John) 1944- .... **CLC 61**
See also CA 97-100; CANR 17, 39, 69; CD 5, 6

Buzzati, Dino 1906-1972 .... **CLC 36**
See also CA 160; CAAS 33-36R; DLB 177; RGWL 2, 3; SFW 4

Byars, Betsy 1928- .... **CLC 35**
See also AAYA 19; BYA 3; CA 183; 33-36R, 183; CANR 18, 36, 57, 102, 148; CLR 1, 16, 72; DLB 52; INT CANR-18; JRDA; MAICYA 1, 2; MAICYAS 1; MTCW 1; SAAS 1; SATA 4, 46, 80, 163; SATA-Essay 108; WYA; YAW

Byars, Betsy Cromer
See Byars, Betsy

Byatt, Antonia Susan Drabble
See Byatt, A.S.

Byatt, A.S. 1936- .... **CLC 19, 65, 136, 223; SSC 91**
See also BPFB 1; BRWC 2; BRWS 4; CA 13-16R; CANR 13, 33, 50, 75, 96, 133; CN 1, 2, 3, 4, 5, 6; DA3; DAM NOV, POP; DLB 14, 194, 319, 326; EWL 3; MTCW 1, 2; MTFW 2005; RGSF 2; RHW; TEA

Byrd, William II 1674-1744 .... **LC 112**
See also DLB 24, 140; RGAL 4

Byrne, David 1952- .... **CLC 26**
See also CA 127

Byrne, John Keyes 1926-
See Leonard, Hugh
See also CA 102; CANR 78, 140; INT CA-102

Byron, George Gordon (Noel) 1788-1824 ..... **DC 24; NCLC 2, 12, 109, 149; PC 16; WLC 1**
See also AAYA 64; BRW 4; BRWC 2; CDBLB 1789-1832; DA; DA3; DAB; DAC; DAM MST, POET; DLB 96, 110; EXPP; LMFS 1; PAB; PFS 1, 14; RGEL 2; TEA; WLIT 3; WP

Byron, Robert 1905-1941 .... **TCLC 67**
See also CA 160; DLB 195

C. 3. 3.
See Wilde, Oscar (Fingal O'Flahertie Wills)

Caballero, Fernan 1796-1877 .... **NCLC 10**

Cabell, Branch
See Cabell, James Branch

Cabell, James Branch 1879-1958 .... **TCLC 6**
See also CA 152; CAAE 105; DLB 9, 78; FANT; MAL 5; MTCW 2; RGAL 4; SUFW 1

Cabeza de Vaca, Alvar Nunez 1490-1557(?) .... **LC 61**

Cable, George Washington 1844-1925 .... **SSC 4; TCLC 4**
See also CA 155; CAAE 104; DLB 12, 74; DLBD 13; RGAL 4; TUS

Cabral de Melo Neto, Joao 1920-1999 .... **CLC 76**
See Melo Neto, Joao Cabral de
See also CA 151; DAM MULT; DLB 307; LAW; LAWS 1

Cabrera Infante, G. 1929-2005 ... **CLC 5, 25, 45, 120; HLC 1; SSC 39**
See also CA 85-88; CAAS 236; CANR 29, 65, 110; CDWLB 3; CWW 2; DA3; DAM MULT; DLB 113; EWL 3; HW 1, 2; LAW; LAWS 1; MTCW 1, 2; MTFW 2005; RGSF 2; WLIT 1

Cabrera Infante, Guillermo
See Cabrera Infante, G.

Ciardi, John (Anthony) 1916-1986 . **CLC 10,**
40, 44, 129; PC 69
See also CA 5-8R; 2; CAAS 118; CANR 5,
33; CLR 19; CP 1, 2, 3, 4; CWRI 5; DAM
POET; DLB 5; DLBY 1986; INT
CANR-5; MAICYA 1, 2; MAL 5; MTCW
1, 2; MTFW 2005; RGAL 4; SAAS 26;
SATA 1, 65; SATA-Obit 46

Cibber, Colley 1671-1757 .... **LC 66**
See also DLB 84; RGEL 2

Cicero, Marcus Tullius
106B.C.-43B.C. .... **CMLC 3, 81**
See also AW 1; CDWLB 1; DLB 211;
RGWL 2, 3; WLIT 8

Cimino, Michael 1943- .... **CLC 16**
See also CA 105

Cioran, E(mil) M. 1911-1995 .... **CLC 64**
See also CA 25-28R; CAAS 149; CANR
91; DLB 220; EWL 3

Cisneros, Sandra 1954- .... **CLC 69, 118, 193;**
HLC 1; PC 52; SSC 32, 72
See also AAYA 9, 53; AMWS 7; CA 131;
CANR 64, 118; CN 7; CWP; DA3; DAM
MULT; DLB 122, 152; EWL 3; EXPN;
FL 1:5; FW; HW 1, 2; LAIT 5; LATS 1:2;
LLW; MAICYA 2; MAL 5; MTCW 2;
MTFW 2005; NFS 2; PFS 19; RGAL 4;
RGSF 2; SSFS 3, 13; WLIT 1; YAW

Cixous, Helene 1937- .... **CLC 92**
See also CA 126; CANR 55, 123; CWW 2;
DLB 83, 242; EWL 3; FL 1:5; FW; GLL
2; MTCW 1, 2; MTFW 2005; TWA

Clair, Rene .... **CLC 20**
See Chomette, Rene Lucien

Clampitt, Amy 1920-1994 .... **CLC 32; PC 19**
See also AMWS 9; CA 110; CAAS 146;
CANR 29, 79; CP 4, 5; DLB 105; MAL 5

Clancy, Thomas L., Jr. 1947-
See Clancy, Tom
See also CA 131; CAAE 125; CANR 62,
105; DA3; INT CA-131; MTCW 1, 2;
MTFW 2005

Clancy, Tom .... **CLC 45, 112**
See Clancy, Thomas L., Jr.
See also AAYA 9, 51; BEST 89:1, 90:1;
BPFB 1; BYA 10, 11; CANR 132; CMW
4; CPW; DAM NOV, POP; DLB 227

Clare, John 1793-1864 .. **NCLC 9, 86; PC 23**
See also BRWS 11; DAB; DAM POET;
DLB 55, 96; RGEL 2

Clarin
See Alas (y Urena), Leopoldo (Enrique
Garcia)

Clark, Al C.
See Goines, Donald

Clark, Brian (Robert)
See Clark, (Robert) Brian
See also CD 6

Clark, (Robert) Brian 1932- .... **CLC 29**
See Clark, Brian (Robert)
See also CA 41-44R; CANR 67; CBD; CD
5

Clark, Curt
See Westlake, Donald E.

Clark, Eleanor 1913-1996 .... **CLC 5, 19**
See also CA 9-12R; CAAS 151; CANR 41;
CN 1, 2, 3, 4, 5, 6; DLB 6

Clark, J. P.
See Clark Bekederemo, J.P.
See also CDWLB 3; DLB 117

Clark, John Pepper
See Clark Bekederemo, J.P.
See also AFW; CD 5; CP 1, 2, 3, 4, 5, 6, 7;
RGEL 2

Clark, Kenneth (Mackenzie)
1903-1983 .... **TCLC 147**
See also CA 93-96; CAAS 109; CANR 36;
MTCW 1, 2; MTFW 2005

Clark, M. R.
See Clark, Mavis Thorpe

Clark, Mavis Thorpe 1909-1999 ...... **CLC 12**
See also CA 57-60; CANR 8, 37, 107; CLR
30; CWRI 5; MAICYA 1, 2; SAAS 5;
SATA 8, 74

Clark, Walter Van Tilburg
1909-1971 .... **CLC 28**
See also CA 9-12R; CAAS 33-36R; CANR
63, 113; CN 1; DLB 9, 206; LAIT 2;
MAL 5; RGAL 4; SATA 8; TCWW 1, 2

Clark Bekederemo, J.P. 1935- . **BLC 1; CLC**
38; DC 5
See Bekederemo, J. P. Clark; Clark, J. P.;
Clark, John Pepper
See also BW 1; CA 65-68; CANR 16, 72;
DAM DRAM, MULT; DFS 13; EWL 3;
MTCW 2; MTFW 2005

Clarke, Arthur C. 1917- .... **CLC 1, 4, 13, 18,**
35, 136; SSC 3
See also AAYA 4, 33; BPFB 1; BYA 13;
CA 1-4R; CANR 2, 28, 55, 74, 130; CLR
119; CN 1, 2, 3, 4, 5, 6, 7; CPW; DA3;
DAM POP; DLB 261; JRDA; LAIT 5;
MAICYA 1, 2; MTCW 1, 2; MTFW 2005;
SATA 13, 70, 115; SCFW 1, 2; SFW 4;
SSFS 4, 18; TCLE 1:1; YAW

Clarke, Austin 1896-1974 .... **CLC 6, 9**
See also CA 29-32; CAAS 49-52; CAP 2;
CP 1, 2; DAM POET; DLB 10, 20; EWL
3; RGEL 2

Clarke, Austin C. 1934- . **BLC 1; CLC 8, 53;**
SSC 45
See also BW 1; CA 25-28R; 16; CANR 14,
32, 68, 140; CN 1, 2, 3, 4, 5, 6, 7; DAC;
DAM MULT; DLB 53, 125; DNFS 2;
MTCW 2; MTFW 2005; RGSF 2

Clarke, Gillian 1937- .... **CLC 61**
See also CA 106; CP 3, 4, 5, 6, 7; CWP;
DLB 40

Clarke, Marcus (Andrew Hislop)
1846-1881 .... **NCLC 19; SSC 94**
See also DLB 230; RGEL 2; RGSF 2

Clarke, Shirley 1925-1997 .... **CLC 16**
See also CA 189

Clash, The
See Headon, (Nicky) Topper; Jones, Mick;
Simonon, Paul; Strummer, Joe

Claudel, Paul (Louis Charles Marie)
1868-1955 .... **TCLC 2, 10**
See also CA 165; CAAE 104; DLB 192,
258, 321; EW 8; EWL 3; GFL 1789 to
the Present; RGWL 2, 3; TWA

Claudian 370(?)-404(?) .... **CMLC 46**
See also RGWL 2, 3

Claudius, Matthias 1740-1815 .... **NCLC 75**
See also DLB 97

Clavell, James 1925-1994 .... **CLC 6, 25, 87**
See also BPFB 1; CA 25-28R; CAAS 146;
CANR 26, 48; CN 5; CPW; DA3; DAM
NOV, POP; MTCW 1, 2; MTFW 2005;
NFS 10; RHW

Clayman, Gregory .... **CLC 65**

Cleaver, (Leroy) Eldridge
1935-1998 .... **BLC 1; CLC 30, 119**
See also BW 1, 3; CA 21-24R; CAAS 167;
CANR 16, 75; DA3; DAM MULT;
MTCW 2; YAW

Cleese, John (Marwood) 1939- .... **CLC 21**
See Monty Python
See also CA 116; CAAE 112; CANR 35;
MTCW 1

Cleishbotham, Jebediah
See Scott, Sir Walter

Cleland, John 1710-1789 .... **LC 2, 48**
See also DLB 39; RGEL 2

Clemens, Samuel Langhorne 1835-1910
See Twain, Mark
See also CA 135; CAAE 104; CDALB
1865-1917; DA; DA3; DAB; DAC; DAM
MST, NOV; DLB 12, 23, 64, 74, 186,
189; JRDA; LMFS 1; MAICYA 1, 2;
NCFS 4; NFS 20; SATA 100; YABC 2

Clement of Alexandria
150(?)-215(?) .... **CMLC 41**

Cleophil
See Congreve, William

Clerihew, E.
See Bentley, E(dmund) C(lerihew)

Clerk, N. W.
See Lewis, C.S.

Cleveland, John 1613-1658 .... **LC 106**
See also DLB 126; RGEL 2

Cliff, Jimmy .... **CLC 21**
See Chambers, James
See also CA 193

Cliff, Michelle 1946- .... **BLCS; CLC 120**
See also BW 2; CA 116; CANR 39, 72; CD-
WLB 3; DLB 157; FW; GLL 2

Clifford, Lady Anne 1590-1676 .... **LC 76**
See also DLB 151

Clifton, Lucille 1936- ... **BLC 1; CLC 19, 66,**
162; PC 17
See also AFAW 2; BW 2, 3; CA 49-52;
CANR 2, 24, 42, 76, 97, 138; CLR 5; CP
2, 3, 4, 5, 6, 7; CSW; CWP; CWRI 5;
DA3; DAM MULT, POET; DLB 5, 41;
EXPP; MAICYA 1, 2; MTCW 1, 2;
MTFW 2005; PFS 1, 14; SATA 20, 69,
128; WP

Clinton, Dirk
See Silverberg, Robert

Clough, Arthur Hugh 1819-1861 .. **NCLC 27,**
163
See also BRW 5; DLB 32; RGEL 2

Clutha, Janet Paterson Frame 1924-2004
See Frame, Janet
See also CA 1-4R; CAAS 224; CANR 2,
36, 76, 135; MTCW 1, 2; SATA 119

Clyne, Terence
See Blatty, William Peter

Cobalt, Martin
See Mayne, William (James Carter)

Cobb, Irvin S(hrewsbury)
1876-1944 .... **TCLC 77**
See also CA 175; DLB 11, 25, 86

Cobbett, William 1763-1835 .... **NCLC 49**
See also DLB 43, 107, 158; RGEL 2

Coburn, D(onald) L(ee) 1938- .... **CLC 10**
See also CA 89-92; DFS 23

Cocteau, Jean 1889-1963 ... **CLC 1, 8, 15, 16,**
43; DC 17; TCLC 119; WLC 2
See also AAYA 74; CA 25-28; CANR 40;
CAP 2; DA; DA3; DAB; DAC; DAM
DRAM, MST, NOV; DLB 65, 258, 321;
EW 10; EWL 3; GFL 1789 to the Present;
MTCW 1, 2; RGWL 2, 3; TWA

Cocteau, Jean Maurice Eugene Clement
See Cocteau, Jean

Codrescu, Andrei 1946- .... **CLC 46, 121**
See also CA 33-36R; 19; CANR 13, 34, 53,
76, 125; CN 7; DA3; DAM POET; MAL
5; MTCW 2; MTFW 2005

Coe, Max
See Bourne, Randolph S(illiman)

Coe, Tucker
See Westlake, Donald E.

Coen, Ethan 1958- .... **CLC 108**
See also AAYA 54; CA 126; CANR 85

Coen, Joel 1955- .... **CLC 108**
See also AAYA 54; CA 126; CANR 119

The Coen Brothers
See Coen, Ethan; Coen, Joel

Cunninghame Graham, R. B.
See Cunninghame Graham, Robert (Gallnigad) Bontine
Cunninghame Graham, Robert (Gallnigad) Bontine 1852-1936 .... **TCLC 19**
See Graham, R(obert) B(ontine) Cunning-hame
See also CA 184; CAAE 119
Curnow, (Thomas) Allen (Monro) 1911-2001 .... **PC 48**
See also CA 69-72; CAAS 202; CANR 48, 99; CP 1, 2, 3, 4, 5, 6, 7; EWL 3; RGEL 2
Currie, Ellen 19(?)- .... **CLC 44**
Curtin, Philip
See Lowndes, Marie Adelaide (Belloc)
Curtin, Phillip
See Lowndes, Marie Adelaide (Belloc)
Curtis, Price
See Ellison, Harlan
Cusanus, Nicolaus 1401-1464 .... **LC 80**
See Nicholas of Cusa
Cutrate, Joe
See Spiegelman, Art
Cynewulf c. 770- .... **CMLC 23**
See also DLB 146; RGEL 2
Cyrano de Bergerac, Savinien de 1619-1655 .... **LC 65**
See also DLB 268; GFL Beginnings to 1789; RGWL 2, 3
Cyril of Alexandria c. 375-c. 430 . **CMLC 59**
Czaczkes, Shmuel Yosef Halevi
See Agnon, S(hmuel) Y(osef Halevi)
Dabrowska, Maria (Szumska) 1889-1965 .... **CLC 15**
See also CA 106; CDWLB 4; DLB 215; EWL 3
Dabydeen, David 1955- .... **CLC 34**
See also BW 1; CA 125; CANR 56, 92; CN 6, 7; CP 5, 6, 7
Dacey, Philip 1939- .... **CLC 51**
See also CA 231; 37-40R, 231; 17; CANR 14, 32, 64; CP 4, 5, 6, 7; DLB 105
Dacre, Charlotte c. 1772-1825(?) . **NCLC 151**
Dafydd ap Gwilym c. 1320-c. 1380 ..... **PC 56**
Dagerman, Stig (Halvard) 1923-1954 .... **TCLC 17**
See also CA 155; CAAE 117; DLB 259; EWL 3
D'Aguiar, Fred 1960- .... **CLC 145**
See also CA 148; CANR 83, 101; CN 7; CP 5, 6, 7; DLB 157; EWL 3
Dahl, Roald 1916-1990 ...... **CLC 1, 6, 18, 79; TCLC 173**
See also AAYA 15; BPFB 1; BRWS 4; BYA 5; CA 1-4R; CAAS 133; CANR 6, 32, 37, 62; CLR 1, 7, 41, 111; CN 1, 2, 3, 4; CPW; DA3; DAB; DAC; DAM MST, NOV, POP; DLB 139, 255; HGG; JRDA; MAICYA 1, 2; MTCW 1, 2; MTFW 2005; RGSF 2; SATA 1, 26, 73; SATA-Obit 65; SSFS 4; TEA; YAW
Dahlberg, Edward 1900-1977 .. **CLC 1, 7, 14**
See also CA 9-12R; CAAS 69-72; CANR 31, 62; CN 1, 2; DLB 48; MAL 5; MTCW 1; RGAL 4
Daitch, Susan 1954- .... **CLC 103**
See also CA 161
Dale, Colin .... **TCLC 18**
See Lawrence, T(homas) E(dward)
Dale, George E.
See Asimov, Isaac
d'Alembert, Jean Le Rond 1717-1783 .... **LC 126**
Dalton, Roque 1935-1975(?) ..... **HLCS 1; PC 36**
See also CA 176; DLB 283; HW 2

Daly, Elizabeth 1878-1967 .... **CLC 52**
See also CA 23-24; CAAS 25-28R; CANR 60; CAP 2; CMW 4
Daly, Mary 1928- .... **CLC 173**
See also CA 25-28R; CANR 30, 62; FW; GLL 1; MTCW 1
Daly, Maureen 1921-2006 .... **CLC 17**
See also AAYA 5, 58; BYA 6; CAAS 253; CANR 37, 83, 108; CLR 96; JRDA; MAICYA 1, 2; SAAS 1; SATA 2, 129; SATA-Obit 176; WYA; YAW
Damas, Leon-Gontran 1912-1978 .... **CLC 84**
See also BW 1; CA 125; CAAS 73-76; EWL 3
Dana, Richard Henry Sr. 1787-1879 .... **NCLC 53**
Daniel, Samuel 1562(?)-1619 .... **LC 24**
See also DLB 62; RGEL 2
Daniels, Brett
See Adler, Renata
Dannay, Frederic 1905-1982 .... **CLC 11**
See Queen, Ellery
See also CA 1-4R; CAAS 107; CANR 1, 39; CMW 4; DAM POP; DLB 137; MTCW 1
D'Annunzio, Gabriele 1863-1938 ... **TCLC 6, 40**
See also CA 155; CAAE 104; EW 8; EWL 3; RGWL 2, 3; TWA; WLIT 7
Danois, N. le
See Gourmont, Remy(-Marie-Charles) de
Dante 1265-1321 .... **CMLC 3, 18, 39, 70; PC 21; WLCS**
See Alighieri, Dante
See also DA; DA3; DAB; DAC; DAM MST, POET; EFS 1; EW 1; LAIT 1; RGWL 2, 3; TWA; WP
d'Antibes, Germain
See Simenon, Georges (Jacques Christian)
Danticat, Edwidge 1969- ... **CLC 94, 139, 228**
See also AAYA 29; CA 192; 152, 192; CANR 73, 129; CN 7; DNFS 1; EXPS; LATS 1:2; MTCW 2; MTFW 2005; SSFS 1; YAW
Danvers, Dennis 1947- .... **CLC 70**
Danziger, Paula 1944-2004 .... **CLC 21**
See also AAYA 4, 36; BYA 6, 7, 14; CA 115; CAAE 112; CAAS 229; CANR 37, 132; CLR 20; JRDA; MAICYA 1, 2; MTFW 2005; SATA 36, 63, 102, 149; SATA-Brief 30; SATA-Obit 155; WYA; YAW
Da Ponte, Lorenzo 1749-1838 .... **NCLC 50**
d'Aragona, Tullia 1510(?)-1556 .... **LC 121**
Dario, Ruben 1867-1916 .... **HLC 1; PC 15; TCLC 4**
See also CA 131; CANR 81; DAM MULT; DLB 290; EWL 3; HW 1, 2; LAW; MTCW 1, 2; MTFW 2005; RGWL 2, 3
Darley, George 1795-1846 .... **NCLC 2**
See also DLB 96; RGEL 2
Darrow, Clarence (Seward) 1857-1938 .... **TCLC 81**
See also CA 164; DLB 303
Darwin, Charles 1809-1882 .... **NCLC 57**
See also BRWS 7; DLB 57, 166; LATS 1:1; RGEL 2; TEA; WLIT 4
Darwin, Erasmus 1731-1802 .... **NCLC 106**
See also DLB 93; RGEL 2
Daryush, Elizabeth 1887-1977 ...... **CLC 6, 19**
See also CA 49-52; CANR 3, 81; DLB 20
Das, Kamala 1934- .... **CLC 191; PC 43**
See also CA 101; CANR 27, 59; CP 1, 2, 3, 4, 5, 6, 7; CWP; DLB 323; FW
Dasgupta, Surendranath 1887-1952 .... **TCLC 81**
See also CA 157

Dashwood, Edmee Elizabeth Monica de la Pasture 1890-1943
See Delafield, E. M.
See also CA 154; CAAE 119
da Silva, Antonio Jose 1705-1739 .... **NCLC 114**
Daudet, (Louis Marie) Alphonse 1840-1897 .... **NCLC 1**
See also DLB 123; GFL 1789 to the Present; RGSF 2
Daudet, Alphonse Marie Leon 1867-1942 .... **SSC 94**
See also CA 217
d'Aulnoy, Marie-Catherine c. 1650-1705 .... **LC 100**
Daumal, Rene 1908-1944 .... **TCLC 14**
See also CA 247; CAAE 114; EWL 3
Davenant, William 1606-1668 .... **LC 13**
See also DLB 58, 126; RGEL 2
Davenport, Guy (Mattison, Jr.) 1927-2005 .... **CLC 6, 14, 38; SSC 16**
See also CA 33-36R; CAAS 235; CANR 23, 73; CN 3, 4, 5, 6; CSW; DLB 130
David, Robert
See Nezval, Vitezslav
Davidson, Avram (James) 1923-1993
See Queen, Ellery
See also CA 101; CAAS 171; CANR 26; DLB 8; FANT; SFW 4; SUFW 1, 2
Davidson, Donald (Grady) 1893-1968 .... **CLC 2, 13, 19**
See also CA 5-8R; CAAS 25-28R; CANR 4, 84; DLB 45
Davidson, Hugh
See Hamilton, Edmond
Davidson, John 1857-1909 .... **TCLC 24**
See also CA 217; CAAE 118; DLB 19; RGEL 2
Davidson, Sara 1943- .... **CLC 9**
See also CA 81-84; CANR 44, 68; DLB 185
Davie, Donald (Alfred) 1922-1995 .... **CLC 5, 8, 10, 31; PC 29**
See also BRWS 6; CA 1-4R; 3; CAAS 149; CANR 1, 44; CP 1, 2, 3, 4, 5, 6; DLB 27; MTCW 1; RGEL 2
Davie, Elspeth 1918-1995 .... **SSC 52**
See also CA 126; CAAE 120; CAAS 150; CANR 141; DLB 139
Davies, Ray(mond Douglas) 1944- ... **CLC 21**
See also CA 146; CAAE 116; CANR 92
Davies, Rhys 1901-1978 .... **CLC 23**
See also CA 9-12R; CAAS 81-84; CANR 4; CN 1, 2; DLB 139, 191
Davies, Robertson 1913-1995 .. **CLC 2, 7, 13, 25, 42, 75, 91; WLC 2**
See Marchbanks, Samuel
See also BEST 89:2; BPFB 1; CA 33-36R; CAAS 150; CANR 17, 42, 103; CN 1, 2, 3, 4, 5, 6; CPW; DA; DA3; DAB; DAC; DAM MST, NOV, POP; DLB 68; EWL 3; HGG; INT CANR-17; MTCW 1, 2; MTFW 2005; RGEL 2; TWA
Davies, Sir John 1569-1626 .... **LC 85**
See also DLB 172
Davies, Walter C.
See Kornbluth, C(yril) M.
Davies, William Henry 1871-1940 ... **TCLC 5**
See also BRWS 11; CA 179; CAAE 104; DLB 19, 174; EWL 3; RGEL 2
Davies, William Robertson
See Davies, Robertson
Da Vinci, Leonardo 1452-1519 ..... **LC 12, 57, 60**
See also AAYA 40
Davis, Angela (Yvonne) 1944- .... **CLC 77**
See also BW 2, 3; CA 57-60; CANR 10, 81; CSW; DA3; DAM MULT; FW

del Valle-Inclan, Ramon (Maria)
    See Valle-Inclan, Ramon (Maria) del
    See also DLB 322
Del Vecchio, John M(ichael) 1947- .. **CLC 29**
    See also CA 110; DLBD 9
de Man, Paul (Adolph Michel)
    1919-1983 .... **CLC 55**
    See also CA 128; CAAS 111; CANR 61;
    DLB 67; MTCW 1, 2
DeMarinis, Rick 1934- .... **CLC 54**
    See also CA 184; 57-60, 184; 24; CANR 9,
    25, 50, 160; DLB 218; TCWW 2
de Maupassant, (Henri Rene Albert) Guy
    See Maupassant, (Henri Rene Albert) Guy
    de
Dembry, R. Emmet
    See Murfree, Mary Noailles
Demby, William 1922- .... **BLC 1; CLC 53**
    See also BW 1, 3; CA 81-84; CANR 81;
    DAM MULT; DLB 33
de Menton, Francisco
    See Chin, Frank (Chew, Jr.)
Demetrius of Phalerum c.
    307B.C.- .... **CMLC 34**
Demijohn, Thom
    See Disch, Thomas M.
De Mille, James 1833-1880 .... **NCLC 123**
    See also DLB 99, 251
Deming, Richard 1915-1983
    See Queen, Ellery
    See also CA 9-12R; CANR 3, 94; SATA 24
Democritus c. 460B.C.-c. 370B.C. . **CMLC 47**
de Montaigne, Michel (Eyquem)
    See Montaigne, Michel (Eyquem) de
de Montherlant, Henry (Milon)
    See Montherlant, Henry (Milon) de
Demosthenes 384B.C.-322B.C. ...... **CMLC 13**
    See also AW 1; DLB 176; RGWL 2, 3;
    WLIT 8
de Musset, (Louis Charles) Alfred
    See Musset, Alfred de
de Natale, Francine
    See Malzberg, Barry N(athaniel)
de Navarre, Marguerite 1492-1549 ... **LC 61;**
    SSC 85
    See Marguerite d'Angouleme; Marguerite
    de Navarre
    See also DLB 327
Denby, Edwin (Orr) 1903-1983 .... **CLC 48**
    See also CA 138; CAAS 110; CP 1
de Nerval, Gerard
    See Nerval, Gerard de
Denham, John 1615-1669 .... **LC 73**
    See also DLB 58, 126; RGEL 2
Denis, Julio
    See Cortazar, Julio
Denmark, Harrison
    See Zelazny, Roger
Dennis, John 1658-1734 .... **LC 11**
    See also DLB 101; RGEL 2
Dennis, Nigel (Forbes) 1912-1989 ...... **CLC 8**
    See also CA 25-28R; CAAS 129; CN 1, 2,
    3, 4; DLB 13, 15, 233; EWL 3; MTCW 1
Dent, Lester 1904-1959 .... **TCLC 72**
    See also CA 161; CAAE 112; CMW 4;
    DLB 306; SFW 4
De Palma, Brian 1940- .... **CLC 20**
    See also CA 109
De Palma, Brian Russell
    See De Palma, Brian
de Pizan, Christine
    See Christine de Pizan
    See also FL 1:1
De Quincey, Thomas 1785-1859 ..... **NCLC 4,**
    87
    See also BRW 4; CDBLB 1789-1832; DLB
    110, 144; RGEL 2

Deren, Eleanora 1908(?)-1961
    See Deren, Maya
    See also CA 192; CAAS 111
Deren, Maya .... **CLC 16, 102**
    See Deren, Eleanora
Derleth, August (William)
    1909-1971 .... **CLC 31**
    See also BPFB 1; BYA 9, 10; CA 1-4R;
    CAAS 29-32R; CANR 4; CMW 4; CN 1;
    DLB 9; DLBD 17; HGG; SATA 5; SUFW
    1
Der Nister 1884-1950 .... **TCLC 56**
    See Nister, Der
de Routisie, Albert
    See Aragon, Louis
Derrida, Jacques 1930-2004 ...... **CLC 24, 87,**
    225
    See also CA 127; CAAE 124; CAAS 232;
    CANR 76, 98, 133; DLB 242; EWL 3;
    LMFS 2; MTCW 2; TWA
Derry Down Derry
    See Lear, Edward
Dersonnes, Jacques
    See Simenon, Georges (Jacques Christian)
Der Stricker c. 1190-c. 1250 .... **CMLC 75**
    See also DLB 138
Desai, Anita 1937- .... **CLC 19, 37, 97, 175**
    See also BRWS 5; CA 81-84; CANR 33,
    53, 95, 133; CN 1, 2, 3, 4, 5, 6, 7; CWRI
    5; DA3; DAB; DAM NOV; DLB 271,
    323; DNFS 2; EWL 3; FW; MTCW 1, 2;
    MTFW 2005; SATA 63, 126
Desai, Kiran 1971- .... **CLC 119**
    See also BYA 16; CA 171; CANR 127
de Saint-Luc, Jean
    See Glassco, John
de Saint Roman, Arnaud
    See Aragon, Louis
Desbordes-Valmore, Marceline
    1786-1859 .... **NCLC 97**
    See also DLB 217
Descartes, Rene 1596-1650 .... **LC 20, 35**
    See also DLB 268; EW 3; GFL Beginnings
    to 1789
Deschamps, Eustache 1340(?)-1404 .. **LC 103**
    See also DLB 208
De Sica, Vittorio 1901(?)-1974 .... **CLC 20**
    See also CAAS 117
Desnos, Robert 1900-1945 .... **TCLC 22**
    See also CA 151; CAAE 121; CANR 107;
    DLB 258; EWL 3; LMFS 2
Destouches, Louis-Ferdinand
    1894-1961 .... **CLC 9, 15**
    See Celine, Louis-Ferdinand
    See also CA 85-88; CANR 28; MTCW 1
de Tolignac, Gaston
    See Griffith, D(avid Lewelyn) W(ark)
Deutsch, Babette 1895-1982 .... **CLC 18**
    See also BYA 3; CA 1-4R; CAAS 108;
    CANR 4, 79; CP 1, 2, 3; DLB 45; SATA
    1; SATA-Obit 33
Devenant, William 1606-1649 .... **LC 13**
Devkota, Laxmiprasad 1909-1959 . **TCLC 23**
    See also CAAE 123
De Voto, Bernard (Augustine)
    1897-1955 .... **TCLC 29**
    See also CA 160; CAAE 113; DLB 9, 256;
    MAL 5; TCWW 1, 2
De Vries, Peter 1910-1993 ..... **CLC 1, 2, 3, 7,**
    10, 28, 46
    See also CA 17-20R; CAAS 142; CANR
    41; CN 1, 2, 3, 4, 5; DAM NOV; DLB 6;
    DLBY 1982; MAL 5; MTCW 1, 2;
    MTFW 2005
Dewey, John 1859-1952 .... **TCLC 95**
    See also CA 170; CAAE 114; CANR 144;
    DLB 246, 270; RGAL 4

Dexter, John
    See Bradley, Marion Zimmer
    See also GLL 1
Dexter, Martin
    See Faust, Frederick (Schiller)
Dexter, Pete 1943- .... **CLC 34, 55**
    See also BEST 89:2; CA 131; CAAE 127;
    CANR 129; CPW; DAM POP; INT CA-
    131; MAL 5; MTCW 1; MTFW 2005
Diamano, Silmang
    See Senghor, Leopold Sedar
Diamond, Neil 1941- .... **CLC 30**
    See also CA 108
Diaz del Castillo, Bernal c.
    1496-1584 .... **HLCS 1; LC 31**
    See also DLB 318; LAW
di Bassetto, Corno
    See Shaw, George Bernard
Dick, Philip K. 1928-1982 ... **CLC 10, 30, 72;**
    SSC 57
    See also AAYA 24; BPFB 1; BYA 11; CA
    49-52; CAAS 106; CANR 2, 16, 132; CN
    2, 3; CPW; DA3; DAM NOV, POP; DLB
    8; MTCW 1, 2; MTFW 2005; NFS 5;
    SCFW 1, 2; SFW 4
Dick, Philip Kindred
    See Dick, Philip K.
Dickens, Charles (John Huffam)
    1812-1870 .... **NCLC 3, 8, 18, 26, 37, 50,**
    86, 105, 113, 161; SSC 17, 49, 88; WLC
    2
    See also AAYA 23; BRW 5; BRWC 1, 2;
    BYA 1, 2, 3, 13, 14; CDBLB 1832-1890;
    CLR 95; CMW 4; DA; DA3; DAB; DAC;
    DAM MST, NOV; DLB 21, 55, 70, 159,
    166; EXPN; GL 2; HGG; JRDA; LAIT 1,
    2; LATS 1:1; LMFS 1; MAICYA 1, 2;
    NFS 4, 5, 10, 14, 20; RGEL 2; RGSF 2;
    SATA 15; SUFW 1; TEA; WCH; WLIT
    4; WYA
Dickey, James (Lafayette)
    1923-1997 .... **CLC 1, 2, 4, 7, 10, 15, 47,**
    109; PC 40; TCLC 151
    See also AAYA 50; AITN 1, 2; AMWS 4;
    BPFB 1; CA 9-12R; CAAS 156; CABS
    2; CANR 10, 48, 61, 105; CDALB 1968-
    1988; CP 1, 2, 3, 4, 5, 6; CPW; CSW;
    DA3; DAM NOV, POET, POP; DLB 5,
    193; DLBD 7; DLBY 1982, 1993, 1996,
    1997, 1998; EWL 3; INT CANR-10;
    MAL 5; MTCW 1, 2; NFS 9; PFS 6, 11;
    RGAL 4; TUS
Dickey, William 1928-1994 .... **CLC 3, 28**
    See also CA 9-12R; CAAS 145; CANR 24,
    79; CP 1, 2, 3, 4; DLB 5
Dickinson, Charles 1951- .... **CLC 49**
    See also CA 128; CANR 141
Dickinson, Emily (Elizabeth)
    1830-1886 ..... **NCLC 21, 77, 171; PC 1;**
    WLC 2
    See also AAYA 22; AMW; AMWR 1;
    CDALB 1865-1917; DA; DA3; DAB;
    DAC; DAM MST, POET; DLB 1, 243;
    EXPP; FL 1:3; MBL; PAB; PFS 1, 2, 3,
    4, 5, 6, 8, 10, 11, 13, 16; RGAL 4; SATA
    29; TUS; WP; WYA
Dickinson, Mrs. Herbert Ward
    See Phelps, Elizabeth Stuart
Dickinson, Peter (Malcolm de Brissac)
    1927- .... **CLC 12, 35**
    See also AAYA 9, 49; BYA 5; CA 41-44R;
    CANR 31, 58, 88, 134; CLR 29; CMW 4;
    DLB 87, 161, 276; JRDA; MAICYA 1, 2;
    SATA 5, 62, 95, 150; SFW 4; WYA; YAW
Dickson, Carr
    See Carr, John Dickson
Dickson, Carter
    See Carr, John Dickson

Duhamel, Georges 1884-1966 .... **CLC 8**
See also CA 81-84; CAAS 25-28R; CANR 35; DLB 65; EWL 3; GFL 1789 to the Present; MTCW 1

Dujardin, Edouard (Emile Louis)
1861-1949 .... **TCLC 13**
See also CAAE 109; DLB 123

Duke, Raoul
See Thompson, Hunter S.

Dulles, John Foster 1888-1959 .... **TCLC 72**
See also CA 149; CAAE 115

Dumas, Alexandre (pere)
1802-1870 .... **NCLC 11, 71; WLC 2**
See also AAYA 22; BYA 3; DA; DA3; DAB; DAC; DAM MST, NOV; DLB 119, 192; EW 6; GFL 1789 to the Present; LAIT 1, 2; NFS 14, 19; RGWL 2, 3; SATA 18; TWA; WCH

Dumas, Alexandre (fils) 1824-1895 ...... **DC 1; NCLC 9**
See also DLB 192; GFL 1789 to the Present; RGWL 2, 3

Dumas, Claudine
See Malzberg, Barry N(athaniel)

Dumas, Henry L. 1934-1968 .... **CLC 6, 62**
See also BW 1; CA 85-88; DLB 41; RGAL 4

du Maurier, Daphne 1907-1989 .. **CLC 6, 11, 59; SSC 18**
See also AAYA 37; BPFB 1; BRWS 3; CA 5-8R; CAAS 128; CANR 6, 55; CMW 4; CN 1, 2, 3, 4; CPW; DA3; DAB; DAC; DAM MST, POP; DLB 191; GL 2; HGG; LAIT 3; MSW; MTCW 1, 2; NFS 12; RGEL 2; RGSF 2; RHW; SATA 27; SATA-Obit 60; SSFS 14, 16; TEA

Du Maurier, George 1834-1896 ..... **NCLC 86**
See also DLB 153, 178; RGEL 2

Dunbar, Paul Laurence 1872-1906 ... **BLC 1; PC 5; SSC 8; TCLC 2, 12; WLC 2**
See also AAYA 75; AFAW 1, 2; AMWS 2; BW 1, 3; CA 124; CAAE 104; CANR 79; CDALB 1865-1917; DA; DA3; DAC; DAM MST, MULT, POET; DLB 50, 54, 78; EXPP; MAL 5; RGAL 4; SATA 34

Dunbar, William 1460(?)-1520(?) .... **LC 20; PC 67**
See also BRWS 8; DLB 132, 146; RGEL 2

Dunbar-Nelson, Alice .... **HR 1:2**
See Nelson, Alice Ruth Moore Dunbar

Duncan, Dora Angela
See Duncan, Isadora

Duncan, Isadora 1877(?)-1927 .... **TCLC 68**
See also CA 149; CAAE 118

Duncan, Lois 1934- .... **CLC 26**
See also AAYA 4, 34; BYA 6, 8; CA 1-4R; CANR 2, 23, 36, 111; CLR 29; JRDA; MAICYA 1, 2; MAICYAS 1; MTFW 2005; SAAS 2; SATA 1, 36, 75, 133, 141; SATA-Essay 141; WYA; YAW

Duncan, Robert 1919-1988 ... **CLC 1, 2, 4, 7, 15, 41, 55; PC 2, 75**
See also BG 1:2; CA 9-12R; CAAS 124; CANR 28, 62; CP 1, 2, 3, 4; DAM POET; DLB 5, 16, 193; EWL 3; MAL 5; MTCW 1, 2; MTFW 2005; PFS 13; RGAL 4; WP

Duncan, Sara Jeannette
1861-1922 .... **TCLC 60**
See also CA 157; DLB 92

Dunlap, William 1766-1839 .... **NCLC 2**
See also DLB 30, 37, 59; RGAL 4

Dunn, Douglas (Eaglesham) 1942- .... **CLC 6, 40**
See also BRWS 10; CA 45-48; CANR 2, 33, 126; CP 1, 2, 3, 4, 5, 6, 7; DLB 40; MTCW 1

Dunn, Katherine 1945- .... **CLC 71**
See also CA 33-36R; CANR 72; HGG; MTCW 2; MTFW 2005

Dunn, Stephen 1939- .... **CLC 36, 206**
See also AMWS 11; CA 33-36R; CANR 12, 48, 53, 105; CP 3, 4, 5, 6, 7; DLB 105; PFS 21

Dunn, Stephen Elliott
See Dunn, Stephen

Dunne, Finley Peter 1867-1936 ...... **TCLC 28**
See also CA 178; CAAE 108; DLB 11, 23; RGAL 4

Dunne, John Gregory 1932-2003 ..... **CLC 28**
See also CA 25-28R; CAAS 222; CANR 14, 50; CN 5, 6, 7; DLBY 1980

Dunsany, Lord .... **TCLC 2, 59**
See Dunsany, Edward John Moreton Drax Plunkett
See also DLB 77, 153, 156, 255; FANT; IDTP; RGEL 2; SFW 4; SUFW 1

Dunsany, Edward John Moreton Drax Plunkett 1878-1957
See Dunsany, Lord
See also CA 148; CAAE 104; DLB 10; MTCW 2

Duns Scotus, John 1266(?)-1308 ... **CMLC 59**
See also DLB 115

du Perry, Jean
See Simenon, Georges (Jacques Christian)

Durang, Christopher 1949- .... **CLC 27, 38**
See also CA 105; CAD; CANR 50, 76, 130; CD 5, 6; MTCW 2; MTFW 2005

Durang, Christopher Ferdinand
See Durang, Christopher

Duras, Claire de 1777-1832 .... **NCLC 154**

Duras, Marguerite 1914-1996 . **CLC 3, 6, 11, 20, 34, 40, 68, 100; SSC 40**
See also BPFB 1; CA 25-28R; CAAS 151; CANR 50; CWW 2; DFS 21; DLB 83, 321; EWL 3; FL 1:5; GFL 1789 to the Present; IDFW 4; MTCW 1, 2; RGWL 2, 3; TWA

Durban, (Rosa) Pam 1947- .... **CLC 39**
See also CA 123; CANR 98; CSW

Durcan, Paul 1944- .... **CLC 43, 70**
See also CA 134; CANR 123; CP 1, 5, 6, 7; DAM POET; EWL 3

d'Urfe, Honore
See Urfe, Honore d'

Durfey, Thomas 1653-1723 .... **LC 94**
See also DLB 80; RGEL 2

Durkheim, Emile 1858-1917 .... **TCLC 55**
See also CA 249

Durrell, Lawrence (George)
1912-1990 ..... **CLC 1, 4, 6, 8, 13, 27, 41**
See also BPFB 1; BRWS 1; CA 9-12R; CAAS 132; CANR 40, 77; CDBLB 1945-1960; CN 1, 2, 3, 4; CP 1, 2, 3, 4, 5; DAM NOV; DLB 15, 27, 204; DLBY 1990; EWL 3; MTCW 1, 2; RGEL 2; SFW 4; TEA

Durrenmatt, Friedrich
See Duerrenmatt, Friedrich
See also CDWLB 2; EW 13; EWL 3; RGHL; RGWL 2, 3

Dutt, Michael Madhusudan
1824-1873 .... **NCLC 118**

Dutt, Toru 1856-1877 .... **NCLC 29**
See also DLB 240

Dwight, Timothy 1752-1817 .... **NCLC 13**
See also DLB 37; RGAL 4

Dworkin, Andrea 1946-2005 ..... **CLC 43, 123**
See also CA 77-80; 21; CAAS 238; CANR 16, 39, 76, 96; FL 1:5; FW; GLL 1; INT CANR-16; MTCW 1, 2; MTFW 2005

Dwyer, Deanna
See Koontz, Dean R.

Dwyer, K. R.
See Koontz, Dean R.

Dybek, Stuart 1942- .... **CLC 114; SSC 55**
See also CA 97-100; CANR 39; DLB 130; SSFS 23

Dye, Richard
See De Voto, Bernard (Augustine)

Dyer, Geoff 1958- .... **CLC 149**
See also CA 125; CANR 88

Dyer, George 1755-1841 .... **NCLC 129**
See also DLB 93

Dylan, Bob 1941- .... **CLC 3, 4, 6, 12, 77; PC 37**
See also CA 41-44R; CANR 108; CP 1, 2, 3, 4, 5, 6, 7; DLB 16

Dyson, John 1943- .... **CLC 70**
See also CA 144

Dzyubin, Eduard Georgievich 1895-1934
See Bagritsky, Eduard
See also CA 170

E. V. L.
See Lucas, E(dward) V(errall)

Eagleton, Terence (Francis) 1943- .. **CLC 63, 132**
See also CA 57-60; CANR 7, 23, 68, 115; DLB 242; LMFS 2; MTCW 1, 2; MTFW 2005

Eagleton, Terry
See Eagleton, Terence (Francis)

Early, Jack
See Scoppettone, Sandra
See also GLL 1

East, Michael
See West, Morris L(anglo)

Eastaway, Edward
See Thomas, (Philip) Edward

Eastlake, William (Derry)
1917-1997 .... **CLC 8**
See also CA 5-8R; 1; CAAS 158; CANR 5, 63; CN 1, 2, 3, 4, 5, 6; DLB 6, 206; INT CANR-5; MAL 5; TCWW 1, 2

Eastman, Charles A(lexander)
1858-1939 .... **NNAL; TCLC 55**
See also CA 179; CANR 91; DAM MULT; DLB 175; YABC 1

Eaton, Edith Maude 1865-1914 .... **AAL**
See Far, Sui Sin
See also CA 154; DLB 221, 312; FW

Eaton, (Lillie) Winnifred 1875-1954 .... **AAL**
See also CA 217; DLB 221, 312; RGAL 4

Eberhart, Richard 1904-2005 ...... **CLC 3, 11, 19, 56; PC 76**
See also AMW; CA 1-4R; CAAS 240; CANR 2, 125; CDALB 1941-1968; CP 1, 2, 3, 4, 5, 6, 7; DAM POET; DLB 48; MAL 5; MTCW 1; RGAL 4

Eberhart, Richard Ghormley
See Eberhart, Richard

Eberstadt, Fernanda 1960- .... **CLC 39**
See also CA 136; CANR 69, 128

Echegaray (y Eizaguirre), Jose (Maria Waldo) 1832-1916 .... **HLCS 1; TCLC 4**
See also CAAE 104; CANR 32; DLB 329; EWL 3; HW 1; MTCW 1

Echeverria, (Jose) Esteban (Antonino)
1805-1851 .... **NCLC 18**
See also LAW

Echo
See Proust, (Valentin-Louis-George-Eugene) Marcel

Eckert, Allan W. 1931- .... **CLC 17**
See also AAYA 18; BYA 2; CA 13-16R; CANR 14, 45; INT CANR-14; MAICYA 2; MAICYAS 1; SAAS 21; SATA 29, 91; SATA-Brief 27

Eckhart, Meister 1260(?)-1327(?) .. **CMLC 9, 80**
See also DLB 115; LMFS 1

Eckmar, F. R.
See de Hartog, Jan

Fukuyama, Francis 1952- .... **CLC 131**
See also CA 140; CANR 72, 125

Fuller, Charles (H.), (Jr.) 1939- .... **BLC 2; CLC 25; DC 1**
See also BW 2; CA 112; CAAE 108; CAD; CANR 87; CD 5, 6; DAM DRAM, MULT; DFS 8; DLB 38, 266; EWL 3; INT CA-112; MAL 5; MTCW 1

Fuller, Henry Blake 1857-1929 .... **TCLC 103**
See also CA 177; CAAE 108; DLB 12; RGAL 4

Fuller, John (Leopold) 1937- .... **CLC 62**
See also CA 21-24R; CANR 9, 44; CP 1, 2, 3, 4, 5, 6, 7; DLB 40

Fuller, Margaret
See Ossoli, Sarah Margaret (Fuller)
See also AMWS 2; DLB 183, 223, 239; FL 1:3

Fuller, Roy (Broadbent) 1912-1991 ... **CLC 4, 28**
See also BRWS 7; CA 5-8R; 10; CAAS 135; CANR 53, 83; CN 1, 2, 3, 4, 5; CP 1, 2, 3, 4, 5; CWRI 5; DLB 15, 20; EWL 3; RGEL 2; SATA 87

Fuller, Sarah Margaret
See Ossoli, Sarah Margaret (Fuller)

Fuller, Sarah Margaret
See Ossoli, Sarah Margaret (Fuller)
See also DLB 1, 59, 73

Fuller, Thomas 1608-1661 .... **LC 111**
See also DLB 151

Fulton, Alice 1952- .... **CLC 52**
See also CA 116; CANR 57, 88; CP 5, 6, 7; CWP; DLB 193; PFS 25

Furphy, Joseph 1843-1912 .... **TCLC 25**
See Collins, Tom
See also CA 163; DLB 230; EWL 3; RGEL 2

Fuson, Robert H(enderson) 1927- .... **CLC 70**
See also CA 89-92; CANR 103

Fussell, Paul 1924- .... **CLC 74**
See also BEST 90:1; CA 17-20R; CANR 8, 21, 35, 69, 135; INT CANR-21; MTCW 1, 2; MTFW 2005

Futabatei, Shimei 1864-1909 .... **TCLC 44**
See Futabatei Shimei
See also CA 162; MJW

Futabatei Shimei
See Futabatei, Shimei
See also DLB 180; EWL 3

Futrelle, Jacques 1875-1912 .... **TCLC 19**
See also CA 155; CAAE 113; CMW 4

Gaboriau, Emile 1835-1873 .... **NCLC 14**
See also CMW 4; MSW

Gadda, Carlo Emilio 1893-1973 ...... **CLC 11; TCLC 144**
See also CA 89-92; DLB 177; EWL 3; WLIT 7

Gaddis, William 1922-1998 ... **CLC 1, 3, 6, 8, 10, 19, 43, 86**
See also AMWS 4; BPFB 1; CA 17-20R; CAAS 172; CANR 21, 48, 148; CN 1, 2, 3, 4, 5, 6; DLB 2, 278; EWL 3; MAL 5; MTCW 1, 2; MTFW 2005; RGAL 4

Gage, Walter
See Inge, William (Motter)

Gaiman, Neil 1960- .... **CLC 195**
See also AAYA 19, 42; CA 133; CANR 81, 129; CLR 109; DLB 261; HGG; MTFW 2005; SATA 85, 146; SFW 4; SUFW 2

Gaiman, Neil Richard
See Gaiman, Neil

Gaines, Ernest J. 1933- .. **BLC 2; CLC 3, 11, 18, 86, 181; SSC 68**
See also AAYA 18; AFAW 1, 2; AITN 1; BPFB 2; BW 2, 3; BYA 6; CA 9-12R; CANR 6, 24, 42, 75, 126; CDALB 1968-1988; CLR 62; CN 1, 2, 3, 4, 5, 6, 7; CSW; DA3; DAM MULT; DLB 2, 33,

152; DLBY 1980; EWL 3; EXPN; LAIT 5; LATS 1:2; MAL 5; MTCW 1, 2; MTFW 2005; NFS 5, 7, 16; RGAL 4; RGSF 2; RHW; SATA 86; SSFS 5; YAW

Gaitskill, Mary 1954- .... **CLC 69**
See also CA 128; CANR 61, 152; DLB 244; TCLE 1:1

Gaitskill, Mary Lawrence
See Gaitskill, Mary

Gaius Suetonius Tranquillus
See Suetonius

Galdos, Benito Perez
See Perez Galdos, Benito
See also EW 7

Gale, Zona 1874-1938 .... **TCLC 7**
See also CA 153; CAAE 105; CANR 84; DAM DRAM; DFS 17; DLB 9, 78, 228; RGAL 4

Galeano, Eduardo (Hughes) 1940- . **CLC 72; HLCS 1**
See also CA 29-32R; CANR 13, 32, 100; HW 1

Galiano, Juan Valera y Alcala
See Valera y Alcala-Galiano, Juan

Galilei, Galileo 1564-1642 .... **LC 45**

Gallagher, Tess 1943- .... **CLC 18, 63; PC 9**
See also CA 106; CP 3, 4, 5, 6, 7; CWP; DAM POET; DLB 120, 212, 244; PFS 16

Gallant, Mavis 1922- ..... **CLC 7, 18, 38, 172; SSC 5, 78**
See also CA 69-72; CANR 29, 69, 117; CCA 1; CN 1, 2, 3, 4, 5, 6, 7; DAC; DAM MST; DLB 53; EWL 3; MTCW 1, 2; MTFW 2005; RGEL 2; RGSF 2

Gallant, Roy A(rthur) 1924- .... **CLC 17**
See also CA 5-8R; CANR 4, 29, 54, 117; CLR 30; MAICYA 1, 2; SATA 4, 68, 110

Gallico, Paul (William) 1897-1976 ..... **CLC 2**
See also AITN 1; CA 5-8R; CAAS 69-72; CANR 23; CN 1, 2; DLB 9, 171; FANT; MAICYA 1, 2; SATA 13

Gallo, Max Louis 1932- .... **CLC 95**
See also CA 85-88

Gallois, Lucien
See Desnos, Robert

Gallup, Ralph
See Whitemore, Hugh (John)

Galsworthy, John 1867-1933 .... **SSC 22; TCLC 1, 45; WLC 2**
See also BRW 6; CA 141; CAAE 104; CANR 75; CDBLB 1890-1914; DA; DA3; DAB; DAC; DAM DRAM, MST, NOV; DLB 10, 34, 98, 162, 330; DLBD 16; EWL 3; MTCW 2; RGEL 2; SSFS 3; TEA

Galt, John 1779-1839 .... **NCLC 1, 110**
See also DLB 99, 116, 159; RGEL 2; RGSF 2

Galvin, James 1951- .... **CLC 38**
See also CA 108; CANR 26

Gamboa, Federico 1864-1939 .... **TCLC 36**
See also CA 167; HW 2; LAW

Gandhi, M. K.
See Gandhi, Mohandas Karamchand

Gandhi, Mahatma
See Gandhi, Mohandas Karamchand

Gandhi, Mohandas Karamchand
1869-1948 .... **TCLC 59**
See also CA 132; CAAE 121; DA3; DAM MULT; DLB 323; MTCW 1, 2

Gann, Ernest Kellogg 1910-1991 ..... **CLC 23**
See also AITN 1; BPFB 2; CA 1-4R; CAAS 136; CANR 1, 83; RHW

Gao Xingjian 1940- .... **CLC 167**
See Xingjian, Gao
See also MTFW 2005

Garber, Eric 1943(?)-
See Holleran, Andrew
See also CANR 89

Garcia, Cristina 1958- .... **CLC 76**
See also AMWS 11; CA 141; CANR 73, 130; CN 7; DLB 292; DNFS 1; EWL 3; HW 2; LLW; MTFW 2005

Garcia Lorca, Federico 1898-1936 ...... **DC 2; HLC 2; PC 3; TCLC 1, 7, 49, 181; WLC 2**
See Lorca, Federico Garcia
See also AAYA 46; CA 131; CAAE 104; CANR 81; DA; DA3; DAB; DAC; DAM DRAM, MST, MULT, POET; DFS 4, 10; DLB 108; EWL 3; HW 1, 2; LATS 1:2; MTCW 1, 2; MTFW 2005; TWA

Garcia Marquez, Gabriel 1928- .... **CLC 2, 3, 8, 10, 15, 27, 47, 55, 68, 170; HLC 1; SSC 8, 83; WLC 3**
See also AAYA 3, 33; BEST 89:1, 90:4; BPFB 2; BYA 12, 16; CA 33-36R; CANR 10, 28, 50, 75, 82, 128; CDWLB 3; CPW; CWW 2; DA; DA3; DAB; DAC; DAM MST, MULT, NOV, POP; DLB 113, 330; DNFS 1, 2; EWL 3; EXPN; EXPS; HW 1, 2; LAIT 2; LATS 1:2; LAW; LAWS 1; LMFS 2; MTCW 1, 2; MTFW 2005; NCFS 3; NFS 1, 5, 10; RGSF 2; RGWL 2, 3; SSFS 1, 6, 16, 21; TWA; WLIT 1

Garcia Marquez, Gabriel Jose
See Garcia Marquez, Gabriel

Garcilaso de la Vega, El Inca
1539-1616 .... **HLCS 1; LC 127**
See also DLB 318; LAW

Gard, Janice
See Latham, Jean Lee

Gard, Roger Martin du
See Martin du Gard, Roger

Gardam, Jane (Mary) 1928- .... **CLC 43**
See also CA 49-52; CANR 2, 18, 33, 54, 106; CLR 12; DLB 14, 161, 231; MAICYA 1, 2; MTCW 1; SAAS 9; SATA 39, 76, 130; SATA-Brief 28; YAW

Gardner, Herb(ert George)
1934-2003 .... **CLC 44**
See also CA 149; CAAS 220; CAD; CANR 119; CD 5, 6; DFS 18, 20

Gardner, John, Jr. 1933-1982 ... **CLC 2, 3, 5, 7, 8, 10, 18, 28, 34; SSC 7**
See also AAYA 45; AITN 1; AMWS 6; BPFB 2; CA 65-68; CAAS 107; CANR 33, 73; CDALBS; CN 2, 3; CPW; DA3; DAM NOV, POP; DLB 2; DLBY 1982; EWL 3; FANT; LATS 1:2; MAL 5; MTCW 1, 2; MTFW 2005; NFS 3; RGAL 4; RGSF 2; SATA 40; SATA-Obit 31; SSFS 8

Gardner, John (Edmund) 1926- .... **CLC 30**
See also CA 103; CANR 15, 69, 127; CMW 4; CPW; DAM POP; MTCW 1

Gardner, Miriam
See Bradley, Marion Zimmer
See also GLL 1

Gardner, Noel
See Kuttner, Henry

Gardons, S. S.
See Snodgrass, W.D.

Garfield, Leon 1921-1996 .... **CLC 12**
See also AAYA 8, 69; BYA 1, 3; CA 17-20R; CAAS 152; CANR 38, 41, 78; CLR 21; DLB 161; JRDA; MAICYA 1, 2; MAICYAS 1; SATA 1, 32, 76; SATA-Obit 90; TEA; WYA; YAW

Garland, (Hannibal) Hamlin
1860-1940 .... **SSC 18; TCLC 3**
See also CAAE 104; DLB 12, 71, 78, 186; MAL 5; RGAL 4; RGSF 2; TCWW 1, 2

Garneau, (Hector de) Saint-Denys
1912-1943 .... **TCLC 13**
See also CAAE 111; DLB 88

Garner, Alan 1934- .... **CLC 17**
See also AAYA 18; BYA 3, 5; CA 178; 73-76, 178; CANR 15, 64, 134; CLR 20; CPW; DAB; DAM POP; DLB 161, 261; FANT; MAICYA 1, 2; MTCW 1, 2; MTFW 2005; SATA 18, 69; SATA-Essay 108; SUFW 1, 2; YAW

Garner, Hugh 1913-1979 .... **CLC 13**
See Warwick, Jarvis
See also CA 69-72; CANR 31; CCA 1; CN 1, 2; DLB 68

Garnett, David 1892-1981 .... **CLC 3**
See also CA 5-8R; CAAS 103; CANR 17, 79; CN 1, 2; DLB 34; FANT; MTCW 2; RGEL 2; SFW 4; SUFW 1

Garnier, Robert c. 1545-1590 .... **LC 119**
See also DLB 327; GFL Beginnings to 1789

Garrett, George (Palmer, Jr.) 1929- . **CLC 3, 11, 51; SSC 30**
See also AMWS 7; BPFB 2; CA 202; 1-4R, 202; 5; CANR 1, 42, 67, 109; CN 1, 2, 3, 4, 5, 6, 7; CP 1, 2, 3, 4, 5, 6, 7; CSW; DLB 2, 5, 130, 152; DLBY 1983

Garrick, David 1717-1779 .... **LC 15**
See also DAM DRAM; DLB 84, 213; RGEL 2

Garrigue, Jean 1914-1972 .... **CLC 2, 8**
See also CA 5-8R; CAAS 37-40R; CANR 20; CP 1; MAL 5

Garrison, Frederick
See Sinclair, Upton

Garrison, William Lloyd
1805-1879 .... **NCLC 149**
See also CDALB 1640-1865; DLB 1, 43, 235

Garro, Elena 1920(?)-1998 .. **HLCS 1; TCLC 153**
See also CA 131; CAAS 169; CWW 2; DLB 145; EWL 3; HW 1; LAWS 1; WLIT 1

Garth, Will
See Hamilton, Edmond; Kuttner, Henry

Garvey, Marcus (Moziah, Jr.)
1887-1940 ... **BLC 2; HR 1:2; TCLC 41**
See also BW 1; CA 124; CAAE 120; CANR 79; DAM MULT

Gary, Romain .... **CLC 25**
See Kacew, Romain
See also DLB 83, 299; RGHL

Gascar, Pierre .... **CLC 11**
See Fournier, Pierre
See also EWL 3; RGHL

Gascoigne, George 1539-1577 .... **LC 108**
See also DLB 136; RGEL 2

Gascoyne, David (Emery)
1916-2001 .... **CLC 45**
See also CA 65-68; CAAS 200; CANR 10, 28, 54; CP 1, 2, 3, 4, 5, 6, 7; DLB 20; MTCW 1; RGEL 2

Gaskell, Elizabeth Cleghorn
1810-1865 .... **NCLC 5, 70, 97, 137; SSC 25, 97**
See also BRW 5; CDBLB 1832-1890; DAB; DAM MST; DLB 21, 144, 159; RGEL 2; RGSF 2; TEA

Gass, William H. 1924- . **CLC 1, 2, 8, 11, 15, 39, 132; SSC 12**
See also AMWS 6; CA 17-20R; CANR 30, 71, 100; CN 1, 2, 3, 4, 5, 6, 7; DLB 2, 227; EWL 3; MAL 5; MTCW 1, 2; MTFW 2005; RGAL 4

Gassendi, Pierre 1592-1655 .... **LC 54**
See also GFL Beginnings to 1789

Gasset, Jose Ortega y
See Ortega y Gasset, Jose

Gates, Henry Louis, Jr. 1950- ... **BLCS; CLC 65**
See also BW 2, 3; CA 109; CANR 25, 53, 75, 125; CSW; DA3; DAM MULT; DLB 67; EWL 3; MAL 5; MTCW 2; MTFW 2005; RGAL 4

Gatos, Stephanie
See Katz, Steve

Gautier, Theophile 1811-1872 .. **NCLC 1, 59; PC 18; SSC 20**
See also DAM POET; DLB 119; EW 6; GFL 1789 to the Present; RGWL 2, 3; SUFW; TWA

Gay, John 1685-1732 .... **LC 49**
See also BRW 3; DAM DRAM; DLB 84, 95; RGEL 2; WLIT 3

Gay, Oliver
See Gogarty, Oliver St. John

Gay, Peter 1923- .... **CLC 158**
See also CA 13-16R; CANR 18, 41, 77, 147; INT CANR-18; RGHL

Gay, Peter Jack
See Gay, Peter

Gaye, Marvin (Pentz, Jr.)
1939-1984 .... **CLC 26**
See also CA 195; CAAS 112

Gebler, Carlo 1954- .... **CLC 39**
See also CA 133; CAAE 119; CANR 96; DLB 271

Gee, Maggie 1948- .... **CLC 57**
See also CA 130; CANR 125; CN 4, 5, 6, 7; DLB 207; MTFW 2005

Gee, Maurice 1931- .... **CLC 29**
See also AAYA 42; CA 97-100; CANR 67, 123; CLR 56; CN 2, 3, 4, 5, 6, 7; CWRI 5; EWL 3; MAICYA 2; RGSF 2; SATA 46, 101

Gee, Maurice Gough
See Gee, Maurice

Geiogamah, Hanay 1945- .... **NNAL**
See also CA 153; DAM MULT; DLB 175

Gelbart, Larry
See Gelbart, Larry (Simon)
See also CAD; CD 5, 6

Gelbart, Larry (Simon) 1928- .... **CLC 21, 61**
See Gelbart, Larry
See also CA 73-76; CANR 45, 94

Gelber, Jack 1932-2003 ...... **CLC 1, 6, 14, 79**
See also CA 1-4R; CAAS 216; CAD; CANR 2; DLB 7, 228; MAL 5

Gellhorn, Martha (Ellis)
1908-1998 .... **CLC 14, 60**
See also CA 77-80; CAAS 164; CANR 44; CN 1, 2, 3, 4, 5, 6 7; DLBY 1982, 1998

Genet, Jean 1910-1986 .. **CLC 1, 2, 5, 10, 14, 44, 46; DC 25; TCLC 128**
See also CA 13-16R; CANR 18; DA3; DAM DRAM; DFS 10; DLB 72, 321; DLBY 1986; EW 13; EWL 3; GFL 1789 to the Present; GLL 1; LMFS 2; MTCW 1, 2; MTFW 2005; RGWL 2, 3; TWA

Genlis, Stephanie-Felicite Ducrest
1746-1830 .... **NCLC 166**
See also DLB 313

Gent, Peter 1942- .... **CLC 29**
See also AITN 1; CA 89-92; DLBY 1982

Gentile, Giovanni 1875-1944 .... **TCLC 96**
See also CAAE 119

Geoffrey of Monmouth c.
1100-1155 .... **CMLC 44**
See also DLB 146; TEA

George, Jean
See George, Jean Craighead

George, Jean Craighead 1919- .... **CLC 35**
See also AAYA 8, 69; BYA 2, 4; CA 5-8R; CANR 25; CLR 1; 80; DLB 52; JRDA; MAICYA 1, 2; SATA 2, 68, 124, 170; WYA; YAW

George, Stefan (Anton) 1868-1933 . **TCLC 2, 14**
See also CA 193; CAAE 104; EW 8; EWL 3

Georges, Georges Martin
See Simenon, Georges (Jacques Christian)

Gerald of Wales c. 1146-c. 1223 ... **CMLC 60**

Gerhardi, William Alexander
See Gerhardie, William Alexander

Gerhardie, William Alexander
1895-1977 .... **CLC 5**
See also CA 25-28R; CAAS 73-76; CANR 18; CN 1, 2; DLB 36; RGEL 2

Gerson, Jean 1363-1429 .... **LC 77**
See also DLB 208

Gersonides 1288-1344 .... **CMLC 49**
See also DLB 115

Gerstler, Amy 1956- .... **CLC 70**
See also CA 146; CANR 99

Gertler, T. .... **CLC 34**
See also CA 121; CAAE 116

Gertsen, Aleksandr Ivanovich
See Herzen, Aleksandr Ivanovich

Ghalib .... **NCLC 39, 78**
See Ghalib, Asadullah Khan

Ghalib, Asadullah Khan 1797-1869
See Ghalib
See also DAM POET; RGWL 2, 3

Ghelderode, Michel de 1898-1962 ..... **CLC 6, 11; DC 15; TCLC 187**
See also CA 85-88; CANR 40, 77; DAM DRAM; DLB 321; EW 11; EWL 3; TWA

Ghiselin, Brewster 1903-2001 .... **CLC 23**
See also CA 13-16R; 10; CANR 13; CP 1, 2, 3, 4, 5, 6, 7

Ghose, Aurabinda 1872-1950 .... **TCLC 63**
See Ghose, Aurobindo
See also CA 163

Ghose, Aurobindo
See Ghose, Aurabinda
See also EWL 3

Ghose, Zulfikar 1935- .... **CLC 42, 200**
See also CA 65-68; CANR 67; CN 1, 2, 3, 4, 5, 6, 7; CP 1, 2, 3, 4, 5, 6, 7; DLB 323; EWL 3

Ghosh, Amitav 1956- .... **CLC 44, 153**
See also CA 147; CANR 80, 158; CN 6, 7; DLB 323; WWE 1

Giacosa, Giuseppe 1847-1906 .... **TCLC 7**
See also CAAE 104

Gibb, Lee
See Waterhouse, Keith (Spencer)

Gibbon, Edward 1737-1794 .... **LC 97**
See also BRW 3; DLB 104; RGEL 2

Gibbon, Lewis Grassic .... **TCLC 4**
See Mitchell, James Leslie
See also RGEL 2

Gibbons, Kaye 1960- .... **CLC 50, 88, 145**
See also AAYA 34; AMWS 10; CA 151; CANR 75, 127; CN 7; CSW; DA3; DAM POP; DLB 292; MTCW 2; MTFW 2005; NFS 3; RGAL 4; SATA 117

Gibran, Kahlil 1883-1931 . **PC 9; TCLC 1, 9**
See also CA 150; CAAE 104; DA3; DAM POET, POP; EWL 3; MTCW 2; WLIT 6

Gibran, Khalil
See Gibran, Kahlil

Gibson, Mel 1956- .... **CLC 215**

Gibson, William 1914- .... **CLC 23**
See also CA 9-12R; CAD; CANR 9, 42, 75, 125; CD 5, 6; DA; DAB; DAC; DAM DRAM, MST; DFS 2; DLB 7; LAIT 2; MAL 5; MTCW 2; MTFW 2005; SATA 66; YAW

Grade, Chaim 1910-1982 .... **CLC 10**
　　See also CA 93-96; CAAS 107; DLB 333;
　　EWL 3; RGHL

Grade, Khayim
　　See Grade, Chaim

Graduate of Oxford, A
　　See Ruskin, John

Grafton, Garth
　　See Duncan, Sara Jeannette

Grafton, Sue 1940- .... **CLC 163**
　　See also AAYA 11, 49; BEST 90:3; CA 108;
　　CANR 31, 55, 111, 134; CMW 4; CPW;
　　CSW; DA3; DAM POP; DLB 226; FW;
　　MSW; MTFW 2005

Graham, John
　　See Phillips, David Graham

Graham, Jorie 1950- .... **CLC 48, 118; PC 59**
　　See also AAYA 67; CA 111; CANR 63, 118;
　　CP 4, 5, 6, 7; CWP; DLB 120; EWL 3;
　　MTFW 2005; PFS 10, 17; TCLE 1:1

Graham, R(obert) B(ontine) Cunninghame
　　See Cunninghame Graham, Robert
　　(Gallnigad) Bontine
　　See also DLB 98, 135, 174; RGEL 2; RGSF
　　2

Graham, Robert
　　See Haldeman, Joe

Graham, Tom
　　See Lewis, (Harry) Sinclair

Graham, W(illiam) S(ydney)
　　1918-1986 .... **CLC 29**
　　See also BRWS 7; CA 73-76; CAAS 118;
　　CP 1, 2, 3, 4; DLB 20; RGEL 2

Graham, Winston (Mawdsley)
　　1910-2003 .... **CLC 23**
　　See also CA 49-52; CAAS 218; CANR 2,
　　22, 45, 66; CMW 4; CN 1, 2, 3, 4, 5, 6,
　　7; DLB 77; RHW

Grahame, Kenneth 1859-1932 ...... **TCLC 64,
　　136**
　　See also BYA 5; CA 136; CAAE 108;
　　CANR 80; CLR 5; CWRI 5; DA3; DAB;
　　DLB 34, 141, 178; FANT; MAICYA 1, 2;
　　MTCW 2; NFS 20; RGEL 2; SATA 100;
　　TEA; WCH; YABC 1

Granger, Darius John
　　See Marlowe, Stephen

Granin, Daniil 1918- .... **CLC 59**
　　See also DLB 302

Granovsky, Timofei Nikolaevich
　　1813-1855 .... **NCLC 75**
　　See also DLB 198

Grant, Skeeter
　　See Spiegelman, Art

Granville-Barker, Harley
　　1877-1946 .... **TCLC 2**
　　See Barker, Harley Granville
　　See also CA 204; CAAE 104; DAM
　　DRAM; RGEL 2

Granzotto, Gianni
　　See Granzotto, Giovanni Battista

Granzotto, Giovanni Battista
　　1914-1985 .... **CLC 70**
　　See also CA 166

Grass, Guenter
　　See Grass, Gunter
　　See also CWW 2; DLB 330; RGHL

Grass, Gunter 1927- .. **CLC 1, 2, 4, 6, 11, 15,
　　22, 32, 49, 88, 207; WLC 3**
　　See Grass, Guenter
　　See also BPFB 2; CA 13-16R; CANR 20,
　　75, 93, 133; CDWLB 2; DA; DA3; DAB;
　　DAC; DAM MST, NOV; DLB 75, 124;
　　EW 13; EWL 3; MTCW 1, 2; MTFW
　　2005; RGWL 2, 3; TWA

Grass, Gunter Wilhelm
　　See Grass, Gunter

Gratton, Thomas
　　See Hulme, T(homas) E(rnest)

Grau, Shirley Ann 1929- .... **CLC 4, 9, 146;
　　SSC 15**
　　See also CA 89-92; CANR 22, 69; CN 1, 2,
　　3, 4, 5, 6, 7; CSW; DLB 2, 218; INT CA-
　　89-92; CANR-22; MTCW 1

Gravel, Fern
　　See Hall, James Norman

Graver, Elizabeth 1964- .... **CLC 70**
　　See also CA 135; CANR 71, 129

Graves, Richard Perceval
　　1895-1985 .... **CLC 44**
　　See also CA 65-68; CANR 9, 26, 51

Graves, Robert 1895-1985 ... **CLC 1, 2, 6, 11,
　　39, 44, 45; PC 6**
　　See also BPFB 2; BRW 7; BYA 4; CA 5-8R;
　　CAAS 117; CANR 5, 36; CDBLB 1914-
　　1945; CN 1, 2, 3; CP 1, 2, 3, 4; DA3;
　　DAB; DAC; DAM MST, POET; DLB 20,
　　100, 191; DLBD 18; DLBY 1985; EWL
　　3; LATS 1:1; MTCW 1, 2; MTFW 2005;
　　NCFS 2; NFS 21; RGEL 2; RHW; SATA
　　45; TEA

Graves, Valerie
　　See Bradley, Marion Zimmer

Gray, Alasdair 1934- .... **CLC 41**
　　See also BRWS 9; CA 126; CANR 47, 69,
　　106, 140; CN 4, 5, 6, 7; DLB 194, 261,
　　319; HGG; INT CA-126; MTCW 1, 2;
　　MTFW 2005; RGSF 2; SUFW 2

Gray, Amlin 1946- .... **CLC 29**
　　See also CA 138

Gray, Francine du Plessix 1930- ..... **CLC 22,
　　153**
　　See also BEST 90:3; CA 61-64; 2; CANR
　　11, 33, 75, 81; DAM NOV; INT CANR-
　　11; MTCW 1, 2; MTFW 2005

Gray, John (Henry) 1866-1934 ...... **TCLC 19**
　　See also CA 162; CAAE 119; RGEL 2

Gray, John Lee
　　See Jakes, John

Gray, Simon (James Holliday)
　　1936- .... **CLC 9, 14, 36**
　　See also AITN 1; CA 21-24R; 3; CANR 32,
　　69; CBD; CD 5, 6; CN 1, 2, 3; DLB 13;
　　EWL 3; MTCW 1; RGEL 2

Gray, Spalding 1941-2004 .... **CLC 49, 112;
　　DC 7**
　　See also AAYA 62; CA 128; CAAS 225;
　　CAD; CANR 74, 138; CD 5, 6; CPW;
　　DAM POP; MTCW 2; MTFW 2005

Gray, Thomas 1716-1771 .... **LC 4, 40; PC 2;
　　WLC 3**
　　See also BRW 3; CDBLB 1660-1789; DA;
　　DA3; DAB; DAC; DAM MST; DLB 109;
　　EXPP; PAB; PFS 9; RGEL 2; TEA; WP

Grayson, David
　　See Baker, Ray Stannard

Grayson, Richard (A.) 1951- .... **CLC 38**
　　See also CA 210; 85-88, 210; CANR 14,
　　31, 57; DLB 234

Greeley, Andrew M. 1928- .... **CLC 28**
　　See also BPFB 2; CA 5-8R; 7; CANR 7,
　　43, 69, 104, 136; CMW 4; CPW; DA3;
　　DAM POP; MTCW 1, 2; MTFW 2005

Green, Anna Katharine
　　1846-1935 .... **TCLC 63**
　　See also CA 159; CAAE 112; CMW 4;
　　DLB 202, 221; MSW

Green, Brian
　　See Card, Orson Scott

Green, Hannah
　　See Greenberg, Joanne (Goldenberg)

Green, Hannah 1927(?)-1996 .... **CLC 3**
　　See also CA 73-76; CANR 59, 93; NFS 10

Green, Henry .... **CLC 2, 13, 97**
　　See Yorke, Henry Vincent
　　See also BRWS 2; CA 175; DLB 15; EWL
　　3; RGEL 2

Green, Julian .... **CLC 3, 11, 77**
　　See Green, Julien (Hartridge)
　　See also EWL 3; GFL 1789 to the Present;
　　MTCW 2

Green, Julien (Hartridge) 1900-1998
　　See Green, Julian
　　See also CA 21-24R; CAAS 169; CANR
　　33, 87; CWW 2; DLB 4, 72; MTCW 1, 2;
　　MTFW 2005

Green, Paul (Eliot) 1894-1981 .... **CLC 25**
　　See also AITN 1; CA 5-8R; CAAS 103;
　　CAD; CANR 3; DAM DRAM; DLB 7, 9,
　　249; DLBY 1981; MAL 5; RGAL 4

Greenaway, Peter 1942- .... **CLC 159**
　　See also CA 127

Greenberg, Ivan 1908-1973
　　See Rahv, Philip
　　See also CA 85-88

Greenberg, Joanne (Goldenberg)
　　1932- .... **CLC 7, 30**
　　See also AAYA 12, 67; CA 5-8R; CANR
　　14, 32, 69; CN 6, 7; NFS 23; SATA 25;
　　YAW

Greenberg, Richard 1959(?)- .... **CLC 57**
　　See also CA 138; CAD; CD 5, 6

Greenblatt, Stephen J(ay) 1943- ...... **CLC 70**
　　See also CA 49-52; CANR 115

Greene, Bette 1934- .... **CLC 30**
　　See also AAYA 7, 69; BYA 3; CA 53-56;
　　CANR 4, 146; CLR 2; CWRI 5; JRDA;
　　LAIT 4; MAICYA 1, 2; NFS 10; SAAS
　　16; SATA 8, 102, 161; WYA; YAW

Greene, Gael .... **CLC 8**
　　See also CA 13-16R; CANR 10

Greene, Graham 1904-1991 .. **CLC 1, 3, 6, 9,
　　14, 18, 27, 37, 70, 72, 125; SSC 29;
　　WLC 3**
　　See also AAYA 61; AITN 2; BPFB 2;
　　BRWR 2; BRWS 1; BYA 3; CA 13-16R;
　　CAAS 133; CANR 35, 61, 131; CBD;
　　CDBLB 1945-1960; CMW 4; CN 1, 2, 3,
　　4; DA; DA3; DAB; DAC; DAM MST,
　　NOV; DLB 13, 15, 77, 100, 162, 201,
　　204; DLBY 1991; EWL 3; MSW; MTCW
　　1, 2; MTFW 2005; NFS 16; RGEL 2;
　　SATA 20; SSFS 14; TEA; WLIT 4

Greene, Robert 1558-1592 .... **LC 41**
　　See also BRWS 8; DLB 62, 167; IDTP;
　　RGEL 2; TEA

Greer, Germaine 1939- .... **CLC 131**
　　See also AITN 1; CA 81-84; CANR 33, 70,
　　115, 133; FW; MTCW 1, 2; MTFW 2005

Greer, Richard
　　See Silverberg, Robert

Gregor, Arthur 1923- .... **CLC 9**
　　See also CA 25-28R; 10; CANR 11; CP 1,
　　2, 3, 4, 5, 6, 7; SATA 36

Gregor, Lee
　　See Pohl, Frederik

Gregory, Lady Isabella Augusta (Persse)
　　1852-1932 .... **TCLC 1, 176**
　　See also BRW 6; CA 184; CAAE 104; DLB
　　10; IDTP; RGEL 2

Gregory, J. Dennis
　　See Williams, John A(lfred)

Gregory of Nazianzus, St.
　　329-389 .... **CMLC 82**

Grekova, I. .... **CLC 59**
　　See Ventsel, Elena Sergeevna
　　See also CWW 2

Grendon, Stephen
　　See Derleth, August (William)

Grenville, Kate 1950- .... **CLC 61**
　　See also CA 118; CANR 53, 93, 156; CN
　　7; DLB 325

Grenville, Pelham
　　See Wodehouse, P(elham) G(renville)

Greve, Felix Paul (Berthold Friedrich)
1879-1948
See Grove, Frederick Philip
See also CA 141, 175; CAAE 104; CANR
79; DAC; DAM MST

Greville, Fulke 1554-1628 .... **LC 79**
See also BRWS 11; DLB 62, 172; RGEL 2

Grey, Lady Jane 1537-1554 .... **LC 93**
See also DLB 132

Grey, Zane 1872-1939 .... **TCLC 6**
See also BPFB 2; CA 132; CAAE 104;
DA3; DAM POP; DLB 9, 212; MTCW 1,
2; MTFW 2005; RGAL 4; TCWW 1, 2;
TUS

Griboedov, Aleksandr Sergeevich
1795(?)-1829 .... **NCLC 129**
See also DLB 205; RGWL 2, 3

Grieg, (Johan) Nordahl (Brun)
1902-1943 .... **TCLC 10**
See also CA 189; CAAE 107; EWL 3

Grieve, C(hristopher) M(urray)
1892-1978 .... **CLC 11, 19**
See MacDiarmid, Hugh; Pteleon
See also CA 5-8R; CAAS 85-88; CANR
33, 107; DAM POET; MTCW 1; RGEL 2

Griffin, Gerald 1803-1840 .... **NCLC 7**
See also DLB 159; RGEL 2

Griffin, John Howard 1920-1980 ..... **CLC 68**
See also AITN 1; CA 1-4R; CAAS 101;
CANR 2

Griffin, Peter 1942- .... **CLC 39**
See also CA 136

Griffith, D(avid) Lewelyn) W(ark)
1875(?)-1948 .... **TCLC 68**
See also CA 150; CAAE 119; CANR 80

Griffith, Lawrence
See Griffith, D(avid) Lewelyn) W(ark)

Griffiths, Trevor 1935- .... **CLC 13, 52**
See also CA 97-100; CANR 45; CBD; CD
5, 6; DLB 13, 245

Griggs, Sutton (Elbert)
1872-1930 .... **TCLC 77**
See also CA 186; CAAE 123; DLB 50

Grigson, Geoffrey (Edward Harvey)
1905-1985 .... **CLC 7, 39**
See also CA 25-28R; CAAS 118; CANR
20, 33; CP 1, 2, 3, 4; DLB 27; MTCW 1,
2

Grile, Dod
See Bierce, Ambrose (Gwinett)

Grillparzer, Franz 1791-1872 .... **DC 14;**
NCLC 1, 102; SSC 37
See also CDWLB 2; DLB 133; EW 5;
RGWL 2, 3; TWA

Grimble, Reverend Charles James
See Eliot, T(homas) S(tearns)

Grimke, Angelina (Emily) Weld
1880-1958 .... **HR 1:2**
See Weld, Angelina (Emily) Grimke
See also BW 1; CA 124; DAM POET; DLB
50, 54

Grimke, Charlotte L(ottie) Forten
1837(?)-1914
See Forten, Charlotte L.
See also BW 1; CA 124; CAAE 117; DAM
MULT, POET

Grimm, Jacob Ludwig Karl
1785-1863 .... **NCLC 3, 77; SSC 36**
See Grimm Brothers
See also CLR 112; DLB 90; MAICYA 1, 2;
RGSF 2; RGWL 2, 3; SATA 22; WCH

Grimm, Wilhelm Karl 1786-1859 .. **NCLC 3,**
77; SSC 36
See Grimm Brothers
See also CDWLB 2; CLR 112; DLB 90;
MAICYA 1, 2; RGSF 2; RGWL 2, 3;
SATA 22; WCH

Grimm and Grim
See Grimm, Jacob Ludwig Karl; Grimm,
Wilhelm Karl

Grimm Brothers .... **SSC 88**
See Grimm, Jacob Ludwig Karl; Grimm,
Wilhelm Karl
See also CLR 112

**Grimmelshausen, Hans Jakob Christoffel
von**
See Grimmelshausen, Johann Jakob Christoffel von
See also RGWL 2, 3

**Grimmelshausen, Johann Jakob Christoffel
von** 1621-1676 .... **LC 6**
See Grimmelshausen, Hans Jakob Christof-
fel von
See also CDWLB 2; DLB 168

Grindel, Eugene 1895-1952
See Eluard, Paul
See also CA 193; CAAE 104; LMFS 2

Grisham, John 1955- .... **CLC 84**
See also AAYA 14, 47; BPFB 2; CA 138;
CANR 47, 69, 114, 133; CMW 4; CN 6,
7; CPW; CSW; DA3; DAM POP; MSW;
MTCW 2; MTFW 2005

Grosseteste, Robert 1175(?)-1253 . **CMLC 62**
See also DLB 115

Grossman, David 1954- .... **CLC 67, 231**
See also CA 138; CANR 114; CWW 2;
DLB 299; EWL 3; RGHL; WLIT 6

Grossman, Vasilii Semenovich
See Grossman, Vasily (Semenovich)
See also DLB 272

Grossman, Vasily (Semenovich)
1905-1964 .... **CLC 41**
See Grossman, Vasilii Semenovich
See also CA 130; CAAE 124; MTCW 1;
RGHL

Grove, Frederick Philip .... **TCLC 4**
See Greve, Felix Paul (Berthold Friedrich)
See also DLB 92; RGEL 2; TCWW 1, 2

Grubb
See Crumb, R.

Grumbach, Doris 1918- .... **CLC 13, 22, 64**
See also CA 5-8R; 2; CANR 9, 42, 70, 127;
CN 6, 7; INT CANR-9; MTCW 2; MTFW
2005

Grundtvig, Nikolai Frederik Severin
1783-1872 .... **NCLC 1, 158**
See also DLB 300

Grunge
See Crumb, R.

Grunwald, Lisa 1959- .... **CLC 44**
See also CA 120; CANR 148

Gryphius, Andreas 1616-1664 .... **LC 89**
See also CDWLB 2; DLB 164; RGWL 2, 3

Guare, John 1938- .... **CLC 8, 14, 29, 67; DC
20**
See also CA 73-76; CAD; CANR 21, 69,
118; CD 5, 6; DAM DRAM; DFS 8, 13;
DLB 7, 249; EWL 3; MAL 5; MTCW 1,
2; RGAL 4

Guarini, Battista 1537-1612 .... **LC 102**

Gubar, Susan (David) 1944- .... **CLC 145**
See also CA 108; CANR 45, 70, 139; FW;
MTCW 1; RGAL 4

Gudjonsson, Halldor Kiljan 1902-1998
See Halldor Laxness
See also CA 103; CAAS 164

Guenter, Erich
See Eich, Gunter

Guest, Barbara 1920-2006 ... **CLC 34; PC 55**
See also BG 1:2; CA 25-28R; CAAS 248;
CANR 11, 44, 84; CP 1, 2, 3, 4, 5, 6, 7;
CWP; DLB 5, 193

Guest, Edgar A(lbert) 1881-1959 ... **TCLC 95**
See also CA 168; CAAE 112

Guest, Judith 1936- .... **CLC 8, 30**
See also AAYA 7, 66; CA 77-80; CANR
15, 75, 138; DA3; DAM NOV, POP;
EXPN; INT CANR-15; LAIT 5; MTCW
1, 2; MTFW 2005; NFS 1

Guevara, Che .... **CLC 87; HLC 1**
See Guevara (Serna), Ernesto

Guevara (Serna), Ernesto
1928-1967 .... **CLC 87; HLC 1**
See Guevara, Che
See also CA 127; CAAS 111; CANR 56;
DAM MULT; HW 1

Guicciardini, Francesco 1483-1540 ..... **LC 49**

Guild, Nicholas M. 1944- .... **CLC 33**
See also CA 93-96

Guillemin, Jacques
See Sartre, Jean-Paul

Guillen, Jorge 1893-1984 . **CLC 11; HLCS 1;
PC 35**
See also CA 89-92; CAAS 112; DAM
MULT, POET; DLB 108; EWL 3; HW 1;
RGWL 2, 3

Guillen, Nicolas (Cristobal)
1902-1989 .... **BLC 2; CLC 48, 79; HLC
1; PC 23**
See also BW 2; CA 125; CAAE 116; CAAS
129; CANR 84; DAM MST, MULT,
POET; DLB 283; EWL 3; HW 1; LAW;
RGWL 2, 3; WP

Guillen y Alvarez, Jorge
See Guillen, Jorge

Guillevic, (Eugene) 1907-1997 .... **CLC 33**
See also CA 93-96; CWW 2

Guillois
See Desnos, Robert

Guillois, Valentin
See Desnos, Robert

Guimaraes Rosa, Joao 1908-1967 .... **HLCS 2**
See Rosa, Joao Guimaraes
See also CA 175; LAW; RGSF 2; RGWL 2,
3

Guiney, Louise Imogen
1861-1920 .... **TCLC 41**
See also CA 160; DLB 54; RGAL 4

Guinizelli, Guido c. 1230-1276 ...... **CMLC 49**
See Guinizzelli, Guido

Guinizzelli, Guido
See Guinizelli, Guido
See also WLIT 7

Guiraldes, Ricardo (Guillermo)
1886-1927 .... **TCLC 39**
See also CA 131; EWL 3; HW 1; LAW;
MTCW 1

Gumilev, Nikolai (Stepanovich)
1886-1921 .... **TCLC 60**
See Gumilyov, Nikolay Stepanovich
See also CA 165; DLB 295

Gumilyov, Nikolay Stepanovich
See Gumilev, Nikolai (Stepanovich)
See also EWL 3

Gump, P. Q.
See Card, Orson Scott

Gunesekera, Romesh 1954- .... **CLC 91**
See also BRWS 10; CA 159; CANR 140;
CN 6, 7; DLB 267, 323

Gunn, Bill .... **CLC 5**
See Gunn, William Harrison
See also DLB 38

Gunn, Thom(son William)
1929-2004 . **CLC 3, 6, 18, 32, 81; PC 26**
See also BRWS 4; CA 17-20R; CAAS 227;
CANR 9, 33, 116; CDBLB 1960 to
Present; CP 1, 2, 3, 4, 5, 6, 7; DAM
POET; DLB 27; INT CANR-33; MTCW
1; PFS 9; RGEL 2

Gunn, William Harrison 1934(?)-1989
See Gunn, Bill
See also AITN 1; BW 1, 3; CA 13-16R;
CAAS 128; CANR 12, 25, 76

Gunn Allen, Paula
See Allen, Paula Gunn
Gunnars, Kristjana 1948- .... **CLC 69**
See also CA 113; CCA 1; CP 6, 7; CWP;
DLB 60
Gunter, Erich
See Eich, Gunter
Gurdjieff, G(eorgei) I(vanovich)
1877(?)-1949 .... **TCLC 71**
See also CA 157
Gurganus, Allan 1947- .... **CLC 70**
See also BEST 90:1; CA 135; CANR 114;
CN 6, 7; CPW; CSW; DAM POP; GLL 1
Gurney, A. R.
See Gurney, A(lbert) R(amsdell), Jr.
See also DLB 266
Gurney, A(lbert) R(amsdell), Jr.
1930- .... **CLC 32, 50, 54**
See Gurney, A. R.
See also AMWS 5; CA 77-80; CAD; CANR
32, 64, 121; CD 5, 6; DAM DRAM; EWL
3
Gurney, Ivor (Bertie) 1890-1937 ... **TCLC 33**
See also BRW 6; CA 167; DLBY 2002;
PAB; RGEL 2
Gurney, Peter
See Gurney, A(lbert) R(amsdell), Jr.
Guro, Elena (Genrikhovna)
1877-1913 .... **TCLC 56**
See also DLB 295
Gustafson, James M(oody) 1925- ... **CLC 100**
See also CA 25-28R; CANR 37
Gustafson, Ralph (Barker)
1909-1995 .... **CLC 36**
See also CA 21-24R; CANR 8, 45, 84; CP
1, 2, 3, 4, 5, 6; DLB 88; RGEL 2
Gut, Gom
See Simenon, Georges (Jacques Christian)
Guterson, David 1956- .... **CLC 91**
See also CA 132; CANR 73, 126; CN 7;
DLB 292; MTCW 2; MTFW 2005; NFS
13
Guthrie, A(lfred) B(ertram), Jr.
1901-1991 .... **CLC 23**
See also CA 57-60; CAAS 134; CANR 24;
CN 1, 2, 3; DLB 6, 212; MAL 5; SATA
62; SATA-Obit 67; TCWW 1, 2
Guthrie, Isobel
See Grieve, C(hristopher) M(urray)
Guthrie, Woodrow Wilson 1912-1967
See Guthrie, Woody
See also CA 113; CAAS 93-96
Guthrie, Woody .... **CLC 35**
See Guthrie, Woodrow Wilson
See also DLB 303; LAIT 3
Gutierrez Najera, Manuel
1859-1895 .... **HLCS 2; NCLC 133**
See also DLB 290; LAW
Guy, Rosa (Cuthbert) 1925- .... **CLC 26**
See also AAYA 4, 37; BW 2; CA 17-20R;
CANR 14, 34, 83; CLR 13; DLB 33;
DNFS 1; JRDA; MAICYA 1, 2; SATA 14,
62, 122; YAW
Gwendolyn
See Bennett, (Enoch) Arnold
H. D. .... **CLC 3, 8, 14, 31, 34, 73; PC 5**
See Doolittle, Hilda
See also FL 1:5
H. de V.
See Buchan, John
Haavikko, Paavo Juhani 1931- .. **CLC 18, 34**
See also CA 106; CWW 2; EWL 3
Habbema, Koos
See Heijermans, Herman
Habermas, Juergen 1929- .... **CLC 104**
See also CA 109; CANR 85; DLB 242
Habermas, Jurgen
See Habermas, Juergen

Hacker, Marilyn 1942- ...... **CLC 5, 9, 23, 72,
91; PC 47**
See also CA 77-80; CANR 68, 129; CP 3,
4, 5, 6, 7; CWP; DAM POET; DLB 120,
282; FW; GLL 2; MAL 5; PFS 19
Hadewijch of Antwerp fl. 1250- ... **CMLC 61**
See also RGWL 3
Hadrian 76-138 .... **CMLC 52**
Haeckel, Ernst Heinrich (Philipp August)
1834-1919 .... **TCLC 83**
See also CA 157
Hafiz c. 1326-1389(?) .... **CMLC 34**
See also RGWL 2, 3; WLIT 6
Hagedorn, Jessica T(arahata)
1949- .... **CLC 185**
See also CA 139; CANR 69; CWP; DLB
312; RGAL 4
Haggard, H(enry) Rider
1856-1925 .... **TCLC 11**
See also BRWS 3; BYA 4, 5; CA 148;
CAAE 108; CANR 112; DLB 70, 156,
174, 178; FANT; LMFS 1; MTCW 2;
RGEL 2; RHW; SATA 16; SCFW 1, 2;
SFW 4; SUFW 1; WLIT 4
Hagiosy, L.
See Larbaud, Valery (Nicolas)
Hagiwara, Sakutaro 1886-1942 .... **PC 18;
TCLC 60**
See Hagiwara Sakutaro
See also CA 154; RGWL 3
Hagiwara Sakutaro
See Hagiwara, Sakutaro
See also EWL 3
Haig, Fenil
See Ford, Ford Madox
Haig-Brown, Roderick (Langmere)
1908-1976 .... **CLC 21**
See also CA 5-8R; CAAS 69-72; CANR 4,
38, 83; CLR 31; CWRI 5; DLB 88; MAI-
CYA 1, 2; SATA 12; TCWW 2
Haight, Rip
See Carpenter, John (Howard)
Haij, Vera
See Jansson, Tove (Marika)
Hailey, Arthur 1920-2004 .... **CLC 5**
See also AITN 2; BEST 90:3; BPFB 2; CA
1-4R; CAAS 233; CANR 2, 36, 75; CCA
1; CN 1, 2, 3, 4, 5, 6, 7; CPW; DAM
NOV, POP; DLB 88; DLBY 1982; MTCW
1, 2; MTFW 2005
Hailey, Elizabeth Forsythe 1938- ..... **CLC 40**
See also CA 188; 93-96, 188; 1; CANR 15,
48; INT CANR-15
Haines, John (Meade) 1924- .... **CLC 58**
See also AMWS 12; CA 17-20R; CANR
13, 34; CP 1, 2, 3, 4, 5; CSW; DLB 5,
212; TCLE 1:1
Ha Jin 1956- .... **CLC 109**
See Jin, Xuefei
See also CA 152; CANR 91, 130; DLB 244,
292; MTFW 2005; SSFS 17
Hakluyt, Richard 1552-1616 .... **LC 31**
See also DLB 136; RGEL 2
Haldeman, Joe 1943- .... **CLC 61**
See Graham, Robert
See also AAYA 38; CA 179; 53-56, 179;
25; CANR 6, 70, 72, 130; DLB 8; INT
CANR-6; SCFW 2; SFW 4
Haldeman, Joe William
See Haldeman, Joe
Hale, Janet Campbell 1947- .... **NNAL**
See also CA 49-52; CANR 45, 75; DAM
MULT; DLB 175; MTCW 2; MTFW 2005
Hale, Sarah Josepha (Buell)
1788-1879 .... **NCLC 75**
See also DLB 1, 42, 73, 243
Halevy, Elie 1870-1937 .... **TCLC 104**

Haley, Alex(ander Murray Palmer)
1921-1992 .... **BLC 2; CLC 8, 12, 76;
TCLC 147**
See also AAYA 26; BPFB 2; BW 2, 3; CA
77-80; CAAS 136; CANR 61; CDALBS;
CPW; CSW; DA; DA3; DAB; DAC;
DAM MST, MULT, POP; DLB 38; LAIT
5; MTCW 1, 2; NFS 9
Haliburton, Thomas Chandler
1796-1865 .... **NCLC 15, 149**
See also DLB 11, 99; RGEL 2; RGSF 2
Hall, Donald 1928- .. **CLC 1, 13, 37, 59, 151;
PC 70**
See also AAYA 63; CA 5-8R; 7; CANR 2,
44, 64, 106, 133; CP 1, 2, 3, 4, 5, 6, 7;
DAM POET; DLB 5; MAL 5; MTCW 2;
MTFW 2005; RGAL 4; SATA 23, 97
Hall, Donald Andrew, Jr.
See Hall, Donald
Hall, Frederic Sauser
See Sauser-Hall, Frederic
Hall, James
See Kuttner, Henry
Hall, James Norman 1887-1951 ..... **TCLC 23**
See also CA 173; CAAE 123; LAIT 1;
RHW 1; SATA 21
Hall, Joseph 1574-1656 .... **LC 91**
See also DLB 121, 151; RGEL 2
Hall, Marguerite Radclyffe
See Hall, Radclyffe
Hall, Radclyffe 1880-1943 .... **TCLC 12**
See also BRWS 6; CA 150; CAAE 110;
CANR 83; DLB 191; MTCW 2; MTFW
2005; RGEL 2; RHW
Hall, Rodney 1935- .... **CLC 51**
See also CA 109; CANR 69; CN 6, 7; CP
1, 2, 3, 4, 5, 6, 7; DLB 289
Hallam, Arthur Henry
1811-1833 .... **NCLC 110**
See also DLB 32
Halldor Laxness .... **CLC 25**
See Gudjonsson, Halldor Kiljan
See also DLB 293; EW 12; EWL 3; RGWL
2, 3
Halleck, Fitz-Greene 1790-1867 .... **NCLC 47**
See also DLB 3, 250; RGAL 4
Halliday, Michael
See Creasey, John
Halpern, Daniel 1945- .... **CLC 14**
See also CA 33-36R; CANR 93; CP 3, 4, 5,
6, 7
Hamburger, Michael (Peter Leopold)
1924- .... **CLC 5, 14**
See also CA 196; 5-8R, 196; 4; CANR 2,
47; CP 1, 2, 3, 4, 5, 6, 7; DLB 27
Hamill, Pete 1935- .... **CLC 10**
See also CA 25-28R; CANR 18, 71, 127
Hamilton, Alexander
1755(?)-1804 .... **NCLC 49**
See also DLB 37
Hamilton, Clive
See Lewis, C.S.
Hamilton, Edmond 1904-1977 .... **CLC 1**
See also CA 1-4R; CANR 3, 84; DLB 8;
SATA 118; SFW 4
Hamilton, Elizabeth 1758-1816 ... **NCLC 153**
See also DLB 116, 158
Hamilton, Eugene (Jacob) Lee
See Lee-Hamilton, Eugene (Jacob)
Hamilton, Franklin
See Silverberg, Robert
Hamilton, Gail
See Corcoran, Barbara (Asenath)
Hamilton, (Robert) Ian 1938-2001 . **CLC 191**
See also CA 106; CAAS 203; CANR 41,
67; CP 1, 2, 3, 4, 5, 6, 7; DLB 40, 155
Hamilton, Jane 1957- .... **CLC 179**
See also CA 147; CANR 85, 128; CN 7;
MTFW 2005

Hamilton, Mollie
See Kaye, M.M.
Hamilton, (Anthony Walter) Patrick
1904-1962 .... **CLC 51**
See also CA 176; CAAS 113; DLB 10, 191
Hamilton, Virginia 1936-2002 .... **CLC 26**
See also AAYA 2, 21; BW 2, 3; BYA 1, 2,
8; CA 25-28R; CAAS 206; CANR 20, 37,
73, 126; CLR 1, 11, 40; DAM MULT;
DLB 33, 52; DLBY 2001; INT CANR-
20; JRDA; LAIT 5; MAICYA 1, 2; MAI-
CYAS 1; MTCW 1, 2; MTFW 2005;
SATA 4, 56, 79, 123; SATA-Obit 132;
WYA; YAW
Hammett, (Samuel) Dashiell
1894-1961 .... **CLC 3, 5, 10, 19, 47; SSC
17; TCLC 187**
See also AAYA 59; AITN 1; AMWS 4;
BPFB 2; CA 81-84; CANR 42; CDALB
1929-1941; CMW 4; DA3; DLB 226, 280;
DLBD 6; DLBY 1996; EWL 3; LAIT 3;
MAL 5; MSW; MTCW 1, 2; MTFW
2005; NFS 21; RGAL 4; RGSF 2; TUS
Hammon, Jupiter 1720(?)-1800(?) .... **BLC 2;
NCLC 5; PC 16**
See also DAM MULT, POET; DLB 31, 50
Hammond, Keith
See Kuttner, Henry
Hamner, Earl (Henry), Jr. 1923- ...... **CLC 12**
See also AITN 2; CA 73-76; DLB 6
Hampton, Christopher 1946- .... **CLC 4**
See also CA 25-28R; CD 5, 6; DLB 13;
MTCW 1
Hampton, Christopher James
See Hampton, Christopher
Hamsun, Knut .... **TCLC 2, 14, 49, 151**
See Pedersen, Knut
See also DLB 297, 330; EW 8; EWL 3;
RGWL 2, 3
Handke, Peter 1942- .... **CLC 5, 8, 10, 15, 38,
134; DC 17**
See also CA 77-80; CANR 33, 75, 104, 133;
CWW 2; DAM DRAM, NOV; DLB 85,
124; EWL 3; MTCW 1, 2; MTFW 2005;
TWA
Handy, W(illiam) C(hristopher)
1873-1958 .... **TCLC 97**
See also BW 3; CA 167; CAAE 121
Hanley, James 1901-1985 ..... **CLC 3, 5, 8, 13**
See also CA 73-76; CAAS 117; CANR 36;
CBD; CN 1, 2, 3; DLB 191; EWL 3;
MTCW 1; RGEL 2
Hannah, Barry 1942- .. **CLC 23, 38, 90; SSC
94**
See also BPFB 2; CA 110; CAAE 108;
CANR 43, 68, 113; CN 4, 5, 6, 7; CSW;
DLB 6, 234; INT CA-110; MTCW 1;
RGSF 2
Hannon, Ezra
See Hunter, Evan
Hansberry, Lorraine (Vivian)
1930-1965 ... **BLC 2; CLC 17, 62; DC 2**
See also AAYA 25; AFAW 1, 2; AMWS 4;
BW 1, 3; CA 109; CAAS 25-28R; CABS
3; CAD; CANR 58; CDALB 1941-1968;
CWD; DA; DA3; DAB; DAC; DAM
DRAM, MST, MULT; DFS 2; DLB 7, 38;
EWL 3; FL 1:6; FW; LAIT 4; MAL 5;
MTCW 1, 2; MTFW 2005; RGAL 4; TUS
Hansen, Joseph 1923-2004 .... **CLC 38**
See Brock, Rose; Colton, James
See also BPFB 2; CA 29-32R; 17; CAAS
233; CANR 16, 44, 66, 125; CMW 4;
DLB 226; GLL 1; INT CANR-16
Hansen, Karen V. 1955- .... **CLC 65**
See also CA 149; CANR 102
Hansen, Martin A(lfred)
1909-1955 .... **TCLC 32**
See also CA 167; DLB 214; EWL 3

Hanson, Kenneth O(stlin) 1922- .... **CLC 13**
See also CA 53-56; CANR 7; CP 1, 2, 3, 4,
5
Hardwick, Elizabeth 1916- .... **CLC 13**
See also AMWS 3; CA 5-8R; CANR 3, 32,
70, 100, 139; CN 4, 5, 6; CSW; DA3;
DAM NOV; DLB 6; MBL; MTCW 1, 2;
MTFW 2005; TCLE 1:1
Hardy, Thomas 1840-1928 .... **PC 8; SSC 2,
60; TCLC 4, 10, 18, 32, 48, 53, 72, 143,
153; WLC 3**
See also AAYA 69; BRW 6; BRWC 1, 2;
BRWR 1; CA 123; CAAE 104; CDBLB
1890-1914; DA; DA3; DAB; DAC; DAM
MST, NOV, POET; DLB 18, 19, 135, 284;
EWL 3; EXPN; EXPP; LAIT 2; MTCW
1, 2; MTFW 2005; NFS 3, 11, 15, 19; PFS
3, 4, 18; RGEL 2; RGSF 2; TEA; WLIT
4
Hare, David 1947- . **CLC 29, 58, 136; DC 26**
See also BRWS 4; CA 97-100; CANR 39,
91; CBD; CD 5, 6; DFS 4, 7, 16; DLB
13, 310; MTCW 1; TEA
Harewood, John
See Van Druten, John (William)
Harford, Henry
See Hudson, W(illiam) H(enry)
Hargrave, Leonie
See Disch, Thomas M.
**Hariri, Al- al-Qasim ibn 'Ali Abu
Muhammad al-Basri**
See al-Hariri, al-Qasim ibn 'Ali Abu Mu-
hammad al-Basri
Harjo, Joy 1951- ..... **CLC 83; NNAL; PC 27**
See also AMWS 12; CA 114; CANR 35,
67, 91, 129; CP 6, 7; CWP; DAM MULT;
DLB 120, 175; EWL 3; MTCW 2; MTFW
2005; PFS 15; RGAL 4
Harlan, Louis R(udolph) 1922- .... **CLC 34**
See also CA 21-24R; CANR 25, 55, 80
Harling, Robert 1951(?)- .... **CLC 53**
See also CA 147
Harmon, William (Ruth) 1938- .... **CLC 38**
See also CA 33-36R; CANR 14, 32, 35;
SATA 65
Harper, F. E. W.
See Harper, Frances Ellen Watkins
Harper, Frances E. W.
See Harper, Frances Ellen Watkins
Harper, Frances E. Watkins
See Harper, Frances Ellen Watkins
Harper, Frances Ellen
See Harper, Frances Ellen Watkins
Harper, Frances Ellen Watkins
1825-1911 ..... **BLC 2; PC 21; TCLC 14**
See also AFAW 1, 2; BW 1, 3; CA 125;
CAAE 111; CANR 79; DAM MULT,
POET; DLB 50, 221; MBL; RGAL 4
Harper, Michael S(teven) 1938- ... **CLC 7, 22**
See also AFAW 2; BW 1; CA 224; 33-36R,
224; CANR 24, 108; CP 2, 3, 4, 5, 6, 7;
DLB 41; RGAL 4; TCLE 1:1
Harper, Mrs. F. E. W.
See Harper, Frances Ellen Watkins
Harpur, Charles 1813-1868 .... **NCLC 114**
See also DLB 230; RGEL 2
Harris, Christie
See Harris, Christie (Lucy) Irwin
Harris, Christie (Lucy) Irwin
1907-2002 .... **CLC 12**
See also CA 5-8R; CANR 6, 83; CLR 47;
DLB 88; JRDA; MAICYA 1, 2; SAAS 10;
SATA 6, 74; SATA-Essay 116
Harris, Frank 1856-1931 .... **TCLC 24**
See also CA 150; CAAE 109; CANR 80;
DLB 156, 197; RGEL 2
Harris, George Washington
1814-1869 .... **NCLC 23, 165**
See also DLB 3, 11, 248; RGAL 4

Harris, Joel Chandler 1848-1908 ..... **SSC 19;
TCLC 2**
See also CA 137; CAAE 104; CANR 80;
CLR 49; DLB 11, 23, 42, 78, 91; LAIT 2;
MAICYA 1, 2; RGSF 2; SATA 100; WCH;
YABC 1
**Harris, John (Wyndham Parkes Lucas)
Beynon** 1903-1969
See Wyndham, John
See also CA 102; CAAS 89-92; CANR 84;
SATA 118; SFW 4
Harris, MacDonald .... **CLC 9**
See Heiney, Donald (William)
Harris, Mark 1922- .... **CLC 19**
See also CA 5-8R; 3; CANR 2, 55, 83; CN
1, 2, 3, 4, 5, 6, 7; DLB 2; DLBY 1980
Harris, Norman .... **CLC 65**
Harris, (Theodore) Wilson 1921- .... **CLC 25,
159**
See also BRWS 5; BW 2, 3; CA 65-68; 16;
CANR 11, 27, 69, 114; CDWLB 3; CN 1,
2, 3, 4, 5, 6, 7; CP 1, 2, 3, 4, 5, 6, 7; DLB
117; EWL 3; MTCW 1; RGEL 2
Harrison, Barbara Grizzuti
1934-2002 .... **CLC 144**
See also CA 77-80; CAAS 205; CANR 15,
48; INT CANR-15
Harrison, Elizabeth (Allen) Cavanna
1909-2001
See Cavanna, Betty
See also CA 9-12R; CAAS 200; CANR 6,
27, 85, 104, 121; MAICYA 2; SATA 142;
YAW
Harrison, Harry (Max) 1925- .... **CLC 42**
See also CA 1-4R; CANR 5, 21, 84; DLB
8; SATA 4; SCFW 2; SFW 4
Harrison, James
See Harrison, Jim
Harrison, James Thomas
See Harrison, Jim
Harrison, Jim 1937- .... **CLC 6, 14, 33, 66,
143; SSC 19**
See also AMWS 8; CA 13-16R; CANR 8,
51, 79, 142; CN 5, 6; CP 1, 2, 3, 4, 5, 6;
DLBY 1982; INT CANR-8; RGAL 4;
TCWW 2; TUS
Harrison, Kathryn 1961- .... **CLC 70, 151**
See also CA 144; CANR 68, 122
Harrison, Tony 1937- .... **CLC 43, 129**
See also BRWS 5; CA 65-68; CANR 44,
98; CBD; CD 5, 6; CP 2, 3, 4, 5, 6, 7;
DLB 40, 245; MTCW 1; RGEL 2
Harriss, Will(ard Irvin) 1922- .... **CLC 34**
See also CA 111
Hart, Ellis
See Ellison, Harlan
Hart, Josephine 1942(?)- .... **CLC 70**
See also CA 138; CANR 70, 149; CPW;
DAM POP
Hart, Moss 1904-1961 .... **CLC 66**
See also CA 109; CAAS 89-92; CANR 84;
DAM DRAM; DFS 1; DLB 7, 266; RGAL
4
Harte, (Francis) Bret(t)
1836(?)-1902 ... **SSC 8, 59; TCLC 1, 25;
WLC 3**
See also AMWS 2; CA 140; CAAE 104;
CANR 80; CDALB 1865-1917; DA;
DA3; DAC; DAM MST; DLB 12, 64, 74,
79, 186; EXPS; LAIT 2; RGAL 4; RGSF
2; SATA 26; SSFS 3; TUS
Hartley, L(eslie) P(oles) 1895-1972 ... **CLC 2,
22**
See also BRWS 7; CA 45-48; CAAS 37-
40R; CANR 33; CN 1; DLB 15, 139;
EWL 3; HGG; MTCW 1, 2; MTFW 2005;
RGEL 2; RGSF 2; SUFW 1
Hartman, Geoffrey H. 1929- .... **CLC 27**
See also CA 125; CAAE 117; CANR 79;
DLB 67

Hartmann, Sadakichi 1869-1944 ... **TCLC 73**
See also CA 157; DLB 54

Hartmann von Aue c. 1170-c.
1210 .... **CMLC 15**
See also CDWLB 2; DLB 138; RGWL 2, 3

Hartog, Jan de
See de Hartog, Jan

Haruf, Kent 1943- .... **CLC 34**
See also AAYA 44; CA 149; CANR 91, 131

Harvey, Caroline
See Trollope, Joanna

Harvey, Gabriel 1550(?)-1631 .... **LC 88**
See also DLB 167, 213, 281

Harwood, Ronald 1934- .... **CLC 32**
See also CA 1-4R; CANR 4, 55, 150; CBD;
CD 5, 6; DAM DRAM, MST; DLB 13

Hasegawa Tatsunosuke
See Futabatei, Shimei

Hasek, Jaroslav (Matej Frantisek)
1883-1923 .... **SSC 69; TCLC 4**
See also CA 129; CAAE 104; CDWLB 4;
DLB 215; EW 9; EWL 3; MTCW 1, 2;
RGSF 2; RGWL 2, 3

Hass, Robert 1941- ... **CLC 18, 39, 99; PC 16**
See also AMWS 6; CA 111; CANR 30, 50,
71; CP 3, 4, 5, 6, 7; DLB 105, 206; EWL
3; MAL 5; MTFW 2005; RGAL 4; SATA
94; TCLE 1:1

Hastings, Hudson
See Kuttner, Henry

Hastings, Selina .... **CLC 44**

Hathorne, John 1641-1717 .... **LC 38**

Hatteras, Amelia
See Mencken, H(enry) L(ouis)

Hatteras, Owen .... **TCLC 18**
See Mencken, H(enry) L(ouis); Nathan,
George Jean

Hauptmann, Gerhart (Johann Robert)
1862-1946 .... **SSC 37; TCLC 4**
See also CA 153; CAAE 104; CDWLB 2;
DAM DRAM; DLB 66, 118, 330; EW 8;
EWL 3; RGSF 2; RGWL 2, 3; TWA

Havel, Vaclav 1936- ..... **CLC 25, 58, 65, 123;**
DC 6
See also CA 104; CANR 36, 63, 124; CD-
WLB 4; CWW 2; DA3; DAM DRAM;
DFS 10; DLB 232; EWL 3; LMFS 2;
MTCW 1, 2; MTFW 2005; RGWL 3

Haviaras, Stratis .... **CLC 33**
See Chaviaras, Strates

Hawes, Stephen 1475(?)-1529(?) .... **LC 17**
See also DLB 132; RGEL 2

Hawkes, John 1925-1998 .. **CLC 1, 2, 3, 4, 7,**
9, 14, 15, 27, 49
See also BPFB 2; CA 1-4R; CAAS 167;
CANR 2, 47, 64; CN 1, 2, 3, 4, 5, 6; DLB
2, 7, 227; DLBY 1980, 1998; EWL 3;
MAL 5; MTCW 1, 2; MTFW 2005;
RGAL 4

Hawking, S. W.
See Hawking, Stephen W.

Hawking, Stephen W. 1942- ..... **CLC 63, 105**
See also AAYA 13; BEST 89:1; CA 129;
CAAE 126; CANR 48, 115; CPW; DA3;
MTCW 2; MTFW 2005

Hawkins, Anthony Hope
See Hope, Anthony

Hawthorne, Julian 1846-1934 .... **TCLC 25**
See also CA 165; HGG

Hawthorne, Nathaniel 1804-1864 ... **NCLC 2,**
10, 17, 23, 39, 79, 95, 158, 171; SSC 3,
29, 39, 89; WLC 3
See also AAYA 18; AMW; AMWC 1;
AMWR 1; BPFB 2; BYA 3; CDALB
1640-1865; CLR 103; DA; DA3; DAB;
DAC; DAM MST, NOV; DLB 1, 74, 183,
223, 269; EXPN; EXPS; GL 2; HGG;
LAIT 1; NFS 1, 20; RGAL 4; RGSF 2;
SSFS 1, 7, 11, 15; SUFW 1; TUS; WCH;
YABC 2

Hawthorne, Sophia Peabody
1809-1871 .... **NCLC 150**
See also DLB 183, 239

Haxton, Josephine Ayres 1921-
See Douglas, Ellen
See also CA 115; CANR 41, 83

Hayaseca y Eizaguirre, Jorge
See Echegaray (y Eizaguirre), Jose (Maria
Waldo)

Hayashi, Fumiko 1904-1951 .... **TCLC 27**
See Hayashi Fumiko
See also CA 161

Hayashi Fumiko
See Hayashi, Fumiko
See also DLB 180; EWL 3

Haycraft, Anna 1932-2005
See Ellis, Alice Thomas
See also CA 122; CAAS 237; CANR 90,
141; MTCW 2; MTFW 2005

Hayden, Robert E(arl) 1913-1980 ..... **BLC 2;**
CLC 5, 9, 14, 37; PC 6
See also AFAW 1, 2; AMWS 2; BW 1, 3;
CA 69-72; CAAS 97-100; CABS 2;
CANR 24, 75, 82; CDALB 1941-1968;
CP 1, 2, 3; DA; DAC; DAM MST, MULT,
POET; DLB 5, 76; EWL 3; EXPP; MAL
5; MTCW 1, 2; PFS 1; RGAL 4; SATA
19; SATA-Obit 26; WP

Haydon, Benjamin Robert
1786-1846 .... **NCLC 146**
See also DLB 110

Hayek, F(riedrich) A(ugust von)
1899-1992 .... **TCLC 109**
See also CA 93-96; CAAS 137; CANR 20;
MTCW 1, 2

Hayford, J(oseph) E(phraim) Casely
See Casely-Hayford, J(oseph) E(phraim)

Hayman, Ronald 1932- .... **CLC 44**
See also CA 25-28R; CANR 18, 50, 88; CD
5, 6; DLB 155

Hayne, Paul Hamilton 1830-1886 . **NCLC 94**
See also DLB 3, 64, 79, 248; RGAL 4

Hays, Mary 1760-1843 .... **NCLC 114**
See also DLB 142, 158; RGEL 2

Haywood, Eliza (Fowler)
1693(?)-1756 .... **LC 1, 44**
See also BRWS 12; DLB 39; RGEL 2

Hazlitt, William 1778-1830 ...... **NCLC 29, 82**
See also BRW 4; DLB 110, 158; RGEL 2;
TEA

Hazzard, Shirley 1931- .... **CLC 18, 218**
See also CA 9-12R; CANR 4, 70, 127; CN
1, 2, 3, 4, 5, 6, 7; DLB 289; DLBY 1982;
MTCW 1

Head, Bessie 1937-1986 ...... **BLC 2; CLC 25,**
67; SSC 52
See also AFW; BW 2, 3; CA 29-32R; CAAS
119; CANR 25, 82; CDWLB 3; CN 1, 2,
3, 4; DA3; DAM MULT; DLB 117, 225;
EWL 3; EXPS; FL 1:6; FW; MTCW 1, 2;
MTFW 2005; RGSF 2; SSFS 5, 13; WLIT
2; WWE 1

Headon, (Nicky) Topper 1956(?)- ..... **CLC 30**

Heaney, Seamus 1939- . **CLC 5, 7, 14, 25, 37,**
74, 91, 171, 225; PC 18; WLCS
See also AAYA 61; BRWR 1; BRWS 2; CA
85-88; CANR 25, 48, 75, 91, 128; CD-
BLB 1960 to Present; CP 1, 2, 3, 4, 5, 6,
7; DA3; DAB; DAM POET; DLB 40,
330; DLBY 1995; EWL 3; EXPP; MTCW
1, 2; MTFW 2005; PAB; PFS 2, 5, 8, 17;
RGEL 2; TEA; WLIT 4

Hearn, (Patricio) Lafcadio (Tessima Carlos)
1850-1904 .... **TCLC 9**
See also CA 166; CAAE 105; DLB 12, 78,
189; HGG; MAL 5; RGAL 4

Hearne, Samuel 1745-1792 .... **LC 95**
See also DLB 99

Hearne, Vicki 1946-2001 .... **CLC 56**
See also CA 139; CAAS 201

Hearon, Shelby 1931- .... **CLC 63**
See also AITN 2; AMWS 8; CA 25-28R;
11; CANR 18, 48, 103, 146; CSW

Heat-Moon, William Least .... **CLC 29**
See Trogdon, William (Lewis)
See also AAYA 9

Hebbel, Friedrich 1813-1863 . **DC 21; NCLC**
43
See also CDWLB 2; DAM DRAM; DLB
129; EW 6; RGWL 2, 3

Hebert, Anne 1916-2000 .... **CLC 4, 13, 29**
See also CA 85-88; CAAS 187; CANR 69,
126; CCA 1; CWP; CWW 2; DA3; DAC;
DAM MST, POET; DLB 68; EWL 3; GFL
1789 to the Present; MTCW 1, 2; MTFW
2005; PFS 20

Hecht, Anthony (Evan) 1923-2004 .... **CLC 8,**
13, 19; PC 70
See also AMWS 10; CA 9-12R; CAAS 232;
CANR 6, 108; CP 1, 2, 3, 4, 5, 6, 7; DAM
POET; DLB 5, 169; EWL 3; PFS 6; WP

Hecht, Ben 1894-1964 ..... **CLC 8; TCLC 101**
See also CA 85-88; DFS 9; DLB 7, 9, 25,
26, 28, 86; FANT; IDFW 3, 4; RGAL 4

Hedayat, Sadeq 1903-1951 .... **TCLC 21**
See also CAAE 120; EWL 3; RGSF 2

Hegel, Georg Wilhelm Friedrich
1770-1831 .... **NCLC 46, 151**
See also DLB 90; TWA

Heidegger, Martin 1889-1976 .... **CLC 24**
See also CA 81-84; CAAS 65-68; CANR
34; DLB 296; MTCW 1, 2; MTFW 2005

Heidenstam, (Carl Gustaf) Verner von
1859-1940 .... **TCLC 5**
See also CAAE 104; DLB 330

Heidi Louise
See Erdrich, Louise

Heifner, Jack 1946- .... **CLC 11**
See also CA 105; CANR 47

Heijermans, Herman 1864-1924 .... **TCLC 24**
See also CAAE 123; EWL 3

Heilbrun, Carolyn G(old)
1926-2003 .... **CLC 25, 173**
See Cross, Amanda
See also CA 45-48; CAAS 220; CANR 1,
28, 58, 94; FW

Hein, Christoph 1944- .... **CLC 154**
See also CA 158; CANR 108; CDWLB 2;
CWW 2; DLB 124

Heine, Heinrich 1797-1856 .... **NCLC 4, 54,**
147; PC 25
See also CDWLB 2; DLB 90; EW 5; RGWL
2, 3; TWA

Heinemann, Larry 1944- .... **CLC 50**
See also CA 110; 21; CANR 31, 81, 156;
DLBD 9; INT CANR-31

Heinemann, Larry Curtiss
See Heinemann, Larry

Heiney, Donald (William) 1921-1993
See Harris, MacDonald
See also CA 1-4R; CAAS 142; CANR 3,
58; FANT

Heinlein, Robert A. 1907-1988 .. **CLC 1, 3, 8,**
14, 26, 55; SSC 55
See also AAYA 17; BPFB 2; BYA 4, 13;
CA 1-4R; CAAS 125; CANR 1, 20, 53;
CLR 75; CN 1, 2, 3, 4; CPW; DA3; DAM
POP; DLB 8; EXPS; JRDA; LAIT 5;
LMFS 2; MAICYA 1, 2; MTCW 1, 2;
MTFW 2005; RGAL 4; SATA 9, 69;
SATA-Obit 56; SCFW 1, 2; SFW 4; SSFS
7; YAW

Helforth, John
See Doolittle, Hilda

Heliodorus fl. 3rd cent. - .... **CMLC 52**
See also WLIT 8

Hellenhofferu, Vojtech Kapristian z
See Hasek, Jaroslav (Matej Frantisek)

Heller, Joseph 1923-1999 . **CLC 1, 3, 5, 8, 11, 36, 63; TCLC 131, 151; WLC 3**
See also AAYA 24; AITN 1; AMWS 4; BPFB 2; BYA 1; CA 5-8R; CAAS 187; CABS 1; CANR 8, 42, 66, 126; CN 1, 2, 3, 4, 5, 6; CPW; DA; DA3; DAB; DAC; DAM MST, NOV, POP; DLB 2, 28, 227; DLBY 1980, 2002; EWL 3; EXPN; INT CANR-8; LAIT 4; MAL 5; MTCW 1, 2; MTFW 2005; NFS 1; RGAL 4; TUS; YAW

Hellman, Lillian 1906-1984 . **CLC 2, 4, 8, 14, 18, 34, 44, 52; DC 1; TCLC 119**
See also AAYA 47; AITN 1, 2; AMWS 1; CA 13-16R; CAAS 112; CAD; CANR 33; CWD; DA3; DAM DRAM; DFS 1, 3, 14; DLB 7, 228; DLBY 1984; EWL 3; FL 1:6; FW; LAIT 3; MAL 5; MBL; MTCW 1, 2; MTFW 2005; RGAL 4; TUS

Helprin, Mark 1947- .... **CLC 7, 10, 22, 32**
See also CA 81-84; CANR 47, 64, 124; CDALBS; CN 7; CPW; DA3; DAM NOV, POP; DLBY 1985; FANT; MAL 5; MTCW 1, 2; MTFW 2005; SUFW 2

Helvetius, Claude-Adrien 1715-1771 .. **LC 26**
See also DLB 313

Helyar, Jane Penelope Josephine 1933-
See Poole, Josephine
See also CA 21-24R; CANR 10, 26; CWRI 5; SATA 82, 138; SATA-Essay 138

Hemans, Felicia 1793-1835 ...... **NCLC 29, 71**
See also DLB 96; RGEL 2

Hemingway, Ernest (Miller) 1899-1961 .... **CLC 1, 3, 6, 8, 10, 13, 19, 30, 34, 39, 41, 44, 50, 61, 80; SSC 1, 25, 36, 40, 63; TCLC 115; WLC 3**
See also AAYA 19; AMW; AMWC 1; AMWR 1; BPFB 2; BYA 2, 3, 13, 15; CA 77-80; CANR 34; CDALB 1917-1929; DA; DA3; DAB; DAC; DAM MST, NOV; DLB 4, 9, 102, 210, 308, 316, 330; DLBD 1, 15, 16; DLBY 1981, 1987, 1996, 1998; EWL 3; EXPN; EXPS; LAIT 3, 4; LATS 1:1; MAL 5; MTCW 1, 2; MTFW 2005; NFS 1, 5, 6, 14; RGAL 4; RGSF 2; SSFS 17; TUS; WYA

Hempel, Amy 1951- .... **CLC 39**
See also CA 137; CAAE 118; CANR 70; DA3; DLB 218; EXPS; MTCW 2; MTFW 2005; SSFS 2

Henderson, F. C.
See Mencken, H(enry) L(ouis)

Henderson, Sylvia
See Ashton-Warner, Sylvia (Constance)

Henderson, Zenna (Chlarson) 1917-1983 .... **SSC 29**
See also CA 1-4R; CAAS 133; CANR 1, 84; DLB 8; SATA 5; SFW 4

Henkin, Joshua .... **CLC 119**
See also CA 161

Henley, Beth .... **CLC 23; DC 6, 14**
See Henley, Elizabeth Becker
See also AAYA 70; CABS 3; CAD; CD 5, 6; CSW; CWD; DFS 2, 21; DLBY 1986; FW

Henley, Elizabeth Becker 1952-
See Henley, Beth
See also CA 107; CANR 32, 73, 140; DA3; DAM DRAM, MST; MTCW 1, 2; MTFW 2005

Henley, William Ernest 1849-1903 .. **TCLC 8**
See also CA 234; CAAE 105; DLB 19; RGEL 2

Hennissart, Martha 1929-
See Lathen, Emma
See also CA 85-88; CANR 64

Henry VIII 1491-1547 .... **LC 10**
See also DLB 132

Henry, O. . **SSC 5, 49; TCLC 1, 19; WLC 3**
See Porter, William Sydney
See also AAYA 41; AMWS 2; EXPS; MAL 5; RGAL 4; RGSF 2; SSFS 2, 18; TCWW 1, 2

Henry, Patrick 1736-1799 .... **LC 25**
See also LAIT 1

Henryson, Robert 1430(?)-1506(?) ..... **LC 20, 110; PC 65**
See also BRWS 7; DLB 146; RGEL 2

Henschke, Alfred
See Klabund

Henson, Lance 1944- .... **NNAL**
See also CA 146; DLB 175

Hentoff, Nat(han Irving) 1925- .... **CLC 26**
See also AAYA 4, 42; BYA 6; CA 1-4R; 6; CANR 5, 25, 77, 114; CLR 1, 52; INT CANR-25; JRDA; MAICYA 1, 2; SATA 42, 69, 133; SATA-Brief 27; WYA; YAW

Heppenstall, (John) Rayner 1911-1981 .... **CLC 10**
See also CA 1-4R; CAAS 103; CANR 29; CN 1, 2; CP 1, 2, 3; EWL 3

Heraclitus c. 540B.C.-c. 450B.C. ... **CMLC 22**
See also DLB 176

Herbert, Frank 1920-1986 ... **CLC 12, 23, 35, 44, 85**
See also AAYA 21; BPFB 2; BYA 4, 14; CA 53-56; CAAS 118; CANR 5, 43; CDALBS; CPW; DAM POP; DLB 8; INT CANR-5; LAIT 5; MTCW 1, 2; MTFW 2005; NFS 17; SATA 9, 37; SATA-Obit 47; SCFW 1, 2; SFW 4; YAW

Herbert, George 1593-1633 . **LC 24, 121; PC 4**
See also BRW 2; BRWR 2; CDBLB Before 1660; DAB; DAM POET; DLB 126; EXPP; PFS 25; RGEL 2; TEA; WP

Herbert, Zbigniew 1924-1998 ..... **CLC 9, 43; PC 50; TCLC 168**
See also CA 89-92; CAAS 169; CANR 36, 74; CDWLB 4; CWW 2; DAM POET; DLB 232; EWL 3; MTCW 1; PFS 22

Herbst, Josephine (Frey) 1897-1969 .... **CLC 34**
See also CA 5-8R; CAAS 25-28R; DLB 9

Herder, Johann Gottfried von 1744-1803 .... **NCLC 8**
See also DLB 97; EW 4; TWA

Heredia, Jose Maria 1803-1839 .... **HLCS 2**
See also LAW

Hergesheimer, Joseph 1880-1954 ... **TCLC 11**
See also CA 194; CAAE 109; DLB 102, 9; RGAL 4

Herlihy, James Leo 1927-1993 .... **CLC 6**
See also CA 1-4R; CAAS 143; CAD; CANR 2; CN 1, 2, 3, 4, 5

Herman, William
See Bierce, Ambrose (Gwinett)

Hermogenes fl. c. 175- .... **CMLC 6**

Hernandez, Jose 1834-1886 .... **NCLC 17**
See also LAW; RGWL 2, 3; WLIT 1

Herodotus c. 484B.C.-c. 420B.C. .. **CMLC 17**
See also AW 1; CDWLB 1; DLB 176; RGWL 2, 3; TWA; WLIT 8

Herr, Michael 1940(?)- .... **CLC 231**
See also CA 89-92; CANR 68, 142; DLB 185; MTCW 1

Herrick, Robert 1591-1674 .... **LC 13; PC 9**
See also BRW 2; BRWC 2; DA; DAB; DAC; DAM MST, POP; DLB 126; EXPP; PFS 13; RGAL 4; RGEL 2; TEA; WP

Herring, Guilles
See Somerville, Edith Oenone

Herriot, James 1916-1995 .... **CLC 12**
See Wight, James Alfred
See also AAYA 1, 54; BPFB 2; CAAS 148; CANR 40; CLR 80; CPW; DAM POP; LAIT 3; MAICYA 2; MAICYAS 1; MTCW 2; SATA 86, 135; TEA; YAW

Herris, Violet
See Hunt, Violet

Herrmann, Dorothy 1941- .... **CLC 44**
See also CA 107

Herrmann, Taffy
See Herrmann, Dorothy

Hersey, John 1914-1993 .. **CLC 1, 2, 7, 9, 40, 81, 97**
See also AAYA 29; BPFB 2; CA 17-20R; CAAS 140; CANR 33; CDALBS; CN 1, 2, 3, 4, 5; CPW; DAM POP; DLB 6, 185, 278, 299; MAL 5; MTCW 1, 2; MTFW 2005; RGHL; SATA 25; SATA-Obit 76; TUS

Herzen, Aleksandr Ivanovich 1812-1870 .... **NCLC 10, 61**
See Herzen, Alexander

Herzen, Alexander
See Herzen, Aleksandr Ivanovich
See also DLB 277

Herzl, Theodor 1860-1904 .... **TCLC 36**
See also CA 168

Herzog, Werner 1942- .... **CLC 16**
See also CA 89-92

Hesiod c. 8th cent. B.C.- .... **CMLC 5**
See also AW 1; DLB 176; RGWL 2, 3; WLIT 8

Hesse, Hermann 1877-1962 ... **CLC 1, 2, 3, 6, 11, 17, 25, 69; SSC 9, 49; TCLC 148; WLC 3**
See also AAYA 43; BPFB 2; CA 17-18; CAP 2; CDWLB 2; DA; DA3; DAB; DAC; DAM MST, NOV; DLB 66, 330; EW 9; EWL 3; EXPN; LAIT 1; MTCW 1, 2; MTFW 2005; NFS 6, 15, 24; RGWL 2, 3; SATA 50; TWA

Hewes, Cady
See De Voto, Bernard (Augustine)

Heyen, William 1940- .... **CLC 13, 18**
See also CA 220; 33-36R; 220; 9; CANR 98; CP 3, 4, 5, 6, 7; DLB 5; RGHL

Heyerdahl, Thor 1914-2002 .... **CLC 26**
See also CA 5-8R; CAAS 207; CANR 5, 22, 66, 73; LAIT 4; MTCW 1, 2; MTFW 2005; SATA 2, 52

Heym, Georg (Theodor Franz Arthur) 1887-1912 .... **TCLC 9**
See also CA 181; CAAE 106

Heym, Stefan 1913-2001 .... **CLC 41**
See also CA 9-12R; CAAS 203; CANR 4; CWW 2; DLB 69; EWL 3

Heyse, Paul (Johann Ludwig von) 1830-1914 .... **TCLC 8**
See also CA 209; CAAE 104; DLB 129, 330

Heyward, (Edwin) DuBose 1885-1940 .... **HR 1:2; TCLC 59**
See also CA 157; CAAE 108; DLB 7, 9, 45, 249; MAL 5; SATA 21

Heywood, John 1497(?)-1580(?) .... **LC 65**
See also DLB 136; RGEL 2

Heywood, Thomas 1573(?)-1641 .... **LC 111**
See also DAM DRAM; DLB 62; LMFS 1; RGEL 2; TEA

Hibbert, Eleanor Alice Burford 1906-1993 .... **CLC 7**
See Holt, Victoria
See also BEST 90:4; CA 17-20R; CAAS 140; CANR 9, 28, 59; CMW 4; CPW; DAM POP; MTCW 1, 2; MTFW 2005; RHW; SATA 2; SATA-Obit 74

Ivanov, Vyacheslav Ivanovich
See Ivanov, Vyacheslav
Ivask, Ivar Vidrik 1927-1992 .... **CLC 14**
See also CA 37-40R; CAAS 139; CANR 24
Ives, Morgan
See Bradley, Marion Zimmer
See also GLL 1
Izumi Shikibu c. 973-c. 1034 .... **CMLC 33**
J. R. S.
See Gogarty, Oliver St. John
Jabran, Kahlil
See Gibran, Kahlil
Jabran, Khalil
See Gibran, Kahlil
Jackson, Daniel
See Wingrove, David
Jackson, Helen Hunt 1830-1885 .... **NCLC 90**
See also DLB 42, 47, 186, 189; RGAL 4
Jackson, Jesse 1908-1983 .... **CLC 12**
See also BW 1; CA 25-28R; CAAS 109;
CANR 27; CLR 28; CWRI 5; MAICYA
1, 2; SATA 2, 29; SATA-Obit 48
Jackson, Laura (Riding) 1901-1991 .... **PC 44**
See Riding, Laura
See also CA 65-68; CAAS 135; CANR 28,
89; DLB 48
Jackson, Sam
See Trumbo, Dalton
Jackson, Sara
See Wingrove, David
Jackson, Shirley 1919-1965 . **CLC 11, 60, 87;**
SSC 9, 39; TCLC 187; WLC 3
See also AAYA 9; AMWS 9; BPFB 2; CA
1-4R; CAAS 25-28R; CANR 4, 52;
CDALB 1941-1968; DA; DA3; DAC;
DAM MST; DLB 6, 234; EXPS; HGG;
LAIT 4; MAL 5; MTCW 2; MTFW 2005;
RGAL 4; RGSF 2; SATA 2; SSFS 1;
SUFW 1, 2
Jacob, (Cyprien-)Max 1876-1944 .... **TCLC 6**
See also CA 193; CAAE 104; DLB 258;
EWL 3; GFL 1789 to the Present; GLL 2;
RGWL 2, 3
Jacobs, Harriet A(nn)
1813(?)-1897 .... **NCLC 67, 162**
See also AFAW 1, 2; DLB 239; FL 1:3; FW;
LAIT 2; RGAL 4
Jacobs, Jim 1942- .... **CLC 12**
See also CA 97-100; INT CA-97-100
Jacobs, W(illiam) W(ymark)
1863-1943 .... **SSC 73; TCLC 22**
See also CA 167; CAAE 121; DLB 135;
EXPS; HGG; RGEL 2; RGSF 2; SSFS 2;
SUFW 1
Jacobsen, Jens Peter 1847-1885 .... **NCLC 34**
Jacobsen, Josephine (Winder)
1908-2003 .... **CLC 48, 102; PC 62**
See also CA 33-36R; 18; CAAS 218; CANR
23, 48; CCA 1; CP 2, 3, 4, 5, 6, 7; DLB
244; PFS 23; TCLE 1:1
Jacobson, Dan 1929- ...... **CLC 4, 14; SSC 91**
See also AFW; CA 1-4R; CANR 2, 25, 66;
CN 1, 2, 3, 4, 5, 6, 7; DLB 14, 207, 225,
319; EWL 3; MTCW 1; RGSF 2
Jacqueline
See Carpentier (y Valmont), Alejo
Jacques de Vitry c. 1160-1240 ...... **CMLC 63**
See also DLB 208
Jagger, Michael Philip
See Jagger, Mick
Jagger, Mick 1943- .... **CLC 17**
See also CA 239
Jahiz, al- c. 780-c. 869 .... **CMLC 25**
See also DLB 311
Jakes, John 1932- .... **CLC 29**
See also AAYA 32; BEST 89:4; BPFB 2;
CA 214; 57-60, 214; CANR 10, 43, 66,
111, 142; CPW; CSW; DA3; DAM NOV,

POP; DLB 278; DLBY 1983; FANT; INT
CANR-10; MTCW 1, 2; MTFW 2005;
RHW; SATA 62; SFW 4; TCWW 1, 2
James I 1394-1437 .... **LC 20**
See also RGEL 2
James, Andrew
See Kirkup, James
James, C(yril) L(ionel) R(obert)
1901-1989 .... **BLCS; CLC 33**
See also BW 2; CA 125; CAAE 117; CAAS
128; CANR 62; CN 1, 2, 3, 4; DLB 125;
MTCW 1
James, Daniel (Lewis) 1911-1988
See Santiago, Danny
See also CA 174; CAAS 125
James, Dynely
See Mayne, William (James Carter)
James, Henry Sr. 1811-1882 .... **NCLC 53**
James, Henry 1843-1916 .... **SSC 8, 32, 47;**
TCLC 2, 11, 24, 40, 47, 64, 171; WLC
3
See also AMW; AMWC 1; AMWR 1; BPFB
2; BRW 6; CA 132; CAAE 104; CDALB
1865-1917; DA; DA3; DAB; DAC; DAM
MST, NOV; DLB 12, 71, 74, 189; DLBD
13; EWL 3; EXPS; GL 2; HGG; LAIT 2;
MAL 5; MTCW 1, 2; MTFW 2005; NFS
12, 16, 19; RGAL 4; RGEL 2; RGSF 2;
SSFS 9; SUFW 1; TUS
James, M. R. .... **SSC 93**
See James, Montague (Rhodes)
See also DLB 156, 201
James, Montague (Rhodes)
1862-1936 .... **SSC 16; TCLC 6**
See James, M. R.
See also CA 203; CAAE 104; HGG; RGEL
2; RGSF 2; SUFW 1
James, P. D. .... **CLC 18, 46, 122, 226**
See White, Phyllis Dorothy James
See also BEST 90:2; BPFB 2; BRWS 4;
CDBLB 1960 to Present; CN 4, 5, 6; DLB
87, 276; DLBD 17; MSW
James, Philip
See Moorcock, Michael
James, Samuel
See Stephens, James
James, Seumas
See Stephens, James
James, Stephen
See Stephens, James
James, William 1842-1910 .... **TCLC 15, 32**
See also AMW; CA 193; CAAE 109; DLB
270, 284; MAL 5; NCFS 5; RGAL 4
Jameson, Anna 1794-1860 .... **NCLC 43**
See also DLB 99, 166
Jameson, Fredric (R.) 1934- .... **CLC 142**
See also CA 196; DLB 67; LMFS 2
James VI of Scotland 1566-1625 .... **LC 109**
See also DLB 151, 172
Jami, Nur al-Din 'Abd al-Rahman
1414-1492 .... **LC 9**
Jammes, Francis 1868-1938 .... **TCLC 75**
See also CA 198; EWL 3; GFL 1789 to the
Present
Jandl, Ernst 1925-2000 .... **CLC 34**
See also CA 200; EWL 3
Janowitz, Tama 1957- .... **CLC 43, 145**
See also CA 106; CANR 52, 89, 129; CN
5, 6, 7; CPW; DAM POP; DLB 292;
MTFW 2005
Jansson, Tove (Marika) 1914-2001 ... **SSC 96**
See also CA 17-20R; CAAS 196; CANR
38, 118; CLR 2; CWW 2; DLB 257; EWL
3; MAICYA 1, 2; RGSF 2; SATA 3, 41
Japrisot, Sebastien 1931- .... **CLC 90**
See Rossi, Jean-Baptiste
See also CMW 4; NFS 18

Jarrell, Randall 1914-1965 .... **CLC 1, 2, 6, 9,**
13, 49; PC 41; TCLC 177
See also AMW; BYA 5; CA 5-8R; CAAS
25-28R; CABS 2; CANR 6, 34; CDALB
1941-1968; CLR 6, 111; CWRI 5; DAM
POET; DLB 48, 52; EWL 3; EXPP; MAI-
CYA 1, 2; MAL 5; MTCW 1, 2; PAB; PFS
2; RGAL 4; SATA 7
Jarry, Alfred 1873-1907 .... **SSC 20; TCLC 2,**
14, 147
See also CA 153; CAAE 104; DA3; DAM
DRAM; DFS 8; DLB 192, 258; EW 9;
EWL 3; GFL 1789 to the Present; RGWL
2, 3; TWA
Jarvis, E. K.
See Ellison, Harlan
Jawien, Andrzej
See John Paul II, Pope
Jaynes, Roderick
See Coen, Ethan
Jeake, Samuel, Jr.
See Aiken, Conrad (Potter)
Jean Paul 1763-1825 .... **NCLC 7**
Jefferies, (John) Richard
1848-1887 .... **NCLC 47**
See also DLB 98, 141; RGEL 2; SATA 16;
SFW 4
Jeffers, (John) Robinson 1887-1962 .. **CLC 2,**
3, 11, 15, 54; PC 17; WLC 3
See also AMWS 2; CA 85-88; CANR 35;
CDALB 1917-1929; DA; DAC; DAM
MST, POET; DLB 45, 212; EWL 3; MAL
5; MTCW 1, 2; MTFW 2005; PAB; PFS
3, 4; RGAL 4
Jefferson, Janet
See Mencken, H(enry) L(ouis)
Jefferson, Thomas 1743-1826 . **NCLC 11, 103**
See also AAYA 54; ANW; CDALB 1640-
1865; DA3; DLB 31, 183; LAIT 1; RGAL
4
Jeffrey, Francis 1773-1850 .... **NCLC 33**
See Francis, Lord Jeffrey
Jelakowitch, Ivan
See Heijermans, Herman
Jelinek, Elfriede 1946- .... **CLC 169**
See also AAYA 68; CA 154; DLB 85, 330;
FW
Jellicoe, (Patricia) Ann 1927- .... **CLC 27**
See also CA 85-88; CBD; CD 5, 6; CWD;
CWRI 5; DLB 13, 233; FW
Jelloun, Tahar ben 1944- .... **CLC 180**
See Ben Jelloun, Tahar
See also CA 162; CANR 100
Jemyma
See Holley, Marietta
Jen, Gish .... **AAL; CLC 70, 198**
See Jen, Lillian
See also AMWC 2; CN 7; DLB 312
Jen, Lillian 1955-
See Jen, Gish
See also CA 135; CANR 89, 130
Jenkins, (John) Robin 1912- .... **CLC 52**
See also CA 1-4R; CANR 1, 135; CN 1, 2,
3, 4, 5, 6, 7; DLB 14, 271
Jennings, Elizabeth (Joan)
1926-2001 .... **CLC 5, 14, 131**
See also BRWS 5; CA 61-64; 5; CAAS 200;
CANR 8, 39, 66, 127; CP 1, 2, 3, 4, 5, 6,
7; CWP; DLB 27; EWL 3; MTCW 1;
SATA 66
Jennings, Waylon 1937-2002 .... **CLC 21**
Jensen, Johannes V(ilhelm)
1873-1950 .... **TCLC 41**
See also CA 170; DLB 214, 330; EWL 3;
RGWL 3
Jensen, Laura (Linnea) 1948- .... **CLC 37**
See also CA 103
Jerome, Saint 345-420 .... **CMLC 30**
See also RGWL 3

Jones, Thom (Douglas) 1945(?)- ..... **CLC 81; SSC 56**
See also CA 157; CANR 88; DLB 244; SSFS 23

Jong, Erica 1942- .... **CLC 4, 6, 8, 18, 83**
See also AITN 1; AMWS 5; BEST 90:2; BPFB 2; CA 73-76; CANR 26, 52, 75, 132; CN 3, 4, 5, 6, 7; CP 2, 3, 4, 5, 6, 7; CPW; DA3; DAM NOV, POP; DLB 2, 5, 28, 152; FW; INT CANR-26; MAL 5; MTCW 1, 2; MTFW 2005

Jonson, Ben(jamin) 1572(?)-1637 . **DC 4; LC 6, 33, 110; PC 17; WLC 3**
See also BRW 1; BRWC 1; BRWR 1; CD-BLB Before 1660; DA; DAB; DAC; DAM DRAM, MST, POET; DFS 4, 10; DLB 62, 121; LMFS 1; PFS 23; RGEL 2; TEA; WLIT 3

Jordan, June 1936-2002 .. **BLCS; CLC 5, 11, 23, 114, 230; PC 38**
See also AAYA 2, 66; AFAW 1, 2; BW 2, 3; CA 33-36R; CAAS 206; CANR 25, 70, 114, 154; CLR 10; CP 3, 4, 5, 6, 7; CWP; DAM MULT, POET; DLB 38; GLL 2; LAIT 5; MAICYA 1, 2; MTCW 1; SATA 4, 136; YAW

Jordan, June Meyer
See Jordan, June

Jordan, Neil 1950- .... **CLC 110**
See also CA 130; CAAE 124; CANR 54, 154; CN 4, 5, 6, 7; GLL 2; INT CA-130

Jordan, Neil Patrick
See Jordan, Neil

Jordan, Pat(rick M.) 1941- .... **CLC 37**
See also CA 33-36R; CANR 121

Jorgensen, Ivar
See Ellison, Harlan

Jorgenson, Ivar
See Silverberg, Robert

Joseph, George Ghevarughese .... **CLC 70**

Josephson, Mary
See O'Doherty, Brian

Josephus, Flavius c. 37-100 .... **CMLC 13**
See also AW 2; DLB 176; WLIT 8

Josiah Allen's Wife
See Holley, Marietta

Josipovici, Gabriel (David) 1940- ...... **CLC 6, 43, 153**
See also CA 224; 37-40R; 224; 8; CANR 47, 84; CN 3, 4, 5, 6, 7; DLB 14, 319

Joubert, Joseph 1754-1824 .... **NCLC 9**

Jouve, Pierre Jean 1887-1976 .... **CLC 47**
See also CA 252; CAAS 65-68; DLB 258; EWL 3

Jovine, Francesco 1902-1950 .... **TCLC 79**
See also DLB 264; EWL 3

Joyce, James (Augustine Aloysius) 1882-1941 .... **DC 16; PC 22; SSC 3, 26, 44, 64; TCLC 3, 8, 16, 35, 52, 159; WLC 3**
See also AAYA 42; BRW 7; BRWC 1; BRWR 1; BYA 11, 13; CA 126; CAAE 104; CDBLB 1914-1945; DA; DA3; DAB; DAC; DAM MST, NOV, POET; DLB 10, 19, 36, 162, 247; EWL 3; EXPN; EXPS; LAIT 3; LMFS 1, 2; MTCW 1, 2; MTFW 2005; NFS 7; RGSF 2; SSFS 1, 19; TEA; WLIT 4

Jozsef, Attila 1905-1937 .... **TCLC 22**
See also CA 230; CAAE 116; CDWLB 4; DLB 215; EWL 3

Juana Ines de la Cruz, Sor 1651(?)-1695 ... **HLCS 1; LC 5, 136; PC 24**
See also DLB 305; FW; LAW; RGWL 2, 3; WLIT 1

Juana Inez de La Cruz, Sor
See Juana Ines de la Cruz, Sor

Juan Manuel, Don 1282-1348 .... **CMLC 88**

Judd, Cyril
See Kornbluth, C(yril) M.; Pohl, Frederik

Juenger, Ernst 1895-1998 .... **CLC 125**
See Junger, Ernst
See also CA 101; CAAS 167; CANR 21, 47, 106; DLB 56

Julian of Norwich 1342(?)-1416(?) . **LC 6, 52**
See also BRWS 12; DLB 146; LMFS 1

Julius Caesar 100B.C.-44B.C.
See Caesar, Julius
See also CDWLB 1; DLB 211

Junger, Ernst
See Juenger, Ernst

Junger, Ernst
See Juenger, Ernst
See also CDWLB 2; EWL 3; RGWL 2, 3

Junger, Sebastian 1962- .... **CLC 109**
See also AAYA 28; CA 165; CANR 130; MTFW 2005

Juniper, Alex
See Hospital, Janette Turner

Junius
See Luxemburg, Rosa

Junzaburo, Nishiwaki
See Nishiwaki, Junzaburo
See also EWL 3

Just, Ward 1935- .... **CLC 4, 27**
See also CA 25-28R; CANR 32, 87; CN 6, 7; INT CANR-32

Just, Ward Swift
See Just, Ward

Justice, Donald (Rodney) 1925-2004 .... **CLC 6, 19, 102; PC 64**
See also AMWS 7; CA 5-8R; CAAS 230; CANR 26, 54, 74, 121, 122; CP 1, 2, 3, 4, 5, 6, 7; CSW; DAM POET; DLBY 1983; EWL 3; INT CANR-26; MAL 5; MTCW 2; PFS 14; TCLE 1:1

Juvenal c. 60-c. 130 .... **CMLC 8**
See also AW 2; CDWLB 1; DLB 211; RGWL 2, 3; WLIT 8

Juvenis
See Bourne, Randolph S(illiman)

K., Alice
See Knapp, Caroline

Kabakov, Sasha .... **CLC 59**

Kabir 1398(?)-1448(?) .... **LC 109; PC 56**
See also RGWL 2, 3

Kacew, Romain 1914-1980
See Gary, Romain
See also CA 108; CAAS 102

Kadare, Ismail 1936- .... **CLC 52, 190**
See also CA 161; EWL 3; RGWL 3

Kadohata, Cynthia (Lynn) 1956(?)- .... **CLC 59, 122**
See also AAYA 71; CA 140; CANR 124; SATA 155

Kafka, Franz 1883-1924 ... **SSC 5, 29, 35, 60; TCLC 2, 6, 13, 29, 47, 53, 112, 179; WLC 3**
See also AAYA 31; BPFB 2; CA 126; CAAE 105; CDWLB 2; DA; DA3; DAB; DAC; DAM MST, NOV; DLB 81; EW 9; EWL 3; EXPS; LATS 1:1; LMFS 2; MTCW 1, 2; MTFW 2005; NFS 7; RGSF 2; RGWL 2, 3; SFW 4; SSFS 3, 7, 12; TWA

Kahanovitch, Pinchas
See Der Nister

Kahanovitsch, Pinkhes
See Der Nister

Kahanovitsh, Pinkhes
See Der Nister

Kahn, Roger 1927- .... **CLC 30**
See also CA 25-28R; CANR 44, 69, 152; DLB 171; SATA 37

Kain, Saul
See Sassoon, Siegfried (Lorraine)

Kaiser, Georg 1878-1945 .... **TCLC 9**
See also CA 190; CAAE 106; CDWLB 2; DLB 124; EWL 3; LMFS 2; RGWL 2, 3

Kaledin, Sergei .... **CLC 59**

Kaletski, Alexander 1946- .... **CLC 39**
See also CA 143; CAAE 118

Kalidasa fl. c. 400-455 .... **CMLC 9; PC 22**
See also RGWL 2, 3

Kallman, Chester (Simon) 1921-1975 .... **CLC 2**
See also CA 45-48; CAAS 53-56; CANR 3; CP 1, 2

Kaminsky, Melvin .... **CLC 12, 217**
See Brooks, Mel
See also AAYA 13, 48; DLB 26

Kaminsky, Stuart M. 1934- .... **CLC 59**
See also CA 73-76; CANR 29, 53, 89; CMW 4

Kaminsky, Stuart Melvin
See Kaminsky, Stuart M.

Kamo no Chomei 1153(?)-1216 .... **CMLC 66**
See also DLB 203

Kamo no Nagaakira
See Kamo no Chomei

Kandinsky, Wassily 1866-1944 .... **TCLC 92**
See also AAYA 64; CA 155; CAAE 118

Kane, Francis
See Robbins, Harold

Kane, Henry 1918-
See Queen, Ellery
See also CA 156; CMW 4

Kane, Paul
See Simon, Paul

Kanin, Garson 1912-1999 .... **CLC 22**
See also AITN 1; CA 5-8R; CAAS 177; CAD; CANR 7, 78; DLB 7; IDFW 3, 4

Kaniuk, Yoram 1930- .... **CLC 19**
See also CA 134; DLB 299; RGHL

Kant, Immanuel 1724-1804 ..... **NCLC 27, 67**
See also DLB 94

Kantor, MacKinlay 1904-1977 .... **CLC 7**
See also CA 61-64; CAAS 73-76; CANR 60, 63; CN 1, 2; DLB 9, 102; MAL 5; MTCW 2; RHW; TCWW 1, 2

Kanze Motokiyo
See Zeami

Kaplan, David Michael 1946- .... **CLC 50**
See also CA 187

Kaplan, James 1951- .... **CLC 59**
See also CA 135; CANR 121

Karadzic, Vuk Stefanovic 1787-1864 .... **NCLC 115**
See also CDWLB 4; DLB 147

Karageorge, Michael
See Anderson, Poul

Karamzin, Nikolai Mikhailovich 1766-1826 .... **NCLC 3, 173**
See also DLB 150; RGSF 2

Karapanou, Margarita 1946- .... **CLC 13**
See also CA 101

Karinthy, Frigyes 1887-1938 .... **TCLC 47**
See also CA 170; DLB 215; EWL 3

Karl, Frederick R(obert) 1927-2004 .... **CLC 34**
See also CA 5-8R; CAAS 226; CANR 3, 44, 143

Karr, Mary 1955- .... **CLC 188**
See also AMWS 11; CA 151; CANR 100; MTFW 2005; NCFS 5

Kastel, Warren
See Silverberg, Robert

Kataev, Evgeny Petrovich 1903-1942
See Petrov, Evgeny
See also CAAE 120

Kataphusin
See Ruskin, John

Katz, Steve 1935- .... **CLC 47**
See also CA 25-28R; 14, 64; CANR 12; CN 4, 5, 6, 7; DLBY 1983

Author Index

Kerrigan, (Thomas) Anthony 1918- .. **CLC 4, 6**
See also CA 49-52; 11; CANR 4

Kerry, Lois
See Duncan, Lois

Kesey, Ken 1935-2001 .... **CLC 1, 3, 6, 11, 46, 64, 184; WLC 3**
See also AAYA 25; BG 1:3; BPFB 2; CA 1-4R; CAAS 204; CANR 22, 38, 66, 124; CDALB 1968-1988; CN 1, 2, 3, 4, 5, 6, 7; CPW; DA; DA3; DAB; DAC; DAM MST, NOV, POP; DLB 2, 16, 206; EWL 3; EXPN; LAIT 4; MAL 5; MTCW 1, 2; MTFW 2005; NFS 2; RGAL 4; SATA 66; SATA-Obit 131; TUS; YAW

Kesselring, Joseph (Otto) 1902-1967 .... **CLC 45**
See also CA 150; DAM DRAM, MST; DFS 20

Kessler, Jascha (Frederick) 1929- ...... **CLC 4**
See also CA 17-20R; CANR 8, 48, 111; CP 1

Kettelkamp, Larry (Dale) 1933- .... **CLC 12**
See also CA 29-32R; CANR 16; SAAS 3; SATA 2

Key, Ellen (Karolina Sofia) 1849-1926 .... **TCLC 65**
See also DLB 259

Keyber, Conny
See Fielding, Henry

Keyes, Daniel 1927- .... **CLC 80**
See also AAYA 23; BYA 11; CA 181; 17-20R, 181; CANR 10, 26, 54, 74; DA; DA3; DAC; DAM MST, NOV; EXPN; LAIT 4; MTCW 2; MTFW 2005; NFS 2; SATA 37; SFW 4

Keynes, John Maynard 1883-1946 .... **TCLC 64**
See also CA 162, 163; CAAE 114; DLBD 10; MTCW 2; MTFW 2005

Khanshendel, Chiron
See Rose, Wendy

Khayyam, Omar 1048-1131 ... **CMLC 11; PC 8**
See Omar Khayyam
See also DA3; DAM POET; WLIT 6

Kherdian, David 1931- .... **CLC 6, 9**
See also AAYA 42; CA 192; 21-24R, 192; 2; CANR 39, 78; CLR 24; JRDA; LAIT 3; MAICYA 1, 2; SATA 16, 74; SATA-Essay 125

Khlebnikov, Velimir .... **TCLC 20**
See Khlebnikov, Viktor Vladimirovich
See also DLB 295; EW 10; EWL 3; RGWL 2, 3

Khlebnikov, Viktor Vladimirovich 1885-1922
See Khlebnikov, Velimir
See also CA 217; CAAE 117

Khodasevich, V.F.
See Khodasevich, Vladislav

Khodasevich, Vladislav 1886-1939 .... **TCLC 15**
See also CAAE 115; DLB 317; EWL 3

Khodasevich, Vladislav Felitsianovich
See Khodasevich, Vladislav

Kielland, Alexander Lange 1849-1906 .... **TCLC 5**
See also CAAE 104

Kiely, Benedict 1919-2007 . **CLC 23, 43; SSC 58**
See also CA 1-4R; CANR 2, 84; CN 1, 2, 3, 4, 5, 6, 7; DLB 15, 319; TCLE 1:1

Kienzle, William X. 1928-2001 .... **CLC 25**
See also CA 93-96; 1; CAAS 203; CANR 9, 31, 59, 111; CMW 4; DA3; DAM POP; INT CANR-31; MSW; MTCW 1, 2; MTFW 2005

Kierkegaard, Soren 1813-1855 ..... **NCLC 34, 78, 125**
See also DLB 300; EW 6; LMFS 2; RGWL 3; TWA

Kieslowski, Krzysztof 1941-1996 .... **CLC 120**
See also CA 147; CAAS 151

Killens, John Oliver 1916-1987 .... **CLC 10**
See also BW 2; CA 77-80; 2; CAAS 123; CANR 26; CN 1, 2, 3, 4; DLB 33; EWL 3

Killigrew, Anne 1660-1685 .... **LC 4, 73**
See also DLB 131

Killigrew, Thomas 1612-1683 .... **LC 57**
See also DLB 58; RGEL 2

Kim
See Simenon, Georges (Jacques Christian)

Kincaid, Jamaica 1949- ...... **BLC 2; CLC 43, 68, 137, 234; SSC 72**
See also AAYA 13, 56; AFAW 2; AMWS 7; BRWS 7; BW 2, 3; CA 125; CANR 47, 59, 95, 133; CDALBS; CDWLB 3; CLR 63; CN 4, 5, 6, 7; DA3; DAM MULT, NOV; DLB 157, 227; DNFS 1; EWL 3; EXPS; FW; LATS 1:2; LMFS 2; MAL 5; MTCW 2; MTFW 2005; NCFS 1; NFS 3; SSFS 5, 7; TUS; WWE 1; YAW

King, Francis (Henry) 1923- .... **CLC 8, 53, 145**
See also CA 1-4R; CANR 1, 33, 86; CN 1, 2, 3, 4, 5, 6, 7; DAM NOV; DLB 15, 139; MTCW 1

King, Kennedy
See Brown, George Douglas

King, Martin Luther, Jr. 1929-1968 . **BLC 2; CLC 83; WLCS**
See also BW 2, 3; CA 25-28; CANR 27, 44; CAP 2; DA; DA3; DAB; DAC; DAM MST, MULT; LAIT 5; LATS 1:2; MTCW 1, 2; MTFW 2005; SATA 14

King, Stephen 1947- .... **CLC 12, 26, 37, 61, 113, 228; SSC 17, 55**
See also AAYA 1, 17; AMWS 5; BEST 90:1; BPFB 2; CA 61-64; CANR 1, 30, 52, 76, 119, 134; CN 7; CPW; DA3; DAM NOV, POP; DLB 143; DLBY 1980; HGG; JRDA; LAIT 5; MTCW 1, 2; MTFW 2005; RGAL 4; SATA 9, 55, 161; SUFW 1, 2; WYAS 1; YAW

King, Stephen Edwin
See King, Stephen

King, Steve
See King, Stephen

King, Thomas 1943- .... **CLC 89, 171; NNAL**
See also CA 144; CANR 95; CCA 1; CN 6, 7; DAC; DAM MULT; DLB 175; SATA 96

Kingman, Lee .... **CLC 17**
See Natti, (Mary) Lee
See also CWRI 5; SAAS 3; SATA 1, 67

Kingsley, Charles 1819-1875 .... **NCLC 35**
See also CLR 77; DLB 21, 32, 163, 178, 190; FANT; MAICYA 2; MAICYAS 1; RGEL 2; WCH; YABC 2

Kingsley, Henry 1830-1876 .... **NCLC 107**
See also DLB 21, 230; RGEL 2

Kingsley, Sidney 1906-1995 .... **CLC 44**
See also CA 85-88; CAAS 147; CAD; DFS 14, 19; DLB 7; MAL 5; RGAL 4

Kingsolver, Barbara 1955- .... **CLC 55, 81, 130, 216**
See also AAYA 15; AMWS 7; CA 134; CAAE 129; CANR 60, 96, 133; CDALBS; CN 7; CPW; CSW; DA3; DAM POP; DLB 206; INT CA-134; LAIT 5; MTCW 2; MTFW 2005; NFS 5, 10, 12, 24; RGAL 4; TCLE 1:1

Kingston, Maxine Hong 1940- .... **AAL; CLC 12, 19, 58, 121; WLCS**
See also AAYA 8, 55; AMWS 5; BPFB 2; CA 69-72; CANR 13, 38, 74, 87, 128; CDALBS; CN 6, 7; DA3; DAM MULT, NOV; DLB 173, 212, 312; DLBY 1980; EWL 3; FL 1:6; FW; INT CANR-13; LAIT 5; MBL; MTCW 1, 2; MTFW 2005; NFS 6; RGAL 4; SATA 53; SSFS 3; TCWW 2

Kinnell, Galway 1927- ..... **CLC 1, 2, 3, 5, 13, 29, 129; PC 26**
See also AMWS 3; CA 9-12R; CANR 10, 34, 66, 116, 138; CP 1, 2, 3, 4, 5, 6, 7; DLB 5; DLBY 1987; EWL 3; INT CANR-34; MAL 5; MTCW 1, 2; MTFW 2005; PAB; PFS 9; RGAL 4; TCLE 1:1; WP

Kinsella, Thomas 1928- .... **CLC 4, 19, 138; PC 69**
See also BRWS 5; CA 17-20R; CANR 15, 122; CP 1, 2, 3, 4, 5, 6, 7; DLB 27; EWL 3; MTCW 1, 2; MTFW 2005; RGEL 2; TEA

Kinsella, W.P. 1935- .... **CLC 27, 43, 166**
See also AAYA 7, 60; BPFB 2; CA 222; 97-100, 222; 7; CANR 21, 35, 66, 75, 129; CN 4, 5, 6, 7; CPW; DAC; DAM NOV, POP; FANT; INT CANR-21; LAIT 5; MTCW 1, 2; MTFW 2005; NFS 15; RGSF 2

Kinsey, Alfred C(harles) 1894-1956 .... **TCLC 91**
See also CA 170; CAAE 115; MTCW 2

Kipling, (Joseph) Rudyard 1865-1936 . **PC 3; SSC 5, 54; TCLC 8, 17, 167; WLC 3**
See also AAYA 32; BRW 6; BRWC 1, 2; BYA 4; CA 120; CAAE 105; CANR 33; CDBLB 1890-1914; CLR 39, 65; CWRI 5; DA; DA3; DAB; DAC; DAM MST, POET; DLB 19, 34, 141, 156, 330; EWL 3; EXPS; FANT; LAIT 3; LMFS 1; MAICYA 1, 2; MTCW 1, 2; MTFW 2005; NFS 21; PFS 22; RGEL 2; RGSF 2; SATA 100; SFW 4; SSFS 8, 21, 22; SUFW 1; TEA; WCH; WLIT 4; YABC 2

Kircher, Athanasius 1602-1680 .... **LC 121**
See also DLB 164

Kirk, Russell (Amos) 1918-1994 .. **TCLC 119**
See also AITN 1; CA 1-4R; 9; CAAS 145; CANR 1, 20, 60; HGG; INT CANR-20; MTCW 1, 2

Kirkham, Dinah
See Card, Orson Scott

Kirkland, Caroline M. 1801-1864 . **NCLC 85**
See also DLB 3, 73, 74, 250, 254; DLBD 13

Kirkup, James 1918- .... **CLC 1**
See also CA 1-4R; 4; CANR 2; CP 1, 2, 3, 4, 5, 6, 7; DLB 27; SATA 12

Kirkwood, James 1930(?)-1989 .... **CLC 9**
See also AITN 2; CA 1-4R; CAAS 128; CANR 6, 40; GLL 2

Kirsch, Sarah 1935- .... **CLC 176**
See also CA 178; CWW 2; DLB 75; EWL 3

Kirshner, Sidney
See Kingsley, Sidney

Kis, Danilo 1935-1989 .... **CLC 57**
See also CA 118; CAAE 109; CAAS 129; CANR 61; CDWLB 4; DLB 181; EWL 3; MTCW 1; RGSF 2; RGWL 2, 3

Kissinger, Henry A(lfred) 1923- ..... **CLC 137**
See also CA 1-4R; CANR 2, 33, 66, 109; MTCW 1

Kittel, Frederick August
See Wilson, August

Kivi, Aleksis 1834-1872 .... **NCLC 30**

Kroetz, Franz
See Kroetz, Franz Xaver
Kroetz, Franz Xaver 1946- .... **CLC 41**
See also CA 130; CANR 142; CWW 2;
EWL 3
Kroker, Arthur (W.) 1945- .... **CLC 77**
See also CA 161
Kroniuk, Lisa
See Berton, Pierre (Francis de Marigny)
Kropotkin, Peter (Aleksieevich)
1842-1921 .... **TCLC 36**
See Kropotkin, Petr Alekseevich
See also CA 219; CAAE 119
Kropotkin, Petr Alekseevich
See Kropotkin, Peter (Aleksieevich)
See also DLB 277
Krotkov, Yuri 1917-1981 .... **CLC 19**
See also CA 102
Krumb
See Crumb, R.
Krumgold, Joseph (Quincy)
1908-1980 .... **CLC 12**
See also BYA 1, 2; CA 9-12R; CAAS 101;
CANR 7; MAICYA 1, 2; SATA 1, 48;
SATA-Obit 23; YAW
Krumwitz
See Crumb, R.
Krutch, Joseph Wood 1893-1970 ..... **CLC 24**
See also ANW; CA 1-4R; CAAS 25-28R;
CANR 4; DLB 63, 206, 275
Krutzch, Gus
See Eliot, T(homas) S(tearns)
Krylov, Ivan Andreevich
1768(?)-1844 .... **NCLC 1**
See also DLB 150
Kubin, Alfred (Leopold Isidor)
1877-1959 .... **TCLC 23**
See also CA 149; CAAE 112; CANR 104;
DLB 81
Kubrick, Stanley 1928-1999 .... **CLC 16;
TCLC 112**
See also AAYA 30; CA 81-84; CAAS 177;
CANR 33; DLB 26
Kumin, Maxine 1925- .... **CLC 5, 13, 28, 164;
PC 15**
See also AITN 2; AMWS 4; ANW; CA
1-4R; 8; CANR 1, 21, 69, 115, 140; CP 2,
3, 4, 5, 6, 7; CWP; DA3; DAM POET;
DLB 5; EWL 3; EXPP; MTCW 1, 2;
MTFW 2005; PAB; PFS 18; SATA 12
Kundera, Milan 1929- . **CLC 4, 9, 19, 32, 68,
115, 135, 234; SSC 24**
See also AAYA 2, 62; BPFB 2; CA 85-88;
CANR 19, 52, 74, 144; CDWLB 4; CWW
2; DA3; DAM NOV; DLB 232; EW 13;
EWL 3; MTCW 1, 2; MTFW 2005; NFS
18; RGSF 2; RGWL 3; SSFS 10
Kunene, Mazisi 1930-2006 .... **CLC 85**
See also BW 1, 3; CA 125; CAAS 252;
CANR 81; CP 1, 6, 7; DLB 117
Kunene, Mazisi Raymond
See Kunene, Mazisi
Kunene, Mazisi Raymond Fakazi Mngoni
See Kunene, Mazisi
Kung, Hans .... **CLC 130**
See Kung, Hans
Kung, Hans 1928-
See Kung, Hans
See also CA 53-56; CANR 66, 134; MTCW
1, 2; MTFW 2005
Kunikida Doppo 1869(?)-1908
See Doppo, Kunikida
See also DLB 180; EWL 3
Kunitz, Stanley 1905-2006 ..... **CLC 6, 11, 14,
148; PC 19**
See also AMWS 3; CA 41-44R; CAAS 250;
CANR 26, 57, 98; CP 1, 2, 3, 4, 5, 6, 7;
DA3; DLB 48; INT CANR-26; MAL 5;
MTCW 1, 2; MTFW 2005; PFS 11;
RGAL 4

Kunitz, Stanley Jasspon
See Kunitz, Stanley
Kunze, Reiner 1933- .... **CLC 10**
See also CA 93-96; CWW 2; DLB 75; EWL
3
Kuprin, Aleksander Ivanovich
1870-1938 .... **TCLC 5**
See Kuprin, Aleksandr Ivanovich; Kuprin,
Alexandr Ivanovich
See also CA 182; CAAE 104
Kuprin, Aleksandr Ivanovich
See Kuprin, Aleksander Ivanovich
See also DLB 295
Kuprin, Alexandr Ivanovich
See Kuprin, Aleksander Ivanovich
See also EWL 3
Kureishi, Hanif 1954- .. **CLC 64, 135; DC 26**
See also BRWS 11; CA 139; CANR 113;
CBD; CD 5, 6; CN 6, 7; DLB 194, 245;
GLL 2; IDFW 4; WLIT 4; WWE 1
Kurosawa, Akira 1910-1998 ..... **CLC 16, 119**
See also AAYA 11, 64; CA 101; CAAS 170;
CANR 46; DAM MULT
Kushner, Tony 1956- .... **CLC 81, 203; DC 10**
See also AAYA 61; AMWS 9; CA 144;
CAD; CANR 74, 130; CD 5, 6; DA3;
DAM DRAM; DFS 5; DLB 228; EWL 3;
GLL 1; LAIT 5; MAL 5; MTCW 2;
MTFW 2005; RGAL 4; RGHL; SATA 160
Kuttner, Henry 1915-1958 .... **TCLC 10**
See also CA 157; CAAE 107; DLB 8;
FANT; SCFW 1, 2; SFW 4
Kutty, Madhavi
See Das, Kamala
Kuzma, Greg 1944- .... **CLC 7**
See also CA 33-36R; CANR 70
Kuzmin, Mikhail (Alekseevich)
1872(?)-1936 .... **TCLC 40**
See also CA 170; DLB 295; EWL 3
Kyd, Thomas 1558-1594 .. **DC 3; LC 22, 125**
See also BRW 1; DAM DRAM; DFS 21;
DLB 62; IDTP; LMFS 1; RGEL 2; TEA;
WLIT 3
Kyprianos, Iossif
See Samarakis, Antonis
L. S.
See Stephen, Sir Leslie
Labe, Louise 1521-1566 .... **LC 120**
See also DLB 327
Labrunie, Gerard
See Nerval, Gerard de
La Bruyere, Jean de 1645-1696 .... **LC 17**
See also DLB 268; EW 3; GFL Beginnings
to 1789
LaBute, Neil 1963- .... **CLC 225**
See also CA 240
Lacan, Jacques (Marie Emile)
1901-1981 .... **CLC 75**
See also CA 121; CAAS 104; DLB 296;
EWL 3; TWA
Laclos, Pierre-Ambroise Francois
1741-1803 .... **NCLC 4, 87**
See also DLB 313; EW 4; GFL Beginnings
to 1789; RGWL 2, 3
Lacolere, Francois
See Aragon, Louis
La Colere, Francois
See Aragon, Louis
La Deshabilleuse
See Simenon, Georges (Jacques Christian)
Lady Gregory
See Gregory, Lady Isabella Augusta (Persse)
Lady of Quality, A
See Bagnold, Enid
**La Fayette, Marie-(Madelaine Pioche de la
Vergne)** 1634-1693 .... **LC 2**
See Lafayette, Marie-Madeleine
See also GFL Beginnings to 1789; RGWL
2, 3

Lafayette, Marie-Madeleine
See La Fayette, Marie-(Madelaine Pioche
de la Vergne)
See also DLB 268
Lafayette, Rene
See Hubbard, L. Ron
La Flesche, Francis 1857(?)-1932 ...... **NNAL**
See also CA 144; CANR 83; DLB 175
La Fontaine, Jean de 1621-1695 .... **LC 50**
See also DLB 268; EW 3; GFL Beginnings
to 1789; MAICYA 1, 2; RGWL 2, 3;
SATA 18
LaForet, Carmen 1921-2004 .... **CLC 219**
See also CA 246; CWW 2; DLB 322; EWL
3
LaForet Diaz, Carmen
See LaForet, Carmen
Laforgue, Jules 1860-1887 . **NCLC 5, 53; PC
14; SSC 20**
See also DLB 217; EW 7; GFL 1789 to the
Present; RGWL 2, 3
Lagerkvist, Paer (Fabian)
1891-1974 ..... **CLC 7, 10, 13, 54; TCLC
144**
See Lagerkvist, Par
See also CA 85-88; CAAS 49-52; DA3;
DAM DRAM, NOV; MTCW 1, 2; MTFW
2005; TWA
Lagerkvist, Par .... **SSC 12**
See Lagerkvist, Paer (Fabian)
See also DLB 259, 331; EW 10; EWL 3;
RGSF 2; RGWL 2, 3
Lagerloef, Selma (Ottiliana Lovisa)
.... **TCLC 4, 36**
See Lagerlof, Selma (Ottiliana Lovisa)
See also CAAE 108; MTCW 2
Lagerlof, Selma (Ottiliana Lovisa)
1858-1940
See Lagerloef, Selma (Ottiliana Lovisa)
See also CA 188; CLR 7; DLB 259, 331;
RGWL 2, 3; SATA 15; SSFS 18
La Guma, Alex 1925-1985 .. **BLCS; CLC 19;
TCLC 140**
See also AFW; BW 1, 3; CA 49-52; CAAS
118; CANR 25, 81; CDWLB 3; CN 1, 2,
3; CP 1; DAM NOV; DLB 117, 225; EWL
3; MTCW 1, 2; MTFW 2005; WLIT 2;
WWE 1
Lahiri, Jhumpa 1967- .... **SSC 96**
See also AAYA 56; CA 193; CANR 134;
DLB 323; MTFW 2005; SSFS 19
Laidlaw, A. K.
See Grieve, C(hristopher) M(urray)
Lainez, Manuel Mujica
See Mujica Lainez, Manuel
See also HW 1
Laing, R(onald) D(avid) 1927-1989 . **CLC 95**
See also CA 107; CAAS 129; CANR 34;
MTCW 1
Laishley, Alex
See Booth, Martin
Lamartine, Alphonse (Marie Louis Prat) de
1790-1869 .... **NCLC 11; PC 16**
See also DAM POET; DLB 217; GFL 1789
to the Present; RGWL 2, 3
Lamb, Charles 1775-1834 ..... **NCLC 10, 113;
WLC 3**
See also BRW 4; CDBLB 1789-1832; DA;
DAB; DAC; DAM MST; DLB 93, 107,
163; RGEL 2; SATA 17; TEA
Lamb, Lady Caroline 1785-1828 ... **NCLC 38**
See also DLB 116
Lamb, Mary Ann 1764-1847 .... **NCLC 125**
See also DLB 163; SATA 17
Lame Deer 1903(?)-1976 .... **NNAL**
See also CAAS 69-72

Lawrence of Arabia
See Lawrence, T(homas) E(dward)

Lawson, Henry (Archibald Hertzberg)
1867-1922 .... **SSC 18; TCLC 27**
See also CA 181; CAAE 120; DLB 230;
RGEL 2; RGSF 2

Lawton, Dennis
See Faust, Frederick (Schiller)

Layamon fl. c. 1200- .... **CMLC 10**
See Laȝamon
See also DLB 146; RGEL 2

Laye, Camara 1928-1980 ..... **BLC 2; CLC 4, 38**
See Camara Laye
See also AFW; BW 1; CA 85-88; CAAS
97-100; CANR 25; DAM MULT; MTCW
1, 2; WLIT 2

Layton, Irving 1912-2006 ..... **CLC 2, 15, 164**
See also CA 1-4R; CAAS 247; CANR 2,
33, 43, 66, 129; CP 1, 2, 3, 4, 5, 6, 7;
DAC; DAM MST, POET; DLB 88; EWL
3; MTCW 1, 2; PFS 12; RGEL 2

Layton, Irving Peter
See Layton, Irving

Lazarus, Emma 1849-1887 ...... **NCLC 8, 109**

Lazarus, Felix
See Cable, George Washington

Lazarus, Henry
See Slavitt, David R(ytman)

Lea, Joan
See Neufeld, John (Arthur)

Leacock, Stephen (Butler)
1869-1944 .... **SSC 39; TCLC 2**
See also CA 141; CAAE 104; CANR 80;
DAC; DAM MST; DLB 92; EWL 3;
MTCW 2; MTFW 2005; RGEL 2; RGSF
2

Lead, Jane Ward 1623-1704 .... **LC 72**
See also DLB 131

Leapor, Mary 1722-1746 .... **LC 80**
See also DLB 109

Lear, Edward 1812-1888 ..... **NCLC 3; PC 65**
See also AAYA 48; BRW 5; CLR 1, 75;
DLB 32, 163, 166; MAICYA 1, 2; RGEL
2; SATA 18, 100; WCH; WP

Lear, Norman (Milton) 1922- .... **CLC 12**
See also CA 73-76

Leautaud, Paul 1872-1956 .... **TCLC 83**
See also CA 203; DLB 65; GFL 1789 to the
Present

Leavis, F(rank) R(aymond)
1895-1978 .... **CLC 24**
See also BRW 7; CA 21-24R; CAAS 77-
80; CANR 44; DLB 242; EWL 3; MTCW
1, 2; RGEL 2

Leavitt, David 1961- .... **CLC 34**
See also CA 122; CANR 50, 62, 101, 134; CPW; DA3; DAM POP;
DLB 130; GLL 1; INT CA-122; MAL 5;
MTCW 2; MTFW 2005

Leblanc, Maurice (Marie Emile)
1864-1941 .... **TCLC 49**
See also CAAE 110; CMW 4

Lebowitz, Fran(ces Ann) 1951(?)- ... **CLC 11, 36**
See also CA 81-84; CANR 14, 60, 70; INT
CANR-14; MTCW 1

Lebrecht, Peter
See Tieck, (Johann) Ludwig

le Carre, John 1931- .... **CLC 9, 15**
See also AAYA 42; BEST 89:4; BPFB 2;
BRWS 2; CA 5-8R; CANR 13, 33, 59,
107, 132; CDBLB 1960 to Present; CMW
4; CN 1, 2, 3, 4, 5, 6, 7; CPW; DA3;
DAM POP; DLB 87; EWL 3; MSW;
MTCW 1, 2; MTFW 2005; RGEL 2; TEA

Le Clezio, J. M.G. 1940- .... **CLC 31, 155**
See also CA 128; CAAE 116; CANR 147;
CWW 2; DLB 83; EWL 3; GFL 1789 to
the Present; RGSF 2

Le Clezio, Jean Marie Gustave
See Le Clezio, J. M.G.

Leconte de Lisle, Charles-Marie-Rene
1818-1894 .... **NCLC 29**
See also DLB 217; EW 6; GFL 1789 to the
Present

Le Coq, Monsieur
See Simenon, Georges (Jacques Christian)

Leduc, Violette 1907-1972 .... **CLC 22**
See also CA 13-14; CAAS 33-36R; CANR
69; CAP 1; EWL 3; GFL 1789 to the
Present; GLL 1

Ledwidge, Francis 1887(?)-1917 .... **TCLC 23**
See also CA 203; CAAE 123; DLB 20

Lee, Andrea 1953- .... **BLC 2; CLC 36**
See also BW 1, 3; CA 125; CANR 82;
DAM MULT

Lee, Andrew
See Auchincloss, Louis

Lee, Chang-rae 1965- .... **CLC 91**
See also CA 148; CANR 89; CN 7; DLB
312; LATS 1:2

Lee, Don L. .... **CLC 2**
See Madhubuti, Haki R.
See also CP 2, 3, 4, 5

Lee, George W(ashington)
1894-1976 .... **BLC 2; CLC 52**
See also BW 1; CA 125; CANR 83; DAM
MULT; DLB 51

Lee, Harper 1926- ... **CLC 12, 60, 194; WLC 4**
See also AAYA 13; AMWS 8; BPFB 2;
BYA 3; CA 13-16R; CANR 51, 128;
CDALB 1941-1968; CSW; DA; DA3;
DAB; DAC; DAM MST, NOV; DLB 6;
EXPN; LAIT 3; MAL 5; MTCW 1, 2;
MTFW 2005; NFS 2; SATA 11; WYA;
YAW

Lee, Helen Elaine 1959(?)- .... **CLC 86**
See also CA 148

Lee, John .... **CLC 70**

Lee, Julian
See Latham, Jean Lee

Lee, Larry
See Lee, Lawrence

Lee, Laurie 1914-1997 .... **CLC 90**
See also CA 77-80; CAAS 158; CANR 33,
73; CP 1, 2, 3, 4, 5, 6; DAB; DAM
POP; DLB 27; MTCW 1; RGEL 2

Lee, Lawrence 1941-1990 .... **CLC 34**
See also CAAS 131; CANR 43

Lee, Li-Young 1957- .... **CLC 164; PC 24**
See also AMWS 15; CA 153; CANR 118;
CP 6, 7; DLB 165, 312; LMFS 2; PFS 11,
15, 17

Lee, Manfred B. 1905-1971 .... **CLC 11**
See Queen, Ellery
See also CA 1-4R; CAAS 29-32R; CANR
2, 150; CMW 4; DLB 137

Lee, Manfred Bennington
See Lee, Manfred B.

Lee, Nathaniel 1645(?)-1692 .... **LC 103**
See also DLB 80; RGEL 2

Lee, Shelton Jackson
See Lee, Spike
See also AAYA 4, 29

Lee, Spike 1957(?)- .... **BLCS; CLC 105**
See Lee, Shelton Jackson
See also BW 2, 3; CA 125; CANR 42;
DAM MULT

Lee, Stan 1922- .... **CLC 17**
See also AAYA 5, 49; CA 111; CAAE 108;
CANR 129; INT CA-111; MTFW 2005

Lee, Tanith 1947- .... **CLC 46**
See also AAYA 15; CA 37-40R; CANR 53,
102, 145; DLB 261; FANT; SATA 8, 88,
134; SFW 4; SUFW 1, 2; YAW

Lee, Vernon .... **SSC 33, 98; TCLC 5**
See Paget, Violet
See also DLB 57, 153, 156, 174, 178; GLL
1; SUFW 1

Lee, William
See Burroughs, William S.
See also GLL 1

Lee, Willy
See Burroughs, William S.
See also GLL 1

Lee-Hamilton, Eugene (Jacob)
1845-1907 .... **TCLC 22**
See also CA 234; CAAE 117

Leet, Judith 1935- .... **CLC 11**
See also CA 187

Le Fanu, Joseph Sheridan
1814-1873 .... **NCLC 9, 58; SSC 14, 84**
See also CMW 4; DA3; DAM POP; DLB
21, 70, 159, 178; GL 3; HGG; RGEL 2;
RGSF 2; SUFW 1

Leffland, Ella 1931- .... **CLC 19**
See also CA 29-32R; CANR 35, 78, 82;
DLBY 1984; INT CANR-35; SATA 65;
SSFS 24

Leger, Alexis
See Leger, (Marie-Rene Auguste) Alexis
Saint-Leger

**Leger, (Marie-Rene Auguste) Alexis
Saint-Leger** 1887-1975 .. **CLC 4, 11, 46;
PC 23**
See Perse, Saint-John; Saint-John Perse
See also CA 13-16R; CAAS 61-64; CANR
43; DAM POET; MTCW 1

Leger, Saintleger
See Leger, (Marie-Rene Auguste) Alexis
Saint-Leger

Le Guin, Ursula K. 1929- ...... **CLC 8, 13, 22,
45, 71, 136; SSC 12, 69**
See also AAYA 9, 27; AITN 1; BPFB 2;
BYA 5, 8, 11, 14; CA 21-24R; CANR 9,
32, 52, 74, 132; CDALB 1968-1988; CLR
3, 28, 91; CN 2, 3, 4, 5, 6, 7; CPW; DA3;
DAB; DAC; DAM MST, POP; DLB 8,
52, 256, 275; EXPS; FANT; FW; INT
CANR-32; JRDA; LAIT 5; MAICYA 1,
2; MAL 5; MTCW 1, 2; MTFW 2005;
NFS 6, 9; SATA 4, 52, 99, 149; SCFW 1,
2; SFW 4; SSFS 2; SUFW 1, 2; WYA;
YAW

Lehmann, Rosamond (Nina)
1901-1990 .... **CLC 5**
See also CA 77-80; CAAS 131; CANR 8,
73; CN 1, 2, 3, 4; DLB 15; MTCW 2;
RGEL 2; RHW

Leiber, Fritz (Reuter, Jr.)
1910-1992 .... **CLC 25**
See also AAYA 65; BPFB 2; CA 45-48;
CAAS 139; CANR 2, 40, 86; CN 2, 3, 4,
5; DLB 8; FANT; HGG; MTCW 1, 2;
MTFW 2005; SATA 45; SATA-Obit 73;
SCFW 1, 2; SFW 4; SUFW 1, 2

Leibniz, Gottfried Wilhelm von
1646-1716 .... **LC 35**
See also DLB 168

Leimbach, Martha 1963-
See Leimbach, Marti
See also CA 130

Leimbach, Marti .... **CLC 65**
See Leimbach, Martha

Leino, Eino .... **TCLC 24**
See Lonnbohm, Armas Eino Leopold
See also EWL 3

Leiris, Michel (Julien) 1901-1990 ..... **CLC 61**
See also CA 128; CAAE 119; CAAS 132;
EWL 3; GFL 1789 to the Present

MST, NOV; DLB 9, 102, 284, 331; DLBD
1; EWL 3; LAIT 3; MAL 5; MTCW 1, 2;
MTFW 2005; NFS 15, 19, 22; RGAL 4;
TUS

Lewis, (Percy) Wyndham
1884(?)-1957 .. **SSC 34; TCLC 2, 9, 104**
See also BRW 7; CA 157; CAAE 104; DLB
15; EWL 3; FANT; MTCW 2; MTFW
2005; RGEL 2

Lewisohn, Ludwig 1883-1955 .... **TCLC 19**
See also CA 203; CAAE 107; DLB 4, 9,
28, 102; MAL 5

Lewton, Val 1904-1951 .... **TCLC 76**
See also CA 199; IDFW 3, 4

Leyner, Mark 1956- .... **CLC 92**
See also CA 110; CANR 28, 53; DA3; DLB
292; MTCW 2; MTFW 2005

Lezama Lima, Jose 1910-1976 .... **CLC 4, 10,
101; HLCS 2**
See also CA 77-80; CANR 71; DAM
MULT; DLB 113, 283; EWL 3; HW 1, 2;
LAW; RGWL 2, 3

L'Heureux, John (Clarke) 1934- ...... **CLC 52**
See also CA 13-16R; CANR 23, 45, 88; CP
1, 2, 3, 4; DLB 244

Li Ch'ing-chao 1081(?)-1141(?) .... **CMLC 71**

Liddell, C. H.
See Kuttner, Henry

Lie, Jonas (Lauritz Idemil)
1833-1908(?) .... **TCLC 5**
See also CAAE 115

Lieber, Joel 1937-1971 .... **CLC 6**
See also CA 73-76; CAAS 29-32R

Lieber, Stanley Martin
See Lee, Stan

Lieberman, Laurence (James)
1935- .... **CLC 4, 36**
See also CA 17-20R; CANR 8, 36, 89; CP
1, 2, 3, 4, 5, 6, 7

Lieh Tzu fl. 7th cent. B.C.-5th cent.
B.C. .... **CMLC 27**

Lieksman, Anders
See Haavikko, Paavo Juhani

Lifton, Robert Jay 1926- .... **CLC 67**
See also CA 17-20R; CANR 27, 78; INT
CANR-27; SATA 66

Lightfoot, Gordon 1938- .... **CLC 26**
See also CA 242; CAAE 109

Lightfoot, Gordon Meredith
See Lightfoot, Gordon

Lightman, Alan P(aige) 1948- .... **CLC 81**
See also CA 141; CANR 63, 105, 138;
MTFW 2005

Ligotti, Thomas (Robert) 1953- ...... **CLC 44;
SSC 16**
See also CA 123; CANR 49, 135; HGG;
SUFW 2

Li Ho 791-817 .... **PC 13**

Li Ju-chen c. 1763-c. 1830 .... **NCLC 137**

Lilar, Francoise
See Mallet-Joris, Francoise

Liliencron, Detlev
See Liliencron, Detlev von

Liliencron, Detlev von 1844-1909 .. **TCLC 18**
See also CAAE 117

Liliencron, Friedrich Adolf Axel Detlev von
See Liliencron, Detlev von

Liliencron, Friedrich Detlev von
See Liliencron, Detlev von

Lille, Alain de
See Alain de Lille

Lillo, George 1691-1739 .... **LC 131**
See also DLB 84; RGEL 2

Lilly, William 1602-1681 .... **LC 27**

Lima, Jose Lezama
See Lezama Lima, Jose

Lima Barreto, Afonso Henrique de
1881-1922 .... **TCLC 23**
See Lima Barreto, Afonso Henriques de
See also CA 181; CAAE 117; LAW

Lima Barreto, Afonso Henriques de
See Lima Barreto, Afonso Henrique de
See also DLB 307

Limonov, Eduard
See Limonov, Edward
See also DLB 317

Limonov, Edward 1944- .... **CLC 67**
See Limonov, Eduard
See also CA 137

Lin, Frank
See Atherton, Gertrude (Franklin Horn)

Lin, Yutang 1895-1976 .... **TCLC 149**
See also CA 45-48; CAAS 65-68; CANR 2;
RGAL 4

Lincoln, Abraham 1809-1865 .... **NCLC 18**
See also LAIT 2

Lind, Jakov .... **CLC 1, 2, 4, 27, 82**
See Landwirth, Heinz
See also CA 4; DLB 299; EWL 3; RGHL

Lindbergh, Anne Morrow
1906-2001 .... **CLC 82**
See also BPFB 2; CA 17-20R; CAAE 193;
CANR 16, 73; DAM NOV; MTCW 1, 2;
MTFW 2005; SATA 33; SATA-Obit 125;
TUS

Lindsay, David 1878(?)-1945 .... **TCLC 15**
See also CA 187; CAAE 113; DLB 255;
FANT; SFW 4; SUFW 1

Lindsay, (Nicholas) Vachel
1879-1931 .... **PC 23; TCLC 17; WLC 4**
See also AMWS 1; CA 135; CAAE 114;
CANR 79; CDALB 1865-1917; DA;
DA3; DAC; DAM MST, POET; DLB 54;
EWL 3; EXPP; MAL 5; RGAL 4; SATA
40; WP

Linke-Poot
See Doeblin, Alfred

Linney, Romulus 1930- .... **CLC 51**
See also CA 1-4R; CAD; CANR 40, 44,
79; CD 5, 6; CSW; RGAL 4

Linton, Eliza Lynn 1822-1898 .... **NCLC 41**
See also DLB 18

Li Po 701-763 .... **CMLC 2, 86; PC 29**
See also PFS 20; WP

Lipsius, Justus 1547-1606 .... **LC 16**

Lipsyte, Robert 1938- .... **CLC 21**
See also AAYA 7, 45; CA 17-20R; CANR
8, 57, 146; CLR 23, 76; DA; DAC; DAM
MST, NOV; JRDA; LAIT 5; MAICYA 1,
2; SATA 5, 68, 113, 161; WYA; YAW

Lipsyte, Robert Michael
See Lipsyte, Robert

Lish, Gordon 1934- .... **CLC 45; SSC 18**
See also CA 117; CAAE 113; CANR 79,
151; DLB 130; INT CA-117

Lish, Gordon Jay
See Lish, Gordon

Lispector, Clarice 1925(?)-1977 .... **CLC 43;
HLCS 2; SSC 34, 96**
See also CA 139; CAAS 116; CANR 71;
CDWLB 3; DLB 113, 307; DNFS 1; EWL
3; FW; HW 2; LAW; RGSF 2; RGWL 2,
3; WLIT 1

Littell, Robert 1935(?)- .... **CLC 42**
See also CA 112; CAAE 109; CANR 64,
115; CMW 4

Little, Malcolm 1925-1965
See Malcolm X
See also BW 1, 3; CA 125; CAAS 111;
CANR 82; DA; DA3; DAB; DAC; DAM
MST, MULT; MTCW 1, 2; MTFW 2005

Littlewit, Humphrey Gent.
See Lovecraft, H. P.

Litwos
See Sienkiewicz, Henryk (Adam Alexander
Pius)

Liu, E. 1857-1909 .... **TCLC 15**
See also CA 190; CAAE 115; DLB 328

Lively, Penelope 1933- .... **CLC 32, 50**
See also BPFB 2; CA 41-44R; CANR 29,
67, 79, 131; CLR 7; CN 5, 6, 7; CWRI 5;
DAM NOV; DLB 14, 161, 207, 326;
FANT; JRDA; MAICYA 1, 2; MTCW 1,
2; MTFW 2005; SATA 7, 60, 101, 164;
TEA

Lively, Penelope Margaret
See Lively, Penelope

Livesay, Dorothy (Kathleen)
1909-1996 .... **CLC 4, 15, 79**
See also AITN 2; CA 25-28R; 8; CANR 36,
67; CP 1, 2, 3, 4, 5; DAC; DAM MST,
POET; DLB 68; FW; MTCW 1; RGEL 2;
TWA

Livy c. 59B.C.-c. 12 .... **CMLC 11**
See also AW 2; CDWLB 1; DLB 211;
RGWL 2, 3; WLIT 8

Lizardi, Jose Joaquin Fernandez de
1776-1827 .... **NCLC 30**
See also LAW

Llewellyn, Richard
See Llewellyn Lloyd, Richard Dafydd Viv-
ian
See also DLB 15

Llewellyn Lloyd, Richard Dafydd Vivian
1906-1983 .... **CLC 7, 80**
See Llewellyn, Richard
See also CA 53-56; CAAS 111; CANR 7,
71; SATA 11; SATA-Obit 37

Llosa, Jorge Mario Pedro Vargas
See Vargas Llosa, Mario
See also RGWL 3

Llosa, Mario Vargas
See Vargas Llosa, Mario

Lloyd, Manda
See Mander, (Mary) Jane

Lloyd Webber, Andrew 1948-
See Webber, Andrew Lloyd
See also AAYA 1, 38; CA 149; CAAE 116;
DAM DRAM; SATA 56

Llull, Ramon c. 1235-c. 1316 .... **CMLC 12**

Lobb, Ebenezer
See Upward, Allen

Locke, Alain (Le Roy)
1886-1954 .... **BLCS; HR 1:3; TCLC 43**
See also AMWS 14; BW 1, 3; CA 124;
CAAE 106; CANR 79; DLB 51; LMFS
2; MAL 5; RGAL 4

Locke, John 1632-1704 .... **LC 7, 35, 135**
See also DLB 31, 101, 213, 252; RGEL 2;
WLIT 3

Locke-Elliott, Sumner
See Elliott, Sumner Locke

Lockhart, John Gibson 1794-1854 .. **NCLC 6**
See also DLB 110, 116, 144

Lockridge, Ross (Franklin), Jr.
1914-1948 .... **TCLC 111**
See also CA 145; CAAE 108; CANR 79;
DLB 143; DLBY 1980; MAL 5; RGAL
4; RHW

Lockwood, Robert
See Johnson, Robert

Lodge, David 1935- .... **CLC 36, 141**
See also BEST 90:1; BRWS 4; CA 17-20R;
CANR 19, 53, 92, 139; CN 1, 2, 3, 4, 5,
6, 7; CPW; DAM POP; DLB 14, 194;
EWL 3; INT CANR-19; MTCW 1, 2;
MTFW 2005

Lodge, Thomas 1558-1625 .... **LC 41**
See also DLB 172; RGEL 2

Mangan, James Clarence
1803-1849 .... **NCLC 27**
See also RGEL 2
Maniere, J.-E.
See Giraudoux, Jean(-Hippolyte)
Mankiewicz, Herman (Jacob)
1897-1953 .... **TCLC 85**
See also CA 169; CAAE 120; DLB 26;
IDFW 3, 4
Manley, (Mary) Delariviere
1672(?)-1724 .... **LC 1, 42**
See also DLB 39, 80; RGEL 2
Mann, Abel
See Creasey, John
Mann, Emily 1952- .... **DC 7**
See also CA 130; CAD; CANR 55; CD 5,
6; CWD; DLB 266
Mann, (Luiz) Heinrich 1871-1950 ... **TCLC 9**
See also CA 164, 181; CAAE 106; DLB
66, 118; EW 8; EWL 3; RGWL 2, 3
Mann, (Paul) Thomas 1875-1955 . **SSC 5, 80,
82; TCLC 2, 8, 14, 21, 35, 44, 60, 168;
WLC 4**
See also BPFB 2; CA 128; CAAE 104;
CANR 133; CDWLB 2; DA; DA3; DAB;
DAC; DAM MST, NOV; DLB 66, 331;
EW 9; EWL 3; GLL 1; LATS 1:1; LMFS
1; MTCW 1, 2; MTFW 2005; NFS 17;
RGSF 2; RGWL 2, 3; SSFS 4, 9; TWA
Mannheim, Karl 1893-1947 .... **TCLC 65**
See also CA 204
Manning, David
See Faust, Frederick (Schiller)
Manning, Frederic 1882-1935 .... **TCLC 25**
See also CA 216; CAAE 124; DLB 260
Manning, Olivia 1915-1980 .... **CLC 5, 19**
See also CA 5-8R; CAAS 101; CANR 29;
CN 1, 2; EWL 3; FW; MTCW 1; RGEL 2
Mannyng, Robert c. 1264-c.
1340 .... **CMLC 83**
See also DLB 146
Mano, D. Keith 1942- .... **CLC 2, 10**
See also CA 25-28R; 6; CANR 26, 57; DLB
6
Mansfield, Katherine .... **SSC 9, 23, 38, 81;
TCLC 2, 8, 39, 164; WLC 4**
See Beauchamp, Kathleen Mansfield
See also BPFB 2; BRW 7; DAB; DLB 162;
EWL 3; EXPS; FW; GLL 1; RGEL 2;
RGSF 2; SSFS 2, 8, 10, 11; WWE 1
Manso, Peter 1940- .... **CLC 39**
See also CA 29-32R; CANR 44, 156
Mantecon, Juan Jimenez
See Jimenez (Mantecon), Juan Ramon
Mantel, Hilary (Mary) 1952- .... **CLC 144**
See also CA 125; CANR 54, 101; CN 5, 6,
7; DLB 271; RHW
Manton, Peter
See Creasey, John
Man Without a Spleen, A
See Chekhov, Anton (Pavlovich)
Manzano, Juan Franciso
1797(?)-1854 .... **NCLC 155**
Manzoni, Alessandro 1785-1873 ... **NCLC 29,
98**
See also EW 5; RGWL 2, 3; TWA; WLIT 7
Map, Walter 1140-1209 .... **CMLC 32**
Mapu, Abraham (ben Jekutiel)
1808-1867 .... **NCLC 18**
Mara, Sally
See Queneau, Raymond
Maracle, Lee 1950- .... **NNAL**
See also CA 149
Marat, Jean Paul 1743-1793 .... **LC 10**
Marcel, Gabriel Honore 1889-1973 . **CLC 15**
See also CA 102; CAAS 45-48; EWL 3;
MTCW 1, 2

March, William .... **TCLC 96**
See Campbell, William Edward March
See also CA 216; DLB 9, 86, 316; MAL 5
Marchbanks, Samuel
See Davies, Robertson
See also CCA 1
Marchi, Giacomo
See Bassani, Giorgio
Marcus Aurelius
See Aurelius, Marcus
See also AW 2
Marguerite
See de Navarre, Marguerite
Marguerite d'Angouleme
See de Navarre, Marguerite
See also GFL Beginnings to 1789
Marguerite de Navarre
See de Navarre, Marguerite
See also RGWL 2, 3
Margulies, Donald 1954- .... **CLC 76**
See also AAYA 57; CA 200; CD 6; DFS 13;
DLB 228
Marie de France c. 12th cent. - ..... **CMLC 8;
PC 22**
See also DLB 208; FW; RGWL 2, 3
Marie de l'Incarnation 1599-1672 ...... **LC 10**
Marier, Captain Victor
See Griffith, D(avid Lewelyn) W(ark)
Mariner, Scott
See Pohl, Frederik
Marinetti, Filippo Tommaso
1876-1944 .... **TCLC 10**
See also CAAE 107; DLB 114, 264; EW 9;
EWL 3; WLIT 7
Marivaux, Pierre Carlet de Chamblain de
1688-1763 .... **DC 7; LC 4, 123**
See also DLB 314; GFL Beginnings to
1789; RGWL 2, 3; TWA
Markandaya, Kamala .... **CLC 8, 38**
See Taylor, Kamala
See also BYA 13; CN 1, 2, 3, 4, 5, 6, 7;
DLB 323; EWL 3
Markfield, Wallace (Arthur)
1926-2002 .... **CLC 8**
See also CA 69-72; 3; CAAS 208; CN 1, 2,
3, 4, 5, 6, 7; DLB 2, 28; DLBY 2002
Markham, Edwin 1852-1940 .... **TCLC 47**
See also CA 160; DLB 54, 186; MAL 5;
RGAL 4
Markham, Robert
See Amis, Kingsley
Marks, J.
See Highwater, Jamake (Mamake)
Marks-Highwater, J.
See Highwater, Jamake (Mamake)
Markson, David M. 1927- .... **CLC 67**
See also CA 49-52; CANR 1, 91, 158; CN
5, 6
Markson, David Merrill
See Markson, David M.
Marlatt, Daphne (Buckle) 1942- .... **CLC 168**
See also CA 25-28R; CANR 17, 39; CN 6,
7; CP 4, 5, 6, 7; CWP; DLB 60; FW
Marley, Bob .... **CLC 17**
See Marley, Robert Nesta
Marley, Robert Nesta 1945-1981
See Marley, Bob
See also CA 107; CAAS 103
Marlowe, Christopher 1564-1593 . **DC 1; LC
22, 47, 117; PC 57; WLC 4**
See also BRW 1; BRWR 1; CDBLB Before
1660; DA; DA3; DAB; DAC; DAM
DRAM, MST; DFS 1, 5, 13, 21; DLB 62;
EXPP; LMFS 1; PFS 22; RGEL 2; TEA;
WLIT 3
Marlowe, Stephen 1928- .... **CLC 70**
See Queen, Ellery
See also CA 13-16R; CANR 6, 55; CMW
4; SFW 4

Marmion, Shakerley 1603-1639 .... **LC 89**
See also DLB 58; RGEL 2
Marmontel, Jean-Francois 1723-1799 .. **LC 2**
See also DLB 314
Maron, Monika 1941- .... **CLC 165**
See also CA 201
Marot, Clement c. 1496-1544 .... **LC 133**
See also DLB 327; GFL Beginnings to 1789
Marquand, John P(hillips)
1893-1960 .... **CLC 2, 10**
See also AMW; BPFB 2; CA 85-88; CANR
73; CMW 4; DLB 9, 102; EWL 3; MAL
5; MTCW 2; RGAL 4
Marques, Rene 1919-1979 .. **CLC 96; HLC 2**
See also CA 97-100; CAAS 85-88; CANR
78; DAM MULT; DLB 305; EWL 3; HW
1, 2; LAW; RGSF 2
Marquez, Gabriel Garcia
See Garcia Marquez, Gabriel
Marquis, Don(ald Robert Perry)
1878-1937 .... **TCLC 7**
See also CA 166; CAAE 104; DLB 11, 25;
MAL 5; RGAL 4
Marquis de Sade
See Sade, Donatien Alphonse Francois
Marric, J. J.
See Creasey, John
See also MSW
Marryat, Frederick 1792-1848 .... **NCLC 3**
See also DLB 21, 163; RGEL 2; WCH
Marsden, James
See Creasey, John
Marsh, Edward 1872-1953 .... **TCLC 99**
Marsh, (Edith) Ngaio 1895-1982 .. **CLC 7, 53**
See also CA 9-12R; CANR 6, 58; CMW 4;
CN 1, 2, 3; CPW; DAM POP; DLB 77;
MSW; MTCW 1, 2; RGEL 2; TEA
Marshall, Allen
See Westlake, Donald E.
Marshall, Garry 1934- .... **CLC 17**
See also AAYA 3; CA 111; SATA 60
Marshall, Paule 1929- .. **BLC 3; CLC 27, 72;
SSC 3**
See also AFAW 1, 2; AMWS 11; BPFB 2;
BW 2, 3; CA 77-80; CANR 25, 73, 129;
CN 1, 2, 3, 4, 5, 6, 7; DA3; DAM MULT;
DLB 33, 157, 227; EWL 3; LATS 1:2;
MAL 5; MTCW 1, 2; MTFW 2005;
RGAL 4; SSFS 15
Marshallik
See Zangwill, Israel
Marsten, Richard
See Hunter, Evan
Marston, John 1576-1634 .... **LC 33**
See also BRW 2; DAM DRAM; DLB 58,
172; RGEL 2
Martel, Yann 1963- .... **CLC 192**
See also AAYA 67; CA 146; CANR 114;
DLB 326; MTFW 2005
Martens, Adolphe-Adhemar
See Ghelderode, Michel de
Martha, Henry
See Harris, Mark
Marti, Jose .... **PC 76**
See Marti (y Perez), Jose (Julian)
See also DLB 290
Marti (y Perez), Jose (Julian)
1853-1895 .... **HLC 2; NCLC 63**
See Marti, Jose
See also DAM MULT; HW 2; LAW; RGWL
2, 3; WLIT 1
Martial c. 40-c. 104 .... **CMLC 35; PC 10**
See also AW 2; CDWLB 1; DLB 211;
RGWL 2, 3
Martin, Ken
See Hubbard, L. Ron
Martin, Richard
See Creasey, John

Meyer, June
See Jordan, June

Meyer, Lynn
See Slavitt, David R(ytman)

Meyers, Jeffrey 1939- .... **CLC 39**
See also CA 186; 73-76, 186; CANR 54, 102, 159; DLB 111

Meynell, Alice (Christina Gertrude Thompson) 1847-1922 .... **TCLC 6**
See also CA 177; CAAE 104; DLB 19, 98; RGEL 2

Meyrink, Gustav .... **TCLC 21**
See Meyer, Gustav
See also DLB 81; EWL 3

Michaels, Leonard 1933-2003 ..... **CLC 6, 25; SSC 16**
See also AMWS 16; CA 61-64; CAAS 216; CANR 21, 62, 119; CN 3, 45, 6, 7; DLB 130; MTCW 1; TCLE 1:2

Michaux, Henri 1899-1984 .... **CLC 8, 19**
See also CA 85-88; CAAS 114; DLB 258; EWL 3; GFL 1789 to the Present; RGWL 2, 3

Micheaux, Oscar (Devereaux) 1884-1951 .... **TCLC 76**
See also BW 3; CA 174; DLB 50; TCWW 2

Michelangelo 1475-1564 .... **LC 12**
See also AAYA 43

Michelet, Jules 1798-1874 .... **NCLC 31**
See also EW 5; GFL 1789 to the Present

Michels, Robert 1876-1936 .... **TCLC 88**
See also CA 212

Michener, James A. 1907(?)-1997 . **CLC 1, 5, 11, 29, 60, 109**
See also AAYA 27; AITN 1; BEST 90:1; BPFB 2; CA 5-8R; CAAS 161; CANR 21, 45, 68; CN 1, 2, 3, 4, 5, 6; CPW; DA3; DAM NOV, POP; DLB 6; MAL 5; MTCW 1, 2; MTFW 2005; RHW; TCWW 1, 2

Mickiewicz, Adam 1798-1855 . **NCLC 3, 101; PC 38**
See also EW 5; RGWL 2, 3

Middleton, (John) Christopher 1926- .... **CLC 13**
See also CA 13-16R; CANR 29, 54, 117; CP 1, 2, 3, 4, 5, 6, 7; DLB 40

Middleton, Richard (Barham) 1882-1911 .... **TCLC 56**
See also CA 187; DLB 156; HGG

Middleton, Stanley 1919- .... **CLC 7, 38**
See also CA 25-28R; 23; CANR 21, 46, 81, 157; CN 1, 2, 3, 4, 5, 6, 7; DLB 14, 326

Middleton, Thomas 1580-1627 ...... **DC 5; LC 33, 123**
See also BRW 2; DAM DRAM, MST; DFS 18, 22; DLB 58; RGEL 2

Migueis, Jose Rodrigues 1901-1980 . **CLC 10**
See also DLB 287

Mikszath, Kalman 1847-1910 .... **TCLC 31**
See also CA 170

Miles, Jack .... **CLC 100**
See also CA 200

Miles, John Russiano
See Miles, Jack

Miles, Josephine (Louise) 1911-1985 .... **CLC 1, 2, 14, 34, 39**
See also CA 1-4R; CAAS 116; CANR 2, 55; CP 1, 2, 3, 4; DAM POET; DLB 48; MAL 5; TCLE 1:2

Militant
See Sandburg, Carl (August)

Mill, Harriet (Hardy) Taylor 1807-1858 .... **NCLC 102**
See also FW

Mill, John Stuart 1806-1873 ... **NCLC 11, 58, 179**
See also CDBLB 1832-1890; DLB 55, 190, 262; FW 1; RGEL 2; TEA

Millar, Kenneth 1915-1983 .... **CLC 14**
See Macdonald, Ross
See also CA 9-12R; CAAS 110; CANR 16, 63, 107; CMW 4; CPW; DA3; DAM POP; DLB 2, 226; DLBD 6; DLBY 1983; MTCW 1, 2; MTFW 2005

Millay, E. Vincent
See Millay, Edna St. Vincent

Millay, Edna St. Vincent 1892-1950 ..... **PC 6, 61; TCLC 4, 49, 169; WLCS**
See Boyd, Nancy
See also AMW; CA 130; CAAE 104; CDALB 1917-1929; DA; DA3; DAB; DAC; DAM MST, POET; DLB 45, 249; EWL 3; EXPP; FL 1:6; MAL 5; MBL; MTCW 1, 2; MTFW 2005; PAB; PFS 3, 17; RGAL 4; TUS; WP

Miller, Arthur 1915-2005 ..... **CLC 1, 2, 6, 10, 15, 26, 47, 78, 179; DC 1; WLC 4**
See also AAYA 15; AITN 1; AMW; AMWC 1; CA 1-4R; CAAS 236; CABS 3; CAD; CANR 2, 30, 54, 76, 132; CD 5, 6; CDALB 1941-1968; DA; DA3; DAB; DAC; DAM DRAM, MST; DFS 1, 3, 8; DLB 7, 266; EWL 3; LAIT 1, 4; LATS 1:2; MAL 5; MTCW 1, 2; MTFW 2005; RGAL 4; RGHL; TUS; WYAS 1

Miller, Henry (Valentine) 1891-1980 .... **CLC 1, 2, 4, 9, 14, 43, 84; WLC 4**
See also AMW; BPFB 2; CA 9-12R; CAAS 97-100; CANR 33, 64; CDALB 1929-1941; CN 1, 2; DA; DA3; DAB; DAC; DAM MST, NOV; DLB 4, 9; DLBY 1980; EWL 3; MAL 5; MTCW 1, 2; MTFW 2005; RGAL 4; TUS

Miller, Hugh 1802-1856 .... **NCLC 143**
See also DLB 190

Miller, Jason 1939(?)-2001 .... **CLC 2**
See also AITN 1; CA 73-76; CAAS 197; CAD; CANR 130; DFS 12; DLB 7

Miller, Sue 1943- .... **CLC 44**
See also AMWS 12; BEST 90:3; CA 139; CANR 59, 91, 128; DA3; DAM POP; DLB 143

Miller, Walter M(ichael, Jr.) 1923-1996 .... **CLC 4, 30**
See also BPFB 2; CA 85-88; CANR 108; DLB 8; SCFW 1, 2; SFW 4

Millett, Kate 1934- .... **CLC 67**
See also AITN 1; CA 73-76; CANR 32, 53, 76, 110; DA3; DLB 246; FW; GLL 1; MTCW 1, 2; MTFW 2005

Millhauser, Steven 1943- ... **CLC 21, 54, 109; SSC 57**
See also CA 111; CAAE 110; CANR 63, 114, 133; CN 6, 7; DA3; DLB 2; FANT; INT CA-111; MAL 5; MTCW 2; MTFW 2005

Millhauser, Steven Lewis
See Millhauser, Steven

Millin, Sarah Gertrude 1889-1968 ... **CLC 49**
See also CA 102; CAAS 93-96; DLB 225; EWL 3

Milne, A. A. 1882-1956 .... **TCLC 6, 88**
See also BRWS 5; CA 133; CAAE 104; CLR 1, 26, 108; CMW 4; CWRI 5; DA3; DAB; DAC; DAM MST; DLB 10, 77, 100, 160; FANT; MAICYA 1, 2; MTCW 1, 2; MTFW 2005; RGEL 2; SATA 100; WCH; YABC 1

Milne, Alan Alexander
See Milne, A. A.

Milner, Ron(ald) 1938-2004 ..... **BLC 3; CLC 56**
See also AITN 1; BW 1; CA 73-76; CAAS 230; CAD; CANR 24, 81; CD 5, 6; DAM MULT; DLB 38; MAL 5; MTCW 1

Milnes, Richard Monckton 1809-1885 .... **NCLC 61**
See also DLB 32, 184

Milosz, Czeslaw 1911-2004 .... **CLC 5, 11, 22, 31, 56, 82; PC 8; WLCS**
See also AAYA 62; CA 81-84; CAAS 230; CANR 23, 51, 91, 126; CDWLB 4; CWW 2; DA3; DAM MST, POET; DLB 215, 331; EW 13; EWL 3; MTCW 1, 2; MTFW 2005; PFS 16; RGHL; RGWL 2, 3

Milton, John 1608-1674 ..... **LC 9, 43, 92; PC 19, 29; WLC 4**
See also AAYA 65; BRW 2; BRWR 2; CDBLB 1660-1789; DA; DA3; DAB; DAC; DAM MST, POET; DLB 131, 151, 281; EFS 1; EXPP; LAIT 1; PAB; PFS 3, 17; RGEL 2; TEA; WLIT 3; WP

Min, Anchee 1957- .... **CLC 86**
See also CA 146; CANR 94, 137; MTFW 2005

Minehaha, Cornelius
See Wedekind, Frank

Miner, Valerie 1947- .... **CLC 40**
See also CA 97-100; CANR 59; FW; GLL 2

Minimo, Duca
See D'Annunzio, Gabriele

Minot, Susan (Anderson) 1956- ...... **CLC 44, 159**
See also AMWS 6; CA 134; CANR 118; CN 6, 7

Minus, Ed 1938- .... **CLC 39**
See also CA 185

Mirabai 1498(?)-1550(?) .... **PC 48**
See also PFS 24

Miranda, Javier
See Bioy Casares, Adolfo
See also CWW 2

Mirbeau, Octave 1848-1917 .... **TCLC 55**
See also CA 216; DLB 123, 192; GFL 1789 to the Present

Mirikitani, Janice 1942- .... **AAL**
See also CA 211; DLB 312; RGAL 4

Mirk, John (?)-c. 1414 .... **LC 105**
See also DLB 146

Miro (Ferrer), Gabriel (Francisco Victor) 1879-1930 .... **TCLC 5**
See also CA 185; CAAE 104; DLB 322; EWL 3

Misharin, Alexandr .... **CLC 59**

Mishima, Yukio ... **CLC 2, 4, 6, 9, 27; DC 1; SSC 4; TCLC 161; WLC 4**
See Hiraoka, Kimitake
See also AAYA 50; BPFB 2; GLL 1; MJW; RGSF 2; RGWL 2, 3; SSFS 5, 12

Mistral, Frederic 1830-1914 .... **TCLC 51**
See also CA 213; CAAE 122; DLB 331; GFL 1789 to the Present

Mistral, Gabriela
See Godoy Alcayaga, Lucila
See also DLB 283, 331; DNFS 1; EWL 3; LAW; RGWL 2, 3; WP

Mistry, Rohinton 1952- ... **CLC 71, 196; SSC 73**
See also BRWS 10; CA 141; CANR 86, 114; CCA 1; CN 6, 7; DAC; SSFS 6

Mitchell, Clyde
See Ellison, Harlan

Mitchell, Emerson Blackhorse Barney 1945- .... **NNAL**
See also CA 45-48

Mitchell, James Leslie 1901-1935
See Gibbon, Lewis Grassic
See also CA 188; CAAE 104; DLB 15

Mitchell, Joni 1943- .... **CLC 12**
See also CA 112; CCA 1
Mitchell, Joseph (Quincy)
1908-1996 .... **CLC 98**
See also CA 77-80; CAAS 152; CANR 69;
CN 1, 2, 3, 4, 5, 6; CSW; DLB 185;
DLBY 1996
Mitchell, Margaret (Munnerlyn)
1900-1949 .... **TCLC 11, 170**
See also AAYA 23; BPFB 2; BYA 1; CA
125; CAAE 109; CANR 55, 94;
CDALBS; DA3; DAM NOV, POP; DLB
9; LAIT 2; MAL 5; MTCW 1, 2; MTFW
2005; NFS 9; RGAL 4; RHW; TUS;
WYAS 1; YAW
Mitchell, Peggy
See Mitchell, Margaret (Munnerlyn)
Mitchell, S(ilas) Weir 1829-1914 .... **TCLC 36**
See also CA 165; DLB 202; RGAL 4
Mitchell, W(illiam) O(rmond)
1914-1998 .... **CLC 25**
See also CA 77-80; CAAS 165; CANR 15,
43; CN 1, 2, 3, 4, 5, 6; DAC; DAM MST;
DLB 88; TCLE 1:2
Mitchell, William (Lendrum)
1879-1936 .... **TCLC 81**
See also CA 213
Mitford, Mary Russell 1787-1855 ... **NCLC 4**
See also DLB 110, 116; RGEL 2
Mitford, Nancy 1904-1973 .... **CLC 44**
See also BRWS 10; CA 9-12R; CN 1; DLB
191; RGEL 2
Miyamoto, (Chujo) Yuriko
1899-1951 .... **TCLC 37**
See Miyamoto Yuriko
See also CA 170, 174
Miyamoto Yuriko
See Miyamoto, (Chujo) Yuriko
See also DLB 180
Miyazawa, Kenji 1896-1933 .... **TCLC 76**
See Miyazawa Kenji
See also CA 157; RGWL 3
Miyazawa Kenji
See Miyazawa, Kenji
See also EWL 3
Mizoguchi, Kenji 1898-1956 .... **TCLC 72**
See also CA 167
Mo, Timothy (Peter) 1950- .... **CLC 46, 134**
See also CA 117; CANR 128; CN 5, 6, 7;
DLB 194; MTCW 1; WLIT 4; WWE 1
Modarressi, Taghi (M.) 1931-1997 .... **CLC 44**
See also CA 134; CAAE 121; INT CA-134
Modiano, Patrick (Jean) 1945- .... **CLC 18,
218**
See also CA 85-88; CANR 17, 40, 115;
CWW 2; DLB 83, 299; EWL 3; RGHL
Mofolo, Thomas (Mokopu)
1875(?)-1948 .... **BLC 3; TCLC 22**
See also AFW; CA 153; CAAE 121; CANR
83; DAM MULT; DLB 225; EWL 3;
MTCW 2; MTFW 2005; WLIT 2
Mohr, Nicholasa 1938- .... **CLC 12; HLC 2**
See also AAYA 8, 46; CA 49-52; CANR 1,
32, 64; CLR 22; DAM MULT; DLB 145;
HW 1, 2; JRDA; LAIT 5; LLW; MAICYA
2; MAICYAS 1; RGAL 4; SAAS 8; SATA
8, 97; SATA-Essay 113; WYA; YAW
Moi, Toril 1953- .... **CLC 172**
See also CA 154; CANR 102; FW
Mojtabai, A(nn) G(race) 1938- ..... **CLC 5, 9,
15, 29**
See also CA 85-88; CANR 88
Moliere 1622-1673 ..... **DC 13; LC 10, 28, 64,
125, 127; WLC 4**
See also DA; DA3; DAB; DAC; DAM
DRAM, MST; DFS 13, 18, 20; DLB 268;
EW 3; GFL Beginnings to 1789; LATS
1:1; RGWL 2, 3; TWA

Molin, Charles
See Mayne, William (James Carter)
Molnar, Ferenc 1878-1952 .... **TCLC 20**
See also CA 153; CAAE 109; CANR 83;
CDWLB 4; DAM DRAM; DLB 215;
EWL 3; RGWL 2, 3
Momaday, N. Scott 1934- ...... **CLC 2, 19, 85,
95, 160; NNAL; PC 25; WLCS**
See also AAYA 11, 64; AMWS 4; ANW;
BPFB 2; BYA 12; CA 25-28R; CANR 14,
34, 68, 134; CDALBS; CN 2, 3, 4, 5, 6,
7; CPW; DA; DA3; DAB; DAC; DAM
MST, MULT, NOV, POP; DLB 143, 175,
256; EWL 3; EXPP; INT CANR-14;
LAIT 4; LATS 1:2; MAL 5; MTCW 1, 2;
MTFW 2005; NFS 10; PFS 2, 11; RGAL
4; SATA 48; SATA-Brief 30; TCWW 1,
2; WP; YAW
Monette, Paul 1945-1995 .... **CLC 82**
See also AMWS 10; CA 139; CAAS 147;
CN 6; GLL 1
Monroe, Harriet 1860-1936 .... **TCLC 12**
See also CA 204; CAAE 109; DLB 54, 91
Monroe, Lyle
See Heinlein, Robert A.
Montagu, Elizabeth 1720-1800 .... **NCLC 7,
117**
See also FW
Montagu, Mary (Pierrepont) Wortley
1689-1762 .... **LC 9, 57; PC 16**
See also DLB 95, 101; FL 1:1; RGEL 2
Montagu, W. H.
See Coleridge, Samuel Taylor
Montague, John (Patrick) 1929- ..... **CLC 13,
46**
See also CA 9-12R; CANR 9, 69, 121; CP
1, 2, 3, 4, 5, 6, 7; DLB 40; EWL 3;
MTCW 1; PFS 12; RGEL 2; TCLE 1:2
Montaigne, Michel (Eyquem) de
1533-1592 .... **LC 8, 105; WLC 4**
See also DA; DAB; DAC; DAM MST;
DLB 327; EW 2; GFL Beginnings to
1789; LMFS 1; RGWL 2, 3; TWA
Montale, Eugenio 1896-1981 ... **CLC 7, 9, 18;
PC 13**
See also CA 17-20R; CAAS 104; CANR
30; DLB 114, 331; EW 11; EWL 3;
MTCW 1; PFS 22; RGWL 2, 3; TWA;
WLIT 7
Montesquieu, Charles-Louis de Secondat
1689-1755 .... **LC 7, 69**
See also DLB 314; EW 3; GFL Beginnings
to 1789; TWA
Montessori, Maria 1870-1952 ...... **TCLC 103**
See also CA 147; CAAE 115
Montgomery, (Robert) Bruce 1921(?)-1978
See Crispin, Edmund
See also CA 179; CAAS 104; CMW 4
Montgomery, L(ucy) M(aud)
1874-1942 .... **TCLC 51, 140**
See also AAYA 12; BYA 1; CA 137; CAAE
108; CLR 8, 91; DA3; DAC; DAM MST;
DLB 92; DLBD 14; JRDA; MAICYA 1,
2; MTCW 2; MTFW 2005; RGEL 2;
SATA 100; TWA; WCH; WYA; YABC 1
Montgomery, Marion H., Jr. 1925- .... **CLC 7**
See also AITN 1; CA 1-4R; CANR 3, 48;
CSW; DLB 6
Montgomery, Max
See Davenport, Guy (Mattison, Jr.)
Montherlant, Henry (Milon) de
1896-1972 .... **CLC 8, 19**
See also CA 85-88; CAAS 37-40R; DAM
DRAM; DLB 72, 321; EW 11; EWL 3;
GFL 1789 to the Present; MTCW 1
Monty Python
See Chapman, Graham; Cleese, John
(Marwood); Gilliam, Terry; Idle, Eric;
Jones, Terence Graham Parry; Palin,
Michael (Edward)
See also AAYA 7

Moodie, Susanna (Strickland)
1803-1885 .... **NCLC 14, 113**
See also DLB 99
Moody, Hiram 1961-
See Moody, Rick
See also CA 138; CANR 64, 112; MTFW
2005
Moody, Minerva
See Alcott, Louisa May
Moody, Rick .... **CLC 147**
See Moody, Hiram
Moody, William Vaughan
1869-1910 .... **TCLC 105**
See also CA 178; CAAE 110; DLB 7, 54;
MAL 5; RGAL 4
Mooney, Edward 1951-
See Mooney, Ted
See also CA 130
Mooney, Ted .... **CLC 25**
See Mooney, Edward
Moorcock, Michael 1939- .... **CLC 5, 27, 58**
See Bradbury, Edward P.
See also AAYA 26; CA 45-48; 5; CANR 2,
17, 38, 64, 122; CN 5, 6, 7; DLB 14, 231,
261, 319; FANT; MTCW 1, 2; MTFW
2005; SATA 93, 166; SCFW 1, 2; SFW 4;
SUFW 1, 2
Moorcock, Michael John
See Moorcock, Michael
Moore, Alan 1953- .... **CLC 230**
See also AAYA 51; CA 204; CANR 138;
DLB 261; MTFW 2005; SFW 4
Moore, Brian 1921-1999 ... **CLC 1, 3, 5, 7, 8,
19, 32, 90**
See Bryan, Michael
See also BRWS 9; CA 1-4R; CAAS 174;
CANR 1, 25, 42, 63; CCA 1; CN 1, 2, 3,
4, 5, 6; DAB; DAC; DAM MST; DLB
251; EWL 3; FANT; MTCW 1, 2; MTFW
2005; RGEL 2
Moore, Edward
See Muir, Edwin
See also RGEL 2
Moore, G. E. 1873-1958 .... **TCLC 89**
See also DLB 262
Moore, George Augustus
1852-1933 .... **SSC 19; TCLC 7**
See also BRW 6; CA 177; CAAE 104; DLB
10, 18, 57, 135; EWL 3; RGEL 2; RGSF
2
Moore, Lorrie .... **CLC 39, 45, 68**
See Moore, Marie Lorena
See also AMWS 10; CN 5, 6, 7; DLB 234;
SSFS 19
Moore, Marianne (Craig)
1887-1972 .... **CLC 1, 2, 4, 8, 10, 13, 19,
47; PC 4, 49; WLCS**
See also AMW; CA 1-4R; CAAS 33-36R;
CANR 3, 61; CDALB 1929-1941; CP 1;
DA; DA3; DAB; DAC; DAM MST,
POET; DLB 45; DLBD 7; EWL 3; EXPP;
FL 1:6; MAL 5; MBL; MTCW 1, 2;
MTFW 2005; PAB; PFS 14, 17; RGAL 4;
SATA 20; TUS; WP
Moore, Marie Lorena 1957- .... **CLC 165**
See Moore, Lorrie
See also CA 116; CANR 39, 83, 139; DLB
234; MTFW 2005
Moore, Michael 1954- .... **CLC 218**
See also AAYA 53; CA 166; CANR 150
Moore, Thomas 1779-1852 .... **NCLC 6, 110**
See also DLB 96, 144; RGEL 2
Moorhouse, Frank 1938- .... **SSC 40**
See also CA 118; CANR 92; CN 3, 4, 5, 6,
7; DLB 289; RGSF 2
Mora, Pat 1942- .... **HLC 2**
See also AMWS 13; CA 129; CANR 57,
81, 112; CLR 58; DAM MULT; DLB 209;
HW 1, 2; LLW; MAICYA 2; MTFW
2005; SATA 92, 134

Nordhoff, Charles Bernard
1887-1947 .... **TCLC 23**
See also CA 211; CAAE 108; DLB 9; LAIT
1; RHW 1; SATA 23

Norfolk, Lawrence 1963- .... **CLC 76**
See also CA 144; CANR 85; CN 6, 7; DLB
267

Norman, Marsha (Williams) 1947- . **CLC 28,**
186; DC 8
See also CA 105; CABS 3; CAD; CANR
41, 131; CD 5, 6; CSW; CWD; DAM
DRAM; DFS 2; DLB 266; DLBY 1984;
FW; MAL 5

Normyx
See Douglas, (George) Norman

Norris, (Benjamin) Frank(lin, Jr.)
1870-1902 .... **SSC 28; TCLC 24, 155**
See also AAYA 57; AMW; AMWC 2; BPFB
2; CA 160; CAAE 110; CDALB 1865-
1917; DLB 12, 71, 186; LMFS 2; MAL
5; NFS 12; RGAL 4; TCWW 1, 2; TUS

Norris, Leslie 1921-2006 .... **CLC 14**
See also CA 11-12; CAAS 251; CANR 14,
117; CAP 1; CP 1, 2, 3, 4, 5, 6, 7; DLB
27, 256

North, Andrew
See Norton, Andre

North, Anthony
See Koontz, Dean R.

North, Captain George
See Stevenson, Robert Louis (Balfour)

North, Captain George
See Stevenson, Robert Louis (Balfour)

North, Milou
See Erdrich, Louise

Northrup, B. A.
See Hubbard, L. Ron

North Staffs
See Hulme, T(homas) E(rnest)

Northup, Solomon 1808-1863 ...... **NCLC 105**

Norton, Alice Mary
See Norton, Andre
See also MAICYA 1; SATA 1, 43

Norton, Andre 1912-2005 .... **CLC 12**
See Norton, Alice Mary
See also AAYA 14; BPFB 2; BYA 4, 10,
12; CA 1-4R; CAAS 237; CANR 2, 31,
68, 108, 149; CLR 50; DLB 8, 52; JRDA;
MAICYA 2; MTCW 1; SATA 91; SUFW
1, 2; YAW

Norton, Caroline 1808-1877 .... **NCLC 47**
See also DLB 21, 159, 199

Norway, Nevil Shute 1899-1960
See Shute, Nevil
See also CA 102; CAAS 93-96; CANR 85;
MTCW 2

Norwid, Cyprian Kamil
1821-1883 .... **NCLC 17**
See also RGWL 3

Nosille, Nabrah
See Ellison, Harlan

Nossack, Hans Erich 1901-1977 .... **CLC 6**
See also CA 93-96; CAAS 85-88; CANR
156; DLB 69; EWL 3

Nostradamus 1503-1566 .... **LC 27**

Nosu, Chuji
See Ozu, Yasujiro

Notenburg, Eleanora (Genrikhovna) von
See Guro, Elena (Genrikhovna)

Nova, Craig 1945- .... **CLC 7, 31**
See also CA 45-48; CANR 2, 53, 127

Novak, Joseph
See Kosinski, Jerzy

Novalis 1772-1801 .... **NCLC 13, 178**
See also CDWLB 2; DLB 90; EW 5; RGWL
2, 3

Novick, Peter 1934- .... **CLC 164**
See also CA 188

Novis, Emile
See Weil, Simone (Adolphine)

Nowlan, Alden (Albert) 1933-1983 ... **CLC 15**
See also CA 9-12R; CANR 5; CP 1, 2, 3;
DAC; DAM MST; DLB 53; PFS 12

Noyes, Alfred 1880-1958 ...... **PC 27; TCLC 7**
See also CA 188; CAAE 104; DLB 20;
EXPP; FANT; PFS 4; RGEL 2

Nugent, Richard Bruce
1906(?)-1987 .... **HR 1:3**
See also BW 1; CA 125; DLB 51; GLL 2

Nunn, Kem .... **CLC 34**
See also CA 159

Nussbaum, Martha Craven 1947- .. **CLC 203**
See also CA 134; CANR 102

Nwapa, Flora (Nwanzuruaha)
1931-1993 .... **BLCS; CLC 133**
See also BW 2; CA 143; CANR 83; CD-
WLB 3; CWRI 5; DLB 125; EWL 3;
WLIT 2

Nye, Robert 1939- .... **CLC 13, 42**
See also BRWS 10; CA 33-36R; CANR 29,
67, 107; CN 1, 2, 3, 4, 5, 6, 7; CP 1, 2, 3,
4, 5, 6, 7; CWRI 5; DAM NOV; DLB 14,
271; FANT; HGG; MTCW 1; RHW;
SATA 6

Nyro, Laura 1947-1997 .... **CLC 17**
See also CA 194

Oates, Joyce Carol 1938- .. **CLC 1, 2, 3, 6, 9,**
11, 15, 19, 33, 52, 108, 134, 228; SSC 6,
70; WLC 4
See also AAYA 15, 52; AITN 1; AMWS 2;
BEST 89:2; BPFB 2; BYA 11; CA 5-8R;
CANR 25, 45, 74, 113, 129; CDALB
1968-1988; CN 1, 2, 3, 4, 5, 6, 7; CP 5,
6, 7; CPW; CWP; DA; DA3; DAB; DAC;
DAM MST, NOV, POP; DLB 2, 5, 130;
DLBY 1981; EWL 3; EXPS; FL 1:6; FW;
GL 3; HGG; INT CANR-25; LAIT 4;
MAL 5; MBL; MTCW 1, 2; MTFW 2005;
NFS 8, 24; RGAL 4; RGSF 2; SATA 159;
SSFS 1, 8, 17; SUFW 2; TUS

O'Brian, E. G.
See Clarke, Arthur C.

O'Brian, Patrick 1914-2000 .... **CLC 152**
See also AAYA 55; BRWS 12; CA 144;
CAAS 187; CANR 74; CPW; MTCW 2;
MTFW 2005; RHW

O'Brien, Darcy 1939-1998 .... **CLC 11**
See also CA 21-24R; CAAS 167; CANR 8,
59

O'Brien, Edna 1932- ..... **CLC 3, 5, 8, 13, 36,**
65, 116; SSC 10, 77
See also BRWS 5; CA 1-4R; CANR 6, 41,
65, 102; CDBLB 1960 to Present; CN 1,
2, 3, 4, 5, 6, 7; DA3; DAM NOV; DLB
14, 231, 319; EWL 3; FW; MTCW 1, 2;
MTFW 2005; RGSF 2; WLIT 4

O'Brien, Fitz-James 1828-1862 ..... **NCLC 21**
See also DLB 74; RGAL 4; SUFW

O'Brien, Flann .... **CLC 1, 4, 5, 7, 10, 47**
See O Nuallain, Brian
See also BRWS 2; DLB 231; EWL 3;
RGEL 2

O'Brien, Richard 1942- .... **CLC 17**
See also CA 124

O'Brien, Tim 1946- .... **CLC 7, 19, 40, 103,**
211; SSC 74
See also AAYA 16; AMWS 5; CA 85-88;
CANR 40, 58, 133; CDALBS; CN 5, 6,
7; CPW; DA3; DAM POP; DLB 152;
DLBD 9; DLBY 1980; LATS 1:2; MAL
5; MTCW 2; MTFW 2005; RGAL 4;
SSFS 5, 15; TCLE 1:2

Obstfelder, Sigbjoern 1866-1900 .... **TCLC 23**
See also CAAE 123

O'Casey, Sean 1880-1964 .... **CLC 1, 5, 9, 11,**
15, 88; DC 12; WLCS
See also BRW 7; CA 89-92; CANR 62;
CBD; CDBLB 1914-1945; DA3; DAB;
DAC; DAM DRAM, MST; DFS 19; DLB
10; EWL 3; MTCW 1, 2; MTFW 2005;
RGEL 2; TEA; WLIT 4

O'Cathasaigh, Sean
See O'Casey, Sean

Occom, Samson 1723-1792 .... **LC 60; NNAL**
See also DLB 175

Occomy, Marita (Odette) Bonner
1899(?)-1971
See Bonner, Marita
See also BW 2; CA 142; DFS 13; DLB 51,
228

Ochs, Phil(ip David) 1940-1976 .... **CLC 17**
See also CA 185; CAAS 65-68

O'Connor, Edwin (Greene)
1918-1968 .... **CLC 14**
See also CA 93-96; CAAS 25-28R; MAL 5

O'Connor, (Mary) Flannery
1925-1964 .... **CLC 1, 2, 3, 6, 10, 13, 15,**
21, 66, 104; SSC 1, 23, 61, 82; TCLC
132; WLC 4
See also AAYA 7; AMW; AMWR 2; BPFB
3; BYA 16; CA 1-4R; CANR 3, 41;
CDALB 1941-1968; DA; DA3; DAB;
DAC; DAM MST, NOV; DLB 2, 152;
DLBD 12; DLBY 1980; EWL 3; EXPS;
LAIT 5; MAL 5; MBL; MTCW 1, 2;
MTFW 2005; NFS 3, 21; RGAL 4; RGSF
2; SSFS 2, 7, 10, 19; TUS

O'Connor, Frank .... **CLC 23; SSC 5**
See O'Donovan, Michael Francis
See also DLB 162; EWL 3; RGSF 2; SSFS
5

O'Dell, Scott 1898-1989 .... **CLC 30**
See also AAYA 3, 44; BPFB 3; BYA 1, 2,
3, 5; CA 61-64; CAAS 129; CANR 12,
30, 112; CLR 1, 16; DLB 52; JRDA;
MAICYA 1, 2; SATA 12, 60, 134; WYA;
YAW

Odets, Clifford 1906-1963 ..... **CLC 2, 28, 98;**
DC 6
See also AMWS 2; CA 85-88; CAD; CANR
62; DAM DRAM; DFS 3, 17, 20; DLB 7,
26; EWL 3; MAL 5; MTCW 1, 2; MTFW
2005; RGAL 4; TUS

O'Doherty, Brian 1928- .... **CLC 76**
See also CA 105; CANR 108

O'Donnell, K. M.
See Malzberg, Barry N(athaniel)

O'Donnell, Lawrence
See Kuttner, Henry

O'Donovan, Michael Francis
1903-1966 .... **CLC 14**
See O'Connor, Frank
See also CA 93-96; CANR 84

Oe, Kenzaburo 1935- .. **CLC 10, 36, 86, 187;**
SSC 20
See also CA 97-100; CANR 36, 50, 74, 126;
DA3; DAM NOV; DLB 182, 331; DLBY
1994; LATS 1:2; MJW; MTCW 1, 2;
MTFW 2005; RGSF 2; RGWL 2, 3

Oe Kenzaburo
See Oe, Kenzaburo
See also CWW 2; EWL 3

O'Faolain, Julia 1932- .... **CLC 6, 19, 47, 108**
See also CA 81-84; 2; CANR 12, 61; CN 2,
3, 4, 5, 6, 7; DLB 14, 231, 319; FW;
MTCW 1; RHW

O'Faolain, Sean 1900-1991 ...... **CLC 1, 7, 14,**
32, 70; SSC 13; TCLC 143
See also CA 61-64; CAAS 134; CANR 12,
66; CN 1, 2, 3, 4; DLB 15, 162; MTCW
1, 2; MTFW 2005; RGEL 2; RGSF 2

O'Flaherty, Liam 1896-1984 .... **CLC 5, 34; SSC 6**
See also CA 101; CAAS 113; CANR 35; CN 1, 2, 3; DLB 36, 162; DLBY 1984; MTCW 1, 2; MTFW 2005; RGEL 2; RGSF 2; SSFS 5, 20

Ogai
See Mori Ogai
See also MJW

Ogilvy, Gavin
See Barrie, J(ames) M(atthew)

O'Grady, Standish (James) 1846-1928 .... **TCLC 5**
See also CA 157; CAAE 104

O'Grady, Timothy 1951- .... **CLC 59**
See also CA 138

O'Hara, Frank 1926-1966 .... **CLC 2, 5, 13, 78; PC 45**
See also CA 9-12R; CAAS 25-28R; CANR 33; DA3; DAM POET; DLB 5, 16, 193; EWL 3; MAL 5; MTCW 1, 2; MTFW 2005; PFS 8, 12; RGAL 4; WP

O'Hara, John (Henry) 1905-1970 . **CLC 1, 2, 3, 6, 11, 42; SSC 15**
See also AMW; BPFB 3; CA 5-8R; CAAS 25-28R; CANR 31, 60; CDALB 1929-1941; DAM NOV; DLB 9, 86, 324; DLBD 2; EWL 3; MAL 5; MTCW 1, 2; MTFW 2005; NFS 11; RGAL 4; RGSF 2

O'Hehir, Diana 1929- .... **CLC 41**
See also CA 245

Ohiyesa
See Eastman, Charles A(lexander)

Okada, John 1923-1971 .... **AAL**
See also BYA 14; CA 212; DLB 312

Okigbo, Christopher 1930-1967 .... **BLC 3; CLC 25, 84; PC 7; TCLC 171**
See also AFW; BW 1, 3; CA 77-80; CANR 74; CDWLB 3; DAM MULT, POET; DLB 125; EWL 3; MTCW 1, 2; MTFW 2005; RGEL 2

Okigbo, Christopher Ifenayichukwu
See Okigbo, Christopher

Okri, Ben 1959- .... **CLC 87, 223**
See also AFW; BRWS 5; BW 2, 3; CA 138; CAAE 130; CANR 65, 128; CN 5, 6, 7; DLB 157, 231, 319, 326; EWL 3; INT CA-138; MTCW 2; MTFW 2005; RGSF 2; SSFS 20; WLIT 2; WWE 1

Olds, Sharon 1942- .. **CLC 32, 39, 85; PC 22**
See also AMWS 10; CA 101; CANR 18, 41, 66, 98, 135; CP 5, 6, 7; CPW; CWP; DAM POET; DLB 120; MAL 5; MTCW 2; MTFW 2005; PFS 17

Oldstyle, Jonathan
See Irving, Washington

Olesha, Iurii
See Olesha, Yuri (Karlovich)
See also RGWL 2

Olesha, Iurii Karlovich
See Olesha, Yuri (Karlovich)
See also DLB 272

Olesha, Yuri (Karlovich) 1899-1960 . **CLC 8; SSC 69; TCLC 136**
See also Olesha, Iurii; Olesha, Iurii Karlovich; Olesha, Yury Karlovich
See also CA 85-88; EW 11; RGWL 3

Olesha, Yury Karlovich
See Olesha, Yuri (Karlovich)
See also EWL 3

Oliphant, Mrs.
See Oliphant, Margaret (Oliphant Wilson)
See also SUFW

Oliphant, Laurence 1829(?)-1888 .. **NCLC 47**
See also DLB 18, 166

Oliphant, Margaret (Oliphant Wilson) 1828-1897 .... **NCLC 11, 61; SSC 25**
See also Oliphant, Mrs.
See also BRWS 10; DLB 18, 159, 190; HGG; RGEL 2; RGSF 2

Oliver, Mary 1935- ... **CLC 19, 34, 98; PC 75**
See also AMWS 7; CA 21-24R; CANR 9, 43, 84, 92, 138; CP 4, 5, 6, 7; CWP; DLB 5, 193; EWL 3; MTFW 2005; PFS 15

Olivier, Laurence (Kerr) 1907-1989 . **CLC 20**
See also CA 150; CAAE 111; CAAS 129

Olsen, Tillie 1912-2007 .... **CLC 4, 13, 114; SSC 11**
See also AAYA 51; AMWS 13; BYA 11; CA 1-4R; CANR 1, 43, 74, 132; CDALBS; CN 2, 3, 4, 5, 6, 7; DA; DA3; DAB; DAC; DAM MST; DLB 28, 206; DLBY 1980; EWL 3; EXPS; FW; MAL 5; MTCW 1, 2; MTFW 2005; RGAL 4; RGSF 2; SSFS 1; TCLE 1:2; TCWW 2; TUS

Olson, Charles (John) 1910-1970 .. **CLC 1, 2, 5, 6, 9, 11, 29; PC 19**
See also AMWS 2; CA 13-16; CAAS 25-28R; CABS 2; CANR 35, 61; CAP 1; CP 1; DAM POET; DLB 5, 16, 193; EWL 3; MAL 5; MTCW 1, 2; RGAL 4; WP

Olson, Toby 1937- .... **CLC 28**
See also CA 65-68; 11; CANR 9, 31, 84; CP 3, 4, 5, 6, 7

Olyesha, Yuri
See Olesha, Yuri (Karlovich)

Olympiodorus of Thebes c. 375-c. 430 .... **CMLC 59**

Omar Khayyam
See Khayyam, Omar
See also RGWL 2, 3

Ondaatje, Michael 1943- ..... **CLC 14, 29, 51, 76, 180; PC 28**
See also AAYA 66; CA 77-80; CANR 42, 74, 109, 133; CN 5, 6, 7; CP 1, 2, 3, 4, 5, 6, 7; DA3; DAB; DAC; DAM MST; DLB 60, 323, 326; EWL 3; LATS 1:2; LMFS 2; MTCW 2; MTFW 2005; NFS 23; PFS 8, 19; TCLE 1:2; TWA; WWE 1

Ondaatje, Philip Michael
See Ondaatje, Michael

Oneal, Elizabeth 1934-
See Oneal, Zibby
See also CA 106; CANR 28, 84; MAICYA 1, 2; SATA 30, 82; YAW

Oneal, Zibby .... **CLC 30**
See Oneal, Elizabeth
See also AAYA 5, 41; BYA 13; CLR 13; JRDA; WYA

O'Neill, Eugene (Gladstone) 1888-1953 ... **DC 20; TCLC 1, 6, 27, 49; WLC 4**
See also AAYA 54; AITN 1; AMW; AMWC 1; CA 132; CAAE 110; CAD; CANR 131; CDALB 1929-1941; DA; DA3; DAB; DAC; DAM DRAM, MST; DFS 2, 4, 5, 6, 9, 11, 12, 16, 20; DLB 7, 331; EWL 3; LAIT 3; LMFS 2; MAL 5; MTCW 1, 2; MTFW 2005; RGAL 4; TUS

Onetti, Juan Carlos 1909-1994 ... **CLC 7, 10; HLCS 2; SSC 23; TCLC 131**
See also CA 85-88; CAAS 145; CANR 32, 63; CDWLB 3; CWW 2; DAM MULT, NOV; DLB 113; EWL 3; HW 1, 2; LAW; MTCW 1, 2; MTFW 2005; RGSF 2

O Nuallain, Brian 1911-1966
See O'Brien, Flann
See also CA 21-22; CAAS 25-28R; CAP 2; DLB 231; FANT; TEA

Ophuls, Max
See Ophuls, Max

Ophuls, Max 1902-1957 .... **TCLC 79**
See also CAAE 113

Opie, Amelia 1769-1853 .... **NCLC 65**
See also DLB 116, 159; RGEL 2

Oppen, George 1908-1984 ..... **CLC 7, 13, 34; PC 35; TCLC 107**
See also CA 13-16R; CAAS 113; CANR 8, 82; CP 1, 2, 3; DLB 5, 165

Oppenheim, E(dward) Phillips 1866-1946 .... **TCLC 45**
See also CA 202; CAAE 111; CMW 4; DLB 70

Oppenheimer, Max
See Ophuls, Max

Opuls, Max
See Ophuls, Max

Orage, A(lfred) R(ichard) 1873-1934 .... **TCLC 157**
See also CAAE 122

Origen c. 185-c. 254 .... **CMLC 19**

Orlovitz, Gil 1918-1973 .... **CLC 22**
See also CA 77-80; CAAS 45-48; CN 1; CP 1, 2; DLB 2, 5

O'Rourke, Patrick Jake
See O'Rourke, P.J.

O'Rourke, P.J. 1947- .... **CLC 209**
See also CA 77-80; CANR 13, 41, 67, 111, 155; CPW; DAM POP; DLB 185

Orris
See Ingelow, Jean

Ortega y Gasset, Jose 1883-1955 ...... **HLC 2; TCLC 9**
See also CA 130; CAAE 106; DAM MULT; EW 9; EWL 3; HW 1, 2; MTCW 1, 2; MTFW 2005

Ortese, Anna Maria 1914-1998 .... **CLC 89**
See also DLB 177; EWL 3

Ortiz, Simon J(oseph) 1941- ... **CLC 45, 208; NNAL; PC 17**
See also AMWS 4; CA 134; CANR 69, 118; CP 3, 4, 5, 6, 7; DAM MULT, POET; DLB 120, 175, 256; EXPP; MAL 5; PFS 4, 16; RGAL 4; SSFS 22; TCWW 2

Orton, Joe ...... **CLC 4, 13, 43; DC 3; TCLC 157**
See Orton, John Kingsley
See also BRWS 5; CBD; CDBLB 1960 to Present; DFS 3, 6; DLB 13, 310; GLL 1; RGEL 2; TEA; WLIT 4

Orton, John Kingsley 1933-1967
See Orton, Joe
See also CA 85-88; CANR 35, 66; DAM DRAM; MTCW 1, 2; MTFW 2005

Orwell, George ..... **SSC 68; TCLC 2, 6, 15, 31, 51, 128, 129; WLC 4**
See Blair, Eric (Arthur)
See also BPFB 3; BRW 7; BYA 5; CDBLB 1945-1960; CLR 68; DAB; DLB 15, 98, 195, 255; EWL 3; EXPN; LAIT 4, 5; LATS 1:1; NFS 3, 7; RGEL 2; SCFW 1, 2; SFW 4; SSFS 4; TEA; WLIT 4; YAW

Osborne, David
See Silverberg, Robert

Osborne, George
See Silverberg, Robert

Osborne, John 1929-1994 .... **CLC 1, 2, 5, 11, 45; TCLC 153; WLC 4**
See also BRWS 1; CA 13-16R; CAAS 147; CANR 21, 56; CBD; CDBLB 1945-1960; DA; DAB; DAC; DAM DRAM, MST; DFS 4, 19; DLB 13; EWL 3; MTCW 1, 2; MTFW 2005; RGEL 2

Osborne, Lawrence 1958- .... **CLC 50**
See also CA 189; CANR 152

Osbourne, Lloyd 1868-1947 .... **TCLC 93**

Osgood, Frances Sargent 1811-1850 .... **NCLC 141**
See also DLB 250

Oshima, Nagisa 1932- .... **CLC 20**
See also CA 121; CAAE 116; CANR 78

Parks, Gordon 1912-2006 .... **BLC 3; CLC 1, 16**
See also AAYA 36; AITN 2; BW 2, 3; CA 41-44R; CAAS 249; CANR 26, 66, 145; DA3; DAM MULT; DLB 33; MTCW 2; MTFW 2005; SATA 8, 108; SATA-Obit 175

Parks, Suzan-Lori 1964(?)- .... **DC 23**
See also AAYA 55; CA 201; CAD; CD 5, 6; CWD; DFS 22; RGAL 4

Parks, Tim(othy Harold) 1954- ...... **CLC 147**
See also CA 131; CAAE 126; CANR 77, 144; CN 7; DLB 231; INT CA-131

Parmenides c. 515B.C.-c. 450B.C. .... **CMLC 22**
See also DLB 176

Parnell, Thomas 1679-1718 .... **LC 3**
See also DLB 95; RGEL 2

Parr, Catherine c. 1513(?)-1548 .... **LC 86**
See also DLB 136

Parra, Nicanor 1914- ... **CLC 2, 102; HLC 2; PC 39**
See also CA 85-88; CANR 32; CWW 2; DAM MULT; DLB 283; EWL 3; HW 1; LAW; MTCW 1

Parra Sanojo, Ana Teresa de la 1890-1936 .... **HLCS 2**
See de la Parra, (Ana) Teresa (Sonojo)
See also LAW

Parrish, Mary Frances
See Fisher, M(ary) F(rances) K(ennedy)

Parshchikov, Aleksei 1954- .... **CLC 59**
See Parshchikov, Aleksei Maksimovich

Parshchikov, Aleksei Maksimovich
See Parshchikov, Aleksei
See also DLB 285

Parson, Professor
See Coleridge, Samuel Taylor

Parson Lot
See Kingsley, Charles

Parton, Sara Payson Willis 1811-1872 .... **NCLC 86**
See also DLB 43, 74, 239

Partridge, Anthony
See Oppenheim, E(dward) Phillips

Pascal, Blaise 1623-1662 .... **LC 35**
See also DLB 268; EW 3; GFL Beginnings to 1789; RGWL 2, 3; TWA

Pascoli, Giovanni 1855-1912 .... **TCLC 45**
See also CA 170; EW 7; EWL 3

Pasolini, Pier Paolo 1922-1975 .. **CLC 20, 37, 106; PC 17**
See also CA 93-96; CAAS 61-64; CANR 63; DLB 128, 177; EWL 3; MTCW 1; RGWL 2, 3

Pasquini
See Silone, Ignazio

Pastan, Linda (Olenik) 1932- .... **CLC 27**
See also CA 61-64; CANR 18, 40, 61, 113; CP 3, 4, 5, 6, 7; CSW; CWP; DAM POET; DLB 5; PFS 8, 25

Pasternak, Boris 1890-1960 ... **CLC 7, 10, 18, 63; PC 6; SSC 31; WLC 4**
See also BPFB 3; CA 127; CAAS 116; DA; DA3; DAB; DAC; DAM MST, NOV, POET; DLB 302, 331; EW 10; MTCW 1, 2; MTFW 2005; RGSF 2; RGWL 2, 3; TWA; WP

Patchen, Kenneth 1911-1972 .... **CLC 1, 2, 18**
See also BG 1:3; CA 1-4R; CAAS 33-36R; CANR 3, 35; CN 1; CP 1; DAM POET; DLB 16, 48; EWL 3; MAL 5; MTCW 1; RGAL 4

Pater, Walter (Horatio) 1839-1894 . **NCLC 7, 90, 159**
See also BRW 5; CDBLB 1832-1890; DLB 57, 156; RGEL 2; TEA

Paterson, A(ndrew) B(arton) 1864-1941 .... **TCLC 32**
See also CA 155; DLB 230; RGEL 2; SATA 97

Paterson, Banjo
See Paterson, A(ndrew) B(arton)

Paterson, Katherine 1932- .... **CLC 12, 30**
See also AAYA 1, 31; BYA 1, 2, 7; CA 21-24R; CANR 28, 59, 111; CLR 7, 50; CWRI 5; DLB 52; JRDA; LAIT 4; MAICYA 1, 2; MAICYAS 1; MTCW 1; SATA 13, 53, 92, 133; WYA; YAW

Paterson, Katherine Womeldorf
See Paterson, Katherine

Patmore, Coventry Kersey Dighton 1823-1896 .... **NCLC 9; PC 59**
See also DLB 35, 98; RGEL 2; TEA

Paton, Alan 1903-1988 ..... **CLC 4, 10, 25, 55, 106; TCLC 165; WLC 4**
See also AAYA 26; AFW; BPFB 3; BRWS 2; BYA 1; CA 13-16; CAAS 125; CANR 22; CAP 1; CN 1, 2, 3, 4; DA; DA3; DAB; DAC; DAM MST, NOV; DLB 225; DLBD 17; EWL 3; EXPN; LAIT 4; MTCW 1, 2; MTFW 2005; NFS 3, 12; RGEL 2; SATA 11; SATA-Obit 56; TWA; WLIT 2; WWE 1

Paton Walsh, Gillian
See Paton Walsh, Jill
See also AAYA 47; BYA 1, 8

Paton Walsh, Jill 1937- .... **CLC 35**
See Paton Walsh, Gillian; Walsh, Jill Paton
See also AAYA 11; CANR 38, 83, 158; CLR 2, 65; DLB 161; JRDA; MAICYA 1, 2; SAAS 3; SATA 4, 72, 109; YAW

Patsauq, Markoosie 1942- .... **NNAL**
See also CA 101; CLR 23; CWRI 5; DAM MULT

Patterson, (Horace) Orlando (Lloyd) 1940- .... **BLCS**
See also BW 1; CA 65-68; CANR 27, 84; CN 1, 2, 3, 4, 5, 6

Patton, George S(mith), Jr. 1885-1945 .... **TCLC 79**
See also CA 189

Paulding, James Kirke 1778-1860 ... **NCLC 2**
See also DLB 3, 59, 74, 250; RGAL 4

Paulin, Thomas Neilson
See Paulin, Tom

Paulin, Tom 1949- .... **CLC 37, 177**
See also CA 128; CAAE 123; CANR 98; CP 3, 4, 5, 6, 7; DLB 40

Pausanias c. 1st cent. - .... **CMLC 36**

Paustovsky, Konstantin (Georgievich) 1892-1968 .... **CLC 40**
See also CA 93-96; CAAS 25-28R; DLB 272; EWL 3

Pavese, Cesare 1908-1950 .... **PC 13; SSC 19; TCLC 3**
See also CA 169; CAAE 104; DLB 128, 177; EW 12; EWL 3; PFS 20; RGSF 2; RGWL 2, 3; TWA; WLIT 7

Pavic, Milorad 1929- .... **CLC 60**
See also CA 136; CDWLB 4; CWW 2; DLB 181; EWL 3; RGWL 3

Pavlov, Ivan Petrovich 1849-1936 . **TCLC 91**
See also CA 180; CAAE 118

Pavlova, Karolina Karlovna 1807-1893 .... **NCLC 138**
See also DLB 205

Payne, Alan
See Jakes, John

Payne, Rachel Ann
See Jakes, John

Paz, Gil
See Lugones, Leopoldo

Paz, Octavio 1914-1998 . **CLC 3, 4, 6, 10, 19, 51, 65, 119; HLC 2; PC 1, 48; WLC 4**
See also AAYA 50; CA 73-76; CAAS 165; CANR 32, 65, 104; CWW 2; DA; DA3; DAB; DAC; DAM MST, MULT, POET; DLB 290, 331; DLBY 1990, 1998; DNFS 1; EWL 3; HW 1, 2; LAW; LAWS 1; MTCW 1, 2; MTFW 2005; PFS 18; RGWL 2, 3; SSFS 13; TWA; WLIT 1

p'Bitek, Okot 1931-1982 .... **BLC 3; CLC 96; TCLC 149**
See also AFW; BW 2, 3; CA 124; CAAS 107; CANR 82; CP 1, 2, 3; DAM MULT; DLB 125; EWL 3; MTCW 1, 2; MTFW 2005; RGEL 2; WLIT 2

Peabody, Elizabeth Palmer 1804-1894 .... **NCLC 169**
See also DLB 1, 223

Peacham, Henry 1578-1644(?) .... **LC 119**
See also DLB 151

Peacock, Molly 1947- .... **CLC 60**
See also CA 103; 21; CANR 52, 84; CP 5, 6, 7; CWP; DLB 120, 282

Peacock, Thomas Love 1785-1866 .... **NCLC 22**
See also BRW 4; DLB 96, 116; RGEL 2; RGSF 2

Peake, Mervyn 1911-1968 .... **CLC 7, 54**
See also CA 5-8R; CAAS 25-28R; CANR 3; DLB 15, 160, 255; FANT; MTCW 1; RGEL 2; SATA 23; SFW 4

Pearce, Philippa 1920-2006
See Christie, Philippa
See also CA 5-8R; CANR 4, 109; CWRI 5; FANT; MAICYA 2

Pearl, Eric
See Elman, Richard (Martin)

Pearson, T. R. 1956- .... **CLC 39**
See also CA 130; CAAE 120; CANR 97, 147; CSW; INT CA-130

Pearson, Thomas Reid
See Pearson, T. R.

Peck, Dale 1967- .... **CLC 81**
See also CA 146; CANR 72, 127; GLL 2

Peck, John (Frederick) 1941- .... **CLC 3**
See also CA 49-52; CANR 3, 100; CP 4, 5, 6, 7

Peck, Richard 1934- .... **CLC 21**
See also AAYA 1, 24; BYA 1, 6, 8, 11; CA 85-88; CANR 19, 38, 129; CLR 15; INT CANR-19; JRDA; MAICYA 1, 2; SAAS 2; SATA 18, 55, 97, 110, 158; SATA-Essay 110; WYA; YAW

Peck, Richard Wayne
See Peck, Richard

Peck, Robert Newton 1928- .... **CLC 17**
See also AAYA 3, 43; BYA 1, 6; CA 182; 81-84, 182; CANR 31, 63, 127; CLR 45; DA; DAC; DAM MST; JRDA; LAIT 3; MAICYA 1, 2; SAAS 1; SATA 21, 62, 111, 156; SATA-Essay 108; WYA; YAW

Peckinpah, David Samuel
See Peckinpah, Sam

Peckinpah, Sam 1925-1984 .... **CLC 20**
See also CA 109; CAAS 114; CANR 82

Pedersen, Knut 1859-1952
See Hamsun, Knut
See also CA 119; CAAE 104; CANR 63; MTCW 1, 2

Peele, George 1556-1596 .... **DC 27; LC 115**
See also BRW 1; DLB 62, 167; RGEL 2

Peeslake, Gaffer
See Durrell, Lawrence (George)

Peguy, Charles (Pierre) 1873-1914 .... **TCLC 10**
See also CA 193; CAAE 107; DLB 258; EWL 3; GFL 1789 to the Present

Pinget, Robert 1919-1997 .... **CLC 7, 13, 37**
See also CA 85-88; CAAS 160; CWW 2;
DLB 83; EWL 3; GFL 1789 to the Present

Pink Floyd
See Barrett, (Roger) Syd; Gilmour, David;
Mason, Nick; Waters, Roger; Wright, Rick

Pinkney, Edward 1802-1828 .... **NCLC 31**
See also DLB 248

Pinkwater, D. Manus
See Pinkwater, Daniel Manus

Pinkwater, Daniel
See Pinkwater, Daniel Manus

Pinkwater, Daniel M.
See Pinkwater, Daniel Manus

Pinkwater, Daniel Manus 1941- .... **CLC 35**
See also AAYA 1, 46; BYA 9; CA 29-32R;
CANR 12, 38, 89, 143; CLR 4; CSW;
FANT; JRDA; MAICYA 1, 2; SAAS 3;
SATA 8, 46, 76, 114, 158; SFW 4; YAW

Pinkwater, Manus
See Pinkwater, Daniel Manus

Pinsky, Robert 1940- .... **CLC 9, 19, 38, 94,
121, 216; PC 27**
See also AMWS 6; CA 29-32R; 4; CANR
58, 97, 138; CP 3, 4, 5, 6, 7; DA3; DAM
POET; DLBY 1982, 1998; MAL 5;
MTCW 2; MTFW 2005; PFS 18; RGAL
4; TCLE 1:2

Pinta, Harold
See Pinter, Harold

Pinter, Harold 1930- .. **CLC 1, 3, 6, 9, 11, 15,
27, 58, 73, 199; DC 15; WLC 4**
See also BRWR 1; BRWS 1; CA 5-8R;
CANR 33, 65, 112, 145; CBD; CD 5, 6;
CDBLB 1960 to Present; CP 1; DA; DA3;
DAB; DAC; DAM DRAM, MST; DFS 3,
5, 7, 14; DLB 13, 310, 331; EWL 3;
IDFW 3, 4; LMFS 2; MTCW 1, 2; MTFW
2005; RGEL 2; RGHL; TEA

Piozzi, Hester Lynch (Thrale)
1741-1821 .... **NCLC 57**
See also DLB 104, 142

Pirandello, Luigi 1867-1936 .. **DC 5; SSC 22;
TCLC 4, 29, 172; WLC 4**
See also CA 153; CAAE 104; CANR 103;
DA; DA3; DAB; DAC; DAM DRAM,
MST; DFS 4, 9; DLB 264, 331; EW 8;
EWL 3; MTCW 2; MTFW 2005; RGSF
2; RGWL 2, 3; WLIT 7

Pirsig, Robert M(aynard) 1928- ... **CLC 4, 6,
73**
See also CA 53-56; CANR 42, 74; CPW 1;
DA3; DAM POP; MTCW 1, 2; MTFW
2005; SATA 39

Pisan, Christine de
See Christine de Pizan

Pisarev, Dmitrii Ivanovich
See Pisarev, Dmitry Ivanovich
See also DLB 277

Pisarev, Dmitry Ivanovich
1840-1868 .... **NCLC 25**
See Pisarev, Dmitrii Ivanovich

Pix, Mary (Griffith) 1666-1709 .... **LC 8**
See also DLB 80

Pixerecourt, (Rene Charles) Guilbert de
1773-1844 .... **NCLC 39**
See also DLB 192; GFL 1789 to the Present

Plaatje, Sol(omon) T(shekisho)
1878-1932 .... **BLCS; TCLC 73**
See also BW 2, 3; CA 141; CANR 79; DLB
125, 225

Plaidy, Jean
See Hibbert, Eleanor Alice Burford

Planche, James Robinson
1796-1880 .... **NCLC 42**
See also RGEL 2

Plant, Robert 1948- .... **CLC 12**

Plante, David 1940- .... **CLC 7, 23, 38**
See also CA 37-40R; CANR 12, 36, 58, 82,
152; CN 2, 3, 4, 5, 6, 7; DAM NOV;
DLBY 1983; INT CANR-12; MTCW 1

Plante, David Robert
See Plante, David

Plath, Sylvia 1932-1963 ..... **CLC 1, 2, 3, 5, 9,
11, 14, 17, 50, 51, 62, 111; PC 1, 37;
WLC 4**
See also AAYA 13; AMWR 2; AMWS 1;
BPFB 3; CA 19-20; CANR 34, 101; CAP
2; CDALB 1941-1968; DA; DA3; DAB;
DAC; DAM MST, POET; DLB 5, 6, 152;
EWL 3; EXPN; EXPP; FL 1:6; FW; LAIT
4; MAL 5; MBL; MTCW 1, 2; MTFW
2005; NFS 1; PAB; PFS 1, 15; RGAL 4;
SATA 96; TUS; WP; YAW

Plato c. 428B.C.-347B.C. .... **CMLC 8, 75;
WLCS**
See also AW 1; CDWLB 1; DA; DA3;
DAB; DAC; DAM MST; DLB 176; LAIT
1; LATS 1:1; RGWL 2, 3; WLIT 8

Platonov, Andrei
See Klimentov, Andrei Platonovich

Platonov, Andrei Platonovich
See Klimentov, Andrei Platonovich
See also DLB 272

Platonov, Andrey Platonovich
See Klimentov, Andrei Platonovich
See also EWL 3

Platt, Kin 1911- .... **CLC 26**
See also AAYA 11; CA 17-20R; CANR 11;
JRDA; SAAS 17; SATA 21, 86; WYA

Plautus c. 254B.C.-c. 184B.C. ...... **CMLC 24;
DC 6**
See also AW 1; CDWLB 1; DLB 211;
RGWL 2, 3; WLIT 8

Plick et Plock
See Simenon, Georges (Jacques Christian)

Plieksans, Janis
See Rainis, Janis

Plimpton, George 1927-2003 .... **CLC 36**
See also AITN 1; AMWS 16; CA 21-24R;
CAAS 224; CANR 32, 70, 103, 133; DLB
185, 241; MTCW 1, 2; MTFW 2005;
SATA 10; SATA-Obit 150

Pliny the Elder c. 23-79 .... **CMLC 23**
See also DLB 211

Pliny the Younger c. 61-c. 112 ...... **CMLC 62**
See also AW 2; DLB 211

Plomer, William Charles Franklin
1903-1973 .... **CLC 4, 8**
See also AFW; BRWS 11; CA 21-22; CANR
34; CAP 2; CN 1; CP 1, 2; DLB 20, 162,
191, 225; EWL 3; MTCW 1; RGEL 2;
RGSF 2; SATA 24

Plotinus 204-270 .... **CMLC 46**
See also CDWLB 1; DLB 176

Plowman, Piers
See Kavanagh, Patrick (Joseph)

Plum, J.
See Wodehouse, P(elham) G(renville)

Plumly, Stanley (Ross) 1939- .... **CLC 33**
See also CA 110; CAAE 108; CANR 97;
CP 3, 4, 5, 6, 7; DLB 5, 193; INT CA-
110

Plumpe, Friedrich Wilhelm
See Murnau, F.W.

Plutarch c. 46-c. 120 .... **CMLC 60**
See also AW 2; CDWLB 1; DLB 176;
RGWL 2, 3; TWA; WLIT 8

Po Chu-i 772-846 .... **CMLC 24**

Podhoretz, Norman 1930- .... **CLC 189**
See also AMWS 8; CA 9-12R; CANR 7,
78, 135

Poe, Edgar Allan 1809-1849 ..... **NCLC 1, 16,
55, 78, 94, 97, 117; PC 1, 54; SSC 1,
22, 34, 35, 54, 88; WLC 4**
See also AAYA 14; AMW; AMWC 1;
AMWR 2; BPFB 3; BYA 5, 11; CDALB
1640-1865; CMW 4; DA; DA3; DAB;
DAC; DAM MST, POET; DLB 3, 59, 73,
74, 248, 254; EXPP; EXPS; GL 3; HGG;
LAIT 2; LATS 1:1; LMFS 1; MSW; PAB;
PFS 1, 3, 9; RGAL 4; RGSF 2; SATA 23;
SCFW 1, 2; SFW 4; SSFS 2, 4, 7, 8, 16;
SUFW; TUS; WP; WYA

Poet of Titchfield Street, The
See Pound, Ezra (Weston Loomis)

Poggio Bracciolini, Gian Francesco
1380-1459 .... **LC 125**

Pohl, Frederik 1919- .... **CLC 18; SSC 25**
See also AAYA 24; CA 188; 61-64, 188; 1;
CANR 11, 37, 81, 140; CN 1, 2, 3, 4, 5,
6; DLB 8; INT CANR-11; MTCW 1, 2;
MTFW 2005; SATA 24; SCFW 1, 2; SFW
4

Poirier, Louis 1910-
See Gracq, Julien
See also CA 126; CAAE 122; CANR 141

Poitier, Sidney 1927- .... **CLC 26**
See also AAYA 60; BW 1; CA 117; CANR
94

Pokagon, Simon 1830-1899 .... **NNAL**
See also DAM MULT

Polanski, Roman 1933- .... **CLC 16, 178**
See also CA 77-80

Poliakoff, Stephen 1952- .... **CLC 38**
See also CA 106; CANR 116; CBD; CD 5,
6; DLB 13

Police, The
See Copeland, Stewart (Armstrong); Summers, Andrew James

Polidori, John William
1795-1821 .... **NCLC 51; SSC 97**
See also DLB 116; HGG

Poliziano, Angelo 1454-1494 .... **LC 120**
See also WLIT 7

Pollitt, Katha 1949- .... **CLC 28, 122**
See also CA 122; CAAE 120; CANR 66,
108; MTCW 1, 2; MTFW 2005

Pollock, (Mary) Sharon 1936- .... **CLC 50**
See also CA 141; CANR 132; CD 5; CWD;
DAC; DAM DRAM, MST; DFS 3; DLB
60; FW

Pollock, Sharon 1936- .... **DC 20**
See also CD 6

Polo, Marco 1254-1324 .... **CMLC 15**
See also WLIT 7

Polonsky, Abraham (Lincoln)
1910-1999 .... **CLC 92**
See also CA 104; CAAS 187; DLB 26; INT
CA-104

Polybius c. 200B.C.-c. 118B.C. ...... **CMLC 17**
See also AW 1; DLB 176; RGWL 2, 3

Pomerance, Bernard 1940- .... **CLC 13**
See also CA 101; CAD; CANR 49, 134;
CD 5, 6; DAM DRAM; DFS 9; LAIT 2

Ponge, Francis 1899-1988 .... **CLC 6, 18**
See also CA 85-88; CAAS 126; CANR 40,
86; DAM POET; DLBY 2002; EWL 3;
GFL 1789 to the Present; RGWL 2, 3

Poniatowska, Elena 1932- . **CLC 140; HLC 2**
See also CA 101; CANR 32, 66, 107, 156;
CDWLB 3; CWW 2; DAM MULT; DLB
113; EWL 3; HW 1, 2; LAWS 1; WLIT 1

Pontoppidan, Henrik 1857-1943 .... **TCLC 29**
See also CA 170; DLB 300, 331

Ponty, Maurice Merleau
See Merleau-Ponty, Maurice

Poole, Josephine .... **CLC 17**
See Helyar, Jane Penelope Josephine
See also SAAS 2; SATA 5

Popa, Vasko 1922-1991 . **CLC 19; TCLC 167**
See also CA 148; CAAE 112; CDWLB 4;
DLB 181; EWL 3; RGWL 2, 3

Pope, Alexander 1688-1744 ...... **LC 3, 58, 60,
64; PC 26; WLC 5**
See also BRW 3; BRWC 1; BRWR 1; CD-
BLB 1660-1789; DA; DA3; DAB; DAC;
DAM MST, POET; DLB 95, 101, 213;
EXPP; PAB; PFS 12; RGEL 2; WLIT 3;
WP

Popov, Evgenii Anatol'evich
See Popov, Yevgeny
See also DLB 285

Popov, Yevgeny .... **CLC 59**
See Popov, Evgenii Anatol'evich

Poquelin, Jean-Baptiste
See Moliere

Porete, Marguerite (?)-1310 .... **CMLC 73**
See also DLB 208

Porphyry c. 233-c. 305 .... **CMLC 71**

Porter, Connie (Rose) 1959(?)- .... **CLC 70**
See also AAYA 65; BW 2, 3; CA 142;
CANR 90, 109; SATA 81, 129

Porter, Gene(va Grace) Stratton .. **TCLC 21**
See Stratton-Porter, Gene(va Grace)
See also BPFB 3; CAAE 112; CWRI 5;
RHW

Porter, Katherine Anne 1890-1980 ... **CLC 1,
3, 7, 10, 13, 15, 27, 101; SSC 4, 31, 43**
See also AAYA 42; AITN 2; AMW; BPFB
3; CA 1-4R; CAAS 101; CANR 1, 65;
CDALBS; CN 1, 2; DA; DA3; DAB;
DAC; DAM MST, NOV; DLB 4, 9, 102;
DLBD 12; DLBY 1980; EWL 3; EXPS;
LAIT 3; MAL 5; MBL; MTCW 1, 2;
MTFW 2005; NFS 14; RGAL 4; RGSF 2;
SATA 39; SATA-Obit 23; SSFS 1, 8, 11,
16, 23; TCWW 2; TUS

Porter, Peter (Neville Frederick)
1929- .... **CLC 5, 13, 33**
See also CA 85-88; CP 1, 2, 3, 4, 5, 6, 7;
DLB 40, 289; WWE 1

Porter, William Sydney 1862-1910
See Henry, O.
See also CA 131; CAAE 104; CDALB
1865-1917; DA; DA3; DAB; DAC; DAM
MST; DLB 12, 78, 79; MTCW 1, 2;
MTFW 2005; TUS; YABC 2

Portillo (y Pacheco), Jose Lopez
See Lopez Portillo (y Pacheco), Jose

Portillo Trambley, Estela 1927-1998 .. **HLC 2**
See Trambley, Estela Portillo
See also CANR 32; DAM MULT; DLB
209; HW 1

Posey, Alexander (Lawrence)
1873-1908 .... **NNAL**
See also CA 144; CANR 80; DAM MULT;
DLB 175

Posse, Abel .... **CLC 70**
See also CA 252

Post, Melville Davisson
1869-1930 .... **TCLC 39**
See also CA 202; CAAE 110; CMW 4

Potok, Chaim 1929-2002 ... **CLC 2, 7, 14, 26,
112**
See also AAYA 15, 50; AITN 1, 2; BPFB 3;
BYA 1; CA 17-20R; CAAS 208; CANR
19, 35, 64, 98; CLR 92; CN 4, 5, 6; DA3;
DAM NOV; DLB 28, 152; EXPN; INT
CANR-19; LAIT 4; MTCW 1, 2; MTFW
2005; NFS 4; RGHL; SATA 33, 106;
SATA-Obit 134; TUS; YAW

Potok, Herbert Harold -2002
See Potok, Chaim

Potok, Herman Harold
See Potok, Chaim

Potter, Dennis (Christopher George)
1935-1994 .... **CLC 58, 86, 123**
See also BRWS 10; CA 107; CAAS 145;
CANR 33, 61; CBD; DLB 233; MTCW 1

Pound, Ezra (Weston Loomis)
1885-1972 .. **CLC 1, 2, 3, 4, 5, 7, 10, 13,
18, 34, 48, 50, 112; PC 4; WLC 5**
See also AAYA 47; AMW; AMWR 1; CA
5-8R; CAAS 37-40R; CANR 40; CDALB
1917-1929; CP 1; DA; DA3; DAB; DAC;
DAM MST, POET; DLB 4, 45, 63; DLBD
15; EFS 2; EWL 3; EXPP; LMFS 2; MAL
5; MTCW 1, 2; MTFW 2005; PAB; PFS
2, 8, 16; RGAL 4; TUS; WP

Povod, Reinaldo 1959-1994 .... **CLC 44**
See also CA 136; CAAS 146; CANR 83

Powell, Adam Clayton, Jr.
1908-1972 .... **BLC 3; CLC 89**
See also BW 1, 3; CA 102; CAAS 33-36R;
CANR 86; DAM MULT

Powell, Anthony 1905-2000 ... **CLC 1, 3, 7, 9,
10, 31**
See also BRW 7; CA 1-4R; CAAS 189;
CANR 1, 32, 62, 107; CDBLB 1945-
1960; CN 1, 2, 3, 4, 5, 6; DLB 15; EWL
3; MTCW 1, 2; MTFW 2005; RGEL 2;
TEA

Powell, Dawn 1896(?)-1965 .... **CLC 66**
See also CA 5-8R; CANR 121; DLBY 1997

Powell, Padgett 1952- .... **CLC 34**
See also CA 126; CANR 63, 101; CSW;
DLB 234; DLBY 01

Powell, (Oval) Talmage 1920-2000
See Queen, Ellery
See also CA 5-8R; CANR 2, 80

Power, Susan 1961- .... **CLC 91**
See also BYA 14; CA 160; CANR 135; NFS
11

Powers, J(ames) F(arl) 1917-1999 ..... **CLC 1,
4, 8, 57; SSC 4**
See also CA 1-4R; CAAS 181; CANR 2,
61; CN 1, 2, 3, 4, 5, 6; DLB 130; MTCW
1; RGAL 4; RGSF 2

Powers, John J(ames) 1945-
See Powers, John R.
See also CA 69-72

Powers, John R. .... **CLC 66**
See Powers, John J(ames)

Powers, Richard 1957- .... **CLC 93**
See also AMWS 9; BPFB 3; CA 148;
CANR 80; CN 6, 7; MTFW 2005; TCLE
1:2

Powers, Richard S.
See Powers, Richard

Pownall, David 1938- .... **CLC 10**
See also CA 89-92, 180; 18; CANR 49, 101;
CBD; CD 5, 6; CN 4, 5, 6, 7; DLB 14

Powys, John Cowper 1872-1963 ... **CLC 7, 9,
15, 46, 125**
See also CA 85-88; CANR 106; DLB 15,
255; EWL 3; FANT; MTCW 1, 2; MTFW
2005; RGEL 2; SUFW

Powys, T(heodore) F(rancis)
1875-1953 .... **TCLC 9**
See also BRWS 8; CA 189; CAAE 106;
DLB 36, 162; EWL 3; FANT; RGEL 2;
SUFW

Pozzo, Modesta
See Fonte, Moderata

Prado (Calvo), Pedro 1886-1952 ... **TCLC 75**
See also CA 131; DLB 283; HW 1; LAW

Prager, Emily 1952- .... **CLC 56**
See also CA 204

Pratchett, Terry 1948- .... **CLC 197**
See also AAYA 19, 54; BPFB 3; CA 143;
CANR 87, 126; CLR 64; CN 6, 7; CPW;
CWRI 5; FANT; MTFW 2005; SATA 82,
139; SFW 4; SUFW 2

Pratolini, Vasco 1913-1991 .... **TCLC 124**
See also CA 211; DLB 177; EWL 3; RGWL
2, 3

Pratt, E(dwin) J(ohn) 1883(?)-1964 . **CLC 19**
See also CA 141; CAAS 93-96; CANR 77;
DAC; DAM POET; DLB 92; EWL 3;
RGEL 2; TWA

Premchand .... **TCLC 21**
See Srivastava, Dhanpat Rai
See also EWL 3

Prescott, William Hickling
1796-1859 .... **NCLC 163**
See also DLB 1, 30, 59, 235

Preseren, France 1800-1849 .... **NCLC 127**
See also CDWLB 4; DLB 147

Preussler, Otfried 1923- .... **CLC 17**
See also CA 77-80; SATA 24

Prevert, Jacques (Henri Marie)
1900-1977 .... **CLC 15**
See also CA 77-80; CAAS 69-72; CANR
29, 61; DLB 258; EWL 3; GFL 1789 to
the Present; IDFW 3, 4; MTCW 1; RGWL
2, 3; SATA-Obit 30

Prevost, (Antoine Francois)
1697-1763 .... **LC 1**
See also DLB 314; EW 4; GFL Beginnings
to 1789; RGWL 2, 3

Price, Reynolds 1933- .. **CLC 3, 6, 13, 43, 50,
63, 212; SSC 22**
See also AMWS 6; CA 1-4R; CANR 1, 37,
57, 87, 128; CN 1, 2, 3, 4, 5, 6; CSW;
DAM NOV; DLB 2, 218, 278; EWL 3;
INT CANR-37; MAL 5; MTFW 2005;
NFS 18

Price, Richard 1949- .... **CLC 6, 12**
See also CA 49-52; CANR 3, 147; CN 7;
DLBY 1981

Prichard, Katharine Susannah
1883-1969 .... **CLC 46**
See also CA 11-12; CANR 33; CAP 1; DLB
260; MTCW 1; RGEL 2; RGSF 2; SATA
66

Priestley, J(ohn) B(oynton)
1894-1984 .... **CLC 2, 5, 9, 34**
See also BRW 7; CA 9-12R; CAAS 113;
CANR 33; CDBLB 1914-1945; CN 1, 2,
3; DA3; DAM DRAM, NOV; DLB 10,
34, 77, 100, 139; DLBY 1984; EWL 3;
MTCW 1, 2; MTFW 2005; RGEL 2; SFW
4

Prince 1958- .... **CLC 35**
See also CA 213

Prince, F(rank) T(empleton)
1912-2003 .... **CLC 22**
See also CA 101; CAAS 219; CANR 43,
79; CP 1, 2, 3, 4, 5, 6, 7; DLB 20

Prince Kropotkin
See Kropotkin, Peter (Aleksieevich)

Prior, Matthew 1664-1721 .... **LC 4**
See also DLB 95; RGEL 2

Prishvin, Mikhail 1873-1954 .... **TCLC 75**
See Prishvin, Mikhail Mikhailovich

Prishvin, Mikhail Mikhailovich
See Prishvin, Mikhail
See also DLB 272; EWL 3

Pritchard, William H(arrison)
1932- .... **CLC 34**
See also CA 65-68; CANR 23, 95; DLB
111

Pritchett, V(ictor) S(awdon)
1900-1997 ... **CLC 5, 13, 15, 41; SSC 14**
See also BPFB 3; BRWS 3; CA 61-64;
CAAS 157; CANR 31, 63; CN 1, 2, 3, 4,
5, 6; DA3; DAM NOV; DLB 15, 139;
EWL 3; MTCW 1, 2; MTFW 2005; RGEL
2; RGSF 2; TEA

Private 19022
See Manning, Frederic

Probst, Mark 1925- .... **CLC 59**
See also CA 130

Procaccino, Michael
See Cristofer, Michael

Proclus c. 412-c. 485 .... **CMLC 81**
Prokosch, Frederic 1908-1989 ...... **CLC 4, 48**
See also CA 73-76; CAAS 128; CANR 82;
CN 1, 2, 3, 4; CP 1, 2, 3, 4; DLB 48;
MTCW 2
Propertius, Sextus c. 50B.C.-c.
16B.C. .... **CMLC 32**
See also AW 2; CDWLB 1; DLB 211;
RGWL 2, 3; WLIT 8
Prophet, The
See Dreiser, Theodore
Prose, Francine 1947- .... **CLC 45, 231**
See also AMWS 16; CA 112; CAAE 109;
CANR 46, 95, 132; DLB 234; MTFW
2005; SATA 101, 149
Protagoras c. 490B.C.-420B.C. ...... **CMLC 85**
See also DLB 176
Proudhon
See Cunha, Euclides (Rodrigues Pimenta)
da
Proulx, Annie
See Proulx, E. Annie
Proulx, E. Annie 1935- .... **CLC 81, 158**
See also AMWS 7; BPFB 3; CA 145;
CANR 65, 110; CN 6, 7; CPW 1; DA3;
DAM POP; MAL 5; MTCW 2; MTFW
2005; SSFS 18, 23
Proulx, Edna Annie
See Proulx, E. Annie
Proust, (Valentin-Louis-George-Eugene)
Marcel 1871-1922 ..... **SSC 75; TCLC 7,**
13, 33; WLC 5
See also AAYA 58; BPFB 3; CA 120;
CAAE 104; CANR 110; DA; DA3; DAB;
DAC; DAM MST, NOV; DLB 65; EW 8;
EWL 3; GFL 1789 to the Present; MTCW
1, 2; MTFW 2005; RGWL 2, 3; TWA
Prowler, Harley
See Masters, Edgar Lee
Prudentius, Aurelius Clemens 348-c.
405 .... **CMLC 78**
See also EW 1; RGWL 2, 3
Prudhomme, Rene Francois Armand
1839-1907
See Sully Prudhomme, Rene-Francois-
Armand
See also CA 170
Prus, Boleslaw 1845-1912 .... **TCLC 48**
See also RGWL 2, 3
Pryor, Aaron Richard
See Pryor, Richard
Pryor, Richard 1940-2005 .... **CLC 26**
See also CA 152; CAAE 122; CAAS 246
Pryor, Richard Franklin Lenox Thomas
See Pryor, Richard
Przybyszewski, Stanislaw
1868-1927 .... **TCLC 36**
See also CA 160; DLB 66; EWL 3
Pseudo-Dionysius the Areopagite fl. 5th
cent. - .... **CMLC 89**
See also DLB 115
Pteleon
See Grieve, C(hristopher) M(urray)
See also DAM POET
Puckett, Lute
See Masters, Edgar Lee
Puig, Manuel 1932-1990 .... **CLC 3, 5, 10, 28,**
65, 133; HLC 2
See also BPFB 3; CA 45-48; CANR 2, 32,
63; CDWLB 3; DA3; DAM MULT; DLB
113; DNFS 1; EWL 3; GLL 1; HW 1, 2;
LAW; MTCW 1, 2; MTFW 2005; RGWL
2, 3; TWA; WLIT 1
Pulitzer, Joseph 1847-1911 .... **TCLC 76**
See also CAAE 114; DLB 23
Purchas, Samuel 1577(?)-1626 .... **LC 70**
See also DLB 151

Purdy, A(lfred) W(ellington)
1918-2000 .... **CLC 3, 6, 14, 50**
See also CA 81-84; 17; CAAS 189; CANR
42, 66; CP 1, 2, 3, 4, 5, 6, 7; DAC; DAM
MST, POET; DLB 88; PFS 5; RGEL 2
Purdy, James (Amos) 1923- .... **CLC 2, 4, 10,**
28, 52
See also AMWS 7; CA 33-36R; 1; CANR
19, 51, 132; CN 1, 2, 3, 4, 5, 6, 7; DLB
2, 218; EWL 3; INT CANR-19; MAL 5;
MTCW 1; RGAL 4
Pure, Simon
See Swinnerton, Frank Arthur
Pushkin, Aleksandr Sergeevich
See Pushkin, Alexander (Sergeyevich)
See also DLB 205
Pushkin, Alexander (Sergeyevich)
1799-1837 .... **NCLC 3, 27, 83; PC 10;**
SSC 27, 55; WLC 5
See Pushkin, Aleksandr Sergeevich
See also DA; DA3; DAB; DAC; DAM
DRAM, MST, POET; EW 5; EXPS; RGSF
2; RGWL 2, 3; SATA 61; SSFS 9; TWA
P'u Sung-ling 1640-1715 .... **LC 49; SSC 31**
Putnam, Arthur Lee
See Alger, Horatio, Jr.
Puttenham, George 1529(?)-1590 ...... **LC 116**
See also DLB 281
Puzo, Mario 1920-1999 .... **CLC 1, 2, 6, 36,**
107
See also BPFB 3; CA 65-68; CAAS 185;
CANR 4, 42, 65, 99, 131; CN 1, 2, 3, 4,
5, 6; CPW; DA3; DAM NOV, POP; DLB
6; MTCW 1, 2; MTFW 2005; NFS 16;
RGAL 4
Pygge, Edward
See Barnes, Julian
Pyle, Ernest Taylor 1900-1945
See Pyle, Ernie
See also CA 160; CAAE 115
Pyle, Ernie .... **TCLC 75**
See Pyle, Ernest Taylor
See also DLB 29; MTCW 2
Pyle, Howard 1853-1911 .... **TCLC 81**
See also AAYA 57; BYA 2, 4; CA 137;
CAAE 109; CLR 22, 117; DLB 42, 188;
DLBD 13; LAIT 1; MAICYA 1, 2; SATA
16, 100; WCH; YAW
Pym, Barbara (Mary Crampton)
1913-1980 .... **CLC 13, 19, 37, 111**
See also BPFB 3; BRWS 2; CA 13-14;
CAAS 97-100; CANR 13, 34; CAP 1;
DLB 14, 207; DLBY 1987; EWL 3;
MTCW 1, 2; MTFW 2005; RGEL 2; TEA
Pynchon, Thomas 1937- .. **CLC 2, 3, 6, 9, 11,**
18, 33, 62, 72, 123, 192, 213; SSC 14,
84; WLC 5
See also AMWS 2; BEST 90:2; BPFB 3;
CA 17-20R; CANR 22, 46, 73, 142; CN
1, 2, 3, 4, 5, 6, 7; CPW 1; DA; DA3;
DAB; DAC; DAM MST, NOV, POP;
DLB 2, 173; EWL 3; MAL 5; MTCW 1,
2; MTFW 2005; NFS 23; RGAL 4; SFW
4; TCLE 1:2; TUS
Pythagoras c. 582B.C.-c. 507B.C. . **CMLC 22**
See also DLB 176
Q
See Quiller-Couch, Sir Arthur (Thomas)
Qian, Chongzhu
See Ch'ien, Chung-shu
Qian, Sima 145B.C.-c. 89B.C. .... **CMLC 72**
Qian Zhongshu
See Ch'ien, Chung-shu
See also CWW 2; DLB 328
Qroll
See Dagerman, Stig (Halvard)
Quarles, Francis 1592-1644 .... **LC 117**
See also DLB 126; RGEL 2

Quarrington, Paul (Lewis) 1953- ..... **CLC 65**
See also CA 129; CANR 62, 95
Quasimodo, Salvatore 1901-1968 .... **CLC 10;**
PC 47
See also CA 13-16; CAAS 25-28R; CAP 1;
DLB 114, 332; EW 12; EWL 3; MTCW
1; RGWL 2, 3
Quatermass, Martin
See Carpenter, John (Howard)
Quay, Stephen 1947- .... **CLC 95**
See also CA 189
Quay, Timothy 1947- .... **CLC 95**
See also CA 189
Queen, Ellery .... **CLC 3, 11**
See Dannay, Frederic; Davidson, Avram
(James); Deming, Richard; Fairman, Paul
W.; Flora, Fletcher; Hoch, Edward
D(entinger); Kane, Henry; Lee, Manfred
B.; Marlowe, Stephen; Powell, (Oval) Tal-
mage; Sheldon, Walter J(ames); Sturgeon,
Theodore (Hamilton); Tracy, Don(ald
Fiske); Vance, Jack
See also BPFB 3; CMW 4; MSW; RGAL 4
Queen, Ellery, Jr.
See Dannay, Frederic; Lee, Manfred B.
Queneau, Raymond 1903-1976 ..... **CLC 2, 5,**
10, 42
See also CA 77-80; CAAS 69-72; CANR
32; DLB 72, 258; EW 12; EWL 3; GFL
1789 to the Present; MTCW 1, 2; RGWL
2, 3
Quevedo, Francisco de 1580-1645 .... **LC 23**
Quiller-Couch, Sir Arthur (Thomas)
1863-1944 .... **TCLC 53**
See also CA 166; CAAE 118; DLB 135,
153, 190; HGG; RGEL 2; SUFW 1
Quin, Ann 1936-1973 .... **CLC 6**
See also CA 9-12R; CAAS 45-48; CANR
148; CN 1; DLB 14, 231
Quin, Ann Marie
See Quin, Ann
Quincey, Thomas de
See De Quincey, Thomas
Quindlen, Anna 1953- .... **CLC 191**
See also AAYA 35; CA 138; CANR 73, 126;
DA3; DLB 292; MTCW 2; MTFW 2005
Quinn, Martin
See Smith, Martin Cruz
Quinn, Peter 1947- .... **CLC 91**
See also CA 197; CANR 147
Quinn, Peter A.
See Quinn, Peter
Quinn, Simon
See Smith, Martin Cruz
Quintana, Leroy V. 1944- ...... **HLC 2; PC 36**
See also CA 131; CANR 65, 139; DAM
MULT; DLB 82; HW 1, 2
Quintilian c. 40-c. 100 .... **CMLC 77**
See also AW 2; DLB 211; RGWL 2, 3
Quintillian 0035-0100 .... **CMLC 77**
Quiroga, Horacio (Sylvestre)
1878-1937 ... **HLC 2; SSC 89; TCLC 20**
See also CA 131; CAAE 117; DAM MULT;
EWL 3; HW 1; LAW; MTCW 1; RGSF
2; WLIT 1
Quoirez, Francoise 1935-2004 .... **CLC 9**
See Sagan, Francoise
See also CA 49-52; CAAS 231; CANR 6,
39, 73; MTCW 1, 2; MTFW 2005; TWA
Raabe, Wilhelm (Karl) 1831-1910 . **TCLC 45**
See also CA 167; DLB 129
Rabe, David (William) 1940- .. **CLC 4, 8, 33,**
200; DC 16
See also CA 85-88; CABS 3; CAD; CANR
59, 129; CD 5, 6; DAM DRAM; DFS 3,
8, 13; DLB 7, 228; EWL 3; MAL 5

Rabelais, Francois 1494-1553 .... **LC 5, 60; WLC 5**
See also DA; DAB; DAC; DAM MST; DLB 327; EW 2; GFL Beginnings to 1789; LMFS 1; RGWL 2, 3; TWA

Rabi'a al-'Adawiyya c. 717-c. 801 .... **CMLC 83**
See also DLB 311

Rabinovitch, Sholem 1859-1916
See Sholom Aleichem
See also CAAE 104

Rabinyan, Dorit 1972- .... **CLC 119**
See also CA 170; CANR 147

Rachilde
See Vallette, Marguerite Eymery; Vallette, Marguerite Eymery
See also EWL 3

Racine, Jean 1639-1699 .... **LC 28, 113**
See also DA3; DAB; DAM MST; DLB 268; EW 3; GFL Beginnings to 1789; LMFS 1; RGWL 2, 3; TWA

Radcliffe, Ann (Ward) 1764-1823 ... **NCLC 6, 55, 106**
See also DLB 39, 178; GL 3; HGG; LMFS 1; RGEL 2; SUFW; WLIT 3

Radclyffe-Hall, Marguerite
See Hall, Radclyffe

Radiguet, Raymond 1903-1923 ...... **TCLC 29**
See also CA 162; DLB 65; EWL 3; GFL 1789 to the Present; RGWL 2, 3

Radnoti, Miklos 1909-1944 .... **TCLC 16**
See also CA 212; CAAE 118; CDWLB 4; DLB 215; EWL 3; RGHL; RGWL 2, 3

Rado, James 1939- .... **CLC 17**
See also CA 105

Radvanyi, Netty 1900-1983
See Seghers, Anna
See also CA 85-88; CAAS 110; CANR 82

Rae, Ben
See Griffiths, Trevor

Raeburn, John (Hay) 1941- .... **CLC 34**
See also CA 57-60

Ragni, Gerome 1942-1991 .... **CLC 17**
See also CA 105; CAAS 134

Rahv, Philip .... **CLC 24**
See Greenberg, Ivan
See also DLB 137; MAL 5

Raimund, Ferdinand Jakob 1790-1836 .... **NCLC 69**
See also DLB 90

Raine, Craig (Anthony) 1944- .. **CLC 32, 103**
See also CA 108; CANR 29, 51, 103; CP 3, 4, 5, 6, 7; DLB 40; PFS 7

Raine, Kathleen (Jessie) 1908-2003 .. **CLC 7, 45**
See also CA 85-88; CAAS 218; CANR 46, 109; CP 1, 2, 3, 4, 5, 6, 7; DLB 20; EWL 3; MTCW 1; RGEL 2

Rainis, Janis 1865-1929 .... **TCLC 29**
See also CA 170; CDWLB 4; DLB 220; EWL 3

Rakosi, Carl .... **CLC 47**
See Rawley, Callman
See also CA 5; CAAS 228; CP 1, 2, 3, 4, 5, 6, 7; DLB 193

Ralegh, Sir Walter
See Raleigh, Sir Walter
See also BRW 1; RGEL 2; WP

Raleigh, Richard
See Lovecraft, H. P.

Raleigh, Sir Walter 1554(?)-1618 .... **LC 31, 39; PC 31**
See Ralegh, Sir Walter
See also CDBLB Before 1660; DLB 172; EXPP; PFS 14; TEA

Rallentando, H. P.
See Sayers, Dorothy L(eigh)

Ramal, Walter
See de la Mare, Walter (John)

Ramana Maharshi 1879-1950 .... **TCLC 84**

Ramoacn y Cajal, Santiago 1852-1934 .... **TCLC 93**

Ramon, Juan
See Jimenez (Mantecon), Juan Ramon

Ramos, Graciliano 1892-1953 .... **TCLC 32**
See also CA 167; DLB 307; EWL 3; HW 2; LAW; WLIT 1

Rampersad, Arnold 1941- .... **CLC 44**
See also BW 2, 3; CA 133; CAAE 127; CANR 81; DLB 111; INT CA-133

Rampling, Anne
See Rice, Anne
See also GLL 2

Ramsay, Allan 1686(?)-1758 .... **LC 29**
See also DLB 95; RGEL 2

Ramsay, Jay
See Campbell, (John) Ramsey

Ramuz, Charles-Ferdinand 1878-1947 .... **TCLC 33**
See also CA 165; EWL 3

Rand, Ayn 1905-1982 ...... **CLC 3, 30, 44, 79; WLC 5**
See also AAYA 10; AMWS 4; BPFB 3; BYA 12; CA 13-16R; CAAS 105; CANR 27, 73; CDALBS; CN 1, 2, 3; CPW; DA; DA3; DAC; DAM MST, NOV, POP; DLB 227, 279; MTCW 1, 2; MTFW 2005; NFS 10, 16; RGAL 4; SFW 4; TUS; YAW

Randall, Dudley (Felker) 1914-2000 . **BLC 3; CLC 1, 135**
See also BW 1, 3; CA 25-28R; CAAS 189; CANR 23, 82; CP 1, 2, 3, 4, 5; DAM MULT; DLB 41; PFS 5

Randall, Robert
See Silverberg, Robert

Ranger, Ken
See Creasey, John

Rank, Otto 1884-1939 .... **TCLC 115**

Ransom, John Crowe 1888-1974 .. **CLC 2, 4, 5, 11, 24; PC 61**
See also AMW; CA 5-8R; CAAS 49-52; CANR 6, 34; CDALBS; CP 1, 2; DA3; DAM POET; DLB 45, 63; EWL 3; EXPP; MAL 5; MTCW 1, 2; MTFW 2005; RGAL 4; TUS

Rao, Raja 1908-2006 .... **CLC 25, 56**
See also CA 73-76; CAAS 252; CANR 51; CN 1, 2, 3, 4, 5, 6; DAM NOV; DLB 323; EWL 3; MTCW 1, 2; MTFW 2005; RGEL 2; RGSF 2

Raphael, Frederic (Michael) 1931- ... **CLC 2, 14**
See also CA 1-4R; CANR 1, 86; CN 1, 2, 3, 4, 5, 6, 7; DLB 14, 319; TCLE 1:2

Raphael, Lev 1954- .... **CLC 232**
See also CA 134; CANR 72, 145; GLL 1

Ratcliffe, James P.
See Mencken, H(enry) L(ouis)

Rathbone, Julian 1935- .... **CLC 41**
See also CA 101; CANR 34, 73, 152

Rattigan, Terence (Mervyn) 1911-1977 .... **CLC 7; DC 18**
See also BRWS 7; CA 85-88; CAAS 73-76; CBD; CDBLB 1945-1960; DAM DRAM; DFS 8; DLB 13; IDFW 3, 4; MTCW 1, 2; MTFW 2005; RGEL 2

Ratushinskaya, Irina 1954- .... **CLC 54**
See also CA 129; CANR 68; CWW 2

Raven, Simon (Arthur Noel) 1927-2001 .... **CLC 14**
See also CA 81-84; CAAS 197; CANR 86; CN 1, 2, 3, 4, 5, 6; DLB 271

Ravenna, Michael
See Welty, Eudora

Rawley, Callman 1903-2004
See Rakosi, Carl
See also CA 21-24R; CAAS 228; CANR 12, 32, 91

Rawlings, Marjorie Kinnan 1896-1953 .... **TCLC 4**
See also AAYA 20; AMWS 10; ANW; BPFB 3; BYA 3; CA 137; CAAE 104; CANR 74; CLR 63; DLB 9, 22, 102; DLBD 17; JRDA; MAICYA 1, 2; MAL 5; MTCW 2; MTFW 2005; RGAL 4; SATA 100; WCH; YABC 1; YAW

Ray, Satyajit 1921-1992 .... **CLC 16, 76**
See also CA 114; CAAS 137; DAM MULT

Read, Herbert Edward 1893-1968 ..... **CLC 4**
See also BRW 6; CA 85-88; CAAS 25-28R; DLB 20, 149; EWL 3; PAB; RGEL 2

Read, Piers Paul 1941- .... **CLC 4, 10, 25**
See also CA 21-24R; CANR 38, 86, 150; CN 2, 3, 4, 5, 6, 7; DLB 14; SATA 21

Reade, Charles 1814-1884 .... **NCLC 2, 74**
See also DLB 21; RGEL 2

Reade, Hamish
See Gray, Simon (James Holliday)

Reading, Peter 1946- .... **CLC 47**
See also BRWS 8; CA 103; CANR 46, 96; CP 5, 6, 7; DLB 40

Reaney, James 1926- .... **CLC 13**
See also CA 41-44R; 15; CANR 42; CD 5, 6; CP 1, 2, 3, 4, 5, 6, 7; DAC; DAM MST; DLB 68; RGEL 2; SATA 43

Rebreanu, Liviu 1885-1944 .... **TCLC 28**
See also CA 165; DLB 220; EWL 3

Rechy, John 1934- ..... **CLC 1, 7, 14, 18, 107; HLC 2**
See also CA 195; 5-8R, 195; 4; CANR 6, 32, 64, 152; CN 1, 2, 3, 4, 5, 6, 7; DAM MULT; DLB 122, 278; DLBY 1982; HW 1, 2; INT CANR-6; LLW; MAL 5; RGAL 4

Rechy, John Francisco
See Rechy, John

Redcam, Tom 1870-1933 .... **TCLC 25**

Reddin, Keith 1956- .... **CLC 67**
See also CAD; CD 6

Redgrove, Peter (William) 1932-2003 .... **CLC 6, 41**
See also BRWS 6; CA 1-4R; CAAS 217; CANR 3, 39, 77; CP 1, 2, 3, 4, 5, 6, 7; DLB 40; TCLE 1:2

Redmon, Anne .... **CLC 22**
See Nightingale, Anne Redmon
See also DLBY 1986

Reed, Eliot
See Ambler, Eric

Reed, Ishmael 1938- ..... **BLC 3; CLC 2, 3, 5, 6, 13, 32, 60, 174; PC 68**
See also AFAW 1, 2; AMWS 10; BPFB 3; BW 2, 3; CA 21-24R; CANR 25, 48, 74, 128; CN 1, 2, 3, 4, 5, 6, 7; CP 1, 2, 3, 4, 5, 6, 7; CSW; DA3; DAM MULT; DLB 2, 5, 33, 169, 227; DLBD 8; EWL 3; LMFS 2; MAL 5; MSW; MTCW 1, 2; MTFW 2005; PFS 6; RGAL 4; TCWW 2

Reed, John (Silas) 1887-1920 .... **TCLC 9**
See also CA 195; CAAE 106; MAL 5; TUS

Reed, Lou .... **CLC 21**
See Firbank, Louis

Reese, Lizette Woodworth 1856-1935 .... **PC 29; TCLC 181**
See also CA 180; DLB 54

Reeve, Clara 1729-1807 .... **NCLC 19**
See also DLB 39; RGEL 2

Reich, Wilhelm 1897-1957 .... **TCLC 57**
See also CA 199

Reid, Christopher (John) 1949- .... **CLC 33**
See also CA 140; CANR 89; CP 4, 5, 6, 7; DLB 40; EWL 3

Reid, Desmond
See Moorcock, Michael

Reid Banks, Lynne 1929-
   See Banks, Lynne Reid
   See also AAYA 49; CA 1-4R; CANR 6, 22,
      38, 87; CLR 24; CN 1, 2, 3, 7; JRDA;
      MAICYA 1, 2; SATA 22, 75, 111, 165;
      YAW
Reilly, William K.
   See Creasey, John
Reiner, Max
   See Caldwell, (Janet Miriam) Taylor
      (Holland)
Reis, Ricardo
   See Pessoa, Fernando (Antonio Nogueira)
Reizenstein, Elmer Leopold
   See Rice, Elmer (Leopold)
   See also EWL 3
Remarque, Erich Maria 1898-1970 . **CLC 21**
   See also AAYA 27; BPFB 3; CA 77-80;
      CAAS 29-32R; CDWLB 2; DA; DA3;
      DAB; DAC; DAM MST, NOV; DLB 56;
      EWL 3; EXPN; LAIT 3; MTCW 1, 2;
      MTFW 2005; NFS 4; RGHL; RGWL 2, 3
Remington, Frederic S(ackrider)
   1861-1909 .... **TCLC 89**
   See also CA 169; CAAE 108; DLB 12, 186,
      188; SATA 41; TCWW 2
Remizov, A.
   See Remizov, Aleksei (Mikhailovich)
Remizov, A. M.
   See Remizov, Aleksei (Mikhailovich)
Remizov, Aleksei (Mikhailovich)
   1877-1957 .... **TCLC 27**
   See Remizov, Alexey Mikhaylovich
   See also CA 133; CAAE 125; DLB 295
Remizov, Alexey Mikhaylovich
   See Remizov, Aleksei (Mikhailovich)
   See also EWL 3
Renan, Joseph Ernest 1823-1892 . **NCLC 26,
   145**
   See also GFL 1789 to the Present
Renard, Jules(-Pierre) 1864-1910 .. **TCLC 17**
   See also CA 202; CAAE 117; GFL 1789 to
      the Present
Renart, Jean fl. 13th cent. - .... **CMLC 83**
Renault, Mary .... **CLC 3, 11, 17**
   See Challans, Mary
   See also BPFB 3; BYA 2; CN 1, 2, 3;
      DLBY 1983; EWL 3; GLL 1; LAIT 1;
      RGEL 2; RHW
Rendell, Ruth 1930- .... **CLC 28, 48**
   See Vine, Barbara
   See also BPFB 3; BRWS 9; CA 109; CANR
      32, 52, 74, 127; CN 5, 6, 7; CPW; DAM
      POP; DLB 87, 276; INT CANR-32;
      MSW; MTCW 1, 2; MTFW 2005
Rendell, Ruth Barbara
   See Rendell, Ruth
Renoir, Jean 1894-1979 .... **CLC 20**
   See also CA 129; CAAS 85-88
Resnais, Alain 1922- .... **CLC 16**
Revard, Carter 1931- .... **NNAL**
   See also CA 144; CANR 81, 153; PFS 5
Reverdy, Pierre 1889-1960 .... **CLC 53**
   See also CA 97-100; CAAS 89-92; DLB
      258; EWL 3; GFL 1789 to the Present
Rexroth, Kenneth 1905-1982 .... **CLC 1, 2, 6,
   11, 22, 49, 112; PC 20**
   See also BG 1:3; CA 5-8R; CAAS 107;
      CANR 14, 34, 63; CDALB 1941-1968;
      CP 1, 2, 3; DAM POET; DLB 16, 48, 165,
      212; DLBY 1982; EWL 3; INT CANR-
      14; MAL 5; MTCW 1, 2; MTFW 2005;
      RGAL 4
Reyes, Alfonso 1889-1959 .... **HLCS 2; TCLC
   33**
   See also CA 131; EWL 3; HW 1; LAW
Reyes y Basoalto, Ricardo Eliecer Neftali
   See Neruda, Pablo

Reymont, Wladyslaw (Stanislaw)
   1868(?)-1925 .... **TCLC 5**
   See also CAAE 104; DLB 332; EWL 3
Reynolds, John Hamilton
   1794-1852 .... **NCLC 146**
   See also DLB 96
Reynolds, Jonathan 1942- .... **CLC 6, 38**
   See also CA 65-68; CANR 28
Reynolds, Joshua 1723-1792 .... **LC 15**
   See also DLB 104
Reynolds, Michael S(hane)
   1937-2000 .... **CLC 44**
   See also CA 65-68; CAAS 189; CANR 9,
      89, 97
Reznikoff, Charles 1894-1976 .... **CLC 9**
   See also AMWS 14; CA 33-36; CAAS 61-
      64; CAP 2; CP 1, 2; DLB 28, 45; RGHL;
      WP
Rezzori, Gregor von
   See Rezzori d'Arezzo, Gregor von
Rezzori d'Arezzo, Gregor von
   1914-1998 .... **CLC 25**
   See also CA 136; CAAE 122; CAAS 167
Rhine, Richard
   See Silverstein, Alvin; Silverstein, Virginia
      B(arbara Opshelor)
Rhodes, Eugene Manlove
   1869-1934 .... **TCLC 53**
   See also CA 198; DLB 256; TCWW 1, 2
R'hoone, Lord
   See Balzac, Honore de
Rhys, Jean 1890-1979 .... **CLC 2, 4, 6, 14, 19,
   51, 124; SSC 21, 76**
   See also BRWS 2; CA 25-28R; CAAS 85-
      88; CANR 35, 62; CDBLB 1945-1960;
      CDWLB 3; CN 1, 2; DA3; DAM NOV;
      DLB 36, 117, 162; DNFS 2; EWL 3;
      LATS 1:1; MTCW 1, 2; MTFW 2005;
      NFS 19; RGEL 2; RGSF 2; RHW; TEA;
      WWE 1
Ribeiro, Darcy 1922-1997 .... **CLC 34**
   See also CA 33-36R; CAAS 156; EWL 3
Ribeiro, Joao Ubaldo (Osorio Pimentel)
   1941- .... **CLC 10, 67**
   See also CA 81-84; CWW 2; EWL 3
Ribman, Ronald (Burt) 1932- .... **CLC 7**
   See also CA 21-24R; CAD; CANR 46, 80;
      CD 5, 6
Ricci, Nino (Pio) 1959- .... **CLC 70**
   See also CA 137; CANR 130; CCA 1
Rice, Anne 1941- .... **CLC 41, 128**
   See Rampling, Anne
   See also AAYA 9, 53; AMWS 7; BEST
      89:2; BPFB 3; CA 65-68; CANR 12, 36,
      53, 74, 100, 133; CN 6, 7; CPW; CSW;
      DA3; DAM POP; DLB 292; GL 3; GLL
      2; HGG; MTCW 2; MTFW 2005; SUFW
      2; YAW
Rice, Elmer (Leopold) 1892-1967 ...... **CLC 7,
   49**
   See Reizenstein, Elmer Leopold
   See also CA 21-22; CAAS 25-28R; CAP 2;
      DAM DRAM; DFS 12; DLB 4, 7; IDTP;
      MAL 5; MTCW 1, 2; RGAL 4
Rice, Tim(othy Miles Bindon)
   1944- .... **CLC 21**
   See also CA 103; CANR 46; DFS 7
Rich, Adrienne 1929- .... **CLC 3, 6, 7, 11, 18,
   36, 73, 76, 125; PC 5**
   See also AAYA 69; AMWR 2; AMWS 1;
      CA 9-12R; CANR 20, 53, 74, 128;
      CDALBS; CP 1, 2, 3, 4, 5, 6, 7; CSW;
      CWP; DA3; DAM POET; DLB 5, 67;
      EWL 3; EXPP; FL 1:6; FW; MAL 5;
      MBL; MTCW 1, 2; MTFW 2005; PAB;
      PFS 15; RGAL 4; RGHL; WP
Rich, Barbara
   See Graves, Robert

Rich, Robert
   See Trumbo, Dalton
Richard, Keith .... **CLC 17**
   See Richards, Keith
Richards, David Adams 1950- .... **CLC 59**
   See also CA 93-96; CANR 60, 110, 156;
      CN 7; DAC; DLB 53; TCLE 1:2
Richards, I(vor) A(rmstrong)
   1893-1979 .... **CLC 14, 24**
   See also BRWS 2; CA 41-44R; CAAS 89-
      92; CANR 34, 74; CP 1, 2; DLB 27; EWL
      3; MTCW 2; RGEL 2
Richards, Keith 1943-
   See Richard, Keith
   See also CA 107; CANR 77
Richardson, Anne
   See Roiphe, Anne
Richardson, Dorothy Miller
   1873-1957 .... **TCLC 3**
   See also CA 192; CAAE 104; DLB 36;
      EWL 3; FW; RGEL 2
**Richardson (Robertson), Ethel Florence
   Lindesay** 1870-1946
   See Richardson, Henry Handel
   See also CA 190; CAAE 105; DLB 230;
      RHW
Richardson, Henry Handel .... **TCLC 4**
   See Richardson (Robertson), Ethel Florence
      Lindesay
   See also DLB 197; EWL 3; RGEL 2; RGSF
      2
Richardson, John 1796-1852 .... **NCLC 55**
   See also CCA 1; DAC; DLB 99
Richardson, Samuel 1689-1761 ...... **LC 1, 44;
   WLC 5**
   See also BRW 3; CDBLB 1660-1789; DA;
      DAB; DAC; DAM MST, NOV; DLB 39;
      RGEL 2; TEA; WLIT 3
Richardson, Willis 1889-1977 .... **HR 1:3**
   See also BW 1; CA 124; DLB 51; SATA 60
Richler, Mordecai 1931-2001 .... **CLC 3, 5, 9,
   13, 18, 46, 70, 185**
   See also AITN 1; CA 65-68; CAAS 201;
      CANR 31, 62, 111; CCA 1; CLR 17; CN
      1, 2, 3, 4, 5, 7; CWRI 5; DAC; DAM
      MST, NOV; DLB 53; EWL 3; MAICYA
      1, 2; MTCW 1, 2; MTFW 2005; RGEL 2;
      RGHL; SATA 44, 98; SATA-Brief 27;
      TWA
Richter, Conrad (Michael)
   1890-1968 .... **CLC 30**
   See also AAYA 21; BYA 2; CA 5-8R;
      CAAS 25-28R; CANR 23; DLB 9, 212;
      LAIT 1; MAL 5; MTCW 1, 2; MTFW
      2005; RGAL 4; SATA 3; TCWW 1, 2;
      TUS; YAW
Ricostranza, Tom
   See Ellis, Trey
Riddell, Charlotte 1832-1906 .... **TCLC 40**
   See Riddell, Mrs. J. H.
   See also CA 165; DLB 156
Riddell, Mrs. J. H.
   See Riddell, Charlotte
   See also HGG; SUFW
Ridge, John Rollin 1827-1867 ...... **NCLC 82;
   NNAL**
   See also CA 144; DAM MULT; DLB 175
Ridgeway, Jason
   See Marlowe, Stephen
Ridgway, Keith 1965- .... **CLC 119**
   See also CA 172; CANR 144
Riding, Laura .... **CLC 3, 7**
   See Jackson, Laura (Riding)
   See also CP 1, 2, 3, 4, 5; RGAL 4
Riefenstahl, Berta Helene Amalia 1902-2003
   See Riefenstahl, Leni
   See also CA 108; CAAS 220
Riefenstahl, Leni .... **CLC 16, 190**
   See Riefenstahl, Berta Helene Amalia

Roiphe, Anne 1935- .... **CLC 3, 9**
See also CA 89-92; CANR 45, 73, 138;
DLBY 1980; INT CA-89-92
Roiphe, Anne Richardson
See Roiphe, Anne
Rojas, Fernando de 1475-1541 ... **HLCS 1, 2;**
LC 23
See also DLB 286; RGWL 2, 3
Rojas, Gonzalo 1917- .... **HLCS 2**
See also CA 178; HW 2; LAWS 1
Roland (de la Platiere), Marie-Jeanne
1754-1793 .... **LC 98**
See also DLB 314
Rolfe, Frederick (William Serafino Austin
Lewis Mary) 1860-1913 .... **TCLC 12**
See Al Siddik
See also CA 210; CAAE 107; DLB 34, 156;
RGEL 2
Rolland, Romain 1866-1944 .... **TCLC 23**
See also CA 197; CAAE 118; DLB 65, 284,
332; EWL 3; GFL 1789 to the Present;
RGWL 2, 3
Rolle, Richard c. 1300-c. 1349 ...... **CMLC 21**
See also DLB 146; LMFS 1; RGEL 2
Rolvaag, O(le) E(dvart) .... **TCLC 17**
See Roelvaag, O(le) E(dvart)
See also DLB 9, 212; MAL 5; NFS 5;
RGAL 4
Romain Arnaud, Saint
See Aragon, Louis
Romains, Jules 1885-1972 .... **CLC 7**
See also CA 85-88; CANR 34; DLB 65,
321; EWL 3; GFL 1789 to the Present;
MTCW 1
Romero, Jose Ruben 1890-1952 .... **TCLC 14**
See also CA 131; CAAE 114; EWL 3; HW
1; LAW
Ronsard, Pierre de 1524-1585 . **LC 6, 54; PC**
11
See also DLB 327; EW 2; GFL Beginnings
to 1789; RGWL 2, 3; TWA
Rooke, Leon 1934- .... **CLC 25, 34**
See also CA 25-28R; CANR 23, 53; CCA
1; CPW; DAM POP
Roosevelt, Franklin Delano
1882-1945 .... **TCLC 93**
See also CA 173; CAAE 116; LAIT 3
Roosevelt, Theodore 1858-1919 ..... **TCLC 69**
See also CA 170; CAAE 115; DLB 47, 186,
275
Roper, William 1498-1578 .... **LC 10**
Roquelaure, A. N.
See Rice, Anne
Rosa, Joao Guimaraes 1908-1967 ... **CLC 23;**
HLCS 1
See Guimaraes Rosa, Joao
See also CAAS 89-92; DLB 113, 307; EWL
3; WLIT 1
Rose, Wendy 1948- . **CLC 85; NNAL; PC 13**
See also CA 53-56; CANR 5, 51; CWP;
DAM MULT; DLB 175; PFS 13; RGAL
4; SATA 12
Rosen, R. D.
See Rosen, Richard (Dean)
Rosen, Richard (Dean) 1949- .... **CLC 39**
See also CA 77-80; CANR 62, 120; CMW
4; INT CANR-30
Rosenberg, Isaac 1890-1918 .... **TCLC 12**
See also BRW 6; CA 188; CAAE 107; DLB
20, 216; EWL 3; PAB; RGEL 2
Rosenblatt, Joe .... **CLC 15**
See Rosenblatt, Joseph
See also CP 3, 4, 5, 6, 7
Rosenblatt, Joseph 1933-
See Rosenblatt, Joe
See also CA 89-92; CP 1, 2; INT CA-89-92
Rosenfeld, Samuel
See Tzara, Tristan

Rosenstock, Sami
See Tzara, Tristan
Rosenstock, Samuel
See Tzara, Tristan
Rosenthal, M(acha) L(ouis)
1917-1996 .... **CLC 28**
See also CA 1-4R; 6; CAAS 152; CANR 4,
51; CP 1, 2, 3, 4, 5, 6; DLB 5; SATA 59
Ross, Barnaby
See Dannay, Frederic; Lee, Manfred B.
Ross, Bernard L.
See Follett, Ken
Ross, J. H.
See Lawrence, T(homas) E(dward)
Ross, John Hume
See Lawrence, T(homas) E(dward)
Ross, Martin 1862-1915
See Martin, Violet Florence
See also DLB 135; GLL 2; RGEL 2; RGSF
2
Ross, (James) Sinclair 1908-1996 ... **CLC 13;**
SSC 24
See also CA 73-76; CANR 81; CN 1, 2, 3,
4, 5, 6; DAC; DAM MST; DLB 88;
RGEL 2; RGSF 2; TCWW 1, 2
Rossetti, Christina 1830-1894 ... **NCLC 2, 50,**
66; PC 7; WLC 5
See also AAYA 51; BRW 5; BYA 4; CLR
115; DA; DA3; DAB; DAC; DAM MST,
POET; DLB 35, 163, 240; EXPP; FL 1:3;
LATS 1:1; MAICYA 1, 2; PFS 10, 14;
RGEL 2; SATA 20; TEA; WCH
Rossetti, Christina Georgina
See Rossetti, Christina
Rossetti, Dante Gabriel 1828-1882 . **NCLC 4,**
77; PC 44; WLC 5
See also AAYA 51; BRW 5; CDBLB 1832-
1890; DA; DAB; DAC; DAM MST,
POET; DLB 35; EXPP; RGEL 2; TEA
Rossi, Cristina Peri
See Peri Rossi, Cristina
Rossi, Jean-Baptiste 1931-2003
See Japrisot, Sebastien
See also CA 201; CAAS 215
Rossner, Judith 1935-2005 .... **CLC 6, 9, 29**
See also AITN 2; BEST 90:3; BPFB 3; CA
17-20R; CAAS 242; CANR 18, 51, 73;
CN 4, 5, 6; DLB 6; INT CANR-18;
MAL 5; MTCW 1, 2; MTFW 2005
Rossner, Judith Perelman
See Rossner, Judith
Rostand, Edmond (Eugene Alexis)
1868-1918 .... **DC 10; TCLC 6, 37**
See also CA 126; CAAE 104; DA; DA3;
DAB; DAC; DAM DRAM, MST; DFS 1;
DLB 192; LAIT 1; MTCW 1; RGWL 2,
3; TWA
Roth, Henry 1906-1995 ..... **CLC 2, 6, 11, 104**
See also AMWS 9; CA 11-12; CAAS 149;
CANR 38, 63; CAP 1; CN 1, 2, 3, 4, 5, 6;
DA3; DLB 28; EWL 3; MAL 5; MTCW
1, 2; MTFW 2005; RGAL 4
Roth, (Moses) Joseph 1894-1939 ... **TCLC 33**
See also CA 160; DLB 85; EWL 3; RGWL
2, 3
Roth, Philip 1933- ... **CLC 1, 2, 3, 4, 6, 9, 15,**
22, 31, 47, 66, 86, 119, 201; SSC 26;
WLC 5
See also AAYA 67; AMWR 2; AMWS 3;
BEST 90:3; BPFB 3; CA 1-4R; CANR 1,
22, 36, 55, 89, 132; CDALB 1968-1988;
CN 3, 4, 5, 6, 7; CPW 1; DA; DA3; DAB;
DAC; DAM MST, NOV, POP; DLB 2,
28, 173; DLBY 1982; EWL 3; MAL 5;
MTCW 1, 2; MTFW 2005; RGAL 4;
RGHL; RGSF 2; SSFS 12, 18; TUS
Roth, Philip Milton
See Roth, Philip

Rothenberg, Jerome 1931- .... **CLC 6, 57**
See also CA 45-48; CANR 1, 106; CP 1, 2,
3, 4, 5, 6, 7; DLB 5, 193
Rotter, Pat .... **CLC 65**
Roumain, Jacques (Jean Baptiste)
1907-1944 .... **BLC 3; TCLC 19**
See also BW 1; CA 125; CAAE 117; DAM
MULT; EWL 3
Rourke, Constance Mayfield
1885-1941 .... **TCLC 12**
See also CA 200; CAAE 107; MAL 5;
YABC 1
Rousseau, Jean-Baptiste 1671-1741 ...... **LC 9**
Rousseau, Jean-Jacques 1712-1778 .... **LC 14,**
36, 122; WLC 5
See also DA; DA3; DAB; DAC; DAM
MST; DLB 314; EW 4; GFL Beginnings
to 1789; LMFS 1; RGWL 2, 3; TWA
Roussel, Raymond 1877-1933 .... **TCLC 20**
See also CA 201; CAAE 117; EWL 3; GFL
1789 to the Present
Rovit, Earl (Herbert) 1927- .... **CLC 7**
See also CA 5-8R; CANR 12
Rowe, Elizabeth Singer 1674-1737 ..... **LC 44**
See also DLB 39, 95
Rowe, Nicholas 1674-1718 .... **LC 8**
See also DLB 84; RGEL 2
Rowlandson, Mary 1637(?)-1678 .... **LC 66**
See also DLB 24, 200; RGAL 4
Rowley, Ames Dorrance
See Lovecraft, H. P.
Rowley, William 1585(?)-1626 ... **LC 100, 123**
See also DFS 22; DLB 58; RGEL 2
Rowling, J.K. 1965- .... **CLC 137, 217**
See also AAYA 34; BYA 11, 13, 14; CA
173; CANR 128, 157; CLR 66, 80, 112;
MAICYA 2; MTFW 2005; SATA 109,
174; SUFW 2
Rowling, Joanne Kathleen
See Rowling, J.K.
Rowson, Susanna Haswell
1762(?)-1824 .... **NCLC 5, 69**
See also AMWS 15; DLB 37, 200; RGAL 4
Roy, Arundhati 1960(?)- .... **CLC 109, 210**
See also CA 163; CANR 90, 126; CN 7;
DLB 323, 326; DLBY 1997; EWL 3;
LATS 1:2; MTFW 2005; NFS 22; WWE
1
Roy, Gabrielle 1909-1983 .... **CLC 10, 14**
See also CA 53-56; CAAS 110; CANR 5,
61; CCA 1; DAB; DAC; DAM MST;
DLB 68; EWL 3; MTCW 1; RGWL 2, 3;
SATA 104; TCLE 1:2
Royko, Mike 1932-1997 .... **CLC 109**
See also CA 89-92; CAAS 157; CANR 26,
111; CPW
Rozanov, Vasilii Vasil'evich
See Rozanov, Vassili
See also DLB 295
Rozanov, Vasily Vasilyevich
See Rozanov, Vassili
See also EWL 3
Rozanov, Vassili 1856-1919 .... **TCLC 104**
See Rozanov, Vasilii Vasil'evich; Rozanov,
Vasily Vasilyevich
Rozewicz, Tadeusz 1921- ...... **CLC 9, 23, 139**
See also CA 108; CANR 36, 66; CWW 2;
DA3; DAM POET; DLB 232; EWL 3;
MTCW 1, 2; MTFW 2005; RGHL;
RGWL 3
Ruark, Gibbons 1941- .... **CLC 3**
See also CA 33-36R; 23; CANR 14, 31, 57;
DLB 120
Rubens, Bernice (Ruth) 1923-2004 . **CLC 19,**
31
See also CA 25-28R; CAAS 232; CANR
33, 65, 128; CN 1, 2, 3, 4, 5, 6, 7; DLB
14, 207, 326; MTCW 1

Sait Faik .... **TCLC 23**
   See Abasiyanik, Sait Faik
Saki .... **SSC 12; TCLC 3; WLC 5**
   See Munro, H(ector) H(ugh)
   See also BRWS 6; BYA 11; LAIT 2; RGEL
   2; SSFS 1; SUFW
Sala, George Augustus 1828-1895 . **NCLC 46**
Saladin 1138-1193 .... **CMLC 38**
Salama, Hannu 1936- .... **CLC 18**
   See also CA 244; EWL 3
Salamanca, J(ack) R(ichard) 1922- .. **CLC 4,
15**
   See also CA 193; 25-28R, 193
Salas, Floyd Francis 1931- .... **HLC 2**
   See also CA 119; 27; CANR 44, 75, 93;
   DAM MULT; DLB 82; HW 1, 2; MTCW
   2; MTFW 2005
Sale, J. Kirkpatrick
   See Sale, Kirkpatrick
Sale, John Kirkpatrick
   See Sale, Kirkpatrick
Sale, Kirkpatrick 1937- .... **CLC 68**
   See also CA 13-16R; CANR 10, 147
Salinas, Luis Omar 1937- ... **CLC 90; HLC 2**
   See also AMWS 13; CA 131; CANR 81,
   153; DAM MULT; DLB 82; HW 1, 2
Salinas (y Serrano), Pedro
   1891(?)-1951 .... **TCLC 17**
   See also CAAE 117; DLB 134; EWL 3
Salinger, J.D. 1919- . **CLC 1, 3, 8, 12, 55, 56,
138; SSC 2, 28, 65; WLC 5**
   See also AAYA 2, 36; AMW; AMWC 1;
   BPFB 3; CA 5-8R; CANR 39, 129;
   CDALB 1941-1968; CLR 18; CN 1, 2, 3,
   4, 5, 6, 7; CPW 1; DA; DA3; DAB; DAC;
   DAM MST, NOV, POP; DLB 2, 102, 173;
   EWL 3; EXPN; LAIT 4; MAICYA 1, 2;
   MAL 5; MTCW 1, 2; MTFW 2005; NFS
   1; RGAL 4; RGSF 2; SATA 67; SSFS 17;
   TUS; WYA; YAW
Salisbury, John
   See Caute, (John) David
Sallust c. 86B.C.-35B.C. .... **CMLC 68**
   See also AW 2; CDWLB 1; DLB 211;
   RGWL 2, 3
Salter, James 1925- .. **CLC 7, 52, 59; SSC 58**
   See also AMWS 9; CA 73-76; CANR 107,
   160; DLB 130
Saltus, Edgar (Everton) 1855-1921 . **TCLC 8**
   See also CAAE 105; DLB 202; RGAL 4
Saltykov, Mikhail Evgrafovich
   1826-1889 .... **NCLC 16**
   See also DLB 238:
Saltykov-Shchedrin, N.
   See Saltykov, Mikhail Evgrafovich
Samarakis, Andonis
   See Samarakis, Antonis
   See also EWL 3
Samarakis, Antonis 1919-2003 .... **CLC 5**
   See Samarakis, Andonis
   See also CA 25-28R; 16; CAAS 224; CANR
   36
Sanchez, Florencio 1875-1910 .... **TCLC 37**
   See also CA 153; DLB 305; EWL 3; HW 1;
   LAW
Sanchez, Luis Rafael 1936- .... **CLC 23**
   See also CA 128; DLB 305; EWL 3; HW 1;
   WLIT 1
Sanchez, Sonia 1934- .... **BLC 3; CLC 5, 116,
215; PC 9**
   See also BW 2, 3; CA 33-36R; CANR 24,
   49, 74, 115; CLR 18; CP 2, 3, 4, 5, 6, 7;
   CSW; CWP; DA3; DAM MULT; DLB 41;
   DLBD 8; EWL 3; MAICYA 1, 2; MAL 5;
   MTCW 1, 2; MTFW 2005; SATA 22, 136;
   WP
Sancho, Ignatius 1729-1780 .... **LC 84**

Sand, George 1804-1876 ..... **NCLC 2, 42, 57,
174; WLC 5**
   See also DA; DA3; DAB; DAC; DAM
   MST, NOV; DLB 119, 192; EW 6; FL 1:3;
   FW; GFL 1789 to the Present; RGWL 2,
   3; TWA
Sandburg, Carl (August) 1878-1967 . **CLC 1,
4, 10, 15, 35; PC 2, 41; WLC 5**
   See also AAYA 24; AMW; BYA 1, 3; CA
   5-8R; CAAS 25-28R; CANR 35; CDALB
   1865-1917; CLR 67; DA; DA3; DAB;
   DAC; DAM MST, POET; DLB 17, 54,
   284; EWL 3; EXPP; LAIT 2; MAICYA 1,
   2; MAL 5; MTCW 1, 2; MTFW 2005;
   PAB; PFS 3, 6, 12; RGAL 4; SATA 8;
   TUS; WCH; WP; WYA
Sandburg, Charles
   See Sandburg, Carl (August)
Sandburg, Charles A.
   See Sandburg, Carl (August)
Sanders, (James) Ed(ward) 1939- .... **CLC 53**
   See Sanders, Edward
   See also BG 1:3; CA 13-16R; 21; CANR
   13, 44, 78; CP 1, 2, 3, 4, 5, 6, 7; DAM
   POET; DLB 16, 244
Sanders, Edward
   See Sanders, (James) Ed(ward)
   See also DLB 244
Sanders, Lawrence 1920-1998 .... **CLC 41**
   See also BEST 89:4; BPFB 3; CA 81-84;
   CAAS 165; CANR 33, 62; CMW 4;
   CPW; DA3; DAM POP; MTCW 1
Sanders, Noah
   See Blount, Roy (Alton), Jr.
Sanders, Winston P.
   See Anderson, Poul
Sandoz, Mari(e Susette) 1900-1966 .. **CLC 28**
   See also CA 1-4R; CAAS 25-28R; CANR
   17, 64; DLB 9, 212; LAIT 2; MTCW 1,
   2; SATA 5; TCWW 1, 2
Sandys, George 1578-1644 .... **LC 80**
   See also DLB 24, 121
Saner, Reg(inald Anthony) 1931- .... **CLC 9**
   See also CA 65-68; CP 3, 4, 5, 6, 7
Sankara 788-820 .... **CMLC 32**
Sannazaro, Jacopo 1456(?)-1530 .... **LC 8**
   See also RGWL 2, 3; WLIT 7
Sansom, William 1912-1976 . **CLC 2, 6; SSC
21**
   See also CA 5-8R; CAAS 65-68; CANR
   42; CN 1, 2; DAM NOV; DLB 139; EWL
   3; MTCW 1; RGEL 2; RGSF 2
Santayana, George 1863-1952 .... **TCLC 40**
   See also AMW; CA 194; CAAE 115; DLB
   54, 71, 246, 270; DLBD 13; EWL 3;
   MAL 5; RGAL 4; TUS
Santiago, Danny .... **CLC 33**
   See James, Daniel (Lewis)
   See also DLB 122
**Santillana, Inigo Lopez de Mendoza,
Marques de** 1398-1458 .... **LC 111**
   See also DLB 286
Santmyer, Helen Hooven
   1895-1986 .... **CLC 33; TCLC 133**
   See also CA 1-4R; CAAS 118; CANR 15,
   33; DLBY 1984; MTCW 1; RHW
Santoka, Taneda 1882-1940 .... **TCLC 72**
Santos, Bienvenido N(uqui)
   1911-1996 ... **AAL; CLC 22; TCLC 156**
   See also CA 101; CAAS 151; CANR 19,
   46; CP 1; DAM MULT; DLB 312; EWL;
   RGAL 4; SSFS 19
Sapir, Edward 1884-1939 .... **TCLC 108**
   See also CA 211; DLB 92
Sapper .... **TCLC 44**
   See McNeile, Herman Cyril
Sapphire
   See Sapphire, Brenda
Sapphire, Brenda 1950- .... **CLC 99**

Sappho fl. 6th cent. B.C.- ... **CMLC 3, 67; PC
5**
   See also CDWLB 1; DA3; DAM POET;
   DLB 176; FL 1:1; PFS 20; RGWL 2, 3;
   WLIT 8; WP
Saramago, Jose 1922- .... **CLC 119; HLCS 1**
   See also CA 153; CANR 96; CWW 2; DLB
   287, 332; EWL 3; LATS 1:2; SSFS 23
Sarduy, Severo 1937-1993 .... **CLC 6, 97;
HLCS 2; TCLC 167**
   See also CA 89-92; CAAS 142; CANR 58,
   81; CWW 2; DLB 113; EWL 3; HW 1, 2;
   LAW
Sargeson, Frank 1903-1982 .... **CLC 31**
   See also CA 25-28R; CAAS 106; CANR
   38, 79; CN 1, 2, 3; EWL 3; GLL 2; RGEL
   2; RGSF 2; SSFS 20
Sarmiento, Domingo Faustino
   1811-1888 .... **HLCS 2; NCLC 123**
   See also LAW; WLIT 1
Sarmiento, Felix Ruben Garcia
   See Dario, Ruben
Saro-Wiwa, Ken(ule Beeson)
   1941-1995 .... **CLC 114**
   See also BW 2; CA 142; CAAS 150; CANR
   60; DLB 157
Saroyan, William 1908-1981 ... **CLC 1, 8, 10,
29, 34, 56; SSC 21; TCLC 137; WLC 5**
   See also AAYA 66; CA 5-8R; CAAS 103;
   CAD; CANR 30; CDALBS; CN 1, 2; DA;
   DA3; DAB; DAC; DAM DRAM, MST,
   NOV; DFS 17; DLB 7, 9, 86; DLBY
   1981; EWL 3; LAIT 4; MAL 5; MTCW
   1, 2; MTFW 2005; RGAL 4; RGSF 2;
   SATA 23; SATA-Obit 24; SSFS 14; TUS
Sarraute, Nathalie 1900-1999 .... **CLC 1, 2, 4,
8, 10, 31, 80; TCLC 145**
   See also BPFB 3; CA 9-12R; CAAS 187;
   CANR 23, 66, 134; CWW 2; DLB 83,
   321; EW 12; EWL 3; GFL 1789 to the
   Present; MTCW 1, 2; MTFW 2005;
   RGWL 2, 3
Sarton, May 1912-1995 ... **CLC 4, 14, 49, 91;
PC 39; TCLC 120**
   See also AMWS 8; CA 1-4R; CAAS 149;
   CANR 1, 34, 55, 116; CN 1, 2, 3, 4, 5, 6;
   CP 1, 2, 3, 4, 5, 6; DAM POET; DLB 48;
   DLBY 1981; EWL 3; FW; INT CANR-
   34; MAL 5; MTCW 1, 2; MTFW 2005;
   RGAL 4; SATA 36; SATA-Obit 86; TUS
Sartre, Jean-Paul 1905-1980 . **CLC 1, 4, 7, 9,
13, 18, 24, 44, 50, 52; DC 3; SSC 32;
WLC 5**
   See also AAYA 62; CA 9-12R; CAAS 97-
   100; CANR 21; DA; DA3; DAB; DAC;
   DAM DRAM, MST, NOV; DFS 5; DLB
   72, 296, 321, 332; EW 12; EWL 3; GFL
   1789 to the Present; LMFS 2; MTCW 1,
   2; MTFW 2005; NFS 21; RGHL; RGSF
   2; RGWL 2, 3; SSFS 9; TWA
Sassoon, Siegfried (Lorraine)
   1886-1967 .... **CLC 36, 130; PC 12**
   See also BRW 6; CA 104; CAAS 25-28R;
   CANR 36; DAB; DAM MST, NOV,
   POET; DLB 20, 191; DLBD 18; EWL 3;
   MTCW 1, 2; MTFW 2005; PAB; RGEL
   2; TEA
Satterfield, Charles
   See Pohl, Frederik
Satyremont
   See Peret, Benjamin
Saul, John (W. III) 1942- .... **CLC 46**
   See also AAYA 10, 62; BEST 90:4; CA 81-
   84; CANR 16, 40, 81; CPW; DAM NOV,
   POP; HGG; SATA 98
Saunders, Caleb
   See Heinlein, Robert A.
Saura (Atares), Carlos 1932-1998 .... **CLC 20**
   See also CA 131; CAAE 114; CANR 79;
   HW 1

Scott, Joanna 1960- .... **CLC 50**
See also CA 126; CANR 53, 92
Scott, Paul (Mark) 1920-1978 ...... **CLC 9, 60**
See also BRWS 1; CA 81-84; CAAS 77-80;
CANR 33; CN 1, 2; DLB 14, 207, 326;
EWL 3; MTCW 1; RGEL 2; RHW; WWE
1
Scott, Ridley 1937- .... **CLC 183**
See also AAYA 13, 43
Scott, Sarah 1723-1795 .... **LC 44**
See also DLB 39
Scott, Sir Walter 1771-1832 .... **NCLC 15, 69,**
110; PC 13; SSC 32; WLC 5
See also AAYA 22; BRW 4; BYA 2; CD-
BLB 1789-1832; DA; DAB; DAC; DAM
MST, NOV, POET; DLB 93, 107, 116,
144, 159; GL 3; HGG; LAIT 1; RGEL 2;
RGSF 2; SSFS 10; SUFW 1; TEA; WLIT
3; YABC 2
Scribe, (Augustin) Eugene 1791-1861 . **DC 5;**
NCLC 16
See also DAM DRAM; DLB 192; GFL
1789 to the Present; RGWL 2, 3
Scrum, R.
See Crumb, R.
Scudery, Georges de 1601-1667 .... **LC 75**
See also GFL Beginnings to 1789
Scudery, Madeleine de 1607-1701 .. **LC 2, 58**
See also DLB 268; GFL Beginnings to 1789
Scum
See Crumb, R.
Scumbag, Little Bobby
See Crumb, R.
Seabrook, John
See Hubbard, L. Ron
Seacole, Mary Jane Grant
1805-1881 .... **NCLC 147**
See also DLB 166
Sealy, I(rwin) Allan 1951- .... **CLC 55**
See also CA 136; CN 6, 7
Search, Alexander
See Pessoa, Fernando (Antonio Nogueira)
Sebald, W(infried) G(eorg)
1944-2001 .... **CLC 194**
See also BRWS 8; CA 159; CAAS 202;
CANR 98; MTFW 2005; RGHL
Sebastian, Lee
See Silverberg, Robert
Sebastian Owl
See Thompson, Hunter S.
Sebestyen, Igen
See Sebestyen, Ouida
Sebestyen, Ouida 1924- .... **CLC 30**
See also AAYA 8; BYA 7; CA 107; CANR
40, 114; CLR 17; JRDA; MAICYA 1, 2;
SAAS 10; SATA 39, 140; WYA; YAW
Sebold, Alice 1963(?)- .... **CLC 193**
See also AAYA 56; CA 203; MTFW 2005
Second Duke of Buckingham
See Villiers, George
Secundus, H. Scriblerus
See Fielding, Henry
Sedges, John
See Buck, Pearl S(ydenstricker)
Sedgwick, Catharine Maria
1789-1867 .... **NCLC 19, 98**
See also DLB 1, 74, 183, 239, 243, 254; FL
1:3; RGAL 4
Sedulius Scottus 9th cent. -c. 874 .. **CMLC 86**
Seelye, John (Douglas) 1931- .... **CLC 7**
See also CA 97-100; CANR 70; INT CA-
97-100; TCWW 1, 2
Seferiades, Giorgos Stylianou 1900-1971
See Seferis, George
See also CA 5-8R; CAAS 33-36R; CANR
5, 36; MTCW 1

Seferis, George .... **CLC 5, 11; PC 66**
See Seferiades, Giorgos Stylianou
See also DLB 332; EW 12; EWL 3; RGWL
2, 3
Segal, Erich (Wolf) 1937- .... **CLC 3, 10**
See also BEST 89:1; BPFB 3; CA 25-28R;
CANR 20, 36, 65, 113; CPW; DAM POP;
DLBY 1986; INT CANR-20; MTCW 1
Seger, Bob 1945- .... **CLC 35**
Seghers, Anna .... **CLC 7**
See Radvanyi, Netty
See also CDWLB 2; DLB 69; EWL 3
Seidel, Frederick (Lewis) 1936- .... **CLC 18**
See also CA 13-16R; CANR 8, 99; CP 1, 2,
3, 4, 5, 6, 7; DLBY 1984
Seifert, Jaroslav 1901-1986 . **CLC 34, 44, 93;**
PC 47
See also CA 127; CDWLB 4; DLB 215,
332; EWL 3; MTCW 1, 2
Sei Shonagon c. 966-1017(?) ..... **CMLC 6, 89**
Sejour, Victor 1817-1874 .... **DC 10**
See also DLB 50
Sejour Marcou et Ferrand, Juan Victor
See Sejour, Victor
Selby, Hubert, Jr. 1928-2004 ..... **CLC 1, 2, 4,**
8; SSC 20
See also CA 13-16R; CAAS 226; CANR
33, 85; CN 1, 2, 3, 4, 5, 6, 7; DLB 2, 227;
MAL 5
Selzer, Richard 1928- .... **CLC 74**
See also CA 65-68; CANR 14, 106
Sembene, Ousmane
See Ousmane, Sembene
See also AFW; EWL 3; WLIT 2
Senancour, Etienne Pivert de
1770-1846 .... **NCLC 16**
See also DLB 119; GFL 1789 to the Present
Sender, Ramon (Jose) 1902-1982 ...... **CLC 8;**
HLC 2; TCLC 136
See also CA 5-8R; CAAS 105; CANR 8;
DAM MULT; DLB 322; EWL 3; HW 1;
MTCW 1; RGWL 2, 3
Seneca, Lucius Annaeus c. 4B.C.-c.
65 .... **CMLC 6; DC 5**
See also AW 1; CDWLB 1; DAM DRAM;
DLB 211; RGWL 2, 3; TWA; WLIT 8
Senghor, Leopold Sedar 1906-2001 ... **BLC 3;**
CLC 54, 130; PC 25
See also AFW; BW 2; CA 125; CAAE 116;
CAAS 203; CANR 47, 74, 134; CWW 2;
DAM MULT, POET; DNFS 2; EWL 3;
GFL 1789 to the Present; MTCW 1, 2;
MTFW 2005; TWA
Senior, Olive (Marjorie) 1941- .... **SSC 78**
See also BW 3; CA 154; CANR 86, 126;
CN 6; CP 6, 7; CWP; DLB 157; EWL 3;
RGSF 2
Senna, Danzy 1970- .... **CLC 119**
See also CA 169; CANR 130
Serling, (Edward) Rod(man)
1924-1975 .... **CLC 30**
See also AAYA 14; AITN 1; CA 162; CAAS
57-60; DLB 26; SFW 4
Serna, Ramon Gomez de la
See Gomez de la Serna, Ramon
Serpieres
See Guillevic, (Eugene)
Service, Robert
See Service, Robert W(illiam)
See also BYA 4; DAB; DLB 92
Service, Robert W(illiam)
1874(?)-1958 ... **PC 70; TCLC 15; WLC**
5
See Service, Robert
See also CA 140; CAAE 115; CANR 84;
DA; DAC; DAM MST, POET; PFS 10;
RGEL 2; SATA 20

Seth, Vikram 1952- .... **CLC 43, 90**
See also BRWS 10; CA 127; CAAE 121;
CANR 50, 74, 131; CN 6, 7; CP 5, 6, 7;
DA3; DAM MULT; DLB 120, 271, 282,
323; EWL 3; INT CA-127; MTCW 2;
MTFW 2005; WWE 1
Seton, Cynthia Propper 1926-1982 .. **CLC 27**
See also CA 5-8R; CAAS 108; CANR 7
Seton, Ernest (Evan) Thompson
1860-1946 .... **TCLC 31**
See also ANW; BYA 3; CA 204; CAAE
109; CLR 59; DLB 92; DLBD 13; JRDA;
SATA 18
Seton-Thompson, Ernest
See Seton, Ernest (Evan) Thompson
Settle, Mary Lee 1918-2005 .... **CLC 19, 61**
See also BPFB 3; CA 89-92; 1; CAAS 243;
CANR 44, 87, 126; CN 6, 7; CSW; DLB
6; INT CA-89-92
Seuphor, Michel
See Arp, Jean
Sevigne, Marie (de Rabutin-Chantal)
1626-1696 .... **LC 11**
See Sevigne, Marie de Rabutin Chantal
See also GFL Beginnings to 1789; TWA
Sevigne, Marie de Rabutin Chantal
See Sevigne, Marie (de Rabutin-Chantal)
See also DLB 268
Sewall, Samuel 1652-1730 .... **LC 38**
See also DLB 24; RGAL 4
Sexton, Anne (Harvey) 1928-1974 ..... **CLC 2,**
4, 6, 8, 10, 15, 53, 123; PC 2; WLC 5
See also AMWS 2; CA 1-4R; CAAS 53-56;
CABS 2; CANR 3, 36; CDALB 1941-
1968; CP 1, 2; DA; DA3; DAB; DAC;
DAM MST, POET; DLB 5, 169; EWL 3;
EXPP; FL 1:6; FW; MAL 5; MBL;
MTCW 1, 2; MTFW 2005; PAB; PFS 4,
14; RGAL 4; RGHL; SATA 10; TUS
Shaara, Jeff 1952- .... **CLC 119**
See also AAYA 70; CA 163; CANR 109;
CN 7; MTFW 2005
Shaara, Michael 1929-1988 .... **CLC 15**
See also AAYA 71; AITN 1; BPFB 3; CA
102; CAAS 125; CANR 52, 85; DAM
POP; DLBY 1983; MTFW 2005
Shackleton, C. C.
See Aldiss, Brian W.
Shacochis, Bob .... **CLC 39**
See Shacochis, Robert G.
Shacochis, Robert G. 1951-
See Shacochis, Bob
See also CA 124; CAAE 119; CANR 100;
INT CA-124
Shadwell, Thomas 1641(?)-1692 .... **LC 114**
See also DLB 80; IDTP; RGEL 2
Shaffer, Anthony 1926-2001 .... **CLC 19**
See also CA 116; CAAE 110; CAAS 200;
CBD; CD 5, 6; DAM DRAM; DFS 13;
DLB 13
Shaffer, Anthony Joshua
See Shaffer, Anthony
Shaffer, Peter 1926- ... **CLC 5, 14, 18, 37, 60;**
DC 7
See also BRWS 1; CA 25-28R; CANR 25,
47, 74, 118; CBD; CD 5, 6; CDBLB 1960
to Present; DA3; DAB; DAM DRAM,
MST; DFS 5, 13; DLB 13, 233; EWL 3;
MTCW 1, 2; MTFW 2005; RGEL 2; TEA
Shakespeare, William 1564-1616 .... **WLC 5**
See also AAYA 35; BRW 1; CDBLB Be-
fore 1660; DA; DA3; DAB; DAC; DAM
DRAM, MST, POET; DFS 20, 21; DLB
62, 172, 263; EXPP; LAIT 1; LATS 1:1;
LMFS 1; PAB; PFS 1, 2, 3, 4, 5, 8, 9;
RGEL 2; TEA; WLIT 3; WP; WS; WYA
Shakey, Bernard
See Young, Neil

Snyder, Gary 1930- . CLC 1, 2, 5, 9, 32, 120; PC 21
See also AAYA 72; AMWS 8; ANW; BG 1:3; CA 17-20R; CANR 30, 60, 125; CP 1, 2, 3, 4, 5, 6, 7; DA3; DAM POET; DLB 5, 16, 165, 212, 237, 275; EWL 3; MAL 5; MTCW 2; MTFW 2005; PFS 9, 19; RGAL 4; WP

Snyder, Zilpha Keatley 1927- .... CLC 17
See also AAYA 15; BYA 1; CA 252; 9-12R, 252; CANR 38; CLR 31; JRDA; MAI-CYA 1, 2; SAAS 2; SATA 1, 28, 75, 110, 163; SATA-Essay 112, 163; YAW

Soares, Bernardo
See Pessoa, Fernando (Antonio Nogueira)

Sobh, A.
See Shamlu, Ahmad

Sobh, Alef
See Shamlu, Ahmad

Sobol, Joshua 1939- .... CLC 60
See Sobol, Yehoshua
See also CA 200; RGHL

Sobol, Yehoshua 1939-
See Sobol, Joshua
See also CWW 2

Socrates 470B.C.-399B.C. .... CMLC 27

Soderberg, Hjalmar 1869-1941 ...... TCLC 39
See also DLB 259; EWL 3; RGSF 2

Soderbergh, Steven 1963- .... CLC 154
See also AAYA 43; CA 243

Soderbergh, Steven Andrew
See Soderbergh, Steven

Sodergran, Edith (Irene) 1892-1923
See Soedergran, Edith (Irene)
See also CA 202; DLB 259; EW 11; EWL 3; RGWL 2, 3

Soedergran, Edith (Irene)
1892-1923 .... TCLC 31
See Sodergran, Edith (Irene)

Softly, Edgar
See Lovecraft, H. P.

Softly, Edward
See Lovecraft, H. P.

Sokolov, Alexander V(sevolodovich) 1943-
See Sokolov, Sasha
See also CA 73-76

Sokolov, Raymond 1941- .... CLC 7
See also CA 85-88

Sokolov, Sasha .... CLC 59
See Sokolov, Alexander V(sevolodovich)
See also CWW 2; DLB 285; EWL 3; RGWL 2, 3

Solo, Jay
See Ellison, Harlan

Sologub, Fyodor .... TCLC 9
See Teternikov, Fyodor Kuzmich
See also EWL 3

Solomons, Ikey Esquir
See Thackeray, William Makepeace

Solomos, Dionysios 1798-1857 .... NCLC 15

Solwoska, Mara
See French, Marilyn

Solzhenitsyn, Aleksandr I. 1918- .. CLC 1, 2, 4, 7, 9, 10, 18, 26, 34, 78, 134; SSC 32; WLC 5
See Solzhenitsyn, Aleksandr Isayevich
See also AAYA 49; AITN 1; BPFB 3; CA 69-72; CANR 40, 65, 116; DA; DA3; DAB; DAC; DAM MST, NOV; DLB 302, 332; EW 13; EXPS; LAIT 4; MTCW 1, 2; MTFW 2005; NFS 6; RGSF 2; RGWL 2, 3; SSFS 9; TWA

Solzhenitsyn, Aleksandr Isayevich
See Solzhenitsyn, Aleksandr I.
See also CWW 2; EWL 3

Somers, Jane
See Lessing, Doris

Somerville, Edith Oenone
1858-1949 .... SSC 56; TCLC 51
See also CA 196; DLB 135; RGEL 2; RGSF 2

Somerville & Ross
See Martin, Violet Florence; Somerville, Edith Oenone

Sommer, Scott 1951- .... CLC 25
See also CA 106

Sommers, Christina Hoff 1950- ...... CLC 197
See also CA 153; CANR 95

Sondheim, Stephen (Joshua) 1930- . CLC 30, 39, 147; DC 22
See also AAYA 11, 66; CA 103; CANR 47, 67, 125; DAM DRAM; LAIT 4

Sone, Monica 1919- .... AAL
See also DLB 312

Song, Cathy 1955- .... AAL; PC 21
See also CA 154; CANR 118; CWP; DLB 169, 312; EXPP; FW; PFS 5

Sontag, Susan 1933-2004 ... CLC 1, 2, 10, 13, 31, 105, 195
See also AMWS 3; CA 17-20R; CAAS 234; CANR 25, 51, 74, 97; CN 1, 2, 3, 4, 5, 6, 7; CPW; DA3; DAM POP; DLB 2, 67; EWL 3; MAL 5; MBL; MTCW 1, 2; MTFW 2005; RGAL 4; RHW; SSFS 10

Sophocles 496(?)B.C.-406(?)B.C. .... CMLC 2, 47, 51, 86; DC 1; WLCS
See also AW 1; CDWLB 1; DA; DA3; DAB; DAC; DAM DRAM, MST; DFS 1, 4, 8; DLB 176; LAIT 1; LATS 1:1; LMFS 1; RGWL 2, 3; TWA; WLIT 8

Sordello 1189-1269 .... CMLC 15

Sorel, Georges 1847-1922 .... TCLC 91
See also CA 188; CAAE 118

Sorel, Julia
See Drexler, Rosalyn

Sorokin, Vladimir .... CLC 59
See Sorokin, Vladimir Georgievich

Sorokin, Vladimir Georgievich
See Sorokin, Vladimir
See also DLB 285

Sorrentino, Gilbert 1929-2006 .... CLC 3, 7, 14, 22, 40
See also CA 77-80; CAAS 250; CANR 14, 33, 115, 157; CN 3, 4, 5, 6, 7; CP 1, 2, 3, 4, 5, 6, 7; DLB 5, 173; DLBY 1980; INT CANR-14

Soseki
See Natsume, Soseki
See also MJW

Soto, Gary 1952- ... CLC 32, 80; HLC 2; PC 28
See also AAYA 10, 37; BYA 11; CA 125; CAAE 119; CANR 50, 74, 107, 157; CLR 38; CP 4, 5, 6, 7; DAM MULT; DLB 82; EWL 3; EXPP; HW 1, 2; INT CA-125; JRDA; LLW; MAICYA 2; MAICYAS 1; MAL 5; MTCW 2; MTFW 2005; PFS 7; RGAL 4; SATA 80, 120, 174; WYA; YAW

Soupault, Philippe 1897-1990 .... CLC 68
See also CA 147; CAAE 116; CAAS 131; EWL 3; GFL 1789 to the Present; LMFS 2

Souster, (Holmes) Raymond 1921- .... CLC 5, 14
See also CA 13-16R; 14; CANR 13, 29, 53; CP 1, 2, 3, 4, 5, 6, 7; DA3; DAC; DAM POET; DLB 88; RGEL 2; SATA 63

Southern, Terry 1924(?)-1995 .... CLC 7
See also AMWS 11; BPFB 3; CA 1-4R; CAAS 150; CANR 1, 55, 107; CN 1, 2, 3, 4, 5, 6; DLB 2; IDFW 3, 4

Southerne, Thomas 1660-1746 .... LC 99
See also DLB 80; RGEL 2

Southey, Robert 1774-1843 .... NCLC 8, 97
See also BRW 4; DLB 93, 107, 142; RGEL 2; SATA 54

Southwell, Robert 1561(?)-1595 .... LC 108
See also DLB 167; RGEL 2; TEA

Southworth, Emma Dorothy Eliza Nevitte
1819-1899 .... NCLC 26
See also DLB 239

Souza, Ernest
See Scott, Evelyn

Soyinka, Wole 1934- .. BLC 3; CLC 3, 5, 14, 36, 44, 179; DC 2; WLC 5
See also AFW; BW 2, 3; CA 13-16R; CANR 27, 39, 82, 136; CD 5, 6; CDWLB 3; CN 6, 7; CP 1, 2, 3, 4, 5, 6 ,7; DA; DA3; DAB; DAC; DAM DRAM, MST, MULT; DFS 10; DLB 125, 332; EWL 3; MTCW 1, 2; MTFW 2005; RGEL 2; TWA; WLIT 2; WWE 1

Spackman, W(illiam) M(ode)
1905-1990 .... CLC 46
See also CA 81-84; CAAS 132

Spacks, Barry (Bernard) 1931- .... CLC 14
See also CA 154; CANR 33, 109; CP 3, 4, 5, 6, 7; DLB 105

Spanidou, Irini 1946- .... CLC 44
See also CA 185

Spark, Muriel 1918-2006 .... CLC 2, 3, 5, 8, 13, 18, 40, 94; PC 72; SSC 10
See also BRWS 1; CA 5-8R; CAAS 251; CANR 12, 36, 76, 89, 131; CDBLB 1945-1960; CN 1, 2, 3, 4, 5, 6, 7; CP 1, 2, 3, 4, 5, 6, 7; DA3; DAB; DAC; DAM MST, NOV; DLB 15, 139; EWL 3; FW; INT CANR-12; LAIT 4; MTCW 1, 2; MTFW 2005; NFS 22; RGEL 2; TEA; WLIT 4; YAW

Spark, Muriel Sarah
See Spark, Muriel

Spaulding, Douglas
See Bradbury, Ray

Spaulding, Leonard
See Bradbury, Ray

Speght, Rachel 1597-c. 1630 .... LC 97
See also DLB 126

Spence, J. A. D.
See Eliot, T(homas) S(tearns)

Spencer, Anne 1882-1975 .... HR 1:3
See also BW 2; CA 161; DLB 51, 54

Spencer, Elizabeth 1921- .... CLC 22; SSC 57
See also CA 13-16R; CANR 32, 65, 87; CN 1, 2, 3, 4, 5, 6, 7; CSW; DLB 6, 218; EWL 3; MTCW 1; RGAL 4; SATA 14

Spencer, Leonard G.
See Silverberg, Robert

Spencer, Scott 1945- .... CLC 30
See also CA 113; CANR 51, 148; DLBY 1986

Spender, Stephen 1909-1995 ..... CLC 1, 2, 5, 10, 41, 91; PC 71
See also BRWS 2; CA 9-12R; CAAS 149; CANR 31, 54; CDBLB 1945-1960; CP 1, 2, 3, 4, 5, 6; DA3; DAM POET; DLB 20; EWL 3; MTCW 1, 2; MTFW 2005; PAB; PFS 23; RGEL 2; TEA

Spengler, Oswald (Arnold Gottfried)
1880-1936 .... TCLC 25
See also CA 189; CAAE 118

Spenser, Edmund 1552(?)-1599 ...... LC 5, 39, 117; PC 8, 42; WLC 5
See also AAYA 60; BRW 1; CDBLB Before 1660; DA; DA3; DAB; DAC; DAM MST, POET; DLB 167; EFS 2; EXPP; PAB; RGEL 2; TEA; WLIT 3; WP

Spicer, Jack 1925-1965 .... CLC 8, 18, 72
See also BG 1:3; CA 85-88; DAM POET; DLB 5, 16, 193; GLL 1; WP

Spiegelman, Art 1948- .... CLC 76, 178
See also AAYA 10, 46; CA 125; CANR 41, 55, 74, 124; DLB 299; MTCW 2; MTFW 2005; RGHL; SATA 109, 158; YAW

Stern, Richard (Gustave) 1928- ... **CLC 4, 39**
   See also CA 1-4R; CANR 1, 25, 52, 120;
   CN 1, 2, 3, 4, 5, 6, 7; DLB 218; DLBY
   1987; INT CANR-25

Sternberg, Josef von 1894-1969 .... **CLC 20**
   See also CA 81-84

Sterne, Laurence 1713-1768 .... **LC 2, 48;**
   WLC 5
   See also BRW 3; BRWC 1; CDBLB 1660-
   1789; DA; DAB; DAC; DAM MST, NOV;
   DLB 39; RGEL 2; TEA

Sternheim, (William Adolf) Carl
   1878-1942 .... **TCLC 8**
   See also CA 193; CAAE 105; DLB 56, 118;
   EWL 3; IDTP; RGWL 2, 3

Stevens, Margaret Dean
   See Aldrich, Bess Streeter

Stevens, Mark 1951- .... **CLC 34**
   See also CA 122

Stevens, Wallace 1879-1955 . **PC 6; TCLC 3,**
   12, 45; WLC 5
   See also AMW; AMWR 1; CA 124; CAAE
   104; CDALB 1929-1941; DA; DA3;
   DAB; DAC; DAM MST, POET; DLB 54;
   EWL 3; EXPP; MAL 5; MTCW 1, 2;
   PAB; PFS 13, 16; RGAL 4; TUS; WP

Stevenson, Anne (Katharine) 1933- .. **CLC 7,**
   33
   See also BRWS 6; CA 17-20R; 9; CANR 9,
   33, 123; CP 3, 4, 5, 6, 7; CWP; DLB 40;
   MTCW 1; RHW

Stevenson, Robert Louis (Balfour)
   1850-1894 ...... **NCLC 5, 14, 63; SSC 11,**
   51; WLC 5
   See also AAYA 24; BPFB 3; BRW 5;
   BRWC 1; BRWR 1; BYA 1, 2, 4, 13; CD-
   BLB 1890-1914; CLR 10, 11, 107; DA;
   DA3; DAB; DAC; DAM MST, NOV;
   DLB 18, 57, 141, 156, 174; DLBD 13;
   GL 3; HGG; JRDA; LAIT 1, 3; MAICYA
   1, 2; NFS 11, 20; RGEL 2; RGSF 2;
   SATA 100; SUFW; TEA; WCH; WLIT 4;
   WYA; YABC 2; YAW

Stewart, J(ohn) I(nnes) M(ackintosh)
   1906-1994 .... **CLC 7, 14, 32**
   See Innes, Michael
   See also CA 85-88; 3; CAAS 147; CANR
   47; CMW 4; CN 1, 2, 3, 4, 5; MTCW 1,
   2

Stewart, Mary (Florence Elinor)
   1916- .... **CLC 7, 35, 117**
   See also AAYA 29, 73; BPFB 3; CA 1-4R;
   CANR 1, 59, 130; CMW 4; CPW; DAB;
   FANT; RHW; SATA 12; YAW

Stewart, Mary Rainbow
   See Stewart, Mary (Florence Elinor)

Stifle, June
   See Campbell, Maria

Stifter, Adalbert 1805-1868 .. **NCLC 41; SSC**
   28
   See also CDWLB 2; DLB 133; RGSF 2;
   RGWL 2, 3

Still, James 1906-2001 .... **CLC 49**
   See also CA 65-68; 17; CAAS 195; CANR
   10, 26; CSW; DLB 9; DLBY 01; SATA
   29; SATA-Obit 127

Sting 1951-
   See Sumner, Gordon Matthew
   See also CA 167

Stirling, Arthur
   See Sinclair, Upton

Stitt, Milan 1941- .... **CLC 29**
   See also CA 69-72

Stockton, Francis Richard 1834-1902
   See Stockton, Frank R.
   See also AAYA 68; CA 137; CAAE 108;
   MAICYA 1, 2; SATA 44; SFW 4

Stockton, Frank R. .... **TCLC 47**
   See Stockton, Francis Richard
   See also BYA 4, 13; DLB 42, 74; DLBD
   13; EXPS; SATA-Brief 32; SSFS 3;
   SUFW; WCH

Stoddard, Charles
   See Kuttner, Henry

Stoker, Abraham 1847-1912
   See Stoker, Bram
   See also CA 150; CAAE 105; DA; DA3;
   DAC; DAM MST, NOV; HGG; MTFW
   2005; SATA 29

Stoker, Bram . **SSC 62; TCLC 8, 144; WLC**
   6
   See Stoker, Abraham
   See also AAYA 23; BPFB 3; BRWS 3; BYA
   5; CDBLB 1890-1914; DAB; DLB 304;
   GL 3; LATS 1:1; NFS 18; RGEL 2;
   SUFW; TEA; WLIT 4

Stolz, Mary 1920-2006 .... **CLC 12**
   See also AAYA 8, 73; AITN 1; CA 5-8R;
   CANR 13, 41, 112; JRDA; MAICYA 1,
   2; SAAS 3; SATA 10, 71, 133; YAW

Stolz, Mary Slattery
   See Stolz, Mary

Stone, Irving 1903-1989 .... **CLC 7**
   See also AITN 1; BPFB 3; CA 1-4R; 3;
   CAAS 129; CANR 1, 23; CN 1, 2, 3, 4;
   CPW; DA3; DAM POP; INT CANR-23;
   MTCW 1, 2; MTFW 2005; RHW; SATA
   3; SATA-Obit 64

Stone, Oliver 1946- .... **CLC 73**
   See also AAYA 15, 64; CA 110; CANR 55,
   125

Stone, Oliver William
   See Stone, Oliver

Stone, Robert 1937- .... **CLC 5, 23, 42, 175**
   See also AMWS 5; BPFB 3; CA 85-88;
   CANR 23, 66, 95; CN 4, 5, 6, 7; DLB
   152; EWL 3; INT CANR-23; MAL 5;
   MTCW 1; MTFW 2005

Stone, Ruth 1915- .... **PC 53**
   See also CA 45-48; CANR 2, 91; CP 5, 6,
   7; CSW; DLB 105; PFS 19

Stone, Zachary
   See Follett, Ken

Stoppard, Tom 1937- ... **CLC 1, 3, 4, 5, 8, 15,**
   29, 34, 63, 91; DC 6; WLC 6
   See also AAYA 63; BRWC 1; BRWR 2;
   BRWS 1; CA 81-84; CANR 39, 67, 125;
   CBD; CD 5, 6; CDBLB 1960 to Present;
   DA; DA3; DAB; DAC; DAM DRAM,
   MST; DFS 2, 5, 8, 11, 13, 16; DLB 13,
   233; DLBY 1985; EWL 3; LATS 1:2;
   MTCW 1, 2; MTFW 2005; RGEL 2;
   TEA; WLIT 4

Storey, David (Malcolm) 1933- . **CLC 2, 4, 5,**
   8
   See also BRWS 1; CA 81-84; CANR 36;
   CBD; CD 5, 6; CN 1, 2, 3, 4, 5, 6; DAM
   DRAM; DLB 13, 14, 207, 245, 326; EWL
   3; MTCW 1; RGEL 2

Storm, Hyemeyohsts 1935- ... **CLC 3; NNAL**
   See also CA 81-84; CANR 45; DAM MULT

Storm, (Hans) Theodor (Woldsen)
   1817-1888 .... **NCLC 1; SSC 27**
   See also CDWLB 2; DLB 129; EW; RGSF
   2; RGWL 2, 3

Storni, Alfonsina 1892-1938 . **HLC 2; PC 33;**
   TCLC 5
   See also CA 131; CAAE 104; DAM MULT;
   DLB 283; HW 1; LAW

Stoughton, William 1631-1701 .... **LC 38**
   See also DLB 24

Stout, Rex (Todhunter) 1886-1975 ..... **CLC 3**
   See also AITN 2; BPFB 3; CA 61-64;
   CANR 71; CMW 4; CN 2; DLB 306;
   MSW; RGAL 4

Stow, (Julian) Randolph 1935- ... **CLC 23, 48**
   See also CA 13-16R; CANR 33; CN 1, 2,
   3, 4, 5, 6, 7; CP 1, 2, 3, 4; DLB 260;
   MTCW 1; RGEL 2

Stowe, Harriet (Elizabeth) Beecher
   1811-1896 ..... **NCLC 3, 50, 133; WLC 6**
   See also AAYA 53; AMWS 1; CDALB
   1865-1917; DA; DA3; DAB; DAC; DAM
   MST, NOV; DLB 1, 12, 42, 74, 189, 239,
   243; EXPN; FL 1:3; JRDA; LAIT 2;
   MAICYA 1, 2; NFS 6; RGAL 4; TUS;
   YABC 1

Strabo c. 64B.C.-c. 25 .... **CMLC 37**
   See also DLB 176

Strachey, (Giles) Lytton
   1880-1932 .... **TCLC 12**
   See also BRWS 2; CA 178; CAAE 110;
   DLB 149; DLBD 10; EWL 3; MTCW 2;
   NCFS 4

Stramm, August 1874-1915 .... **PC 50**
   See also CA 195; EWL 3

Strand, Mark 1934- .. **CLC 6, 18, 41, 71; PC**
   63
   See also AMWS 4; CA 21-24R; CANR 40,
   65, 100; CP 1, 2, 3, 4, 5, 6, 7; DAM
   POET; DLB 5; EWL 3; MAL 5; PAB;
   PFS 9, 18; RGAL 4; SATA 41; TCLE 1:2

Stratton-Porter, Gene(va Grace) 1863-1924
   See Porter, Gene(va Grace) Stratton
   See also ANW; CA 137; CLR 87; DLB 221;
   DLBD 14; MAICYA 1, 2; SATA 15

Straub, Peter 1943- .... **CLC 28, 107**
   See also BEST 89:1; BPFB 3; CA 85-88;
   CANR 28, 65, 109; CPW; DAM POP;
   DLBY 1984; HGG; MTCW 1, 2; MTFW
   2005; SUFW 2

Straub, Peter Francis
   See Straub, Peter

Strauss, Botho 1944- .... **CLC 22**
   See also CA 157; CWW 2; DLB 124

Strauss, Leo 1899-1973 .... **TCLC 141**
   See also CA 101; CAAS 45-48; CANR 122

Streatfeild, (Mary) Noel
   1897(?)-1986 .... **CLC 21**
   See also CA 81-84; CAAS 120; CANR 31;
   CLR 17, 83; CWRI 5; DLB 160; MAI-
   CYA 1, 2; SATA 20; SATA-Obit 48

Stribling, T(homas) S(igismund)
   1881-1965 .... **CLC 23**
   See also CA 189; CAAS 107; CMW 4; DLB
   9; RGAL 4

Strindberg, (Johan) August
   1849-1912 ... **DC 18; TCLC 1, 8, 21, 47;**
   WLC 6
   See also CA 135; CAAE 104; DA; DA3;
   DAB; DAC; DAM DRAM, MST; DFS 4,
   9; DLB 259; EW 7; EWL 3; IDTP; LMFS
   2; MTCW 2; MTFW 2005; RGWL 2, 3;
   TWA

Stringer, Arthur 1874-1950 .... **TCLC 37**
   See also CA 161; DLB 92

Stringer, David
   See Roberts, Keith (John Kingston)

Stroheim, Erich von 1885-1957 ..... **TCLC 71**

Strugatskii, Arkadii (Natanovich)
   1925-1991 .... **CLC 27**
   See Strugatsky, Arkadii Natanovich
   See also CA 106; CAAS 135; SFW 4

Strugatskii, Boris (Natanovich)
   1933- .... **CLC 27**
   See Strugatsky, Boris (Natanovich)
   See also CA 106; SFW 4

Strugatsky, Arkadii Natanovich
   See Strugatskii, Arkadii (Natanovich)
   See also DLB 302

Strugatsky, Boris (Natanovich)
   See Strugatskii, Boris (Natanovich)
   See also DLB 302

Strummer, Joe 1952-2002 .... **CLC 30**

Strunk, William, Jr. 1869-1946 ...... **TCLC 92**
 See also CA 164; CAAE 118; NCFS 5
Stryk, Lucien 1924- .... **PC 27**
 See also CA 13-16R; CANR 10, 28, 55,
 110; CP 1, 2, 3, 4, 5, 6, 7
Stuart, Don A.
 See Campbell, John W(ood, Jr.)
Stuart, Ian
 See MacLean, Alistair (Stuart)
Stuart, Jesse (Hilton) 1906-1984 ... **CLC 1, 8,**
 11, 14, 34; SSC 31
 See also CA 5-8R; CAAS 112; CANR 31;
 CN 1, 2, 3; DLB 9, 48, 102; DLBY 1984;
 SATA 2; SATA-Obit 36
Stubblefield, Sally
 See Trumbo, Dalton
Sturgeon, Theodore (Hamilton)
 1918-1985 .... **CLC 22, 39**
 See Queen, Ellery
 See also AAYA 51; BPFB 3; BYA 9, 10;
 CA 81-84; CAAS 116; CANR 32, 103;
 DLB 8; DLBY 1985; HGG; MTCW 1, 2;
 MTFW 2005; SCFW; SFW 4; SUFW
Sturges, Preston 1898-1959 .... **TCLC 48**
 See also CA 149; CAAE 114; DLB 26
Styron, William 1925-2006 .. **CLC 1, 3, 5, 11,**
 15, 60, 232; SSC 25
 See also AMW; AMWC 2; BEST 90:4;
 BPFB 3; CA 5-8R; CANR 6, 33, 74, 126;
 CDALB 1968-1988; CN 1, 2, 3, 4, 5, 6,
 7; CPW; CSW; DA3; DAM NOV, POP;
 DLB 2, 143, 299; DLBY 1980; EWL 3;
 INT CANR-6; LAIT 2; MAL 5; MTCW
 1, 2; MTFW 2005; NCFS 1; NFS 22;
 RGAL 4; RGHL; RHW; TUS
Su, Chien 1884-1918
 See Su Man-shu
 See also CAAE 123
Suarez Lynch, B.
 See Bioy Casares, Adolfo; Borges, Jorge
 Luis
Suassuna, Ariano Vilar 1927- .... **HLCS 1**
 See also CA 178; DLB 307; HW 2; LAW
Suckert, Kurt Erich
 See Malaparte, Curzio
Suckling, Sir John 1609-1642 . **LC 75; PC 30**
 See also BRW 2; DAM POET; DLB 58,
 126; EXPP; PAB; RGEL 2
Suckow, Ruth 1892-1960 .... **SSC 18**
 See also CA 193; CAAS 113; DLB 9, 102;
 RGAL 4; TCWW 2
Sudermann, Hermann 1857-1928 .. **TCLC 15**
 See also CA 201; CAAE 107; DLB 118
Sue, Eugene 1804-1857 .... **NCLC 1**
 See also DLB 119
Sueskind, Patrick 1949- .... **CLC 44, 182**
 See Suskind, Patrick
Suetonius c. 70-c. 130 .... **CMLC 60**
 See also AW 2; DLB 211; RGWL 2, 3;
 WLIT 8
Sukenick, Ronald 1932-2004 ..... **CLC 3, 4, 6,**
 48
 See also CA 209; 25-28R, 209; 8; CAAS
 229; CANR 32, 89; CN 3, 4, 5, 6, 7; DLB
 173; DLBY 1981
Suknaski, Andrew 1942- .... **CLC 19**
 See also CA 101; CP 3, 4, 5, 6, 7; DLB 53
Sullivan, Vernon
 See Vian, Boris
Sully Prudhomme, Rene-Francois-Armand
 1839-1907 .... **TCLC 31**
 See Prudhomme, Rene Francois Armand
 See also DLB 332; GFL 1789 to the Present
Su Man-shu .... **TCLC 24**
 See Su, Chien
 See also EWL 3
Sumarokov, Aleksandr Petrovich
 1717-1777 .... **LC 104**
 See also DLB 150

Summerforest, Ivy B.
 See Kirkup, James
Summers, Andrew James 1942- .... **CLC 26**
Summers, Andy
 See Summers, Andrew James
Summers, Hollis (Spurgeon, Jr.)
 1916- .... **CLC 10**
 See also CA 5-8R; CANR 3; CN 1, 2, 3;
 CP 1, 2, 3, 4; DLB 6; TCLE 1:2
Summers, (Alphonsus Joseph-Mary
 Augustus) Montague
 1880-1948 .... **TCLC 16**
 See also CA 163; CAAE 118
Sumner, Gordon Matthew .... **CLC 26**
 See Police, The; Sting
Sun Tzu c. 400B.C.-c. 320B.C. ...... **CMLC 56**
Surrey, Henry Howard 1517-1574 ... **LC 121;**
 PC 59
 See also BRW 1; RGEL 2
Surtees, Robert Smith 1805-1864 .. **NCLC 14**
 See also DLB 21; RGEL 2
Susann, Jacqueline 1921-1974 .... **CLC 3**
 See also AITN 1; BPFB 3; CA 65-68;
 CAAS 53-56; MTCW 1, 2
Su Shi
 See Su Shih
 See also RGWL 2, 3
Su Shih 1036-1101 .... **CMLC 15**
 See Su Shi
Suskind, Patrick .... **CLC 182**
 See Sueskind, Patrick
 See also BPFB 3; CA 145; CWW 2
Suso, Heinrich c. 1295-1366 .... **CMLC 87**
Sutcliff, Rosemary 1920-1992 .... **CLC 26**
 See also AAYA 10; BYA 1, 4; CA 5-8R;
 CAAS 139; CANR 37; CLR 1, 37; CPW;
 DAB; DAC; DAM MST, POP; JRDA;
 LATS 1:1; MAICYA 1, 2; MAICYAS 1;
 RHW; SATA 6, 44, 78; SATA-Obit 73;
 WYA; YAW
Sutro, Alfred 1863-1933 .... **TCLC 6**
 See also CA 185; CAAE 105; DLB 10;
 RGEL 2
Sutton, Henry
 See Slavitt, David R(ytman)
Suzuki, D. T.
 See Suzuki, Daisetz Teitaro
Suzuki, Daisetz T.
 See Suzuki, Daisetz Teitaro
Suzuki, Daisetz Teitaro
 1870-1966 .... **TCLC 109**
 See also CA 121; CAAS 111; MTCW 1, 2;
 MTFW 2005
Suzuki, Teitaro
 See Suzuki, Daisetz Teitaro
Svevo, Italo .... **SSC 25; TCLC 2, 35**
 See Schmitz, Aron Hector
 See also DLB 264; EW 8; EWL 3; RGWL
 2, 3; WLIT 7
Swados, Elizabeth (A.) 1951- .... **CLC 12**
 See also CA 97-100; CANR 49; INT CA-
 97-100
Swados, Harvey 1920-1972 .... **CLC 5**
 See also CA 5-8R; CAAS 37-40R; CANR
 6; CN 1; DLB 2; MAL 5
Swan, Gladys 1934- .... **CLC 69**
 See also CA 101; CANR 17, 39; TCLE 1:2
Swanson, Logan
 See Matheson, Richard (Burton)
Swarthout, Glendon (Fred)
 1918-1992 .... **CLC 35**
 See also AAYA 55; CA 1-4R; CAAS 139;
 CANR 1, 47; CN 1, 2, 3, 4, 5; LAIT 5;
 SATA 26; TCWW 1, 2; YAW
Swedenborg, Emanuel 1688-1772 ..... **LC 105**
Sweet, Sarah C.
 See Jewett, (Theodora) Sarah Orne

Swenson, May 1919-1989 ...... **CLC 4, 14, 61,**
 106; PC 14
 See also AMWS 4; CA 5-8R; CAAS 130;
 CANR 36, 61, 131; CP 1, 2, 3, 4; DA;
 DAB; DAC; DAM MST, POET; DLB 5;
 EXPP; GLL 2; MAL 5; MTCW 1, 2;
 MTFW 2005; PFS 16; SATA 15; WP
Swift, Augustus
 See Lovecraft, H. P.
Swift, Graham 1949- .... **CLC 41, 88, 233**
 See also BRWC 2; BRWS 5; CA 122;
 CAAE 117; CANR 46, 71, 128; CN 4, 5,
 6, 7; DLB 194, 326; MTCW 2; MTFW
 2005; NFS 18; RGSF 2
Swift, Jonathan 1667-1745 ..... **LC 1, 42, 101;**
 PC 9; WLC 6
 See also AAYA 41; BRW 3; BRWC 1;
 BRWR 1; BYA 5, 14; CDBLB 1660-1789;
 CLR 53; DA; DA3; DAB; DAC; DAM
 MST, NOV, POET; DLB 39, 95, 101;
 EXPN; LAIT 1; NFS 6; RGEL 2; SATA
 19; TEA; WCH; WLIT 3
Swinburne, Algernon Charles
 1837-1909 ... **PC 24; TCLC 8, 36; WLC**
 6
 See also BRW 5; CA 140; CAAE 105; CD-
 BLB 1832-1890; DA; DA3; DAB; DAC;
 DAM MST, POET; DLB 35, 57; PAB;
 RGEL 2; TEA
Swinfen, Ann .... **CLC 34**
 See also CA 202
Swinnerton, Frank (Arthur)
 1884-1982 .... **CLC 31**
 See also CA 202; CAAS 108; CN 1, 2, 3;
 DLB 34
Swinnerton, Frank Arthur
 1884-1982 .... **CLC 31**
 See also CAAS 108; DLB 34
Swithen, John
 See King, Stephen
Sylvia
 See Ashton-Warner, Sylvia (Constance)
Symmes, Robert Edward
 See Duncan, Robert
Symonds, John Addington
 1840-1893 .... **NCLC 34**
 See also DLB 57, 144
Symons, Arthur 1865-1945 .... **TCLC 11**
 See also CA 189; CAAE 107; DLB 19, 57,
 149; RGEL 2
Symons, Julian (Gustave)
 1912-1994 .... **CLC 2, 14, 32**
 See also CA 49-52; 3; CAAS 147; CANR
 3, 33, 59; CMW 4; CN 1, 2, 3, 4, 5; CP 1,
 3, 4; DLB 87, 155; DLBY 1992; MSW;
 MTCW 1
Synge, (Edmund) J(ohn) M(illington)
 1871-1909 .... **DC 2; TCLC 6, 37**
 See also BRW 6; BRWR 1; CA 141; CAAE
 104; CDBLB 1890-1914; DAM DRAM;
 DFS 18; DLB 10, 19; EWL 3; RGEL 2;
 TEA; WLIT 4
Syruc, J.
 See Milosz, Czeslaw
Szirtes, George 1948- .... **CLC 46; PC 51**
 See also CA 109; CANR 27, 61, 117; CP 4,
 5, 6, 7
Szymborska, Wislawa 1923- ... **CLC 99, 190;**
 PC 44
 See also CA 154; CANR 91, 133; CDWLB
 4; CWP; CWW 2; DA3; DLB 232, 332;
 DLBY 1996; EWL 3; MTCW 2; MTFW
 2005; PFS 15; RGHL; RGWL 3
T. O., Nik
 See Annensky, Innokenty (Fyodorovich)
Tabori, George 1914- .... **CLC 19**
 See also CA 49-52; CANR 4, 69; CBD; CD
 5, 6; DLB 245; RGHL

CWRI 5; DA; DA3; DAB; DAC; DAM
MST, NOV, POP; DLB 15, 160, 255; EFS
2; EWL 3; FANT; JRDA; LAIT 1; LATS
1:2; LMFS 2; MAICYA 1, 2; MTCW 1,
2; MTFW 2005; NFS 8; RGEL 2; SATA
2, 32, 100; SATA-Obit 24; SFW 4; SUFW;
TEA; WCH; WYA; YAW

Toller, Ernst 1893-1939 .... **TCLC 10**
See also CA 186; CAAE 107; DLB 124;
EWL 3; RGWL 2, 3

Tolson, M. B.
See Tolson, Melvin B(eaunorus)

Tolson, Melvin B(eaunorus)
1898(?)-1966 .... **BLC 3; CLC 36, 105**
See also AFAW 1, 2; BW 1, 3; CA 124;
CAAS 89-92; CANR 80; DAM MULT,
POET; DLB 48, 76; MAL 5; RGAL 4

Tolstoi, Aleksei Nikolaevich
See Tolstoy, Alexey Nikolaevich

Tolstoi, Lev
See Tolstoy, Leo (Nikolaevich)
See also RGSF 2; RGWL 2, 3

Tolstoy, Aleksei Nikolaevich
See Tolstoy, Alexey Nikolaevich
See also DLB 272

Tolstoy, Alexey Nikolaevich
1882-1945 .... **TCLC 18**
See Tolstoy, Aleksei Nikolaevich
See also CA 158; CAAE 107; EWL 3; SFW
4

Tolstoy, Leo (Nikolaevich)
1828-1910 . **SSC 9, 30, 45, 54; TCLC 4,
11, 17, 28, 44, 79, 173; WLC 6**
See Tolstoi, Lev
See also AAYA 56; CA 123; CAAE 104;
DA; DA3; DAB; DAC; DAM MST, NOV;
DLB 238; EFS 2; EW 7; EXPS; IDTP;
LAIT 2; LATS 1:1; LMFS 1; NFS 10;
SATA 26; SSFS 5; TWA

Tolstoy, Count Leo
See Tolstoy, Leo (Nikolaevich)

Tomalin, Claire 1933- .... **CLC 166**
See also CA 89-92; CANR 52, 88; DLB
155

Tomasi di Lampedusa, Giuseppe 1896-1957
See Lampedusa, Giuseppe (Tomasi) di
See also CAAE 111; DLB 177; EWL 3;
WLIT 7

Tomlin, Lily 1939(?)-
See Tomlin, Mary Jean
See also CAAE 117

Tomlin, Mary Jean .... **CLC 17**
See Tomlin, Lily

Tomline, F. Latour
See Gilbert, W(illiam) S(chwenck)

Tomlinson, (Alfred) Charles 1927- .... **CLC 2,
4, 6, 13, 45; PC 17**
See also CA 5-8R; CANR 33; CP 1, 2, 3, 4,
5, 6, 7; DAM POET; DLB 40; TCLE 1:2

Tomlinson, H(enry) M(ajor)
1873-1958 .... **TCLC 71**
See also CA 161; CAAE 118; DLB 36, 100,
195

Tonna, Charlotte Elizabeth
1790-1846 .... **NCLC 135**
See also DLB 163

Tonson, Jacob fl. 1655(?)-1736 .... **LC 86**
See also DLB 170

Toole, John Kennedy 1937-1969 ..... **CLC 19,
64**
See also BPFB 3; CA 104; DLBY 1981;
MTCW 2; MTFW 2005

Toomer, Eugene
See Toomer, Jean

Toomer, Eugene Pinchback
See Toomer, Jean

Toomer, Jean 1894-1967 .. **BLC 3; CLC 1, 4,
13, 22; HR 1:3; PC 7; SSC 1, 45;
TCLC 172; WLCS**
See also AFAW 1, 2; AMWS 3, 9; BW 1;
CA 85-88; CDALB 1917-1929; DA3;
DAM MULT; DLB 45, 51; EWL 3; EXPP;
EXPS; LMFS 2; MAL 5; MTCW 1, 2;
MTFW 2005; NFS 11; RGAL 4; RGSF 2;
SSFS 5

Toomer, Nathan Jean
See Toomer, Jean

Toomer, Nathan Pinchback
See Toomer, Jean

Torley, Luke
See Blish, James (Benjamin)

Tornimparte, Alessandra
See Ginzburg, Natalia

Torre, Raoul della
See Mencken, H(enry) L(ouis)

Torrence, Ridgely 1874-1950 .... **TCLC 97**
See also DLB 54, 249; MAL 5

Torrey, E. Fuller 1937- .... **CLC 34**
See also CA 119; CANR 71, 158

Torrey, Edwin Fuller
See Torrey, E. Fuller

Torsvan, Ben Traven
See Traven, B.

Torsvan, Benno Traven
See Traven, B.

Torsvan, Berick Traven
See Traven, B.

Torsvan, Berwick Traven
See Traven, B.

Torsvan, Bruno Traven
See Traven, B.

Torsvan, Traven
See Traven, B.

Tourneur, Cyril 1575(?)-1626 .... **LC 66**
See also BRW 2; DAM DRAM; DLB 58;
RGEL 2

Tournier, Michel 1924- .... **CLC 6, 23, 36, 95;
SSC 88**
See also CA 49-52; CANR 3, 36, 74, 149;
CWW 2; DLB 83; EWL 3; GFL 1789 to
the Present; MTCW 1, 2; SATA 23

Tournier, Michel Edouard
See Tournier, Michel

Tournimparte, Alessandra
See Ginzburg, Natalia

Towers, Ivar
See Kornbluth, C(yril) M.

Towne, Robert (Burton) 1936(?)- ..... **CLC 87**
See also CA 108; DLB 44; IDFW 3, 4

Townsend, Sue .... **CLC 61**
See Townsend, Susan Lilian
See also AAYA 28; CA 127; CAAE 119;
CANR 65, 107; CBD; CD 5, 6; CPW;
CWD; DAB; DAC; DAM MST; DLB
271; INT CA-127; SATA 55, 93; SATA-
Brief 48; YAW

Townsend, Susan Lilian 1946-
See Townsend, Sue

Townshend, Pete
See Townshend, Peter (Dennis Blandford)

Townshend, Peter (Dennis Blandford)
1945- .... **CLC 17, 42**
See also CA 107

Tozzi, Federigo 1883-1920 .... **TCLC 31**
See also CA 160; CANR 110; DLB 264;
EWL 3; WLIT 7

Tracy, Don(ald Fiske) 1905-1970(?)
See Queen, Ellery
See also CA 1-4R; CAAS 176; CANR 2

Trafford, F. G.
See Riddell, Charlotte

Traherne, Thomas 1637(?)-1674 .. **LC 99; PC
70**
See also BRW 2; BRWS 11; DLB 131;
PAB; RGEL 2

Traill, Catharine Parr 1802-1899 .. **NCLC 31**
See also DLB 99

Trakl, Georg 1887-1914 .... **PC 20; TCLC 5**
See also CA 165; CAAE 104; EW 10; EWL
3; LMFS 2; MTCW 2; RGWL 2, 3

Trambley, Estela Portillo .... **TCLC 163**
See Portillo Trambley, Estela
See also CA 77-80; RGAL 4

Tranquilli, Secondino
See Silone, Ignazio

Transtroemer, Tomas Gosta
See Transtromer, Tomas (Goesta)

Transtromer, Tomas (Gosta)
See Transtromer, Tomas (Goesta)
See also CWW 2

Transtromer, Tomas (Goesta)
1931- .... **CLC 52, 65**
See Transtromer, Tomas (Goesta)
See also CA 129; 17; CAAE 117; CANR
115; DAM POET; DLB 257; EWL 3; PFS
21

Transtromer, Tomas Gosta
See Transtromer, Tomas (Goesta)

Traven, B. 1882(?)-1969 .... **CLC 8, 11**
See also CA 19-20; CAAS 25-28R; CAP 2;
DLB 9, 56; EWL 3; MTCW 1; RGAL 4

Trediakovsky, Vasilii Kirillovich
1703-1769 .... **LC 68**
See also DLB 150

Treitel, Jonathan 1959- .... **CLC 70**
See also CA 210; DLB 267

Trelawny, Edward John
1792-1881 .... **NCLC 85**
See also DLB 110, 116, 144

Tremain, Rose 1943- .... **CLC 42**
See also CA 97-100; CANR 44, 95; CN 4,
5, 6, 7; DLB 14, 271; RGSF 2; RHW

Tremblay, Michel 1942- .... **CLC 29, 102, 225**
See also CA 128; CAAE 116; CCA 1;
CWW 2; DAC; DAM MST; DLB 60;
EWL 3; GLL 1; MTCW 1, 2; MTFW
2005

Trevanian .... **CLC 29**
See Whitaker, Rod

Trevor, Glen
See Hilton, James

Trevor, William .. **CLC 7, 9, 14, 25, 71, 116;
SSC 21, 58**
See Cox, William Trevor
See also BRWS 4; CBD; CD 5, 6; CN 1, 2,
3, 4, 5, 6, 7; DLB 14, 139; EWL 3; LATS
1:2; RGEL 2; RGSF 2; SSFS 10; TCLE
1:2

Trifonov, Iurii (Valentinovich)
See Trifonov, Yuri (Valentinovich)
See also DLB 302; RGWL 2, 3

Trifonov, Yuri (Valentinovich)
1925-1981 .... **CLC 45**
See Trifonov, Iurii (Valentinovich); Trifonov, Yury Valentinovich
See also CA 126; CAAS 103; MTCW 1

Trifonov, Yury Valentinovich
See Trifonov, Yuri (Valentinovich)
See also EWL 3

Trilling, Diana (Rubin) 1905-1996 . **CLC 129**
See also CA 5-8R; CAAS 154; CANR 10,
46; INT CANR-10; MTCW 1, 2

Trilling, Lionel 1905-1975 ..... **CLC 9, 11, 24;
SSC 75**
See also AMWS 3; CA 9-12R; CAAS 61-
64; CANR 10, 105; CN 1, 2; DLB 28, 63;
EWL 3; INT CANR-10; MAL 5; MTCW
1, 2; RGAL 4; TUS

Trimball, W. H.
See Mencken, H(enry) L(ouis)

Tristan
See Gomez de la Serna, Ramon

Tristram
See Housman, A(lfred) E(dward)

Author Index

Urquhart, Jane 1949- .... **CLC 90**
See also CA 113; CANR 32, 68, 116, 157; CCA 1; DAC

Usigli, Rodolfo 1905-1979 .... **HLCS 1**
See also CA 131; DLB 305; EWL 3; HW 1; LAW

Usk, Thomas (?)-1388 .... **CMLC 76**
See also DLB 146

Ustinov, Peter (Alexander) 1921-2004 .... **CLC 1**
See also AITN 1; CA 13-16R; CAAS 225; CANR 25, 51; CBD; CD 5, 6; DLB 13; MTCW 2

U Tam'si, Gerald Felix Tchicaya
See Tchicaya, Gerald Felix

U Tam'si, Tchicaya
See Tchicaya, Gerald Felix

Vachss, Andrew 1942- .... **CLC 106**
See also CA 214; 118, 214; CANR 44, 95, 153; CMW 4

Vachss, Andrew H.
See Vachss, Andrew

Vachss, Andrew Henry
See Vachss, Andrew

Vaculik, Ludvik 1926- .... **CLC 7**
See also CA 53-56; CANR 72; CWW 2; DLB 232; EWL 3

Vaihinger, Hans 1852-1933 .... **TCLC 71**
See also CA 166; CAAE 116

Valdez, Luis (Miguel) 1940- ..... **CLC 84; DC 10; HLC 2**
See also CA 101; CAD; CANR 32, 81; CD 5, 6; DAM MULT; DFS 5; DLB 122; EWL 3; HW 1; LAIT 4; LLW

Valenzuela, Luisa 1938- .... **CLC 31, 104; HLCS 2; SSC 14, 82**
See also CA 101; CANR 32, 65, 123; CDWLB 3; CWW 2; DAM MULT; DLB 113; EWL 3; FW; HW 1, 2; LAW; RGSF 2; RGWL 3

Valera y Alcala-Galiano, Juan 1824-1905 .... **TCLC 10**
See also CAAE 106

Valerius Maximus fl. 20- .... **CMLC 64**
See also DLB 211

Valery, (Ambroise) Paul (Toussaint Jules) 1871-1945 .... **PC 9; TCLC 4, 15**
See also CA 122; CAAE 104; DA3; DAM POET; DLB 258; EW 8; EWL 3; GFL 1789 to the Present; MTCW 1, 2; MTFW 2005; RGWL 2, 3; TWA

Valle-Inclan, Ramon (Maria) del 1866-1936 .... **HLC 2; TCLC 5**
See del Valle-Inclan, Ramon (Maria)
See also CA 153; CAAE 106; CANR 80; DAM MULT; DLB 134; EW 8; EWL 3; HW 2; RGSF 2; RGWL 2, 3

Vallejo, Antonio Buero
See Buero Vallejo, Antonio

Vallejo, Cesar (Abraham) 1892-1938 .... **HLC 2; TCLC 3, 56**
See also CA 153; CAAE 105; DAM MULT; DLB 290; EWL 3; HW 1; LAW; RGWL 2, 3

Valles, Jules 1832-1885 .... **NCLC 71**
See also DLB 123; GFL 1789 to the Present

Vallette, Marguerite Eymery 1860-1953 .... **TCLC 67**
See Rachilde
See also CA 182; DLB 123, 192

Valle Y Pena, Ramon del
See Valle-Inclan, Ramon (Maria) del

Van Ash, Cay 1918-1994 .... **CLC 34**
See also CA 220

Vanbrugh, Sir John 1664-1726 .... **LC 21**
See also BRW 2; DAM DRAM; DLB 80; IDTP; RGEL 2

Van Campen, Karl
See Campbell, John W(ood, Jr.)

Vance, Gerald
See Silverberg, Robert

Vance, Jack 1916-
See Queen, Ellery; Vance, John Holbrook
See also CA 29-32R; CANR 17, 65, 154; CMW 4; MTCW 1

Vance, John Holbrook .... **CLC 35**
See Vance, Jack
See also DLB 8; FANT; SCFW 1, 2; SFW 4; SUFW 1, 2

Van Den Bogarde, Derek Jules Gaspard Ulric Niven 1921-1999 .... **CLC 14**
See Bogarde, Dirk
See also CA 77-80; CAAS 179

Vandenburgh, Jane .... **CLC 59**
See also CA 168

Vanderhaeghe, Guy 1951- .... **CLC 41**
See also BPFB 3; CA 113; CANR 72, 145; CN 7

van der Post, Laurens (Jan) 1906-1996 .... **CLC 5**
See also AFW; CA 5-8R; CAAS 155; CANR 35; CN 1, 2, 3, 4, 5, 6; DLB 204; RGEL 2

van de Wetering, Janwillem 1931- ... **CLC 47**
See also CA 49-52; CANR 4, 62, 90; CMW 4

Van Dine, S. S. .... **TCLC 23**
See Wright, Willard Huntington
See also DLB 306; MSW

Van Doren, Carl (Clinton) 1885-1950 .... **TCLC 18**
See also CA 168; CAAE 111

Van Doren, Mark 1894-1972 .... **CLC 6, 10**
See also CA 1-4R; CAAS 37-40R; CANR 3; CN 1; CP 1; DLB 45, 284; MAL 5; MTCW 1, 2; RGAL 4

Van Druten, John (William) 1901-1957 .... **TCLC 2**
See also CA 161; CAAE 104; DLB 10; MAL 5; RGAL 4

Van Duyn, Mona 1921-2004 .... **CLC 3, 7, 63, 116**
See also CA 9-12R; CAAS 234; CANR 7, 38, 60, 116; CP 1, 2, 3, 4, 5, 6, 7; CWP; DAM POET; DLB 5; MAL 5; MTFW 2005; PFS 20

Van Dyne, Edith
See Baum, L(yman) Frank

van Itallie, Jean-Claude 1936- .... **CLC 3**
See also CA 45-48; 2; CAD; CANR 1, 48; CD 5, 6; DLB 7

Van Loot, Cornelius Obenchain
See Roberts, Kenneth (Lewis)

van Ostaijen, Paul 1896-1928 .... **TCLC 33**
See also CA 163

Van Peebles, Melvin 1932- .... **CLC 2, 20**
See also BW 2, 3; CA 85-88; CANR 27, 67, 82; DAM MULT

van Schendel, Arthur(-Francois-Emile) 1874-1946 .... **TCLC 56**
See also EWL 3

Vansittart, Peter 1920- .... **CLC 42**
See also CA 1-4R; CANR 3, 49, 90; CN 4, 5, 6, 7; RHW

Van Vechten, Carl 1880-1964 ... **CLC 33; HR 1:3**
See also AMWS 2; CA 183; CAAS 89-92; DLB 4, 9, 51; RGAL 4

van Vogt, A(lfred) E(lton) 1912-2000 . **CLC 1**
See also BPFB 3; BYA 13, 14; CA 21-24R; CAAS 190; CANR 28; DLB 8, 251; SATA 14; SATA-Obit 124; SCFW 1, 2; SFW 4

Vara, Madeleine
See Jackson, Laura (Riding)

Varda, Agnes 1928- .... **CLC 16**
See also CA 122; CAAE 116

Vargas Llosa, Jorge Mario Pedro
See Vargas Llosa, Mario

Vargas Llosa, Mario 1936- .. **CLC 3, 6, 9, 10, 15, 31, 42, 85, 181; HLC 2**
See Llosa, Jorge Mario Pedro Vargas
See also BPFB 3; CA 73-76; CANR 18, 32, 42, 67, 116, 140; CDWLB 3; CWW 2; DA; DA3; DAB; DAC; DAM MST, MULT, NOV; DLB 145; DNFS 2; EWL 3; HW 1, 2; LAIT 5; LATS 1:2; LAW; LAWS 1; MTCW 1, 2; MTFW 2005; RGWL 2; SSFS 14; TWA; WLIT 1

Varnhagen von Ense, Rahel 1771-1833 .... **NCLC 130**
See also DLB 90

Vasari, Giorgio 1511-1574 .... **LC 114**

Vasilikos, Vasiles
See Vassilikos, Vassilis

Vasiliu, George
See Bacovia, George

Vasiliu, Gheorghe
See Bacovia, George
See also CA 189; CAAE 123

Vassa, Gustavus
See Equiano, Olaudah

Vassilikos, Vassilis 1933- .... **CLC 4, 8**
See also CA 81-84; CANR 75, 149; EWL 3

Vaughan, Henry 1621-1695 .... **LC 27**
See also BRW 2; DLB 131; PAB; RGEL 2

Vaughn, Stephanie .... **CLC 62**

Vazov, Ivan (Minchov) 1850-1921 . **TCLC 25**
See also CA 167; CAAE 121; CDWLB 4; DLB 147

Veblen, Thorstein B(unde) 1857-1929 .... **TCLC 31**
See also AMWS 1; CA 165; CAAE 115; DLB 246; MAL 5

Vega, Lope de 1562-1635 ... **HLCS 2; LC 23, 119**
See also EW 2; RGWL 2, 3

Veldeke, Heinrich von c. 1145-c. 1190 .... **CMLC 85**

Vendler, Helen (Hennessy) 1933- ... **CLC 138**
See also CA 41-44R; CANR 25, 72, 136; MTCW 1, 2; MTFW 2005

Venison, Alfred
See Pound, Ezra (Weston Loomis)

Ventsel, Elena Sergeevna 1907-2002
See Grekova, I.
See also CA 154

Verdi, Marie de
See Mencken, H(enry) L(ouis)

Verdu, Matilde
See Cela, Camilo Jose

Verga, Giovanni (Carmelo) 1840-1922 .... **SSC 21, 87; TCLC 3**
See also CA 123; CAAE 104; CANR 101; EW 7; EWL 3; RGSF 2; RGWL 2, 3; WLIT 7

Vergil 70B.C.-19B.C. ... **CMLC 9, 40; PC 12; WLCS**
See Virgil
See also AW 2; DA; DA3; DAB; DAC; DAM MST, POET; EFS 1; LMFS 1

Vergil, Polydore c. 1470-1555 .... **LC 108**
See also DLB 132

Verhaeren, Emile (Adolphe Gustave) 1855-1916 .... **TCLC 12**
See also CAAE 109; EWL 3; GFL 1789 to the Present

Verlaine, Paul (Marie) 1844-1896 .. **NCLC 2, 51; PC 2, 32**
See also DAM POET; DLB 217; EW 7; GFL 1789 to the Present; LMFS 2; RGWL 2, 3; TWA

3; EXPS; HGG; LAIT 3; MAL 5; MBL; MTCW 1, 2; MTFW 2005; NFS 13, 15; RGAL 4; RGSF 2; RHW; SSFS 2, 10; TUS

Welty, Eudora Alice
See Welty, Eudora

Wen I-to 1899-1946 .... **TCLC 28**
See also EWL 3

Wentworth, Robert
See Hamilton, Edmond

Werfel, Franz (Viktor) 1890-1945 ... **TCLC 8**
See also CA 161; CAAE 104; DLB 81, 124; EWL 3; RGWL 2, 3

Wergeland, Henrik Arnold
1808-1845 .... **NCLC 5**

Wersba, Barbara 1932- .... **CLC 30**
See also AAYA 2, 30; BYA 6, 12, 13; CA 182; 29-32R, 182; CANR 16, 38; CLR 3, 78; DLB 52; JRDA; MAICYA 1, 2; SAAS 2; SATA 1, 58; SATA-Essay 103; WYA; YAW

Wertmueller, Lina 1928- .... **CLC 16**
See also CA 97-100; CANR 39, 78

Wescott, Glenway 1901-1987 .. **CLC 13; SSC 35**
See also CA 13-16R; CAAS 121; CANR 23, 70; CN 1, 2, 3, 4; DLB 4, 9, 102; MAL 5; RGAL 4

Wesker, Arnold 1932- .... **CLC 3, 5, 42**
See also CA 1-4R; 7; CANR 1, 33; CBD; CD 5, 6; CDBLB 1960 to Present; DAB; DAM DRAM; DLB 13, 310, 319; EWL 3; MTCW 1; RGEL 2; TEA

Wesley, Charles 1707-1788 .... **LC 128**
See also DLB 95; RGEL 2

Wesley, John 1703-1791 .... **LC 88**
See also DLB 104

Wesley, Richard (Errol) 1945- .... **CLC 7**
See also BW 1; CA 57-60; CAD; CANR 27; CD 5, 6; DLB 38

Wessel, Johan Herman 1742-1785 .... **LC 7**
See also DLB 300

West, Anthony (Panther)
1914-1987 .... **CLC 50**
See also CA 45-48; CAAS 124; CANR 3, 19; CN 1, 2, 3, 4; DLB 15

West, C. P.
See Wodehouse, P(elham) G(renville)

West, Cornel 1953- .... **BLCS; CLC 134**
See also CA 144; CANR 91, 159; DLB 246

West, Cornel Ronald
See West, Cornel

West, Delno C(loyde), Jr. 1936- .... **CLC 70**
See also CA 57-60

West, Dorothy 1907-1998 ...... **HR 1:3; TCLC 108**
See also BW 2; CA 143; CAAS 169; DLB 76

West, (Mary) Jessamyn 1902-1984 ... **CLC 7, 17**
See also CA 9-12R; CAAS 112; CANR 27; CN 1, 2, 3; DLB 6; DLBY 1984; MTCW 1, 2; RGAL 4; RHW; SATA-Obit 37; TCWW 2; TUS; YAW

West, Morris L(anglo) 1916-1999 ..... **CLC 6, 33**
See also BPFB 3; CA 5-8R; CAAS 187; CANR 24, 49, 64; CN 1, 2, 3, 4, 5, 6; CPW; DLB 289; MTCW 1, 2; MTFW 2005

West, Nathanael 1903-1940 .. **SSC 16; TCLC 1, 14, 44**
See also AMW; AMWR 2; BPFB 3; CA 125; CAAE 104; CDALB 1929-1941; DA3; DLB 4, 9, 28; EWL 3; MAL 5; MTCW 1, 2; MTFW 2005; NFS 16; RGAL 4; TUS

West, Owen
See Koontz, Dean R.

West, Paul 1930- .... **CLC 7, 14, 96, 226**
See also CA 13-16R; 7; CANR 22, 53, 76, 89, 136; CN 1, 2, 3, 4, 5, 6, 7; DLB 14; INT CANR-22; MTCW 2; MTFW 2005

West, Rebecca 1892-1983 ... **CLC 7, 9, 31, 50**
See also BPFB 3; BRWS 3; CA 5-8R; CAAS 109; CANR 19; CN 1, 2, 3; DLB 36; DLBY 1983; EWL 3; FW; MTCW 1, 2; MTFW 2005; NCFS 4; RGEL 2; TEA

Westall, Robert (Atkinson)
1929-1993 .... **CLC 17**
See also AAYA 12; BYA 2, 6, 7, 8, 9, 15; CA 69-72; CAAS 141; CANR 18, 68; CLR 13; FANT; JRDA; MAICYA 1, 2; MAICYAS 1; SAAS 2; SATA 23, 69; SATA-Obit 75; WYA; YAW

Westermarck, Edward 1862-1939 . **TCLC 87**

Westlake, Donald E. 1933- .... **CLC 7, 33**
See also BPFB 3; CA 17-20R; 13; CANR 16, 44, 65, 94, 137; CMW 4; CPW; DAM POP; INT CANR-16; MSW; MTCW 2; MTFW 2005

Westlake, Donald Edwin
See Westlake, Donald E.

Westmacott, Mary
See Christie, Agatha (Mary Clarissa)

Weston, Allen
See Norton, Andre

Wetcheek, J. L.
See Feuchtwanger, Lion

Wetering, Janwillem van de
See van de Wetering, Janwillem

Wetherald, Agnes Ethelwyn
1857-1940 .... **TCLC 81**
See also CA 202; DLB 99

Wetherell, Elizabeth
See Warner, Susan (Bogert)

Whale, James 1889-1957 .... **TCLC 63**
See also AAYA 75

Whalen, Philip (Glenn) 1923-2002 .... **CLC 6, 29**
See also BG 1:3; CA 9-12R; CAAS 209; CANR 5, 39; CP 1, 2, 3, 4, 5, 6, 7; DLB 16; WP

Wharton, Edith (Newbold Jones)
1862-1937 ... **SSC 6, 84; TCLC 3, 9, 27, 53, 129, 149; WLC 6**
See also AAYA 25; AMW; AMWC 2; AMWR 1; BPFB 3; CA 132; CAAE 104; CDALB 1865-1917; DA; DA3; DAB; DAC; DAM MST, NOV; DLB 4, 9, 12, 78, 189; DLBD 13; EWL 3; EXPS; FL 1:6; GL 3; HGG; LAIT 2, 3; LATS 1:1; MAL 5; MBL; MTCW 1, 2; MTFW 2005; NFS 5, 11, 15, 20; RGAL 4; RGSF 2; RHW; SSFS 6, 7; SUFW; TUS

Wharton, James
See Mencken, H(enry) L(ouis)

Wharton, William (a pseudonym)
1925- .... **CLC 18, 37**
See also CA 93-96; CN 4, 5, 6, 7; DLBY 1980; INT CA-93-96

Wheatley (Peters), Phillis
1753(?)-1784 ... **BLC 3; LC 3, 50; PC 3; WLC 6**
See also AFAW 1, 2; CDALB 1640-1865; DA; DA3; DAC; DAM MST, MULT, POET; DLB 31, 50; EXPP; FL 1:1; PFS 13; RGAL 4

Wheelock, John Hall 1886-1978 .... **CLC 14**
See also CA 13-16R; CAAS 77-80; CANR 14; CP 1, 2; DLB 45; MAL 5

Whim-Wham
See Curnow, (Thomas) Allen (Monro)

Whisp, Kennilworthy
See Rowling, J.K.

Whitaker, Rod 1931-2005
See Trevanian
See also CA 29-32R; CAAS 246; CANR 45, 153; CMW 4

White, Babington
See Braddon, Mary Elizabeth

White, E. B. 1899-1985 .... **CLC 10, 34, 39**
See also AAYA 62; AITN 2; AMWS 1; CA 13-16R; CAAS 116; CANR 16, 37; CDALBS; CLR 1, 21, 107; CPW; DA3; DAM POP; DLB 11, 22; EWL 3; FANT; MAICYA 1, 2; MAL 5; MTCW 1, 2; MTFW 2005; NCFS 5; RGAL 4; SATA 2, 29, 100; SATA-Obit 44; TUS

White, Edmund 1940- .... **CLC 27, 110**
See also AAYA 7; CA 45-48; CANR 3, 19, 36, 62, 107, 133; CN 5, 6, 7; DA3; DAM POP; DLB 227; MTCW 1, 2; MTFW 2005

White, Elwyn Brooks
See White, E. B.

White, Hayden V. 1928- .... **CLC 148**
See also CA 128; CANR 135; DLB 246

White, Patrick (Victor Martindale)
1912-1990 ...... **CLC 3, 4, 5, 7, 9, 18, 65, 69; SSC 39; TCLC 176**
See also BRWS 1; CA 81-84; CAAS 132; CANR 43; CN 1, 2, 3, 4; DLB 260, 332; EWL 3; MTCW 1; RGEL 2; RGSF 2; RHW; TWA; WWE 1

White, Phyllis Dorothy James 1920-
See James, P. D.
See also CA 21-24R; CANR 17, 43, 65, 112; CMW 4; CN 7; CPW; DA3; DAM POP; MTCW 1, 2; MTFW 2005; TEA

White, T(erence) H(anbury)
1906-1964 .... **CLC 30**
See also AAYA 22; BPFB 3; BYA 4, 5; CA 73-76; CANR 37; DLB 160; FANT; JRDA; LAIT 1; MAICYA 1, 2; RGEL 2; SATA 12; SUFW 1; YAW

White, Terence de Vere 1912-1994 ... **CLC 49**
See also CA 49-52; CAAS 145; CANR 3

White, Walter
See White, Walter F(rancis)

White, Walter F(rancis) 1893-1955 ... **BLC 3; HR 1:3; TCLC 15**
See also BW 1; CA 124; CAAE 115; DAM MULT; DLB 51

White, William Hale 1831-1913
See Rutherford, Mark
See also CA 189; CAAE 121

Whitehead, Alfred North
1861-1947 .... **TCLC 97**
See also CA 165; CAAE 117; DLB 100, 262

Whitehead, Colson 1970- .... **CLC 232**
See also CA 202

Whitehead, E(dward) A(nthony)
1933- .... **CLC 5**
See Whitehead, Ted
See also CA 65-68; CANR 58, 118; CBD; CD 5; DLB 310

Whitehead, Ted
See Whitehead, E(dward) A(nthony)
See also CD 6

Whiteman, Roberta J. Hill 1947- ...... **NNAL**
See also CA 146

Whitemore, Hugh (John) 1936- .... **CLC 37**
See also CA 132; CANR 77; CBD; CD 5, 6; INT CA-132

Whitman, Sarah Helen (Power)
1803-1878 .... **NCLC 19**
See also DLB 1, 243

Whitman, Walt(er) 1819-1892 .. **NCLC 4, 31, 81; PC 3; WLC 6**
See also AAYA 42; AMW; AMWR 1; CDALB 1640-1865; DA; DA3; DAB; DAC; DAM MST, POET; DLB 3, 64,

Wollstonecraft, Mary 1759-1797 .... **LC 5, 50,**
    90
    See also BRWS 3; CDBLB 1789-1832;
    DLB 39, 104, 158, 252; FL 1:1; FW;
    LAIT 1; RGEL 2; TEA; WLIT 3
Wonder, Stevie 1950- .... **CLC 12**
    See also CAAE 111
Wong, Jade Snow 1922-2006 .... **CLC 17**
    See also CA 109; CAAS 249; CANR 91;
    SATA 112; SATA-Obit 175
Wood, Mrs. Henry 1814-1887 ...... **NCLC 178**
    See also CMW 4; DLB 18; SUFW
Woodberry, George Edward
    1855-1930 .... **TCLC 73**
    See also CA 165; DLB 71, 103
Woodcott, Keith
    See Brunner, John (Kilian Houston)
Woodruff, Robert W.
    See Mencken, H(enry) L(ouis)
Woolf, (Adeline) Virginia 1882-1941 .. **SSC 7,**
    79; TCLC 1, 5, 20, 43, 56, 101, 123,
    128; WLC 6
    See also AAYA 44; BPFB 3; BRW 7;
    BRWC 2; BRWR 1; CA 130; CAAE 104;
    CANR 64, 132; CDBLB 1914-1945; DA;
    DA3; DAB; DAC; DAM MST, NOV;
    DLB 36, 100, 162; DLBD 10; EWL 3;
    EXPS; FL 1:6; FW; LAIT 3; LATS 1:1;
    LMFS 2; MTCW 1, 2; MTFW 2005;
    NCFS 2; NFS 8, 12; RGEL 2; RGSF 2;
    SSFS 4, 12; TEA; WLIT 4
Woollcott, Alexander (Humphreys)
    1887-1943 .... **TCLC 5**
    See also CA 161; CAAE 105; DLB 29
Woolrich, Cornell .... **CLC 77**
    See Hopley-Woolrich, Cornell George
    See also MSW
Woolson, Constance Fenimore
    1840-1894 .... **NCLC 82; SSC 90**
    See also DLB 12, 74, 189, 221; RGAL 4
Wordsworth, Dorothy 1771-1855 . **NCLC 25,**
    138
    See also DLB 107
Wordsworth, William 1770-1850 .. **NCLC 12,**
    38, 111, 166; PC 4, 67; WLC 6
    See also AAYA 70; BRW 4; BRWC 1; CD-
    BLB 1789-1832; DA; DA3; DAB; DAC;
    DAM MST, POET; DLB 93, 107; EXPP;
    LATS 1:1; LMFS 1; PAB; PFS 2; RGEL
    2; TEA; WLIT 3; WP
Wotton, Sir Henry 1568-1639 .... **LC 68**
    See also DLB 121; RGEL 2
Wouk, Herman 1915- .... **CLC 1, 9, 38**
    See also BPFB 2, 3; CA 5-8R; CANR 6,
    33, 67, 146; CDALBS; CN 1, 2, 3, 4, 5,
    6; CPW; DA3; DAM NOV, POP; DLBY
    1982; INT CANR-6; LAIT 4; MAL 5;
    MTCW 1, 2; MTFW 2005; NFS 7; TUS
Wright, Charles 1935- ... **CLC 6, 13, 28, 119,**
    146
    See also AMWS 5; CA 29-32R; 7; CANR
    23, 36, 62, 88, 135; CP 3, 4, 5, 6, 7; DLB
    165; DLBY 1982; EWL 3; MTCW 1, 2;
    MTFW 2005; PFS 10
Wright, Charles Stevenson 1932- ..... **BLC 3;**
    CLC 49
    See also BW 1; CA 9-12R; CANR 26; CN
    1, 2, 3, 4, 5, 6, 7; DAM MULT, POET;
    DLB 33
Wright, Frances 1795-1852 .... **NCLC 74**
    See also DLB 73
Wright, Frank Lloyd 1867-1959 .... **TCLC 95**
    See also AAYA 33; CA 174
Wright, Harold Bell 1872-1944 .... **TCLC 183**
    See also BPFB 3; CAAE 110; DLB 9;
    TCWW 2
Wright, Jack R.
    See Harris, Mark

Wright, James (Arlington)
    1927-1980 .... **CLC 3, 5, 10, 28; PC 36**
    See also AITN 2; AMWS 3; CA 49-52;
    CAAS 97-100; CANR 4, 34, 64;
    CDALBS; CP 1, 2; DAM POET; DLB 5,
    169; EWL 3; EXPP; MAL 5; MTCW 1,
    2; MTFW 2005; PFS 7, 8; RGAL 4; TUS;
    WP
Wright, Judith 1915-2000 ... **CLC 11, 53; PC**
    14
    See also CA 13-16R; CAAS 188; CANR
    31, 76, 93; CP 1, 2, 3, 4, 5, 6, 7; CWP;
    DLB 260; EWL 3; MTCW 1, 2; MTFW
    2005; PFS 8; RGEL 2; SATA 14; SATA-
    Obit 121
Wright, L(aurali) R. 1939- .... **CLC 44**
    See also CA 138; CMW 4
Wright, Richard (Nathaniel)
    1908-1960 ... **BLC 3; CLC 1, 3, 4, 9, 14,**
    21, 48, 74; SSC 2; TCLC 136, 180;
    WLC 6
    See also AAYA 5, 42; AFAW 1, 2; AMW;
    BPFB 3; BW 1; BYA 2; CA 108; CANR
    64; CDALB 1929-1941; DA; DA3; DAB;
    DAC; DAM MST, MULT, NOV; DLB 76,
    102; DLBD 2; EWL 3; EXPN; LAIT 3,
    4; MAL 5; MTCW 1, 2; MTFW 2005;
    NCFS 1; NFS 1, 7; RGAL 4; RGSF 2;
    SSFS 3, 9, 15, 20; TUS; YAW
Wright, Richard B(ruce) 1937- .... **CLC 6**
    See also CA 85-88; CANR 120; DLB 53
Wright, Rick 1945- .... **CLC 35**
Wright, Rowland
    See Wells, Carolyn
Wright, Stephen 1946- .... **CLC 33**
    See also CA 237
Wright, Willard Huntington 1888-1939
    See Van Dine, S. S.
    See also CA 189; CAAE 115; CMW 4;
    DLBD 16
Wright, William 1930- .... **CLC 44**
    See also CA 53-56; CANR 7, 23, 154
Wroth, Lady Mary 1587-1653(?) .... **LC 30;**
    PC 38
    See also DLB 121
Wu Ch'eng-en 1500(?)-1582(?) .... **LC 7**
Wu Ching-tzu 1701-1754 .... **LC 2**
Wulfstan c. 10th cent. -1023 .... **CMLC 59**
Wurlitzer, Rudolph 1938(?)- ... **CLC 2, 4, 15**
    See also CA 85-88; CN 4, 5, 6, 7; DLB 173
Wyatt, Sir Thomas c. 1503-1542 . **LC 70; PC**
    27
    See also BRW 1; DLB 132; EXPP; PFS 25;
    RGEL 2; TEA
Wycherley, William 1640-1716 ...... **LC 8, 21,**
    102, 136
    See also BRW 2; CDBLB 1660-1789; DAM
    DRAM; DLB 80; RGEL 2
Wyclif, John c. 1330-1384 .... **CMLC 70**
    See also DLB 146
Wylie, Elinor (Morton Hoyt)
    1885-1928 .... **PC 23; TCLC 8**
    See also AMWS 1; CA 162; CAAE 105;
    DLB 9, 45; EXPP; MAL 5; RGAL 4
Wylie, Philip (Gordon) 1902-1971 ... **CLC 43**
    See also CA 21-22; CAAS 33-36R; CAP 2;
    CN 1; DLB 9; SFW 4
Wyndham, John .... **CLC 19**
    See Harris, John (Wyndham Parkes Lucas)
    Beynon
    See also DLB 255; SCFW 1, 2
Wyss, Johann David Von
    1743-1818 .... **NCLC 10**
    See also CLR 92; JRDA; MAICYA 1, 2;
    SATA 29; SATA-Brief 27
Xenophon c. 430B.C.-c. 354B.C. ... **CMLC 17**
    See also AW 1; DLB 176; RGWL 2, 3;
    WLIT 8

Xingjian, Gao 1940-
    See Gao Xingjian
    See also CA 193; DFS 21; DLB 330;
    RGWL 3
Yakamochi 718-785 .... **CMLC 45; PC 48**
Yakumo Koizumi
    See Hearn, (Patricio) Lafcadio (Tessima
    Carlos)
Yamada, Mitsuye (May) 1923- .... **PC 44**
    See also CA 77-80
Yamamoto, Hisaye 1921- .... **AAL; SSC 34**
    See also CA 214; DAM MULT; DLB 312;
    LAIT 4; SSFS 14
Yamauchi, Wakako 1924- .... **AAL**
    See also CA 214; DLB 312
Yanez, Jose Donoso
    See Donoso (Yanez), Jose
Yanovsky, Basile S.
    See Yanovsky, V(assily) S(emenovich)
Yanovsky, V(assily) S(emenovich)
    1906-1989 .... **CLC 2, 18**
    See also CA 97-100; CAAS 129
Yates, Richard 1926-1992 .... **CLC 7, 8, 23**
    See also AMWS 11; CA 5-8R; CAAS 139;
    CANR 10, 43; CN 1, 2, 3, 4, 5; DLB 2,
    234; DLBY 1981, 1992; INT CANR-10;
    SSFS 24
Yau, John 1950- .... **PC 61**
    See also CA 154; CANR 89; CP 4, 5, 6, 7;
    DLB 234, 312
Yearsley, Ann 1753-1806 .... **NCLC 174**
    See also DLB 109
Yeats, W. B.
    See Yeats, William Butler
Yeats, William Butler 1865-1939 . **PC 20, 51;**
    TCLC 1, 11, 18, 31, 93, 116; WLC 6
    See also AAYA 48; BRW 6; BRWR 1; CA
    127; CAAE 104; CANR 45; CDBLB
    1890-1914; DA; DA3; DAB; DAC; DAM
    DRAM, MST, POET; DLB 10, 19, 98,
    156, 332; EWL 3; EXPP; MTCW 1, 2;
    MTFW 2005; NCFS 3; PAB; PFS 1, 2, 5,
    7, 13, 15; RGEL 2; TEA; WLIT 4; WP
Yehoshua, A(braham) B. 1936- .. **CLC 13, 31**
    See also CA 33-36R; CANR 43, 90, 145;
    CWW 2; EWL 3; RGHL; RGSF 2; RGWL
    3; WLIT 6
Yellow Bird
    See Ridge, John Rollin
Yep, Laurence 1948- .... **CLC 35**
    See also AAYA 5, 31; BYA 7; CA 49-52;
    CANR 1, 46, 92; CLR 3, 17, 54; DLB 52,
    312; FANT; JRDA; MAICYA 1, 2; MAI-
    CYAS 1; SATA 7, 69, 123, 176; WYA;
    YAW
Yep, Laurence Michael
    See Yep, Laurence
Yerby, Frank G(arvin) 1916-1991 ..... **BLC 3;**
    CLC 1, 7, 22
    See also BPFB 3; BW 1, 3; CA 9-12R;
    CAAS 136; CANR 16, 52; CN 1, 2, 3, 4,
    5; DAM MULT; DLB 76; INT CANR-16;
    MTCW 1; RGAL 4; RHW
Yesenin, Sergei Aleksandrovich
    See Esenin, Sergei
Yevtushenko, Yevgeny (Alexandrovich)
    1933- ...... **CLC 1, 3, 13, 26, 51, 126; PC**
    40
    See Evtushenko, Evgenii Aleksandrovich
    See also CA 81-84; CANR 33, 54; DAM
    POET; EWL 3; MTCW 1; RGHL
Yezierska, Anzia 1885(?)-1970 .... **CLC 46**
    See also CA 126; CAAS 89-92; DLB 28,
    221; FW; MTCW 1; RGAL 4; SSFS 15
Yglesias, Helen 1915- .... **CLC 7, 22**
    See also CA 37-40R; 20; CANR 15, 65, 95;
    CN 4, 5, 6, 7; INT CANR-15; MTCW 1
Yokomitsu, Riichi 1898-1947 .... **TCLC 47**
    See also CA 170; EWL 3

Literary Criticism Series
Cumulative Topic Index

This index lists all topic entries in Thompson Gale's *Children's Literature Review* (CLR), *Classical and Medieval Literature Criticism* (CMLC), *Contemporary Literary Criticism* (CLC), *Drama Criticism* (DC), *Literature Criticism from 1400 to 1800* (LC), *Nineteenth-Century Literature Criticism* (NCLC), *Short Story Criticism* (SSC), and *Twentieth-Century Literary Criticism* (TCLC). The index also lists topic entries in the Gale Critical Companion Collection, which includes the following publications: *The Beat Generation* (BG), *Feminism in Literature* (FL), *Gothic Literature* (GL), and *Harlem Renaissance* (HR).

Topic Index

NCLC Cumulative Nationality Index

Nationality Index

ISBN-13: 978-0-7876-9851-5
ISBN-10: 0-7876-9851-2